KB185858

믿고보는 멘토스의

All New 미드영어 단숨에 따라잡기

CHRIS SUH

MENTORS

믿고보는 멘토스의 All New
미드영어 단숨에 따라잡기

2024년 11월 18일 인쇄
2024년 11월 25일 개정판 포함 26쇄 발행

지 은 이 Chris Suh
발 행 인 Chris Suh
발 행 처 **MENTORS**
경기도 성남시 분당구 황새울로 335번길 10 598
TEL 031-604-0025 FAX 031-696-5221
mentors.co.kr
blog.naver.com/mentorsbook
* Play 스토어 및 App 스토어에서 '멘토스북' 검색해 어플다운받기!
등록일자 2005년 7월 27일
등록번호 제 2009-000027호
I S B N 979-11-989667-6-6
가 격 33,000원(MP3 무료다운로드)

미드, 그 다양성에 빠지다

〈미드영어 단숨에 따라잡기〉가 최초로 나온지 수년이 흘렀다. 많이 부족함에도 독자분들의 많은 관심과 사랑을 받아왔다. 이제 다시 그때 담지 못한 표현들을 대폭 보강하여 〈믿고보는 멘토스 미드영어 단숨에 따라잡기 Episodes 01-50〉이라는 제목의 개정판을 내놓게 되었다. Friends, Desperate Housewives, Sex and the City 그리고 CSI 등 대작의 시대가 가는 대신 Game of Thrones, Walking Dead, The Big Bang Theory, Breaking Bad, Homeland, 그리고 Blacklist, Gotham 등 스토리가 탄탄한 중견작품들이 다양하게 나와 각자 취향에 따라 골라 보는 시대가 되었다.

미드로 쭉쭉쭉 영어실력 늘리기

'포스트 시험영어' 시대의 미덕은 바로 '영어듣기 말하기'이며 이러한 면에서 미드는 최고의 영어학습 자료이다. 미드는 미국 드라마의 줄임말로 미국 드라마란 미국 생활을 있는 그대로 보여준다는 점에서 미국에 가지 않고 미국을 가장 유사하게 경험할 수 있는 영어학습자료이다. 그렇다면 미국을 우리 안방으로 들여놓은 듯한 수많은 미드를 보면서 '어떻게 영어공부를 해야 하나'라는 방법론적 의문이 생긴다. 아는 표현도 들리지도 않고 들려도 모르는 표현도 많고 . 미드가 좋다는 것은 알지만 그래서 남들이 추천하듯 자막없이 듣고, dictation을 해보기도 한다. 하지만 이것도 어느 정도 실력이 있는 사람에게나 가능한 일이고 그렇지 않은 사람의 경우에는 동네 야산에나 오르던 사람보고 에베레스트 산에 올라가라는 것과 매한가지이다. 실력과 지속력이라는 부분에서 자신없는 사람들에게는 다음과 같은 방법을 추천하고 싶다.

❶ 읽는단계 : 영어자막을 켜놓고 많은 미드를 보고 자막을 정신없이 읽는다 ···› 생활영어표현에 익숙해진다
❷ 학습단계 : 미드영어표현을 많이 학습한다 ···› 정신없던 자막이 속도를 늦춘 듯 놓치지 않고 다 읽힌다
❸ 실전단계 : 학습한 미드표현으로 무장한 채 자막없이 미드를 듣는다 ···› 들리는 단어와 들리는 문장이 점점 많아지면서 미드영어에 자신감이 생긴다

물론 자막없이 보고 dictation을 하면 빠르게 영어를 습득할 수 있는 건 사실이지만 금방 지쳐 포기할 방법이라면 좀 여유있게 돌아서 가는 것도 좋을 것이다. 최선은 미드표현을 많이 먼저 알아야 한다는 것이다. 알아야 영어자막을 놓치지 않고 읽을 수 있고 또한 궁극적으로는 귀로 들을 수도 있게 되기 때문이다. 그렇게 되면 어느덧 미드의 재미에 제대로 빠질 수 있고 자신도 모르게 영어실력이 쭉쭉쭉 늘어나는 것을 느낄 수 있을 것이다.

미드영어 단숨에 따라하기

〈믿고보는 멘토스 미드영어 단숨에 따라하기 Episodes 01-50〉은 인기 미드에서 자주 등장하는 표현들을 총집합하였다. 주요 표현만 2,500여 개, 거기에 활용표현 및 More expressions까지 합하면 무려 5,500여 개 이상의 미드표현들이 수록되어 있다. 또한 예문의 경우 다이알로그 2,500여 개 외에 미드에 실제 자주 나오는 예문 7,000여 문장을 수록하여 미드족이 미드영어에 정말 제대로 푹 빠질 수 있도록 기획되었다. 〈믿고보는 멘토스 미드영어 단숨에 따라잡기〉는 무늬만 미드인 책이 아니라 실제 미드의 핵심을 관통하고 있어 미드영어공부를 조금이나마 해본 사람이라면 그 가치를 느낄 수 있을 것이다. 이제 영어실력의 척도는 찍는 시험이 아니라 실제 듣고 말하는 능력이다.
그 점에 있어서 미드는 더할 나위없이 소중한 학습소스이다. 어렵다 미루지 말고 하나하나씩 배워나가면 영어회화실력이 남과 달리 출중해질 것이다.
뭐든지 처음이 어려운 법이다. 이책 〈믿고보는 멘토스 미드영어 단숨에 따라잡기〉가 미드족 여러분들이 처음 '미드재미'에 빠지는데, 빠져서 헤어나오지 못하는데 큰 도움이 되기를 확신한다.

미드영어 단숨에 따라잡기란?

특징

1. 50개의 테마

미드에 가장 자주 등장하게 되는 상황 50개를 선정하여 동일 문맥에서 사용되는 빈출표현들을 집중적으로 모았다.

2. 미드표현총정리

인기 미드에 자주 나오는 영어표현을 총망라하였다. 주요 표현 2,500여 개를 포함 총 5,500여 개 이상의 표현을 수록하였다.

3. English Definition

주요 표현 2,500여 개를 쉬운 영어로 설명함으로써 미드표현의 의미를 감각적으로 정확하게 느낄 수 있다.

4. Drama Expressions

표현만 달랑 알아서는 실제 미드를 보고 이해하는데 도움이 되지 않는다. 그 표현이 어떻게 응용되고 변형되어 쓰이는지 알 수 있도록 현장감 있는 생생한 미드표현들을 수록하였다.

5. Native 녹음

주요 표현 2,500여 개의 대화 및 Drama Expressions 전량이 원어민의 녹음으로 수록되어 눈으로 읽을 뿐만 아니라 귀로도 들으면서 미드를 보고 즐길 수 있는 실력을 향상시킬 수 있다.

구성

1. 50개의 테마

미드에 자주 등장하는 50개의 상황에 총 5,500여 개 이상의 표현을 수록하였다. 비슷한 문맥의 표현들을 함께 모아 학습함으로써 미드영어를 따라잡는 속도를 배가시킬 수 있다.

2. 의미(English definition)

미드표현을 우리말 뜻으로 받아들이는 것보다는 영어로 이해하는 것이 훨씬 정확하고 빠르다. 주요 미드표현은 모두 영영사전처럼 영어로 쉽게 설명되어 있어 미드표현이 어떤 상황에서 어떻게 쓰이는지를 잘 알 수 있도록 하였다.

3. Point

주요 표현의 응용표현 혹은 관련표현들을 수록하여 함께 많은 표현을 섭취할 수 있도록 하였으며 또한 필요한 경우에는 부가설명을 달아 이해를 쉽게 하였다.

4. 다이알로그

실제 미드표현이 쓰이는 가장 유사한 대화를 수록하여 그 표현의 실전활용법을 습득하고 아울러 원어민의 생동감있는 음성을 들으면서 귀를 미드에 익숙하게 할 수 있다.

5. 미드표현

미드 표현을 아는 것과 이를 실제 미드에서 듣고 이해하는 것은 별개다. 이 표현들이 실제 미드에서는 어떻게 활용되는지 앞뒤 어떤 문맥에서 사용되는지 그 활용되는 경우들을 미드에서 콕콕 집어내 '미드 이해'와 학습에 도움이 되도록 했다.

6. 미드에선 이렇게 쓰인다!

실제 미드에서 쓰인 현장을 목격하는 순간. 해당 표현이 들어간 부분의 장면 대사를 수록함으로써 그 때 그 장면을 연상하면서 표현이 어떻게 쓰이는지를 확인할 수 있다.

미드영어 단숨에 따라잡기란?

엔트리 표현
미드에 자주 나오는 비중있는 표현들과 이에 대한 친절한 우리말 의미설명.

다이알로그
실제 대사를 통해 주요 표현의 쓰임새를 확인한다.

POINT
주요 표현과 연관된 관련표현 및 부가설명이 수록되어 있다.

의미
주요 미드표현들의 의미를 영어로 자세히 설명하여 의미파악을 정확히 할 수 있다.

미드표현
실제 주요 표현들이 미드에서 어떻게 사용됐나 확인하는 자리. 인위적인 문장이 아니라 사실적인 미드 문장들 속에서 미드표현들을 만나본다.

001 You got it? 알았어?

the speaker is asking "Did you understand the meaning of what was said?" He wants to know if he was clearly understood

| Point | You got that? 잘 들었어?

A: You need to be at the airport at 7am. You got it? 오전 7시까지 공항에 와야 돼. 알았어?
B: Sure, I got it. I'll be there on time. 어, 알았어. 제때 갈게.

미드표현
Watch her closely, you got it? 걔를 주의해서 봐. 알았지?
Nobody moves. You got that? 다들 꼼짝마. 알겠어?
Now, lock the door. You got it? 이제 문을 잠그라고. 알았어?
You don't ever talk to me again, you got it? 넌 다시는 내게 말걸지마. 알았어?

002 You got me 내말 알아들었지

usually this is a way for a speaker to express that he wants to be sure something was clearly understood. It means that he feels he is saying something important. It is a way to say "Did you understand that?"

| Point | get sb …의 말을 이해하다, 알아듣다

A: I don't want anyone smoking in the house. You got me. 집에서는 어느 누구도 금연이야. 알아들었지.
B: Sure. I will tell everyone to smoke outside. 물론. 다들 나가서 담배피라고 할게.

미드표현
I'm telling you. Talk to someone. You got me? 정말이야. 누구한테 말해봐. 알았어?
You stay away from him, or you'll be one sorry individual. You got me? 걔 근처에 얼씬하지마, 그렇지 않으면 넌 후회하게 될거야. 알겠어?
Do it now! You got me? 지금 당장 그걸 해! 알았어?
I will break every bone in your body. You got me? 내가 네 몸안의 모든 뼈를 부셔놓을거야. 알았어?

003 Do you hear me? 1. (내가 한 말) 알았지? 2. (무선통신) 내 말 들려?

this is a way of asking if a person has physically heard something that has been said. It is similar to asking "Am I loud enough to be heard?"

| Point | Did you hear me? 내 말 들었어?
(Do) You hear? 1. 들리니? 2. (내가 한 말) 알겠니?

A: This place needs to be cleaned before you leave. Do you hear me? 가기 전에 여기 청소해놔. 알았지?
B: Yeah. It's impossible not to hear you because you're shouting so loud. 그렇게 소리치는데 못들을 수없지.

미드표현
I want an explanation, James, do you hear me? 제임스, 설명을 해줘야지. 알겠어?
Helen, you're history! Do you hear me? 헬렌, 넌 한물 갔어! 알겠어?
You're everything to me, you hear? 넌 내 전부야. 알겠어?
Did you hear me? I said she is married. 내 말 알겠어? 걔 결혼했다고.

004 You know what I mean? 1. 무슨 말인지 알겠어? 2. (평서문) 너도 알겠지만

this is a way of asking if a person has understood an idea that was expressed by the speaker. It is like asking "Do you understand my idea?"

| Point | If you know what I mean 내가 무슨 말 하는지 안다면 말야

A: I'd really like to be rich in the future. You know what I mean? 앞으로 정말 부자가 되고 싶어. 무슨 말인지 알겠어?
B: I think a lot of people dream of having money. 많은 사람들이 돈을 갖는 꿈을 꾸는 것 같아.

미드표현
I need more time. You know what I mean? 시간이 더 필요해. 무슨 말인지 알지?
Hey, man, just let it go. You know what I mean? 야, 그냥 잊어버려. 무슨 말인지 알겠지?
I had great time with Jill last night, if you know what I mean. 어젯밤에 질과 끝내주는 시간을 보냈어. 내가 무슨 말을 하는 건지 안다면 말야.

12 | 미드영어 단숨에 따라잡기

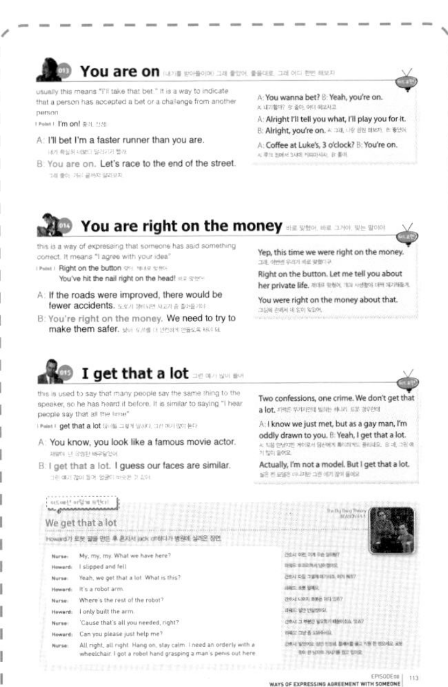
You are on
usually this means "I'll take that bet." It is a way to indicate that a person has accepted a bet or a challenge from another person.
A: I'll bet I'm a faster runner than you are.
B: You are on. Let's race to the end of the street.
A: You wanna bet? B: Yeah, you're on.
A: Alright I'll tell you what, I'll play you for it. B: Alright, you're on.
A: Coffee at Luke's, 3 o'clock? B: You're on.

You are right on the money
this is a way of expressing that someone has said something correct. It means "I agree with your idea"
| Point | Right on the button
You've hit the nail right on the head!
A: If the roads were improved, there would be fewer accidents.
B: You're right on the money. We need to try to make them safer.
Yep, this time we were right on the money.
Right on the button. Let me tell you about her private life.
You were right on the money about that.

I get that a lot
this is used to say that many people say the same thing to the speaker, so he has heard it before. It is similar to saying "I hear people say that all the time"
| Point | get that a lot
A: You know, you look like a famous movie actor.
B: I get that a lot. I guess our faces are similar.
Two confessions, one crime. We don't get that a lot.
A: I know we just met, but as a gay man, I'm oddly drawn to you. B: Yeah, I get that a lot.
Actually, I'm not a model. But I get that a lot.

We get that a lot

EPISODE 06 | 113
WAYS OF EXPRESSING AGREEMENT WITH SOMEONE

미드에선 이렇게 쓰인다!
실제 미드에서 쓰이는 장면을 생생하게 들여다보는 공간.

01 What can I say?
<Friends 2-18>
Monica: Alright, before I tell you, uh, why don't you tell me how many women you've been with.
Richard: Two.
Monica: Two? TWO? How is that possible? I mean, have you seen you?
Richard: Well, I mean what can I say? I, I was married to Barbara for 30 years. She was my high school sweetheart, now you, that's two.
Monica: Two it is. Okay, time for bed, I'm gonna go brush my teeth.
Richard: Woah, woah, no wait a minute now. C'mon it's your turn. Oh c'mon. Ya know, I don't need the actual number, just a ballpark.
Monica: Okay, it is definitely less than a ballpark.

02 What do you want from me?
<Sex and the City 1-7>
Carrie: How many women are you dating?
BIG: In the tri-state area?
Carrie: Well, let's see, there's me, um, Julia, and let's not forget international Melissa.
BIG: I'm not doing this here.
Carrie: Fine.
BIG: Can't we just enjoy the party?
Carrie: I don't know.
BIG: Come on, I mean, what do you want from me?

730 | 미드영어 단숨에 따라잡기

Supplement : 미드 속 "미드영어 단숨에 따라잡기 37"
37개의 미드 명장면을 통해서 미드단숨에 따라잡기의 표현들이 어떻게 쓰였는지를 확인하는 자리.

CONTENTS

Ways to communicate well with each other(1)

서로의 말을 이해하기 위해 의사소통하기 (1)

Are you with me?

001 You got it? 알았어?

the speaker is asking "Did you understand the meaning of what was said?" He wants to know if he was clearly understood

| Point | You got that? 알아 들었어?

A: You need to be at the airport at 7am. **You got it?** 오전 7시까지 공항에 와야 돼. 알았어?

B: Sure, I got it. I'll be there on time. 어, 알았어. 제때 갈게.

Watch her closely, you got it? 걔를 주의해서 봐. 알았지?

Nobody moves. You got that? 다들 꼼짝마. 알겠어?

Now, lock the door. You got it?
이제 문을 잠그라고. 알았어?

You don't ever talk to me again, you got it? 넌 다시는 내게 말걸지마, 알았어?

002 You got me 내말 알아들었지

미드표현

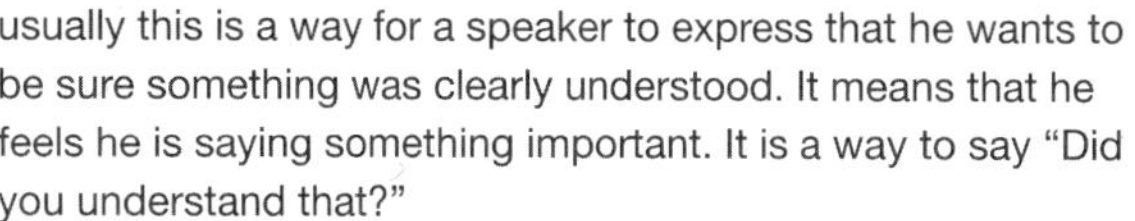

usually this is a way for a speaker to express that he wants to be sure something was clearly understood. It means that he feels he is saying something important. It is a way to say "Did you understand that?"

| Point | get sb …의 말을 이해하다, 알아듣다

A: I don't want anyone smoking in the house. **You got me.** 집에서는 어느 누구도 금연이야. 알아들었지.

B: Sure. I will tell everyone to smoke outside.
물론. 다들 나가서 담배피라고 할게.

I'm telling you. Talk to someone. You got me?
정말이야. 누구한테 말해봐. 알았어?

You stay away from him, or you'll be one sorry individual. You got me?
걔 근처에 얼씬하지마, 그렇지 않으면 넌 후회하게 될거야. 알겠어?

Do it now! You got me? 지금 당장 그걸 해! 알았어?

I will break every bone in your body. You got me? 내가 네 몸안의 모든 뼈를 부셔놓을거야. 알았어?

003 Do you hear me? 1. (내가 한 말) 알았지? 2. (무선통신) 내 말 들려?

미드표현

this is a way of asking if a person has physically heard something that has been said. It is similar to asking "Am I loud enough to be heard?"

| Point | Did you hear me? 내 말 들었어?
(Do) You hear? 1. 들리니? 2. (내가 한 말) 알겠니?

A: This place needs to be cleaned before you leave. **Do you hear me?** 가기 전에 여기 청소해놔. 알았지?

B: Yeah. It's impossible not to hear you because you're shouting so loud. 그렇게 소리치는데 못들을 수없지.

I want an explanation, James, do you hear me? 제임스, 설명을 해줘야지, 알겠어?

Helen, you're history! Do you hear me?
헬렌, 넌 한물 갔어! 알겠어?

You're everything to me, you hear?
넌 내 전부야, 알겠어?

Did you hear me? I said she is married.
내 말 알겠어? 걔 결혼했다고.

004 You know what I mean? 1. 무슨 말인지 알겠어? 2. (평서문) 너도 알겠지만

미드표현

this is a way of asking if a person has understood an idea that was expressed by the speaker. It is like asking "Do you understand my idea?"

| Point | If you know what I mean 내가 무슨 말 하는지 안다면 말야

A: I'd really like to be rich in the future. **You know what I mean?** 앞으로 정말 부자가 되고 싶어. 무슨 말인지 알겠어?

B: I think a lot of people dream of having money.
많은 사람들이 돈을 갖는 꿈을 꾸는 것 같아.

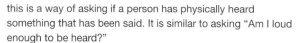

I need more time. You know what I mean?
시간이 더 필요해. 무슨 말인지 알지?

Hey, man, just let it go. You know what I mean? 야, 그냥 잊어버려. 무슨 말인지 알겠지?

I had a great time with Jill last night, if you know what I mean.
어젯밤에 질과 끝내주는 시간을 보냈어, 내가 무슨 말을 하는 건지 안다면 말야.

005 (Do you) Know what I'm saying?

무슨 말인지 알겠니?, 네 생각은 어때?

it asks "Do you understand what I said?" The speaker wants to know if a person has understood the idea or concept that was expressed

| Point | See what I'm saying? 무슨 말인지 알지?
If you know what I'm saying 내가 하는 말이 무슨 말인지 안다면 말야

A: I think we need to get some sleep now. **Know what I'm saying?** 이제 우리 좀 자야 돼. 내 말 알아들었어?

B: But I'm not tired enough to go to bed yet.
하지만 아직 잘 정도로 피곤하진 않아.

You have to get this done by Friday. Know what I'm saying?
금요일까지 이거 끝내야 돼. 내 말 알아 들었어?

I'm probably gonna be in the mood for dance. You know what I'm saying?
춤추고 싶어질 것 같아. 무슨 말인지 알지?

Do you understand what I'm saying?
내 말 알아들었어?

006 Do I have to spell it out (for you)?

도대체 어떻게 해야 이해가 되겠니?

this is a question that asks if someone needs something explained more deeply in order to understand it. It is like asking "Should I say it to you more clearly?"

| Point | I have got to spell it out for you 내 자세히 설명해줄게
Do I have to spell it out for you? 다시 분명히 설명해야 돼?

A: Why are Bob and Martha looking so sad?
밥과 마사가 왜 그리 슬퍼보여?

B: **Do I have to spell it out for you?** They've been arguing. 꼭 꼬치꼬치 얘기해야 알아? 다퉜다고.

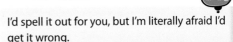

I'd spell it out for you, but I'm literally afraid I'd get it wrong.
너한테 자세히 설명해줄 수 있지만 내가 틀릴까봐 정말 걱정 돼.

Look, let me spell it out for you, Avery.
이봐, 에이버리, 내가 자세히 설명해줄게.

He didn't spell it out, but I think that means you're gonna have to have a funeral without the body.
걔는 자세히 말은 안했지만 내 생각은 그 말은 네가 시신없이 장례를 치러야 할거야.

007 Are you with me?

1. 내 말 이해돼? 2. 내 편이 돼 줄테야?, 나랑 같이 할거지?

this asks "Have you understood me so far?" The speaker wants to know if someone has understood what was said

| Point | We're with you 이해돼, 난 네 편이야

A: How are we going to pass this exam?
이 시험 통과하려면 어떻게 해야 돼?

B: We'll just have to study all night. **Are you with me?** 그냥 밤새 공부해야 돼. 내 말 이해돼?

Are you with me on this? 이거 알아듣겠니?

So are you with me or not? 그럼 나랑 같은 편 할래 말래?

Are you with me? Leave her alone, Larry.
내 말 이해돼? 래리야, 걔를 괴롭히지마.

008 I get the point

무슨 말인지 이해했어

this usually indicates that the speaker has completely understood something. It is a way of saying "I see what you mean"

| Point | You take my point? 내 말뜻을 알겠어?

A: I don't want anyone smoking in this building.
이 건물에서는 아무도 담배피지마.

B: **I get the point.** I won't do that. 알겠어. 안 그럴게.

I just never really got the point of it.
난 정말이지 그걸 전혀 이해하지 못했어.

Stop explaining. I get the point.
그만 설명해. 무슨 말인지 알겠어.

You don't want to go with me. I get the point.
넌 나와 가기 싫어하는구나. 무슨 뜻인지 알겠어.

009 Do I make myself clear? 내 말 알아 들었지?, 내 말 이해하겠어?

this is asking "Have you understood?" The speaker wants to know if everyone has understood something important that was said

| Point | I didn't make myself clear 내 말 뜻을 이해시키지 못했구만

A: I don't allow cell phones to be used in class. **Do I make myself clear?**
수업중엔 핸드폰 사용금지다. 내 말 알아들었지?

B: But sir, what if there is an emergency call from my parents? 하지만 선생님, 부모님한테서 긴급전화가 오면은요?

Did I make myself clear? I'll say it again.
내 말 알아 들었지? 다시 말해줄게.

I'm going to need a little bit more compensation. Do I make myself clear?
난 더 보상이 필요해. 내 말 이해하겠어?

A: Do I make myself clear? B: It won't happen again. A: 내말 알아들었지? B: 다시는 그러지 않을게요.

010 Is that clear? 내 말 알겠지?, 무슨 뜻인지 알겠지?

미드표현

this is similar to the previous phrase. It is asking if an important thing the speaker said was understood. It is like asking "Did you understand what I said?"

| Point | Is that clear? 내말 알겠지?

A: I don't ever want to see you again. **Is that clear?** 널 다신 보고 싶지 않아. 알겠어?

B: Fine! Here is your engagement ring back.
좋아! 자 여기 약혼반지 다시 가져가.

This is just sex. Is that clear?
이건 그냥 섹스일 뿐이야. 내 말 알겠어?

You can't have a vacation this year. Is that clear? 금년에 휴가없어. 알겠어?

Is that clear? Do you have any questions for us? 내말 알겠지? 우리한테 뭐 질문있어?

011 I can't get through to her 난 걔를 이해시킬 수가 없어

미드표현

this means that the speaker has tried to convince someone of something, but he has been unable to. He probably feels unhappy, because he thinks what he is saying makes sense. In other words, "I tried to make her understand my way of thinking, but she won't listen"

| Point | get through to sb …에게 이해시키다. …와 말이 통하다. 전화가 통하다

A: Haven't you warned Alice about drinking too much? 앨리스에게 과음에 대해 경고를 하지 않았어?

B: Yes, but **I can't get through to her.**
했는데 걜 이해시킬 수가 없어.

I don't think you're gonna get through to him.
난 네가 걔를 이해시킬거라 생각하지 않아.

We've done everything we could to try and get through to him.
우리는 걔를 이해시키기 위해 안해본 짓이 없어.

Every day is a battle. I don't know how to get through to her.
매일매일이 전쟁야. 어떻게 걔하고 말이 통할지를 모르겠어.

012 Get the message? (무슨 말인지) 알아들었어?

this is a somewhat rude and curt way of asking if someone understood something clearly. It means "Do you understand what I said?"

| Point | get the message 알아듣다, 메시지를 받다

A: Sara, why don't you ever talk to me anymore?
새라야, 왜 더 이상 나랑 얘기 안 하는 거야?

B: Because you're a loser. I don't like you. **Get the message?** 넌 머저리니까. 네가 싫다고. 알겠어?

All right, I get the message. 좋아, 알아들었어.

I'm so sorry, I didn't get the message.
미안, 무슨 말인지 못 알아들었어.

Ziva, call us as soon as you get the message.
지바, 이 메시지 받으면 바로 전화해.

Didn't you get the message? He's not going.
메시지 못 받았어? 걔 안가.

013 Don't you see? 모르겠어?, 그거 몰라?

often this is a way of asking a person "Can't you understand?" The speaker may not be sure if someone understands something

| Point | Don't you see how[when] S+V?
…을 몰랐어?(= Isn't it clear that S+V?)

A: How are we going to get enough money to buy a house? 어떻게 해야 집을 살 충분한 돈을 갖게 될까?

B: **Don't you see?** We'll both have to get jobs and save our salaries. 모르겠어? 맞벌이 하면서 월급을 저축해야 돼.

This won't help, don't you see?
이건 도움이 안될거야, 모르겠어?

I do love you. Don't you see? Don't you understand? You're the love of my life.
널 사랑해. 그거 몰라? 모르냐고? 넌 내 인생의 유일한 사랑이야.

This won't help, don't you see?
이건 도움이 안될거야, 모르겠어?

014 Don't you know? 몰랐어?

usually this expresses surprise that a person doesn't have information. It is similar to saying "I can't believe that you didn't get that information"

| Point | Don't you know? 몰랐단 말야?

A: Have you seen Jenna around the office recently? 최근 사무실에서 제나 본 적 있어?

B: **Don't you know?** She had an accident and is in the hospital. 몰랐어? 사고나서 병원에 있어.

What, what don't you know? I've explained the entire thing to you.
뭐라고, 몰랐다고? 너한테 모든 거 다 설명해줬잖아.

Don't you know she was arrested last night?
걔가 어젯밤에 잡힌 걸 몰랐어?

Don't you know fast food will make you fat?
패스트푸드 먹으면 살찐다는 걸 몰랐어?

Don't you know cars cost a lot of money?
자동차가 비싸다는 걸 몰랐어?

015 I got it 알았어, 알아들었어, 무슨 말인지 알겠어

this is a way to say "I understand now." It indicates that an idea or meaning has been understood

| Point | Got it 알았어, 이해해
I get it 알겠어

A: Do you need some more help understanding your homework? 숙제 이해하는 거 좀 도와줄까?

B: No thank you. **I got it** now. 고맙지만 됐어. 이해했어.

It's fine[okay]. I got it. 좋아. 알았어.

A: I think that I'm going to be sick.
B: I got it. Go get some fresh air.
A: 속이 좀 안 좋아. B: 무슨 말인지 알겠어. 가서 바람 좀 쐬고 와.

Oh, God! I'm sorry! I got it.
맙소사! 미안해! 무슨 말인지 알겠어.

I got it. Seven digits... It's a phone number.
알았어. 일곱자리라…. 이건 전화번호야.

016 You got it 1. 알았어 2. 맞아, 바로 그거야

this expresses "I'll do it for you." The speaker is saying yes to something that was asked for. Also this means "That's right." The speaker is indicating that a person understood something correctly

| Point | You got it 알았어, 바로 그거야

A: Can I borrow your CD player tomorrow?
낼 시디플레이어 좀 빌려줄래?

B: **You got it.** I'd be glad to lend it to you.
알았어. 기꺼이 빌려줄게.

I think you got it. 알아들었을텐데.

You want my attention, Jack? You got it.
내 관심을 원한다고, 잭? 알았어.

A: Is this the subway station we will get off at?
B: You got it. Let's get going.
A: 이 전철역이 우리가 내릴 곳야? B: 맞아. 가자고.

017 You get the idea 너도 이해할거야, 무슨 말인지 알겠지

this speaker is expressing that a listener has understood the main point that has been talked about. It is a way to say "I think you understand"

| Point | I get the idea 알겠어

A: So you want me to find some people who can join the club? 그럼 클럽 함께 할 사람을 찾아달라는거야?

B: Yeah. **You get the idea.** We need new members. 어, 맞아. 새로운 회원들이 필요해.

미드표현

It's still kind of a mess, but I think you get the idea. 아직 좀 복잡하지만 넌 이해했을거야.

Be romantic, send her flowers. You get the idea. 로맨틱하게 행동해, 걔한테 꽃도 보내고. 무슨 말인지 알겠지.

I don't trust Jim, he creeps me out. You get the idea. 난 짐을 믿지 않아. 소름이 끼쳐. 너도 이해할거야.

018 I can see that 알겠어, 알고 있어, 알아

this means "That is clear to me." It indicates that a person understands something well

| Point | I can see that S+V …임을 알겠다, …이구나

A: **I can see** that Jack has a new suit. 잭이 새로운 옷을 입었네.

B: Yes, he bought it for his graduation ceremony. 그래, 졸업식 때 입으려고 샀대.

미드표현

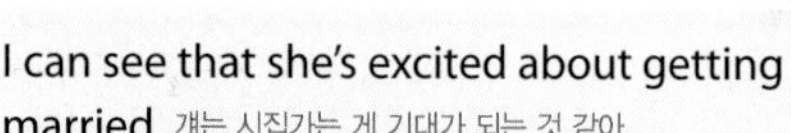

I can see that she's excited about getting married. 걔는 시집가는 게 기대가 되는 것 같아.

A: She can't stop crying.
B: I can see that! What did you guys do to her?
A: 걔가 울음을 멈추지 않아 B: 알고 있어! 도대체 무슨 짓을 한거야?

A: Get the fuck out of my yard!
B: Okay, I can see that you're upset.
A: 내 집에서 꺼져! B: 알았어, 너 화났구나.

019 I can imagine 무슨 말인지 알겠어, 그래 이해해

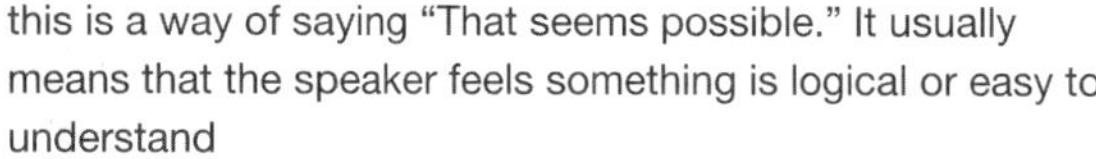

this is a way of saying "That seems possible." It usually means that the speaker feels something is logical or easy to understand

| Point | I can imagine (that) S+V …을 짐작하겠어

A: It's really difficult when a family member is sick. 가족이 아프면 정말 힘들어.

B: **I can imagine.** You must be very worried about your mom. 무슨 말인지 알겠어. 엄마걱정이 많이 되겠구나.

미드표현

I can imagine it must have been like a nightmare. 악몽과 같았을거라고 짐작돼.

A: Sorry about the mess. It's been busy lately.
B: I can imagine.
A: 좀 정신없지, 미안해. 요새 바빠서 말야. B: 그래 무슨 말인지 알겠어.

020 I get your point 무슨 말인지 알아들었어, 알겠어

this is usually said when someone wants to indicate that an idea has been understood. It means "I see what you mean"

| Point | I (can) see your point 무슨 말인지 알겠어

A: I hope you understand what I've been explaining. 내가 뭘 설명하는지 알겠지.

B: Oh, yes, I do. **I get your point.** 어, 그래. 알겠어.

미드표현

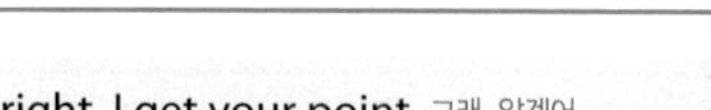

All right, I get your point. 그래, 알겠어.

A: Okay! Okay! I get your point.
B: All righty, then, my work here is done.
A: 알겠어! 무슨 말을 하는지 알겠다고. B: 그래 그럼 내가 할 일은 끝났네.

021 I know[hear] what you're saying 무슨 말인지 알아

미드표현

this is a way of agreeing with a statement that has been made. It is similar to saying "Yes, that's right"

| Point | I know what you're talking about 그럴만도 해
I know where you're coming from
어떻게 해서 그 말이 나왔는지 알겠어, 네 말에 동의해

A: I've been freezing in this winter weather we've been having. 이번 겨울 날씨에 얼어붙겠어.

B: **I know what you're saying.** Everyone feels cold these days. 무슨 말인지 알겠어. 요즘 다들 추워해.

Oh, yeah, I know what you're saying. You want my money. 무슨 말인지 알겠어. 내 돈이 필요하다 이거지.

I hear what you're saying, and truth be told, I am a little nervous.
그래, 네가 하는 말이 뭔지 알겠어. 솔직히 조금 긴장돼.

I know what you're saying. Hey, you know what I should do?
무슨 말인지 알겠어. 야, 내가 뭘 해야 되는지 알아?

022 I've been there 1. 나도 그런 적 있어, 정말 그 심정 이해해 2. 가본 적 있어

미드표현

the speaker wants to say "It was the same for me." It indicates that the speaker has shared a similar experience

| Point | We have all been there 우리도 모두 그런 적 있잖아
Been there? 그런 적 있어?, 가본적 있어?

A: My salary is so small that I can't pay my bills.
월급이 너무 적어서 공과금도 못내겠어.

B: **I've been there.** You need to look for something better. 그 심정 이해해. 더 좋은 걸 찾아봐.

Believe me, I understand. I've been there.
정말이야. 이해해. 나도 그런 적 있어.

I've been there. We're human.
나도 그런 적 있어. 우린 다 사람이잖아.

I've been there more times than I can remember. 기억못할 정도로 여러 번 가봤어.

Been there done that. (전에도 해본 것이어서) 뻔할 뻔자지.

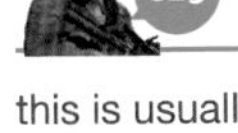

023 I know what you mean 무슨 말인지 알아, 나도 그렇게 생각해

미드표현

this is usually said to express agreement with someone. It is often indicating "I had a similar experience"

| Point | I know what you mean 무슨 말인지 알겠어
I know what you meant 무슨 말이었는지 알겠어

A: I hope we can have a nice vacation this year.
금년에 멋진 휴가를 갔으면 해.

B: **I know what you mean.** It's refreshing to get away for a while. 무슨 말인지 알아. 잠시 벗어나 있는 것도 재충전이 돼.

I know what you mean. My father does the same thing. 무슨 말인지 알아. 아버지도 그래.

I know what you mean. I do that too.
무슨 말인지 알아. 나도 그래.

Yes, it's all right. I know what you meant.
그래 괜찮아. 무슨 말이었는지 알겠어.

024 I get the picture 알겠어, 이해됐어

미드표현

this is a way of saying "It's clear to me." It means that something has been understood

| Point | Now you're getting the picture 이제 (상황이 어떻게 돌아가는지) 아는구만
I get the hint 나 눈치챘어

A: I want you to have your homework done in an hour. Understood? 한 시간내로 숙제마쳐. 알았어?

B: Sure, Mom. **I get the picture.** 네, 엄마. 알겠어요.

I think you get the picture. 네가 이제 이해할 것 같아.

I think I'm beginning to get the picture.
이제 내가 이해를 하기 시작하는 것 같아.

I get the picture, but I'm a little fuzzy on how this makes your client insane.
알겠지만 어떻게 이 일로 네 고객의 꼭지가 돌았는지 알쏭달쏭해.

My history teacher is also the football coach, get the picture? 내 역사 선생님이 미식축구 감독야, 알겠어?

025 I can tell 알고 있어, 그렇게 보여

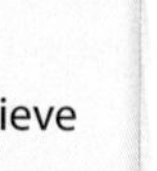

this is used often when someone wants to express that something is obvious. It's like saying "I know that"

| Point | I can tell (that) S+V ···을 알겠어
From what I can tell 내가 보는 바로는
As far as I can tell 내가 보는 한

A: I felt sick yesterday. 어제 아팠어.
B: **I can tell.** You still look kind of unhealthy.
그렇게 보여. 아직 안좋아 보여.

I can tell. A real man always stands out in a crowd. 알아. 진정한 남자는 군중 속에서도 드러나는 법이지.

I can tell by your tone that you don't believe me. 네 목소리로 날 믿지 않는다는 걸 알겠어.

From what I can tell, he was shot once in the chest. 내가 보기에 그 사람은 가슴에 총 한 방을 맞았어.

026 Duly noted (무슨 말인지) 알아

this means "I understood your opinion." We can understand that the speaker may or may not agree with that opinion

| Point | duly noted 무슨 말인지 알아

A: We need to update the software we are using.
우리가 쓰는 소프트웨어 업데이트 해야 돼.
B: **Duly noted.** I will check up on it. 알았어. 확인해볼게.
A: May I say how lovely you look today?
오늘 굉장히 예뻐 보이는 거 알아?
B: **Duly noted.** 응, 알았어.

Duly noted. And I'll stay out of your business too. 무슨 말인지 알겠어. 네 일을 방해하지 않을게.

Okay. Was not aware of that. Duly noted.
알았어. 난 그걸 모르고 있었어. 이제 알겠어.

Not what the psychic in the subway told me, but duly noted.
전철에서 심령술사가 내게 말한 것은 아니지만 무슨 말인지 알겠어.

027 Say no more 더 말 안해도 알아, 무슨 말인지 말 안 해도 알겠어

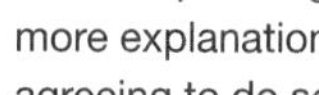

this is expressing that something has been understood and no more explanation is necessary. It can also mean the person is agreeing to do something. Another way to say it is "Yes, I see what you mean"

| Point | Say no more 더 말안해도 알아

A: Would you be willing to substitute for me at work tomorrow? 내일 직장에서 내대신 일 좀 해줄테야?
B: Yeah. **Say no more.** I know it's your daughter's birthday. 그래, 알겠어. 딸 생일이지.

Well, say no more. You know it takes guts to bring this up.
더 말 안해도 돼. 이걸 얘기하는 건 굉장히 용기있는 일이야.

Got it. Say no more. Really say no more.
알았어. 무슨 말인지 말 안해도 알겠어.

Say no more, it'll be our little secret.
더 말 안해도 알아. 그건 우리의 비밀로 하자.

028 Now I understand 이제 알겠어, 이제 이해돼

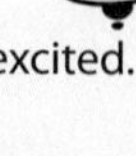

this a way to say "OK, I know what it means." It indicates that the speaker finally gets the main point of something that was said

| Point | I understand S+V ···라는 걸 알겠어

A: I need to get my car repaired this weekend.
이번주에 차 수리해야 돼.
B: OK, so you'll be busy. **Now I understand.**
그래, 그럼 바쁘겠네. 이제 알겠어.

Now I understand why people are so excited.
사람들이 왜 그토록 흥분되어 있는지 이제야 알겠어.

Now I understand what he was talking about.
이제야 그 친구의 말이 이해돼.

Now I understand why you want your vacation time. 네가 휴식이 필요하다고 한 이유를 이제야 알겠다.

029 I'll do that (알았어) 그럴게, 그렇게 할게

this usually means "I'm going to finish this job." It is said to confirm that something is going to be done or completed by the speaker

| Point | Will do 그럴게 = I'll do that
I think I'll do that 내가 할게

A: We really need someone to help us move to another apartment.
다른 아파트로 이사가는데 도와줄 사람이 정말 필요해.

B: Really? I didn't know you needed help. **I'll do that.** 정말? 도움을 필요로 하는 줄 몰랐어. 내가 도와줄게.

미드표현

A: If I'm gonna give myself to you, you better worship me! B: And I will do that.
A: 내가 너한테 가면 잘해주어야 돼! B: 그럴게.

A: False alarm. You can go back to sleep.
B: Oh, I think I'll do that.
A: 잘못 울린 알람이었어. 다시 자도 돼. B: 그렇게 할게.

I'll do that. It'll be faster, I type ninety words a minute. 내가 할게. 난 분당 90타를 치기 때문에 더 빠를거야.

030 Yeah, that'll be happening 어 그럴거야, 응 알았어, 응 그렇게 될거야

this is a way of saying that some event is going to occur in the future. The speaker wants to say "It will take place"

| Point | will be happening 그렇게 될거야

A: I heard you're getting a new computer delivered.
새 컴퓨터 온다며?

B: Yeah, **that'll be happening** tomorrow. 어, 낼 올거야.

None of this would be happening.
이 중 어떤 것도 일어나지 않을거야.

If I had only left you alone from the beginning, none of this would be happening.
내가 첨부터 널 내버려뒀다면 이 중 어떤 일도 일어나지 않았을거야.

All of this will just be happening for her all over again. 이 모든 일이 전부 다시 그녀에게 일어날거야.

If it weren't for you, none of this would be happening to me.
네가 아니라면 이 어떤 일도 나한테 일어나지 않을거야.

031 Point well taken 무슨 말인지 잘 알았어

the speaker is saying "I see what you mean." This is expressing that an idea was understood and thought about

| Point | Point well taken 무슨 말인지 잘 알겠어

A: If you get a job overseas, you'll be lonely and miss your family. 해외 취업하면 외롭고 가족이 그리울거야.

B: **Point well taken.** I'll have to discuss it with them. 무슨 말인지 잘 알겠어. 가족과 상의해봐야겠어.

Point well taken! I'll bring the wine.
무슨 말인지 잘 알았어! 와인을 가져올게.

Point well taken. I'll call you tomorrow.
무슨 말인지 잘 알았어. 내일 전화할게.

I don't agree, but your point is well taken.
난 동의하지 않지만 네 말이 무슨 말인지 잘 알겠어.

I see what you are saying. Point well taken.
무슨 말인지 잘 알겠어. 잘 알아들었어.

032 That explains it 그럼 설명이 되네, 아 그래서 이런 거구나, 이제 알겠네

this is a way to indicate that the reason for something happening can now be understood. It is like saying "I see the reason why"

| Point | It all adds up 앞뒤가 들어 맞아

A: I left a bottle of wine outside your door last night. 간밤에 너네집 문밖에 와인 한병을 놔두었어.

B: I wondered where it came from. **That explains it.** 어디서 온건가 그랬어. 이제 알겠구만.

Well, I guess that explains it. 어, 그럼 설명이 되는 것 같아.

It all adds up! You have a major crush on her.
이제 알겠다! 너 걔한테 완전히 반했구나.

Oh, okay that explains it. I got a call at two in the morning.
어, 그래 그래서 그런거구만. 새벽 2시에 전화가 왔었거든.

033 Fill in the blanks 빈칸을 채우시오, 네가 맞춰봐, 결론이 어떻게 되는지 감이 잡혀

the speaker wants to say that something can be understood if it's thought about carefully. It's another way to say "Think about it and you'll understand"

I Point I fill in the blanks 서류의 빈 곳에 채워넣다, 기입하다, 알아맞추다

A: Why are Carla and Dave getting a divorce?
칼라와 데이브가 왜 이혼한대?

B: Did you see Carla's boyfriend? Come on, **fill in the blanks.** 칼라의 애인 봤어? 자, 감잡아봐.

You're trying to fill in the blanks? 알아 맞춰볼래?

Can you fill in the blanks? 알아 맞출 수 있어?

You want to fill in the blanks? 알아 맞출래?

034 I think I know the answer to that 알 것 같아, 왜인지 알 것 같아

this is a way to express "I know why that is." It indicates that the speaker probably understands the reason for something

I Point I know the answer to …의 답을 알다

A: Why do you think the earth has gotten hotter recently? 왜 지구가 최근에 더 온난해진다고 생각해?

B: **I think I know the answer to that.** 알 것 같아.

I don't think I'm gonna know the answer to that for a while. 얼마 동안 그에 대한 답이 없을 것 같아.

I think I know the answer to this question.
이 문제 답 알 것 같아.

It'd be nice to know the answer to everything.
모든 문제에 답을 알고 있다면 얼마나 멋질까?

035 (I hear you) Loud and clear 1. (무선통신) 잘 들려 2. 잘 알았어

this is a way of expressing that the speaker has understood or agrees with something. Another way to say it is "I know how you feel"

I Point I Roger that (무선통신) 상대방 이야기를 잘 알았다, 오바
Do you read me? 1. (무선통신) 내 말 들려? 2. 무슨 말인지 알겠어?

A: I'd like you to finish the report asap.
가능한 한 빨리 이 보고서를 끝내 줘.

B: Alright, I hear you **loud and clear.** 그래, 잘 알았어.

We heard you loud and clear.
네가 하는 말 아주 분명히 잘 들었어.

A: Do you read me? B: Yes, sir. Loud and clear.
A: 내 말 잘 들리나? B: 네, 아주 잘 들립니다.

Message received, loud and clear.
메시지 아주 잘 알아들었어.

His prints speak loud and clear.
걔 지문은 아주 분명하게 말해주고 있어.

036 He knows what's what 걘 (뭐가 뭔지) 진상을 알아, (…에 대해) 아주 잘 알아

usually this is a way to express "He understands about that." It indicates that the person being spoken about has a lot of knowledge about something

I Point I He knows the score 그 사람은 사정을 알고 있어
What's what? 뭐가 뭔데? 뭐가 뭐라니?

A: Call Tom over. **He knows what's what** with electronic gadgets. 탐불러. 전기기구에 대해 잘 알아.

B: Oh yeah? Do you think he can fix my MP3 player? 어 그래? 내 MP3도 고칠 수 있을 것 같아?

Ask Jack about the computer program. He knows what's what.
컴퓨터 프로그램은 잭에게 알아봐. 걔가 아주 잘 알아.

He knows what's what. He helps everyone out. 걔가 사실을 잘 알고 있어. 걔가 사람들을 도와주고 있어.

He will be giving the tour because he knows what's what. 걔가 잘 알기 때문에 둘러보여줄거야.

037 That's what I'm saying 내 말이 바로 그거야

this means "That is the idea I have been talking about." It indicates that a person has understood what a a speaker has been saying

Point That's what I say 내 생각이 그래
(*That's what I'm saying은 상대방이 자기와 같은 의견임을, That's what I say는 자신의 의견을 표현)

A: We really need to work harder here.
정말 여기서 열심히 일해야 돼.

B: **That's what I've been saying.** Everyone is too lazy. 내말이 바로 그거야. 다들 너무 게을러.

That's what I'm saying. She's a little old for me.
내 말이 바로 그거야. 걘 나에게 나이가 좀 많아.

You see? That's what I'm saying.
알았지? 내 말이 바로 그 말이야.

That's what I'm saying. Of course they didn't.
내 말이 바로 그 말이야. 당연히 걔네들이 그러지 않았어.

038 All I'm saying is I can do it 단지 내 말은 내가 할 수 있다는 거야

미드표현

this indicates the speaker thinks he's able to complete something. It's like saying "I can take care of that"

Point All I'm saying is+N/ do/ (that) S+V 내가 말하고자 하는 건 …이다
That's all I'm saying 내 말이 그거야

A: Do you have enough experience to do this job?
이 일을 할 수 있는 경험이 충분해?

B: I don't know. **All I'm saying is I can do it.**
몰라. 내가 말할 수 있는건 내가 할 수 있다는 거야.

All I'm saying is five days is what I need.
단지 내가 하고자 하는 말은 5일이 필요하다는 거야.

All I'm saying is just talk to Angela. Okay?
내가 하고자 하는 말은 안젤라에게 말하라는 거야. 응?

All I'm saying is don't judge Bill before you get to know him. All right?
내가 말하고자 하는 건 빌을 알기 전엔 판단하지 말라는거야. 알았어?

039 (It's) Just what I need 바로 그게 내가 필요한거야

미드표현

usually this expresses that the speaker has received something useful. It's like saying "I can really use that"

Point That's all I need to do~ 내가 필요한 건 …하는 것 뿐이야
All I need is ~ 내가 필요한 건 …야

A: Did you like the new coat I bought for you?
내가 사준 새 코트 맘에 들어?

B: Sure. **It's just what I need** for the winter weather. 그럼. 겨울철에 딱 필요한건데.

It was just what I needed. 바로 그게 내가 필요한 거였어.

I know that sounds selfish, but it's just what I need. 이기적으로 들리겠지만 그게 바로 내가 원하는 거야.

You're just what I need. 넌 바로 내가 원하는 사람야.

040 You took the words right out of my mouth
내 말이 그 말이야

미드표현

the speaker is saying that someone said what he has been thinking. It is like saying "Your thoughts are the same as mine about this"

Point take the words right out of one's mouth …가 하려는 말을 해버리다

A: I think it is time to take a coffee break right now.
이제 커피 좀 마시면서 쉬자.

B: **You took the words right out of my mouth.** Let's go! 내말이 그말야. 가자!

You took the words right out of my mouth. I couldn't have said it better.
내말이 바로 그 말이야. 정말 동감이야.

That's just what I was thinking. You took the words right out of my mouth.
내가 생각하던게 바로 그거야. 내말이 바로 그 말이라고..

041 That's my point 내 말이 그거야, 바로 그거야

this means "That was what I was trying to explain." The speaker is saying that someone understood the main idea he talked about

I Point I That's my point 내말이 바로 그거야

A: So you think that we need to have a better government? 그래 넌 더 나은 정부를 가져야 한다는 거지?

B: Yes, **that's my point.** A better government will help everyone.
그래, 바로 그거야. 더 나은 정부가 모두에게 도움이 될거야.

That's my point. I didn't do it.
그게 바로 내 말이야. 난 안그랬다니까.

That's my point. I'm getting old.
내 말이 바로 그거야. 내가 늙어간다고.

A: A call girl can't get raped?
B: Yeah, that's my point.
A: 창녀는 강간당할 수가 없다고? B: 어, 내말이 바로 그거야.

A: It's hard to find a man when you're a single mom. B: That's my point.
A: 싱글맘이면 남자를 찾기가 어려워. B: 내말이 바로 그거야.

042 That's the thing! 그거라니까!, 그렇지!, 바로 그게 문제야!

this means "You talked about what I was thinking about." It is a way to indicate someone understood what the speaker wanted to say

I Point I That's the thing about sth 그게 바로 …의 다른 점(특징)이야
That's the stuff[spirit, ticket]! 바로 그거야!, 잘했어!

A: I know we need to be careful when we invest our money. 돈을 투자할 때는 주의해야 된다는 걸 알아.

B: **That's the thing!** If you aren't careful, you can lose everything. 그렇지! 신중하게 안하면 모든 걸 잃을 수 있어.

That's the thing. I don't know what I want to do. 바로 그게 문제야. 내가 원하는 게 뭔지 모르겠어.

That's the thing about Las Vegas. You never know what's around the corner.
바로 그게 라스베거스가 다른 점이지. 눈앞의 일도 전혀 모르거든.

That's the thing about really good friends.
그게 바로 진정한 친구가 다른 점이지.

043 That's who~ 그게 바로 …한 사람이야

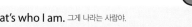

this is a way to mention what a person did. It is another way to say "He was the person that S+V"

I Point I That's that~ …해서 그래

A: You said that your uncle and aunt traveled here from Canada. 네 삼촌과 숙모가 캐나다에서 이리로 여행오셨다고 했지.

B: **That's who** I was taking out for dinner last weekend. 지난 주말 내가 모시고 나가서 식사하신 분들이야.

That's who I am. 그게 나라는 사람야.

That's who he talked to. 그가 얘기를 나누던 사람야.

That's who you are, you son of a bitch!
이게 바로 너라는 인간이구나, 이 빌어먹을 자식!

044 That's the idea 바로 그거야, 바로 그럴 생각야, 좋은 생각이야

this is a way to say that someone is thinking in the right way. It indicates "Yes, your thinking is right"

I Point I That's the idea 바로 그거야, 좋은 생각이야

A: Do you want us to stack the boxes over in the corner? 이 박스들은 코너에 쌓아놓을까요?

B: **That's the idea.** We need to clear an area for people to walk around.
좋은 생각야. 사람들이 걸어다니는 공간을 비워둬야지.

Of course they are joining our club. That's the idea. 물론 걔네들 우리 클럽에 가입해. 좋은 생각이야.

That's the idea. We need more customers.
바로 그거야. 우리는 더 많은 고객이 필요해.

I'm losing weight and getting in shape. That's the idea. 나 살이 빠지고 몸상태가 좋아지고 있어. 바로 그거야.

Ways to communicate well with each other(2)

서로의 말을 이해하기 위해 의사소통하기 (2)

What's your point?

001 I don't know what you mean 그게 무슨 말이야

미드표현

this expresses that the speaker doesn't understand something. It's a way to say "I don't understand that"

| Point | I'm not sure what you mean 무슨 말하는 건지 잘 모르겠어
I'm not sure what you mean when you say~
…를 말할 때 그게 무슨 말이야

A: **I'm not sure what you mean** when you say I don't work hard. 내가 열심히 일 안한다는 말이 무슨 말이죠?

B: I mean that I think you are pretty lazy.
자네가 꽤나 게으르다는 거지.

I'm not sure what you mean when you say you're leaving. 네가 떠난다고 말하는 게 무슨 말인지 모르겠어.

I'm just not sure what to do. 뭘 해야할 지 모르겠어.

I don't know what you mean. Why did you say like that? 무슨 말하는지 모르겠어. 왜 그런 식으로 말하는 거야?

002 What do you mean by that? 그게 무슨 말[뜻]이야?

미드표현

this is asking someone to explain a statement that has been made. It's similar to saying "Tell me what that means"

| Point | What do you mean by + ~ing/N? …라니 그게 무슨 말이야?
What do you mean S+V? …라는 그게 무슨 말이야?

A: You need to change your hairstyle. 머리스타일 바꿔.

B: **What do you mean by that?** Do you dislike the way it's cut? 무슨 말야? 자른 게 맘에 안든다는 거야?

What do you mean by telling everyone that I'm gay? 사람들에게 내가 게이라고 말하는 의도가 뭐야?

What do you mean by special treatment?
특별대우라니 그게 무슨 말이야?

What do you mean all your friends know me? Are you saying I'm a whore? 네 친구들이 모두 다 날 알고 있다니 그게 무슨 말이야? 내가 창녀라고 말하는거야?

003 What does that mean? 그게 무슨 뜻이야?, 그게 무슨 말이야?

미드표현

the speaker is asking someone to give more details to make something clear. It is like asking "Can you tell me more?"

| Point | What do you call that[this]? 저걸 뭐라고 하니?

A: You said you need more friends. **What does that mean?** 친구가 더 필요하다고 했는데 그게 무슨 말이야?

B: It means we should try to be more social with people. 사람들과 더 잘 어울리도록 해야 한다는 말야.

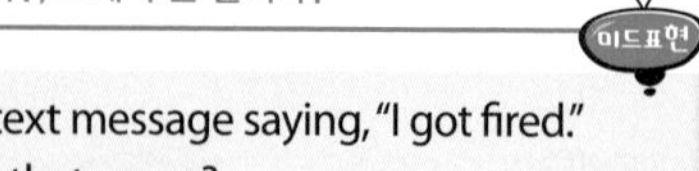

I got your text message saying, "I got fired." What does that mean?
내가 잘렸다는 문자를 받았는데 그게 무슨 말이야?

What do you call a girl who isn't married but had a baby? 처녀지만 애를 낳은 여자를 뭐라고 하니?

No, I want to know. What does that mean?
싫어, 알고 싶어. 그게 무슨 말이야?

004 What are you getting at? 무슨 말을 하려는 거야?

미드표현

this is a way of saying "Tell me that directly." The speaker is asking a person to clearly express something he is speaking about

| Point | I don't know[see] what you're getting at
무슨 말을 하려는 건지 모르겠어
What're you getting into[driving at]? 무슨 일을 하려는 거야?

A: We need to be careful about making noise tonight. 오늘 밤 시끄럽지 않도록 조심해야 돼.

B: **What are you getting at?** Do you think I'm too noisy? 무슨 말 하는 거야? 내가 시끄럽다고?

What on earth is this? What are you getting at? 도대체 이게 뭐야? 무슨 말을 하려는 거야?

I'm not sure I know what you're getting at.
네가 무슨 말을 하려는 건지 잘 모르겠어.

I see what you're getting at. You want to keep me away from her.
무슨 말 하는지 알겠어. 걔하고 가까이 못있게 하려는 거지.

005 I don't follow (you) 무슨 말인지 모르겠어, 무슨 말인지 잘 이해 못하겠어

미드표현

this indicates the speaker hasn't understood something. It is a way of saying "Please explain what you mean"

| Point | Are you following me? 1. 알아듣고 있지? 2. 날 미행하는 거야?

A: You should put these boxes over there. **Are you following me?** 이 상자들 여기에 놔. 알았지?

B: Yes. I understood all of your instructions.
네. 지시한 거 다 알아들었어요.

What do you mean? Are you following me?
그게 무슨 말이야? 내 말 알아듣고 있어?

I don't follow you. Can you explain it to me?
무슨 말이야? 나한테 설명해줄 수 있어?

Hold on, this is confusing. I don't follow you.
잠깐, 이거 헷갈리네. 무슨 말인지 이해 못하겠어.

I don't follow you. Are you saying you committed the crime?
무슨 말하는거야? 범죄를 저질렀단 말야?

006 What're you saying? 그게 무슨 말이야?

미드표현

this is a way to say "I don't think that is right." The speaker is expressing surprise and some disagreement with something that was said

| Point | What're you saying that S+V? …하다니 그게 무슨 말이야?

A: You don't seem to work very hard these days.
너 요즘 열심히 일 안하는 것 같아.

B: **What are you saying?** Do you think I'm lazy?
그게 무슨 말이야? 내가 게으르단 말이야?

What are you saying? Am I fat or am I skinny?
무슨 말이야? 뚱뚱하다는 거야 말랐다는 거야?

So what are you saying? It's now or never?
그래 무슨 말이야? 지금 아니면 기회가 없는거야?

So, what are you saying, that his father murdered her?
그래 무슨 말이야, 걔 아버지가 그 여자를 죽였다는 거야?

007 What're you talking about?
(놀라거나 의아[황당]해하며) 무슨 말을 하는 거야?

미드표현

often this is a way of saying "That idea is wrong." It can be a way to express "I don't understand what you mean." The speaker may be disagreeing with someone, or he may be expressing that he would like something to be explained more clearly

| Point | I don't know what you're talking about 무슨 소리를 하는 거야
What are we talking about? 우리 무슨 얘기하고 있는거지?

A: I told Cindy that you are going to travel to China.
신디한테 네가 중국여행간다고 했어.

B: **What are you talking about?** I'm not going to China! 그게 무슨 말이야? 나 중국 안가!

What're you talking about? Everybody loves you. 그게 무슨 말이야? 다들 널 좋아하는데.

What are you talking about? I have done nothing wrong. 무슨 말하는 거야? 난 잘못 하나도 안했는데.

008 Is that what I think it is? 내가 생각하는 그거 맞지?, 이게 정말 맞아?

미드표현

this is expressing surprise at seeing something unexpected. The speaker is asking someone else to confirm that he is really seeing whatever unusual sight is in front of him. People sometimes ask this when they mean "I can't believe what I see. Is it real?"

| Point | Is that what I think it is? 내가 생각하는 그거 맞지?
Is that who I think it is? 내가 생각하는 그 사람 맞지?

A: I can't believe it. **Is that what I think it is?**
믿을 수가 없네. 내가 생각하는 그거 맞아?

B: Yeah, my boyfriend bought me a huge diamond ring. 어, 남친이 커다란 다이아 반지를 사줬어.

A: Is that who I think it is? B: Who?
A: 내가 생각하는 그 사람 맞지? B: 누구?

A: Is that who I think it is? B: It can't be.
A: 내가 생각하는 그 사람 맞지? B: 그럴 리가 없어.

A: Is that what I think it is? B: Oh, yes.
A: 내가 생각하는 그거 맞지? B: 어, 그럼.

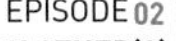

009 What're you trying to say? 무슨 말을 하고 싶은 거야?

미드표현

this is a way to say "Tell it to me directly." The speaker wants to know clearly what message a person intends to speak about

| Point | What're you trying to say? 무슨 말을 하려는거야?

A: I miss being with my ex-girlfriend.
옛 여친과 있을 때가 그리워.

B: **What are you trying to say?** Do you want to break up with me? 무슨 말 하는 거야? 나하고 헤어지고 싶어?

What are you trying to say? Do I look fat?
무슨 얘기를 하려는 거야? 살쪄보인다구?

A: What are you trying to say?
B: Well, maybe we should just take a break.
A: 무슨 말을 하고 싶은 거야? B: 우리 잠시 헤어지는 게 좋을 것 같아.

A: What are you trying to say?
B: I'm trying to say I want you to come to dinner tomorrow night.
A: 무슨 말을 하고 싶은거야? B: 내일 저녁 식사에 네가 오기를 바란다는 말야.

010 Did I miss it? 내가 놓쳤어?, 내가 못봤니?, 벌써 지나갔어?

미드표현

the speaker wants to know if some event has already happened and is now over. It is a way to say "Has it happened already?"

| Point | Did I miss something? 내가 뭐 놓친거야?
What did I miss? 내가 놓친게 뭐야?, 지나간게 뭔데

A: Hurry up! Your dad is on the TV news!
서둘러! 네 아빠가 TV뉴스에 나왔어!

B: Where is he? **Did I miss it?** 어디? 벌써 지나갔어?

Sorry I'm late. Did I miss anything?
늦어서 미안해. 내가 뭐 놓쳤어?

Has it happened? Did I miss it?
그렇게 된거야? 내가 그걸 놓친거야?

Good, that'll make it easier. So, what did I miss? 좋아. 그러면 더 쉬워질거야. 그래 내가 뭘 놓친거지?

How was the movie? Did I miss something amazing? 영화는 어땠어? 내가 멋진 부분을 놓친거야?

011 I don't know where you're going with this

이걸로 뭘 말하려는지 모르겠네

미드표현

this is a way to say that the speaker has become confused by what a person was saying. This is said when the reason someone is speaking is not very clear. In other words, the speaker is saying "I don't understand what point you are trying to make"

| Point | Where (are) you going with this?
이거 가지고 어디가는거야?, 무슨 말을 하려는거야?

A: Fred has become an important doctor at the hospital. 프레드는 병원에서 권위있는 의사가 되었어.

B: So what? **I don't know where you're going with this.** 그래서 뭐 어쨌다고? 뭘 말하려고 하는건지 모르겠네.

Where are you going with this, Leonard?
레너드, 무슨 말을 하려는거야?

Hang on. Let's see where he's going.
잠깐. 무슨 말 하는지 좀 더 들어보자.

A: You have a daughter? B: Where are you going with this? A: 딸이 있어? B: 무슨 말을 하려고?

A: I haven't had sex in a year. B: Where are you going with this?
A: 난 일년간 섹스 못했어. B: 무슨 말하려는거야?

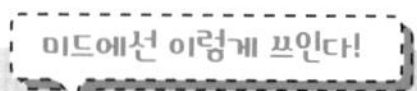

Where are you going with this, Raj?

The Big Bang Theory
SEASON#3-20

애인이 없어 외로운 Raj가 역시 Penny와 헤어져 상심이 큰 Leonard에게 일년동안 섹스를 해보지 못했다고 푸념하는 장면.

Raj: I haven't had sex in a year.
Leonard: Where are you going with this, Raj?
Raj: Don't flatter yourself, dude. I want to go out and meet a woman.
Leonard: So, go.
Raj: Well, I need a wingman. I don't want to come off like a lonely loser.
Leonard: And you think my presence will help with that?

라지: 일년동안 섹스를 못해봤어.
레너드: 무슨 말을 하려는거야, 라지?
라지: 이상한 생각하지마. 이 친구야. 나가서 여자를 만나고 싶다고.
레너드: 그럼 나가.
라지: 바람잡이가 필요해. 외로운 패배자처럼 보이기 싫어.
레너드: 내가 있으면 도움이 될 것 같아?

012 What's your point? 하고 싶은 말이 뭐야?

the speaker wants to say "Tell me your main idea." He is indicating that someone should be clear about the message or point that is being made

I Point I What's the point of ~ing/N? 뭐하러 …하는 거야?
What's the point of sb ~ing? …가 뭐하러 …하는거야?
Get to the point 요점을 말해, 요점이 뭐야

A: I don't think I'd like traveling overseas.
해외 여행 하고 싶지가 않아.

B: **What's your point?** Don't you want to go to Europe with me? 무슨 말야? 나랑 유럽가기 싫다는 거야?

What's the point of this? 이게 무슨 말야?

What's the point of talking about it right now? 지금 이 순간 그걸 이야기 하는 의미가 뭐야?

Get to the point. I don't want to waste time.
요점만 말해. 시간낭비하기 싫으니까.

What's the point of us going to live with him?
우리가 뭐하러 걔와 함께 살려고 가는거야?

013 You can't be serious 정말이야, 말도 안돼, 그럴 리가, 장난하는 거지?

this can be expressed as "Are you kidding?" Usually this is said when someone hears something that sounds strange or unbelievable

I Point I Are you serious? 정말이야?, 장난아냐?
You are not serious, are you? 농담이지, 그렇지?
Seriously? 정말 이럴거야?

A: I decided that I'm going to try skydiving.
스카이다이빙을 해보기로 결정했어.

B: **You can't be serious.** Why would you do something so dangerous? 정말? 왜 그렇게 위험한 걸 하려고 해?

Oh, you can't be serious. That's too much.
아, 말도 안돼. 이건 너무해.

Oh my God! Are you serious?! 맙소사! 정말이야?!

Are you serious? You still see Dr. Gate?
정말이야? 아직도 게이트 의사를 만나는 거야?

014 Are you sure? 정말이야? 확신해?

this is a way of asking whether a person is certain of something. It is the same as asking "Is that really true?"

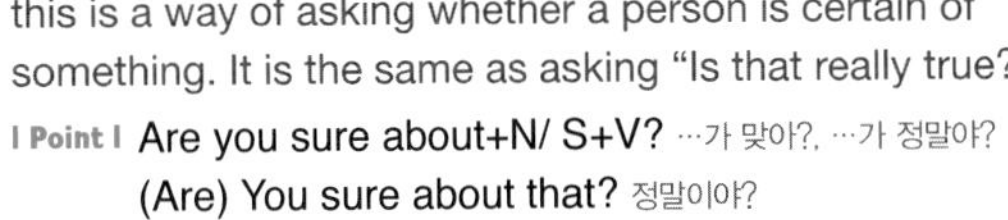

I Point I Are you sure about+N/ S+V? …가 맞아?, …가 정말야?
(Are) You sure about that? 정말이야?

A: I heard that a new movie theater is going to be built here. 여기에 새로운 극장이 세워질거래.

B: **Are you sure?** I haven't heard anything about that. 정말? 전혀 그런 소식 못들었는데.

Are you sure you're okay[all right]? 정말 괜찮은거야?

Are you sure you're gay? 너 정말 게이 맞아?

Are you sure this is the right address?
이 주소 정말 맞는거야?

Are you sure we're in the right place?
이 장소가 확실한거야?

015 You're kidding! (불신) 그럴 리가!, (놀람) 정말!, (불확실) 너 농담이지!

this usually expresses "That sounds like a joke!" It means that the speaker is not sure whether a statement was said seriously or jokingly

I Point I You're kidding me, right? 거짓말(장난)이지, 맞지?

A: I'm going to be on a quiz show on TV.
TV 퀴즈쇼에 나갈거야.

B: **You're kidding!** How did you get chosen for that? 정말! 어떻게 나가게 된거야?

You're kidding. When did you decide that?
정말, 언제 결정했는데?

A: The paper has a story about your restaurant. B: You're kidding! What does it say?
A: 신문에 네 식당에 관한 이야기가 나왔어. B: 정말! 뭐라고 쓰여 있어?

016 You('ve) got to be kidding me! 농담말아!, 웃기지마!

this indicates that the speaker has just heard something he either didn't believe or else something he didn't want to hear. It is similar to saying "That seems crazy"

| Point | You must be kidding! 말도 안돼!

A: We aren't going to get a raise in salary this year.
금년에 급여인상이 없을거래.

B: **You have got to be kidding!** I deserve more money. 농담마! 난 급여를 더 많이 받아야 돼.

미드표현

Oh. Uh, you have got to be kidding. I do not believe this. 말도 안돼. 난 도저히 믿을 수가 없어.

A: I don't think it was the same killer. B: You gotta be kidding me.
A: 동일범이라고 생각하지 않아. B: 말도 안돼.

You gotta be kidding me. That many?
농담말아. 그렇게나 많이?

017 Are you kidding (me)? 농담하는 거야?, 장난해?, 무슨 소리야?

this is often a way to check whether a statement was said seriously or not. It is like asking "Really?"

| Point | Are you kidding me with this? 이거 농담하는 거야?
I'm just kidding 농담야

A: I don't think I want to date you anymore.
더 이상 너랑 데이트하기 싫어.

B: **Are you kidding?** Why not? 무슨 소리야? 왜 싫어?

미드표현

Are you kidding me? You want me to feel sorry for you? 장난해? 나보고 너한테 미안해하라고?

Are you kidding me with this?! I'm not gonna do your homework for you.
이거 장난해?! 니 숙제 안해줄거야.

Are you kidding me? This isn't about terrorism. 장난해? 이건 테러에 관한게 아냐.

No, I'm just kidding. It was a joke.
아냐. 농담야. 장난였어.

018 No kidding 1. 설마? 2. 너 농담하냐! 3. 진심(정말)이야 4. 맞아, 그렇지

this usually is a way of saying "Yeah, that's right." It is often said when a speaker wants to express agreement with something. It can also be a way to double check if something is real or true

| Point | No kidding? (놀람, 사실 확인) 설마?, 정말?
No kidding! (남들 다 아는 이야기를 이제 알았다는 사람에게)
너 장난(농담)하냐!, 이제야 알았어?
No kidding (내 말을 강조) 진심이야, 장난아냐 (동의) 맞아, 그렇지

A: Gee, this room looks really dirty.
어휴, 이 방이 정말 지저분해 보인다.

B: **No kidding.** It needs to be cleaned soon.
맞아. 어서 치워야 돼.

미드표현

No kidding, really, it's a great butt.
진심이야, 정말, 정말 멋진 엉덩이야.

A: You are the living embodiment of the beautiful Princess Punchali. B: Oh, no kidding? Oh, who is that?
A: 넌 아름다운 펀찰리 공주의 살아있는 화신이야. B: 정말? 어, 그게 누군데?

No kidding, you speak English really well.
설마, 너 영어 정말 잘 말하는데.

019 (Do) You mean it? 정말이야?, 진심이야?

this indicates that the speaker wants to be sure that someone was being serious when something was said. It is similar to asking "Is that really true?"

| Point | You don't mean that 그 말 사실 아니겠지, 진심은 아니겠지

A: I'd like you to join me on a vacation to Hawaii.
하와이 여행에 같이 가자.

B: **You mean it?** It'd be terrific to go traveling with you. 정말이야? 너와 여행가면 정말 멋지겠다.

미드표현

Oh, you mean it? That would be so fun!
어, 정말이야? 무척 재미있겠다!

Really? You mean that? You wouldn't mind?
정말? 진심이야? 괜찮겠어?

A: They won't be able to keep up with you.
B: You mean it?
A: 걔네들은 너를 따라잡을 수 없을거야. B: 정말이야?

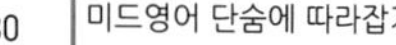

020 Is this some kind of joke? 장난하는 거지?, 나 놀리는 거지?

usually this expresses the speaker's surprise or unhappiness over something that has happened. It is like saying "This can't be real."

| Point | You must be joking 농담하는 거지?
Is this a joke? 농담야?
Are you pulling my leg? 누구 놀리는 거야?

A: I think someone damaged your car in the parking lot. 주차장의 네 차가 파손되었던데?
B: **Is this some kind of a joke?** I just bought that car! 장난하는 거야? 새차인데!

What is that, some kind of joke?
저게 뭐야, 장난하는거야?

A: I thought you said she was cool with this.
B: You must be joking.
A: 걔가 이거 괜찮다고 말한걸로 아는데. B: 너 농담하는거지.

A: You must be joking! B: No. No joke.
A: 너 농담하는거지! B: 아니, 농담아냐.

Is this a joke, is this a long, boring joke that I'm not going to get?
내가 이해할 수 없는 지루하고 긴 농담인거야?

021 Tell me another (one) 말도 안되는 소리하지마, 거짓말 마, 헛소리 하지마

this is a way of saying "That sounds like bullshit." The speaker believes something is a lie, and is waiting to hear the next lie that will be told

A: I am really good friends with Nicole Kidman.
니콜 키드만과 정말 친한 친구야.
B: Oh yeah, sure you are. **Tell me another one.**
어 그래, 어련하시겠어. 거짓말 마.

That's a lie, but go on and tell me another.
거짓말, 하지만 더 지껄여봐.

I don't believe what you said, but tell me another one. 네가 한 말 믿기지 않지만 더 씨부려봐.

You think UFOs are real? Tell me another one.
UFO가 실제 있다고 생각한다고? 말도 안되는 소리마.

022 I'm not buying your story 네 얘기는 못 믿겠어, 네 거짓말에 안 속아

this is a very blunt way of saying that the speaker doesn't believe something. It is a way to say "I don't think that's true."

| Point | I don't buy it 못 믿어(buy = believe or accept)
You're not buying all this 이걸 곧이곧대로 믿지는 않지?

A: At the nightclub, all of the girls wanted to dance with me. 나이트클럽에서 모든 여자들이 나랑 춤출려고 했어.
B: Oh no, **I'm not buying your story.**
어 그러지마, 네 얘기는 못 믿겠어.

I don't buy it. You're a big liar.
안 속아, 넌 거짓말쟁이니까.

You're going to church? I don't buy it.
네가 교회를 간다고? 못 믿겠어.

But what I don't buy is them taking such a big risk. 하지만 내가 못믿는 건 걔네들이 그런 엄청난 위험을 감수하는거야.

023 Don't give me that! (변명하거나 거짓말하는 상대에게) 그런 말 마!, 변명하지마!

this means "I'm not going to believe that." The speaker is objecting or disagreeing strongly with something that was said

| Point | I'm not making it up 얘기를 꾸며대는 게 아니야
I made up a story about that 그거 꾸며낸거야
Is that something you're making up? 네가 만들어낸 이야기지?

A: I'm sorry I was late. There was a big traffic jam on the highway. 미안, 늦었네. 고속도로에 차가 많이 막혔어.
B: **Don't give me that.** You could have taken the subway this morning. 그러지마. 아침에 전철탈 수도 있었잖아.

Don't give me that. I'm mad at you.
그런 말 마. 열받잖아.

Don't give me that. I'm mad at you. You have robbed me, and I'll never get it back.
변명하지마. 나 지금 굉장히 화났어. 넌 내게서 빼앗아갔고, 난 그걸 다시 돌려받지 못할거야.

That's why you made up that robbery story?
그래서 네가 강도 이야기를 꾸며낸거야?

024 You're lying to me 거짓말하지마

this means "You aren't being honest." It is a simple way of saying the speaker thinks someone is not telling the truth

| Point | Don't lie to me 거짓말 마
Would I lie? 내가 거짓말하겠냐?
You're not a very good liar 거짓말이 서투르구만

A: I can't give you my homework because my dog ate it. 개가 먹어서 숙제를 낼 수가 없어요.

B: **You're lying to me.** I don't think you did your homework. 거짓말마. 숙제하지도 않아놓구선.

Please just stop, I know that you're lying to me.
제발 그만해, 거짓말하는거 알아.

Don't lie to me. I've seen you flirt with him.
거짓말 마. 네가 그 남자랑 집적대는 걸 봤어.

You lied to Chris and now you are lying to me.
넌 크리스에게 거짓말을 했고 이제는 나한테 거짓말을 하고 있어.

I don't believe you, you're lying to me.
난 널 믿지 않아, 거짓말하지마.

025 (Do) You mean to tell me ~? 그 말 진심야?, 그 말에 대해 후회하지 않지?

usually this indicates that the speaker is very surprised or finds it difficult to believe something. It is like asking "Is that really true?"

| Point | You mean to tell me S+V? 그 말 진심이야?

A: I had a party at my house this weekend.
이번 주말에 집에서 파티했어.

B: **Do you mean to tell me** I wasn't invited?
내가 초대받지 않았다는 게 사실야?

You mean to tell me that Smith had nothing to do with the murder?
스미스 씨가 그 살인사건과 관계없다는 게 사실야?

You mean to tell me you can't find the restaurant you went before?
전에 갔던 레스토랑을 못찾겠다는 거야?

Do you mean to tell me that none of you has any notion of where he is?
그가 어디에 있는지 너희들 중 아무도 모른다는게 진심이야?

027 (I) Wouldn't count on it
그렇지 않을 걸, 그렇게 되지 않을 걸, 기대 안하는게 좋을 걸

this is often said to indicate "It's not likely." The speaker thinks that something is either probably not true, or probably won't occur.

| Point | count on = depend on = bank on = rely on 의지하다

A: The big picnic is scheduled to take place on Saturday. 큰 규모의 피크닉이 일요일에 열릴 예정이야.

B: **I wouldn't count on it.** It's going to rain all weekend. 그렇게 안될 걸. 주말 내내 비온대.

You shouldn't count on me. 넌 나를 믿으면 안돼.

I knew I could count on you Tom.
탐, 난 넌 믿을 수 있다는 걸 알았어.

We can't count on circumstantial evidence to carry this case.
정황증거를 믿고서 이 사건을 계속 끌고 갈 수는 없어.

Every time you tried to count on someone, they let you down, so you go it alone. 누군가를 믿으려고 할 때마다, 넌 실망을 할거고 그래서 결국 혼자 가게 될거야.

MEMO

Ways of saying you (don't) completely understand something

알거나 혹은 모르거나

You got me

001 You have a really good grasp on this
넌 정말 이걸 잘 알고 있어

this indicates that the speaker thinks a person understands something very well. It is a nice thing to say, and we can assume the speaker thinks the listener is intelligent.

I Point I have a good grasp on~ …을 잘 알고 있다

A: So this is the way to check the exam scores.
그럼 이게 시험성적을 확인하는 방법이야.

B: **You have a really good grasp on this**
넌 정말 이거 잘 알고 있구나.

미드표현

I may not have a firm grasp on sarcasm.
난 비꼬는 말에 대해 완벽하게 알고 있지 못할 수도 있어.

The cops had a good grasp on the facts of the case. 경찰은 사건의 진상에 대해 잘 알고 있었어.

I have a good grasp on the test questions.
난 시험문제를 잘 알고 있어.

002 She knows her way around a mattress
걔는 섹스에 대해 잘 알고 있어

this seems to mean that a woman has had a lot of sexual encounters. To know your way around something is an idiom that means a person is experienced, and a mattress usually signifies sleeping or sex.

I Point I know one's way around 사정을 훤히 알고 있다, 자기 할 일을 잘 알고 있다.

A: Has she screwed a lot of guys?
걔는 많은 남자와 섹스를 했어?

B: **She knows her way around a mattress.**
걔는 섹스에 대해 해박해.

미드표현

I understand you already know your way around, probably better than I do.
넌 내가 아는 것보다 더 많이 잘 알고 있을 거라고 이해해.

You seem to know your way around here!
넌 여기를 아주 잘 알고 있는 것 같아!

You still know your way around a ship?
너 아직 배에 대해서 잘 알고 있어?

003 I know it backwards and forwards 난 그걸 낱낱이 알고 있어

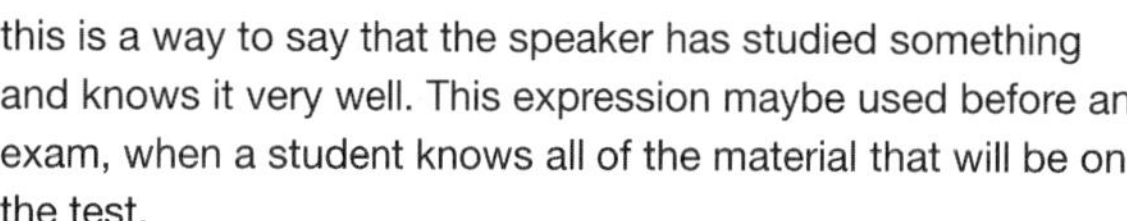

this is a way to say that the speaker has studied something and knows it very well. This expression maybe used before an exam, when a student knows all of the material that will be on the test.

I Point I know sth backwards and forwards 낱낱이 알다, 훤히 잘 알다

A: Are you ready to take the exam to become a lawyer? 변호사 자격시험 볼 준비됐어?

B: Yes I am. **I know the whole thing backwards and forwards.** 어. 난 시험 볼 내용을 낱낱이 알고 있어.

미드표현

A: Have you memorized the manual?
B: Backwards and forwards.
A: 매뉴얼 다 암기했어? B: 완벽하게 했어.

Yes, it's daunting. But I know the Massachusetts penal code backwards and forwards.
어, 그건 힘에 겨운 일이지만, 난 매사추세츠 형법을 훤히 꿰차고 있어.

004 Who's to say that Chris is a alien?
크리스가 외계인인 줄 누가 알겠어?

this is a way of implying that something is not certain or not clear. The speaker is indicating that there is a possibility that something is true, but not confirming it.

I Point I Who's to say that~? …을 누가 알겠어?(확실하지 않다)

A: Ann doesn't want to become a housewife.
앤은 주부가 되는 걸 싫어해.

B: **Who's to say** she'll ever get married?
걔가 결혼할 지 누가 알겠어?

미드표현

Who's to say this gun was the gun?
이 총이 그 총인 것을 누가 알겠어?

Who's to say what it will be tomorrow?
그게 내일일지 누가 알겠어?

Who's to say he won't kill you first?
걔가 너를 먼저 죽이지 않을지 누가 알겠어?

Who's to say he won't come for you again?
걔가 다시 너에게로 오지 않을지 누가 알겠어?

005 He's done everything there is to do in show business 걘 쇼업계에서 잔뼈가 굵은 사람이야

this indicates that a person has held many different jobs in the entertainment industry. Perhaps the person is old, because he has done so many things. Another way to say this is "He has experience in most aspects of the entertainment business"

I Point I do everything there is to do~ 해야 될 것은 다 해보다

A: Why was Mr. Talbot selected to manage the stage show? 왜 탈보트 씨가 무대공연을 책임지도록 뽑혔어?

B: **He's done everything there is to do** in show business. 그 사람은 쇼비즈니스 업계에서 잔뼈가 굵은 사람이거든.

미드표현

I feel as if I know everything there is to know about you. 너에 대해 알 것은 다 알고 있다는 느낌이 들어.

Gail knows everything there is to know about me. 게일은 나에 대해 알고 있을 것은 다 알고 있어.

I know everything there is to know about Shakespeare. 세익스피어에 관한 모든 것을 알고 있어.

006 When did you pick up on that? 언제 알아차렸어?

this is used to ask someone about when he began to understand or comprehend something important. Often this might be asked when people are working together to figure out what they don't know, and they are looking for clues.

I Point I pick up on sth (빨리) 알아차리다, 이해하다

A: I am pretty sure the suspect has been lying to us. 용의자가 우리에게 거짓말하고 있다는게 확실해.

B: Really? **When did you pick up on that?**
정말? 언제 알아차렸는데?

미드표현

We try to pick up on the behavior of the killer.
우리는 살인범의 행동을 빨리 알아차리려고 하고 있어.

I don't usually pick up on those things. Good for me. 난 보통 그런 것들을 알아차리지 못해. 나한테 잘 된 일이지.

Mom, I'm not an idiot. I pick up on things.
엄마, 나 바보 아냐. 상황을 이해한다고.

007 That's a good question 좋은 질문이야, 그러게나 말야

often this is said when a person thinks a question is intelligent or it is seeking important information. Sometimes it also indicates the speaker doesn't know the answer to a question. Usually it is said just before someone tries to answera question that was asked.

I Point I That's a (very) good question (진짜) 좋은 질문이야.
(답을 모르거나 생각이 안날 때) 그러게나 말야, 나도 모르겠는데

A: Do you think that a person here committed the crime? 여기 있는 사람이 범죄를 저질렀다고 생각해?

B: **That's a good question.** Yes, I think the criminal is still here. 좋은 질문이야. 어, 범인은 아직 여기 있다고 생각해.

미드표현

I don't know. That's a good question.
모르겠어. 좋은 질문이야.

That's a good question. I don't know why.
그러게나 말야. 그 이유를 모르겠어.

A good question. I asked myself the same thing. 좋은 질문이야. 나도 같은 문제를 자문해봤어.

008 Beats me 글쎄 잘 모르겠네, 내가 어떻게 알아?

this means "I don't know." It's a way of saying the speaker doesn't know the answer or solution to something

I Point I Search me 난 몰라

A: Is your sister coming to the party tonight?
오늘 밤 네 누이 파티에 와?

B: **Beats me.** I haven't talked to her. 몰라. 얘기 안해봤어.

미드표현

A: Where has Greg been all day? B: Beats me, why don't you ask him?
A: 그렉은 하루 종일 어디 있었던 거야? B: 몰라, 걔한테 물어봐

A: Where's David go? B: Beats me. His car's still in the parking lot.
A: 데이빗이 어디 간거야? B: 몰라, 걔 차는 차고에 있는데.

009 Don't ask me 나한테 묻지마, 나도 몰라

this indicates the person doesn't have the answer to something and doesn't want to be bothered about it. It's a way to say "Go ask someone else about that"

| Point | Don't ask me why[how] 나 한테 이유[방법]를 묻지마
Don't ask me why S+V …한 이유를 묻지마
*Don't ask!는 "묻지마 다쳐," "모르는게 나아"라는 의미

A: How can I get to the post office from here?
여기서 우체국 어떻게 가요?

B: **Don't ask me.** I just moved to this town.
저도 몰라요. 여기 방금 이사와서요.

Don't ask me why I remember that.
내가 왜 그걸 기억하는지 묻지마.

Don't ask me how to do it. 그걸 하는 방법을 내게 묻지마.

You don't ask me about that. 그거에 대해 내게 묻지마.

010 I can't say 잘 몰라, 확실히 말 못하겠어

미드표현

usually this means someone doesn't know something, although it can also mean someone has to keep a secret and is not allowed to tell about something

| Point | (I) Can't say for sure 확실히는 몰라

A: Do you think it will snow tomorrow? 내일 눈올 것 같아?

B: **I can't say.** It certainly feels like it might.
몰라. 그럴지도 모르지.

Without the body, I can't say. 시신이 없으면 잘 몰라.

A: What would you do in my place? B: I can't say. A: 내 입장이라면 어떻게 하겠어? B: 잘 모르겠어.

A: Why would her fever be back? B: I can't say.
A: 왜 걔가 열이 다시 나는거죠? B: 확실히는 말씀 못드리겠습니다.

A: Where did you get this? B: I can't say.
A: 이거 어디서 난거야? B: 잘 모르겠어.

011 I wonder if~ …인지 잘 모르겠어, …인지 궁금해

미드표현

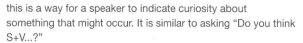

this is a way for a speaker to indicate curiosity about something that might occur. It is similar to asking "Do you think S+V...?"

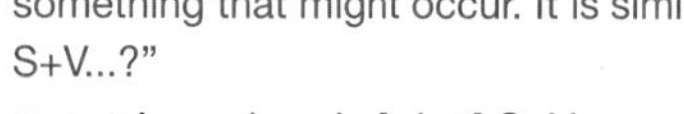

| Point | I wonder why[what] S+V 왜[무엇이] …인지 궁금해
I wonder 글쎄

A: **I wonder what** I would do if I won the lottery.
로또에 당첨되면 뭘 할지 모르겠어.

B: Stop dreaming. You're never going to win anything. 꿈깨. 아무 것도 못 탈거야.

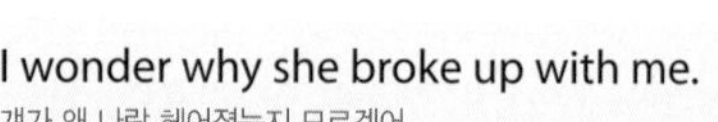

I wonder why she broke up with me.
걔가 왜 나랑 헤어졌는지 모르겠어.

I wonder where she works. 걔가 어디서 일하는지 궁금해.

I wonder what he needed the money for.
걔가 돈을 뭐 때문에 필요한지 모르겠어.

012 I have no idea 몰라, 전혀 모르겠어

this is almost always a way of saying that a person has no answer to something. It usually means "I don't know"

| Point | I have no idea what[when/how]~ …을 모르겠어
You have no idea what[how]~ …을 넌 모를거야

A: How are you going to get the money to buy a house? 집 살 돈 어떻게 마련할거야?

B: **I have no idea.** It is going to be really difficult for me. 몰라. 정말 어려울 것 같아.

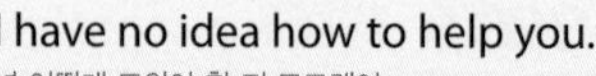

I have no idea how to help you.
널 어떻게 도와야 할 지 모르겠어.

I have no idea what you're talking about.
네가 무슨 말 하는지 모르겠어.

I have no idea whose side you're on.
네가 누구 편이지 모르겠어.

You have no idea how much I miss her.
내가 얼마나 걔를 그리워하는지 넌 모를거야.

013 I don't know about that 글쎄, 잘 모르겠어

generally this means the speaker is gently disagreeing with something that has been said. Another way to express it is "That seems incorrect"

| Point | I don't know for sure 확실히 모르겠어
I don't know what/why~ …을 몰라

A: The economy is supposed to improve soon.
경제가 곧 좋아질거래.

B: **I don't know about that.** It's still doing rather poorly. 글쎄. 아직도 안 좋던데.

I don't know what that means.
그게 무슨 의미인지 몰라.

I don't know what happened.
무슨 일이 일어났는지 몰라.

I don't know what to say. 뭐라 말해야 할지 모르겠어.

I don't know what the hell you're talking about! 네가 도대체 무슨 말을 하는지 모르겠어!

014 You're talking to the wrong man 딴데가서 얘기해

this means that the speaker doesn't know something. He is indicating "I'm not responsible for that" or "I don't know about that"

| Point | You should speak to sb …에게 말씀하세요

A: Where is the nearest post office?
가장 가까운 우체국이 어딥니까?

B: **You're talking to the wrong man.** I just moved here. 다른 사람한테 물어보시죠. 방금 이사와서요.

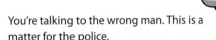

You're talking to the wrong man. This is a matter for the police.
번지수가 틀렸어. 경찰이 다룰 문제야.

If you don't mind my suggestion, you should speak to your boss.
내가 제안해도 된다면, 네 사장한테 말해야지.

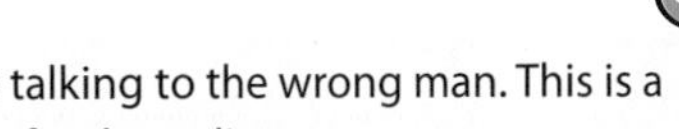

015 I do not know a thing 난 아무 것도 몰라

this is a way of indicating "I have no information about it." We can understand that the speaker either doesn't know something, or doesn't want to talk about something

| Point | I don't know anything about ~ …에 대해 아무 것도 몰라
I don't know him from Adam 나 그 사람 전혀 몰라

A: Come on, tell us more about the Christmas presents. 자, 성탄선물에 대해 더 말해줘.

B: I can't. **I do not know a thing about** them.
몰라. 난 아무 것도 몰라.

I just realized I don't know a thing about you.
난 내가 너에 대해 아무것도 모른다는 사실을 깨달았어.

I don't know nothing about that case.
그 사건에 대해 아무 것도 몰라.

I don't know anything about the murder.
그 살인사건에 대해 난 아무것도 몰라.

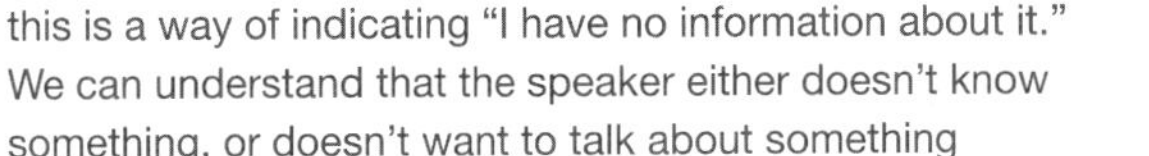

016 I don't know what to make of it 무슨 일인지 모르겠어

this is a way to express that something is confusing, and the speaker doesn't understand it. When a person says this, we know that he cannot explain what has happened, and it may be a mystery. It can be a way to say "I'm not really sure of what happened"

| Point | don't know what to make of it 어떻게 생각해야 할지 모르겠다

A: Why do you think Steve decided not to get married? 왜 스티브는 결혼하지 않기로 한거야?

B: **I don't know what to make of it.** Maybe he's gay. 어떻게 된건지 도통 모르겠어. 아마 게이일지도 몰라.

And frankly, I don't know what to make of Barry. 솔직히 배리를 어떻게 생각해야 할지 모르겠어.

I don't know what to make of her today.
오늘 걜 어떻게 생각해야 될지 모르겠어.

Rachel looks around, not quite sure what to make of it.
레이첼은 어떻게 생각해야 될지 몰라 주위를 둘러보고 있어.

017 You got me 1. 난 모르겠는데 2. 내가 졌어

this usually indicates the speaker isn't sure what the answer to something is. It is like saying "I don't know." It can also mean that someone gave someone something or that a person persuaded another person to do something

| Point | *You got me+N/ adj/ to do의 형태가 되면 의미가 달라진다.
You got me+N 나한테 …를 준거야
You got me+adj/ to do 나를 …하게 하다

A: Which singer is singing this song? 이 노래 누가 불러?
B: **You got me.** I've never heard it before.
몰라. 처음 들어봐.

Oh, all right, you got me.
아, 알았어, 내가 거짓말을 좀 했는데, 알아차렸군.

Okay, you got me. What do you want?
그래, 내가 졌어. 원하는 게 뭐야?

You got me this for Christmas. Don't you remember? 이거 네가 성탄절 때 내게 준거야. 기억안나?

You got me to think. 넌 내가 생각하도록 해줬어.

018 You got me there 1. 모르겠어(I don't know) 2. 네 말이 맞아(You're right)

this means "I don't know the answer." It's a way of expressing that the speaker doesn't know something

| Point | You got me there 모르겠어, 네 말이 맞아

A: How is the food in the new Thai restaurant?
이 새로운 태국식당 음식 어때?
B: **You got me there.** None of my friends have eaten there. 몰라. 친구들 중 아무도 먹어보질 않아서.

I have no way to answer that. You got me there. 그거에 대답할 방법이 없어. 모르겠어.

You got me there. I never heard of that game.
모르겠어. 난 그런 게임 들어본 적이 없어.

You got me there. I'll ask someone to research it. 네 말이 맞아. 다른 사람에게 그걸 조사해보라고 할게.

019 I can't imagine that 상상도 안돼, 전혀 모르겠어

this often is a way to say "That doesn't seem right." It is usually a way for a speaker to say that something is unlikely to happen

| Point | I can't imagine S+V …가 상상이 안돼
I can't imaging ~ing …을 상상할 수 없어

A: The doctor said your dad should give up smoking this year. 의사가 니네 아빠 올해 금연해야 된다고 했어.
B: **I can't imagine** he'll quit cigarettes after all this time. 아빠가 여짓껏 피우셨는데 끊으실지 모르겠어.

I can't imagine that's true.
그게 사실이라는 게 상상도 못하겠어.

I can't imagine why you like her.
왜 네가 걔를 좋아하는지 도통 모르겠어.

Honey, I can't imagine what you're going through. 자기야, 난 네가 무슨 일을 겪었는지 상상이 안가.

020 I didn't catch what you said 무슨 말인지 못 알아들었어요, 잘못 들었어요

this is most often a way of saying that the speaker couldn't hear something. It is very similar to asking "Could you repeat that?"

| Point | catch what sb said …가 한 말을 이해하다

A: Are you going to be staying in a hotel?
호텔에 머물거야?
B: **I didn't catch what you said.** Can you repeat it? 뭐라고? 다시 말해줘.

Speak louder. I didn't catch what you said.
큰 소리로 말해. 무슨 말인지 못알아들었어.

I didn't catch what you said. Can you repeat that? 무슨 말인지 못알아들었어. 다시한번 말해줄래?

I didn't catch what you said. Stop mumbling!
무슨 말인지 못알아들었어. 그만 좀 중얼거려!

021 I don't get it[that] 모르겠어, 이해가 안돼

this is a way to say "I can't understand it." The speaker is expressing that he is confused about something

| Point | I didn't (quite) get that (전혀) 못 알아 들었어 (그러니 다시 말해줘)
You don't get it 못 알아듣는구만

A: Are we going to invite Jack to come along on the trip? 잭한테 여행같이 가자고 할거야?
B: **You don't get it.** He and I are no longer friends.
못알아듣는구만. 걔하고 난 더이상 친구가 아냐.

미드표현

She's going out with Jim. I don't get it. He's so dorky. 걔가 짐하고 데이트하는데 이해가 안돼. 짐은 얼간이잖아.

You don't get it, do you? 넌 못 알아들었지, 그지?

I don't get it. What's so funny?
이해가 안돼, 뭐가 우습다는 거야?

022 You tell me 그거야 네가 알지, 네가 더 잘 알지

this is a way for a speaker to say "I think you know the answer." It indicates the listener probably has an answer for a question that has been asked

| Point | You tell me+N/ what[why] S+V …을 말해봐

A: Is it interesting to live in California?
캘리포니아에서 사는 게 재미있지?
B: **You tell me.** You're from L.A.
그거야 네가 알지. LA 출신이잖아.

미드표현

I don't know, you tell me. 난 모르지, 네가 알잖아.

You're the lawyer. You tell me.
네가 변호사니까 네가 더 잘 알지.

You tell me what happened here.
여기 무슨 일이 있었는지 말해봐.

A: Well, then, where are we gonna work?
B: You tell me.
A: 그럼 우리 어디서 일하게 되는거야? B: 그거야 네가 알지.

023 You('ve) got it all wrong 잘못 알고 있는 거야, 잘못 이해하고 있어

usually this is said to indicate that someone has incorrect thinking about something. It expresses "Your ideas are not right"

| Point | You('ve) got this all wrong 잘못 알고 있는 거야
She got it all wrong 걔가 잘못 알고 있는 거야

A: You went on a date with my boyfriend!
내 남친하고 데이트했지!
B: **You've got it all wrong!** He wanted to ask questions about you. 아냐! 너에 대해 물어보려 했어.

미드표현

You've got it all wrong. I'm telling you. Nothing happened. 완전 오해야. 정말이야. 아무 일도 없었어

Last night, when you were talking about the accident, you got it all wrong.
네가 어젯밤에 사건에 대해 얘기할 때, 다 잘못 알고 있었어

You got it all wrong, man. I barely even know her. 네가 잘못 알고 있는거야. 난 걜 알지도 못해.

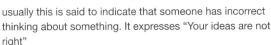

024 Nobody knows (what~) (…는) 아무도 몰라

this is usually said when the people in the group don't have the answer to something. Another way to say this is "We aren't sure what S+V."

| Point | Who knows (what S+V)? (…를) 누가 알겠어?
God (only) knows (what S+V)! (…는) 누구도 알 수 없지!
God knows (that) S+V 정말이지…
Who can tell? 누가 알겠어?

A: Where is Bob at these days? 요즘 밥 어디 있는거야?
B: **Nobody knows.** He just disappeared.
아무도 몰라. 그냥 사라졌어.

Nobody knows what they're doing.
걔들이 뭘하는지 누가 알겠어.

God only knows what your mother is gonna say. 네 엄마가 뭐라 할지 누가 알겠어.

God knows I owe you so much.
정말이지 너한테 신세진 게 많아.

Who knows what could happen?
무슨 일이 일어날지 아무도 몰라.

025 He doesn't (even) have a clue 걘 하나도 몰라, 아무 것도 눈치 못 챘어

미드표현

this is a way of saying "He doesn't know anything." The speaker is indicating that a person is either foolish or uninformed about something

| Point | I haven't got a clue (about that) 난 전혀 몰랐어
I'm clueless (about~) (…에 대해) 난 전혀 몰라

A: Has Bob found out about his surprise birthday party? 밥이 깜짝 파티 여는 거 알아챘어?
B: No way. **He doesn't have a clue.** 전혀. 아무 것도 몰라.

I just thought you might have a clue where your son is. 네가 네 아들이 어디 있는지 알지도 모른다고 생각했어.

You don't have a clue what I'm feeling. 넌 내 기분이 어떤지 전혀 몰라.

You think he suspects? I'm sure he doesn't have a clue. 걔가 의심한다고? 걘 전혀 모르고 있는게 확실해.

026 You don't know the first thing about it
쥐뿔도 모르면서, 아무 것도 모르면서

미드표현

this expresses "You have no knowledge of that." It is a slightly insulting way of saying that a person has no information on a topic

| Point | You don't know the half of it 얼마나 심각한지 네가 아직 몰라서 그래
You don't know shit 아무 것도 모르면 가만히 있어. 네가 알긴 뭘 알아

A: I heard that you have been arguing with your girlfriend. 여친하고 다퉜다며.
B: **You don't know the first thing about it!** Just leave me alone! 쥐뿔도 모르면서! 그냥 나 좀 놔둬!

You don't know the first thing about having a business! 사업체를 운영하는게 뭔지 넌 아무 것도 몰라!

You don't know the first thing about tough. 넌 터프함이 어떤 건지 쥐뿔도 몰라.

Because she's a young girl, she won't know the first thing about managing that money. 걔는 어린 소녀여서, 그 돈을 관리하는거에 대해 아무 것도 모를거야.

I'm pretty sure you don't know the first thing about my life. 내 확신하는데 넌 내 삶에 대해 아무 것도 몰라.

027 Your guess is as good as mine 모르긴 나도 매한가지야

미드표현

the speaker is saying that he doesn't know anything about something. It means "I'm not sure."

| Point | That's[It's] anybody's guess 그건 아무도 몰라
S+be anybody's guess …은 아무도 몰라

A: How long is this movie supposed to last? 이 영화 상영시간이 어떻게 되는거야?
B: I haven't heard. **Your guess is as good as mine.** 몰라. 나도 마찬가지야.

Your guess is as good as mine. I think we should check his arms for needle marks. 나도 모르긴 마찬가지야. 내 생각은 걔팔에 주사자국이 있는지 확인해봐야 될 것 같아.

A: Where's Walt? I haven't seen him since this morning. B: Your guess is as good as mine. A: 월트가 어디 있어? 아침이후로 보이지 않네. B: 나도 모르긴 마찬가지야.

028 I don't see why~ 왜 …인지 모르겠어

미드표현

this is usually said when the speaker doesn't understand the reason for something. It expresses "That doesn't make sense to me."

| Point | I don't see why 이유를 모르겠어
I don't see why not 그래 I don't see that 그런 것 같지 않아

A: **I don't understand why** I wasn't invited to Perry's party. 내가 왜 페리 파티에 초대 못 받았는지 모르겠어.
B: I think that Perry doesn't like you very much. 페리가 널 별로 좋아하지 않나봐.

I don't see why he wouldn't do it again. 왜 걔가 그걸 안 하려고 하는지 모르겠어.

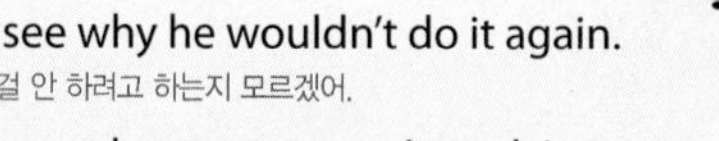

I don't see why you two can't work it out. 왜 너희들이 잘 안 되는지 모르겠어.

She needs rest. But I don't see why she can't go home soon. 걘 쉬어야 되는데 곧 집으로 가면 왜 안되는지 모르겠어.

029 (I) Wouldn't know 알 도리가 없지, 그걸 내가 어떻게 알겠니, 나도 모르지

this is a way of expressing that the person doesn't have an answer to something. It is similar to saying "I have no idea."

| Point | I wouldn't know+N/ what[if] S+V …을 알 리 없어
You wouldn't know+N/ what[if] S+V 네가 …을 알 리가 없지

A: How is Jake doing after being fired from his job?
잭이 직장에서 잘린 후에 뭐해?

B: **I wouldn't know.** I haven't spoken with him.
낸들 어떻게 알겠어. 얘기해본 적이 없어.

I wouldn't know anything about that.
내가 그걸 알 리가 없지.

I wouldn't know what to do without you.
너없이 내가 뭘해야 할지 어찌 알겠어.

I just wouldn't know where they might get off the plane. 걔네들이 어디서 비행기에서 내릴지 어떻게 알겠어.

You wouldn't know anything about that either, would you? 너도 그거에 대해 알 리가 없지, 그지?

030 I didn't know that 전혀 몰랐었어, 몰랐네, 모르고 있었지 뭐야

this is a way to say "I never heard that before." It indicates that a person has just received new information

| Point | I didn't know (that) S+V …을 몰랐어

A: This house is where Brad Pitt was born.
이 집이 브래드 피트가 태어난 곳이야.

B: How interesting. **I didn't know that.** 재밌네, 몰랐어.

What're you looking at me for? I didn't know that. 뭐 때문에 그렇게 날 쳐다보는 거야? 난 몰랐다니까.

I didn't know that you knew that.
네가 그걸 알고 있다는 걸 몰랐어.

I didn't know that she was gonna be that hot.
걔가 그렇게 섹시하리라고는 몰랐어.

031 There's no way to tell 알 길이 없어, 그건 아무도 몰라

미드표현

this is usually a way of saying that something will remain uncertain. Another way to express this is "We can't be sure about it."

| Point | There's no way to tell what[who] S+V …을 알 방법이 없어

A: Will your parents be angry when they see your school grades? 부모님이 네 성적보시고 화내실까?

B: **There's no way to tell.** They know I have difficult classes. 알 수 없지. 내가 어려운 거 배운다는 건 아셔.

There's no way to tell who. 그게 누구인지는 알 길이 없어.

So there's no way to tell where he went before he died. 걔가 죽기 전에 어디에 갔는지 알 길이 없어.

There's no way to tell whether it was forcible.
그게 강제적이었는지는 아무도 몰라.

032 There's no telling 알 수가 없지, 모르지

미드표현

like the previous expression, this indicates there is uncertainty about what will happen in the future. It is often said to mean "We can't know about that."

| Point | There's no telling(knowing) what[how]~ …을 알 수가 없어

A: Do you think I should marry my girlfriend?
내가 여친과 결혼해야 된다고 생각해?

B: **There's no telling.** Just see what happens in the future. 알 수 없지. 앞으로 어떻게 되나 봐.

There's no telling where the lies begin and end. 거짓말의 시작과 끝이 어디인지 알 길이 없어.

There's no telling how her family might handle that. 걔네 가족이 어떻게 그거에 대처할지는 알 수가 없어.

There's no telling how long it's going to take to clean up that chaos. 저 혼란을 정리하는데 얼마나 시간이 걸릴지는 알 수가 없어.

033 I'm not sure about this 잘 몰라, 이건 잘 모르겠어

this is usually indicating "I am uncertain." It's a way of expressing that the speaker doesn't know something absolutely

| Point | I'm not sure of+N/ that(if)~ …을(인지) 확실히 모르겠어
I'm not sure (yet) (아직) 잘 모르겠어

A: I heard your husband is being promoted.
남편이 승진했다면서.

B: **I'm not sure about that.** We'll find out next week. 잘 몰라. 다음 주에 알게 될거야.

미드표현

I'm not sure about any of this. 이건 전혀 모르겠어.

I'm not sure if he's done with it yet.
걔가 그걸 마쳤는지 모르겠어.

Not sure what it is. 그게 뭔지 모르겠어.

Sometimes I'm not sure of anything.
간혹 모든 게 확실하지 않을 때가 있어.

034 How should I know? 내가 어떻게 알아?, 난 전혀 몰라, 난들 어찌 알겠어?

this simply means "I don't know." It is a rude way of expressing that the speaker doesn't have the answer to something

| Point | How can I tell? 내가 알 수 없지(What way could I be sure?)
You can never tell 단정할 순 없지

A: Will you see Gina at the office? 사무실에서 지나 볼거야?

B: **How should I know?** I don't know her schedule. 낸들 어찌 알아? 걔 일정을 모르는데.

미드표현

You can never tell. They look totally normal.
알 수 없는 노릇이야. 아주 정상으로 보이거든.

A: Do you think I should invite him? B: How should I know? When I'm done with them, I'm done with them.
A: 내가 걜 초대해야 될까? B: 내가 어떻게 알아? 걔네들과 난 이미 끝난 사이야.

035 You don't know what it's like to~ …가 어떤 건지 넌 이해 못해

this is indicating that the listener can't understand the speaker's feelings or experiences. It is a way to say "You can't understand how+V"

| Point | You have no idea what it's like to~ …하는게 어떤 건지 넌 몰라
You remember what it's like to do/~ing?
…하는 것이 어떤 건지 기억나?

A: I really envy you for living overseas for so long.
그렇게 오랫동안 외국에서 살다니 정말 부러워.

B: **You don't know what it's like to** live away from your family for years.
그렇게 오랫동안 가족과 떨어져 산다는 게 어떤 건지 넌 몰라.

미드표현

You don't know what it's like to have a baby.
애기 낳는 게 어떤 건지 넌 몰라.

You remember what it's like to be eighteen years old? 18살이 된다는 게 뭔지 기억나?

You remember what it's like to work a sixty hour week? 주당 60시간 일한다는 게 뭔지 기억나?

036 I know[understand] what it's like to~
…하는 것이 어떤 건지 알아

This indicates that the speaker has had an experience similar to what someone else is going through, and so he may have a special understanding of it. It is another way to say "I recognize the things that are happening to you."

| Point | know[understand] what it's like to~ …하는 것이 어떤 걸지 알다

A: How come you were so kind when I was sick?
내가 아팠을 때 왜 그렇게 잘해준거야?

B: **I know what it's like to** have a serious illness.
중병을 앓는게 어떤건지 알거든.

I know what it's like to be a teenager.
10대라는 게 어떤 건지 알아.

If you understand what it's like to have a daughter, then how can you threaten to kill someone else's?
딸이 있다는 것이 어떤 것인지 안다면, 어떻게 다른 사람의 딸을 죽이겠다고 협박을 할 수가 있어?

I want you to know what it's like to love someone, to truly love someone.
다른 사람을 사랑하는게, 진정으로 사랑하는게 어떤건지 알아줬으면 해.

037 I can't quite put my finger on it 딱히 뭐라고 하지 못하겠어

미드표현

this is a way of indicating that something is hard to describe or hard to express in words

| Point | put one's finger on
어떤 상황이 왜 틀렸고 이상한지 알고 있거나 혹은 설명하다

A: Why do you have such an unhappy look on your face? 왜 얼굴이 그렇게 안좋아?

B: **I can't quite put my finger on it,** but something is upsetting me. 딱히 뭐라고는 못하겠지만 뭐가 많이 혼란스러워.

There's something about Jerry. I can't put my finger on it. 제리에겐 뭔가가 있는데 딱히 뭐라고 하지 못하겠어.

I can't put my finger on it, but he seems more like your type.
딱 뭐라고 하지 못하겠지만 걔는 너랑 같은 유형인 듯해.

Ways of expressing certainty
내 말이 정말이라고 확실하다고 할 때

Take my word for it

001 I mean it 정말이야, 진심이야, 분명히 말했어

usually this is a way to say "This is true." The speaker is confirming that he is serious about something

| Point | I mean business 진심이야, 농담 아니야
I don't mean maybe! 대충 하는 말 아냐!, 진심으로 하는 말이야!
This time I mean it 이번엔 진짜 진심야

A: I don't want you to come home late again. **I mean it.** 다신 늦게 집에 오지마. 진심이야.

B: You can't control what time I choose to come home. 내 귀가시간을 네가 이래라 저래라 할 수 없어.

미드표현

Stop talking. I mean it. 그만 얘기해. 분명히 말했어.

I am serious. I mean it. 장난아냐. 진심이야.

That was a wonderful speech. I mean it.
정말 멋진 연설이었어. 정말이야.

002 I'm (dead) serious 정말이야, 진심이야, 나 굉장히 진지해

like the previous phrase, this is a way of saying that the speaker is earnest about what is being said. It expresses "I mean what I am saying"

| Point | I'm (so/ quite/ hundred percent) sure 정말 확신해

A: I'm going to quit this job. **I am dead serious.**
그만 둘래. 진심이야.

B: But what will you do without a salary?
월급도 없이 어떻게 할건데?

미드표현

Yes. I'm serious, Mike. I packed my things and I'm leaving. 그래, 진심야 마이크. 짐쌌고 나 떠나.

I'm serious. I've never seen these before.
정말이야. 이런 건 처음봐.

Don't do it again. I'm serious. 다시는 그러지마. 정말이야.

003 I'll bet 1. (상대방에 동조) 그럴거야, 확실해(I'm pretty sure) 2. (빈정) 그러겠지(sarcastically I agree)

this is usually a way to say that the speaker thinks something is true. It is like saying "Yeah, that's right"

| Point | I('ll) bet you (너한테) 맹세해
I'd bet my life[my last dollar] on~/that~
…라는 데 내 전 재산을 걸겠다, …라는 건 확실해
I('ll) bet S+V 틀림없어, 확실해

A: **I'll bet** rich people can go on vacation several times a year. 부자는 일년에 여러 번 휴가가는 게 확실해.

B: It sounds like you envy their lifestyle.
걔네들 사는 거가 부러운가 보군.

미드표현

I'll bet all I got. 정말 틀림없어.

I'll bet he's totally over me, I'll bet he's fine.
걘 날 잊은 게 확실해, 정말이지 괜찮을 거야.

I'll bet your Mom doesn't think so.
네 엄마는 그렇게 생각하지 않는 게 확실해.

I'll bet you 50 bucks that you can't do that.
네가 그거 못하는데 50달러 걸지.

004 You bet 1. (긍정) 확실해, 물론이지, 응 걱정마 2. (의문) 진짜야? 틀림없어?

this is like saying "Sure." It is said to confirm that something is true

| Point | You bet your life[your boots/ your ass]
확실해, 단연코, 틀림없어!, 물론!, 그럼!
You bet S+V 틀림없이 …야

A: Are you going to be at the meeting tonight?
오늘 밤 회의에 나올거야?

B: **You bet.** I wouldn't miss it. 물론이지, 꼭 갈게.

You bet your ass, I'm gonna fire you!
그렇고 말고, 넌 해고야!

You bet it did. 정말이지 그랬어.

You bet I am! 정말 그래!

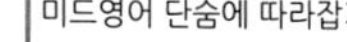

005 You can bet on it 그럼, 물론이지, 정말야, 걱정할 필요없어

often this is said to confirm that the speaker will be doing something in the future. It is similar to saying "That's going to happen" or "That will be done"

| Point | You can bet S+V …가 틀림없어

A: Will you be flying to Europe this summer?
이번 여름에 유럽에 갈거야?

B: **You can bet on it.** I've planned this trip for months. 물론이지. 여러 달 동안 이번 여행을 계획했는데.

Yeah, yeah, absolutely, you can bet on that.
그래, 그래, 물론이고 말고, 정말이야.

You can bet he's gonna use it.
걔가 그걸 이용할 것은 틀림없어.

If he did it once before, you can bet that he's done the same thing to other women.
걔가 전에 한 번 그랬다면, 걘 다른 여자들에게도 같은 짓을 한게 틀림없어.

006 [That's] For sure 맞아, 확실해, 물론야

미드표현

this is a way of agreeing or expressing certainty about something. It expresses "You are right about that"

| Point | for sure 확실히

A: I think the weather has gotten a lot colder this week. 날씨가 이번 주에 좀 더 추워진 것 같아.

B: **That's for sure.** I've worn a winter coat every day. 맞아. 매일 겨울 코트 입고 있어.

Well, she's got some breast implants. That's for sure. 저기 걘 가슴수술받았어. 확실해.

A: Maybe we should come up with a set of ground rules. B: Yeah, for sure.
A: 우리 사이에 규칙을 만드는 건 어떨까. B: 그래, 그러자.

And you don't have to worry about him cheating. That's for sure.
그리고 넌 걔가 바람피는 걸 걱정할 필요가 없어. 확실해.

007 Believe me 정말이야, 날 믿어 확실해

미드표현

this is a way for the speaker to say "Trust what I say." The speaker wants to express that what is being said is true and should be trusted

| Point | Believe you me 정말 진심이야(You really should believe me)
You'd better believe it 정말 맞는 말이야, 그럼, 그렇고 말고

A: Are you sure there is a meeting scheduled for today? 오늘 회의있는게 확실해?

B: **Believe me.** It will take place at 3 p.m.
정말이야. 오후 3시에 있어.

Believe me, I didn't want to hurt anyone.
진심이야, 누구에게도 해를 끼치고 싶지 않았어.

Believe me, it'll never happen again.
진심이야, 다시는 그런 일 없을거야.

Believe you me, I've been listening!
정말 진심이야, 듣고 있었다고!

008 I'll say 그러게 말이야, 맞아, 정말이야

this is usually a way for a speaker to say "Yes, that's right." He is expressing agreement with something that was said

| Point | I'll say 그러게 말이야, 정말이야

A: Anita is sure looking beautiful tonight.
애니타가 정말 오늘 밤 아름다워 보여.

B: **I'll say.** She seems like a movie star.
정말이야. 영화배우 같아.

I'll say. That's what everyone thinks.
그러게 말야. 모든 사람들이 바로 그렇게 생각해.

I'll say. You have a way with words.
맞아. 넌 입심이 좋아.

You think taxes are too high? I'll say.
세금이 너무 높다고 생각한다고? 정말이야.

009 I'm not kidding 정말이야, 장난아냐

this is indicating that the speaker is serious about what has been said. It is like saying "This is not a joke"

| Point | I kid you not 정말이야, 장난으로 하는 말 아냐

A: I am about ready to quit school. **I'm not kidding.** 학교 그만 둘려고. 장난아냐.

B: Come on. You need to stay in school so you can get a good job. 야아, 학교를 계속 다녀야 좋은 직장을 얻지.

미드표현

I'm not kidding, we lost the deal.
정말이야, 계약을 못했어.

I certainly am not kidding. This is serious.
정말이지 장난아냐. 이거 심각해.

I'm not kidding, we could lose our jobs over this. 정말이야, 우리는 이 일로 해서 직장을 잃을 수도 있어.

010 That's the truth 그건 사실이야, 맞는 말이야, 정말이야

this means "That is right." It is a simple way of agreeing with something that has been said

| Point | That's true 사실이야, 정말이야
I'm telling the truth 정말이야

A: I'm so tired of having to work late every night.
매일 밤 야근해야 하는 게 정말 힘들어.

B: **That's the truth.** When will it end?
맞는 말이야. 언제 끝날까?

미드표현

That's the truth, and you know it.
그건 사실이야 그리고 너도 알잖아.

I don't know if that's true or not.
그게 맞는지 아닌지 모르겠어.

That's true. We did a good thing.
정말이야. 우린 좋은 일 한거야.

I'm telling the truth. I wasn't there. I didn't kill Adam. 정말이지 난 거기에 없었어. 애덤을 죽이지 않았어.

011 I'm telling you (앞서 말한 내용강조) 진짜라니까, 정말이야

usually this is a way of saying "Believe what I say." The speaker is expressing that he is certain of something he stated before.

| Point | I'm telling you S+V …는 틀림없어

A: Are you saying that they're going to film a movie here? 여기서 영화촬영을 할거란 말이야?

B: **I'm telling you.** I heard the news from the press. 정말이야. 언론에서 뉴스를 들었어.

미드표현

I'm telling you, something's wrong!
잘 들어, 뭔가 이상해!

I'm telling you. I think she thinks I'm foxy.
정말이야. 걔가 날 섹시하다고 생각하는 것 같아.

I'm telling you, Jimmy, she's not right for me!
잘 들어봐, 지미, 걘 나하고 안맞아!

I'm telling you now

Friends
SEASON#10-18

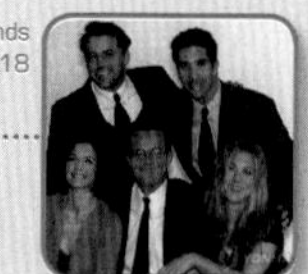

〈프렌즈〉 시즌 10의 마지막 에피소드, 파리행 비행기를 타는 Rachel에게 Phebe와 함께 온 Ross가 사랑한다며 남아달라고 하는 장면.

Ross: Please, please stay with me. I am so in love with you. Please, don't go.
Rachel: Oh my God.
Ross: I know, I know. I shouldn't have waited 'till now to say it, but I'm.. That was stupid, okay? I'm sorry, but I'm telling you now. I love you. Do not get on this plane.
Gate attendant #2: Miss? Are you boarding the plane?
Ross: Hey, hey. I know you love me. I know you do.
Gate attendant #2: Miss?
Rachel: I - I have to get on the plane.

로스: 제발 나와 함께 있어줘. 난 정말 널 사랑해. 제발이지 가지마.
레이첼: 아 이런.
로스: 알아, 알아. 진작 말했어야 했는데, 내가... 참 바보같지, 응? 미안해 하지만 지금 말하잖아. 널 사랑해. 이 비행기 타지마.
출입구안내원: 손님, 비행기 타실건가요?
로스: 네가 날 사랑하는거 알아. 네가 그렇다는거 알아.
출입구안내원: 손님?
레이첼: 나 비행기 타야 돼.

012 How true 정말 그래, 딱 맞는 말이야, 맞아

이드표현

this is expressing agreement with a statement that has been made. It is like saying "I think that is correct too"

A: The weather in the spring feels so nice.
봄 날씨는 정말 좋아.

B: **How true.** I love warm temperatures.
정말 그래. 온도가 따스해서 좋아.

How true. These snacks are delicious.
정말 그래. 이 스낵들은 정말 맛있어.

How true. He seemed guilty to me too.
정말 그래. 나도 걔가 유죄인 것 같았어.

How true. The traffic in this city is terrible.
맞는 말이야. 이 도시의 교통은 아주 끔찍해.

013 Take my word for it 진짜라니까, 믿어줘, 내 말 믿어

this is a way of saying "Believe me." It indicates that the speaker thinks something is absolutely true

I Point I (You can) Take it from me 내 말을 믿어 (Believe me)

A: You'll do fine on the exam. **Take my word for it.**
시험 잘 볼거야. 진짜라니까.

B: But I'm really worried about getting a bad grade.
하지만 성적이 나쁠까봐 정말 걱정되는데.

Take my word for it, he's the worst in the class.
진짜야, 걔는 반에서 최악이야.

Take it from me, Dad loves you.
그 점은 내 말을 믿어도 돼, 아빠는 널 사랑하셔.

Dad, I'm telling you the truth, okay you have to take my word for it, I don't smoke!
아빠, 진짜예요, 내 말을 믿어줘요, 난 담배를 피지 않아요!

014 I'm not lying 거짓말 아냐, 진짜야

이드표현

usually this is a way of protesting and saying something is true that has not been believed. In other words, it is like saying "I'm being honest"

I Point I I'm not lying for you 널 위해 거짓말하지 않을거야

A: I don't think you know anyone who is famous.
네가 아는 유명한 사람이 아무도 없을거야.

B: **I'm not lying.** I know a lot of celebrities.
거짓말 아냐. 내가 아는 유명인이 많아.

A: I know you're lying to me. Because you don't look me in the eye. B: I'm not lying.
A: 너 나한테 거짓말 하지. 내 눈을 바로 못 보잖아. B: 거짓말아냐.

A: You're lying to your wife? B: I'm not lying.
A: 네 아내한테 거짓말 해? B: 거짓말 안해.

015 I'd be lying if I said~ …라고 말하면 그건 거짓말이지

this is like saying "I'll admit that I didn't...." This is a way for the speaker to talk about his feelings on something

I Point I I would be lying if I said S+V …라고 말하면 그건 거짓말이겠지

A: How did you like the concert tonight?
오늘 밤 콘서트 어땠어?

B: **I'd be lying if I said** I enjoyed it.
좋았다고 하면 거짓말이겠지.

I'd be lying if I said I regret what happened.
내가 일어난 일을 후회한다고 말하면 그건 거짓말이지.

I'd be lying if I said I haven't thought about it myself. 내가 그거에 대해 생각해보지 않았다고 하면 거짓말이지.

I'd be lying if I said this hasn't been fun.
이게 재미없었다고 말한다면 그건 거짓말이지.

I would be lying if I said I wasn't disappointed.
내가 실망하지 않았다고 말하면 그건 거짓말이겠지.

016 No joke! 농담아니야!, 정말이라니까!

this is similar to saying "It's true." The speaker is telling people to believe what he says

| Point | This[That] is no joke 장난(농담)아니야, 웃을 일 아니야

A: So is the company offering you a good salary?
그래서 회사가 네게 월급을 많이 준다고?

B: Yeah, they are going to make me rich. **No joke!**
그래, 날 부자로 만들어준대. 농담아니야!

미드표현

This is no joke. She hit me. 농담아냐. 걔가 날 때렸어.

A man was killed. That's no joke.
한 남자가 죽었다고. 농담아냐.

Hey, no joke, I'm serious. 야, 농담아냐, 나 진지하다고.

No joke. He scammed all of us. He just wanted money. 농담아냐. 걔가 우리 모두에게 사기를 쳤어. 걘 돈을 원했어.

017 (There's) No question about it 의문의 여지가 없어, 확실해

this indicates that something is clearly true. It is like saying "It's certain"

| Point | No question about it 의문의 여지가 없어

A: Are you sure that David stole the computer?
데이빗이 컴퓨터를 훔친게 확실해?

B: **There's no question about it.** We found it in his apartment. 의심할 여지가 없어. 걔 아파트에서 컴퓨터를 발견했거든.

미드표현

No question about it, we'll have to fly to Boston. 의문의 여지가 없어, 우리는 보스톤으로 날아가야 돼.

No question about it, it's going to snow tomorrow. 확실해, 내일 눈이 올거야.

No question about it, your new clothes look great. 정말이야, 네 새 옷은 정말 멋져.

018 I couldn't have said it better 동감이야, 더 이상 어떻게 말을 해, 진짜야

this expresses "That is the way I was thinking." The speaker strongly agrees with something that was said

| Point | couldn't have+pp+비교 더 이상 …할 수 없었을거야, 정말 …해

A: I wish the snow was gone and summer was here. 겨울이 가고 여름이 왔으면 좋겠어.

B: **I couldn't have said it better.** I hate winter weather. 누가 아니래. 겨울날씨가 싫어.

미드표현

I couldn't have said it better. You knew the company's policy well.
내가 더 어떻게 말을 해. 너 회사 방침 잘 알잖아.

That couldn't have been cuter. 정말이지 귀여웠어.

I couldn't have been more clear. 정말 확실해.

MEMO

Ways of checking other's speaking and avoiding the misunderstanding

상대방 말을 다시 확인하거나 오해를 피하기

Don't take it personally

001 That's what they all say 다들 그렇게 말하겠지

when people say this, they are anticipating that most people will respond to an event in a certain way. Often it means that the person expects gossip about something that happened.

| Point | Well that's what we all say 다들 그렇게 말하지
That's what you all say 너 맨날 그렇게 말하지

A: People may start to think you're having an affair with Tom. 사람들은 네가 탐과 바람을 핀다고 생각하기 시작할지 몰라.

B: **That's probably what they'll say,** but we're just good friends. 다들 그렇게 말하겠지만 우린 그냥 친구사이야.

"The victim was asking for it." Isn't that what they all say?
"피해자는 스스로 자초한거야." 다들 이렇게 말하지 않겠어?

That's what you all say. You just don't want to go out with me because I have an off-putting personality.
너희들은 그렇게 말하겠지. 난 정이 안가는 사람이기 때문에 너희들은 나하고 놀고 싶지 않다고 말야.

002 Don't get me wrong 오해하지마

this means "Don't misunderstand me." It is said when a person wants to explain something clearly

| Point | Don't get me wrong, but~ 오해하진 마시구요 하지만…
Don't take this wrong (but ~) 오해하지마 (하지만 …)
Don't take this the wrong way (but~) 오해하지 말고 (하지만 …)

A: So you think that the war was a good idea?
그래 네 생각은 전쟁이 좋은 방법이었다는 거야?

B: **Don't get me wrong.** I hate to see so many people get killed.
오해하지마. 그렇게 많은 사람들이 죽어가는 걸 보는 건 정말 싫어.

Don't get me wrong, you're better than she is.
오해하지마, 넌 걔보다 나아.

Don't get me wrong, you're a great guy, maybe the best guy I know.
오해하지마, 넌 좋은 놈야 아마도 내가 아는 사람 중에서 가장 좋은 놈야.

Don't take this the wrong way, but how old are you? 이상하게 받아들이지 말고 몇 살이야?

003 Don't take it personally 기분 나쁘게 받아들이지마

this is a way to say "Don't get angry about this." It is said so someone won't feel insulted by something

| Point | Don't take it personally, but ~ 기분나쁘게 생각하지마, 하지만…

A: This article says that I have no talent.
이 기사에 의하면 내가 능력이 없대.

B: **Don't take it personally.** Not everyone understands your artwork.
기분나빠하지마. 다 네 예술작품을 이해하는 건 아냐.

Don't take it personally, but I'm not going to take your word for that.
기분 나쁘게 생각마, 하지만 거기에 대해선 네 말 듣지 않을 거야.

Don't take it personally. It's the doctor-thing.
기분 나쁘게 생각마. 이건 의사가 해야 할 일이잖아.

004 I didn't mean it 고의로 그런 건 아냐

this indicates the speaker didn't want to make anyone angry. It is like saying "Please don't be upset by what I did or said"

| Point | I didn't mean that like that 그러려고 그런 것 아니었어
I didn't mean any harm 다치게 할 생각은 없었어
I really didn't mean any offense
정말이지 기분나쁘게 하려고 한 게 아니야

A: Jean is still angry about what you said to her.
진은 네가 걔한테 한 말 때문에 아직 화나 있어.

B: **I didn't mean it.** I was just joking with her. 고의로 그런 건 아냐. 그냥 걜 놀린 것 뿐인데.

Whatever I said, I was drunk, I didn't mean it.
내가 뭐라 했든, 난 취했었어. 고의로 그런 게 아냐.

I just said that to upset you. I didn't mean it.
단지 널 화나게 할려고 말한거야. 정말 그런 뜻은 아니었어.

I didn't mean it last time. I mean it this time.
지난번에는 그럴 뜻이 아니었지만, 지금은 진심이야.

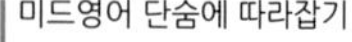

005 I didn't mean to do that 그럴려고 그런 게 아니었어

often this is a way to say "Sorry for doing that." The speaker wants to tell people he didn't want to make anyone unhappy or angry

| Point | I didn't mean to do~ …하려고 그런 건 아니야

A: You made a mess outside of my house.
너 집 밖을 난장판을 만들어놨어.

B: **I didn't mean to do that.** Let me clean it up.
그럴려고 그런 게 아닌데. 내가 치울게.

I didn't mean to offend you.
기분 나쁘라고 한 말은 아니었어.

I didn't mean to come up and ruin your weekend. 와서 네 주말을 망칠 생각은 아니었어.

I'm sure she didn't mean to hurt your feelings.
걔는 네 감정을 아프게 할 생각은 아니었던 게 확실해.

006 I don't mean to do that 그럴 생각은 없어

this is a way to say "Pardon me , but..." The speaker is apologizing for saying or doing something that could cause a small problem

| Point | I don't mean to do ~ …하려는 게 아니야
I don't mean it 그걸 생각은 아냐

A: I just lost my job today. 오늘 직장을 잃었어.

B: **I don't mean to** make things worse, but we have a lot of bills to pay.
더 힘들게 하려는 건 아니지만 내야할 청구서가 많아.

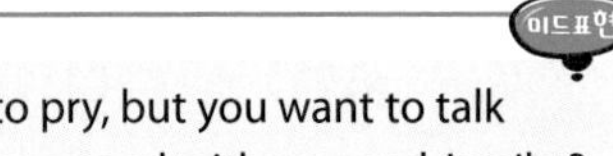

I don't mean to pry, but you want to talk about what happened with you and Jessika?
꼬치꼬치 파고 들고 싶진 않지만 너랑 제시카와 무슨 일이었는지 말해야지?

I don't mean to cut you off.
말을 끊으려고 했던 건 아니에요.

I don't mean to make things worse, but I don't want to live with him anymore.
사태를 더 나쁘게 만들려는 것은 아니지만 걔랑은 더 이상 같이 못 살겠어.

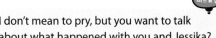

007 That's not what I mean 실은 그런 뜻이 아냐

this indicates "You didn't understand what I said." Usually this is a way for the speaker to explain more about his thoughts

| Point | That's not what I meant 그런 뜻이 아니었어
That's not what I said 내 말은 그런 게 아냐
That's not how I mean it 그런 뜻이 아니야

A: I think you feel that we should get a divorce.
우리가 이혼해야 된다고 네가 생각하는 것 같아.

B: **That's not what I mean.** I just think we're fighting too much.
그런 뜻은 아냐. 그냥 우리가 너무 많이 싸운다고 생각해.

That's not what I mean. I agree with you about that. 그런 뜻이 아냐. 그 점에 있어 너랑 동감야.

A: I thought you thought he was still a lawyer.
B: No, no, that's not what I meant.
A: 나는 네가 걔를 변호사로 생각하는 줄 알았어. B: 아냐 그런 뜻이 아냐.

That's not what I mean. I wanna marry you.
실은 그런 뜻이 아냐. 난 너랑 결혼하고 싶어.

008 No hard feelings (on my part) 악의는 아냐, 기분 나쁘게 생각마

this tells people that everything is OK. The speaker wants to say "I'm not angry"

| Point | (There's) No hard feelings for[about]~ …한 거에 악의는 없어

A: I'm sorry that I yelled at you this afternoon.
오늘 오후에 소리쳐서 미안해.

B: You were upset. **There are no hard feelings.**
너 화났잖아. 나쁜 감정은 없어.

I know you tried, so no hard feelings, okay?
네가 노력했다는 거 알아. 그러니 기분 나쁘게 생각하지마. 알았지?

I wanted to call and tell you that there's no hard feelings for firing you.
널 해고한 건 아무 악의도 없다는 말하려고 전화한 거야.

No offense 악의는 없었어, 기분 나빠하지마

this is a way of saying "I didn't mean to insult you." The speaker wants to tell someone that he hopes that person isn't angry

I Point I No offense to~ …에게 악의는 없었어
No offense, but~ 악의는 없지만 …
None taken (대답으로) 오해하지 않았어

A: I think that shirt isn't a good match for you. **No offense.** 그 셔츠가 너와 안 어울리는 것 같아. 기분나빠하지마.

B: Do you think I should wear another one?
다른 거 입어봐야 될까?

No offense, but that sounds nothing like her.
기분 나빠 하지마, 하지만 걔답지 않았어.

No offense, but can I see some kind of identification? 기분 나빠하지말고 신분증 좀 볼 수 있을까?

No offense, but I've got work to do.
기분 나빠하지마, 하지만 나 일해야 돼.

Am I right? 그렇지 않니?, 내 말이 맞지?

this is a way of asking "Is that correct?" The speaker wants to be sure everyone thinks he is correct

I Point I Am I right? 내 말이 맞아?

A: We should start a club for computer gamers. **Am I right?** 컴퓨터 게임 클럽을 시작하자. 내 말이 맞지?

B: Sure, there are a lot of people who would join.
그럼, 가입하는 사람이 많을 거야.

You love me and you want me to be happy. Am I right? 넌 날 사랑하고 내가 행복하길 바라지. 내 말 맞지?

I bet you always wanted to be a cop, am I right? 넌 늘 경찰이 되고 싶어 했지, 그렇지 않아?

I'm gonna have to trade you in for a newer model. Am I right, buddy?
널 새로운 모델과 교환해야 될 것 같아. 친구야 내 말이 맞지?

Like what? 예를 들면?, 어떤 거?

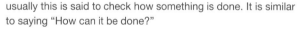

usually this is said to check how something is done. It is similar to saying "How can it be done?"

I Point I Such as? 예를 들면?
Like this? 이렇게 하면 돼?(Is this right?)
Yes, like that 그래 그렇게
No, not like that 아니 그렇게 아니고

A: You need to change the way you write reports.
넌 글 쓰는 법을 바꿔야 돼.

B: **Like what?** How should I change my writing style? 예를 들면? 어떻게 내 작문스타일을 바꿔야 돼?

Like this? Is this okay? 이렇게 하면 돼? 괜찮아?

Like this? Am I doing it correctly?
이렇게? 내가 제대로 하고 있는 거야?

Like what, for instance? I'm sure Donna would like to know. 예를 들면 어떤 거? 분명 도나는 알고 싶어할거야.

You did? 그랬어?, 정말?

often this is a way to ask "Really?" The speaker will say this when he is very surprised and wants to make sure he understood something

I Point I You do? 그래? You are? 그래?
You were? 그랬어? You have? 그래?

A: I went to the president's office this afternoon.
오늘 오후에 사장실에 갔었어.

B: **You did?** Why did you go there? 그랬어? 왜 갔는데?

You did? I can't believe it. 그랬어? 믿을 수 없구만.

You did? How? 그랬어? 어떻게?

A: I reached out to him, you know, to let him know it's okay to be gay. B: You did?
A: 난 걔한테 다가가서 게이라도 괜찮다는 것을 알려줬어. B: 그랬어?

013 You're just saying that 빈말인 거 알아, 그냥 해보는 말이지, 괜한 소리지

this is said when a person doesn't think another person is being honest. It indicates "I don't believe you"

| Point | You're just saying to do~ 그냥 …하려고 하는 소리지
You're just saying that S+V 그냥 …라고 하는 거지?

A: You are the most beautiful woman in the room.
넌 이 방에서 제일 예뻐.

B: **You're just saying that.** There are more beautiful women here. 괜한 소릴. 더 예쁜 여자들이 여기에 있구만.

That's a lie. You're just saying that to hurt me.
거짓말. 날 아프게 하려고 하는 말이지.

You're just saying that to make me feel better.
나 기분 좋아지라고 그냥 하는 말이지.

You're just saying that 'cause it's obvious.
그게 뻔하니까 그냥 하는 말이지.

014 Let's double check 다시 한번 보자

the speaker is saying that something should be looked at again to see if it is right. It is a way to say "Let's look at that a second time"

| Point | double check 다시 확인하다, 재확인하다
I'll check back 다시 한번 확인할게

A: I bought enough food for the party.
파티에 쓸 음식을 충분히 샀어.

B: **Let's double check** the amount. There will be many guests. 양을 다시 확인해보자. 손님이 많을거야.

So Eli can double check her story?
그럼 일라이가 자신의 이야기를 재확인해 줄 수 있어?

I just wanted to double check everything for tomorrow. 난 내일 건으로 모든 것을 다시 확인하고 싶었을 뿐이야.

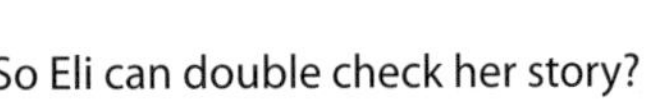

You can double check the guest list with the invitations. 넌 초대장과 손님리스트를 다시 한번 확인해보도록 해.

015 I'll make it clear 분명히 말해 줄게

this indicates the speaker will explain more about something. It is a way to say "I'll help you understand it"

| Point | make it clear (that S+V) (…을) 분명히 하다

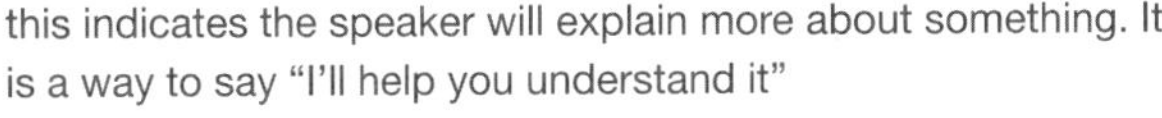

A: How are we supposed to submit this report?
이 보고서를 어떻게 제출해야 되는 건가요?

B: **I'll make it clear.** Just listen to me.
분명하게 얘기해줄게요. 제 말을 잘 들어요.

We didn't make it clear enough.
우리가 그걸 충분하게 분명히 하지 못했어.

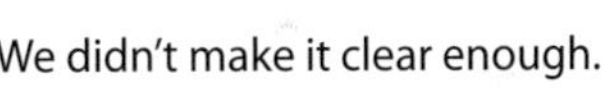

Get in touch with the local dispatch. Make it clear that we want this man in custody.
근처 경찰서에 연락해. 이 남자를 감금시켜야 된다고 말야.

That's right, he did make it clear, and he was wrong. 맞아. 걔는 그걸 분명히 했는데 걔가 틀렸어.

016 Let me get this straight 이건 분명히 해두자, 얘기를 정리해보자고

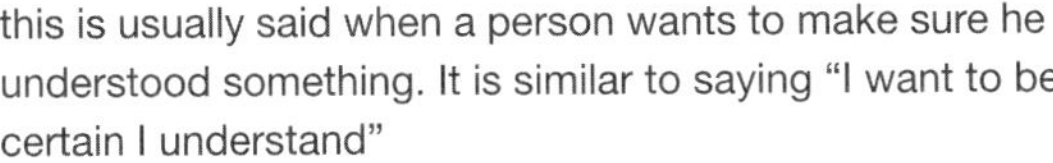

this is usually said when a person wants to make sure he understood something. It is similar to saying "I want to be certain I understand"

| Point | Let's just get one thing straight 이거 하나는 분명히 해두자
We got this straight 확실히 해야겠어

A: So I'll be running in the marathon on Saturday.
그래 내가 토요일에 마라톤 뛸거야.

B: **Let me get this straight.** You plan to run 26 miles? 얘기를 분명히 해보자고. 네가 26마일을 달릴거라고?

So let me get this straight. You just assumed my paper would be bad so you wrote one for me?
얘기를 정리해보자고. 내 레포트가 형편없을거라 생각해서 날 위해 새로운 레포트를 썼다고?

So let me get this straight. You use me to get back at your ex, and now you're dumping me for some other guy?
이건 분명히 하자고. 넌 날 이용해 네 전처에 복수하고 나서 이제는 다른 놈 때문에 나를 차버린다는거야?

017 Is that what you're saying? 네가 말하는 게 이 말이야?

this means "Do you mean this?" It checks to see if the speaker understood correctly

| Point | Is that a yes or not? 예스야 노야?

A: The amount of this bill is much too high.
이 청구서금액이 너무 높아요.

B: You want your bill reduced. **Is that what you're saying?** 청구서금액을 깍아 달라고요? 그 말씀예요?

미드표현

Have I become a burden? Is that what you're saying? 내가 네게 짐이 된다고? 네가 말하는 게 이 말이야?

I need to know how many people will be there. Is that a yes or a no?
몇 명 올지 알아야 돼. 온다는 거야 아님 못 온다는 거야?

I just need a yes or a no.
그러겠다는 건지 안 그러겠다는 건지 대답해줘.

018 Is that it? 그런 거야?, 그걸로 끝이야?

this is a way to ask "Was I right?" It checks to see if the speaker had the right idea

| Point | Is that all? 그게 다야? 그것 밖에 안돼?
Is that so? 맞아?, 그래?, 과연 그럴까?
That's it? 이걸로 끝이야?

A: I think you want to move to another city. **Is that it?** 네가 다른 도시로 이사가고 싶어하는 것 같아. 그건 거야?

B: Well, I have been thinking of going elsewhere.
어, 다른 곳으로 가는 걸 생각해왔어.

미드표현

You're just not gonna talk to me, is that it?
나하고 이야기하지 않겠다, 그런 거야?

So you stalked him? Is that it?
그래서 걔를 스토킹했어? 그런 거야?

You asked her to leave? That's it?
걔보고 떠나라고 했어? 그걸로 끝이야?

019 Is that what this is (about)? 그 때문에 이런 거니?

this is usually said to check if something is correct or understood. He is asking "Do you mean it is....?"

| Point | That's what it is 그게 바로 그런 거야
That's where it's at 상황이 바로 그런거야

A: I keep my collection of stamp books here.
내 우편 수집책을 여기 보관해.

B: These books? **Is that what this is?**
이 책들? 그게 이거야?

미드표현

Oh, my god! Is that what this is all about?
오, 맙소사! 그래서 그런 거야?

Is that what this is all about? Your desire to make love to me?
이게 그 때문에 그런 거야? 나랑 자고 싶어서?

Do you like Mona? Is that what this is about? Do you have a crush on her?
모나를 좋아하는 거야? 그래서 다 그런 거야? 걔한테 반했어?

020 Excuse me? 뭐라구?, 못 들었어

this is a polite way of saying "What?" It means that someone should repeat something

| Point | I'm sorry? 예? (말을 못 알아들었을 때) 뭐라고 했어?
Come again? 뭐라구요?
Pardon me? 뭐라고 하셨죠?
I'm sorry I missed that 미안해요 못 들었어요

A: **Excuse me?** I didn't hear you. 뭐라구요? 못 들었어요.

B: I asked if you would move your car. 차 좀 치워달라고요.

미드표현

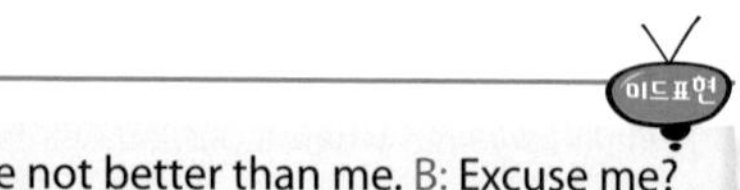

A: You are not better than me. B: Excuse me?
A: 넌 나보다 못해. B: 뭐라고?

A: How do you feel about working undercover?
B: I'm sorry? A: 잠복근무에 대해 어떻게 생각해? B: 뭐라구?

A: We just lost a million dollars on that deal.
B: Come again?
A: 우리 그 거래에서 백만 달러를 손해봤어요. B: 뭐라구요?

021 How's that? 뭐라고?

usually this is a question that is either asking for more information, or it is asking for someone to repeat himself. When asking for more information, it is like saying "I don't understand. Explain it to me." When asking for someone to repeat something, it is like saying "Tell me that again, because I didn't hear you"

I Point I How's that? 뭐라고?, 다시 말해봐?
How's that again? 다시 한번 말해줄래?
What was that again? 뭐라고 했죠?

A: I plan to study psychology in school.
난 학교에서 심리학을 공부할 생각이야.

B: **How's that?** Did you say you work in radiology?
다시 말해봐? 방사선과에서 일한다고 했어?

How's that? You need to talk louder.
뭐라고? 좀 더 큰 소리로 말해봐.

So you got a visa to the US? How's that?
그럼 미국비자를 얻었다고? 뭐라고 그런거야?

How's that? I can't hear anything you said.
뭐라고? 네가 한 말 하나도 들리지 않아.

You want to start a business? How's that?
사업을 시작하고 싶다고? 다시 말해봐.

022 You did what? 네가 뭘 어쨌다구?

this is asking someone "What did you do?" It is often said when someone is shocked or surprised about something that was said

I Point I You went where? 어디 갔었다고? Which is which? 뭐가 뭐라고?
You did it when? 언제 했다고? Who did what? 누가 뭘 했다고?

A: I went to Africa last year with Bill.
작년에 빌과 아프리카에 갔었어.

B: **You did what?** You really went to Africa?
네가 뭘 어쨌다고? 정말 아프리카에 갔었어?

A: I went to the police station and filed a complaint against you. B: You did what?
A: 경찰서에 가서 널 고발했어. B: 뭘 했다구?

A: I invited him over tomorrow anyway. You can find out what he wants then. B: You did what?
A: 어쨌든 난 걔를 내일 초대했어. 그럼 넌 걔가 뭘 원하는지 알아낼 수 있어. B: 뭘 어쨌다고?

A: I took Grace and Zach to see Peter. B: You did what? A: 그레이스와 잭을 데리고 피터를 만나러 갔어. B: 뭘 했다고?

023 You're what? 뭘 어떻게 하겠다고?, 뭘 어쩐다고?, 뭐라고?

like the previous phrase, this indicates surprise. It is like saying "Tell me again"

I Point I You what? 뭘 어떻게 했다고?, 뭐라고?,
Yes, what? 네, 뭐라구요?

A: I'm moving to Paris in a month. 한달 후에 파리로 이사가.

B: **You're what?** You're going to move to Paris?
뭐라고? 파리로 이사간다고?

So you're what? Protecting him?
그래서? 걔를 보호하겠다고?

A: I'm pregnant. B: You're what?
A: 임신 중이야. B: 뭐라고?

You're what? What is wrong with you?
뭘 어쩌겠다고? 너 도대체 왜 그러냐?

024 Tell her what? 걔에게 뭐라고 하라고?, 뭐를 말하라고?

this means "What do you want me to tell her?" Often this is a way of asking someone to repeat something

I Point I Tell her what? 걔한테 무슨 말을 한다고?
Tell me what? 나한테 무슨 말을 한다고?

A: Tell Lisa that she needs to practice the piano.
리사에게 피아노 연습을 해야 한다고 말해.

B: **Tell her what?** I didn't understand what you said.
뭐라고 하라고? 네가 하는 말 이해못했어.

A: Okay, when are you gonna tell her? B: Tell her what? A: 걔한테 언제 말할거야. B: 뭐를?

Tell me what? What is it that you need to tell me? 나한테 무슨 말을 한다고? 나한테 할 말이 뭔데?

A: But shouldn't we just tell Larry? B: Tell him what? A: 하지만 래리에게 말해야 되지 않을까? B: 걔한테 뭐라고 말해?

A: He wants me to tell you somethin'. B: Tell me what? A: 걘 나보고 너에게 뭐 좀 얘기하래. B: 나한테 무슨 말을?

025 Say what? 뭐라고?, 다시 말해줄래?

this is not commonly used because it is slang, but it means "What did you say?" It indicates the speaker is surprised

| Point | Say what? 뭐라고?, 뭘 말할건데?

A: I want you to help me steal some things.
뭐 좀 훔치는 거 도와줘.

B: **Say what?** I'm not going to help steal anything.
뭐라고? 어떤 것도 훔치는 걸 도와주지 않을 거야.

A: Maybe I just need to say it out loud. B: Say what? A: 내가 분명하게 말해야 될지도 모르겠네. B: 뭐라고?

A: He fell into me. We're engaged! B: Say what? A: 걘 나한테 빠졌어. 우린 약혼했어! B: 뭐라고?

A: You're so immature. You're going to make me say it? B: Say what?
A: 너 참 미숙하다. 나보고 얘기하라는거야? B: 뭘 말할건데?

026 Say it again? 뭐라구?, 다시 한번 말해줄래?

this is asking someone to repeat something. Often this is the same as saying "What did you say?"

| Point | (Can you) Say that again? 뭐라구?
*say that again 두말하면 잔소리지

A: Grandpa, we need to go to the grocery store.
할아버지, 식품점에 가야 돼요.

B: **Say it again?** I couldn't hear you. 뭐라고? 못 들었어.

I didn't really hear what you said. Could you just say it again? 무슨 말인지 안 들려. 다시 말해 줄래?

Can you say that again? The signal's really bad.
다시 말해 줄래? 신호가 잘 안 잡혀.

Do I need to say it again? Let's move.
두말하면 잔소리지. 자 가자고.

I can't hear you. Say that again.
잘 못들었어. 다시 말해주라.

027 Run it[that] by (me) again 다시 한번 설명해줘

usually this means someone wants to hear something again so he can try to understand it. It is like saying "I'd like you to tell me that once more"

| Point | run A by B B에게 A에 대한 상의하다, A를 허락받기 위해 B에게 설명하다
You'd better run it by me 내게 먼저 상의해(Give me the details)

A: Do you think the sales plan is a good one?
그 판매계획이 좋다고 생각해?

B: **Run it by me again.** I need to think about it.
다시 한번 말해줘봐. 생각을 해봐야겠어.

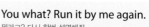

You what? Run it by me again.
뭐라고? 다시 한번 설명해줘.

I'm going to let you run that by the D.A.
지방검사에 그걸 설명하도록 해주지.

So before I turn this in, I wanted to run it by Vince. 내가 이걸 제출하기 전에 빈스와 상의하고 싶었어.

I think I would have to run it by Chris first.
먼저 크리스에게 상의를 해야 될 것 같았어.

028 What did you say? 뭐라고 했는데?, 뭐라고?

this is a simple way to tell someone "Say it again." It usually means the person didn't hear what was said

| Point | What did you say? 뭐라고?, 뭐라고 했어?

A: I'm sorry. **What did you say?** 미안. 뭐라고 했어?

B: I said that your hearing aid needs new batteries.
네 보청기 배터리를 갈아야 한다고 했어.

What did you say? I don't understand what you're saying. 뭐라고? 네가 말하는 걸 이해못하겠어.

I'm sorry Jane. I couldn't hear you. What did you say? 제인, 미안해. 잘 안 들려. 뭐라고 했어?

What did he say? He said marry me?
걔가 뭐라고 했다고? 나랑 결혼한다고?

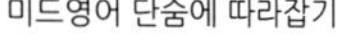

029 You lost me 못 알아들었어

this often means "I don't understand what you mean. It indicates the speaker wants something explained more

| Point | You lost me there 못 알아들었는데(fail to hear, see, understand)
You lost me at~ …할 때부터 못 들었어

A: That is how a car's engine works.
이렇게 해서 자동차 엔진이 작동하는 거야.

B: **You lost me.** I don't understand mechanical things. 못 알아들었어. 기계적인 것들은 이해가 안돼.

You lost me when you talked about scientific theory. 니가 과학이론 얘기하는 부분에서 못알아들었어.

You lost me at the start of your speech.
네 연설 처음부터 무슨 말인지 못알아들었어.

You lost me when you started talking crazy.
네가 말도 안되는 소리할 때부터 무슨 소리인지 모르겠어.

030 How's that again? 다시 한번 말해줄래?, 뭐라고?

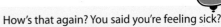

this is a way to tell someone to repeat something. It means "I couldn't hear you"

| Point | What was that again? 뭐라고 했어?
Once again, please 다시 한번 말해줘

A: Would you like some more food? 음식 좀 더 들래?

B: **How's that again?** Speak louder. 뭐라고? 크게 얘기해봐.

How's that again? You said you're feeling sick?
뭐라고? 몸이 아프다고 말했어?

How's that again? I didn't hear you.
뭐라고? 네 말 못들었어.

How's that again? It's really loud in this room.
다시 한번 말해줄래? 이 방 정말 시끄럽네.

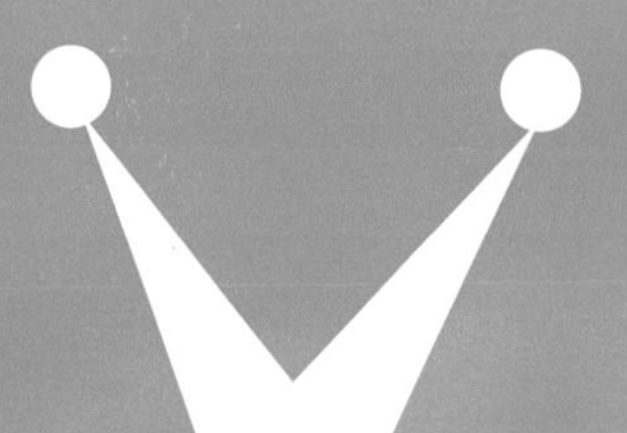

331

Things that are said when someone starts to talk about or explain something

말을 시작하거나 얘기를 나누고자 할 때

Listen to me

001 (Do) You hear that? 1. (바로 전에 한 말) 들었지? 2. (이상한 소리) 저 소리 들리니?

this is usually a way for the speaker to ask "What was that noise?" It is asking others to confirm that they heard the same sound as he did

| Point | You hear that? 내 말 들었지?, 저 소리 들려?

A: **Do you hear that?** It sounds like a thunderstorm. 저 소리 들려? 천둥소리같아.

B: I think it was just the noise from a passing airplane. 비행기 지나가는 소리인 것 같아.

미드표현

Shh! You hear that? 쉿! 저 소리 들려?

Oh, yeah, Sara, you hear that? I'm going to be a Dad! 와 새라, 들었지? 내가 아버지가 된대!

You hear that? What is that? 들었지? 저게 무슨 소리지?

You hear that? The phone's off the hook. 들었지? 수화기가 제대로 안꼽혀 있나봐.

002 Did you hear that? (얘기) 들었지?, 너도 들었니?

like the previous expression, this may be a way to confirm something that was heard. It is like the speaker is saying "Are we hearing the same thing?"

| Point | Did you hear (S+V)? …얘기(소식) 들었니?
Where did you hear that? 너 그 얘기 어디서 들었니?
You heard that? 그 얘기 들었어?

A: I think school has been canceled. **Did you hear that?** 학교가 휴교래. 얘기 들었지?

B: Yes, the radio reported that there was no school today. 어. 라디오에서 오늘 수업없다고 하더라.

Did you hear that? Karen's hurt. 얘기 들었지? 카렌이 아프대.

Did you hear that?! My Dad's proud of me! 너 들었지?! 아빠가 날 자랑스러워 하신대!

Did you hear that? Nick had a crush on me!! 그 얘기 들었지? 닉이 날 좋아한대!!

003 Have you heard (that~)? 그 말(소식) 들어봤니?

often this is a way to ask "Did you know S+V?" The speaker is checking if others have received some important news or information

| Point | Have you heard about~? …에 대한 소식 들어봤어?
Have you heard from~? …로부터 소식 들어봤어?
Have you heard of~? …소식 들어봤어?
What have you heard? 무슨 이야기를 들은거야?

A: **Have you heard** that we will have a special meeting today? 오늘 특별회의 있는 거 들었어?

B: No, I haven't. What time will it take place? 아니, 못 들었어. 언제 한대?

Have you heard that Julie is dropping out? 줄리가 그만둔다는 얘기 들어봤어?

Have you heard from Jamie? 제이미에게서 연락있어?

Have you heard about Sandy's secret boyfriend? 샌디의 비밀 남친에 대해 들어봤어?

Have you heard of them? 걔네들 이야기 들어봤어?

004 I didn't hear that 못 들었어

미드표현

this is a way of expressing that the speaker hasn't been told about something. He is saying "I never got that information"

| Point | I didn't hear that 그런 얘기 못 들었어
I didn't hear sb V …하는 것을 듣지 못했어
I didn't hear that S+V …이야기를 들은 적이 없어

A: Everyone is planning to attend the wedding on Saturday. 다들 토요일 결혼식에 갈거야.

B: Is that right? **I didn't hear that.** 정말 맞아? 얘길 못들어서.

I'm going to pretend I didn't hear that. 못 들은 척 할거야.

Hey! I didn't hear you come in. 야, 너 들어오는 소리 못들었어.

Honey, I didn't hear you come downstairs. You couldn't sleep, either? 자기야, 일층으로 내려오는 소리 못들었어. 자기도 잠이 오지 않는거야?

005 I can't[couldn't] hear you 안 들려, 못 들었어

this is the same as saying "You weren't loud enough." It indicates that the speaker couldn't understand what was said and wants it repeated

I Point I I can't[couldn't] hear you 안 들려, 못 들었어

A: What? **I can't hear you.** 뭐라고? 안 들려.

B: I said Steve wants to see you now.
스티브가 널 지금 보고 싶다고 말했어.

I can't hear you. You'll have to speak up.
못 들었어. 크게 말해봐.

I can't hear you! What? 안들려! 뭐라고!

I'm sorry Linda. I couldn't hear you. What did you say? 린다야 미안해. 못 들었거든. 뭐라고 했어?

006 I heard about it second hand 전해 들었어

미드표현

this means that the speaker got information from someone who was not directly involved. It is a way to say "Another person told me about it"

I Point I I heard about it 얘기 들었어
I've heard all about it (다른 누군가가 알려주어서) 이미 다 알고 있어

A: When did Gail decide she was going to get married? 게일은 결혼하기로 언제 결정했어?

B: I don't know. **I heard about it second hand.**
몰라. 전해들은 거야.

We heard about what happened.
어떤 일이 있었는지 들었어.

I heard about that, man. Everybody's talking about it. 다 들었어. 모두가 그 얘기 하더라.

I heard about the bombing. I'm here to help.
폭탄에 대해 들었어. 도와주려고 왔어.

007 I was told that (누군가 내게) 그걸 말해 줬어, 그렇게 들었어, 전해 들었어

미드표현

usually this indicates the speaker was given specific information. He is saying "Someone gave me that information"

I Point I I was [I've been] told (that) S+V …라고 들었어, 내가 듣기론…
So I've been told/ So I hear 그렇다고 들었어

A: **I was told** that department stores would be having sales today. 백화점이 오늘 세일한다고 들었어.

B: Yes, traditionally this is the time when they hold sales. 어, 늘상 세일하는 때야.

I've been told by more than one man that I am gorgeous. 내가 멋지다고 한 사람 이상으로부터 들어왔어.

I was told that the doors close at ten.
내가 듣기로 문은 10시에 닫힌대.

I was told you had a question. 너 질문있다며.

008 Word travels fast 발없는 말이 천리 가, 소문은 빨리 돌잖아

미드표현

this is a way of saying "People spread news quickly." It indicates that news reaches many people in a rapid way

I Point I Word gets around 소문 따위가 널리 퍼진다

A: I heard you've been promoted to manager.
매니저로 승진되었다며.

B: Yeah, it was just announced. **Word travels fast.**
어, 방금 발표났어. 소문 빠르네.

A: Word around the office is you've reopened the case. B: Who told you? A: Word travels.
A: 네가 사건을 다시 수사한다는 소문이 돌던대. B: 누가 그래? A: 소문은 빨리 돌잖아.

A: How'd you know we were here? B: Sam called. A: Wow! Word travels fast.
A: 우리가 여기에 있다는 것을 어떻게 알았어? B: 샘이 전화했어. A: 소문 한번 엄청 빠르다.

009 From what I hear[heard] 내가 들은 바로는, 내가 듣기로는

this is a way to say "I heard this information." It expresses that the speaker got information that made him think in a specific way

| Point | From what I hear[heard] 내가 듣기로는

A: What kind of weather are we going to have tomorrow? 내일 날씨가 어떨거래?

B: **From what I hear,** it's supposed to snow.
내가 들은바로는 눈이 올거래.

미드표현

These streets ain't safe in this part of town from what I hear.
내가 듣기로는 시내의 이 지역에서 이 거리들은 안전하지 않대.

I grew up on a farm, okay, from what I heard they're having sex or Howard's caught in a milking machine. Do you mind if I stay here tonight?
내가 농장에서 자랐잖아. 내가 듣기로는 걔네들 섹스를 하고 있거나 하워드가 착유기를 착용하고 있는거야. 나 오늘 여기서 자도 될까?

010 I got wind of it 그 얘기를 들었어, 그런 얘기가 있더라

this is usually said when someone learns of new information, or possibly rumors. In other words, it means "I have heard about it"

| Point | I heard it through the grapevine 소문으로 들었어
A little bird told me 그냥 누가 알려줬어
What's the buzz? 무슨 소문이니?

A: **I got wind of** the possibility our company will be sold. 우리 회사가 매각될 지도 모른다는 소문을 들었어.

B: Is that right? I wonder if our jobs will be safe.
정말야? 우리 자리가 안전할 까 궁금하네.

미드표현

What happened? You got wind of the party?
무슨 일이야? 파티에 대해 들었어?

It didn't take the media long to get wind of this. Make sure no one contaminates my crime scene.
언론이 바로 그 얘기를 들었어. 내 범죄현장을 아무도 모르게 해.

011 Rumor has it~ …라는 소문을 들었어

often this communicates something that people are talking about and believe to be true. It is like saying "I have heard many people say that S+V"

| Point | Rumor has it (that) S+V …라는 소문을 들었어

A: **Rumor has it** you will be leaving for Australia.
호주 간다는 소문을 들었어.

B: That's silly. I have no plans to travel there.
어처구니 없구만. 거기 갈 계획없어.

미드표현

Rumor has it you used to be a pretty funny guy. 너 예전엔 꽤 재미있는 녀석이었다며.

Rumor has it he's going to quit
걔가 그만둘 거라는 얘기가 있어.

Rumor has it that Jack was busy hazing one of his interns today.
소문에 의하면 잭은 오늘 자기 인턴 중 한 명을 괴롭히는데 바빴다고 하던데.

012 You heard me 내가 말했지, 명심해, 말한 그대로야

often this means "I meant it when I said..." It is usually said when the speaker wants to repeat something, especially instructions, and say it strongly

| Point | I believe you heard me 내가 말해잖아
I don't think you heard me 내 말 못들었구만

A: Do I have to do my homework? 숙제를 해야 돼요?

B: **You heard me.** You can't watch TV until your homework is complete. 내가 말했지. 숙제 다 할 때까지는 TV 못봐.

You heard me. Go to your room.
내 말 들었지. 방으로 가.

You heard me. I don't want you dating him.
명심해. 걔랑 데이트하지마.

You heard me. Get out! 내 말 들었지. 꺼져!

013 That ain't the way I heard it
내가 듣기로는 그게 아닌데, 나는 다르게 들었는데

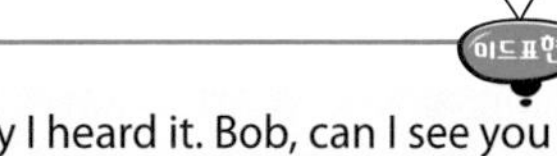

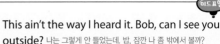

the grammar here is incorrect, but it is a way of expressing disagreement with something that was said. It means "I heard something that was different"

| Point | Little different from the way I heard it 내가 들은 거랑 좀 다르네

A: Sharon broke up with Ben because she didn't like his friends. 샤론이 벤의 친구들을 싫어해서 벤과 헤어졌대.

B: **That ain't the way I heard it.** I heard she had another boyfriend. 내가 듣기론 다른 남자가 생겼다는대.

This ain't the way I heard it. Bob, can I see you outside? 나는 그렇게 안 들었는데. 밥, 잠깐 나 좀 밖에서 볼까?

Little different from the way I heard it. Cindy. You want to tell me what happened here? 내가 듣기로는 그게 아닌데. 신디, 무슨 일인지 설명 좀 해주겠어?

014 Now I've heard[seen] everything
살다 보니 별 말[걸]을 다 듣[보]겠네

미드표현

often this is used to express "That is very unusual or strange." It shows amazement at some form of news that has been received

| Point | You[We] live and learn 살다 보니 별 걸 다 알게 되네
I've heard everything 별소리를 다 듣네
I heard everything 모든 얘기를 다 들었어

A: Soon every car will have Internet service in it. 곧 모든 차에서 인터넷이 가능할거야.

B: **Now I've heard everything.** Do people really want Internet in their cars? 별소릴 다 듣네. 사람들이 정말 차에서 인터넷 하기를 원할까?

You were a beauty queen? Now I've heard everything. 네가 미인대회우승했다고? 살다보니 별말 다 듣네.

Now I've heard everything. I don't believe you were ever rich. 살다보니 별말 다 들어보네. 네가 부자였다는 말 못믿겠어.

He's supposed to be innocent? Now I've heard everything. 걔가 무죄여야 된다고? 살다보니 별말 다 듣네.

015 Mark my word! 내 말 잘들어!

미드표현

the speaker is telling a listener to believe what he says because it will be shown to be true in the future. It is like saying "Remember what I said and you'll see I'm right"

| Point | Mark my word 내 말을 잘 들어

A: Are you sure the stock market is a good place to invest? 주식시장이 투자하기에 정말 좋을까?

B: **Mark my word.** You can make a lot of money there. 내 말대로 해. 그러면 돈 많이 벌 수 있어.

You'll turn against me, you mark my words. 넌 내게서 등을 돌리게 될거야. 내 말을 잘 기억해두라고.

But mark my words, I will destroy him and whatever wedding he thinks he's planning. 하지만 내 말을 잘 들으라고. 난 걔와 걔가 계획하는 무슨 결혼식이든 다 망가뜨릴거야.

016 I'm talking to you! 내 말 안들려!, 너한테 말하는 거야!, 내가 하는 말 좀 잘 들어봐!

미드표현

often this is expressing "I want you to listen to me." It is said when the speaker wants to get the attention of a listener

| Point | Read[Watch] my lips 내 말 잘 들어

A: Hey Gloria, **I'm talking to you!** Did you hear me? 야 글로리아, 너한테 말하는 거야! 내 말 들려?

B: No, I'm sorry. I was paying attention to something else. 아니, 미안. 딴데 신경쓰느라고.

Are you peeing while I'm talking to you? (전화) 너 쉬하면서 나하고 이야기하는 거야?

You heard me, all right? Read my lips. 명심해, 알았지? 내 말을 잘 들으라고.

I'm talking to you. Now hurry up and get out of the bathroom. 내말 안들려. 빨리 서둘러 화장실에서 나와.

017 I'm getting to it 바로 얘기해줄게

usually this is a way to tell others that the speaker is going to start talking about a subject. It reassures listeners that he hasn't forgotten it and hasn't intentionally avoided talking about it. Another way to say this would be "I'm ready to start talking about it now"

| Point | get (right) to it …을 바로 시작하다, 말하다(get right to the point)
get right down to 요점[핵심]을 말하다(get to the point quickly)
Let me just get right to it 직접적으로 말할게

A: When will you tell us about the result of the audit? 감사결과를 언제 우리에게 말해줄거야?

B: **I'm getting to it,** just be patient for a while. 바로 얘기해줄게, 좀 참으라고.

I'm going to get right to it. Jack's semen was found all over your kitty costume.
요점을 말할게요. 잭의 정액이 당신 고양이 의상 곳곳에서 발견되었어요.

I know how valuable your time is, so I'll get right to it. 네 시간이 얼마나 소중한지 아니까 바로 이야기할게.

018 I'll come to that 나중에 얘기해줄게

this is a way to tell people that a subject will be discussed soon. Sometimes when a person is giving information to a group of people, he is asked for additional or extra information. This phrase can be used to say "Let me finish what I'm talking about and then I will discuss that"

| Point | (sb) come to that 얘기하다, (새로운 토픽을) 다루기 시작하다

A: Can you show us how to use these computers? 이 컴퓨터 어떻게 쓰는지 알려줄래?

B: Sure. **I'll come to that** in a few minutes. 그럼. 잠시 후에 알려줄게.

I'll come to that in a few minutes.
몇분 후에 얘기해줄게.

After we conclude the presentation, I'll come to that. 발표회를 끝낸 후에 얘기해줄게.

I'll come to that when you calm down a bit.
네가 좀 진정하면 얘기해줄게.

I'll come to that if there is a private place for us to talk. 우리가 조용히 얘기할 곳이 있으면 얘기해줄게.

019 Listen to me 내 말 좀 들어봐

this is a way of saying "I have something to say to you." It is urging someone to pay attention to whatever is being spoken about

| Point | He listens to me 걘 내 말을 잘 들어

A: Why do you enjoy hanging around Antonio? 왜 앤토니어와 어울리는 걸 좋아해?

B: He's nice, and he **listens to me.** 걔 좋아, 내 말도 잘 듣고.

I want you to listen to me very carefully.
내 말 좀 잘 들어봐.

Listen to me Nina. That's never gonna happen.
니나야 내 말 들어봐. 그건 절대 안 될거야.

I don't have to listen to this. And you can't shove me around.
난 당신이 지껄이는 말을 들을 필요가 없어. 당신은 나를 이래라 저래라 할 수도 없고.

020 Are you listening to me? 듣고 있는 거야?, 내 말 듣는 거야?

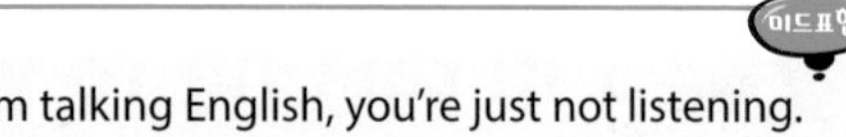

this is often said to check whether someone has been paying attention. It is like asking "Have you heard what I said to you?"

| Point | You don't seem to be listening 내 말 안 듣는 것 같으네
Do you have something else on your mind? 뭐 딴 생각하는 거야?
You're just not listening 내 말 안 듣고 뭐해

A: I've been talking for 10 minutes. **Are you listening to me?** 10분간 이야기했는데, 듣고 있는거야?

B: Yeah, I've heard every word that you have been saying. 어. 네 말 빠지지 않고 다 들었어.

I'm talking English, you're just not listening.
난 영어로 말하고 있는데 넌 안듣고 있어.

You are not going to believe the evening I've had. Are you listening to me?
오늘 저녁에 무슨 일이 일어났는지 믿지 못할거야. 내 말 듣고 있어?

Charlotte, are you listening to me? Give me the number. 샬롯, 내 말 듣고 있는거야? 전화번호 달라니까.

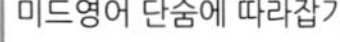

021 All right, get this 알겠어, 이거 들어봐봐

this is another way to tell people that they should listen to something because it will interest them. The speaker is trying to draw people's attention. Another way of saying it would be "Listen up everyone, you will be interested in what I have to say"

| Point | Get this (관심유도) 이것 좀 들어봐

A: **All right, get this.** Taxes are going up again.
알겠어, 이것 좀 들어봐. 세금이 또 올라가고 있어.

B: I can't believe it. Everything costs so much.
이럴 수가. 돈이 안들어가는데가 없구만.

Get this, the rapist's semen came back positive for cocaine.
이것 좀 들어봐, 강간범의 정액이 코카인 양성반응으로 나왔어.

Get this, Charlie here walked into our bedroom and saw Serena naked. 이것 좀 들어봐, 찰리는 우리 침대로 걸어 들어와 세레나의 벗은 몸을 봤어.

And get this, I waited up for Tony to call me last night, and he never did.
이거 들어봐봐, 어젯밤에 토니가 전화하기를 내내 기다렸는데 전화가 오지 않았어.

022 Listen up! (명령조로) 잘 들어!

this is a slightly impolite way to say "Be quiet and hear what I want to say." It is said to get everyone to pay attention, especially when there is an important announcement for a group

| Point | Listen good! 잘 들어!

A: **Listen up!** The bus will be leaving in ten minutes. 자 들어봐! 버스는 10분 후에 출발할거야.

B: I guess that means we'd better get on it now.
그럼 지금 타야겠네.

Okay, everybody, listen up. 좋아, 다들 잘 들어.

All right, everybody, listen up. 자, 모두들 잘 들어봐.

Listen up, Tom, this is real important.
탐, 잘 들어, 중요한 문제야.

023 (Just) Hear me out 내 말 끝까지 들어봐

often this is asking someone to consider the speaker's opinion before making a judgment on it. In other words, "Listen to me before you decide"

| Point | Now hear this 자, 주목해봐

A: I don't think that is a very good idea. 좋은 생각같지 않아.

B: **Hear me out.** I'll explain why I think it is.
내 말 끝까지 들어봐. 내가 왜 그렇게 생각하는지 설명해줄게.

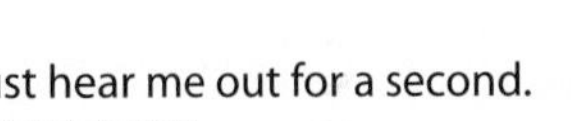

Listen, just hear me out for a second.
저기, 잠시만 내 얘기 좀 들어봐.

Please, hear me out. This is important.
제발 내 말 좀 끝까지 들어봐. 중요한 문제라고.

I'm glad you decided to hear me out.
내 말을 끝까지 들어주기로 해서 고마워.

024 Can I talk to you(for) a second? 잠깐 얘기 좀 할까?

this is asking someone for time to talk. It is similar to saying "I'd like to talk to you"

| Point | Can I talk to you about+N? …에 대해 잠깐 얘기 좀 할까?
Can we talk? 얘기 좀 할까?
Can we have a talk? 얘기 좀 할 수 있겠니?

A: **Can I talk to you for a second?** 잠깐 얘기 좀 할까?

B: OK. Tell me what's on your mind. 그래, 무슨 얘기인데.

Can I talk to you real quick? 잠깐 얘기 좀 할까?

Can I talk to you about it? 그거에 대해 잠깐 얘기 좀 할까?

Can I talk to you inside for a second?
안에서 잠깐 얘기 좀 할까?

Can I talk to you outside for just a second?
밖에서 잠깐 얘기 좀 할까?

025 Can I have a word (with you)? 잠깐 얘기 좀 할까?

this is said to ask someone if there is time to talk. It is like asking "Can we talk?"

| Point | Can I have a quick word (with you)? 잠깐만 얘기 할까?

A: **Can I have a word with you?** It's important.
잠깐 얘기 좀 할까? 중요한 거야.

B: You look serious. Is everything OK?
심각해보이는데, 무슨 일 없는거지?

미드표현

Can I have a word with you, alone?
단 둘이서 얘기 좀 할까?

Can I have a word with you outside... please?
밖에서 좀 얘기 좀 할까?

Jessy can I have a word with you in my office?
제시 내 사무실에서 얘기 좀 할까?

Can I have a word with you in private?
잠깐 조용히 얘기 좀 할까?

026 (You) Got a minute? 시간돼?, (잠깐) 얘기 좀 할 수 있을까?

this is a way of asking "Do you have time to talk?" A person says this when he wants some time to talk about something

| Point | Got a sec? 시간있어?

A: **Got a minute?** We need to discuss the schedule. 시간돼? 일정 논의 좀 해야 돼.

B: I'm busy, but I can meet you for lunch.
바쁘지만 점심 때 볼 수 있어.

미드표현

Hey, Tony, you got a minute? I really need to talk to you. 야 토니야, 시간있어? 너랑 얘기 좀 하자.

Hey, you got a minute? I need your help with something. 야 시간돼? 뭐 좀 도와줘.

How's it going? You got a minute? 안녕? 시간돼?

027 I want to talk to you (about that) 얘기 좀 하자

this is a way of saying "I must say something to you." It indicates the speaker needs to tell someone something.

| Point | I want to talk to you about~ …에 관해 너와 얘기하고 싶어

A: I heard you looked at my final test score.
네가 내 기말시험 성적을 봤다며?

B: Yes I did. **I want to talk to you about that.**
어, 봤어. 그거 얘기 좀 하자.

미드표현

Come here. I want to talk to you for a sec.
이리와. 잠깐 얘기 좀 하자.

I want to talk to you about this.
너랑 이거 얘기 좀 나누자.

Where have you been?! I tried to call you! I want to talk to you! 어디갔었어? 전화했는데! 얘기 좀 하자!

028 We need to talk (to you about that) 우리 얘기 좀 하자

this is often said when there is important information to give. It means "We have something to say to you"

| Point | We need to talk about something 우리 …에 대해 얘기해야 돼
We have to talk (about~) (…에 관해) 얘기하자

A: **We need to talk.** What are you doing this afternoon? 얘기 좀 하자. 오늘 오후에 뭐해?

B: I will be in a meeting for several hours.
몇 시간 동안 회의할거야.

미드표현

We need to talk to her right away.
당장 걔하고 얘기해야 돼.

This is not good, we have to talk about this.
이건 아닌데, 이 문제 얘기 하자.

We have to talk about her relationship.
걔의 관계에 대해 얘기해야 돼.

029 Let's talk 같이 이야기해보자

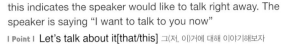

this indicates the speaker would like to talk right away. The speaker is saying "I want to talk to you now"

| Point | Let's talk about it[that/this] 그(저, 이)거에 대해 이야기해보자

*talk about something에서 about을 뺀 talk something도 같은 의미.

A: **Let's talk.** I think you are having personal problems. 이야기해보자. 네가 개인적인 문제가 있는 것 같은데.

B: I don't want to discuss them with you.
너랑은 이야기하기 싫어.

Let's talk about this in my office.
내 사무실에서 이 문젤 이야기하자고.

Let's talk about something else.
다른 거 이야기해보자고.

Let's talk motive. 동기에 대해 말해보자고.

We're talking our friendship here.
우린 지금 우정에 대해 말하고 있는 거야.

030 Can I get a word? 얘기 좀 할 수 있을까?

this is a basic way of asking someone if they have a little time to talk about something important. Often we can infer that the speaker wants to talk privately, and it may be about something confidential.

| Point | get a word 얘기를 하다 get word to …에게 말을 전해주다

A: Larry, **can I get a word** with you?
래리, 잠깐 얘기해도 될까?

B: Sure. Let's go to my office. 물론. 내 사무실로 가자고.

Can I get a word with you, Dr. Hunt?
헌트 박사, 잠깐 얘기 좀 할까요?

Can I get a word with you in private?
조용히 잠깐 얘기할까?

The manager needs to get a word with you today. 매니저는 오늘 너와 얘기를 좀 해야 돼.

031 Let's let someone else get a word in

다른 사람이 말할 기회를 주자

this indicates the speaker thinks someone has been dominating a conversation, and he thinks other people should have the opportunity to speak too. In other words, he is saying "You've talked a lot, so let someone else talk now"

| Point | get a word in 자기 의견을 말하다
get a word in edgewise 말할 기회를 잡다

A: Darin, **let's let someone else get a word in.**
다린, 다른 사람이 말할 기회를 주자.

B: Why? Have I been talking too much?
왜? 내가 너무 말을 많이 했나?

You don't even let me get a word in edgewise.
넌 내가 말할 기회도 잡지 못하게 해.

I'll be lucky if I get a word in edgewise.
내가 말할 기회를 잡는다면 행운일거야.

A: After all, you're the one who just walked out of here last week without saying a word.
B: Because I couldn't get a word in.
A: 결국, 넌 지난주에 말한마디도 없이 여기를 걸어나간 사람야.
B: 말할 기회가 주어지지 않았기 때문이야.

032 He was gonna strike up a conversation with Jill

걔는 질과 대화를 시작하려고 했었어

this tells us that someone planned to go and start talking to a woman named Jill. Sometimes it might be the case that the person wants to be involved romantically with Jill, so he is trying to get closer to her by talking with her. A similar way of expressing this is "He wanted to have time to talk with Jill"

| Point | strike up a friendship with ~ 난 …와 친구가 되다, 친해지다

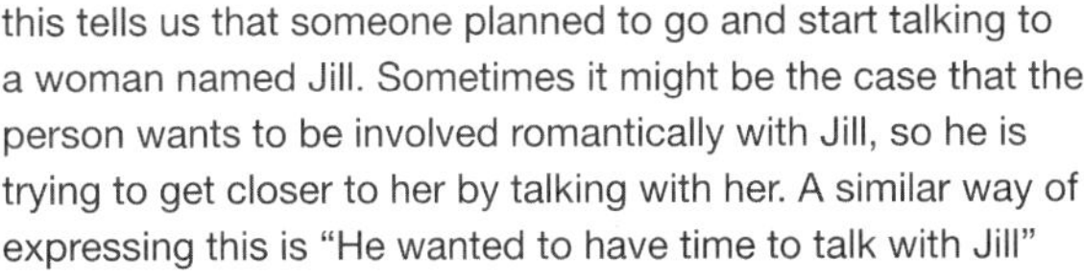

A: Why did Rob go to sit at that table?
랍은 왜 저 테이블에 가 앉은거야?

B: **He was going to strike up a conversation with Jill.** 걔는 질과 대화를 시작하려고 했었어.

It was all a setup. Brad was going to strike up a conversation with Scott at the club.
그런 전부 함정이었어. 브래드는 클럽에서 스캇과 대화를 나누려고 했어.

Well, then you'll just have to strike up a conversation with him and find out what kind of a man he is.
그럼 넌 걔와 대화를 해서 그가 어떤 종류의 사람인지 알아내야 될거야.

033 I'm having a little chat with her 걔랑 잠깐 이야기하는 중이야

미드표현

the speaker is saying "I'm talking to her now." It means that he is saying something to the person

| Point | chew the fat 오랫동안 잡담하다
It was just small talk 그냥 잡담이야
have a chat with 잡담하다, 수다떨다
chit chat 잡담

A: Did you hear what Jessica said last night?
제시카가 지난 밤에 뭐라 했는지 들었어?

B: I did. **I'm having a little chat with** her about it.
어. 그거에 대해 걔하고 잠깐 이야기하는 중야.

My lawyer would like to have a little chat with you. 내 변호사가 너랑 잠깐 이야기하고 싶대.

I didn't exactly have time to sit around and chew the fat. 죽치고 앉아 잡담할 시간 없어.

You've spent most of the hour engaging in small talk. 잡담하면서 대부분의 시간을 보내는 구나.

034 Let's cut to the chase 단도직입적으로 물어볼게, 요점만 말하자고

미드표현

this is a way of saying "Let's talk about the main subject." The speaker doesn't want to waste time talking about other things

| Point | Just cut to the chase 단도직입적으로 물어볼게
I'll cut to the chase 까놓고 이야기할게

A: This product will improve the way you live.
이 제품은 여러분의 삶의 방식을 향상시켜 줄 것입니다.

B: **Let's cut to the chase.** How much does it cost?
본론으로 들어갑시다. 얼마요?

I'm going to cut to the chase here.
이거 단도직입적으로 물어볼게

Let's cut to the chase, Bob. Can you prove your case? 단도직입적으로 물어볼게, 밥. 네 사건 증명할 수 있어?

Let's just cut to the chase here. Okay? Jill, who do you like?
까놓고 이야기하자고, 알았지? 질, 누구를 좋아하는 거야?

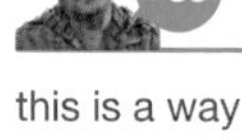

035 Spare me the details 요점만 말해, 자세히 말하지마

미드표현

this is a way for the speaker to say that he doesn't want to hear any more information about something. Often this is said when the details about something are unpleasant to hear. Basically, the speaker is saying "I don't want you to tell me anything else about that"

| Point | spare sb the details 지겹거나 불쾌해서 자세한 내용을 …에게 말하지 않다
spare sb sth 불쾌하거나 힘든 상황을 면하게 해주다

A: My boyfriend and I broke up again last night.
나 남친과 간밤에 헤어졌어.

B: **Spare me the details.** You guys are always breaking up. 그만 말해. 너희들 맨날 헤어지잖아.

Spare me the lecture and just book me another job quick.
잔소리를 그만두고 빨리 다른 일이나 잡아줘.

Oh spare me the speech, Paul, would you please? 폴, 연설은 그만둘래, 제발?

Why don't you spare me the sermon and get to why you're here?
설교는 그만두고 네가 왜 여기 있는지 말해봐.

036 I can't get into that right now 나중에 이야기하자

미드표현

usually this is said when a speaker doesn't want to talk about something. It is like saying "I don't want to discuss it"

| Point | get into sth 이야기하다, 문제를 논하다

A: Why did your parents move away from Chicago? 왜 너희 부모님이 시카고에서 이사가셨어?

B: **I can't get into that right now.** It's private.
나중에 이야기하자. 사적인 거라서.

I can't get into this with you now.
지금은 당신과 이 문제를 따질 수 없어.

I don't want to get into that right now.
지금 당장 그 문제를 따지고 싶지 않아

Let's not get into that right now.
지금 당장 그 문제를 이야기하지 말자

037 You know what? 저기 말야?, 근데 말야?, 근데 있지?

often this is a way of starting a conversation. It is like saying "I want to tell you something."

| Point | (Do) You know something? 그거 알려나?
Do you know about this? 이거 아니?
Know what? 너, 그거 알아?, 저, 그거 말야

A: **You know what?** I feel like having pizza for lunch. 근데 말야, 점심으로 피자 먹고 싶어.

B: Well let's go out and order a pizza and some beer. 그럼 나가서 피자하고 맥주 주문하자.

You know what? Let's have coffee sometime. When are you free?
저 말야, 언제 한번 커피마시자고, 언제 시간돼?

You know what? I can't do this. 근데 말야, 난 이거 못해.

You know what? I am sick of this!
저 말야, 나 이거 지긋지긋해!

038 I'll tell you what 이게 어때, 저기 있잖아, 이러면 어떨까

this is a way to say "I'm going to give you my opinion." It's often said when the speaker starts talking

| Point | Tell you what 이러면 어때
*I'll tell you what S+V …을 말해줄게

A: **I'll tell you what.** I think every summer feels hotter. 저기 있잖아, 매년 여름이 더 더워지는 것 같아.

B: Me too. Is it an effect of global warming?
나도 그래. 지구 온난화 현상인가?

I'll tell you what. I'll buy you a new pair of gloves. 이러면 어떨까, 새 장갑 사줄게.

I'll tell you what. How about I cook dinner at my place? 이럼 어때, 우리 집에서 저녁 해먹자.

I'll tell you what I want. 내가 원하는 게 뭔지 말해줄게.

I'll tell you what they were fighting over.
걔네들이 무엇 땜에 싸웠는지 말해줄게.

039 Guess what? 저기 말야, 그거 알아

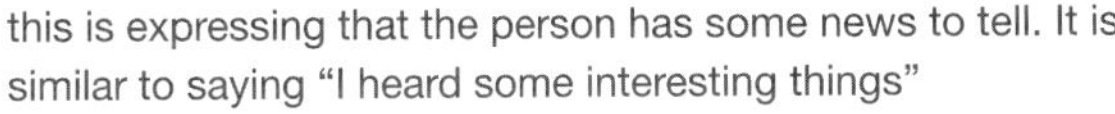

this is expressing that the person has some news to tell. It is similar to saying "I heard some interesting things"

| Point | Guess what? 저기 말야, 그거 알아

A: **Guess what?** George and Andrea are going to get married. 저기 말야, 조지와 앤드리아가 결혼할거래.

B: That's great. They are such a nice couple.
잘됐다, 아주 좋은 커플이야.

Guess what? I have a date with Mike.
그거 알아? 나 마이크랑 데이트해.

Guys, guess what? She just bought me a boat! 얘들아, 그거 알아? 걔가 내게 배를 사줬어!

And guess what? It's her birthday tomorrow, and I'm throwing her a party.
그거 알아? 내일 걔 생일이고 난 걜 위해 파티를 열어줄거야.

040 I have to tell you (something) 진지하게 할 말이 있어

this is a way of saying "I need to give you some information." The speaker wants to talk to someone

| Point | I have to[gotta] tell you this 이거 말해두는데

A: **I have to tell you something.** It's about your son. 할 말이 있어. 네 아들에 관련된 거야.

B: Has he been causing problems at school again?
학교에서 또 말썽폈대?

I have to tell you this. If you ever hurt my little sister, I will hunt you down.
이거 하나 말해두는데, 내 누이를 아프게 하면 쫓아가서 혼내줄거야.

A: I have to tell you something. B: I'm too fat to be wearing this?
A: 할 말이 있어. B: 내가 이거 입기엔 너무 뚱뚱하다고?

Wait. Sit down. I have to tell you something.
기다려봐. 앉으라고, 내가 할 말이 있어.

041 Let me tell you something (내 의견을) 말할게 있는데

미드표현

often this is used when a speaker starts to disagree or state a strong opinion. It means "I'm going to tell you what I think"

I Point I Let me tell you (something) about …에 대해 말하겠어
Can I tell you something? 알려줄까?, 말해도 돼?

A: These cookies are the best I've ever tasted.
이 쿠키는 여태껏 먹은 거 중에서 최고야.

B: **Let me tell you something.** I can bake better cookies than these. 저말야. 이보다 더 맛난 쿠키를 구울 수 있어.

Let me tell you something. Your baby isn't even that cute.
말할게 있는데. 네 애기는 그렇게까지 귀엽지도 않아.

Can I tell you something? I'm a little mad at him now. 알려줄까? 지금 걔한테 좀 열받았어.

But let me tell you something, work is not about fun. 하지만 내가 하나 말해두겠는데, 일하는건 재미가 아냐.

042 Get a load of this 이것 좀 (들어)봐

미드표현

this means "Look at this." The speaker has seen something interesting and wants to draw the attention of others to it

I Point I get a load of …을 주시하다, 보다
Look here (자기가 할 말을 강조) 이것 봐, 중요한 건 이거지

A: **Get a load of this.** It's the newest cell phone from Nokia. 이것 좀 봐. 노키아 휴대폰 최신제품이야.

B: Whoa. That looks like it has a lot of extra features. 와. 부가기능이 많은 것 같아.

Look here. I need to use a computer because mine broke.
이봐. 내 컴퓨터가 고장나서 그러는데 네 것 좀 써야겠어.

Wow! Get a load of you! You look so pretty. I hardly recognize you.
와! 너좀봐! 너무 예뻐졌어. 못알아봤잖아.

Hey, did you hear about the new guy that just moved in? Well, get a load of this.
너네 얼마전에 이사온 사람알지? 이것 좀 들어봐.

043 Can I(just) ask you a question?
질문 하나 해도 돼?, 뭐 좀 물어봐도 돼?

미드표현

this is like saying "Could you answer something I ask?" It means the speaker wants to get some information from someone

I Point I Can I ask you a question about~ ? …에 관한 질문 하나 해도 돼?
I have a question for you 질문 있는데요

A: **Can I ask you a question?** 질문 하나 해도 돼?

B: You can ask me anything you want to. 뭐든 물어 봐.

Can I ask you a question? It's kind of personal.
질문 하나 해도 돼? 좀 개인적인데.

A: Can I ask you a question? B: Sure. You can ask me anything.
A: 질문하나 해도 돼? B: 그럼 아무거나 물어봐.

Could I ask you a question? It's critical.
뭐 좀 물어봐도 돼. 심각한건데.

044 Let me ask you something 뭐 좀 물어볼게, 뭐하나 물어봐도 돼

미드표현

this is a way of saying "I'm going to ask a question." It is said when the speaker wants to find out more information

I Point I Let me ask (you something) 뭐 좀 물어볼게
Let me ask you a question 질문 하나 할게

A: **Let me ask you something.** Have you ever been in love? 뭐 좀 물어볼게. 사랑해본 적 있어?

B: I fell in love a few years ago, with another student. 몇 년 전에 다른 학생과 사랑해본 적 있어.

Let me ask you something. Will you do a threesome with me? 뭐 좀 물어볼게. 나랑 쓰리섬할래?

Let me ask you something. When we were together, it was good, right?
뭐 좀 물어볼게. 우리 함께 있을 때 좋았지, 그래?

Let me ask you something. Do you think it's okay for Penny to have an ex-boyfriend sleep on her couch?
뭐 좀 물어볼게. 페니가 전 남친을 소파에서 재워도 된다고 생각해?

045 I'll just fire away 바로 질문할게

this indicates the speaker plans to start asking questions as he feels like it. He is saying "I'll start talking when I have questions"

| Point | Fire away (질문하겠다는 상대방에게) 어서 해, 쏴, 던져

A: Did you have some questions to ask me?
내게 뭐 물어볼 거 있어?

B: Yeah. I'll just fire away. 어, 바로 질문할게.

A: It's my turn to ask you some questions.
B: Fire away. A: 내가 너에게 질문 좀 할 차례네. B: 어서 해봐.

A: I'm gonna make three assumptions.
B: Fire away. A: 내가 세가지 가정을 해볼게. B: 어서 해봐.

A: Mind if I ask you a couple questions about the election? B: Not at all. Fire away.
A: 선거에 대해 몇가지 질문을 해도 될까요? B: 그럼요. 어서 해보세요

046 Let me (just) say 말하자면

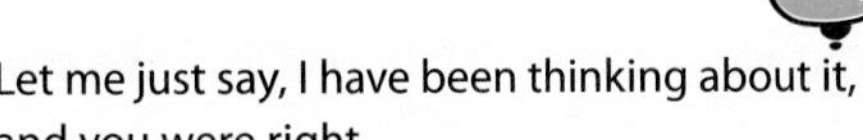

this means "I'm going to say something quickly." It is said when the speaker doesn't want to talk a long time

| Point | Just let me say 말하자면
Let me say this 한 마디할세, 한 말씀느리죠
Let me say (that) S+V …라고 말해둘게

A: Let me just say I'm tired of waking up early.
말하자면 아침 일찍 일어나는게 짜증난다고.

B: But you need to be at your job early every morning. 하지만 넌 매일 아침 일찍 출근해야 되잖아.

Let me just say, I have been thinking about it, and you were right.
말하자면 내가 생각을 해봤는데 네가 맞았어.

Let me say this. We're one of the greatest team of all the contestants.
이것만 말하자. 우린 참가팀들 중에서 가장 뛰어나.

First let me say I very much regret involving you in this.
우선 난 네가 이 일에 관련되게 해서 매우 유감이라는 말을 해둘게.

047 Let me see 그러니까 (내 생각엔), 저기, 글쎄

this gives a speaker a chance to stop and think about something. It has a similar meaning to "Wait a minute"

| Point | Let me[Let's] see 뭐랄까, 그러니까 그게
Let me see+N …을 보자
Let me see if S+V …인지 보자

A: When was the last time you ate steak?
마지막으로 고기 먹은 게 언제지?

B: Let me see. I think it was about seven months ago. 그러니까, 7개월 전인 것 같아.

What is it? Let me see. 뭐야? 한번 보자.

Let me see if she's here. 걔가 왔는지 보자.

Let me see if I can get that for you.
내가 너에게 그걸 갖다줄 수 있는지 보자고.

So let me see if I understand this.
내가 이걸 이해했는지 보자고.

048 You won't believe this 이거 믿지 못할 걸, 넌 짐작도 못할 걸

this often means "This is very surprising." It is said when there is information about some unusual thing

| Point | You wouldn't believe what I ~ 내가 뭘 …했는지 믿을 수 없을 거야
You'll never guess what I heard
내가 무슨 얘기를 들었는지 넌 짐작도 못 할 걸

A: You won't believe this, but I saw a UFO.
믿지 못하겠지만 UFO를 봤어.

B: That's crazy. I don't think UFOs exist.
미쳤구만. UFO는 존재하지 않아.

You won't believe this, but Terry has disappeared. 이거 믿지 못하겠지만 테리가 사라졌어.

You won't believe this, but I heard he was dead. 이건 믿지 못하겠지만, 걔가 죽었대.

You won't believe this, but we may have won the lottery.
이거 믿지 못하겠지만, 우리가 로또에 당첨되었을지도 몰라.

049 How should I put it? 뭐랄까?, 어떻게 얘기할까?

this often indicates the speaker can't explain something easily. It is like saying "It will take time to explain this"

I Point I put it another way = put another way 달리 표현하다
To put it simply[shortly/briefly] 간단히 말하자면
Let's put it this way 이렇게 표현해보자고

A: What was your opinion of Tom Robbin's new book? 탐 로빈의 신간에 대해 어떻게 생각해?

B: **How should I put it?** Reading it made me feel disappointed. 뭐라고 할까? 실망했어.

미드표현

Let me put it this way: If you are still seeing Will you need to stop.
이렇게 표현해보자고, 네가 아직 윌을 만나고 있다면 넌 그만둬야 돼.

Okay, let me put it this way, if you're really David's friend you will support him no matter who he wants to be with. 좋아, 이렇게 표현해보자고, 네가 데이빗의 진정한 친구라면 걔가 누구와 함께 있든지 걔를 지지해줘야 돼.

050 Let me get back to you (on that) 나중에 이야기할게, 나중에 전화할게

usually this means the speaker wants time to decide something. It is a way of saying "I'll tell you later"

I Point I get back to sb 나중에 이야기하다, 나중에 전화하다
get back to sth ...로 돌아가다
I'll get back to you 나중에 이야기(전화)할게
Get back to me (on this) 나중에 이야기하자, 나중에 전화해

A: I need to know if you are going to move to another apartment. 다른 아파트로 이사갈 건지 알아야겠어.

B: **Let me get back to you** on that. I haven't decided. 나중에 이야기하자고, 아직 결정못했어.

미드표현

I'll get back to you as soon as I have something. 뭔가 알게 되는대로 바로 이야기할게.

If we have any more questions, we'll get back to you. 궁금한 게 더 있으면 전화할게.

We need to get back to the crime scene.
범죄현장으로 돌아가야 돼.

051 Where was I? 내가 무슨 얘길 했어?, 내가 어디까지 이야기했지?

often this means "I forgot the place I stopped talking." The speaker is saying he doesn't remember where he stopped talking

I Point I Where were we? 우리 어디까지 이야기했지?
What was I saying? 내가 무슨 말하고 있었지?

A: **Where was I?** I've lost my place. 내가 어디까지 얘기했지?

B: You were talking about Korean history, professor. 한국 역사에 대해 말씀하셨어요, 교수님.

I'm sorry. Where were we?
미안, 우리 어디까지 이야기했지?

So where were we? I believe you were asking me some kind of a question.
그래 우리 어디까지 이야기했지? 네가 뭐 질문했었지.

Where was I? Oh yeah. Lane. Will you marry me? 내가 무슨 얘길 하고 있었지? 어 그래, 레인, 나와 결혼해줄래?

052 I was somewhere else 잠시 딴 생각했어

this is a way to communicate that the speaker was distracted and not concentrating on what was going on in the present. Often this is said by a person who is daydreaming. A similar way to say this would be "I was thinking of other things."

A: Hey, Ursula, are you paying attention to what I'm saying? 우르술라야, 내 말 듣고 있는거야?

B: I'm so sorry. **I was somewhere else** for a minute. 미안해, 잠시 딴 생각했어.

미드표현

I was somewhere else when I was sitting in church. 교회에 앉아있을 때 잠시 다른 생각을 했어.

Can you repeat that? I was somewhere else. 다시 한번 말해줄래? 잠시 딴 생각했어.

I was somewhere else and didn't catch any of that. 내가 잠시 딴 생각을 해서 그 얘기를 전혀 못 들었어.

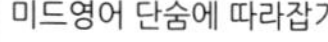

053 Like I said (before) (전에) 말했듯이

this is a way of repeating something important. It can be similar to "I want to tell you again"

I Point I as I said (before) 내가 (전에) 말했듯이
as[like] I told you (before) (전에) 내가 말했듯이
as I mentioned before 내가 전에 말했듯이

A: Have you been on a visit to China yet?
중국 방문해봤어?

B: **As I mentioned before,** I'll go there this summer. 전에 말했듯이, 이번 여름에 갈거야.

Like I said, it's none of your concern.
내가 말한 것처럼, 네가 관여할 문제가 아냐.

Like I told you, it was an accident.
내가 말했듯이, 그건 사고였어.

It's like I told you, there's nothing I can do.
내가 말한대로야, 내가 어찌할 수 있는 게 없어.

As I was saying, take as much time as you want! 내가 말했듯이 원하는 만큼 시간을 가져!

054 Check this[it] out 이것 좀 봐, 들어봐

this is like saying "Look at this, it's very interesting." It is said when a person wants to show another person something

I Point I check it[this] out 확인하다

A: **Check this out.** It's an IQ test. 이것 좀 봐. IQ 테스트야.

B: I want to see how smart I am.
내가 얼마나 똑똑한 지 알고 싶어.

You need to check this out. 이것 좀 봐야 돼.

Hey, come here. Check this out. 야, 이리와. 이것 좀 봐.

Judy, check it out. This is amazing.
주디야, 이것 좀 봐. 끝내줘.

055 Just so we're clear 분명히 하겠는데

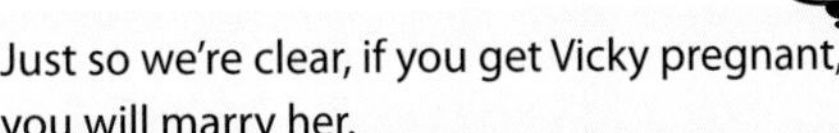

this is used to say "I want to make sure you understand me." The speaker would like to be understood clearly

I Point I Just so we're clear 분명히 하겠는데

A: **Just so we're clear,** we'll meet tomorrow at 6 am. 분명히 하겠는데, 우리 내일 오전 6시에 만나자.

B: Do we have to be here so early? 여길 그렇게 일찍 와야 돼?

Just so we're clear, if you get Vicky pregnant, you will marry her.
분명히 해두겠는데 비키를 임신시키면 결혼해야 돼.

Just so we're clear, don't say a word of what you heard to anyone.
분명히 해두겠는데 들은 걸 누구에게도 절대 한마디도 하지마.

Just so we're clear. We're over.
분명히 하겠는데. 우린 끝이야.

미드에선 이렇게 쓰인다!

Just so we're clear

The Big Bang Theory
SEASON#1-5

괴짜인 여성 과학자인인 Lesley가 4중주 연주하는데 대타로 Leonard에게 첼로 연주를 해달라고 부탁한다. 그리고 Leonard의 집에서 연주연습을 하는데, 연습을 끝내고 Lesley가 남아서 Leonard를 유혹하는 장면에서 서두를 꺼내는 표현이 바로 이 just so we're clear이다.

Lesley: Just so we're clear, you understand that me hanging back to practice with you is a pretext for letting you know that I'm sexually available.

Leonard: Really?

Lesley: Yeah, I'm good to go.

Leonard: I thought you weren't interested in me.

레슬리: 분명히 해두는데, 내가 남아서 너랑 연습하는 것은 나랑 섹스할 수 있다는 것을 알려주기 위한 핑계라고.

레너드: 정말?

레슬리: 난 준비 다됐어.

레너드: 난 네가 내게 관심없는 줄 알았는데.

056 Make no mistake (about it)! 경고하는데!, 분명히 얘기해두는데!

this is a way of saying "Let me say this clearly." It is said when someone wants everyone to understand what he is saying

| Point | ~ make no mistake = make no mistake about it

A: **Make no mistake about it.** We need to clean this place up. 분명히 얘기해두는데 여기 깨끗이 해놔야 돼.

B: But that will take days to do. 하지만 며칠 걸릴텐데요.

Make no mistake, our friendship is over.
분명히 얘기하는데, 우리 우정은 끝났어.

And make no mistake. He wants me there.
분명히 얘기하는데 걔가 나보고 그리로 오래.

Make no mistake, I'm a good mother.
분명히 얘기해두지만 난 좋은 엄마야.

057 We were just talking about you 안 그래도 네 얘기하고 있었어

this tells someone that the people were discussing him. It means "We were interested in you"

| Point | We were just talking about~ 안그래도 …을 얘기하고 있었어

A: Hey ladies. What is going on? 야, 얘들아. 무슨 일야?

B: Hi Joan. **We were just talking about you.**
안녕, 조앤. 안 그래도 네 얘기하고 있었어.

Actually we were just talking about me not going to your party.
안 그래도 내가 너 파티에 안가는 거 얘기하고 있었어.

Yeah, we were just talking about that.
어, 그거에 대해 이야기하고 있었어.

I thought we were just talking about a newspaper story.
난 우리가 신문기사 얘기하고 있는 걸로 생각했어.

We were just talking about your daughter-in-law. 안그래도 우리는 네 며느리 얘기하고 있었어.

058 We're talking~ 그러니까 내 말은…

this is like saying "I mean..." It is said when a person wants to explain an important part of an idea

| Point | We're talking~ 그러니까 내 말은…
We're talking about~ 우리는 …에 대해 말하는거야

A: The tour lasts 3 months. **We're talking** a long trip. 여행은 3주간 계속돼. 그러니까 내 말은 장기여행이란 말야.

B: That sounds like a long time to be away from home. 집에서 오랜 시간 떠나있겠네.

We're talking about my future happiness here. 그러니까 내 말은 나의 앞으로의 행복에 대해 말하는 거야.

Hey, We're talking about our friendship here.
야, 그러니까 내 말은 우리 우정을 말하는 거야.

It's my principles! We're talking about my principles!
그건 내 원칙들이야! 우리는 내 원칙들에 대해서 말하고 있는거야!

059 I was just about to say that 안 그래도 그 얘기하려고 했어

this is usually a way of saying "I was thinking the same way." It indicates the speaker understands someone else's ideas

| Point | I was just about to say that 안 그래도 그 얘기 하려고 했어

A: You need to go home and get some rest.
집에 가서 좀 쉬어.

B: **I was just about to say that.** I'm really tired.
막 그 얘기 하려던 참이었어. 정말 피곤해.

I was about to say I'm the one to blame.
안 그래도 내가 비난받을 사람이라고 말하려고 했어.

Okay, I was just about to say "just like you," And then I changed my mind.
좋아, 난 "너처럼"이라고 말하려고 하다가 내가 맘을 바꿨어.

I was about to say the very same thing.
안그래도 나도 똑같은 얘기를 하려고 했어.

060 Deep down (인정하긴 싫지만, 모르고 있었지만) 사실은

this refers to the way a person truly feels. It is like saying "in your heart"

I Point I Deep down, 사실은,

A: My sister and I argue a lot these days.
누이와 내가 요즘 많이 다퉈.

B: That's common. **Deep down** you know you love her. 흔한 일이지. 사실은 누이 사랑하잖아.

Deep down, I know it's wrong, and so do you!
사실은, 그게 틀리다는 걸 나도 알고 있고 너도 그렇지?

Deep down you're still really sad.
사실은 너 여전히 슬퍼하고 있어.

Deep down, you just know she's a bitch.
사실은 걔가 나쁜 년이라는 거 알지.

061 Here's the thing 내 말은 말야, 그게 말야, 문제가 되는 건

this expresses "This is the important point." It is said so people understand something should be listened to

I Point I Here's the thing 내 말은 말야, 그게 말야

A: I want to help poor people after I graduate.
졸업 후에 가난한 사람들을 도와주고 싶어.

B: **Here's the thing.** It's very hard to improve their lives. 그게 말야. 그 사람들 삶을 향상시키는 건 정말 어려워.

Here's the thing. I really like you.
내 말은 말야. 난 정말 네가 좋다구.

Here's the thing. We're both really enjoyed each other. 내말은 말야. 우린 서로 모두 정말 즐거웠어.

Here's the thing I do know about your exes, and frankly, sometimes it sucks. 내 말은 말야. 난 네 전처들에 잘 알고 있지만 솔직히 말해서 가끔은 엿같아.

Okay, here's the thing. Danny and I don't hang out. 좋아. 그게 말야. 대니와 난 같이 놀지 않아.

062 I don't know how to tell you this, but~
어떻게 이걸 말해야 할지 모르겠지만,

this is often a way of giving bad news. It can also be said as "I have something bad to say to you"

I Point I I don't know how to tell you this, but~
이걸 어떻게 말해야 할지 모르겠지만

A: **I don't know how to tell you this,** but your dad is in the hospital. 어떻게 말해야 할지 모르겠지만 네 아빠가 병원에 계셔.

B: Why? Is he having some sort of health problem? 왜? 건강에 뭐 좀 이상있으셔?

I don't know how to tell you this but I think she's cheating on you.
이걸 어떻게 말해야 할 지 모르겠기만 걔가 바람피는 것 같아.

I don't know how to tell you this, but we are broke. 어떻게 말해야 할지 모르겠지만 우리 빈털털이야.

I don't know how to tell you this, but your dad is in the hospital.
어떻게 말해야 할지 모르겠지만 네 아빠는 병원에 계셔.

063 I don't wanna make any trouble, but~
소란피고 싶지는 않지만…

this expresses that the speaker hopes someone will be calm when he talks about something. It is similar to saying "I'm sorry to tell you this, but..."

I Point I I don't mean to complain, but~ 불평하려는 것은 아니지만…
I won't say any more, but~ 한마디만 할게
(I don't want to talk about this for a long time)

A: **I don't want to make trouble, but** you need to move your car. 소란피고 싶진 않지만 차 좀 빼주시죠.

B: No way! I'm not going to move it from that parking space. 안돼요! 저 주차자리에서 빼지 않을겁니다.

I don't wanna make any trouble, but I'm in a lot of pain. 소란피고 싶지는 않지만 많이 아파.

I won't say any more, but he brought her flowers yesterday.
한마디만 할게. 걔가 어제 꽃을 갔다주더라고.

064 I don't want to rain on your parade 산통깨기 싫은데

usually this is a way for someone to indicate he does not want to make a person feel bad, but he feels like saying something that the listener may consider negative, and it may also make the listener upset.

| Point | rain on one's parade …의 일을 망치다, …의 하루를 망치다, 산통깨다

A: I think I'll be able to be rich by the time I'm forty.
내가 40세가 되면 부자가 될 수 있을 것 같아.

B: **I don't want to rain on your parade,** but it's not going to happen. 산통깨고 싶지 않지만 그렇게 되지 않을거야.

미드표현

Who rained on your parade? 누가 네 일을 망쳤어?

You who have no dreams rain on those who do. 꿈이 없는 사람은 꿈이 있는 사람에게 불평해.

I don't want to rain on your parade, but he just totally manipulated you.
산통을 깨고 싶지 않지만 걘 널 완전히 조종했어.

065 Far be it from me to call her a liar

개를 거짓말쟁이라고 부를 맘은 조금도 없지만

this expression is slightly complex. The speaker is saying that he is not going to say that a woman is lying, but sometimes we may understand that he is implying that he still believes that she is telling lies.

| Point | far be it from me to+V (반대나 비난하기 전) …할 마음은 조금도 없지만

A: Do you think Rachel faked getting pregnant?
레이첼이 임신인 척 했던 것 같아?

B: **Far be it from me to call her a liar,** but I never saw her baby. 걔를 거짓말쟁이라고 부를 맘은 없지만 걔 애기를 전혀 본 적이 없어.

미드표현

Well, far be it from me to stand in the way of that. 음, 난 그것을 반대하고 싶은 맘은 전혀 없어.

Why would somebody do something like this? Far be it from me to understand the minds of hooligans. 왜 사람들이 이런 짓을 하는걸까? 난 훌리건의 마음을 이해할 생각이 추호도 없어.

066 That's all well and good 그것도 괜찮기는 하지만

this is often said when a speaker wants to indicate that he agrees with a part of a statement, but disagrees with another part of it. Often we hear this just before people start talking about what they don't agree with.

| Point | That's all well and good, but~ 그것도 괜찮기는 하지만…

A: Jim promised that he would quit drinking beer.
짐은 맥주를 끊겠다고 약속했어.

B: **That's all well and good,** but he'll still drink whiskey and wine. 그것도 괜찮기는 하지만, 걘 위스키와 와인을 여전히 마실거야.

미드표현

Charm is all well and good, but in the real world, knowledge is power.
매력도 괜찮기는 하지만 실제 세계에서는 아는게 힘이지.

That's all well and good, but our employers are going to ask us about the risks involved in cooperating with an FBI investigation.
그것도 좋기는 하지만, 고용주들은 FBI 수사에 협조해서 생기는 위험에 대해 우리에게 물어볼거야.

067 I hate to admit it, but I like your theory

인정하고 싶지 않지만 네 말이 맞아

this is a way of saying "I'm surprised that I like something." It indicates the speaker thought he would not like it.

| Point | I hate to admit it, but~ 인정하고 싶지 않지만…

A: I feel that more girls would date me if I wore nice clothes. 내가 멋진 옷을 입으면 더 많은 여자들이 나랑 데이트할 것 같아.

B: **I hate to admit it,** but I like your theory.
인정하긴 싫지만 네 말이 맞아.

미드표현

And I hate to admit it, but I think the kid is right. 그리고 인정하기는 싫지만 그 애가 맞는 것 같아.

I hate to admit it, but I think that Betty has made the smart move.
인정하기 싫지만, 베티가 현명하게 행동한 것 같아.

I hate to admit it, but I wish they were all dead. 인정하기 싫지만, 난 걔네들이 모두 죽었으면 해.

068 I may be way out on a limb here, but~

이런 말해도 괜찮을 지 모르겠지만,

미드표현

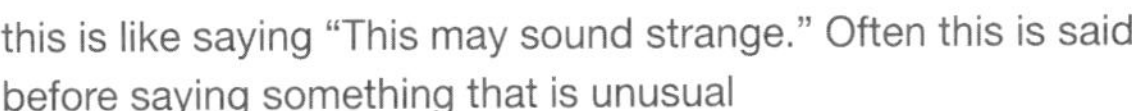

this is like saying "This may sound strange." Often this is said before saying something that is unusual

I Point I I'm probably out of line here 이렇게 말해도 좋을지 모르겠지만

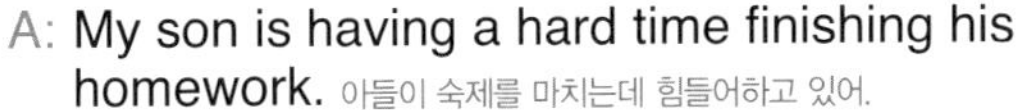

A: My son is having a hard time finishing his homework. 아들이 숙제를 마치는데 힘들어하고 있어.

B: **I may be way out on a limb here, but** I think you should forbid computer games. 맞는 말인지 모르겠지만, 컴퓨터 게임을 금지해야 할거야.

I may be way out on a limb here, but do you have a problem with your mom?
이게 맞는 말인지 모르겠지만, 엄마랑 무슨 문제있어?

I hope I'm not out of line here, but did you ever spend any time in prison?
이런 말 해도 될지 모르겠지만 감방 살아봤어?

069 Dare I say

감히[굳이] 말하자면, …라고 해도 될까

미드표현

this is said to mean "This is a suggestion, but I don't know if I should say it." The speaker is not sure if it is a good idea to suggest something

I Point I I dare say 아마도(I suppose)

A: How are we going to get to the airport?
어떻게 공항에 갈거야?

B: **Dare I say** that we need to take a taxi there?
거기에 택시타야 한다고 해도 될까?

So, your argument is, dare I say it, a fumble, correct? 그래 네 논증이 감히 말하자면 틀렸다는 거야, 맞아?

Sam just landed, dare I say it, a big whale.
샘은 방금 굳이 말하자면 커다란 고래를 잡았어.

He's recently made some unauthorized, and dare I say, reckless trades.
걔는 최근 금지된, 굳이 말하자면 무모한 거래를 좀 했어.

070 I'm sorry I didn't tell you this before[sooner], but~

미리[좀 더 일찍] 이걸 말하지 않아 미안하지만,

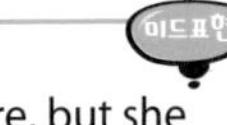

미드표현

this expresses that the speaker is saying something late. It means "I wish I had told you before now"

I Point I I've never told you this but~ 전에 이걸 말한 적이 없지만…
I don't know if I've told you this, but~ 내가 이걸 말했는지 모르겠지만 …

A: Why am I being fired just before the Christmas holiday? 내가 왜 성탄휴가 바로 전에 잘려야 되는 겁니까?

B: **I'm sorry I didn't tell you this before, but** the boss asked me not to. 미리 얘기 못해 미안하지만, 사장이 그러지 말라고 했어.

I'm sorry I didn't tell you this before, but she isn't coming back.
미리 말하지 않아 미안하지만, 걔는 돌아오지 않을거야.

I'm sorry I didn't tell you this before, but I have been divorced three times.
미리 말안해 미안하지만, 나 세번 이혼했어.

I'm sorry I didn't tell you this before, but the cops are looking for you.
미리 말하지 않아 미안하지만, 경찰이 너를 찾고 있어.

071 This is really hard for me to say, but~

나도 이런 얘기하기 정말 힘들지만,

미드표현

this is like saying "I don't like saying this." It is usually said when the speaker must give bad news

I Point I I don't want to get all sentimental on your asses, but~ 아양떠는 것은 아니지만…

A: **This is really hard for me to say, but** I don't want to hang around with you.
이런 말 꺼내게 돼서 안됐지만 너랑 놀기 싫어.

B: Why is that? Have you found other friends to hang around with? 왜? 다른 놀 친구들이 생긴거야?

This is really hard for me to say, but we need to break up. 이런 얘기하기 정말 힘들지만, 우리 헤어져야 되겠어.

This is really hard for me to say, but you can't work here anymore.
이런 얘기 정말 힘들지만, 그만 나가줘야겠어.

This is really hard for me to say, but I need my money back. 이런 얘기 정말 힘들지만 내 돈 좀 돌려줘.

072 I hate myself for doing this 이렇게 하고 싶지 않아

this is a way to say "Although I'm doing it, I don't like it." The speaker thinks he is doing something bad

| Point | hate oneself for~ …로 후회하다
I'm sorry to have to tell you this, but~ 이런 말해서 안됐지만 …

A: **I hate myself for doing this, but** can I borrow some money? 이러고 싶지는 않지만 돈 좀 빌려줄래?

B: You are always trying to borrow money from me. 넌 늘상 나한테 돈을 빌릴려고 하냐.

미드표현

I hate myself for what we did! Okay? I can't sleep at night! 우리가 한 짓이 후회돼! 알아? 밤에 잠도 못자!

I'm sorry to have to tell you this, but your dad's been shot. 이런 말씀드리게 돼 유감입니다만 아버님이 총에 맞았습니다.

I'm sorry to have to tell you this, but your boyfriend is cheating on you. 이런 말해서 안됐지만 네 남친이 바람펴.

073 If you ask me 내 생각은, 내 생각을 말한다면

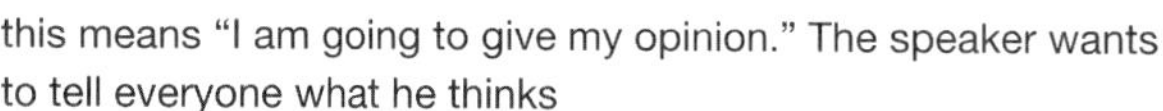

this means "I am going to give my opinion." The speaker wants to tell everyone what he thinks

| Point | If you'll excuse me (자리를 뜨면서) 괜찮다면
If that's the case 실제 그렇다면
If worst comes to worst 설상가상

A: Everyone seems to like Raymond. 다들 레이몬드를 좋아하는 것 같아.

B: **If you ask me,** I think he complains too much. 내 생각은 걔가 불평을 너무 많이 하는 것 같아.

미드표현

If you ask me, he was way off base. 내 생각엔 쟤가 잘못 짚었어.

If I were you, I'd be worried. 내가 너라면 걱정했을 텐데.

If that's the case, she was shot by somebody 11 to 14 feet tall. 그게 사실이라면 걔는 11피트나 14피트 키의 사람에게 당한 거구만.

074 If you don't mind 당신이 괜찮다면

this is usually said before requesting something. It is like saying "I'd like you to..."

| Point | If it's okay[all right] with you 괜찮다면
If you insist 네가 정 그렇다면 If you must 네가 꼭 해야만 한다면
If it's too much trouble 수고스럽지 않다면

A: **If you don't mind,** I'd like to have a cigarette. 괜찮다면 담배 한대 피고 싶어.

B: Can you smoke it outside? 밖에서 피울래?

미드표현

If you don't mind, I'm busy. 괜찮다면, 내가 바빠서.

If you don't mind, I'd like to ask you both a few questions. 괜찮다면 너희 둘에게 몇 가지 질문할게.

If it's not too much trouble, can you close the door? 수고스럽지 않다면 문 닫아줄래?

075 That being said, 그래도,

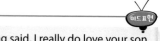

many times this is said after a statement is made, and the speaker is going to say something that contradicts that statement. To use an example, we might hear "The weather here is usually hot. That being said, the forecast is for snow tomorrow". This is like using the phrase "In spite of that..."

| Point | That being said 그래도, 그렇지만 That being so 그래서, 그렇다면

A: It has been fun talking with you. **That being said,** I am leaving. 너랑 얘기해서 재미있었어. 그렇지만 나 그만 갈게.

B: But why? Do you have to get up early tomorrow? 하지만 왜? 낼 일찍 일어나야 돼?

Well, that being said, I really do love your son. 저기 그렇지만 전 정말 당신 아들을 사랑해요.

Now that being said, this baby is ours so we get to make all those parenting decisions together. Right? 그렇지만 이 아이는 우리 애니까 우리가 모든 육아결정사항들을 함께 하는 거지, 맞지?

076 I'll boil it down for you 간단히 얘기할게, 요점만 얘기할게

usually this means "I'm going to tell you just the facts." A speaker often does this so his meaning is clear

I Point I boil it down 간단히 말하다
In a nutshell 간단히 말하자면, 요컨대

A: Can you explain this math problem?
이 수학문제를 설명할 수 있어?

B: Sure I can. **I'll boil it down for you.**
물론. 간단히 설명해줄게.

미드표현

This is the report. I'll boil it down for you.
이게 보고서인데 내가 간단히 요점만 얘기할게.

I'll boil it down for you if you have time to listen. 들을 시간이 있다면 내가 간단히 얘기할게.

077 Suffice it to say she's my ex 걔는 내 전처라고만 말해둘게

this expresses that the speaker does not want to give a lot of details, he just wants to give basic information that he was once together with a woman. Generally, this expression means a person is reluctant to talk about something. In other words, "All I want to tell you is that we were a couple in the past"

I Point I suffice it to say (that~) …라고만 말해두자

A: What can you tell me about Polly Clark?
폴리 클락에 대해 뭐 말해줄거 있어?

B: **Suffice it to say** she's my ex. 내 전처라고만 말해두자.

미드표현

Suffice it to say, Tony is a bit of a con man.
토니는 약간 사기성이 있다라고만 말해둘게.

Could it be him? Suffice it to say, that's not possible. 그게 걔일까? 그건 불가능하다고만 말해둘게.

Suffice it to say she is my generation's Audrey Hepburn. 걔는 우리 시대의 오드리 헵번이라고만 말해둘게.

078 Last but not least 끝으로 중요한 말 더하자면

this is said when the speaker doesn't want people to forget something. It is like saying "I want you to remember this too"

I Point I Last but not least 끝으로 중요한 말 더하자면, 끝으로 한가지 더

A: **Last but not least,** remember to be nice to other people.
끝으로 중요한 말 더하자면 다른 사람들에게 착하게 대하는 걸 기억해.

B: I hope everyone takes time to do that.
다들 그랬으면 좋겠어.

미드표현

Last but not least, we have to review these reports.
끝으로 중요한 말 더하자면, 우리는 이 보고서들을 검토해야 돼.

Last but not least, remember to buy a gift for your mom. 끝으로 한가지 더, 네 엄마줄 선물 사는거 잊지 마라.

Last but not least, we need some groceries.
끝으로 한가지 더, 우리 식료품을 좀 사야 돼.

079 Before I forget, you got a call from Tom
잊기 전에 말해두는데 탐이 전화했었어

this is a way for a speaker to say that he needs to tell the listener that Tom phoned him. The speaker is afraid that he might not remember to give the message later on. It is like saying "I just remembered, Tom called you"

I Point I before I forget 잊기 전에 말해두는데

A: **Before I forget,** you got a call from Tom.
잊기 전에 말해두는데 탐이 전화했었어.

B: Oh really? Did he say why he was calling?
정말? 전화한 이유를 말했어?

미드표현

Ah! Before I forget, I got you a present.
아! 잊기 전에 말해두는데, 너한테 줄 선물있어.

Oh, before I forget, I have one more thing for you. 오, 잊기 전에 말하는데, 너에게 줄게 하나 더 있어.

Before I forget, I'd like your opinion on the menus I've prepared for the Halloween party.
내가 잊기 전에 말해두는데, 할로윈 파티에 내가 준비한 메뉴에 대한 의견을 좀 줘봐.

080 (I was) Just wondering (질문 후) 그냥 물어봤어

often this is a way of starting a question. It means "I'd like to know..."

| Point | I was just wondering if[weather/when/how~]
= I wonder if~ 1. 단지 …가 궁금해서 물어봤어 2. …을 해주시겠어요?

A: What's your hometown? **I was just wondering.**
고향이 어디야? 그냥 궁금해서.

B: I was born in Chicago. 시카고야.

I was just wondering how you'd feel if I went out with him.
내가 걔랑 데이트해도 네가 어떻게 생각할지 생각해봤어.

I was just wondering why you're here.
왜 네가 여기 있는지 생각해봤어.

I'm just wondering if that's how you killed him. 네가 그 사람을 그렇게 죽였나하고 생각해봤어.

It's me again. Just wondering where you're at.
또 나야. 뭐 하는지 그냥 궁금해서.

081 It's a long story 말하자면 길어

this means "It is complicated or hard to explain." Speakers say this when something would take a long time to explain

| Point | It's a long story 말하자면 길어
to make a long story short 간단히 말하자면

A: How did you meet your husband? 남편을 어떻게 만났어?

B: **It's a long story.** How much time do you have?
말하자면 길어. 시간이 얼마나 있어?

It's a long story. I'll tell you later.
얘기하자면 길어. 나중에 이야기할게.

It's a long story. Just do me a favor?
얘기하려면 길어. 그냥 도와줄테야?

I told you, it's a long story, I don't wanna talk about it. 내 말했잖아, 얘기하면 길어. 얘기하기 싫어.

Well, to make a long story short, Jim's family hates me. 간단히 말해서, 짐의 가족은 날 싫어해.

082 Speaking of~ …얘기가 나와서 말인데

this shifts a conversation to a similar subject. It is like saying "I'd like to talk about something that is related to that"

| Point | Speaking of which 그 말이 나와서 말인데, 말이 나왔으니 말인데

A: The summer is nearly finished. 여름이 거의 끝나가.

B: **Speaking of** summer, did you go on vacation this year? 여름 얘기가 나와서 그런데, 금년에 휴가갔다 왔어?

미드표현

Speaking of Mona, I have some big news.
모나 얘기가 나와서 말인데 아주 놀라운 소식이 있어.

Speaking of which, are you ready to go to lunch? 말이 나왔으니 말인데, 점심 먹으러 갈 준비됐어?

So, speaking of which, we have another big event coming up.
말이 나와서 그런데, 우리는 큰 이벤트가 다가오고 있어.

083 Now that you mention it
말이 나온 김에, 말을 하니까 말인데요, 얘기가 나와서 그런데

this is a way of saying "That made me remember something." This is said when the speaker has been reminded of something by someone else

| Point | now that you mention it 얘기가 나와서 그런데

A: She looks a lot like my mother does.
걔 우리 엄마하고 무척 닮았어.

B: **Now that you mention it,** she does seem similar. 얘기가 나와서 그런데 정말 비슷해.

미드표현

Now that you mention it, yeah, it was very offensive. 말이 나와서 하는데, 그건 정말 불쾌했어.

And now that you mention it, it does sound fun. 말이 나와서 그런데, 그거 정말 재미있게 들리더라.

Now that you mention it, I was thinking tomorrow might not be great.
얘기가 나와서 그런데, 내일이 그렇게 좋지 않을거라 생각하고 있었어.

Now that you mention it, maybe these fellas can help you out, too.
말이 나온 김에 말하는데 이 친구들이 너를 도와줄 수도 있어.

084 Come to think of it 생각해보니까 말야, 말이 나왔으니 말인데

like the previous phrase, this means the speaker has been reminded of something. He is saying "Yes, now I remember"

| Point | When it comes to …로 말하자면
Off the top of my head 지금 막 생각해보니
By the way 참, 그런데, 참고로, 덧붙여서(I also want to say)

A: Have you ever been to this restaurant before?
전에 이 식당에 와본 적 있어?

B: **Come to think of it,** I was here several years ago. 생각해보니까 말야, 몇 년 전에 와봤어.

When it comes to love, what does age matter? 사랑에 관해 말하자면, 나이가 무슨 상관야?

When it comes to psychology I know what I'm talking about. 심리학으로 말하자면 난 자신있어.

By the way, I wanted to ask you something.
그런데, 네게 뭐 좀 물어보고 싶었어.

085 I've got news for you 새로운 소식있어, 놀랄만한 소식이 있어

often this means the speaker is telling a person something he didn't know. It is like saying "I'm going to tell you some new information"

| Point | I have a surprise for you 널 위해 깜짝 놀랄만한 걸 준비한 게 있어

A: **I've got news for you.** You're going to be promoted! 새로운 소식있어. 네가 승진될거래!

B: Oh, that really makes me feel great! 정말 기분 좋다!

I got news for you. There were forty other survivors of this plane crash.
놀랄만한 소식이 있어. 비행기 사고에서 40명이나 살았대.

Well, I got news for you. You can't have him, because he's mine!
새로운 소식이 있어. 넌 걔를 못가져. 내꺼니까!

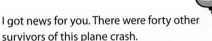

086 That's about it 그게 다야, 대강 그 정도야

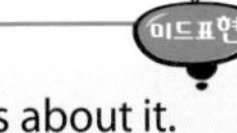

this means the person has finished. It is similar to saying "I'm done"

| Point | ~ that's about it (앞에 나열한 후에) 뭐 그런 거야

A: Do we have anything else to talk about?
다른 논의할 게 있나요?

B: No, **that's about it** for this meeting.
아뇨, 이번 회의로는 그게 다예요.

We'll arrest the suspect, and that's about it.
우리는 용의자를 체포할건데, 그게 다야.

That's about it. We're finished for today.
그게 다야. 우린 오늘 일은 마쳤어.

That's about it. I'll let you know if I need more help. 그게 다야. 내가 도움이 더 필요하면 내가 말할게.

087 It's like that 응 맞아, 그 경우와 비슷해, 그런 셈이야, 그런 거야

this means "It's a similar situation." It is said when someone wants to say one thing is like another

| Point | It's like that 그런 셈이야

A: Has your business trip to Hawaii been like a vacation? 하와이출장 휴가같아?

B: Yeah, **it's like that.** The weather here is really beautiful. 어, 그런 셈이야. 여기 날씨가 정말 좋아.

Well, it's like that. With feelings.
그래, 그거야. 딱 그 때 그 느낌이야.

A: Put your hands out in front of you. B: Oh, it's like that, huh? A: 손 앞으로 내봐. B: 어, 이렇게, 응?

You know how a cobra can swallow an entire pig? It's like that.
코브라가 어떻게 돼지 한 마리를 통째로 먹는 줄 알아? 그 경우와 비슷해.

088 It's stuff like that 그 비슷한 거야

this is an informal way to say "It's similar to those things." It indicates something is similar to a group of things

Point It's stuff like that 그 비슷한거야

A: The children are always making a lot of noise.
얘들은 항상 무척 시끄럽게 해.

B: **It's stuff like that** which makes it hard to study here. 그런 것들 때문에 여기서 공부하기가 어려워.

It's stuff like that, isn't it? 그 비슷한 거지, 그렇지 않아?

You think about stuff like that?
그런 비슷한 거 생각하는 거야?

Don't say stuff like that. 그런 건 말하지마.

089 That means~ 그 말은…, …라는 말이지

this is a way to explain the significance of something. It is like saying "The reason for it is this..."

Point That means~ …라는 말이지

A: The snow has been falling all night. 밤새 눈이 내렸어.

B: **That means** it will be cold outside.
밖이 추울거라는 말이지.

That means no sleeping with your girlfriend.
다시 말해 네 여친과 잘 수 없다는 뜻이지.

That means no more water.
물은 그만 마셔야 한다는 말야.

That means I'll have to quit smoking.
내가 금연해야 한다는 말이네.

090 ~ for all we(I) know 우리가 아는 바로는, …이런 거 아닌가, …인지 누가 알아

this usually means "We don't have all of the information." When this is said, we can understand the speaker is not sure about something

Point ~ for all I care …하든 말든 난 상관없다, 혹시 …인지도 모른다

A: Have your parents called you today? 네 부모님이 오늘 전화하셨어?

B: No, but they may call tomorrow, **for all we know.** 아니, 하지만 내일 전화하실 수도 있는 거지 누가 알겠어.

For all we know, this is animal blood.
동물 피인지 누가 알아.

For all we know, Jerry is who she was meant to be with. 제리가 걔가 운명으로 생각하는 애인지 알 바 아니지.

She could be his new daughter, for all I care.
걔가 그 사람의 새로운 딸이든 말든 상관없어.

091 for what it's worth 맞는지 모르겠지만, 어쨌든, 그건 그렇다치고

often this is said when someone gives his opinion. It is like saying "You might not agree with me"

Point for what it's worth 어쨌든, 그런 그렇다치고

A: I think you should take a long vacation, **for what it's worth.** 어쨌든 장기휴가를 갔다 오는 게 좋을 것 같아.

B: I'd rather continue working until this project is finished. 이 프로젝트가 끝날 때까지 계속 일하겠어.

That night Mike gave Kate multiple orgasms, for what it's worth. 그날 밤 마이크는 케이트에게 모르긴 해도 오르가즘을 여러 번 느끼게 해주었어.

And for what it's worth, you got nothing to be nervous about. You were wonderful.
어쨌든, 넌 걱정할게 없어. 넌 대단했어.

For what it's worth I was very fond of your mother. 그건 그렇다치고, 난 네 엄마를 무척 좋아했어.

092 or words to that effect 뭐 그 비슷한 말이었어, 뭐 그런 얘기였어

미드표현

this means "Or something similar." It indicates something may not be exactly the same, but it is very similar

| Point | or something to that effect 그 비슷한 거야

A: He said we must move, **or words to that effect.** 걘 우리가 이사해야 된대, 뭐 그런 얘기였어.

B: Do you think you'll be able to find another apartment? 다른 아파트를 찾을 수 있을 거라고 생각해?

She promised to bring the money, or words to that effect. 걔는 돈을 가져온다고 약속했어, 뭐 그런 얘기였어.

Rob said he'll call tonight, or words to that effect. 랍이 오늘 밤에 전화할거라고 했는데 뭐 그런 비슷한 말이었어.

The contract says we'll be hired, or words to that effect. 계약서에 따르면 우리는 고용될거래, 뭐 그런 얘기였어.

093 or something …인지 무엇인지, …하던지 하지 뭐, 뭐 그런 거 등

미드표현

often this means that the speaker is saying that a thing is unknown. It is like saying "I'm not sure what else"

| Point | ~and stuff 기타 등등 다른 것도

A: What are you going to do tomorrow? 내일 뭐 할거야?

B: I'll go hiking with friends **or something.**
친구들과 하이킹인지 무엇인지 할거야.

Are you a drug dealer or something?
당신 마약상이나 뭐 그런거야?

Why don't we hire a manager or something?
매니저나 뭐 그런 사람 고용하자.

It's just my books and stuff.
그냥 내 책들하고 다른 것들야.

094 ~ or what? 1. 그게 아니면 뭐야?, …아니면 어쩔건데? 2. 그렇지 않아?, 그런 거 아냐?

미드표현

this means "Tell me more." The speaker is asking someone to give more information

| Point | ~or what? 그게 아니면 뭐야?, 그런 거 아냐?

A: Are we going to the festival **or what?**
축제갈거지 그렇지 않아?

B: Just wait. We'll go to the festival soon.
기다려. 곧 축제갈거야.

So, are we gonna get together, or what?
그럼 우리 만날거야, 그런 거 아냐?

Are you guys arresting me or what?
날 체포할거야 뭐야?

Are we gonna do this or what? 이거 할거야 뭐야?

095 (~ and) that's that 이게 전부야, 그걸로 끝이야

미드표현

this means "It's all finished." This is said when something is over and nothing about it can be changed

| Point | ~ that's what 그래서 그런 거야(= that is what happened)

A: You shouldn't have let her talk badly to you.
걔가 널 험담 못하도록 했어야 됐어.

B: Well, she did, **and that's that.**
저기, 걔가 험담을 했는데 그걸로 끝이었어.

I'm gonna tell him that he had his chance, and that's that!
걔한테 기회가 있었다고 말할거야, 그리고 그게 끝이었다고!

That's that. I got some packing to do.
다 끝났어. 짐싸야겠어.

She showed up, that's what.
걔가 나타났고 그래서 그렇게 된 거야.

096 (The) Cat got your tongue? 왜 말이 없어?

this is asking "Why aren't you speaking?" It is usually said when someone is too quiet

| Point | She's tongue-tied 걔는 할 말을 잃었어

A: Why are you so quiet? **The cat got your tongue?** 왜 그렇게 조용해? 왜 말이 없어?

B: I was just thinking about some things.
뭐 좀 생각하는 중이었어.

미드표현

Nothing more to say? Cat got your tongue?
더 할 말 없어? 왜 말이 없어?

Why are you so quiet tonight? Cat got your tongue? 오늘밤 왜 이렇게 조용한거야? 왜 말이 없는거야?

Cat got your tongue? Or are you ignoring me? 왜 말이 없는거야? 아니면 날 무시하는거야?

You don't have to remain silent. Cat got your tongue? 넌 침묵할 필요가 없어. 왜 말이 없는거야?

097 It's on the tip of my tongue 혀 끝에서 뱅뱅도네, 생각이 날듯 말듯해

this means "I forgot what it was but I will remember soon." It is said to explain why a person can't answer

| Point | be on the tip of one's tongue 혀 끝에서 뱅뱅도네

A: What is the capital of Portugal? 포르투갈의 수도가 어디지?

B: I know it, but **it's on the tip of my tongue.**
아는데 혀 끝에서 뱅뱅도네.

미드표현

The name of the restaurant is on the tip of my tongue. 그 식당이름이 혀끝에서 뱅뱅도네.

I can't tell you because it's on the tip of my tongue. 생각이 날듯 말듯해서 말을 해줄 수가 없어.

A: Who am I thinking of? You know. B: Oh, it's on the tip of my tongue.
A: 내가 누굴 생각하게? 넌 알아. B: 생각이 날듯 말듯하네.

098 It was a slip of the tongue 실언했어, 말이 잘못 나왔네

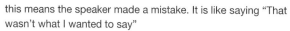

this means the speaker made a mistake. It is like saying "That wasn't what I wanted to say"

| Point | a slip of the tongue 말 실수

A: You told me that you didn't like John. 존을 싫어한다고 내게 말했잖아.

B: I didn't mean to say that. **It was a slip of the tongue.** 그렇게 말할려는 게 아니었어. 말이 잘못 나온거야.

미드표현

I'm sorry, it was a slip of the tongue.
미안, 말이 잘못 나왔네.

Telling them the secret was a slip of the tongue. 걔네들에게 비밀얘기한 건 실수였어.

And a slip of the tongue won't go on the record. 그리고 말실수는 기록으로 남지 않을거야.

099 He let it slip that he was love with Jane
갠 제인을 사랑한다는 걸 무심결에 말해버렸어

to let something slip is to tell a secret. It is another way to say "He confided that..."

| Point | let sth slip (out) (to sb) (…에게) 무심결에 말을 뱉어버리다, 얼떨결에 말하다

A: Abe **let it slip** that I didn't get the job.
에이브는 무심결에 내가 일을 못 맡았다고 말했어.

B: That's too bad. Did he tell you who got it?
안됐네. 누가 맡았는지 말했어?

I let it slip out to the police that she's recently gotten into drugs.
무심결에 걔가 최근에 다시 마약을 한다고 경찰에 말해 버렸어.

Rinda got drunk one night and let it slip about her secret Internet chat buddy.
린다는 취해서 얼떨결에 자신의 은밀한 채팅상대에 대해 말했어.

Catherine let it slip that she was gonna be here today. 캐서린은 무심결에 오늘 여기에 온다고 말해버렸어.

100 I spoke out of turn 말이 잘못 나왔어, 내가 잘못 말했어, 하지 말아야 될 말을 했어

this means "I shouldn't have said that and I'm sorry." Often this is said when a person is wrong about something

I Point I Please don't speak out of turn 경솔하게 말하지 좀 마

A: You've made Julia very angry with you.
네가 줄리아를 열받게 만들었어?

B: **I spoke out of turn.** I didn't mean to upset her.
말이 잘못 나왔어. 걜 화나게 할려는 건 아니었어.

I apologized after I spoke out of turn.
말이 잘못 나온 다음에 난 사과했어.

I spoke out of turn and everyone got upset.
하지 말아야 할 말을 내가 해서 다들 당황해 했어.

My father scolded me after I spoke out of turn. 하지 말아야 될 말을 했다고 아버지한테 혼났어.

101 I spoke too soon 잘 알지도 못하면서 함부로 말했어

this means the person was wrong and wishes he had waited to say something. It is like saying "I made a mistake by saying that"

I Point I Don't speak too soon 미리 속단하지 말라구

A: You said that MP3 players would never become popular. MP3가 결코 유행하지 않을 거라고 말했지?

B: **I spoke too soon.** It seems like every kid has one. 잘 알지도 못하면서 말했네. 모든 애들이 하나씩 갖고 있는 것 같아.

I spoke too soon and realized I was mistaken.
잘 알지도 못하고 말했다가 내가 틀렸다는 걸 깨달았어.

I spoke too soon and it created many problems.
내가 잘 알지도 못하면서 함부로 말했다가 많은 문제들이 생겼어.

I spoke too soon and my prediction was wrong. 내가 경솔하게 말을 했고 나의 예측은 틀렸어.

102 I'm not being flip 내 말 진심이야

미드표현

this is a way for the speaker to say he is being serious, and that he is not joking around. A person may say this if he thinks people do not think he is sincere. Basically the speaker is saying "I'm being earnest, so please listen to me seriously"

I Point I be flip(=be flippant) 경솔하다, 건방지다, 무례하다

A: I can't believe you'd joke about marrying me.
나와 결혼한다고 농담하다니 믿을 수가 없어.

B: **I'm not being flip.** I'm being totally serious.
그냥 하는 말이 아니야. 정말 진심이야.

I'm not being flip, I'm just pointing out a reality. 그냥 얘기하는게 아냐. 단지 현실을 알려주고 싶을 뿐이야.

I don't mean to be flip, but you came here because you were troubled and then you refuse any help we give you.
내 진심으로 말하는데, 넌 힘들어서 여기 왔는데 우리의 도움을 전부 거절하고 있어.

I'd really appreciate it if you wouldn't be flip about this. 네가 이거에 대해 너무 경솔하지 않으면 정말 고맙겠어.

I don't mean to be flippant. 기분나쁘게 하려는 것은 아냐.

미드에선 이렇게 쓰인다!

I'm not being flip

Desperate Housewives SEASON#1-3

Mary가 자살하기 전에 열겠다고 한 파티를 어떻게 할 것인가를 놓고 남은 네 명이 대화를 나누고 있는 장면.

Susan: How could we have all forgotten about this?
Lynette: We didn't exactly forget. It's just usually, when the hostess dies, the party is off.
Bree: Lynette!
Lynette: I'm not being filp, I'm just pointing out a reality.
Gabrielle: Mary Alice was so excited about it. It's so sad.
Susan: I think we should go through with it.

수잔: 어떻게 우리 모두가 이걸 잊고 있었지?
르넷: 잊은 건 아니지, 보통 파티 주최자가 죽은 파트는 없는거지.
브리: 르넷!
르넷: 나쁜 뜻은 없어, 난 현실이 그렇다는 말이지.
가브리엘: 매이 앨리스가 정말 좋아했었는데, 정말 슬프다.
수잔: 우리가 그 파티를 열어야 될 것 같아.

103 The words just wouldn't come out of my mouth 말이 안 나왔을 뿐이야

미드표현

this is a way of explaining why the speaker couldn't talk. It means "I couldn't think of what to say"

I Point I come out of one's mouth 말이 …의 입에서 나오다

A: Why didn't you invite Randy to the party?
왜 랜디를 파티에 초대하지 않았어?

B: **The words just wouldn't come out of my mouth** and I was embarrassed.
말이 안 나왔을 뿐이고 내가 당황했었어.

I tried to break up with her, but because I wasn't sure you wanted me back, the words just wouldn't come out of my mouth.
걔랑 헤어질려고 했지만 네가 날 다시 원하는 지 확신이 없어서 그냥 말이 안 나왔을 뿐이야.

I mean, why wouldn't I want to hear those words come out of his mouth?
내 말은 걔 입에서 그런 말들이 나오는 것을 내가 왜 원하지 않았겠어?

104 I lost my train of thought 잠시 정신을 놓았어, 생각이 끊겨버렸어, 하려던 말을 잊었어

미드표현

this is a way of saying "I couldn't concentrate." People say this when they forget what they were talking about

I Point I lose one's train of thought 말하려던 말을 잊어버리다

A: **I lost my train of thought.** What was I saying?
하려던 말을 잊었어. 내가 뭐 얘기하고 있었어?

B: You were talking about the presidential election.
대통령 선거에 대해 얘기하고 있었어.

This is where I always lose my train of thought. 항상 이 부분에서 내가 하려면 말을 잊어버려.

I don't know. I lost my train of thought.
몰라. 잠시 정신을 놓았어.

I knew this conversation was really about you, so I just gave you an answer so you could get back to your train of thought.
이 대화는 너에 대한 것임을 알고 있어. 내가 네게 답을 줄테니 넌 다시 네가 하려던 말을 하면 돼.

105 You don't mean to say that 진심으로 하는 말은 아니겠지

미드표현

this is usually a way to indicate that the speaker has heard someone say something, but he likely thinks that they don't mean it because it was said when the person was upset or angry. This can also be expressed as "I think you are just saying that because you're mad"

I Point I You don't mean to say (that) S+V …라 말하는게 진심은 아니지
You don't mean to say that 진심으로 하는 말은 아니겠지

A: I really hate all the students here.
여기 학생들 모두 다 정말 싫어.

B: **You don't mean to say that.** They are nice.
진심으로 하는 말은 아니겠지. 걔네들 착한데.

You don't mean to say that the performance is cancelled. 공연이 취소되었다는 말은 아니지?

You don't mean to say that you met the president. 네가 사장을 만났다는 말은 진심이 아니지?

You don't mean to say that he came on to you. 걔가 너한테 추근댔다는 것은 진심이 아니지?

You don't mean to say that Sarah ate the whole cake. 새라가 케익을 다 먹었다는게 진심은 아니지?

MEMO

Ways of saying something was surprising and of talking about new things

어떻게 그럴 수 있어, 놀람과 충격

How could that be?

001 I can't believe it (놀람) 설마!, 말도 안돼!, 그럴 리가, 이럴 수가!, 믿지지 않아

this is usually a way of expressing surprise about something. It means "It was surprising to me"

| Point | I can't believe+N/ S+V …한 것이 믿어지지 않아, …는 말도 안돼
I don't believe it (사실부정) 사실이 아니잖아, 못 믿겠어
I don't believe this! (충격, 놀람) 이건 말도 안돼!

A: **I can't believe** that Tim wants to marry Joanne.
팀이 조앤과 결혼을 원한다는 게 믿기지 않아.

B: Well, maybe he is really in love with her.
글쎄, 아마 걔를 정말 사랑하나봐.

I can't believe you did that. 네가 그랬다니 말도 안돼.

I can't believe it's real. 이게 사실이라는게 믿기지 않아.

I can't believe it. I'm so glad you came.
이럴 수가, 네가 와서 너무 기뻐.

002 Would you believe (it)! 믿어지지가 않아!

often, this means "I was surprised by that." It is a way of expressing that something which has occurred wasn't expected

| Point | Would you believe me if I said~? 내가 …한다고 하면 날 믿겠어?

A: I'm being transferred to New York next month. **Would you believe it?** 담달에 뉴욕으로 전근가, 믿기지 않아!

B: It sounds like your life is going to be pretty busy.
사는 게 꽤 바빠지겠구나.

Would you believe me if I said I was sorry?
내가 사과하면 내 말 믿겠어?

Would you believe me if I said I can't stop thinking of you, and I came here to make love to you?
내가 너에 대한 생각을 멈출 수가 없고 너와 사랑을 나누기 위해 왔다고 하면 믿겠니?

003 (This is) Unbelievable! 정말 놀라워라!, 말도 안돼!

this expresses "I'm very surprised about that." The speaker learned something that he didn't expect.

| Point | It was unbelievable 정말 놀라웠어
You are unbelievable 너 정말 놀라워, 대단해

A: So Jim is being promoted to department manager. 그래, 짐이 백화점 매니저로 승진돼.

B: **Unbelievable!** He has never worked very hard.
정말 놀라워라! 열심히 일한 적도 없는데.

Oh, my god, that's unbelievable! What happened? 맙소사, 믿을 수 없네! 무슨 일이야?

I know, it's unbelievable. 그래 알아 놀라운 일이지.

Unbelievable. This is even bigger than the Feds thought.
정말 놀라워. 이건 FBI가 생각했던 것보다 훨씬 크네.

004 Gee, how could that be? 이런, 어떻게 그럴 수 있어?

this is usually said when a speaker is confused or surprised about something. He may say this after he is told something that he did not expect to hear. Another way to say this would be "I feel really surprised to hear that"

| Point | How could that be? 어떻게 그럴 수 있어?
How could sb be? …가 어떻게 그럴 수 있어?
How could sb be~? …는 어떻게 …할 수가 있어?

A: A big snowstorm is coming this weekend.
이번 주말에 폭설이 내린대.

B: **Gee, how could that be?** It's so warm today.
이런, 어떻게 그럴 수 있대? 오늘 이렇게 따뜻한데.

How could you be? You're on a vendetta against her.
네가 어떻게 그럴 수 있어? 넌 걔한테 복수심을 품고 있잖아.

How could you be that stupid?
넌 어떻게 그렇게 멍청할 수 가 있어?

How could that be? I mean, I didn't know what the hell I was doing.
어떻게 그럴 수 있지? 내 말은 나도 어떻게 해야 할 줄 몰랐단말야.

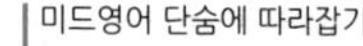

005 You're really starting to creep me out 너 정말 겁나기 시작해

미드표현

this is said in order to tell someone that he is making others feel nervous or afraid of his behavior. It is a very negative thing to creep people out, because they don't like it. A different way to say this would be "Your actions are making everyone feel anxious"

| Point | creep sb out …를 겁[놀]나게 하다, 오싹하게 하다
give sb the creeps …을 소름 끼치게 하다

A: I like hanging out in cemeteries at night.
난 밤에 묘지에서 노는 것을 좋아해.

B: **You're really starting to creep me out.**
너 정말 겁나기 시작하네.

Why would the baby creep me out?
왜 난 애를 보면 겁나는걸까?

This place looks abandoned. Gives me the creeps. 이 곳은 방치된 것 같아. 오싹 소름이 돋아.

This whole thing creeps me out.
이 모든 것이 아주 기분을 안좋게 해.

006 You don't say 1. (가벼운 놀람, 불확실) 설마!, 그럴리가!, 정말? 2. (다 아는얘기) 뻔한 거 아냐?

often this is used as a way of expressing mild interest or surprise over some news. It is very similar to saying "Oh really?"

| Point | You don't say+N …말하지 말라(금지표현)

A: I hear the weather is due to get really cold next week. 날씨가 담주에 무척 추워질거래.

B: **You don't say.** Well, I better get out my winter clothes. 설마. 음, 겨울 옷 꺼내놔야겠구만.

These diamonds are priceless? You don't say?
이 다이아몬드가 엄청 비싸다며? 정말야?

You don't say? I've never heard that before.
그럴리가? 처음 들어보는데.

You've been on TV before? You don't say?
전에 TV에 출연했다고? 설마?

007 I can't get over it[this] 정말 놀라워라, 놀랍군, 아직도 못 잊겠어

usually this is a way of indicating "That shocked me." We can understand that something was so surprising that the speaker still can't believe it

| Point | I can't get over how ~ 얼마나 …한지 놀라워

A: It was really shocking to hear that John died.
존이 죽다니 정말 충격적이었어.

B: Yeah. **I can't get over it.** 그래, 정말 놀라워.

I can't get over how old you are. You've really changed. 정말이지 너 나이 참 많이 먹었네. 정말 변했어.

I can't get over Donna and Chris making out like that.
도나와 크리스가 저렇게 성적 행위를 하다니 정말 놀라워.

Doris, I can't get over how lovely that jacket looks on you.
도리스, 저 재킷이 너한테 얼마나 예쁘게 어울리는지 몰라.

008 I didn't see that coming 그럴 줄 몰랐어

미드표현

this expresses that a person was very surprised by something that happened, and he had no hint that it would occur. Often it means that the surprise was bad or unwelcome. A similar way to say this is "This was not something that I expected"

| Point | see that coming 그럴 줄 알다

A: Randy and Melissa ran off to Vegas to get married. 랜디와 멜리사가 결혼하려고 베거스로 도망쳤어.

B: Oh my God! **I didn't see that coming.**
맙소사! 그럴 줄 몰랐네.

Sorry. I didn't see it coming. 미안해. 그럴 줄 몰랐어.

And how did we not see this coming?
어떻게 이렇게 될 줄 몰랐을까?

You set me up, and I didn't even see it coming. 넌 날 함정에 빠뜨렸어, 그리고 난 그런 줄 꿈에도 몰랐어.

I didn't see that coming! You're-you're asking me out! 이런 날이 올 줄은 몰랐어! 네가 네가 데이트를 신청하다니!

009 I don't want to freak him out 걔를 놀래키고[기분상하게 하고] 싶지 않아

the speaker is expressing the wish that a person will not get very upset about something. It is saying "I hope he won't get too angry or worried"

| Point | freak sb out 놀래키다
You freaked me out 너 때문에 놀랬어

A: Have you told Tom that he wasn't accepted into Yale? 예일에 떨어졌다고 탐에게 말했어?
B: Not yet. **I don't want him to freak out.** 아직. 놀래키고 싶지 않아서.

I don't want to freak you out, but I think I just saw a rat in your cupboard. 놀래키려는 건 아니지만, 방금 찬장에서 쥐를 봤어.

Let me guess. My parents sent you here to freak me out. 어디 보자. 내 부모님이 날 놀래키려고 널 보냈구나.

Yeah, well, I don't like bugs, okay? They freak me out. 난 벌레를 싫어해. 알았어? 벌레보면 난 기겁을 해.

010 I'm not freaking out 안 놀랬어, 난 괜찮아

미드표현

this means "Don't worry, I'm alright." The speaker is saying he has remained calm, without getting upset

| Point | Sb+freak out (a little) …가 (좀) 놀래다, 기겁하다
I got so freaked out 내가 정말이지 기겁했어

A: How have you been getting along at your new job? 새로운 일은 어떻게 해나가고 있어?
B: Well, **I'm not freaking out,** but it is very stressful. 음, 난 괜찮지만 스트레스를 많이 받아.

A: I'm not freaking out. B: Then why are you laughing? A: 난 괜찮아. B: 그럼 왜 웃는거야?

I'm not freaking out. Why would I be freaking out? 난 놀라지 않았어. 내가 왜 놀래겠어?

I got so freaked out that I hung up the phone. 너무 놀라 전화를 끊었어.

011 It's gonna knock your socks off 넌 깜짝 놀랄거야

미드표현

this is a way of saying that something is going to be very impressive. We can understand that the listener is experiencing it for the first time, and the speaker is sure he will like it. Another way to say this would be "You are really going to like this"

| Point | knock sb's socks off 너무 놀라다, 기쁘다, 감동받다

A: How was the new sci-fi movie? 새로운 공상과학영화 어땠어?
B: **It's going to knock your socks off.** 넌 아주 깜짝 놀랄거야.

I didn't exactly knock his socks off, did I? 난 걔를 감동시키지 못했어, 그지?

You give me ten minutes, I'll whip up a spaghetti carbonara that'll knock their socks off. 10분만 줘봐, 걔네들을 놀라게 할 까르보라나 스파게티를 준비할게.

If the explosion had knocked his socks off, that would be impressive, wouldn't it? 그 폭발로 걔가 놀랐었다면, 기억에 오래 남았을텐데, 그렇지 않을까?

012 It comes as a bit of shock 받아들이기 힘들었지만, 정말 놀라워

미드표현

this often expresses that something was a surprise to the speaker. It is a way of saying "It was difficult to believe"

| Point | That comes as quite a surprise 상당히 놀라운 일이야
Isn't that a bit shocking? 충격적이지 않아?
This may[might] come as a shock to you, but~ 네겐 충격일지 모르겠지만…

A: How did you feel when Randy broke up with you? 랜디가 너랑 헤어졌을 때 기분 어땠어?
B: **It came as a bit of a shock,** but I'm over it now. 정말 놀라웠지만 지금은 다 잊었어.

I know this may come as a shock to you, but your mother dumped you when you were a child. 받아들이기 힘들겠지만 네 엄만 네가 어렸을 때 널 버렸어.

Did that come as a shock to you? 충격적이야?

013 He was taken by surprise 걔는 깜짝 놀랐어, 걔는 예상도 못했어

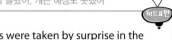

this often indicates that something happened to a person that wasn't expected. Another way to say it is "He didn't know it would happen"

| Point | Don't take me by surprise 놀라게 하지마
I'm not surprised 당연하지, 놀랠 일도 아니구만

A: Had Frank known that he was going to be fired?
프랭크가 자기가 잘릴 줄 알았어?

B: Absolutely not. **He was taken by surprise.**
전혀 몰랐어. 걘 깜짝 놀랐어.

미드표현

The thieves were taken by surprise in the apartment. 그 도둑들은 아파트에서 깜짝 놀랐어.

We were taken by surprise when the cops arrived. 우리는 경찰이 도착했을 때 정말 깜짝 놀랐어.

I'm usually cautious, but I was taken by surprise. 내가 보통 조심스럽지만 예상도 못할 정도로 깜짝 놀랐어.

014 I'm speechless (기쁨, 놀람 따위로) 할 말을 잃었어, 말문이 막히네

this is usually said when a person is shocked or surprised. It is like saying "I don't know what to say"

| Point | I'm absolutely at a loss for words 기가 막혀 말이 안 나오네

A: For your birthday we got you a new car.
생일선물로 우리가 너한테 주는 새 차야.

B: **I'm speechless.** How could you afford this?
말문이 막히네. 어떻게 이걸 사줄 수가 있었어?

미드표현

I can't believe he dropped his pants. I'm speechless.
걔가 자기 바지를 밑으로 내렸다니 믿기지 않아. 할 말을 잃었어.

I'm speechless. I never suspected he was a criminal. 할 말을 잃었어. 걔가 범죄자라고는 전혀 의심하지 않았거든.

Sara didn't tell me she was leaving. I'm speechless. 새라는 떠난다는 말도 내게 하지 않았어. 할 말을 잃었어.

015 Who could[would] have thought?
누가 생각이나 했겠어?, 상상도 못했네

this is used to express surprise that something occurred. It is like saying "I can't believe..."

| Point | Who could[would] have thought (that) S+V?
…을 누가 상상이나 했겠어?

A: **Who would have thought** a tsunami would have killed so many people?
쓰나미가 그렇게 많은 인명을 해칠 줄 누가 상상이나 했겠어?

B: I know. It was a really tragic event for Southeast Asia. 그래, 동남아시아의 정말 비극적인 일이었어.

미드표현

Who would have thought there could be a thief in my house?
우리 집에 도둑이 들줄 누가 상상이나 했겠어?

Who's have thought that you could be in jail for murder?
네가 살인죄로 감방에 있으리라고 누가 상상이나 했겠어?

Who would have thought it was you?
그게 너였다는 걸 누가 상상이나 했겠어?

016 That will make your head spin 그 때문에 네 머리가 돌게 될거야

this means that something will be overwhelming or confusing to someone. We can understand that the person got a lot of important information at one time and is having difficulty understanding it all. A similar way to say this would be "That will blow your mind"

| Point | make a person's head spin[go around, swim]
사람의 머리를 혼란하게 하다, 어리둥절하게 하다

A: I heard the new sci-fi movie has great special effects. 그 새로운 공상과학영화에는 굉장한 특수효과들이 나온대.

B: Yeah, it's true. **They will make your head spin.**
어, 정말야. 그 때문에 머리가 빙빙 돌거야.

미드표현

All the information we were taught made my head spin. 우리가 들은 모든 정보로 머리가 빙빙 돌아.

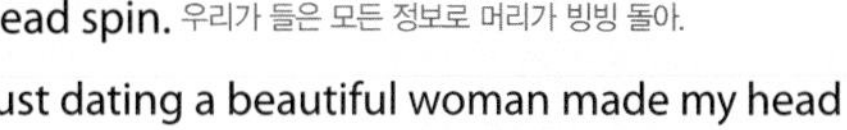

Just dating a beautiful woman made my head spin. 아름다운 여인과 데이트만 해도 내 머리가 어지러워.

017 Don't[Never] tell me (상대방 말이 말도 안되는 말이라며) 설마, …아니겠지

usually this means "I'm surprised that..." It expresses a feeling of surprise or shock over something the speaker has just heard

| Point | Don't tell me S+V 설마 …는 아니겠지

A: I was just considering enlisting in the army.
군입대를 생각하고 있었어.

B: **Don't tell me** you're going to become a soldier!
설마 군인이 되려는 건 아니겠지!

Don't tell me you don't remember.
잊어버린 건 아니겠지.

Don't tell me you can't. 못하는 건 아니겠지.

Don't tell me you didn't sign a lease.
임대계약서 사인안했다는 건 아니겠지.

Don't tell me that it's over. 끝난 거라고 말하지마.

018 What do you know? 1. (비아냥) …에 대해 네가 뭘 알어? 2. (놀람) 정말

in a sarcastic way, this expresses "I don't think you know much about that." It is an impolite way to indicate that someone's ideas may seem foolish. And most often, this is a way of showing mild surprise over something. Another way to express the same feeling is by saying "That's interesting"

| Point | What do you know about+N/S+V …에 대해 네가 뭘 알아?

A: I think Rachel and Peter are going to break up.
레이첼과 피터가 헤어질 것 같아.

B: **What do you know?** You'll never understand their relationship. 무슨 소리? 걔네들 관계가 어떤지 몰라서 그래.

What do you know? Shut up. 네가 뭘 안다고? 입닥쳐

What do you know about marriage? You married a lesbian!
네가 결혼에 대해 뭘 안다고? 레즈비언하고 결혼해놓고서

What do you know about this guy? You've been on one date.
네가 걔에 대해 뭘 알아? 데이트 한 번 해놓고.

019 It threw me for a loop 기겁했다니까, 상상도 못했어, 그럴 줄 몰랐어

this means "I didn't think it could happen." It is a way of indicating that something that happened was completely unexpected

| Point | throw sb for a loop …를 놀라게(기겁하게)하다

A: I'll bet it was difficult when you got ill during the final exam week. 기말고사때 아파서 정말 힘들었겠네.

B: Yes it was. **It really threw me for a loop.**
정말 그랬어. 정말 예상도 못했다니까.

Her whole bisexual thing is throwing me for a loop. 걔의 양성애관련 일 때문에 놀랐어.

Yeah, that kind of threw me for a loop.
그래 그 때문에 좀 놀랬어.

It threw me for a loop, but I think we can get passed this. 놀랠 놀자였지만 잊을 수 있을 것 같아.

020 You scared the crap[shit, hell] out of me
깜작 놀랐네, 간 떨어질 뻔 했네

this is a somewhat rude way of saying "What you did made me afraid." The speaker was shocked or made afraid by something the listener did

| Point | You scared me 걱정했잖아, 놀랐잖아
I'm scared to death 무서워 죽겠어

A: It turns out that I'm not pregnant after all.
임신이 아닌 것으로 판명됐어.

B: God, **you scared the shit out of me.**
휴, 간 떨어질 뻔 했네.

What are you doing? You scared the crap out of me! 뭐하는 거야? 간 떨어질 뻔 했잖아!

I'm not going! I'm too scared to visit a prison!
난 안가! 감옥은 가보기에 너무 무서워!

What the hell, Danny? You scared the crap out of me! 이런 젠장, 대니? 너 때문에 간 떨어질 뻔 했잖아!

021 Isn't it amazing? 정말 놀랍구나!, 대단하지 않냐?, 굉장하지?

미드표현

frequently this is a way of showing a feeling of happy surprise over something. It is like saying "That's great"

| Point | Isn't that[it] great? 대단하지 않니?
You're amazing 너 참 대단해

A: I am so happy we found such a nice house to rent. 저렇게 멋진 집을 임대하게 돼 넘 기뻐.

B: Me too. **Isn't it amazing?** 나도 그래. 대단하지 않아?

He's gonna be a free man. Isn't that great?
걘 자유의 몸이 될거야. 놀랍지 않아?

I hated it! But I still like you. isn't that great?
정말 짜증나지만 네가 아직 좋아. 놀랍지 않아?

My dream house is done! Isn't it amazing?
내가 꿈에 그리던 집이 완성됐어! 대단하지 않아?

022 What a coincidence! 이런 우연이!

미드표현

usually this means that someone thinks that a very unusual or special circumstance has taken place. The speaker is expressing "It's surprising that these things happened"

| Point | coincidence 우연

A: I think my father attended the same high school as your mom. 내 아빠가 네 엄마랑 고교동문같아.

B: **What a coincidence.** I wonder if they remember ever meeting each other.
이런 우연이. 서로 만났다 하더라도 기억할까.

I think it's nothing, a coincidence.
그건 아무 것도 아냐. 우연일 뿐이야.

Do you think it's a coincidence she disappeared the same night Jeffrey died?
제프리가 죽은 날 저녁에 걔가 사라진 게 우연이라고 생각해?

Wait, so you and that guy knew each other, too? What a coincidence!
잠깐, 그럼 너와 저 사람과 서로 아는 사이였어? 이런 우연이!

023 What a small world! 세상 참 좁네!

미드표현

most commonly, this means "I'm surprised that these things are related." It is usually a way of expressing that two people have been linked by an interesting or unusual circumstance

| Point | It's a small world 세상 정말 좁네
Small world, isn't it? 세상 한번 좁네, 그렇죠?

A: I think I met your sister while I was vacationing in Thailand. 태국 휴가때 네 누이를 만난 것 같아.

B: **What a small world!** She was traveling with a tour group there in January.
세상 참 좁네! 1월에 거기에 단체여행갔었어.

It's a small world, isn't it? 참 세상 좁네, 그지 않아?

What a small world. Conrad. Why didn't you tell me you knew Emily?
콘라드야, 세상 정말 좁다. 너 왜 에밀리를 알고 있다고 내게 말하지 않았어?

Small world, huh? Just assumed you two knew each other.
세상 참 좁지? 너희 둘이 서로 알고 있을거라 짐작했었어.

024 What (in) the hell? 도대체 뭐야?

미드표현

This is a way to express surprise and curiosity about something. It means "What was that?"

| Point | What/Who/Where the hell~? 의문문에 the hell이 삽입되어 강조문이 된다.

A: Look at all those police cars. **What the hell?**
저 경찰차들 봐. 도대체 뭐야?

B: I think someone robbed the bank downtown.
누가 시내에서 은행을 털었나봐.

What the hell?! What are you doing here?
도대체 네가 여기 왜 있어?

What the hell is going on? 도대체 무슨 일이야?

Who the hell are you? 당신은 도대체 누구야?

025 I've never seen anything like it[this, that]
그런 건 처음 봐

미드표현

the speaker wants to express that something is unique or out of the ordinary. It is another way to say "This is special" or "This is unusual"

A: It's winter time, yet the weather is still quite warm. 겨울인데 날씨가 여전히 꽤 더워.

B: I know. **I've never seen anything like it.** 그래. 이런 것 처음야.

I've never seen anything like that in the business world. 비즈니스 세계에서 이런 건 처음 봐.

Please tell me that you've never seen anything like that before. 너도 저런 건 처음 보는거지.

It's complete chaos out here. I've never seen anything like it. 정말 난장판이구만. 이런 건 처음 봐.

026 That[It]'s a new one for me! 이런 일은 처음이야!, 이런 적 없었는데!

미드표현

this is a way of expressing "This is the first time I had it happen." We can understand that something has occurred for the first time for the speaker

I Point I It's a new one for me, too 나도 이런 건 처음이야

A: Have you ever experienced anything like the circus acts we saw? 이 서커스의 묘기들을 본 적 있어?

B: Nope. **That was a new one for me.** 아니. 이런 건 처음이야.

You think there's gold in the cave? That's a new one for me. 동굴에 금이 있다고? 난 처음 듣는 얘기인데.

People say the business is failing. That's a new one for me. 사업이 안된다고 사람들이 그래. 이런 적이 없었는데.

We're being charged an admission fee? That's a new one for me. 우리가 입장료를 내야 된다고? 이런 일 처음인데.

027 I never heard of such a thing 그런 얘긴 처음 들어봐, 말도 안돼

미드표현

often this is a way for a speaker to express mild disbelief in something. It is a way of indicating "I'm not sure if it's true"

A: They say the museum has an exhibit with many strange animals. 박물관이 기이한 동물들을 전시한대.

B: I can't believe it. **I've never heard of such a thing.** 설마. 말도 안돼.

Where did you hear this from? I never heard of such a thing. 그걸 어디서 들었어? 난 처음 듣는데.

Stop saying like that. I never heard of such a thing. 그런 말 하지마. 말도 안돼.

Sex swing? I've never even heard of such a thing. 섹스 그네? 그런 얘기 처음 들어봐.

028 You startled me! 놀랐잖아!

미드표현

this means "I didn't expect to see you." It is a way of saying that one person surprised the speaker by being somewhere unexpected

I Point I startle 깜짝 놀라게 하다

A: Geez, **you startled me!** What are you doing here? 이런, 놀랐잖아! 여기서 뭐하는 거야?

B: I found your key and let myself into your apartment. 열쇠를 찾아서 집안으로 들어왔어.

You startled me. Your house is crawling with rats. 놀랐잖아! 너네 집에 쥐떼가 있어.

Tom is startled and cuts his finger. 톰이 놀라서 손가락을 베었어.

A: Sorry we startled you. B: Oh, uh, that's okay. I, I just didn't expect to see anybody up here. A: 놀래켜서 미안. B: 아냐. 위에 사람이 있는 줄 몰랐어.

029 I did a double take 놀라 다시 한번 쳐다봤어, 깜짝 놀랐어

the speaker is expressing a feeling of surprise that made him look at something a second time to check if he was seeing it accurately. It is a way to say "I looked again to see if it was real"

| Point | do a double take 말이나 상황 등을 뒤늦게 깨달았을 때 '아차하다, 다시 한번 보다'라는 뜻

A: When you drove up in your new Porsche sports car, **I did a double take.**
네가 포르쉐 스포츠 새차로 달릴 때 깜짝 놀라 다시 한번 쳐다봤어.

B: I know. Most of my friends can't believe I bought it. 알아. 친구들 대부분이 내가 산 걸 못믿더라.

He walked into the office and did a double take when he saw Cindy.
걘 사무실에 들어가서 신디를 보자 깜작 놀랐어.

I did a double take when I saw my ex-wife.
내 전처를 봤을 때 깜짝 놀랐어.

When Sam ate a bug, I did a double take.
샘이 벌레를 먹을 때 난 깜짝 놀라 다시 한번 쳐다봤어.

030 How could you do this[that]? 어떻게 그럴 수가 있어?

this is a way of asking "Why did you do that?" It is asked when someone has done something that was strange or bad

| Point | How could you do this to me[us]? 어떻게 내게 그럴 수 있어?

A: I ate the birthday cake that was in the fridge.
냉장고에 있는 생일케익 먹었어.

B: **How could you do this?** You knew it was for the party! 어떻게 그럴 수 있어? 파티에 쓸 건지 알고 있었잖아!

You pierced his ears? How could you do this without telling me?
걔 귀에다 피어싱했다고? 어쩜 내게 말도 없이 그럴 수 있어?

How could you do this to him... after all he has done for you?
걔가 네가 해준 걸 생각하면 어떻게 걔한테 그럴 수 있는 거야?

How could you do that, after you promised me? 내게 약속해놓고 어떻게 그럴 수가 있나?

031 How could this happen? 어떻게 이럴 수가 있어?, 이런 일이 있을 수가?

this is usually asked when something unusual happens. It is away of asking "Why did it happen?"

| Point | How could this happen to me? 내게 어떻게 이런 일이 생긴단 말야
How can this happen[be happening]? 어떻게 이런 일이 일어나?
How could that happen? 어떻게 그럴 수가 있니?

A: I think there is a big rainstorm on the way.
센 폭우가 오고 있는 것 같아.

B: But today is our picnic day. **How could this happen?** 하지만 오늘은 피크닉가는 날이잖아. 어떻게 이럴 수가?

There's nothing we can do? Well, how could this happen?
우리가 할 수 있는 게 아무 것도 없다고? 어떻게 이럴 수가 있어?

How could that happen to a perfectly healthy young man? 어떻게 완벽하게 건강한 젊은이에게 그럴 수가 있어?

How can this be happening? What are we going to do?
어떻게 이런 일이 일어나는 거야? 우리 어떻게 할거야?

032 This can't be happening 이건 있을 수가 없는 일이야, 이럴 수가

this is often said when something so unusual happens that it doesn't seem real. It is similar to saying "I can't believe this is happening"

A: **This can't be happening.** 이건 있을 수 없는 일이야.

B: Calm down. We'll find a way to fix it. 진정해. 그걸 수리할 방법을 찾을게.

This can't be happening. My husband is dead? I don't know how I'm going to tell my kids. 이럴 리가 없어. 남편이 죽었다고요? 어떻게 애들에게 말해야 하나.

This can't be happening. This is a misunderstanding. Oh, this can't happen to me. 이럴 리가 없어. 오해야. 어. 나한테 이런 일이 일어날 리 없어.

033 You wouldn't do that! 그렇게 못할거면서!, 절대 못할걸!, 이럴 수는 없지!

the speaker is stating he thinks someone won't do something. It is similar to saying "I can't believe you'll do that"

A: I might join the Marines next year. 내년에 해병대에 입대할까 해.

B: **You wouldn't do that!** You aren't tough enough. 그렇게 못할거면서! 그렇게 강인하지도 않잖아.

미드표현

If you were really his friend, you wouldn't do this. 네가 진정으로 걔친구라면, 이럴 수 없을거야.

You wouldn't do anything illegal, right? 불법적인 건 하지 않겠지, 그지?

You wouldn't do that if you weren't gonna say yes. 네가 찬성할게 아니라면 그렇게는 할 수 없지.

034 How can you say that? 어떻게 그렇게 말할 수 있냐?

this means "I don't agree with what you said." It is usually said when the speaker is angry about something he heard

| Point | How can you say that to me? 어떻게 내게 그렇게 말할 수 있어?
How can you say that S+V? 어떻게 …라고 말할 수 있어?
How could you say that? 어떻게 그렇게 말할 수 있어?

A: I don't enjoy eating the food you cook. 네가 요리한 거 맛 없게 먹었어.

B: **How can you say that?** You are so rude! 어떻게 그렇게 말할 수 있어? 정말 싸가지 없네!

미드표현

How can you say that? You endangered my life today. 어떻게 그런 말을? 오늘 내 생명을 위험하게 해놓고서.

I am hurt. How can you say something like that? 상처받았다고. 어떻게 그런 말을 내게 할 수 있어?

How can you say your life has no meaning? 어떻게 네 인생이 의미없다고 말할 수 있어?

035 How could you say such a thing? 네가 어떻게 그런 말을 할 수 있니?

this indicates the speaker is very upset about something that was said. It is like saying "You shouldn't have said that"

| Point | say such a thing 그런 말을 하다

A: I think you all are a bunch of jerks! 너희들 모두 다 멍청한 놈들야!

B: **How could you say such a thing?** I'll never invite you here again! 어떻게 그런 말을 할 수 있냐? 다신 널 여기 초대하지 않겠어!

미드표현

I heard you said Alice is ugly. How could you say such a thing? 앨리스가 못생겼다고 말했다며. 어떻게 그런 말을 할 수 있어?

How could you say such a thing? You knew they'd get angry. 어떻게 그런 말을 할 수 있어? 걔네들이 화낼거라는 걸 알고 있었잖아.

Did you call Ray stupid? How could you say such a thing? 레이를 멍청이라고 했어? 어떻게 그런 말을 할 수 있어?

036 How could you not tell us? 어떻게 우리에게 말하지 않을 수 있지?

this is asking "Why didn't you tell us (something)?" It is said when a person is upset about not being told some information

| Point | How could you not tell me[us] that S+V? 어떻게 …을 내게(우리에게) 말하지 않을 수 있어?
How could you tell her? 어떻게 걔한테 말할 수 있어?

A: Oh, I forgot to mention that I am married. 오, 내가 유부남이라는 걸 깜박하고 말 못했네.

B: **How could you not tell us?** We thought you were single! 어떻게 말하지 않을 수 있어? 우린 네가 독신인 줄 알았다구!

미드표현

How could you not tell me you worked here? 여기서 일한다는 말을 왜 내게 말하지 않을 수 있어?

How could you not tell me about this? 왜 내게 그거에 관해 말하지 않을 수 있어?

How could you not tell me that? We share everything. 어떻게 내게 말하지 않을 수 있어? 우린 다 공유하잖아

037 Can you believe this is already happening?

이런 일이 있는게 믿겨지니?

this is a way of expressing surprise that something is happening. It is the same as saying "I'm very surprised it is happening"

| Point | I guess I just can't believe this is happening, again!
이런 일이 내게 또 생기다니! 이런 일이 생기다니 믿을 수가 없어!

A: Wow, look at the snow falling outside.
와, 밖에 눈 내리는 것 봐.

B: **Can you believe this is already happening?** It's only October. 벌써 이러는 게 믿어져? 겨우 10월인데.

미드표현

They are getting married tomorrow. Can you believe this is already happening?
걔네들 내일 결혼해. 벌써 이렇게 되다니 믿겨져?

Can you believe this is already happening? It's so soon. 벌써 이렇게 되다니 믿겨져? 금방야.

Our business is ready to open. Can you believe this is already happening?
사업시작할 준비됐어. 벌써 이렇게 되다니 믿겨지니?

038 How is that possible? 어떻게 그럴 수가 있지?

this asks "What made that happen?" It is a way of asking why something occurred

| Point | How is this possible? 이게 가능해?

A: There is no money in your bank account, Mr. LaRue. 라뤼씨, 은행계좌에 잔고가 없는데요.

B: **How is that possible?** I put money in last week. 어떻게 그럴 수가 있죠? 지난 주에 입금했는데요.

미드표현

How is that possible? You barely know her! 어떻게 그럴 수가 있어? 넌 걔를 거의 모르잖아!

A: You're telling me my daughter might actually be a boy? B: How is that possible?
A: 제 딸이 사실은 아들일 수도 있다구요? B: 어떻게 이런 일이 가능하죠?

Hold on, but how is that possible? Chris never let any of his victims live.
잠깐, 하지만 어떻게 그럴 수 있어? 크리스는 절대 자신의 피해자를 살려둔 적이 없어.

039 That can't be 뭔가 잘못된 거야, 그럴 리가 없어

this is a way to say "I don't believe it." It is said when the speaker is very surprised

| Point | That can't be+adj/N …일리가 없어
It can't be (+adj/N) 이럴 수가!, …일리가 없어

A: All of the tickets for the movie have been sold.
영화표가 다 팔렸어.

B: **That can't be.** I made reservations!
그럴 리가. 예매했는데!

미드표현

That can't be right. 그럴 리가 없어.

That can't be good for her. 걔한테 좋을 리가 없어.

No, that's not right. It can't be.
아냐, 그게 아니야. 그럴 리가 없어.

It can't be you. 너일 리가 없어.

040 How dare you do~ ! 어떻게 …할 수가 있냐!

this expresses anger that someone did something. It is another way of saying "I'm very angry because of your actions"

| Point | How dare you! 네가 뭔데!, 네가 감히!
You wouldn't dare! 어떻게 그럴 수 있어!

A: You children sit down and shut up!
너희 얘들 앉아서 조용히 해!

B: **How dare you** treat them so badly!
어떻게 그렇게 못되게 다룰 수 있어!

How dare you talk to me like that?
어떻게 내게 그렇게 말할 수 있냐?

How dare you do this? 어떻게 이럴 수가 있냐?

How dare you reveal secrets from our marriage bed? 어떻게 결혼 성생활의 비밀을 폭로할 수 있어?

You wouldn't dare to tell him that!
네가 어떻게 그럴 수 있겠어!

041 Who are you to~ ? 네가 뭔데 …라고 하는 거야?

this means "You shouldn't have done something." The speaker is angry because of something that a person did

A: I want everyone to stay several extra hours at work tonight. 다들 오늘 저녁 몇 시간 야근해.

B: **Who are you to** try and make everyone stay late? 네가 뭔데 다들 늦게까지 남으라는 거야?

미드표현

Who are you to say something like that?
네가 뭔데 감히 그런 말을 해?

Who do you think you are? Who are you to decide what's best for me?
네가 뭔데? 뭔데 감히 뭐가 내게 가장 좋다고 결정하는 거야?

I hate that you know me so well. But who are you to judge, Stacy?
네가 날 넘 잘 아는 게 싫어. 하지만 스테이시, 네가 뭔데 판단하려는 거야?

042 How do you do that? 어쩜 그렇게 잘하니?, 어떻게 해낸 거야?

this is a way of asking for information how someone did something. It is asking "Can you show me ?"

I Point I How do you know that? 어떻게 안 거야?

A: This is my most popular magic trick.
이게 내가 가장 잘하는 마술이야.

B: That's great. **How do you do that?**
멋지다. 어떻게 한거야?

미드표현

How do you do that? How do you take that theory and put it in practice?
어떻게 해낸거야? 어떻게 그 이론을 실행에 옮긴거야?

How do you forget a wife and three kids? How-how do you do that?
어떻게 아내와 자식 셋을 잊는거야? 어떻게 그런거야?

How do you do that? You've been here, like, two minutes. 어떻게 해낸거야? 넌 여기 2분 정도 있었는데.

043 How[Why] ~ is beyond me …을 이해할 수가 없어, 나로선 알 수 없어

this indicates that the speaker doesn't understand why something happened. It is similar to saying "I really don't know how-----"

I Point I It's beyond me 나로선 알 수 없어, 나로선 할 수 없어

A: **How** Henry could leave his wife and kids is **beyond me.** 헨리가 처자식을 떠난 건 이해할 수 없어.

B: I think he is just a selfish man. 참 이기적인 사람인 것 같아.

미드표현

Why anybody would choose to be homeless is beyond me. 왜 누구는 노숙자가 되려는지 이해가 안 가.

Why some guy hasn't snapped you up is beyond me. 왜 사람들이 널 채가지 않는지 이해가 안돼.

How you can sit there and be so casual is beyond me. 어떻게 거기 앉아 그렇게 태연한 지 이해가 안돼.

MEMO

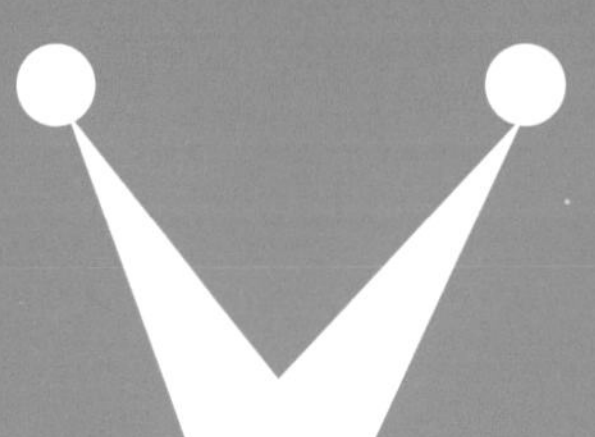

Ways of expressing agreement with someone

상대방의 말에 동의하고 찬성하고

You're telling me

001 You can say that again 그렇고 말고, 정말 그래, 동감이야

this indicates that the speaker thinks a statement that was made was completely correct. It means "I agree with you"

| Point | You could[might] say that 그렇게 말할 수도 있겠지

A: I think that restaurant is too expensive.
저 식당은 너무 비싸.

B: **You can say that again.** I can't afford to eat there. 그러게나 말야. 거기서 먹을 여유가 안돼.

I thought you might say that.
그렇게 말할 수도 있을 것 같아.

I guess you could say that. 그렇게 말할 수도 있을 걸.

You could say that she shot herself in the living room. 그 여자가 거실에서 자살했다고 할 수 있지.

002 You said it 네 말이 맞아, 내 말이 그말이야

like the previous phrases, this means "I think you're right." It is a way of expressing strong agreement with something

| Point | You said S+V …라고 말했지, …라고 말했잖아

A: Romantic movies seem really boring to me.
로맨틱 영화는 난 정말 지루해.

B: **You said it.** I prefer to see action movies.
정말 그래. 액션 영화보는 게 더 좋아.

You said it was urgent! 급한 거라고 했잖아!

I asked you and you said it was okay.
내가 물었고 넌 괜찮다고 말했어.

I thought you said it was okay.
괜찮다고 말한 줄로 알고 있었어.

003 You're telling me 1.(강한 동의) 누가 아니래!, 정말 그래! 2. 나도 알아

this is a way of saying "Yeah, that is right" or 'I know that." The speaker is agreeing with something that was said

| Point | You're telling me (that) S+V …라고 말하는 거야?

A: I can't believe how hot it is today. 오늘 정말 무지 덥구만.

B: **You're telling me.** Let's find someplace cool.
정말 그래. 어디 시원한 곳 좀 찾아보자고.

You're telling me there's a million dollars in here? 여기에 백만 달러가 있다는 말야?

You're telling me you didn't try to hit him?
넌 걔를 치려고 하지 않았다는 말야?

You're telling me I can't see her?
내가 걔를 만날 수 없다는 말야?

004 (It) Suits me (fine) (상대방 제안에 찬성) 난 좋아, 내 생각에 괜찮은 것 같아

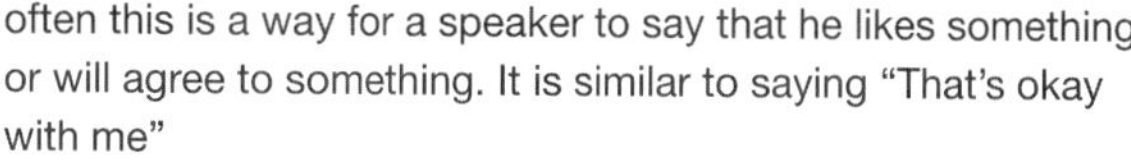

often this is a way for a speaker to say that he likes something or will agree to something. It is similar to saying "That's okay with me"

| Point | This[It] doesn't quite suit me 그다지 썩 맘에 들지 않아

A: How do you like the neighborhood you live in?
네가 사는 주변 어때?

B: **It suits me fine.** I love living in that area.
난 좋아. 그 곳에 사는 게 좋아.

Look, it doesn't suit me to kill her.
걔를 죽이는 게 내겐 썩 좋지 않은 것 같아.

The weather is getting cold, but it suits me fine. 날씨가 점점 추워지지만 난 괜찮아.

You want to cancel the contract? Suits me fine. 계약서를 취소하고 싶다고? 난 괜찮아.

Suits me fine. Do whatever you want to do.
난 괜찮아. 너 하고 싶은대로 해.

005 That's nice (상대방의 말이나 제안에) 좋아, 괜찮은데

this is a way of expressing that the speaker understood what was said and doesn't disagree with it. It is like saying "It sounds good"

| Point | Wonderful! 아주 좋아!

A: I'd like to go to New York to study design.
디자인 공부하러 뉴욕에 가고 싶어.

B: **That's nice.** New York has many good universities. 좋은 생각야. 뉴욕에는 좋은 대학이 많아.

That's nice. Where is it? 좋은데. 그게 어디 인데?

Well, that's nice of you to offer.
네가 제안을 해줘서 좋아.

Well, that's nice. I didn't know that. She's a sweet kid. 괜찮은데. 난 몰랐어. 걘 다정한 아이야.

006 (It) Looks that way 그런 것 같아

this is indicating "I think so." The speaker feels that something is likely or seems to be true

| Point | It certainly looks that way 확실히 그래 보여
Most likely 아마도 그럴 거야

A: Are you going to get a new car this year?
금년에 차 새로 뽑을거야?

B: **It looks that way.** My old car is worn out.
그럴 것 같아. 내 오래된 차가 낡아빠졌어.

A: You think that was on purpose? B: Well, sure looks that way. Take a look at this.
A: 저거 일부러 그런 것 같아? B: 그런 것 같아. 이거 한번 봐봐.

A: It looks like we're the first ones here.
B: Yeah, looks that way. First ones here!
A: 우리가 제일 먼저 도착한 것 같아. B: 그래, 그런 가봐! 제일 먼저 왔다고!

007 I'm afraid so (안타깝게도) 그런 것 같아, (아무래도) 그런 것 같아

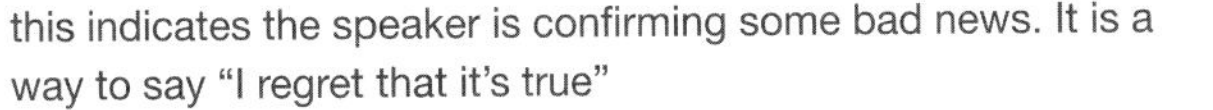

this indicates the speaker is confirming some bad news. It is a way to say "I regret that it's true"

| Point | I think so 그럴 걸 / I guess so 아마 그럴 걸
I believe so 그럴 거야 / I suppose (so) 아마 그럴 걸

A: Do you think we'll have to move somewhere else? 어디 다른 곳으로 이사해야 할 것 같아?

B: **I'm afraid so.** This apartment building has been sold. 그럴 것 같아. 이 아파트가 팔렸어.

A: Is Karen the kid who got raped at the Kastner Center? B: I'm afraid so. Yes.
A: 카렌이 캐스트너 센터에서 강간당한 아이야? B: 그런 것 같아. 맞아.

A: Is Steven really dead? B: I'm afraid so.
A: 스티븐이 정말로 죽었어? B: 그런 것 같아.

A: Mom, has dad gone crazy? B: I'm afraid so dear. A: 엄마, 아빠가 미쳤어? B: 그런 것 같구나 얘야.

008 Now you're talking 이제야 말이 통하네!, 그래 바로 그거야!, 그렇지!

usually this is used to say "I like that." It expresses approval of something that has been said

A: Let's head to the beach and do some camping this weekend. 이번 주에 해변가로 가서 캠핑하자.

B: **Now you're talking.** I could use some time away from the city. 바로 그거야. 도시에서 벗어나 시간을 좀 보내야 돼.

A: I'd rather go to a nightclub. B: Now you're talking! I haven't danced in months.
A: 나는 차라리 나이트클럽에 가겠어. B: 바로 그거야! 난 몇 달동안 춤을 못췄거든.

A: I say we fly there for the weekend. B: Now you're talking!
A: 저기, 주말에 거기 갈 때 비행기 타고 가자. B: 이제야 말이 통하는군!

009 All right 1. 알았어 2. (자기 말 확인) 알았어? 3. 좋아, 그래

this is way of saying "OK" or "Go ahead." Usually the speaker is either agreeing or giving permission to do something

| Point | All right then 좋아 그럼
All right already 좋아 알았다구!, 이제 됐어!

A: Dad, is it OK if I go to visit Marcia today?
아빠, 오늘 마르샤 집에 가도 돼요?

B: **All right.** But you'll have to do it later this afternoon. 그래. 하지만 오늘 오후 늦게 가거라.

All right, I'll see you guys later. 알았어 나중에 보자.

Apologize to your Mom, all right?
엄마한테 사과해. 알았어?

All right, how about this? 그래, 이건 어때?

010 (I) Couldn't agree more 정말 네 말이 맞아 , 네 말에 전적으로 동의해

this is usually said to indicate that a statement was correct. It means "I think you're right"

| Point | (I) Couldn't agree with you more 네 말이 백 번 옳고 말구
I agree with you 100% 전적으로 동감야

A: Kids need to be taught how to have good study habits. 얘들은 좋은 학습습관을 갖는 거에 대해 교육받아야 돼.

B: **I couldn't agree with you more.** It's so important to be a good student.
정말 네 말이 맞아. 좋은 학생이 되는 게 중요해.

I couldn't agree more. So, now what?
정말 네 말이 맞아? 그래서?

I couldn't agree more. But it might be difficult too. 나도 동의해. 근데 좀 어려울지도 모르겠어.

A: It's hard to know who to trust when it comes to money. B: Couldn't agree more.
A: 돈에 관련된 일에서는 누구 믿어야 할지 참 어려워. B: 정말 네 말이 맞아.

011 That's right (상대방 말에 동의하면서) 맞아, 그래

this either confirms something, or it expresses complete agreement with something that was said. It simply means "Yes"

| Point | You're right 그래, 맞아
You're right about that 네 말이 맞아

A: So you would like to borrow some money?
그래 돈 좀 빌려달라고?

B: **That's right.** I'm planning to buy a house.
그래. 집을 살려고.

That's right, honey, I'm a police officer.
자기야 맞아. 난 경찰관이야.

That's right. We had another appointment.
맞아. 우리는 다른 약속이 있어.

Oh, that's right. It's not my fault.
오 맞아. 그건 내 잘못이 아냐.

That's right, you're only responsible for yourself. 맞아. 스스로를 책임지는 건 자신 뿐이야.

012 You got that right 네 말이 맞아

this is a way of saying "I think you're correct." The speaker is expressing agreement

| Point | Right you are 맞아
You're right on 좋아!, (네 말이) 맞아!(That's what I think too)

A: I really like the food in this restaurant.
이 식당 음식 정말 맛있어.

B: **You got that right.** It's the best pizza in town.
네 말이 맞아. 시내에서 가장 맛있는 피자야.

You're right on. They are very good for your body. 네 말이 맞아. 네 몸에 무척 좋아.

A: You commit a crime, you pay the price. B: You got that right.
A: 죄를 저질렀으면 상응하는 대가를 치르는거야. B: 네 말이 맞아.

You got that right. You should have listened to Chris. 네 말이 맞아. 넌 크리스의 말을 들었어야 했는데.

013 You are on (내기를 받아들이며) 그래 좋았어, 좋을대로, 그래 어디 한번 해보자

usually this means "I'll take that bet." It is a way to indicate that a person has accepted a bet or a challenge from another person

I Point I I'm on! 좋아, 찬성!

A: I'll bet I'm a faster runner than you are.
내가 확실히 너보다 달리기가 빨라.

B: **You are on.** Let's race to the end of the street.
그래 좋아. 거리 끝까지 달려보자.

A: You wanna bet? B: Yeah, you're on.
A: 내기할까? B: 좋아, 어디 해보자고

A: Alright I'll tell you what, I'll play you for it.
B: Alright, you're on. A: 그래, 나랑 한판 해보자. B: 좋았어.

A: Coffee at Luke's, 3 o'clock? B: You're on.
A: 루크 집에서 3시에 커피마시자. B: 좋아.

014 You are right on the money 바로 맞혔어, 바로 그거야, 맞는 말이야

this is a way of expressing that someone has said something correct. It means "I agree with your idea"

I Point I Right on the button 맞아, 제대로 맞혔어
You've hit the nail right on the head! 바로 맞혔어!

A: If the roads were improved, there would be fewer accidents. 도로가 정비되면 사고가 좀 줄어들거야.

B: **You're right on the money.** We need to try to make them safer. 맞아. 도로를 더 안전하게 만들도록 해야 돼.

Yep, this time we were right on the money.
그래, 이번엔 우리가 바로 맞혔다구.

Right on the button. Let me tell you about her private life. 제대로 맞혔어. 걔의 사생활에 대해 얘기해줄게.

You were right on the money about that.
그점에 관해서 네 말이 맞았어.

015 I get that a lot 그런 얘기 많이 들어

this is used to say that many people say the same thing to the speaker, so he has heard it before. It is similar to saying "I hear people say that all the time"

I Point I get that a lot 많이들 그렇게 말하다, 그런 얘기 많이 듣다

A: You know, you look like a famous movie actor.
저말야, 넌 유명한 배우닮았어.

B: **I get that a lot.** I guess our faces are similar.
그런 얘기 많이 들어. 얼굴이 비슷한 것 같아.

Two confessions, one crime. We don't get that a lot. 자백은 두가지인데 범죄는 하나라, 드문 경우인데.

A: I know we just met, but as a gay man, I'm oddly drawn to you. B: Yeah, I get that a lot.
A: 처음 만났지만 게이로서 당신에게 특이하게도 끌리네요. B: 네, 그런 얘기 많이 들어요.

Actually, I'm not a model. But I get that a lot.
실은 전 모델은 아니지만 그런 얘기 많이 들어요.

미드에선 이렇게 쓰인다!

We get that a lot

The Big Bang Theory
SEASON#4-1

Howard가 로봇 팔을 만든 후 혼자서 jack off하다가 병원에 실려온 장면.

Nurse: My, my, my. What we have here?
Howard: I slipped and fell.
Nurse: Yeah, we get that a lot. What is this?
Howard: It's a robot arm.
Nurse: Where's the rest of the robot?
Howard: I only built the arm.
Nurse: 'Cause that's all you needed, right?
Howard: Can you please just help me?
Nurse: All right, all right. Hang on, stay calm. I need an orderly with a wheelchair. I got a robot hand grasping a man's penis out here.

간호사: 이런, 이게 무슨 일이람?
하워드: 미끄러져서 넘어졌어요.
간호사: 다들 그렇게 얘기하죠. 이게 뭐죠?
하워드: 로봇 팔예요.
간호사: 나머지 로봇은 어디 있죠?
하워드: 팔만 만들었어요.
간호사: 그 부분만 필요했기 때문이겠죠, 맞죠?
하워드: 그냥 좀 도와주세요.
간호사: 알았어요. 잠깐 진정해. 휠체어를 끌고 직원 한 명오세요. 로봇 팔이 한 남자의 거시기를 잡고 있어요.

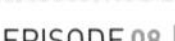

016 Tell me about it! 내말이!, 그러게나 말야, 누가 아니래, 그렇고 말고

this is a way of saying "I agree with that statement." The speaker is saying that something is correct

A: I never seem to have enough money.
항상 돈이 부족한 것 같아.

B: Tell me about it. There are too many things to spend money on. 누가 아니래. 돈을 써야 할 데가 넘 많아.

미드표현

A: Men...always have sex on their minds. B: Tell me about it.
A: 남자들은 언제나 섹스생각을 하고 있어. B: 누가 아니래.

Tell me about it! He made everyone upset.
누가 아니래! 걔 때문에 다들 어리둥절했어.

Tell me about it! We weren't allowed to leave the building. 물론이야! 우리는 이 빌딩을 나가는게 금지됐어.

017 (It) Sounds like a plan 좋은 생각이야

usually this means that the speaker thinks something is a good idea. It is a way to say "I think that will be fine"

| Point | Sounds good (to me) 좋은 것 같은데
Sounds like a good idea 좋은 생각 같은데
Sounds like fun 재미있을 것 같은데

A: I'd like to take you out to dinner on Friday.
금요일에 저녁 외식시켜줄게.

B: Sounds like a plan. I'm free then.
좋은 생각이야. 나 시간 돼.

미드표현

A: We can grab a bite to eat before we go.
B: Sounds like a plan.
A: 가기 전에 뭐도 좀 먹자. B: 그거 좋지.

That sounds like a good idea. 좋은 생각이야.

He sounds like a smart man. 걘 무척 똑똑한 사람같아.

Sounds like a good theory to me. 괜찮은 이론인데.

018 Okey-dokey[Okie-dokie] 좋아, 됐어, 알았어

this often means that the speaker has understood something. It is like saying "I got it"

| Point | (That's) Okay by me 괜찮으니 그렇게 해

A: If you just want to talk about anything, you can call me any time, okay?
뭔가 얘기하고 싶으면 언제든 전화해, 알았지?

B: Okey-dokey. 알았어.

미드표현

Okie-dokie, I'll get it started right away.
좋아, 바로 당장 그걸 시작할게.

You need my help moving? Okie-dokie.
이사하는데 내 도움이 필요하다고? 알았어.

Okie-dokie, we're ready for our lunch now.
좋아, 우리 이제 점심먹을 준비됐어.

019 I'm for it 난 찬성이야

this means "I think it's good." It indicates that a speaker is in favor of some idea

| Point | I'm in favor of it 찬성이야

A: What do you think of the plan to develop the downtown area? 시내 개발하는 계획에 대해 어떻게 생각해?

B: I'm for it. I'm sure it will bring a lot of business to the merchants. 찬성야. 상인들이 많은 장사를 할 수 있을거야.

미드표현

Are you kidding? I'm for it! 장난하니? 당연히 찬성이지!

A: What's your position? B: I'm for it.
A: 네 생각은 어때? B: 난 찬성이야.

020 (I'm) Right behind you 나도 네 말에 찬성야, 네 말에 동의해

this is a way of saying "I will back you up." We can understand the speaker will support someone's idea

| Point | I'm (100%) behind you 난 (전적으로) 네 편이야
We're behind you all the way 우리는 너를 끝까지 지지할 거야

A: I've really got to talk to the boss about some problems here. 여기 문제 좀 사장한테 말해야겠어.

B: **I'm right behind you.** We have to correct the things that are going wrong. 찬성야. 잘못된 걸 바로 잡아야 돼.

Let's get going. I'm right behind you.
자 가자. 내가 바로 뒤따를게.

I'm right behind you. Don't worry about a thing. 널 전적으로 지지하니까 하나도 걱정하지마.

If you want to talk to the boss, I'm right behind you. 사장에게 얘기하고 싶으면 내가 함께 할게.

021 Right back at ya 너도 그래, 너와 동감이야

미드표현

this is not frequently used, and when it is, it is used in a joking way to tell a person that the speaker feels the same way. It is not uncommon to hear it said on sit-coms. This is similar to saying "Yeah, I have the same feelings you just expressed"

| Point | Right back at ya[you] 너도 그래, 너도 마찬가지야, 너와 동감이야

A: I have really enjoyed spending time together.
함께 정말 즐거운 시간 보냈어.

B: **Right back at you.** It's been fun.
너와 동감이야. 재미있었어.

A: You're my friend! B: Right back at ya!
A: 넌 내 친구야! B: 너와 동감이야!

A: I think you're a great, cool kid, and the best friend a girl could have. B: Right back at ya.
A: 넌 정말 괜찮은 아이면서 남친으로서도 최고야. B: 너도 그래.

A: God, you look fantastic. You haven't aged a day. B: Right back at ya.
A: 야, 너 멋져 보인다. 하나도 안늙었네. B: 너도 그래

A: Go to hell! B: Right back at ya!
A: 나가 뒈져라! B: 너도 마찬가지야!

022 Right there with ya 나도 같은 생각이야

미드표현

usually this is used to say that the speaker feels the same way, or that he can understand very clearly what someone is talking about. It is very much like saying "That's exactly what I was thinking too"

| Point | (I'm) Right there with you 나도 동감이야
I'm right there with sb~ …와 함께 있다

A: I was thinking we could visit her house.
우리가 걔 집을 방문할 수도 있을거라 생각했었어.

B: Good idea. **I'm right there with you.**
좋은 생각이야. 나도 같은 생각이야.

A: I guess I was just confused. B: Yeah, I'm right there with you.
A: 내가 혼동했던 것 같아. B: 그래, 나도 같은 생각이야.

A: It's hard to believe I'm actually having this conversation with you. B: Right there with you. A: 내가 너와 이런 대화를 하다니 믿기지 않아. B: 나도 그래.

Oh, hey, copy that. I'm right there with you.
어, 알았어. 나도 같은 생각이야.

I'm right there with her most of the time.
난 대부분 걔와 함께 시간을 보내.

023 Well said 맞아, 바로 그거야, 말 한번 잘했다, 나도 동감야

미드표현

this is a way of expressing "I like the things you were saying." It shows approval of a statement that was made

A: If he doesn't act nicer, I'm going to hit him!
걔가 더 똑바로 행동못하면 칠거야!

B: **Well said.** I think he deserves to be hit because of his behavior. 나도 동감야. 걘 행실 땜에 맞아 싸.

A: It's hard to tell where the human ends and the animal begins. B: Well said.
A: 어디가 인간의 끝이고 어디서부터 짐승이 시작되는 건지 모르겠어.
B: 나도 동감야.

A: You ached to feel his naked body pressed up against yours. B: Yes. Well said.
A: 그의 벗은 몸을 느끼고 싶어서 안달이 났구나. B: 그래, 바로 맞아.

024 I'm with you 동감야, 그러자, 알았어

the speaker wants to offer support and assistance for someone's idea. It's like saying "That's what I think too"

| Point | I'm with you there 그 말에 공감해
I'm with you all the way 전적으로 동감이야
I feel like you do 나도 너랑 같은 생각이야

A: I'd really like to return to school and get a higher degree. 학교로 돌아가서 높은 성적을 정말 받고 싶어.

B: **I'm with you.** I'd love to resume my studies. 동감야. 공부를 다시 시작하고 싶어.

I'm with you all the way! Let's go talk to him. 전적으로 당신 편이에요! 말씀드리러 갑시다.

I'm with you on that one. 그 점에 나도 동감야.

025 I'm on your side 난 네 편이야

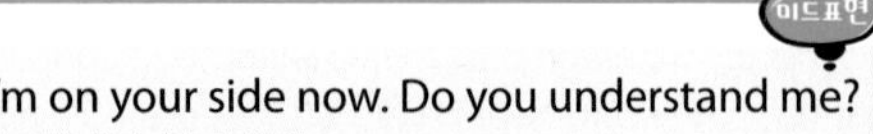

usually this is expressing "I support your ideas." The speaker is showing a strong agreement with or support of someone

| Point | be on sb's side …의 편이다

A: Do you really think I can win an argument with her? 내가 걔와의 논쟁에서 이길거라고 정말 생각해?

B: Of course you can. **I'm on your side.** 물론 그렇지. 난 네 편이야.

I'm on your side now. Do you understand me? 난 이제 네 편이야. 알겠어?

Jack, the law is completely on your side. 잭, 법은 네 편이야.

I'm on your side, whatever you tell me. 네가 뭐라고 해도 난 네편이야.

026 Big time 1. 그렇고 말고 2. 많이

the speaker wants to say that some statement is correct. It is a way to express "That's right"

A: Man, I just love attending baseball games. 휴, 야구장에 가고 싶어.

B: **Big time.** It's the most enjoyable part of summer. 그렇고 말고, 여름에 가장 흥미로운 건데.

You owe me big time. 너 나한테 신세 크게 진거야.

I am gonna change -- big time. 난 변화할거야 – 아주 많이.

Thanks, you guys, so much. I owe you big time. 너희들, 정말 고마워. 정말 큰 신세졌어.

We screwed up. Big time. 우리는 망했어. 아주 많이.

027 (There is) No doubt about it! 틀림없어!, 확실히 그렇지!

this is a way of indicating that something is very certain. It is saying "I'm sure of it"

| Point | Without a doubt 틀림없이, 그럼요, 그렇고 말구

A: Do you think there is life on other planets? 다른 행성에 생명이 있을 것 같아?

B: Sure I do. **There is no doubt about it!** 물론이지. 확실해 그래!

There is no doubt about it, he's going to file for bankruptcy. 의심할 여지가 없이 그 사람은 파산신청을 할 거야.

No doubt about it -- it's a fake. 틀림없이– 그건 가짜야.

There's no doubt about it. These guys are blood relatives. 틀림없어. 이 사람들은 피를 나눈 혈족이야.

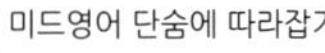

028 It sure is 그렇고 말고, 맞고 말고

usually this is used to say "Yes it is." It expresses strong agreement with something

| Point | Sure 물론, 당연하지
Sure thing 물론이지, 그럼

A: That is one of the most beautiful sunsets I've ever seen. 저건 내가 본 가장 아름다운 노을 중의 하나야.

B: **It sure is.** I wonder what causes the sky to become so red.
그렇고 말고, 뭐 때문에 하늘이 저렇게 붉어지는지 궁금해.

미드표현

It sure is. She hired my son to do her yard work. And also, she raped him. 그렇고 말고, 그 여자가 내 아들을 정원사로 고용했어 그리고 나서 걜 강간했다고.

Yeah, it sure is. This is the biggest department store that I've ever seen.
맞아, 내가 본 백화점 중에서 가장 큰 것 같아.

A: It's nice to be with family. B: It sure is.
A: 가족과 함께 있으면 정말 좋아. B: 정말 그래.

029 Positive 물론야, 그럼

often this is a way to answer a question and state something is certain. It is very similar to saying "Yes"

A: Are you sure Jill was supposed to meet us here tonight? 질이 오늘 밤 여기에서 우릴 만나기로 한거 맞아?

B: **Positive.** She's probably just late because of a traffic jam. 물론, 차가 막혀서 좀 늦을거야.

미드표현

A: You sure? B: Positive. A: 확실해? B: 물론.

A: And you're sure you didn't see her walk out?
B: Positive. A: 걔가 나가는 걸 못본게 확실해? B: 그럼.

Positive. I could tell that he recognized me.
확실해. 걔가 날 알아보는 걸 알 수 있었어.

030 So be it 그렇게 되라지, 그래 그렇게 해, 맘대로 해

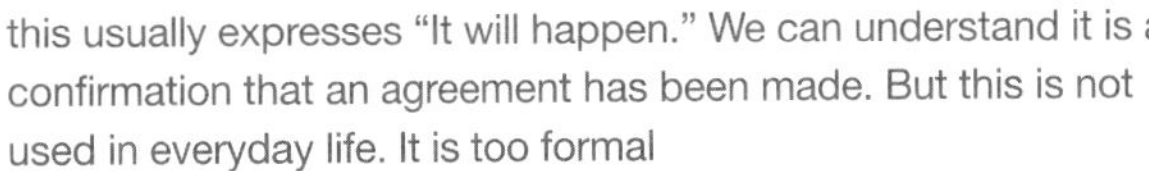

this usually expresses "It will happen." We can understand it is a confirmation that an agreement has been made. But this is not used in everyday life. It is too formal

A: We will hold the festival on the third week of October this year. 올해 10월 3번째 주에 페스티발을 열거야.

B: **So be it.** Let's announce the schedule to all of our students. 그렇게 해. 우리 학생들에게 일정을 알리자.

미드표현

If that gets me sued, so be it.
그걸로 고소를 당한다면 그래도 좋습니다.

They want to play dirty? So be it!
더럽게 나오겠다고? 그럼 그렇게 하라고 해!

If that means we can't be friends at work, then so be it.
그래서 우리가 직장에서 친구가 될 수 없다면 그렇게 해.

031 (It) Works for me 난 괜찮아, 난 좋아, 찬성이야

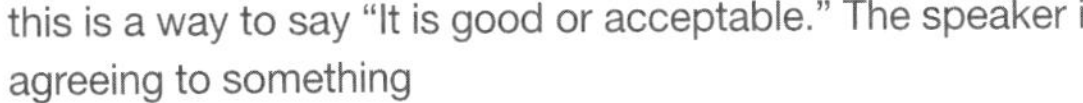

this is a way to say "It is good or acceptable." The speaker is agreeing to something

| Point | Somebody works for A A밑에서 일하다
시간명사 +works for me (약속일정 정할 때) …가 괜찮다

A: Could you stop by at 3 o'clock today?
오늘 3시에 들릴 수 있어?

B: Sure, that time **works for me.** 물론, 난 괜찮아.

미드표현

Well, the truth works for me. I like the truth.
어, 난 진실이 통해. 진실이 좋아.

November works for me. 11월은 괜찮아.

A: How about a month from tonight? That would be the 20th. Good for everyone?
B: Works for me.
A: 오늘부터 한달 뒤에 어때? 20일인데 다들 괜찮아? B: 난 좋아.

032 Fair enough (제안에 대해) 좋아, 됐어, 이제 됐어, 그만하면 됐어

this means that someone agrees with something. It is like saying "That's OK with me"

| Point | Good enough! 좋아!, 그만하면 됐어!

A: I can work for you starting next week.
다음 주부터 일할 수 있어요.

B: **Fair enough.** I really need your help.
좋아요. 당신 도움이 정말 필요해요.

미드표현

Fair enough, fair enough. Everything's okay.
좋아, 좋아. 다 괜찮아.

Fair enough. Where are you going?
좋아 됐어. 어딜 가?

Good enough for me. Want to go get something to eat? 난 그만하면 됐어. 뭐 좀 먹으러 갈까?

033 I'll drink to that! 옳소!, 찬성이오!

usually this is a very informal way of stating that something is agreeable. It means "That sounds good to me"

| Point | I'll drink to that 동감이야, 찬성이야

A: Let's hope we have good luck in the upcoming year. 다가오는 해에 행운이 있길 바라자.

B: **I'll drink to that.** Good luck everyone!
좋아. 다들 행운이 있기를!

미드표현

A: What do you say we take the entire week off between Christmas and New Year's as my Christmas present to you? B: I'll drink to that.
A: 크리스마스 선물로 성탄절과 설날 사이에 아예 1주일을 쉬면 어떨까? B: 찬성이야.

A: Hey, here's to you. B: I'll drink to that.
A: 야, 너를 위하여. B: 동감이야.

034 Same here 1. 나도 그래, 동의해 2.(식당) 같은 걸로

this is a way of indicating "I have a similar opinion." The speaker has the same feelings as another person

| Point | Me too 나도 그래

A: Personally, I think that we need to elect better leaders. 개인적으로 더 나은 지도자를 뽑을 필요가 있다고 생각해.

B: **Same here.** The politicians we have are not doing a good job. 나도 그래. 현 정치가들은 일을 제대로 못해.

미드표현

Oh, same here. Good luck with Harvard.
어, 나도 그래. 하바드 대학은 잘 되기를 바래.

Same here. Boredom stinks.
나도 그래. 지겨운 것은 정말 그지 같아.

A: Thanks. I'm glad we had this talk. B: Yeah, same here.
A: 고마워. 우리가 이런 대화를 나누어서 기뻐. B: 어, 나도 그래.

035 I don't see why not 그럼, 안 될 이유가 어딨어

the speaker wants to say "It is okay." He feels that there is no reason to disagree with something

A: Do you think we could stop at a grocery store tonight? 오늘 밤 마트에 좀 들릴까?

B: **I don't see why not.** We need to buy some food for our house. 그럼. 음식 좀 사야 돼.

미드표현

I don't see why not. Let's go get some ice cream. 그럼. 가서 아이스크림 좀 먹자.

A: I don't see why not. Shall I wait here, then? B: Yeah, you wait right there.
A: 안될 이유야 없지. 여기서 기다릴까? B: 그래 기다리고 있어.

A: Can you do that? B: I don't see why not.
A: 그렇게 해줄 수 있어? B: 그럼.

036 I feel the same way 나도 그렇게 생각해, 나도 그래

미드표현

this is usually said when a person wants to express agreement with a statement. He is saying "Me too"

| Point | feel the same way about ~ …에 대한 같은 생각이다

A: For some reason I feel very sleepy today.
왠지 모르겠지만 오늘 정말 졸려.

B: **I feel the same way.** Maybe we need to take a nap. 나도 그래. 낮잠 좀 자야 되겠어.

I assumed that you would feel the same way.
너도 같은 생각일거라 생각했어.

I hope that you feel the same way about that.
너도 그 문제에 같은 생각이기를 바래.

You need to show him you feel the same way.
너도 같은 생각이라는 점을 개한테 보여줄 필요가 있어.

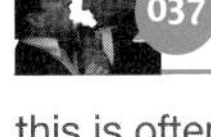

037 I'll go along with that 난 찬성야, 동의해

미드표현

this is often a way to say that the speaker will follow someone else's plan or idea. It is similar to saying "That's fine with me"

| Point | go along with sb[sth] …에 찬성[동의]하다

A: I think the best thing to do would be to arrive at the airport early. 일찍 공항에 도착하는게 최선인 것 같아.

B: **I'll go along with that.** We need to make sure we catch the flight. 찬성야. 비행기 타는 거 확실히 해야지.

How can you be so sure he's gonna go along with this? 걔가 이거에 동의할 거라는 걸 어떻게 확신할 수 있어?

Why did you go along with that? 왜 이거에 찬성했니?

Do you really think I'd go along with it? Well, no. 내가 그거에 찬성할거라 생각해? 저기, 아냐.

038 I can't[won't] argue with that 두말하면 잔소리지, 물론이지

미드표현

this is a way of saying "It seems correct." We can understand that someone is right and that the speaker doesn't disagree

| Point | I wouldn't say no 아니라고는 말하지 않을게
(basically, the speaker is telling someone he will say yes to something)

A: I think Terri is the prettiest girl in our class.
테리가 우리 반에서 가장 이쁜 것 같아.

B: **I won't argue with that.** 두말하면 잔소리지.

It's best if you go to university, I can't argue with that. 네가 대학에 진학하면 그게 최고지, 두말하면 잔소리야.

I can't argue with that, you are absolutely right. 두말하면 잔소리지, 네 말이 정말 맞아.

Can't argue with that. I'll get the tickets.
물론이지. 내가 표를 가져올게.

039 That would be great 그거 좋지

미드표현

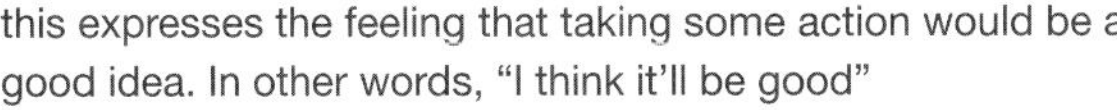

this expresses the feeling that taking some action would be a good idea. In other words, "I think it'll be good"

A: Can I make you some breakfast this morning?
오늘 아침에 아침 좀 만들어줄까?

B: **That would be great.** I'm really hungry.
그러면 좋지. 정말 배고파.

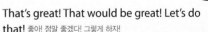

That's great! That would be great! Let's do that! 좋아! 정말 좋겠다! 그렇게 하자!

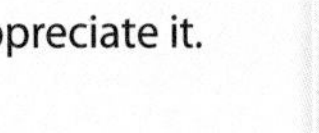

That would be great. I really appreciate it.
그럼 좋지. 정말 고마워.

Yeah, that'd be great. I'd love it.
그래, 그럼 좋지. 정말 좋겠다.

040 So am I 나도 그래

this is a way for the speaker to say "Me too." It expresses that he feels or thinks in a similar way

| Point | So do I 나도 그래, 나도 마찬가지야
So are you 너도 그래
So is he 걔도 그래

A: I'm bored with all of this studying.
이 놈의 공부하는 거 정말 지루해.

B: **So am I.** Let's take a break. 나도 그래. 잠깐 쉬자.

미드표현

Yeah, so is my Dad. 어, 아빠도 그러셔.

Apparently so do I. It's okay.
나도 마찬가지이고 말고. 괜찮아.

A: I know, I'm so excited! B: So am I!
A: 맞아. 굉장히 기대돼! B: 나도 그래!

041 That[It] makes sense 일리가 있군

this is a way of saying "I understand why that is true." The speaker means that the reason for something is easy to understand

| Point | That does make sense (강조) 정말 일리가 있어
That makes no sense 말도 안돼
Does that make any sense? 그게 말이 되나?

A: If we fix this old house, we can sell it for a higher price. 이 낡은 집을 수리하면 더 비싸게 팔 수 있어.

B: **That makes sense.** Do you know how to repair houses? 말되네. 집수리 어떻게 하는 지 알아?

미드표현

That logic makes no sense at all. 그 논리는 말도 안돼.

This game makes no sense! 이 게임은 말이 안돼!

That doesn't make any sense. I mean, that's the last thing a depressed person would take.
그건 말도 안돼. 우울증에 걸린 사람이 정말 그러겠어.

042 That's a good point 좋은 지적이야, 맞는 말이야

this means that the speaker thinks someone has said something intelligent or useful. It is another way to say "It's a smart idea"

| Point | Good point 맞는 말이야, 바로 그거야

A: It is really important for us to exercise several times a week. 한 주에 여러 번 운동하는게 정말 중요해.

B: **That's a good point.** Why don't we join a health club? 맞는 말이야. 헬스클럽 다니자.

미드표현

That's a good point, But the important thing is that you're healthy.
맞는 말이야. 하지만 중요한 것은 네가 건강하다는거야.

That's a good point. My time is much too valuable. 좋은 지적이야. 내 시간은 너무나도 소중해.

That's a good point. You ever get the feeling she does this intentionally?
맞는 말이야. 걔가 일부러 그랬다는 생각이 혹 들어?

043 You got[have] a point there 네 말이 맞아, 네 말에 일리가 있어

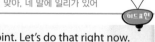

like the previous expression, the speaker is saying "That idea is good." It means someone has said something useful

| Point | You've got a point 네 말에 일리가 있어

A: None of these programs has gotten rid of my computer virus. 이 프로그램 중 어떤 것도 내 컴의 바이러스를 못 없앴어.

B: **You have a point there.** Maybe you need a new computer. 네 말이 맞아. 컴퓨터를 새로 사야 되겠구만.

You've got a point. Let's do that right now.
네 말이 맞아. 지금 그렇게 하자.

A: It's only going to make matters worse for us. B: You've got a point there.
A: 그건 우리의 상황을 더 악화시킬 따름이야. B: 네 말에 일리가 있어.

044 You've made your point 너의 주장이 뭔지 알겠어, 무슨 말인지 알겠어

this is a way to indicate that everyone has understood the idea that someone expressed. It is like saying "We see what you mean"

| Point | make one's point 자기 주장을 말하다, 목적을 달성하다

A: The behavior of some students has made me angry recently. 일부 학생들의 행동으로 최근 열받았어.

B: **You've made your point.** I think everyone understands why you're upset.
알아듣게 말했잖아. 다들 왜 네가 화났는지 이해할거야.

Look, I think you've made your point.
이봐, 너의 주장이 뭔지 알겠어.

You made your point. Now how about letting us do our jobs?
네 생각은 알아들었으니, 이제 우리가 우리 일을 하도록 해주면 어떨까?

If you are doing this to scare me, you made your point. 이걸로 우리를 겁주려했다면, 넌 네 목적을 달성한거야.

045 We're talking the same language
이제 얘기가 된다, 이제야 말이 통하는 군

usually this is a way of indicating "We are having similar ideas." We can understand that the speaker is thinking in a way that is similar to someone else

| Point | You're talking my language 넌 나하고 말이 통해
speak my language 나와 말이 통하다

A: I'd like to complete this deal today.
이 계약건을 오늘 마치고 싶어.

B: **We're talking the same language.** So would I.
나랑 얘기가 되네. 나도 그러고 싶어.

We have absolutely nothing in common and we don't even speak the same language.
우린 공통점도 전혀 없고 말도 안통해.

That night, for the first time, we spoke the same language. 그날 밤 우린 처음으로 말이 통했어.

046 You and me both 너나 나나 똑같아, 나도 그래

this is a way of indicating that the speaker feels the same way as someone else. In other words, it expresses "We have the same opinion"

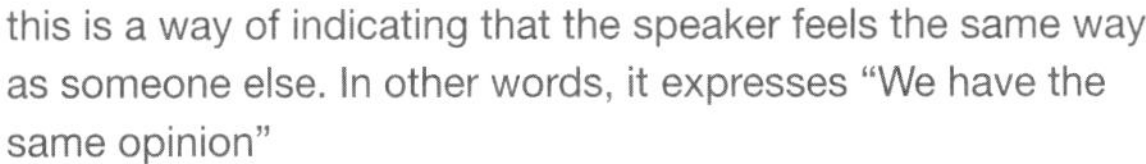

A: I really hope this rainy weather will go away soon. 이 비오는 날씨가 가버렸으면 해.

B: **You and me both.** I hate cloudy days.
너나 나나 똑같아. 흐린 날씨는 정말 싫어.

A: Sometimes I even wonder how I got through it. B: You and me both.
A: 가끔 내가 어떻게 그걸 해결했나 싶어. B: 나도.

A: I so needed this vacation. B: You and me both. A: 이 휴가가 꼭 필요했어. B: 나도 그래.

A: I feel like shit. B: Yeah, you and me both.
A: 기분 더럽네. B: 어, 너나 나나 똑같아.

047 Whatever you say (다 따를테니) 뭐든 말만 해

this usually indicates that the speaker is willing to do anything that is requested. It is like saying "I'll agree to any of your suggestions"

| Point | Whatever you ask 다 들어줄 테니까 뭐든 말만 해
Whatever it takes 필요한 것은 뭐든지
Whatever turns you on (네가 좋다면야) 뭐든 좋을 대로, 뭐든 간에

A: Can you help me with my project for art class?
미술 수업 프로젝트 좀 도와줄래?

B: Sure I can. **Whatever you ask.** 물론, 뭐든 말만 해.

Whatever you say, I'll believe you.
무슨 말을 하든 난 널 믿어.

Whatever you say. But just be careful, all right? 맘대로 해. 하지만 조심하고 알았지?

She'll do whatever you say.
걔는 네가 하자는 대로 할거야.

I wouldn't like that, but whatever turns you on. 그렇게 하지 않았으면 좋겠지만 뭐 좋을 대로 해.

048 Be my guest! (상대방 요청을 허락하며) 그럼, 그렇게 해!, 좋을대로 해!

often this is a way to say "Go ahead." The speaker is expressing that a person is free to try something or to do something

A: May I use your telephone to make a quick call?
잠깐 전화할려고 네 핸드폰 써도 돼?

B: **Be my guest.** It's on the stand next to the fridge. 그럼 그렇게 해. 냉장고 옆 스탠드에 있어.

미드표현

But if you want to give it a shot, be my guest.
하지만 한번 해보고 싶다면, 그렇게 해.

Be my guest. But I don't think it'll do you any good. 그렇게 해. 하지만 네게 도움될 것 같진 않아.

You want to stay here? Be my guest.
여기 남겠다고? 그럼 그렇게 해.

049 Right away (상대방의 지시를 바로 따르겠다면서) 지금 당장

usually this is said to indicate something will be done quickly, or should be done quickly. In some cases, it is similar to saying "Immediately"

A: Get me a glass of water. **Right away!**
물 한잔 갖다 줘. 지금 당장!

B: Why? Are you having some kind of problem swallowing? 왜? 삼키는데 뭐 문제있어?

미드표현

Let's get her to the OR right away!
이 환자 지금 당장 수술실로 옮기자!

Peter, I have to tell you something right away.
피터야, 지금 바로 네게 얘기할 게 있어.

I'm not gonna keep this a secret. We have to let the government know. Right away.
난 이걸 비밀로 하지 않을거야. 우리는 정부에 알려야 돼. 지금 당장.

050 You name it 말만 해, 누구든지[뭐든지] 말만 해

the speaker is saying "Whatever you want will be done." It expresses that any request will be agreed to

| Point | to name a few 몇 개 대자면, 몇몇 이름을 대자면

A: If I marry you, will you buy me a cute sports car? 너랑 결혼하면 멋진 스포츠카 사줄거야?

B: **You name it.** Anything you'd like, I'll get for you.
뭐든 말만해. 네가 좋아하는 거라면 뭐든지 사줄게.

미드표현

You name it. What can I do for you?
말해 봐. 뭘 도와줘야 하지?

What's it gonna take? Cash? Uh, free pizza for the rest of your life? You name it.
로 원하는데? 현금? 평생동안 먹을 피자? 말만해.

You name it. It's done. I promise.
말만 해, 다 해줄게. 약속할게.

051 You're the boss 분부만 내리십시오, 시키는 대로 하죠, 맘대로 해요

this is a way of saying that the speaker will follow the orders of the person he is talking to. It is like saying "I'll follow your directions"

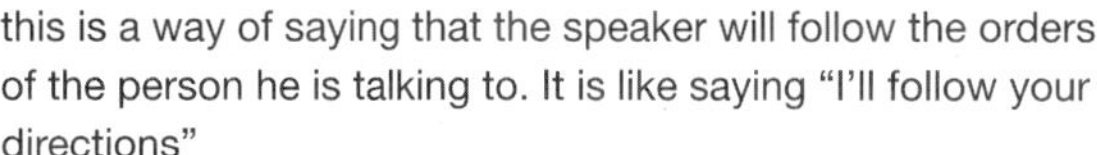

| Point | You're the doctor 네 조언대로 따를게
Whatever he says goes 그 사람 말이면 통해
Anything you say 시키는 대로 하죠, 동감이야

A: I need you to paint my kitchen a different color.
부엌엔 다른 색으로 칠해요.

B: **You're the boss.** What color did you have in mind? 그렇게 하죠. 맘에 둔 색깔이 있나요?

미드표현

Right. You're the boss. I'm just your love slave.
맞아. 맘대로 해. 난 너의 사랑의 노예야.

A:Go work up some new ideas and then we'll go over it during lunch. Okay? B:You're the boss.
A: 새로운 아이디어를 내봐. 점심때 상의하게 말야, 알았지? B: 시키는대로 하죠.

052 Anytime 1. (초대받고) 언제든지 2. (상대방이 감사할 때) 언제라도 3. (준비) 언제라도

미드표현

often this is a way of indicating the speaker will help someone whenever it is needed. It is like saying "Whenever"

| Point | Anytime you are ready 너만 준비되면 언제든지

A: Thank you so much for coming over and helping me out. 와서 날 도와줘 정말 고마워.

B: **Anytime.** I hope you won't feel shy about asking for help in the future.
언제든지. 앞으로 부탁하는데 꺼리지 말고.

A: Anyway, thank you for looking after Sammy.
B: Anytime. A: 어쨌든 새미를 돌봐줘서 고마워. B: 언제든지.

A: Thanks for coming with me. B: Anytime.
A: 나와 함께 와줘서 고마워. B: 언제든.

053 I'm all yours 네가 원한다면 언제든지

미드표현

this means "I will listen to everything you say." It indicates that the speaker is giving his complete attention to someone

A: Can you spare a few minutes of your time?
시간 좀 내줄 수 있어?

B: Of course I can. **I'm all yours.** 물론이지. 언제든지.

Yeah, whenever you feel like it. I mean, if I'm alone, I'm all yours.
그래, 네가 원할 때 아무때나. 내말은 내가 혼자라면 네가 원한다면 언제든지.

I play today and then I'm all yours!
경기에 나가고 그 뒤는 마음대로 하세요!

I promise, once the deal is done, I'm all yours.
내 약속하는데, 일단 거래가 이루어지면 네 맘대로 해.

054 Now there you have me 1. 모르겠어 2. 내가 졌어

미드표현

usually this means that the speaker is not sure of what the answer to a question is, as in "I don't know that." In some cases it means that another person has won some type of competition against the speaker, as in "You won the bet we had"

A: Where does Cindy work? 신디가 어디서 일해?

B: **Now there you have me.** I'm not sure.
몰라. 잘 모르겠어.

You want to know why the sky is blue? Now there you have me.
하늘이 왜 파란지 알고 싶다고? 나 모르겠어.

Now there you have me. I don't know the answer to that question. 모르겠어. 난 그 질문의 답을 몰라.

Now there you have me. Go ask someone else. 모르겠어. 가서 다른 사람에게 물어봐봐.

055 That's what I thought 나도 그렇게 생각했어, 나도 그 생각이야

미드표현

this is usually said when the speaker has confirmed something is true. It often means "I was sure that was correct"

| Point | That's what I thought about ~ …에 대해 그렇게 생각했었어
That's what I think 내 생각도 바로 그래

A: I think John was lying about being sick.
존이 아프다고 거짓말 한 것 같아.

B: **That's what I thought.** I wonder why he skipped work today.
나도 그렇게 생각했어. 왜 걔가 오늘 결근했는지 궁금해.

That's what I thought at first.
처음에 나도 그렇게 생각했어.

Exactly. That's what I thought.
바로 그래. 내 생각도 그랬어.

She seems great. That's what I thought when I dated her. 걔 굉장히 예뻐. 걔랑 데이트할 때 그 생각을 했어.

Ways to disagree or say something might not be true

상대방의 말을 부정하거나, 반대, 거절할 때

It's not what you think

001 It's not what you think 네가 생각하는 그런게 아냐, 속단하지 마라

the speaker wants to say "You don't understand it." It means that something is different than it seems to be

| Point | It's not that 그런 건 아냐

A: I heard you were at Joe's house all night on Friday. 금요일 밤새 조의 집에 있었다며.

B: **It's not what you think.** We were studying. 네 생각과 달라. 우린 공부했어.

미드표현

It's not! It's not what you think! 아니야! 그런 게 아니야!

It's not what you think. I mean it is just not an affair. 속단하지마. 바람핀게 아니야.

That thing is not what you think it is anyway. You don't understand, man. You don't have any idea.
하여간 저건 네가 생각하는 그런게 아냐. 너 이해못해. 넌 생각도 못하는 거라고.

002 (It's) Not likely 아마 안될 걸, 그럴 것 같지 않아, 아닐 걸

this means that "It probably won't happen." The speaker doubts something will take place

A: I'm planning a hike in the woods tomorrow. Will it rain? 낼 숲속에서 하이킹할거야. 비가 올까?

B: **Not likely.** We are supposed to have hot and sunny weather. 아닐 걸. 따뜻하고 화창한 날이 될거래.

미드표현

No, and it's not likely to happen soon.
아니 그리고 실현가능성도 희박해.

I'm not saying that we can't win Peter. I'm saying it's not likely and that we should settle.
우리가 피터를 못이길 것 같단 소리는 아냐. 그럴 확률이 없으니 그냥 해결하자고.

A: Think she'll come out today? B: Not likely.
A: 걔가 오늘 나올 것 같아? B: 아닐 걸.

003 You couldn't do that! 넌 절대 못할걸!

often we can understand this to mean that the speaker thinks doing something is impossible, or that doing it would cause many serious problems. It is a strong recommendation not to try to do something. A similar way to express this is "That's not something that should be done"

| Point | You couldn't (do that)! 넌 절대 못할걸!, 그럼 안되지!

A: I may decide not to go to work tomorrow.
내일 일하러 가지 않을 수도 있어.

B: **You couldn't do that.** Your boss would be angry. 그러면 안되지! 그럼 사장이 화를 낼텐데.

미드표현

Oh. Let me guess. You couldn't do it.
어, 어디 보자. 넌 그렇게 절대 못할거야.

Chris, you couldn't do that. It would be embarrassing.
크리스, 넌 그렇게 못할거야. 그렇게 하면 매우 황당할거야.

I hear you want to leave your wife. You couldn't do that.
네 아내와 헤어지고 싶어 한다며. 넌 그렇게 못할거야.

004 I don't see it that way 난 그렇게 생각하지 않아, 그런 것 같지 않아

this implies that someone has a different opinion. It usually means "I think it is different"

| Point | I don't see it[that] 안 보여, 그렇지 않아

A: I think your son is lazy. 네 아들 게으른 것 같아.

B: **I don't see it that way.** I think he's bored with schoolwork. 난 그런 것 같지 않아. 숙제가 지겨워서 그럴거야.

I put it in here and I don't see it.
여기다 두었는데 보이지 않아.

I don't see it here. What's the patient's name?
여기 어디 있는거야. 환자이름 뭐야?

005 I don't see that happening 그렇게는 안될 걸

this is a way to say that the speaker thinks something won't happen. It means "I think that won't occur"

A: I think you will get married next year, Jack.
잭, 너 내년에 결혼하게 될거야.

B: **I don't see that happening.** I don't even have a girlfriend. 그렇겐 안될 걸. 여친도 없는데.

미드표현

Well, I don't see that happening. You see that happening? 음, 그렇게 되지는 않을 걸. 그렇게 될 것 같아?

A: Since you saw my boobies, I think, uh, you're gonna have to show me your weenie.
B: You know, I don't see that happening.
A: 넌 내 가슴을 봤으니 넌 내게 네 거시기를 보여줘. B: 글쎄, 그렇게는 안 될 걸.

006 I don't think so 그런 것 같지 않은데, 그렇지 않아, 아닐 걸

this is a way for the speaker to say the answer is probably no. It is very similar to saying "Probably not"

| Point | I guess not 아닌 것 같아
I don't believe so 그렇지 않아
I expect not 아닐 듯
I suppose not 아닐 걸
I'm afraid not 아닐 거야

A: Have your parents ever been to New York?
부모님들이 뉴욕에 가본 적 있으셔?

B: **I don't think so.** I have never heard them talk about visiting there. 아닐 걸. 가보셨다는 얘기 못들어봤어.

My daughter? Nah. I don't think so.
내 딸이? 아냐. 그렇지 않아.

A: Are you sure we haven't met before?
B: I don't think so.
A: 정말 우리 전에 만난 적이 없나요? B: 그럴거요.

No, I don't think so. That looks physiological.
아니, 난 그렇게 생각안해. 저건 생리적인 것으로 보여.

A: But did anybody see you? B: No. I don't think so. A: 누가 너 본 사람있어? B: 없어. 그런 것 같지 않아.

007 (You) Want to bet? 그렇지 않을 걸?, 내기할래?

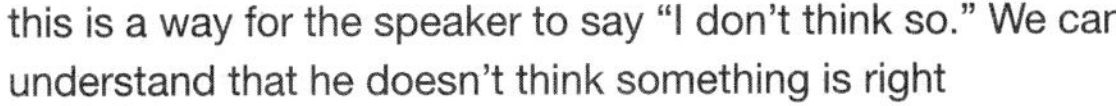

this is a way for the speaker to say "I don't think so." We can understand that he doesn't think something is right

| Point | What do you want to bet S+V? (정말이라니까) …에 뭘 걸래?
How much do you want to bet S+V? (정말야) …얼마 걸래?

A: You never met Ricky Martin. 리키마틴 만난 적 없잖아.

B: **You want to bet?** I have his picture right here.
내기 할래? 여기 걔 사진있다고.

미드표현

What do you want to bet Carol will date me?
캐롤이 나와 데이트하는데 뭘 걸래?

How much you want to bet? 얼마를 걸래?

How much do you want to bet the party will be canceled? 파티가 취소된다는데 얼마걸래?

008 I don't believe it 사실이 아니잖아, 못믿어

the speaker is saying "I don't think it's true." It indicates he feels something is wrong or false

A: The economy is supposed to improve next year.
경제가 내년에 좋아질거래.

B: **I don't believe it.** I think it will continue to be bad. 사실이 아닐 걸. 계속 나쁠거야.

미드표현

You're joking! I don't believe it! 농담이지! 못믿겠어!

I don't believe it! That's great, honey!
정말이니! 잘 했다, 얘야!

Wait a second, you were a band geek? Oh, I don't believe it. 잠깐, 네가 밴드에 있었단 말야? 어, 못믿겠어.

009 I can't say~ …라고 할 수는 없지, …하지는 않았어, …는 아니지

this is a polite way to say the speaker is uncertain. The speaker means "I'm not sure S+V"

A: Do you like to eat hamburgers? 햄버거 먹는 거 좋아해?

B: **I can't say** that I do. They are too greasy for me. 그렇지는 않아. 너무 기름져서.

미드표현

I can't say I blame them. 걔네들을 비난할 수는 없지.

I can't say I understand what you're going through. 네가 겪을 어려움을 안다고 말할 수는 없지.

I can't say for certain she'll recover completely. 걔가 완전히 회복될 거라고는 확실히 말 못해.

010 I wouldn't say that 그렇지도 않던데

this usually means "I don't agree." Often it indicates the speaker thinks someone is wrong

| Point | I wouldn't bet on it 그럴 일은 없을 거야

A: These are the best shoes that you can buy.
이 구두들은 지금 나온 것중에서 최고입니다.

B: **I wouldn't say that.** Some other shoes are better. 그렇지도 않던데. 다른 구두들 중 더 좋은 것도 있어요.

미드표현

A: Well, sorry I couldn't help. B: I wouldn't say that. A: 못 도와줘서 미안. B: 그렇지도 않아.

A: I know I haven't been your favorite friend over the few years. B: I wouldn't say that.
A: 내가 근 몇년 동안 네가 좋아하는 친구가 되지 못한 것 같아. B: 그렇지도 않아.

011 It's not like that 꼭 그런 건 아냐, 그런 것 같지는 않아

this is often said when a speaker wants to say something is different. It is like saying "It's different than what you're thinking"

| Point | It's not like S+V …처럼인 것은 아니다, 꼭 …는 아니다

A: Have you enjoyed your summer vacation?
여름 휴가 잘 갔다왔어?

B: Not very much. **It's not like** we did a lot of fun things. 별로 그렇지 않아. 많이 재미있게 보낸 것은 아냐.

미드표현

No, it's not like that. You don't understand.
아니, 그런 건 아냐. 네가 이해못해.

It's not like there's anything that interesting going on. 뭐 재미난 일이 있는 것은 아냐.

It's not like you've never slept with a guy you weren't married to.
결혼하지 않은 사람과는 자지 않는다는 것과는 달라.

012 No, nothing like that 아니, 그런 건 아냐

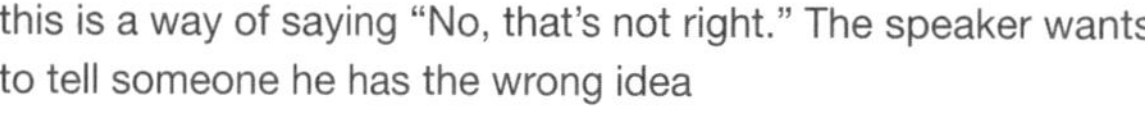

this is a way of saying "No, that's not right." The speaker wants to tell someone he has the wrong idea

| Point | There's nothing like that! 저 만하게 없지!(That thing is very special)

A: Are you going to buy a house this year?
금년에 집을 살거야?

B: No, **nothing like that.** I don't have the money for a house. 아니, 그런 건 아냐. 집살 돈이 없어.

미드표현

No, nothing like that. He's harmless.
아니, 전혀 그런 게 아냐. 걘 해를 끼치지 않아.

Oh, it's nothing like that. 그런 얘기가 아니야.

A: Has his behavior changed recently, drug use, alcohol, things like that? B: No, no, nothing like that.
A: 최근에 술을 마신다든가 마약을 한다는 식으로 걔가 변했니? B: 아니, 그런 건 아냐.

013 That's easy for you to say 그렇게 말하기는 쉽지, 말이야 그렇지

this is a way of saying "I think it will be hard to actually do that." It means that something may be more difficult to do than to talk about

A: I don't think that it is very hard to climb Mount Everest 에베레스트 등산은 무척 어렵지는 않을 것 같아.

B: **That's easy for you to say.** You've never even been mountain climbing. 말하긴 쉽지. 등산 안 해봤잖아.

Oh, come on, honey, that's easy for you to say. 어, 이봐 자기야, 네가 말하기는 쉽지.

That's easy for you to say, you weren't almost just killed. 그렇게 말하기는 쉽지, 넌 거의 죽을 뻔했잖아.

014 I doubt it 과연 그럴까, 그럴 것 같진 않아

this is a way for the speaker to say he disagrees. It is like saying "I don't think so"

I Point I I doubt that 그럴 리 없어
I doubt if[that]~ …아닐거라고 의심하다
I suspect that~ …일거라고 의심하다

A: I think I may be getting an A in this class.
이 수업에서 A를 받을 것 같아.

B: **I doubt it.** You haven't been a very good student. 그럴까. 그리 좋은 학생은 아니잖아.

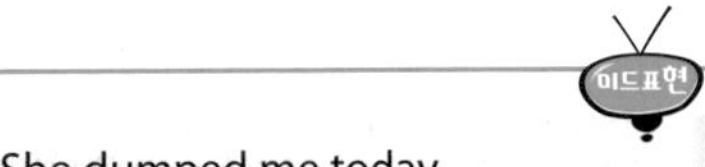

I doubt it. She dumped me today.
그럴 리 없어. 걔가 날 오늘 찼거든.

I doubt it. All I know is her name is Amy. I didn't even get a phone number.
과연 그럴까. 걔 이름이 에이미라는 것 밖에 몰라. 전화번호도 모르는 걸.

I doubt it. You haven't seen him since he was 4. 과연 그럴까. 넌 걔가 네 살 이후로 본 적이 없잖아.

015 Speak for yourself 그건 그쪽 얘기죠, 너나 그렇지

this means "I don't agree with that." We can understand that the speaker has a different opinion

A: I think that it's a good idea to exercise every day. 매일 운동하는 게 좋은 생각인 것 같아.

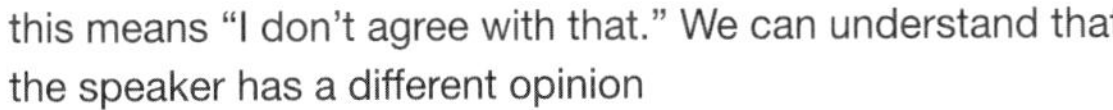

B: **Speak for yourself.** I really hate to exercise.
너나 그렇지. 난 정말 운동하는 게 싫어.

Speak for yourself. I don't feel the same way.
너나 그렇지. 난 공감하지 않아.

I know you hate Indian food, but speak for yourself. 너 인도 음식을 싫어하는 걸 알지만 그건 너나 그런거지.

Speak for yourself. To me, this apartment is fine. 그쪽 얘기지. 내게 이 아파트는 멋져.

016 It's not that 그런 건 아냐

this is like saying "It isn't very..." The speaker is saying something is different than it seems

I Point I It's not that+adj 그 정도로 …는 아니다
It's not that S+V …하기 때문이 아니야

A: I heard you won't be coming to the meeting.
회의에 오지 못한다며.

B: **It's not that** I don't want to come. I have another appointment. 가기 싫은게 아냐. 다른 약속이 있었어.

It's not that fun. 그렇게 재미있지 않아.

It's not that simple. 그렇게 단순하지 않아.

It's not that I don't love you.
내가 널 사랑하지 않아서가 아니야.

It's not that we don't have confidence in you.
너를 못 믿어서가 아니야.

017 It's not about that 그런 문제가 아냐, 요점은 그게 아니야

the speaker is saying "That is not the main point." It indicates that something has a different meaning or importance

A: I guess your job must pay you a lot of money.
직장이 급여를 많이 주나보구만.

B: **It's not about that.** I really love the work I do.
그런 문제가 아냐. 정말 내가 하는 일을 좋아해.

A: I didn't want your dad living in the same building. B: You know it's not about that.
A: 난 네 아버지가 같은 빌딩에 사는 걸 원치 않았어. B: 문제는 그게 아니잖아.

We both know it's not about that.
우리 둘다 그게 문제는 아니라는 걸 알아.

A: Are you signing my paychecks? Are you hiring or firing? B: This is not about that.
A: 내 급여수표에 사인할건가요? 절 고용하시나요 해고하시나요? B: 문제는 그게 아닙니다.

018 Me neither 나도 안 그래

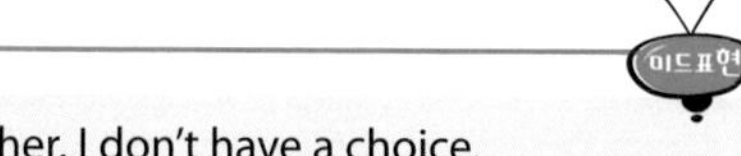

this is a way to agree that something is not good or should not be done. It is the same as saying "Nor do I"

| Point | Neither did I 나도 안 그랬어
Neither do I 나도 안 그래
Neither will I 나도 안 그럴 거야

A: I don't want to attend the meeting this afternoon.
오늘 오후 미팅에 가기 싫어.

B: **Me neither.** But we need to go or our boss will be angry. 나도 그래. 하지만 안 가면 사장이 열받을거야.

Me neither. I don't have a choice.
나도, 하지만 선택의 여지가 없잖아.

To tell you the truth, neither did I.
사실대로 말하자면, 나도 뜻밖이야.

Me neither, but as you said, we need to get to know each other better.
나도 안그래. 하지만 네가 말한 것처럼 우리는 서로 더 잘 알도록 해야 돼.

019 Don't look at me 내가 안 그랬어, 나 아니야

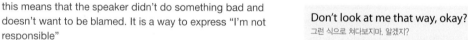

this means that the speaker didn't do something bad and doesn't want to be blamed. It is a way to express "I'm not responsible"

| Point | Don't look at me like that 그런 식으로 날 쳐다보지마
Don't give me that look 날 그렇게 쳐다보지마

A: Did you eat all of the cookies that were in the kitchen? 부엌에 있던 쿠키 다 먹었어?

B: **Don't look at me.** I didn't touch any of the cookies. 내가 안 그랬어. 쿠키에 손도 안댔어.

Don't look at me that way, okay?
그런 식으로 쳐다보지마, 알겠지?

Well, don't look at me. I quit smoking twenty years ago. 나 아냐. 20년 전에 담배 끊었어.

A: How did you let this happen? B: Don't look at me like that.
A: 어떻게 이렇게 된거야? B: 날 그런 식으로 쳐다보지마.

020 I beg to differ 내 생각은 달라, 그렇지 않아, 네 말에 동의하지 않아

this is a very polite way to say "I disagree." The speaker has a different opinion than someone else

A: Everyone here thinks that the plan is a good idea. 여기 사람들은 모두 그 계획이 좋다고 생각해.

B: **I beg to differ.** There are some serious problems with it. 내 생각은 달라. 몇몇 중요한 문제가 있다고.

Oh! No, I beg to differ. Of the three of us, I was by far the most supportive.
아냐. 그렇지 않아. 우리 세 명중에서 내가 가장 도와주는데 적극적이었어.

I think every delivery boy in town would beg to differ. 시내의 모든 배달소년들은 네 말에 동의하지 않을거야.

I beg to differ. I'm five weeks older than you.
내 생각은 달라. 난 너보다 5주 먼저 태어났어.

021 That's not gonna happen 그럴 일 없을거야, 난 그러지 않을거야

미드표현

this could mean that the speaker is predicting that something will not happen in the future, or it could mean the speaker is refusing to do something. In other words, sometimes it means "I don't think that will occur" and other times it means "No, I am not going to do that"

| Point | (That's) Not gonna happen 그런 일은 없을거야, 그렇게는 안될거야.
(It'll) Never happen! 절대 안돼!, 말도 안돼!
That can't happen 말도 안돼, 그렇게는 안돼

A: Maybe some day you and I will get married.
언젠가 너와 내가 결혼할지도 모르지.

B: **That's not gonna happen.** We are too different. 그럴 일 없을거야. 우린 너무 달라.

That's not gonna happen. I can't let you question the suspect.
그렇게는 안돼. 네가 용의자를 심문하도록 하지 않을거야.

Well, forget it! It's not gonna happen.
저기, 그만두라고! 그럴 일 없을거니까.

I think we both know that's not gonna happen. 우리 둘 다 그런 일은 없을거라는 걸을 알고 있을 것 같아.

022 Don't even think about (doing) it 꿈도 꾸지마, 절대 안돼

미드표현

the speaker wants to tell someone strongly not to do something. It is like giving a warning "Don't do it"

| Point | Don't even think about ~ing …할 생각은 꿈도 꾸지마

A: Come on, let's go out and drink a few beers tonight. 자, 오늘 밤 나가서 맥주 몇 잔 하자.

B: **Don't even think about it.** We've got a lot of work to do. 절대 안돼. 할 일이 너무 많아.

Don't even think about blaming me.
날 비난할 생각일랑 꿈도 꾸지마.

Shut up and move over there! Don't even think about it! Let's go!
입닥치고 저리가! 꿈도 꾸지마! 자 가자!

023 You've got to put your foot down 넌 결사 반대를 해야 돼

this means that the speaker thinks someone has to be very strict and stop someone's bad behavior. Often when a parent or authority figure becomes very strict, we say they are putting their foot down. A way to say the same thing would be "You've gotta tell them strongly that they have to stop"

| Point | put one's foot down 결사반대하다, 단호하게 거절하다

A: My son has been staying out drinking all night.
내 아들은 밤새 술마시며 집에 들어오지 않았어.

B: **You've got to put your foot down** and stop this behavior. 넌 단호하게 안된다고 하고 이런 행동을 금지시켜야 돼.

I am putting my foot down. You'd better start treating her with some respect.
난 강력히 반대야. 넌 걔를 존경심을 좀 가지고 대하기 시작하라고.

You're gonna have to put your foot down?
넌 강하게 반대할거야?

Drugs are wrong! I'm putting my big foot down on drugs!
마약은 잘못된거야! 난 강력하게 마약을 반대할거야!

024 Not that I know of 내가 알기로는 그렇지 않아

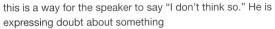

this is a way for the speaker to say "I don't think so." He is expressing doubt about something

| Point | Not that I remember 내 기억으로는 아냐
Not that I recall 내가 기억하기로는 아냐

A: Have you met any famous people in your life?

B: **Not that I know of.** Most people I know have normal lives. 내가 알기론 없지. 내가 아는 대부분의 사람들은 평범하게 살아.

Not that I know of, but I'll go check.
내가 아는 한은 없지만 가서 확인해 볼게.

Not that I know of. Why? 내가 알기로는 아냐, 왜?

A: Do you have something you want to say to me? B: Not that I know of.
A: 나한테 뭐 하고 싶은 말 있어? B: 아니 없는데.

025 (It's) Not even close 어림도 없어

this is usually said to tell someone they are wrong. It is a way to say "That is certainly not right"

| Point | You're not even close

A: I would say that you are around 27 years old.
넌 한 스물 일곱 살 쯤으로 보이는데.

B: **Not even close.** I'm actually almost 40 years old. 어림도 없어. 실은 거의 40이 다 돼가.

You're wrong. It's not even close to being over.
틀렸어. 아직 끝날려면 어림도 없어.

You're not even close to getting it done.
일을 다 맞추려면 아직 멀었어.

A: I've been waiting for ten minutes. B: Sorry, not even close to the record.
A: 난 10분이나 기다렸어. B: 미안, 하지만 기록에 미치지도 못하네.

026 Not a thing 전혀, 아무 것도

this generally means "Nothing." The speaker is saying that nothing occurred or happened

| Point | Not a drop 전혀 안그래
Not always 항상 그런 건 아니다
Not in a million years 절대로 안돼

A: What did you do on Christmas day? 성탄절에 뭐했어?

B: **Not a thing.** My family doesn't celebrate that holiday. 아무 것도. 우리 가족은 그 날을 기념하지 않아.

It was a kiss, not a thing. 그건 키스였어, 아무 것도 아녔어.

A: Is there anything I need to know, Danny?
B: Nope. Not a thing.
A: 대니, 내가 뭐 알아야 될게 있어? B: 아니, 전혀.

A: What did you do to my sperm? B: Not a thing. A: 내 정자를 어떻게 한거야? B: 아무 것도 안했어.

A: What's wrong with you? B: Nothing. Not a thing. A: 너 뭐가 문제야? B: 전혀, 아무 것도 아냐.

027 Not that way! 그런 식으론 안돼!, 그렇게는 아냐!

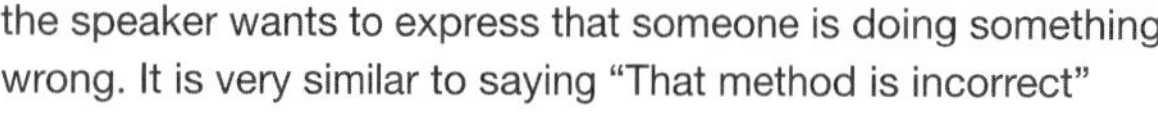

the speaker wants to express that someone is doing something wrong. It is very similar to saying "That method is incorrect"

A: Is this how I put a CD into your new stereo?
이렇게 CD를 네 새 스테레오에 넣는거야?

B: No! **Not that way!** You're going to break it!
아니! 그렇게 하는 거 아냐! 망가뜨리겠다!

Stack the books over there. Not that way!
저기에다 책을 쌓아. 그런 식으로 말고!

Not that way! You are going in the wrong direction! 그 길이 아냐! 방향이 틀렸어!

Over there, go! Not that way. 저쪽으로 가! 그 쪽 말고.

028 No way! 절대 안돼!, 말도 안돼!

this speaker wants to say "No." He is denying something strongly

| Point | (There's) No way to do/S+V …할 수가 없어
No dice! 절대 아냐!, 그런 건 못하겠어!

A: Have you ever been to a DVD room while on a date? 데이트하면서 DVD방에 가본 적 있어?

B: **No way!** I'd never do something like that!
절대 없어! 난 그런 건 절대 안해!

There's no way to repair what was lost.
잃은 걸 회복할 방법이 없어.

There's no way that we're gonna have sex together. 우리가 앞으로 함께 섹스할 일이 없을거야.

There's no way she will help us.
절대로 걔가 우리를 도울 일을 없을거야.

There's no way we will be able to go on vacation. 우리는 휴가를 갈 수 없을거야.

029 (It's) Out of the question 그건 안돼, 불가능해, 절대 안돼

미드표현

this means that someone is saying no to something. It is a way to say "I would not do that"

A: Why don't we buy a new computer to do work with? 사용할 새로운 컴퓨터를 사자.

B: **It's out of the question.** New computers are much too expensive. 안돼. 새 컴퓨터는 너무 비싸.

I guess that's out of the question, right?
그건 안될 걸, 맞지?

That's out of the question. 말도 안돼.

Out of the question. It's taking up space and I can't have it here. 그건 안돼. 그게 공간을 차지하기 때문에 내가 여기에 가지고 있을 수가 없어.

030 Over my dead body 내 눈에 흙이[목에 칼이] 들어가기 전엔 안돼

미드표현

this is a way for the speaker to say "I'll never allow it." In other words, he won't let something happen

| Point | Not on your life 절대 안돼
That can be arranged 그럼 그렇게 해주지. *Over my deal body의 대답으로 죽기 전에는 안 된다고 하니 "내가 죽어주면 되겠네"라는 뜻.

A: Dad, I'd really like to get a new motorcycle.
아빠, 새 오토바이 사고 싶어요.

B: **Over my dead body.** Those things are dangerous! 절대 안돼. 그건 건 너무 위험해!

I told her no way is she borrowing my stuff. Over my dead body!
내 눈에 흙이 들어오더라도 걔한테 내 물건 안 빌려줄거야!

I made a promise to myself that the next time I would talk to her would be over my dead body. 내 목에 칼이 들어와도 걔하곤 절대 얘기하지 않을거야.

031 Not under any circumstances 결코 그렇지 않아

미드표현

this is used to say "It won't happen." The speaker wants to express that something will never happen

| Point | under no circumstances 절대 안돼

A: Mom, should I open our door to a person who seems strange? 엄마, 낯선 사람에게 문열어줘야 돼요?

B: No, don't do that. **Not under any circumstances.** 아니, 그러면 안돼. 절대 그러면 안돼.

Do not under any circumstances let him be alone with her. 어떤 경우에도 걔가 재와 단둘이 있게 하지마.

I repeat, do not under any circumstances enter this apartment.
다시 말하는데 결코 이 아파트에 들어오지마.

032 Who said anything about talking? 누가 얘기만 한대?

미드표현

this indicates the person does not want to talk. At times, this may indicate the speaker wants to do something physical or sexual instead of talking. We might understand this to mean "I want to do something else besides talk"

| Point | Who said anything about+N[~ing] 누가 …을 한대?(안할건대)

A: You invited me to your apartment just to talk?
단지 얘기하자고 네 아파트에 날 초대한거야?

B: No. **Who said anything about** talking?
아니, 누가 얘기만 한대?

Who said anything about talking? 누가 얘기한대?

Who said anything about renting?
누가 임대를 한다고 그래?

Who said anything about taking him?
누가 걔를 데려간대?

A: I don't want to kill myself. B: Who said anything about killing yourself, man?
A: 난 자살하고 싶지 않아. B: 누가 너한테 자살하라고 했어?

033 I'm against[for] the plan 그 계획에 반대[찬성]야

usually this means "I don't like it." We can understand the speaker disagrees with something

| Point | I'm dead against it 절대 반대야
I'm dead set against it 절대 반대야

A: What is your opinion of the agreement?
그 협의에 네 의견은 뭐야?

B: **I'm against the plan.** It seems like a bad idea.
난 그 계획에 절대 반대야. 안 좋은 생각같아.

Sam, you know I'm against hunting.
샘, 알잖아 나 사냥 반대하는 거.

I didn't do anything. I'm against this whole project. 아무 것도 안했어. 난 이 프로젝트 전반에 걸쳐 반대야.

I'm for it. 찬성야.

034 Not by a long shot 어떠한 일이 있어도 아냐, 절대로 싫어, 전혀 아니야

this is usually said when someone has the wrong idea. The speaker is saying "That is the wrong sort of thinking"

A: I always thought that you were in love with Kate.
난 네가 케이트를 사랑하는 줄 알았어.

B: **Not by a long shot.** She and I were only friends. 전혀 아니야. 걔하고 난 그냥 친구야.

A: Is it the worst film you've ever seen? B: No. Not by a long shot.
A: 네가 본 영화중에 최악이야? B: 아니, 그렇지 않아.

A: Are we done? B: Not by a long shot.
A: 우리 끝났어? B: 아직 멀었어.

A: Are we through here, Detective? B: Not by a long shot, Lawson.
A: 형사님, 우리 이제 끝났나요? B: 로슨, 아직 멀었어.

A: We're even now. B: Not by a long shot, buddy.
A: 우린 이제 비겼어. B: 친구야, 전혀 아니야.

035 Not for me 난 싫어, 난 아냐

미드표현

this indicates the speaker doesn't want something. In other words "No, thank you"

| Point | That's[It's] not for me 그건 나한테는 안 어울려, 내게는 아냐, 싫어

A: How about a little more coffee? 커피 좀 더 들래?

B: **Not for me.** I must leave here soon. 됐어. 곧 가야 돼.

What? It's not for me. 뭐라고? 내꺼 아냐.

But it's not for me, it's for Mindy. 내꺼아냐, 멘디꺼야.

I guess not for me. 난 싫어.

036 Not a chance! 절대 안돼!, 어림없는 소리!

미드표현

this is similar to saying "No way." It means that someone has the wrong idea

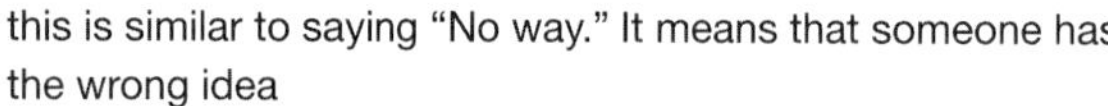

| Point | (There is) No chance 절대 안돼, 그럴 리가 없어
There is no chance of~ing/ S+V …할 리가 없다

A: Are you traveling to Hawaii this winter?
이번 겨울에 하와이 여행갈거야?

B: **Not a chance.** I don't have that much extra money. 어림없는 소리. 그럴 여분의 돈이 없어.

There's no chance she walked outside by herself? 걔가 혼자 걸어 나갔을 리가 없지?

There is no chance. Really. I mean... look where we are.
어림없는 소리. 정말이야. 내 말은 우리 처지를 보라고.

Not a chance, the MRI was clean.
그럴 리가 없어, MRI는 아무 이상없이 나왔어.

037 What gives you the right? 네가 무슨 권리로?

this is a way of asking why a person is allowed to do something. Generally this is asked when someone thinks another person is doing something that they are not allowed to do. It is very similar to asking "Who gave you permission to do that?"

| Point | What gives you the right to~ ? 네가 무슨 권리로 …하는거야?

A: You can't bring coffee into the classroom.
교실에 커피를 갖고 오면 안돼.

B: **What gives you the right to** take away my drink? 네가 무슨 권리로 내 커피를 뺐어간다는거야?

What gives you the right? Look at me!
네가 무슨 권리가 있다고? 날 봐봐!

What gives you the right to break down my door? 네가 무슨 권리로 내 문을 부수는거야?

So what gives you the right to judge what I do? Why do you even care?
네가 무슨 권리로 내 행동을 비판하는거야? 무슨 상관인데?

038 I wish I could, but I can't 그러고 싶지만 안되겠어

this means "I'm not able to." The speaker is indicating he is not going to do something

| Point | I'd love to, but ~ 그러고 싶지만…
Sorry, but I can't 미안하지만 못하겠어

A: Can you come and visit us for dinner tonight?
오늘밤 와서 저녁 먹을래?

B: **I wish I could, but I can't.** I'm quite busy.
그러고 싶지만 안돼. 많이 바빠서.

I wish I could, but I can't. I have too much pride. 그러고 싶지만 안돼. 자존심이 너무 강해서 말야.

I'd love to, but I'm a little tired.
그러고는 싶지만 좀 피곤해.

I'd love to, but it's really getting late.
그러고는 싶지만 정말 늦었어.

I'm sorry, but I can't handle this project.
미안하지만 이번 프로젝트는 못하겠어.

039 This is where I draw the line 여기까지가 내 한계야

this is a way to say the speaker has done something up to a point, but he is not going to continue with it. We can also understand that he is very firm in his decision, and will not change his mind. In other words, he is saying "I have had enough, and I have decided I don't want to do this"

| Point | This is where you draw the line 여기까지가 내 한계야(더 이상은 안돼)
draw the line 선을 긋다, 거부하다

A: Your girlfriend asked me to borrow $1,000.
네 여친이 내게 천 달러를 빌려달라고 했어.

B: **This is where I draw the line.** She can't do that. 여기까지가 내 한계야. 걔가 그러면 안되지.

Five kids are tough enough, but your husband makes six. And that's where I draw the line.
아이 다섯도 힘든데, 네 남편도 아이 같아. 여기까지가 내 한계야.

Vacationing with your harlot is where I draw the line. 네 창녀와 함께 휴가를 보내는 것은 못하겠네.

We know where to draw the line.
언제 거부를 해야 되는지 우리는 알고 있어.

040 That's the limit 더 이상 못참아

this is most commonly used to indicate that the speaker has become tired or annoyed with someone's bad behavior, and he is no longer willing to put up with that behavior. It is another way to say "I won't tolerate that anymore"

| Point | That's the limit 더는 못참아, 더 이상은 안돼

A: Our boss says we can't take time for lunch.
사장이 그러는데 점심식사시간을 없앤대.

B: **That's the limit.** I'm quitting this job.
더 이상 못참아. 나 그만 둘거야.

Moe wants more money? No, that's the limit.
모가 돈을 더 원한다고? 안돼, 더 이상은 안돼.

That's the limit. I can't do it anymore.
더 이상은 안돼. 더는 그렇게 할 수 없어.

This has to end. That's the limit.
이건 끝이 나야 돼. 더 이상은 못참아.

That's the limit. We have used up our reserves.
더 이상은 못참아. 우린 비축해놓은 걸 다 썼어.

041 That's not a good idea 별로 좋은 생각이 아냐

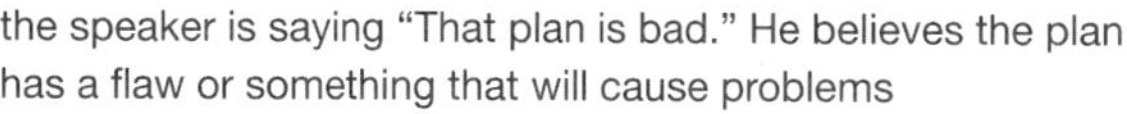

the speaker is saying "That plan is bad." He believes the plan has a flaw or something that will cause problems

| Point | It's not a good idea to~ …하는 것은 좋은 생각이 아냐

A: I think if we complain about the manager, he will be fired. 부장에 대해 불만을 털어놓으면 잘릴지 몰라.

B: **That's not a good idea.** Try to solve your problem another way. 바람직하지 않아. 다른 방식으로 문제를 풀어보자.

A: I'm coming with you. B: That's not a good idea, Micheal.
A: 너와 같이 가겠어. B: 별로 좋은 생각이 아닌 것 같아, 마이클.

It's not a good idea for the patient to be here.
그 환자가 여기 있는 것은 좋은 생각같지 않아.

I think I know what's going on here, and I gotta tell you, it's not a good idea.
여기서 무슨 일이 일어나는지 알 것 같은데, 내 말하지만 그건 좋은 생각이 아냐.

042 I'd rather not 그렇고 싶지 않아

this is usually said when a speaker doesn't prefer something. It is the same as saying "I don't want to"

A: Could you call my mom and tell her I'll be late?
엄마한테 전화해서 내가 늦는다고 말해줄테야?

B: **I'd rather not.** She may yell at me.
별로 그렇고 싶지 않아. 나한테 소리지르실텐데.

You know what? I'd rather not. 글쎄. 그러고 싶지 않아.

A: Feel free to ask. B: I'd rather not.
A: 뭐든지 물어봐. B: 아니야.

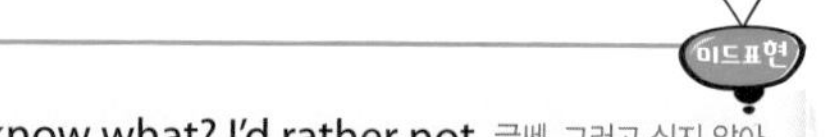

A: Well, Why don't we go back to my place. B: I'd rather not.
A: 우리 집으로 돌아가는게 어때. B: 그러고 싶지 않아.

043 I think I will pass 난 사양할게, 난 됐어

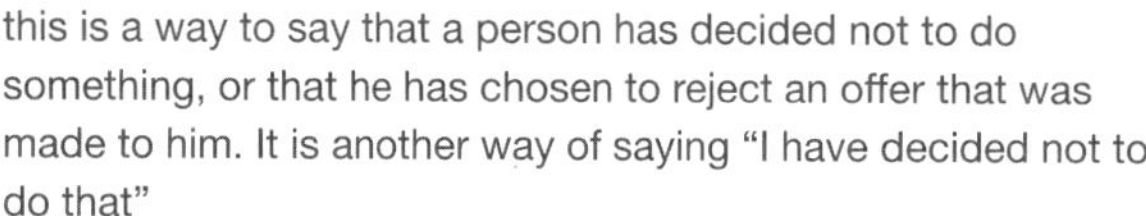

this is a way to say that a person has decided not to do something, or that he has chosen to reject an offer that was made to him. It is another way of saying "I have decided not to do that"

| Point | (I think) I'll pass 난 사양할게, 난 됐어
I'll pass on~ 난 …은 됐어

A: Want to come to the nightclub with us?
우리랑 함께 나이트클럽에 갈래?

B: **I think I will pass.** I'm really tired.
난 됐어. 정말 피곤하거든.

I'll pass. Hang on a second. 난 됐어. 잠깐만 기다려봐.

I think I'll pass on that, John. 존 난 그만 사양할게.

A: I think I'll pass. B: How can you pass? It's a tradition. A: 난 됐어. B: 어떻게 그래? 전통인데.

A: You want to see me make a mangina? B: Oh, that's sexy, but I'll pass.
A: 내가 여자몸처럼 만들어볼까? B: 섹시하겠지만 사양할게

044 Maybe some other time 나중을 기약하지, 다음 기회에 하죠

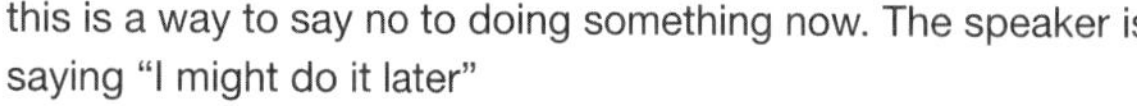

this is a way to say no to doing something now. The speaker is saying "I might do it later"

| Point | We'll try again some other time 다음을 기약하죠

A: We could use your help putting together this report. 이 보고서를 준비하는데 너의 도움이 필요해.

B: I can't help right now. **Maybe some other time.**
지금은 도울 수 없어. 나중에 도와줄게.

I gotta go to work. Maybe some other time.
일하러 가야 돼. 나중을 기약하자고.

Some other time then. 그럼 다음에 하자.

If you give me your number I will call you some other time. 전번주면 나중에 전화할게.

045 I don't feel like it 됐어, 사양할래

the speaker is refusing to do something because he chooses not to. In other words, "I don't want to do it now"

| Point | I don't feel like ~ing/S+V …하고 싶지 않아

A: Why don't you wash your car? It's dirty.
세차해라. 더러워.

B: **I don't feel like it.** I have other things to do.
됐어. 다른 할 일이 있어서.

미드표현

I don't feel like I want to drink. 술마시고 싶지 않아.

I don't feel like talking. 얘기하기 싫어.

I don't feel like kissing anyone tonight.
오늘 밤은 누구하고도 키스하기 싫어.

046 I'll take that as a no 반대한 것으로 알겠어

this is said by a speaker when he gets a response to a question, but the response is not as clear as it should be. The speaker guesses that the response means either being yes or no, and asks for confirmation that his interpretation is correct. It is similar to saying "I think you mean no. Right?"

| Point | I'll take that as~ …로[한 것으로] 알겠어
I'll take that as a "yes." 승낙한 것으로 알다
I'll take that as a compliment. 칭찬으로 받아들이다

A: It might cause trouble if we used her car.
우리가 걔 차를 사용하면 문제가 될거야.

B: So you don't want to borrow it? **I take that as a no.** 그럼 빌리지 말자는거야? 반대한 것으로 알겠어.

미드표현

I'll take that as a yes. Where you from?
승낙한 것으로 알겠어. 어디 출신이야?

Well, thank you, Randy. I'll take that as a compliment. 고마워 랜디. 칭찬으로 받아들일게.

Okay, don't take this as a criticism.
좋아, 이걸 비난으로 받아들이지마.

Can we take that as a yes? 그걸 승낙으로 받아들여도 돼?

047 I couldn't ask you to do that (고맙지만) 그러지 않아도 돼

usually this means the speaker doesn't want to burden someone. He is expressing "I don't want to ask you for that favor"

A: I can loan you some money until you've paid.
갚을 때까지 돈 좀 빌려줄게.

B: **I couldn't ask you to do that.** 고맙지만 그러지 않아도 돼.

미드표현

That is a very kind offer, but I would not ask you to do that. 매우 친절한 제의지만 그러지 않으셔도 돼요.

I couldn't ask you to do that. It wouldn't be fair. 그러지 않아도 돼. 그럼 공평하지가 않을거야.

It was kind of you to try to lend me money, but I couldn't ask you to do that.
나한테 돈을 빌려주려고 해서 정말 고마웠지만 그러지 않아도 돼.

048 I have[I've got] better things to do
시간낭비야, 그걸 할 바에는 다른 걸 하겠어

미드표현

this is usually said when a speaker explains why he won't do something. It is similar to saying "That's not important enough for me to do"

| Point | I have[I've got] better things to do than (to) do~
…할 바에는 …을 하겠어

A: I'm not going to the festival. **I've got better things to do.** 축제에 안 갈거야. 시간낭비야.

B: But the festival is a lot of fun. You shouldn't miss it. 하지만 축제는 재미잖아. 꼭 가봐.

I'd really love to, honey, but I have better things to do. 자기야, 정말 그러고 싶은데, 그럴바엔 다른 걸 하겠어.

We're here to visit her, and she can't show up? I've got better things to do!
우린 걜 방문하러 왔는데 없단말야? 시간낭비야!

Don't you think I have better things to do than to bring you checks every day?
매일 네게 수표를 갖다주는 것보단 다른 할 일이 있다고 생각되지 않니?

049 I'd have to say no 안되겠는데, 아마 안될거야

this is a way to say "No." The speaker is declining to do something

| Point | I'm going to have to say no 안 되겠다고 할거야

A: Wouldn't you like to move to another country?
다른 나라로 이민가고 싶진 않아?

B: **I'd have to say no.** I like living here.
아니지. 난 여기 사는게 좋아.

Speaking for my family, I'd have to say no.
내 가족을 생각해볼 때 안되겠어.

I think I'm gonna have to say no to that.
안 되겠다고 해야 될 것 같아.

050 I'm not like you 난 너랑 달라

미드표현

this is usually said to show that two people have different ideas. It indicates "Our opinions are different"

| Point | I'm not like that 난 그렇지 않아
You're not like that 너는 그렇지는 않아
He's always like that? 쟤 맨날 저래?

A: Why don't you like to go to department stores?
백화점에 가자.

B: **I'm not like you.** I hate to go shopping.
난 너랑 달라. 쇼핑을 싫어해.

I'm not like you, Eva. I just can't say anything that pops into my head.
에바, 난 너랑 달라. 머리에 떠오르는 대로 이야기 못한다고.

I'm not like that anymore. 난 더 이상 그렇지 않아.

I'm not like you. I care what they think.
난 너랑 달라. 난 걔네들이 뭐 생각하는지 신경을 써.

051 No can do 안 되겠는걸

미드표현

this is a way to say that the speaker won't do something. It simply means "No"

A: Can you take care of my dog while I'm away?
내가 없는 동안 내 개 좀 봐줄테야?

B: **No can do.** My husband doesn't like to be around dogs. 안 되겠어. 남편이 개하고 있는 걸 싫어해.

No can do. Sorry, we're through. I was only using you to get what I wanted. Now that I got that, what do I need you for? 안 되겠는걸, 우린 끝이야. 난 널 이용했었고, 이제 이용가치가 없으니, 넌 쓸모없어.

I can't go for that. No can do. 그럴 순 없어. 안되겠는 걸.

052 With all due respect (반대의견을 말하면서 공손함을 표시) 그렇긴 한데요

미드표현

often this is a polite way of stating that the speaker disagrees with someone. It is a way to say "I'm afraid I don't agree"

| Point | with all due respect 그렇기 한데요, 그렇기는 하지만

A: **With all due respect,** I think you don't understand the issues.
그렇긴 한데요, 문제를 이해 못하시는 것 같네요.

B: I have studied the issues for a long time and know them very well! 오랫동안 연구해서 아주 잘 안다고!

Mrs. Walker, with all due respect, you're crazy.
워커부인, 그렇기는 해도 당신은 미쳤네요.

Well, with all due respect, sir, it's not a baked potato. 어, 그렇기는 하지만 이건 구운 감자가 아닌데요.

With all due respect, you have failed.
그렇기는 하지만 넌 실패했어.

MEMO

Ways of expressing like or dislike of something
좋거나 싫거나 혹은 하고 싶거나 하기 싫거나

I like this part

001 I like that 그거 좋은데, 맘에 들어

this is usually a way to say "That's fine with me." The speaker thinks something is good

Point I'd like that 그렇게 한다면 난 좋아, 그러면 난 좋지
I like+N[to do~, ~ing] …가 맘에 들어
I love it! 정말 좋다, 내 맘에 꼭 들어 I'd love it 그럼 좋지

A: How's the new employee in your office? 신입어때?

B: He works really hard every day. **I like that.**
매일 정말 열심히 일해. 맘에 들어.

미드표현

You're smart. I like that. 너 똑똑하구나. 맘에 들어

I like that place. 저 곳이 맘에 들어.

I like that idea. 그 생각 맘에 들어.

I like that you're a good friend. 네가 좋은 친구여서 좋아.

002 I don't like it 싫어, 그러지 말자

this shows a displeasure or dislike of something. It is a way to express "This is not good"

Point I don't like it either 나도 역시 싫어
I hate+N[to do~, ~ing] …을(하는 걸) 싫어해
I hate it when S+V …할 때 싫어 I didn't care for it 난 싫어

A: Have you heard any of the current popular music? 요즘 유행하는 음악 들어본 것 있어?

B: Yes, I hear it on the radio from time to time. **I don't like it.** 어, 때때로 라디오로 들어. 맘에 안들어.

미드표현

I don't like it when you take food off of my plate. 네가 내 접시에서 음식 뺐어가는 게 싫어.

Stop invading my privacy, I don't like it.
내 프라이버시를 침해하지마, 싫단 말야.

I hate all that shit. 저 모든 게 싫어.

I hate it when they do that. 걔네들이 저럴 때 싫어.

I hate drinking alone. 혼자 술 마시는 게 싫어.

003 I like this part 난 이런게 좋더라

this is a very literal phrase. It expresses that the speaker enjoys a certain part of something. Often we hear this used when people are watching a movie that they have seen before, and someone wants to express appreciation for a specific scene. It means "I think this portion is very good"

Point like this part 이 부분을 좋아하다

A: This is the section of the movie where they fall in love. 영화의 이 부분이 걔네들이 사랑에 빠지는 장면이야.

B: Wonderful. Romance is great. **I like this part.**
멋져. 사랑은 위대한거야. 이 부분이 좋더라.

미드표현

What about the scene with the kangaroo? Did-did you like that part?
캥거루가 나오는 장면은 어땠어? 그 부분도 좋았어?

This is where I give you advice and pretend you're going to listen to it. I like this part.
이 부분에서 내가 네게 조언하고 네가 그걸 들을거라고 하는 척하지. 난 이 부분이 좋더라.

004 That's more like it 그게 더 낫네, 바로 그거야

this usually means "I'm happy with how things have changed." It is a way to indicate that the speaker is satisfied with the progress or development of something

Point be (more) like~ (더) …답다

A: The neighbors have certainly made their house look nice. **That's more like it!**
이웃사람들이 확실히 집단장을 했네. 더 좋네!

B: Yeah, it looks so much better than it did in the past. 그래, 옛날보다 훨씬 더 좋아 보여.

미드표현

This hotel is luxurious. That's more like it.
이 호텔이 고급스럽네. 그게 더 낫네.

A: Screw this up, and I'll kill you. B: That's more like it. A: 이 일 망치면 죽일거야. B: 그게 더 낫네.

A: There's nothing to worry about. Your secret's safe with me. B: That's more like it.
A: 걱정할 거 하나 없어. 네 비밀을 꼭 지킬게. B: 바로 그거야.

005 It's not that bad 괜찮은데, 그렇게 나쁘지 않아

often this expresses a mild approval of something. It is very similar to saying "It is okay"

| Point | This is not that bad 그리 나쁘지 않아
I'm not that bad 내가 그렇게 나쁜 사람 아니야

A: How is the yoga class going for you? 요가수업 어때?
B: **It's not that bad.** I think they are helping me lose weight. 괜찮아. 살 빼는데 도움될 것 같아.

Look, it's not that bad. 그렇게 나빠 보이지 않아.

You guys, I am not that bad!
애들아, 나 그렇게 나쁜 사람 아니야!

Well, Jill, you're not that bad, and, believe me, I'm not that good.
저기 질, 넌 그렇게 나쁜 사람 아니야, 그리고 정말이지 내가 그렇게 좋은 사람도 아니고 말야.

006 She has an appetite for rap music 걘 랩음악을 좋아해

this means "She really likes rap music." We can understand that the person ehjoys listening to this type of music

| Point | have an appetite for …을 좋아하다

A: Why is Karen always watching the music channel on TV? 왜 카렌은 늘상 TV에서 음악채널을 보는 거야?
B: **She has an appetite for** rap music. 걘 랩음악을 좋아해.

Leroy has an appetite for sci fi movies.
르로이는 공상과학 영화를 좋아해.

I have an appetite for pasta tonight.
오늘밤은 파스타를 먹고 싶어.

The killer has an appetite for violence.
살인자는 폭력을 좋아해.

007 You're a sucker for a hot dancer 넌 섹시한 댄서에 사족을 못써

this implies that the listener is attracted to people who can dance well. A hot dancer is either someone who is talented at dancing or someone who is physically attractive, and can also dance. In other words "You're tempted by dancers who are good looking"

| Point | be a sucker for~ …에 사족을 못쓰다, …이 없이는 못살아, …에 약해

A: She is the best looking girl at this club.
쟤는 이 클럽에서 가장 외모가 뛰어나.
B: **You're a sucker for** a hot dancer.
너 섹시한 댄서라면 사족을 못쓰잖아.

I'm a sucker for these Buicks.
난 이 뷰익차 없이는 못살아.

You always were a sucker for a hot dancer, weren't you, Sam?
샘, 넌 항상 섹시한 댄서엔 사족을 못썼잖아, 그지 않았어?

Does it involve candy? Because I'm a sucker for chocolates.
그거 캔디도 포함되나? 나 초콜렛에 사족을 못쓰잖아.

008 I have a weakness for younger women
난 젊은 여자라면 사족을 못써

미드표현

this indicates that the speaker is attracted to younger women much more than any other type of women. We can understand that he probably is more responsive when interacting with women who are under thirty years old. Another way to say this is "I am very fond of women who are younger"

| Point | have a weakness for~ …을 좋아하다, 사족을 못쓰다

A: Your new girlfriend is a total babe.
네 새 여친 정말 매력 덩어리야.
B: **I have a weakness for** younger women.
난 젊은 여자라면 사족을 못써.

It seems that she has some inexplicable weakness for Chris.
뭐라 설명할 수 없지만 걔는 크리스에게 사족을 못쓰는 것 같아.

She was so beautiful. I have a weakness for younger women.
걘 너무 아름다웠어. 난 젊은 여자라면 사족을 못써.

I was a croupier for forty years, and as you can see, I had a weakness for showgirls.
난 40년간 딜러였으니 니가 알다시피 쇼걸을 보면 난 사족을 못써.

009 You've got a soft spot for this guy 넌 이 사람을 좋아하지

this is a way to say the speaker thinks the listener favors a specific guy. Having a soft spot for someone means being more lenient and nice to that person.

I Point I have a soft spot for~ …에 사족을 못쓰다, …에 약하다

A: We can let Ralph join our committee.
우리는 랠프가 우리 위원회에 들어오게 할 수 있어.

B: **You've got a soft spot for** this guy.
넌 이 친구에게 약하구만.

It's not often that you meet a lawyer with a soft spot for cross-dressers.
복장도착자를 좋아하는 변호사를 만나기는 쉽지 않아.

The parents said that Tracy's always had a soft spot for Zack.
부모님에 따르면 트레이시는 잭을 항상 좋아했다고 그래.

No, don't tell me you've got a soft spot for this guy. 아냐, 넌 이 사람을 좋아한다는 것은 아니겠지.

010 It kinda grows on you 넌 그걸 점점 좋아하는구나

this expresses that something becomes better the more it is done. It often means that the speaker didn't like it at first, but grew to like it over time. We can say this in a similar way as "The more you do it, the more you'll enjoy it"

I Point I ~grow on sb …가 주어를 좋아하게 되다

A: Do you like eating Vietnamese food?
베트남 음식 먹는 걸 좋아해?

B: Yeah, **it kind of grows on** you.
어, 너 그거 점점 좋아하는구나.

I'm gonna grow on you. 넌 나를 좋아할거야.

Maybe it's starting to grow on me.
아마도 내가 그걸 좋아하기 시작할거야.

Come on, just give her a chance. Maybe she'll grow on you.
그러지말고, 걔한테 기회를 줘봐. 네가 걔를 좋아하게 될거야.

Despite our differences, you were beginning to grow on me.
우리 차이점에도 불구하고, 난 너를 좋아하기 시작했어.

011 He'll get a kick out of it 걘 그걸 무척 좋아할거야

this means that the speaker thinks someone will get special enjoyment from doing or seeing something specific. Whatever it is will be a special treat for that person. It is like saying "I'm sure he's really going to love this"

I Point I get a kick out of~ing[N] 무척 좋아하다, …로 기쁨을 맛보다
get a kick out of sb ~ing …가 …하는 것을 좋아하다
get one's kicks from …로 쾌감을 얻다

A: I got Louie this joke book for his birthday.
난 루이에게 생일선물로 이 유머집을 사줬어.

B: It's a perfect gift. **He'll get a kick out of it.**
정말 좋은 선물이다. 걘 그걸 무척 좋아할거야.

I thought you'd get a kick out of it.
난 네가 그걸 무척 좋아할거라 생각했어.

Don't worry about it. I'm getting a kick out of being here. 걱정하지마. 여기 있는게 아주 즐거워.

He got his kicks from inflicting pain on others.
걔는 다른 사람들에게 고통을 주는데 쾌감을 느껴.

012 I got a thing about this 난 이게 무척이나 좋아

usually this is a way for a speaker to say he is very interested in something. To have a thing for something means that the person has an unusually high amount of interest in it.

I Point I have [get] a thing about[for]~ (이유없이) 몹시 좋아하거나 싫어하다

A: Every time I see you, you talk about League of Legends. 너 볼 때마다, 너 리그오브레전드 얘기하더라.

B: Yeah, it's true. I **got a thing about** this game.
어, 그래. 나 이 게임을 엄청 좋아해.

You really have a thing about weddings, don't you? 너 결혼식 무척이나 좋아하지, 그지 않아?

Just stop it. This really freaks me out. I got a thing about this, OK?
그만해. 정말 섬뜩하다. 나 정말 이거 싫어하거든, 알았어?

Maybe she has a thing about sex offenders.
아마 걔는 이상하게도 성범죄자들에게 끌리나봐.

013 You get off on that psych stuff, don't you?

너 비과학적인 것들을 즐기는구나, 그렇지 않아?

미드표현

this can be somewhat unclear, but we can understand that it probably means that someone thinks using psychological techniques is very useful. Perhaps that person is a policeman using those techniques to catch a criminal. The speaker is asking "You enjoy using psychology, right?"

| Point | get off on 성적으로 흥분하다, 즐기다
get off (on) 풀려나다, (…의 이유로) 풀려나다, (…에서) 내리다

A: The suspect likely has a bad relationship with his mom. 용의자는 자기 엄마와 관계가 안좋을 것 같아.

B: You **get off on** that psych stuff, don't you?
너 심리학적인 기술들을 즐기는구나, 그렇지 않아?

You get off on that? Sniffing on the things of others? 너 그런 걸로 꼴려? 다른 사람들의 물건 냄새를 맡는데?

You get off on the brutal torture of others.
너 다른 사람들을 잔인하게 고문하는 것에 흥분하는구나.

Did I get off on the wrong floor?
내가 다른 층에 내렸나?

014 I'm not just big on Mexican food

난 멕시코 음식을 그다지 좋아하지 않아

미드표현

this is a simple way for the speaker to say he doesn't like Mexican food. If a person is not big on something, it is a polite way to say he dislikes it. We can say the same thing like this "I prefer not to eat Mexican food"

| Point | be big on sth[~ing] …를 무척 좋아하다, 무척 관심을 갖다

A: Why aren't you coming to the restaurant?
왜 식당에 오지 않는거야?

B: I'**m just not big on** Mexican food.
난 멕시코 음식을 그다지 좋아하지 않아.

Unfortunately, she was crazy. Not so big on taking medication.
안타깝게도 걔는 미쳤어. 약물을 먹을 정도는 아니고.

You know, my mother, she was big on pro bono surgeries.
저기, 우리 엄마는 무료수술에 무척 관심이 있으셨어.

Jessica is not big on eye contact, so don't be surprised if she doesn't look at you.
제시카는 눈마주치는 걸 좋아하지 않아, 그러니 걔가 널 쳐다보지 않아도 놀라지마.

015 Are you happy now? 이제 맘에 들어?, 만족하니?, 이제 됐어?

this indicates that the speaker has done a lot of work to satisfy someone, and he wants to know if that person is finally satisfied. It is like asking "Do you feel good now?"

A: I spent hours helping you arrange your furniture. **Are you happy now?**
네 가구 정리하는데 오랫동안 도와줬는데 이제 됐어?

B: No, I think there are several things that still need to be moved around. 아니, 아직 이동해야 될 게 몇 개 더 있어.

I'm a bad mother! Are you happy now?
난 못된 엄마다! 이제 됐냐?

You kicked Dad in the ass! Are you happy now? 아버지의 엉덩이를 걷어차다니! 이제 만족하니?

That's great. Are you happy now?
잘됐네. 이제 맘에 드니?

016 I'm not happy about this 만족 못하겠어, 불만이야

미드표현

this is a way to say "I feel upset." It is expressing that the speaker is unhappy about some situation

| Point | be happy with[about] …에 만족하다

A: My boss said I have to work all weekend. **I'm not happy about this.** 사장이 주말내내 일해야 된대. 정말 싫어.

B: Didn't he give you any choice in the matter?
그 건으로 네게 선택권을 주지 않았지?

Quite frankly, we're not happy about it.
솔직히 말해서 우린 그거에 만족 못해.

He's not happy with the result.
걔는 결과에 만족 못하고 있어.

You're not happy with me, are you?
나한테 불만이라 이거지?

017 (It's) Better than nothing 없는 것보단 낫네

this indicates that although the result may not be what was expected, it was not bad. In other words "I think this could have been worse"

| Point | can't be better than this 이것보다는 좋을 순 없어
There's none better 아주 좋아

A: We worked hard all day and all we got paid was $20. 종일 일하고 겨우 20달러 받았어.

B: Come on, cheer up. **It's better than nothing.**
자, 기운내. 없는 것 보다 낫네.

미드표현

Something's better than nothing.
좀 있는게 없는 것보단 나아.

But there's a chance. it's better than nothing.
찬스는 있어. 없는 것보다 낫잖아.

Well, minimum wage is better than nothing.
최소 임금이 없는거 보다는 나아.

018 I hate your guts 정말 너 싫어

this is a way to say "I really don't like you. The speaker wants to express a very strong dislike for someone

| Point | hate one's guts 정말 싫어하다, 증오하다

A: Why do you always treat me so mean?
왜 날 그렇게 비열하게 대하는 거야?

B: Because you are garbage. **I hate your guts.**
왜냐면 넌 쓰레기니까. 네가 정말 넌더리가 나.

미드표현

I hate your guts, you idiot! 네가 정말 싫어! 이 머저리야!

He's going to hate your guts. 걔가 정말 너 싫어할거야.

I was going to say I still pretty much hate your guts, Mike.
마이크, 난 아직 너를 증오한다고 말하려고 했어.

019 He always has it in for me 걘 늘 나를 미워해

the speaker is saying that a person dislikes him and does things to try to make his life more difficult. This means "He tries to cause problems for me"

| Point | A have it in for B A가 B를 싫어해

A: Our supervisor has given you another difficult assignment. 우리 감독관은 네게 또 다른 어려운 과제를 줬어.

B: I know. **He has it in for me.** 알아. 걘 늘 날 싫어해.

미드표현

Your boss has it in for you. 네 사장은 널 싫어해.

The president has it in for his enemies.
사장은 자신의 적들을 미워해.

Dan has it in for the man who hurt him.
댄은 자신을 해코지 한 사람들을 싫어해.

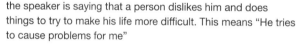

020 That's not my thing 난 그런 건 질색이야, 내 관심사 밖이야, 내 취향이 아니야

this indicates "I don't like to do that." It is a way to say that something is not enjoyed by the speaker, or he has no talent for it

| Point | That's not my cup of tea 내 취향이 아냐
It isn't to my taste 내 취향이 아냐
That's not my dish 그런 건 나와는 거리가 멀어
It's just not my field 그건 정말 내 분야가 아니야

A: Have you ever tried snowboarding? 스노우보딩 해봤어?

B: Yeah, but **that's not my thing.** 어, 하지만 내 취향이 아냐.

미드표현

I don't drink whiskey. That's not my thing.
난 위스키를 안 마셔. 내 취향이 아냐.

You have pets? Sorry, but that's not my thing.
애완동물 기른다고? 미안, 내 관심사밖이야.

Why do I have to do this? I'm not a public speaker. It's not my thing.
내가 왜 이렇게 해야 돼? 난 대중연설가가 아냐. 그런 건 질색이야.

021 I've seen better 별로던데, 그저 그래

this is usually said to indicate that the speaker has witnessed something nicer or of higher quality. It is a way to express "That is not as nice as other things"

| Point | I've seen worse 아직은 괜찮은 편이야
I've seen better days 별로였어

A: How did you feel about last night's concert?
지난 밤 콘서트 어때?

B: To be honest, **I've seen better.** 솔직히 말해서, 별로였어.

It's a nice house, but I've seen better.
멋진 집이기는 하지만 그저 그래.

I don't like this painting. I've definitely seen better. 이 그림은 맘에 안들어. 평범하거든.

A: Nice day, isn't it? B: I've seen better.
A: 좋은 날이지, 그지 않아? B: 그저 그래.

022 I wouldn't be caught dead~ …는 절대로[죽어도] 하지 않겠어

this means "I would never..." The speaker is saying strongly that he wouldn't do something

A: I just love some of the fashions made by Gucci.
구치 패션 중에서 좀 좋아하는 게 있어.

B: Are you kidding? **I wouldn't be caught dead** in a Gucci dress! 정말야? 난 구치 옷은 절대 안 입을거야!

She always said she's never be caught dead in red. 걘 항상 붉은 옷을 절대로 입지 않을 거라고 말했어.

I wouldn't be caught dead at that meeting.
난 그 회의에 절대로 가지 않을 거야.

I wouldn't be caught dead in those bras.
난 그런 브라자는 하지 않을 거야.

023 I can't wait to~ 지금 당장이라고 …을 하고 싶어

this means "I really want to..." It means the speaker is very excited and happy to do something

| Point | can't wait to = be eager to = be dying to 몹시 …하고 싶다

A: **I can't wait to** go to Laurie's house tonight.
오늘 밤에 로리네 정말 가고 싶어.

B: I know. She always cooks such good food.
알아. 걘 언제나 요리를 무척 잘해.

I can't wait to tell you this.
당장 네게 이 얘기를 해주고 싶어.

I just can't wait to be married to you.
너랑 당장이라도 결혼하고 싶어.

I can't wait for you to try this.
네가 빨리 이것을 했으면 해.

I can't wait for that day. 그 날이 빨리 왔으면 좋겠어.

I can't wait till I'm old enough to move out of here. 빨리 커서 독립했으면 좋겠어.

024 I'm dying to know 알고 싶어 죽겠어

this is a way of say of saying that the speaker really wants to find out about something. In other words "I would like information on that"

| Point | have been dying to do~ 몹시 …하고 싶어해왔다

A: **I'm dying to** know what happened on Pam and Tom's date. 팜과 탐의 데이트가 어떻게 됐는지 알고 싶어 죽겠어.

B: You mean she hasn't called you and told you yet? 걔가 아직 전화해서 말하지 않았단 말야?

Bring your girlfriend. I'm dying to meet her.
애인 좀 데려와. 보고 싶어 죽겠어.

I have 3 different people dying to marry me.
나랑 결혼 못해서 죽겠다는 사람이 세 명야.

Truth is I was dying to sleep with him.
사실은 내가 걔랑 자고 싶어 죽겠었어.

025 I'm willing to do that 기꺼이 그걸 하고 싶어

this is a way for the speaker to say "I'll do it." The speaker is saying he can do some type of activity

| Point | be willing to~ 기꺼이 …하다

A: If you join the basketball team, you will have to exercise every day. 농구팀에 들어가면 매일 운동해야 돼.

B: **I'm willing to do that.** I really want to be on the team. 정말 그러고 싶어. 정말 팀에 들어가고 싶어.

I wasn't willing to take a risk so I put it in a bank. 모험은 전혀 하기 싫어서 은행에 넣어두었어.

You weren't willing to do that? 그걸 하고 싶은 마음이 없었단 말야?

I am willing to make that sacrifice. 기꺼이 내가 그 희생을 하겠어.

026 I could do with a beer 맥주를 마시고 싶어

this can simply indicate that the speaker wants alcohol. It can also mean that the speaker has had a stressful day and is asking for a beer to help him relax. In other words, "I need a beer to make myself feel better"

| Point | I could do with~(I'd like~) …을 하고 싶어
What I could do with~ ? …가 있으면 얼마나 좋을까?

A: You look like you had a rough day. 오늘 힘들었나 보네.

B: Yeah, it sucked. **I could do with** a beer. 어, 지랄같았어. 맥주마시고 싶다.

I could do with a cognac. 코냑을 마시고 싶어.

Oh, my God. What I could do with this house. 맙소사. 이 집을 가질 수 있다면 좋겠어.

Boy, what I could do with a car like this. 어휴, 이런 차를 가질 수 있다면 얼마나 좋을까.

027 I'd love to~ …을 하고 싶어

this expresses that the speaker would really enjoy doing something. It is similar to saying "I'd enjoy..."

| Point | I'd like to! 좋아!, 그러고 싶어!

A: **I'd love to** have a big meal of steak and lobster right now. 스테이크와 가재가 나오는 식사를 하고 싶어.

B: Yeah, but where would you get the money to pay for it? 그래, 하지만 그거 지불할 돈이 어디 있어?

I'd love to have sex with him, but I'm not sure I'm ready yet. 난 걔랑 섹스를 하고 싶지만 난 아직 준비가 안된 것 같아.

I'd love to get a policeman's opinion on that. 난 그거에 대한 경찰관의 의견을 듣고 싶어.

Well, sure, I'd love to hang out with you. Come on over. 물론, 난 너랑 놀고 싶어. 어서 와.

028 I'm really looking forward to this 정말 무척 기대하고 있어

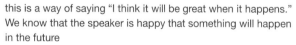

this is a way of saying "I think it will be great when it happens." We know that the speaker is happy that something will happen in the future

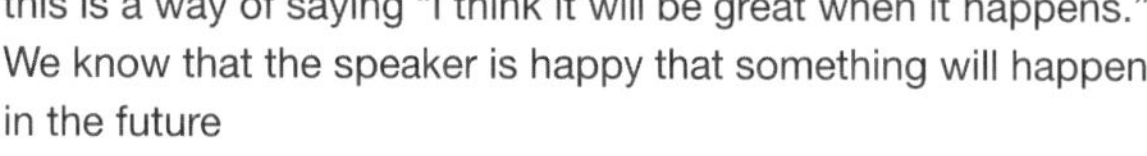

| Point | look forward to+N/ ~ing …을 학수고대하다
I'm looking forward to A ~ing A가 …하기를 학수고대하고 있어

A: Well, today is the day that we'll finally graduate from high school. 자, 오늘은 드디어 고등학교 졸업하는 날야.

B: **I'm really looking forward to this.** I want to enter university next year. 정말 기다렸어. 내년에 대학가고 싶어.

Looking forward to working with you. 너랑 함께 무척 일하고 싶어.

I thought you were looking forward to this trip. 난 네가 이번 여행을 무척 기다리는 줄 알았어.

These are some friends of mine looking forward to getting to know you. 너랑 만나고 싶어 안달이 난 내 친구들이 몇 있어.

029 You up for it? 하고 싶어?, 같이 할래?

미드표현

this asks if someone would like to do something that was suggested. It is similar to asking "Are you ready to do it?"

| Point | be up for …을 하고 싶다, …을 의도하다

A: We're planning to take a long hike on Sunday. **You up for it?** 일요일 장시간 하이킹할 예정야. 같이 갈래?

B: No, I don't think so. I've been feeling tired lately. 아니, 안돼. 요즘 피곤해서.

I don't think I'm up for it. 별로 생각이 없어.

I'm just not up for it right now. 지금은 그걸 하고 싶지 않아.

I'm not going. I'm not up for it. 난 안가. 별 생각이 없어.

030 I wanna do it right 이거 지금 하고 싶어

미드표현

the speaker is indicating that he wants to do a good job on some work he must finish. It is like saying "I hope to do it correctly"

| Point | I wanna do this now 지금 이걸 하고 싶어

A: You can finish up that report in about an hour or so. 한 시간 전후에서 이 보고서를 끝내.

B: No, it will take longer. **I want to do a good job on it.** 안돼요. 시간이 더 걸려요. 제대로 하고 싶은 걸요.

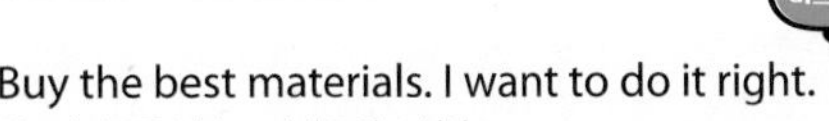

Buy the best materials. I want to do it right. 최고의 재료를 사라고. 제대로 하고 싶어.

I want to do it right. Let's take our time. 난 제대로 그걸 하고 싶어. 시간을 갖고 하자고.

I am careful because I want to do it right. 난 그걸 제대로 하고 싶기 때문에 조심스러워.

031 All I want to do is~ 내가 원하는 것은 …하는 거야

미드표현

this is a way of saying "The main activity for me is..." The speaker is telling people what he thinks is important to do

| Point | What I wanna do is~ 내가 하고 싶은 것은 …이야

A: What do you plan to do after graduating? 졸업 후에 뭐할 거야?

B: **All I want to do is** find a job with a great salary. 내가 원하는 건 단지 급여가 좋은 직장을 찾는 거야.

All I wanna do is tell you that I love you. 내가 바라는 건 사랑한다고 네게 말하는 거야.

All I wanna do right now is go to New York. 지금 내가 하고 싶은 건 뉴욕에 가는 거야.

What I wanna do right now actually is take you to the doctor. 내가 지금 당장 하고 싶은 건 널 병원에 데려가는 거야.

032 I have a taste for danger 난 모험을 즐겨

미드표현

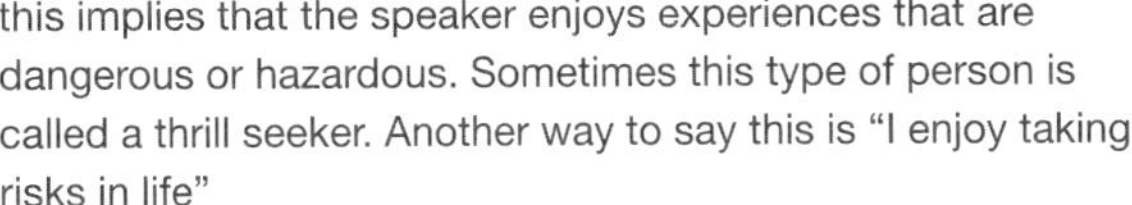

this implies that the speaker enjoys experiences that are dangerous or hazardous. Sometimes this type of person is called a thrill seeker. Another way to say this is "I enjoy taking risks in life"

| Point | have a taste for~ …을 좋아하다, …을 보는 눈이 있다
have a taste of~ 음식 등을 조금 맛보다

A: Why do you choose to ride motorcycles and go skydiving? 넌 왜 오토바이를 타고 스카이다이빙을 하는거야?

B: I love that stuff. **I have a taste for** danger. 난 그런게 좋아. 모험을 즐기거든.

I have a taste for danger. 난 모험을 좋아해.

One of my exes had a taste for fine jewelry. 내 전 애인 중 한 명이 보석류를 보는 눈이 있어.

The guests had a taste of a different culture. 손님들은 문화적 기호가 다양했어.

033 I don't want to get in the way 방해되고 싶지 않아

this expresses that the speaker doesn't want to slow down someone who is working. It means "I don't want to cause you to work less"

| Point | get[be, stand] in the way of …에 방해가 되다

A: Are you helping Andrew build his house?
너 앤드류가 집 짓는거 도와주고 있어?

B: A little bit. **I don't want to get in the way,** so I mostly watch the work. 조금. 방해될까 구경만 했어.

Don't pay attention to me. I don't want to get in the way. 나한테 신경쓰지마. 방해가 되고 싶지 않아.

I don't want to get in the way. I'll stand off to the side. 방해가 되고 싶지 않아. 옆쪽으로 비켜 서 있을게.

Do you want me here? I don't want to get in the way. 내가 필요하다고? 난 방해가 되고 싶지 않은데.

034 I will have my way 내 방식대로 살겠어, 내 좋은대로 살거야

this is a way of saying "I'm going to do it using my method." It expresses that the speaker plans to do things without thinking about what other people think or want

| Point | I'm going on my way 내 갈 길을 가야지
I'll do it your way 네 방식대로 할게(do one's way …의 방식대로 하다)

A: Have you thought about the opinions of Sue and Ted? 수와 테드의 의견에 대해 생각해봤어?

B: Not really. **I will have my own way** on this project. 아니. 이 프로젝트는 내 방식대로 할거야.

We have our ways. 우린 우리 식이 있어.

Damn, you're right. Okay, we'll do it your way.
제기랄, 네가 맞아. 좋아, 네 방식대로 할게.

If my way doesn't work, then we'll do it your way. 내 방식이 안 들으면 네 방식대로 할게.

035 I'd rather~ 차라리 …할거야

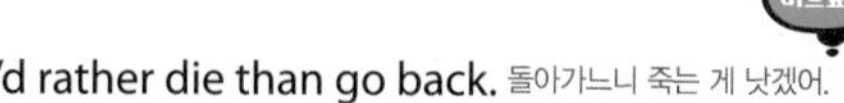

this expresses "I like this better." It shows that the speaker favors one thing more than another thing

| Point | I'd rather not 안하는 게 낫겠어
I'd rather not do 차라리 …하지 않는 게 낫겠어
I'd rather A than B A하기 보다는 차라리 B하겠어
I'd rather S+V …하지 않는 게 좋겠어

A: **I'd rather** have fun than make a lot of money.
돈을 많이 벌기 보다는 차라리 재미있는게 나아.

B: Don't forget that money can be very important in life. 돈이 인생에서 매우 중요하다는 걸 잊지마.

I'd rather die than go back. 돌아가느니 죽는 게 낫겠어.

Believe me, I'd rather follow the evidence.
정말이야, 증거를 믿는 게 나아.

I'd rather not say. 말 안하는 게 낫겠어.

I'd rather you didn't. 그러지 않는 게 낫겠어.

036 I'd kill for this job 이 일만 할 수 있다면 뭐든지 하겠어

this indicates the speaker wants to work somewhere very much. It's a way to express "I really want this job"

| Point | would kill for+N …을 얻기 위해서 무슨 일이라도 하겠다,
…한다면 소원이 없겠어

A: The offices of this company are very impressive.
이 회사의 사무실은 매우 인상적이야.

B: I know it. **I'd kill for** this job.
알고 있어. 여기서 일할 수만 있다면 뭐든지 하겠어.

I'd kill for a cold beer right now.
지금 당장 시원한 맥주를 마실 수 있다면 소원이 없겠다.

I'd kill for a chance to sleep a few hours.
몇시간 잘 수 있는 기회가 있다면 소원이 없겠어.

Hey, uh, morphine's cool, but I'd kill for something to eat.
야, 모르핀도 좋지만, 뭐 좀 먹을게 있으면 좋겠어.

037 It'd be nice if~ …한다면 좋을텐데

this is used to say the speaker would prefer something to happen. It means "I'd like it if..."

Point I just thought it'd be nice if S+V …하면 얼마나 좋을까 그냥 생각해봤어
It'll be nice to~ …하면 멋질거야

A: **It'd be nice if** the sun came out and the temperature was warm. 태양이 비춰 온도가 올라가면 좋을텐데.
B: Well, maybe the weather will improve a bit this afternoon. 음, 오후에 날씨가 좀 좋아질거야.

It'd be nice if you visited your grandmother. 네가 네 할머니를 방문한다면 좋을텐데.
It'd be nice if you attended the wedding. 네가 결혼식에 참석한다면 좋을텐데.
It'd be nice if the weather was sunny tomorrow. 내일 날씨가 맑으면 좋을텐데.

038 If only I could~ …할 수 있다면 좋을 텐데

this is a way of wishing for something, especially if it is something that is difficult to get. It is like saying "I really wish I could..."

A: **If only I could** get into Harvard University, I would be happy. 하바드에 들어갈 수 있다면 행복할텐데.
B: But I think it's pretty stressful to study there. 하지만 거기서 공부하는게 꽤 스트레스 받을텐데.

If only I could be sure. 확실하다면 좋을 텐데.
If only I could put into words how I feel. 내 느낌을 말로 표현할 수 있으면 좋을 텐데.
If only I could've controlled the weather. 내가 날씨를 조종할 수 있다면 좋을 텐데.

039 I wish~ …면 좋을 텐데

this is a way to say "I'd like it if S+V." Usually it expresses a sadness or unhappiness over something that happened

Point I wish I had …였으면 좋을 텐데

A: **I wish** he hadn't asked me out on a date. 걔가 데이트 신청 안했더라면 좋을 텐데.
B: What's the matter? Don't you think you'll have a good time? 뭐가 문제야? 좋은 시간 보낼거라고 생각되지 않아?

I wish we were together. 우리가 함께면 좋을 텐데.
I wish I hadn't asked. 내가 묻지 않았더라면 좋을 텐데.
I wish I'd said that. 그 얘기를 내가 했더라면 좋을 텐데.

040 Hopefully! 바라건대!, 그랬음 좋겠어!

like the phrase above, this indicates that the speaker wishes that something will happen. It means "It would be great if that happened"

Point I hope so 그러면 좋겠어, 그래야지
I hope not 그러지 말았으면 좋겠다

A: Are you going to get married soon? 곧 결혼할거야?
B: **Hopefully.** I plan to propose to my girlfriend tonight. 그랬음 좋겠어. 오늘 밤에 여친에게 결혼신청하려고.

Hopefully she won't need any more surgery. 바라건대 걔가 수술을 더 안 받았으면 좋겠어.
Hopefully, John's making some progress. 바람직하게도 존의 일이 좀 진척이 있어.

041 I hope you like it 마음에 들기 바래

this is used to say "I want you to enjoy this." It is said when someone gives a gift and wishes that it will be thought of as nice

A: Wow! You gave me a really nice necklace for my birthday. 와! 내 생일이라고 정말 멋진 목걸이를 주네.

B: It took a long time for me to find it. **I hope you like it.** 찾는데 시간 많이 걸렸어. 맘에 들기 바래.

미드표현

A: Thank you for the gift you sent on my birthday. B: Oh, it was my pleasure. I hope you like it.
A: 내 생일에 보내준 선물 고마워. B: 뭘 그런 걸 가지고. 네 맘에 들었으면 좋겠다.

I hope you like tuna fish sandwiches, 'cause that's all we got.
참치 샌드위치 마음에 들기 바래. 그게 가진 거 전부거든

042 That's all I ask 내가 바라는 건 그 뿐이야

this is a way to say the speaker has only one request that he wants to make. It is like saying "This is the one thing I'd like"

A: Please be quiet so I can sleep. **That's all I ask.**
좀 자게 조용히 해줘. 내가 바라는 건 그뿐야.

B: But I have my friends here and we are having a good time. 하지만 친구들하고 재미난 시간 보내고 있는데.

미드표현

I don't want you to meet my daughter again, never! That's all I ask.
내 딸을 다시는 만나지 마! 내가 바라는 건 그뿐이야.

Just one minute. That's all I ask.
아주 잠깐만. 내가 바라는 건 그것 뿐이야.

Think about it. That's all I ask.
그거 생각해봐. 내가 바라는 건 그 뿐이야.

043 I'm hoping for the best 잘 되길 빌고 있어

this means "I want the result to be good." It shows the speaker wishes that a good thing will happen

I Point I hope for the best 어려운 역경 속에서도 잘 되기를 기대하다
God willing 사정이 허락한다면(I hope it happens)

A: Have you gotten the results from your exam back yet? 시험결과 나왔어?

B: No, not yet. **I'm hoping for the best** with the results. 아니, 아직. 잘 나오길 바래.

미드표현

We're hoping for the best but preparing for the worst. 잘되기를 바라지만 최악도 준비하고 있어.

We wait for the storm to pass hoping for the best. 무사하길 바라면서 태풍이 지나가길 기다리고 있어.

044 Not if I can help it 할 수만 있다면 피하고 싶어

this is a way of saying that the speaker will try to stop something from happening. In other words "I'll prevent it if I can"

A: I heard that a factory is supposed to be built in your neighborhood. 공장이 네집 주변에 건설될거래.

B: **Not if I can help it.** A factory would make everything here really dirty. 할 수만 있다면 피하고 싶어. 공장이 들어서면 이곳이 다 정말 더러워질텐데.

미드표현

He said he'll steal the money, but not if I can help it.
걘 자기가 돈을 훔칠거라고 말했지만 나야 왜 그런 짓을 하겠어.

I won't let her run away. Not if I can help it.
걔가 도망못가게 할거야. 내가 왜 그렇게 하겠어.

Not if I can help it. There's no way I'll allow it.
내가 왜 그렇게 하겠어. 난 절대로 그걸 허락하지 않을거야.

MEMO

Ways of talking about things that someone is interested in

함께 하거나 혹은 상관이 있거나 없거나

I'm in on it

001 That's interesting 흥미롭네

this is a way to say "It makes me curious." We can understand that the speaker wants to know more about something

| Point | (That) Sounds interesting 흥미롭네

A: These are very old items that were found in China. 이것들은 중국에서 발견된 오래된 것들이야.

B: **That's interesting.** What were they used for? 흥미롭구만. 어디에 쓰던 거야?

미드표현

Well, that's interesting because according to his phone records, he never called the cops. 흥미롭네, 왜냐하면 기록에 의하면 갠 경찰에 전화한 적이 없거든.

Wow. That's interesting. You've fallen in love with a woman. 와, 흥미롭네. 네가 여자와 사랑에 빠졌구나.

You're lying to me, that's interesting. 넌 내게 거짓말하고 있어, 흥미롭구만.

002 I'm not interested in that 그거에 관심없어

this is a way to express that the speaker doesn't want to know about something. It is like saying "I don't need to hear about that"

| Point | I'm not interested in+N/~ing …에 관심이 없어
What are you interested in? 무슨 일에 흥미가 있어?
What are your interests? 뭐에 흥미있어?

A: It's nice to meet you. **What are your interests?** 만나서 반가워. 뭐에 흥미있어?

B: Well, I like computer games and I do a lot of chatting on the Internet. 컴퓨터겜 좋아하고 채팅많이 해.

미드표현

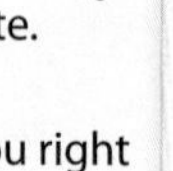

I'm not interested in going out on a date. 데이트에 흥미가 없어.

I'm really not interested in talking to you right now. 정말이지 지금 너랑 얘기하기 싫어.

Tell me more about yourself. What are your interests? 너 얘기 좀 더 해봐. 뭐에 흥미있어 해?

003 I'm in on it 난 알고 있어, 난 관련되어 있어

this means that the speaker knows about something, or is a part of it. It is a way to say "That's something I know about" or "That's something I'm involved with"

| Point | be in on …에 관련되어 있다

A: Have you heard about the new club that is being started? 새롭게 시작하는 클럽에 대해 들어봤어?

B: Yeah, **I'm in on it.** It was formed by my friends. 어, 나도 일원이야. 내 친구들이 만들었어.

미드표현

There is a scam going on, and I'm in on it. 사기사건이 벌어지고 있는데 나도 관련되어 있어.

If you want to play poker, I'm in on it. 포커치고 싶으면 나도 할게.

Have you heard about the new blog? I'm in on it. 새로운 블로그에 관한 소식들었어? 나도 관련되어 있어.

004 I got hooked on TV TV에 중독됐어

this indicates the person watches a lot of TV, maybe more than most people. It is a way to say "I like to watch TV a lot"

| Point | hooked = addicted 중독된 get hooked on …에 중독되다
get sb hooked on …을 …에 중독시키다

A: **I got hooked on** TV. Now I stay at home every night to watch different programs. TV에 중독됐어. 매일 저녁 집에서 여러 프로그램을 봐.

B: I think you need some healthier habits in your life. 인생에서 좀 더 건강한 습관을 가져야 될 것 같아.

미드표현

Nicole got hooked on drugs. 니콜은 약물에 중독됐어.

She's gotten really hooked on Age of Conan, she's playing non-stop. 걘 Age of Conan에 정말 중독됐어. 쉬지 않고 게임을 해.

Her parents ignored her and her boyfriend got her hooked on drugs. 부모님은 걔한테 무관심했고 남친은 걔를 약물에 중독시켰어.

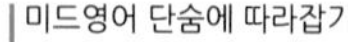

005 I'm into this stuff 이런 걸 정말 좋아해, 요새 이거에 빠졌어

this expresses "I enjoy this." We can understand that the speaker likes something he is talking about very much, especially in the case of a hobby

Point be into something …에 열중하다, 심취하다
be into somebody …에 푹 빠져있다

A: Why do you have so many pictures of airplanes and helicopters? 왜 그렇게 비행기와 헬리콥터 그림을 많이 갖고 있어?

B: **I'm into this stuff.** I really want to be a pilot when I get older. 이런 거 정말 좋아해. 나이들면 파일럿이 되고 싶어.

I'm not into it. 그런 건 안 해요.

I had no idea you are into this stuff.
이런 걸 좋아하는지 몰랐군.

You're not telling me you're into this stuff?
이런 걸 좋아한다고 말 안했잖아?

I'm so into you. 난 너한테 푹 빠져 있어.

006 I'm intrigued 흥미로와

this is a way for the speaker to say "It makes me curious." He is saying he is very interested or wants to know more about something

A: Did you go to the lecture about ancient Egypt?
고대이집트 강의 들으러 갔어?

B: Yes I did. **I'm intrigued** by the pyramids that they built. 어 그랬어. 이집트인이 세운 피라미드가 흥미로와.

Are you intrigued? 흥미로와?

I'd be lying if I said I wasn't intrigued.
내가 흥미롭지 않았다고 하면 거짓말이지.

I'm intrigued. Continue. 흥미롭구만. 계속해봐.

Now I'm intrigued. Tell me more.
흥미롭구만. 더 얘기해봐.

007 Are you in? 너도 할래?, 너도 낄래?

미드표현

this is a way of asking if someone wants to be part of something. It means "Are you joining us?"

Point I'm in 나 할게 = I will do it
You're in 너도 하자
You game? 너도 할래?
Are you game? 할 생각 있어?
You want in? 들어올래?

A: Our card game will start at 10 pm tonight. **Are you in?** 카드게임 오후 10시에 할거야. 너도 할래?

B: Sure I am. I really enjoy playing cards with you.
그래. 너랑 카드게임 하고 싶어.

I'll be there. Just let me know when and where. I'm in. 나도 갈게. 장소하고 시간 알려줘. 나도 갈 테니까.

Nina's out. You're in. You are our new member.
니나가 그만뒀어. 네가 들어와. 넌 신입멤버가 되는 거야.

I'm in if you're in. 네가 하면 나도 할게.

Things have changed. I want in.
상황이 변했어. 난 낄래.

008 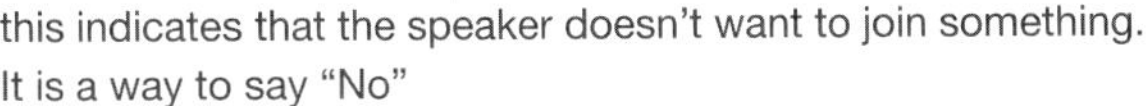 (You can) Count me out! 난 빠져!

미드표현

this indicates that the speaker doesn't want to join something. It is a way to say "No"

Point (You can) Count me in 나도 끼워줘
Leave me out of it 난 빠져

A: We're planning to go out and have a few drinks after we stop working. 그만하고 나가 술 좀 하려고.

B: **You can count me out.** My wife gets angry when I drink too much. 난 빠져. 술 많이 마시면 아내가 화내.

I've done enough today already, so count me out. 난 오늘 충분히 할 것 했으니 난 빠져.

Well, you can count me out. I won't face a girl when I ditch her.
난 빠져. 여자를 찰 때 난 보면서 하지 않을거야.

Count me out! I don't want to break the law.
난 빠져! 난 범법행위를 하고 싶지 않아.

009 (You) Mind if I join you? 내가 껴도 돼?

this asks if someone can sit down with one person, or enter a group of people and talk or do whatever they are doing. Another way to say this is "Can I be a part of this group?"

Point Care if I join you? 내가 껴도 돼?
Care to join me? 함께 갈래?
May[Can] I join you? 합석해도 될까?, 끼어도 되겠어?

A: How are you doing? **Do you mind if I join you?**
잘 지내? 내가 껴도 돼?

B: Well, I was waiting for my boyfriend and he'll be here soon. 음, 남친기다리고 있는데 곧 올거야.

Oh, are we drinking? I'll join you.
어, 술마시는 거야? 함께 가자.

Okay, then let me join you. 그래 그럼 같이 가자.

I thought I might join you. Is that okay?
너랑 같이 같이 가도 될 것 같아. 괜찮겠어?

Join me, won't you? 같이 가자, 그럴래?

010 He was out of the picture 걘 더 이상 관심의 대상이 아냐

this means "He wasn't considered important anymore." We can understand that the person was not around much after time passed

Point be out of the picture 고려대상이 아니어서 관심에서 제외하다

A: After he lost his job, **Josh was out of the picture.** 직장을 잃은 후 조쉬는 관심대상이 아니었다.

B: That's too bad. Do you know what he is doing these days? 안됐네. 요즘 뭐하는지 알아?

Why are we still talking about him? He hurt her. He's out of the picture.
왜 아직 걔 얘길하는 거야? 걘 걔한테 아프게 했어. 말 꺼내지도 말자.

Scott's out of the picture. He's left out in the cold. 스캇 얘긴 하지 말자. 걘 왕따야.

I want Mona out of the picture.
모나를 더 이상 언급하지 말자.

011 I got your number 네 속셈을 알겠어, 네 의중을 알았어

This is a way for the speaker to say that he understands a person's intentions and the reasons why he is doing something. We can understand that the person may be trying to do something that is not good or not fair. Another way to say this is "I know what you are up to."

A: I see you cheating. **I've got your number.**
네가 컨닝하는 것 봤어. 네 속셈 알았어.

B: I'm only doing it so I can pass this test.
이번 시험 통과하려고 그렇게 하는 거야.

I got your number and I'll be watching you closely. 네 속셈을 알겠어. 널 자세히 지켜보고 있겠어.

Don't think you can trick me. I got your number. 날 속일 수 있다고 생각마. 네 속셈을 알거든.

I got your number. You'd better behave yourself. 네 속셈을 알아. 행동 조심하라고.

012 (It's) None of your business 남 일에 신경쓰지마, 참견마, 네 알바 아니야

this is a way to tell people that they are being impolite and that they should not try to find out about private things

Point That's really my business 그건 정말 내 일이야
Keep[Get] your nose out of my business 내일에 참견하지마

A: Who did you go out with last night?
지난 밤에 누구랑 데이트했어?

B: **It's none of your business.** 네 알 바 아니야.

That's none of your business. But it is my business. 남일에 신경꺼. 이건 내 일이야.

My experience with women is none of your business. 내 여성편력은 네가 알 바 아니야.

I can't talk to you about this. This is none of your business. So just please just stay out of this. 그 얘기는 해줄 수 없어. 참견 마. 그러니 끼어들지 말라고.

013 Mind your own business! 상관마!, 신경꺼!, 네 일이나 신경써!

this means someone is trying to become involved in something that is private. It is a way of saying "Go away because this has nothing to do with you"

| Point | (I'm just) Minding my own business 내 일에 신경쓰는 거야

A: I think that Melanie is having personal problems. 멜라니에게 개인적인 문제가 있는 것 같아.

B: **Mind your own business.** I like Melanie. 상관마. 내가 멜라니 좋아하니까.

미드표현

Why can't you mind your own business? What is your problem? 왜 신경을 못 끄는 거야? 문제가 뭐야?

I'm sitting in the lounge minding my own business. 라운지에 앉아서 내 일에 신경쓰고 있어.

I'll thank you to mind your own business. 남의 일에 참견 말아줬으면 좋겠어.

014 Not my problem 상관없어, 내 알 바 아니지

this is said to indicate "I don't care." The speaker is saying he doesn't want to be involved with something

A: The bathroom in this place is really dirty. 여기 화장실은 정말 더러워.

B: **Not my problem.** Harry is supposed to clean it. 상관없어. 해리가 청소하기로 되어 있어.

미드표현

It's not my business. Not my problem. 내가 간섭할 일이 아니야. 상관없어.

It's not my problem. It's yours. 내 알 바 아냐. 네 문제지.

I'm sorry but, that's really not my problem. 미안하지만 그건 내 문제가 아니야.

015 Stay out of this! 끼어들지마!

this is a way to tell someone to go away and not interfere with private things. It is used to tell someone "Don't get involved"

| Point | You stay out of it! 넌 끼어 들지마!
Keep out of this! 당신 일 아니니까 끼어들지마!
Stay out of my way! 비켜!, 방해하지마!

A: I think you should spend more time with your family. 넌 가족과 더 많은 시간을 보내야 돼.

B: **Stay out of this!** I don't need advice. 끼어들지마! 네 조언은 필요없어.

미드표현

Tammy, stay out of this. It's none of your business. 태미야 끼어들지 마. 네 일이 아니야.

I asked you to stay out of this. 끼어들지 말라고 말했는데.

Chris, I told you before to stay out of this. 크리스, 내가 전에 끼어들지 말라고 했는데.

016 He just horned in on the girl I wanted to date
걘 내가 데이트하고픈 애와 데이트를 하려고 해

this is expressing that someone intruded when the speaker planned to ask a girl on a date, and that person likely asked the girl out himself. The speaker is probably angry, and he thinks the person had bad manners to do this type of thing. It is like saying "He moved in on that girl before I could ask her out"

| Point | horn in on (말리는데도) 참견하다, 관련되다

A: Why are you so angry at Simon tonight? 너 오늘 밤 사이몬에게 왜 그렇게 화난거야?

B: **He just horned in on** the girl I wanted to date. 내가 데이프하고픈 애와 데이트를 하려고 했잖아.

미드표현

I wasn't trying to horn in on your business. 네 사업에 참견하려고 하는게 아니었어.

Please, Gale, stop trying to horn in on my new friends. 게일 내 새로운 친구들에게 끼어들려고 하지마.

He horned in on their private dinner. 걔는 그들의 사적인 저녁식사에 끼어들었어.

017 Don't you get in the middle of us! 우리 일에 끼어들지마!

this is warning someone that it could cause problems if he gets involved. It is like saying "keep out of this"

| Point | I don't want to get in the middle of anything
난 어떤 일에도 끼어들고 싶지 않아

A: Look guys, try to calm down. OK? 얘들아, 진정해. 알았어?
B: **Don't you get in the middle of us!**
우리 일에 끼어들지마!

I just don't wanna get in the middle of something so complicated.
너무 복잡한 일에는 끼어들고 싶지 않아.

I don't want to get in the middle of it.
난 거기에 끼어들고 싶지 않아.

Please don't butt in. You'll get yourself in trouble. 끼어들지마. 네가 곤란해질거야.

018 I want no part of it 난 그 일에 관여하고 싶지 않아

this is said when a person wants to say he absolutely does not want to participate in something. It is common to use this expression when someone disapproves of an activity, or thinks it is wrong. It is another way to say, "No, I refuse to be involved"

| Point | want no part of ~ …에 관여하고 싶지 않다
have no part of~ …에 관여하지 않다

A: If you help us steal computer passwords, we can get rich.
우리가 컴퓨터 비밀번호 훔치는걸 네가 도와주면 우린 부자가 될거야.
B: That's not something I'd do. **I want no part of it.** 난 그런 일 하지 않아. 그 일에 관여하고 싶지 않아.

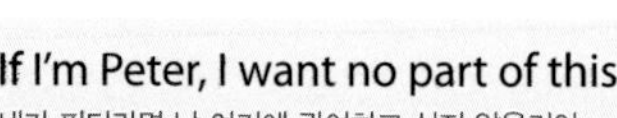

If I'm Peter, I want no part of this.
내가 피터라면 난 여기에 관여하고 싶지 않을거야.

I don't know what kind of sick game you're playing, but I want no part of it.
네가 어떤 이상한 게임을 하려는지 모르겠지만 난 관여하고 싶지 않아.

I want no part of your ruthless, money-grubbing schemes.
잔인하고 악착같이 돈을 모으는 네 계획에는 참여하고 싶지 않아.

019 Please don't butt in 끼어들지마

This is a way of asking someone not to intrude in a personal matter. Many times we can understand that the speaker wants privacy and does not want interference from any other people. In other words, "Please don't try to get involved with this."

| Point | butt in 간섭하다, 끼어들다
Butt out! 참견말고 꺼져, 가서 네 일이나 잘해!

A: I know how to help with your marriage problems. 네 결혼문제를 어떻게 도와야 할지 내가 알고 있어.
B: It's none of your business. **Please don't butt in.**
네가 알바 아냐, 참견하지마.

Please don't butt in when the neighbors are arguing. 이웃들이 다툴 때는 제발 끼어들지마.

The point is that Annie is our daughter, and you had no right to butt in.
핵심은 애니는 우리 딸이고 넌 참견할 권한이 없었다는거야.

020 What's it to you? 그게 너랑 무슨 상관이지?

this asks "Why does it matter to you personally?" The speaker wants to know why someone is interested in something

| Point | What's it got to (do with) you? 네가 무슨 상관이야?

A: Didn't I see you out drinking late last night?
지난 밤에 늦게까지 너 술먹는 거 내가 보지 않았나?
B: **What's it to you?** That is my own business.
그게 너랑 무슨 상관야? 그건 내 일이라고.

Of course she's gay. What's it to you?
물론 걔는 게이야. 그게 너랑 무슨 상관이야?

We like playing League of Legend. What's it to you?
우리는 리그 오브 레전드 게임하는 걸 좋아해. 그게 너랑 무슨 상관야?

What's it to you? No one else cares!
그게 너랑 무슨 상관이야? 다른 사람은 아무도 신경쓰지 않는데!

021 How is that relevant? 그게 무슨 관련이 있어?, 그게 뭐가 중요해?

미드표현

this is asking why something matters or is important to a specific discussion. Often it is asked when people are talking about a subject and someone says something that seems like it is unimportant to the discussion. It is very much like asking "Why would that matter to us?"

| Point | be relevant 적절하다, 관련있다

A: Jay and I had breakfast before the meeting.
제이와 난 회의 전에 아침을 먹었어.

B: I understand, but **how is that relevant?**
그래, 근데 그게 무슨 관련이 있는거야?

Not that any of that information is relevant.
그 정보의 어느 하나도 적절한게 없어.

Do you have any more information that might be relevant? 관련있는 정보가 더 없어?

The suffering of the victim isn't relevant?
피해자의 고통은 상관없다고?

022 Why[What] do you care? 무슨 상관이야?, 왜 그리 신경쓰는데?

미드표현

It is asking "Why are you interested in this?"

| Point | Why do you care about~ …관해 왜 신경쓰는데?
Why do you care what[that] S+V …을 왜 신경써?
What do you care what S+V? …가 무슨 상관이야?

A: I think you are having difficulty making friends.
네가 친구 사귀는 데 어려움이 있는 것 같아.

B: **Why do you care?** I can make friends if I want to. 무슨 상관인데? 내가 원하면 친구를 사귈 수 있다고.

Why do you care about her so much?
왜 그렇게 걔한테 신경을 많이 쓰는 거야?

Why do you care what other people think?
다른 사람이 무슨 생각이든 왜 상관해?

What do you care what people call you?
사람들이 널 뭐라고 부르든 무슨 상관이야?

023 Who cares? 알게 뭐람?, 무슨 상관이야?, 누가 신경이나 쓴대?

This is a way to say "I don't care at all." The speaker wants to indicate he has no opinion about something

| Point | See if I care 내가 끄덕이나 할 줄 알아
Who cares about~? …에 신경이나 쓴데?
Who cares if[what/who]~? …에 무슨 상관이야?

A: I think Toyota is going to make a new sports car.
도요타가 새로운 스포츠카를 만들 것 같아.

B: **Who cares?** I don't have enough money for a new car. 알게 뭐람? 난 차 바꿀 돈도 없는데.

Who cares? I didn't like her anyway.
알게 뭐람? 난 어쨌거나, 걔 싫어.

Who cares? The bottom line is she loves you.
무슨 상관이야? 요점은 걔가 널 좋아한다는 거야

Who cares who's had more sex?
누가 섹스를 더한 게 무슨 상관이야?

024 I don't care (about it) 상관없어, 신경안써

미드표현

this is like the previous 2 phrases. It is a way to say "It means nothing to me"

| Point | I don't care about~ …상관없어
I don't care if[what, how much~]~ …이든 아니든 상관없어
I couldn't care less 알게 뭐람, 전혀 상관없어

A: What would you like for dinner tonight?
오늘 밤에 저녁 뭐 먹을래?

B: **I don't care.** Anything in the fridge will be fine.
신경안써. 냉장고 있는 거 아무거나 좋아.

I don't care what you think. I don't care what anybody thinks.
네 생각 관심없어. 누가 어떻게 생각하든 신경 안쓴다고.

I don't care if she's fat or thin.
난 걔가 뚱뚱하든 날씬하든 상관안해.

I don't care who he sleeps with.
걔가 누구랑 자는지 관심없어.

I couldn't care less. I don't like politics.
알게 뭐람. 정치를 싫어해서.

025 I don't give a shit 알게 뭐야

미드표현

this is a very rude and angry way to say "I don't care about it"

I Point I I didn't give a damn[fuck, crap] 대체 무슨 상관이야
I don't give a rat's ass 상관없어

A: The students are having a big party tonight.
학생들이 오늘 밤 파티를 크게 열거래.

B: **I don't give a shit.** I hate them all.
알게 뭐야. 난 걔네들 다 싫어해.

The FBI doesn't give a shit about you.
FBI는 너에 대해 신경도 안써.

I don't give a shit, because I'm broke.
난 돈이 다 떨어져서 신경도 안써.

026 What's the difference? 그게 무슨 상관이야?

미드표현

this asks why something is important. It is like saying "Does it really matter?"

I Point I What difference does it make? 그게 무슨 차이가 있어?
What's the difference between A and B? A와 B의 차이점이 뭐지?

A: We could go hiking or we could take a walk.
하이킹 갈 수도 있고 산보할 수도 있어.

B: **What's the difference?** They are both pretty similar. 그게 무슨 상관이야? 둘 다 비슷한 걸.

I don't remember. What's the difference?
기억이 안나. 무슨 상관이야?

What's the difference? She's dead.
무슨 상관이야? 걔는 죽었잖아.

Well, what's the difference? I mean, it's not important. 그게 무슨 상관이야? 내 말은 그건 중요한 거 아니잖아.

027 It's not gonna make any difference

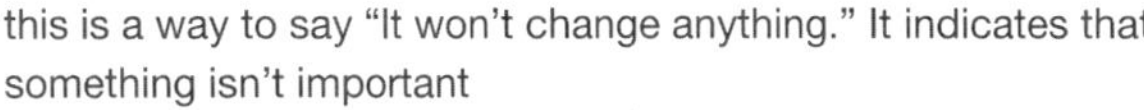
전혀 상관없어, 그래봤자 달라질 것 없어

미드표현

this is a way to say "It won't change anything." It indicates that something isn't important

I Point I (It) Makes no difference to me 상관없어
Does it make any difference? 상관있어?

A: I am going to try my best in this interview.
이번 인터뷰에서 최선을 다할거야.

B: **It's not going to make any difference.** You won't get the job. 그래봤자 달라질 거 없어. 너 취직 안 될거야.

I'm afraid your efforts aren't gonna make any difference. 노력해봤자 달라질 것 없어.

I've given her everything she ever wanted, but it doesn't seem to make a difference.
걔가 원하는 걸 다 해줬지만 달라지는 것 같지가 않아.

It doesn't matter what you say. It's not gonna make a difference anyway, so you can just go.
네가 무슨 말 하든 상관없어. 그래봤자 달라지는 거 아무 것도 없으니 그냥 가버려.

028 It's gonna make a difference 차이가 있을 거야, 달라질거야

미드표현

this means something will cause a change. It is a way to say "This will change things"

I Point I That makes a difference 그거 확실히 다른데

A: What do you think of the new plan to help poor people? 가난한 사람들을 돕는 새로운 계획 어때?

B: **It's going to make a difference.** They need our help. 달라질거야. 그들은 우리 도움을 필요로 해.

The students have new computers. It's going to make a difference.
학생들에게 새로운 컴퓨터가 지급됐어. 이제 많이 달라질거야.

It's going to make a difference. We know it will be helpful.
많이 차이가 날거야. 우리는 그게 도움이 될거라는 걸 알고 있어.

So many people are protesting. It's going to make a difference.
그럼 많은 사람들이 항의하고 있는거네. 달라지겠는데.

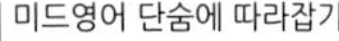

029 It doesn't matter to me 난 아무래도 상관없어, 난 신경쓰지 않아

미드표현

this is a way to say "I have no opinion." It is said when the speaker doesn't have a strong feeling about something

| Point | (It, That) doesn't matter 별거 아니예요
It doesn't matter what[who~] …이든 상관없어

A: Would you like to have lunch today? 오늘 점심할래?
B: **It doesn't matter to me.** I'm free all week.
난 아무래도 상관없어. 이번 주 내내 한가해.

I suppose that doesn't matter to you, does it?
너한테 상관없잖아, 그지?

If you wanna be lesbian, be lesbian. Doesn't matter to me.
네가 레즈비언이 되고 싶으면 그렇게 해. 난 상관없어.

Doesn't matter. I love you, baby, and I am so proud of you. 상관없어. 자기야 난 널 사랑하고 네가 자랑스러워.

030 Does it matter? 그게 중요해?, 그게 무슨 상관이야?

미드표현

this asks "Is it important?" The speaker wants to know if something has any value

| Point | Does it matter that~? …가 중요해?
What does it matter (what, where~)? …하는 게 그게 뭐가 중요해?

A: This was the most expensive suit in the store.
이 가게에서 제일 비싼 옷이었어.
B: **Does it matter?** It looks like the other suits.
그게 무슨 상관야? 다른 옷들하고 같아 보이는데.

Why does it matter so much to you?
그게 왜 그렇게 중요해?

What does it matter? We're all on the same team. 그게 뭐가 중요해? 우린 한 팀이잖아.

Does it matter that I may have loved him?
내가 걔를 사랑했을 지도 모른다는 사실이 중요해?

What does it matter where we go?
우리가 어디로 가는 게 그리 중요해?

031 What's that got to do with anything? 그게 무슨 상관이야?

미드표현

the speaker is asking why something is important. It is similar to saying "Why are you talking about that?"

| Point | What has it got to do with sb[sth]? …와 무슨 상관이야?

A: Tomorrow I am going fishing with my dad.
내일 아빠와 낚시하러 갈거야.
B: **What's that got to do with anything?** I don't even know your dad. 그게 무슨 상관야? 난 너 아빠도 모르는데.

What's it got to do with us? 우리와 무슨 상관이죠?

What's all this got to do with the little dead girl, anyway? 어쨌든 이 모든 게 죽은 소녀와 무슨 상관이죠?

That's my kid sister, Julie. Why? What's she got to do with it? 여동생 줄리예요. 왜요? 걔가 그거와 무슨 상관이죠?

032 What does it have to do with Chris?

그게 크리스와 무슨 관련이 있어?

미드표현

this is a way of asking how something relates to a specific person. We can understand that there may be some confusion, perhaps something strange happened, and the speaker wants to know if it involves a person named Chris. It is similar to asking "Is this associated with Chris?"

| Point | What does it have to do with~? 그게 …와 무슨 관계가 있어?
Does it have to do with~? …와 관련이 있어?

A: The robbers took everything in the apartment.
도둑들이 아파트를 싹 털었어.
B: I know, but **what does it have to do with Chris?** 알아, 하지만 그게 크리스와 무슨 상관이야?

And what does this have to do with us?
그리고 이게 우리랑 무슨 관계야?

Excuse me, what does this have to do with our son? 실례지만, 이게 우리 아들과 무슨 관련이 있나요?

Does it have to do with drugs? 이게 약물과 관련있어?

033 Does this have anything to do with you?

이게 너와 무슨 관련이 있어?

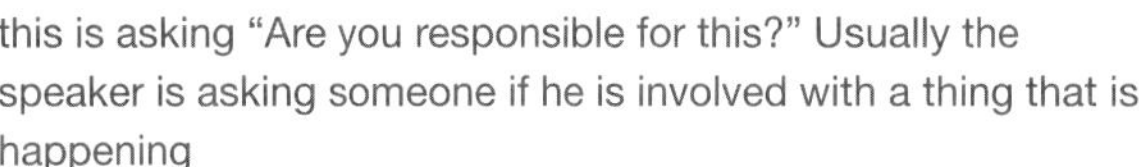

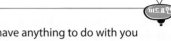

this is asking "Are you responsible for this?" Usually the speaker is asking someone if he is involved with a thing that is happening

| Point | Does A have anything to do with B? A가 B와 무슨 관련이 있어?
Does A have anything to do with sb ~ing?
A는 …가 …하는 것과 연관이 있는거야?

A: The police called this morning. **Does this have anything to do with you?**
아침에 경찰전화왔는데 너와 무슨 관련있는거야?

B: No, I haven't done anything that would make the police call you. 아냐, 경찰이 날 찾을 짓을 한 게 없는데.

미드표현

Does this have anything to do with you making her do housework?
네가 걔 집안일 시키는 것과 연관이 있는거야?

Did you have anything to do with this?
너 이거랑 무슨 관련있어?

Did this emergency have anything to do with Jill? 이 위급한 상황이 질하고 관련있어?

Does this have anything to do with the bruises on your face? 이게 얼굴에 난 멍과 관련이 있어?

034 It doesn't have anything to do with me

난 모르는 일이야, 난 신경안써

this means the speaker doesn't feel involved with something. It is a way to say "I don't care because it doesn't involve my life"

A: The factory workers are on strike this week.
공장근로자들이 이번 주 파업해.

B: **It doesn't have anything to do with** me.
나하곤 상관없는 일이야.

미드표현

I want you to understand it doesn't have anything to do with you.
그건 너와 전혀 상관없다는 것을 알아줬으면 해.

He didn't have anything to do with it.
걔는 그거와 아무 상관없어.

What are you looking at me for? I didn't have anything to do with this.
왜 날 그렇게 쳐다보는 거야? 난 그거와 아무 관련없어.

035 I have nothing to do with this 난 아무 관련이 없어

미드표현

the speaker thinks something is private and doesn't want to be involved. He's saying "I want to stay out of this"

| Point | I had nothing to do with this 난 아무 짓도 안 했어
It's got nothing to do with you 너하곤 상관없는 일이야

A: Are you part of the NGO office here?
여기 NGO 사무실 일원입니까?

B: No, **I have nothing to do with this.** 아뇨, 전 관련없어요.

I have nothing to do with casting.
난 캐스팅하고는 관련이 없어.

Those things have nothing to do with what happened with Jackson.
그 일들은 잭슨에게 일어난 일들과는 관련이 없어.

We both know why we got married and it had nothing to do with affection.
우리 둘 다 우리 결혼이유를 알고 있고 그건 애정하고는 거리가 멀잖아.

036 It doesn't mean anything to me 난 상관없어

this is said to indicate something has no meaning to the speaker. It means "That doesn't involve my life"

| Point | Does it mean anything to you that S+V? …가 무슨 의미가 있어?

A: Wow, these decorations are really beautiful.
와, 이 장식물들은 정말 예뻐.

B: **They don't mean anything to me.** They were here when I moved in. 난 몰라. 이사올 때 있었어.

미드표현

Does this mean anything to you?
이게 네게 무슨 의미가 있어?

Does the name Steve Charlton mean anything to you? 스티브 칼튼이라는 이름이 무슨 의미가 있어?

Did it mean anything to you that we were all in the office today?
오늘 우리 모두가 사무실에 있다는 게 네게 무슨 의미가 있었어?

037 You decide 네가 결정해

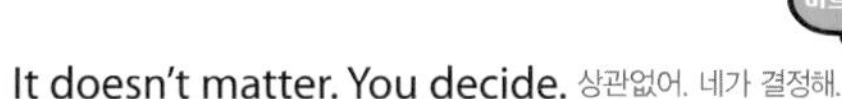

this tells someone to make a choice. It's a way to say 'The decision is up to you"

| Point | I'm happy either way 난 아무래도 좋아

A: What should we get Mom for her birthday?
엄마에게 생일선물로 뭘 줘야 할까?

B: **You decide.** I'm terrible at buying gifts.
네가 결정해. 난 선물사는데 젬병야.

미드표현

It doesn't matter. You decide. 상관없어. 네가 결정해.

You decide who's going to stay and who's going to go. 누가 남고 누가 갈 건지 네가 결정해.

Well, you're the lawyer. You decide.
저기, 네가 변호사잖아. 네가 결정해.

038 It's not my place 내가 상관할 바가 아니다, 내가 나설 자리가 아냐

this means "It's not my responsibility." The speaker doesn't think he needs to participate in something

| Point | It's not my place to do~ …하는 건 내가 말 할 입장이 아니야

A: Don't you think you should tell your boss about the problems? 사장님께 문제를 얘기해야 되지 않겠니?

B: **It's not my place.** He might get angry at me.
내가 나설 자리가 아냐. 내게 화낼 지도 몰라.

미드표현

I know it's probably not my place but can I give you a piece of advice?
내가 나설 자리가 아니라는 걸 알지만 조언하나 해도 될까?

Forget I mentioned it. It is not my place.
내가 말했던 거 잊어. 내가 나설 자리가 아니야.

It's not my place to judge. 내가 판단할 입장은 아닌데.

039 Whatever! 뭐든지 간에!, 아무렴 어때!

this is usually said when someone is unhappy with something. It means "I don't agree with that"

A: I don't think I can go to your party. 네 파티에 못 갈 것 같아.

B: **Whatever!** That isn't what you said to me yesterday. 하여튼! 어제 나한테 한 말하고 다르네.

미드표현

Whatever! You'll never be successful!
뭐든지간에! 넌 성공할 수 없을거야!

You don't want to work with me? Whatever!
넌 나랑 함께 일하기 싫어한다고? 아무래도 좋아!

I can't believe you insulted me. Well, whatever! 네가 나를 모욕하다니 믿겨지지 않아. 그래, 아무렴 어때!

040 The hell with that! 알게 뭐람!, 맘대로 해!

this often means "I won't do that." It is a way to express unhappiness and disagreement with something when the speaker feels angry

| Point | to hell with ~ …알게 뭐야, 상관없어, …는 끝이야

A: We are going to have to pay more taxes this year. 금년에 세금을 더 내야 할거야.

B: **To hell with that!** I'm not going to pay higher taxes! 알게 뭐람! 더 많은 세금은 내지 않을거야!

미드표현

To tell with that! 그게 끝이야! 더는 없어!

To hell with tradition! 전통 따윈 알게 뭐야!

To hell with her! 걔는 알게 뭐람!

But to hell with that bitch. 저 나쁜 년은 이제 끝이야.

041 So shoot me 그래서 어쨌다는 거야, 배째

this is a way to say "You have no power to change what I do." This is said when the speaker wants to indicate that he doesn't care if people disagree with him

| Point | So what? 그래서 뭐가 어쨌다고?
What of it? 그게 어쨌다는 거야?
Does that mean something (to you)? 그래서?, 그게 어쨌다구?

A: I don't think you have chosen the right major to study. 네가 공부할 전공을 잘못 선택한 것 같아.

B: **So shoot me.** I can study what I want.
그래서 뭐 어쨌다고. 내가 원하는 걸 공부하는 거지.

So your sex life isn't so great. So what?
그래 네 성생활이 그저 그렇다. 그래서 뭐가 어쨌다고?

We had sex. So what? 우린 섹스했어. 그래서?

I admit I was there. So what?
그래 난 거기 있었어. 그래서?

042 You want to cut the cord? 관계를 끝내고 싶어?

this person is asking if someone wants to separate from something, or to end something. In other words, the person is asking "Do you want to stop this?" or "Do you want to disconnect from this?"

| Point | cut the cord 관계 등을 끝내다, 독립적으로 되다(be independent)

A: This business partnership has been a disaster for us. 이 사업협력관계는 우리에게 재앙이었어.

B: I agree, so maybe we should stop it. **You want to cut the cord?** 맞아, 그럼 우리 그만 두어야겠어. 관계를 끝낼래?

You want to cut the cord, Dr. Grey?
그레이 박사, 우리 관계를 끝내고 싶어?

You need to cut the cord with Penny.
넌 페니와의 관계를 끝내야 돼.

Which means you freak out? Julie, just cut the cord. Go nuts. Come on. Let's do shots. Come on!
그럼 너도 걱정한다는거야? 줄리야, 그냥 걱정그만하고 미친듯 놀자. 어서. 술마시자고. 어서!

SHERIFF'S
DEPT.

Ways to do things and ways to suggest doing things

뭔가 제안을 하거나 받을 때

I'll take you up on that

001 Here's the deal 이렇게 된 거야

미드표현

this is a way to say "I'm going to tell you everything." It means that the speaker is going to explain something

Point Here's the plan 자, 이렇게 하자
*Here is a deal은 거래시 낮은 가격을 제시하면서 하는 표현(It's good price)

A: Can you tell me the secret to being successful?
성공의 비밀을 말해줄래?

B: **Here's the deal.** If you work hard, you are going to be successful. 이렇게 되는거야. 열심히 일하면 성공할거야.

Okay, here's the plan. Call Jane and tell her to meet you tonight.
좋아, 이렇게 하자. 제인한테 전화해서 오늘 밤에 보자고 해.

Here's the plan. I'm booking a hotel for the weekend. 이렇게 하자. 주말동안 지낼 호텔을 예약할게.

A: Here's a deal. This radio is only nine dollars.
B: That sounds like a bargain. Let's buy it.
A: 좋은 가격이죠. 라디오가 겨우 9달러예요. B: 아주 싼 것 같네. 사자고.

002 Here's a thought 좋은 생각이 있어, 이렇게 해봐, 이건 어때?

미드표현

this is a way for the speaker to say something that he thinks is a good idea. It is like saying "I'm going to suggest this..."

A: What is the best place to go on my vacation?
나 휴가가기에 가장 좋은 곳이 어디야?

B: **Here's a thought.** Why not take a trip around Southeast Asia? 좋은 생각이 있어. 극동지역을 여행해봐.

Here's a thought. Why don't you try telling her directly? 좋은 생각이 있어. 걔한테 직접 말해.

Here's a thought. Quit following me!
좋은 생각이 났어. 그만 날 따라 다녀!

003 The offer's still on the table? 그 제안 아직 유효한거지?

미드표현

this is a way of asking if a deal that was proposed is still valid, or whether the person that offered the deal decided to cancel it. If an offer is still on the table, a person can still decide to accept it. It is like asking "Can I still say yes to that proposal?"

Point be on the table 아직 유효하다, 논의중이다 be off the table 제외되다

A: Are you going to accept the terms of the contract? 넌 계약 조건을 받아들일거야?

B: **The offer's still on the table?** I thought they withdrew it. 그 제안 아직 유효해? 걔네들이 철회한 줄 알았어.

What exactly was on the table?
정확히 뭐가 논의 중이었던거야?

I thought it was on the table. But we haven't even discussed that.
난 그게 논의중인걸로 알았는데 우린 토의조차 하지 않았어.

Unfortunately, it's no longer on the table.
안타깝게도, 그건 더이상 논의사항이 아냐.

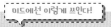

Sex is off the table, right?

The Big Bang Theory
SEASON#5-9

헤어진 후 데이트가 아닌 친구로서 함께 영화를 본 Leonard와 Penny. 섹스없는 만남을 하는데 서로 계속 언쟁을 한다. 집에 올라오면서 다시 한번 다투는 장면.

Leonard: Okay. So, we went out, saw a movie, met some nice people, said horrible things about each other in public, all in all, a pretty magical night.

Penny: Okay, I'm not innocent in all this, but you basically called me stupid, you asthmatic dumbass.

Leonard: I know, I crossed a line. And I'm sorry. No, no, no, hang on. I really mean it. And it's not like when we were going out, I'd just apologize for everything so we could end up in bed. This is a 100% sex-is-off-the-table I'm sorry.

Penny: All right. Thank you. I'm sorry, too.

Leonard: Just to be clear, sex is off the table, right?

Penny: Way off.

레너드: 좋아, 우리는 나가서 영화를 보고 좋은 사람들을 만났고 사람들 있는데서 서로를 헐뜯었어. 그래도 아주 멋진 밤이었어.

페니: 나도 잘한 것은 없지만 넌 날 바보라고 불렀어, 이 한심한 천식쟁이야.

레너드: 알아, 내가 선을 넘었어. 미안해. 잠깐만. 진심이라고. 그리고 우리가 데이트할 때와는 달라. 섹스하기 위해서 모든 것에 사과하는. 이건 정말이지 섹스를 염두에 두지 않은거야. 미안해.

페니: 좋아. 고마워. 나도 미안해.

레너드: 분명히 해두겠는데, 섹스는 없는거지, 맞지?

페니: 당근이지.

004 Why don't you~ ? …좀 해봐

this is a way to say "You could...." The speaker is suggesting doing something

| Point | Why don't we do~? = Let's do~ …하자

A: I'm so worried because my boyfriend and I have been arguing a lot. 남친과 많이 싸워서 걱정야.

B: **Why don't you** give him a call? He may be worried too. 전화해봐. 걔도 걱정하고 있을지 몰라.

Well, why don't you say something?
어, 뭐 얘기 좀 해봐.

So, why don't you just do it? I mean, what are we waiting for? 그럼 그냥 해봐. 내 말은 뭘 기다리냐고?

Why don't you think twice before you start?
시작하기 전에 신중히 생각해봐

005 Why not? 1. 왜 안해?, 왜 안되는 거야? 2. (상대방 제안에) 좋아, 그러지 뭐

미드표현

usually this is a way of asking "What would stop you from...?" The speaker is wondering why someone should not do something. Also this can mean "Sure, that's fine." We can understand that the speaker is agreeing to something

| Point | Why not+N? 왜 …는 안돼?
Why not do~? …하는 게 어때?

A: I'd say you shouldn't go to the new restaurant.
저 새 식당엔 가지 말지.

B: **Why not?** Does the food taste bad there?
왜 가지 말라고? 음식 맛이 나빠?

Why not? It's a good chance. 왜 안돼? 좋은 기회인데.

Why not her? 왜 걔는 안돼?

Why not ask her about it? 걔한테 그거 물어보는 게 어때?

May I ask you why not? 왜 안되는지 물어도 될까요?

006 Do you want me to~? 내가 …할까?, …을 바라는 거야?

미드표현

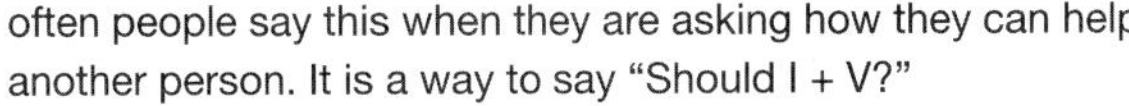

often people say this when they are asking how they can help another person. It is a way to say "Should I + V?"

A: Why do you look so sad? **Do you want me to** stay with you? 왜 그렇게 슬퍼보여? 내가 함께 있을까?

B: No, that's OK. I'd really prefer to be alone.
아니, 괜찮아. 정말 혼자 있고 싶어.

Do you want me to call? 내가 전화할까?

Do you want me to page him? 걔를 호출할까?

Do you want me to quit? 그만두라는 말인가요?

Do you want me to say that I'll stop seeing her? 걔를 만나지 않겠다는 말을 하라는 거야?

007 Let's make a deal 이렇게 하자, 우리 협상하자

미드표현

this is a way of saying that two people can agree on something. It's the same as saying "Let's agree to this"

| Point | Let's meet halfway 타협하자

A: **Let's make a deal.** If you help with my homework, I'll help with your report. 이렇게 하자. 내 숙제 도와주면 네 리포트 도와줄게.

B: That sounds good. But my report will be a lot harder to finish. 좋아. 하지만 내 리포트가 끝내기 더 어려울걸.

Let's make a deal. I'll give you ten bucks for it.
이렇게 하자. 내가 그 대가로 10 달러를 줄게.

I want to buy that car. Let's make a deal.
난 저 차를 사고 싶어. 우리 이렇게 하자.

Let's make a deal. How much do you want for the company?
우리 협상하자. 회사 매각대금으로 얼마를 원하는거야?

008 That gives me an idea 그러고 보니 좋은 수가 떠올랐어

this expresses "I just thought of something new." It is a way to tell people that the speaker will suggest something

A: Everyone loves these new dolls.
다들 이 새로운 인형을 좋아해.

B: **That gives me an idea.** We should sell them ourselves.
그러고 보니 좋은 수가 떠올랐어. 우리가 직접 이것들을 판매하는 거야.

Wait a minute. That gives me an idea. Can you say that again?
잠깐 그 말 들으니 좋은 생각이 떠올랐어. 다시 한번 말해줄래?

None of this was my idea. 이건 어떤 것도 내 생각이 아냐.

Any good ideas? 뭐 좋은 생각 있어?

009 I'll take you up on that 네 제안을 받아들일게

this means "I'll accept your offer." We can understand that someone offered to do something and the speaker agreed to it

| Point | take sb up on~ …을 받아들이다
*on 다음에는 주로 제안, 초대, 약속 관련어가 나온다.

A: I'd be glad to help you prepare for your party.
기쁜 맘으로 너 파티준비하는 걸 도와줄게.

B: **I'll take you up on that.** I need some extra help. 좋아 그렇게 해. 도움이 더 좀 필요하니까.

Did he take you up on your offer?
걔가 네 제안을 받아들였어?

Maybe I'll take you up on that.
아마도 네 제안을 받아들일지 몰라.

I'm going to take you up on your offer.
난 네 제안을 받아들일거야.

010 (I) Don't mind if I do 그럼 기꺼이, 좋아, (제안에 긍정적으로 답하면서) 그래도 된다면야

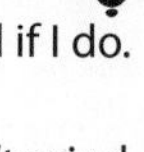

this is a way of saying "I'm going to do that." It is said when someone says yes to another person's offer

A: Please help yourself to some food. 음식 맘껏 들어.

B: **I don't mind if I do.** This looks delicious.
그래도 된다면야. 이거 맛있게 보이는데.

A: Want to find out why? B: Don't mind if I do.
A: 이유를 알고 싶어? B: 그래도 된다면야.

A: Why don't you join us, Mike? B: Don't mind if I do. A: 마이크 우리랑 함께 가자. B: 그럼 좋아.

011 Let's just play it by ear (그때그때) 상황에 맞게 행동하자

this means "I want to wait and see what will happen." We can understand the speaker wants to see how the situation changes

| Point | play it by ear 상황 돌아가는 거에 따라 맞춰 행동하다

A: Have you planned anything for us this weekend? 이번 주말 우릴 위해 뭐 계획잡은 거 있어?

B: No, I haven't. **Let's just play it by ear.**
아니, 없어. 그때 그때 상황에 맞춰 놀자.

I'll have to play it by ear. 봐가면서 할 거야.

Why don't we play it by ear? 상황봐가면서 하자.

Can we just play it by ear? 상황봐가면서 하자.

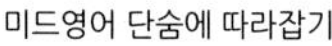

012 Let's do it[that] 자 하자, 그렇게 하자

this means "Let's start something right away." The speaker is agreeing to begin something

I Point I Show time 어디 한번 해보자

A: Would you like to play some on-line games?
온라인 게임할래?

B: Yeah, definitely. **Let's do it.** 어, 그렇고 말고. 자 하자.

미드표현

All right, let's do it. 좋아, 그러자.

I want to live with you too! Let's do that!
나도 너랑 함께 살고 싶어! 그렇게 하자!

You remember that pie you wanted to make? Let's do that tonight.
네가 만들고 싶어했던 파이 기억나? 오늘 밤에 만들어보자.

Yeah, let's do that. You... you do everything, and I'll do nothing.
어, 그렇게 하자. 네가 모든 일 다 하고 난 아무 것도 안할거야.

013 Let's not get ahead of ourselves 너무 앞서서 생각하지 말자

this is a way to tell people not to proceed too quickly, because if they go too quickly, it could be confusing. People sometimes say this at meetings, meaning "Let's slow down and finish this topic before we jump ahead to the next thing we want to discuss"

I Point I get ahead of sb 앞지르다, 앞서다, 능가하다
get ahead of oneself 앞서가다

A: After I get rich, I'll buy a big house and a BMW.
내가 부자가 된 후에 큰 집과 BMW를 살거야.

B: **Let's not get ahead of ourselves.** We're not rich yet. 너무 앞서가지 말자고. 우리는 아직 부자가 아니야.

No, let's not get ahead of ourselves.
아니, 우리 너무 앞서가지 말자고.

Just want to make sure that we don't get ahead of ourselves.
우리가 앞서가지 않게끔 확실히 하고 싶어.

You think it's gonna work? Well, let's not get ahead of ourselves.
그게 될거라 생각해? 자, 우리 앞서가지 말자고.

014 You (will) do that 그렇게 해

this is a way of saying that someone has the ability to do something and should go ahead. It is similar to saying "Go ahead and try it"

A: I think I'm going to try snow boarding this year.
금년에 스노우보딩 해볼려고 해.

B: **You do that.** It should be a lot of fun.
그렇게 해. 정말 재미있을거야.

You do that every night, don't you?
너 매일 그러지, 그렇지 않아?

Really?! You do that? 정말?! 그래?

A: I'll find you something, Larry, don't sweat it.
B: You do that.
A: 래리야 내가 뭐 찾아줄테니, 걱정마. B: 그렇게 해줘.

015 Let's go get~ …하러 가자

this indicates that the speaker wants to do something in another place. It is like saying "I want to do~"

I Point I go + 동사 …하러 가다

A: It feels really hot today. 오늘 정말 더운 것 같아.

B: **Let's go get** some ice cream to cool down.
가서 아이스크림 좀 먹고 식히자.

Let's go get some sleep. 가서 잠 좀 자자.

Let's go get some dinner, okay?
가서 저녁 좀 먹자, 좋아?

Let's go have a drink. 가서 술 한잔하자.

I'm gonna go take a shower. 가서 샤워할거야.

016 How about ~? …은 어때?, …어떻게 생각해?

미드표현

this is a way to suggest "Let's ....." Often it is a way to suggest doing something

| Point | How about + N/~ing/S+V? …은 어때?, …하는 건 어때?

A: Where can I go for my birthday party?
생일파티 어디서 할까?

B: **How about** a nice place that serves snacks and beer? 스낵과 맥주를 제공하는 멋진 곳이 어때?

How about dinner tomorrow night?
내일 저녁 저녁먹자고

How about I let you sleep on it? We'll talk about morning tomorrow.
하루 더 생각해봐. 내일 아침에 이야기하자고.

How about you don't tell her? 걔한테 이야기하지마.

017 I suggest you take it 그렇게 하도록 해, 그렇게 하면 좋을 것 같은데

미드표현

this is a way to say that the speaker thinks something is good to have. It is like saying "I think that would benefit you"

| Point | I suggest (that) S+V …하지 그래

A: So AT&T offered me a job with a good salary.
AT&T가 급여가 센 일자리를 제시했어.

B: AT&T is a good company. **I suggest** you take it.
AT&T는 좋은 회사야. 그렇게 해.

If you're not hiding anything I suggest you answer their questions.
숨기는 게 아무것도 없다면 걔네들 질문에 답을 하지 그래.

I suggest you join me in the bathroom.
나와 함께 욕실로 가지 그래.

018 How would that be? 그러면 어떨까?, 그러면 좋겠어?

미드표현

this is a way of asking "Would you like it?" The speaker wants to know if a person would enjoy something

A: I didn't get an e-mail from you. 이메일을 못받았어.

B: I'll send you one tonight. **How would that be?**
저녁에 보낼게. 그럼 어떻겠어?

I'll get you a notebook. How would that be?
내가 노트북을 사줄게. 그러면 어떨까?

I'll make some coffee for you. How would that be? 내가 커피를 좀 타줄게. 그러면 좋겠어?

From now on you'll just have to keep your expenses low. And I could get you some work. Right away, how would that be?
지금부터 넌 지출을 최소로 줄여. 그리고 난 너한테 일거리를 좀 줄게. 지금부터 바로, 그러면 어떨까?

019 (You) Want to~? …할래?

미드표현

this is a way of asking if a person would like to do something. It is like asking "Would you like to do...?"

| Point | You first 당신 먼저, 먼저 해(You try to do it before I will)

A: I'm hungry. **You want to** go out to eat?
배고파. 나가서 식사할래?

B: No, I can cook up some food right here.
아니, 여기서 음식 좀 요리할게.

Do you want to meet me there? 거기서 나 볼래?

You want to talk about it? 그 얘기하고 싶어?

Want to get some air? 바람 좀 쐴래?

Want to know why? 이유를 알고 싶어?

So, let's get to know each other. You first.
그럼 서로에 대해 이야기해보죠. 당신 먼저요.

MEMO

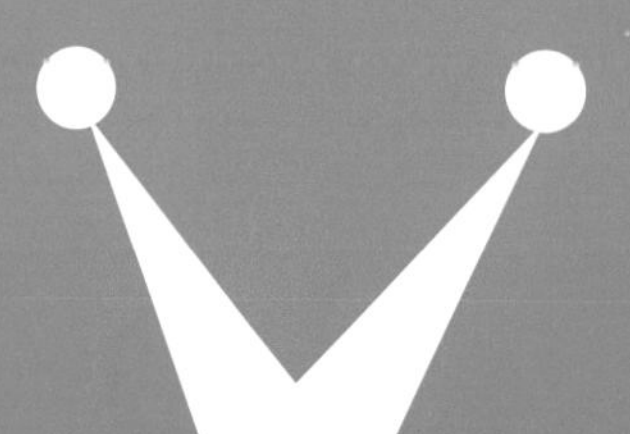

Ways of offering advice to others

상대방에게 충고하기

That's not how it works

001 Watch out! 조심해!

this is usually said to mean "There is some danger." It indicates that a possible problem is around

| Point | Watch out for+N …을 조심해 Watch what S+V …을 조심해
Watch it! (진행중인 위험 상황하에서) 조심해!
Watch your step 발 조심해 Look out! 조심해!, 정신 차리라고!

A: **Watch out.** There are some big holes in the sidewalk. 조심해. 보도에 큰 구멍이 좀 있어.

B: I'll be very careful when I walk here. 여기 걸을 때 매우 조심할게.

Watch out for the thorns. 가시 조심해.

You should watch out for her. She's a liar. 걔 조심해. 거짓말쟁이야.

Watch what you say. You never know who's listening. 말 조심해. 누가 듣는지 모르잖아.

Hey! Watch it lady! 이봐, 조심하라고 아가씨야!

Look out! The baseball is coming toward you! 조심해! 야구공이 네게 날라와!

002 Use your head! 머리를 좀 써라!, 생각 좀 해봐!

this means "Consider it carefully." We can understand that a person should think more about something before doing it

| Point | Where's your head at? 머리는 두었다가 어디에 쓰려고 그래?
Use your brain 생각해봐

A: I may join the army later this year. 올 후반기에 입대할지몰라.

B: Are you sure that is a good idea? **Use your head!** 좋은 생각이라고 확신해? 머리를 좀 써봐!

Use your head! I'm not going to let you ruin my family! 머리를 좀 써봐! 네가 내 가정을 망치게 놔두지 않을거야!

I expect you to use your brain. 머리를 좀 써봐.

003 You have to get used to it 적응해야지

usually this means something new is happening and people must accept it. It is a way to say "You have to accept the situation"

| Point | You better get used to it 익숙해지는 게 좋을걸
You'll get the hang of it 금방 손에 익을거야, 익숙해질거야
You'll get the knack of it 요령이 붙을거야

A: The noise from the construction is making me feel crazy. 건설현장 소음이 날 미치게 해.

B: **You have to get used to it.** The construction will be going on for months. 적응해야지. 몇 달간 계속될텐데.

I guess it'll take while to get used to this. 이거 적응하는데 어느 정도 시간이 걸릴 것 같아.

Well, you know what? You better get used to it. 응, 저 말이야, 적응하는 게 좋을 거야.

Don't give up. You'll get the hang of it. 낙담하지마. 익숙해질거야.

004 Do yourself a favor 너 자신을 (위해) 생각 좀 해봐

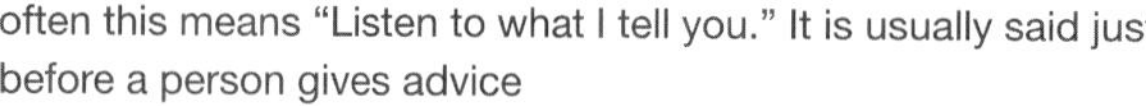

often this means "Listen to what I tell you." It is usually said just before a person gives advice

A: Rick is always the laziest person on our team. 릭은 항상 우리 팀에서 가장 굼떠.

B: **Do yourself a favor.** Don't let him upset you. 네 자신을 생각해야지. 걔 신경 건드리지마.

Do yourself a favor. If you don't know enough about something, stay out of it. 너 자신을 위해 뭘 모르면 끼어들지마.

So do yourself a favor. And don't try to fight this! 너 자신을 위해 생각 좀 해봐. 그리고 이것과 싸우려들지마!

Do yourself a favor and learn to take yes for an answer. 너 자신을 위해 그냥 받아들이는 법을 좀 배워봐.

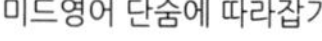

005 Brace yourself 마음 단단히 먹고 들어, 각오해 둬

this usually indicates that the speaker is going to give bad news. He is saying "Be strong when I tell you this"

I Point I brace oneself 각오하다, 마음을 다잡다

A: I have some bad news for you. You'd better **brace yourself.** 안 좋은 소식이 있어. 단단히 각오해.

B: Oh no! Am I going to get fired or something? 어, 이런! 나 잘리는 거야 뭐야?

미드표현

Ok, brace yourself. Here it comes. Just stay calm. 각오해 둬. 긴장말고.

Honey, brace yourself. Your husband's having an affair. 마음 단단히 먹고 들어. 네 남편이 바람폈어.

Well if it's a divorce you want, you better brace yourself for a fight. 네가 이혼을 원한다면, 싸울 준비를 단단히 해두라고

006 Try to put a positive spin on it 긍정적으로 바라보도록 해

when this is said, it means that someone is trying to make something seem very good, even though it might not be good. Sometimes we can understand that a 'positive spin' tricks people into thinking something is better than it really is. It is a way to say "Try to make it look as good as possible"

I Point I put a ~ spin on …에 …한 의미나 해석을 하다
*spin 앞에는 weird, positive 등의 형용사가 온다

A: I've got bad news. I have to tell Joan she's fired. 안좋은 소식이 있어. 조앤에게 해고사실을 말해야 돼.

B: **Put a positive spin on it.** Tell her she'll get a better job. 긍정적으로 바라보도록 해. 걔한테 더 나은 직장을 구할거라고 말해.

미드표현

Well, excuse me for putting a good spin on a traffic jam! 교통혼잡에 대해 좋게 말해서 미안해!

You don't have to put a good spin on everything. 모든 일을 좋게 말할 필요는 없어.

If you find out something really bad, just try to put a positive spin on it. 뭔가 안좋은 일을 알게 되면, 긍정적으로 바라보도록 해.

007 Be careful what you wish for 뭘 원하는지 신중히 생각해

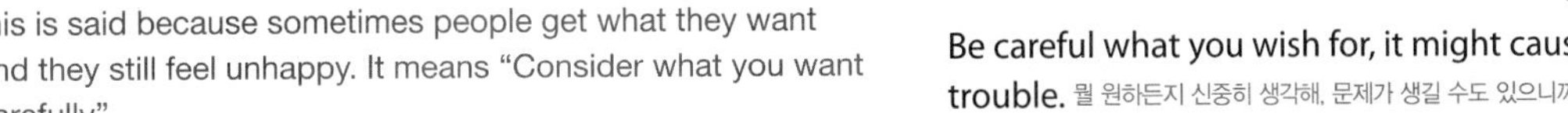

this is said because sometimes people get what they want and they still feel unhappy. It means "Consider what you want carefully"

A: Many rich people I know seem like they are unhappy. 내가 아는 많은 부자들은 불행해보여.

B: **Be careful what you wish for.** Money can cause problems. 신중하게 생각해. 돈은 많은 문제를 낳을 수 있어.

미드표현

Be careful what you wish for, it might cause trouble. 뭘 원하든지 신중히 생각해, 문제가 생길 수도 있으니까.

Be careful what you wish for because you might not want it. 뭘 원하든지 신중히 생각해, 네가 원하지 않는 것일 수도 있어.

Be careful what you wish for, because you could get your wish. 뭘 원하든지 신중히 생각해, 네가 원하는 것을 얻을 수도 있으니까.

008 Be nice 얌전하게 굴어, 친절하게 좀 행동해

this is a way to tell someone "Be kinder." The speaker wants someone to behave in a good way

I Point I Be a man 남자답게 행동해
Be a good boy 착하게 굴어라

A: Nina is wearing the ugliest make-up I've ever seen. 니나는 지금껏 본 것 중 최악의 화장을 하고 있어.

B: **Be nice.** Nina is very sensitive about her appearance. 착하게 굴어. 니나는 자기 외모에 매우 민감하잖아.

미드표현

Be nice if he got somebody who can actually work here. 실제로 여기서 일할 사람이 있다면 잘해줘라.

Be nice. It took me 20 minutes to find my opera cloak. 얌전하게 굴어. 내 야회용 외투를 찾는데 20분이나 걸렸어.

Make friends. Be nice to people. 친구들을 사귀고 사람들을 잘 대해주라고.

009 Follow your heart 마음가는대로 해라

this is usually said to make someone do what they really desire. In other words "Do what you really want to do"

A: All of my life I have wanted to be an airplane pilot. 평생 비행기 조종사가 되고 싶어했어.

B: **Follow your heart.** You can become a pilot if you want to. 하고 싶은대로 해. 원하면 될 수 있잖아.

미드표현

What's more important? What people think or how you feel, huh? Tammy, you gotta follow your heart.
뭐가 중요해? 사람들 생각 아님 너의 느낌, 어? 태미야 마음가는대로 해야 돼.

I think you gotta follow your heart on this one, even if it isn't the easiest thing to do.
가장 쉽지 않은 일이라 할지라도 네 마음가는대로 가야 된다고 생각해.

010 Let that[this, it] be a lesson to you

그 이야기를 교훈 삼아라

this indicates a person should learn something from a bad experience. The speaker is saying "This bad thing will teach you to act differently"

| Point | I've learned my lesson (나쁜 경험을 통해) 교훈을 얻었어

A: I bought Sandra a lot of expensive gifts, and then she broke up with me.
샌드라에게 비싼 선물 많이 사줬는데 나하고 헤어졌어.

B: **Let that be a lesson to you.** True love is not about money. 그걸 교훈삼아. 진정한 사랑은 돈하고 상관없어.

미드표현

Let this be a lesson to all of you, all right?
너희들 모두 이걸 교훈 삼거라, 알았지?

What happened to us is a tragedy but let it be a lesson to all of us.
우리에게 일어난 일은 비극야, 하지만 이를 우리 모두 교훈 삼자.

011 Let's face it 현실을 직시하자

this indicates the speaker is going to say something very honestly. It is another way to say "Let's be very honest with ourselves"

| Point | face the music 당당히 맞서다, 죄값을 치루다

A: **Let's face it.** Our business is going to fail.
현실을 직시하자고, 우리 사업은 망할거야.

B: But can't we do anything that would save it?
하지만 회사를 살릴 뭐라도 할 수 없나요?

미드표현

But let's face it. She's a whore. She cheated on her husband.
하지만 현실을 바로 보자고, 걔는 창녀야. 걔는 자기 남편한테 부정을 저질렀다고.

Let's face it, he may not be a handsome man.
현실을 직시하자고 그 남자는 잘 생기지 않을 수도 있어.

But let's face it. Boys will be boys.
하지만 현실을 직시하자고, 남자애들이 그렇지 뭐.

012 Get your head out of your ass! 정신 좀 차려라!

this is a very rude way to tell someone that he must stop being self-absorbed and start paying attention to what is going on around him. A different way to say this would be "Stop daydreaming and start paying attention"

| Point | get[pull] your head out of your ass 똑똑히 하다, 정신차리다

A: I'm sorry I made so many mistakes. 실수를 많이 해서 미안해요.

B: **You'd better get your head out of your ass.**
정신 좀 차려라.

미드표현

She can't seem to get her head out of her ass.
걘 정신을 못차릴 것 같아.

Get your head out of your ass before you hurt someone. 누구 다치게 하기 전에 정신차리라고.

My advice is to get your head out of your ass.
내 충고는 정신차리라는거야.

He will be fired if he doesn't get his head out of his ass. 걔가 정신차리지 못하면 해고될거야.

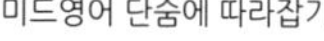

013 That is how it's done 이렇게 하는거야

this is said after showing someone the way to do something. It is like saying "This is the correct way to do it"

| Point | That's how S+V 저렇게[이렇게] …해

A: I just ran a virus scan for your computer.
방금 네 컴퓨터 바이러스 스캔돌렸어.

B: **That is how it's done.** I was wondering about that. 저렇게 하는 거구나. 궁금했었어.

That's how it's gotta be. If you want it.
저렇게 되어야 돼. 네가 그걸 원한다면.

Yeah, that's how babies are made.
어, 저렇게 해서 아이가 만들어져.

That's how we do it down here.
여기서도 이렇게 하고 있어.

That's how I got all these bruises.
그렇게 해서 내가 이 모든 타박상이 생긴거야.

014 That's not how it[this] works 그렇게는 안돼

this usually indicates "You did it wrong." The speaker is saying someone's idea about something is incorrect

| Point | That's not the way it works 그렇게는 안돼
That's not really how it works 정말 그렇게 되는게 아냐
That's not how we do things here 여기서는 그렇게 하는게 아냐
That's (pretty much) how it works 그렇게 해야 되는거야

A: So if I get in a fight, the other guy will get arrested? 그래 내가 싸우게 되면 상대방이 체포될거라고?

B: **That's not how it works.** You'll probably both be arrested. 그렇게는 아니지. 너희들 모두 체포돼.

That's not how this works, okay? I mean we have to make decisions together.
이건 그렇게 하는게 아냐, 알았어? 내 말은 우리가 함께 결정을 내려야 한다는거야.

That is not how it works. Everybody's supposed to submit their proposals in writing.
그렇게 하는게 아냐. 다들 서류상으로 제안서를 제출해야 돼.

015 Get with the program 정신차리라고

this expresses that the speaker feels someone has been lazy or has fallen behind the other people in a group, and it is causing problems. He is warning someone that they need to start doing as well as everyone else. It is like saying "You need to do better or you'll be in trouble"

| Point | get with the program (뒤쳐지지 않도록) 참여하다, 시작하다, (규칙을 따르지 않은 사람을) 이해하다, 주목하다

A: You're always making mistakes. **Get with the program.** 넌 맨날 실수투성이야. 정신 좀 차리라고.

B: I'm sorry, I'll have to try to do better. 미안, 더 열심히 하도록 할게.

Now you get with the program, and fast.
이제 다른 사람들처럼 시작해, 그리고 빨리.

Get with the program, Folks! This guy is as guilty as sin! 정신차려, 사람들아! 이 친구는 확실한 유죄라고!

We just have to get with the program.
우리는 다른 사람들처럼 참여해야 돼.

This will all be taken care of if we all just stick with the program.
우리 모두가 다른 사람들처럼 한다면 모든게 다 처리될거야.

미드에선 이렇게 쓰인다!

Get with the program

Sex and the City SEASON#2-1

주인공 네 명이 식당에서 얘기를 한다. Charlotte의 애인이 공공장소에서 계속 거시기부분을 만진다고 고민을 털어놓는데…

Charlotte: I don't know how long they are.
Samantha: Wait a minute. You've been dating this guy for 3 weeks and you haven't seen his balls yet? Oh, come on, get with the program.
Charlotte: But why do men do this? I mean, how would they feel if we stood around in public touching ourselves?
Both: They'd love it.
Miranda: What are we talking about?
Carrie: Charlotte's boyfriend's balls.

샬롯: 난 그것들이 얼마나 늘어져 있는지 몰라.
사만다: 잠깐, 3주간 지금 남친과 사귀는데 고환을 아직 못봤다고? 그러지말고 정신 좀 차리라고.
샬롯: 하지만 왜 남자들은 그러는거야? 내 말은 우리가 공공장소에 서서 우리 몸을 만진다면 남자들은 어떻게 생각할까?
캐리&사만다: 걔네들은 좋아할거야.
미란다: 무슨 얘기하고 있어?
캐리: 샬롯 남친의 고환.

016 You can't go wrong with this 이건 잘못되는 법이 없어

the speaker is saying that he approves of an idea or plan to do something. It is a way of saying "This is good," or "I would recommend this" or "Go ahead and do it"

I Point I You can't go wrong with sth …는 항상 만족스러워, …는 잘못되는 법이 없어

A: Do you think that this is a good notebook computer to buy? 이 노트북 사도 좋을 것 같아?

B: Absolutely. **You can't go wrong with this model.** 그럼. 이 모델 사도 돼.

You know, can't go wrong with a garden, right? 저기, 정원을 꾸리는건 언제나 만족스러워, 그지?

How about chicken? You can't go wrong with chicken. 닭요리는 어떨까? 닭요리는 항상 맛있잖아.

You cannot go wrong with either one. 어느 쪽을 선택해도 잘못되지 않을거야.

Hey, did something go wrong with Lisa's surgery? 야, 리사 수술 뭐 잘못됐어?

017 Better late than never 아예 안 하는 거보단 늦는 게 나아, 늦더라고 하는 게 나아

this is way to say "It is good something was done, even though it's late." The speaker feels that it is good that it was completed

I Point I Better than nothing 없는 것 보다 낫지

A: This report is overdue by two weeks! 이 보고서는 2주나 늦었어!

B: Well, **better late than never,** sir! 저기, 아예 안하는 것보단 낫지요!

Well, better late than never, I suppose. 음, 안 하는 거보다는 낫지 않겠어.

A: A little late. B: Well, better late than never, right? A: 좀 늦었네 B: 늦더라도 하는게 낫지?

018 Get a life! 정신차려!, 인생 똑바로 살아!

미드표현

the speaker is saying "Grow up." It indicates someone should act like an adult, not a child

I Point I Get real! 정신 좀 차리라구!

A: I played computer games for 6 hours yesterday. 어제 6시간동안 컴퓨터 게임을 했어.

B: **Get a life.** That is a huge waste of time. 정신차려. 엄청난 시간낭비야.

Stop bothering me. Get a life! 그만 나 좀 괴롭히고 정신 좀 차려!

Get a life! All you do is criticize other people. 똑바로 좀 살아! 네가 하는 일이라곤 다른 사람 비난하는 것밖에 없잖아.

You think everyone is worse than you. Get a life! 넌 모든 사람이 너보다 못하다고 생각해. 정신차리라고!

019 Don't do anything I wouldn't do
내가 안 할 것 같은 일은 너도 하지 마, 나쁜 짓 하지 말고

미드표현

this is way to say goodbye to someone and also to advise them to act nicely. The speaker is saying "You need to behave well"

A: I'm off to the airport to fly to Miami Beach. 마이애미 해변가려고 공항에 가.

B: That sounds great! **Don't do anything I wouldn't do.** 멋지다! 잘 행동하고.

And listen. When you're on workshop, don't do anything I wouldn't do. 들어봐, 워크샵에 가면 내가 안할 것 같은 일은 너도 하지마.

Don't do anything I wouldn't do on your date. 너 데이트 때 내가 안할 것 같은 일은 너도 하지마.

I hear you're going to a nightclub. Don't do anything I wouldn't do. 너 나이트클럽에 간다며, 나쁜 짓은 하지 말라고.

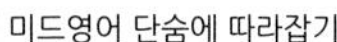

020 I wouldn't if I were you 내가 너라면 그렇게 하지 않겠어

this is a way of giving someone advice. It is similar to saying "It isn't a good idea

| Point | I wouldn't do that if I were you 네가 너라면 그러지 않을텐데

A: I'm just about to purchase a new BMW.
신형 BMW를 사려고 해.

B: **I wouldn't if I were you.** Those cars are too expensive. 내가 너라면 안 살텐데. 너무 비싸.

I know he asked you to take a job, but I wouldn't if I were you.
걔가 너보고 취직하라고 했다는 걸 알아. 하지만 내가 너라면 그렇게 하지 않겠어.

I wouldn't if I were you. It could be very dangerous.
내가 너라면 그렇게 하지 않겠어. 매우 위험할 수도 있는 일이야.

Are you going to Russia? I wouldn't if I were you. 러시아에 간다고? 내가 너라면 그렇게 하지 않겠어.

021 Don't get carried away 너무 흥분하지마, 너무 신경쓰지 마

speaker wants to tell someone "Calm down." He is warning that they shouldn't get too excited or upset

| Point | get carried away …에 몰입하다

A: How will we do this work? It's not possible!
이 일을 우리가 어떻게 해? 불가능해!

B: **Don't get carried away.** We'll get it done.
너무 신경쓰지마. 우린 끝마칠거야.

I guess I've gotten carried away.
제가 너무 정신없이 제 얘기만 했군요.

I'm understanding, but let's not get carried away. 이해해, 하지만 너무 빠져들진 말자.

I mean don't get carried away.
내 말은 너무 몰두하지 말라고.

022 You don't want to know 모르는 게 나아, 안 듣는게 좋을 걸

this usually indicates the speaker doesn't want to talk about something. It is another way to say "I'd rather not tell you about it"

| Point | Don't ask 모르는 게 나아 / You don't want it 안하는 게 좋을거야 / You just watch 두고 봐 / You'll see 두고 봐

A: How was your interview at the new company?
새로운 회사 인터뷰 어땠어?

B: **You don't want to know.** It went very badly.
모르는 게 나아. 정말 안 좋았어.

And believe me, you don't want to know how bad that hurts! 정말이야, 넌 이게 얼마나 아픈지 모르는게 나아!

So, you don't want to know what she looks like. 걔가 어떻게 생겼는지 모르는게 나아.

A: You had sex with her, what, ten times, 20 times? B: You don't want to know the details of what I did.
A: 넌 걔랑 섹스했잖아, 열 번, 이십 번했어? B: 내가 한 행동을 자세히 모르는게 좋아.

미드에선 이렇게 쓰인다!

I'm gonna let you off with a warning this time

Desperate Housewives SEASON# 1-2

Lynette이 극성떠는 아이들을 차로 데리고 가다가 속도위반에 걸렸을 때 경찰이 충고를 하자, 가사와 아이들에게 지치고 지친 Lynette의 분노가 폭발한다.

Lynette:	Are you saying I'm a bad mother?	르넷: 내가 나쁜 엄마라는 말예요?
Cop:	Ma'am you need to get back in your car, please.	경찰: 부인, 차안으로 다시 돌아가십시오.
Lynette:	I have no help. My husband is always away on business.	르넷: 난 도움도 못받아요. 남편은 항상 출장 중이구요.
Cop:	I'm gonna have to ask you to step back now.	경찰: 뒤로 물러서라고 말씀드려야겠네요.
Lynette:	My baby-sitter joined the witness relocation program. I haven't slept through the night in six years. And for you to stand there and judge me.	르넷: 내 보모는 증인보호프로그램에 들어갔고, 난 6년간 밤에 잠을 못잤어요. 그래 당신이 거기 서서 날 비난해요.
Cop:	Okay. I'm not gonna give you a ticket. I'm just gonna let you off with a warning.	경찰: 좋아요. 딱지 끊지는 않을게요. 이번에는 경고만 할게요.
Lynette:	I accept your apology.	르넷: 사과를 받아들이지요.

023 I'm gonna let you off with a warning
경고만 하고 보낼게

this is something usually said by a police officer who is checking how fast cars are going. When he stops people for going too fast, he can give them a speeding ticket or he can let them off with a warning to slow down. People prefer a warning because they don't have to pay money. It is a way of saying "Slow down or I'll give you a ticket next time"

| Point | let sb off with a warning 경고만 주고 봐주다

A: Please don't give me a ticket for speeding.
속도위반 딱지를 끊지 말아 주세요.

B: **I'm gonna let you off with a warning** this time.
이번만은 경고만 하고 보내줄게요.

That was so sweet, you let him off with a warning! 정말 고마웠어요. 경고만하고 놔줘서요!

I'm not gonna give you a ticket. I'm gonna let you off with a warning.
딱지는 끊지 않을게요. 주의만 줄게요.

If you promise not to do it again, I'll let you off with a warning.
다시는 그러지 않겠다고 약속하면 훈방조치할게.

Okay, what if I let her off with a warning, you know, just this one time.
그래. 알겠지만 딱 이번만 걔를 주의만 주면 어떨까.

024 You'll have to make do with it 이걸로라도 때워야 하겠는데

this means "You need to do the best you can." It often indicates someone has a difficult situation and may not get much help

| Point | make do with 그런대로 …로 때우다, 변통하다

A: Dad, my car is old and keeps breaking down.
아빠, 제 차가 낡아서 자꾸 고장나요.

B: **You'll have to make do with it** until you have money to buy another car.
다른 차 살 돈이 생길 때까지 그걸로 때워야 돼.

I'm afraid you'll have to make do with me.
나로 그냥 해야 할 거예요.

We'll make do with what we have here.
있는 것으로 그냥 해야 할거야.

025 Do your job 네 일이나 잘해

this is a way of saying "You need to work with more effort." It indicates someone should work harder

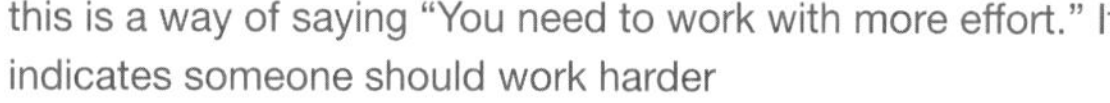

A: There have been complaints about my work here. 여기서 내 일에 대해 불만들이 있었어.

B: **Do your job.** Then everyone will be happy.
네 일이나 잘 해. 그럼 다들 좋아할거야.

You get in there and you do your job.
그곳에 가서 일 잘해.

I've got to do my job, you got to do your job.
난 내 일을 해야 하고 넌 네 일을 해야지.

You're supposed to help the victims. Do your job. 넌 피해자들을 돕기로 되어 있어. 네 일을 잘 하라고.

026 There will be hell to pay 나중에 몹시 성가시게 될거야, 뒤탈이 생길텐데

this means "Someone is going to be very angry." We can understand that a big problem has been created

| Point | be hell to pay 골치 아픈 일이 생기다

A: **There will be hell to pay** when my mom comes home. 엄마가 집에 오시면 엄청 화나실텐데.

B: Yeah, she'll find out you broke the TV!
그래, 네가 TV를 망가트린 걸 아시게 될거야!

If you're not going to show up, there will be hell to pay. 너 안 오면 뒤탈이 생길거야.

If you ever come near her again, there will be hell to pay. Do you understand?
걔 근처에 다시 얼씬하기만 하면 각오해. 알았어?

027 You're gonna have to do a lot better than that 그거 갖고는 턱도 없어

this means that the effort to do something was not good enough, and the person will have to try much harder to be successful. We can understand that the speaker is saying "That's not good enough, you can't succeed unless your effort gets a lot better"

| Point | have to do a lot better than that 그 이상으로 잘해야 된다

A: My report on the company's finances is three pages long. 회사재정에 관한 레포트는 3장 짜리야.

B: That's not enough information. **You're gonna have to do a lot better than that.**
그걸로는 정보가 부족해. 그거 갖고는 턱도 없다고.

미드표현

If you wanna threaten me, you're gonna have to do a lot better than that.
날 협박하려면 그 정도로는 턱도 없어.

If you want me to sign this release, you're gonna have to do a lot better than that.
내가 이 발표문에 서명하기를 바란다면 이 정도로는 턱도 없을거야.

I really want to help you out, but you're gonna have to do a lot better than that.
난 정말 널 돕고 싶지만 넌 그 이상으로 잘해야 돼.

028 Someone is out to get you 누가 널 해칠거야

this expresses that a person is intending to harm or somehow damage another person. We can understand that the speaker is warning the other person that someone may try to do something bad. It means "You better be careful because someone may try to hurt you"

| Point | be out to get sb …을 힘들게 하다(want to cause trouble for sb), …을 해치게 하다

A: I keep finding threatening e-mails in my in-box.
날 협박하는 이멜이 계속 오고 있어.

B: It sounds like **someone is out to get you.** Be careful. 누가 널 해칠려는 것 같은데. 조심해.

미드표현

I think Emily's out to get me.
난 에밀리가 날 힘들게 할 것 같아.

Have you ever felt someone was out to get you? 누군가 너를 곤경에 빠트리고 있다고 느낀 적이 있어?

She thought that somebody was out to get her. 걔는 누군가가 자기를 곤경에 빠트리고 있다고 생각했어.

029 You're better off without me 나 없는 게 너한테 더 좋을거야

this means "Things will be better for you when I leave." The speaker thinks he may be creating problems

A: John, I want you to stay here with me.
존, 나와 함께 있자.

B: That's foolish. **You're better off without me.**
어리석은 일이야. 나 없는게 더 좋을거야.

You're better off without me, so I'm leaving.
나 없는게 너한테 더 좋을거야. 그러니 나 갈게.

Everyone says you're better off without me.
다들 그러는데, 너한테 내가 없는게 더 좋대.

You're better off without me, don't you think?
나없는게 너한테는 더 좋지, 그렇게 생각하지 않아?

You're gonna have to do a lot better than that

Desperate Housewives
SEASON#2-9

Gabrielle은 Carlos가 수녀 Mary와 사이가 가까워지자 Mary에게 경고를 하다가 오히려 큰 코를 다친다.

Gabrielle: What the hell kind of nun are you? Look, if you try to come between me and my husband, I will take you down.

Sister Mary: I grew up on the south side of Chicago. If you wanna threaten me, you're gonna have to do a lot better than that.

Gabrielle: You listen to me, you little bitch. You do not want to start a war with me.

Sister Mary: Well, I have God on my side, Bring it on.

가브리엘: 무슨 수녀가 이래요? 이봐요, 당신이 나와 내 남편사이에 끼어들면 가만두지 않을거예요.
메리 수녀: 전 시카고 남부에서 자라났어요. 협박을 하려면 그 정도로는 턱도 없지요.
가브리엘: 내 말들어, 이 못된 년아. 나와 싸울 생각을 아예 하지 말라고.
메리 수녀: 하나님이 내 편이니 어디 해볼테면 해봐요.

030 (It) Doesn't make it right 그렇다고 그게 옳은 것은 아냐

often this is said when someone does something bad but is not punished for it. The speaker may be angry and feel that it is unfair, and that the person should be punished. It can also be expressed "When someone doesn't get caught doing bad things, that person is still wrong to do them"

| Point | sth doesn't make it right 그걸 정당화하지 못하다
sb make it right …을 바로잡다

A: It's easy to make money selling these fake products. 이 위조상품을 팔아서 돈을 버는 건 쉬운 일이야.

B: It may be profitable, but **that doesn't make it right.** 돈이 될지 모르지만 그렇다고 그게 옳은 것은 아냐.

Just because something's legal doesn't make it right. 합법적이라고 해서 그게 옳은 것은 아냐

Taking the blame for something you didn't do may be noble, but it doesn't make it right.
하지 않은 일에 책임을 지는건 고상할지 모르겠으나 그렇다고 그게 옳은 것은 아니다.

She does good-naturedly to all professors? That doesn't make it right.
그녀가 모든 교수에게 친절하게 대한다고? 그렇다고 그게 옳은 것은 아냐.

031 It's in your best interest not to go there

거기에 안 가는 게 너한텐 최선야

미드표현

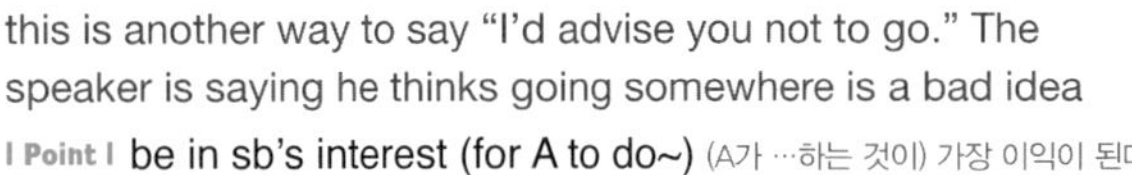

this is another way to say "I'd advise you not to go." The speaker is saying he thinks going somewhere is a bad idea

| Point | be in sb's interest (for A to do~) (A가 …하는 것이) 가장 이익이 된다

A: Do you think it's safe to visit Iraq?
이라크를 방문하는 게 안전할 것 같아?

B: No. **It's in your best interest not to go there.**
아니. 거기에 안 가는 게 좋아.

She realized it was in her best interest to lie to the boss. 걘 사장에게 거짓말하는 게 가장 이익이 된다고 깨달았다.

Is this all really in the best interest of Jessica?
이게 다 정말 제시카를 위한 걸까?

It would be in the best interest of all if this situation didn't become public.
따라서 이 상황이 공개되지 않는 게 모두의 이익을 위해 최선일 겁니다.

032 Heads up! 조심해!

미드표현

this is a way of warning people that something dangerous might be happening. For example, someone might say this if he sees a tree is about to fall over. It is another way to say "Look out!" or "Be careful, something bad is about to happen"

| Point | Heads up! 조심해! heads-up 경고, 충고

A: **Heads up!** A baseball is flying into the stands.
조심해! 야구공이 스탠드로 날아 들어오고 있어.

B: Thanks, that almost hit me in the head.
고마워, 내 머리를 거의 칠 뻔했네.

Heads up. The press is going to be all over this one. 조심하라고, 언론이 이걸로 도배를 할거야.

Heads up. Watch your back, watch your back.
조심해, 뒤를 조심해, 뒤를.

Heads up. Here comes the bus.
조심해, 버스가 들어온다.

I'll give him a heads up. 난 걔한테 경고를 할거야.

033 Do damage control 피해를 최소화해라, 인기 관리를 해라

미드표현

the speaker wants someone to limit the problems that may be caused. It is a way of saying "Try to make things better"

| Point | damage control 피해대책
do damage control 피해를 봐야 하는 상황에서 가장 피해를 줄일 수 있는 방법을 강구하는 것

A: How can I stop the gossip that people say about me? 사람들이 나에 대해 말하는 소문을 어떻게 멈추게 해?

B: **Do damage control.** Tell them the gossip isn't true. 피해를 최소화해. 소문이 사실이 아니라고 말해.

We have to do damage control. 피해를 최소화해야 돼.

You're not terminal, you just need some damage control. 넌 아직 가망있어, 단지 피해를 최소화해야 돼.

First thing we gotta do, damage control.
제일 먼저 해야 할 일은 피해를 줄이는 일이야.

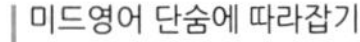

034 Don't put yourself down 자신을 낮추지마

this is a way of urging a person not to be pessimistic about himself. When a person says bad things about himself, he is putting himself down. The speaker is telling that person "Don't diminish yourself, because I think you are better than that," or possibly "Don't talk bad about yourself because you're a good person"

Point put oneself down 자기를 낮추다
put sb down …을 비난하다

A: My parents always said I'd be a failure.
내 부모님은 늘상 내가 실패작이 될거라고 말했어.

B: **Don't put yourself down.** You'll do fine.
너무 자신을 비하하지마. 넌 잘해낼거야.

Don't put yourself down. You're a very attractive man. 자신을 낮추지마. 넌 무척 매력적인 남자야.

It's sad, but Frank constantly puts himself down. 슬프지만 프랭크는 계속해서 자기비하를 해.

It's not so bad. Just remember not to put yourself down.
그거 그렇게 나쁘지 않아. 자신을 낮추지 않도록 해.

035 She's got another thing coming 걘 그러다 큰 코 다칠거야

this indicates that a woman is mistaken about something and something else will happen other than what she is expecting. It is a rebuke, and more or less it is saying to someone "You are not correct about what you think will happen"

Point have got another thing coming 그렇게 하다가는 큰 코 다칠 수 있어

A: Lisa is sure she is going to win the contest.
리사는 자기가 일등할거라 확신하고 있어.

B: I don't think so. **She's got another thing coming.** 안 그럴걸. 그러다 큰 코 다치지.

If you think I'll help, you've got another thing coming. 내가 도와줄거라 네가 생각한다면 큰 코 다칠거야.

He is sure he'll win, but he's got another thing coming. 걘 자기가 이길거라고 확신하고 있지만 큰 코 다치게 될거야.

If he thinks he's playing with 'em when he visits, he's got another thing coming.
걔가 방문해서 자기가 걔네들을 갖고 논다고 생각한다면 걔 큰 코 다칠거야.

036 Deal with it 할 수 없지

this is a way of saying "You must accept the situation." Sometimes it also means that the situation may be difficult or troublesome

Point Get with it! 정신바짝차려!(try harder and stop doing dumb things)

A: This stove is not working correctly.
이 난로는 제대로 작동하지 않아.

B: **Deal with it.** I have other problems to worry about. 할 수 없지. 다른 문제들이 걱정야.

You don't have a choice. Deal with it.
선택여지가 없어. 받아들여.

Confront the situation. Deal with it head-on.
그 상황에 맞서라고. 정면으로 대처하라고.

A: Get your hand off my boob! B: Deal with it.
A: 내 가슴에서 손떼! B: 받아들이라고.

I'm from Asia. I'm mysterious. Deal with it.
난 아시아에서 왔고 신비로와. 받아들이라고.

037 Don't be so sure 모르는 소리

this is usually a way to indicate someone's thinking may be wrong. It means "That is probably not right"

A: These new machines don't work very well.
이 새로운 기계는 잘 돌아가지 않아.

B: **Don't be so sure.** I think you're using them wrong. 모르는 소리. 잘못 사용하는 것 같은데.

Don't be so sure. It's not easy. 모르는 소리. 만만치 않아.

Don't be so sure. He's not like you.
모르는 소리. 걘 너랑 달라.

A: We're gonna win this game easily. B: Don't be so sure. A: 이 게임을 쉽게 이길거야. B: 모르는 소리.

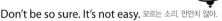

038 Do it right 제대로 해

this means "Use the correct method." The speaker is telling someone not to make mistakes

| Point | I wanna do it right 제대로 해결하고 싶어
We can do it right! 우린 제대로 할 수 있어
Let's just do it right 제대로 좀 하자
Do your job right 일에 차질없이 제대로 해

A: Your math formulas are all wrong. **Do them right.** 네 수학공식은 다 틀려. 제대로 해.

B: But I thought this was the right way to do them. 하지만 제대로 하는 맞는 방법이라 생각했는데.

미드표현

Maybe you didn't do it right.
아마 네가 일을 제대로 안한 것 같아.

If we're gonna do this we're gonna do it right.
이걸 하려면 제대로 해야 돼.

Either way, you gotta do it right now.
어떤 방식이든 이제 넌 제대로 해야 돼.

I have to be there. I want to go back and do it right. 난 거기 가야 돼. 난 돌아가서 그 일을 제대로 해야 돼.

039 You need to get clear on this right now
넌 지금 이걸 확실히 짚고 넘어가야 돼

often this is a way to tell someone that it is very important for him to understand something clearly. This is something that may be said when a person has been causing problems because he doesn't know things well enough. It is like saying "You had better learn that information quickly"

| Point | get clear on 확실히 짚고 넘어가다

A: I am ready to quit this job if things don't change. 상황이 바뀌지 않으면 난 회사를 그만둘거야.

B: **You need to get clear on this now.** No one cares. 지금 넌 이걸 확실히 짚고 넘어 가야 돼. 아무도 신경안쓰거든.

미드표현

Okay, let's get clear on something.
좋아. 뭐 좀 확실히 짚고 넘어가자.

I just wanted to see if I could get clear on what Leo was saying.
난 단지 레오가 한 말을 확실히 짚고 넘어갈 수 있는지 알고 싶었어.

You need to get clear on this right now. I am in charge of this project.
넌 지금 이걸 확실히 짚고 넘어가야 돼. 내가 이 프로젝트 책임자야.

040 Don't take no for an answer 상대방이 거절해도 끈질기게 설득해라

this is a way of telling someone not to give up. It means "Don't allow people to refuse you"

A: How can I get Shelia to go on a date with me? 어떻게 쉴라가 나와 데이트하게 만들 수 있을까?

B: Keep asking her out. **Don't take no for an answer.** 계속 데이트 신청해. 거절해도 끝까지 밀어붙여.

미드표현

I won't take no for an answer.
싫다고는 말하지 못하게 할거야.

I told her no, but she just wouldn't take no for an answer. 걔한테 아니라고 말했는데도 받아들이지 않으려고 해.

Maybe somebody wouldn't take no for an answer. 아마도 누군가는 거절을 받아들이지 않을 거야.

041 It's all or nothing 이판사판야, 모 아니면 도야

this is used to say that something will either be very successful or be a failure. It is another way to say "The result will be very important"

A: I've invested my savings in this company. **It's all or nothing.** 이 회사에 저금을 다 투자했어. 이판사판야.

B: I sure hope this company does well on the stock market. 이 회사가 주식시장에서 잘 나가길 바랄게.

미드표현

It's all or nothing when it comes to love.
사랑에 관해서는 모 아니면 도야.

Does it have to be all or nothing?
그건 모 아니면 도여야 되는거야?

It feels like it's all or nothing. 모 아니면 도인 것 같아.

042 They always fear the worst 걔네들은 항상 최악을 걱정하고 있어

this expresses the feeling that some people are pessimistic or negative in their thinking, and always expect that the worst possible outcomes of things will occur. Another way of saying this is "They are always expecting bad things to happen"

| Point | fear the worst 최악의 상황을 걱정하다, 최악의 경우를 염두에 두다

A: The economic committee says it will be a bad year. 경제위원회가 그러는데 올 한해 안좋을거래.

B: Don't believe them. **They always fear the worst.** 걔네들 말 믿지마. 항상 최악의 경우를 말한다니까.

I feared the worst, immediately called 911.
최악의 상황을 걱정하여, 즉시 911에 전화했어.

And though we hope for the best, we fear the worst. 비록 가장 잘되기를 희망하지만 우린 최악을 대비해.

If I have no one I can open up to, then I fear the worst.
내 맘을 열어보일 사람이 하나도 없다면 난 최악을 걱정할거야.

Military families, they always fear the worst.
군인 가족들은 언제나 최악의 상황을 걱정하고 있어.

043 It's every man for himself (누가 도와주지 않으니) 각자 알아서 해야지

this means "All people need to be selfish now." We can understand the situation is bad and people aren't being kind to each other

A: Too many employees are getting fired here.
너무 많은 사람들이 잘려나가고 있어.

B: I know. **It's every man for himself.**
알아. 이젠 각자 알아서 챙겨야지.

Now it's a whole new ball game. It's every man for himself.
자 이제 전부 새롭게 시작하니까 모두 각각 알아서 해야 돼.

Every man for himself is not gonna work.
각자 알아서 한다는 것은 깨졌어.

Now it's every man for himself? Looks like it.
이제 각자 알아서 해야 돼? 그렇게 보여.

044 You'd better nip this in the bud 애초에 싹을 잘라야 해

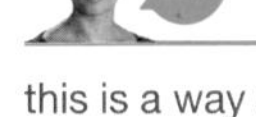

this is a way of saying "Something must be stopped right now." The speaker is trying to stop something before it becomes a big problem

| Point | nip sth in the bud 애초에 싹을 잘라버리다
put the breaks on …에 제동을 걸다

A: I've heard the kids are planning to bring alcohol to the party. 얘들이 파티에 술을 가져 온다며.

B: That's no good. **You'd better nip this in the bud.** 안 좋은데. 애초에 싹을 잘라.

You'd better nip this in the bud right now and I am not kidding. 지금 당장 싹을 잘라야 돼 장난아냐.

He's going to put the brakes on the investigation. 걔가 조사에 제동을 걸거야.

So put the brakes on this thing. 그럼 이 일을 그만둬.

045 (It's) Too late for that 그러기엔 너무 늦었어

this indicates that something can't be changed. In other words "We can't stop it now"

A: Can you go get your umbrella? 가서 네 우산 좀 가져올래?

B: **Too late for that.** I think we're going to get wet.
넘 늦었어. 비를 맞을 것 같아.

It's too late for apologies. 사과하기엔 너무 늦었어.

No, it's too late for that now. 그러기엔 너무 늦었어.

Well, it's too late for that. We need your DNA. Open wide.
그러기엔 너무 늦었어요. 너의 DNA가 필요하니 입을 벌려요.

046 Where're your manners? 버릇이 그게 뭐야, 매너가 없구나

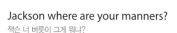

this is usually said when someone is being rude. It is a way of asking "Why are you being so impolite?"

| Point | Mind your manners! 행동 조심해!
Mind your P' and Q'! 행동거지 조심해!
Remember your manners 버릇없이 굴지마, 예의를 지켜야지

A: Give me a sandwich and something to drink! 샌드위치하고 마실 것 좀 줘!

B: **Where are your manners?** Don't talk to me like that! 버릇없기는, 나한테 그런 식으로 말하지마!

Jackson where are your manners? 잭슨 너 버릇이 그게 뭐냐?

You will mind your manners, you will do your chores. 넌 행동거지를 조심하고 네 집안일을 해.

047 Don't make a big deal out of it 과장하지마

this is usually said to ask someone to be calm about something. The speaker is telling the person "Don't create a problem"

| Point | make a big deal out of~ …을 과장하다

A: Someone just took the cart I was using! 내가 사용하는 카트를 누가 가져갔어!

B: **Don't make a big deal out of it.** I'll get you another 소란 떨지마. 다른 거 갖다줄게.

The reason we didn't tell anyone was because we didn't want to make a big deal out of it. 우리가 아무에게도 얘기하지 않는 건 이걸 너무 과장하지 않기 위해서야.

I didn't want to make a big deal out of this. 너무 이거 과장하고 싶지 않아.

Let's not make a big deal out of this! It doesn't even matter! 과장하지 말자고! 문제가 되지도 않는 건데!

048 Where does she get off having all that attitude? 걘는 어떻게 태도가 저따위야?

here the speaker is asking why someone acts so arrogant. We can understand that the speaker may be upset that the person is arrogant. It is like asking "Why does she act like a jerk so often?"

| Point | Where does sb get off ~ing? (상대의 비정상적인 행동에 놀라며) …는 어떻게 그런 식으로 …하나?

A: Betty treats her friends like they are her servants. 베티는 자기 친구들을 하인인 것처럼 대해.

B: **Where does she get off** having all that attitude? 걔 행동을 어떻게 그 따위로 하는거야?

Where do you get off telling me what to do? 넌 어떻게 나한테 이래라저래라 말하는거야?

Where do you get off telling Dick he's not good enough to raise a child? 넌 어떻게 딕이 아이를 기르지 못할거라는 그런 말을 하는거야?

Where do you get off talking to me like that? 어떻게 그딴 식으로 내게 말하는거야?

Where in the hell do you get off telling people that I am bad in bed! 어떻게 내가 섹스에 서툴다고 사람들에게 말하는거야?

Why are you making such a big deal out of this?

Homeland SEASON#1-1

Jessica(Brody의 아내)는 남편의 전화를 받고 남편친구와 하던 섹스를 급마무리하고 집에 가서 자식들에게 알려주려고 가는데… 딸 Dana는 남친과 마리화나를 피고 있다.

Dana: Why are you making such a big deal out of this, Mom?

Jessica: Gee, Dana, I don't know. It's either the lying or the drugs. You're supposed to be looking after your brother.

Dana: Well, he didn't burn down the house.

데이나: 엄마, 별일도 아닌데 이렇게 소란을 피워요?

제시카: 맙소사, 데이나, 모르겠다. 거짓말 때문인지 마리화나 때문인지. 넌 네 동생을 돌보기로 되어 있잖아.

데이나: 걔가 집을 태우는 것도 아닌데요.

049 Behave yourself 버릇없이 굴면 안돼(아이들에게), 점잖게 행동해

this is a way to tell someone "Be good and kind." The speaker wants a person to use good manners

| Point | Your behavior is out of place 네 행동은 무례한 짓이야

A: You'll spend the weekend at your grandmother's. **Behave yourself.**
할머님댁에서 주말을 보낼거야. 점잖게 행동해.

B: I promise that I am going to be very nice to Grandma. 할머니한테 착하게 행동할게요.

Will you behave yourself? 점잖게 행동할테야?

Hey, make sure you behave yourself out there. 야, 거기서 확실히 행동조심해.

Now behave yourself and eat your dinner. Maybe later, if you're lucky, you get to sleep with a college girl.
행동 바르게 하고 저녁을 먹어. 나중에 혹 네가 운이 좋다면 넌 여대생과 잠자리를 하게 될거야.

050 You might want to do that 그걸 하는 게 좋을거야

this indicates the speaker thinks something is a good idea. It is a way of saying "That seems like the right thing to do"

| Point | You might want to~ …하는게 좋아
Why don't you do that? 그거 하지
You'd better do that 그거 해라

A: I was thinking about buying insurance for my house. 집에 보험을 들까 생각중이었어.

B: Yeah, **you might want to do that.** It's a good idea. 어, 그렇게 하는 게 좋을거야. 좋은 생각야.

I just thought you might want to do it. You're the one that saved her life.
네가 하길 원하는 줄 알았어. 걔의 생명을 살린 건 너잖아.

This is one thing you might want to consider.
이건 네가 고려해보는게 좋은 일 중의 하나야.

Scott, you might want to take a look.
스캇, 한번 점검해보는게 좋을거야.

051 You can't have it both ways 둘 다 할 순 없잖아, 결정해야지

this usually means "You must decide about this." It is said to indicate a person must choose one thing

A: I don't know if I want to live in Japan or Australia. 일본에 살지 호주에 살지 모르겠어.

B: You have to choose one. **You can't have it both ways.** 하나를 선택해야지. 두 군데서 살 순 없잖아.

You know you don't want me to help. You can't have it both ways!
내가 도와주는게 싫지? 빨리 결정해!

You can't have it both ways, guys. A judge will laugh me out of court.
둘다 할 수는 없잖아. 판사가 날 법원에서 날 쫓아내거야.

052 You gotta do what you gotta do 할 일은 해야지

this means "Sometimes people must do things that they don't want to do." The speaker is indicating that difficult tasks must be done at times

A: Eventually, I had to fire my best friend because he was always late. 결국, 난 친한 친구가 항상 지각을 해서 잘랐어.

B: That must have been difficult. Well, **you have got to do what you have got to do.**
힘들었겠구나. 음, 그래도 할 일은 해야지.

It's no big deal. You do what you gotta do. Right? 별일아냐. 할 일은 해야지, 아냐?

I gotta do what I gotta do, you gotta do what you gotta do, you just do it.
내가 할 일은 내가 하고 네가 할 일은 네가 해야지. 그냥 해.

053 I'm just gonna talk you out of it 널 설득해서 못하게 할거야

this means "I will convince you not to do something." To talk someone into something means to convince that person to do something. To talk someone out of something means the person will be convinced that doing something is a bad idea

| Point | talk sb out of sth 설득하여 …하지 못하게 하다
talk sb into sth …을 설득하여 …하게 하다

A: I don't want to show Mom my low test score.
엄마에게 낮은 점수 성적표를 보여주고 싶지 않아.

B: Yeah, you won't be able to **talk her out of** punishing you. 어, 널 혼내지 말아달라고 설득하지 못할거야.

미드표현

I can't talk you out of this? I'm a lawyer, I'm very good at this sort of thing.
널 설득해서 이걸 못하게 하지 못한다고? 난 변호사야. 이런 종류의 일에 아주 능숙해.

You want me to talk you out of it?
내가 널 설득해서 그걸 못하게 해달라고?

She only had to talk me into it because she first talked me out of it.
걔가 처음에 내가 못하게 했으니 걔만이 날 설득해서 하게 할 수 있어.

054 Do you have to do that? 꼭 그래야 돼?

this question is used to show that the speaker wants someone to stop doing something because he considers it to be upsetting or annoying. A different way to say the same thing would be "Could you please stop doing that?"

| Point | Do you have to do that? 꼭 그래야 돼?
Why do you have to do that? 왜 꼭 그래야 돼?

A: I am practicing for tomorrow's piano recital.
내일 피아노 연주회 준비로 연습하고 있어.

B: **Do you have to do that?** It's giving me a headache. 꼭 그래야 돼? 그 때문에 머리가 아파.

미드표현

Do I have to do that? Don't I have the right to not incriminate myself?
내가 그래야 돼? 나한테 무죄를 주장하는 권리가 있지 않아?

Do you have to do that? It's Saturday!
꼭 그래야 돼? 토요일이잖아!

You're removing part of my skullcap? Do you really have to do that?
내 두개골 일부를 제거한다고? 꼭 그래야만 해?

055 Don't try to pin it on me! 나한테 뒤집어 씌우지마!

this means "Don't blame me." The person is saying something is not his fault

| Point | pin sth on sb …에게 …에 대한 책임을 뒤집어 씌우다

A: I think that you broke the window! 네가 창문을 부셨지!

B: **Don't try to pin it on me.** I didn't do it.
내게 뒤집어 씌우지마! 난 안 그랬어.

미드표현

You can't pin that on me. 나한테 뒤집어 씌울 수 없지.

A guy gets murdered at my shop, you want to pin it on me?
내 가게에서 살인이 일어났다고 나한테 뒤집어 씌우고 싶은 건가?

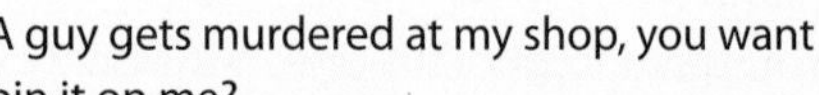

Don't pin that on me. 나한테 뒤집어 씌우지 마.

056 Don't dump your problems into my lap
네 문제를 내가 책임지게 하지마

this is a means of telling another person not to try to transfer unwanted work to the speaker. The speaker can see there are many problems involved in the work, and he doesn't want the responsibility for it. It is another way to say

| Point | dump sth in sb's lap …를 …가 책임지도록 하다

A: Would you mind doing my homework for me?
날 위해 숙제를 해줘도 될까?

B: No way. **Don't dump your problems into my lap.** 말도 안돼. 네 문제를 나한테 떠넘기지마.

Don't expect to dump your work in my lap.
나한테 네 일을 떠맡기는 건 생각도 마.

Peter's boss dumped the whole project in his lap. 피터의 사장은 그 전체 프로젝트를 걔한테 맡겼어.

The new recruits were just dumped in my lap.
신입사원들은 내 책임하에 있게 됐어.

057 You're barking up the wrong tree 잘못 짚었네

this is said when a person has the wrong idea. It is a way to say "You are wasting your time because that is wrong"

| Point | You're on the wrong track 헛짚었어

A: I heard that you work as a doctor. 네가 의사라며.

B: **You're barking up the wrong tree.** I'm a teacher. 잘못 짚었네. 난 선생님이야.

If you think I'll help, you're barking up the wrong tree. 내가 도울거라 생각한다면 큰 오산이야.

You're barking up the wrong tree. It will never work. 너 잘못 짚었어. 그거 절대로 그렇게 되지 않을거야.

Everyone has told you that you're barking up the wrong tree. 다들 너한테 번지수 잘못 짚었다고 말했잖아.

058 I'll try not to slip up 실수하지 않도록 할게

this person wants to say "I'll be careful not to make a mistake." It is a way of saying he plans to do his best

| Point | slip up 실수하다(make a mistake)

A: You have to make sure this is perfect.
이거 확실하게 완벽하도록 해.

B: **I'll try not to slip up.** 실수하지 않도록 할게.

She's going to slip up. She's going to leave a piece of evidence that can't be refuted.
걘 실수할거야. 반박할 수 없는 증거를 남겨놓을 거야.

Maybe they're trying to rattle you, hoping you'll slip up.
걔네들이 네가 실수하기를 바라며 너를 당황하게 만들지 몰라.

You're right. But teenagers sometimes slip up.
네 말이 맞아. 하지만 십대들은 종종 실수를 하잖아.

059 You're to blame 네 책임이야

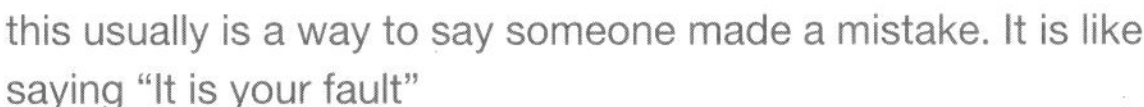

this usually is a way to say someone made a mistake. It is like saying "It is your fault"

| Point | I have myself to blame 모두 내 탓으로 돌리다
I'm not in charge (of~) (…의) 책임자가 아니야
put sb in charge of …에게 …을 책임지우다

A: If you dated other guys, **you're to blame** for the relationship failing.
네가 다른 놈들과 데이트하면 관계를 망친 게 네 책임이야.

B: But he dates other women too!
하지만 걔도 다른 여자들하고 데이트하는데!

You're not to blame for this, Harry.
해리야 이건 네 잘못이 아냐.

So I'm to blame for this? 그럼 이게 내 책임야?

It was an accident, there's no one to blame.
그건 사고였어 아무도 비난하면 안돼.

I'm the one who stole. I'm the one to blame, not you. 내가 훔친 사람이야. 네가 아니라 내가 비난 받을 사람이지.

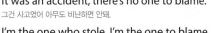

060 Don't blame me 나한테 그러지 마

this indicates "I'm not at fault." This person doesn't want people to think something was his mistake

| Point | Don't blame sb for~/if S+V …했다고 …을 비난하지 마라
Don't place[lay] the blame on me 내 탓하지 마
Let's blame me for this 내 잘못으로 치자

A: This cake tastes very strange. 이 케익 정말 맛이 이상해.

B: **Don't blame me.** I didn't cook it.
나한테 그러지마. 내가 만든 거 아냐.

Well, don't blame me for that.
그게 내 잘못이라고 하지마.

Don't blame me. It's your mom's fault.
나한테 그러지마. 네 엄마의 잘못이야.

Hey, don't blame me. I'm not the one who jumped into a relationship without thinking about the consequences.
야, 나한테 그러지마. 결과를 생각하지도 않고 성급하게 관계를 맺은 것은 내가 아냐.

061 I take full responsibility for that 그거에 대한 모든 책임을 지겠어

미드표현

this means the person accepts blame for something bad. It is a way to say "It happened because of me"

| Point | take responsibility for~ …에 대한 책임을 지다
accept responsibility for~ …에 대한 책임을 받아들이다
It's my responsibility (to do~) (…을 하는 게) 나의 책임이야

A: This fire happened while you were working.
네가 일하고 있을 때 불이 났어.

B: **I take full responsibility for that.**
내가 그에 대한 모든 책임을 질게.

There comes a time when you have to take responsibility for yourself.
스스로를 책임져야 할 때가 올거야.

Taking responsibility for it is more than just saying "Sorry."
단지 '미안'하다고 말하는 것보다는 책임을 지는 게 나아.

It's my responsibility to tell you the truth about her! 걔한테 너에 관한 진실을 말하는 게 내 책임야!

062 I take it back 취소할게

미드표현

this means "Please forget what I said." It is used when someone wants to say that he didn't mean something he just said

| Point | take sth back (잘못 인정후 한 말) 취소하다, 되돌리다

A: You said I was beautiful last year.
작년에 내가 아름답다고 했잖아.

B: **I take it back.** You've gotten kind of fat.
취소할게. 너 살이 좀 쪘어.

You can't take it back. You already said it.
취소할 수 없어. 벌써 말해버렸잖아.

I'm sorry, I'm just gonna have to take it back.
미안해 내 말 취소해야겠어.

If you do it, you can never take it back.
그걸 하면 절대 다시 되돌릴 수 없어.

Why don't you just take it back to where you got it? 가져 온 곳으로 다시 돌려줘.

063 I'm looking over my shoulder every day
난 매일 조심하고 있어

미드표현

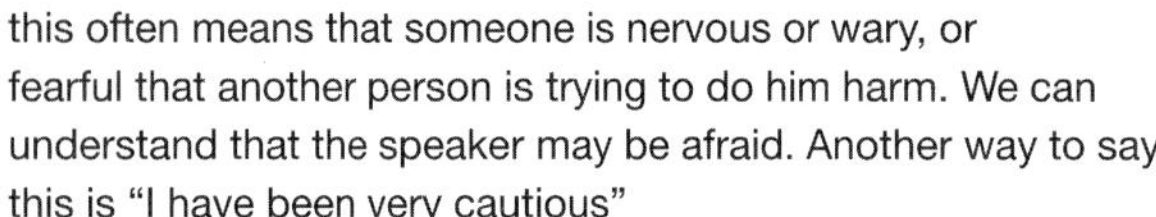

this often means that someone is nervous or wary, or fearful that another person is trying to do him harm. We can understand that the speaker may be afraid. Another way to say this is "I have been very cautious"

| Point | look over one's shoulder (위험을 대비하며) 걱정하다, 조심하다, 감시하다

A: Are you still worried about getting mugged?
넌 아직도 강도당할까봐 걱정하고 있어?

B: Yes I am. **I'm looking over my shoulder every day.** 어 그래, 난 매일 조심하고 살아.

I've spent the last ten years looking over my shoulder every day.
난 지난 10년간 매일 조심하면서 살았어.

I don't need you looking over my shoulder! I'll find them and kill them.
내 걱정하지 않아도 돼! 난 걔네들을 찾아서 죽일거야.

Porter's ducking a subpoena and I'm looking over my shoulder.
포터는 소환장을 회피하고 있고 난 조심할거야.

MEMO

Ways of saying you're not happy with something or someone

실망과 후회하기 혹은 상대방에게 불만있는지 물어보기

Don't bitch about it

001 Do you have a problem with me?

나한테 뭐 불만있는 거야? 내 말에 뭐 문제라도 있어?

this is a way of asking "Are you upset with me?" The speaker wants to know why someone doesn't like him

| Point | Do you have a problem with sb? …에게 불만있어?
I think you have a problem 너 불만 있나본데

A: You keep looking at me. **Do you have a problem with me?** 날 계속 쳐다보는데 뭐 불만있어?

B: Yeah. I think you used my parking space without asking. 넌 내게 묻지도 않고 내 주차자리를 차지했어.

미드표현

I liked her. Maybe you're the one who has a problem with her.
난 걔를 좋아해. 너만 걔한테 불만갖고 있을 거야.

I heard you're having a problem with one of the boys in your class. 네 반 친구 한명과 문제가 생겼다며.

Is there a problem with me or with you?
나한테 불만이 있는거야 아님 너한테 문제있는거야?

002 Do you have a problem with that?

그게 뭐 문제있어?, 그게 불만야?

this means that the speaker wants to know if someone will become angry. It is another way to ask "Will this upset you?"

| Point | Does anybody have a problem with that? 누구 문제있어?
You got a problem with that? 그게 뭐 문제 있어?

A: I'm going to sit here. **Do you have a problem with that?** 여기 앉을거야. 뭐 문제 있어?

B: No, go ahead and have a seat if you want to.
아니, 그래 원하면 앉아.

미드표현

If you're having a problem with the sex, you should just say it now. 섹스에 불만있으면 지금 그냥 얘기해.

If you've got a problem with that, then maybe we should find another chef.
문제가 있으면 다른 주방장을 찾자고.

I am so glad you don't have a problem with this. 이거에 별 불만이 없어서 기뻐.

003 Don't bitch about it 그거 가지고 징징대지마

this is a rude way to say "Don't complain about it." The speaker doesn't want to hear people say bad things

| Point | bitch about = complain about 불평하다, 투덜대디
You know what the real bitch of it is?
이거에서 제일 엉터리가 뭔지 아나? *여기서 bitch는 명사로 엉터리라는 의미.

A: It's really cold and wet in this campground.
이 캠프장은 정말 춥고 축축하네.

B: You chose to come camping. **Don't bitch about it.** 네가 캠핑오자고 했잖아. 투덜대지마.

미드표현

Want to have some coffee, sit around, bitch about our kids?
커피 좀 마실래? 앉아서 자식들 푸념이나 할까?

I can't take it anymore. I'm gonna bitch about the neighbor's loud music.
더 이상 못 참아. 이웃집의 시끄러운 음악소리에 항의할거야.

I used to bitch about the fact that there weren't any great girls out there.
멋진 아가씨들이 없다는 사실에 투덜거리곤 했어.

004 Don't complain about it 불평하지마

the speaker is telling someone he doesn't want to hear bad things said. In other words "Don't talk about that problem"

A: This has to be the worst food I've ever tasted.
내가 먹어본 것 중 가장 최악의 음식야.

B: **Don't complain about it.** We can't send it back. 투덜대지마. 취소할 수도 없잖아.

I'm here to complain about the noise.
시끄럽다고 항의하러 왔는데요.

Don't complain about my smoking.
내가 담배피는 것 불평하지마.

Well, I can't complain about my boss. He's right here. 난 내 상사에 대해 불평을 할 수 없어. 지금 여기 있거든.

005 I've got a bone to pick with you 너한테 불만 있어

this indicates the speaker wants to talk about a problem someone caused. He is saying "I want to discuss something we disagree about"

A: **I've got a bone to pick with you** about the work you did.네가 한 일로 너한테 불만 있어.

B: Why is that? Were you unhappy about the way it turned out? 뭔데? 결과가 맘에 안들어?

That reminds me, I have a bone to pick with you. 그러고보니 생각나는데, 나 너한테 불만이 있어.

I've got a bone to pick with you, and I'm about to do it in front of all your friends.
나 너한테 따질게 있는데 네 모든 친구들 앞에서 이제 따질거야.

A: Okay, I got a bone to pick with you. B: What did I do now?
A: 좋아, 나 너한테 따질게 있어. B: 내가 뭘 어쨌는데?

006 It stinks 엉망이야, 영 아니야

this means "Something is very bad." It indicates that the speaker really doesn't like it. It can also mean that something has a bad smell

| Point | stink 고약한 냄새가 나다, 뭐가 좋지 않다, 엉망이다
stink of …의 냄새가 나다
stink at+N/~ing …에 서투르다
What stinks? 뭐가 그렇게 지독한데?

A: How do you like the apartment building you moved to? 이사간 아파트 어때?

B: **It stinks.** It's noisy and the neighbors are impolite. 으악야, 시끄럽고 이웃들도 불친절하고.

Something stinks. 뭔가 수상한 냄새가 나.

Service here always stinks. 여기 서비스는 늘상 엉망야.

Let's call a spade a spade, this party stinks.
솔직히 말하자고, 이 파티는 영 아냐.

I don't stink. I'm a good chef.
난 엉망이 아냐, 능력있는 주방장이라고.

You stink at lying. 너 거짓말은 영 아니잖아.

007 It sucks! 밥맛이야!, 젠장할!, 최악이야!

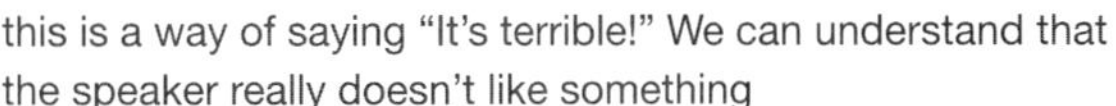

this is a way of saying "It's terrible!" We can understand that the speaker really doesn't like something

| Point | You suck! 재수없어! That sucks! 빌어먹을! 젠장할!
It doesn't suck 봐줄 만 한데, 나쁘지 않은데

A: Have you seen the new Bruce Willis film? **It sucks!** 브루스 윌리스 나오는 새 영화 봤어? 끔직해!

B: Yeah, I've heard that it was kind of boring.
그래, 좀 지겹다고 하던대.

Your life doesn't suck, you have a woman who really loves you.
네 인생은 나쁘지 않아, 널 진정으로 사랑하는 여자가 있잖아.

They're all like that. Or worse. Men suck.
걔네들은 다 똑 같아, 더 나쁘거나, 남자들은 밥맛이야.

You guys suck! I hate you!
니네들은 밥맛이야! 니네들이 정말 싫어!

008 Talk about selfish! 이기적이라면 그 사람 따라갈 수가 없어!

this indicates someone was not thinking about others. It's a way to say "That person only thinks of himself"

| Point | Talk about ~ …라니 터무니없구만, …라는 게 어디 있냐, …치곤 최고구만

A: John ate all of the spaghetti I made for the party.
존은 파티용으로 만든 스파게티를 다 먹어버렸어.

B: That's awful. **Talk about selfish!** 굉장하네, 정말 이기적이라니깐!

He failed every class. Talk about stupid!
걔 모든 과목에서 낙제했어, 멍청한 건 누가 따라갈 수가 없어!

Talk about expensive. I'll never be able to afford it. 정말 엄청 비싸네, 난 절대로 그걸 살 여유가 없을거야.

Talk about strange. Tim never talks to anyone.
정말이지 진짜 이상하네, 팀은 절대로 누구와도 얘기를 하지 않아.

009 Is that [it] too much to ask? 내가 너무 많이 요구하는 거야?

usually this means the speaker wants to know if something seems impossible to do. He is asking "Is it too difficult?"

| Point | Is it too much to ask to do~? …해달라고 하는 게 무리한 요구야?
Do I expect too much? 내가 너무 많은 걸 기대하나?

A: All I want is a nice wife and a good job. **Is that too much to ask?**
단지 내가 바라는 건 좋은 아내와 번듯한 직장야. 내가 넘 요구하는 건가?

B: No, I think you'll be able to have both of those things. 아니, 그 두개 다 갖을 수 있을거야.

미드표현

I'm having a real bad day. Is this too much to ask? 오늘 정말 힘들었는데 이게 너무 무리한 부탁이야?

Is that too much to ask after ten years?
10년 만인데 이게 너무 무리한 부탁인가?

Is it too much to ask to have dinner with me tonight? 오늘 밤 저녁 같이하자는 게 무리한 부탁이야?

010 What's it gonna take (for you) to get it done 어떻게 하면 그걸 끝낼 수 있겠니?

this is asking what the person wants or needs to complete a job. It's like asking "What do you need to do it?"

| Point | What's it gonna take (for you) to do~
…하는 데 필요한 게 뭐야?, 어떻게 하면 …하겠니?

A: My computer needs to be fixed. **What's it going to take to get it done?** 컴퓨터 수리해야 하는데 어떻게 하면 돼죠?

B: I need a few hours to fix it, and it will be expensive. 몇시간 소요되고요 수리비가 비싸요.

미드표현

What is it gonna take to make you happy?
어떻게 하면 널 행복하게 해줄 수 있겠니?

Let's talk turkey. What is it gonna take for you to give up the baby?
솔직히 얘기하자. 어떻게 해야 아이를 포기할래?

What's it gonna take for you to forgive me? I'll do anything you want.
어떻게 해야 날 용서하겠니? 네가 원하는 뭐든지 할게.

011 You'll be the death of me (yet) 너 때문에 내가 못살아

the speaker is saying "You're causing many problems for me." He is indicating someone is making his life more difficult and stressful

A: I'm sorry Dad, but I crashed the car.
미안 아빠, 하지만 차를 망가트렸어요.

B: Oh Tom, **you'll be the death of me** yet.
어, 탐, 너 땜에 내가 내 명에 못 죽겠다.

미드표현

You'll be the death of me. You're giving me too much stress.
너 때문에 내가 못살겠다. 너 나한테 스트레스를 너무 많이 줘.

This is the second time you wrecked my car. You'll be the death of me.
내 차를 망가트린게 이번이 두번째야. 너 때문에 내가 못살겠어.

My mom always said that you'll be the death of me. 우리 엄마는 늘상 나 때문에 못살겠다고 하셔.

012 That's not fair 그건 공평하지가 않아

this is a way to say "Something is not equal or not right." We can understand the speaker is upset because of this situation

| Point | This is so unfair 이거 정말 불공평해
No fair! 불공평해!, 이건 공정하지 않아!

A: I can buy ice cream for her, but not for you.
걜 위해 아이스크림을 사줘도 넌 안돼.

B: **That's not fair!** We should both get ice cream!
불공평해! 우리 모두 아이스크림을 사줘야지!

미드표현

That's not fair! It's not our fault!
불공평해! 우리 잘못이 아니란말야!

You think that's me? That's not fair.
그게 나라고 생각해? 그건 공평하지 않아.

How could this happen? I mean, this is so unfair! 어떻게 이런 일이? 너무 불공평하단 말야!

Dad, you can't do that. This is so unfair.
아빠, 그러시면 안돼요. 너무 불공평해요.

013 He didn't even stick up for me 걔는 내 편을 들어주지도 않았어

this is said when someone didn't assist the speaker in a fight or disagreement. In other words "He didn't help me when I needed it"

I Point I stick up for sb (아무도 도와주지 않는 상황에서 비난받는 사람) 편을 들어주다, 지지하다

A: Why are you angry at Michael today?
오늘 마이클한테 왜 화났어?

B: **He didn't even stick up for me** when people were being unkind.
사람들이 내게 불친절한데도 내 편을 들어주지 않았어.

You don't have to stick up for her.
넌 걔 편을 들어주지 않아도 돼.

If there's one thing I learned in prison, it's to stick up for myself because nobody else will.
감옥에서 배운 게 하나 있다면, 아무도 나의 편이 돼주지 않기 때문에 스스로를 챙기는 것이야.

014 What do I get? 내가 얻는 게 뭔대?, 난 얻는 게 없어, 내가 바보냐?

this is usually said when someone wants to know what they will be given. It expresses "What will I receive?"

A: I know that the kids got gifts, but **what do I get?**
아이들은 선물을 받는 걸 알겠는데 난 얻는게 뭐야?

B: Just be patient. I have presents for you too.
좀 침착해. 너 줄 선물도 있어.

What do I get if I win? 내가 이기면 얻는 게 뭔데?

And what do I get in return? Nothing!
그럼 그 보답으로 얻는 게 뭔데? 아무 것도 없다구!

What do I get, besides a headache?
두통말고 내가 얻는게 뭔데?

015 What have I got? 나에겐 뭐가 남지?

this is often a way to ask what was gained, or what profit came from doing something. Sometimes we can understand that the speaker is expressing regret because he did not receive more profit. Another way to say this is "What good did this do me?"

I Point I What have I got? 내게 남는게 뭐지?

A: What are you so angry about? 뭐 때문에 그렇게 화가 난거야?

B: I started this company and it failed. **What have I got now?** 이 회사를 창업했는데 실패했어. 내게 남는건 뭘까?

I worked twenty years and what have I got?
20년 넘게 일했는데 내게 남는게 뭐지?

What have I got? Nothing of value. 내겐 뭐가 남지? 돈되는 건 아무것도 없어.

Someone stole all of my money. Now what have I got? 누가 내 돈 전부를 훔쳐갔어. 이제 내게 뭐가 남지?

What have I got? No one has paid me.
내게 뭐가 남겠어? 아무도 내게 지불해주지 않는데.

016 What's in it for me? 내가 얻는 게 뭔데?, 내게 무슨 득이 되는데?

this is asking "What benefit do I get?" The speaker wants to know if he will be rewarded if he does something

I Point I What's in it for him? 걔가 얻는 게 뭔데?

A: Can you help me mow my lawn? 내 잔디 깎는 거 도와줄래?

B: **What's in it for me?** I don't work for free.
내가 얻는 게 뭔데? 난 무료봉사는 안 한다고.

That's good for you. But what's in it for me?
너한테는 잘 된 일인데 내가 얻는 건 뭔데?

How did I become a part of this? What's in it for me? 내가 어쩌다 이렇게 됐을까? 내게 무슨 득이 된다고?

A: Will you just come over and fix it? B: What's in it for me?
A: 이리와서 그것 좀 수리해줄테야? B: 내가 얻는 게 뭔데?

017 Don't let me down (믿었던 상대방이 실망시켰을 때) 날 실망시키지마

this is a way to tell people to do their best. It means "I trust you and want you to do a good job"

I Point I let sb down …을 실망시키다
What a letdown! 야, 참 실망이다!
Don't disappoint[fail] me 실망시키지마
You failed me 넌 날 실망시켰어

A: You have to study hard. **Don't let me down.**
공부 열심히 해야 돼. 날 실망시키지마.

B: I'll do my best Dad. Believe me. 최선다할게요. 믿으세요.

I'm tired of you acting like a kid. You let me down. 애들처럼 행동하는 네가 지겨워. 실망했어.

I'm sorry I let you down, Dad.
아빠 실망시켜드려 죄송해요.

You disappoint me. I thought you were smarter than that.
날 실망시켰어. 그러지 않을 정도로 똑똑하다고 생각했는데.

You're not going to disappoint me, are you, Jimmy? 날 실망시키지 않을거지, 지미?

018 That's a downer 김빠지네, 실망스럽네, 암울해

this refers to something that made people feel sad. It expresses that "That made me feel unhappy." It can also describe a person or event that has made people sad

I Point I Tom was a real downer last night 탐은 어젯밤 정말 실망스러웠어
What a downer! 야, 참 실망이네!(that is very sad or depressing)

A: My father said we have to move to another city.
아버지가 다른 도시로 이사해야 한다고 하셨어.

B: **That's a downer.** You'll miss all of your friends.
실망스럽네. 네 친구들을 다 그리워하게 될거야.

I know prison's supposed to be a deterrent, but does it have to be such a downer? It's so gross and scary.
감옥이 죄를 억제한다고는 하지만 왜 그렇게 분위기가 암울해? 역겹고 무시무시해.

No matter how much make-up you wear, you're still a downer. 네가 아무리 많이 화장을 해도 넌 안돼.

019 I'm bummed out 실망이야

this means "I feel bad/sad." The speaker is indicating that he is feeling gloomy about something

I Point I be bummed out 실망하다

A: Hey Frank, what's the matter? 프랭크, 무슨 일야?

B: I had an argument with my best friend. **I'm bummed out.** 친한 친구와 다투었어. 실망하고 있어.

I just get a little bummed when my birthday's over. 내 생일이 끝났을 때 좀 실망했어.

This blows his mind and he's extremely bummed out. 이것 때문에 걔 정신이 나갔고 절망했어.

I'm sure he's not more bummed out than I am. 걔가 나보다 좀 덜 실망했을 게 확실해.

020 I was frustrated with you! 너 땜에 맥이 풀렸어!

this means "I was unhappy with your behavior." It expresses an upset feeling with someone

I Point I be[get] frustrated with …때문에 좌절하다, 실망하다

A: Why did you leave the room so suddenly?
왜 그렇게 급히 방을 나간 거야?

B: **I was frustrated with you!** You talk too much!
너 땜에 진이 빠졌어! 넌 말이 너무 많아!

She looks frustrated with herself for what she did. 걔는 자기가 한 일로 스스로 좌절하고 있는 것 같아.

How on earth can you be frustrated with me right now? 넌 도대체 왜 지금 나한테 실망을 할 수 있는거야?

I knew he was frustrated with me, and I was definitely frustrated with him.
걔가 나한테 실망한 걸 알고 있었고 난 확실히 걔 때문에 실망했어.

021 It's not all it's cracked up to be 사람들의 말처럼 그런 건 아냐

often this is a way to say "It's not good." It means the speaker was disappointed with something

| Point | It's not what it's cracked up to be 소문난 대로는 아냐

A: How was the new movie you saw?
네가 본 새로 개봉한 영화 어땠어?

B: Not so good. **It's not all that it's cracked up to be.** 별로야. 사람들 말처럼 그렇지 않아.

Divorce isn't all it's cracked up to be, is it?
이혼이란 게 사람들 말처럼 그런 게 아니지 그지?

This whole motherhood thing, it's not all it's cracked up to be?
엄마가 해야 할 이 모든 게 사람들 말처럼 그런 게 아니지?

Honesty's not all it's cracked up to be.
정직이라는게 사람들 말처럼 꼭 그런 것은 아냐.

Having a job is not all it's cracked up to be. Working at the hospital is very hard work!
직장다는게 다 그런 것은 아냐. 병원에서 하는 일은 정말 힘들어!

022 It's a major bummer 정말 기운 빠지네, 정말 영 아닌데, 정말 기대에 못 미치는데

미드표현

this indicates something bad happened. It is a way to say "That really makes me feel unhappy"

| Point | What a bummer! 정말 맥 빠지는구먼! *bummer는 원래 게으름뱅이

A: I heard that the team's star player is injured.
그 팀의 스타플레이어가 부상이래.

B: **It's a major bummer.** Now we can't win the tournament. 정말 맥 빠지는데. 이제 우승 못하겠네.

Wow, that is really a bummer. 와, 정말 실망스럽네.

So things didn't work out with Julie, huh? Bummer. 그래 줄리에게 상황이 안 좋게 돌아갔지, 응? 영 아니네.

023 I shouldn't have done that 그러면 안 되는 거였는데, 내가 왜 그랬을까

미드표현

this is a way of showing regret. It means "I wish I had done something else"

| Point | should have+p.p. …했어야 했는데 (…하지 못했다)

A: I don't think you should have hit Tom.
네가 탐을 때리지 말았어야 했는데.

B: Yeah, you're right. **I shouldn't have done that.**
그래, 맞아. 그러면 안 되는 거였는데.

I shouldn't have asked. 묻지 말았어야 했는데.

I shouldn't have said. 말하지 말았어야 했는데.

You shouldn't have done it! 그러면 안 되는 거였는데!

I screwed up. I shouldn't have lied.
내가 망쳤어. 거짓말하면 안 되는 거였는데.

024 What was I thinking? 내가 왜 그랬을까?

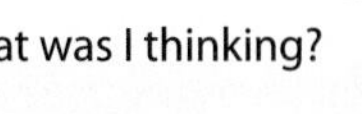

this is a way of expressing regret about something that happened in the past. The speaker is not actually asking a question, but rather saying out loud, "I'm not sure why I did that. I should have thought about it more carefully before I acted"

| Point | What was I thinking? 내가 왜 그랬을까?, 내가 무슨 생각으로 그랬을까?

A: So you stayed in your room all day?
그럼 너 종일 방에 있었단 말야?

B: Yeah. **What was I thinking?** I could've gone to the beach. 어, 내 왜 그랬을까? 해변에라도 갈 수 있었을텐데.

Oh, right, of course, what was I thinking?
어, 맞아, 물론이야, 내가 왜 그랬을까?

What was I thinking? I should've stayed out of it. 내가 왜 그랬을까? 난 빠졌어야 했는데.

Honey, you're right. This scarf doesn't go with this outfit at all. What was I thinking?
자기 말이 맞아. 이 스카프는 이 옷과 어울리지 않아. 내가 무슨 생각으로 그랬을까?

What was I thinking? I'm an idiot.
내가 무슨 생각으로 그랬을까? 난 바보 멍충이야.

025 You'll live to regret this decision
넌 앞으로 이 결정을 후회하게 될거야

this is a way to say that the speaker thinks someone is making a bad decision, and in the future that person will feel a lot of sadness and remorse because of it. In other words "This is a dumb thing to do, and you will be unhappy if you choose do it"

| Point | live to regret 앞으로 후회하다

A: I'm going to get married, no matter what anyone says. 누가 뭐라든 난 결혼을 할거야.

B: It's a bad idea. **You'll live to regret this decision.** 좋은 생각이 아냐. 넌 이 결정을 앞으로 후회하게 될거야.

You'll live to regret it if you do.
네가 그러면 앞으로 후회하게 될거야.

You'll only live to regret them.
넌 단지 그것들을 앞으로 후회하게 될거야.

Let's not say things we'll live to regret.
나중에 후회하게 될 일들은 말하지 말자.

You mean the world to me. I know you'll live to regret this decision.
넌 내게 정말 소중한 사람이야. 넌 이 결정에 대해 앞으로 후회하게 될거라는 걸 알고 있어.

026 Sorry (that) I asked 물어보지 말걸

this is a way to say the person got more information than they wanted. It is similar to saying "I wish I hadn't questioned you"

A: I split up with my wife because we always fought. She was bad!
항상 싸워서 마누라하고 갈라섰어. 걘 정말 나빠!

B: Oh, that makes me feel sad. **I'm sorry that I asked.** 어, 안됐네. 물어보지 말걸.

That's too personal. Sorry I asked.
그거 너무 개인적인 일이야. 물어보지 말걸.

Sorry I asked. I thought I was being helpful.
물어보지 말걸. 난 내가 도움이 된다고 생각했어.

I needed to know the answer, but I'm sorry I asked. 난 답을 알아야 했었지만 그래도 물어보지 말걸.

027 I'm ashamed of you 부끄러운 일이야, 부끄러워 혼났어, 너 때문에 너무 창피해

this means "I think your behavior was bad." It expresses a bad feeling about what the person did

| Point | You should be ashamed of yourself 스스로 부끄러운 줄 알아라
You embarrass me 너 때문에 창피해

A: You stole this toy. **I'm ashamed of you.**
네가 이 장난감을 훔쳤어. 부끄러운 일이야.

B: I'm sorry Dad. I'll take it back to the store.
죄송해요 아빠. 가게에 다시 갖다 놓을게요.

I never said I was ashamed of you!
너를 부끄러워한다고 말한 적이 전혀 없어!

I'm not ashamed of anyone I've slept with.
내가 잔 사람들을 부끄러워하지 않아.

I'm ashamed of myself. Allow me to make this right.
내 자신이 부끄럽기 한이 없어. 내가 이 일을 바로 잡을 수 있도록 해줘.

028 The shame of it (all)! 부끄러운 일이야!, 부끄러워서 혼났네!

this indicates someone is very unhappy about something. It means "That was a bad thing"

| Point | The shame of it is (that) S+V 부끄러운 일은 …이야
For shame 부끄러운 줄 알아야지, 창피한 일이야

A: This war was started so companies could profit.
이 전쟁이 시작되어서 회사들이 이익을 남길 수 있을거야.

B: **The shame of it all.** It really upsets me.
참 한심하구만. 정말 열받네.

The shame of it is you didn't do that.
부끄러운 일은 네가 그걸 하지 않은거야.

The shame of it is an innocent kid got killed.
부끄러운 일은 어린 아이가 살해당했다는 거야.

029 Shame on you! 부끄러운 줄 알아야지!, 창피한 일이야!

미드표현

this is a way of criticizing someone. It is saying "Your actions were bad"

A: I took this apple from my teacher's desk.
선생님 책상에서 이 사과를 가져왔어.

B: **Shame on you!** That was bad behavior.
창피한 줄 알아야지! 그건 안 좋은 행동이야.

Shame on you! You should know better.
창피해라! 더 좀 알아야지.

You fool me once, shame on you. You fool me twice shame on me. 네가 날 한 번 속이면 네가 쪽 팔리는 거고 날 두 번 속이면 내가 쪽 팔리는 거지.

I didn't hire the prostitute, she was a gift from him. Shame on you, Raj. 내가 매춘부를 부른게 아니고 걔가 선물해준 여자였어. 부끄러운 줄 알아야지, 라지.

030 There's nothing to be ashamed of
창피하게 생각할 건 하나도 없어

미드표현

this means "Don't worry about it." It is used to say that the person't behavior was correct or OK

| Point | You have nothing to be ashamed of 창피하게 생각할 거 없어
I have nothing to be ashamed of 난 떳떳해, 난 하나도 부끄럽지 않아

A: Some of my exam scores were low.
시험 성적 일부가 안 좋아.

B: **There's nothing to be ashamed of.** You did your best. 창피하게 생각하지마, 넌 최선을 다했잖아.

I know it's nothing to be ashamed of.
하나도 부끄러울 게 하나도 없다는 거 알아.

She's a good student, nothing to be ashamed of. 걔는 훌륭한 학생이야, 하나도 부끄러울게 없어.

Look, having a crush is nothing to be ashamed of. 이봐, 사랑에 빠지는 건 부끄러워 할 일이 아냐.

031 What have I done? 내가 무슨 짓을 한거야?

미드표현

often a speaker asks this as a way to express that he feels he is innocent, and has done nothing bad to anyone else. At times it can also be expressing regret for having done something. A different way to express innocence would be "What have I done that was harmful or bad? Nothing." A different way to express regret would be "I am so sorry for what I've done"

| Point | What have I[we] done? 내가 무슨 짓을 한거야?, 내가 뭘 어쨌는데?
What have you done to~ ? …을 어떻게 한거야?, 이게 무슨 짓이야?

A: Are you upset with me? **What have I done?**
나한테 화났어? 내가 뭘 어쨌다고?

B: I heard you were kissing another woman.
네가 다른 여자하고 키스했다며.

Oh my God, what have I done?
맙소사, 내가 무슨 짓을 한거야?

All right, let's see, what have I done? What do I want to do?
좋아, 글쎄, 내가 무슨 짓을 한거지? 내가 하고 싶은 일은 뭘까?

What have I done? I quit my job.
내가 무슨 짓을 한거지? 내가 직장을 그만뒀어.

What are you doing? What have you done?
너 뭐하는거야? 이게 무슨 짓이야?

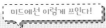

미드에선 이렇게 쓰인다!

What have we done?

The Big Bang Theory
SEASON#3-23

설마 있을까라고 생각하며 Sheldon의 짝을 만남사이트를 통해 소개시켜주는데 그만 서로 다른 차원의 천생연분이라… 자신이 해놓은 일에 놀라서 Howard가 하는 말….

Amy: Noted. Now, before this goes any further, you should know that all forms of physical contact up to and including coitus are off the table.
Sheldon: May I buy you a beverage?
Amy: Tepid water, please.
Howard: Good God, what have we done?

에이미: 알아들었어요. 더 진도가 나가기 전에, 성교를 포함한 모든 종류의 육체적 접촉은 고려 대상이 아니라는 점을 알아둬야 해요.
쉘든: 마실거 사줄까요?
에이미: 미지근한 물 주세요.
하워드: 맙소사, 우리가 무슨 짓을 한거지?

032 I am so humiliated 너무 모욕적이었어, 쪽 팔려 죽겠어, 창피해 죽겠어

this is a way of expressing shame. It expresses "I feel embarrassed about something"

A: **I am so humiliated.** Everyone knows about my problems. 정말 쪽 팔려. 다들 내 문제를 알고 있어.

B: Try not to think about that right now. 신경쓰지 않도록 해봐.

미드표현

I looked like an idiot! And I was humiliated.
난 바보같았어! 너무 쪽 팔렸어.

You just humiliated me in front of my friends.
내 친구들 앞에서 날 쪽 팔리게 했어.

She humiliated me, I wanted revenge.
걔가 날 쪽 팔리게 했고 난 복수를 원했지.

033 After all[everything] I have done for you 얼마나 네게 잘해주었는데

this speaker is saying "You did something bad to me after I helped you." It expresses disappointment

A: I'm sorry Tom, but I have fallen in love with another man. 탐 미안해, 하지만 나 다른 남자와 사랑에 빠졌어.

B: I can't believe it. **After everything I have done for you!** 말도 안돼. 얼마나 네게 잘해주었는데!

미드표현

So, you're ending our friendship, after everything I've done for you?
그렇게 잘 해줬는데 관계를 끝내자는 거야?

I'm really hurt. After all I've done for you.
정말 맘이 아파. 얼마나 잘해줬는데.

MEMO

Ways of telling someone not to do something

해도 된다고 허락하거나, 안된다고 금지하기

Don't you dare!

001 (Please) Don't do that 제발 그러지마

this is a polite way of telling someone to stop something. It is similar to saying "Please stop that"

| Point | Don't do that anymore 더는 그러지 마
Don't ever do that again 두 번 다시 그러지마
Don't ever try to do it 절대로 그러지마

A: I'm going to continue singing a song.
계속해서 노래를 부를거야.

B: **Please don't do that.** I don't like your voice.
제발 그러지마. 네 목소리 듣기 싫어.

Oh my God, don't do that! 맙소사, 그러지마!

Don't do that to yourself. 너한테 그렇게 하지마.

Don't do that. You listen to me. I mean what I say. You understand?
그러지마, 내 말 들어. 정말이야. 알았어?

Don't do that. Don't give me that fake confused look.
그러지마. 그 혼란스러워 하는 척 하는 표정 좀 짓지마.

002 You can't do that! 그러면 안되지!

this means that something is not allowed. The speaker is saying that doing something is against the rules

| Point | We can't do that 우리가 그럼 안되지
She can't do that 걔가 그러면 안되지

A: I'm going to get up and leave now. 일어나서 가려고.

B: **You can't do that!** The host of the party will become angry. 그럼 안되지! 파티 주최한 사람이 열받지.

You can't do that, because mom will freak out. 그러면 안돼, 엄마가 기겁할거야.

That's crazy! You can't do that! 미쳤군! 그러지마!

What? What are you talking about? You can't do that. 뭐라고? 무슨 말하는거야? 너 그러면 안되지.

003 Don't you dare! 당치도 않아!, 까불지마!

this is a way of saying "Don't do that." The speaker is telling someone strongly not to do something

| Point | Don't you dare do~ ! 감히…를 하지마!, …할 생각은 꿈도 꾸지마!

A: I'm going to cheat on the final exam.
기말고사에서 컨닝할거야.

B: **Don't you dare!** You should study harder instead. 그러지마! 대신 공부를 열심히 해야지.

Don't touch me. Don't you dare touch me!
만지지 마. 만질 생각은 꿈도 꾸지마!

Don't you dare give me that attitude.
그런 태도는 내게 짓지마.

Don't you dare leave this house!
이 집을 나갈 생각은 꿈도 꾸지마!

Don't you dare say that I wanted this

Desperate Housewives SEASON#3-7

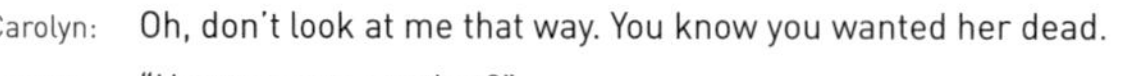

Grocery에서 남편의 바람핀 거에 분해 총질을 해대는 Carolyn의 총에 Nora가 죽자 Lynette이 분노해서 Carolyn과 나누는 대화.

Carolyn: Oh, don't look at me that way. You know you wanted her dead.
Lynette: "How can you say that?"
Carolyn: Well, you told me about her and your husband after I made it pretty clear where I stand on whores.
Lynette: I did not want this. Don't you dare say that I wanted this."
Carolyn: Shut up!"
Lynette: No, I will not shut up! What's the matter with you?!"
Carolyn: Have you not been paying attention? My husband cheated on me!"
Lynette: Who cares?! Who cares? We all have pain! Everyone in here has pain, but we deal with it! We swallow it and get going with our lives! What we don't do is go around shooting strangers!"

캐롤린: 오, 그런 식으로 날 쳐다보지마. 걔가 죽기를 바랬잖아.
르넷: 어떻게 그렇게 말할 수 있어?
캐롤린: 내가 창녀들을 어떻게 생각하는지 분명히 말한 후에 넌 걔와 네 남편에 대해서 말했어.
르넷: 난 이걸 원하지 않았어. 어떻게 감히 내가 이걸 원했다고 말하는거야?
캐롤린: 입닥쳐!
르넷: 안돼, 난 입다물지 않을거야! 넌 도대체 뭐가 문제야?!
캐롤린: 지금까지 내 말 못들었어? 내 남편이 바람을 폈다고!
르넷: 그래서? 누가 신경이나 쓴대? 우리 모두 아픔을 갖고 있어. 여기 있는 모든 사람은 아픔이 있지만 헤쳐나가고 있다고. 우리는 맘속으로 삼키고 삶을 살아가고 있다고. 우리가 하지 않는 것은 돌아다니면서 총을 쏘는 일이라고!

004 I can't tolerate it 용납이 안돼, 그러면 안돼

this indicates the person won't accept some behavior. It is a way to say "You can't do that"

| Point | tolerate 참다, 견디다

A: Can I smoke in here? 여기서 담배펴도 돼?
B: No. **I can't tolerate it.** 아니, 그럼 안돼.

She was with the only man she could tolerate.
그 여자는 자신이 용납할 수 있는 남자하고만 있었어.

I will not tolerate this kind of behavior. Do you understand? 이런 행동은 안돼. 알겠어?

005 Don't say it! (상대방의 말을 끝으며) 그만해!, 말하지마!

this indicates the speaker doesn't want to hear something. It is said to stop someone from saying this information

A: Wait until you hear what Melanie did yesterday.
멜라니가 어제 뭘 했는지 들을 때까지 기다려.
B: **Don't say it!** I don't like gossip.
그만해! 소문은 좋아하지 않는다고.

No, don't say it! Don't even think it!
아니, 그만 말해! 생각도 하지마!

You're right! You're right. Don't say it.
맞아! 네 말이 맞아. 그만해.

006 Don't let him~ 걔가 …하지 못하게 해

the speaker is saying that a person should not be allowed to do something. It is like telling someone "Stop him[her] from doing ..."

A: Mark really drank a lot of beer tonight.
마크가 오늘 밤에 정말 술 많이 마셨어.
B: I know. **Don't let him** drive his car home.
말아. 집에 차 못 갖고 가게 해.

Don't let her drink anymore! 걔 술 더 못 마시게 해!

Don't let her in. 걔 들여보내지마.

Don't let her drive. 걔 운전 못하게 해.

Don't let him kiss you. 걔가 너한테 키스 못하게 해.

007 You're not supposed to do that 그러면 안돼

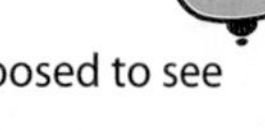

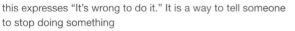

this expresses "It's wrong to do it." It is a way to tell someone to stop doing something

| Point | I'm not supposed to~ 난 …하면 안돼

A: I like to have a few beers during our lunch break. 점심시간에 맥주 몇 병 마시고 싶어.
B: **You're not supposed to do that.** You'll get in trouble. 그러면 안돼. 문제 생길거야.

Get out of here! You're not supposed to see the bride before the wedding!
나가! 결혼식 전에 신부 보면 안돼!

What are you doing here? You're not supposed to be back till Sunday.
여기서 뭐해? 일요일까지 오면 안돼.

I am not supposed to be here.
난 여기 있으면 안 되는데.

008 That's off limits 거긴 가면 안돼, 그건 절대 금지야

this is said when something is not allowed. When a thing is off limits, people shouldn't do it

| Point | She's off limits 걔한테는 접근 금지야
The OR is off limits 수술실은 접근금지야

A: Can your brother come home from the army base this weekend? 이번 주말에 형이 부대에서 집으로 올 수 있어?

B: No, **that's off limits.** He'll come home next month. 아니, 금지됐어. 다음 달에 올거야.

That's off limits. Don't talk about it.
그건 절대 금지야. 그것에 관해서는 얘기하지마.

No questions about my sex life. That's off limits. 내 성생활에 대해서는 물어보지마. 그건 절대 금지야.

That's off limits. We are forbidden from going there. 거긴 가면 안돼. 우리는 거기 가는게 금지됐어.

009 I talked him out of it 걔를 설득해서 못하게 했어

this means that the speaker changed another person's mind. To talk someone out of something means to convince someone not to do something

| Point | talk sb into+N/ ~ing …를 설득해서 …하게 하다
talk sb out of+N/ ~ing …를 설득해서 …하지 못하게 하다

A: Why didn't Ray go out with Tina last Saturday?
왜 지난 일요일에 레이가 티나와 데이트 안했어?

B: **I talked him out of it.** Tina isn't a nice girl.
걔한테 하지 말라고 했어. 티나는 안 좋은 애야.

I can't believe you talked me into doing this.
나보고 이걸 하라고 했다니 믿을 수가 없어.

Jim wanted to go after her again but I talked him out of it.
짐은 걔를 쫓아가려고 했는데 내가 말렸어.

Jane talked you out of it? Mike told me that he talked you out of it.
제인이 널 말렸다고? 마이크는 자기가 말렸다고 하던대.

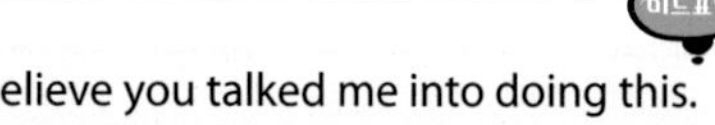

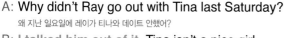

010 I'm not allowed to do that 난 그거 하면 안돼

this indicates a person isn't permitted to do something. It is similar to saying "It's against the rules for me to do that

| Point | be allowed to do …하는 게 허용되다
You're not allowed to do~ …를 하면 안돼

A: Come on, let's drink some whiskey together!
자, 위스키 함께 마시자!

B: **I'm not allowed to do that.** My parents don't like me to drink alcohol. 안돼. 부모님이 술마시는 거 싫어해.

That's not allowed. 그건 안돼.

You're not allowed to sleep with any of your students. 네 학생 누구와도 자면 안돼.

We're not allowed to talk to strangers.
우린 모르는 사람과 이야기 하면 안돼.

011 I took the liberty of declining it 난 내 맘대로 그걸 취소했어

this means that a person chose to do something without asking for permission to do it. In many situations it may be common to ask someone to be allowed to do something, but a person who takes the liberty of doing something just does it. It is like saying "I decided to do that without asking anyone"

| Point | take the liberty of~ 실례를 무릅쓰고 …하다, 제멋대로 …하다, 마음대로 …하다, 허락도 없이 …하다

A: Darnell said he invited both of us to his New Year's party. 다넬은 자기 송년파티에 우리 둘을 다 초대했다고 하던대.

B: That's right. **I took the liberty of** declining his invitation. 맞아. 내가 맘대로 걔 초대를 거절했어.

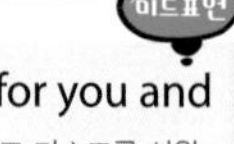

I took the liberty of buying masks for you and your brother. 내가 내키는 대로 너와 네 형 주려고 마스크를 사왔어.

I took the liberty of packing up your suite and checking you out.
내가 맘대로 네 스위트룸 짐을 싸고 체크아웃을 했어.

I took the liberty of scripting a new outgoing voice mail message for both of us.
내가 맘대로 음성사서함 메시지를 새롭게 바꿨어.

012 Stay out of trouble 말썽 피지마, 문제 일으키지마

this is a way to say "Don't do something bad"

A: I'm off on my vacation to Las Vegas.
휴가로 라스베거스에 가.

B: **Stay out of trouble.** Make sure you behave yourself. 문제 일으키지마. 행동거지 확실히 잘하고.

You just have to promise me you'll stay out of trouble. 문제 안 일으키겠다고 내게 약속해.

Now, all I have to do is stay out of trouble.
이제 난 문제 일으키지 않기만 하면 돼.

I made a promise to my parents that I'd stay out of trouble. 부모님께 말썽 안 핀다고 약속했어.

013 You don't belong here 여기에 오면 안돼

this is said when a person is in the wrong place. It means they should leave and go to the correct place

I Point I belong to …에 속하다

A: Is this the class that I am supposed to attend?
이게 내가 들어야 하는 수업야?

B: No, it isn't. **You don't belong here.**
아니, 그렇지 않아. 여기 아냐.

I feel like we don't belong here. 우리 잘못 온 것 같아.

What makes you think you belong here?
왜 여기에 와야 된다는 생각이 드는거야?

This is a crime scene. You don't belong here.
여긴 범죄현장이야. 오면 안돼.

014 Get your hands off! 건드리지 마!

this is a very strong and rude way to tell someone not to touch something. It is like saying "Don't touch"

I Point I get your hands off~ …에게서 손을 떼다

A: Oh, let me see your new diamond ring!
어, 새로 산 다이아몬드 반지 보여줘!

B: **Get your hands off!** You'll damage it! 만지지마! 기스나!

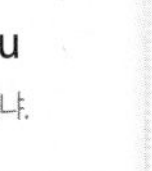

Please get your hands off my breasts!
내 가슴에서 손 좀 치워!

Get your hands off of her! 걔한테서 손 떼!

Get your hands off me! Let go of me. You don't own me. 나 건드리지마! 날 놔둬. 난 네 소유가 아냐.

Stop it! Get your hands off me! 그만해! 나 건드리지마!

015 Is it all right if~ ? …해도 돼?

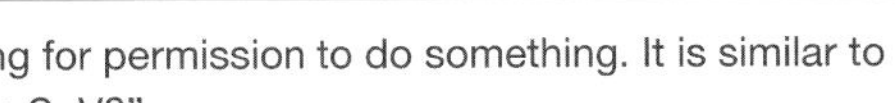

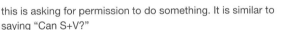

this is asking for permission to do something. It is similar to saying "Can S+V?"

A: **Is it all right if** I smoke a cigarette? 담배펴도 돼?

B: Sure. I'm not bothered by people smoking.
물론. 사람들 담배피는 건 난 괜찮아.

Is it all right if I come? 내가 가도 돼?

Is it all right if I go with you? 내가 너와 함께 가도 돼?

Is it all right if I stay in New York for a few more days for a vacation?
휴가 동안 뉴욕에서 며칠 더 머물러도 괜찮아요?

016 Feel free to~ 언제든 …해

this is a way to tell someone it is OK to do something. It is like saying “Go ahead and do~”

| Point | Feel free to ask 뭐든 물어봐

A: **Feel free to** wear your shoes inside my house.
내 집에서는 편하게 신발 신고 있어.

B: But isn't that impolite to do in Asia?
하지만 아시아에서는 결례 아냐?

미드표현

Please feel free to do it. 마음대로 그걸 해.

Feel free to drop by anytime. 언제든 들러.

Feel free to use my cellphone. 언제든 내 핸드폰 써.

017 (Do you) Mind if~ ? …해도 돼?

this is a way to ask if something is allowed. We can consider this similar to “Is it OK to S+V?”

| Point | Would you mind if~ = Do you mind if~
= You mind if~ = Mind if~ …해도 돼?

A: **Would you mind if** I took a look around?
둘러봐도 돼요?

B: Be my guest. 맘대로 하세요

Mind if I try? 해도 돼?

You mind if I ask you a few questions?
질문 몇 개 좀 해도 돼?

You wouldn't mind if I examined your room, would you? 네 방 조사해도 괜찮겠지, 그지?

Hey, anyone mind if I take my boob out for a second? 이봐, 잠깐 내 가슴 좀 내놔도 괜찮겠지?

018 By all means 물론이지, 그렇고 말고, 그 정도야

미드표현

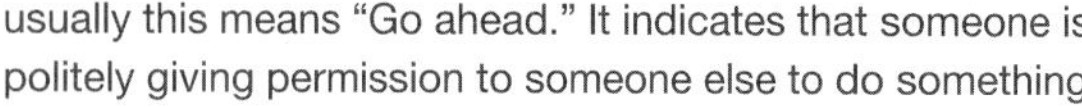

usually this means “Go ahead.” It indicates that someone is politely giving permission to someone else to do something.

A: May I smoke a cigarette while we wait?
기다리는 동안 담배펴도 돼요?

B: **By all means.** It won't bother me at all.
물론. 전혀 괜찮아.

A: Mind if I take a look? B: By all means.
A: 좀 봐도 되겠니? B: 물론.

A: Do you mind if we ask you a few more questions? B: By all means.
A: 몇가지 질문을 더해도 될까? B: 그럼.

MEMO

Things that are said when someone is upset

화를 내고 짜증을 내기

Cut the crap!

001 Don't be a baby 어린애처럼 굴지마

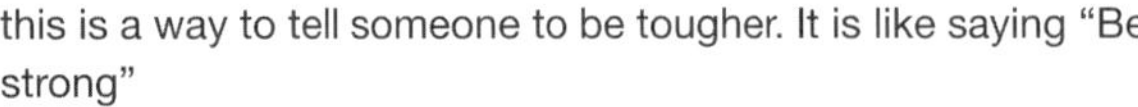

this is a way to tell someone to be tougher. It is like saying "Be strong"

| Point | Act your age! 나이 값 좀 해라!, 철 좀 들어라!
You have to grow up 철 좀 들어
Grow up already 이제 철 들 때도 되지 않았어

A: My stomach is really hurting me! 정말 배가 아파 죽겠어!
B: **Don't be a baby.** It's not that bad.
애처럼 굴지마. 그렇게 안좋지는 않은데.

미드표현

You shouldn't have done such a stupid thing. Act your age!
왜 그렇게 유치한 짓을 했어. 나이 값 좀 해!

This is our apartment and you can not behave this way. Now if you can't act your age then you'll in trouble.
여긴 우리 아파트고 이런 식으로 행동하면 안돼. 제대로 행동못하면 혼날줄 알아.

002 You're one to talk 사돈 남 말 하네, 웃기고 있네

this is saying "Your actions are similar." It means the person may be doing some of the things that he has been complaining about

| Point | Look who's talking 사돈 남 말하네
*You're the one to talk 네가 얘기할 차례

A: It seems like Jack is drinking a lot of alcohol these days. 잭이 요즘 술을 많이 마시는 것 같아.
B: **You're one to talk.** I think you drink every night.
사돈 남 말 하네. 넌 매일밤 술 마시잖아.

미드표현

Oh you're one to talk. Sleeping with two men.
사돈 남 말하네. 두 명의 남자하고 자놓고서.

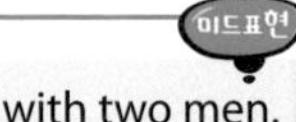

I know you're the one to talk to.
네가 이야기나눌 수 있는 사람인 걸 알아.

003 It[That] doesn't make any sense 무슨 소리야, 말도 안돼

미드표현

this means that something can't be understood. It is like saying something is foolish or unclear

| Point | It makes [no] sense 말이 (안)된다
You're not making sense 무슨 소리야, 말도 안돼
Does that make any sense? 말이 돼?

A: This is the new textbook you will study from.
네가 공부할 새로운 교과서야.
B: The information in the book is wrong. **It doesn't make any sense.** 책의 내용이 틀려. 말도 안돼.

I can't make any sense of any of it.
난 그게 조금도 이해가 되질 않아.

It's not gonna make any sense! 전혀 말도 안될거야!

How does that make any sense?
그게 어떻게 말이 되냐?

She fell 7 storeys and lived. It doesn't make any sense. 7층에서 떨어지고 살다니, 말도 안돼.

Nothing you say makes sense to me.
네가 말하는 건 이해가 안돼.

004 This is crazy 말도 안돼, 엉망이구만, 개판이네

this speaker wants to say "This is a bad idea." He feels there is some big problem with what is happening

| Point | This is insane! 미친 짓이야!
This is ridiculous 황당하구만

A: I'm sorry that I got us lost. 나 땜에 길잃어 미안해.
B: **This is crazy.** We should have been home long ago. 말도 안돼. 오래 전에 집에 도착했어야 하는데.

미드표현

This is crazy! I can't do this! 말도 안돼! 난 못해!

What is going on? This is crazy. 무슨 일이야? 개판이네.

What? I didn't kill anybody. This is crazy.
뭐라고? 난 아무도 안 죽였어. 말도 안돼.

005 Don't tell me (that) ~ …라고 말하지마, 설마 …라는 얘기는 아니겠지?

미드표현

this means a speaker doesn't want to listen. When he says this he thinks "I don't want to hear that information"

| Point | Don't tell me 말하지마

A: The repairs on your car are going to be really expensive. 차 수리비가 정말 많이 나올거예요.

B: **Don't tell me that.** I am already low on money. 설마, 벌써 돈이 부족한데.

Don't tell me men are nice. 남자들이 착하다고 말하지마.

Don't tell me you believe that. 설마 그걸 믿는 건 아니겠지?

Don't tell me. Let me guess. 말하지마. 맞춰볼게.

006 Very funny! (화난 어조로) 장난해!, 그래 우습기도 하겠다!, 말도 안돼!, 안 웃기거든!

미드표현

this is usually said in a sarcastic way, and it means the speaker thinks something is not funny. It is similar to saying "I didn't like your joke"

| Point | What's so funny? 뭐가 그렇게 우스워?
Did I say something funny? 내 말이 웃겨?

A: Who put hot sauce in my sandwich? **Very funny!** 누가 내 샌드위치에 핫소스를 넣었어? 안 웃기거든!

B: Come on Norm, don't get angry at us. 그러지마 놈, 우리한테 화내지마.

Someone put salt in my coffee? Very funny! 누가 내 커피에 소금을 넣었다고? 장난하냐!

Very funny! That really made me laugh. 정말 웃긴다! 그 때문에 정말 웃었어.

Oh, did someone make a farting noise? Very funny! 누가 방귀소리냈어? 되게 웃긴다!.

007 I don't believe this! (원치 않는 혹은 뭔가 이상한 상황에서) 이건 말도 안돼!

미드표현

this is said when someone is very surprised. It means "It's really surprising this happened"

| Point | I don't believe it 어떤 사실을 '못 믿겠다'
I don't believe this 놀람과 화난 감정이 섞인 표현으로 당황과 황당함이 서려있다.

A: I have to go to the dentist this afternoon. 오늘 오후에 치과에 가야돼.

B: **I don't believe this.** You want to leave early again? 말도 안돼. 또 이렇게 일찍 가겠다고?

I don't believe this. You called the police? 이건 말도 안돼. 경찰을 불렀다고?

I don't believe this. You're setting me up? 이게 뭐야. 날 함정에 빠트렸다고?

I don't believe this. ou look so completely different. 말도 안돼. 너 정말 완전히 다르게 보인다.

I don't believe this. Aren't you listening to me? 이건 말도 안돼. 내 말 안듣고 있는거야?

008 She's being super stuck up 걘 정말 거만해

미드표현

this indicates a woman is being arrogant or acting as if she is better than other people. Most commonly this is used by younger people who dislike the unkind way someone is behaving. In other words, "She acts as if she is superior to everyone else"

| Point | be super stuck up 정말 거만하다(be arrogant), 잘난 척하다
be[get] stuck up~ …에 갇힌다, 끼이다

A: Why does Edna treat everyone so poorly? 왜 에드나가 사람들에게 그렇게 못되게 구는거야?

B: **She's being super stuck up.** She's a real bitch. 걘 정말 거만해. 정말 못된 년이야.

Ann comes off a little stuck up when you first meet her. 앤은 처음 만나면 좀 거만하게 보여.

She had a boyfriend and she was kind of stuck up. 걘 남친이 있었고 좀 잘난 척을 했어.

Brook is known for being super stuck up and totally twofaced. 브룩은 엄청 거만하고 위선적인 사람으로 알려져 있어.

009 Cut the crap 바보 같은 소리마, 쓸데 없는 이야기 좀 그만둬

this is a way of telling someone to be serious. It is similar to telling someone "Stop joking around"

| Point | crap 배설물, 허풍
Come off it! (잘난 척 혹은 거짓말하는 상대방에게) 집어쳐!, 건방떨지마!
Cut the shit 쓸데없는 소리 그만해, 본론으로 들어가

A: Let's play a joke on Lenny today. 오늘 레니 놀리자.
B: **Cut the crap.** You guys should be working.
쓸데 없는 얘기 그만둬. 너희들 일해야지.

You better cut the crap and tell me the exact date and time. 잡소리 그만하고 정확한 날짜와 시간을 말해.

You got to cut the crap. Okay? Come on, tell me what happened.
쓸데 없는 소리 그만해. 알았어? 자, 무슨 일이 있었는지 말해.

Cut the crap and answer my questions.
쓰잘데 없는 소리 집어치우고 내 질문에 답해.

010 You're so full of crap 넌 완전 엉터리야

this means that a person often lies. It is like saying "I don't believe you"

| Point | full of crap 허풍으로 가득찬
I'm full of crap 쓸데없는 말만 잔뜩 늘어놓았네
That's a load of crap 그건 엉터리 얘기야

A: Yeah, I often go to Hollywood to hang out with stars. 어, 종종 할리우드에 가서 스타들과 어울려.
B: **You're so full of crap.** I don't believe you at all.
이런 뻥쟁이. 넌 전혀 못 믿겠어.

I told you she was full of crap.
내가 걔는 완전히 엉터리라고 말했잖아.

You even think your boss is full of crap.
사장이 완전 엉터리라고 생각하는구나.

I still think you're full of crap.
난 아직도 네가 엉터리라고 생각해.

That's a load of crap, and you know it.
말도 안 되는 이야기야 너도 알잖아.

011 It's a piece of shit 거짓말이야, 엉망이야

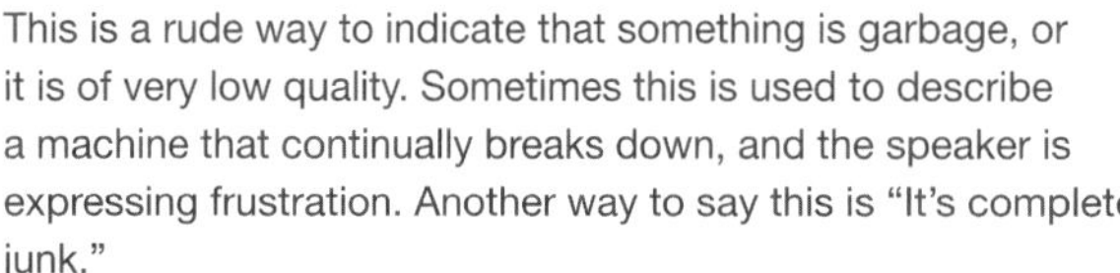

This is a rude way to indicate that something is garbage, or it is of very low quality. Sometimes this is used to describe a machine that continually breaks down, and the speaker is expressing frustration. Another way to say this is "It's complete junk."

| Point | You're full of shit 넌 거짓말만 해대잖아
be a piece of shit[crap] 말도 안되는 거짓말이다, 엉망이다, 개떡같다

A: Do you like the car that you bought?
네가 산 차 맘에 들어?
B: I hate it. **It's a piece of shit** that always breaks.
정말이지 싫어. 허구헌날 고장만 나는 고물단지야.

Some people like I-phones, but I think they are pieces of shit.
아이폰을 좋아하는 사람들도 있지만 난 그거 쓰레기같아.

What are you looking at, you piece of shit!
뭘 보는거야, 이 한심한 놈아!

Where's that little piece of shit?
저 작은 고물 어디에 있는거야?

012 Cut it out 그만둬, 닥쳐, 하지마

this is a way to say "Stop that." The speaker wants someone not to continue doing something

| Point | Would you cut it out? 좀 그만 둬라?

A: You are too noisy. **Cut it out.** 넌 너무 시끄러워. 그만둬.
B: I was just talking to my friend on my cell phone.
핸드폰으로 친구와 그냥 얘기중이었어.

Cut it out! You're really making people mad.
그만해! 너 때문에 사람들이 화를 내잖아.

Fuck! Wake up! Wake up! Stop it! Cut it out!
젠장! 일어나! 일어나라고! 그만두고! 그만하라고!

Cut it out, you're bugging me. 그만둬, 너 때문에 피곤해.

013 Listen to yourself 멍청한 소리 그만해

this is a way of telling people that their thinking is wrong. It means "Think about what you are saying"

| Point | Will you listen to yourself? 방금 뭐라고 했지?

A: You complain all the time. **Listen to yourself.**
넌 늘상 불평하냐. 말도 안 되는 얘긴 그만해.

B: Do you really think I do it a lot? 정말 내가 불평을 많이 해?

Listen to yourself. That's not you.
정신차려. 너답지 않아.

A: God, would you listen to yourself?
B: Yeah, I know. I've become one of those women we hate.
A: 네가 무슨 말을 하는지 좀 들어봐. B: 알아 내가 싫어하는 그런 여자가 됐어.

014 You wish! 행여나!, 바랠 걸 바래야지!

this means "That is what you want, but you can't have it." This is said when people desire something they can't get

| Point | In your dreams 꿈도 꾸지마
Not in your wildest dreams 그런 건 꿈도 꾸지 마
Dream on! 꿈 깨!
Dare to dream 그건 꿈에서나 있는 일이지

A: I want to buy a sports car when I graduate.
내가 졸업하면 스포츠카를 사고 싶어.

B: **You wish.** You'll never have that much money.
행여나. 그만한 돈이 없을 걸.

You think Cindy would date you? You wish!
신디가 너와 데이트할거라 생각해? 행여나!

You wish! There's no way you'll get rich.
바랄 걸 바래야지. 네가 부자가 될 일은 전혀 없어.

I heard you're trying to buy a Corvette. You wish! 네가 콜벳 자동차를 사려고 한다며. 바랄 걸 바래야지!

015 Don't make me laugh! 웃기지 좀 마!, 바보 같은 얘기 하지마!

this is a way of saying "That was a foolish idea." It is said to indicate some idea or plan is silly

| Point | You make me laugh 너 때문에 웃는다

A: I think I'm going to build a house for myself.
내 스스로 집을 지을까봐.

B: **Don't make me laugh.** You don't know about building things. 웃기지 마. 집을 짓는 게 뭔지도 모르면서.

Knock it off. Don't make me laugh.
그만둬. 웃기지 좀 마.

Don't make me laugh. It's tragic.
웃기지마. 슬픈 일이야.

Don't make me laugh. I'm being photographed. 웃기지마. 사진 찍고 있어.

016 Don't kid yourself 장난해?

this is a way to tell someone "Be honest with yourself." The speaker wants to say someone must be realistic and not live in a fantasy

A: Do you think I could become a fighter jet pilot?
내가 전투기 조종사가 될 수 있을 것 같아?

B: **Don't kid yourself.** It's very difficult for a woman to qualify as a military pilot.
장난해? 여자가 군조종사가 되는 건 엄청 어려워.

Don't kid yourself, honey. I didn't do it for you. 자기야, 장난해? 널 위해 그런 게 아냐.

A: You didn't do me a favor. B: Don't kid yourself. A: 넌 날 도와주지 않았어. B: 너 지금 장난해?

017 Spare me 헛소리하지마, 집어치워, 그런 말은 듣고 싶지 않아, 설마 그럴라구

the speaker is saying "I don't want to hear any more." This is usually said when someone is speaking foolishly

| Point | spare sb sth …에게 …을 덜어주다 spare sb …살려주다, 봐주다
spare one's feelings 감정을 상하지 않게 하다

A: Let me tell you about my plan to open a restaurant. 식당을 개업할 내 계획을 말해줄게.

B: **Spare me.** I don't want to hear your crazy plan. 집어치워. 말도 안 되는 얘긴 듣고 싶지 않아.

I was trying to spare your feelings. 네 감정을 상하지 않게 하려고 했어.

Oh spare me the speech, Mike, would you please? 헛소리 그만해, 마이크 제발.

Spare me the sales pitch. We're investigating a homicide. 그런 말 듣고 싶지 않아. 지금 살인 사건을 수사해야 돼.

018 I didn't want to mess with his head 난 걔를 열받게 하고 싶지 않았어

this is saying that the speaker didn't want to do something that would cause confusion or unexpected happiness for someone else. It is another way to say "I didn't want to screw things up for him"

| Point | mess with sb's head 많이 화나게 하거나 혼란스럽게 하다

A: Why didn't you go out with Gary's girlfriend? 너 왜 게리의 여친과 데이트하지 않았어?

B: **I didn't want to mess with his head.** 걔 열받게 하고 싶지 않았어.

Rachel, if you go, you're just gonna mess with his head and ruin his wedding! 레이첼, 네가 가면, 넌 걔 맘을 혼란스럽게 하고 걔 결혼식을 망칠거야!

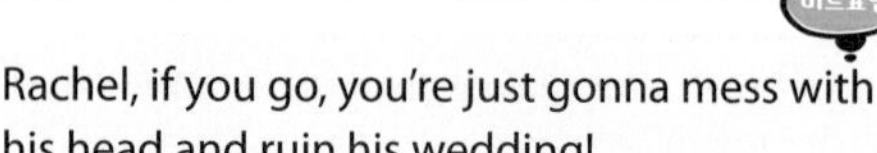

That's the kind of thing that could really mess with someone's head. 그건 누군가를 열받게 할 수도 있는 그런 종류의 일이야.

And rapists use the body's response against the victims to mess with their head, to make them believe that they were asking for it. 그리고 강간범들은 피해자들의 머리 속을 혼란스럽게 하기 위해 몸의 반응을 이용하여 피해자들이 원하는 거라고 믿게 끔 해.

019 She flipped out 걔가 화를 벌컥 냈어

this is usually a way to say that a woman got very angry quickly, although occasionally it might mean someone got excited quickly. We can understand that the woman's anger was probably too much for the situation, and she may have acted in a crazy, frightening way. It's similar to saying "She went nuts"

| Point | flip (out) 매우 화내다, 열광하다

A: Did your girlfriend find out you got arrested? 네가 체포된 걸 여친이 알게 된거야?

B: Yeah, then **she flipped out** and broke up with me. 어, 벌컥 화를 내더니 나와 헤어졌어.

I mean, no wonder she flipped out. 내 말은 걔가 벌컥 화를 내는 것도 당연하다는 말야.

When Larry first came to live with us, I completely flipped out. 래리가 처음 우리와 살려고 왔을 때 난 완전히 정신이 팽 돌았어.

Then she got a voice mail ... checked it and flipped out. 그런 다음 갠 보이스 멜을 확인하더니 핵 돌아버렸어.

020 Don't bite my head off! 나한테 화내지마!

this means that a person has reacted to someone else in an overly angry way. Usually the anger is unexpected, and frightening or upsetting. The speaker is saying "Don't get so angry at me, because I don't deserve it"

| Point | bite one's head off (이유없이) 신경질 내다, 갑자기 화를 내다

A: You'd better get this problem fixed or you're fired! 너 이 문제를 해결하라고 아니면 해고야!

B: **Don't bite my head off!** I'm working on it. 나한테 신경질내지 말아요! 지금 하고 있어요.

I'm scared to open my mouth for fear you're gonna bite my head off. 네가 아무 이유없이 화낼까봐 말하기가 무서워.

Look, I know this is my fault, so if you wanna bite my head off, go ahead. 내 잘못인지 알고 있으니 날 씹으려면 어서 씹으라고.

You were just trying to be nice, and I bit your head off. 넌 그냥 친절을 베풀려고 했는데 내가 마구 쏘아붙였지.

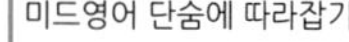

021 You had it coming! 그럴 줄 알았어!, 네가 자초한 거야!

this means that something bad happened to the person after he acted badly. It means "What happened was your fault"

| Point | He had it coming! 제 놈이 자초했어
Who had it coming? 누가 초래한거야?

A: I can't believe I failed that exam. 내가 시험에 떨어지다니.
B: **You had it coming.** You refused to study. 네가 자초한 거야. 공부하기 싫어했잖아.

Perhaps she had it coming. 걔가 자초한 일이겠지.

Oh, God, she had it coming. And you were careful, right? 맙소사. 그럴 줄 알았어. 넌 조심했지, 맞아?

She ruined my life. And she ruined yours. And she had it coming.
걘 너와 나의 인생을 망쳤어. 그럴 줄 알았어.

022 You asked for it 자업자득이지, 네가 자초한 일이잖아,그런 일을 당해 싸다

this means "Your actions caused this problem." This is said when someone creates problems for himself because of something he did

| Point | You asked for sth~ 네가 …을 요청했나

A: Do you know that my wife is very angry with me? 아내가 나한테 엄청 화난 거 알아?
B: **You asked for it** when you went out with those other girls. 다른 걸들하고 싸돌아 다녔으니 자업자득이지.

I'm warning you, idiot. Don't you remember! You asked for it.
내 경고하잖아. 이 바보야. 기억안나! 네가 자초한 일이잖아.

That info that you asked for is on your desk.
네가 부탁한 자료는 책상위에 있어.

023 That'll teach her! 그래도 싸지!, 당연한 대가야!, 좋은 공부가 될 거야!

this means that the speaker thinks actions that caused bad results will teach someone not to do them again. It is like saying "This will change her behavior"

| Point | That'll teach sb to do …가 …하는데 도움이 될 거야

A: When Linda went to the party, no one talked to her. 린다가 파티에 갔을 때 아무도 걔한테 말을 걸지 않았어.
B: **That'll teach her** not to talk badly about her friends. 이젠 친구 험담을 하지 않게 되겠지.

That'll teach him not to trust you.
그 덕에 걔가 널 믿지 않을거야.

That'll teach me to try and be clever.
그 덕에 내가 똑똑해지려고 할거야.

Well, that'll teach me to fight with my lovely wife. 그럼 그 덕에 내가 내 사랑하는 아내와 싸우는데 도움이 될거야.

024 It serves you right! 넌 그런 일 당해도 싸!, 꼴 좋다!, 샘통이다!

this means "You deserved the bad thing that happened." This is used when people creates problems because of bad actions

| Point | It served me right 난 당해도 싸지

A: Oh God, my head really hurts today.
맙소사, 오늘 머리가 너무 아파.
B: **It serves you right!** You shouldn't have had all that beer last night. 꼴 좋다! 간밤에 그 맥주를 다 마시지 말았었야지.

You got sick after overeating? It serves you right! 과식한 후에 탈났다고? 샘통이다!

It serves you right! You shouldn't be so nasty.
꼴좋다! 그렇게 비열하게 행동하는게 아니지.

Your wife wants a divorce after you cheated. It serves you right!
네 아내는 네가 바람핀 후에 이혼을 원하고 있어. 당해도 싸다!

025 You're in for it! 네가 자초한 일이니 후회해도 소용없어!, 너 큰일 났어!

this is a way of telling someone "You are going to have big problems soon." It is said when someone is going to have trouble, or possibly some sort of surprise, in the future

| Point | Sb be in for~ …가 …을 경험하게 되다

A: Dad saw all of your low test scores. **You're in for it!** 아빠가 네 시험성적 안 나온 걸 다 보셨어. 너 큰일났어!

B: That's not good. Did he seem really angry?
좋지 않구만. 정말 화 나신 것 같아?

You're in for a big surprise. 엄청 놀라게 될거야.

You're in for a lifetime of heartache.
평생 머리가 아플거야.

026 You('ve) brought this on yourself 이건 네가 자초한거야

this means a person created his own problems. It is like saying "You caused this"

| Point | I brought this on myself 내가 스스로 자초한 거야

A: Why do I owe the credit card company so much money? 카드 값이 왜 이리 많이 나왔어?

B: **You've brought this on yourself.** You bought too many things. 네가 자초한거야. 너무 많은 걸 사잖아.

What do you expect me to do? You brought this on yourself. 나보고 어찌라고? 네가 자초한거잖아.

You brought this on yourself. Now, the next time you want to play with me, maybe you'll think twice. 네가 자초한거야. 담부터 날 건드릴 생각하지마.

027 You'll pay for that! 어디 두고 보자!, 대가를 치뤄야 할거야!

this is said to indicate someone will have problems because of something he did. It is like saying "That's going to create problems in the future"

| Point | You're gonna pay for that 대가를 치뤄야 돼

A: My friends and I were up all night playing computer games. 친구들과 난 밤새 컴퓨터 게임을 했어.

B: **You'll pay for that.** You're going to be sleepy all day. 대가를 치뤄야 할 걸. 종일 졸릴거야.

If you kill someone, and you're going to have to pay for that the rest of your life.
살인을 한다면 평생동안 대가를 치뤄야 할 것이야.

You can't keep lying to everyone. You'll pay for that! 너 사람들한테 계속 거짓말하면 안돼. 대가를 치뤄야 할거야!

If you keep eating fast food you'll pay for that!
패스트푸드를 계속 먹어대면 대가를 치뤄야 될거야!

028 I did it out of spite 난 분풀이로 그랬어

미드표현

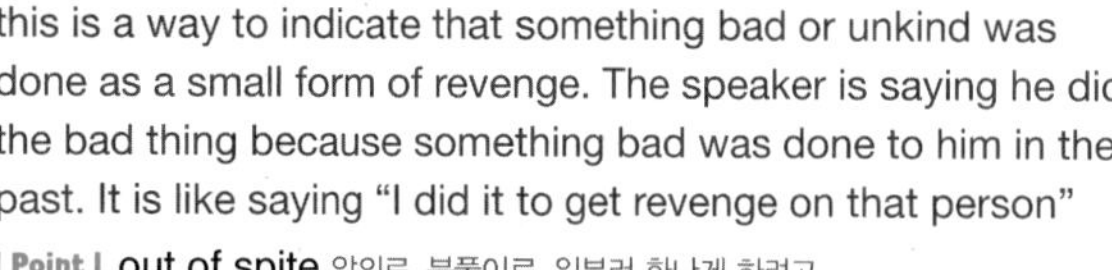
this is a way to indicate that something bad or unkind was done as a small form of revenge. The speaker is saying he did the bad thing because something bad was done to him in the past. It is like saying "I did it to get revenge on that person"

| Point | out of spite 악의로, 분풀이로, 일부러 화나게 하려고

A: Why did you break the window in the bar?
왜 술집 유리창을 깬거야?

B: **I did it out of spite.** The owner had insulted me. 분풀이로 했어. 주인이 나를 모욕했거든.

You are so just doing this out of spite.
넌 정말 악의로 이걸 하는구나.

Morgan was jealous of Neal, sleeps with Sam out of spite.
모건은 닐을 시샘했고 분풀이로 샘과 잠자리를 하고 있어.

My mom'll be booking the big room at the Holiday Inn just out of spite!
엄마는 화풀이로 홀리데이인에 큰 방을 예약할거야!

029 You'll be sorry later 나중에 후회할거야

this is a way to say "That will cause trouble for you soon." It indicates the person will soon be unhappy because of his actions

I Point I You'll be sorry S+V …하면 후회하게 될 거야
You're heading for trouble 너 불구덩이에 들어가는구나

A: Sometimes I eat a lot of junk food before I go to sleep at night. 때때로 밤에 자기 전에 많은 정크푸드를 먹어.

B: **You'll be sorry later.** I bet you'll get fat.
나중에 후회할 걸. 뚱뚱해질거야.

You'll be sorry you harassed my son.
내 아들 괴롭힌 걸 후회하게 될거야.

You'll be sorry for this. I promise you will.
넌 나중에 이 때문에 후회하게 될거야. 분명히 그렇게 될거야.

A: One day I will show you my penis. B: And you'll be sorry.
A: 언젠가 내 거시기 보여줄게. B: 그럼 넌 후회하게 될거야.

030 What do you want from me? 내게 뭘 원하는거야?, 나보고 어쩌라는거야?

this is asking what kind of help a person wants to get. It means "What do you think I should do for you?"

I Point I What do you want me to say? 무슨 말을 하라는 거야?, 나보고 어쩌라고?

A: You always follow me around. **What do you want from me?** 항상 날 따라다니는데 나보고 어쩌라고?

B: I was hoping that we could become friends.
우리가 친구가 될 수 있지 않나 해서.

What do you want from me? You want me to quit my job? 날 보고 어찌라고? 직장 그만 두라고?

What do you want from me? I've never met the guy. 날 보고 어쩌란 말야, 난 걔 만난 적이 없어.

What do you want me to say? You want me to say I'm a bad mother?
나보고 어쩌라고? 내가 나쁜 엄마라고 말하라는 거야?

031 Who do you think you're kidding? 날 바보로 알아?

this is a way of saying that a person can't hide his true goals, even if he tries. It's similar to saying "You can't trick me"

I Point I Who do you think you're talking to? 내가 그렇게 바보로 보여?

A: I just bought this wig for my head. 나 가발 샀어.

B: **Who do you think you're kidding?** Everyone knows you're bald. 그 말 믿으라고? 네가 대머리인 줄 다 알아.

Who do you think you're talking to? Quit trying to pretend you're best friends with Cameron Diaz!
내가 바보인 줄 알아? 카메론 디아즈와 친한 친구인 척 그만해!

Who do you think you're kidding here? Jack, you're not gonna shoot me. Put the gun down. 날 바보로 알아? 잭, 넌 날 못쏴. 총 내려놔.

032 Who do you think you are? 네가 도대체 뭔데 그래?

this asks "Why are you acting that way?" It is said when someone is acting arrogant or strangely

A: You never talk to me anymore. **Who do you think you are?** 더 이상 내게 말도 안 하는데 네가 도대체 뭔데 그래?

B: I know that I am better than you are.
너보단 잘 난건 알지.

Over?! Who do you think you are? It's not over until I say it is!
끝났다고? 네가 뭔데? 내가 끝났다고 할 때까지 아냐!

Who do you think you are? Get out of my face right now! 네가 도대체 뭔데? 당장 꺼져!

Excuse me, who do you think you are?
잠깐만, 네가 도대체 뭔데 그래?

033 You can't do this to me 나한테 이러면 안되지, 이러지마

this means someone has done something bad to the speaker. It is a way to say "I'm very unhappy about what you did"

| Point | Why are you doing this to me? 내게 왜 이러는 거야?

A: Jason, get out of here. You're fired.
제이슨, 꺼져. 넌 해고야.

B: **You can't do this to me.** I've worked here a long time! 제게 이러시면 안돼죠. 오랫동안 일해왔는데.

You can't do this to people! Have you lost your minds? 사람들한테 이러면 안돼! 정신나갔어?

She can't do this to us. We're leaving.
걔가 우리한테 그러면 안되지. 우리 간다.

You can't do this to me. I'm not doing anything to you.
내게 이러면 안되지. 난 네게 아무 짓도 하지 않잖아.

034 Get off my tail 귀찮게 굴지말고 나 좀 내버려둬

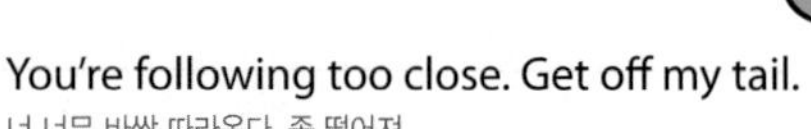

usually this means the speaker wants someone to stop following him so closely, or to stop nagging or bothering him. We can understand that he is upset. It is very similar to saying "Back off and leave me alone for a while"

| Point | get off one's tail …의 뒤를 쫓는 것을 그만두다, …을 괴롭히는 것을 그만두다

A: Are you taking a coffee break again? 커피 한잔 더 할래?

B: **Get off my tail!** You've been bothering me all day! 그만 좀 괴롭혀! 종일 귀찮게 구네!

You're following too close. Get off my tail.
너 너무 바싹 따라온다. 좀 떨어져.

Get off my tail! I need some space.
그만 좀 떨어져! 난 공간이 좀 필요해.

Why don't you get off my tail? I don't need your help. 나 좀 내버려둬. 난 네 도움이 필요없어.

035 Don't screw with me 나한테 장난치지마

this means "Don't cause trouble for me." It is a warning that someone should behave nicely

| Point | make trouble for sb = cause trouble for sb 문제를 만들다, 물의를 일으키다
Don't make trouble for me 내게 장난치지마, 내게 문제 일으키지마
Don't make trouble for yourself 사서 고생하지마

A: **Don't screw with me.** If I get angry, you'll regret it. 장난치지마. 내가 화나면 넌 후회할거야.

B: Calm down. No one wants to make trouble for you. 진정해. 아무도 너한테 문제일으키는 걸 원치않아.

You're right. I need you. I also need you to know you can't screw with me.
네 말이 맞아. 난 네가 필요해. 또한 내게 장난치면 안된다는 사실을 알아두었으면 해.

You're saying that just to screw with me.
너 나 골리려고 그렇게 말하는거지.

It's been a rough weekend. Don't screw with me. 힘든 주말이었어. 나 골리지마.

036 Don't tell me what to do! 나에게 이래라 저래라 하지마!

this is a way to say "You can't control me." The speaker doesn't want anyone to have power over him

| Point | Don't tell me what S+V …라고 말하지마

A: Go get me a cup of coffee and a donut.
가서 커피하고 도넛 좀 가져와라.

B: **Don't tell me what to do.** You're not my boss.
내게 이래라 저래라 하지마. 사장도 아니면서.

You don't tell me what to do! I tell you what to do! 내게 명령하지마! 명령하는 건 나야!

Don't tell me what to do, okay?
이래라 저래라 하지마, 알겠지?

No, don't tell me what I can't do.
나보고 이래라 저래라 하지마.

037 What's the catch? 속셈이 뭐야?, 무슨 꿍꿍이야?, 조건이 뭔데?

this is a way of asking if a bad surprise is waiting. It means "What is the hidden problem with this?"

A: They say I can get a new car for $3000.
3천 달러에 새 차를 살 수 있다고 하네.

B: **What's the catch?** I think you'll have to pay a lot more than that. 무슨 꿍꿍이야? 그보단 돈을 더내야 될 걸.

미드표현

A: What's the catch? B: There's no catch. It's yours, Tom. No strings attached.
A: 무슨 꿍꿍이야? B: 아무 것도 없어. 네꺼야, 탐. 아무 조건도 없고.

Loan me a 100 dollars? What's the catch?
100불을 빌려준다고? 조건이 뭔데?

038 Don't play dumb[coy] with me 날 바보 취급하지마, 내가 바보같아

this means "Tell me everything." It is said to someone who is trying to hide something from the speaker

I Point I play dumb 멍청한 척하다
Don't play dumb 어리석게 굴지마
How dumb do you think I am? 내가 바보인줄 알아?

A: I don't ever remember meeting Simon.
사이몬을 만난 기억이 전혀 없어.

B: **Don't play dumb with me.** I know you dated him. 날 바보로 아는 거야. 걔랑 데이트한 거 알고 있어.

미드표현

Don't play coy with me. You've got something to say, then just say it. 내숭떨지마. 말할 게 있으면 그냥 말해.

Don't play coy with me. You read that report.
내숭떨지마. 그 보고서 읽었잖아.

What the fuck are you talking about? Don't play dumb with me.
도대체 너 무슨 말을 하는거야? 내가 바보인 줄 알아?

039 Don't play games with me 날 갖고 놀 생각 마, 나한테 수작부리지마

this is very similar to the previous phrase. It is telling someone to be honest and give all of the information

I Point I I don't play games 수작 부리는 거 아니야

A: I might tell you the gossip if you're nice to me.
나한테 잘해주면 소문이야기 해줄게.

B: **Don't play games with me.** Tell me right now.
날 갖고 놀 생각 마. 지금 당장 말해.

미드표현

She wanted to play games with my son's life.
걔는 내 아들의 목숨을 갖고 수작을 부리려고 했었어.

Well, Nolan, you do not want to play games with me. 놀란, 나한테 수작부리지마.

Don't you fucking play games with me.
날 갖고 놀 생각은 하지마.

040 I know what you're up to 네 속셈 다 알아

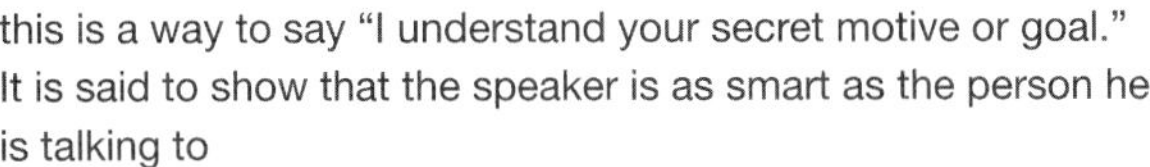

this is a way to say "I understand your secret motive or goal." It is said to show that the speaker is as smart as the person he is talking to

I Point I What are you up to? 뭐해?, 무슨 수작이야?
They're up to something 걔들 뭔가 꾸미고 있어

A: **I know what you're up to.** You want to cheat on the exam. 네 속셈 다 알아. 시험에서 커닝하고 싶은 거지.

B: I would never do something like that.
그런 거 절대로 하지 않을 거야.

미드표현

So what are you up to? Doing a little shopping? 그래 뭐해? 쇼핑 좀 하는 거야?

A: I see what you're up to. You planned this whole thing. B: What are you talking about?
A: 네 속셈알겠어. 이 모든 걸 네가 꾸몄지. B: 무슨 말 하는 거야?

041 She has an ax to grind 걘 딴 속셈이 있어

this indicates the woman is angry about something. It is a way to say "She wants revenge because she is angry"

| Point | have an ax to grind 딴 속셈이 있다, 따질게 있다

A: Why does Sally always look so angry?
왜 샐리는 늘 화나 있어?

B: **She has an ax to grind** with her husband.
남편에게 따질게 있어서 그래.

미드표현

These days, everyone has an ax to grind.
요즘에는 사람들 모두가 딴 속셈이 있어.

She got angry because she has an ax to grind.
걔는 따질 것이 있기 때문에 화를 냈어.

I have an ax to grind with the person who left garbage here. 여기에 쓰레기를 투척한 사람에게 난 따질게 있어.

042 You're making fun of me? 너 지금 나 놀리냐?, 장난하냐?

this is asking if someone is trying to make another person seem foolish. It is like saying "Are you treating me like an idiot?"

| Point | Don't make fun of me, okay? 너 지금 나한테 장난치냐?

A: You look like you eat enough food for 2 people.
너 2인분 식사는 충분히 할 것 같아 보여.

B: **You're making fun of me?** That isn't very nice.
나 놀리는 거야? 그럼 기분 안좋지.

미드표현

I know what it feels like to be made fun of, and I know it's not a good feeling.
놀림받는게 어떤 기분이지 이해해. 굉장히 맘 아프지.

What happened, honey? Did she make fun of your pot belly? 무슨 일이야? 너 배나온 거 갖고 걔가 놀렸댔어?

You have to apologize for making fun of my culture. 넌 내 나라의 문화를 조롱한 거에 대해 내게 사과해야 돼.

043 I am nobody's fool 날 물로 보지마

this means "You can't trick me." It is a way to say it is very difficult to fool the speaker

| Point | He is nobody's fool 걔는 빈틈이 없어

A: If you buy this, it will be very useful.
이걸 사면 매우 유용할거야.

B: **I'm nobody's fool.** That is too expensive.
날 물로 보지마. 이건 너무 비싸.

미드표현

Don't try to trick me. I am nobody's fool.
날 속이려고 하지마. 날 물로 보지 말라고.

I am nobody's fool, and I don't believe what you say. 날 물로 보지마. 난 네가 하는 말 믿지 않아.

They tried to scam me and found out I am nobody's fool.
그들은 나한테 사기치려다 내가 만만치 않은 사람이라는 걸 알게 됐어.

044 You're putting words in my mouth
넌 내가 하지도 않은 말을 했다는 거야

this is said when someone has the wrong idea about what was said. It is similar to saying "You didn't understand me correctly"

| Point | put words in sb's mouth …가 하지도 않은 말을 했다고 하다

A: You always want me to be more stylish.
넌 항상 나보고 좀 더 세련되라고 해.

B: **You're putting words into my mouth.** I think you look fine.
넌 내가 하지도 않은 말을 했다는 거야. 난 네가 보기 좋다고 생각해.

미드표현

Don't you put words in my mouth. I never said that.
하지도 않은 말을 했다고 하지마. 절대 그렇게 말한 적 없어.

She's putting words in your mouth!
걔는 네가 하지도 않을 말을 했다고 해!

045 What do you take me for? 날 뭘로 보는 거야?

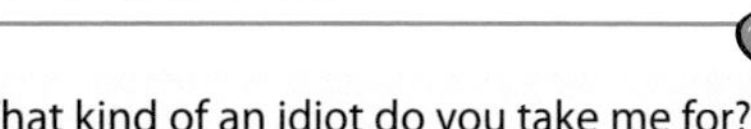

this is a way to say "Do you think I'm foolish?" It is said when the speaker is angry about being treated a certain way

I Point I take A for B A를 B로 생각하다, 잘못 알다

A: Come up to my apartment and we'll have a drink together. 내 아파트로 올라와 술 같이하자.

B: **What do you take me for?** I'm a nice girl!
날 뭘로 보는 거야? 난 착한 여자라고!

미드표현

What kind of an idiot do you take me for?
날 도대체 무슨 멍청이로 생각하는 거야?

A: Do you take me for a complete idiot? B: I take you for a total nut job!
A: 날 바보로 아니? B: 아니, 머저리로 알아!

A: I just want to make sure you understand that. B: What do you take me for?
A: 네가 확실히 그걸 이해해주기를 바래. B: 날 뭘로 보는거야?

046 That's enough! 이제 그만!, 됐어 그만해!, 그만 좀 해!

this means "Stop it." It is usually said when someone is angry about something and wants to stop it fast

I Point I Enough of that 이제 됐어, 그만해
That's enough for now 이제 됐어, 당분간은 괜찮을 것 같아
That's enough about that 그건 그 정도로 충분해

A: Sheila is pulling my hair, Mom!
쉴라가 머리카락을 잡아 댕겨요, 엄마!

B: **That's enough!** You children stop fighting!
그만해! 너희들 그만 싸워라.

미드표현

That's enough! I've had it! All right?
이제 그만! 이젠 지겨워! 알았어?

That's enough! It's over! 이제 됐어! 끝났다고!

047 Stop it! 그만 둬!

this is like the phrase above. It means "Don't do that"

I Point I Just drop it 그만 둬
Can you[we] drop this? 이 얘기 좀 그만 할 수 없어?

A: **Stop it!** You are making too much noise.
그만해! 너무 시끄럽잖아.

B: Oh really? I'm sorry that I bothered you.
어 정말? 귀찮게 해서 미안.

미드표현

You know what you're doing. Stop it.
네 행동 네가 알지. 그만 둬.

Let go of me! Stop it! 날 놔줘! 그만 둬!

Can we just drop this? I'm not gonna smoke again. 그만 좀 하자? 난 다시 흡연 안 할거야

048 Knock it off 그만해, 귀찮게 굴지마

this means "Stop it." It is usually said when the speaker wants something to stop right away

A: You are bothering me. **Knock it off.** 참 귀찮네. 그만해라.

B: Can't I play with my friends? 내 친구들과 놀지도 못해?

미드표현

Stop it! Knock it off! 그만해!

All right, guys, knock it off. 얘들아, 그만해.

Knock it off! Do you hear what I'm saying?
그만 좀 하라고! 내가 하는 말 안들려?

049 Could you lay off, please? 그만 좀 할래?

this is a polite way of asking someone to stop something. It means the speaker doesn't want something to happen right now

| Point | lay off 그만두다

A: I see you're late again, like you always are.
언제나처럼 또 너 늦었구나.

B: **Can you lay off please?** I know I'm late.
그만 좀 하실래요? 늦은 거 안다구요.

미드표현

Why don't you lay off, you little bitch, before I slap your face. 싸대기 때리기 전에 그만해, 이년아.

Could you just lay off, please? All right? My life is an chaos! 그만 좀 할래? 내 인생은 개판이야!

050 Don't get me started 난 빠질래, 그 얘긴 꺼내지도 마

this indicates if the speaker begins to talk about something, he will continue talking until everyone is bored. It means "It's better not to talk about that subject"

| Point | Don't get me started on~ …는 말도 마. …얘기는 꺼내지마

A: I hear that you're angry about the new rules.
새로운 규칙에 화났다고 들었어.

B: **Don't get me started.** They are so stupid.
그 얘긴 꺼내지도 마. 걔네들 정말 멍청해.

미드표현

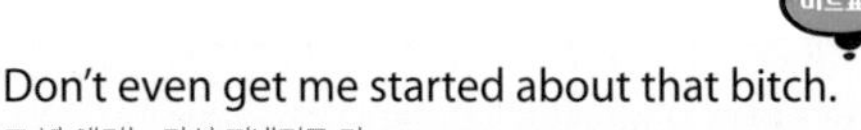

Don't even get me started about that bitch.
그 년 얘기는 다시 꺼내지도 마.

Don't get me started on your sex life.
네 성생활 얘기는 꺼내지마.

Don't get me started on that. 그건 난 빠질래.

051 Don't go there 그 문제는 언급하지마, 그 얘긴 하지마

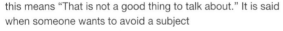

this means "That is not a good thing to talk about." It is said when someone wants to avoid a subject

| Point | Don't go there 그 얘기 꺼내지 마라(Don't bring that topic!), 그렇게 하지마

A: Maybe we should discuss the things you should pay for. 네가 돈을 지불해야 되는 것을 얘기해봐야 될 것 같아.

B: **Don't go there.** I don't have enough money right now. 그 얘긴 하지마. 지금 돈이 없다고.

미드표현

Don't go there. I don't want to talk about it.
그 얘긴 꺼내지마. 난 그 얘기하고 싶지 않아.

That's too personal. Don't go there.
그건 너무 개인적인 일인데. 그 문제는 언급하지마.

Don't go there. It's off limits.
그 문제는 얘기하지마. 절대 금지야.

052 Leave it at that 더 이상 말하지마, 그만 두자

this is a way to say "Let's stop talking about it now." It is saying that they have talked enough about something

| Point | Let's leave it at that 그건 그렇다 치고, 그만 하자

A: I think that Penny has been punished enough.
페니가 혼날 만큼 혼났다고 생각해.

B: Then her punishment is finished. **Leave it at that.** 그럼 벌은 끝내고 더 이상 말하지 말자.

미드표현

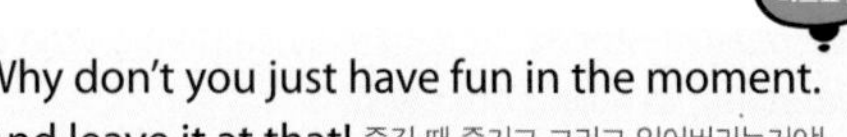

Why don't you just have fun in the moment. And leave it at that! 즐길 때 즐기고 그리고 잊어버리는거야!

I think we can just leave it at that.
더 이상 말하지 말자.

Can we leave it at that? I spent the last six days in prayer asking God why this has happened.
더 이상 말하지 말자. 난 지난 6일간 왜 이런 일이 일어났는지 신에게 물으면 기도했어.

053 Give it a break! 그만 좀 하지 그래!

미드표현

this is a way to tell someone they have talked too much about something. It means "Stop talking about that"

Point Give it a rest 그만 좀 해둬

A: I don't want to see you drinking so much.
네가 그렇게 술 많이 마시는 거 싫어

B: **Give it a break.** I hardly drink at all.
그만 좀 해라. 거의 술 안 마시잖아.

A: Show us your tits! B: No. Give it a rest. You guys have seen enough of my tits.
A: 가슴을 보여줘! B: 그만 좀 해. 내 가슴은 이미 많이 봤잖아.

Why don't you give it a rest, Mr. Hobson.
홉슨 선생님 그만 좀 하시죠.

She'll be here. Just give it a rest, okay?
걔가 곧 여기 올거야. 그만 좀 할래, 응?

054 I'll put a stop to that 내가 중단시킬게

미드표현

this indicates the speaker won't let something continue. He is saying "I won't let that happen anymore"

Point I have got to put a stop to this 중단시켜야 되겠어

A: She seems to be spending your salary quickly.
걘 네 월급을 빨리 쓰는 것 같아.

B: **I'll put a stop to that.** She won't spend any more money! 그렇게 못하게 할게. 걘 돈을 더 이상 쓰지 못할 거야!

Are you saying that we should put a stop to this? 이거 중단시켜야 되는 거야?

You can put a stop to this right now if you want to. 원한다면 지금 당장 멈춰도 돼.

I don't care if you are my boss, I'm gonna put a stop to this.
당신이 내 상사든 말든 상관없어. 난 이걸 중단시킬거야.

055 So much for that 얘기하면 한도 끝도 없어, 얘기가 길어져, 물건너 갔네

미드표현

this is a way of saying "That didn't work." Often this is said when something is tried and it fails

A: I think the new project was a failure.
새로운 프로젝트가 실패한 것 같아.

B: **So much for that.** What went wrong with it?
물 건너 갔구만. 뭐가 잘못된 거지?

So much for the steak. I'll take the coffee.
스테이크는 그만 됐어요. 커피주세요.

A: So much for the race. B: Well, at least we didn't come in last.
A: 경주가 끝났네. B: 그래도 꼴등은 아니잖아.

056 Give it up! 그래봐야 시간 낭비야!, 그만해!

this is a way to say "Stop trying because you won't be successful." This is said when something has clearly failed

Point give up 포기하다

A: I keep trying to get a date with Pam.
팸하고 데이트할려고 계속 시도중이야.

B: **Give it up.** She only dates rich guys.
그만해. 걘 돈 많은 놈들하고만 데이트 해.

Give it up. You're not getting any.
포기해. 아무 것도 얻는 게 없을거야.

Give it up, Mom. We're leaving.
그만 해요 엄마. 우리 가요.

For God's sake, give it up. She doesn't love me. 제발 포기해. 걘 날 사랑하지 않아.

057 She finally threw in the towel 걘 마침내 포기했어

this is a way of saying someone quit. It is like saying "She gave up trying something"

| Point | throw in the towel 포기하다
I threw in the towel 난 포기했어
Don't throw in the towel 포기하지마

A: I guess Tracy decided not to become an artist.
트레이시가 예술가가 되는 것을 단념한 것 같아.

B: Yeah, **she finally threw in the towel.**
어, 마침내 포기했어.

I'm not ready yet to throw in the towel.
아직 포기할 준비가 안 되었어.

Listen, look at me. You want to throw in the towel? 자, 날 봐봐. 너 포기하고 싶다고?

This is not going to work. I think we're just gonna have to throw in the towel.
이건 안될거야. 내가 포기를 해야 될 것 같아.

058 You've gone too far 네가 너무했어, 심했어

this is a way to say "Your behavior will get you in trouble this time." It is said when a person does something that makes others upset

| Point | You go too far 너무하네
You're going too far 넌 지금 너무 지나쳤어
I have gone too far 내가 너무 했어

A: **You have gone too far.** You can't insult your father! 네가 너무했어. 아버지를 모욕하면 안돼!

B: But he made me very angry when we were arguing. 하지만 다툴 때 날 열받게 했어.

It's bad enough you stole a kiss from my girlfriend, but this has gone too far.
내 여친에 기습키스를 하는 건 정말 못된 짓이지만 이건 너무 심했어.

But now, you've gone too far. Do you know what this is about?
하지만 네가 너무 지나쳤어. 이게 뭐에 관한 일인지 알아?

I've gone too far to pretend to be anything else. 내가 다른 것인 양 하려고 너무 지나쳤어.

059 He went overboard 걔가 좀 너무했어, 걔가 좀 심했어

this means a person did too much and caused problems. It's like saying "He got a little crazy with this"

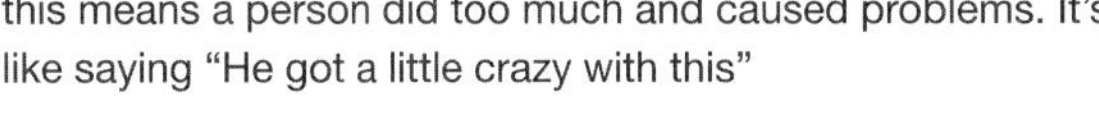

| Point | go overboard 심한 말이나 행동을 하다 *overboard 배밖으로
throw something overboard …을 없애버리다
Don't overdo it 그건 너무 심하게 하지마

A: Gosh, Max spent a lot of money for his wedding.
아이고, 맥스가 결혼식 비용으로 돈을 너무 많이 썼어.

B: **He went overboard.** This is going to be hard to pay for. 걔가 좀 너무했어. 갚기가 쉽지 않을걸.

Don't go overboard. 너무 많이 하지마.

Is someone going overboard with this holiday? 휴일준비 넘 과하게 하는 거야?

Don't you think he went a little overboard?
걔가 좀 심했다고 생각하지 않아?

Man overboard! I think he's drowning.
사람이 배밖으로 빠졌어! 물에 빠진 것 같아.

060 That's (just) too much! 1. 해도 해도 너무해! 2. 그럴 필요없는데!

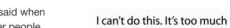

this means "I can't tolerate that behavior" It is said when someone has done something that upsets other people

| Point | This is too much 이건 너무해
This is too much for+N/to do~ …에게는 (하기가) 너무 힘들다
You're too much 정말 너무해

A: Some of our students have been smoking in the bathrooms. 우리 학생들 중 일부는 화장실에서 흡연해.

B: **That's too much.** We need to stop that behavior. 너무 하는구만. 못하게 해야겠어.

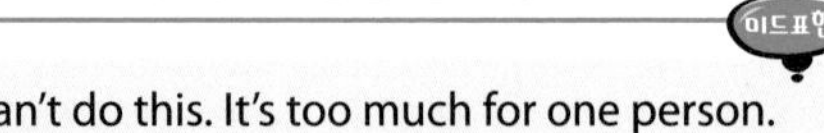

I can't do this. It's too much for one person.
이거 못하겠어. 한 사람이 하기에는 너무 힘들어.

Sounds like it was too much for her.
걔한테는 너무 심했던 것 같아.

You don't think it's too much?
너무 한다고 생각하지 않아?

061 That's the last straw 해도해도 너무 하는군, 더 이상 못 참아

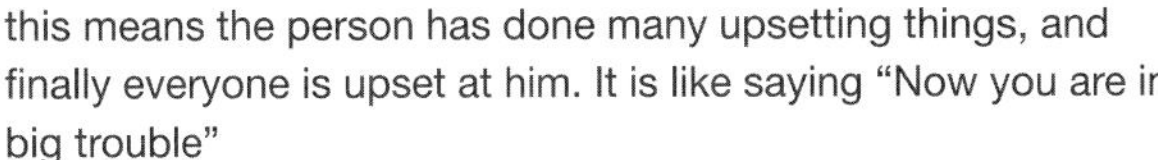

this means the person has done many upsetting things, and finally everyone is upset at him. It is like saying "Now you are in big trouble"

| Point | It was the last straw 그것은 마지막 결정타였어

A: I can hear the neighbors making noise again.
이웃들이 다시 시끄럽게 하네.

B: **That's the last straw.** It's after 2 am!
더 이상 못 참아. 새벽 2시가 지났는데!

미드표현

That's the last straw. Get him out of here!
더 이상 못참아. 걔를 끌어내라고!

When we lost the house, and I had to drop out of school, it was the last straw, and Mom left him.
우리가 집을 잃고 내가 학교를 중퇴해야 했을 때가 마지막이었어. 엄마는 아빠를 떠났어.

When Perry rapes her again, it's the last straw, so she kills herself.
페리가 걔를 다시 강간했을 때, 더 이상 참지 못하고 자살을 했어.

062 That does it 더는 못 참아, 이제 그만

this means "I can't tolerate this anymore." This is said when someone is very angry and taking action against something

A: Kurt says that you are afraid of him.
커트가 말하는데 네가 걜 무서워한다며.

B: **That does it.** I'm going to hit him in the face!
더는 못 참겠구만. 면상을 한대 갈길거야!

미드표현

All right. That does it. 좋아. 더는 못참아.

Okay, people. That does it. Thank you very much. 그래. 다들 이제 그만. 감사했어요.

That does it. Kid, get her out of here.
더는 못 참겠네. 쟤 좀 끌어내.

063 I can't take it anymore 더 이상 못 견디겠어

this means "Something is driving me crazy." A speaker says this when he feels very angry or frustrated by something

A: My life is too stressful. **I can't take it anymore.**
사는 게 넘 힘들어. 더 이상 못 참겠어.

B: You need to take time to relax. 좀 시간을 갖고 긴장을 풀어봐.

미드표현

I can't take it anymore. I am out of here!
더 이상 못 참겠어. 나 갈래!

I can't take it anymore. I'm gonna confront her. 더는 못 참아. 걔한테 맞서야겠어.

I can't take it anymore! I'm putting an end to this! 더는 못 참겠어! 종지부를 찍을거야!

064 I just can't stand your friends 네 친구들은 정말 지겨워[못 봐주겠어]

this means the speaker doesn't like the other people someone is close to. It is similar to saying "I don't enjoy the people you are close to"

| Point | I can't stand+N/ ~ing …를 못 참겠어, …가 …하는 것을 못 참겠어
I can't stand to do~/ ~ing …하는 걸 못 참아
I can't stand (that) S+V …을 못 참아

A: Why do you avoid going to parties with me?
나랑 파티에 가는 걸 왜 피해?

B: **I just can't stand your friends.** I'm sorry about that. 단지 네 친구들이 정말 지겨워. 미안해.

미드표현

I can't stand it[this]. 이건 못 참겠어.

I can't stand the thought of you with another woman! 난 네가 다른 여자랑 있다는 생각만 해도 못 참겠어!

She just can't stand you two fighting over her! 걔는 자기를 두고 니네 둘이 싸우는 걸 지겨워 해!

You really can't stand to lose, can you?
넌 정말 지는 걸 못 참아, 그지?

I can't stand that I hurt her.
내가 걔한테 상처를 줬다는 것을 못 참겠어.

065 It's totally out of line 도가 지나쳤어

this is a way of saying some action is wrong. It means "That shouldn't have been done"

Point You are so out of line 넌 정말 도가 지나쳤어

A: You were rude to everyone. **It's totally out of line.** 넌 모두에게 무례했어. 도가 지나쳤어.

B: But that was because I was drunk. 하지만 그건 내가 취해서였는데.

I hope this isn't out of line, but are you a jerk?
주제넘은 말인지 모르겠지만 너 멍청이야?

I am not proud of what I did. I admit, I was way out of line.
내가 한 일이 자랑스럽지 못해. 인정하지. 내가 지나쳤어.

I realize that I was out of line that night, but I was upset. 내가 지나쳤다는 것을 알아. 하지만 열받았었다고.

066 You are too cocky 너무 건방져

this is telling someone he is acting arrogant. What the speaker means is "I don't like the way you're acting now"

Point Don't get cocky 자만하지 마라

A: I can beat any of these guys in a fight.
난 이 자식들 아무나 다 싸워 이길 수 있어.

B: **You are too cocky.** People are not going to like you. 너무 건방지네. 사람들이 널 좋아하지 않을 거야.

Don't get too cocky! Remember I won the last one! 너무 건방지게 굴지마! 지난 번에는 내가 이겼다는 걸 잊지 말라고!

You're cocky, arrogant, and bossy
넌 건방지고, 교만하고, 우쭐대.

067 Get over yourself! 작작 좀 해라!, 주제파악 좀 해라!

often this means "Don't be so arrogant." It is telling someone that he is not as great as he thinks he is

Point Get over it 극복해, 잊어버려(stop feeling sad or upset about something)

A: I think I must be the most handsome guy around. 내가 주위에서 가장 멋지다고 생각해.

B: **Get over yourself.** You're not a movie star.
주제파악 좀 해라. 영화배우도 아니면서.

Then get over yourself! Grow up!
애들처럼 행동하지 말고, 철 좀 들어!

Well, he's a big boy, he'll get over it
그 사람도 다 큰 어른이니까, 잘 이겨낼거야.

I'm gonna have to get over it. 이제 그만 정신차려야지.

068 You're weighing me down 너 땜에 내가 죽는다

this indicates the speaker thinks someone is a burden, and may be holding him back from being successful. Because of this, we can understand the speaker may feel some anger or resentment toward that person. It is somewhat like saying "I could do a lot better if you were not around me"

Point weigh down 짓누르다, 무겁게 누르다, 억누르다

A: Please tell me why you want to break up.
왜 헤어지고 싶은지 내게 말해봐.

B: I feel so unhappy. **You're weighing me down.**
나 불행해. 네가 부담돼.

I've got a couple of accounts that are weighing me down.
날 무겁게 짓누르는 사건 두어 개가 있어.

Perp must have put something heavy in the bag to weigh it down.
범인은 가방을 무게나가게 하기 위해 뭔가 무거운 것을 넣었음에 틀림없어.

She had rocks tied to her to weigh her down.
그녀의 몸에는 무게가 나가도록 큰 돌들이 묶여져 있었어.

069 She's bluffing 걘 허풍떠는 거야, 뻥이야

this is a way to say "She's saying something but it's not true." This might be said about someone who says something when others think it is a lie

| Point | bluff 허세부리다, 엄포놓다
call the[person's] bluff 상대방의 허풍에 맞서다, 해볼테면 해보다

A: My wife says she will leave me if I don't stop drinking beer. 아내가 금주하지 않으면 날 떠나겠다고 해.

B: **She's bluffing.** I think she'll stay with you.
뻥이지. 네 아내는 널 떠나지 않을 거야.

I thought you were bluffing! 난 네가 뻥치는 줄 알았어!

It's a trick, I know he's bluffing.
그건 사기야. 걔가 뻥치는 거 알고 있어.

You think I'm lying? You think this is a bluff?
내가 거짓말한다고 생각하는 거야? 이게 뻥이라고 생각해?

You don't believe me? Call my bluff. See what happens. 날 못 믿겠다고? 해볼테면 해봐. 어떻게 되는지 보라고.

070 He comes on strong 걘 거만해, 너무 으시대

often this means that a person's personality might make some people dislike him. It is similar to saying "Sometimes he seems arrogant"

| Point | come on strong 으시대다

A: There are a lot of people who don't like Dick.
딕을 싫어하는 사람들이 많아.

B: **He comes on strong.** Sometimes it's hard to take. 걘 대담한 데가 있어. 때론 참기 힘들어.

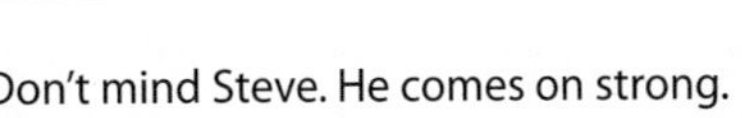

Don't mind Steve. He comes on strong.
스티브는 신경쓰지마. 걘 너무 으시대.

He comes on strong and many people don't like it. 걔는 거만하고 많은 사람들이 그걸 싫어해.

He comes on strong during business meetings. 걔는 업무회의 중에 너무 으시대.

071 Stop bragging about it 제발 잘난 척 좀 그만해

this is a way to tell someone to stop talking too proudly. It can be similar to saying "You are making others angry by talking that way"

| Point | brag (about) 자랑하다, 뽐내다

A: My car is the most expensive car being sold.
내 차가 지금 팔리는 차 중에서 가장 비싼 차야.

B: I know you are rich. **Stop bragging about it.**
네가 부자라는 거 알아. 잘난 척 좀 그만해.

Bragging about it? 자랑하는 거야?

He's always bragging about all the famous people he's met.
걘 자기가 만난 모든 유명인에 대해 항상 떠벌리고 다녀.

She was bragging about her sex life.
걘 자기의 성생활을 뽐냈어.

Your son kept me up all night bragging about his hickey.
네 아들이 키스마크 자랑하느라 밤새 날 잠못자게 했어.

072 Don't be a smart-ass 잔꾀 부리지마, 건방지게 굴지마, 잘난 척 하지마

this means "Don't make jokes right now." The speaker is indicating that someone needs to be serious

| Point | smart ass 건방진 녀석

A: If you aren't tough, you can go cry to your mother. 네가 강하지 못하면 네 엄마한테 가서 울어라.

B: **Stop being a smart ass.** I'm tough enough.
잘난 척 하지마. 난 충분히 강하다고.

Don't even think about getting cute, smart-ass. 잔꾀 부리지마.

You'd better be a smart ass. We have a lot of job to do. 빨리 일하자. 할 일이 많아.

073 Don't be judgmental 비난하지마

this is a command, and it is telling someone that it is bad to be disapproving or critical of the behavior of others. A speaker may say this if he thinks someone is being unfairly negative about other people and the way they live their lives. A different way to say this would be "Don't act like you can criticize them"

| Point | judgmental 비난을 잘하는, 비판적인

A: Most people in rural areas are kind of stupid.
시골지역의 사람들은 대부분 좀 멍청해.

B: You don't know that. **Don't be judgmental.**
모르는 일이야. 비난하지 말라고.

미드표현

People can be so judgmental about men who have served time.
사람들은 전과자에 비판적일 수 있어.

You are extremely judgmental, Chris.
크리스, 넌 극단적으로 비판적이야.

It was awful and mean and judgmental, as you said.
네가 말한 것처럼 그건 끔찍하고 비열하고 그리고 비판적이야.

You are a drug addict. You go to prostitutes. You can't be judgmental.
넌 약물중독자이고 성매매도 하잖아. 네가 남을 비난할 자격은 없어.

MEMO

Ways to express when people are fighting

욕하고 싸우고 그리고 화해하기

I'm gonna take her down

001 What do you think you're doing? 이게 무슨 짓이야, 너 정신 나갔냐?

this is a way of asking "Why are you doing that?" It is scolding someone for doing something wrong

| Point | What the hell[fuck] do you think you're doing?
도대체 너 뭐하는 짓거리야?
What do you think you're doing here? 네가 왜 여기 있는 거지?

A: **What do you think you're doing?** Those clothes don't belong there! 뭐하는 짓야? 이 옷은 저기 두면 안돼!

B: Really? Well, where am I supposed to put them? 정말요? 어, 어디에 놔야 돼죠?

미드표현

Are you out of your mind? What do you think you're doing? 너 미쳤냐? 뭐하는 짓이야?

What do you think you're doing? You're supposed to be grounded.
뭐하는 짓이야? 너 외출금지잖아.

What do you think you're doing? Howard, you never showed up, I was worried about you.
이게 무슨 짓이야? 하워드, 넌 나오지도 않고, 걱정했잖아.

002 What was he thinking? 걔는 무슨 생각을 했던 걸까?, 무슨 생각으로 그랬을까?

this is like saying "I don't understand him." The speaker wants to indicate that someone did something strange or confusing

| Point | What is he thinking? 걔는 무슨 생각을 하는 걸까?

A: Jack ate garlic before he went out on a date.
잭은 데이트가기 전에 마늘을 먹었어.

B: **What was he thinking?** His breath must have smelled terrible. 걘 무슨 생각을 했을까? 냄새가 끔찍했을거야.

미드표현

I mean, what was he thinking, leaving me?
내 말은 걘 뭘 생각했던 걸까, 날 떠나는 거?

I can't believe Sam did this. I mean, what was he thinking?
샘이 이랬다는게 믿기지가 않아. 내 말은 걔가 무슨 생각으로 그랬을까?

What was he thinking? This is not even real gold. 걔가 무슨 생각으로 그랬을까. 이건 진짜 금도 아닌데.

003 You never learn 넌 구제불능이야

this is said when a person keeps making the same mistakes. It implies "You are dumb because you make that mistake again and again"

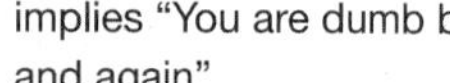

| Point | You're hopeless 넌 안돼

A: Last weekend my new boyfriend broke up with me. 지난 주에 새 남친하고 나랑 헤어졌어.

B: You always date bad guys. **You never learn!**
넌 늘상 나쁜 자식들하고 데이트해. 구제불능야!

미드표현

You never learn. You always make the same mistakes. 넌 구제불능이구나. 늘상 같은 실수를 반복하니.

This is the third time you've been in trouble. You never learn.
네가 곤경에 처한게 이번에 세번째야. 넌 구제불능이야.

You never learn. You must be kind of dumb.
넌 구제불능이야. 넌 좀 멍청한게 틀림없어.

004 How pathetic! 정말 딱하네!, 한심해!

this expresses that something seemed very stupid or foolish. It is similar to say "That's just stupid"

| Point | pathetic 딱한, 처량한, 한심한

A: Sam asked me to go out with him six times.
샘은 여섯번이나 내게 데이트신청했어.

B: **How pathetic.** Doesn't he understand you don't like him? 정말 딱해. 네가 자길 싫어하는 걸 모르나봐?

Can you see how pathetic that is? You shouldn't be jealous.
정말 얼마나 한심한 지 알겠지? 부러워할 필요 없어.

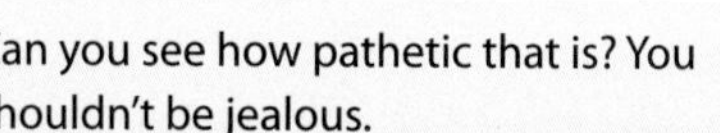

A: She doesn't seem to think so. B: That's pathetic. A: 그녀는 그렇게 생각 안 하던데. B: 한심하네

Does that make me sad and weak and pathetic? 그 때문에 내가 슬프고 연약하고 처량해지는거야?

005 How many times do I have to tell you?

도대체 몇 번을 말해야 알겠어?

미드표현

this is a way of saying "I have said the same things many times but your behavior didn't change." We can understand the speaker is angry because of this situation

| Point | If I've told you once, I've told you a thousand [hundred] times 한번만 더 말하면 천 번째 말하는거다

A: Don't be late! **How many times do I have to tell you?** 늦지마! 내가 몇 번이나 말해야 들어먹겠어?

B: I'm sorry. It's hard for me to wake up in the morning. 미안. 아침에 일어나는 게 넘 힘들어서.

How many times do I have to tell you, I'm fine being alone. I even prefer it.
몇 번이나 말했니, 난 혼자있어도 괜찮아. 더 좋기도 해.

How many times have I told you to stay out of my house? 내 집에 얼씬거리지 말라고 몇 번이나 말했니?

How many times have I told you not to bother me when I'm at work?
내가 직장에 있을 때 방해하지 말라고 몇 번이나 말했니?

006 Don't make me say it[tell you] again!

두 번 말하게 하지 말라구

미드표현

this indicates the speaker is angry because he has had to repeat something many times. It is a way to say "It makes me upset to say this over and over"

| Point | Don't make this harder than it is 더 이상 난처하게 만들지마

A: You students stop talking! **Don't make me say it again!** 너희 학생들 그만 얘기해! 두번 말하게 하지마!

B: Well, I think we need to shut up now.
저기. 우리도 이제 조용해야겠어요.

You know the thing. Don't make me say it.
네가 알잖아. 두번 말하게 하지마.

Don't make me say it twice. 내가 두 번 말하게 하지마.

A: Holly, please, tell me what's wrong?
B: Don't make me say!
A: 홀리야 제발 뭐가 잘못되었는지 말해줘. B: 말해달라고 하지마!

007 Why am I doing all the giving here?

왜 내가 다 이해해줘야 해?

미드표현

this is a way for the speaker to say that he thinks he has always been generous, and the listener has not been generous at all. Often this question means the speaker is angry. Another way to ask this question would be "Why are you always selfish when you know I have been very kind to you?"

| Point | do all the giving 다 이해해주다, 받아주다

A: I want you to clean the house, and then go buy some food. 집청소도 한 다음 가서 음식 좀 사와.

B: **Why am I doing all the giving here?** You should help out too. 왜 내가 다 받아줘야 돼? 너도 도와야 돼.

You're so greedy. Why am I doing all the giving here? 너 참 욕심많다. 왜 내가 항상 다 이해해줘야 돼?

Why am I doing all the giving here? I need help. 왜 내가 항상 이해해줘야 돼? 난 도움이 필요하다고.

008 I'll teach him a lesson

버르장머리를 고쳐놓을 거야, 혼내줘야겠어

미드표현

this means the speaker is going to do something bad to someone who has caused a problem. It's very similar to saying "I'm going to do something for revenge"

| Point | You tell him! (제 3자와 다투는 You에게) 그래 네 말이 맞네!

A: The neighbor's music is too loud again.
이웃집 음악소리가 또 넘 크게 나네.

B: I'm calling the police. **I'll teach him a lesson!**
경찰을 부를거야. 버릇을 고쳐놔야지!

You're right Red. We should teach him a lesson. 레드 네 말이 맞아. 우린 걔를 혼내줘야겠어.

You said you wanted to teach Chris a lesson.
넌 크리스 버르장머리를 고쳐놓고 싶다고 했지.

They were just holding them to teach 'em a lesson. 그들은 걔네들을 혼내주기 위해 데리고 있었어.

009 I'm going to kick some ass 혼 좀 내줘야겠어

this is a rude way of saying "I'm going to beat a person in a fight." We can understand the speaker plans to be violent and fight someone

| Point | kick sb's ass 혼내다, 쳐부수다, 이기다
get sb's ass kicked 혼나다, 패배하다

A: **I'm going to kick some ass** if he bothers me again. 날 다시 귀찮게 하면 혼 좀 내줄거야.

B: I think you will get in trouble if you do. 그렇게 하면 문제가 생길텐데.

미드표현

I will track him down and kick his ass! 걔를 쫓아가 혼 줄 낼거야!

Are you ready to get your ass kicked? 질 준비 됐냐?

I got my ass kicked in front of everyone. 모두들 있는데 혼 줄 났어.

010 I'm gonna take her down 걜 혼내줄거야

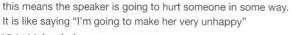

this means the speaker is going to hurt someone in some way. It is like saying "I'm going to make her very unhappy"

| Point | take sb down 혼내다, 콧대를 꺾다

A: Susan is a pain. I'm going to **take her down.** 수잔이 골칫거리야. 혼내줘야겠어.

B: What will you do to her? 걔한테 어떻게 할건데?

미드표현

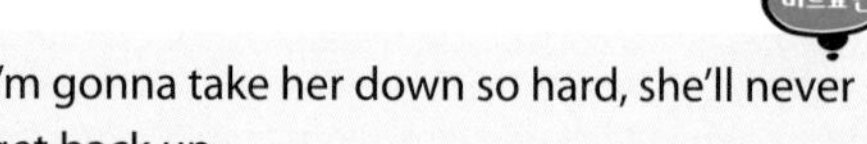

I'm gonna take her down so hard, she'll never get back up. 걔를 아주 따끔하게 다루어서 다시는 일어서지 못하게 할거야.(신체적으로 망치게 혹은 경제적으로 망하게)

If you try to come between me and my husband, I will take you down. 나와 내 남편 사이에 끼어든다면 혼내줄거야.

011 I'm not gonna let it get me down 난 그 때문에 좌절하지 않을거야

This is a way for the speaker to say that something bad that has happened to him, but he will not allow it to make him feel sad or disappointed. In other words, "I won't let that discourage me."

| Point | get sb down 기죽이다, 비난하다

A: I heard your boyfriend left you. 남친이 널 떠났다며.

B: He did, but **I'm not going to let it get me down.** 그랬지만 그 때문에 좌절하지 않을거야.

미드표현

I'm not going to let it get me down just because I have no money. 돈이 없다고 기죽지 않을거야.

It rained during the picnic, but I'm not going to let it get me down. 피크닉 도중에 비가 내렸지만 난 기죽지 않을거야.

Some bad things happened but I'm not going to let it get me down. 좀 안좋은 일들이 일어났지만 난 그 때문에 좌절하지 않을거야.

012 He's a dead man 걘 이제 죽었다

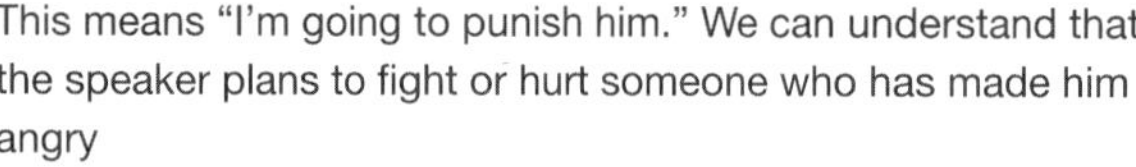

This means "I'm going to punish him." We can understand that the speaker plans to fight or hurt someone who has made him angry

| Point | You're a dead (man) 넌 죽었다 / Party's over 이제 넌 죽었다
It's your funeral 그날로 넌 끝이야 / We're doomed 큰일났다

A: Bob has been hanging around your girlfriend again. 밥이 또 네 여친 주변에 얼쩡거렸어.

B: **He's a dead man.** Wait until I see him on the street. 걘 이제 죽었다. 걔를 보기만 해봐.

미드표현

You're a dead man Scott, you hear me? 스캇, 넌 죽었어, 알았어?

If my wife catches me wearing this, I'm a dead man. 아내가 이거 입은 거 알면 난 죽은 목숨이야.

I'm a dead man if they see me talking to you. 걔네들이 내가 너하고 얘기하는 걸 보게 되면 난 죽은 목숨이야.

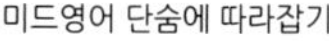

013 When I get my hands on her, she'll be sorry

다음에 만나면 걘 후회할거야

미드표현

this means "The next time I meet him." We can understand that the speaker has some control over the punishment of someone, and the next time they meet, he wants to punish that person

| Point | get one's hands on sth[sb] …을 얻다, 붙잡다, 혼내다

A: I see your son damaged your new car.
네 아들이 네 새 차를 부셨구만.

B: Yeah. **When I get my hands on him,** he'll be sorry. 그래. 잡히기만 하면 후회하게 될거야.

You tell my husband when I get my hands on him, he's a dead man! Do you hear me?
만나기만 하면 죽은 목숨이라고 남편에게 전해 줘요. 알았어요?

I would just love to get my hands on a brochure. 그 팜플렛을 꼭 갖고 싶어.

I'm going to need to get my hands on the original. 원본을 봐야겠어.

I can't get my hands on anything!
마음이 붕 떠 있어서 일이 손에 안 잡혀!

014 You know better than that

알만한 사람이 왜 그런 짓을 해

미드표현

this is usually said to scold someone for doing something that was clearly bad. It means "You shouldn't do those bad things"

A: Why did you steal from that store? **You know better than that!**
왜 그 상점에서 도둑질했어? 알만한 사람이 왜 그랬어!

B: I wanted the handbag, but I didn't have enough money for it. 핸드백을 사고 싶었는데 돈이 부족했어.

Don't drink so much alcohol. You know better than that. 과음하지마. 알만한 사람이 왜 그래.

Don't struggle. You know better than that, don't you?
싸우려 들지마. 그 정도는 알만한 사람이잖아. 그렇지 않아?

You can't take these on the plane. You know better than that.
이것들은 비행기에 갖고 못들어갑니다. 그 정도는 아시겠죠.

015 You can't get away with it

그렇게 못할거야, 절대 못 도망갈거야

미드표현

this is a way of saying "You will be caught and punished for doing something bad." The speaker feels the person won't escape punishment

| Point | get away with 나쁜 짓을 하고도 잡히지 않고 도망가다
You'll never get away with it 넌 그걸 피할 수 없어

A: I'll get an A if I cheat on the exam.
시험에서 커닝하면 A 맞을 수 있어.

B: **You can't get away with it.** You'll be punished.
걸리게 되어 있어. 벌 받을거야.

You're not smart enough to get away with murder. 넌 살인을 저지르고 잡히지 않을 정도로 똑똑하지 않아.

He's lying! Are you gonna let him get away with this crap?
걘 거짓말하고 있어! 그 말도 안되는 걸 보고 그냥 넘어갈거야?

You think I'd let you get away with that?
네가 그러고도 무사히 넘어가게 될거라고 생각해?

016 You think you're so smart

네가 그렇게 똑똑한 줄 알아

미드표현

this is a way to say someone is arrogant. It means "You think you are better than you really are"

| Point | You think you're such a big shot 네가 그렇게 거물급인 줄 알아?
She thinks she can dance 제 딴에는 춤 좀 춘다고 생각해 (하지만 실제는 아니다)
You think you have problems 너만 문제가 있는 줄 알아?

A: The professor likes me better than the other students. 교수님이 다른 얘들보다 날 더 좋아하셔.

B: **You think you're so** big. No he doesn't.
넌 네가 대단하다고 생각하는데 교수님은 그렇게 생각안하셔.

You think you're so great. 네가 그렇게 대단한 줄 알아.

You think you're so much better than everyone.
너 다른 모든 사람들보다 네가 훨씬 낫다고 생각하는거야?

You think you're so talented and unique, don't you?
넌 네가 아주 능력있고 독특하다고 생각하고 있지, 그렇지 않아?

017 Don't be silly 바보같이 굴지마

this is a way to say "You are doing something foolishly." It means a person should think more deeply before acting

| Point | Don't be ridiculous 웃기지마, 말도 안돼
Don't be foolish 바보 같이 굴지마
That's stupid 어리석구만, 말도 안돼

A: Are you planning to visit Europe? 유럽에 갈거야?
B: **Don't be silly.** I don't have that much money.
말도 안되는 소리. 그럴 만한 돈이 없어.

Oh, don't be silly. It's nice to have a new friend. 바보같이 굴지마. 새로운 친구를 사귀는 건 좋은 일이야.

Ohh, no. Don't be silly. He's gonna be thrilled.
바보같이 굴지마. 걘 무척 좋아할거야.

No, don't be silly. George said you were the best. 바고같이 굴지마. 조지는 네가 최고라고 말했어.

018 You're breaking my heart

거 참 안됐군요(비아냥거림), 너 때문에 내 가슴이 찢어져

this is a sarcastic way to say "I don't care about what is being said." The speaker is indicating something is not important to him

| Point | You broke my heart 내맘을 갈기갈기 찢어놨어(= You destroyed me)
heartbreaking 마음아픈

A: I was absent yesterday because my stomach was hurting. 어제 배가 아파서 못왔어요.
B: **You're breaking my heart.** Now you have a lot more work to do. 참 안됐구만. 이제 할 일이 더 많아졌네.

Broke my heart when I found out he was dirty. 걔가 더럽다는 알고서 마음이 찢어졌어.

The bastard broke my heart.
저 나쁜 자식이 내 맘을 찢어놨어.

I split up with a bitch who broke my heart.
내 맘을 찢어 놓은 년과 깨졌어.

019 Don't make a scene 소란 피우지마

this means "Don't become angry." Usually this is said when people are in a public place

| Point | make a scene 소란을 피우다

A: Why do you always treat me so badly?
넌 늘상 내게 짖궂게 대하니?
B: **Don't make a scene.** Let's talk about this when we get home. 소란 피지마. 이 문젠 집에 가서 얘기하자.

Let's not make a scene. It's not worth it.
소란피지 말자고. 그럴 가치가 없어.

Just don't make a scene, okay? 소란 피지마, 알았지?

You made a scene in my bar.
넌 내 바를 난장판을 만들었어.

020 That takes the cake 너무 뻔뻔해, 정말 어처구니가 없군

this usually indicates that something surprising or shocking has happened. It often expresses the feeling "That was really strange"

| Point | take the cake (비꼬는 말투) 보통이 아니다, 대단하다

A: He is dating his friend's wife? Oh, **that takes the cake!** 걘 자기 친구 아내와 바람펴. 어, 너무 뻔뻔해!
B: I know it does. It's really terrible. 알아. 정말 끔직해.

I've heard far-out excuses for not giving sex, but this one takes the cake.
섹스를 안하기 위한 여러가지 변명을 들었지만 이건 너무 하는 군.

We have to stay here all weekend. That takes the cake. 우린 주말 내내 여기에 있어야 돼. 정말 어처구니가 없어.

You aren't coming to work today? That takes the cake. 오늘 출근하지 않겠다고? 정말 어처구니가 없군.

021 You've got a lot of nerve 참 뻔뻔스럽군

this is a way of saying "That was very impolite or not good." The speaker is scolding someone for his actions

I Point I have got a nerve ~ing 뻔뻔하게도 …하다
What a nerve? 참 뻔뻔스럽군
The nerve of you! 뻔뻔스럽네!

A: You want to borrow a lot of money again? **You've got a lot of nerve!**
또 돈을 많이 빌려달라고? 참 뻔뻔하네!

B: But I promise to pay you back this time.
하지만 이번에 꼭 갚을게.

She's got a nerve asking for more sex.
걔는 뻔뻔하게도 더 많이 섹스해달라고 요구해.

You have a lot of nerve walking in my chambers accusing me of murder.
나를 살인자로 비난하며 내 방에 들어오다니 참 뻔뻔하구나.

You got a lot of nerve coming here! How did you even get in?
여기까지 오다니 참 뻔뻔하군! 어떻게 들어왔니?

022 Suit yourself! 네 멋대로 해!, 맘대로 해!, 좋을대로 해!

this is used to say "Do whatever you want." It indicates that the speaker doesn't care what someone does

I Point I Have it your way 네 맘대로 해, 좋을 대로 해(Do what you want to do)

A: I'm investing all my money in that company.
난 그 회사에 내 돈 다 투자하고 있어.

B: **Suit yourself.** I think it's a really bad idea.
맘대로 해. 정말 안 좋은 생각인 것 같아.

You think that'll do the trick? Fine, suit yourself. 그게 먹힐 거라고 생각해? 좋아, 맘대로 해.

Have it your way. They have always been good friends to me.
좋을 대로 해. 걔네들은 내게 항상 좋은 친구였어.

A: I'm not gonna discuss this with you. B: Suit yourself. A: 난 너랑 이 문제를 얘기하지 않을거야. B: 맘대로 해.

023 What's (there) to know? 뻔하잖아?

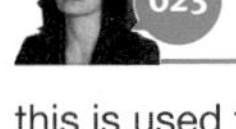

this is used to say the speaker thinks he already has all of the important information. It is similar to saying "I believe I know the information right now"

A: Did you study for the test today? 오늘 시험 공부했어?

B: **What's there to know?** I remember everything we learned in class. 뻔해. 수업시간에 배운 거 다 기억해.

You want to test us? What's there to know?
우리를 테스트하고 싶다고? 뻔하잖아?

What's there to know? Everyone understands the material. 뻔하잖아? 다들 재료를 알고 있다고.

This stuff is easy to learn. What's there to know? 이건 배우기 쉬워. 뻔하잖아.

024 Who died and made you king[boss]? 왜 이리 거만한거야?

this is a way of asking "Why are you acting arrogant?" It is a way to remind a person to be more humble

A: You should make me some dinner, and get me a beer too. 저녁 좀 해주고 맥주도 좀 줘.

B: **Who died and made you king?** 왜 이리 거만해?

Stop giving orders. Who died and made you boss? 명령 좀 그만 내려. 왜 이리 거만한거야?

Who died and made you boss? Just sit down and shut up! 왜 이리 거만한거야? 그냥 앉아서 입닥치라고!

I don't have to obey you. Who died and made you boss?
내가 너한테 복종할 필요가 없지. 너 왜 이렇게 거만한거야?

025 You sound like a broken record 계속 같은 말을 반복하잖아

this is said to stop someone from repeating the same thing. It means "You keep saying that again and again"

| Point | broken record (망가진 레코드 판이 튀면서 계속 같은 부분을 반복하듯이) 같은 말을 자꾸 반복하는 사람

A: Don't forget to buy milk at the store.
가게에서 우유사오는 건 잊지마.

B: You said that 3 times. **You sound like a broken record.** 3번 얘기했어. 계속 같은 말을 반복하잖아.

미드표현

I sound like a broken record, but you work too hard. 같은 말을 계속 하는 것 같지만 넌 일을 너무 열심히 해.

Babies, babies, babies. You sound like a broken record. I just had a miscarriage. It's gonna take some time before I'm ready to get pregnant again.
아기, 아기, 아기. 계속해서 같은 말만 되풀이하잖아. 난 유산해서 다시 임신하기까지는 시간이 걸릴 것 같아.

026 I thought we had an understanding
우리 서로 얘기가 된 걸로 알았는데

this is usually said when a speaker felt he had an agreement, but the other person doesn't think he has an agreement with the speaker. It is a way to ask "didn't we make an agreement?"

A: I plan to move to another apartment next month.
다음 달에 다른 아파트로 이사할 계획야.

B: **I thought we had an understanding** you'd stay here for six months.
6개월간 여기서 지내는 걸로 얘기가 된 줄 알았는데.

미드표현

I thought we had an understanding. I thought this was what we both wanted.
서로 얘기가 된 걸로 알았는데. 이게 바로 우리 모두가 원하는 것이라고 생각했었는데.

Are you insane? I thought we had an understanding. 미쳤니? 우리 서로 얘기가 된 것 아니었어?

027 My mom gave it to me 엄마한테 한소리 들었어

this is a way to say "Mom yelled at me for acting badly." We can understand the mother was trying to change her child's bad behavior

| Point | My mom is angry at me 엄마는 내게 화나셨어
My mother will chew me out 엄마가 나를 혼쭐낼거야
My parents grounded me 부모님이 나를 외출 금지시켰어
You're grounded 너 외출금지야

A: How did your mom react when you broke the lamp? 램프를 깨트렸을 때 엄마의 반응은 어땠어?

B: **My mom gave it to me.** She yelled at me for a long time. 혼내셨지. 한동안 내게 소리치셨어.

미드표현

My mom gave it to me when I got home at 3 am. 내가 새벽 3시에 집에 왔을 때 엄마한테 혼났어.

I just failed my math exam, and my mom gave it to me. 수학시험에서 낙제를 해서 엄마한테 혼났어.

After I broke my cell phone, my mom gave it to me. 내가 핸드폰을 고장낸 다음에 엄마한테 혼났어.

028 You call yourself~ 자칭 …라는 사람이

this is a way to say the speaker may not believe someone should call themselves something. It is similar to saying "I don't think you are~"

A: I can't even ride a horse. 난 말도 못타.

B: Really? And **you call yourself** a cowboy?
정말? 그러고도 자칭 카우보이라고 하는 거야?

미드표현

What kind of profit is that?! And you call yourself an accountant.
무슨 수익이 저래?! 자칭 회계사라는 사람이 말야.

How could you not know that? You call yourself a writer.
어떻게 저걸 모를 수가 있어? 자칭 작가라는 작자가.

I can't believe you call yourself Russian.
자칭 러시아인이라고 하는 사람이 믿기지가 않아.

029 What were you thinking about?

정신을 어디다 놓고 다녀?, 도대체 무슨 생각을 한거야?

미드표현

this is a way to say "You made a foolish decision." The speaker is indicating that someone did something wrong

A: How could you marry him after only a month? **What were you thinking about?** 어떻게 한 달만에 결혼할 수 있어? 제 정신 있는거야?

B: Well, I guess that was a pretty bad decision to make. 음, 바보 같은 결정이었던 것 같아.

You weren't thinking about anybody. Then, what were you thinking about?
아무도 신경을 안쓰고 있었지. 그럼 도대체 무슨 생각을 한거야?

A: I wasn't thinking about killing her. B: What were you thinking about?
A: 난 걔를 죽일 생각을 하지 않았어. B: 그럼 무슨 생각을 하고 있었던거야?

030 What would you call it? 그걸 뭐라고 할테야?, 그럼 그게 뭐야?

this is a way to ask the opinion of someone who is disagreeing. It's saying "Tell me your thoughts on this"

A: I don't think that you live in a luxury apartment.
넌 고급 아파트에 사는 게 아냐.

B: It's very big and very expensive. **What would you call it?** 아파트가 크고 비싼데 그럼 그게 뭐야?

Really? What would you call it, then?
정말? 그럼 그게 뭐야?

A: So, what? You were using me? B: Well, I wouldn't call it using you. A: Then, what would you call it?
A: 그래서 날 이용했다는 거니? B: 아니, 꼭 그런건 아니고. A: 그럼 뭔데?

031 You and your~ ! 또 너의 …야!

미드표현

this is a way of indicating that something a person has causes extra trouble at times. It is like saying "Your ________ creates problems at times"

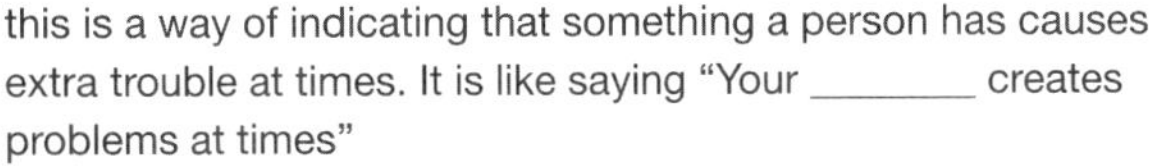

A: I have to go get my car fixed. 가서 차 수리해야겠어.

B: **You and your** old car. Just buy a new one!
너의 또 그 낡은 차야. 새차 뽑아라!

You and your big mouth! 너의 왕이빨 또 시작이구나!

You and your stupid fear. I hate your fear.
너의 그 말도 안되는 두려움. 너의 두려움이 싫어.

You and your macho pride!
너의 그 남성우월주의 또 시작이구나!

032 Wouldn't you just know it? 그런 건 예상했어야지?

미드표현

this is saying "It was expected to happen and it did." It is often said in a cynical way

A: I got a big bill for my dental work.
치과비용이 엄청 많이 나왔어.

B: **Wouldn't you just know it?** Now you won't have any extra money.
그건 예상했어야지? 이제 돈 여유가 없을거야.

Wouldn't you just know it? It rained during our festival. 그런 건 예상했어야지? 축제 중에 비가 왔잖아.

Wouldn't you just know it? We're out of toilet paper! 그런 건 알고 있어야지? 화장실 휴지가 떨어졌잖아!

Wouldn't you just know it? The car is broken again. 그런 건 예상했어야지? 차가 다시 고장났잖아.

033 Shove it 집어치워, 그만둬

this speaker is very rudely and angrily telling someone that he doesn't want or need anything from the person he is talking to. This also signals that the conversation has ended. The speaker is saying "No way, forget about it"

| Point | shove it 꺼지다, 집어치우다, 말도 안되는 소리를 하다

A: If you want to remain here, you have to take a pay cut. 여기 남고 싶으면 급여삭감을 받아들여야 돼.

B: You can take this job and **shove it!**
너나 다녀라, 말도 안되는 소리말고!

미드표현

She told her ex-boyfriend to shove it.
걔는 전 남친보고 꺼지라고 말했어.

If you want more from me, you can shove it.
내게서 뭘 더 원하다면 꿈깨라고.

I told her to shove it when she tried to borrow money. 난 걔가 돈을 빌려달라고 했을 때 집어치우라고 했어.

When she said I was a bad person, I told her to shove it.
걔가 나보고 나쁜 사람이라고 했을 때, 난 걔한데 헛소리하지 말라고 했어.

034 Shove[Stick] it up your ass 엿이나 먹어라

this is a very very rude way of telling someone that the speaker won't do something. It is so rude that it is almost never used. It means "I really don't like you and I won't do that"

A: I want you to stay till midnight tonight.
오늘 밤 자정까지 있어.

B: **Shove it up your ass.** I quit! 엿이나 먹어. 난 간다!

미드표현

Shove the medal up your ass, all right?
메달은 엿이나 바꿔먹어, 알았어?

Shove this marriage up your ass!
이 결혼 엿이나 먹어라!

035 It was a cheap shot 비열한 짓이야, 유치한 짓이야

means "That seems unfair or more unkind than it should have been." We can understand that the speaker is upset about it

| Point | do the nasty with~ …에게 비열하게 대하다

A: Eric said that Helen has had many boyfriends.
에릭은 헬렌이 남친을 여러 사귄다고 말했어.

B: **That was a cheap shot.** Helen is a nice person.
그건 비열한 짓이야. 헬렌은 착한 사람이야.

미드표현

I know it was a cheap shot, but I feel so much better now.
비열한 짓이라는 걸 알았지만 지금은 기분이 많이 좋아졌어.

Yeah, but still, cheap shot!
맞아, 하지만 그래도 비열한 짓이야!

He has a heart attack when he sees her wife doing the nasty with the pool man.
그 남자는 자기 부인이 풀장청소부와 자는 걸 보고 심장마비에 걸렸어.

036 How rude! 참 무례하구만!

this is a way of saying "That's impolite." The speaker thinks someone's behavior has been very bad

| Point | How rude (of me) 이런 무례를 (죄송합니다)

A: Joe never showed up for our date last night.
조는 지난 밤에 데이트에 안나왔어.

B: **How rude.** He is a very selfish man.
정말 무례하구만. 걘 정말 이기적이야.

I'm sorry! How rude! I always forget that men can be nurses.
미안해요! 이런 무례가! 남자도 간호사가 될 수 있다는 걸 항상 잊어서.

You haven't even been offered a drink. How rude. I'm so sorry.
마실거 대접도 못했네요. 이런 무례가. 미안해요.

037 Leave me alone 나 좀 내버려둬, 귀찮게 좀 하지마

미드표현

this indicates the person doesn't want another person near him. It is like saying "Go away"

Point Leave me in peace 나 좀 가만히 냅둬
Give me a rest 날 좀 그만 내버려둬. 나도 좀 쉬자
Give me a minute alone 잠시 혼자 있고 싶어

A: **Leave me alone.** I don't want you near me.
귀찮게 하지마. 가까이 오지 말고.

B: But Rita, I think that I am in love with you.
하지만 리타, 널 사랑하는 것 같아.

Why don't you just leave me alone?!
그냥 나 좀 놔둬?!

Quit being a baby and leave me alone!
애들처럼 굴지 말고 나 좀 가만히 둬!

Just leave me alone, all right? You are not my mother! 나 좀 그냥 가만히 둬, 알았어? 내 엄마도 아니잖아!

038 Let go of me 놔줘, 날 가게 해줘, 풀어줘

미드표현

this is said when a person is holding onto the speaker. It says to that person "release me"

Point let go of me = let me go

A: Hey, you can't leave me now. 야, 지금 가면 안되지.

B: **Let go of me.** I'm going home. 가게 해줘. 집에 갈 거야.

Let go of me! What's the matter with you?
날 놔줘! 너 왜 그래?

Honey, don't squeeze my hand so hard! Let go of my hand! 자기야, 손 꽉잡지마! 놔줘!

Let go of me! Let go of me, can't you see he's sick? 날 놔줘! 놔주라고, 걔가 아픈게 보이지 않아?

039 Stop bothering me 나 좀 가만히 놔둬, 그만 괴롭혀

미드표현

this means "Don't upset me." It is said when a person is getting angry about another person's behavior

Point Don't bother me 저리 가, 나 좀 내버려둬
Stop picking on me 날 못살게 굴지 마, 놀리지 마
Stop bugging me 나 좀 귀찮게 하지마
Stop pestering me 귀찮게 좀 하지마

A: Can we go out and play baseball now?
나가서 야구할래?

B: No we can't. **Stop bothering me.**
아니 안돼. 나 좀 가만히 둬.

I'm a friend of David, and I want you to stop picking on him. 난 데이빗의 친구인데 제발 그만 좀 놀려.

It's okay. These photos don't bother me.
괜찮아. 이 사진들은 신경 안쓰여.

040 You know what you can do with it! 꺼져버려! 알아서 해!

미드표현

this is said when someone wants to express their feeling of contempt or anger. It is similar to the expression "You can shove it." Usually it is said during an argument or disagreement

Point You know what you can do with it? (논쟁 중 화내며서) 알아서 해!, 집어치워!, 꺼져버려
You can go to hell! 꺼져버려!
You can shove[stick] it! 집어치워!

A: I want to end our engagement to be married.
결혼하겠다는 약혼 끝내고 싶어.

B: Fine! Here is your ring back. **You know what you can do with it!** 좋아! 여기 반지돌려줄게. 꺼져버려!

Here's your phone, and you know what you can do with it. 여기 네 핸드폰, 알아서 해.

You can go to hell if you feel that way!
그렇게 느껴진다면 꺼져버려!

Take this contract back, and you know what you can do with it.
이 계약서 도로 가지고 가서 알아서 해.

You can take your money and shove it.
네 돈 가지고 가고 꺼져버려.

041 Get out of[outta] here! 1. 꺼져! 2. 웃기지 마!, 말도 안돼

this is a way to strongly say "Leave." It is used when the speaker doesn't want to be around another person

| Point | Get out of my face 혼자 좀 내버려둬, 내 눈 앞에서 사라져
Let's get out of here 나가자

A: **Get out of here!** I don't want you around.
꺼져! 가까이 오지마.

B: Please let me stay just a while longer.
제발 좀 더 있게 해줘.

I'm calling the police! Get out of here!
경찰 부르겠어! 꺼져!

I want you to leave! Get outta here! 나가줘! 꺼지라고!

Get outta here! I can't believe it! 말도 안돼! 그럴 리가!

042 Get out of my way 1. 비켜 2. 방해하지마

this tells another person "Don't block my path." It means that someone shouldn't try to stop another person't movements

| Point | Keep[Stay] out of my way 귀찮게 하지마
(don't bother or interfere with me)

A: Don't go out drinking tonight. 오늘 밤에 나가서 술마시지 마.

B: **Get out of my way.** I'll go if I want to.
비키라고. 내가 원하면 나가는 거지.

미드표현

Get out of my way! I've got to get in there!
비켜! 저기에 들어가야 돼!

You need to get out of my way right now, so I can do my job. 지금 당장 방해하는 걸 그만둬, 내가 일 좀 하게.

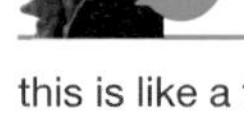

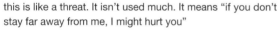

043 Get out of town 그만 꺼져, 다른 데로 가버려

this is like a threat. It isn't used much. It means "if you don't stay far away from me, I might hurt you"

A: You better **get out of town** if you want to stay safe. 안전하고 싶으면 꺼지는 게 좋아.

B: Your threats don't scare me at all.
네 협박은 전혀 무섭지 않은데.

미드표현

How quick can you get out of town?
얼마나 빨리 떠날 수 있어?

Pack up your bags and get out of town.
짐 챙기고 꺼져.

Did you tell her to get out of town?
걔한테 떠나라고 했니?

044 Get off my back (귀찮게 하지 말고) 날 좀 내버려둬

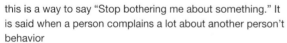

this is a way to say "Stop bothering me about something." It is said when a person complains a lot about another person't behavior

| Point | Get off my case! 귀찮게 좀 하지마!
Get off my property 내 집에서 나가(Get out of my yard)

A: I keep telling you to mow the lawn.
잔디 깎으라고 계속 말했잖아.

B: **Get off my back.** I'll do it this afternoon.
날 좀 내버려둬. 오후에 할게.

미드표현

Will you get off my back? 그만 나 좀 내버려둘래?

A: You wanna get off my back? B: You wanna get out of my face? A: 날 좀 내버려둘래? B: 꺼져줄래?

Okay, I get it. Please get off my back, and stop talking like this.
그래, 알았어. 이제 그만 좀 날 내버려두고 그런 식으로 말하지마.

045 Get lost! (그만 좀 괴롭히고) 꺼져라!, 그만 괴롭혀!

this tells a person to go. It is a rude way of saying "Leave right now"

I Point I Get out! 꺼져! 나가　　Go away! 냅둬, 저리가
Beat it! 빨리 꺼져!, 비켜!

A: Stop following me! **Get lost!** 그만 쫓아와! 꺼져!
B: But what else can I do today? 하지만 오늘 달리 할게 없어.

John, get lost. I'm not done!
존, 나가. 나 아직 안 끝났다고!

Get out of my room! Get out! 방에서 나가! 꺼져!

Go away! I don't want to see anybody.
가! 아무도 보고 싶지 않아.

046 Go to your room 나가, 꺼져

this is said to children when they are punished. It tells them "You must stay alone in your room as punishment

I Point I go to one's room …의 방으로 가다

A: You have been very rude. **Go to your room.**
넌 너무 무례했어. 방으로 들어가.
B: I don't want to do that. I want to stay right here.
그러기 싫어. 여기 있고 싶어.

Go to your room! You're grounded.
방으로 들어가! 넌 외출금지야.

Go to your room and finish packing.
방으로 가서 짐싸는 거 끝내.

This conversation is over. Go to your room!
이 대화는 끝이야. 네 방으로 가라!

Sweetie, why don't you go to your room? And I'll be there in a sec. 자기야, 네 방에 가있어. 내 곧 들어갈게.

047 Take a hike! 가버려!, 꺼져 버려!

this is an old expression telling someone "Go away." It is said when a person is rudely told to leave

A: Would you like to buy some jewelry?
보석 좀 사시겠어요?
B: **Take a hike.** I don't buy anything while riding the subway. 꺼져요. 지하철 탈 동안은 물건 안 사요.

I'm telling you, one of us has got to take a hike. 정말이야, 우리들 중 한 명이 가야 돼.

I'm gonna tell him to take a hike.
걔한테 꺼지라고 얘기하겠어.

048 Go to hell! 뒈져라!, 꺼져!, 지옥에나 가버려!, 그만 좀 놔둬!

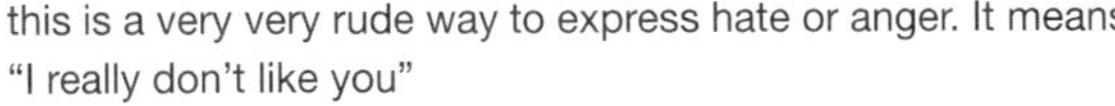

this is a very very rude way to express hate or anger. It means "I really don't like you"

I Point I Sth[Sb]+goes to hell 망치다, 실패하다, 지옥에 가다
Fuck off! 꺼져!
Fuck me! 젠장! 입닥쳐! 꺼져!

A: You are the ugliest girl I have ever seen.
너 같이 못생긴 앤 첨 봐.
B: **Go to hell.** You are just a jerk. 꺼져, 머저리 같은 놈.

Swear to God, we're gonna go to hell.
정말이지, 우린 큰일 났어.

She told him to go to hell. 걘 나보고 나가 뒈지라고 했어.

My relationship with Anita went to hell.
애니터와의 관계가 엉망이 됐어.

049 Why don't you go fuck yourself 좀 꺼져주지 그래

this is a very rude and unpleasant thing to say, and it is only said when someone is very angry. The speaker is very strongly telling someone to go away and never come back. This can be similarly expressed when saying things like "Go to hell" or "Fuck off"

| Point | go fuck oneself 나가 뒈지다, 꺼지다

A: You are the biggest jerk I ever met.
너같은 머저리 같은 놈은 처음본다.

B: **Why don't you go fuck yourself!** 좀 꺼져주지 그래!

미드표현

You want a ransom for Carl? Go fuck yourself!
칼의 몸값을 원한다고? 나가 뒈져라!

Everybody go fuck themselves and fix their own problems. 다들 꺼져버리고 각자의 문제점들 고쳐.

So you can tell him to go fuck himself.
그럼 넌 걔보고 꺼지라고 해.

Why don't you go fuck yourself. I won't be doing it again, ever.
좀 꺼져주라. 절대로 다시는 그 일을 하지 않을거야.

050 I'm pissed off 열받아, 진절머리나

this is a very common way to say "I'm very angry." People say this in a rude way to talk about how they are feeling

| Point | piss off sb …을 열받게 하다
be pissed off (with/at+N) (…에게) 열받다
hit the roof = hit the ceiling = go through the roof 열받다

A: You look really upset, Raul. 라울, 너 정말 화난 것 같아.

B: **I'm pissed off.** People have been treating me badly. 열받았어. 사람들이 내게 짖궂게 굴어.

미드표현

Piss off. 썩 꺼져라.

That pissed you off. So you killed him.
그것 땜에 열받아 걔를 죽인거구만.

I was really pissed off at Dick when I heard about the whole thing.
자초지종을 들었을 때 딕에게 정말 화났었어.

051 I'm really ticked off 정말 열받았어, 화났어

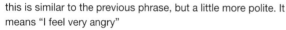

this is similar to the previous phrase, but a little more polite. It means "I feel very angry"

| Point | be ticked off at …에게 화나다
That burns me up 정말 열받네, 정말 화나네
That makes me angry 그것 때문에 열받아

A: **I'm really ticked off.** I didn't get a vacation this year. 정말 화났어. 금년에 휴가를 못 갔어.

B: Maybe you can go on one next year.
내년엔 갈 수 있겠지.

You're really starting to tick me off.
정말 날 열받게 하네.

I'm ticked off at Susie. 수지한테 화났어.

It hurts me, and it makes me angry. 아파서 열받아.

052 It bothers me 정말 짜증나

this indicates the speaker is feeling upset or worried. It is similar to saying "I'm troubled by that"

| Point | It bothers me (that) S+V …가 정말 짜증나
What bothers you the most ~? …에서 가장 불편한 점이 뭐야?
Does it bother you? 짜증나?

A: How do you feel about the price of gas?
기름값이 어떤 것 같아?

B: **It bothers me.** I think it's too expensive.
정말 짜증나. 너무 비싸.

미드표현

It bothers me that I'm never gonna have that feeling. 내가 그런 감정을 절대로 느끼지 못한다는게 짜증나.

It really bothers me when people try to deceive me like that.
사람들이 그런 식으로 나를 속이려 할 때 정말 짜증이 나거든.

It bothered me when he slept with other women. 걔가 다른 여자랑 잘 때가 정말 짜증났어.

053 It's really getting to me 그것 때문에 정말 화나, 정말 신경질 나 죽겠어

this is a way of saying "I am thinking about that problem a lot" or "It's getting on my nerves." People say this when they feel unhappy about some problem

I Point I get to sb …을 신경쓰게 하다, 거슬리게 하다, 화나게 하다
It really got to me 진짜 짜증났어
She got to you 그 여자에게 걸려든거야(she affected the way you are thinking)
You got to me 너한테 말려들었어

A: The weather has become very cold this year.
금년에 날씨가 무척 춥네.

B: I agree. **It's really getting to me.**
맞아. 그 때문에 정말 짜증나.

He's using Betty to get to me and I am not falling for it.
걘 베티를 이용해서 날 건드리려고 하는데 난 안 넘어가.

I guess the pressure does get to me a little.
압력이 좀 날 거슬리게 하는 것 같아.

The girl really got to me. I worry about her all the time. 걘 정말 맘이 쓰여. 항상 걔 걱정하고 있어.

054 He got worked up 걔 열 받았어, 걔 대단했어

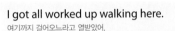

this means the person got upset or emotional. When someone gets worked up, we can say "He got very agitated"

I Point I work oneself up 화내다(get angry), 흥분하다(get excited)
get (all) worked up (about/over) =
get oneself (all) worked up (부정) 화내다, 열받다 (긍정) 흥분하다, 들뜨다

A: How did Richard react when Joan broke up with him? 조앤이 헤어지자고 했을 때 리차드의 반응은 어땠어?

B: **He got worked up.** He couldn't believe it.
열받았지. 믿기지 않는 듯 했어.

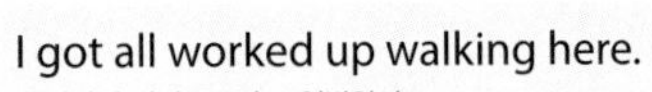

I got all worked up walking here.
여기까지 걸어오느라고 열받았어.

We're all friends. This isn't something to get worked up over. 우리 모두 친구야. 이런 건 열받을 일이 아니야.

All right, don't get yourself all worked up here. 그래, 이걸로 너무 열받지마.

The soccer fans worked themselves up before the match. 축구팬들은 경기시작전 들떠있었어.

055 If you blow up, you'll blow it 화를 내면 일을 망쳐

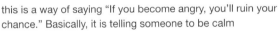

this is a way of saying "If you become angry, you'll ruin your chance." Basically, it is telling someone to be calm

I Point I blow up (at) (…에) 화내다, 폭발하다

A: My boss has really been bothering me this month. 사장은 이번 달에 정말 날 힘들게 해.

B: Stay calm and remember, **if you blow up, you'll blow it.** 침착하고 명심해, 화내면 일을 망쳐.

Unless you want to blow up, I'm coming with you. 네가 화내지 않으면 같이 갈게.

Engine's smoking pretty bad, looks like it could blow up any second.
엔진이 언제 터져도 이상하지 않은 상황이야.

056 He's up in arms~ (…로) 걔 열받았어

this indicates someone is angry about something. It means "He's very upset about something"

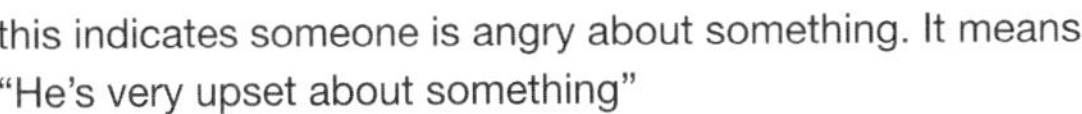

I Point I be up in arms (about/over~) (…에) 매우 화내다

A: Why does our teacher seem so angry these days? 왜 요즘 우리 선생님이 화난 것 같아?

B: **He's up in arms over** the new tests the school is requiring. 학교가 요구하는 새로운 시험으로 열받아계셔.

He's up in arms about the rent increase.
걘 임대로 인상으로 열받았어.

He's up in arms because he wasn't invited.
걔는 초대를 받지 못해서 열받았어.

He's up in arms over the political scandal.
걘 정치적 스캔들로 열받았어.

057 Gross! 역겨워!, 구역질나!

this is said when people see or smell something they don't like. It is like saying "That seems terrible!"

| Point | Gross me out! 열받아! Nasty! 역겨워!
You're so mean 비열해 How annoying! 짜증나!

A: The water from the toilets is cleaned and recycled as drinking water. 화장실물은 정화되어 식수로 재생돼.

B: **Gross!** I don't want to drink anything like that.
구역질나! 그런 건 마시고 싶지 않아.

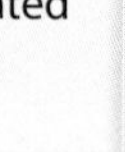

That's so gross! 정말 구역질나!

Did you see it? It was gross! 봤어? 정말 역겨웠어!

My teacher was mean to me. She humiliated me in front of the whole class.
선생님이 내게 못되게 굴었어. 반에서 다들 있는데 날 창피줬어.

058 You're driving me crazy 너 때문에 미치겠어

this is the same as saying "You are bothering me." The speaker wants someone to stop the behavior that is causing him to feel upset

| Point | You're driving me up the wall 너 때문에 내가 미치겠어
You've got me going crazy 너 때문에 미쳐
It drives me nuts (the way S+V) (…에) 내가 미칠 지경이야

A: Mom, can we go eat at McDonald's tonight?
엄마, 오늘 밤에 맥도날드에서 먹을 수 있어요?

B: No, stop asking me. **You're driving me crazy.**
아니, 그만 좀 해라. 미치겠다.

That bitch is driving me crazy. 저년 때문에 내가 미쳐.

This is driving me crazy. 이게 날 미치게 해.

I'm dying to get out of there. He's driving me crazy. 거기서 벗어나고 싶어. 걔가 날 미치게 해.

You used to drive me nuts before.
전에 네가 날 돌게 하곤 했지.

059 You've been on my ass all day 종일 귀찮게 하는군

this is a way to say "You have been too critical of me." It indicates that someone has watched the speaker and complained about his mistakes

| Point | be on sb's ass all day …을 종일 귀찮게 하다

A: Hey, quit bothering me. **You've been on my ass all day.** 야, 그만 좀 괴롭혀라. 종일 귀찮게 하네.

B: I want to make sure you are doing a good job.
네가 일을 잘 하는지 확인하고 싶어서.

What's wrong with you? You've been on my ass all day. 너 왜 그래? 종일 나를 귀찮게 하네.

You've been on my ass all day. I need some space. 너 종일 나를 귀찮게 구네. 난 공간이 좀 필요해.

Why don't you fuck off? You've been on my ass all day. 좀 꺼져주시지. 너 종일 날 귀찮게 하네.

060 You're pushing my buttons 날 건드리네, 귀찮게 하네

this means "You are bothering me." It is said when one person is making another person upset

| Point | push one's buttons …을 화나게 하다, 열받게 하다

A: Can I turn on the TV now? TV 켜도 돼?

B: **You're pushing my buttons.** I need a quiet place to study now. 날 건드리네. 공부하게 조용해야 한다고.

You made fun of my job and you just pushed my buttons. 넌 내 직업을 조롱했어, 넌 날 건드린거라고.

You look for ways to push my buttons.
날 화나게 할 방법을 찾고 있구만.

Alex knew just how to push his buttons.
알렉스는 어떻게 걔를 화나게 하는 방법을 알고 있었어.

You can't let him push your buttons.
걔가 널 화나게 하도록 놔두지마.

061 You're pain in the ass 넌 정말 골칫거리야, 참 성가시네

this means "You have caused a lot of problems." It is said when someone does things that upset others

| Point | pain in the ass[neck] 골칫덩어리

A: Why don't most people like me?
왜 대부분의 사람들이 날 싫어해?

B: **You're a pain in the neck.** 네가 골칫덩어리니까.

미드표현

You guys are a real pain in the ass, you know that? 니네들 정말 골칫덩어리들이야, 그거 알어?

I know that sometimes I can be a pain in the ass, but you just have to talk to me.
때때로 내가 성가시게 한다는 거 알지만 내게 말해야 돼.

I want a boyfriend whose roommate isn't a giant pain in the ass.
난 룸메이트가 엄청난 골칫덩어리가 아닌 남자 친구를 원해.

062 You've gone off the deep end 넌 정신나갔어, 자제력을 잃었어

this indicates someone is acting very strangely. It is a way of saying "You are acting crazy these days"

| Point | go off the deep end 자제력을 잃다, 이유없이 화를 버럭 내다

A: I think **you've gone off the deep end,** Rob.
랍, 네가 자제력을 잃은 것 같아.

B: Stress makes me act in strange ways.
스트레스 때문에 내 행동이 이상해졌어.

미드표현

The kid liked it, but she just went off the deep end. 애는 좋아했는데 걔는 불같이 화를 냈어.

You went off the deep end. What is your problem? 화를 버럭 내는데 문제가 뭔데?

The last time he went off the deep end, he got really messed up.
걔가 지난번에 자제력을 잃었을 때 정말 일이 엉망이 되었어.

063 You're trying my patience 너 정말 짜증난다

this is a way to say "I will become angry soon because of your behavior." It is a way of warning someone to change his behavior before it causes problems

| Point | try sb's patience …의 인내심을 테스트하다, 화나게 하다

A: I want to go to Hawaii right now. 지금 하와이 가고 싶어.

B: **You're trying my patience.** We can't go right now. 너 정말 짜증난다. 지금 당장 갈 수 없잖아.

Stop nagging me. You're trying my patience.
그만 날 괴롭혀. 너 정말 짜증난다.

You're trying my patience. I've had enough of you. 너 정말 짜증난다. 네가 지겨워.

I don't like your attitude. You're trying my patience. 네 태도가 마음에 안들어. 너 정말 짜증나.

064 What're you getting so bent out of shape for?
왜 그렇게 화를 내?

this is a way of asking "Why are you getting angry?" It is said when the speaker doesn't understand why someone is upset

| Point | get bent out of shape 화내다(get upset)

A: I really hate waiting in line so long.
이렇게 긴 줄을 서는 건 정말 짜증나.

B: **What are you getting so bent out of shape for?** Be patient. 그렇게 열 받지마. 조급하게 굴지마.

미드표현

What're you getting so bent out of shape for? It's not like we agreed to get married.
뭐 때문에 그리 화를 내? 결혼하기로 약속한 것도 아니잖아.

I'm sorry you're so bent out of shape. I didn't mean to upset you.
네가 그렇게 화를 내다니 미안해. 널 화나게 할 생각은 아니었어.

065 Not again! 어휴 이런 또 야!, 어떻게 또 그럴 수 있어!

미드표현

this is a way of saying the person doesn't want something to repeat. He feels "I wish this would stop happening"

I Point I Oh, no, not again 오, 안돼, 또야

A: I think someone hit your car. 누가 네 차를 친 것 같아.

B: **Not again!** This happened a few months ago!
또야! 몇 달전에도 그랬는데!

Good lord, Karl, not again! 맙소사, 칼, 또야!

I am not going through this alone. Not again.
나 혼자 이걸 겪지는 않을거야. 다시는 안그래.

066 She's gonna totally freak out! 걔, 완전히 돌아버릴걸!

미드표현

this is expressing that a woman will become very upset. We could say that "She's going to go crazy"

A: Mary's files were thrown away in the garbage yesterday. 메리의 파일들이 어제 쓰레기통에 버려졌어.

B: **She's going to totally freak out.** Those were important. 걔 완전히 돌겠네. 중요한 거였는데.

It's nothing to freak out about. 난리 칠 사항은 아니야.

He's still mourning, Kim. He'd probably freak out. 아직 상중인데, 킴. 아마도 정신 못차릴거야.

I freaked out and screwed everything up with Max, remember?
내가 난리를 쳤고 맥스와의 모든 것을 망쳐버렸어, 기억나?

067 I've had enough of you 이제 너한테 질렸어

미드표현

usually this indicates "I don't want to see you anymore." It is said when a person wants to indicate he doesn't like someone

I Point I have enough of~ …에 질리다

A: You need to work harder. 좀 더 열심히 해라.

B: **I've had enough of you.** Leave me alone.
너한테 질린다. 좀 가만히 놔둬.

I think I've had enough of arts and crafts.
미술 공예품에 질린 것 같아.

Alright, that's it. I've had enough of this.
알았어, 그만해. 그 정도면 충분하니 그만해라.

You know what? I've had enough of your advice, and your help.
저 말이야, 난 네 충고나 도움에 질렸어.

068 I've had it[enough]! 이제 그만!, 참을 만큼 참았어!

미드표현

this is used when someone has become angry and is ready to take some action. It means "I am going to do something to change this"

I Point I Enough is enough! 이젠 충분해!

A: **I've had it.** I really hate staying here.
이제 그만. 정말 여기 있는 게 싫어.

B: Let's move to another apartment complex.
다른 아파트 단지로 이사가자.

That's it. I've had it. Really, I can't have this conversation one more time.
이제 됐어. 그만해. 정말이지 난 이런 대화는 더 이상 못해.

All right, enough is enough. I'm not buying it.
좋아, 이젠 그만. 난 안 믿어.

069 I've had it with you guys 너희들한테 질려버렸어, 이제 진절머리 나

usually this indicates "I'm getting unhappy with the way you act." It is said when someone wants to express his feelings about the way others act

| Point | have it with sb[sth] 지나치게 경험하다
I've had it up to here (with~) (…라면) 진절머리 나

A: Hey baby, you look so cute today. 아가씨, 오늘 아주 귀여운데.
B: **I've had it with you guys.** Stop bothering me!
너희들 질린다. 그만 좀 괴롭혀라!

I've had it with you guys and your cancer.
너희들과 니네들이 말하는 암에 질렸어.

I've had it with both of you. 니네 둘 모두에게 질렸어.

I've had it up to here with you two! Neither of you can come to the party!
니네 둘 모두 지겹다! 둘 다 파티에 오지마!

070 If I had a nickel for every time he did that
개는 지겨울 정도로 그랬어

this is a way to indicate that something happens very frequently. A nickel is a very small amount of money. Sometimes people say "If I had a nickel for every time that happened, I'd be rich." What that means is "That thing occurs very, very often here, and if I got a small amount of money every time it happened, eventually it would become a lot of money"

| Point | If I have a nickel for every time S+V
정말 수없이 …했다, 지겨울 정도로 수도 없이 …했다
(…할 때마다 5센트를 모았다면 엄청 부자가 되었을거야)

A: Your brother got into a fight after drinking too much. 네 형은 과음을 한 후에 싸움을 벌였어.
B: **If I had a nickel for every time** he did that, I'd be rich. 형은 지겨울 정도로 싸움질을 해.

If I had a nickel for every time I puked at school, you know how much money I'd have?
나 학교에서 셀 수도 없이 토했어.

If I had a nickel for every time you've said "Big bucks," I'd have big bucks.
네가 "거금"이라는 말은 정말 수도 없이 들어 지겹다.

071 I'm bored out of my mind 지겨워 죽겠어

this means that the speaker is not interested in something that is happening, and he wants to be doing something else. Usually when someone is bored out of their mind, they dislike what they are doing and want to stop it. The speaker is saying "I hate doing this because it is so dull"

| Point | be bored out of one's mind 지겨워[지루해] 죽겠다

A: **I'm bored out of my mind** these days. 요즘 지겨 죽겠어.
B: Maybe you should try to find a new hobby.
새로운 취미를 찾아보도록 해.

I'm starved and bored out of my mind.
나 배도 고프고 지겨워 죽겠어.

You'll be bored out of your mind.
넌 지겨워 미칠 지경이 될거야.

Oh, please, I'm already so bored out of my mind. 제발, 이미 지겨워서 미칠 지경이야.

072 I'm fed up with you! 너한테 질렸어!, 더 이상 못 참겠어!

It means "I'm upset with the way you have acted

| Point | be[get] fed up with~ …에 질리다
I'm fed up with people who complain about how hard~
…가 너무 힘들다고 투덜대는 사람들이 지긋지긋해

A: You spend too much money on clothes. **I'm fed up with you.** 너 옷에 돈을 넘 많이 써. 더 이상 못 참겠어.
B: But you always said I could buy anything I want.
하지만 사고 싶은 거 아무거나 사라고 늘 말했잖아.

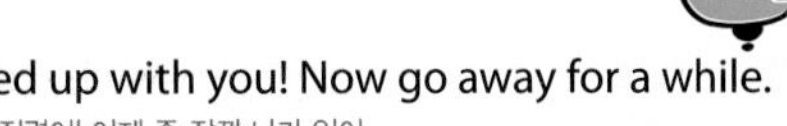

I'm fed up with you! Now go away for a while.
너한테 질렸어! 이제 좀 잠깐 나가 있어.

You need to chill out. I'm fed up with you!
진정 좀 하라고. 난 더 이상 못참겠어!

I'm fed up with you! Why are you such a jerk?
너한테 질렸어! 너 왜 그렇게 머저리같아?

073 I'm not taking this lying down 난 이걸 참지 않을거야

this means that the person is upset about something and is promising to react to it. It is very likely he will try to change or control whatever is happening. It is a way of expressing "I'm going to fight this"

| Point | take sth lying down …을 감수하다, 참다, 가만히 있다

A: These papers say that your money is being seized. 신문보니까 네 돈이 동결된다고 하던대.

B: That's not fair at all! **I'm not taking this lying down!** 정말이지 불공평해! 가만히 있지 않을거야!

Which is why I want to sue. I will not take this lying down.
그래서 난 소송을 원해. 난 가만히 있지 않을거야.

Burke decided he wasn't going to take this stand-up lying down.
버크는 이렇게 바람맞은 걸 참지 않을거라고 결심했어.

And she had decided she would not take it lying down. 그리고 걔는 그것을 참지 않으리라고 결심을 했었어.

074 That's sick 말도 안돼, 역겨워

the speaker wants to say "That is disgusting." This is said when the speaker sees something he really doesn't like

| Point | This is (just too) sick 이건 (넘) 역겨워
It is disgusting 역겨워

A: We looked at dead mice in biology class.
생물 수업시간에 죽은 쥐를 쳐다봤어.

B: **That's sick.** I hate to see dead things.
역겨워. 죽은 거 보는 거 정말 싫은데.

미드표현

You shouldn't cut yourself. That's sick.
넌 칼로 자해를 하면 안되지. 역겨워.

That's sick. Why would anyone do that?
정말 역겨워. 왜 사람들이 그런 짓을 할까?

That's sick. This murderer did some evil things. 정말 역겨워. 이 살인범은 사악한 짓을 했어.

075 You make me sick 너 정말 역겨워

this is like saying "I hate to be around you." The speaker is expressing that he really dislikes someone

| Point | It makes me sick to think~ …을 생각하면 정말 역겨워
This makes me sick 역겨워 It made me sick 역겨웠어

A: My parents gave me a brand new car.
부모님이 새 차를 사주셨어.

B: **You make me sick.** You're too lazy to earn money to get a car yourself.
기가 차네. 넌 너무 게을러 스스로 차살 돈을 안벌지.

미드표현

I know what you did. It makes me sick. I'm going to tell.
네가 무슨 짓을 했는지 알아. 역겨워. 난 폭로할거야.

Stop saying you're sorry when you're not. You make me sick.
시도 때도 없이 미안하다고 하지마. 진짜 역겨워.

It makes me sick to think how cruel I was to my own mother.
내가 어머니에게 얼마나 잔인했나 생각하면 역겨워.

076 I'm sick of this 진절머리가 나

this is a way of saying "This is tiring or boring me." It means that the speaker wants things to change

| Point | be sick[tired] of+N/~ing …가 짜증나, 진절머리 나
be getting sick of+N/~ing …에 신물이나

A: **I am sick of this.** I'm leaving. 진절머리가 나. 나 갈게.

B: But the movie hasn't finished yet.
하지만 영화가 아직 안 끝났어.

All I'm saying is I'm getting sick of being treated like that.
내가 말하고 싶은 건 그렇게 취급당하는 데 짜증난다는 거야.

I'm getting a little tired of this okay?
이거에 신물이 나, 알았어?

I'm tired of dating. I'm ready to get married.
데이트하는 데 짜증나. 결혼준비가 되었다고.

077 That's getting on my nerves 신경 거슬려, 열받아

usually this means something is bothering the speaker. It is like saying "That is upsetting me"

Point get on sb's nerve …를 화나게 하다
It's getting on my nerves 신경거슬려
You're getting on my nerves 넌 날 짜증나게 해

A: Can you hear the noise from the construction site? 건설현장에서 나는 소음 들려?
B: Yeah. **That's getting on my nerves.** 정말 신경거슬려.

If he starts to get on your nerves, say something.
걔가 널 짜증나게 하기 시작하면 뭐라고 말을 좀 해.

Fine, fine, fine. He's just kind of getting on my nerves a little, you know.
괜찮아. 니가 알다시피 걘 뭐 조금 나를 귀찮게 할 뿐이야.

All right, now you're really getting on my nerves. 좋아, 이제 너 정말 날 신경거슬리게 해.

078 That's a drag 지겨운거야, 짜증나는거야

미드표현

Something that is a drag is a thing that is depressing or which makes a person unhappy. It is like saying "That's too bad." The speaker is saying he's sad to hear some bad news

Point a drag 짜증나는 거 혹은 사람
take a drag 담배 한 모금을 빨다

A: I think I'm getting a cold. 감기 걸린 것 같아.
B: **That's a drag.** Maybe you need to go get some sleep. 안 됐네. 너 좀 쉬어야겠어

You made me find you twice, Tony. That's a drag. 토니 널 두번이나 찾게 만들었어. 짜증나.

It is such a drag to be here in detention instead of going home.
집에 못가고 학교에 벌로 남아있는 건 정말이지 짜증나.

She took drag from her cigarette.
그 여자는 담배를 한 모금 빨았다.

079 Don't be upset! 화내지마!

미드표현

this is a way of saying "Calm down." The speaker wants to stop someone from being angry

Point Don't get[be] mad (at me) (나한테) 열받지마

A: There was a mistake on my credit card bill.
신용카드 청구서에 잘못된 게 있어요.
B: **Don't be upset.** We'll fix it tomorrow.
화내지 마세요. 내일 고쳐드릴게요.

I'm sorry, please don't be upset, it could happen to anyone.
미안, 화내지마, 그럴 수도 있는 일이야.

Don't get mad. She was just trying to make you feel better.
화내지마. 걔는 너 기분좋게 해줄려는 것이었어.

Don't be mad at him, it's our fault.
걔한테 화내지마, 우리 잘못이야.

080 Don't take it out on me 내게 분풀이 하지마, 왜 나한테 화풀이야

미드표현

When "A takes out something on B," it means that A is blaming or acting angry at B for a problem. The problem may or may not have been caused by B. It is similar to saying "to act like B has caused a problem"

Point take it out on sb …에게 화(분)풀이 하다, 몰아붙이다

A: Why is the electric bill so expensive this month?
이번 달에 왜 그렇게 전기세가 많이 나왔어?
B: **Don't take it out on me.** You use the computer all the time. 내게 그러지마. 늘상 컴퓨터했잖아.

I shouldn't be taking it out on you. I apologize.
네게 화풀이 하면 안 돼지. 사과할게.

Don't take it out on me because you feel guilty. 네가 죄의식을 느낀다고 내게 화풀이 하지마.

I know we're fighting, but there's no reason to take it out on the children.
우리가 싸운다고 얘들한테 화풀이 해선 안돼.

081 Let her blow off some steam 걔가 화를 좀 풀게 놔둬

미드표현

this indicates that someone is very angry, and that people need to leave her alone so that she can have time to calm down and relax a bit. Sometimes angry people do something physical to blow off steam, which helps them become calm. In other words "Don't bother her for a while, and she can have some time to get over her anger"

| Point | blow off (some) steam 화를 (좀) 표출하다, 스트레스를 풀다

A: Katie is really pissed off about the missing money. 케이티는 돈을 잃어버려서 열받았어.

B: **Let her blow off some steam.** We'll talk to her tomorrow. 화를 풀게 가만 놔둬. 낼 걔와 얘기하자.

Oh, no, he just needs to blow off some steam.
아니야, 걘 단지 화를 좀 표출하는게 필요해.

I'm just going to hang back. Let him blow off some steam. 난 좀 남아 기다릴테니 걔 화 좀 풀게 놔둬.

I've been working so hard this semester. I really need to blow off some steam.
이번 학기에 정말 열심히 공부했어. 난 스트레스 좀 풀어야 돼.

082 Why are you still miffed at me? 넌 왜 아직도 나한테 화나있는거야?

미드표현

this is asking why someone is still angry. We can understand the person is angry about something that happened in the past, and maybe they should have calmed down. It is a way of asking "Why are you still acting so upset at me?"

| Point | be miffed at sb[about sth] 화를 내다

A: Why are you frowning? **Are you still miffed at me?** 왜 얼굴을 찌푸리는거야? 아직도 나한테 화나있는거야?

B: I can't forget the time you cheated with another woman. 네가 다른 여자와 바람핀 때를 잊을 수가 없어.

You're miffed enough to ruin my meal.
네가 씩씩거리는 바람에 밥맛이 다 떨어졌어.

Alex was miffed at his classmates.
알렉스는 같은 반 친구들에게 화가 났어.

Why are you so miffed at your brother?
넌 왜 형에게 화가 나 있는거야?

She gets miffed at people very easily.
걘 사람들에게 쉽게 화를 내.

083 Says who? 누가 그래?, 누가 어쨌다구?

this is usually a way of challenging someone. It is said to mean "Who disagrees with me?"

| Point | Says me! 나한테 한 소리야!, 내 얘기다!
(Says who에 대한 답으로 다분히 싸움 날 대꾸)
Says you! 바로 네 얘기라니까!

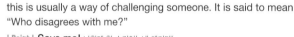

A: You can't live without having a job.
직장을 다니지 않고 살 수는 없어.

B: **Says who?** I can do that if I want to.
누가 그래? 난 원하면 그렇게 할 수 있어.

Says who? I'm allowed to do whatever I want.
누가 어쨌다구? 난 내가 하고 싶은대로 한다고.

A: Of course you're going to wear white. Brides wear white. That's the rule. B: Says who?
A: 물론 너 하얗게 입을거야. 신부는 하얀 옷을 입잖아. 그게 원칙이야. B: 누가 그래?

Says who? This is nuts. 누가 그래? 이건 미친 짓이야.

084 Do you mind? (상대방의 말과 언행에 화나) 그만해줄래?, (상대방의 의사를 물으며) 괜찮겠어?

this is a way of expressing that the speaker would like someone to stop doing something. It is like saying "Please stop that." And this is also used to ask "Is it OK if this is done?" The speaker wants to make certain someone will permit something

A: You've been talking throughout the movie. **Do you mind?** 영화내내 떠드네. 그만 좀 할래?

B: Oh, sorry, I didn't mean to bother you.
어 미안. 방해하려는 건 아니었어.

I need to leave early. Do you mind?
나 일찍 일어나야돼. 괜찮겠지?

Jackie, we're trying to have lunch here do you mind? 잭키, 여기서 점심 먹으려고 하는데, 괜찮겠어?

Can I show you something? Do you mind?
내가 뭐 좀 보여줄까? 괜찮겠어?

085 Bring it on 어디 덤벼봐, 어디 한번 해보자구

this means "I'm strong enough to win a fight or competition with you." It is said when the speaker wants to indicate that he is ready to start the fight or competition

A: Jack says he wants to challenge you to a tennis match. 잭은 네게 테니스 시합 도전하고 싶대.

B: **Bring it on.** You know that I'll beat him easily.
덤비라고 해. 쉽게 이길 수 있는 거 너도 알잖아.

I have God on my side. Bring it on.
하느님이 내 편이셔. 어디 덤벼봐.

A: Well you better be good, because when I'm finished with this, you'll be in trouble. B: Bring it on! A: 이것만 끝나면 넌 끝장이야. B: 어디 덤벼봐!

086 Bite me! 배 째라!, 어쩌라구!, 꺼져!, 그만둬!, 네 맘대로 해!

this is a way of saying that the speaker doesn't respect someone and doesn't care about that person's opinion. This is usually only used by young people, like teenagers. It is similar to saying "It doesn't matter what you think"

| Point | Up yours 그만, 젠장할　　Blow me 제기랄

A: You kids are always causing trouble around here. 너희 놈들은 항상 여기서 사고를 쳐.

B: **Bite me.** I don't cause any problems.
어쩌라고. 난 사고치지 않거든.

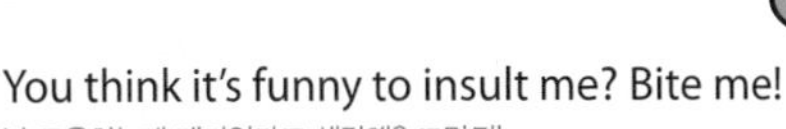

You think it's funny to insult me? Bite me!
날 모욕하는게 재미있다고 생각해? 그만둬!

Bite me! I don't want to see you ever again.
그만둬! 다시는 널 보고 싶지 않아.

If you choose to act like that, you can bite me!
그렇게 행동하기로 했으면 맘대로 해!

087 What about it? 그래서 어쩔건데?, 그게 어때서?

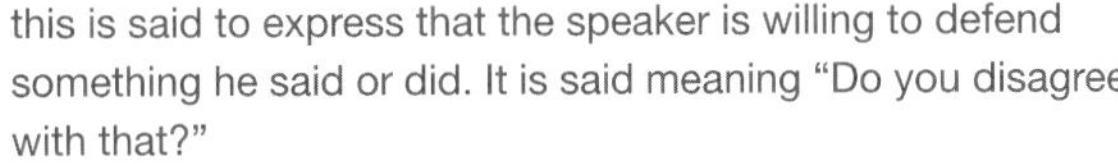

this is said to express that the speaker is willing to defend something he said or did. It is said meaning "Do you disagree with that?"

A: You said you wanted a new manager.
새로운 매니저를 원했다며.

B: **What about it?** Our current manager is terrible.
그게 어때서? 지금 매니저는 으악이야.

I heard of the crime he committed. What about it? 걔가 저지른 범죄에 대해 들었는데 그게 어때서?

What about it? Is there more to the story?
그게 어때서? 얘기 아직 안끝난거야?

Yes, that's my car. What about it?
어, 저 차 내껀데. 그게 어때서?

088 You want a piece of me, boy? 한번 맛 좀 볼래?, 한 판 붙을래?

this phrase is not used, except in video games and movies. It expresses anger and asks "Do you want to fight me?"

| Point | (Do you) Want to make something of it? 나랑 한 판 붙자구?

A: **You want a piece of me,** boy? 한 판 붙어볼래?

B: No, I don't really want to fight you. 아니, 너랑 싸우기 싫어.

You want a piece of me? Is that what you're saying? 나랑 한 판 붙자고? 그 말이 맞아?

Why are you trying to make something of it?!
왜 한판 붙어보려고?!

A: Hey, you are sitting in my seat! B: Want to make something of it? I'll sit here if I want to.
A: 야, 거기 내 자리야! B: 나랑 한 판 붙자구? 내가 원하면 앉는거지.

089 What're you going to do? Shoot me?

어떻게 할 건데? 날 쏘기라도 할거야?

미드표현

this asks how a person will act if the speaker does something. It is like saying "You can't stop me if I do this"

A: You need to stop shouting right now.
지금 당장 소리지르는거 멈춰.

B: **What're you going to do? Shoot me?**
어떻게 할 건데? 날 쏘기라도 할거야?

You're going to shoot me? 날 쏠거야?

Get away from me! Settle down, bitch! You gonna shoot me?
꺼지라고! 진정해, 이 못된년아! 날 쏠거야?

A: You're not gonna shoot me. B: I will if I have to. A: 넌 날 쏘지 못해. B: 그래야 된다면 쏠거야.

090 So, sue me 그럼 고소해 봐, 맘대로 해

미드표현

this expresses "I don't care what you think." It means the speaker is going to do something even if others don't want him to

I Point I sue sb …을 고소하다

A: You always park in my parking space.
넌 항상 내 주차공간에 주차하더라.

B: **So sue me.** You can park somewhere else.
그럼 고소해. 다른 곳에 주차하면 되잖아.

If I don't sign it, you'll sue me? 사인 안 하면 고소할거야?

What are you gonna do? Sue me?
어쩔 건데? 고소할거야?

I wanted something different. So sue me.
난 다른 걸 원했어. 맘대로 해.

I'm loose with the rules. So sue me.
난 규칙에 그렇게 빡빡하지 않아. 그럼 맘대로 해.

091 You wanna play hardball? 세게 나오시겠다?

미드표현

this asks if someone is strong enough to compete with the speaker. It means "Are you strong enough to defeat me?"

I Point I play hardball 원하는 걸 얻기 위해 단호하게 입장을 취하다
He's playing hardball (법적문제 혹은 비즈니스 거래에서)
그 사람은 아주 깐깐하게 나와

A: I think I can defeat you if I try hard.
내가 열심히 하면 널 이길 것 같아.

B: Really? **You want to play hardball?**
정말? 세게 나오겠다 이거야?

A: I'm sure it's what you thought I always I wanted. B: You trying to play hardball with me, Ben?
A: 내가 항상 원했던 거 너도 알잖아. B: 그렇게 나오시겠다, 벤?

Look, I'm not saying another word till I talk to a lawyer. I pay my dues and these guys play hardball.
이봐, 변호사가 올때까지 아무 말도 하지 않을거야. 내 할 도리는 했는데 이 친구들이 세게 나오네.

092 (Do) You want to step outside? 밖으로 나가서 붙어보자고?

미드표현

this is a way of asking "Do you want to go outside and fight?" It is a polite way to start a physical fight with someone

I Point I Step out! 한판붙자, 나와!

A: Your girlfriend is too beautiful for you.
네 여친은 너에겐 너무 예뻐.

B: Oh yeah? **You want to step outside?**
어 그래? 밖에 나가서 한판 하자고?

A: I'm not sacred of you. B: Want to step outside, then?
A: 난 네가 안 무서워. B: 그럼 밖으로 나가서 한번 붙어보자고?

Would you care to step outside for a moment, Luke? 루크야, 잠깐 밖으로 나와볼테야?

Why don't you just step outside here for a second? 잠깐 여기 밖으로 나와 봐.

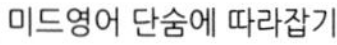

093 You wanna start with me? 너 나하고 한판 붙고 싶어?

this is asking if someone is starting a fight. It is like a warning, meaning "Don't start a fight with me right now"

| Point | Don't start with me 내 성질 돋구지마

A: **You want to start with me?** 나랑 한판 하자고?

B: Calm down. We don't need to argue.
진정해. 다툴 필요 없잖아.

You want to start with me? You want to fight now? 너 나하고 한판 붙고 싶어? 나하고 싸우겠다는거야?

What are you bitching for? You want to start with me? 무슨 불평을 해대는거야? 나하고 한판하자는거야?

You want to start with me? I've had it with you. 나하고 한판하자고? 너 참을만큼 참았어.

094 You're going down 널 때려 눕히고 말겠어, 넌 끝장이야

미드표현

this often indicates "You will be defeated." It is a way to tell someone that he will suffer some problem or defeat

A: I am a much better player of Warcraft than you.
난 너보다 워크래프트 훨씬 잘 해.

B: No you aren't. **You're going down** next time we play. 아니 그렇지 않아. 다음 게임할 땐 널 때려 눕히고 말겠어.

That's it. You're going down!
바로 그거야. 널 때려 눕히겠어!

A: Hey, why don't we arm wrestle. You're going down. B: Oh, yeah? You're going further down! A: 팔씨름 해보자. 넌 끝이야. B: 누가 할 소리!

095 Don't call me names! 험담하지마!, 욕하지마!

미드표현

this means "I don't like the way you talked about me." The person is angry because of something that was said about him

| Point | call sb names …을 험담하다, 욕하다

A: Hey, why do you eat so much food, fatty?
왜 밥많이 먹어? 뚱띵아?

B: **Don't call me names.** I'm not fat.
험담하지마. 난 뚱뚱하지 않다고.

Didn't I warn you about calling me names? 욕하지 말라고 내가 경고하지 않았니?

I know I've given you a lot of grief over the years. Abused you, called you names.
내가 너 험담하면서 스트레스 준거 알아.

A: You're calling him names? B: I didn't call him names.
A: 너 걔 욕을 한거야? B: 난 걔네들에게 욕하지 않았어.

096 Don't cuss at me! 내게 욕 좀 하지마!

미드표현

this expresses that someone is upset because profane or rude language was used to insult him. He does not like this, and is telling the listener not to use the insulting words. It is just like saying "Don't use that rude language around me"

| Point | cuss 욕하다
cuss sb out 호되게 꾸짖다, 욕을 퍼붓다

A: That is the shittiest dress I have ever seen.
이런 엿같은 옷은 처음 보네.

B: There's no need to be rude. **Don't cuss at me!**
무례할 필요는 없잖아. 내게 욕하지 말라고!

You know he's cussing you out in there now.
걔는 지금 너한테 욕을 퍼붓고 있잖아.

Whenever she ran into him upstairs, he'd cuss her out.
걔는 위층에서 그와 부딪칠 때마다 그녀에게 욕을 퍼부어.

You couldn't wait till summer to cuss out the principal?
넌 교장에게 욕을 퍼붓는데 여름까지 기다릴 수가 없었구나.

He got really mad and cussed me out.
걔는 정말 화가 치밀어 올라 내게 욕을 퍼부었어.

097 We'll have it out in a second 우리 빨리 결판을 짓자

this is a way of saying that the speaker is going to argue or fight with someone very soon. It is possible that the speaker is waiting for a person that he is upset with to arrive. We can also say "We are going to go at it soon"

| Point | have it out (with sb) (이견, 불화) 담판을 짓다, 결판짓다, 언쟁하다

A: Aren't you angry about the way Ray treats you?
레이가 널 대하는 태도에 화나지 않아?

B: Yeah, and **we'll have it out in a second.**
그래, 우리는 곧 담판을 지을거야.

I sometimes wish he would just have it out with me. 난 때때로 걔가 나와 터놓고 얘기를 했으면 해.

So we're going to have it out in public?
그럼 사람들 많은데서 담판을 짓자고?

We're not in public, Logan! We're in my house! Yeah, we're going to have it out here!
로건, 우린 공공장소에 있는게 아냐! 우린 내 집에 있는거야! 그래, 우린 여기서 담판을 지을거야!

098 You had a beef with him 넌 걔한테 불만이 있어, 넌 걔랑 다퉜어

this indicates the two people didn't like each other for some reason. It is similar to saying "You were angry at him"

| Point | get into a beef …와 다투게 되다 beef about 매우 불만하다
whine about 징징대다, 푸념하다

A: Remember that guy I was arguing with last week? 지난 주에 내가 다투었던 저 녀석 기억나?

B: Yes I do. **You had a beef with him.**
어 그래, 걔랑 다투었지.

Did you have a beef with the victim?
피해자에게 불만이 있었지?

You have a beef with the rental car company?
렌터카 회사에 불만이 있었지?

He got into a beef with the dealer.
걔는 딜러와 다투었어.

099 I had a run-in with the manager 매니저하고 한바탕했어

this means that two people fought or argued about something. Often it is like saying "I had a disagreement with him"

| Point | have a run-in with sb …와 한바탕하다, 다투다

A: I heard you **had a run-in with** the office manager. 실장하고 다투었다며.

B: That's right. I think he plans to fire me.
맞아, 날 해고할 것 같아.

I heard about your run-in with Paul.
폴과 한바탕 했다며.

How many run-ins have you had with this photographer? 이 사진 작가와 몇 번이나 다툰거야?

I had a little, you know, run-in with a car.
저기 말야, 차사고가 나서 좀 한바탕 했어.

100 Why are you trying to make something of it?
왜 별것도 아닌 것 같고 싸우려하는거야?

this question is usually asked when someone is trying to start an argument or fight over something. The speaker is indicating that he thinks the matter is not very important, and he doesn't understand why it should be argued about.

| Point | make something of it 싸우다

A: I still don't believe she couldn't attend our party.
난 아직도 걔가 우리 파티에 올 수 없었다는 걸 믿을 수가 없어.

B: Why are you trying to **make something of it?** Forget it. 별일도 아닌데 왜 싸우려해? 잊어버려.

Billy got pissed and tried to make something out of it. 빌리는 열받아서 싸우려고 했어.

You want to make something out of it, you jackass? 이 멍청아, 한번 붙어보고 싶어?

Forget it. Don't try to make something out of it. 신경쓰지마, 그 일로 싸우려 하지마.

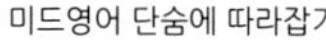

101 You guys have a fight? 너희들 싸웠니?

this is a way to ask if two people have argued or fought each other. Basically, it means "Are you angry at that person?"

| Point | We had a fight 우린 싸웠어
I got slapped 뺨을 맞았어

A: Why didn't you say hello to Tina? **You guys have a fight?** 티나에게 왜 인사 안 해? 둘이 싸웠어?

B: We had a disagreement about something last night. 지난 밤에 의견일치가 안 되는 게 있었어.

미드표현

Did you guys have a fight, or something?
너희들 싸운거야, 뭐야?

What happened to Jill? You guys have a fight?
질한테 무슨 일이야? 너희들 싸웠니?

We had a big fight and then I got slapped.
우린 싸웠고 난 뺨을 맞았어.

102 Break it up! (싸움) 그만둬!, 다투지마!

this is another way to say "Stop fighting." It is said when separating two people who are fighting

A: **Break it up!** I want both of you to leave.
그만둬! 둘 다 가 봐.

B: But he was the one causing problems!
하지만 쟤가 문제를 일으켰어!

미드표현

Hey, come on! Break it up! 야 이봐! 그만해!

Break it up! Bob, stop it! 밥! 그만둬! 그만하라고!

Hey what are you guys doing? Break it up!
너네 뭐하는 거야? 당장 그만둬!

103 I'll get even with you 앙갚음 해줄테다, 되갚아 주겠어

this means "I'm going to get revenge for something." The speaker is angry and plans to do something bad to the person that made him angry

| Point | get even with …에게 보복하다

A: You broke my heart. **I'll get even with you!**
내 맘을 찢어놓았어. 갚아주고 말테다!

B: I'm sorry, but I fell in love with another man.
미안, 하지만 다른 남자를 사랑해.

미드표현

Our goal is to get even. 똑같이 되갚아 주는게 우리 목표야.

Oh, I might have told him to get even with some kids.
난 걔한테 어떤 애들에게는 보복을 하라고 얘기했을지도 몰라.

Tom is going to kill me when he finds out what I did to get even with him.
탐은 내가 걔한테 보복하기 위해 한 짓을 알게 되면 날 죽일거야.

104 He has a score to settle against a guard
걔는 교도관에게 해결해야 될 문제가 있어

this indicates that the person wants revenge against a guard for some reason. We can assume the guard did something in the past to hurt or anger the person, and he now plans to get vengeance. It is like saying "He really wants to get back at that guard"

| Point | settle a score (with~) 앙갚음하다, 보복하다
have a score to settle with[against]~
…에게 갚아야 할 원한이 있다, 해결해야 될 문제가 있다

A: What the hell is Steve hanging around the jail for? 스티브는 도대체 뭣 때문에 감옥주변을 어슬렁거리는거야?

B: **He has a score to settle against** a guard.
교도관에게 앙갚음해야 할게 있대.

I have a score to settle with the guy who hit me.
날 때린 놈에게 갚아야 될게 있어.

Penny must settle a score with her old roommate. 페니는 예전 룸메이트와 해결해야 될 문제가 있어.

This is a prisoner who has a score to settle against a guard.
이 사람은 교도관에게 갚아야 할 원한이 있는 죄수야.

105 I'll blow your head off 네 머리를 날려보내겠어

this is a threat to someone. The speaker is holding a gun and telling the listener that he will shoot him in the head. We can understand this threat is to control the listener's actions. It's like saying "I'll shoot you (if you...)"

| Point | blow one's head off 총으로 머리를 날려버리다, 죽이다, 혼내다
chop my head off 목을 자르다, 목을 베다
take one's head off 목을 자르다, 해고하다

A: Don't move or **I'll blow your head off!**
꼼짝마 그렇지 않으면 머리를 날려버릴테야!

B: Put that gun down. I'm not a criminal.
총 내려놔. 난 범죄자가 아냐.

I'm going to go down there and blow the cunt's head off.
내 그리로 가서 그년의 머리를 날려버릴거야.

Try and make a sound, I'll blow your head off.
소리내려고 해봐, 네 머리를 날려버릴테니.

I'll blow both your heads straight off. You understand me?
너희 둘 다 머리를 바로 날려버리겠어. 알아들었어?

106 I don't want you to take sides 너는 편들지마

this expresses that the speaker wants someone to remain neutral and not support one person over another person in a disagreement. Another way to say this is "You have to remain fair and unbiased toward anyone"

| Point | take one's side 어느 한 쪽 편을 들다
pick sides 편을 들다
be on sb's side …의 편이다

A: Betty and Frank have been having a serious argument. 베티와 프랭크는 아주 심하게 다투었어.

B: I know, but **I don't want you to take sides.**
알아, 하지만 넌 어느 편도 들지마.

A: Don't take sides, Mom. B: I'm not taking sides. A: 엄마, 편들지 마요. B: 난 편드는게 아냐.

I'm not asking you to take sides against your mother. 네 엄마 반대편에 서라고 하는게 아냐.

And you're supposed to be on my side.
그리고 넌 내 편이 되어야 하잖아.

I will never again pick sides against the family.
난 절대로 가족과 반대되는 쪽을 편들지 않을거야.

MEMO

Ways of saying people are making mistakes and deceiving or being deceived

잘못하고 실수하고 그리고 속이고 배신하고

It doesn't feel right

001 It doesn't feel right 뭔가 이상해

this is a way for a speaker to indicate that he thinks something strange is going on. Most often it means a person feels very uneasy about a situation and could be expecting something bad or strange to happen. A similar way to say this would be "I have a very strange feeling about this"

| Point | It doesn't feel right 뭔가 이상해, 허전해
I don't feel right (~ing) 썩 내키지 않아, 뭔가 잘못됐어

A: Why won't you come inside the apartment?
아파트 안으로 들어오지 않을래?

B: **It doesn't feel right.** Something weird is going on. 뭔가 이상해. 뭔가 이상한 일이 벌어지고 있어.

I just don't know! It just doesn't feel right.
모르겠어! 뭔가 이상해.

I'm thinking something doesn't feel right here. 여기 뭔가 이상하다는 생각이 들어.

I don't know. I mean, I don't really feel right.
잘 모르겠어. 내 말은, 썩 내키지 않아.

I just didn't feel right telling you this over there. 거기서 이 얘기를 네게 한게 잘못한 것 같아.

002 It is my fault 내 잘못이야

this is a way to admit the person caused a problem. It is like saying "I am responsible for the problem"

| Point | It's (not) my fault that S+V …한 건 내 잘못이야(잘못이 아니야)
It's not your fault 네 탓이 아냐
Not my fault either 내 잘못도 아냐

A: Why didn't anyone make coffee?
왜 아무도 커피를 안 만들었어?

B: **It's my fault.** I forgot to do it. 내 잘못야. 내가 잊었어.

Are you implying that it's my fault that he left? 걔가 떠난 게 내 잘못이라는 말야?

She thinks it's my fault that you haven't called her. 네가 걔한테 전화한 게 내 잘못이라고 걔는 생각해.

I'll call her and tell her it was totally my fault.
걔한테 전화해서 그건 모두 내 잘못이라고 말할거야.

003 It was my mistake 내 잘못이야, 나의 실수였어

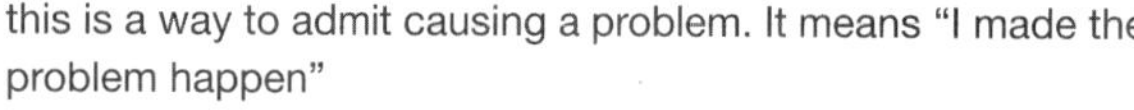

this is a way to admit causing a problem. It means "I made the problem happen"

| Point | I made a mistake 내가 실수했어
My mistake 내 잘못이야
It was a simple mistake 단순한 실수였어

A: Who caused the computer to crash?
누가 컴퓨터 망가트렸어?

B: **It was my mistake.** I'm sorry. 내 잘못이야. 미안해.

This is my mistake, not yours.
이건 내 잘못이야, 네 잘못이 아냐.

Oops sorry, my mistake. 아이고 미안, 내 잘못이야.

Honey don't worry, it was my mistake.
자기야 걱정마, 내 실수였어.

004 (That's) My bad 내가 잘못했어

this means "I am at fault." It is a way to admit that the person caused the problem

A: You caused the machine to break. 네가 기계 망가트렸구나.

B: **My bad.** I'll see if I can fix it. 내가 잘못했어. 고칠 수 있나 볼게.

I'm so sorry. That's my bad. My bad.
미안. 내가 잘못했어. 내 잘못야.

Did I leave my underwear lying around again? I'm so sorry Angie. It's my bad.
내가 내 속옷을 아무데나 놔두었어? 미안해 앤지. 내 잘못이야.

005 I did it wrong 내가 잘못했어, 내가 실수했어

this is a way of admitting the person did something incorrectly. It indicates "I made a mistake"

I Point I I was wrong (about+N) 내가 (…에 관해) 틀렸어
I was wrong to do~ …한 것은 내가 틀렸어
You're dead wrong 넌 완전히 틀렸어
I guessed wrong 짐작이 빗나갔어

A: How can I change this report? **I did it wrong.**
어떻게 이 보고서를 수정하지? 내가 실수했어.

B: You need to use a different format. 다른 포맷을 이용해봐.

I was being selfish and I was wrong.
내가 이기적이었고 내가 잘못했어.

I guess I was wrong. 내가 틀린 것 같아.

I was wrong to assume that she's lonely.
걔가 외롭다고 생각한 건 틀렸어.

I don't know what I'm doing wrong.
내가 무얼 잘못하고 있는지 모르겠어.

006 You (have) got the wrong idea 잘못 짚었네

this usually means "You don't understand correctly." It is said when a person is thinking of something in a way that is not right

I Point I You got the wrong idea about~ …에 대해 잘못 생각하고 있는거야

A: I want to ask Wanda out on a date.
완다에게 데이트 신청하고 싶어.

B: **You got the wrong idea.** She already has a boyfriend. 잘못 짚었어. 걘 이미 남친이 있어.

I think you got the wrong idea. 잘못 짚은 것 같아.

I think you've got the wrong idea about me.
나에 대해 잘못 생각하고 있는 것 같아.

You got the wrong place. 잘못 찾아오신 것 같은데요.

007 You were mistaken 네가 틀렸어

this is a very basic way to tell someone that he was wrong about something. Generally, it is considered polite, and not rude, to point out an error this way. It is very similar to saying "Sorry to say it, but I think you were incorrect"

I Point I You were mistaken 네가 틀렸어, 네가 잘못한거야
You're mistaken 네가 잘못 생각하고 있어, 네가 틀린거야
You're forgiven 내가 용서할게

A: Didn't I meet your sister a few years ago?
내가 몇 년전에 네 누이를 만나지 않았었나?

B: No, **you are mistaken.** She's never met you.
어, 네가 틀렸어. 누이는 널 만난 적이 없어.

I guess you were mistaken. 난 네가 잘못이었던 같은데.

Is it possible that you were mistaken?
네가 틀렸을 수도 있는거야?

If you think you can trick him into giving you some DNA, you're mistaken.
걔를 속여서 DNA를 채취할 수 있다고 생각하다면 그건 네 오산이야.

008 You wouldn't know it to look at her
개 겉모습만 봐서는 알 수가 없을거야

this is something that is said when a person appears to be okay, but they are really experiencing something different, possibly something that is bad or unhealthy. Sometimes it is the same as saying "She looks okay, but really she has been having a lot of trouble"

I Point I You wouldn't know it to look at~ …의 겉모습만 봐서는 모를거야

A: Margie has been addicted to drugs for a decade. 마지는 십 년동안 마약에 중독됐었어.

B: **You wouldn't know it to look at her.** She seems healthy. 겉모습만 봐서는 알 수가 없네. 건강해 보이는데.

You wouldn't know it to look at him but Sam's got very nimble fingers.
걔 겉만 봐서는 모르겠지만 샘의 손은 무척 빨라.

Alice is very rich. You wouldn't know it to look at her. 앨리스는 매우 부자야. 겉모습만 봐서는 알 수 없을거야.

She's only fifteen. You wouldn't know it to look at her.
걔는 겨우 열다섯 살이야. 겉모습만 봐서는 알 수 없을거야.

009 That's not (quite) right 그렇지 않아, 그게 아니야 , 그건 옳지 않아

미드표현

this is a way for a speaker to talk about a mistake. It is the same as saying "It's wrong"

A: This is a picture of a painting done by Monet.
이건 모네가 그린 그림이야.

B: **That's not right.** That painting was done by Manet. 그렇지 않아. 이 그림은 마네가 그린 거야.

You can't leave a mess here. That's not right.
넌 여기를 어지럽혀놓으면 안되지. 그건 옳지 않아.

She treated you very badly. That's not right.
걔는 너한테 매우 못되게 굴었어. 그건 옳지 않아.

That's not right. We'll have to fix it.
그건 옳지 않아. 우리는 그걸 고쳐야 돼.

010 I was way off (base) 완전히 잘못 짚었네, 내 생각[행동]이 틀렸네

this is a way of saying "My idea about that was wrong." People say this when they admit they misunderstood something

| Point | I'm off base 내가 잘못 알았네
You're way off base 넌 완전히 틀렸어
You're a bit off base 네 얘기는 사실과 거리가 있어

A: I think Sam graduated from Harvard.
샘이 하바드를 졸업한 것 같아.

B: Really? **I was way off base.** I thought he was dumb. 정말? 잘못 생각했네. 난 걔가 바본줄 알았는데.

Your calculations are way off. 네 계산은 많이 틀렸어.

You two are both way off base.
너희 둘 다 완전히 잘못 짚었어.

Leslie, you are way off base here.
레슬리, 넌 이거 완전히 틀렸어.

We are a long way off from that.
그러기까지는 아직 시간이 많이 걸릴거야.

011 I guess I dropped the ball 내가 큰 실수를 한 거 같아

미드표현

this phrase indicates the speaker made an important mistake, and maybe other people are angry at him. It is like saying "The big mistake was my fault"

| Point | drop the ball 큰 실수하다

A: This mistake cost us a lot of money.
이번 실수로 비용이 많이 들어.

B: Sorry. **I guess I dropped the ball.**
미안. 내가 큰 실수를 한 것 같아.

The boss has a strong suspicion that you dropped the ball on that project.
사장은 네가 그 프로젝트에서 큰 실수를 했다고 의심하고 있어.

I guess I dropped the ball there.
내가 거기서 큰 실수를 한 것 같아.

012 I just made a complete fool of myself
내가 아주 멍청한 짓을 했어

this means "I made a mistake that everyone saw. We can understand the person did something to embarrass himself.

| Point | make a fool of sb …을 기만하다, 바보취급하다
make a fool of oneself 웃음거리가 되다, 멍청한 짓을 하다

A: **I just made a complete fool of myself.**
내가 아주 멍청한 짓을 했어.

B: Yeah, everyone saw you fall down.
그래, 다들 네가 넘어지는 걸 봤어.

He made a fool of me. 걔가 날 바보취급했어.

You're making a fool of yourself.
멍청한 짓을 하는 거야.

She made a fool of herself by marrying someone she doesn't really love.
걔는 진정으로 사랑하지 않는 사람과 결혼하는 멍청한 짓을 했어.

013 She had the goods on me 내가 나쁜 짓한 걸 걔가 잘 알고 있어

this might be said when a woman has evidence that will get the speaker in trouble. The speaker is fearful of the woman and may have to bribe her or do things that will make her happy. It is similar to saying "She could cause problems for me if she wanted to"

| Point | have[get] the goods on sb 나쁜 짓 한 증거를 갖고 있다.

A: You shouldn't have done what she told you to do. 넌 걔가 하라는 것을 하지 말았어야 했는데.

B: Yeah, but **she had the goods on me** and could have gotten me in trouble.
알아, 하지만 내 약점을 알고 있어서 내가 곤경에 처할 수도 있었을거야.

미드표현

Boy, and she had the goods on me, too. 아이구, 걔도 내 약점을 잘 알고 있었어.

I had to pay him because he had the goods on me. 걘 내 약점을 쥐고 있어서 돈을 줘야 했어.

Have you got the goods on the guy you're blackmailing? 네가 협박하고 있는 사람의 약점은 갖고 있는거야?

014 I stand corrected 내가 잘못했다는 거 인정해, 틀렸다는 거 인정해

this indicates "You are right and I was wrong." It is a way to admit the other person was correct

A: This CD was made in 2014, not 2010.
이 CD는 2010년이 아니라 2014년에 만들어졌어.

B: **I stand corrected.** 내가 틀렸다는 거 인정해.

미드표현

I stand corrected. I always get that wrong.
내가 틀렸다는 거 인정해. 항상 그걸 오해해.

A: I stand corrected. DNA is what we are, not who we are. B: What we are never changes. Who we are never stops changing.
A: 내가 틀렸어. DNA는 사람의 구성요소일뿐 인성은 아니지. B: 구성요소는 바뀌지 않지만 인성은 끊임없이 바뀌지.

015 That's where you're wrong 그 점이 틀린 거야, 넌 거기서 잘못 생각하는거야

this phrase is used to point out the mistake of someone else. It is similar to saying "This part is not right"

| Point | Where did we go wrong? 우린 어디서 잘못된 거지?

A: I think that all Africans are poor.
모든 아프리카 사람들은 가난한 것 같아.

B: **That's where you're wrong.** There are some very rich Africans. 그 점이 네가 틀렸어. 부유한 아프리카 사람들도 있어.

미드표현

That's where you're wrong. I am going.
그 점이 네가 틀린거야. 나 간다.

See, that is where you're wrong! She's better off with you.
거봐, 그 점이 네가 틀린거야! 갠 너와 있을 때 더 잘 지내.

I can't believe she fired me! Where did I go wrong? 걔가 날 해고하다니! 내가 뭘 잘못한거지?

016 Don't go behind my back 뒤통수치지마

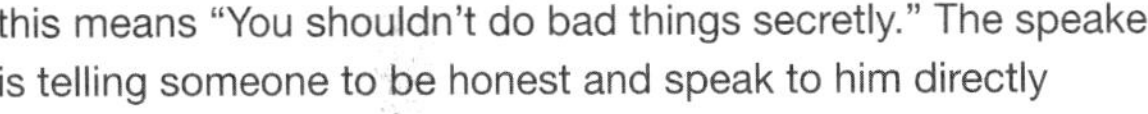

this means "You shouldn't do bad things secretly." The speaker is telling someone to be honest and speak to him directly

| Point | behind one's back …몰래
go behind one's back …의 뒤통수를 치다
talk about[say stuff]~ behind one's back 뒤에서 딴소리하다
Don't act innocent! 시침떼지마!

A: I heard you were spreading gossip about me. **Don't go behind my back** and do that.
내 소문을 퍼뜨리고 다녔다며. 뒤통수치면서 그러지마.

B: But I was only repeating the things everyone else is saying. 하지만 다들 말하는 걸 말했을 뿐야.

미드표현

You went behind my back. 네가 뒤통수쳤잖아.

You went behind my back! I would never do that to you!
넌 내 뒤통수를 쳤어! 난 결코 네게 그렇지 않을건데!

She likes to say stuff behind my back.
걔는 내 뒤에서 딴소리하는 걸 좋아해.

017 How dare you throw it back in my face?

어떻게 그렇게 뒤통수를 치고 있어?

this is something that might be said in an argument. We can understand that during an argument, the listener has said something that is personally hurtful to the speaker, and it has upset him. It is like asking "Why are you saying personal things that insult me?"

I Point I throw sth back in sb's face 과거에 잘해준 사람에게 도리어 비난을 하다, 배은망덕하다, 도리어 욕을 먹이다

A: I can't trust you. You told me sometimes you lie.
널 믿을 수가 없어. 때때로 거짓말한다고 내게 말했잖아.

B: **How dare you throw that back in my face?** I said that because I trusted you.
어떻게 나한테 그렇게 뒤통수를 치고 있어? 난 널 믿었기 때문에 한 말이었는데.

It gets thrown back in my face.
그게 도리어 내게 화가 되었어.

He's the one who insisted I move in with him, and now he throws it back in my face, like I'm some kind of leech.
걔는 나랑 동거하자고 주장해놓고 이제와서는 내가 뭐 거머리라도 되는 양 내 뒤통수를 치고 있어.

018 She lied to cover her ass

걘 다치지 않기 위해 거짓말을 했어

미드표현

this indicates that a woman told a lie so that she could escape from some type of trouble. We can understand that the speaker thinks the woman can't be trusted since she is not honest. Another way to say this is "She avoided punishment by being dishonest"

I Point I cover one's (own) ass[butt] (위험, 비난, 손해) 대비하다, 뒤를 봐주다, 치부를 가려주다, 변명으로 발뺌하다 = cover one's back

A: Why do you think Isabelle is a bad person?
왜 이자벨이 나쁜 사람이라고 생각하는거야?

B: **I know she lied to cover her ass.**
걘 거짓말을 해서 어려움을 피했거든.

I was facing criminal charges. And lied to cover my ass.
난 형사고발을 당할 상황였어. 난 벗어나기 위해 거짓말을 했어.

Put a gun in my hand, I'll cover your ass too.
총을 내게 넘겨, 내가 엄호해줄게.

Do you have any idea how many mistakes doctors make, how many times I've covered their asses?
의사들이 얼마나 많이 실수를 하는지 그리고 내가 얼마나 많이 걔네들 뒤를 봐줬는지 알기나 해?

019 I screwed up!

완전히 망쳤어!, 내가 망쳤어!

미드표현

this is said to indicate "I made a mistake." People say this when they regret the mistake they made

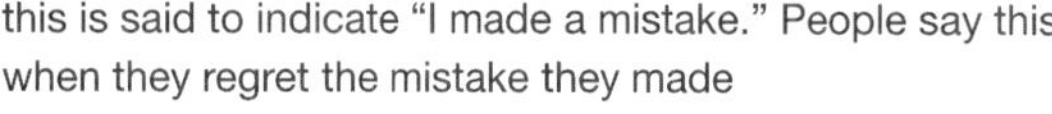

I Point I screw up (sth) 일을 망치다(*screw up은 명사로 실수)
screw sb up …을 망치게 하다 You screwed up 네가 일을 망쳤어

A: **I screwed up!** I forgot about our exam.
망했네! 시험있는 걸 잊어버렸어.

B: Oh no. You're going to have a bad grade.
맙소사. 성적이 나쁘게 나오겠네.

I'm not the only guy in the world that's ever screwed up. 세상에서 나만 실수하는 건 아니잖아.

This thing is really screwed up! 이건 완전히 망쳤잖아!

I screwed up. I broke into the building and almost got caught.
망쳤어. 건물에 침입했다가 거의 잡힐 뻔했어.

I'm screwed up so bad, but it isn't your fault.
정말 완전히 망쳤지만 네 잘못은 아니야.

020 I got screwed

완전히 속았어, 완전히 망했어

미드표현

this is indicating that the speaker was treated unfairly. He is saying "I was tricked or cheated out of something"

I Point I screw sb (over) …을 속여넘기다 You screwed me 날 속였군
I'm totally screwed! 난 이제 죽었다!

A: How did your investment turn out? 투자결과 어땠어?

B: **I got screwed.** They stole all of my money!
속았어. 내 돈을 다 날렸어!

We're screwed. Ok, this will not work.
우린 망했다. 그래 이건 되지 않을 거야.

You've lost all your clients, we're screwed.
고객도 다 잃었으니 우린 망했네.

We're screwed, either way, aren't we?
어느 식으로든 우린 망했어, 그렇지 않아?

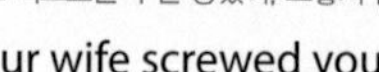

Your wife screwed your best friend.
네 부인이 너의 가장 절친한 친구를 속여먹었어.

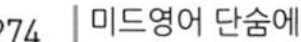

021 I got wise to their game 난 걔네들 속셈을 알아차렸어

this is a way to say that the speaker was being tricked, and he was able to figure that out. We can also understand that he did something to make sure he would not get tricked in the same way again.

| Point | get wise to …을 알아내다, 탐지해내다
get wise to what you are doing 네가 하는 일을 알게 되다

A: Why did you break up with Gina?
너 왜 지나하고 헤어진거야?

B: She was cheating on me, but **I got wise to her game.** 날 속이고 바람폈는데 내가 알아차렸지.

미드표현

It took a while, but I got wise to their game.
시간이 좀 걸렸지만 난 걔들의 속셈을 알아차렸어.

The cops got wise to the planned bank robbery. 경찰은 계획된 은행강도건을 알아냈어.

That's too bad. You should get wiser about dating. 안됐네. 넌 데이트에 대해서 좀 더 잘 알아야겠네.

022 He set me up 걔가 날 속였어, 함정에 빠졌어

this is a way of saying "He made me seem bad or guilty." When a person is set up, it means that person was made to seem guilty when he was not guilty

| Point | set sb up …을 속이다 *set sb up with …을 …에게 소개시키다

A: I heard you got in trouble for giving Jerry alcohol. 제리에게 술을 준 일로 곤경에 처했다며.

B: **He set me up!** He told his parents it was my idea to drink! 걔가 날 속였어! 부모한테 내가 술마시자고 했대!

미드표현

You set me up. This whole thing was a setup.
네가 날 속였어. 이 모든 게 다 함정야.

Why would somebody set you up?
왜 누가 너를 함정에 빠트릴까?

Are you trying to tell me that your own father set you up? 네 친아버지가 널 함정에 빠트렸다는 말야?

023 You should set a trap 넌 함정을 놓아야 돼

this is a way of advising someone to find a way to trick someone so they make a mistake, and they can't escape from their mistake. Sometimes this means that a person who is lying can be tricked into revealing the truth about something. This can be expressed as "You should find a way to catch (him/her)"

| Point | set a trap 함정을 놓다 fall into the trap of~ …의 함정에 빠지다

A: How are we going to catch the burglar?
그 절도범을 어떻게 잡지?

B: **You should set a trap** in the areas he's robbed.
걔가 절도하는 지역에 함정을 파놓아 봐.

미드표현

It was horrible. I couldn't do anything. But then I set a trap.
끔찍했어. 난 아무 일도 할 수 없었지만 난 함정을 팠어.

The police set a trap for the car thieves.
경찰은 차량도둑을 잡기 위해 함정을 놓았어.

Don't fall into the trap of complaining all the time. 늘상 불평만 하는 함정에 빠지지마.

024 He felt trapped 걘 함정에 걸려든 느낌였어

this expresses that a man felt that he was not free to act as he wanted to. It has a negative meaning, since no one wants to be trapped somewhere. Sometimes people feel trapped by a relationship or a job. It is very much like saying "He felt like there was no way to escape"

| Point | feel[be] trapped 갇히다, (함정에) 걸리다, 빠지다

A: Why did Jim decide to quit his job?
짐은 왜 직장을 그만두기로 한거야?

B: It paid well, but **he felt trapped** doing the same thing every day. 급여는 좋은데 맬 같은 일을 반복하는 것 같은 느낌였대.

미드표현

There was a man trapped on the 27th floor. 27층에 갇힌 남자가 한 명 있었어.

Jane is trapped in an ambulance in the middle of the highway.
제인은 고속도로 한 가운데 앰뷸런스에 갇혀 있어.

When you're gone, it's like I'm this prisoner trapped in a cell of loneliness.
네가 가버리면 난 고독한 감방에 갇힌 죄수같아.

025 She framed me 걘 나에게 누명을 씌웠어

this means that a woman did something to make the speaker seem guilty, even though the speaker was really innocent. When someone is framed, they may be sent to jail for a crime they did not commit. Another way to say this is "She falsely made me look guilty"

Point be framed 함정에 빠지다, 누명쓰다

A: Are you saying your wife poisoned the old man?
네 아내가 네 아빠를 독살했다는거야?

B: Yes, and then **she framed me** for the crime.
어, 그리고는 나한테 그 죄를 뒤집어 씌웠어.

My mother was framed for a crime she didn't commit. 어머니는 자신이 저지르지 않은 죄를 뒤집어 쓰셨어.

Why didn't you tell us her father framed you for her murder?
그녀의 아버지가 그녀를 살인했다고 너한테 누명씌웠다는 것을 우리에게 왜 말하지 않은거야?

You've been framed just like Jack.
넌 잭처럼 누명을 쓰게 된거야.

He framed me with a drug charge.
걔는 내가 마약을 했다고 누명을 씌웠어.

026 Don't mess with me 나 건드리지마

this is a warning. It means "Don't make me angry or you will regret it"

Point mess with 쓸데없이 간섭하다, 속이거나 말썽을 일으키다

A: **Don't mess with me.** I get angry easily.
나 건드리지마. 나 화 잘 내.

B: OK, OK, just stay calm. 알았어, 알았어, 그냥 진정하라고.

They're trying to mess with us. 우릴 엿먹일려고해.

I know he's a bad guy. So, please, don't mess with him. 걔는 나쁜 자식이야 그러니 제발 걔 건드리지마.

I'm a dangerous woman. You don't wanna mess with me. 나 위험한 여자야. 건드리지 말라고.

027 You messed up 네가 망쳐놓았어

this usually indicates "You made a mistake." It is a way of saying that someone possibly caused a problem

Point mess up (계획) 망치다, 더럽히다, 실수하다(잘못하다)
make a mess of+N/~ing …을 망쳐놓다, 제대로 못하다

A: Isn't the big party supposed to happen tonight?
오늘 밤에 성대한 파티가 열리는 거 아니었어?

B: **You messed up.** The party happened last night.
네가 실수했어. 파티는 어제 밤에 열렸어.

You completely messed up! 너 완전히 일을 망쳤구나!

If you mess up once, then you'll get nervous because you know you'll probably mess up again.
한 번 망치면 다시 망칠 수도 있다는 걸 알기 때문에 긴장하게 돼.

You made a mess of things. I think we'll have to fire you. 네가 이 일을 망쳐놓았어. 널 해고해야 될 것 같아.

028 I blew it 망쳤어, 기회를 날려버렸어

this means "I failed." When a person blows something, it means they didn't succeed

Point blow it 부주의나 실수로 기회를 놓치다

A: How was your interview today? 오늘 인터뷰어땠어?

B: **I blew it.** They really didn't like me.
망쳤어. 정말 날 싫어하더라.

How'd it go? Thanks to you, I blew it!
어땠냐고? 네 덕에 망쳤다!

Don't ask me, I had it and I blew it!
말도 마. 기회를 잡았는데 망쳤어!

029 I had to go over her head 난 걔를 제끼고 윗사람과 얘기해야만 했어

this is a way for the speaker to say that he had to go to someone who had more authority than a particular woman. When people don't resolve something with one authority, sometimes they go over that person's head to speak to someone more powerful. What the speaker wants to say is "I had to talk to someone that was more powerful than she was"

| Point | go over sb's head …을 거치지 않고 위사람과 얘기하다
sth go over sb's head …의 능력 밖이다, 이해가 안되다

A: How did you get your boss to change the schedule? 어떻게 네 상사가 일정을 변경하도록 했어?

B: **I had to go over her head** to make it happen.
상사 윗사람과 얘기해서 그렇게 했어.

미드표현

I'm sorry for going over your head and putting you in a difficult position during the surgery.
너를 거치지 않고 네가 수술하는 동안 곤란한 상황에 빠트려 미안해.

We want you to go over Burke's head to the chief. 우린 네가 버크를 제끼고 과장에게 바로 가서 얘기해봐.

He just went over my head to you.
갠 나를 거치지 않고 바로 너에게로 갔어.

030 Don't blow me off 나 무시하지마

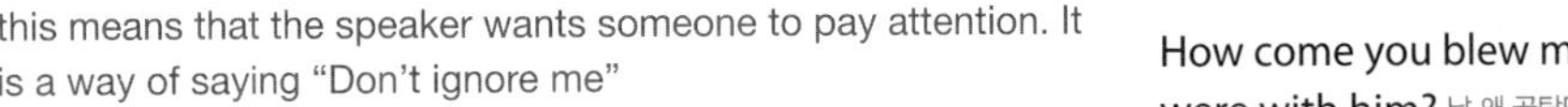

this means that the speaker wants someone to pay attention. It is a way of saying "Don't ignore me"

| Point | blow sb off …을 무시하다, 골탕먹이다

A: There isn't time on my schedule to meet with you. 일정에 널 만날 시간이 없는데.

B: **Don't blow me off.** I want to talk with you personally. 날 무시하지마. 개인적으로 얘기하고 싶어.

미드표현

How come you blew me off? How come you were with him? 날 왜 골탕먹인거야? 왜 걔랑 있었던거야?

I'm mad that you blew me off. 날 골탕먹여서 화가 나.

I can't believe you blew me off! Where the hell were you? 날 골탕먹이다니! 지금 어디냐?

031 She's trying to get into your head 걔는 너를 통제하려는거야

this means that a woman is doing things that will help her influence someone's behavior. We can usually understand that getting into someone's head is using psychology to control another person, and it is considered a negative thing. A similar way to express this is "She is trying to influence your actions"

| Point | get into sb's head …의 행동[사고] 통제하거나 영향을 주다

A: Why has she been reading my e-mails?
왜 걔는 내 이멜을 읽는거야?

B: **She's trying to get into your head.**
걔는 너를 통제하려고 해.

미드표현

He's just trying to get into your head.
걔는 너를 통제하려고 하고 있어.

I want to get into your head 'cause you're the one I love.
넌 내가 사랑하는 사람이니까 너의 행동에 영향을 주고 싶어.

She just overreached. She got into your head.
갠 도가 지나쳤어. 너를 통제했어.

032 You can't let her get into your head 넌 걔한테 당하지 않도록 해

this is a warning to the listener. He is being told that he needs to be careful not to let a woman influence the things he is doing. The speaker probably thinks the woman is a bad person and may use her influence to damage or abuse the listener in some way.

| Point | let ~ get in sb's head …에게 당하다, 영향을 받다

A: Every time I look up, Nancy is glaring at me.
내가 볼 때마다 낸시는 날 응시하고 있어.

B: **You can't let her get into your head.** 걔한테 영향을 받지 않도록 해.

미드표현

You can't let 'em get into your head.
걔네들에게 당하지 않도록 해.

Don't let her get into your head.
걔가 너를 통제하지 못하도록 해.

You cannot allow those images to get into your head. 그런 이미지들에 영향을 받지 않도록 해.

033 She played right into their hands 걔는 그들의 손에 놀아났어

this indicates that the woman did something that gave an advantage to her opponents or enemies. If a person plays into someone's hands, it weakens him and puts him in a bad position. In other words, "She did something that strengthened her enemies"

| Point | play into sb's hands (주어가 …의 손에) 놀아나다
play sb …를 갖고 놀다

A: Tammy gave them all of her money.
태미는 걔들에게 자기 돈을 다 줬어.

B: **She played right into their hands.**
걘 그들의 손아귀에 놀아났구만.

미드표현

Karen could play right into Carl's hands.
카렌은 칼의 손아귀에 놀아날 수도 있을거야.

You're playing right into their hands.
넌 걔네들 손아귀에 놀아나고 있어.

She played us, Liz. 리즈야, 걘 우리를 갖고 놀았어.

You played me from the beginning.
넌 처음부터 나를 갖고 놀았어.

034 You fucked up my life 너 때문에 내 인생이 망쳤어, 네가 내 인생 망쳐놨어

this is a very rude way to criticize someone. It means "You made many problems for me"

| Point | fuck up 망쳐놓다, 실수하다

A: **You fucked up my life.** I hate you!
너 때문에 내 인생이 망쳤어. 정말 네가 싫어!

B: Well, I guess that is why we're getting a divorce.
음, 그래서 우리가 이혼하는 거잖아.

미드표현

We're fucked. 망했다.

My life is so fucked up. 내 인생은 아주 망쳤어.

All I managed to do was fuck up our friendship.
내가 겨우 한 짓은 우리 우정을 엉망진창으로 만들어 놓은 것 밖에 없어.

035 I pulled a fast one on her 내가 걔한테 사기쳤어

this means that the speaker is saying he deceived someone. Often we can understand this phrase indicates that the person was tricked out of money or material goods. It is like saying "I got one over on her"

| Point | pull a fast one on sb …을 속이다, 사기치다, 등치다

A: How did you get Sue to give you $500?
어떻게 수한테서 500 달러를 받아낸거야?

B: **I pulled a fast one on her.** I told her it was for charity. 내가 돌려먹었지. 자선단체에 낼거라고 했어.

미드표현

Jessica would never forgive me if I pulled a fast one on her.
내가 제시카를 속이면 날 절대로 용서하지 않을거야.

Careful, or she'll pull a fast one on you.
조심해, 그렇지 않으면 걔가 너 등쳐먹을거야.

He pulled a fast one on the old lady and stole her money. 걔는 노부인한테 사기쳐서 돈을 훔쳐갔어.

The con men pulled a fast one on the business owner. 사기꾼들이 그 사업주를 속여먹었어.

미드에선 이렇게 쓰인다!

I pulled a fast one on her

Modern Family
SEASON#1-4

아버지 재혼식을 망친 Mitchell의 엄마가 캐나다로 이주하기 전에 저녁식사에 와서 전남편 Jay와 Gloria에게 사과하겠다고 할 때 아들 Mitchell과 아버지의 대화.

Jay: I would love to get this things behind us. Gloria would never forgive me if I pulled a fast one on her. That's why you're going to pull a fast one on her, and I'm not going to like it one bit.

Mitchell: Okay, that's just great. So it's all up to me.

Jay: I can't hear you because you're back home and I'm taking a nap.

제이: 나도 이 일들을 다 잊고 싶어. 내가 글로리아를 속여 넘기면 날 절대로 용서하지 않을거야. 그러니 그런 말은 네가 글로리아에게 직접하고 난 아주 맘에 들어하지 않을거야.

미첼: 좋아요, 아주 좋아요. 그럼 모두 다 내가 알아서 해야 되네요.

제이: 넌 집에 갔고 난 낮잠을 자고 있으니 네 말이 들리지 않는다.

036 You did a number on me 내가 당했어

this indicates that someone was hurt or upset by the way another person treated him. It is a way of saying "You acted badly towards me"

| Point | do a number on sb …속이다, 이용하다, 다치게 하다

A: **You did a number on me.** I can't believe how badly I was treated. 당했어. 내가 그렇게 당하다니 믿기지 않아.

B: I really didn't mean to make you miserable.
널 비참하게 할려고 한 건 아냐.

Your sister's done a number on you.
네 누이가 널 속인거구만.

She did a number on me. She made me buy this house. 걔한테 속았어. 걔 땜에 이 집을 산거라고.

037 You're tricking me 넌 날 속이고 있어

this is indicating that the speaker thinks he is being fooled by someone, and he no longer trusts them. It can be said in an angry way, and it may also be said in a joking way. A similar way to say this is "You have been trying to fool me"

| Point | You're tricking me 너 날 속이고 있지
I'm not tricking you 널 속이는거 아냐

A: I forgot to bring the money to pay you.
너 줄 돈 깜박 잊고 안가져왔어.

B: **You're tricking me.** I see some money in your pocket. 놀리고 있네. 네 지갑에 돈이 보이던데.

A: You're tricking me. B: You're too smart for that. A: 넌 날 속이고 있어. B: 그러기에 넌 너무 똑똑해.

You're tricking me. You tell me the truth, what do we get? 사기치지말고, 사실대로 말해봐, 우리 상황이 어때?

A: Don't you try to trick me! B: No one's tricking you.
A: 날 속일 생각하덜 말아! B: 아무도 너를 속이지 않아.

038 I suckered her into taking the kids for a while
걔한테 사기쳐서 잠시 애들을 돌보게 했어

this most likely was said by a man who has children, and he has gotten his wife to care for them for a short amount of time. We can understand that he played a small trick on her to get her to take the children and give him free time.

| Point | sucker ~ into~ 사기쳐서 …가 하기 싫은 일을 하도록 하다
be[get] suckered into~ 속아서 …을 하다, 말려들다

A: Didn't your wife want you to help her?
네 아내는 네가 도와주기를 바라지 않았어?

B: **I suckered her into taking** the kids for a while.
아낼 속여서 잠시 애들을 돌보도록 했어.

She suckered you, too, didn't she?
걔가 너도 사기쳤지, 그렇지 않아?

I can't believe I got suckered into that whole thing I mean for so long.
내 말은 내가 그렇게 오랫동안 그 모든 일에 속아 넘어갔다는게 믿어지지 않아.

039 It's stacking the deck 그건 속임수야

this means that someone is trying to increase the chances that something happens by a type of cheating. Originally, this phrase was used to refer to cheating at card games. To stack the deck meant to unfairly putting cards in an order that increased the chance of winning.

| Point | stack the deck 속임수를 쓰다

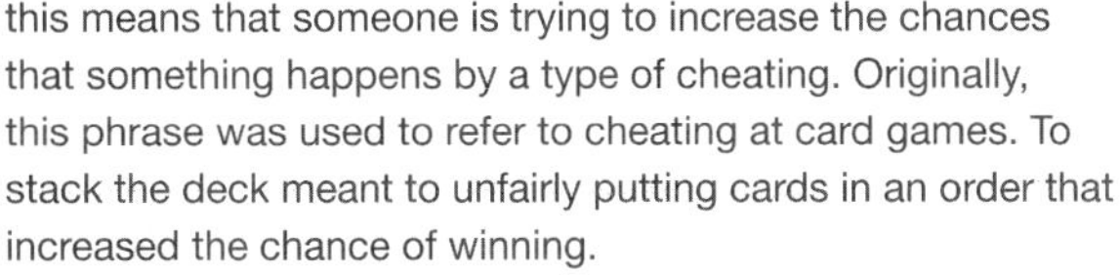

A: Why can't politicians give people money to vote? 왜 정치인들은 사람들에게 투표하라고 돈을 줄 수 없는거야?

B: **It's stacking the deck.** The election would be unfair. 그건 속임수야. 그러면 선거는 공평해지지 못할거야.

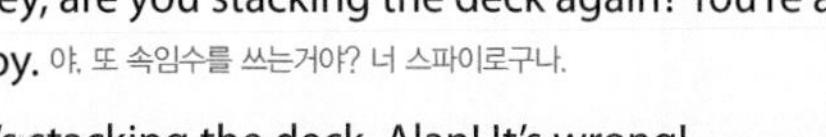

Hey, are you stacking the deck again? You're a spy. 야, 또 속임수를 쓰는거야? 너 스파이로구나.

It's stacking the deck, Alan! It's wrong!
그건 속임수야, 알랜! 그건 나쁜 짓이야!

Then, stack the deck. Cheat. Lie. I don't care.
그럼, 속임수를 써. 사기치고, 거짓말하고, 난 상관안해.

040 She wormed her way into my family

걘 교묘하게 우리 가족의 환심을 샀어

this expresses that a woman was able to become close to members of a family. When it is phrased this way, we can understand that the speaker is suspicious of the woman and thinks she has become close to the family in order to profit personally. This can be similarly expressed as "She wriggled into the family"

| Point | worm one's way into~ 교묘하게 빌붙다, 교묘하게 환심을 사다

A: Why did Rachel marry your brother?
왜 레이첼이 네 오빠하고 결혼한거야?

B: **She wormed her way into my family.**
걔가 교묘하게 우리 가족의 환심을 샀어.

For three years, you've tried to worm your way into our world.
3년간, 넌 우리 세계에 교묘하게 스며들려고 했어.

You just manipulate. You wormed your way into my family.
넌 교묘하게 사람들을 조종해서 우리 가족의 환심을 샀어.

Kevin tried to worm his way into our social circle. 케빈은 교묘하게 사교계에 파고 들었어.

041 Don't fall for it

1. 그 말에 혹하지마, 넘어가지마 2. 사랑에 빠지면 안돼

usually this expresses "Don't be fooled." It is a warning that something may be a trick. And when this is used to refer to love, it can mean "Don't fall in love with that person." The speaker is warning someone to be careful of his emotions

A: He says I can get a lot of money even if I invest a little. 걔말이 돈을 조금 투자해도 많이 벌 수 있다고 해.

B: **Don't fall for it.** He'll only steal your money.
혹하지마. 네 돈을 훔칠려는 거야.

You fall for it every time! 넌 매번 넘어가냐!

Do you really think he's gonna fall for that?
걔가 정말 넘어갈 것 같아?

My sister told me you said you could really fall for her. Now is that true? Or are you just getting over your ex-girlfriend by groping my sister?
내 동생이 네가 자길 좋아한다고 했다며. 사실야 아니면 옛 여친 잊으려고 그러는거야?

042 We can't leave her out in the cold

걔를 제외시킬 수는 없어

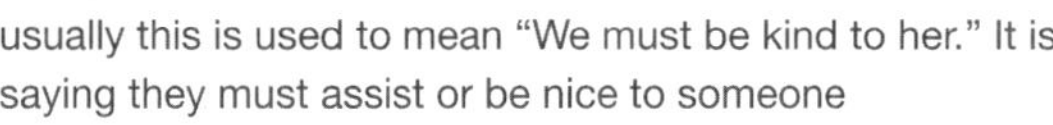

usually this is used to mean "We must be kind to her." It is saying they must assist or be nice to someone

| Point | leave sb out in the cold …를 따돌리다

A: I don't want to have Maria at our wedding.
마리아가 우리 결혼식에 안 왔으면 해.

B: **We can't leave her out in the cold.** We have to invite her. 걜 뺄 수는 없어. 초대해야 돼.

She is one of our people. We can't leave her out in the cold.
걔는 내 사람 중 하나야. 걔를 빼놓을 수는 없어.

You left us out in the cold when you made the deal. 넌 그 거래를 맺을 때 우리를 제외시켰어.

043 You sold me out!

넌 날 배신했어!

this is used to say "You treated me badly so you could benefit." A person who is sold out has been treated unfairly by someone he trusted, while that person has gotten an advantage

| Point | sell sb out 배신하다　　sell sb down the river 배신하다

A: **You sold me out!** You took the job I wanted to get! 넌 날 배신했어! 내가 원했던 일을 빼앗었어!

B: Hey, they chose me because they liked me more. 야, 날 더 좋아하기 때문에 날 뽑은거지.

He sold us out. 걔가 우릴 배신했어.

I can't believe that you sold me out!
네가 날 배신하다니!

(I'm) Sold again. 또 감쪽같이 속아넘어갔어.

I'm telling you, the company is selling me down the river. 정말야, 회사가 날 뒤통수 때릴려고 해.

044 Did you walk out on your family? 넌 가족을 버렸어?

this is a blunt way to ask if a parent unexpectedly moved out of the house where his spouse and children lived and didn't come back. It has a negative meaning, as we can understand the family went through hardships because of his absence. In other words, the question is "Did you leave your family without helping them?"

| Point | walk out on sb (필요로 하는데도) 버리고 가다, 가버리다

A: **Did you walk out on your family?**
넌 가족을 돌보지 않고 버렸어?

B: No, but my wife and I did go through a divorce.
아니, 하지만 아내와 난 이혼을 겪었어.

미드표현

I don't need your crap! You walk out on us, you walk out on your wife!
말같지 않은 얘기는 그만둬! 넌 우리를 버렸어, 네 아내를 버리고 가버렸다고!

How could you just walk out on us without an explanation?
넌 어떻게 설명도 없이 우리를 버리고 갈 수 있어?

Maybe she can have sex with him, and then walk out on him the next morning.
걘 그와 섹스를 할 수 있고 그런 다음에 담날 아침에 그를 놔두고 가버릴 수 있지.

045 Gotcha 1. 잡았다! 2. 속았지!, 당했지! 3. 알았어

this is a way of expressing that someone was only joking. It means "I wasn't serious, I was teasing"

| Point | (I) Gotcha = (I've) Got you

A: I didn't know you planned a surprise birthday party. 서프라이즈 파티를 준비할 줄 몰랐어.

B: **Gotcha!** I worked really hard to keep it a secret.
속았지! 이거 비밀로 하는데 정말 힘들었어.

미드표현

Gotcha. Okay, let's do me now.
알았어. 좋아, 이제 내가 할게.

Gotcha. It won't happen again. 알았어. 다시 안 그럴게.

Gotcha. Watch your back. 알았어. 조심해.

Gotcha. It says here, there's a history of drug abuse. 찾았다. 여기 적혀 있네, 약물과용이력이 있어.

046 You're up to no good 쓸데없는 짓을 하고 있구만, 또 이상한 짓을 꾸미고 있구나

this simply means "You are doing something bad." This is said when the speaker doesn't like what someone is doing

| Point | up to no good 쓸모 없는
(I've) Been up to no good (아무짝에도 쓸모없이) 별 일 없이 그냥 지냈어

A: **You're up to no good.** I can see it in your eyes.
쓸데없는 짓 하고 있구만. 네 눈을 보면 알아.

B: I don't think you have ever trusted me, Sam.
샘 너마저 날 믿지 않을 줄 몰랐어.

미드표현

I can see it in your eyes. You're up to no good.
네 눈을 통해 알 수 있어. 너 또 이상한 짓을 꾸미고 있지.

You're up to no good. You'd better not do something bad.
쓸데없는 짓을 하고 있어. 나쁜 짓을 하지 않도록 해.

미드에선 이렇게 쓰인다!

Did you walk out on your family?

Criminal Minds SEASON#4-16

자신의 아버지처럼 가정을 버린 기업의 CEO들을 살해하는 여성 연쇄살해범 Megan과 Hotch와의 대화

Megan: I thought I could trust you, Aaron.
Hotch: Who says you can't?
Megan: I want to. I even looked you up online. Is that strange?
Hotch: No. It's flattering to be noticed by a woman like you.
Megan: And I thought you were so...upstanding. I watched the presentation you gave on school shootings. I found it posted on youtube. And for a moment, I actually thought there were still good people in the world.
Hotch: But I've disappointed you, haven't I? Just like all the other men in your life who've walked out on their families, who deserves to be punished.
Megan: Did you walk out on your family? **Hotch:** No. My wife left me.

메건: 애런, 난 당신을 믿을 수 있다고 생각했는데요.
하치: 날 믿을 수 없다고 누가 그래요?
메건: 나도 믿고 싶어요. 인터넷에서 당신을 찾아보기까지 했어요. 이상하죠?
하치: 아뇨. 당신같은 여자가 날 알아봐주다니 제가 고맙죠.
메건: 그리고 난 당신은 매우 곧은 사람일거라 생각했어요. 학교총기난사 사건에 대해 발표한 성명서를 봤어요. 유투브에 올려진거요. 잠시 동안 세상에 아직 좋은 사람들이 있다는 것을 진짜 믿었어요.
하치: 하지만 내가 당신을 실망시켰군요 그지 않나요? 자신의 가정을 버리고 당연히 벌받아야 하는 당신이 아는 다른 남자들처럼요.
메건: 당신도 가족을 버렸나요? 하치: 아뇨. 내 아내가 나를 떠났어요.

047 He pulled the rug out from under me 날 곤란하게 만들었어

미드표현

this is something that is said when someone is shocked and harmed by another person's actions. It indicates "You suddenly did something that created many problems for me"

| Point | pull the rug out from under sb …의 입장을 곤란하게 하다

A: I heard your partner stole your money and left the country. 파트너가 돈을 훔쳐서 우리나라를 떴다며.

B: Right. **He pulled the rug out from under me.** 맞아. 날 황당하게 만들었어.

Nobody is gonna be able to pull the rug out from under my life.
누구도 내 인생을 난처하게 만들 수 없어.

He wanted me to talk dirty, I got into it, then he pulled the rug out from under me.
나보고 야한 말을 하라고 해서 했는데 그런 다음 날 아주 곤란하게 만들었어.

048 You ruined my weekend 네가 내 주말을 망쳐놨어

미드표현

this is saying "You made my weekend bad." It is used when someone's actions have created a bad situation

| Point | ruin sth …을 망치다

A: **You ruined my weekend** by being drunk all the time. 네가 줄곧 술취해 있어서 주말이 망쳤졌어.

B: I'm sorry that it caused problems for you. 네게 문제일으켜 미안해.

You've ruined my life. 너 땜에 내 인생이 망쳤어.

You ruined everything. 네가 다 망쳐놨어.

You ruined the surprise party.
서프라이즈 파티를 네가 망쳤어.

You almost ruined a perfectly happy fake marriage. 넌 완벽하게 행복을 가장한 결혼생활을 거의 망칠 뻔했어.

049 It's a disaster 최악이었어, 커다란 실패야, 큰 불행이야, 엉망이야

미드표현

this expresses that there have been too many problems with something. It means "It is really bad"

A: How was the new TV show? TV 쇼 어땠어?

B: **It's a disaster.** I don't want to watch it again. 끔직해. 다신 보고 싶지 않아.

This is going to be a disaster. 큰 불행일거야.

This whole day has been a disaster.
오늘 하루는 다 엉망이야.

I married him. It was a disaster.
걔하고 결혼했는데 불행이었어.

050 The relationship has gone to pot 관계가 안 좋아졌어

미드표현

this is a way of saying "This has become very bad." When a relationship has gone to pot, people usually end it

| Point | go to pot(= go to the dogs) (사물주어가 돌보지 않아)실패하다, 나빠지다

A: Mike and Lisa seem to always be fighting. 마이크와 리사는 항상 싸우는 것 같아.

B: I know. **The relationship has gone to pot.** 알아. 관계가 안 좋아졌어.

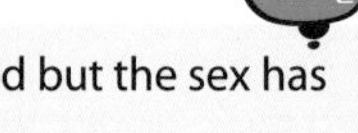

The conversation is still good but the sex has gone to pot.
서로 대화는 아직 괜찮은 상태인데 성생활은 엉망이 되었어.

Man, this place is going to pot.
어휴, 여기는 안 좋아질거야.

I heard your case has gone to the dogs.
네가 맡은 사건이 안 좋아졌다며.

051 She's trying to butter up her boss 걔는 사장에게 아부하려고 해

this is a way to say a woman is trying to flatter her boss so that she receives more favorable treatment from him. In other words, she is probably telling him how great he is, but she is not sincere. This can be like saying "She praises her boss so that he'll treat her better"

| Point | butter up[away 아부하다

A: Why is Linda bringing in doughnuts to Mr. Wilford? 왜 린다가 윌포드 씨에게 도너츠를 가져다주는거야?

B: **She's trying to butter up her boss** to get a raise. 걘 사장에게 아부해서 급여인상을 받으려고 해.

미드표현

I had to butter up your dippy freshman counselor. 네 멍청한 신입생 카운슬러에게 아부해야만 했어.

She's trying to butter up her professor.
걔는 교수님에게 아부를 하려고 해.

He's just trying to butter you up.
걔는 네게 아부를 하려고 해.

052 I've been putting on a brave face for one week 난 일주일 동안 태연한 척 했어

this indicates that the speaker has had problems but has been acting as if he didn't have problems when he is around people. To put on a brave face means to act as if everything is fine when it isn't. A different way to say this would be "I've been pretending everything is okay for a week"

| Point | put on a brave face 태연한 척하다

A: I didn't know you were diagnosed with cancer.
네가 암진단을 받은 줄 몰랐어.

B: **I've been putting on a brave face** for a week. I didn't tell anyone. 일주일간 태연한 척 했어. 아무한테도 말하지 않았고.

미드표현

I've been putting on a brave face for eight months. 난 8개월동안 아무일도 없었던 것처럼 행동했어.

Look at you, putting on a brave face.
너 좀 봐라. 태연한 척을 좀 하고.

Vicky is holding a dish and is near tears but she tries to put on a brave face.
비키는 접시를 들고서 눈물이 나려고 했으나 태연한 척하고 있어.

053 The jig is up (계략이) 뽀록났어, 들통났어, 들켰다

this means "Something that has gone on for a long time has ended." When the jig is up, it has finished

A: **The jig is up.** The police caught the head gangster. 속임수가 들통났어. 경찰이 갱두목을 잡았어.

B: I hope he goes to jail for a long time.
오랫동안 감옥에 있기를 바래.

미드표현

I have a child. The jig is up. Right. I'm not a virgin. 난 사실 애가 있어. 들통났네. 그래, 난 처녀가 아니야.

The cops are here for you. The jig is up.
경찰이 널 잡으러 여기 와 있어. 들통났어.

The jig is up. There is no way to escape.
들통났어. 도망갈 길이 없어.

The jig is up. We've caught you red handed.
계략이 들통났어. 우리는 널 현장범으로 잡았어.

054 This is getting us nowhere 이건 아무 소용이 없어

this is usually said when something isn't working. It is another way to say "This is a waste of time"

| Point | get nowhere 아무 소용없다

A: **This is getting us nowhere.** We need someone to help us. 아무 소용이 없어. 우릴 도와줄 사람이 필요해.

B: Can we hire someone to work here?
여기서 일할 사람을 뽑을까?

미드표현

Well, talking to him is getting us nowhere.
걔한테 말하는 건 아무 소용이 없어.

I got nowhere negotiating with Larry.
래리와 협상하는데 아무런 진전이 없어.

The police are getting nowhere in the murder investigation.
경찰은 살인사건 수사에서 아무런 진전도 못하고 있어.

055 I'm just teasing you 그냥 장난으로 한 말이야

this means "I'm joking." It is said when a person doesn't understand that the speaker is joking about something

| Point | tease sb(about sth) (…을) 짓궂게 장난치다, (…을) 놀리다
Don't tease me 날 놀리지 마(= Stop teasing me)
I'm fucking with you 너한테 장난친거야

A: You are starting to make me angry. 날 열받게 하네.
B: **I'm just teasing you.** Don't get upset.
그냥 장난한거야. 화내지마.

They used to tease me about my eyes. They called me names. 걔들은 내 눈을 놀리곤 했고 욕도 했어.

You know, kids get teased, and they get over it. 저 말야, 애들은 놀림 당하기도 하고 또 그걸 극복하기도 해.

She's a bitch and a tease. 재는 나쁜 년이고 날 갖고 놀아.

056 It went just down the drain

헛수고가 됐다, 그냥 날라갔어, 실패했어, 물거품이 됐어

this is a way to say "It was wasted." It is said when something was not used correctly

| Point | go down the drain 1. (시간, 노력, 돈) 수포로 돌아가다, 헛수고가 되다
2.(기관/나라) 실패하다, 악화되다

A: Where did the money Sharon inherited go to?
샤론이 유산으로 받은 돈이 어디갔어?
B: **It went down the drain.** She bought a lot of foolish things. 다 날라갔어. 엉뚱한 것들을 많이 샀어.

All the money I saved, it just went down the drain. 내가 저축한 모든 돈이 날라가버렸어.

It just went down the drain and we'll never see it again. 그건 물거품이 되어서 다시는 볼 수 없을거야.

Remember the stock that you bought? It just went down the drain.
네가 산 주식 기억나? 다 물거품이 됐어.

057 Don't lead me down the garden path 날 속이지마

미드표현

this means "Don't try to fool me by making me believe something nice." It indicates the speaker doesn't want to get tricked

| Point | lead sb down the garden path 의도적으로 …를 속이다

A: If you marry me, I will treat you like a princess every day. 나랑 결혼하면 매일 공주처럼 모실게.
B: **Don't lead me down the garden path.** I know how marriage is. 속이지마. 결혼이 어떤건지 나도 알아.

I don't like being lied to. Don't lead me down a garden path.
누가 나한테 거짓말하는거 싫어해. 날 속이지 말라고.

Don't lead me down a garden path. What's going on here? 날 속이지 말라고. 여기 무슨 일이야?

Don't lead me down a garden path. Just tell me the truth. 날 속이지 말라고. 진실을 말해줘.

058 It was all for nothing 모든 일이 수포로 돌아갔어

미드표현

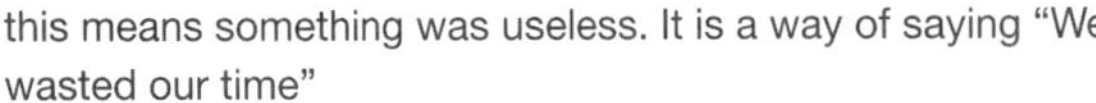

this means something was useless. It is a way of saying "We wasted our time"

A: Did you finally complete the book you were writing? 쓰던 책 다 끝냈어?
B: No, I stopped writing it. **It was all for nothing.**
아니, 그만 뒀어. 다 수포로 돌아갔어.

Do you have any idea how scared I was? It was all for nothing!
내가 얼마나 놀랐는지 알아? 다 수포로 돌아갔어!

So at least it wasn't all for nothing.
그럼 적어도, 그건 모두 수포로 돌아간 건 아니네.

I've--I've failed. It was all for nothing.
난 실패했어. 모든 일이 수포로 돌아갔어.

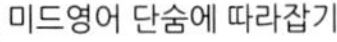

059 (You) Could have fooled me! 바보 될 뻔했잖아!

this indicates the speaker was tricked by something. It is a way of saying "I was surprised by the truth"

I Point I You can't fool me 날 속이려고 하지마

A: My mom is 68 years old. 우리 엄마는 68세야.

B: **You could have fooled me.** She looks much younger. 속을 뻔 했잖아. 훨씬 젊어보이셔.

I thought I could have fooled one of you with that. 너희들 중 하나는 속일 수 있을 줄 알았는데.

A: Those things are dangerous. B: Adrian, you can't fool me.
A: 그 일들은 위험해. B: 에이드리안, 날 속이려고 하지마.

060 Don't spy on me 날 훔쳐보지마

this speaker is telling someone not to secretly watch him. When people are spied on, they don't like it. They have no privacy because they are often being observed. It is like saying "Stop trying to monitor me"

I Point I spy on 몰래 보다, 감시하다

A: I saw you taking Anne out on a date.
네가 앤을 데리고 나가 데이트하는 걸 봤어.

B: Hey, **don't spy on me.** I don't like it.
야, 날 훔쳐보지마. 나 그거 싫다고.

You're gonna spy on him? 너 걔를 감시할거야?

I'm not gonna spy on my kids.
난 내 아이들을 감시하지 않을거야.

Who hired you to spy on Daniel?
다니엘을 감시하라고 누가 널 고용했어?

As I suspected, Carl is using him to spy on me.
내가 의심한대로, 칼은 걔를 이용해 날 감시하고 있어.

061 I just wanted to sneak a peek 난 단지 슬쩍 엿보려는거였어

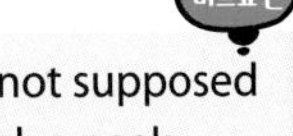

this is a way to say that the speaker wanted to see something before other people were able to see it. Often a sneak peak refers to seeing a film before it is officially released in movie theaters. It is like saying "I wanted to get an early look at it"

I Point I sneak a peek 훔쳐보다
take[get] a peek 잠깐 살펴보다

A: Why did you come to the museum early?
넌 왜 박물관에 일찍 온거야?

B: **I just wanted a sneak peek** at the exhibit.
전시회를 먼저 좀 살펴보고 싶었어.

Don't tell him I stopped by. I'm not supposed to be here. I just wanted to sneak a peek.
걔한테 내가 들렀다고 말하지마. 난 여기 있으면 안되거든. 단지 슬쩍 살펴보려는거였어.

You thought he might try to sneak a peek at the evidence?
넌 걔가 증거를 몰래 훔쳐보려 할 지도 모른다고 생각했지?

You're trying to sneak a peek at my watch.
넌 내 시계를 슬쩍 보려고 하고 있어.

Why don't you take a peek inside here before you go? 가기 전에 여기 안을 잠깐 살펴봐.

Ways of saying you can't control something and expressing nervousness

어쩔 수 없는 상황, 초조해하고 절망도 하고

I don't know what to do with myself

001 I don't know what to do with myself
어떻게 해야 할 줄 모르겠어

this expresses that the speaker has too much free time and is unsure of what he should be doing. This is sometimes said by people who have lost their job or stopped going to school unexpectedly. It is like saying "I'm not sure what I should do with this extra time"

| Point | I don't know what to do with myself
(남는 시간을) 어떻게 해야 할 줄 모르겠어
I don't know what to do with sth …을 어떻게 해야 할 줄 모르겠어

A: I heard you lost your job. How are you doing?
직장을 잃었다며. 어떻게 지내?
B: **I don't know what to do with myself** during the day. 낮에 뭘 어떻게 해야 할 지 모르겠어.

미드표현

You don't know what to do with yourself.
넌 어떻게 해야 할 지 모르고 있어.

Don't exactly know what to do with that information. 저 정보를 어떻게 해야 할지 정확히 모르겠어.

You wouldn't know what to do with a good girl if you had one.
너에게 착한 소녀가 있다면 넌 어떻게 할 줄 모를거야.

Ever since the business closed, you've got all this free time, and you don't know what to do with yourself.
가게 문을 닫은 후로 시간이 엄청 나는데 넌 어떻게 해야 할 줄을 모르고 있어.

002 (I) can't help it
나도 어쩔 수가 없어

this means that the speaker couldn't control something. It would be similar to say "It happened automatically"

| Point | (It) can't be helped 어쩔 수 없는 상황이야

A: Stop acting so nervous. 그렇게 초조해하지마.
B: **I can't help it.** It's the way I feel. 어쩔 수가 없어. 그렇게 돼.

미드표현

I can't help it, I'm just crazy about you.
어쩔 수가 없어. 네가 넘 좋아.

I can't help it. When people talk about it, I just get emotional.
어쩔 수 없어. 사람들이 그 얘길하면 감정적으로 돼.

I promised I wouldn't say anything, but I can't help it! It is so wonderful.
아무 말도 하지 않겠다고 약속했지만 어쩔 수가 없어. 정말 멋져.

003 I can't help myself
내 감정을 억제할 수가 없어, 어쩔 수가 없어

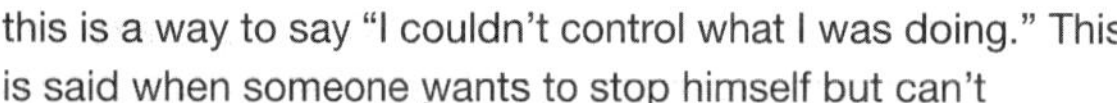

this is a way to say "I couldn't control what I was doing." This is said when someone wants to stop himself but can't

A: Why do you flirt with so many girls?
왜 그렇게 많은 여자들에게 작업들어가는 거야?
B: **I cannot help myself.** It's what I like to do.
나도 어쩔 수가 없어. 내가 하고 싶은 것인 걸.

미드표현

I couldn't help myself because she was acting so hot. 걔가 너무 섹시하게 행동해서 나도 어쩔 수가 없었어.

I'm an idiot, I was weak, I couldn't help myself!
난 바보야, 나약하고, 어쩔 수가 없었어!

004 I can't help ~ing[but~]
…하지 않을 수 없어

this means the person can't stop doing something, even if he tries. It usually indicates that "Even if I wanted to stop, I couldn't"

| Point | can't help ~ing … 하지 않을 수 없다

A: **I can't help** snacking between meals.
식사 사이사이 간식을 먹지 않을 수 없어.
B: That means you'll probably get fat.
그 얘긴 곧 살이 찐다는 거구만.

미드표현

You can't help but break the law, can you?
불법을 저지를 수밖에 없지, 그렇지?

I can't help but take it personally.
개인적으로 받아들일 수밖에 없어.

I can't help being cautious. 조심할 수 밖에 없어.

005 I have no choice but to~ …하지 않을 수밖에 없어

this is a way to say "I must do something." It indicates that the speaker has a duty to complete

Point You have no choice in this matter 이 문제에 넌 선택권이 없어
It's not like I have a choice here 나도 어쩔 수 없는 일이야
leave sb no choice but to~ …가 …할 수밖에 없게 하다

A: **I have no choice but to** pay her the money.
걔한데 돈을 갚을 수밖에 없어.

B: That's going to be really expensive.
돈이 정말 많이 들텐데.

I had no choice but to reveal it out.
밝힐 수 밖에 없었어.

You had no choice but to go with your policy.
너는 네 방침대로 밀고 나갈 수 밖에 없었어.

I will have no choice but to dismiss the case.
이 사건을 기각하는 수밖에 없을거야.

You leave me no choice but to change. My clothes, not my mind.
너 때문에 난 바꿀 수밖에 없어. 내 옷들, 내 생각은 아니고.

006 It's just one of those things
흔한 일야, 어쩔 수 없는 일야, 있는 일들 중 하나야

this phrase usually indicates something is very common and not special. It is like saying "It's very typical" And less commonly, this is used to say "It can't be changed." The speaker is indicating that he isn't able to help with or change a problem

Point Is this one of those things where S+V …하게 되는 것들 중의 하나야?

A: You made Patty quit the school's club. Why?
패티가 학교 동아리를 그만 두게 했지. 왜 그랬어?

B: The other students didn't like her. **It's just one of those things.** 다른 학생들이 걜 싫어했어. 어쩔 수 없었어.

It is one of those things where everyone dresses formally.
모든 사람들이 정장 옷을 입는 그런 행사들 중 하나야.

It is one of those things where people bring their kids to play together.
사람들이 함께 놀리기 위해 아이들을 데려오는건 흔한 일이야.

It's one of those things…just forget about it
어쩔 수 없는 일이야… 그냥 잊어버려

007 There's nothing you can do about it 네가 어쩔 수 없는 일이야

this means "You can't change it." This is said to mean a person can't control something

A: I wish my wife didn't want to divorce me.
아내가 나와의 이혼을 원치 않았으면 좋을텐데.

B: **There's nothing you can do about it.** It's just one of those things.
네가 어쩔 수 있는 일이 아니잖아. 부득이한 일이야.

My sex life is my own business. Not yours. And there's nothing you can do about it anyway.
내 성생활은 나의 문제야. 네 문제가 아니라고. 네가 어떻게 할 수 있는 일이 아니라고.

Get out of here! This is my house. And there's nothing you can do about it.
꺼져! 여긴 내 집이야. 네가 뭘 어떻게 해볼 수 있는 게 없다고.

008 I couldn't keep a straight face 웃음을 참을 수 없었어

this is said when someone can't be serious at a time when he should be serious because he doesn't think the words seem important enough. It means "I couldn't believe the things that were being said"

Point keep a straight face 웃지 않다, 진지한 표정을 짓다

A: **I couldn't keep a straight face** when he told me how rich he was.
걔가 내게 자기가 얼마나 부자인지 말할 때 웃지 않을 수가 없었어.

B: Everyone knows he doesn't have any money.
다들 걔 돈 없는 거 다 아는데 말야.

It's not easy to lie. I couldn't keep a straight face. 거짓말하는 것은 쉽지가 않아. 웃음을 참을 수가 없었어.

I couldn't keep a straight face when I told the jokes. 내가 농담을 할 때 웃음을 참을 수가 없었어.

I have the hardest time keeping a straight face when it pops up.
그게 갑자기 튀어나왔을 때 웃음을 참을 수가 없었어.

009 It's out of my hands 내 손을 떠났어, 나도 어쩔 수 없어

this is a way to say "I can't control it anymore." It means the speaker has no power in the matter

Point Sth is out of sb's hands …의 손을 떠난 일이다, …는 어쩔 수가 없다

A: Can you please help me fix this problem?
이 문제 푸는 거 도와줄테야?

B: No, I can't. **It's out of my hands.** 안돼. 어쩔 수 없어.

미드표현

I have a court order. It's out of my hands.
법원명령이라 어쩔 수가 없어.

I'm sorry, but it's out of my hands.
미안하지만 내 손을 떠난 일이야.

It's out of our hands, it's up to the lawyers now. 우리 손을 떠난 일이야. 이젠 변호사가 알아서 할 일이야.

010 You can't help yourself 너도 어쩔 수가 없잖아

often this indicates that a person does something that can't be controlled. It is like saying "You do it naturally"

Point You can't undo what's happened 이미 일어난 일은 어쩔 수 없어
(Just concentrate on the future)

A: I'm really sorry I ate all of the cake.
내가 케익을 모두 다 먹어서 정말 미안해.

B: **You can't help yourself.** You love snacks.
너도 어쩔 수가 없잖아. 너 스낵 좋아하잖아.

미드표현

You can't help yourself. You've got a problem.
너도 어쩔 수가 없잖아. 문제 있으니.

You can't help yourself. You were born nasty.
너도 어쩔 수가 없잖아. 비열하게 타고 났으니.

You can't undo what's happened. It was a bad mistake. 이미 일어난 일은 어쩔 수 없어. 안 좋은 실수였어.

011 It'll totally freak her out! 그것 때문에 걔 정신 못 차릴 거야!, 엄청 놀랄거야!

this is said to mean "She'll be upset or excited by this." It means some event is going to change the person's feelings

Point freak sb out …을 정신없게 하다
You freaked me out 너 땜에 놀랐잖아
You freaked out 너 정신없더라, 열받았지(S+ freak out = be upset)

A: This letter for Jenna is from her ex-boyfriend.
이 제나한테 온 편지는 걔 옛 남친이 보낸거야.

B: Oh no! **It'll totally freak her out.**
어 안돼! 걔가 정신 못 차릴텐데.

미드표현

It's nothing to freak out about. 놀랄 일 아니야.

Public bathrooms freak me out, I can't even pee. 공중화장실은 정말 으악야, 난 소변도 못누겠어.

You just make her think you wanna have sex with her! It'll totally freak her out!
넌 네가 걔와 섹스하고 싶다는 생각을 걔가 하게끔 했어! 걔가 그 땜에 정신 못차릴거야!

You freaked out in my house. You screamed, you threw furniture around.
내 집에서 난리쳤잖아. 비명지르고 가구들은 여기저기 던지고 말야.

012 I'm all mixed up 너무 혼란스러워, 모든 게 복잡해졌어

this indicates the person is not thinking clearly. It's another way to say "I'm confused(I'm at a loss)"

Point be mixed up 혼란스럽다(= be confused)
You're mixing me up with ~ 나를 …와 혼동한 것 같네
get sb mixed up with 얽혀놓다

A: I don't know what to do. **I'm all mixed up.**
어떻게 해야 할지 모르겠어. 넘 혼란스러워.

B: Maybe you should ask your parents for some advice. 부모님께 조언 좀 부탁하지 그래.

I got it mixed up. 혼동했네.

He says he got his days mixed up.
걔는 요즘 사는 게 혼란스럽다고 해.

Obviously, you've got me mixed up with someone else. 분명히 날 다른 사람과 혼동한거야.

I'm confused. Who's teaching the class now?
혼란스럽네. 지금 수업은 누가 하고 있는건가?

013 She won't know what hit her 걔는 너무 놀라 어쩔 줄 모를거야

this is a way to say that someone will be totally surprised when something happens. We can understand that it is usually a bad surprise that may cause shock or confusion. Another way to say this would be "She'll never expect this"

| Point | not know what hit sb 너무 놀라 어쩔 줄을 모르다, 너무 놀라고 혼란스러워하다

A: Connie doesn't know she's going to be sued.
코니는 소송을 당할걸 모르고 있어.

B: **She won't know what hit her.** 엄청 놀랄텐데.

Got it. She won't know what hit her.
알았어. 걔는 놀라 당황할거야.

Your father didn't know what hit him, did he?
네 아빠는 놀라서 어쩔 줄 모르셨어, 그랬지?

We do it quick, they'll never know what hit them. 우리가 빨리 해치우면 걔네들은 놀라 당황할거야.

Poor guy probably didn't know what hit him.
불쌍한 그 친구는 아마 놀라서 어쩔 줄을 몰랐을거야.

014 She was stumped (대답을 못 찾아) 걔는 쩔쩔맸어, 난처해졌어

this means "She didn't have the answer." It is said when someone is not sure of something

| Point | be stumped (for+N) 답(대답)을 찾지 못하다

A: Was Tracey able to solve the math problem?
트레이시가 그 수학문제를 풀었어?

B: No. **She was stumped.** 아니. 몰라 쩔쩔맸어.

I'm stumped on the first question.
첫번째 질문부터 난처했어.

Now I have to worry about being stumped for conversation? 대화에서조차 쩔쩔매야 돼?

015 I'm just a little stunned 좀 어리둥절해, 좀 충격적이었어

this is said to show a person is shocked or surprised. It can mean "I can't believe it"

A: Why are you surprised that I want to get married? 내가 결혼하고 싶다는 거에 왜 놀래?

B: **I'm just a little stunned.** I didn't expect this.
좀 어리둥절해서. 예상을 못했어.

She stands up and kisses him. He is stunned.
걔가 키스를 하자 남자는 놀랐어.

He is stunned. Are you out of your mind?
걔가 충격먹었잖아. 너 정신나갔어?

She is stunned into silence. 걔 충격먹어서 조용해졌어.

016 I was a basket case 절망적이었지

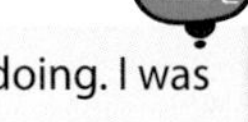

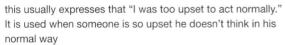

this usually expresses that "I was too upset to act normally." It is used when someone is so upset he doesn't think in his normal way

| Point | a basket case 무능력한 사람, 신경과민한 사람

A: How did you feel when you failed the entrance exam? 입학시험 떨어졌을 때 기분이 어땠어?

B: **I was a basket case.** I couldn't eat or drink anything. 절망적이었지. 아무 것도 먹지도 마시지도 못했어.

I didn't know what the hell I was doing. I was a basket case.
내가 도대체 뭘하고 있는지 몰랐어. 정신이 없었어.

It was a horrible experience. I was a basket case. 정말 끔찍한 경험이었어. 난 절망적이었어.

I was a basket case when my wife was giving birth. 내 아내가 출산을 할 때 난 신경이 아주 예민해졌어.

017 You're so uptight 너무 소심해, 너무 긴장하고 있어

this expresses that someone can't relax. It is like saying "You are always stressed"

| Point | get uptight about 초조하고 걱정이 돼 화를 내다
Don't get[be] uptight 긴장하지 말아

A: This nightclub is too noisy for me.
이 나이트클럽이 너무 시끄러워.

B: **You're so uptight.** Try to relax and enjoy it.
넌 너무 소심해. 긴장풀고 즐기라고.

미드표현

Why are you so uptight? 너 왜 그렇게 까칠한거야?

Why is everyone so uptight about answering a few questions?
왜 다들 질문 몇 개에 답하는 데 긴장하고 있는거야?

What are you getting so uptight about?
뭐 때문에 그렇게 긴장하고 있어?

018 He's always on edge (안 좋은 일이 생길 걸 예상하며) 걔는 늘 초조해

this indicates the person is never calm. We could say "He is a very uptight guy"

| Point | be on pins and needles 초조하다, 떨다(be stressed about something)

A: Gee, I think Joseph is acting kind of nasty.
저런, 조셉이 좀 불쾌하게 행동하는 것 같아.

B: **He's always on edge.** Don't worry.
걘 늘 안절부절야. 걱정마.

All right, I'm just a little on edge today.
그래, 나 오늘 좀 예민한 상태야.

I was on pins and needles when I proposed to her. 내가 걔한테 청혼했을 때 매우 떨렸어.

A: He's a little on edge right now. B: Cut him some slack.
A: 걘 지금 좀 초조해하고 있어. B: 느슨하게 좀 풀어줘.

019 It blows my mind! 정신을 못차리겠어!, 마음이 설레네!

this is a way of saying "It's a very new and exciting idea." It is said when someone is very excited about something he is considering

| Point | blow one's mind 흥분하거나 당황하여 어쩔 줄 모르다, 놀래키다
It blew my mind 당황스러웠어

A: I heard you won the lottery. How does it feel?
복권 당첨했다며. 기분이 어때?

B: **It blows my mind.** I can't believe it.
정신없지. 믿기지 않아.

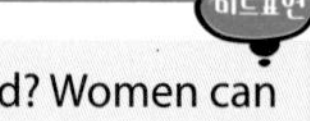

You know what blows my mind? Women can see breasts any time they want.
뭐가 날 정신 못 차리게 하는 줄 알아? 여자들은 원할 때 아무 때나 가슴을 볼 수 있잖아.

I'm fairly sure it's gonna blow your mind.
네가 깜짝 놀랄거라고 난 확신해.

A: I'm about to blow your mind, Lynette.
B: Oh, don't. I like my mind the way it is.
A: 르넷, 너를 깜짝 놀래켜줄게. B: 어, 그러지만. 난 이대로가 좋아.

020 I'm in over my head 너무 걱정이 돼, 감당이 안돼

this indicates the speaker can't do everything he is supposed to do. It is similar to saying "This is too much for me"

| Point | be in over one's head 감당이 안되다, 걱정이 되다

A: Now that I'm dating a famous actress, I feel **I'm in over my head.** 유명 여배우와 데이트하니 넘 걱정돼.

B: Yeah, there must be a lot of competition from other guys. 그래, 다른 사람들로부터 많은 경쟁이 있을거야.

I was in over my head. I got scared.
너무 걱정했었어. 무서웠어.

I'm in over my head. Where are you?
너무 걱정이 돼. 너 어디야?

021 I was worried sick 무척 걱정했잖아

this expresses that someone worried a great deal about something that might happen, and it caused a lot of stress. Often this is said when someone thinks a loved one may be in danger. In other words "I was very stressed over what might happen"

| Point | be worried sick (about)~ 무척 걱정하다(be sick with worry)
be out of one's mind with worry 무척 걱정하다

A: Sarah survived the accident with minor injuries.
새라는 가벼운 부상만 입고 그 사고에서 살아남았어.

B: Thank God. **I was worried sick** about her.
다행이네. 엄청 걱정했는데.

미드표현

Where have you been? We've been worried sick about you! 어디갔었어? 걱정 무척 많이 했잖아!

I was up all night worried sick, digging through medical books.
난 극도로 걱정하며 의학서적들을 뒤져가면서 밤을 샜어.

The doctors wouldn't tell me anything. I was sick with worry.
의사들은 내게 아무말도 하지 않으려 해. 난 몹시 걱정됐어.

022 You had me worried 걱정했잖아

this is often said when a person has behaved in an unusual way, and the speaker felt worried because it seemed strange. It is like saying "I didn't understand what you were doing, and it made me feel very concerned about you"

| Point | have[get] sb worried (sick)~ …가 (매우) 걱정하다
have sb worried (that) S+V …가 …을 걱정하다

A: It took me weeks to get over my illness.
내 병을 이겨내는데 수 주일이 걸렸어.

B: **You had me worried.** I thought you'd never get better. 너 땜에 걱정했잖아. 난 네가 회복되지 못할 줄 알았어.

미드표현

Mom, you're getting me worried. What's going on? 엄마, 걱정되잖아. 무슨 일이야?

You officially have me worried. Please call me back as soon as you get this.
정말이지 너 때문에 걱정돼. 이거 듣는 즉시 내게 전화해줘.

For a moment, you had me worried you weren't gonna be coming.
잠시동안, 네가 오지 않을거라는 걱정을 했었어.

023 I don't know what to do 어떻게 해야 할 지 모르겠어

this means the speaker isn't sure what action he should choose. It's a way of saying "I'm not sure"

| Point | I don't know what else to do 달리 어떻게 해야 할 지 모르겠어
I don't know what to do about[with] this 이거 어떻게 해야 할 지 모르겠어

A: How are you going to tell your parents about this? 이거 부모님께 뭐라 할거야?

B: **I don't know what to do.** Maybe I won't tell them. 어떻게 해야 할 지 모르겠어. 아마 얘기 안 할 수도 있어.

미드표현

I don't know what to do. Would you please help me? 어떻게 해야 할 지 모르겠어. 도와줄래?

I don't know what to do. I'm completely freaked out. 어떻게 해야 할 지 모르겠어. 완전히 정신이 나갔어.

I don't know what to do. I had to do something, but I didn't know what to do.
어떻게 해야 할지 모르겠어. 뭔가 해야 했는데 뭘 어떻게 해야 할 줄 몰랐어.

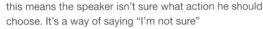

024 I don't know what to say (감사 혹은 실망하여) 뭐라고 말해야 할지

this is said to mean "I can't express what I'm thinking." It is said when a person can't think of words he wishes to say.

| Point | I don't know what to say to her 걔한테 뭐라 말해야 할지 모르겠어

A: I'm sorry, but **I don't know what to say.**
미안하지만 뭐라 해야 할 지 모르겠어.

B: Maybe you should apologize to me. 내게 사과해야지.

미드표현

I don't know what to say. I'll never meet another woman like you.
뭐라 해야 할지. 너 같은 여자애는 다신 안 만날거야.

I don't know what to say. I'm disappointed in you, Jack. 뭐라 해야 할지. 잭 네게 실망했어.

025 I don't know what I'm doing 어떻게 해야 할 지 모르겠어

this means the speaker is confused about something. It is like saying "I'm not sure if this is right"

| Point | I know what I'm doing 내가 알아서 하니까 걱정마

A: How are you doing on the project?
그 프로젝트 어떻게 돼가?

B: **I don't know what I'm doing.** Can you help me? 어떻게 해야 할지 모르겠어. 도와줄테야?

미드표현

I've never done this before. I don't know what I'm doing. 이거 해본 적 한번도 없어. 어떻게 해야 할지 모르겠어.

I don't know what I'm doing here. Peter could show up any minute and kick my ass.
어떻게 해야 할지 모르겠어. 피터는 언제든 나타나서 나를 혼낼거야.

I don't know what I'm doing here. I just missed you. I wanted to see you.
난 어떻게 해야 할지 모르겠어. 난 단지 네가 그리워. 너를 보고 싶었어.

026 Where does that leave us? 그럼 우린 어떻게 되는 거야?

this is a way to say "What is our situation?" It asks about how things are

A: The company is losing a lot of money this year.
회사가 금년도에 많은 돈을 잃었어.

B: That's bad. **Where does that leave us** for next year? 안됐네. 그럼 우린 어떻게 되는 거야?

미드표현

A: There's no sign of struggle. Any prints would have been washed away. B: Where does that leave us?
A: 싸운 흔적은 없는데. 뭔가 흔적이 있었다 하더라도 물에 떠내려갔을거야. B: 그럼 어떻게 되는 거지?

027 What can I say? 1. 할 말이 없네 2. 나더러 어쩌라고 3. 뭐랄까?

this just means "I'm not sure what to say." It is used when a person is asked to explain his actions, and he is not certain how to explain them

A: This is the worst grade of all of the exams.
모든 시험 중에서 최악의 점수야.

B: **What can I say?** I studied hard for it.
할 말이 없어. 열심히는 공부했는데.

미드표현

You're cute when you sleep, what can I say?
너 잘 때 이쁘더라, 어쩌겠어?

What can I say? You were right, I was wrong.
글쎄 뭐라고 할까? 네가 맞았고 내가 틀렸어.

What can I say? I like her. 뭐랄까? 난 걔가 좋아.

What can I say, you missed your chance.
뭐랄까, 넌 기회를 놓쳤어.

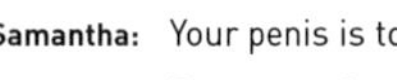

미드에선 이렇게 쓰인다!

What can I say?

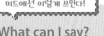

Sex and the City
SEASON#2-2

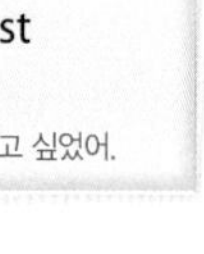

사만다의 남친 James는 다 좋은데 거시기가 tiny하다. 육체적인 사랑에 비중을 두는 사만다의 입장에서는 참기 힘든 고민이나 말을 할 수는 없다. 그래서 어쩔 수 없이 상담을 받는데 한계에 다다르며 마침내 자신의 고민을 털어놓는다.

Samantha: Your penis is too small.
James: Excuse me?
Samantha: It doesn't--and it just--it can't. I can't. It's just too damn small.
James: Did you ever stop to think that maybe your vagina is too big.
Samantha: What can I say? I need a big dick.

사만다: 네 거시기가 너무 작아.
제임스: 뭐라고?
사만다: 섹스를 해도 느낌이 없어. 그게 너무 작아.
제임스: 네 거시기가 크다는 생각을 해보지 않았어?
사만다: 어쩌겠어. 난 큰 거시기가 좋은걸.

028 What can I tell you? 어찌라고?, 뭐라고 해야 하나?

this is said to indicate "I don't have an excuse." Often it means a speaker can't explain what he did

A: This TV is broken again. TV가 다시 고장났어.

B: **What can I tell you?** I accidentally broke it.

뭐라 해야 하나? 뜻하지 않게 망가트렸어.

미드표현

What can I tell you? It all happened so fast.
어찌라고? 모든 게 넘 빨리 벌어졌어.

What can I tell you? I'm a bastard in more ways than one. 뭐라고 해야 하나? 난 여러 면에서 개자식이야.

Danny and I broke up a long time ago, and I wasn't at the party. So what can I tell you?
대니와 난 오래 전에 헤어졌고 난 그 파티에 가지도 않았어요. 그러니 난들 뭐라고 해야 하나?

029 What can I do? 난들 어쩌겠어?, 어떻게 해줄까?

this expresses the feeling "I don't think I can do anything." It is used when a person feels helpless

I Point I What can I do for you? 뭘 도와줄까?
What more[else] can I do? 내가 달리 어쩌겠어?

A: Jim is marrying a very unkind woman.
짐은 싸가지없는 여자와 결혼해.

B: **What can I do?** It is his choice.
난들 어쩌겠어? 걔의 선택인데.

미드표현

What can I do? He won't talk to me.
난들 어쩌겠어? 나한테는 말을 하려 하지 않는데.

I'm sorry. How can I help? What can I do?
미안해요. 뭘 도와줄까요? 어떻게 해줄까요?

What else can I do? I love him. I have to go.
내가 달리 어쩌겠어? 난 걔를 사랑해. 가야 돼.

030 What should I do? 어떻게 해야 하지?, 어떻게 하면 좋을까?

this is a way of asking for advice. It is another way to say "Can you tell me your opinion?"

I Point I What should I do about~ …는 어떻게 해야 하지?
What should I do to do~ …하려면 어떻게 해야 하지?
What do we do now? 이제 어쩌지?

A: I've been offered a job in Australia. **What should I do?**
호주에 있는 일자리를 제안받았어. 어떻게 해야 하지?

B: I think you should take it and move there.
받아들이고 그곳으로 이사가.

미드표현

What should I do to make him jealous?
걔를 질투나게 하려면 어떻게 해야 하지?

There's an unreliable witness. So what do we do now? 증인이 신뢰할 수 없는데 이제 어쩌지?

What am I going to do if he dies?
걔가 죽으면 어떻게 하지?

Ways of saying someone is acting strange and telling someone to relax

상대방이 제 정신이 아닌 것처럼 보일 때

I'm losing my mind

001 Are you out of your mind? 너 제정신이야?, 미쳤니?

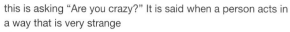

this is asking "Are you crazy?" It is said when a person acts in a way that is very strange

| Point | You're out of your head 넌 제 정신이 아냐
You've got to be out of your mind! 제정신이 아니구나!

A: I decided to quit my job and travel around the world. 회사 그만두고 세계일주 여행하기로 했어.

B: **Are you out of your mind?** You can't do that! 너 제정신이야? 그러면 안돼!

미드표현

Are you out of your mind? Do you know what you've done? 너 제 정신이야? 니가 뭘 했는지 알기나 해?

What are you doing? Are you out of your mind? 너 뭐하는 거야? 미쳤냐?

You can't bring Michael to dinner! Are you out of your mind?
넌 마이클을 저녁식사에 데려오면 안돼. 너 제 정신이야?

002 I'm losing my mind 내가 제 정신이 아냐

this indicates a person is feeling very stressed. It is like saying "I'm feeling much too stressed these days"

| Point | lose one's mind(= lose it) 정신나가다, 제 정신이 아니다
lose one's mind over sb …때문에 돌다
I'm losing it 미쳐가고 있다

A: Look at all of these bills! **I'm losing my mind** trying to pay them! 이 청구서들 좀 봐! 갚느라 정신없겠구만!

B: We'll find a way for you to make some money. 네가 돈을 벌 수 있는 방법을 찾아볼게.

미드표현

If I don't find out what's wrong with me soon, I'm gonna lose my mind.
내게 무슨 문제가 있는지 곧 밝혀내지 못하면 정신이 나갈 것 같아.

Have you completely lost it? 너 완전히 정신 나갔구나?

003 Are you insane? 너 돌았니?

this asks if a person is thinking normally because his actions are odd. It is similar to saying "Why are you acting this way?"

A: I stole these shoes from that store. 가게에서 이 신발들을 훔쳤어.

B: **Are you insane?** You'll get arrested! 너 미쳤니? 잡힐거야!

미드표현

What?! Are you insane? 뭐?! 너 제정신이야?

Are you insane? We're in an elevator. Don't try to undress me.
미쳤니? 엘리베이터 안이잖아. 왜 옷을 벗기려고 그래.

What were you thinking? Staying out all night! Are you insane?
무슨 생각으로 그런거야? 밤새 들어오지 않다니! 너 미쳤어?

004 She is nuts, right? 그 여자 미쳤지, 맞지?

This is a way of asking "Is she crazy?." The speaker wants to know if a person is usually strange

| Point | go[be] nuts 미치다, 무척 화나다
This is nuts 이건 미친 짓이야
I must be nuts 내가 정신나간 게 틀림없어
Are you nuts? 너 미쳤니?

A: Jessica told me she wanted to date three guys at the same time. 제시카가 자긴 동시에 3명과 데이트를 하고 싶다고 했어.

B: No way! **She is nuts,** right? 말도 안돼! 걔 미쳤구만, 맞지?

Kevin, will you stop? This is nuts.
케빈, 그만 좀 할래? 이건 미친 짓이야.

He's gonna go nuts. 걔가 무척 화낼거야.

He's a nut case. He's been driving my boss crazy. 걘 미치광이야. 내 사장을 돌게 만들어.

005 Are you all there? 너 제 정신이야?

this often means "Do you have some mental problem?" It is an unkind way to tell people they are weird

| Point | He's not all there 잰 정신나갔나봐

A: **Are you all there?** 너 제 정신이야?

B: Yeah, sorry I've been acting strangely.
어, 이상하게 행동해서 미안.

미드표현

Are you all there? You are acting strange.
너 제정신이야? 너 이상하게 행동하잖아.

People think you are a bit odd. Are you all there? 사람들이 너 좀 이상하대. 너 제 정신이야?

Are you all there? Do you need me to call a shrink? 너 제 정신이야? 내가 정신과 의사에 전화해줄까?

006 You are not yourself 제 정신이 아니네, 평소랑 다르네

this tells people that they are behaving unusually on a certain day. It is similar to saying "You seem odd today"

| Point | I'm not myself 난 지금 제 정신이 아니야

A: I need to go home early today. 오늘 집에 일찍 가야 돼.

B: Good idea. **You are not yourself.**
좋은 생각야. 평소의 너답지 않구나.

미드표현

You're not yourself right now. 너 지금 제 정신이 아니야.

You have to face it. You're not yourself.
피하지마. 넌 제 정신이 아니야.

You're just coming off the surgery and you're not yourself yet.
당신은 수술 회복중이어서 아직 정상 상태가 아녜요.

007 A little 'Girls gone wild?' 여자들이 좀 광분했다는거지?

this refers to a DVD titled 'Girls Gone Wild' that was popular about ten years ago, featuring young women who were drinking and who took off their clothes. It was not porn because there was no sex and the girls were not professional actresses, but it showed nudity. People jokingly mention the videos title sometimes when they are thinking of women getting drunk and naked

| Point | go wild 열광하다, 미쳐날뛰다

A: Why did those women strip down to their underwear? 왜 저 여자들이 속옷까지 벗은거야?

B: I don't know. Maybe they drank too much and wanted to imitate **Girls Gone Wild?**
몰라. 아마 술을 진창먹고 <Girls Gone Wild>를 흉내내고 싶었나보지.

미드표현

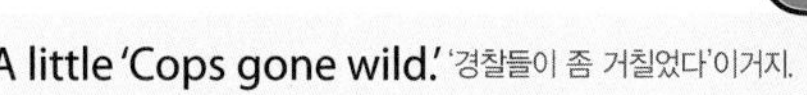

A little 'Cops gone wild.' '경찰들이 좀 거칠었다'이거지.

I mean, what's next, Sam? 'Girls gone wild?'
내 말은 이제 어떻할거야, 샘? "여자들이 깡총깡총뛰는거?"

I know I was a big bitch but you gotta know my hormones are going wild.
난 정말 못된 년인지는 알지만 내 호르몬이 미쳐 날뛰고 있다는 걸 넌 알아야 돼.

008 He's out to lunch 요즘 얼이 빠져있구만

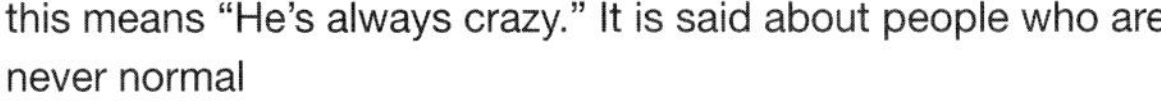

this means "He's always crazy." It is said about people who are never normal

| Point | be out to lunch 1. 점심식사하러 나가다 2. 정신나가다, 정신팔리다

A: Whenever I talk to Brad, he says nothing to me.
브래드에게 말할 때마다 갠 아무 말도 안해.

B: **He's out to lunch.** He doesn't talk to anyone.
얼이 빠졌어. 갠 아무한테도 말 안해.

미드표현

I hate going out to lunch with you CSIs. You notice everything.
너네 CSI 요원들하고 점심먹으러 가는거 짜증나. 모든 걸 눈치채잖아.

He's out to lunch. We don't pay attention to him. 걔 요즘 얼 빠졌어. 걔 신경안써.

Don't worry about Melvin. He's out to lunch.
멜빈 걱정하지마. 걔 요즘 정신없어.

009 I totally spaced 정신이 딴 데 가 있었나 봐

this is a way to say a person couldn't think clearly. It is like saying "I couldn't concentrate"

| Point | You seem spaced out 너 정신이 나간 것 같구나

A: Why couldn't you answer his questions?
왜 걔의 질문에 답을 못한거야?

B: I got nervous and **I totally spaced.**
초조해서 정신이 나가 있었어.

I'm sorry, I totally spaced.
미안해, 정신이 완전히 나가 있어서 말이야.

Shit! I totally spaced. I forgot to buy her a present. 젠장헐! 정신이 완전히 나갔네. 걔 선물 사주는 걸 잊었어.

010 There's nobody home! 정신 어디다 두고 있는 거야!

this is said when it is impossible to communicate with someone. It means "I can't get him to act normally with me"

| Point | Nobody home? 너 제정신이야?(*Anybody home? 집에 아무도 없어?)
The lights are on but nobody's home 정신 어디다 두고 있는 거야

A: Don't bother talking to Jack. **There's nobody home.** 굳이 잭하고 얘기하려고 하지마. 제 정신아냐.

B: He seems a bit crazy these days. 요즘 좀 미친 것 같아.

I look into his eyes and I can see there's nobody home. 걔 눈을 검사했는데 정신이 없다는 걸 알 수 있어.

There's nobody home. You won't get through to Stacey.
정신을 어디다 두고 다니는거야. 넌 스테이시를 이해시키지도 못할거야.

There's nobody home. He's not right in the head. 정신없구만. 걘 분별력이 없어.

011 Take it easy 1. 좀 쉬어가면서 해, 천천히 해 2. 진정해 3. 잘 지내

this is a way to tell someone to "Just calm down." It is used when someone is starting to become upset. And this is also used to tell a person not to work hard. It is like saying "Relax." Finally this is often used as a way to say "Goodbye" when two people leave each other. It is a casual thing to say when parting

| Point | Would you take it easy? 진정 좀 하지?

A: I need to get laid. 한번 자야되겠어.

B: **Take it easy,** lady. I'm married.
진정해요, 부인. 난 유부남인데요.

Hey, take it easy. There's a music box in that bag. 야, 조심해. 가방에 뮤직박스가 들어있어.

You should take it easy for the next few days.
앞으로 몇 일간 좀 쉬어가면서 해.

You only have to be here overnight, but you do have to take it easy for a little bit.
넘 하룻밤만 여기 있어야 되니까 좀 진정하라고.

012 Easy does it 1. 천천히 해, 조심조심 2. 진정해

this is a way of saying "Take your time and go slowly." It indicates that the person should be very careful not to make mistakes

| Point | Easy 천천히, 조심조심 Ease up 진정해
Go easy 천천히 해

A: We have to hurry to complete this report.
이 보고서를 서둘러 끝내야 돼.

B: **Easy does it.** We want the report to be good.
천천히 해. 보고서를 잘 만들어야지.

Easy does it. We don't want to break the machine. 조심해. 우리는 그 기계가 부서지면 안되잖아.

People are getting worried. Easy does it.
사람들이 점점 걱정을 하잖아. 진정하라고.

Easy does it. Just go as slow as possible.
천천히 해. 가능한 천천히 가라고.

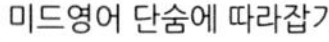

013 Be cool 진정해라, 침착해

미드표현

this means "Stay calm." It is said so someone won't get upset or angry

| Point | Cool down 진정해 Cool it 진정해, 침착해
Cool off 진정해 Play it cool 침착하게 굴어
Stay cool 진정해 Keep cool 진정해

A: I am going to beat him up. 걜 혼내줄거야.
B: **Be cool.** You'll get in trouble if you do that.
진정해. 그렇게 하면 곤란해질거야.

He's coming. Be cool. 걔가 온다. 진정해라.
I'll tell you about it later. Be cool.
나중에 이야기해줄게. 진정해.
I'm gonna play it cool and let him come to me. 침착하게 굴 테니 걔 내게 보내.
Stay cool until I get back. 내가 돌아올 때까지 진정해.

014 Calm down 진정해

미드표현

this is what people say to someone who is upset. It is a way to tell that person "relax"

| Point | Settle down 신성해

A: I can't believe what she just said to me.
걔가 방금 내게 말한 게 믿기지 않아.
B: **Calm down.** Tell me why you feel upset.
진정해. 왜 화났는지 이유를 말해봐.

Will you calm down? 침착 좀 할래?
Just calm down. What's going on?
침착해. 무슨 일이야?
Relax a little bit. Settle down. 좀 긴장을 풀어봐. 진정해.

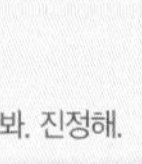

015 Get a grip (on yourself) 진정해

미드표현

this usually means "You need to control yourself. It is said if a person seems like he is starting to act crazy or foolishly

| Point | Get a hold of yourself! 진정해!

A: **Get a grip on yourself.** You're acting crazy.
진정해. 너 행동이 이상해.
B: That's because I feel very angry. 내가 매우 화가 나서 그래.

Get a grip. You're acting too jealous.
진정하라고. 너 너무 질투심을 부리네.
Hey Miles, just calm down. Get a grip.
야 마일즈, 흥분을 가라앉히라고. 진정해.
Get a grip. You can't get so angry.
진정해. 그렇게 화내지마.

016 Are you on crack? 너 약 먹었어?

미드표현

this is an almost joking way to ask why someone is acting oddly. Crack is a form of cocaine, and people who use it are known to behave very strangely. The speaker is not actually asking the listener if he is using cocaine, but rather saying in a kidding way "Hey, your behavior is not normal, so why are you acting that way?"

| Point | be on crack 약을 하다

A: I figure I'll quit school and travel around for a while. 학교그만두고 잠시 여행을 할까봐.
B: **Are you on crack?** You'll never get a good job if you do that. 너 약 먹었니? 너 그러면 절대로 좋은 직장을 못얻어.

With all due respect, Dr. Cooper, are you on crack? 죄송한 말씀이지만, 쿠퍼 박사님 약하셨어요?
If Dan was a gang kid with no dad and a mother who was on crack, we wouldn't blame them for using an environment defense.
댄이 마약하는 편모와 사는 갱단이라면 우리는 그들이 환경을 이용한 변호를 비난하지 못할거야.

017 Keep your shirt[pants] on 진정해

usually this is a way to tell someone that they need to be more patient. The speaker is indicating that the listener needs to relax and wait for a while. In other words, the person is saying "Calm down, you really don't need to be so impatient."

| Point | keep[put] one's shirt on 진정하다, 참다

A: Isn't it time to leave for the meeting?
회의하러 가야 할 때 되지 않았어?

B: **Keep your shirt on.** It doesn't start for another hour. 진정하라고, 앞으로 한 시간 내에 시작하지 않으니까.

I'm right here! Keep your shirt on.
나 여기 있어! 진정하라고.

Put your shirt on. 진정해.

Keep your shirt on. We're leaving! 진정해, 우리 간다!

Tell your friend to keep his shirt on.
네 친구보고 진정 좀 하라고 해.

018 Take a load off 진정하고 앉아

미드표현

this is a way for someone to tell another person to sit down and relax. Often a speaker will say this when someone looks very tired and the speaker wants that person to rest and feel better. Another way to say this would be "Come over here and sit down for a while"

| Point | take a load off 앉다, 안심하다, 마음의 짐을 덜다
There's a load off my mind. 이제 한 짐 덜었다

A: This has been the longest day of my life.
오늘이 내 인생에서 가장 힘든 날이야.

B: Well come inside and **take a load off.**
어서 들어와 앉아서 쉬어.

Why don't you take a load off? You must be tired. 앉지 그래, 피곤할텐데.

Come on in, buddy. Take a load off.
친구야, 어서 들어와, 자리에 앉아.

Have a seat. Take a load off. 자리에 앉아, 긴장을 풀라고.

Can't I just sit down and take a load off before you start in on me!
네가 압력을 가하기 전에 내가 앉아서 좀 쉬면 안될까?

019 Just be yourself 평소대로 자연스럽게 해, 원래대로 행동해

often this means "relax and don't act strangely because you are nervous." Many people think it is better for someone to act naturally

A: Do you have any advice for my interview?
나 인터뷰하는데 뭐 조언해줄 거 있어?

B: **Just be yourself.** They will like you.
평소대로 해, 널 좋아할거야.

I want you to be yourself. 자연스럽게 해.

You just have to be yourself. 자연스럽게 해라.

You can just relax, you know? Be yourself.
그냥 진정하라고, 알았어? 평소대로 행동해.

020 I'm just taking one day at a time 그냥 쉬고 있는 거야

미드표현

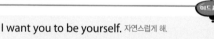

this indicates the person has a difficult situation and is only thinking about the present, not the future. It is a way of saying "I just react to what is happening right now.

| Point | (Take) One day at a time 너무 서두르지 말고 차근차근히 하다

A: I heard that your husband died this year.
금년에 남편이 죽었다며.

B: Yes. **I'm just taking one day at a time** because it's so difficult. 어, 너무 힘들어서 좀 쉬고 있는거야.

Don't get so worked up. Just take it one day at a time. 너무 무리하지마, 서서히 해.

All I can do is take it one day at a time.
내가 하는 거라고는 그냥 서서히 쉬어가면서 하는 거야.

A: What am I going to do? B: You're going to take it one day at a time.
A: 나 어떻게 해야 돼? B: 너무 서두르지 말고 차근차근 해.

021 Take a deep breath 숨을 깊게 들이쉬어, 진정해

this means "Take a moment and calm down." It is usually said when someone is nervous

| Point | Take a breath 진정해

A: **Take a deep breath** and concentrate.
숨을 깊게 들이쉬고 집중을 해.

B: Thanks, coach. I'll do that. 고마워요, 감독님. 그럴게요.

Take a deep breath and think about this.
진정하고 이거 생각해봐.

Why don't you take a deep breath and tell me what happened here.
진정하고 여기 무슨 일이 일어났는지 말해봐.

Take a deep breath before you go inside.
안에 들어가기 전에 숨 한번 깊게 들이쉬어.

022 Just go with it 그냥 그렇게 해

this is a way of telling someone "Relax and enjoy yourself." It indicates the speaker thinks someone should not get stressed

A: Should I be worried about the new culture in this country? 이 나라의 새로운 문화에 대해 걱정해야 돼?

B: No way. Relax and **just go with it.**
전혀. 긴장풀고 그냥 지내.

Just go with it. We have to be supportive.
그냥..이해해줘. 협조해줘야 해.

Don't worry about her weird behavior. Just go with it. 걔의 이상한 행동을 걱정하지마, 신경쓰지마.

Just go with it. There's nothing to get upset about. 그냥 긴장 풀어. 화낼게 아무 것도 없어.

He made you an offer, so just go with it.
걔가 너한테 제의를 했잖아, 그러니 그냥 그렇게 해.

023 Please don't freak out 침작하라고, 흥분하지마

this asks a person not to get too upset. It is similar to saying "Try to stay calm"

| Point | Don't freak me out 놀라게 하지마

A: I have some bad news. **Please don't freak out.**
안 좋은 소식이 있어. 침착하고.

B: Tell me what the bad news is. 안 좋은 소식이 뭔지 말해.

Don't freak out. I'm going to Afghanistan.
놀라지마. 나 아프카니스탄에 갈거야.

Now don't freak out about getting us a present. 우리에게 선물 사주는 걸로 정신없어 하지마.

Don't freak out. Nothing happened.
침작해. 아무 일도 없었어.

024 Lighten up 심각하게 생각하지마, 긴장풀어, 얼굴 좀 펴

this means "Relax." It is often said to someone who is tense

| Point | He'll lighten up 괜찮아질거야
Hang loose 편히 쉬어

A: There is just so much work to be done.
해야 할 일이 너무 많아.

B: **Lighten up.** You deserve a night off.
긴장풀어. 밤에는 쉬어야지.

It's two in the morning. Lighten up Tom.
새벽 2시야. 탐, 긴장풀어.

I know your wife's dead, but it's been six months. Lighten up.
아내가 죽은 거 알지만 6개월 됐으니 그만 얼굴 좀 펴라.

It's a joke. Lighten up. 농담이야, 심각하게 생각하지마.

025 Loosen up! 진정해

This is telling a person that he needs to relax and enjoy things more. Often it is said to a person who commonly acts tense or uneasy and does not seem happy. In other words, the speaker is saying "You need to unwind and have fun."

| Point | loosen up 긴장을 풀다, 늦추다, 맘을 느슨하게 갖다

A: Do you think the restaurant will overcharge us?
식당이 우리에게 바가지를 씌울 것 같아?

B: Why are you always worrying? **Loosen up!**
왜 그렇게 늘상 걱정이 태산이야? 진정하라고!

미드표현

Okay, the whole point of this is to loosen you up a little. 좋아, 이거의 요점은 너의 긴장을 좀 풀어주는 거야.

I said she needed a good banging to loosen her up.
난 걔가 긴장을 풀기 위해서는 멋진 섹스가 필요하다고 말했어.

Loosen up. You always look so unhappy.
긴장풀어. 넌 항상 불행해 보여.

026 Be patient 조바심내지마, 인내심을 가져

this indicates the person should relax and wait for some time. It is a way to advise "It's good to wait"

A: When can I speak to the president?
언제 사장님에게 말할 수 있어?

B: **Be patient.** He is a very busy man.
조바심내지마. 엄청 바쁜 분이잖아.

미드표현

Can't you just be patient? Can't you wait just a little bit longer?
좀 참을 수 없겠니? 좀 더 기다리면 안되겠어?

Not yet. Let's be patient. See what happens.
아직. 인내심을 갖자고. 어떻게 되는지 지켜보자고.

Be patient. It takes time. 인내심을 가져. 시간이 걸려.

027 (You) Back off! 꺼져!, 비켜!, 물러서!, 진정해!

this is a way of saying "Calm down and don't get so upset." People say this when a person seems like he can't control his anger

| Point | back off 뒤로 물러서다, 진정하다

A: I am going to kill Kevin when I find him.
내가 케빈을 찾으면 죽일거야.

B: **Back off.** You need time to cool down.
진정해. 넌 진정할 시간이 필요해.

I'm not talking to you. Back off!
너한테 말하는 거 아냐. 꺼져!

Why should I back off? You back off dude. 왜 내가 물러서야 돼? 네가 물러서라고.

Back off! I need him for right now but you can have him when I'm done. As usual.
진정해! 당장은 걔가 필요한데 나 끝나면 네가 데려가. 언제나처럼.

028 I just lost my head 좀 허둥댔어, 내가 좀 정신없었어

this means "I acted crazy during that time." It is often said when a person wants to explain his strange behavior

| Point | lose one's head 냉정을 잃다, 정신없이 행동하다

A: Why were you acting so badly yesterday?
어제 왜 그렇게 이상하게 행동했어?

B: **I just lost my head.** I was in a very bad mood.
좀 정신이 없었어. 기분이 엄청 안 좋았거든.

I really lost my head last night!
어젯밤에 너무 정신없었어!

I just lost my head. What am I supposed to do now? 너무 허둥댔어. 이젠 뭘 어떻게 하지?

MEMO

Things that are said after someone makes a mistake
잘못했다고 미안하다고 사과하기

I wish I was dead

001 I owe you an apology 내가 사과할게

this is a way of saying the person is sorry. It means "I'm sorry for what I did"

| Point | You owe me an apology 너 나한테 사과해야 돼
Do I owe her an apology? 내가 걔에게 사과해야 하는 건가?
I accept your apology 네 사과를 받아들일게
Tell her, apology accepted 걔한테 말해, 사과가 받아들여졌다고

A: You really hurt my feelings.
너 때문에 내 감정이 상처를 많이 받았어.
B: **I owe you an apology.** 내가 사과할게.

I suppose I do owe you an apology.
내가 사과해야겠지.

I owe you an apology. It's my fault Amy took off last summer.
내가 사과할게. 에이미가 지난 여름에 떠난 건 내 잘못이야.

I owe you an apology. I don't know how I can make it up to you.
사과할게. 어떻게 보상해야 할 지 모르겠어.

002 I came to apologize to you 사과하러 왔어

미드표현

this means "I want to say I am sorry." People do this after they do something wrong

| Point | apologize for+N/~ing to sb …에게 ~을 사과하다
I just want to apologize for that 내 사과할게
Will you accept my apology? 내 사과를 받아줄래요?
Please accept my apologies 내 사과를 받아주라

A: **I came to apologize to you.** 사과하러 왔어.
B: It's OK. I'm not angry anymore. 괜찮아. 화풀렸어.

I have been trying to apologize to him all week! 일주일 내내 걔한테 사과하려고 했다구!

I was just coming over here to apologize for my behavior! 내 행동을 사과하려고 여기 왔다구!

I really think that you should apologize to Bob. 넌 밥에게 사과해야 한다고 생각해.

003 Please forgive me 용서해줘

미드표현

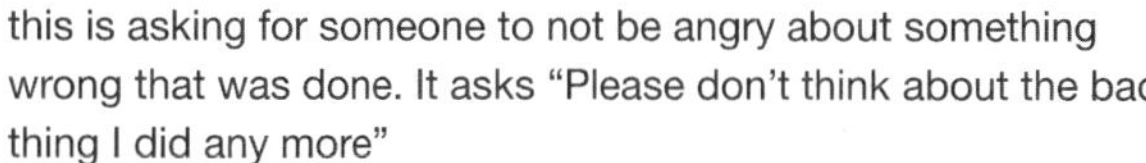

this is asking for someone to not be angry about something wrong that was done. It asks "Please don't think about the bad thing I did any more"

| Point | forgive sb (for~) (… 한 것에 대해) …을 용서하다

A: **Please forgive me** for the bad things I did.
내가 한 못된 짓을 용서해줘.
B: I don't think I can ever forgive you. 절대 용서못하지.

I'm sorry. Do you think you could ever forgive me? 미안. 날 용서해줄 수 있다고 생각해?

Can you ever forgive me for what I did to you? 내가 네게 한 짓을 용서해줄 수 있어?

So, do you think you can forgive me?
그럼 날 용서해줄 수 있을 것 같아?

004 Excuse me 1. 실례지만 2. 미안 3. (불만) 뭐라고? 4. 다시 말해줘?

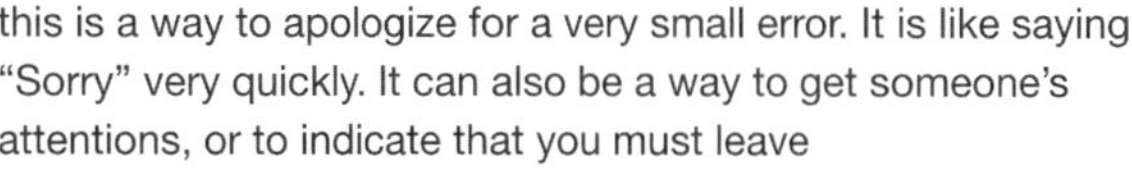

this is a way to apologize for a very small error. It is like saying "Sorry" very quickly. It can also be a way to get someone's attentions, or to indicate that you must leave

| Point | Excuse me "실례지만"의 경우 "말을 걸 때," "자리를 뜰 때,"
그리고 "사람들 틈을 빠져나갈 때" 사용된다
excuse A (for B) A를 용서하다, A가 B한 것을 용서하다

A: I stepped on your foot. **Excuse me.**
발을 밟았네요. 미안해요.
B: Oh, don't worry about it. 어, 괜찮아요.

(Could you) Excuse me for a minute?
잠시만 실례할게요.

Excuse me, I have a question for you.
실례지만 질문할 게 있는데요.

Excuse me, I'm looking for Sheldon Cooper's apartment. 실례지만 쉘든의 아파트를 찾고 있는데요.

005 I'm sorry about that 미안해, … 에 대해 유감이야

like the previous phrases, this is a way to apologize. It means "Forgive what I did"

I Point I be sorry about[for]~ …미안하다, 유감이다

A: You created many problems for me.
넌 내게 많은 문제를 일으켰어.

B: **I am sorry about that.** 그 점 미안해.

I'm sorry about what happened. 이렇게 돼서 미안해.

I'm sorry about this afternoon. 오늘 오후에 미안했어.

I'm so sorry about what I said. I was dead wrong. 내가 말한 거 미안해. 내가 완전히 틀렸어.

That's the truth and I'm sorry about it.
그게 사실이야, 미안하게 됐어.

006 You can't believe how sorry I am 뭐라 사과해야 할지 모르겠어

this is a way to express very deep sadness over doing something wrong. It is a very strong way to say "I apologize"

I Point I Words can't describe how sorry I am 얼마나 미안한지 몰라
I can't tell you how sorry I am 내가 얼마나 미안하지 모르겠어

A: **You can't believe how sorry I am.**
뭐라 사과해야 할지 모르겠어.

B: But you forgot my birthday! 하지만 내 생일 잊었잖아!

I really wanted to tell you how sorry I am.
정말이지 얼마나 미안한지 모르겠어.

I just want you to know how sorry I am.
정말 얼마나 미안한지 알아주었으면 해.

I can't explain how sorry I am about your mom. 네 엄마에게 얼마나 미안하지 말로 못하겠어.

007 I wish I was dead (잘못하고나서) 죽었으면 좋겠어

this is said when a person is very embarrassed or ashamed over something he did. It is similar to saying "I hate myself now because of this"

A: **I wish I was dead!** 내가 죽어야지!

B: Calm down. It's not that bad. 진정해, 그리 나쁘지 않아.

My girlfriend left me. I wish I was dead.
여친이 날 떠났어. 죽었으면 좋겠어.

I wish I was dead. I wish this was all gone.
죽었으면 좋겠어. 이게 모두 끝나버렸으면 좋겠어.

No one seems to like me anymore. I wish I was dead.
더 이상 아무도 날 좋아하는 것 같지 않아. 내가 죽었으면 좋겠어.

008 Pardon my french 욕해서 미안한데

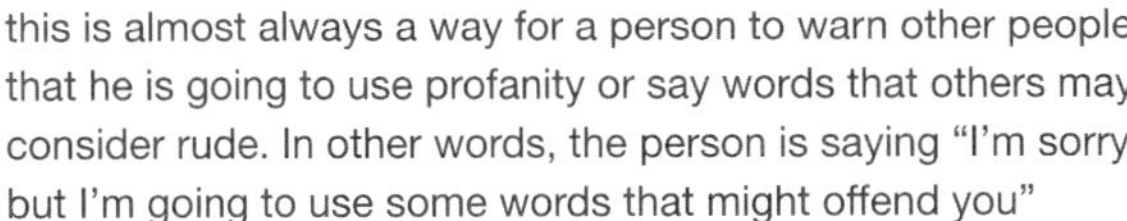

this is almost always a way for a person to warn other people that he is going to use profanity or say words that others may consider rude. In other words, the person is saying "I'm sorry, but I'm going to use some words that might offend you"

I Point I pardon [excuse] my french 상스러운 말이나 욕을 한 후 혹은 하기 전에 사과하다
pardon the expression [language] 이런 말을 써도 될지 모르겠지만

A: **Pardon my French,** but this food tastes like shit. 상스러운 말을 해서 미안한데, 이 음식 맛이 엿같아.

B: Yeah, I don't think we should eat at this restaurant again. 맞아, 다신 이 식당에 오지 말자.

He's an asshole, if you'll pardon the expression. 이런 말 써도 될지 모르겠지만, 걔 머저리야.

Pardon my french, but what's french for 'kiss my ass'?
비어를 써서 미안하지만 '엿먹어라'를 프랑스어로 뭐라고 해?

009 I want to try to make it up to you 내가 다 보상해줄게

this means "I want to do something so you can forgive me." It is said to show someone how sorry the speaker is

| Point | make up 돈이나 빌린 것을 갚다
We'll make it up to you 이 일은 보상해줄게
Let me make it up to you 내가 갚아줄게

A: I am still angry because you shouted at me.
네가 내게 소리쳐서 아직도 화가 나.

B: **I want to try to make it up to you.** 내가 보상해줄게.

미드표현

I screwed up. I'll make it up to you.
내가 망쳤어. 내가 보상해줄게.

What could I do to make it up to you?
보상해주려면 어떻게 해야 돼?

Don't leave. Let me make it up to you. Let me buy you a drink. 가지마. 보상해줄게. 술 한잔 살게.

010 I won't let it happen again 다신 그런 일 없을 거야

this is a way of saying "I'll be careful so the same thing doesn't happen." Often this is part of a way to say a person is sorry

| Point | It won't happen again 다신 그런 일 없을 거야
Don't let it happen again 다신 그러지 마

A: You insulted many of our guests!
넌 많은 손님들을 모욕했어!

B: **I won't let it happen again.** 다신 그런 일 없을거야.

미드표현

I'm not gonna let that[it] happen again.
다신 그런 일 없을 거야.

I just think that Paul will never let it happen.
폴이 다시는 그러지 않을거야.

I know what's going on here, and I'm not gonna let it happen.
여기 무슨 일인지 알아. 다시는 그런 일 없을거야.

011 That's no excuse 그건 변명거리가 안돼

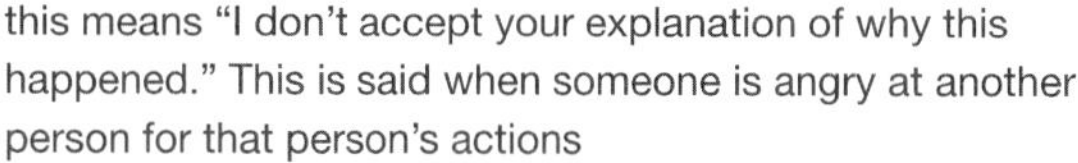

this means "I don't accept your explanation of why this happened." This is said when someone is angry at another person for that person's actions

| Point | That's no excuse for~ 그건 …한 변명이 되지 않아.
I have no excuse 할 말이 없어
I just ran out of excuses 이젠 변명거리도 다 떨어졌어요

A: I couldn't come because my car broke down.
차가 고장나서 올 수 없었어.

B: **That's no excuse.** You should have taken a taxi. 그건 변명이 안돼. 택시를 탈 수도 있었잖아.

미드표현

That's no excuse. I should be punished.
그건 변명이 안돼. 내가 벌 받아야 해.

You're right, I have no excuses! I was totally over the line.
네가 맞아. 할 말이 없어! 내가 전적으로 선을 넘어섰어.

012 There is no excuse for it 그건 변명의 여지가 없어

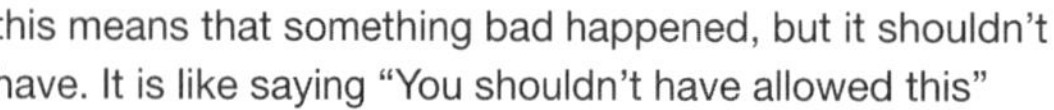

this means that something bad happened, but it shouldn't have. It is like saying "You shouldn't have allowed this"

| Point | That doesn't excuse your behavior 네 행동을 봐줄 수 없어
That hardly explains your actions 그건 네 행동에 대한 변명이 안돼

A: Dad, I'm really sorry that I wrecked the car. I fell asleep. 아빠, 차 망가트려서 죄송해요. 졸았어.

B: **There's no excuse for it.** You shouldn't have been driving. 변명의 여지가 없다. 운전을 하면 안되는 거였는데.

미드표현

That's no excuse for standing me up.
그건 날 바람맞힌 변명이 되지 않아.

This work is sloppy. There is no excuse for it.
이 일은 너무 엉성해. 변명의 여지가 없어.

My salary is late yet again. There is no excuse for it. 내 급여가 또 늦게 나오네. 그건 변명의 여지가 없어.

There is no excuse for it. You just can't do that. 그건 변명의 여지가 없어. 넌 그렇게 하면 안돼.

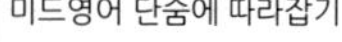

013 Save it 말할 필요가 없어, 변명하지마, 핑계대지마

미드표현

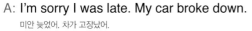

this means "You don't need to explain it to me." It is often said when someone doesn't want to hear excuses from another person

A: I'm sorry I was late. My car broke down.
미안 늦었어. 차가 고장났어.

B: **Save your breath.** You are fired. 그만해. 넌 해고야.

George, save it. I'll be out in ten minutes.
조지, 그만 말해. 10분 후에 나갈거야.

Save it. I know what you're going to say.
그만해. 무슨 말 하려는지 알아.

Save it. I know why you did it.
그만해. 네가 무슨 짓을 했는지 알아.

014 I won't hold it against you 널 원망하진 않을 거야

미드표현

this is a way of saying "I won't be angry at you." It is said when the speaker wants to indicate he won't be upset by some behavior

I Point I hold sth against sb (과거에 받은 상처로) 잊지 않고 계속 싫어하다
Are you still holding that against me? 너 아직 내게 꽁해있니?

A: I'm sorry I didn't come to your wedding.
네 결혼식에 못 가서 미안해.

B: No problem. **I won't hold it against you.**
괜찮아. 원망하지 않을게.

I don't think you should hold that against him. 걔 말 꽁하게 마음 속에 담아두지마.

I said I didn't hold it against her.
난 걔한테 감정 없다고 말했어.

He won't hold it against you. After all, I'm his daughter. 아버진 날 원망하진 않을거야. 어쨌거나 내가 딸이니까.

015 She put me up to it 걔가 선동해서 그 짓을 하게 된거야

미드표현

this indicates "She made me do it." The speaker is saying that doing something wasn't his idea or responsibility

I Point I put sb up to sth …에게 (멍청한 짓)을 하도록 부추키다

A: Why did you choose not to go to school yesterday? 왜 어제 학교 안 가기로 한 거야?

B: It was Andrea's idea. **She put me up to it.**
그건 앤드리아의 생각였어. 걔가 날 그렇게 하게 했어.

Your dad put me up to it.
네 아버지가 날 그렇게 하게 한 거야.

He didn't put me up to this. He was trying to protect me.
걔가 날 이렇게 만든게 아냐. 걔는 날 보호하려고 했어.

He put her up to it? Can you prove that?
걔가 그녀를 그렇게 하게 한거야? 증명할 수 있어?

Ways to comfort people and tell them everything is OK

그럴 수도 있다고 위로하고 걱정말라고 하기

It could happen

001 It happens 그럴 수도 있지

this is a way to express that something occurs normally, and isn't a problem. It is similar to saying "Don't worry"

| Point | It happens to everybody 누구에게나 그럴 수 있어
That happens [happened] 그럴 수도 있지, 그런 일도 있기 마련이지
Shit happens 재수없는 일도 생기는 법이야

A: I think my boyfriend is upset with me.
내 남친이 내게 화난 것 같아.

B: **It happens.** All people in relationships have problems at times.
그럴 수도 있지. 관계를 맺고 있는 사람들 다 때때로 문제를 겪고 있어.

Don't worry about that. That happens.
걱정마, 그럴 수도 있어.

It happens all the time. 항상 그래.

That's OK. It happens sometimes. 괜찮아. 가끔 그래.

It's not unusual, it happens every day.
특별한 것도 아냐, 늘상 그래.

That happens a lot? 자주 그래?

002 It could happen 그럴 수도 있겠지, 그런 일이 있을 수도 있지

this means there is a chance something will occur. It is a way to say "That might occur"

| Point | It could happen to anyone 누구나 그럴 수 있어

A: Do you think that this storm will shut off the electric? 이 폭풍으로 전기가 나갈 것 같아?

B: **It could happen.** Some storms can damage power stations. 그럴 수 있지. 폭풍이 발전소를 손상시키기도 해.

It was a simple mistake. It could happen to anyone. 간단한 실수야. 누구나 그럴 수 있어.

Who knows what could happen?
무슨 일이 일어날지 누가 알겠어?

You never know what could happen.
무슨 일이 일어날 지 모르는 거야.

003 It's not unheard of 새삼스러운 일도 아냐, 흔히 있는 일야

this means that something is not rare, and it may be common or usual. In other words, it has a similar meaning to saying "That thing has happened before" or "I've experienced that in the past"

| Point | It's not unheard of 새삼스러운 일도 아냐, 흔히 있는 일야
It's not unheard of for sb to~ …가 …하는 건 특별한 것도 아냐

A: The weather is very cold. Does it ever snow here in October? 날씨가 매우 춥네요. 10월에 눈이 내린 적이 있나요?

B: **It's not unheard of.** One year we got a snowstorm in September.
흔히 있는 일이죠. 한 해는 9월에 눈보라가 친 적도 있어요.

Outbursts of rage aren't unheard of in a sexual abuse victim.
성적으로 학대받은 피해자에게서 분노폭발은 흔히 있는 일이야.

Mob attack isn't unheard of. 집단폭행은 흔한 일이야.

It's not unheard of for a one-night stand to turn into a relationship.
하룻밤 사랑이 진지한 관계로 변하는 건 드문 일이 아니야.

He's sixteen. It's not unheard of.
걘 열 여섯살이야. 새삼스러운 일도 아니지.

004 I don't blame you 그럴 만도 해, 네가 어쩔 수 없었잖아

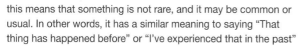

this is like saying "I'm not angry at you." It tells someone everything is OK

| Point | I don't blame you 그럴 만도 해
I don't blame you for~ing 네가 …할 만해

A: Gee Terry, I'm really sorry I spilled coffee on you. 저런 테리, 너한테 커피 쏟아서 정말 미안해.

B: **I don't blame you.** It was an accident.
그럴 수도 있지. 실수였는데.

I don't blame you for being angry. 네가 화낼 만도 해.

I don't blame you for wanting to leave. 네가 가려고 하는 것도 이해가 돼.

A: I don't blame him. B: You know he didn't mean to hurt her.
A: 걔도 어쩔 수 없어. B: 알잖아, 걔가 그녀를 해치려고 했던 것은 아니잖아.

005 What a relief! 아, 다행이야!

this usually means someone is happy at the result of something. It is similar to saying "I feel good that happened"

| Point | I'm relieved to do/(that) S+V~ …하니 다행이야
That's a relief 안심이 된다

A: Mrs. Johnson, I found your glasses.
존슨 부인, 안경 찾았습니다.

B: **What a relief.** I thought I'd have to buy another pair. 다행이네. 안경 사야 돼나 생각했는데.

I'm out of the woods! What a relief!
와 이제 어려운 고비는 넘겼다! 참 다행이야!

I'm relieved to hear that. 그 이야기를 들으니 맘이 놓여.

I'm so relieved you're safe. 네가 안전해서 참 다행이야.

006 That's a load off my mind 그럼 안심이야, 다행이야, 마음이 좀 놓이네

this is a way to say "It's a relief to me." The speaker is saying he feels much better about something

| Point | be a load off one's mind 마음이 편해지다
take a load off (your feet) 앉다, 눕다

A: We have canceled tonight's camping trip.
오늘 밤 캠핑여행 취소했어.

B: **That's a load off my mind.** I wasn't prepared to go. 다행이야. 난 준비가 안 되었었거든.

That is a load off my mind. Well, thank you.
마음이 놓이네. 어 고마워.

It must be quite a load off to finally say it out loud. 마침내 얘길 하고 나면 마음이 한결 편해지는 거야.

Have a seat. Take a load off. 자리에 앉아. 앉아.

007 What a shame! 안됐구나!, 안타깝다!

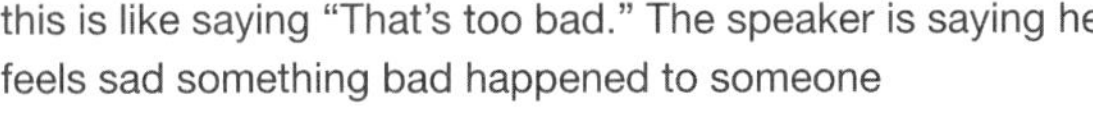

this is like saying "That's too bad." The speaker is saying he feels sad something bad happened to someone

| Point | What a pity! 그것 참 안됐구나!

A: Jack fell and broke his leg while skiing.
잭이 스키타다 넘어져 다리가 부러졌어.

B: **What a shame!** How long will it take him to get better? 안됐네! 나아지는데 얼마나 걸릴까?

Would you look at this? What a shame.
이것 좀 봐. 너무 안됐다.

What a shame. I really wanted her to have a chance to get to know you.
이런, 걔한테 널 소개시켜주고 싶었는데.

008 You're not alone 너만 그런 게 아니야, 넌 혼자가 아이냐

this is usually said when one person feels he is in a similar situation as another person. It expresses the feeling "Me too"

A: I have to study hard tonight. 오늘 밤에 공부해야 돼.

B: **You're not alone.** I have a big exam tomorrow.
너만 그런 게 아냐. 내일 난 중요한 시험이 있어.

If you're looking for someone to talk to, you're not alone. 누군가 얘기할 사람을 찾는다면 넌 혼자가 아니야.

You're not alone. Don't pretend to be.
넌 혼자가 아니야. 그런 척 하지마.

You're not alone in this. We are all here for you. 여긴 넌 혼자가 아니야. 우리 모두 널 위해 여기 있어.

009 That's too bad 저런, 안됐네, 이를 어쩌나

미드표현

this is similar to the phrase "That's a shame." It means the speaker feels sad because someone had bad luck

| Point | It's too bad (that S+V) (…가) 안됐네

A: None of my friends e-mailed me today.
오늘 내 친구들 아무도 내게 이메일을 안 보냈어.

B: **That's too bad.** Are you feeling lonely?
안됐네. 외로워?

That's too bad. I was really looking forward to meeting her. 안됐네. 걜 정말 보길 원했는데.

That's too bad that didn't work out.
그게 잘 안돼서 안됐네.

It's too bad you're leaving. 네가 떠나서 안됐어.

010 I pity you 네가 불쌍해, 네가 안됐어

미드표현

this expresses sadness for the difficult situation that someone else is in. Often people say this when they see someone has experienced bad luck doing something. It is like saying "I'm sorry to see you having problems"

| Point | pity sb …을 동정하다, 불쌍해하다

A: I've been assigned to work with Mr. Shore.
쇼어 씨와 함께 일하라고 배정받았어.

B: **I pity you.** That guy is a real jerk.
안됐네. 그 사람은 완전 머저리인데.

Oh, I don't hate you, Pam. I pity you.
팸, 난 널 싫어하지 않아. 동정해.

You have to pity any woman who makes that mistake. 저런 실수를 하는 여자는 누구나 불쌍히 여겨야 돼.

Don't pity this kid, I envy him.
이 아이를 동정하지마, 난 부러워하는데.

No one likes to be pitied.
동정받기를 좋아하는 사람은 없어.

011 That hurts 그거 안됐네, 마음이 아파

미드표현

this is often a way to say something seems sad or painful. It is like saying "It seems like a bad thing"

| Point | It hurts (sb) to do/ that S+V …하는 것이 아프다
It hurts like hell 엄청 아파

A: My dad is very disappointed with my career.
아빠가 내가 하는 일에 매우 실망하셨어.

B: **That hurts.** Why doesn't he like what you do?
안됐다. 왜 아빠가 네 일을 싫어하셔?

Do you have any idea how much that hurts?
그게 얼마나 아픈지 알기나 해?

It hurts that he's gone. 걔가 가서 마음이 아파.

So you're not going to tell me where it hurts?
그럼 어디가 아픈지 말 안할거야?

012 I'm sorry to hear that 안됐네, 유감이야

미드표현

this is indicating the speaker feels pity for someone. It is like saying "That's too bad"

| Point | I'm sorry to hear about ~/that S+V …가 안됐네

A: My mother got really sick this weekend.
엄마가 이번 주에 정말 아프셨어.

B: **I'm sorry to hear that.** Is she feeling better now? 안됐네. 지금은 좀 좋아지셨어?

I'm sorry to hear that. I was hoping you both would get married. 안됐네. 너희들 결혼하길 바랐었는데.

I'm sorry to hear about your tragedy.
네가 불행을 겪어 안됐어.

I'm sorry to hear that he was murdered.
걔가 살해되다니 안됐네.

013 That's not good 안됐구나, 안 좋군

미드표현

this indicates that there is some problem. It's like saying "Something is bad"

A: The doctor said I should come in and spend the day in the hospital.
의사가 내가 병원에 와서 하루 종일 보내야 한다고 했어.

B: **That's not good.** What problems are you having? 안 좋구만. 어디가 안 좋대?

I guess he's taking Thursday afternoons off now. That's not good.
걔는 목요일 오후들을 휴가내는 것 같아. 별로 좋지 않은데.

That's not good. I thought I handled it.
좋지 않은데. 난 내가 처리했다고 생각했어.

A: They found explosive residue in Tariq's garage. B: Well, that's not good.
A: 타리크의 차고에서 폭발잔여물이 발견됐어. B: 그거 안 좋은데.

014 Don't be so hard on yourself 너무 자책하지마

미드표현

the speaker is saying "Don't be sad because you made a mistake." It is a way of telling someone to relax and not be stressed about something that was done wrong

I Point I be hard on~ …을 힘들게 하다

A: I made my baseball team lose the game.
나 때문에 내 야구팀에 게임에서 졌어.

B: **Don't be so hard on yourself.** It wasn't your fault. 너무 자책하지마. 네 잘못이 아냐.

Don't be so hard on yourself. You were only sixteen. 넘 자책마. 넌 아직 열 여섯 살이잖아.

Don't be so hard on yourself. You are a good person. 넘 자책마. 넌 좋은 얘야.

Don't be so hard on yourself. Everybody makes mistakes. 넘 자책마. 다들 실수하는 거야.

015 Stop[Quit] beating yourself up 그만 자책해, 너무 죄책감 느끼지마

미드표현

like the previous phrase, this tells someone that everything is OK. It means "Don't worry about your mistake"

I Point I Stop torturing yourself 자학하지마

A: I feel like I can't do anything right these days.
요즘 아무 것도 제대로 못할 것 같아.

B: **Stop beating yourself up.** You do things just fine. 그만 자책해. 괜찮게 하는 구만.

Quit beating yourself up and just do it.
그만 자책하고 그냥 해봐.

Stop beating yourself up! People make mistakes! These things happen!
그만 자책해! 사람들 실수하는 거야! 이런 일들 생기게 마련이야!

Steve, you gotta stop beating yourself up.
스티브, 그만 죄책감 느끼라고.

016 Don't feel so bad about it 너무 속상해하지마, 너무 맘아파 하지마

미드표현

this is said to tell someone to "Cheer up." It means that person's problem is not too big

I Point I feel (so) bad about + N/~ing …에 기분이 몹시 상하다
Don't be so serious 그렇게 심각해할 거 없어

A: The bank said that I have almost no money left.
은행은 내 잔고가 거의 없다고 했어.

B: **Don't feel so bad about it.** A lot of people don't have money. 속상해하지마. 많은 사람들이 돈 없다고.

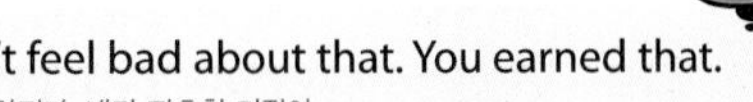

Don't feel bad about that. You earned that.
속상해하지마. 네가 자초한 거잖아.

Does anybody else feel bad about him?
걔한테 속상해있는 사람 누구 있어?

I feel bad about the way he treated me.
걔가 날 대하는 태도에 속상해.

017 I know the feeling 그 심정 내 알겠어, 그 기분 이해해, 무슨 느낌인지 알아

this is a way for the speaker to say "I understand the way you are thinking now." The speaker wants to say he has had the same feeling in the past

I Point I know the feeling 기분을 이해하다

A: My favorite sports team has been losing games lately. 내가 가장 좋아하는 스포츠팀이 최근 지고 있어.

B: **I know the feeling.** My team isn't doing well either. 그 심정 알겠어. 내가 좋아하는 팀도 역시 잘 못해.

A: I never thought a woman would ever even want me. B: I know the feeling.
A: 여자들이 날 절대 좋아하지 않을 거라고 생각했었어. B: 나도 그 느낌 알아.

I know the feeling. It's like accidentally walking into a gay bar and then having no one hit on you.
그 심정 알아. 우연히 게이바에 들어갔는데 아무도 집쩍대지 않는거와 같아.

018 I know just how you feel 어떤 심정인지 알겠어

like the previous phrase, this means "I've had that feeling too." It is a way to show that the speaker understands the person he is talking to

A: Sometimes I miss talking to my ex-girlfriend.
때때로 옛 여친하고 이야기나누고 싶어.

B: **I know just how you feel.** I haven't dated anyone in a while. 그 심정 알아. 한 동안 나도 데이트를 해보질 못했어.

I know just how you feel. I had a tough teacher once.
어떤 심정인지 알아. 나도 예전에 엄한 선생 경험해본 적이 있어.

I don't see her anymore because I know how you feel about her.
네가 걔에 대한 심정이 어떤지 알기 때문에 난 더 이상 걔랑 만나지 않아.

Okay, you're right. I know how you feel.
좋아. 네 말이 맞아. 네 심정이 어떤지 알아.

I know how you feel. I miss Leonard, too.
네 심정이 어떤지 알겠어. 나 역시 레너드가 보고 싶어.

019 Join the club 같은 처지이네

this is a very simple way for the speaker to say that his situation is similar to someone else's. Most often it means that two people are having the same type of experience, and that experience is usually not good. It is very much like saying "Yes, me too"

I Point I Join the club (상대방이 같은 안좋은 처지에 놓였을 때) 같은 처지이네

A: This year I was diagnosed with a heart problem.
금년에 나 심장병 진단을 받았어.

B: **Join the club.** I have to go to the hospital every month. 같은 처지이네. 난 매달 병원에 가야 돼.

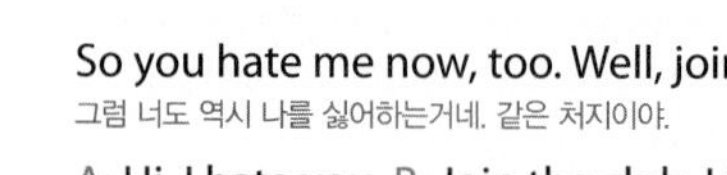

So you hate me now, too. Well, join the club.
그럼 너도 역시 나를 싫어하는거네. 같은 처지이야.

A: Hi, I hate you. B: Join the club, I hate me, too. A: 난 네가 싫어. B: 나도 그래. 나도 내가 싫어.

020 Welcome to my world 나와 같은 처지이네

like the expression "join the club", this means that two people are having similar negative experiences and each one can understand the situation of the other. A similar way to say this would be "That is just like what I have to deal with"

I Point I welcome to my world 같은 처지이네. 나도 그래

A: It's not easy getting up at 5 am daily.
매일 새벽 5시에 일어나는 것은 어려워.

B: **Welcome to my world.** I do it all the time.
나도 그래. 나 매일 그래.

Welcome to my world. We have the same situation now. 나와 같은 처지네. 우린 이제 같은 상황이야.

Welcome to my world. I hope you aren't disappointed. 나와 같은 처지이네. 실망하지 않기를 바래.

A: Ah. I'm an embarrassment to my son.
B: Welcome to my world.
A: 아. 난 아들에게 부끄러운 존재야. B: 나도 같은 처지야.

021 (It's) No big deal 별거 아냐, 대수롭지 않은 일이야

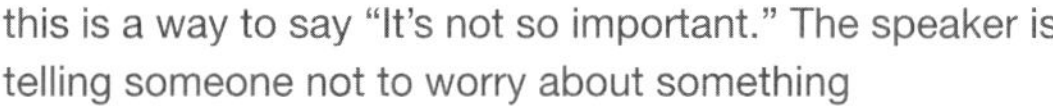

this is a way to say "It's not so important." The speaker is telling someone not to worry about something

| Point | (It's) No biggie 별거 아냐
(It's a) Big fucking deal! 거 참 대단하군!, 별거 아니군!

A: I'm sorry, but I got your magazine wet.
미안해, 네 잡지가 젖었어.

B: **No big deal.** I was finished reading it anyhow.
괜찮아. 뭐 다 읽었는데.

미드표현

It's no big deal, I do it all the time.
별일 아냐, 난 항상 그러는데.

Don't worry about it, no big deal. 걱정마, 별일 아냐.

Everybody knew about it. It was really no big deal. 다들 알고 있었어. 정말 별일 아니었어.

022 What's the big deal? 그게 어때서?, 웬 야단?, 별일 아닌데?

this is asking "Why is there a problem?" The speaker doesn't understand what has caused the problem

| Point | What's the deal? 현재 무슨 일이 벌어지는지 그 이유를 묻는 표현

A: The workers' union is on strike today.
오늘 노조가 파업해.

B: **What's the big deal?** Do they want a higher salary? 웬 야단? 급여인상해달래?

미드표현

I just want to watch a little television. What is the big deal? 그냥 TV보려는 건데 그게 어때서?

What's the big deal? It's just sex.
뭐 대수롭다고. 그냥 섹스야.

What's the big deal about coveting somebody else's spouse?
다른 배우자를 탐하는 게 뭐 대수로운 일이라고 그러는 거야?

023 Don't worry 걱정마, 괜찮아, 미안해할 것 없어

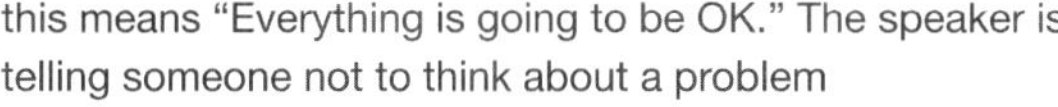

this means "Everything is going to be OK." The speaker is telling someone not to think about a problem

| Point | Don't worry about~ …은 걱정하지마
Don't worry about it 걱정마
Don't worry about a thing 걱정마

A: It's going to be difficult to drive in the snow.
눈길에 운전하기 어려울거야.

B: **Don't worry.** A plow will clear the road off.
걱정마. 제설기가 길을 치울거야.

미드표현

Don't worry about us. We don't drink.
우리 걱정은 마. 술 안마셔.

Don't worry. It's all part of the plan.
걱정마. 계획대로 돼가고 있어.

Don't worry about it. It's not a problem.
걱정마. 문제도 아냐.

024 Not to worry 걱정 안 해도 돼

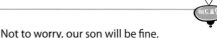

this is said to make people relax. It means "There is no problem"

| Point | not to worry about~ …에 걱정하지 않다

A: I spilled some milk on your new carpet.
너 새로 산 카펫에 우유를 좀 엎질렀어.

B: **Not to worry.** I can clean it up.
걱정 안 해도 돼. 깨끗이 씻을 수 있어.

미드표현

Not to worry, our son will be fine.
걱정 안 해도 돼, 우리 애는 괜찮을 거야.

Not to worry, I have a plan. 걱정 안 해도 돼, 계획이 있어.

He said not to worry about that.
걔가 그거 걱정 안 해도 된다고 했어.

025 There's nothing to worry about

걱정할 것 하나도 없어, 다 잘 될거야

미드표현

this usually means "You are stressed for no reason." The speaker is telling someone that there is no reason to be upset.

| Point | You got[have] nothing to worry about 걱정할 것 없어
You don't have to worry 걱정할 필요가 없어

A: The plane has been delayed for 2 hours.
비행기가 2시간 연착되고 있어.

B: **There's nothing to worry about.** We'll get home in time. 걱정할 것 없어. 집에 늦지않게 도착할거야.

You got nothing to worry about. It's you I'm marrying. 걱정할 것 없어. 내가 결혼하는 사람은 너야.

Trust me, you got nothing to worry about, all right? 날 믿어, 걱정하나도 하지 말고, 알았지?

If that's true, you got nothing to worry about.
그게 사실이라면, 걱정할 것 없지.

026 Don't give it a second thought

걱정하지마, 두번 생각할 필요없어

미드표현

this is telling someone not to worry about something. It indicates "Everything is taken care of"

| Point | give it a second thought 걱정하다, 자꾸 생각하다

A: I am not sure how to cook a Western breakfast.
서양 아침식사를 어떻게 요리하는지 모르겠어.

B: **Don't give it a second thought.** I'll cook it.
걱정마. 내가 할게.

It's no problem. Don't give it a second thought. 그건 문제도 아니니 걱정하지마.

Don't give it a second thought. I'll take care of everything. 걱정하지마. 내가 다 알아서 할게.

Don't give it a second thought. We hired someone to drive you.
걱정하지마, 널 차로 데려다 줄 사람을 구했어.

027 No problem

(감사에) 뭘, (사과에) 괜찮아, (부탁에) 그럼, 기꺼이, (걱정) 문제 없어

미드표현

often this is said to indicate "It's okay." People say this when they want someone to know that everything is good

| Point | No problem at all 괜찮고 말고
(It's) No trouble 아무 문제없어, 걱정마
No[Never] fear 걱정마, 문제 없어(내가 할게)

A: Were you able to finish the work? 일끝낼 수 있었어?

B: **No problem.** It only took me a short time.
그럼, 잠깐걸려 했어.

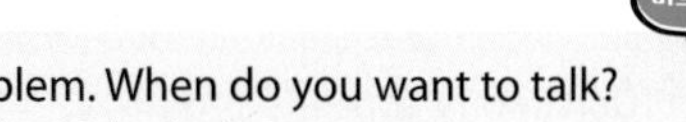

No problem. When do you want to talk?
그러죠, 언제쯤 얘기하고 싶으세요?

No problem. Let's make it at five.
문제 없어요. 그럼 5시로 하죠.

Sure, no problem. How about Thursday?
그럼요 괜찮구말구요, 목요일은 어떠세요?

028 No sweat

걱정마, 힘든 일 아니야, 문제 없어

미드표현

usually this means "It was easy." It is a way to say some task wasn't difficult

A: What did you think of the university entrance exam? 대학입학시험 어떻게 생각했어?

B: **No sweat.** It wasn't as difficult as people said it would be. 쉬웠어. 사람들이 그러는 것보다 안 어려웠어.

No sweat. We can try again tomorrow.
걱정마, 우리 내일 다시 시도해보면 돼.

No sweat. The workers will fix everything.
걱정마. 근로자들이 모든 것을 고칠거야.

I can help with your homework. No sweat.
내가 너 숙제하는거 도와줄게. 걱정마.

029 Don't sweat it! (별일 아니니) 걱정하지 마라!, 그런 일로 진땀빼지마!, 신경쓰지마!

this tells people "Don't be stressed." It is said when someone is worrying too much about something

A: I wasn't able to fix the coffee machine.
커피메이커를 수리할 수가 없었어.

B: **Don't sweat it.** We can buy another one.
걱정하지마. 다른 거 사지.

Don't sweat it. Call me anytime.
걱정마. 아무 때나 전화해.

Don't sweat it, amigo. I know which way they went. 걱정마. 친구. 걔들이 어디로 갔는지 알아.

Don't sweat it. I've got bigger things to worry about now. 신경쓰지마. 더 중요한 일들이 있어.

030 What's the worst(thing) that could happen?

무슨 나쁜 일이야 생기겠어?

미드표현

this is usually said when the speaker thinks "Everything will be OK." He doesn't think anything bad will happen

A: I don't think Jason should go to Tokyo alone.
제이슨이 혼자 도쿄에 가서는 안될 것 같아.

B: **What's the worst that could happen?** Do you think he'll have problems? 무슨 나쁜 일이야 생기겠어? 문제가 생길거라고 생각해?

Take a chance, I mean, what's the worst that could happen? 한 번 해봐, 내 말은 무슨 나쁜 일이야 있겠어?

Just ask her out. What's the worst thing that could happen? 걔하고 데이트 신청해봐. 뭐 나쁜 일이야 있겠어?

What's the worst that could happen, you kill him? 무슨 나쁜 일이야 생기겠어, 네가 걜 죽일거야?

031 It was nothing 별일 아녔어, 아무 것도 아녔어

미드표현

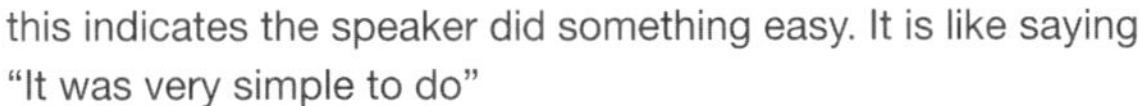

this indicates the speaker did something easy. It is like saying "It was very simple to do"

I Point I Nothing in particular 별일 아냐
Nothing special 별일 아냐
There's nothing to it 그거 별거 아니야, 간단한 일이야

A: Thank you for cleaning up after the party.
파티 후에 깨끗이 청소해줘 고마워.

B: **It was nothing.** I wanted to help you out.
별것도 아닌데. 도와주고 싶었어.

I'm fine. It was nothing. 난 괜찮아. 별일 아냐.

It was nothing. I just called to see how you were doing. 별일 아냐. 그냥 안부 전화한 거야.

It was nothing. It was no big deal.
아무 일도 아냐. 별일 아녔어.

032 Don't bother 소용없어, 신경쓰지마, 괜한 고생하지마, 그럴 필요없어

미드표현

this is a way to tell someone "Don't do it." It is a way to cancel something that was going to happen

I Point I Don't bother ~ing 괜히 …하지마

A: I think I should call Sara and see how she is feeling. 새라에게 전화해서 기분이 어떤지 물어봐야겠어.

B: **Don't bother.** I already did it this afternoon.
그러지마. 오늘 오후에 내가 했어.

Do it right or don't bother doing it at all.
제대로 하거나 아니면 아예 하지를 말고.

Don't bother. I'm not hungry. 신경쓰지마. 나 안 배고파.

Okay, you know what? Don't bother coming over tonight. 좋아, 저 말이야. 괜히 오늘밤에 들르지마.

Don't bother looking. Whatever you order, they'll just bring you something different.
괜히 쳐다보지마. 네가 뭘 주문하든 걔네들은 다른 것을 가져올거야.

033 Don't let it bother you 너무 신경 쓰지마, 그냥 무시해

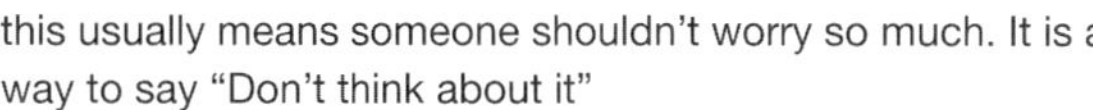

this usually means someone shouldn't worry so much. It is a way to say "Don't think about it"

| Point | Does it bother you (to do~)? (…하는 게) 거슬리니?
Don't let sth[sb] get you down 그 사람 (그것) 때문에 괴로워하지마
Don't let sth[sb] get to you 그 사람(그것) 때문에 신경쓰지마

A: Those boys were saying that I'm ugly.
저 얘들이 내가 못생겼다고 그래.

B: They're just teasing. **Don't let it bother you.**
그냥 놀리는 거야. 너무 신경쓰지마.

미드표현

Does that smell bother you? 저 냄새 때문에 신경쓰여?

This doesn't bother you? Any of this?
이거 때문에 신경거슬리지 않아? 조금도?

Don't let the bastards wear you down.
(싸움) 지면 안 돼.

Don't let him get to you. He can be a real S.O.B.
걔 때문에 신경쓰지마. 걘 정말 개자식이야.

034 Don't fret! 걱정하지마, 너무 초조해하지마

this tells someone "relax." It means that the person shouldn't think much about a problem

| Point | Fret not 걱정마

A: I can't sleep because of all the stress in my life right now. 지금 스트레스 때문에 잠을 못자겠어.

B: **Don't fret.** You'll find a way to solve your problems. 너무 초조해하지마, 해결할 길을 찾을거야.

미드표현

Honey, don't you fret about that deposit.
자기야, 보증금은 걱정마.

Don't fret. Things will work out in the end.
걱정마, 결국 일들이 잘 해결될거야.

Everything is already under control. Don't fret. 모든 게 다 잘 관리되고 있어. 걱정마.

The kid is tech savvy, but fret not, I am tech savvier.
그 아이는 기술에 능통하지만 걱정하지마 내가 더 능통하니까.

035 Never mind 신경쓰지마, 맘에 두지마

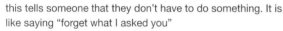

this tells someone that they don't have to do something. It is like saying "forget what I asked you"

| Point | Never mind sth …을 신경쓰지마
Never you mind 신경쓸 거 없어, 네 알 바 아니야
Think nothing of it (감사 혹은 미안하다고 하는 상대방에게) 마음쓰지마

A: Do you still want to go to the zoo on Saturday?
아직도 토요일에 동물원가고 싶어?

B: **Never mind.** I decided to go somewhere else.
신경쓰지마. 다른 곳으로 가는 걸로 정했어.

미드표현

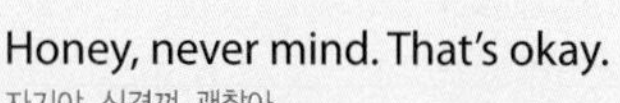

Honey, never mind. That's okay.
자기야, 신경꺼, 괜찮아.

Never mind, I don't want to know.
신경쓰지마, 알고 싶지 않아.

Never mind what I want. What do you want?
내가 원하는 건 신경쓰지마, 네가 원하는 건 뭐야?

Think nothing of it. It was a simple problem.
마음쓰지마, 간단한 문제였는걸.

036 Forget (about) it! 잊어버려, 됐어

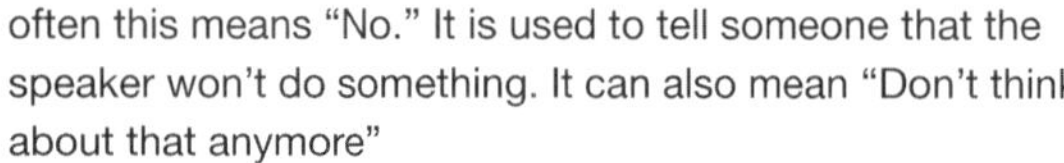

often this means "No." It is used to tell someone that the speaker won't do something. It can also mean "Don't think about that anymore"

A: Can I borrow your new sports car tonight?
오늘 저녁에 새로 산 네 스포츠카 빌려줄래?

B: **Forget about it.** I never lend it to anyone.
됐네, 절대 아무에게도 빌려주지 않아.

Oh, forget it. It's not that important.
저기 잊어버려, 그리 중요한 것도 아냐.

Forget about it. It's not gonna be that easy.
잊어버려, 그렇게 쉽지 않을 거야.

I think it's best that we just forget about it.
잊어버리는 게 최선인 것 같아.

037 Ignore it 신경꺼

this is like saying "Pretend it isn't there." Often it means the person should relax and not worry about the thing that is being ignored

I Point I ignore 무시하다, 신경쓰지 않다

A: I think those people are talking badly about me.
저 사람들이 날 험담하는 것 같아.

B: **Ignore it.** They are just foolish old women.
무시해. 멍텅구리 할망구들인데.

No matter how hard we try to ignore it or deny it, eventually the lies fall away.
우리가 아무리 힘들게 무시하고 거부를 해도 결국 거짓말은 들키기 마련이야.

The threat came from some fool on the Internet. Ignore it.
협박은 인터넷의 어떤 멍청이들로부터 온거잖아. 무시해.

That noise is from a garbage truck. Ignore it.
저 소음은 쓰레기 트럭에서 나는 소리야. 신경쓰지마.

038 Are you all right? 괜찮아?

this is asking if someone has a problem. It is similar to asking "What's the matter?"

A: You look kind of sick. **Are you all right?**
너 좀 아파보여. 괜찮아?

B: I think I got food poisoning at the restaurant.
식당에서 먹고 식중독에 걸린 것 같아.

You all right? You seem injured. 괜찮아? 다친 거 같아.

Michael? Are you all right? You look awful.
마이클 괜찮아? 안 좋아보여.

You look like a man who just rolled out of bed. You all right? 방금 침대에서 나온 사람 같아. 괜찮아?

039 I'm all right with that 난 괜찮아

this is a way to say "That is OK with me." It indicates someone's feeling about something is good

I Point I They seem all right with that 그들은 괜찮은 거 같아

A: Is it alright if I give Tim your old tennis shoes?
팀에게 네 낡은 테니스화 줘도 돼?

B: **I'm all right with that.** I don't use them anymore. 난 괜찮아. 더 이상 신지도 않는데.

I'm all right. I'm okay. 난 괜찮아.

I see your point. I'm all right with it.
네가 무슨 말하는지 알겠어, 괜찮아.

You-you all right with this meeting?
너 이 회의 괜찮아?

A: You're really all right with all of this? B: Yeah, yeah, it's cool.
A: 너 정말 이 모든 거에 괜찮아? B: 어, 그래, 좋은데.

040 That's all right (사과 혹은 감사하다는 말에) 괜찮아, 됐어

this usually means the speaker thinks something has no problems. It is like saying "Everything is fine"

I Point I It's all right 괜찮아

A: I'm sorry I made so much noise last night.
지난 밤에 너무 시끄럽게 해서 미안해.

B: **That's all right.** I still slept well. 괜찮아. 잘 잘 잤어.

That's all right, honey, I understand.
괜찮아. 자기야, 이해해.

That's all right. You didn't mean it, did you?
괜찮아. 그럴려고 그런 건 아니잖아. 그지?

It's all right. You don't have to explain.
괜찮아. 설명 안 해도 돼.

041 You're doing OK? 잘 지내?, 별 일 없지?

this is a way of asking if someone is feeling alright. It is like asking "how are you?"

| Point | Are you okay? 괜찮아?
I'm doing okay 잘 지내

A: I heard you were in the hospital. **You're doing OK?** 병원에 입원했었다며. 괜찮아?

B: To be honest, I'm still feeling pretty sick.
사실, 아직 많이 아파.

So are guys doing okay? 너희들 괜찮아?

I'm doing okay. I think it's going well.
난 괜찮아. 잘 되는 것 같아.

What about your kids? Are they doing okay?
너희 애들은 어때? 잘 지내고 있어?

I know this wasn't easy. You doing okay?
이게 쉽지 않았다는 걸 알아. 너 별 일 없지?

042 I'm cool with[about] that 난 괜찮아, 상관없어

미드표현

this is similar to saying "Yes, I agree with that." Usually this is said when a person wants to say something is OK

| Point | be cool with[about] sth …가 괜찮다, 상관없다
be cool with sb(~ing) (…가) …하는 게 괜찮다

A: Can you come here for an interview tomorrow?
내일 이곳으로 인터뷰 오실 수 있어요?

B: Sure, **I'm cool with that.** 물론요. 괜찮아요.

You're cool with this, right? 이거 괜찮아, 그래?

Are you cool with the three of us hanging out? 우리 셋이 놀아도 되겠어?

It's cool with me. It's fine. 난 상관없어. 괜찮아.

043 I'm in good[bad] shape 난 컨디션이 좋아[나빠]

미드표현

this is a way to say "Things are OK with me." The speaker is telling others not to worry about him

| Point | be in bad[good] shape 상태가 나쁘다[좋다]
be in no shape to~ 전혀 …할 상태가 아니다

A: How have things been going with you? 상황이 어땠어?

B: **I'm in good shape.** Everything seems just fine.
난 괜찮아. 다 괜찮아.

Dr. Robbins said she was in good shape.
로빈슨 박사가 걔 상태가 좋다고 말했어.

I was in bad shape back then.
난 그 당시에 몸 상태가 안 좋았어.

She's in bad shape, but she's stable.
걔는 상태가 안좋지만 그래도 안정적이야.

She's in no shape to make that decision.
걔는 그런 결정을 할 상태가 아냐.

044 That's fine by [with] me 난 괜찮아

미드표현

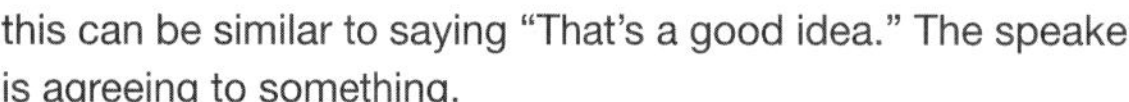

this can be similar to saying "That's a good idea." The speaker is agreeing to something.

| Point | Sth is fine by[with] me …가 난 괜찮아
That's fine=That'll be fine 괜찮을거야

A: We plan to meet at the restaurant at 10 am.
오전 10시에 식당에서 만나기로 했어.

B: **That's fine with me.** I'll see you then. 괜찮아. 그때봐.

That's fine. I'm happy to do it. 괜찮아. 기꺼이 할거야.

That's fine. You didn't do it on purpose.
괜찮아. 일부러 그런 게 아니잖아.

Whoever you're with in there, it's fine by me.
거기에 누구랑 있던지 간에 난 괜찮아.

I think anything that makes you happy is fine by me. 네가 기쁘다면 그 무엇이든지 난 좋아.

045 I have no problem with that 난 괜찮아, 전혀 문제없어

this is said when the speaker thinks something is OK. He is saying "Sure, that's fine"

| Point | have no problem with sb ~ing …가 …해도 괜찮아

A: I would like to take the mirror to my office.
저 거울 사무실로 가져가고 싶어.

B: **I have no problem with that.** 난 괜찮아.

I got no problem with that. 난 괜찮아.

I have no problem with you borrowing this, but you've just gotta understand it means a lot to me.
네가 이거 빌려가도 괜찮은데 이게 나에게 의미가 크다는 걸 명심해.

You've no problem with my talking to him?
내가 걔하고 이야기해도 괜찮겠지?

046 I can live with that 괜찮아, 참을 만해

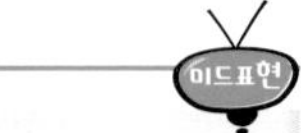

this indicates the speaker feels something is fair. It is like saying "That's OK with me"

| Point | live with sth[sb] 1. (오랜 곤경) …을 참고 견디다, 받아들이다 2. 동거하다 3. 기억 속에 오래 남아있다
Can you both live with that? 그 정도 선에서 둘이 합의하면 인돼?
I could live without it 없어도 돼, 필요없어

A: The lawyer says you need to pay her $2,000.
변호사가 네가 걔한테 2천 달러를 갚아야 한대.

B: **I can live with that.** 그렇게 하지.

I'll just have to learn to live with it.
견디는 법을 배워야 할거야.

I know. And I have to live with that.
알아. 그래 견뎌야지 뭐.

Your mother can come live with us.
네 엄마 오셔서 같이 살아도 돼.

047 No damage 손해본건 없어, 괜찮아

this is said as a reply when a person says they are sorry. It means "Everything is OK"

| Point | (There's) No damage to sth …에 아무 손상이 없어
No harm (done) 괜찮아

A: I'm sorry we caused a problem for you.
너한테 문제를 일으켜서 미안해.

B: **No damage.** Everything turned out alright.
손해본거 없고 다 괜찮아.

No damage to the car, no injuries.
자동차 손상도 없고 다친 데도 없어.

There's no damage to the fuel line.
연료선에는 아무 손상이 없어.

048 What's the harm? 손해볼 게 뭐야?, 밑질 거 없어

this is a way of saying "I don't think this will hurt anything." It is said when a person is going to do something that he thinks won't hurt anyone

| Point | What's the harm in+N/~ing? …해서 손해보는 게 뭔데?

A: You shouldn't eat so much chocolate.
초콜렛 그렇게 많이 먹으면 안돼.

B: **What's the harm?** I'm not getting fat.
밑질 것 없어. 살도 안쪄.

What's the harm in that?
그렇게 한다고 무슨 손해볼 게 있어?

What's the harm in believing? 믿어서 손해볼 게 있어?

What's the harm in telling us that much?
우리에게 그렇게 많이 이야기한다고 손해보는 거 있어?

049 Don't mind me 난 신경쓰지마, 신경꺼, 없다고 생각해

this indicates the speaker is not going to get involved. It is like saying "Go ahead and do what you want to"

A: We're going to the park this afternoon.
오늘 오후에 공원에 갈거야.

B: **Don't mind me.** I just plan to stay home.
난 신경쓰지마. 그냥 집에 있을래.

Don't mind me. I'm not here. 신경쓰지마. 없다고 생각해.

Don't mind me. I'm just getting some ice for my injury. 신경쓰지마. 다친 데 찜질할 얼음이 필요해서.

Keep going, don't mind me. 계속해, 난 신경쓰지말고.

050 I think I can manage 괜찮아, 혼자 할 수 있을거야

this is a polite way to say "I don't need help." People say this to let other people know that they are fine

A: Do you need help unloading your car?
차에서 짐내리는 거 도와줘?

B: No, thank you. **I think I can manage.**
고맙지만, 됐어. 혼자 할 수 있을거야.

I really don't need help. I think I can manage.
난 정말 도움이 필요없어. 혼자 할 수 있을 것 같아.

I think I can manage, but thank you for thinking of me.
혼자 할 수 있을 것 같지만 날 생각해줘서 고마워.

Don't worry about anything. I think I can manage. 걱정하지마. 내가 혼자 할 수 있을 것 같아.

051 You deserve it 1. 넌 그럴 자격이 돼 2. 넌 그래도 싸

this is a way to say someone has worked very hard and should have a reward. It is a way to say "You earned that"

| Point | You more than deserve it 너 정도면 충분히 그러고도 남아

A: I got several prizes for my work.
내가 한 일로 상을 여러 개 받았어.

B: **You deserve it.** It was really excellent.
넌 그럴 자격이 돼. 정말 훌륭했어.

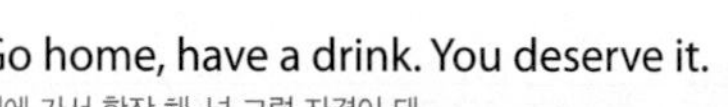

Go home, have a drink. You deserve it.
집에 가서 한잔 해. 넌 그럴 자격이 돼.

I caught her in bed with another guy. Go ahead. Do your happy dance. You deserve it.
걔가 다른 남자랑 자는 걸 봤어. 어서 잘난 척해라. 넌 그럴 자격이 돼.

Well, some people praise children even when they don't deserve it.
어떤 사람들은 자격이 안되는 아이들을 칭찬하지.

052 It's going to be okay 잘 될거야, 괜찮을거야

this is a way to express that later there will be no problems. It means "It will be good in the future"

| Point | It's going to be great 잘 될 거야
You're going to be great 넌 잘 될 거야
This year is going to be great 올해는 다 잘 될 거야

A: I may not be able to come to work because I'm sick. 내가 아파서 출근 못할 수도 있어.

B: Just take the time to rest. **It's going to be okay.**
천천히 쉬어. 괜찮을거야.

It's going to be okay, honey. I'm on my way.
자기야 괜찮을거야. 내가 지금 가고 있어.

You'll see, it's gonna be great for you.
두고 봐, 넌 잘 될거야.

The sex is gonna be great, because you two are in love. 니네들은 사랑하고 있으니까 섹스가 잘 될거야.

053 That'll be fine 잘 될거야, 괜찮을거야

this is a way to say "I agree to that." The person is saying that something is OK with him

I Point I Everything will be fine 다 괜찮을거야
Everything is going to be fine 다 잘될거야
It's going to be fine 괜찮아질거야
I'll be fine in no time 곧 좋아질거야

A: Can I meet with you at 3pm? 오후 3시에 만날 수 있을까?
B: **That'll be fine.** I have free time then.
괜찮아. 그때 시간 돼.

I'm a little unprepared, but it'll be fine.
좀 준비부족이지만 괜찮을거야.

Don't cry. You wife will be fine.
울지마. 네 부인은 괜찮을거야.

He was very eager to get home. Don't worry. He'll be fine. 걘 정말 집에 가고 싶어했어. 걱정마. 괜찮을거야.

054 Everything's gonna be all right 다 잘 될거야

this means that things will be OK in the future. It's a way of saying "It will be better soon"

I Point I She gonna be all right 걔는 괜찮아질거야

A: My daughter is entering high school this year.
딸애가 금년에 고등학교 들어가.
B: **She's going to be all right.** She's a good student. 걘 잘 할거야. 좋은 학생이잖아.

미드표현

Don't worry. The doctor said everything was going to be all right. 걱정마. 의사가 다 잘 될거라고 했어.

Now let's go. It's going to be all right.
자 이제 가자. 잘 될거야.

You're going to be all right. Just hang in there, okay? 넌 괜찮아질거야. 참고 견뎌, 알았지?

055 It's (all) for the best 다 잘되려고 그런 거야, 차라리 잘된 일이야

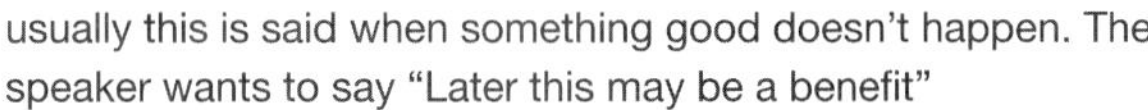
usually this is said when something good doesn't happen. The speaker wants to say "Later this may be a benefit"

A: Bill and Susan decided to split up.
빌과 수잔은 헤어지기로 했어.
B: **It's all for the best.** They were fighting a lot.
차라리 잘 된 일이야. 엄청 싸웠거든.

미드표현

It's all for the best. I mean, I really like Tom, but maybe he's not what I need.
차라리 잘된 일이야. 내 말은 정말이지 탐을 좋아하지만 아마도 내가 필요로 하는 사람은 아닐 수도 있을 것 같아.

I don't know. Maybe it's for the best.
모르겠지만 아마 그게 최선이야.

056 We'll make it through this 우린 이걸 이겨낼거다

this is a way to say "It's difficult, but we will survive." It indicates the people are tough enough to survive hard times

I Point I make it through 어려운 상황을 잘 이겨내다, 견뎌내다
We'll get through it 괜찮아질거야

A: Are you sure you can pay off our debts?
우리 빚을 확실히 갚을 수 있어?
B: Of course. **We'll make it through** these problems.물론, 이 문제들을 이겨낼거야.

미드표현

Don't worry about it. You'll make it through.
걱정마. 넌 잘 견뎌낼거야.

The doctor said she wouldn't make it through the night. 의사가 밤을 넘기지 못한다고 했어.

He does what he has to do to get through it.
걘 이겨내기 위해 뭐든 하는 애야.

057 I'm not gonna hurt you 해치지 않을테니 걱정마

the speaker is saying "Your are safe." He doesn't plan to harm the person he is speaking to

| Point | It's not gonna hurt you 너한테 해롭지 않을거야

A: Sometimes you get angry and scare me.
때때로 넌 화를 내 날 무섭게 해.

B: Don't worry. **I'm not going to hurt you.**
걱정마. 해치지 않을테니.

We're not going to hurt you. We're the police.
해치지 않을테니 걱정마요. 우린 경찰예요.

If you refuse to cooperate, I'm going to hurt you. 협조를 거부하면 널 해칠거야.

Just sit down, Allan. Nobody's going to hurt you. 앉아. 앨런. 아무도 널 해치지 않아.

058 I'm so sorry for your loss 상심에 위로 드립니다

this is said to a person whose family member has died. It is like saying "I feel sad because of this bad event in your life"

| Point | She dropped dead 그 여자는 갑자기 죽었어
He was a goner 그 사람은 가버렸어, 끝장났어
Rest in peace 평화롭게 고이 쉬소서
He's done for 그 사람 죽었어

A: My father died suddenly last week.
아버지가 지난 주에 갑자기 돌아가셨어요.

B: I didn't know that. **I'm so sorry for your loss.**
몰랐네요. 얼마나 상심이 크세요.

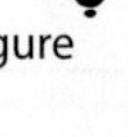
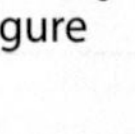

I'm sorry for your loss. We're trying to figure out who did this.
얼마나 상심이 크시겠어요. 누가 그랬는지 밝혀내겠습니다.

He was a car salesman and dropped dead at work. Apparent heart attack.
자동차 딜러였는데 근무중에 돌연사했어. 심장마비같아.

Despite his neighbor's best efforts, he was a goner. 이웃이 많이 노력했지만 그는 이미 세상을 떠났어.

I don't think there is any reason he took his own life. 걔가 자살할 아무런 이유가 없어.

059 Things will work out all right 잘 될거야

this indicates the speaker thinks everything will be fine. He is saying "It will all be OK in the future"

| Point | work out all right[for the best, in the end] 일이 잘 되다
Everything will work out (all right) 다 잘 될 거야
It didn't work out 잘 안되었어, 일이 잘 안 풀렸어
It never would have worked out 애초에 가망이 없었어

A: I'm nervous because I owe so much money.
빚이 너무 많아 짜증나.

B: **Things will work out all right.** Just relax.
다 잘 될 거야. 진정하라고.

I'm sorry it didn't work out for you.
네 일이 잘 안되어서 어쩌니.

I was engaged last year, but it didn't work out. 작년에 약혼했는데 잘 안 되었어.

The DNA didn't pan out, huh? DNA가 잘 안됐지, 그지?

060 This perks him up 이걸로 해서 걔가 기운이 날거야

this means that something causes a person to feel happier and more energetic. In some cases it may be an activity, or it may be something like a cup of coffee. A different way to say the same thing would be "This makes him feel more cheerful"

| Point | sb[sth] perk up 기운나다, 기운을 차리다
perk sb up 기운나게 하다, 활기차게 하다

A: I see you bring your boss coffee every morning.
너 매일 아침 상사에게 커피갖다 주던데.

B: Yeah, **I think it perks him up.** 어, 그거 먹고 기운차리는 것 같아.

I gave her some chocolate. It perks her up.
걔한테 초콜릿을 줬는데 그걸로 기운을 차릴거야.

Visiting my grandparents perks them up.
할머니를 방문하면 걔네들 기운이 날거야.

We should also mention how he always perks up when we watch "Big Bang Theory."
우리가 〈빅뱅이론〉을 볼 때마다 걔가 얼마나 기운이 차리는지도 말을 해야 돼.

Ways of talking about information

정보가 필요하니 계속 알려줘, 말해줘, 그리고 설명해줘

I'll walk you through it

001 Keep me posted 계속 알려줘, 소식을 알려줘

this means "Let me know what is happening." It is a way to say that the speaker wants to know all of the news

| Point | Keep me informed 계속 소식 알려줘

A: Steve is still in the hospital after his accident.
스티브는 사고 후 아직 병원에 있어.

B: **Keep me posted** on how he is doing.
걔가 어떤지 계속 알려줘.

미드표현

Keep me posted on how he's doing, OK?
걔가 어떻게 지내는지 계속 알려줘, 알았지?

You'll keep me posted, right? 계속 알려줄거지, 그지?

I got to go. Keep me posted. 나 가야 돼. 계속 알려줘.

I'll keep you posted with any developments.
무슨 변화있으면 알려 줄게.

002 He filled me in 걔가 알려줬어

this means the speaker was given information. It is like saying "He told me what happened"

| Point | fill sb in …에게 최근 상황을 이야기해주다
Please fill me in 나한테 말해줘

A: Did you get information on the meeting you missed? 네가 참석 못 한 회의에 대한 정보얻었어?

B: Yeah, I met with Doug. **He filled me in.**
어, 더그를 만났는데, 걔가 알려줬어.

미드표현

I ran into the D.A. He filled me in on your case.
지방검사를 만났는데 그 사람이 네 사건에 대해 알려줬어.

She filled me in on your situation.
걔가 네 상황에 대해 말해줬어.

Wherever you're going, please fill me in.
어딜 가던지 내게 말해줘.

003 I'll walk you through it 그걸 어떻게 하는지 방법을 알려줄게

this is a way for the speaker to tell someone that he will show the method of doing something. We can understand the listener is inexperienced at whatever they are doing. Another way to say this is "Watch me and I'll show you how to do it"

| Point | walk sb through sth 어떤 일의 과정이나 방법을 상세히 …에게 알려주다
I'll walk you through it 자세히 알려줄게

A: How do these new computers work?
이 새로운 컴퓨터 어떻게 작동하는거야?

B: Come over here and **I'll walk you through it.**
이리와봐, 내가 어떻게 하는지 알려줄게.

미드표현

I can walk you through it.
내가 그거 자세히 알려줄 수 있어.

We gotta go walk her through the procedure.
우리는 걔에게 그 절차를 상세히 알려줘야 돼.

I'll walk you through the process.
내가 너에게 그 과정에 대해 자세히 알려줄게

You'll walk me through your thought process as a courtesy? 네 사고과정을 내게 자세히 말해줄래?

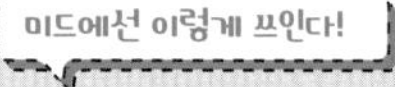

미드에선 이렇게 쓰인다!

Walk him through this

The Big Bang Theory
SEASON#4-15

Sheldon은 Leonerd에게 노부인에게 몸바쳐 섹스하고 학교와 과학을 위해 기부받으라고 하는데…. Sheldon은 이런 몸파는 일(?)에 익숙한 Penny보고 Leonerd에게 방법을 알려주라고 한다.

Sheldon: Penny, you're an expert on trading sexual favors for material gains, walk him through this.
Leonerd: Well, no, hold on a second, I'm not going to sleep with her.
Sheldon: But we need cryogenic centrifugal pump.
Leonerd: Well, forget it! It's not gonna happen.

쉘든: 페니야, 넌 성적인 호의를 베풀어 주고 물질적인 이득을 얻는데 선수잖아, 재한테 자세히 방법을 알려줘.
레너드: 저기, 잠깐만, 난 그녀와 자지 않을거야.
쉘든: 하지만 우리는 극저온 원심분리기 펌프가 필요하다고.
레너드: 잊어버려! 그럴 일 없을거야.

004 I'll pass that along 내가 그거 건네줄게

this is a way of telling someone that important information which was learned will be given to someone else who needs that information. In other words, it is saying "I'll tell other people about this information"

I Point I pass sth along (to sb) (물건, 정보) 넘겨주다, 건네주다

A: Look, people say the cops have been investigating your partner.
이봐, 사람들이 그러는데 경찰이 네 파트너를 수사하고 있대.

B: Thank you for telling me. **I'll pass that along.**
말해줘서 고마워. 다른 사람에게도 알려줄게.

I was asked to pass this along to you.
이걸 네게 건네주라고 누가 내게 부탁했어.

I was told to pass it along to you.
이걸 네게 주라고 얘기들었어.

Fin was kind enough to pass it along to me.
핀은 친절하게도 그걸 내게 건네주었어.

If there's anything of interest, I'll pass it along.
뭔가 관심있는게 있으면 알려줄게.

005 (Here's) A little tip 뭐 하나 알려줄게, 충고하나 해줄게

this is a way to say "Here is some good advice" It is said to someone who may need some help

I Point I Let me give you a little tip 뭐 하나 알려줄게

A: How can I make more money? 어떻게 돈을 더 벌 수 있을까?

B: **Here's a little tip.** You need to work very hard.
하나 알려줄게. 열심히 일하는 거야.

But look, can I give you a little tip?
하지만 이봐, 내가 뭐하나 팁 알려줄까?

You have to spend money to make money, my friend. It's a little tip from me to you.
친구야, 돈을 벌려면 돈을 써야 돼. 내가 너에게 주는 팁이야.

Well, let me give you a little tip.
저기, 내가 뭐 하나 알려줄게.

006 I want you to know that I'm dealing with it
내가 지금 처리하고 있다는 걸 알아둬

this is a way to express that the speaker is trying to solve some kind of problem. We can understand that he is reassuring someone that everything is okay, and he will resolve the problem as quickly as possible. It is like saying "Don't worry, I'm doing my best to fix it"

I Point I I want you to know that~ 네가 …을 알아둬
I just wanted you to know that~ 단지 네가 …을 알아줬으면 했어

A: People have said you are having money problems. 사람들이 그러는데 너 돈 문제가 있다며.

B: **I want you to know that I'm dealing with them.** 내가 지금 문제를 해결하고 있으니 걱정마.

Paul, I want you to know how sorry I am.
폴, 내가 얼마나 미안해하는지 알아줬으면 해

I want you to know that I support whatever you want to do.
네가 뭘 하고 싶어하든 내가 도울거라는 걸 알아줬으면 해.

I just wanted you to know that I don't think Jerry's gonna confess.
제리는 자백하지 않을거라는 내 생각을 네가 알고 있었으면 했어.

007 That would be telling 그런 말이겠구나, 그러면 되겠구나

this is usually said when people are looking for information. An event or action may not tell them everything, but when it might provide some clues, it is telling, meaning that they can guess about some of the information. What the speaker wants to say is "That would allow us to imagine what some of the information is"

I Point I That would be telling 그런 말이겠구나, 그러면 알겠구나.

A: Let's see if she acts nervous when we question her. 그녀를 심문할 때 초조해하는지 보자고.

B: **That would be telling.** It may show us she's guilty. 그러면 알겠구나. 걔가 죄를 졌는지 알려줄 수도 있어.

If he steals something, that would be telling.
걔가 뭔가 훔친다면 그게 뭔가 말해줄거야.

The doctor says if I have chest pains, that would be telling.
의사가 그러는데 내가 가슴통증이 있다면 그게 뭔가 말해주는걸거래.

If your date smiles at you, that would be telling. 네 데이트 상대가 너한테 웃는다면 뭔지 알게 될거야.

008 All I can tell you is we do have a plan

내가 말해줄 수 있는 건 우리에게 계획이 있다는거야

미드표현

this is a way to say "This is the information I can give you." The speaker is saying that the information he can give is limited

| Point | All[What] I can tell you is (that) S+V
내가 말해줄 수 있는 거라고는 …뿐이야

A: Why didn't the bus come today? 왜 오늘 버스가 안왔어?
B: **All I can tell you is that** there was some accident. 내가 말해줄 수 있는 건 사고가 있었다는거야.

All I can tell you is cause of death.
내가 말해줄 수 있는 건 사인뿐이야.

What I can tell you is that you'll see things there that you never imagined.
내가 말해줄 수 있는 건 거기서 상상도 못한 것들을 보게 될거란 거야.

What I can tell you about that is I'm impressed.
내가 그거에 대해 말해줄 수 있는 건 내가 감동받았다는거야.

009 Why don't we just go poke around? 가서 캐물어보자

미드표현

this speaker is telling someone that he thinks it would be a good idea to go look around to see what they can find. Most commonly, this would be said at a crime scene where police want to look for clues. What the speaker is saying is "Let's take a look and see if we are able to find anything important"

| Point | poke around (뭔가 찾으려, 알아내려) 뒤지다, 꼬치꼬치 캐묻다, 조사하다

A: I think this house holds important clues.
난 이집이 중요한 단서라고 생각해.
B: **Why don't we just go poke around?** 가서 파헤쳐보자.

If you poke around a little bit, I bet you could find something.
좀 더 뒤져보면 넌 확실히 뭔가 찾을 수 있을거야.

You should call in a favor from your police detective pal. Have him poke around.
네 경찰 친구에게 도와달라고 해봐. 그 사람이 조사를 해보게 해봐.

I'll ask him a few questions, poke around his story a little.
내가 걔한테 질문 몇 개 던져보고 걔 얘기를 좀 더 파헤쳐볼게.

010 You do all the talking 네가 얘기 다 해봐

미드표현

this speaker is telling someone that he will remain silent, and he expects that person to say everything in the situation they are entering. Often this is said before a meeting, when one person is afraid that if he speaks, he will make a mistake. It can also be expressed as "I'm going to be quiet and let you explain everything"

| Point | do (all) the talking 상황설명을 하다, 얘기를 다 하다
let sb do the talking …가 대변하도록 하다

A: This is the most important meeting we've ever had. 이 회의는 지금껏 어느 회의보다 가장 중요한 회의야.
B: You know the information well, so **you do all the talking.** 네가 정보를 잘 알고 있으니 네가 쭉 얘기를 해봐.

As usual, I did all the talking.
언제나처럼 내가 상황설명을 다 했어.

You guys do all the talking you want.
너희들 원하는 대로 얘기를 해봐.

Let me do all the talking, okay?
내가 얘기를 하도록 할게, 알았어?

011 She put the word out 걔가 사람들에게 얘기를 했어

미드표현

this is a way of saying that a woman told a lot of people about something. It is possible that the woman said something bad about someone, or warned others of some danger. Another way of saying this would be "She told everyone she knows about it"

| Point | put the word out (on~/that S+V) 말을 꺼내다, 사람들에게 알리다

A: How did you know that Nancy's brother got arrested? 낸시의 오빠가 체포된 것을 어떻게 알았어?
B: **She put the word out** that the cops came and got him. 경찰이 와서 그를 데려갔다고 걔가 알렸어.

It gave me time to put the word out on your victim.
그렇게 되면 내가 네 피해자에 관해 말을 꺼낼 시간을 갖게 될거야.

What'd I tell you, Susan? We just had to put the word out.
내가 뭐라고 했는데, 수잔? 우리는 단지 얘기를 해야 했어.

It would help to just put the word out there that we have a dog.
우리가 개를 키우고 있다는 말을 하는게 도움이 될거야.

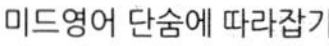

012 It's gonna be all over the news 뉴스마다 그 얘기야

this is often a way to say that something important happened and the news media is going to do a lot of reporting on it. Often this type of thing is something very unusual or unexpected. It can be similarly expressed by saying "This will be covered by many news reporters"

| Point | be all over the news 뉴스마다 계속 나오다

A: I can't believe the mayor was killed.
시장이 살해당하다니 믿기지 않아.

B: **It's going to be all over the news.**
뉴스마다 그 얘기로 도배하겠구만.

미드표현

His face is all over the news. We've got him cornered.
걔 얼굴이 뉴스마다 나오고 있어. 우린 걔를 궁지에 몰았어.

We got reporters outside of the school. This thing is all over the news.
학교밖에 기자들이 와있어. 이 일을 뉴스로 도배할거야.

That girl, she survived. It's all over the news.
저 여자, 살아남았대. 지금 뉴스마다 나오고 있어.

Let's turn then to a subject that's been all over the news lately.
최근에 뉴스마다 나오는 주제로 넘어가보자.

013 I can tell you~ …라고는 말할 수 있어, …하기는 해

usually this indicates that a person is willing to share some information that he has. It is similar to saying "This is the information I can give"

| Point | I can't tell you~ …라고는 말할 수 없다(말하는 내용을 가볍게 부정)

A: Do you think it is a good time to invest in real estate? 부동산에 투자하기에 좋은 때라고 생각해?

B: **I can tell you** that the prices of houses are very low right now. 주택가격이 지금 무척 낮기는해.

미드표현

I can tell you one thing for sure.
확실히 한 가지는 말할 수 있어.

I can tell you what he's going to find.
걔가 무엇을 찾을 지는 말할 수 있어.

I was popular with the people then, I can tell you that. 그 당시 사람들에게 난 인기있었어. 그렇긴 했어.

014 I wanted to keep you in the loop
네게도 알려야겠다고 생각했을 뿐이야

'in the loop' often this means that the person has been informed of all the news. When someone is "in the loop," they are aware of the latest news

| Point | keep sb in the loop …에게 정보를 알려주다

A: Thank you for telling me about the surprise exam. 깜작시험에 대해 말해줘서 고마워.

B: **I wanted to keep you in the loop.**
네게도 알려야겠다고 생각했어.

미드표현

You guys get over there. Keep me in the loop. Keep the media out of it.
너희들 저리로 가. 내게는 알리고 언론에는 비밀로 해.

Maybe if I were in the loop I could be more helpful. 나도 알고 있으면 도움이 될 수 있을텐데.

015 Let me break it down for you 내가 그거 설명해줄게

this expresses that the person is going to carefully give an explanation, possibly about the way something works. It is a way of saying "Let me tell you all about this"

| Point | break it down 설명해주다, 부수다

A: How are we going to organize the fall festival?
가을 축제를 어떤 식으로 할까?

B: Have a seat and **let me break it all down for you.** 자리에 앉아봐, 너한테 설명해줄게.

미드표현

Break it down for me guys, and don't be afraid to be honest.
너희들 내게 설명해봐, 솔직해지는 걸 두려워말고.

Okay then, break it down. List your concerns.
좋아 그럼, 설명해봐. 네 관심사항들을 나열해봐.

Well, let me break it down for you, Mikey.
그래, 마이키, 내가 설명을 해줄게.

016 Do you know anything about ~? …에 대해 뭐 아는 거 있어?

this is asking "Can you tell me about...?" The speaker wants information on something

I Point I Do you know anything about+N/~ing? …에 대해 뭐 알어?
Do you know how to do~? …하는 방법을 아니?

A: **Do you know anything about** playing the violin? 바이올린 연주하는 법 아는 거 있어?

B: I studied violin for a few years when I was young. 어렸을 때 몇 년간 바이올린 공부했어.

Do you know anything about that?
그거에 대해 뭐 아는 거 있어?

Do you know anything about fishing?
낚시에 대해 뭐 아는 거 있어?

Do you know how to cut hair? 머리 자르는 거 알아?

017 Do you have any idea what [who]~? …을 알아?

this speaker is asking if someone has specific information about something. It is like asking "do you know...?" But sometimes "Do you have any idea how~?" can be used for scolding someone

I Point I Do you have any idea how S+V? 얼마나 …한지 알아?
Do you have any idea how painful it is to do~
…하는게 얼마나 괴로운 줄 알아?
Do you have any idea? 뭐 좋은 생각있어?

A: **Do you have any idea what** our class schedule will be? 수업일정이 어떻게 되는지 알아?

B: I think we'll have math class this morning and English this afternoon. 아침에 수학, 오후에 영어가 있을걸.

Do you have any idea what this means?
이게 무슨 의미인지 알아?

Do you have any idea what happened to David last night?
어젯밤에 데이빗에게 무슨 일이 있었는지 알아?

Do you have any idea how dangerous those are?! 저것들이 얼마나 위험한 줄 알기나 해?!

018 Let me know 알려줘, 나중에 알게 되면 얘기해줘

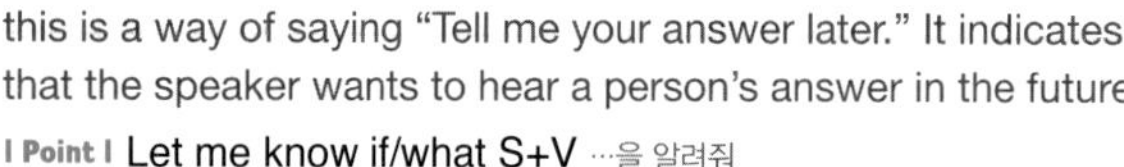

this is a way of saying "Tell me your answer later." It indicates that the speaker wants to hear a person's answer in the future

I Point I Let me know if/what S+V …을 알려줘

A: I'm not sure if I want any coffee. 커피를 먹을까.

B: **Let me know.** I'd be glad to make some.
알려줘. 기꺼이 만들어줄게.

If there's anything else you need, you just let me know. 뭐 다른 필요한 게 있으면 알려줘.

If you hear anything, let me know.
뭐라도 듣게 되면 내게 알려줘.

Let me know what you think. 네 생각이 어떤지 알려줘.

019 You want to catch me up? 무슨 일인지 알려줄래?

this question is asked when someone has not gotten all of the new information about something. The speaker is asking someone else to tell him everything that happened that he doesn't know about. We might understand him to mean "I'd like you to tell me about whatever new information there is"

I Point I catch sb up sb가 없었던 순간에 일어난 일을 말하다

A: We got to the crime scene an hour before you did. 너보다 한 시간 빨리 범죄현장에 도착했어.

B: I know. **You want to catch me up?**
알아. 무슨 일인지 말해봐.

Why don't you catch us up?
무슨 일인지 우리에게 알려줄래?

I think I need to take a little rest. Will you catch me up? 나 좀 쉬어야겠어. 일어나는 일 얘기해줄거지?

How have you been? Catch me up.
어떻게 지냈어? 얘기해봐.

Why don't you catch me up on everything that's been going on, yeah? 무슨 일이었는지 다 내게 말해봐.

020 How so? 어째서 그래?

this is used to ask for more information. It is like asking "Can you explain it to me?"

A: These plants are good for curing sickness.
이 식물들은 병을 치료하는데 도움이 돼.

B: **How so?** How can people use them for that?
어째서 그래? 어떻게 식물들을 치료하는데 써?

미드표현

Really, how so? How badly do you want that coffee? 정말, 어째서? 저 커피를 얼마나 마시고 싶은거야?

A: Well, I'm very surprised by this. B: How so?
A: 나 이거에 정말 놀랐어. B: 어째서 그래?

A: Okay, I'm sorry, but that makes me a little uncomfortable. B: How so?
A: 좋아, 미안하지만 그 때문에 내가 좀 불편하네. B: 어째서 그래?

021 Now what? 그래서 다음엔 어떻게 할 건데?, 이제 어쩌지?

this asks "What will happen next?" It indicates the speaker wants to know what will occur in the future

| Point | Now what? = What now? Then what? 그러고 나서는?, 그럼 뭐야?, 그러면 뭔데?(What'll be next?)

A: I think the fire alarm is ringing. 화재경보가 울리는 것 같아.

B: **Now what?** Are we supposed to go outside?
이제 어쩌지? 밖으로 나가야 하는 거야?

미드표현

So what now? What are we supposed to do?
이제 어쩔거야? 우리 어떻게 해야 되는 거지?

So what now? Should I tell him that I know?
그래 이제 어쩌지? 내가 알고 있다고 걔한테 말해야 되나?

If Susie doesn't approve, then what?
수지가 인정 안 하면 그럼 뭐야?

Let's say that she is gonna be there. Then what? 걔가 거기에 갈 거라고 하자. 그럼 어떻게 되는데?

022 I can't give specifics 세세히 말하고 싶지 않아, 자세히 말 못해

this is said when a person doesn't want to talk about everything. He is saying "I won't tell you the details of it"

| Point | We owe them an explanation 그들에게 해명을 해야 돼

A: Tell me about the work you do. 네가 하는 일에 대해 말해봐.

B: **I can't give specifics.** It's top secret.
세세히 말하고 싶지 않아. 극비야.

미드표현

I can't give specifics, but we're going to have big problems.
자세히는 말 못하지만 우리 앞으로 큰 문제가 닥칠거야.

I know some of the information, but I can't give specifics. 일부 정보를 알고 있지만 자세히는 말 못해.

I can't give specifics. I'm sorry if that's what you were expecting.
자세히는 말 못해. 네가 바라던 게 그거라면 미안해.

023 What does that tell us? 이게 무슨 말이겠어?

this question is asking how much information the speaker and others were able to get from something. It may be a question that is asked after finding a clue. In other words, the speaker wants to know "What did we learn from the information we now have?"

| Point | What does that tell you? 그게 무슨 의미이겠어?
What does that tell us about~? …에 대해 뭘 말해주는거겠어?

A: There is blood on the door. **What does that tell us?** 문에 피가 묻어 있어. 이게 무슨 말이겠어?

B: It looks like the crime was committed here.
범죄가 여기서 벌어진 것 같네.

미드표현

What does that tell us? You can talk now.
이게 무슨 말이겠어? 이제 말해도 돼.

So what does that tell us about the unsub?
그럼 이게 용의자에 대해 뭘 말해주는거겠어?

The minute he got in the same room with my mom they ended up in bed together. What does that tell you?
그가 엄마랑 같은 방에 들어오자마자 서로 침대에서 뒹굴었어. 이게 무슨 의미이겠어?

024 What does it look like I'm doing? 내가 뭐하는 걸로 보여?

this speaker is expressing that what he is doing is very evident, and that anyone observing him should clearly be able to understand what he is up to.

| Point | What does it look like? 그게 뭐같이 보여?, 그게 뭘로 보여?
What does it look like S+V? 그게 뭘 …하는 것처럼 보여?

A: I want to know what you've done for the last hour. 지난 한시간동안 무슨 일을 했는지 알고 싶어.

B: **What does it look like I'm doing?** I'm cleaning the house. 내가 뭐하는 걸로 보여? 집청소하잖아.

미드표현

What does it look like? I'm coming with you.
그게 뭐같이 보여? 내가 너랑 함께 가잖아.

What does it look like he's doing?
걔가 뭐하는 걸로 보여?

What does that look like to you? Opportunities. 네게는 그게 뭘로 보여? 기회들이야.

025 What else is new? 1. (다 아는 사실여서) 그야 뻔한 거 아냐 2. 뭐 더 새로운 거 없어?

this is sometimes a way to say "I know that already." The speaker is saying he knows that something usual has happened or will happen. And this is also a way of asking "Is there anymore new information?" The speaker wants to know if there are any other important thing

| Point | Anything else? 다른 건 없어?
What's the scoop? 새로운 소식이 뭐야?

A: I think it's going to snow again. 또 눈이 내릴 것 같아.

B: **What else is new?** It seems to snow every day.
뻔한 거잖아. 매일 눈이 내리는 것 같은데.

If it makes you angry, well, what else is new?
그 때문에 화가 난다면, 그거 뻔한 거 아냐?

What else is new? Has anything interesting happened? 뭐 다른 소식없어? 뭐 좀 흥미로운 일 일어난거 있어?

Mr. Wilson is complaining again. What else is new? 윌슨 씨가 또 불평을 하고 있어. 그야 뻔한거 아냐?

026 Need I say more? 더 말 안해도 알지?

this is a way for a speaker to indicate that he thinks what he said is clearly right. Because his point is so clear, he feels he does not need to give any more information now. When we hear this, we know the speaker is saying "I don't need to say anything else. You understand what I mean"

| Point | Need I say more? 더 말안해도 알지?

A: So you think we shouldn't hire Chris?
그럼 넌 크리스를 고용하지 말아야 한다고 생각해?

B: No. He's been fired from three jobs. **Need I say more?** 어. 걔는 3번이나 잘렸다고. 더 말 안해도 알지?

미드표현

I'll tell you. I'm from Texas. Need I say more?
내 말하는데 난 텍사스출신이야. 더 말 안해도 알지?

She refuses to co-operate. Need I say more?
걔는 협력을 반대했어. 더 말 안해도 알지?

The company is bankrupt. Need I say more?
회사가 파산했어. 더 말 안해도 알지?

Kelly lied to us many times. Need I say more?
켈리는 우리에게 엄청 거짓말해댔어. 더 말 안해도 알지?

027 I'm springing this on you at the last minute
임박해서[닥쳐서] 말하는데

often this is a way to say "Sorry, but I had no time to warn you." It indicates that something happened very quickly and everyone must react to it

| Point | spring sth on sb …가 예상도 못하고 준비도 안된 상태에서 말을 꺼내다

A: **I'm springing this on you at the last minute, but** we need volunteers for tomorrow.
닥쳐서 말하는데, 내일 자원봉사자가 필요해.

B: What are the volunteers going to be doing?
자원봉사자가 하게 되는 일은 뭐야?

미드표현

Why are you springing this on me now?
왜 이 얘기를 지금에서야 하는 거야?

I cannot believe you are springing this on me an hour before we have to go.
어떻게 가기 한 시간 전에 이걸 말하는 거야.

028 I'll see what I can do 알아보죠, 어디 한번 알아볼게요, 어떻게든 해보다

this is indicating "I will try to fix that problem." The speaker is saying he will try to improve something

A: I think the heater in my apartment is broken.
아파트 히터가 고장난 것 같아.

B: **I'll see what I can do** to fix it. 수리할 수 있나 내가 한번 볼게.

미드표현

I do know what it's like. I'll see what I can do.
그게 어떤 건지 알아. 한번 가능한지 알아볼게.

I will talk to my boss and I will see what I can do. 사장한테 말해서 가능한지 알아볼게.

I know how it works. I'll see what I can do.
난 그게 어떻게 돌아가는지 알아. 어떻게든 해볼게.

029 Isn't it obvious? 뻔하지 않아?

often this expresses that something should be easy or simple to see or understand. People say this when they want to ask "Isn't that easy to understand?"

| Point | Isn't it[that] obvious? 뻔하지 않아?
It is obvious that S+V …는 뻔하다

A: Why is Linda acting like such a jerk today?
린다가 왜 오늘 저렇게 바보처럼 행동하는거야?

B: **Isn't it obvious?** She got bad news from her boss. 뻔할 뻔자지. 사장한테 안 좋은 얘길 들은거야.

미드표현

Isn't it obvious? The bastard nearly raped her to death.
뻔하지 않아? 그 개자식이 그녀를 거의 죽도록 강간을 했어.

Isn't it obvious? I want another kid.
당연한 거 아냐? 난 아이 하나를 더 원해.

Isn't it obvious to you what Tim is planning? He's going to use you to replace me.
팀이 꾸미고 있는게 뻔히 보이지 않아? 걘 너를 이용해 나를 대체하려고 할거야.

030 I think I see where this is going 안봐도 비디오다

this indicates that the speaker understands what is being communicated, and probably doesn't need any more explanation. He wants to let people know that the point is clear to him. It is like saying "I've got what you are trying to say, you don't need to waste more time explaining"

| Point | see where this is going 이 상황이 어떻게 돌아가는지 알다, 얘기 안해도 알다

A: You don't treat me well, and you're always mean. 넌 날 푸대접해, 언제나 야비하게 굴어.

B: **I think I see where this is going.** You want to start a fight. 얘기 안해도 알겠다. 싸움을 걸고 싶은거구만.

미드표현

I'd like to see where this is going.
이게 어떻게 될지 알고 싶어.

She's trying to liquor me up. I can see where this is going. 걔는 날 취하게 하려고 하고 있어. 어떻게 될지 뻔해.

I honestly don't know where this is going. Just following the clues.
이게 어떻게 될지 솔직히 몰라. 그냥 단서를 쫓아갈 뿐이야.

031 What's to know? 뻔한거 아냐?

this is a way for a speaker to express confidence in his own knowledge. It may be said in response to someone who asks him if he knows about something. In responding "What's to know?," we can understand he feels that "I'm not worried about that, I already know everything I need to know"

| Point | What's to know? 뻔한 거 아냐?

A: Have you prepared for today's science test?
오늘 보는 과학시험 준비했어?

B: **What's to know?** It's all just basic information.
뻔한거 아냐? 다 기본지식인데.

미드표현

What's to know? He preyed on young boys.
뻔한거 아냐? 그는 어린 소년들을 먹잇감으로 했어.

What's to know? I was at the top of my class.
뻔한거 아냐? 난 반에서 탑이었어.

This will be easy. What's to know?
이건 되게 쉬울거야. 뻔한거 아냐?

Ways of telling someone to keep or tell a secret

솔직히 말하거나 비밀을 지키거나

Not a word

001 Just keep it down 조용히 좀 해

미드표현

this is asking someone to be quieter. It is similar to saying "Please quiet down"

I Point I keep it down 목소리를 낮추다, 조용히 하다
Please keep your voices down 제발, 목소리 좀 낮춰
Hold it down 조용히 해

A: Would you **keep it down?** 조용히 좀 해줄래?
B: Sure. I can turn this music off. 그래. 이 음악을 끌게.

Shh-shh-shh! Just keep it down. You'll wake up, Mom. 쉿! 조용히 좀 해. 엄마. 깨우겠다.

We'll try to keep it down. 조용히 지내도록 할게요.

Could you guys just keep it down? I'm trying to concentrate. 조용히 좀 해줄래? 나 집중하려고 하고 있어.

I'm gonna have to ask you to keep it down while we're doing our work.
우리 일을 하는 동안은 조용히 해달라고 부탁해야겠네.

002 Shut your mouth! 입닥쳐!

미드표현

this is a rude way to say "Stop talking." It often indicates the speaker is angry

I Point I Shut your trap! 조용히 해!, 입 다물어!

A: You are the ugliest woman I've ever seen.
너같이 못 생긴 여자는 처음 봐.
B: **Shut your mouth!** You are both rude and foolish. 입닥쳐! 넌 무례하고 멍청하잖아.

If you wanna stay here. Then shut your mouth! 여기 머무르고 싶으면 입닥치고 있어!

A: Now you're acting like you still in charge.
B: Shut your mouth, bitch.
A: 아직도 명령만 내리네. B: 입닥쳐!

You shut your mouth, or I'll shut it for you.
너 입닥쳐, 아니면 내가 닥치게 해줄게.

003 Shut the fuck up! 아가리 닥쳐!

미드표현

like the previous phrase, this is a very very rude way to tell a person not to talk, and it usually indicates someone is very angry. It means "Don't talk anymore!"

I Point I Shut up! 입닥쳐!, 조용히 좀 하란 말야!
Shut up about it 누구에게도 말하면 안돼, 입 꽉 다물고 있으라구

A: I really hate being around you.
네가 내 옆에 있는 거 정말 싫어.
B: **Shut the fuck up!** You're a loser! 입닥쳐! 한심한 놈아!

I owe you nothing. Shut up. Get outta here.
네 덕본 거 하나도 없어. 입닥치고 꺼져.

Then shut up about it and eat your lunch.
그럼 입 다물고 점심이나 먹지.

Did I not just say shut up about it already?
그건 누구에게도 말하면 안 된다고 이미 말하지 않았어?

004 Stop saying that! 닥치라고!, 그만 좀 얘기해! , 그 얘기 좀 그만해!

미드표현

this is a way to say "Don't repeat it anymore." We can understand that something has been said that the speaker doesn't want to hear

I Point I Stop talking! 그만 얘기해!

A: You can't get a job! You can't get a job!
넌 취직 안 될 거야! 넌 취직 안 될거야!
B: **Stop saying that!** I'm trying hard to get a job!
닥치라고! 취직하려고 열심히 하고 있어!

Stop saying that like it means something.
뭔가 있는 것처럼 이야기하지마.

Would you stop? Stop saying that. OK?
그만 할래? 그만 얘기해. 알았지?

You gotta stop saying that, now. It's no big deal. 이제 그만 얘기 좀 해. 별일 아니잖아.

005 Watch your tongue! 말 조심해!

this means "Be careful of what you say because you are saying bad things." This is said to children a lot when they say something unkind or rude

| Point | Watch your mouth[language]! 말 조심해!
Hold your tongue 입다물어(this is a very old way to say stop talking)
Bite your tongue 입 조심해, 말이 씨가 되는 수가 있어

A: I think my dad is kind of stupid. 아빠가 좀 멍청한 것 같아.
B: **Watch your tongue.** You're going to be punished. 말 조심해. 혼나겠다.

Maybe you should watch your mouth.
자네 입 조심해야 할 걸.

Watch your language. There are ladies present. 말 조심해. 숙녀들 있잖아.

You'd better watch your tongue! 너 말 조심해라!

006 (That is) Better left unsaid

말 안 하는 게 좋겠어, 입다물고 있는게 낫겠어, 말하지 말자

this indicates that it is good manners not to say something. It is like saying "Don't talk about it or you might upset someone

A: Should I tell Carrie why people didn't like her party? 캐리에게 사람들이 걔 파티를 싫어하는 이유를 말해야 할까?
B: No, **that is better left unsaid.** 아니, 말 안하는 게 좋겠어.

I know she's a bitch, but that is better left unsaid. 걔가 못된 년이라는 건 알고 있지만 입 다물고 있는게 낫겠어.

That is better left unsaid. It would only upset people. 말 안하는게 좋겠어. 사람들 화만 돋구게 될거야.

The job is unsatisfactory, but that is better left unsaid. 일자리가 마음에 안들지만 입 다물고 있는게 낫겠어.

007 Keep quiet (about it) 입다물고 있어

this means "It's a secret." We can understand that the speaker doesn't want people to know this information

| Point | keep quiet about~ …에 대해 입다물다

A: I'm glad we left school early today.
오늘 학교가 일찍 끝나서 좋아.
B: **Keep quiet about it.** I don't want my parents to find out. 입 다물어. 부모님이 아시면 안돼.

Keep quiet. You're making a scene!
조용히 해. 너무 소란스럽잖아!

If you were smart, you'd better keep quiet about that. 네가 현명하면 조용히 입다물고 있는 게 나아.

Why did she keep quiet about it?
걔는 왜 그거에 대해 입다물고 있었던 거야?

008 Not another word! 더 이상 한마디도 하지마!

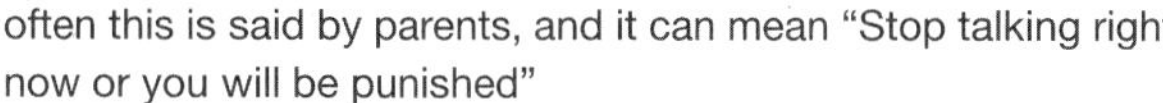

often this is said by parents, and it can mean "Stop talking right now or you will be punished"

| Point | Not another word from[out of] you 넌 더 이상 한 마디도 하지마

A: Mom, Tommy pushed me! 엄마, 토미가 날 밀었어요!
B: You children stop fighting. **Not another word!**
너희들 그만 싸워. 더 이상 한마디도 하지마!

Not another word outta you. You don't have anything to be sorry about?
한 마디도 하지마. 넌 후회할 일을 한 적이 한 번도 없어?

Enough! Stop! Not another word from any of you! 충분해! 그만! 니네들 더 이상 한 마디도 하지마!

Not another word, Conrad. I am warning you.
더 이상 한마디도 하지마, 콘래드, 경고야.

009 You're such a big talker 넌 너무 말이 많아, 말만 앞서는구나

this is a way of saying that a person talks a lot but that person doesn't do much to prove what he has said. Often it indicates "I don't believe most of what you say"

I Point I He has got a big mouth 입이 엄청 싸구만, 저 놈은 입만 살았어

A: I plan to climb Mount Everest in my lifetime.
내 평생에 에베레스트 산을 오를 계획이야.

B: **You're such a big talker.** I bet you'll never do that. 정말 말만 앞서는구나. 네가 절대 안 그럴걸 확신해.

Dale got a big mouth, but he's harmless.
데일은 입이 싸지만 해를 끼치지는 않아.

You're such a big talker. Why can't you just shut up? 넌 너무 말이 많아. 왜 입다물지 못하는거야?

Some people can't be trusted because they have a great big mouth.
어떤 사람들은 입이 너무 싸서 신뢰를 받지 못해.

010 Keep your mouth shut 누구한테도 말하면 안돼, 비밀이야

this means "Don't tell anyone." It is said when there is a secret to be kept

I Point I Keep your mouth shut about~ …에 대해 입을 다물어라

A: I heard Beth's surprise birthday party is Sunday.
베스의 서프라이즈 파티가 일요일이라며.

B: **Keep your mouth shut** about that. I don't want her to find out. 아무한테도 말하지마. 걔 알면 안돼.

You keep your mouth shut unless I give you permission to open it. Understood?
내가 허락할 때까지는 함구해라. 알았어?

You keep your mouth shut, no one here cares what you think! 입 다물고 있어. 아무도 네 생각에 관심없다구!

You keep your mouth shut about the ring.
반지에 대해서 누구에게도 말하면 안돼.

011 Keep this to yourself 이건 비밀인데, 너만 알고 있어야 해, 아무한테도 말하지마

this usually means something is private. It is like saying "Please don't tell anyone else"

I Point I I'll keep it private 비밀로 할게

A: **Keep this to yourself.** I'm planning to retire.
이건 비밀인데 나 퇴직할려고.

B: But the company needs you here to run things.
하지만 회사는 네가 남아서 일을 해주길 바래.

You keep this to yourself while we work it out.
우리가 해결하는 동안 이거 너만 알고 있어야 해.

You keep this to yourself! Not a word. We do not speak of this again. You understand?
이거 비밀이야! 한 마디도 하지마. 다신 이 얘기하지 않는다. 알았지?

012 Not a word 한 마디도 하지마

this is a simple way to say "Don't talk about it." The speaker doesn't want the person to discuss the subject

I Point I Not a word about[to]~ …에 관해서[에게] 한 마디도 하지마

A: I heard you started working for the CIA.
네가 CIA일을 시작했다며.

B: Yes I have. But **not a word** to anyone about it.
어 그래. 하지만 아무한테도 말하지마.

Not a word to anyone. 누구한테도 아무 말도 하지마.

Try not speaking for the rest of the day. Not a word. 오늘이 가기 전까지는 더 이상 말하지 않도록 해. 한 마디도.

So not a word about us having been married.
그럼 우리가 결혼한 거에 대해 입도 뻥긋하지마.

013 My lips are sealed 비밀 지켜줄게, 나 입 무거워

this is like promising to keep a secret. It is the same as saying "I won't tell anyone"

A: Please don't tell anyone I've had plastic surgery.
내가 성형수술했다는 거 아무한테도 말하지마.

B: **My lips are sealed.** I won't tell anyone at all.
비밀 지킬게. 아무한테도 말하지 않을게.

It's cool, a little porn on a Saturday night. My lips are sealed. 좋구만, 토요일 저녁 야동이라, 비밀지켜줄게.

I have to go. So, I'll talk to you later. Lips are sealed, promise.
나 가야 돼. 그럼, 나중에 얘기해. 비밀은 지켜줄게, 정말야.

014 I'm not one to kiss and tell (신의를 저버리고) 비밀을 떠벌리는 사람은 아냐

this usually means "I keep secrets well." A person will say this to indicate he can be trusted

| Point | kiss and tell 비밀을 떠들고 다니다

A: Who was your big date with last night?
지난 밤 에 누구랑 거창하게 데이트한 거야?

B: It's a secret. **I'm not one to kiss and tell.**
비밀야. 난 떠벌리는 사람아니거든.

I don't kiss and tell. 비밀을 떠벌리고 다니지 않아.

I'm not one to kiss and tell, but I'm also not one to have sex and shut up.
비밀을 떠벌리는 사람도 아니지만 그렇다고 섹스하고 비밀을 지키는 사람도 아냐.

I think I've already proven. I'm not one to kiss and tell. 이미 증명되었지만 난 비밀을 떠벌리는 사람은 아냐.

Well, Daniel and I aren't ones to kiss and tell.
다니엘과 나는 비밀을 떠들고 다니는 사람은 아냐.

015 Mum's the word 비밀야, 아무한테도 말하지마

this is usually said when something shouldn't be discussed. It's a way of saying "Keep it secret."

A: These documents are confidential. Understand?
이 서류들은 비밀야, 알겠어?

B: Yes I do. **Mum's the word.**
어 알았어. 아무한테도 말하지 않을게.

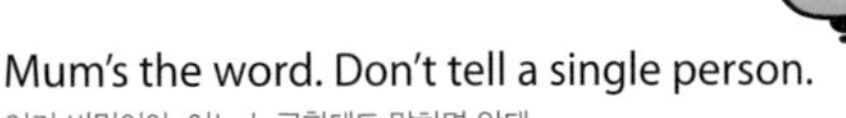

Mum's the word. Don't tell a single person.
이거 비밀이야. 어느 누구한테도 말하면 안돼.

Mum's the word until we are ready to reveal the secret.
우리가 비밀을 말할 준비가 될 때까지는 아무한테도 말하지마.

And in the meantime, mum's the word, all right? 그리고 그러는 동안은 비밀이다, 알았지?

016 Just between us[you and me] 우리끼리 비밀인데

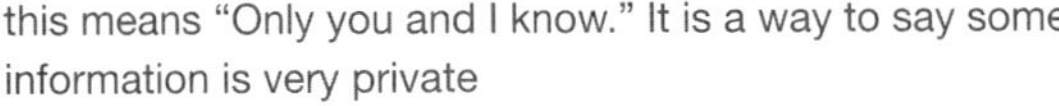

this means "Only you and I know." It is a way to say some information is very private

| Point | It stays between us 우리끼리 이야기야

A: **Just between us,** my marriage isn't going so well. 우리끼리 비밀인데, 결혼생활이 썩 잘 되지 않아.

B: Are you fighting a lot with your husband?
남편하고 많이 싸워?

This is between you and me. 이건 우리끼리 이야기인데.

Alright, I got an idea. But it stays between us. Agreed?
좋아, 나한테 좋은 생각이 있어. 하지만 우리끼리만 하는 얘기니까 비밀을 지켜야 돼, 알았지?

What is said here, stays here.
여기서 한 말은 모두 비밀을 지켜야 돼.

017 Don't tell a soul 소문내지마, 무덤까지 가져가

this warns someone not to tell anyone else. It is like saying "Don't discuss this with anyone"

I Point I Don't repeat any of it 조금도 그것에 대해 말하지마
I won't tell a soul 입 꼭 다물고 있을게

A: These letters are from the Yakuza. **Don't tell a soul.** 이 편지들은 야쿠자에서 온 것들이야. 소문내지마.

B: Alright. What do they say inside?
알았어. 안에 뭐라고 쓰여있는데?

미드표현

You're not going to tell a soul. 아무한테도 얘기하지마.

Don't tell a soul, not even your mom.
아무한테도 말하지마, 엄마한테도.

I can't tell a soul unless you authorize me to.
당신이 허가를 해주지 않으면 아무한테도 말하지 않아요.

018 Could you keep a secret? 비밀 지킬 수 있어?

the speaker is asking "Can I trust you?" He wants to know if a person can listen to private information and not tell it

I Point I This is top secret 이건 절대 비밀이야

A: **Could you keep a secret?** 비밀 지킬 수 있어?

B: Sure. I'd never tell anyone what you said.
물론. 네가 말한 거 아무한테도 말하지 않을게.

미드표현

Don't worry. I can keep a secret.
걱정마. 비밀 지킬 수 있어.

I can keep a secret. I promise I will never tell her. 비밀 지킬 수 있어. 걔한테 절대로 말 안할게.

She never could keep a secret.
걘 절대로 비밀 지키지 못해.

019 Your secret's safe with me 비밀 지켜줄게

this means "I won't tell anyone." It is a way of saying that the speaker can be trusted

A: Actually I only have a high school education.
실은 나 고졸야.

B: **Your secret's safe with me.** I thought you've been to university. 비밀 지켜줄게. 대학나온 줄 알았어.

미드표현

Don't worry, Jane. Your secret's safe with me.
걱정마, 제인. 비밀은 지켜줄게.

Your secret is safe with us, my lady.
부인, 우리는 당신의 비밀을 발설하지 않습니다.

020 The cat's out of the bag 비밀이 들통났어

this indicates "Someone told that secret." Often it is a way to say now many people know that secret

I Point I let the cat out of the bag 어떤 사실, 비밀 등을 폭로하다

A: That movie star and his wife are divorcing.
저 영화배우가 아내하고 이혼중이래.

B: **The cat's out of the bag.** Now everyone knows. 비밀이 들통났네. 이제 다들 알고 있구만.

미드표현

Oh, great, now the cat's out of the bag. Oh, You might as well tell her.
이런, 들통났네. 걔한테 얘기해주는게 낫겠어.

She knows about the surprise party. The cat's out of the bag.
걔는 깜짝파티에 대해 알고 있어. 비밀이 들통났어.

He told everyone my secret? Well, the cat's out of the bag.
걔가 사람들에게 내 비밀을 말했다고? 이제 다들 알고 있겠구만.

021 I won't say a word 비밀은 꼭 지킬게

this is a way for the speaker to say he will keep a secret and not talk about it. It is similar to saying "I'm not going to tell anyone"

| Point | I won't breathe a word (of it) 누구에게도 말하지 않을게
Don't breathe a word of this to anyone 아무한테도 말하지마, 비밀 지켜

A: You can't tell anyone about this.
이거 누구한테도 말하면 안돼.

B: Trust me. **I won't say a word.** 날 믿어. 아무 말도 안할게.

Don't say a word. Pretend it never happened.
한 마디도 하지마. 없었던 걸로 해.

I promise I won't say a word.
정말 한 마디도 하지도 않을게.

You can trust me. I won't say a word. I promise. 날 믿어도 돼. 정말이지 아무 말도 하지 않을게.

022 Let's get this out in the open 백일하에 드러내놓자, 그냥 얘기해버리자

this is a way of saying "I want to talk about this honestly." Usually it is a way of saying that the speaker wants to talk about something that is private

| Point | get sth out in the open ...을 드러내다

A: **Let's get this out in the open.** I'm unhappy working here. 까놓고 얘기해서, 여기서 일하는 게 싫어.

B: Is there anything we can do to get you to stay?
네가 계속다니도록 우리가 뭐 할게 있니?

I wanted to get everything out in the open.
모든 것을 드러내놓기를 원했어.

Everybody's got a secret. Just be glad yours is out in the open. 다들 비밀이 있는데 너의 비밀이 드러나서 기뻐.

023 I'm going to have to get this off my chest
이거 털어놓고 말해야겠어

this is a way of saying "I'm going to confess to you." We can understand that the speaker is going to admit to something that might be difficult to talk about

| Point | get sth off one's chest 속에 있는 걸 털어놓다[reveal something (usually a confession or complaint) that has been bothering you]

A: I heard you dated girls other than your girlfriend.
여친아닌 여자와 데이트 했다며.

B: It's true. **I'm going to have to get this off my chest.** 사실야. 털어놓고 말해야겠어.

Glad to get that off my chest. Thank you.
속에 있는 걸 털어놔서 기뻐. 고마워.

I'm not gonna be any kind of company until I get something off my chest.
속 이야길하지 않고서는 기분이 계속 안 좋을거야.

I'm just gonna have to get this off my chest. You made me feel really bad the other day.
이거 털어놓고 말해야겠어. 네가 요전 날 진짜 날 화나게 했어.

024 Tell me something 말해봐, 말 좀 해봐

this is often said before a question is asked. It is like saying "Give me some information"

| Point | Tell me something 말 좀 해봐
You've got to tell me something 말 좀 해봐

A: **Tell me something.** Do you like the dress I'm wearing? 말 좀 해봐. 내가 입은 이 드레스 맘에 들어?

B: Yes. I think it looks very sexy on you.
어. 네가 아주 섹시하게 보여.

You've got to tell me something. You've got to tell me what side you're on.
말 좀 해봐. 너 어느 편인지 말해봐.

Tell me something. Why didn't you take the ring? 말 좀 해봐. 왜 이 반지를 끼지 않았어?

Tell me something. How are things with you and Emily? 말 좀 해봐. 너와 에밀리 상황은 어때?

025 So, tell me 자 말해봐, 얘기해봐

like the previous phrase, this means "I want to know something." It is said before asking for information

I Point I Do tell (흥미롭구만) 어서 말해봐(That's interesting)

A: **So, tell me,** what kind of work do you do?
그래 말해봐요, 무슨 일을 해요?

B: I work as a teacher in a high school.
고등학교에서 교편을 잡고 있어요.

So, tell me, where did I go wrong?
자 말해봐, 내가 어디서 잘못 한거야?

So, tell me, are his friends cute?
자 말해봐, 걔 친구들 귀여워?

026 Tell me what happened 무슨 일이 있었는지 말해

this is a way of saying "I want to know what occurred." It means the speaker wants to know about some event

I Point I Tell me what you're thinking 네 생각이 뭔지 말해봐

A: I went on a date with Alan last night.
지난 밤에 앨런하고 데이트했어.

B: Alan is so handsome. **Tell me what happened.**
앨런은 정말 잘 생겼는데, 어떻게 됐는지 말해봐.

Then talk to me. Tell me what happened. Where did you go?
그럼 내게 말해. 무슨 일이 있었어? 어디 갔었어?

Excuse me, can you tell me what happened?
저기 무슨 일이 있었는지 말해줄래?

You want to tell me what happened here?
여기 어떻게 된 건지 말해볼래?

027 You want to tell me what happened here? 무슨 일인지 말해볼래?

this a way to ask "What caused this?" The speaker wants to know why something happened

I Point I You tell me+N/ what[why] S+V …을 말해봐

A: **You want to tell me what happened here?**
여기 무슨 일인지 말해볼래?

B: I had a small accident when I was driving your car. 네 차를 몰다가 조그만 사고를 냈어.

미드표현

You want to tell me what happened here?
무슨 일인지 말해볼래?

You want to tell me what that was all about?
그게 다 무슨 일이었는지 말해줄래?

You want to tell me what's going on with you? 너 무슨 일인지 말해볼래?

You want to tell me what that was about?
그게 뭐에 관한 건지 말해볼래?

028 Keep talking 계속 얘기해 봐

this indicates the speaker is interested. It expresses "I want to hear what else you will say"

I Point I Start talking 말해봐

A: Do you want to hear more about what I did today? 오늘 내가 한 일에 대해 더 듣고 싶어?

B: **Keep talking.** It sounds like you had fun.
계속 얘기해 봐. 재미좋았던 것 같아.

미드표현

I need you to keep talking. Can you do that?
계속 얘기해봐. 그럴 수 있지?

So what happened? Start talking.
그래 어떻게 된 거야? 얘기해봐.

Elizabeth, why don't you start talking first.
엘리자베스야 네가 먼저 말해봐라.

029 Let's have it 1. 어서[빨리] 말해봐, 한 번 들어보자 2. 내게 줘

the speaker wants to know the full story of something. He is saying "Tell me about it now"

I Point I Let me have it 어서 말해봐, 내게 줘봐

A: I don't want to tell you why I was punished.
내가 왜 벌을 받았는지 말하기 싫어.

B: **Let's have it.** The teacher is very upset with you. 어서 말해봐. 선생님이 너한테 무지 화나셨어.

You've been wanting to tell me something. Let's have it. 넌 내게 뭔가 말하고 싶어했지. 어서 말해봐.

Let's have it. What do you know about this crime? 어디 한번 들어보자. 이 범죄에 대해 뭘 알고 있어?

Let's have it. Tell everyone about the bad things you did.
어서 말해봐. 네가 저지른 나쁜 짓들에 대해 사람들에게 말해.

030 I'm listening 듣고 있어, 어서 말해

this is a way of saying "I am waiting to hear what you say." We can understand the speaker wants to know about something

I Point I I'm not listening to you 난 네 말 안 듣는다구
I am all ears 귀 쫑긋 세우고 들을게
I'll bite 모르겠어, 어디 들어보자(I don't know, so you can tell me)

A: I want to know why you were fighting. **I'm listening.** 네가 왜 싸웠는지 알고 싶어. 어서 말해봐.

B: Someone was bothering me, so I hit him.
누가 날 괴롭혀서 때렸어.

I'm listening. Talk fast. 듣고 있어, 빨리 말해.

When she has a problem, everyone's all ears.
걔가 문제있으면 다들 신경 써서 듣잖아.

Okay, I'll bite. Why are you so lucky?
좋아, 어디 들어보자. 왜 운이 좋은 거야?

I'll bite. Tell me why the sky is blue.
몰라. 왜 그런지 말해봐.

031 It's not good to keep that bottled up inside
맘속에 담아두는 건 안 좋아

this is a way of saying that a person has to talk about something to release stress. It is a way to say "You should talk with someone about that problem"

I Point I keep sth bottled up (inside) 마음 속에 담아두다
(keep sth that has been bothering you inside)

A: I have been really unhappy with my boss lately.
최근 사장 때문에 정말 기분나빠.

B: Tell me about it. **It's not good to keep that bottled up inside.** 내게 말해봐. 맘속에 담아두면 안좋아.

I'm not the type of person that can keep things bottled up inside.
난 마음 속에 할 말을 담아두는 사람은 아니야.

I just feel like I have so much emotion just bottled up inside of me.
내 맘속에 너무 많은 감정을 담아둔 것 같아.

032 Truth be told 솔직히 말하면, 사실대로 말하자면

this means "I'm going to say it honestly." This is not a common phrase, and often it means someone will give his opinion

I Point I (You) Tell me the truth 진실을 말해
Speaking(quite) candidly 솔직히 말하면

A: You look very sick today. 너 오늘 무척 아파 보여.

B: **Truth be told,** I'm not feeling very good.
사실대로 말하면 몸이 썩 좋지 않아.

Truth be told, I am a little nervous.
솔직히, 난 조금 떨려.

You tell me the truth. You tell me why I can't see her. 진실을 말해봐. 내가 왜 걜 볼 수 없는지 말해봐.

033 Spit it out! 숨기지 말고 다 털어놔!, 까놓고 얘기해봐!

usually this is a way to say "hurry up and tell me everything" We can understand the speaker wants to hear the information quickly.

| Point | Cough it up 자백해, 털어놔봐

A: This isn't easy for me to tell you.
너한테 이걸 말하는 건 쉽지 않아.

B: **Spit it out.** I'm dying to know about that.
사실대로 말해. 털어놔. 알고 싶어 죽겠어.

Yeah, what's the problem? Spit it out.
무슨 문제야? 털어놔봐.

What are you thinking? Spit it out!
무슨 생각하고 있어? 얘기해봐!

I thought he'd never spit it out.
난 걔가 절대 털어놓지 않을거라 생각했어.

034 Give it to me straight 솔직하게 말해줘

미드표현

this person is asking to be told something honestly, even if it is something he doesn't like to hear. It is like saying "Tell me everything"

| Point | give it to sb straight 단도직입적으로 말하다
I'll give it to you straight from the shoulder 진심으로 한마디 할게
(Tell me) Straight up 솔직히 말해, (내 말) 사실야

A: I have some bad news for you. 안 좋은 소식이 있어.

B: **Give it to me straight.** I can take it. 솔직히 말해. 괜찮아.

How about you give it to me straight?
솔직하게 말해주지?

Straight up, am I going to die?
솔직히 말해, 내가 죽게 되는 거야?

035 Level with me 솔직히 말해봐

미드표현

this means "Tell me it honestly." Often this is said when the speaker wants to know a person's real feelings

| Point | I'll level with you 솔직히 말할게
What does your heart tell you? 솔직하게 말해봐

A: **Level with me.** You don't want to date me, right? 솔직히 말해봐. 나랑 데이트하기 싫지, 맞지?

B: Yeah, I really don't think you are attractive.
그래, 난 정말 내가 매력적이라고 생각하지 않아.

Level with me. Who do you think killed her?
솔직해 말해봐. 누가 걜 죽인 것 같아?

I'm going to level with you. 너한테 솔직히 말할게.

I think it's time to level with him.
걔한테 솔직히 말할 때인 것 같아.

036 Be honest 솔직히 털어놔, 진심을 말해봐

people say this when they mean "I want to hear something truthfully." Often it indicates the truth may not be nice to hear

| Point | I'll be honest with you 너한테 솔직히 털어놓을게
Let's be honest (with each other) 우리 서로 솔직해지자
You have to be honest with me 너 내게 솔직히 말해
To be honest (with you) (네게) 솔직히 말해서

A: Have you ever been arrested? **Be honest.**
체포된 적 있어? 솔직히 털어놔.

B: I've never had a problem with the police. Really.
경찰과 문제가 된 적이 한 번도 없어. 정말.

To be honest I didn't even know you were here. 솔직히 말해서 네가 여기 있다는 것조차 모르고 있었어.

But as your friend, I'm gonna be honest with you. 하지만 네 친구로서 내가 솔직히 말할게.

I need you to be honest with me, please.
난 네가 나한테 솔직해지기를 바래.

We're starting fresh, and I wanna be honest with you.
우리 새롭게 시작하자고 그리고 난 너한테 솔직해지고 싶어.

037 You have got to come clean with me!

나한테 실토해!, 속시원히 내게 털어놔

this is a way to say "You need to tell me the truth." It is often said when someone has lied

| Point | Why don't you come clean? 실토하는 게 어때?
If the shoe fits, wear it 그게 사실이면 인정하라구

A: **You have got to come clean with me.** You're seeing other women. 내게 실토해. 딴 여자 만나고 있지.

B: Yeah, I have been on a few dates recently.
어, 최근에 몇 번 만났어.

You gotta come clean with her! This is not right! 걔한테 털어놔야 돼! 이건 옳지 않아!

What you need is to come clean and cooperate. 네가 필요한 것은 솔직히 털어놓고 협조하는 거야.

I know who did this. So, you might as well come clean. 누가 했는지 알아. 그러니 깨끗이 털어놓는 게 나아.

038 Put[Lay] your cards on the table

속마음을 꺼내봐, 다 털어놔봐

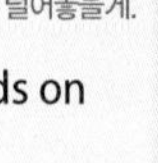

this means "Tell the whole truth." The speaker is telling someone to say everything honestly.

| Point | Don't beat around the bush 말 돌리지 마, 핵심을 말해, 빙빙 돌려 얘기하지마(Tell me what you want to talk about)

A: I want to ask Sara to marry me. 새라에게 청혼할래.

B: **Lay your cards on the table.** See what she says. 생각을 다 털어놔봐. 그리고 걔가 뭐라 하는지 보라고.

I'm gonna lay my cards on the table. 다 털어놓을게.

Susan, we're both adults, put your cards on the table. 수잔, 우리 다 어른이잖아. 다 털어놔봐.

Don't beat around the bush. Tell me what's on your mind. 말 돌리지 마. 네 생각을 말해봐.

039 Out with it!

다 털어놔봐, 말해 봐

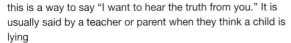

this is a way to say "I want to hear the truth from you." It is usually said by a teacher or parent when they think a child is lying

| Point | Please don't hold back 감추지 말고 다 얘기해(Tell me everything)

A: Mom, I can't tell you what Jerry said about you.
엄마, 제리가 엄마에게 뭐라 했는지 말 못하겠어.

B: **Out with it!** I want to know everything.
다 털어놔! 다 알아야겠어.

Tell me who broke the window. Out with it!
누가 창문을 깨트렸는지 말해. 털어놔봐!

Out with it! The teacher needs you to tell her what happened.
말해봐! 선생님은 네가 무슨 일이 있었는지 말해주기를 원해.

What do you know about this? Out with it!
이거에 대해 뭘 알고 있어? 털어놔봐!

040 Just come out and say it

솔직하게 털어놔봐

this is a way of saying "Tell me something, even if it is not nice." Sometimes people don't want to say something unkind, so the speaker can say this so they speak

A: I'd rather not tell you everything.
네게 다 말하지 않는 게 낫겠어.

B: **Just come out and say it.** Be honest.
솔직히 털어놔봐. 정직하게.

I'm just going to come out and say it. Beckham is an English treasure.
솔직히 말해볼게. 베컴은 영국의 보배야.

I'm just gonna come out and say it. I think I love you. 솔직히 말해볼게. 널 사랑하는 것 같아.

041 Come on, spill it 자 어서 말해봐

this usually means that the speaker wants the listener to tell him something that is secret or private. It is probably true that the listener is trying to avoid telling whatever he knows. It is like saying "Come on, tell me everything about that"

| Point | spill it 말하다, 털어놓다 spill the beans 비밀을 누설하다

A: I don't know if I should tell you about my date.
내 데이트에 대해서 너한테 말해야 할지 모르겠어.

B: **Come on, spill it.** Tell me why you had a bad time. 그러지말고, 어서 말해봐. 왜 데이트가 좋지 않았는지 말해봐.

미드표현

Well, that wasn't statutory rape, so spill it.
그래, 그건 법적강간이 아니었으니까 어서 말해봐.

So, come on, spill it. Did you join the club?
그래 어서 말해봐. 너 그 클럽에 가입했어?

Mom, spill it. What's wrong?
엄마, 말해봐요. 무슨 일이예요?

042 She's not shy about her porn 걘 거리낌없이 포르노를 갖고 있다고 말해

this is an unusual phrase, and apparently it is saying that a woman owns a lot of porn showing people having sex, and now she is not embarrassed by it. We can understand that she has no problem telling others about it. It is like saying "She is honest about the porn that she has"

| Point | be not shy about N[~ing] 기꺼이 …하다, 전혀 거리낌없이 …하다
be[feel] shy of[about]~ing …까지는 하지 않다
be shy of N …수량이 모자라다

A: Sarah was showing me DVDs of different pornography. 새라는 내게 다양한 종류의 포르노 DVD를 보여줬어.

B: I believe it. **She's not shy about her porn.**
그래, 갠 거리낌없이 포르노갖고 있다고 말해.

미드표현

You weren't shy about making other decisions for me. 넌 날 위해 기꺼이 결정을 다르게 했어.

And he's not exactly shy about outing those achievements.
걔는 그러한 성과를 드러내는데 전혀 거리낌이 없어.

Chuck died one day shy of his wedding.
척은 결혼식 하루 전날 죽었어.

043 Look me in the eye and tell me nothing happened 내 눈 똑바로 쳐다보면서 아무 일도 없었다고 이야기해봐

some people think if a person looks them in the eye, they will not lie. Here the speaker is telling someone "Look in my eyes and be truthful"

| Point | Please tell it like it is 있는 그대로 말해줘, 사실대로 말해줘

A: Come on Tracey. Jenny and I are just friends.
야야, 트레이시, 제니와 난 그냥 친구야.

B: **Look me in the eye and tell me nothing happened** when you went to her house.
내 눈 똑바로 쳐다보고 걔집에 가서 아무일도 없었다고 말해봐.

미드표현

You look me in the eye and tell me that you're not breaking up with her.
내 눈을 똑바로 쳐다보면서 걔하고 헤어지지 않는다고 말해봐.

If you can look me in the eye and tell me that when we kissed, you felt nothing, then I'll just go.
내 눈을 똑바로 쳐다보면서 우리가 키스했을 때 아무 느낌이 없었다고 말할 수 있으면 난 가버리겠어.

You look me in the eye and you swear to me that you didn't kill anybody.
내 눈을 똑바로 쳐다보면서 아무도 안 죽였다고 내게 맹세해봐.

044 (Is there) Anything you want to say? 내게 뭐 할 말 있어?

this is asking if someone wants to talk more about something. It is like saying "Do you want to talk more about this?"

| Point | Anything you want to say to me? 내게 뭐 할 말이라도 있어?

A: **Anything more you want to say to me?**
내게 뭐 더 할 말 있어?

B: No, I think I said everything. 아니, 다 말한 것 같아.

미드표현

We're going to be placing you under arrest for murder. Is there anything you want to say?
당신을 살인죄로 체포합니다. 할 말 있습니까?

A: Anything you want to say to me? B: As a matter of fact, yes. A: 할 말있니? B: 응 사실 있어.

Ways of asking about what someone is thinking

내 생각은… 그리고 네 생각은?

What do you think?

001 What do you say? (상대방의 동의를 구하며) 어때?, 네 생각은?

this is another way to say "Give me your answer." The speaker is expecting a person to say yes or no

| Point | What do you say to +N/~ing ? …하는 거 어때?
What do you say (that) S+V …가 어때?
What do you say to that? 그거 어때?

A: Come with us to the party tomorrow. **What do you say?** 내일 파티에 우리랑 함께 가자. 어때?

B: That sounds like a lot of fun to me. 정말 재미있겠다.

> So what do you say? Can I be your girlfriend again? 그래 어때? 나랑 다시 사귈래?
>
> What do you say to going for a drink? 한잔 하러 가는 게 어때?
>
> What do you say we call it a day? 오늘 일은 그만하는 게 어때?

002 What would you say? 어떻게 할 거야?, 넌 뭐라고 할래?

this is used when people are talking about something that is possible. It is like saying "If that happened, how would you react?"

| Point | What would you say to+N/~ing? …한다면 넌 뭐라고 할래?
What would you say if S+V? …한다면 어떨까?

A: **What would you say if** someone offered you a job on the stock market? 증권일을 제안받으면 어떻게 할래?

B: I'd probably turn it down because it would be stressful. 너무 스트레스가 많기 때문에 아마 거절할거야.

> What would you say to bringing your boys over to my house and letting them hang out with mine some time? 언제 한번 얘들 데리고 우리 집에 와서 우리 얘들과 놀리면 어때?
>
> What would you say if she stayed with us all night? 걔가 우리랑 밤샌다면 어떨까?

003 How do you like that? (놀람) 저것 좀 봐, 황당하지 않냐?, (의견) 어때?

usually this is a way to express surprise. It often means "I'm really surprised it happened." Sometimes this is also asking "What is your opinion of that?" The speaker wants to know how someone feels about something

| Point | How do you like+N? [의견]…는 어때?
How would you like+N? …를 어떻게 해줄까?
How would you like to do~? [제안] 어떻게 …할 거야?, …을 하자
How would you like it if S+V? …한다면 어떻겠어?

A: I heard that Kyle moved to LA. 카일이 LA로 이사간다며?

B: **How do you like that?** I thought he wanted to stay here. 의외네? 여기 사는 걸 원하는지 알았는데.

> So tell me. How'd you like the picture? 그래 말해봐. 이 그림 어때?
>
> How do[would] you like it -- Medium rare? 미디엄과 레어중간으로 해드릴까요?
>
> How would you like to go out on a date with me? Right now. 나랑 데이트 하자. 지금 바로.
>
> How would you like to get together? Say next Saturday? 한 번 만나자. 담주 토요일로 할까?

004 How's that going? 어때?, 잘 돼가?

this is asking if a thing has been good or if it has had problems. It is a way of asking "Have you had a good or bad experience?"

| Point | How's that? 어째서 그래? 뭐라고?, 그거 어때?
How's that sound (to you)? 어떻게 생각해?, 그거 네 맘에 드니?

A: My new job is buying and selling houses. 새로운 일은 집을 매매하는 거야.

B: Sounds interesting. **How is that going?** 재밌겠다. 어때?

> How's that going, by the way? 그런데 그건 어떻게 돼가?
>
> I heard you're getting married. How's that going? 너 결혼했다는 얘기 들었어. 잘 돼가?
>
> We're friends. How's that? 우린 친구잖아. 어때서 그래?
>
> How's that? Is that better? 그거 어때? 나아졌어?

005 How's that working out for you?

그러니까 어때?, 너한테 잘 되어가니?

미드표현

like the previous phrase, this is asking "Has everything been OK?" The speaker wants to know the person's feeling about something

| Point | work out 잘 되어가다

A: I started a new diet in October.
10월에 새로운 다이어트를 시작했어.

B: Oh really? **How's that working out for you?**
어 정말? 그러니까 어때?

This is working out for you? 이게 너한테 잘 돼?

So, things are really working out for you two?
사정이 너희 둘에게 좋아진거야?

So glad it worked out for you. 너한테 잘 되어가서 기뻐.

Let me know how that works out for you.
그게 어떻게 네게 잘 되어갔는지 알려줘.

006 How was it? 어땠어?

미드표현

this is asking for an opinion on something. It is like asking "Did you like it?"

| Point | How was it with your friends? 네 친구들은 어땠니?

A: We went out to a Mexican restaurant last night.
지난 밤에 멕시코 식당에 갔었어.

B: **How was it?** I heard Mexican food has a lot of fat. 어땠어? 멕시코 음식은 지방이 많다며.

So, how was it? Did you have a good time?
그래, 어땠어? 좋은 시간 보냈어?

You took that trip to the Grand Canyon. How was it? 그랜드 캐넌 여행했지. 어땠어?

Hey, you're back. How was it? 어, 돌아왔구나. 어땠어?

I'm glad that you went. Um, that's great. How was it? 네가 갔다와서 기뻐. 대단해. 어땠어?

007 How'd it go? 어떻게 됐어?, 어땠어?

미드표현

this is a way of asking someone to rate something he did. We could also ask "Did you have a good time?"

| Point | How did it go with+N? …하고는 어떻게 됐어?

A: Doreen and I went to visit her mother.
도린하고 난 걘 엄마를 방문하러 갔어.

B: **How'd it go?** Did she like you? 어땠어? 널 좋아하셨어?

How did it go? Please tell me it went okay.
어땠어? 잘 됐다고 제발 말해줘.

Did you talk to Brad? How did it go?
브래드에게 말했어? 어떻게 됐어?

How did it go with the dancer?
댄서하고는 어떻게 됐어?

008 What do you have in mind? 뭘 생각하고 있어?, 하려는 말이 뭐야?

미드표현

the speaker wants to know what another person wants. He is saying "Tell me what you want to do"

| Point | What did you have in mind? 말하려는 게 뭐였어?
That's not what I had in mind 내가 생각한 것은 그게 아냐

A: I want to cook a special cake for him.
걔한테 특별 케익을 만들어주고 싶어.

B: **What do you have in mind?** He loves chocolate cake. 뭘 생각하고 있는데. 걘 초콜릿 케익을 좋아해.

A: Hi. You're sleeping at my place tonight. B: Really? What did you have in mind?
A: 오늘 밤 내 집에서 자. B: 정말? 뭘 원하는 거야?

A: Okay, what do you have in mind? B: Well, I thought you might enjoy a night at a hotel.
A: 좋아, 하려는 말이 뭐야? B: 네가 호텔에서의 하룻밤을 좋아할거라 생각했어.

009 What do you think? 네 생각은 어때?, 무슨 말이야, 그걸 말이라고 해?

this is asking "How do you feel about it?" The speaker wants someone to give him an honest opinion

| Point | What do you think S+V? …하다고 생각해?

A: I like that painting. **What do you think?**
난 저 그림이 좋아. 넌 어때?

B: I don't like modern art much. 난 현대미술은 별로야.

미드표현

What do you think? Should we show them the room? 네 생각은 어때? 걔네한테 방을 보여줘야 돼?

What do you think she's gonna do?
걔가 뭘 할거라고 생각해?

What do you think that is? 그게 뭐라고 생각해?

What do you think happened? 무슨 일인 것 같아?

010 What do you think of that? 넌 그걸 어떻게 생각해?

this is almost exactly the same as the previous phrase. It is asking for someone's opinion

| Point | What do you think of[about]+N/~ing~? …에 대해 어떻게 생각해?

A: I lived in Japan for a year. **What do you think of that?** 일년간 일본에서 살았어. 어떻게 생각해?

B: You must have had a fun time there.
거기서 즐거운 시간 보냈겠구나.

미드표현

What do you think of this weather? 날씨 어때?

What do you think of my breasts?
내 가슴 어떻게 생각해?

What do you think about me staying the night? 내가 밤새는 것 어떻게 생각해?

011 What did you come up with? 뭐 좋은 아이디어 생각해냈어?

this is a way of asking if someone had a new idea. It is very similar to saying "Did you think of an idea about this?"

| Point | come up with …을 고안해내다

A: I was working all last night to create a new schedule. 새로운 일정을 짜느라 밤새 일했어.

B: That's great. **What did you come up with?**
잘했군. 뭐 좀 좋은 생각 떠올랐어?

미드표현

That's the best you could come up with?
네가 생각해 낸 최고의 것이야?

I couldn't come up with anything good, so they fired me.
뭐 좋은 거 하나도 생각해내지 못했고 그래서 잘렸어.

I promise we'll come up with something. Just give us a little more time.
뭔가 좋은 거 생각해낼게. 조금만 시간 더 줘.

012 How about you? 네 생각은 어때?

this is a way to say "What is your opinion?" It is like asking what someone is feeling about something

| Point | What about you? 넌 어때?

A: I'm feeling very hot right now. **How about you?**
지금 무척 더운 것 같은데, 넌 어때?

B: Me too. Let's open up a window.
나도 그래. 창문을 열어놓자.

미드표현

I haven't felt this happy in a long time. How about you? Are you happy?
오랫동안 이런 행복을 느끼지 못했었어. 넌 어때? 행복해?

What about you? You like being single?
넌 어때? 싱글인 게 좋아?

What about you? What do you think?
넌 어때? 네 생각은 어때?

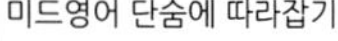

013 Looks like~ …인 것 같아

this is a way to say "It seems like S+V." It is used when someone talks about a thing that is happening

| Point | Looks like+N/(that) S+V …인 거 같아
Sounds like+N/(that) S+V …인 것 같아

A: We don't have any rice or milk.
밥도 없고 우유도 다 떨어졌어.

B: **Looks like** we should go shopping. 쇼핑가야겠구만.

It looks like I'm gonna be here all night.
밤새 여기 있을 것 같아.

She seems really nice. Good kisser.
걘 정말 좋아보여. 키스도 잘해.

Really? It seems like yesterday to me.
정말? 난 어제인 것 같아.

It seems like yesterday they just got engaged.
걔들이 약혼한 게 어제같아.

014 I sensed that~ …인 것 같아

the speaker is talking about how he felt. It is similar to saying "I thought that S+V"

A: Henry and Shirley looked very unhappy.
헨리와 셜리는 매우 불행해보여.

B: **I sensed that** they were arguing before.
걔들이 앞서 다투었던 것 같아.

I sensed that you didn't want me to do that.
너는 내가 그거 하지 않기를 바랬던 것 같았어.

I sensed it was you. 그게 너인 것 같았어.

015 Does it[that] work for you? 네 생각은 어때?, 너도 좋아?, 너한테 괜찮아?

usually this means "Do you like it?" It is a way of asking if something is OK

| Point | Sth works for~ …가 …에게도 괜찮냐(*Sb works for~ …을 위해 일하다)

A: I'd like to meet you at 3. **Does that work for you?** 3시에 만나자. 너도 괜찮아?

B: Sure, I can fit that into my schedule.
물론, 내 스케줄에 맞출 수 있어.

Interesting. Brian, would that work for you?
흥미롭구만. 브라이언, 너도 괜찮겠어?

Go along with this and it'll work for you.
이걸로 해 너한테 괜찮을거야

Does he work for you? 걔가 너 밑에서 일하니?

016 Did you like it? 좋았어?

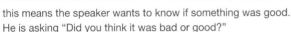

this means the speaker wants to know if something was good. He is asking "Did you think it was bad or good?"

| Point | Was it good? 좋았어?
Did you have fun? 재밌었어?

A: Is that a new perfume you are wearing?
새로운 향수 바른거야?

B: Yes it is. **Do you like it?** 어 그래. 좋아?

What about you, Ray? Did you like it?
넌 어때, 레이? 좋았어?

Thank you so much for coming again. Did you like it tonight? 다시 와줘서 고마워. 오늘밤 좋았어?

017 I have a hunch~ …한 느낌이 들어, …인 것 같아

this is like saying "I think that S+V is true." The speaker is saying that he believes something

I Point I hunch 예감, 육감 on a hunch 예감에 따라

A: **I have a hunch** you will win the contest.
네가 컨테스트에서 우승할 것 같아.

B: It is very nice to hear you say that.
그렇게 말해줘서 정말 고마워.

I have a hunch he's lying to me.
걔가 거짓말하는 느낌이 들어.

That's a hunch talking. Where's the evidence?
그건 느낌이 그렇단 말이지. 증거는 어디 있어?

On a hunch, I asked him about her cell phone.
예감에 따라, 난 걔에게 핸드폰에 대해 물어봤어.

018 I have[got] a feeling~ …할 것 같아

like the previous phrase, this is a way to say that the speaker thinks a thing is true. It is a way of indicating "This is what I believe"

I Point I have a feeling S+V …인 것 같아, 할 것 같아

A: **I've got a feeling** Jim is going to be late.
짐이 늦을 것 같아.

B: Jim is always late for everything. 걘 만사에 항상 늦어.

I have a feeling you did it for me.
네가 날 위해 그랬다는 생각이 들어.

I got a feeling she's coming over. 걔가 올 것 같아.

I get the feeling that he's more interested in the video than me.
걘 나보다 비디오에 더 관심이 많은 것 같아.

019 Let's just say~ …라고 해두자, …인 셈치자

this is similar to saying "I'm going to tell you this in a simple way." It is used when a person wants to say something clearly and directly

A: How was your son's score on the exam?
네 아들 시험성적 어때?

B: **Let's just say** it was one of the best in the class. 반에서 최고에 속한다고 말해두지.

Let's just say that I owe you one.
내가 신세 졌다고 하자.

Let's just say I had a good night last night.
간밤에 잘 지냈다고 치자.

020 I'm just saying~ 내 말은 단지 …라는거야, 그냥 그렇다는거지

this often indicates that the speaker wants to repeat or talk about an important point. It would be like saying "The main thing I want you to remember is..."

A: I don't think you understand what is going on.
네가 돌아가는 일을 이해못하고 있는 것 같아.

B: **I'm just saying** that everyone seems very confused. 내 말은 단지 다들 매우 혼란스러워한다는거야.

I'm not blaming you. I'm just saying it wasn't my fault.
널 비난하는 게 아냐. 내 말은 단지 내 잘못이 아니라는 거지.

I'm just saying maybe I don't need your help.
내 말은 단지 네 도움이 필요없을 수도 있다는 거야.

I'm just saying that it's one of the possibilities.
내 말은 단지 그게 하나의 가능성이라는 거지.

021 It dawned on me~ …라는 생각이 들었어, …가 이해되기 시작했어

this is usually said to indicate the person understands something clearly now. It is similar to saying "I realized S+V"

I Point I dawn on sb 이해되기 시작하다

A: So you let your kids go camping alone?
그래 네 얘들만 캠핑보낼 거야?

B: Yeah. **It dawned on me that** they could take care of themselves. 스스로 돌볼 수 있다는 생각이 들었어.

미드표현

It never dawned on me. 전혀 몰랐어요.

As he walked away, it dawned on me that he didn't have my phone number.
걔가 걸어 갈 때 걔가 내 전화번호를 모른다는 사실을 떠올랐어.

022 It hit me that~ …라는 생각이 갑자기 들었어, 갑자기 떠올랐어

like the previous phrase, this is a way of saying the person suddenly understood something

I Point I It occurred to me that S+V 나에게 …라는 생각이 갑자기 떠올랐어

A: Why did you start your new business?
왜 새로운 사업을 시작한거야?

B: Well, **it hit me that** this is a good place for a restaurant. 여기가 식당을 하기에 좋은 장소라는 생각이 들었어.

It hit me that this isn't going to work.
이거는 제대로 될 수가 없을 거라는 생각이 들었어.

It occurred to me that I was really rude at the meeting. 내가 회의에서 무척 무례했다는 생각이 문득 들었어.

It occurred to Sue this was the nicest compliment she had ever received.
수는 문득 이거는 자기가 받은 찬사 중에서 최고의 찬사라는 생각이 들었어.

023 Let me sleep on it 곰곰이 생각해봐야겠어, 하룻밤 더 생각해볼게

미드표현

this is a way to say "I need to think about it before giving you an answer." People say this when they want time to make a decision

I Point I Sleep on it 신중을 기해서 생각하라구

A: I need to know if you are willing to marry me.
네가 나랑 기꺼이 결혼해줄지 알아야겠어.

B: **Let me sleep on it.** I will call you tomorrow.
좀 더 생각해보고, 내일 전화할게.

Come on, just keep an open mind. In fact, why don't you sleep on it?
그러지 말고 열린 맘을 가지라고, 하룻밤 더 생각해봐.

I told her I'd sleep on it.
난 걔한테 하루 더 생각해보겠다고 말했어.

Go home. Sleep on it. We'll talk more tomorrow. 집에 가서 곰곰이 생각해봐. 내일 더 얘기하자고.

024 We're having second thoughts about it
다시 생각해봐야겠어

미드표현

this means "We might change our minds." It indicates the people thought something was a good idea, but now they are not sure.

I Point I have[give] seconds thought(s) about~ (…에 대해) 생각이 바뀌다, 다시 생각하다, 의구심이 들다
On second thought (결정을 바꾸면서) 다시 생각해보니

A: **I'm having second thoughts about** getting married. 결혼에 대해 다시 생각해봐야겠어.

B: Really? Do you want to cancel the wedding?
정말? 결혼식 취소하고 싶어?

I'm having second thoughts about her death.
그 여자의 죽음에 의구심이 들어.

You're not having second thoughts?
생각을 바꾸는 건 아니겠지?

On second thought, I won't be driving you to school. The walk will do you good.
다시 생각해보니, 차로 학교 데려다 주지 않을거야. 걷는 게 네게 도움이 될거야.

025 Is that what you think? 그게 네 생각이야?, 네가 생각하는 게 이거야?

this expresses surprise over someone's opinion. It is like saying "Do you really feel that way?"

| Point | Is that what you think S+V~? 네 생각이 바로 …라는 거야?
Is that what you think this is? 이걸 그렇게 생각하는 거야?
(=You don't know what this is)
Is that what you think I'm saying? 내가 한 말을 그렇게 생각하는 거야?
(=You don't understand what I'm saying)
That's what you think 그건 네 생각이고

A: There are a lot of dangerous Muslims around.
위험한 이슬람교도들이 주위에 많아.

B: **Is that what you think?** I don't agree with you.
정말 그렇게 생각하는 거야? 그렇지 않아.

You're gonna leave me? Is that what you think?! 날 떠난다고? 네가 생각하는 게 바로 이거야?!

Is that what you think? That once an addict, always an addict?
네 생각이 고작 이거야? 한번 중독자는 영원한 중독자라고?

Is that what you think, that life with me will be crap?
네 생각은 바로 나와 함께 하면 인생이 엉망이 될거라는 거야?

026 Wouldn't it be better to~ ? …하는 게 더 낫지 않을까?

미드표현

this is a way to say "I think it would be better if S+V." The speaker wants to say he thinks he has a good idea

| Point | Wouldn't it be better if S+V~ ? …하는 것이 더 낫지 않을까?

A: I plan to walk downtown today. 오늘 시내에 걸어갈려고.

B: **Wouldn't it be better if** you went on the bus?
버스타고 가는 게 더 낫지 않을까?

Wouldn't it be better to keep it covered up for a while? 잠시 그걸 비밀에 부치는 게 더 낫지 않을까?

I was thinking, wouldn't it be better if the staff wore uniforms?
생각해봤는데, 직원들이 유니폼을 입는 게 더 낫지 않을까?

027 The way I see it 내가 보기엔

미드표현

this means "This is my opinion." It is a way for the speaker to tell people about his feelings

| Point | As I see it 내가 보기에 In my opinion 내 생각에
The way I look at it is ~ 내가 보기엔 …이다

A: We need to buy a gift for your sister.
네 누이한테 줄 선물을 사야 돼.

B: **The way I see it,** we can do that tomorrow.
내가 보기엔, 내일 사도 돼.

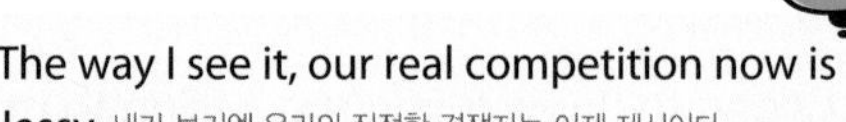

The way I see it, our real competition now is Jessy. 내가 보기엔 우리의 진정한 경쟁자는 이제 제시이다.

The way I see it, somebody did us a favor.
내가 보기에 누군가가 우리에게 호의를 베풀었어.

The way I see it, you're diligent, tidy and detail-oriented.
내가 보기엔, 넌 부지런하고 깔끔하고 꼼꼼한 것 같아.

028 That's how I take it 그렇게 생각하고 있는데

미드표현

this is a slightly complex way to express that the speaker has listened to someone talking about his opinion on or feeling about something, and the speaker wants to indicate that he agrees. His response is a way of saying "I have the same opinion as you about that"

| Point | That's how I take it 나도 그렇게 받아들이는데, 그렇게 생각하고 있는데

A: I think she stole the dress from the store.
걔가 가게에서 옷을 훔친 것 같아.

B: **That's how I take it.** She didn't think she'd be caught. 나도 그렇게 생각하고 있어. 걔는 잡히지 않을거라고 생각했나봐.

He wants to be left alone. That's how I take it.
걔는 혼자 있고 싶어해. 나는 그렇게 생각하고 있어.

The whole place needs to be shut down. That's how I take it.
그곳 전체는 폐쇄되어야 돼. 난 그렇게 생각해.

He wants a cup of black coffee. That's how I take it. 걘 블랙커피를 마시고 싶어해. 난 그렇게 생각하고 있어.

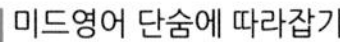

029 You do the math 잘 생각해봐, 계산해봐

this indicates that something is easy to understand. It is like saying "Look at this and you will understand it clearly"

A: Why is Steve being so nice to his grandmother?
스티브가 왜 할머니에게 그렇게 잘하는 거야?

B: She's rich and very old. **You do the math.**
할머니가 부자시면서 늙으셨거든. 잘 생각해봐.

미드표현

You're a man. Do the math. 너 남자잖아. 잘 계산해봐.

What am I going to do, sue for a restaurant? I used to make five million a year. You do the math.
어떻게 해, 레스토랑을 고발할까? 일년에 오백만 불 벌었으니 한번 계산해봐.

030 We'll see 좀 보자고, 두고 봐야지

this indicates that the answer to something will come later. Often it is a way to say "I'll decide later on"

| Point | We'll see what[how]~ …인지 좀 보자고

A: Can we visit the circus this weekend Dad?
이번 주말에 서커스 갈 수 있어요?

B: We'll see. Maybe we can if you act nicely.
좀 두고보자. 네가 착하게 굴면 갈 수도 있지.

미드표현

We'll see what's up. 무슨 일인지 두고보자고.

We'll see what we can do.
우리가 할 수 있는 게 뭔지 좀 보자고.

We'll see how it goes. 어떻게 되어가는지 좀 보자고.

031 when it comes (right) down to it 모든 점을 고려해볼 때

the speaker is saying "The basic facts are..." This is said to express that something is clearly true

| Point | When you get right down to it 모든 걸 고려해볼 때
When all is said and done 모든 일이 끝나면, 모든 걸 고려해볼 때
When it comes down to sth …을 고려해볼 때

A: I think that Teddy is a little strange.
테디가 좀 이상한 것 같아.

B: **When it comes right down to it,** most people feel that way. 모든 점을 고려해볼 때 다들 그렇게 느껴.

미드표현

When it comes down to it, you would risk your life for your wife before you would for your Mom. That's the bottom line.
그런 상황이 오면 어머니보다는 아내가 더 중요해져. 그게 핵심이지.

When it comes down to the environment, it doesn't matter who's going to win.
환경에 관해서 누가 이기든지 중요하지 않아.

032 We're on the same page 우린 같은 생각이야

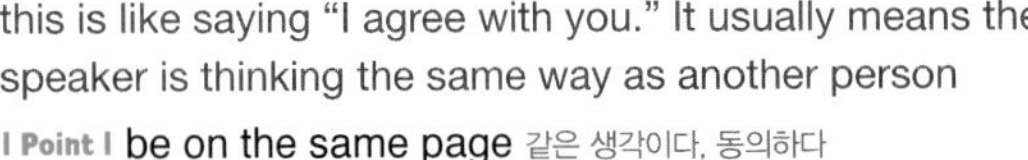

this is like saying "I agree with you." It usually means the speaker is thinking the same way as another person

| Point | be on the same page 같은 생각이다, 동의하다

A: What do you think about the offer I made to you? 내가 제안한 제의 어때?

B: **We're on the same page,** but can you offer a little more? 같은 생각이지만 좀 더 쓰지 그래?

미드표현

I wanted to make sure we were on the same page. 우리가 생각이 같다는 걸 확인하고 싶었어.

Chris and James were finally on the same page. 크리스와 제임스가 마침내 같은 생각을 하게 된거야.

We're on the same page now, so we should just focus on that.
이제 우리 생각이 같으니 그거에만 집중하자고.

033 Has that ever occurred to you? 그런 생각 든 적 없어?

this question is asking if the listener has ever considered something that may be possible. Often it is a way to encourage someone to think with a different point of view. It is very similar to asking someone "Did you ever think about this?"

| Point | Has that ever occurred to you? 그런 생각 든 적 없어?, 이해하겠어?
Has that ever occurred to you that S+V? …라는 생각이 든 적 없어?

A: I am always arguing with my roommates. 난 늘상 룸메이트와 다퉈.

B: Maybe you should move. **Has that ever occurred to you?** 너 이사가야겠다. 그런 생각해본 적 없어?

미드표현

This is inappropriate. Has that ever occurred to you? 이건 부적절해. 그런 생각이 든 적 없어?

Has it ever occurred to you that you might be the problem? 네가 문제거리일 수도 있다는 생각이 든 적 없어?

Has it ever occurred to you I might know my own mind better than you?
내가 너보다 내 맘을 더 잘 알 수도 있다는 생각 든 적이 없어?

034 Don't get hung up on it 너무 신경쓰지마

this is a way to tell someone that some problem is not too important, so he shouldn't get too stressed or bothered by it. In other words, it is saying "Relax, don't give it too much thought"

| Point | get[be] hung up on[about]~ 잊지못하다, 매우 걱정하다, 신경쓰다
hang up on sb 전화를 도중에 끊다(cut off one's phone call)

A: My girlfriend says I need to get a better job.
내 여친은 내가 더 좋은 직장을 얻어야 한대.

B: **Don't get too hung up on it.** You can do it.
너무 걱정마. 넌 할 수 있어.

미드표현

Baby, let's not get hung up on costs, all right?
자기야, 비용은 너무 신경쓰지 말자, 알았어?

I got hung up on the details of the contract.
난 계약서의 세부내용에 대해 매우 걱정하고 있어.

Don't you hang up on me! This is important.
전화끊지마! 중요한 건이야.

035 She will figure a way out 걘 문제를 해결할 방법을 찾아낼거야

this implies that a woman will be able to find a solution for a difficult problem she has. It probably also means the woman is clever, since she is able to solve the problem. Another way to say this is "She can work out the best way to do it"

| Point | figure out 이해하다, 알아내다, 생각해내다

A: Do you think Terry can overcome being fired?
테리가 해고된 것을 극복할 수 있을까?

B: Sure, **she will figure a way out.** 물론, 걘 방법을 찾아낼거야.

미드표현

You want me to help you figure it out?
네가 그걸 알아내는데 내가 도와줄까?

Well you better figure it out because he is not gonna be able to wait forever.
걔는 영원히 기다려주지 않을테니 네가 그걸 알아내는게 나을거야.

I apologize for the noise, and we will try to figure out a way to be quieter.
시끄럽게 해서 죄송해요, 좀 더 조용히 할 방법을 찾도록 할게요.

036 It didn't cross my mind 생각이 나지 않았어

this implies that the speaker did not take the time to remember something. It could mean the speaker was forgetful, or that he was possibly busy thinking of other things. In other words, "I didn't even think of it at all"

| Point | sth cross one's mind …가 생각나다

A: Why didn't you pick up groceries on the way home? 왜 집에 올 때 식료품을 사오지 않았어?

B: I'm sorry, **it didn't cross my mind to do that.**
미안해, 그럴 생각이 전혀 나지 않았어.

미드표현

Didn't cross your mind to tell us you had a DEA agent for a brother-in-law?
처남이 만약 단속반요원이라는 걸 우리에게 말해줄 생각이 전혀 안났어?

Yeah, that thought did cross my mind.
그래 그 생각이 났었어.

Honestly, that never even crossed my mind.
솔직히 말해서 그 생각이 난 적은 전혀 없었어.

037 I got to thinking about safe sex 세이프 섹스에 대해 생각을 해봤어

this speaker is saying that he was considering or wondering about the different aspects of having sex so that no one becomes pregnant and no sexual diseases are transmitted. It is like saying "I was considering the ways a person has to be careful when having sex"

| Point | I got to thinking about[that ~] 생각하기 시작하다.

A: Why are you buying so many condoms?
넌 왜 그렇게 많은 콘돔을 사는거야?

B: **I got to thinking about** safe sex and wanted to be prepared. 세이프 섹스에 대해 생각을 하기 시작했고 항상 준비된 상태로 있고 싶었어.

미드표현

I got to thinking that you never really get any time to yourself.
넌 자신만의 시간을 갖지 못한다는 생각을 하기 시작했어.

We got to thinking about who could have ordered these things, And your name came up.
누가 이 같은 일들을 지시할 수 있었을까 궁리를 해봤는데 네 이름이 떠올랐어.

038 How's that for a suspect? 용의자로 어때?

this is asking what a person feels about something. We can understand the speaker wants to know the listener's opinion or personal feelings. It is similar to asking, "So, what do you think about this?"

| Point | How's that for sth~? …를 어떻게 생각해?

A: You arrested my neighbor for the crime?
넌 범죄를 저질렀다고 내 이웃을 체포했어.

B: That's right. **How's that for** a suspect?
맞아. 용의자로 어때?

미드표현

The meal will be steak and lobster. How's that for a dinner? 식사는 고기와 랍스터야. 저녁식사로 어때?

We got him a Rolex watch. How's that for a gift? 걔한테 롤렉스 시계를 사줬어. 선물로 어때?

He was sentenced to 20 years in prison. How's that for punishment? 걘 20년 형을 받았어. 벌로 어때?

039 Where do we stand on this marriage?
이 결혼에 대한 너의 생각은 어때?

usually this is a way to ask how people feel about a marriage. The speaker is asking for people's opinions, and he probably wants to know whether they think the marriage is good or bad.

| Point | Where do we stand on~? …에 대한 우리의 입장은 어때?

A: **Where do we stand on** this marriage?
이 결혼에 대한 우리 입장은 어때?

B: I think it's shaky and may not last.
불안해서 오래 못갈 수 있을 것 같아.

미드표현

Where do you stand on physicians-assisted suicide? 의사를 통한 자살에 대한 너의 입장은 뭐야?

Leonard, where do you stand on the anthropic principle?
레너드, 넌 이 인간중심원리에 대해 어떤 입장이야?

I just explained it to you. Now, where do you stand on it?
내가 너한테 그걸 설명해주었는데. 이제 그에 대한 네 입장은 뭐야?

040 That didn't strike you as odd? 그게 이상하다는 느낌이 들지 않았어?

this speaker is asking if someone considered something to be weird or unusual. Often this is asked when something out of the ordinary happens, and the speaker wants to know how people reacted to it. What the speaker wants to ask is "Didn't you think that was strange?"

| Point | strike sb as (being)~ …가 …하다는 느낌을 받다, …에게 …한 느낌을 주다
It strikes sb as odd that~ …가 이상하다는 느낌을 …가 느끼다

A: I saw the man fall over into the street.
그 남자가 거리로 떨어지는 것을 봤어.

B: Really? **That didn't strike you as odd?**
정말? 좀 이상하다는 생각이 들지 않았어?

미드표현

Doesn't it strike you as odd that the bullets that killed Tyler came from Emily's gun?
타일러를 죽인 탄환이 에밀리의 총에서 발사됐다는거에 넌 이상한 느낌이 들지 않아?

That doesn't strike you as suspicious? It strikes me as unfortunate.
그게 의심스럽다는 느낌이 들지 않아? 난 안됐다라는 느낌이 들어.

041 You would think it was a dumb idea

그건 어리석은 생각이었다고 생각하고 싶겠지

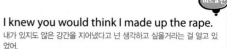

this usually is a way to say that although something seems to be true initially, it probably isn't. The speaker may be expressing a feeling of confusion. It is like saying "It seems dumb, but really it is not"

Point You would think that~ (사실이 아니지만) …라 생각하고 싶을거야

A: Your friend is selling used vacuum cleaners?
네 친구가 중고 진공청소기를 판다고?

B: **You would think** it was a dumb idea, but he's made a lot of money.
어리석은 생각이라고 생각하겠지만 걔 돈 많이 벌어.

I knew you would think I made up the rape.
내가 있지도 않은 강간을 지어냈다고 넌 생각하고 싶을거라는 걸 알고 있었어.

You would think that we've pushed him to change what he's doing.
우리가 강요해서 걔가 자기 일을 바꿨다고 생각하고 싶을거야.

You would think that Scott would have left a suicide note.
넌 스캇이 자살할 때 유서를 남겼을거라고 생각하고 싶겠지.

042 He racked his brain to find a solution

갠 해결책을 찾기 위해 머리를 쥐어 짜냈어

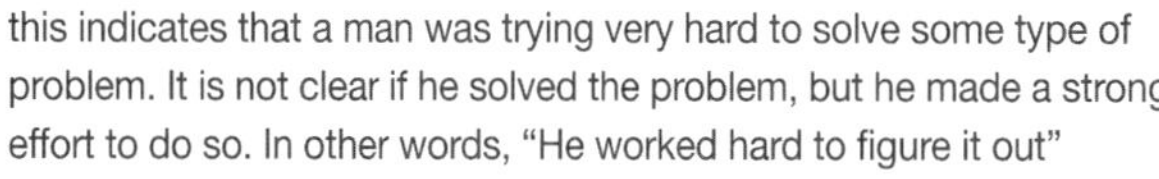

this indicates that a man was trying very hard to solve some type of problem. It is not clear if he solved the problem, but he made a strong effort to do so. In other words, "He worked hard to figure it out"

Point rack[wrack] one's brain to~ …하기 위해 궁리하다, 깊이 생각하다

A: I'm impressed that Brian solved the puzzle.
브라이언이 퍼즐을 푸는 걸 보고 인상적이었어.

B: **He racked his brain to** find a solution.
퍼즐을 풀려고 머리를 쥐어 짜냈어.

Rack your brain. 깊이 생각해봐.

Okay, well why don't you rack your brain?
좋아, 그럼 머리를 쥐어 짜봐.

Try to rack your brain a little. 좀 더 궁리를 해봐.

Wrack your brain. I mean, we've really gotta think here.
머리를 쥐어 짜내봐. 내 말은 우린 정말 여기서 생각을 해내야 돼.

043 I'll get some thoughts to you

내 생각을 말해줄게

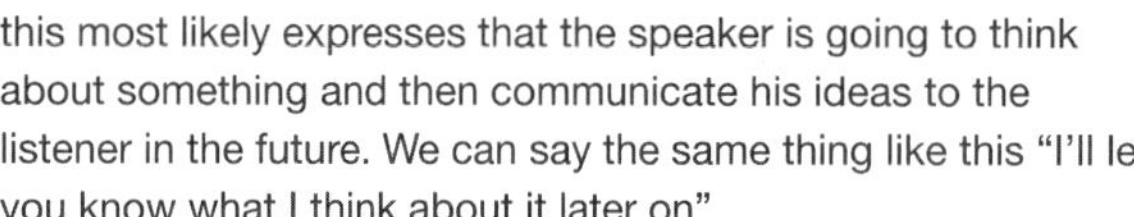

this most likely expresses that the speaker is going to think about something and then communicate his ideas to the listener in the future. We can say the same thing like this "I'll let you know what I think about it later on"

Point get some thoughts (to, on)~ 생각을 …에게 전하다[말해주다]
have some thoughts~ …라는 생각을 좀 하다

A: Let me know what you think about the report.
보고서 어떻게 생각하는지 알려줘.

B: **I'll get some thoughts to you** when I've read it. 읽고 나서 내 생각을 말해줄게 .

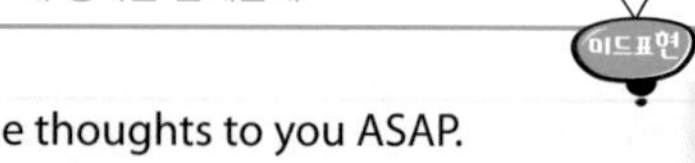

I'll get some thoughts to you ASAP.
가능한 빨리 내 생각을 전해줄게.

Get some of your thoughts to the floor manager. 매장 관리자에게 네 생각을 말해봐.

Did you get some thoughts to the club president? 클럽회장에게 네 생각을 전했어?

044 I'll give it some thought

내가 좀 생각을 해볼게

this means that the speaker is going to think about something and then make a decision about it. He is not going to say yes or no immediately. It is very much like saying "I need some time to consider this before giving you an answer"

Point give sth some thought …을 생각 좀 해보다(give some thought to)

A: Are you planning to join our club? 클럽에 가입하실 건가요?

B: Maybe. **I'll give it some thought.** 아마도요. 생각 좀 해보고요.

You might want to give that some thought. 넌 그거에 대해 좀 생각해보는게 좋을거야.

You know, I've given the matter some thought. 저 말이야, 난 그 문제에 대해 생각을 해봤어.

I've given some thought to your offer.
난 네 제의에 대해 생각을 좀 해봤어.

045 Think outside the box 창의적으로 생각해봐

this is a way to say something can be done in an unusual or unconventional way, but it will still be successful. It is like saying "Think of an alternative way to do this"

| Point | think outside the box 창의적으로 생각하다

A: It's getting harder to compete with businesses.
다른 회사들과 경쟁하는게 점점 더 힘들어져.

B: That means you need to **think outside the box** to make a profit. 그러면 넌 창의적으로 생각을 해서 수익을 내야 돼.

Well it's definitely thinking outside the box.
그건 정말이지 창의적인 생각이야.

She is not strong at thinking outside the box.
걘 창의적으로 생각하는데 좀 약해.

It is so refreshing to be with someone who likes to fuck outside the box.
섹스를 창의적으로 하는 걸 좋아하는 사람과 같이 있으니 정신이 다 개운하네.

046 I had a lot on my mind 머리 속이 복잡해

this expresses that the person was distracted because he had things to worry about. It is also usually an indicator that the person may be experiencing a lot of stress in his life. A different way to say this is "I have a lot of troubles I've been thinking about"

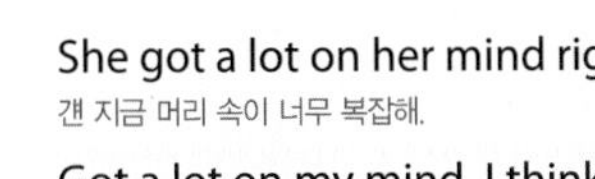

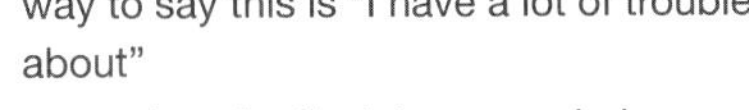

| Point | have[get] a lot on my mind 생각이 복잡하다

A: No one could get in touch with you yesterday.
어제 아무도 네게 연락이 되지 않더라.

B: **I had a lot on my mind** and I decided to shut off my phone. 머리 속이 복잡해서 전화기를 꺼놨어.

She got a lot on her mind right now.
걘 지금 머리 속이 너무 복잡해.

Got a lot on my mind. I think I'm pregnant.
생각이 좀 많아. 나 임신한 것 같아.

You got a lot on your mind-- three kids and a newborn, it sounds like a new job.
생각이 복잡하겠다, 아이 셋에 태어난 애도 있고, 새로운 일을 맡은 것 같아.

047 You got a gut feeling on this? 직감이 오니?

this is asking if someone has a strong personal belief that something will happen. It is similar to asking "What is your instinct on this?"

| Point | gut feeling 직감, 육감

A: We should buy a lottery ticket today.
오늘 로또를 사야겠어.

B: Oh really? **You got a gut feeling on this?**
어 정말? 필이 오는 게 있어?

I don't know, I mean, this is just my initial gut feeling. 모르겠어. 이건 그냥 내 육감인데.

I just have this gut feeling that it would be dangerous. 그게 위험할거라는 육감이 들었어.

I just have a gut feeling that it's her.
그게 걔라는 직감이 들었어.

048 That makes two of us 동감이야, 나도 마찬가지야, 나도 그렇게 생각해

often this indicates "I agree with you." It is said when someone wants to say he has an idea that is similar to another person's

A: I just want to live an interesting life.
단지 재미나게 살고 싶을 뿐이야.

B: **That makes two of us.** 나도 그렇게 생각해.

You like the taste of the spaghetti? That makes two of us. 너 스파게티 맛을 좋아하지? 나도 마찬가지야.

That makes two of us. I'm in total agreement.
나도 그렇게 생각해. 나도 완전히 동의해.

I love this beach resort, so that makes two of us. 난 이 해변 휴양지가 좋아, 그럼 우리 같은 생각이네.

049 What do you expect to~? 뭘 …하기를 바라는 거야?

this is like saying "What do you think will happen when you do that?" It is asking for a person to give his opinion about what the result of his actions will be

| Point | What do you expect me to do~? 내가 …하기를 바라니?
How do you expect to do~? 어떻게 …하겠다는 거야?
How do you expect me to do~? 어떻게 내가 …하기를 바래?

A: I want to visit Hollywood. 할리우드에 가고 싶어.
B: **What do you expect to** see there? 가서 뭘 보려고?

미드표현

What do you expect to happen right now, Terry? 테리야 지금 뭘 바라는 거야?

What do you expect me to do? You brought this on yourself. 내가 뭘 하길 바래? 네가 자초한 거잖아.

How do you expect to earn anyone's trust if you don't keep your word? 약속도 못지키면서 어떻게 남의 신뢰를 받기를 바래?

050 Give or take a few minutes[seconds, hours]

(앞에 말한 숫자가 대강임을 말하며) 대략 그 정도

the speaker wants to say he isn't sure of the time exactly, but it is nearly correct. It means that there could be some changes in the amount of time something takes

A: I think we'll arrive at 7:30, **give or take** a few minutes. 7시 30분 대략 그 정도에 도착할거 같아.
B: I'll be very happy to get off this airplane.
이 비행기에서 내리면 정말 좋겠어.

미드표현

A: How long have you been sitting here?
B: I don't know. Five hours, give or take a few minutes. A: 여기 얼마나 있었니? B: 잘몰라. 한 5시간 가량.

Give or take a yard or two. 1, 2 야드 오차가 있을 수 있어.

051 This is a little more than she bargained for

이건 걔가 예상했던 것보다 조금 심해

this is a way to indicate the person had something happen that was bigger or more than she thought it would be. It means "This isn't what she expected"

| Point | A little more than he bargained for 걔가 예상했던 거 이상

A: Susan seems really busy since she became president of the horse club.
수잔은 승마클럽회장이 된 이후 정말 바쁜 것 같아.
B: Yeah, this is **a little more than she bargained for.** 그래, 걔가 예상했던거 이상야.

미드표현

I think she's more than you bargained for.
걘 네가 예상했던 것 이상일거라 생각해.

Well, you're gonna get a lot more than you bargained for.
넌 네 예상보다 더 많은 걸 얻게 될거야.

Doug and Mr. Francis clearly got more than they bargained for.
더그와 프랜시스 씨는 자신들의 예상보다 훨씬 많이 얻었어.

052 Oh, you just caught me off guard!

굉장히 놀랬어!, 생각도 못한 일이야!

this is a way to say "You surprised me." The person wasn't expecting something that happened

| Point | catch[throw] sb off guard …을 놀래키다, …가 예상 밖의 행동을 하다
Sb be caught off guard (by~) (…로) …가 깜짝 놀라다
It was the last thing I expected 생각도 못했어(It really surprised me)

A: You looked shocked when I spoke to you.
내가 말할 때 놀란 것 같았어.
B: **Oh, you just caught me off guard.** 어, 깜짝 놀랬어.

It just kind of caught me off guard.
생각도 못해 본 일이야.

Sam caught me off guard. 샘 때문에 놀랬어.

Andy was caught off guard by her honesty.
걔의 정직함에 앤디가 놀랬어.

You just caught us off guard with the lesbian thing. 레즈비언건으로 네가 우릴 놀래켰어.

053 (Would you) Let it go 그냥 잊어버려, 그냥 놔둬, 신경 꺼

this is telling someone to stop thinking so much about something. It is like saying "Try to forget it"

| Point | Let it be 내버려 둬 Give it a go 그냥 둬

A: I can't believe that she treated me that way.
개가 날 그렇게 취급했다니 믿어지지가 않아.

B: **Let it go.** It was just a mistake. 그냥 잊어버려. 실수였잖아.

It's not too late to let it go and start over.
잊어버리고 새로 시작하기에 늦지 않았어.

Paul, let it go. This is not a problem.
폴, 잊어버려. 이건 문제도 아니잖아.

Chris. She's got a boyfriend. Just let it go.
크리스, 걘 남친이 있어. 그냥 잊어버려.

She's with me now, I told you that. Let it go.
걘 지금 나와 함께 있어, 내가 말했잖아. 잊어버려.

054 Go with the flow 마음을 가라앉혀, 그냥 내버려 둬, 하는 대로 해

this is a way of telling someone "Relax and don't be stressed." It is also a way of telling that person not to fight or get angry about small things

| Point | go with the flow 대세에 따르다 ↔ go against the flow

A: How do you always stay so calm?
어떻게 그렇게 항상 차분한거야?

B: **Go with the flow.** It's unhealthy to get upset.
그냥 내버려 둬. 화내는 건 건강에 안좋아.

I'm just going with the flow.
물 흘러가는 대로 따라갈 뿐이야.

Can't you relax and go with the flow?
그냥 쉬면서 되는대로 해.

055 Go with your gut 너 끌리는대로 해

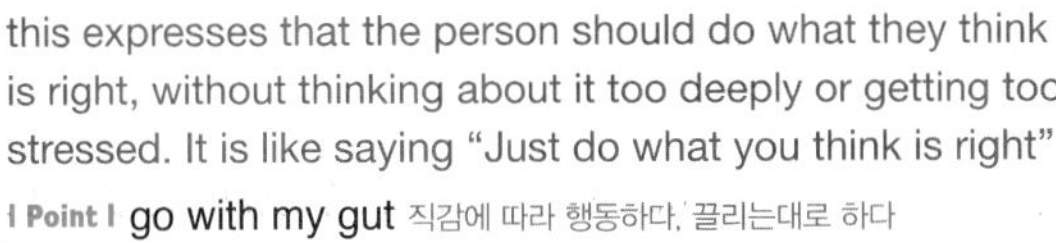

this expresses that the person should do what they think is right, without thinking about it too deeply or getting too stressed. It is like saying "Just do what you think is right"

| Point | go with my gut 직감에 따라 행동하다, 끌리는대로 하다

A: I'm not sure it's a good idea for me to get married right now. 지금 결혼하는게 좋은 생각인지 모르겠어.

B: **Go with your gut.** If you think it's wrong, don't do it. 끌리는대로 해. 아니라고 생각되면 하지마.

Go with your gut. Follow your instincts.
너 끌리는대로 해. 네 본능에 따라 행동하라고.

In your gut you know I'm better than you. Go with your gut.
직관적으로 내가 너보다 뛰어나다는 걸 알거야. 네 직관을 따르라고.

I'd rather go with scientific evidence than with your gut. 네 직감보다는 과학적 증거를 따르겠어.

056 I just can't get past it 그걸 잊을 수가 없어, 아직도 못 잊겠어

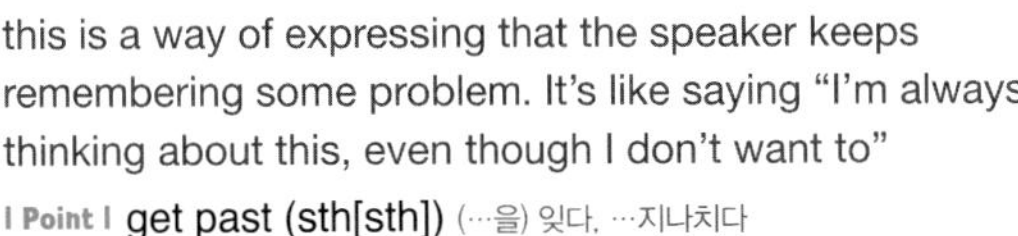

this is a way of expressing that the speaker keeps remembering some problem. It's like saying "I'm always thinking about this, even though I don't want to"

| Point | get past (sth[sth]) (…을) 잊다, …지나치다

A: Are you still missing the relationship with your former boyfriend? 아직도 헤어진 남친과 사귀었던 게 그리워?

B: Yeah. **I just can't get past it.** 어. 잊을 수가 없어.

She will get past it. 걘 잊을 거야.

Can we please get past this?
제발 지나간 일로 치면 안될까?

Could you get past yourself for a second?
다른 사람 생각 좀 해줄 수 없어?

I just can't get past it. I can't get her out of my mind. 잊을 수가 없어. 걜 머리속에서 지울 수가 없어.

057 Put today behind us 오늘 일은 잊어버리자

often this means "Let's forget this bad time." It is a way of saying that it is better to think about the future

| Point | put sth behind sb …을 잊다

A: I had an awful time in this place.
여기서 아주 끔직한 시간을 보냈어.

B: Well, we should try to **put today behind us.**
저기, 오늘은 잊어버리도록 하자.

미드표현

I forgave you. Can't we just put this behind us? 용서했으니까 그냥 이거 잊어버리자

I'm perfectly willing to put it all behind us, if you will just give me a simple, "I'm sorry."
그냥 내게 "미안"이라고만 하면 난 기꺼이 다 잊을거야

058 Let's move on 다음으로 넘어가자고

this expresses that the speaker has finished with something and wants to go on to something else. It is frequently used in discussions. When someone says this, it often means "We have finished with that topic and are ready to talk about the next one"

| Point | move on 담으로 넘어가자, 잊다

A: I think we are done discussing the project.
우린 그 프로젝트에 대한 토의를 끝낸 것 같아.

B: Very well, **let's move on** to other things.
좋아, 다음 사항으로 넘어가자고.

미드표현

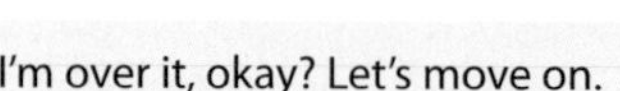

I'm over it, okay? Let's move on.
난 극복했다고, 알았어? 다음 단계로 넘어가자고.

So let's move on to our next subject.
그럼 다음 주제로 넘어가자고.

It took her a long time to move on.
걔는 잊는데 시간이 많이 걸렸어.

I'm not ready to move on.
난 다음으로 넘어갈 준비가 되지 않았어.

059 (That's) Water under the bridge 지나간 건 잊어야지

this is a way of saying "Let's forget about it." It is said to indicate something happened in the past and should be forgotten

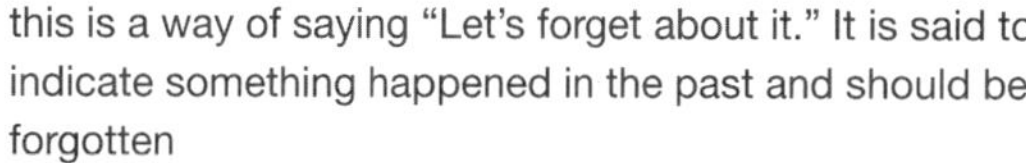

A: Weren't you angry with Bob last year?
작년에 밥한테 화나지 않았었어?

B: I was, but **that's water under the bridge now.**
그랬지만 다 지나간 건 잊어야지.

미드표현

Oh it's water under the bridge. Forget it!
다 지나간 일이야, 잊어버려!

You suspected me of murdering my husband? Detective, that is all water under the bridge now.
내가 남편 살해 혐의자라고요? 형사양반, 그건 이미 다 지나간 일이예요.

060 You just need to get your mind off it 넌 그걸 잠시 잊어야 돼

this expresses that someone has been thinking or worrying too much about something, and it is having a negative effect. The speaker thinks that the person should try to distract himself with other things. It is like saying "You have to stop worrying about it for a while"

| Point | get one's mind off~ 걱정하지 않다, 잠시 잊다

A: I have been stressed about my job.
내 직장문제로 스트레스를 많이 받았어.

B: **You just need to get your mind off it.**
넌 그 문제를 잠시 잊어야 돼.

미드표현

We thought that this would take your mind off things.
이거면 네가 잠시 머리를 식힐 수 있을거라 생각했어.

It'll help you take your mind off the baby.
그건 네가 애걱정을 잠시나마 잊는데 도움을 줄거야.

You need to do something else, get your mind off it. 넌 뭔가 다른 일을 해야 돼, 걱정을 잠시 잊으라고.

061 Help me take my mind off things 내가 현재 일들을 잊도록 도와줘

미드표현

this is a way of asking for someone to distract or entertain the speaker, so that he doesn't keep thinking about the personal problems he is having. What he is saying is "Please do something that makes my mind feel relaxed for a while"

| Point | take one's mind off sth[sb] 불쾌한 일을 잠시 잊어버리다

A: It seems like you've had a stressful month.
너 참 힘든 달을 보낸 것 같아.

B: Yes I have. I hope you'll help me **take my mind off things.** 어 그래. 나 좀 즐겁게 해줘서 일들을 좀 잊게 해줘.

Why don't we take him somewhere to take his mind off it, hmm?
걔가 그 일을 잊도록 다른데로 데려가자.

Get a job! It'll help you take your mind off the baby. 직장을 다녀! 그럼 아기 생각을 잊는데 도움이 될거야.

I think it'll be a great way to take my mind off everything that's happened.
난 그게 일어난 모든 일을 잊게 해주는 아주 좋은 방법이라고 생각해.

Maybe I need something to get my mind off of him. 난 걔를 잊기 위해 뭐가 필요한지 모르겠어.

062 I seem to have lost track of it 잊어버린 것 같아, 까먹은 것 같아

미드표현

this indicates something was forgotten or not kept in touch with. It is like saying "I don't remember where it is" or "I didn't stay in touch"

| Point | lose track of sth …에 두었는지 기억못하다
lose track of sb …와 연락(소식)이 끊기다

A: Can I borrow your English dictionary?
영어사전 좀 빌려줄래?

B: I'm not sure where it is. **I seem to have lost track of it.** 어디있는지 몰라. 어디에다 두었는지 기억이 안나.

I'm sorry, I guess I lost track of time.
미안, 시간 가는 줄 몰랐어.

I lost track of you, but I always read your column. 소식은 끊겼지만 네 칼럼을 항상 읽어.

063 It (completely) slipped my mind 깜박 잊었어

미드표현

this means "I forgot it." Usually this is said as an apology that the person didn't remember something

| Point | Sth slips one's mind …가 …을 깜박 잊다

A: Don't you have a dentist appointment today?
오늘 치과 예약되어 있지 않아?

B: Oh yeah! **It completely slipped my mind.**
어 그래! 깜박 잊었네.

I'm sorry. It slipped my mind. 미안. 깜박 잊었어.

It slipped my mind. I got tons to do, you know? 깜박 잊었어. 난 할 일이 엄청 많아, 알지?

It slipped my mind that we're in the most beautiful city in the world!
세상에서 가장 아름다운 도시에 우리가 있다는 사실을 깜박했어!

064 I can't get that moment out of my mind
난 그 순간을 잊을 수가 없어

미드표현

this speaker is saying that he always remembers an event that happened. We can assume the event was something very bad, and that although he wants to forget it, he can't. Another way to say this is "I keep remembering that incident"

| Point | get sth out of one's mind 잊다, 그만 생각하다
put sth out of one's mind 잠시라도 불쾌한 일을 잊으려 하다

A: So you witnessed the airplane crash?
그럼 너 비행기 추락사고를 목격했다는말야?

B: Yes, and **I can't get that moment out of my mind.** 어, 그 순간을 잊을 수가 없어.

I can't even get the image out of my mind.
그 모습을 잊을 수가 없어.

You gotta put it out of your mind.
넌 그것을 잊어버려야 돼.

I couldn't get the smell of you out of my mind. 네 향기를 잊을 수가 없었어.

I can't get Karen getting hit by that car out of my mind. 난 저 차에 치인 카렌을 잊을 수가 없어.

065 Let me remind you 알려줄게 있어, 명심해, 다시 한번 말할게

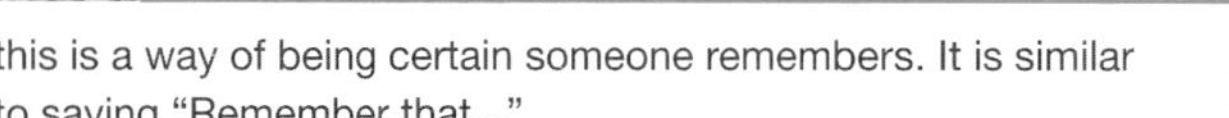

this is a way of being certain someone remembers. It is similar to saying "Remember that..."

Point Let me remind you of[that]~ …을 명심해라
Don't forget to do~ 잊지 말고 …해라(I want you to remember~)

A: **Let me remind you** that you need to clean your room. 네 방 청소하는 거 잊지마라.

B: OK, Mom, I'll do it this afternoon.
알았어요 엄마, 오늘 오후에 할게요.

미드표현

Let me remind you that I am the boss here.
내가 여기 사장이라는 거 명심해.

Let me remind you again of the rules of your probation. 네 보호감찰 규칙을 다시 말해주지.

Don't forget to invite us to the wedding.
결혼식에 초대하는 거 잊지마.

Don't forget to get me a present.
선물 사다 주는 거 잊지마.

066 Do I have to remind you I quit?
내가 그만뒀다는 걸 다시 말해줘야겠어?

this is a way of asking someone to remember something. We can understand that the speaker thinks the listener should know the information already. It is almost like saying "You should be able to recall this"

Point Do I have to remind you (that) S+V? 내가 …을 기억나게 해줘야 되겠어?, …을 다시 말해야겠어?
Need I remind you of/that~ …라는 걸 꼭 상기시켜 주어야 알겠어?

A: **Do I have to remind you** to shut off the TV?
TV를 끄라는 말을 또 해줘야 돼?

B: No, I'll shut it off before I leave. 아니, 가기 전에 끌게.

미드표현

Do I have to remind you what happened last time? 지난 번에 어땠는지 다시 말해야겠어?

Do I have to remind you it's potluck week?
포트럭 주간이라는 걸 상기시켜줘야겠어?

Do I have to remind you how serious this situation is? 이 상황이 얼마나 위중한지 다시 말해줘야겠어?

Do I have to remind you about them, huh?
걔네들에 대해 다시 말해줘야겠어, 어?

067 That reminds me 그러고 보니 생각나네, 그 말을 듣고 보니

this means "I just remembered something." It is usually said when a person has just thought of something that is important to talk about

Point That reminds me 그러고 보니 생각나네
That reminds me of~ 그 말을 듣고 보니 …가 생각나네

A: How is your grandmother doing these days?
요즘 네 할머니 어떻게 지내셔?

B: She's OK. **That reminds me.** I haven't called her in a while. 잘 지내셔. 그러고 보니 한동안 전화 못 드렸네.

That reminds me, I gotta call Robert.
그 말을 듣고 보니, 로버트에게 전화해야 돼.

That reminds me. I have to confirm my appointment at the City Hall.
그러고 보니 시청에 약속을 확인해야 돼.

Oh, that reminds me. Your mother called.
어, 그러고 보니 생각나네. 네 엄마가 전화했었어.

068 Don't remind me 그 얘기 꺼내지마, 생각나게 하지마

this expresses that the speaker has just been told something that has reminded him of something unpleasant. We can understand it has made him unhappy. It is another way to say "Stop telling me about that because I really don't like to remember it"

Point Don't remind me 생각나게 하지마, 기억나게 하지마

A: You have to submit the report by midnight.
자정까지는 보고서를 제출해야 돼.

B: **Don't remind me.** I'm already very stressed.
그 얘긴 꺼내지마. 이미 스트레스 많이 받았으니까.

미드표현

Don't remind me. This bitch boosted my wallet. 그 얘기 꺼내지마. 이 년이 내 지갑을 훔쳤어.

Don't remind me. I asked her to come, and she just kept saying "Get out of my room!"
그 얘기 꺼내지도 마. 난 걔한테 와달라고 했는데 걘 "내 방에서 꺼져!"라고만 되풀이했어.

That reminds me. I have to go.
그러고 보니 생각나네. 나 가야 돼.

069 That rings a bell 얼핏 기억이 나네, 문득 떠오르는 게 있어

this expresses the feeling "That is familiar to me." It is said when a person wants to indicate that he has heard or seen something before

| Point | (Does that) Ring a bell? 잊었어? 기억나?
(No, It) doesn't ring a bell (아니) 기억 안나

A: Have you seen the movie "My Left Foot"?
나의 왼발이란 영화 봤어?

B: **That rings a bell,** but I'm not sure.
얼핏 기억은 나는데 잘 모르겠어.

미드표현

It's David Cutter. Ring a bell? 데이빗 커터야. 기억나?

That might ring a bell. So what?
얼핏 기억나는데, 그래서 어쨌다는 거야?

It does not ring a bell with me. 난 못 들어 봤는데.

070 Now I remember 이제 생각이 났어

the speaker is saying he had forgotten something but now he knows it. It can also be said as "I recall that"

| Point | You can't remember 기억이 안 날 거야
You gotta remember~ 기억을 되살려봐
You remembered wrong 잘못 기억하는 거야

A: We met at Sam's house last year.
우린 작년에 샘의 집에서 만났지.

B: **Now I remember.** It was at a Christmas party.
이제 생각이 나네. 성탄파티였었지.

미드표현

She dumped me. You remember what that feels like. 걔가 날 찼어. 넌 그게 어떤건지 기억하지.

Now I remember when I let you sneak into my parties.
내 파티에 너를 살짝 들여보냈던 때가 이제 기억이 나네.

071 That's a blast from the past 옛 생각 많이 나게 하네

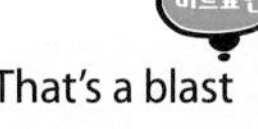

this phrase is used to indicate that something has reminded the speaker of the past. It is similar to saying "That brings back many memories"

| Point | That's(It's) a blast from the past 그거 기억나

A: Wow, I think that is a song by the group Wham.
와, 그룹 왬의 노래인 것 같아.

B: **That's a blast from the past.** They were popular in the 1980s. 옛 생각이 많이 나게 하네. 1980년대에 유명했었지.

미드표현

I've totally forgotten about her! That's a blast from the past!
걔에 대해 아예 잊고 있었는데! 옛 생각이 많이 나네!

Wow, that was a blast from the past-- my old temp agency. 와, 옛 생각이 많이 나네… 내 예전 임시 에이전시.

072 If (my) memory serves me correctly[right]
내 기억이 맞다면, 내가 기억하는 바로는

the speaker is trying to recall something. He is saying "I hope the details I remember are right"

A: **If my memory serves me correctly,** you are from Ontario. 내 기억이 맞다면 너 온타리오 출신이지.

B: Yes. My family comes from Toronto.
맞아. 내 가족은 토론토 출신야.

미드표현

If my memory serves me correctly, we met a few years ago. 내 기억이 맞다면, 우린 몇년 전에 만났어.

If my memory serves me correctly, Larry served time in prison.
내 기억이 맞다면 래리는 감옥살이를 했어.

If my memory serves me correctly, I still owe you fifty dollars. 내 기억이 맞다면 내가 너한테 50달러 줄게 있어.

073 It's like it never happened 마치 없던 일처럼

미드표현

often this is a way to express that something has been either forgotten or forgiven. It is very similar to saying "Let's just forget about it"

| Point | pretend like it never happened 없었던 것처럼 하다

A: Are your parents still angry about your problem?
네 부모님은 네 문제로 아직 화나 있으셔?

B: No. **It's like it never happened.** 아니. 다 잊으셨을거야.

We'll just pretend like it never happened.
우린 시치미 딱 뗄거야.

I turned around and pretended like it never happened. 돌아서서 아무 일도 없었던 척 할거야.

Sometimes it feels like it never happened.
간혹 아무 일도 없었던 것 같아.

MEMO

Ways of asking about the reason for something

이유나 원인을 말할 때

What has come over you?

001 What has come over you? 왜 그런거야?

this is asking for an explanation for unusual behavior. We can understand the speaker is surprised about someone's behavior and wants to know why that person has behaved that way. It is a way to ask "What made you do the things you did?"

| Point | What has come over you? 너 왜 그런거니?

A: **What has come over you?** Your grades suck.
왜 그런거야? 네 성적이 형편없네.

B: I just lost interest in doing school work.
학교공부하는데 흥미를 잃었어요.

What has come over you? Are you feeling sick? 왜 그런거야? 너 몸이 안좋아?

You act so angry. What has come over you?
너 아주 화난듯 행동하네. 무슨 일이야?

What has come over you? Why are you being stubborn? 왜 그런거야? 왜 그렇게 완강한거야?

002 Why does it come to this? 어쩌다 이 지경에 이르렀어?

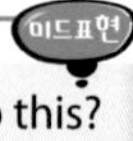

this is asking for the reason something negative happened. Often when this question is asked, something bad has occurred, and it has caused a lot of regret and unhappiness.

| Point | come to this 이 지경에 이르다, 이런 상황이 되다

A: There is nothing we can do to stop the war.
전쟁을 막기 위해 우리가 할 수 있는 일이 없어.

B: War is so terrible. **Why does it come to this?**
전쟁은 끔찍해. 어떡하다 이 지경에 이르렀나?

You're dating a convict? Does it come to this?
죄수하고 데이트를 하고 있다고? 그렇게 된거야?

I hoped it wouldn't come to this, but, uh, maybe it would be helpful if I told you my sexual secrets first.
이렇게 되지 않길 바랬지만 너한테 내 섹스에 관한 비밀을 먼저 말하는게 도움이 될 것같아.

003 Where did you get that idea? 어떻게 그런 생각을 하게 된거야?

this question is asked when someone has an unusual and possibly mistaken idea about something. Often we can understand that this is a way of trying to correct the mistaken idea. It is similar to saying "I don't know why you think that, but you are wrong"

| Point | Where did you get the idea to~? 어쩌다 …할 생각을 하게 된거야?

A: I understand that you sleep with a lot of men.
넌 많은 남자들하고 자는 걸로 아는데.

B: No I don't! **Where did you get that idea?**
아냐 난 안그래! 어떻게 그런 생각을 하게 된거야?

I'm just concerned. Where did you get the idea to do this?
그냥 걱정이 돼서. 어쩌다 이렇게 할 생각을 하게 된거야?

Where did you get this idea that I would only date white guys?
어떻게 내가 백인남자들하고만 데이트할 거라는 생각을 하게 된거야?

004 What have you got to say for yourself? 너 뭐라고 변명할거야?

this is a way of asking for an explanation from someone for their unusual behavior, which possibly caused a problem. Usually this is said by someone like a boss speaking to an employee, or a parent speaking to a child. We might understand this to mean "Tell me why you did that"

| Point | say for oneself 변명하다

A: The window is broken. **What have you got to say for yourself?** 유리창이 깨졌어. 뭐라고 변명할거야?

B: We accidentally broke it while we were playing baseball. 야구를 하다가 실수로 깨뜨렸어요.

Why don't we see what Tom has to say for himself? 탐이 뭐라고 변명하는지 보자고.

He has informed me of your grand deception. Do you have anything to say for yourself?
걔가 네 거대한 사기극에 대해 내게 알려줬어. 뭐 변명할 거리가 있어?

005 What brought that on? 어떻게 그렇게 된거야?

this is a way of asking what made something start happening. We can understand that something unusual occurred that might have been bad, and the speaker wants to know why it happened. Another way of saying this would be "What was the cause of this?"

| Point | bring sth on 초래하다, 야기하다

A: Peter had a heart attack and was taken to the hospital. 피터는 심장마비가 와서 병원으로 이송됐어.

B: I can't believe it. **What brought that on?**
그럴 수가. 왜 그렇게 된거야?

Why? What brought this on?
왜? 뭐 때문에 이렇게 된거야?

I don't know! I mean, what brought that on?
몰라! 내 말은, 어떻게 그렇게 된거야?

I don't understand. What bought that on?
이해가 안돼, 어쩌다 이렇게 된거야?

And what brought you on to that boat, Ben?
벤, 왜 저 보트에 오게 된거였어?

006 There's got to be a reason for that 뭔가 그 이유가 있을거야

this indicates that the speaker thinks that an occurrence was specifically or intentionally caused by something. In other words, it was not a random thing that can not be explained. Basically, the speaker is saying "There is an explanation for what happened here"

| Point | There's got to be~ …가 있을거야

A: The killer left his umbrella at the crime scene.
살인범은 범죄현장에 우산을 남겨두었어.

B: **There's got to be a reason for that.**
뭔가 그 이유가 있을거야.

I've been doin' this ten years and I haven't gotten anywhere. There's gotta be a reason.
10년간 이 일을 하는데 아무런 성과가 없었어. 뭔가 이유가 있을거야.

There's got to be a better way to avoid frostbite. 동상을 피하는 방법이 뭔가 있을거야.

There's got to be a way. There's got to be a different way. 뭔가 방법이 있을거야. 뭔가 다른 방법이 있을거야.

007 You still had a hand in her death 넌 여전히 걔 죽음에 한몫했어

this is a way of accusing someone of helping to cause another person's death. It would likely only be said by a policeman accusing a suspect of helping with a murder. We can express something similar by saying "I think you helped to kill her"

| Point | have a[one's] hand in~ …에 관여하다, 연루되다, 한몫하다, 영향을 미치다

A: I wasn't the person who shot Mrs. Hinkley.
난 힝클리 부인을 쏜 사람이 아녜요.

B: It doesn't matter. **You still had a hand in her death.** 상관없이, 넌 그녀의 죽음에 한몫했잖아.

I'm told you had a hand in planning it.
그것을 계획하는데 네가 한몫했다고 들었어.

If he had a hand in it, then he needs to be punished. 걔가 관여되었다면, 처벌받아야 해.

Whenever something bad happens to me, I assume it's my sister that had a hand in it.
뭔가 나쁜 일이 내게 생길 때마다, 난 누이가 그 일에 개입했다고 생각하고 있어.

008 He stripped which is why we found him naked 옷벗고 있어서 걜 발견했을 때 나체였어

this is saying that a man took off all of his clothes, which was very unusual behavior. We can also understand the man was probably in public because he was found naked somewhere. It is like saying "When we found him, he had no clothes on"

| Point | which is why~ 그래서 …하다, 그것이 …한 이유야

A: I heard the suspect was behaving strangely.
용의자가 이상하게 행동한다며.

B: He stripped, **which is why** we found him naked.
옷을 벗고 있어서 발견했을 때 나체였어.

I know you love his daughter, which is why I don't want you involved in this.
넌 걔 딸을 좋아하잖아, 그래서 난 네가 여기에 연루되지 않기를 바래.

They're not gonna leave me alone. Which is why I didn't want you to come here.
걔네들은 날 놔두지 않을거야. 그래서 나는 네가 여기 오지 않기를 바랬어.

009 Where does it say that? 무슨 근거로 그렇게 말하는거야?, 어디에 그렇게 씌여 있어?

this is a way of asking for clarification of something. The speaker did not see some detail in something that was written. When someone else points out that detail, the speaker may not believe it and wants to double check to make sure it's correct. It's a way of saying "Show me where that is written." It can also have a figurative meaning, in that the speaker is wondering why he should have to conform to an unwritten rule. For example, someone may ask "Where does it say I can't eat cake for breakfast?"

| Point | Where does it say that S+V? 무슨 근거로 …라고 말하는거야?

A: The contract states that your salary will be lowered. 계약서에 의하면 네 급여는 삭감 될거야.

B: Is that right? **Where does it say that?**
정말요? 어디 그렇게 씌여있어요?

미드표현

This painting's a forgery? Where does it say that? 이 그림이 위조라고? 무슨 근거로 그렇게 말하는거야?

This expires tomorrow? Where does it say that? 이거 유효기간이 내일이야? 어디에 그렇게 써있는거야?

010 It's what got me~ 바로 그 때문에 내가 …된거야

this is a way to say "That caused me to..." It explains the reason something happened

| Point | It's what got me to+V 그 때문에 내가 …하게 된거야

A: Was it worth your time to study at a university overseas? 외국대학에서 공부할 가치가 있었어?

B: Yes it was. **It's what got me** my job at the international company.
어 그렇지. 그 덕에 다국적 기업에 취직된거거든.

미드표현

Stupid phonecall. It's what got me caught.
망할 전화 때문에 내가 걸렸어.

It's what got me to start weight lifting.
바로 그 때문에 내가 근력운동을 하게 되었어.

It's what got me to give up drinking.
바로 그 때문에 내가 술을 끊게 되었어.

It's what got me to move to Los Angeles.
바로 그 때문에 내가 LA로 이사가게 되었어.

011 How come? 어째서?, 왜?

this simply means "Why?" The person is asking someone to explain the reason for something

| Point | How come S+V? 어째서 …해?

A: We need to be very quiet right now.
지금 무척 조용히 해야 돼.

B: **How come?** Is someone sleeping? 왜? 누가 자?

미드표현

How come nobody heard her scream?
어째서 걔가 비명지르는 걸 아무도 못들었지?

How come you're single? A pretty woman like you! What's your problem?
어째서 결혼 안했어? 너처럼 멋진 여자가! 무슨 문제 있어?

How come he doesn't like us? 어째서 걘 우릴 싫어해?

How come you never said she was pregnant?
넌 왜 걔가 임신했다는 것을 말하지 않은거야?

012 What for? 왜? , 무슨 이유 때문에?

like the previous phrase, this means "Tell me the reason." The speaker wants to know why something is

| Point | What's it for? 무슨 이유로?, 무엇 때문에?
What the hell for? 도대체 뭣 때문에?
For what? 뭐 때문에?

A: Stop playing those computer games.
그 컴퓨터 게임 좀 그만해라.

B: **What for?** I've already finished my school work.
왜요? 학교공부는 다 끝냈는데.

You want a sample of my DNA? What for?
DNA 샘플이 필요하다고? 무엇 때문에?

What the hell for? What did I do?
도대체 뭣 때문에? 내가 뭘 어쨌다고?

What for? It's not going to rain.
뭣 때문에? 비는 내리지 않을건데.

013 What brings you here? 무슨 일로 왔어?

this is a way of asking "Why did you come?" The speaker is asking about the reason someone came out

I Point I Why are you here? 여기는 왜 왔지?

A: Hi Sam. **What brings you here?** 야 샘, 여긴 웬 일야?

B: I have to talk to you about some important business. 너와 중요한 사업얘기 좀 해야 돼서.

미드표현

What a pleasant surprise. What brings you here? 진짜 반가워. 무슨 일로 왔어?

So, honey, what are you doing here? Why are you here? 그래 자기야, 여긴 웬 일이야? 여긴 왜 왔어?

Why are you here? Is Sally in trouble again? 여긴 왜 왔어? 샐리가 또 사고쳤어?

014 What makes you think so? 1. 왜 그렇게 생각해? 2. 꼭 그런 건 아니잖아?

this is asking for a person to explain his thinking. It's a way of saying "Please tell me why you think that way"

I Point I What makes you think S+V? 왜 …라고 생각해?

A: It looks like this company is going to fail. 이 회사는 망할 것 같아.

B: Really? **What makes you think so?** 정말? 왜 그렇게 생각해?

미드표현

What makes you think I even want you back? 왜 네가 돌아오길 내가 바란다고 생각해?

What makes you think she's seeing someone? 왜 걔가 누굴 만난다고 생각해?

What makes you think we're gonna break up? 왜 우리가 헤어질 거라고 생각해?

You said Shelia looks sick. What makes you think so? 쉴라가 아파보인다고 했는데, 왜 그렇게 생각하는거야?

015 What makes you so sure? 너 무슨 믿는 데라도 있니?, 어떻게 그렇게 확신해?

this is a way to challenge someone's opinion. It is like saying "You need to explain why you believe that"

I Point I What makes you so sure S+V? 왜 …라고 확신하는거야?

A: Jack is likely to get fired this year. 잭은 금년에 잘릴 것 같아.

B: **What makes you so sure?** 어떻게 그렇게 확신해?

미드표현

What makes you so sure? Do you have any proof? 뭐 믿는 데라도 있어? 증거라도 있는거야?

What makes you so sure I don't have talent? 내가 재능없다고 어떻게 그렇게 확신해?

What makes you so sure she would fall in love with me again? 걔가 나와 다시 사랑에 빠질거라고 어떻게 확신해?

016 What makes him tick? 걔가 왜 그렇게 행동하는거야?

this is a way of asking "Why does he act that way?" The speaker is trying to understand someone's way of thinking

I Point I What makes you tick? 뭣 때문에 그렇게 행동하는기야?, 너 왜 그러는거야?

A: Einstein was a genius, but he was kind of strange. 아인슈타인은 천재야 하지만 좀 이상했지.

B: I heard that. I wonder **what made him tick.** 알아. 왜 그렇게 행동했던 걸까?

Who is Cathy? What makes her tick? 캐시가 누구야? 걔가 왜 그렇게 행동하는거야?

Just trying to figure out what makes you tick. 네가 왜 그렇게 행동하는지 알아내려고 하고 있어.

Tell me all about yourself, who you are, what makes you tick. 너 자신에 대해 말해봐. 넌 누구며 왜 그렇게 행동하는건지.

017 You made me want to write 네 덕에 글을 쓰고 싶어졌어

although this might have many different meanings, most commonly we can understand that the speaker is saying that he was inspired to write by the listener. Perhaps he is writing creatively, as in writing a novel, or perhaps he is writing just to communicate personal feelings. In other words, he is saying "I was motivated to write by you"

I Point I You make me want to~ 너 때문에 …하고 싶어져

A: Why have you sent me so many e-mails?
왜 그렇게 많은 이멜을 보낸거야?

B: **You make me want to** write to you.
너 때문에 내가 글을 쓰고 싶어져.

You make me want to kill myself.
너 때문에 내가 자살하고 싶어.

Yeah, it's what makes me want to punch you in the neck right now.
그래, 그 때문에 지금 당장 네 목을 때리고 싶어져.

Well, that just makes me want to stay and see how this whole thing works out.
그 때문에 남아서 이 모든 일이 어떻게 되는지 보고 싶어져.

018 That's why! 바로 그거야!, 그게 이유야!

미드표현

this means "That was the answer." It indicates that the reason for something was just talked about

I Point I That's why S+V 그래서 …한거야(S+V에는 결과를)
That's because S+V 그건 …때문이야(S+V에는 이유를)

A: The weather is getting cold outside.
밖에 날씨 점점 추워지고 있어.

B: **That's why** I am wearing my heavy coat.
그래서 내가 두터운 코트를 입고 있는거야.

Brandon was not a good person. That's why he wasn't on the list.
브랜든은 좋은 친구가 아냐. 그래서 걘 명단에 없었던거야.

Do I look good? That's because I'm wearing a dress that accents my boobs.
좋아보인다구? 그건 가슴을 돋보이게 하는 옷을 입어서 그래.

That's why you came back to New York?
그래서 네가 뉴욕으로 돌아온거야?

019 Why would you say that? 왜 그런 소리를 해?, 무슨 이유로 그런 말을 해?

미드표현

this is usually said when the speaker wants the reason something was said. It is another way to say "What made you talk that way?"

I Point I Why would you say S+V? 왜 …하다고 말하는거야?
Why do you say that? 왜 그런 말을 하는거야?

A: Mary and Tom will probably divorce soon.
메리와 탐이 아마 곧 이혼할 것 같아.

B: **Why would you say that?** Have they been fighting? 왜 그런 소리를 하는거야? 계속 싸웠어?

Why would you say that? That's just mean.
왜 그런 소리를 해? 정말 야비하다.

Why do you say that? I'm not cute.
왜 그런 말을 해? 난 귀엽지 않다고.

Why would you say you are losing your mind?
왜 네가 정신없다고 말하는거야?

020 Why did you do this[that]? 무슨 이유 때문에 그런거야?, 왜 그런거야?

미드표현

this is asking for a person to explain his actions. The speaker wants to know "What is the reason for your actions?"

A: These dishes are all broken. **Why did you do this?** 이 접시들이 다 부서졌어. 왜 그런거야?

B: I got really jealous when you were gone.
네가 없는 동안 정말 질투심이 났어.

I've done everything you wanted me to do. Why did you do this? Why?
네가 원하는 건 다 해주었는데, 왜 그랬어? 왜?

Then why did you do it? 그럼 왜 그랬어?

Why did you do it? Why did you think she might be right?
왜 그런거야? 왜 걔가 맞을 수도 있다고 생각한거야?

021 Seeing as~ …한 것 같으니

this means "Because S+V." It is said when a person is giving a reason for something

I Point I Seeing as S+V …한 것 같으니, …하기 때문에

A: **Seeing as** work is finished, we can all go home.
일이 끝난 것 같으니 모두 집에 가도 돼.

B: I'm really looking forward to eating some dinner.
저녁 좀 먹기를 정말 기다리고 있어.

미드표현

Seeing as you're intent on breaking my balls, let me ask you a question.
나를 괴롭히기로 작정한 것 같으니까, 그럼 나도 질문하나 할게.

There isn't going to be a wedding today, seeing as we have no priest and now, no bride.
신부님도 안계시고 신부도 없으니 오늘 결혼식은 없을 것 같습니다.

Seeing as you've got the most experience, I want you to take care of this.
자네가 가장 경험이 있는 듯하니 이걸 맡아주게.

022 Seeing as how you sleep in the nude,
네가 다벗고 자는 것으로 봐서,

this indicates that the speaker is going to say something that is directly related to the fact the listener sleeps with no clothing on. We can understand him to be saying, "Because you sleep with no clothes…"

I Point I seeing as how~ …인 것으로 봐서

A: You are welcome to sleep on my couch.
넌 소파에서 자도 돼.

B: **Seeing as how** you sleep in the nude, I think I'll go home. 네가 다벗고 자는 걸로 봐서는 나 집에 가는게 나을 것 같아.

미드표현

We're totally incompatible seeing as how she's crazy and I'm not.
걔는 미쳤고 나는 아닌 걸로 봐서 우리는 서로 전혀 맞지 않는 것 같아.

That's probably true, seeing as how you have a brain tumor.
당신이 뇌종양인 걸로 봐서 그게 맞을 수도 있어요.

It's important that we be on good terms, seeing as how he's gonna be living with me now.
걔가 이제 나와 함께 살 것으로 봐서 우리가 서로 잘 지내는게 중요해.

023 It's just that~ 하지만 … 때문에 걸려, … 라고 해서

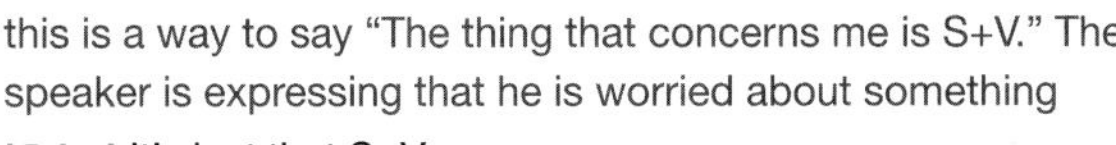

this is a way to say "The thing that concerns me is S+V." The speaker is expressing that he is worried about something

I Point I It's just that S+V 하지만 …때문에 걸려, …라고 해서

A: You can come over to my house on Friday.
금요일에 우리 집에 와.

B: I could. **It's just that** my husband would get angry. 그러고 싶은데, 남편이 화를 낼 것 같아서.

미드표현

It's just that he told us that your husband had been gone for years.
걔가 네 남편이 떠난지 오래되었다고 해서.

It's just that everybody you pay for sex ends up dead. 너에게 성매매한 사람은 다 결국 죽어서 말야.

It's just that you and your tattoos don't add up. 너와 네 문신은 잘 안 맞는 것 같아.

Ways to talk about the main point, idea, or choices
중요한 일을 결정하고 판단하고 또 선택하기

That leaves us with two options

001 That leaves us with two options
그렇게 되면 우리에겐 남는 것은 두가지 옵션이야

this expresses that there are now only two things that can be done, and we can understand that there were probably more choices available previously. It can express frustration at times, since the choices are so limited. It is similar to saying "There are only two choices we can make now"

| Point | That leaves us with~ 그렇게 되면 우리에게는 …가 남는다

A: The bank decided not to lend us any money.
은행은 우리에게 융자해주지 않기로 결정했어.

B: **That leaves us with two options,** sell the business or go bankrupt.
그럼 우리에겐 두가지 옵션이 남네. 사업체를 매각하거나 파산하거나.

So that leaves us with one choice.
그럼 우리가 선택할 수 있는 것은 하나밖에 없어.

Okay, that leaves us with two possibilities, Sara and Almani.
좋아, 그렇게 되면 우리에게는 두 개의 가능성이 있어, 새라하고 알마니.

002 We should exhaust every possibility
모든 가능성을 검토해야 돼

this is a way for the speaker to say that everything should be considered carefully. It can be used in many situations in order to imply that people need to take care and examine things closely before making a choice.

| Point | exhaust a subject 문제를 충분히 검토하다
exhaust an appeal 항소나 상고를 다 해보다, 더 이상 기댈 재판이 없다

A: People are saying we may have to shut down the business. 사람들이 그러는데 회사 문닫아야 할지 모른대.

B: We should **exhaust every possibility** to keep it open. 회사를 유지하기 위해 모든 가능성을 검토해야 돼.

I'm not giving up until I exhaust all my options. 난 내 모든 옵션을 검토하기까지는 포기하지 않을거야.

I've exhausted all my appeals.
난 내가 할 수 있는 항소는 다 해봤어.

He wanted me to exhaust every possible treatment option.
걔는 모든 가능 치료방법을 내가 검토하기를 바랬어.

003 We've got bigger fish to fry
우린 더 중요한 일이 있어

this is a way of saying that there are more important things to worry about. We can understand that the speaker heard about something and thinks it is not so important, and so he feels "We have things that are more significant which concern us"

| Point | have got bigger fish to fry 더 중요한 일이 있다

A: Shall I go pick up some lunch? 내가 가서 점심 사올까?

B: No, we **have bigger fish to fry** right now.
아니, 짐 더 중요한 문제가 있어.

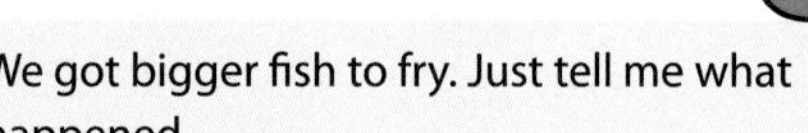

We got bigger fish to fry. Just tell me what happened.
우리는 더 중요한 일이 있어. 어떻게 됐는지 얘기나 해봐.

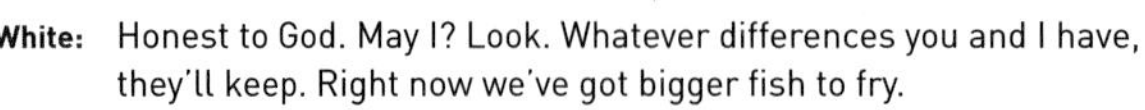

미드에선 이렇게 쓰인다!

We've got bigger fish to fry

Breaking Bad SEASON#5-1

화학선생 Walter White와 제자인 Jesse는 판매상 Gustavo가 자신들의 마약제조과정을 다 녹화했으며 이 영상은 경찰의 증거물 보관소에 있다는 사실을 알게 된다. 그들은 Gustavo의 수하인 Mike를 찾아가 이 영상을 제거할 계획을 세우는데…

White: Honest to God. May I? Look. Whatever differences you and I have, they'll keep. Right now we've got bigger fish to fry.
Mike: Bigger fish.
Jesse: The video cameras.
White: Gus kept cameras on us at the lab, at the laundry, God only knows where else. And, of course, when I say "us," including you.

화이트: 진심이야. 말해도 될까? 너와 내가 다른 점은 뭐든 그냥 놔두자고. 지금 현재 우리에게 더 큰 문제가 있어.
마이크: 더 큰 문제라.
제시: 비디오 카메라요.
화이트: 거스가 실험실과 세탁소, 그리고 어딘지 모르겠지만 우리들을 카메라에 담았어. 물론 내가 '우리'라고 말할 때는 너도 포함되는거야.

004 Keep your eye on her 걔를 잘 지켜봐

this is a way to say that someone needs to pay special attention to someone else. It may be in a negative way, because the person might be suspicious, or it may be in a positive way, because the person might be more talented than others. It is like saying "Pay attention to what she does"

| Point | keep[have] one's eye on sth[sb] 눈을 떼지 않다, 경계하다, 주의하다
keep one's eye on sth 일이 잘못되지 않도록 지켜보다

A: I think that woman might be a thief.
저 여자가 도둑일 수도 있을 것 같아.

B: **Keep your eye on** her and tell me if she steals something. 저 여자 잘 지켜보다 뭐 훔치면 내게 말해.

You make sure you keep an eye on it.
너 그거 잘 지켜보도록 해

Keep an eye on Carl while we're gone.
우리가 나간 사이에 칼을 잘 지켜봐.

Listen, do you mind keeping an eye on Zack for a minute? 저기, 잠깐 잭 좀 봐줄테야?

005 That's all you got? 그게 다야?

미드표현

this would typically be asked when someone is surprised at the small amount of something that a person has. It may be material items, or it may refer to the person's energy or ability to do something. We can understand the speaker is disappointed. In other words, it's like asking "Don't you have any more?"

| Point | That's all you got to do 넌 그것만 하면 돼
Is that all you got? 그게 다야?, 그것뿐이야?

A: This is the money I withdrew from the bank.
내가 은행에서 인출한 돈이야.

B: **That's all you got?** It's not very much. 더없어? 너무 적어.

That's all you got to say. 넌 얘기만 하면 돼.

You don't know? Is that all you got?
너 모른다고? 그게 다야?

What? Is this all you got, huh? 뭐라고? 그것 뿐이야, 응?

Women wearing skirts? Is that all you got?
여자들은 치마를 입는다고? 그것뿐이야?

006 What else could I say? 달리 무슨 말을 할 수 있겠어?

미드표현

when this is said, a person is indicating that he could not think of any other way to respond. Sometimes a person is criticized for something he said, and in his own defense he will say "What else could I say?" It means "That was the only thing I could think of saying then"

| Point | What else could[can] I say? 달리 무슨 말을 할 수 있겠어?.

A: Did you really tell Alex that he's an idiot?
너 알렉스에게 멍청한 놈이라고 말했어?

B: **What else could I say?** He's the dumbest man I know. 그렇게 말할 수 밖에 없지. 걔는 내가 아는 애 중에서 가장 멍청한 걸.

What else can I say? I love a big cock!
달리 뭐라고 할 수 있겠어? 난 대물을 좋아해!

She wanted me to marry her. What else could I say? 걘 나보고 자기와 결혼하재. 달리 무슨 말을 할 수 있겠어?

What else could I say? I was trapped.
달리 무슨 말을 할 수 있겠어? 난 함정에 빠졌다고.

007 Who's running the place? 누가 책임자야?

미드표현

this question is asking who is the leader, or who controls a place. Most commonly we hear this used in reference to a business, when a person wants to find the owner or manager. In other words, the speaker wants to know "Who is the boss here?"

| Point | run the place 운영하다, 책임지다

A: I haven't gotten paid by the company yet.
난 아직 회사로부터 급여를 받지 못했어.

B: Call the manager. **Who's running the place?**
매니저를 불러. 누가 여기 책임자야?

I worked my way up. I run the place now.
승진했어요. 이제 제가 운영하고 있구요.

She's the rather eccentric woman who runs the place. 걔는 여기를 운영하고 있는 좀 별난 여자야.

You would have to have Dick himself running the place in order to break even.
너는 수지타산을 맞추기 위해 딕이 직접 운영을 하도록 해야 할거야.

008 I have half a mind to call my boss 사장에게 전화를 할까

this is a way to say the person is considering calling his boss, but he hasn't made up his mind to do that yet. When a person has half a mind to do something, they haven't decided what to do. Basically the speaker is saying "I might call my boss"

| Point | have[get] half a mind to~ …을 할까(말까) 생각하다
have a mind to~ …할 마음이 있다

A: Someone took the office supplies.
누가 사무용품을 가져갔어.

B: I **have half a mind to** call my boss and report this. 사장한테 전화해서 보고할까 말까.

I got half a mind to call Steve right now and take that offer.
스티브에게 당장 전화해 그 제의를 받아들일까하는 생각이 있어.

I have half a mind to throw this martini right in your face!
이 마티니를 네 얼굴에 쏟아부을까라는 생각이 드네.

009 Judging from the crime scene photos,
범죄현장사진으로 미루어 보건대,

미드표현

this indicates that the police are looking at pictures of a murder or other serious crime, and they are trying to find clues about who committed the crime in those pictures. In other words, "We are studying pictures of where the crime happened so we can catch the criminal"

| Point | Judging from~ …로 미루어보아

A: The murder took place last night. 살인은 지난 밤에 일어났어.

B: **Judging from** the crime scene photos, there was a brutal fight. 범죄사진으로 미루어 보건대, 격렬한 싸움이 있었어.

Judging from your husband's response he knew nothing about it.
네 남편의 반응으로 보아, 남편은 그것을 전혀 모르고 있었어.

Judging from this place, he wasn't making any extra money running drugs.
이 장소로 보건대, 걔는 마약으로 여분의 돈을 벌지는 않았어.

Judging from the things you and other folks have written about him, your dad must be quite a guy.
너와 다른 사람들이 쓴 것으로 보건대, 네 아빠는 틀림없이 대단하신 분이야.

010 All right, we'll do it your way 좋아, 우린 네 방식대로 할게

this means the speaker is agreeing to follow another person's directions or way to do something. Often this is said when two people have disagreed over who would be the leader. It is like saying, "Go ahead, you can be the leader"

| Point | do sth one's own way 제멋대로 하다, 자기 방식대로 하다
do sth one's way …의 방식대로 하다

A: My plan is going to work better than your plan.
내 계획이 네 것보다 더 잘 돌아갈거야.

B: All right, **we'll do it your way.** 좋아, 네 방식대로 하자.

But this time we're gonna do it my way.
하지만 이번에는 우리는 내 방식대로 할거야.

We can either do this the easy way, or we can do it your way.
우리는 이걸 쉬운 방법으로 하거나 아니면 네 방식대로 할 수 있어.

You each do things your own way. But you both get it done.
너희들 각각의 방식대로 하지만 둘 다 모두 그걸 끝내.

011 You always get your way 넌 항상 네 멋대로 해

미드표현

this is a way to say that someone is allowed to do any of the things he wants to do. Usually this is said by a person who is jealous because another person is permitted to do so many things. Another way to say this would be "People let you do whatever you want"

| Point | get one's way …가 하고 싶은대로 하다, …멋대로 하다

A: The boss agreed to let me have a week off.
사장은 내가 일주일 휴가가는걸 허락해줬어.

B: I can't believe it. **You always get your way.**
그럴 수가. 넌 항상 하고 싶은대로 다하네.

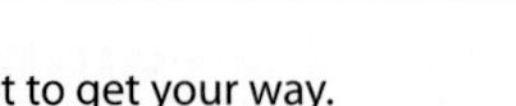

You use it to get your way.
넌 그걸 이용해서 네 맘대로 하고 있어.

You always let her get her way.
넌 항상 걔 멋대로 하도록 놔두더라.

Are you accusing me of manipulating you to get my way?
내 멋대로 하기 위해 널 이용했다고 날 비난하는거야?

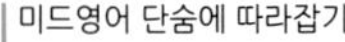

012 I wanted to play her game 난 걔의 방식에 따르고 싶었어

this indicates that someone is willing to do something the way that another person wants him to do it. The speaker is saying he will follow another person's rules. In other words, "I wanted to do things her way"

| Point | play sb's game …의 방식에 따르다

A: Don't you get upset when Joan tells you what to do? 조앤이 너보고 이래라저래라 하는데 화나지 않아?

B: No, **I'll play her game** for a while.
아니, 한동안 걔방식대로 하려고.

No, I wanna play my game.
아니, 난 내 방식대로 하고 싶어.

He mostly just wants to play his game.
걘 대부분 자기 방식대로 하고 싶어해.

Do not play his games, because you will lose.
걔 방식에 따르지마, 넌 질테니까.

013 You got him right where you want him
넌 걔를 완전히 장악했어

this indicates that the person has a strong advantage over someone else. We can understand some type of competition is going on, and this person is likely to be the winner of it. This can also be expressed "You have the upper hand now"

| Point | have sb just where you want sb …을 장악하다, 맘대로 하다
Sth be not where S want sth to be~ …가 뜻대로 되지 않다

A: The suspect says he wants to confess.
용의자가 자백을 하고 싶다는데.

B: **You've got him right where you want him.**
너 걔를 완전히 장악했구만.

Well, then you got him right where you want him. Trust me.
그럼, 넌 걔를 완전히 장악한거야, 날 믿어.

My life is not where I want it to be.
내 인생은 내 맘대로 되지 않아.

Raul is ready to give in. You've got him right where you want him.
라울은 포기할 준비가 됐어. 넌 걔를 완전히 압도했어.

You've got your suspect right where you'll want him. He'll confess.
넌 용의자를 완전히 휘어잡았어. 걘 자백할거야.

014 The heart wants what it wants 내키는 대로 하다

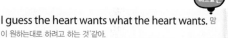

this is often a way to say that a person cannot control the feelings of attraction or love that he may have for another person. In other words "Even though I probably shouldn't be in love with this person, I have no choice about the emotions I feel"

| Point | the heart wants what it wants 하고 싶은대로 하다

A: Isn't it strange that they decided to get married?
걔네들이 결혼하기로 한게 이상하지 않아?

B: **The heart wants what it wants.** 맘 내키는대로 하는거지.

I guess the heart wants what the heart wants. 맘이 원하는대로 하려고 하는 것 같아.

What can I say, Jenny? The heart wants what it wants.
뭐라 말해야 될까, 제니? 맘은 하고 싶은 대로 하는거야.

I'm certainly wise enough to know that the heart wants what the heart wants.
맘은 하고 싶은 대로 한다는 것을 알 정도로 똑똑해.

015 I expect you to do what you always do
난 네가 항상 하던 식으로 하기를 바래

this speaker is saying that he thinks the listener is going to do the same things he has done in the past. We can understand that the speaker anticipates consistency. In other words, "I don't expect you to change at all"

| Point | do what you always do 늘 하던 식으로 하다, 늘 그런 식으로 하다
You always do that 넌 항상 그래

A: Do you have any special instructions for me?
내게 뭐 특별히 지시할 사항이 있어요?

B: **I expect you to do what you always do.**
난 네가 항상 하던 식으로 하기를 바래.

Why do you always do this? 넌 왜 항상 이런 식이야?

It's important that you do exactly what you always do. 항상 하던 식으로 하는게 중요해.

If you always do what you've always done, then you'll always get what you always got.
늘 하던 식으로만 하면 항상 결과는 똑같을거야.

016 Where do you think this is going? 이거 어떻게 되어가는거야?

this is a way of asking what the listener thinks is going to happen in the future. It signifies that the speaker is not sure what will occur next. It's like asking "What do you think the result of this will be?"

A: This relationship, **where do you think it is going?** 이 관계는 어떻게 되어가는거야?
B: I guess someday it will lead to marriage. 언젠가 결혼으로 이르겠지.

Where do you think this conversation is going? 이 대화가 결국 어떻게 될 것 같아?

I saw the contract. Where do you think this is going? 계약서 봤어? 어떻게 될 것 같아?

I'm unhappy, you're unhappy. Where do you think this is going? 나도 불행하고 너도 불행하고. 앞으로 어떻게 될까?

017 I made a snap judgment 내가 너무 성급히 판단했어

this expresses that the speaker had to decide something quickly without much time to think about it. Sometimes people regret these decisions because they haven't had the chance to consider them carefully. It's similar to saying "I had to make a decision quickly"

| Point | make a snap decision 성급한 결정을 하다
It was a snap judgment 그건 성급한 판단였어

A: How could you get married to someone a few days after you met? 어떻게 만난지 며칠 만에 결혼을 할 수 있는거야?
B: Maybe it was a mistake. **I made a snap judgment.** 실수였을지 몰라. 내가 성급히 판단했어.

It will take a while. I can't make a snap judgment. 시간이 좀 걸릴거야. 난 성급한 결정을 내릴 수가 없어.

Taking a vacation in Moscow was a snap decision. 모스코바에서 휴가를 보내는 건 성급한 결정였어.

Fine! I judged you. I made a snap judgment. 좋아! 내가 널 비난했지. 내 판단이 성급했어.

018 Skip it 다음으로 넘어 가자, 그건 빼고

this is a way to say "Let's not do this or talk about this now." It means the speaker wants to do or talk about other things now

| Point | skip 빼먹다, 넘어가다

A: Can we discuss the plans for tomorrow? 내일 계획을 말해볼까?
B: **Skip it.** I don't want to think about it now. 그건 넘어가자. 지금 그거 생각하고 싶지 않아.

So let's skip it. 그래 그냥 넘어가자.

I think I'm gonna skip it. 다음으로 건너 뛰어야겠어.

Skip it? Why would we do that? 넘어가자고? 왜 우리가 그래야 하는거지?

I hate funerals. Let's skip it. 난 장례식은 질색이야. 그냥 건너뛰자고.

019 Work comes first 일이 우선이야

this indicates that a job must be finished. The speaker is saying "It's very important that we finish this job"

| Point | You come first 네가 더 중요해
What comes first? 뭐가 우선이야?

A: Why do you get up so early? 왜 이리 일찍 일어났어?
B: **Work comes first.** I always have a lot to do. 일이 우선이야. 난 늘 할 일이 많아.

My kids come first. 내 자식들 말고 또 누가 있담.

When you're a waiter, you must always be aware, that the customer comes first. 웨이터할 때는 항상 손님이 우선이라는 걸 명심해야 돼.

You always come first with me. Do I still come first with you? 난 항상 널 먼저 생각하는데 넌 아직도 날 먼저 생각해?

020 That's all that matters 바로 그게 중요한거야, 가장 중요한 거지

this is a way of saying "This is the most important thing." It means everything else is less important

| Point | matter (to~) (…에게) 중요하다

A: I try to take care of my family. 내 가족을 돌보려고 해.

B: **That's all that matters.** You should treat them well. 그게 가장 중요한거지. 가족들을 잘 대해야 돼.

I'm free. That's all that matters.
난 자유로와. 바로 이게 중요한거지.

That is real. And that's all that matters.
그건 현실이야. 그게 바로 가장 중요한거야.

I want to keep him safe. That's all that matters.
난 걔를 안전하게 지키고 싶어. 그게 가장 중요한거야.

You're my girl, and that's all that matters.
넌 내 여자야, 그게 가장 중요한거야.

021 It matters to me 나한테 중요해

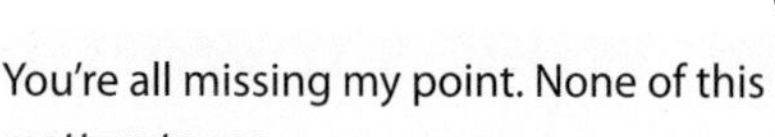

usually this is a way to say "I really care about this." The speaker wants to tell others that something is important to him

| Point | (It) doesn't matter to sb[what S+V] […하는 건] …에게 상관없다
It won't matter to me 내게는 중요하지 않을거야

A: I don't care if people recycle things. 사람들이 재활용하는데 관심없어.

B: **It matters to me.** We should try to conserve things. 내겐 중요해. 환경을 보존하도록 해야 돼.

You're all missing my point. None of this matters to me.
내 말은 전혀 못 알아 듣는구만. 이 어떤 것도 나하고 상관없어.

Is that what matters to you? 그게 너에게 중요한거야?

It seems to matter to you that she had a date with Tony.
걔가 토니하고 데이트하는 게 네겐 중요한가 보구나.

It doesn't really matter to me what you think.
네가 어떻게 생각하든 상관없어.

022 It's the thought that counts 중요한 건 마음이야

this is often said when something is disappointing, especially a gift. The speaker wants to remind everyone that the most important thing is that someone wanted to give a great gift, and his good intentions are more important than the actual gift. It is like saying "The gift may not be great, but remember that the most important thing is what is in the person's heart"

| Point | It's ~ that counts 중요한 것은 …이다

A: The birthday gift Lonnie gave me was a cheap tie. 로니가 내게 준 생일선물은 싸구려 넥타이였어.

B: She is quite poor. **It's the thought that counts** anyhow. 걔 가난하잖아. 어찌됐든 중요한 건 마음이야.

The narcissist believes he's the only one that counts. 나르시스트는 자기만이 중요하다고 생각해.

You know what they say -- it's what's on the inside that counts.
뭐라고들 하는지 알지. 중요한 것은 내면에 있는 것이야.

It's all the people that mattered to her.
걔한테 중요한 것은 모든 사람들이야.

023 It's worth it 가치가 있어

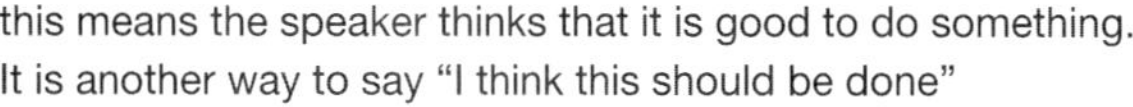

this means the speaker thinks that it is good to do something. It is another way to say "I think this should be done"

| Point | It's worth it to~ …할 가치가 있어
It isn't worth it 그럴 만한 가치가 없어, 쓸데없는 짓이야
Is it worth it? 그럴 만한 가치가 있어?

A: Do you think I should continue at university? 내가 대학교를 계속 다녀야 한다고 생각해?

B: **It's worth it.** You'll get a better job. 그럴 가치가 있지. 좋은 직업을 갖게 될거야.

It's too hard. It's not worth it. I quit.
넘 어려워. 쓸데없는 짓이야. 그만둘래.

It's painful sometimes, but it's worth it.
가끔 힘들지만 그럴 가치가 있어.

I know the process is frustrating, but it's so worth it. 과정이 짜증나지만 그럴만한 가치가 충분해.

024 (It's) Worth a shot 해볼 가치는 있어

usually this means "Let's try it." We can understand that the speaker thinks something should be attempted

| Point | It isn't worth the trouble 괜히 번거롭기만 할거야
It's not worth the effort 굳이 그럴 필요까진 없어

A: I wonder if I should enter the race.
이 경주에 참가할 가치가 있을까.

B: **It's worth a shot.** You are fast, so you might win. 해봐. 넌 빠르니까 이길 수도 있어.

I don't know what a stripper could teach me, but it's worth a shot.
스트리퍼가 내게 뭘 가르쳐줄지 모르겠지만 한번 해볼 가치는 있겠지.

A: Oh, I'm sorry, was that a serious suggestion? B: Hey, it's worth a shot.
A: 어, 미안해, 그거 진지한 제안이었어? B: 야, 그거 한번 해볼 가치는 있어.

I don't know, but it's worth a shot.
잘 모르겠지만 한번 해볼만해.

025 What's it worth to you? 그게 너한테 무슨 가치가 있어?

this question is asking how much someone is willing to pay for something. We can assume the speaker is a seller talking to a buyer and trying to make a deal. He wants to know "How much would you pay to buy this?"

| Point | What's it worth (to you)? 그거의 값어치가 뭐냐?, 무슨 소용이 있는거니?

A: Do you have a gold necklace to sell? 금목걸이 있어요?

B: Yes I do. **What's it worth to you?** 예. 얼마짜리 찾아요?

This old car, what's it worth to you?
이 낡은 차가 너한테 무슨 가치가 있어?

What's it worth to you if I take care of the problem? 내가 그 문제를 처리하면 네게 무슨 가치가 있는거야?

He can fix the computer. What's it worth to you?
걔가 컴퓨터를 수리할 수 있어. 그게 네게 얼마의 값어치가 있는거야?

What's it worth to you if I can cure your cancer? 내가 네 암을 치료할 수 있다면 값어치가 얼마나 되는거야?

026 That's not the point 핵심은 그게 아니라고, 그게 중요한 게 아냐, 요점은 그게 아니야

usually this is expressing that someone misunderstood something. It is like saying "I don't think you understood what I meant"

A: I don't like homeless people in the subway.
지하철의 노숙자들이 못마땅해.

B: **That's not the point.** We need to help them.
핵심은 그게 아니고, 그들은 우리가 도와야 해.

I know it's not. It's not the point.
그렇지 않다는 걸 알지만 그게 핵심은 아냐.

That's not the point, mother. The point is that thanksgiving is a family holiday.
엄마, 그게 중요한게 아냐. 핵심은 추수감사절은 가족휴일이라는거야.

Yes, but that's not the point! Get me out of here. 맞아. 그렇지만 그게 중요한게 아냐! 날 여기서 보내줘.

027 Which brings me to my point 그게 내 요지를 말해주는거야

this is said after a person has spent a long time explaining something. When concluding, he is telling people that he wants them to listen to the main idea he is expressing. In other words, he wants to say "This explanation takes me to the main idea of my talk, which I want to tell you about now"

| Point | which brings me to~ 그게 …을 말해주는거야

A: Your lecture about Africa was very detailed.
네 아프리카 강연은 매우 디테일했어.

B: Africa is interesting, **which brings me to my point** about charity work. 아프리카는 흥미로와, 그게 자선사업에 대한 내 요점을 말해주는거야.

Which brings me to our next order of business. 바로 그게 우리의 다음 사업과제를 말해주는거야.

Which brings me to my second issue.
바로 그게 나의 두번째 이슈에 대해 말해주는거야.

Which brings me to the first question I actually need an answer to.
그게 바로 내가 실제적으로 대답을 원하는 첫번째 질의를 말해주는거야.

028 I don't know what the big deal is

왜 호들갑이야, 뭐가 문제인지 모르겠어

this speaker is saying "I can't understand why there is a problem." This is said when a problem occurs and the speaker either feels there shouldn't be a problem, or wants to know the reason the problem is occurring

A: You shouldn't eat ice cream while you're dieting.
다이어트 할 때는 아이스크림을 먹어서는 안돼.

B: **I don't understand what the big deal is.** I'm just eating a little bit. 뭐가 대수인지 모르겠어. 단지 조금 먹을 뿐인데.

미드표현

I don't know what the big deal is about celebrities.
유명인들에게 대해서 왜 그렇게 호들갑을 떠는지 모르겠어.

I don't know what the big deal is about porn.
포르노가 뭐가 좋다고 다들 그러는지 모르겠어.

I broke up with her. I don't know what the big deal is. 난 걔하고 헤어졌어. 별 일도 아닌데.

029 The point is~

중요한 건 …이야, 핵심(요점)은 …이야

this is a way of saying "This is the thing I want you to

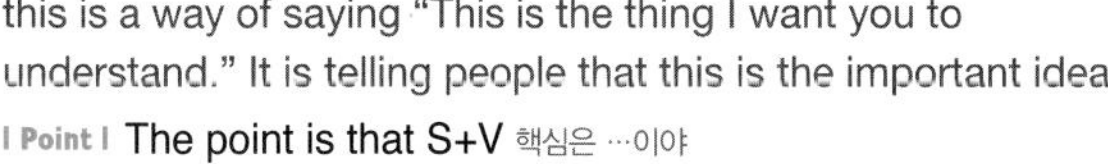

understand." It is telling people that this is the important idea

Point The point is that S+V 핵심은 …이야

A: **The point is** that we need to fix this house.
중요한 건 이 집을 수리해야 한다는거야.

B: I know, but we don't have enough money.
알아, 하지만 돈이 충분하지 않아.

미드표현

The point is Gale wants to be with his wife. He misses her so much.
핵심은 게일이 자기 아내와 함께 있기를 원하다는거야. 몹시 그리워 해.

The point is I don't need this right now.
중요한 건 난 지금 이게 필요없다는거야.

The point is what he did at the gas station.
요점은 그가 주유소에서 무슨 짓을 했냐는거지.

030 The thing is~

중요한 건 …이야, 요는 …이야, 문제의 요점은 …이야

this is used to talk about what is important to the speaker. He is saying "I'd like you to remember..."

Point The thing is that S+V 문제는 …이야

A: Can you drop by tomorrow afternoon?
내일 오후에 들릴 수 있어?

B: **The thing is** that I'll be quite busy then.
중요한 건 그때가 내가 무척 바쁠 때야.

미드표현

The thing is that you're married to Jane.
요는 네가 제인과 결혼했다는거지.

The thing is that they might be able to help you. 문제의 요점은 걔네들이 너에게 도움이 될 수도 있다는거야.

The thing is I don't really believe it.
요는 내가 그걸 안 믿는다는거야.

031 The whole point is to~

진짜 목적은 …하는 것이야

this often means "The reason for this is..." The speaker is explaining why something happens

Point The whole point of A is to~/that S+V …의 진짜 목적은 …하는거야
That's the whole point (S+V) (…하려는) 요점이 바로 그거야

A: I think it'll be fun to travel to South America.
남아메리카 여행하는 게 재미있을 것 같아.

B: **The whole point of** going **is to** improve your Spanish language skills.
네가 가는 진짜 이유는 스페인어 실력을 늘리려는거야.

미드표현

I thought the whole point of the party was to announce our engagement.
파티의 진짜 목적은 우리 약혼을 발표하려는 것인 줄 알았어.

I don't want to be working together. That's the whole point I'm trying to make.
같이 일하고 싶지 않아. 내가 말하려고 하는 요점이 바로 그거야.

032 They mean a lot to me 그건 나한테는 의미가 많아, 큰 도움이 될거야

this indicates that something has a lot of worth to the speaker. He is saying "I think they are very valuable"

I Point I mean a lot to sb …에게 큰 의미가 있다

A: These jewels are very beautiful. Are they from your family? 이 보석들은 무척 아름다워. 집안에서 물려받은거야?

B: Yes they are. **They mean a lot to me.**
어 맞아. 내겐 의미가 커.

It would mean a lot to me if you would attend my engagement.
내 약혼식에 참석해준다면 큰 도움이 될거야.

I hope you know you still mean a lot to me.
아직 네가 내겐 큰 의미가 된다는 걸 알아주길 바래.

I'm sure it would mean a lot to her.
걔한테 그게 큰 도움이 될 게 확실해.

033 What is the bottom line? 요점이 뭐야?

this is a way of asking what the basic idea of something is. It is similar to saying "Just tell me the facts here"

I Point I Here's the bottom line 요지는 이거야
The bottom line is S+V 요점은 …이야

A: This service is going to be very expensive.
이 서비스는 비용이 무척 비싸요.

B: **What is the bottom line?** How much will it cost? 요점이 뭡니까? 얼마예요?

Bottom line, he killed Ben.
요점은 걔가 벤을 죽였다는거야.

The bottom line is she loves you.
요는 걔가 널 사랑한다는거야

The bottom line here is that you love her.
여기서 요점은 네가 걜 사랑한다는거야.

The bottom line is that you have to help me.
요점은 네가 날 도와야 한다는거야.

034 It's one of a kind 아주 귀한 것이야, 유일무이한거야, 독특해, 굉장히 희귀해

this often means "It is very rare." Many people say this about items that are very valuable

I Point I We're two of a kind 우리는 똑 같아

A: I've never seen a painting like this one.
이 같은 그림은 본 적이 없어.

B: **It's one of a kind.** I paid a lot for it.
아주 희귀한거야. 돈 엄청 지불했어.

What I know is that these are masterpieces. One of a kind.
내가 아는 건 이것들이 걸작이라는거야. 유일무이한거야.

You really are one of a kind. 너 정말 독특하다.

She's not weird, she just wants her stuff to be one of a kind.
걘 이상한 게 아냐. 자기 것이 독특하기를 바라는거야.

035 I'm going with it 난 그것으로 하겠어

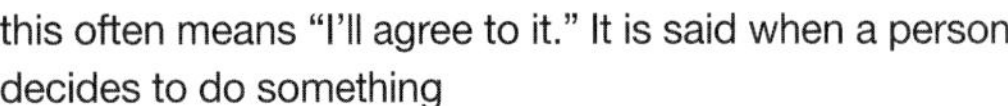

this often means "I'll agree to it." It is said when a person decides to do something

I Point I go with = choose 선택하다

A: Did you like our proposal? 우리 제안이 좋았어?

B: Yes I did. **I'm going with it.** 어 그래. 그걸로 할게.

He offered me a job, and I'm going with it.
걔가 네게 일자리를 제안했고 난 그렇게 하기로 했어.

I'm going with it. I won't worry about the future. 그렇게 하기로 할게. 미래에 대해 걱정하지 않을게.

It's just a romantic fling. I'm going with it.
그건 그냥 불장난 연애야. 그렇게 하기로 했어.

I decided to go with a blue dress for the dance. 난 댄스파티에 푸른색 드레스를 입고 가기로 했어.

036 I got my heart set on it 나 그거 하기로 했어

미드표현

this expresses that the speaker really wants something to happen. We can understand that he is saying that he will be very disappointed if it doesn't occur. A different way to say the same thing is "I desire this very much"

I Point I have one's heart set on~ …을 하기로 맘먹다, (굳게) 결심하다

A: Is this the diamond necklace you want?
이 다이아몬드 목걸이가 네가 원하는거야?

B: It is. **I've got my heart set on it.** 맞아, 꼭 갖고 싶은거야.

He had his heart set on going to Space Camp.
걔는 우주정거장에 가기로 맘먹었어.

I had my heart set on that teddy bear.
난 저 테디베어를 사기로 맘먹었어.

I never really had my heart set on being a cop. 난 절대로 경찰이 되기로 맘먹은 적이 없어.

I had my heart set on doing research tonight.
난 오늘 밤에 조사를 하기로 결심했어.

037 I got my eye on her 난 걔를 점찍어뒀어

미드표현

this means that the speaker has been watching someone carefully. He could be doing it because he is interested, or he could be doing it because he doesn't trust the person. A way to say the same thing would be "I'm monitoring her closely"

I Point I have(get) one's eye on~ 눈독들이다, 눈여겨보다, 지켜보다, 탐내다, 점찍어두다

A: I think our new student may be stealing things.
새로 전학 온 학생이 절도를 하는 것 같아.

B: I know. **I've got my eye on her.** 알아, 눈여겨보고 있어.

I got my eye on you. 난 너를 눈여겨보고 있어.

And I got my eye on a condo in Lincoln Park.
난 링컨파크에 있는 콘도를 점찍어두고 있어.

I was watching the boys. I had my eye on them. 난 그 소년들을 지켜보고 있었어. 내가 눈여겨봤어.

She's got her eye on a beige chair.
갠 베이지색 의자를 점찍어뒀어.

038 I'm calling the shots 내가 결정할래, 내가 지시할게

미드표현

this is said to indicate "I'm the boss." The speaker is saying he controls things

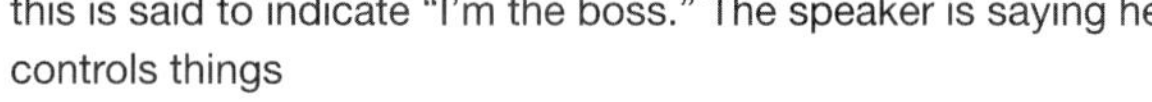

I Point I call the shots 결정하다, 책임지다
Who's calling the shots here? 여기 책임자는 누구야?

A: John says you were wrong about the merger.
존이 네가 합병에 관해 틀렸다고 말해.

B: **I'm calling the shots.** He doesn't understand anything. 내가 결정하는거야. 갠 아무 것도 몰라.

You listen to me! Now, I'm calling the shots!내 말 좀 들어! 이제 내가 결정내릴거야!

You can't give it up for a second, can you? You always have to call the shots! Always!
잠시라도 그냥 놔두지 못하지, 맞지? 항상 네가 주도해야 돼! 항상!

No one calls the shots. Jason and I make decisions together.
아무도 혼자 결정내리지 않아. 제이슨과 내가 함께 결정내리지.

039 I called dibs on her at that party! 난 파티에서 걔를 찜했어!

미드표현

this is a somewhat unusual expression, which likely means that a man met a woman at a party, and he said that he wants to be the first person to date her. To call dibs on something means to casually reserve the right to do something first. In other words "I told you I wanted to be able to ask her on a date before anyone else"

I Point I call[get] dibs on …에 대해 찜을 해두다, …를 찍어두다
have got dibs on …을 먼저 차지하다, …을 찜하다

A: Why do you get to ask Andrea out?
왜 네가 앤드리아에게 데이트를 신청해야 되는데?

B: Because **I called dibs on** her at that party.
내가 파티에서 걔를 찍었거든.

I got dibs on the breast. 난 가슴을 찜했어.

You've now called dibs on everything.
넌 이제 모든 걸 다 찍어뒀다고 하는구나.

You know I have first dibs on designer everything. 디자이너 제품은 내가 먼저 찜해놓은거 너 알잖아.

Hey, I had dibs on being the bitch tonight.
오늘밤은 내가 못된년할 차례였는데.

040 It's your call 네가 결정할 몫이야

미드표현

This is way to tell someone that he can make the decision about something. Often we can understand that the decision may be difficult and may lead to some problems in the future. It is like saying "You choose what to do."

Point That's your call 네가 결정할 문제야. 네 뜻에 따를게

A: Should we search for the murder weapon?
우리가 살인무기를 찾아야 될까?

B: I think the weapon is gone, but **it's your call.**
무기는 못찾을 것 같은데 네가 결정해.

Either way, it's your call. 어떤 경우든지, 네가 결정할 일이야.

Why are you so attached to this girl? It's your call.
왜 이 여자아이에게 그렇게 집착하는거야? 하긴 네가 결정할 문제지.

It's your call whether to fire her or not.
걔를 해고하든지 말든지는 네가 알아서 해.

You can stay or go, it's your call.
남거나 가거나, 네가 결정해.

041 It's up to you 네가 결정할 일이야, 알아서 해

미드표현

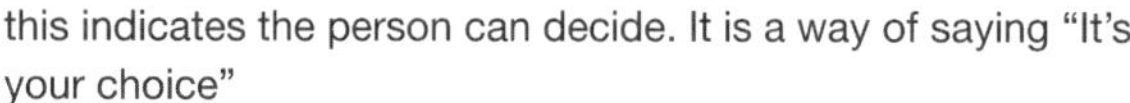

this indicates the person can decide. It is a way of saying "It's your choice"

Point It's not up to me 어쩔 수 없어
The choice is up to you 선택은 네게 달렸어

A: Where should we go to eat lunch? 점심 어디 가서 먹을까?

B: **It's up to you.** I could go anywhere.
네가 결정해. 난 아무데나 갈게.

Well, it's up to you? You can take it out if you want. 네가 알아서 한다고? 원하면 꺼내놔.

I wish you would have the surgery. But it's up to you, Dad. It's your life.
아빠가 수술을 했으면 좋겠지만 좋을대로 하세요. 아빠 인생이잖아요.

It's up to you. Whatever you want to do, I'll do it. 네가 알아서 해. 네가 뭘 하고 싶든지 난 할테니까.

042 The ball's in your court 이제 결정은 네 몫이야

미드표현

this usually means someone can choose what he wants to do next. It is very similar to saying "The choice is up to you"

A: This is the salary we're offering. **The ball's in your court.** 이게 우리가 제안하는 급여입니다. 이제 결정하시죠.

B: I think this offer is much too low for me to accept. 받아들이기에는 너무 적은 액수인 것 같아요.

The ball's in your court. If you sign, I'll sign.
네 손에 달렸어. 네가 서명하면, 나도 할게.

So the ball's pretty much in your court.
그래 결정은 정말이지 네가 해야 돼.

What does this mean, the ball's in my court or something? 이게 무슨 말이야, 내가 결정해야 된다는거야 뭐야?

043 I'm easy (to please) 네 결정에 따를게, 난 어느 쪽도 상관없어

미드표현

this means the speaker is happy without a lot of effort. He is saying "Many things make me happy"

Point I'm easy to+V …하는데 난 까다롭지 않아

A: What kind of wine do you like? 어떤 와인을 좋아해?

B: **I'm easy.** Any French wine will be good.
난 상관없어. 프랑스 와인이라면 어떤 것도 좋아.

I'm easy to live with. 난 같이 살기 까다롭지 않아.

A: Just tell me what you need. B: I'm easy.
A: 네가 원하는 것을 말해봐. B: 어느 쪽도 상관없어.

You guys decide. I'm easy. 너희들이 결정해. 난 상관없어.

044 That's a toughie 어려운 결정이네(=That's a tough decision to make)

this is a way of saying "That's very difficult to answer." This is what people say when they are not sure what the answer is

| Point | toughie 어려운 문제, 건달

A: What will you do if you can't find work?
일을 찾지 못하면 어떻게 할거야?

B: **That's a toughie.** Maybe I'll have to emigrate.
어려운 결정이네. 아마 이민 가야 될거야.

I'd better warn you, I'm a toughie.
너한테 경고해야겠구만, 나 건달이야.

I'm not sure what the answer is. That's a toughie. 정답이 뭔지 모르겠어. 어려운 문제야.

That's a toughie. Go ask Tim about it.
어려운 결정이네. 가서 팀에게 물어봐봐.

That's a toughie. Let's look it up on Google.
어려운 문제네. 구글에서 찾아보자.

045 I'll take this one 이걸로 할게

this means "I want that item." The speaker is saying he prefers a specific item more than other items. And this can also mean "I'll answer." In this case, the speaker is saying he knows what kind of answer to give

| Point | I will take it 이걸로 할게

A: Do you know the answer to that question Dave?
데이브 이 질문의 답을 알고 있어?

B: Yes I do. **I'll take this one.** 네 알아요. 이걸로 할게요.

You take this one. I'll do the next one.
너 이걸로 해. 난 다음 걸로 할게.

I'll take this one. It looks very good.
난 이걸로 할게. 아주 좋아 보이는데.

You gonna take this one, Doctor?
의사 선생님, 이걸로 하시겠어요?

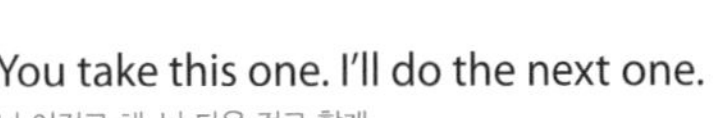

046 Take it or leave it 선택의 여지가 없어, 받든지 말든지 알아서 해

this expresses that this is the last offer. The speaker is indicating "If you don't accept this offer, I don't want to make a deal with you"

| Point | Like it or lump it! 고르고 말 것도 할 것 없어!

A: I'll give you $5,000 for your car. **Take it or leave it.** 차 값으로 5천 달러 줄게요. 하던지 말던지 해요.

B: I guess I can sell it to you for that price.
그 가격에 팔게요.

A: What did you say to him? B: I told him he can take it or leave it.
A: 그 남자한테 뭐라고 했니? B: 이걸 받아들이든지 아님 그만 두자고 했어.

None of your business. Take it or leave it.
상관하지마. 받든지 말든지 알아서 해.

That's all I know, ma'am. Take it or leave it.
부인 더는 아는게 없는데요. 선택의 여지가 없습니다.

That's our offer; Take it or leave it.
그게 우리의 제안이야. 받든지 말든지 알아서 해.

047 You can take your pick 골라서 가져가

this indicates that a person can choose what he wants. It is like saying "Which one would you like?"

| Point | I couldn't pick and choose 골라잡을 수 없었어

A: Which puppy can I have? 어떤 강아지를 살 수 있죠?

B: You can choose any of them. **Take your pick.**
아무 거나 골라요. 고르세요.

A: On what charges? B: Sexual abuse, endangering the welfare of a child. Take your pick. A: 무슨 혐의로? B: 성적 학대, 아동보호를 위태롭게 한거. 골라봐.

Look them over and take your pick.
그것들을 검토해보고 골라.

We have newspapers all around the world. You can take your pick.
전세계 모든 신문이 있습니다. 고르시면 됩니다.

048 We'll get to the bottom of this

이 일에 대해 짚고 넘어갈거야, 진상을 밝혀낼거야

this means "We'll learn why or how this happened." The speaker plans to find out what caused something

| Point | get to the bottom of this 어떤 문제나 상황의 원인을 밝혀내다, 규명하다

A: Someone stole money from my purse.
누가 지갑에서 돈을 훔쳐갔어.

B: I'll find the thief. **We'll get to the bottom of this.** 내가 도둑을 찾을게. 이 일을 짚고 넘어갈거야.

미드표현

There's still time for you to get to the bottom of this thing. 이거의 진상을 밝힐 시간이 아직 네겐 있어.

I'm not leaving here till I get to the bottom of this. 이거의 진상을 규명하기 전에 여길 떠나지 않을거야.

I'm just trying to get to the bottom of what happened here. 여기서 무슨 일이 일어났는지 진상을 밝힐거야.

MEMO

Ways to ask someone for help and say thank you to someone

도와달라는 부탁에 도움을 주고

I got your back

001 I'll help you in any way I see fit
내가 적절하다고 생각한 방법으로 널 도와줄게

this is a way for the speaker to say he will assist the listener, but only if he judges that it is something that will be helpful. In other words, the speaker is saying "I'll decide on what I want to do to give you help"

| Point | see fit 적절하다고 생각하다, …가 맞다고 생각하다
as I see fit 내가 적절하다고 생각한대로

A: Can't you just give me some money?
내게 돈 좀 주면 안돼?

B: No, but **I'll help you in any way I see fit.**
어, 하지만 내식대로 널 도와줄게.

미드표현

I'm not a child, I'm a grown man capable of living my life as I see fit.
난 애가 아냐, 난 하고 싶은대로 내 삶을 살 수 있는 성인이라고.

I'm still the chief of surgery, so I will deal with him as I see fit.
난 아직 외과과장이야 그러니 내 방식대로 걔를 치료할거야.

We will redecorate it as we see fit.
우리가 적절하다고 생각하는대로 다시 실내장식을 할거야.

My detectives will conduct their investigation in any manner they see fit.
내 휘하의 형사들은 자신들이 맞다고 생각하면 그 어떤 방식으로도 그들을 심문할겁니다.

002 I got your back 내가 뒤를 봐줄게

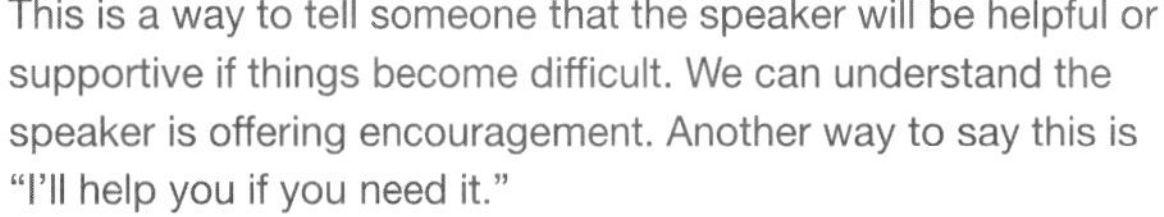

This is a way to tell someone that the speaker will be helpful or supportive if things become difficult. We can understand the speaker is offering encouragement. Another way to say this is "I'll help you if you need it."

| Point | get sb's back …의 뒤를 봐주다, 도와주다
get sb back …을 데려다주다, 데려오다

A: I have to confront Tim about insulting me.
팀이 나를 모욕해서 내가 맞서야 돼.

B: When you do it, **I got your back.**
네가 그럴 때 네 편이 되어줄게.

미드표현

You got my back? 내 뒤를 봐주겠다고?

Don't worry. I've got your back. 걱정마, 내가 도와줄게.

Good to know you've got my back.
나를 도와준다고 하니 넘 좋아.

Okay, honey, let's get you back to group, okay? 좋아, 자기야, 사람들 있는데로 데려다줄게, 알았지?

003 Can you give me a hand? 좀 도와줄래?

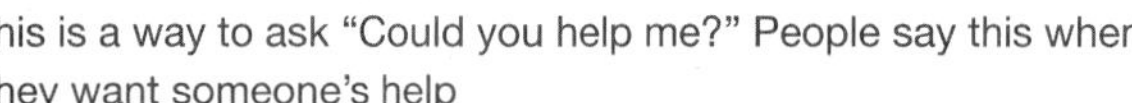

this is a way to ask "Could you help me?" People say this when they want someone's help

| Point | give sb a hand (with~) …을 도와주다 Need a hand? 도와줄까?

A: **Can you give me a hand** moving this sofa?
이 소파 이동하는 거 좀 도와줄래?

B: Sure. It looks kind of heavy though.
그래, 근데 좀 무거워 보인다.

미드표현

Give me a hand with this mattress.
이 매트리스 옮기는 거 도와줘.

Why don't you give me a hand? 나 좀 도와주라.

I'll give you a hand. 도와줄게.

Let me give you a hand, okay? 도와줄게, 알았지?

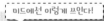

미드에선 이렇게 쓰인다!

Just let me know if you need a hand!

Friends
SEASON#9-21

Monica와 Chandler가 fertility test를 받기 위해 병원에 있다. Chandler는 내키지 않지만 간호사가 준 작은 컵에 정액을 받아와야 하는데 이때 우연히 만난 Janice가 컵을 보면서 도움이 필요하면 알려달라고 한다. 여기서 need a hand는 컵에다 Chandler가 손으로 해야 될 것을 상상해보면 중의적으로 쓰였다는 것을 알 수 있다.

Janice: Oh! Someone's a little cranky today cuz they have to do it in a cup! Oh! They gave you the kiddy size.
Chandler: What!?
Monica: This was fun! But I've got an invasive vaginal exam to get to!
Chandler: I'd love to stay, but I have eh, got a hot date.
Janice: Please... go! Just let me know if you need a hand!

재니스: 누군 좀 짜증나겠네, 컵에다 해야 되고! 오, 아동용 컵을 줬네.
챈들러: 뭐라고!?
모니카: 재밌었어. 하지만 외과자궁검사를 받아야 돼!
챈들러: 나도 더 있고 싶지만 음, 멋진 데이트가 있어서.
재니스: 어서 가! 손이 필요하면 말해!

004 You saved my ass 네가 날 살렸어

This means that the speaker was helped out in some way by the listener. We can understand that the speaker is grateful because with this help, he has avoided possible trouble. It is like saying "You really bailed me out."

| Point | save one's ass …을 구해주다

A: You **saved my ass** when you did that research.
네가 그 조사를 해줘서 내가 살았어.

B: I knew it would help you write your report.
네가 보고서를 쓰는데 그게 도움이 될거라는 걸 알았어.

He saved my ass in there 걔가 거기서 날 구해줬어

I sure as hell wouldn't drive to Queens to save your ass. 난 분명코 널 구하기 위해 차로 퀸즈로 가지 않을거야.

It's my way of trying to save your ass.
그건 내가 널 구하려고 하는 내 방식이야.

I really appreciate you letting me use your computer. You saved my ass.
네 컴퓨터를 쓰게 해줘서 정말 고마워. 너 때문에 살았어.

005 Could you do me a favor? 내 부탁 좀 들어줄래?

미드표현

the speaker is asking if someone will do something for him. It is like saying "Can you do something that will help me?"

| Point | do me a favor 부탁이 있다
Can I ask you for a favor? 부탁 하나 해도 될까?

A: **Can you do me a favor?** I need something to drink. 부탁 좀 들어줄래? 마실 게 좀 필요해.

B: I'll bring you some water from the kitchen.
부엌에서 물 갖다 줄게.

Listen, do me a favor. You're the only one who knows about this.
이봐, 부탁이 있어. 이걸 아는 사람은 너밖에 없잖아.

I'm asking you to do me a favor. 부탁 좀 들어 줘.

Can you do me a favor? I have a friend who needs a reservation for two tonight at 8:00.
부탁 좀 들어줄래? 오늘 저녁 8시에 2명 예약이 필요한 친구가 있어.

006 Could you do me a favor and do~? (제발) 부탁인데 …좀 해줄래?

미드표현

this is asking someone to help. It is like asking "Can you help me to do..?"

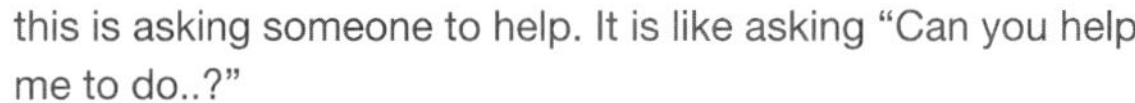

| Point | do sb a favor and+V …에게 …을 해주다

A: **Could you do me a favor and** bring me a drink? 부탁인데 마실 것 좀 갖다 줄테야?

B: Sure. What kind of drink would you like?
그래. 어떤 거 마실래?

Just do me a favor and please don't go in her room. 제발 부탁인데 걔 방에는 들어가지마.

Can you do me a favor and maybe not wear the green suit? 제발 부탁인데 그 초록색 옷은 입지 않아줄래?

Can you do me a favor and drop this off at the lab? 부탁인데 이거 좀 실험실에 갖다줄래?

007 Back me up 도와줘, 지원해줘

미드표현

often this is a way of saying "Help me by agreeing with me." To back a person up is to tell other people he is right

| Point | back sb (on sth) (…에) …을 지지하다, 도와주다.

A: This is the best sandwich I've ever eaten. **Back me up** on this. 여태 먹어본 샌드위치 중 가장 맛있다. 맞다고 해줘.

B: Yeah, I agree with you. It tastes really good.
어, 네 말이 맞아. 정말 맛좋아.

I cannot believe that you didn't back me up in there. 네가 거기서 날 지원해주지 않았다는게 믿을 수가 없어.

Ask him, I bet he'd back me up on that.
걔한테 부탁해봐, 걔가 그거 널 확실히 도와줄거야.

I really need the two of you to back me up on this. 정말이지 너희 둘이 이거 나 도와줘야 돼.

008 You gotta help me out here 이거 좀 도와줘야겠어

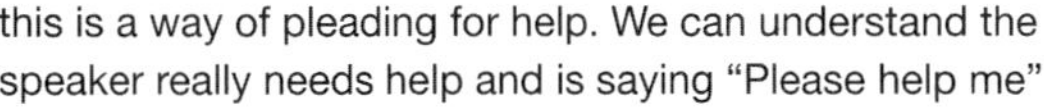

this is a way of pleading for help. We can understand the speaker really needs help and is saying "Please help me"

| Point | help sb out (with~) …에게 …을 도와주다
Can you help me out? 나 좀 도와주라

A: I need a job. **You have got to help me out here.** 일이 필요해요. 이거 좀 도와주셔야 돼요.

B: I'm really sorry but I can't give you a job.
정말 미안하지만 일을 줄 수가 없어요.

미드표현

You've gotta help me out. It's not safe out here. 좀 도와줘야겠어. 이곳은 안전하지 못해.

I don't know how to talk about that stuff. You gotta help me out!
이거 어떻게 말해야 될지 모르겠어. 좀 도와줘야겠어!

Come on, George. Help me out here.
이것 봐, 조지. 나 좀 도와줘.

009 I'd appreciate it if you~ …해주면 정말 고맙겠어

often this means "I hope that you will…" The speaker is asking someone to do something

| Point | I'd like you to do~ …해주라

A: **I'd appreciate it if you would** make less noise while I sleep. 내가 자는 동안 시끄럽게 하지 않았으면 좋겠어.

B: I'm sorry. I'll try to be more quiet.
미안, 더 조용하도록 할게요.

미드표현

I would really appreciate it if you didn't tell her. 걔한테 얘기안했으면 고맙겠어.

We'd appreciate it if no one told him yet.
아무도 걔한테 아직 얘기 안했으면 고맙겠어.

I bought a restaurant and I'd like you to be the head chef. 식당하나 샀는데 네가 주방장이 되어주라.

I'd appreciate it if you wouldn't tell anyone.
아무한테도 얘기안했으면 고맙겠어.

010 I was wondering if[whether] ~ 혹 …해줄래?

usually this expression is used to ask if it is OK to do something. It is very similar to saying "Could I do this?"

| Point | I was wondering if[whether]~ 혹 …해줄래?

A: **I was wondering if** I could take tomorrow off.
내일 쉬어도 돼요?

B: Well, I guess it would be OK to miss one day of work. 어, 하루 결근해도 될 것 같아.

미드표현

I was wondering if I could ask you something.
혹 뭐 좀 물어봐도 될까요.

I was wondering if I could talk to you for a moment. 잠시 이야기해도 될까.

I was wondering if you would like to go to dinner with me. 나와 저녁 먹으러 가시겠어요.

011 (Sometimes) That helps (간혹) 도움이 돼

this indicates that there are times something is useful, and at other times it isn't useful. It is like saying "It might work"

| Point | It might help 도움이 될지도 몰라
These don't help 이것들은 도움이 되지 않아
That didn't help! 그건 도움이 안되었어!

A: Do you think that drinking tea will allow me to sleep better? 차를 마시면 숙면하게 된다고 생각해?

B: **Sometimes that helps.** How long have you had a problem sleeping?
때때로 도움이 돼. 얼마동안 수면장애를 겪고 있는데?

미드표현

That helps a lot. Thanks. 도움이 많이 되었어. 고마워.

I think it might help. 도움이 될 수 있을거야.

She says aspirin didn't help.
걔가 아스피린은 도움이 안됐대.

You're lending me some money. That helps.
내게 돈을 좀 빌려준다고. 그럼 도움이 되지. .

012 I could use a little help here 여기 좀 도와줬으면 해

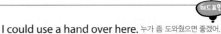

this is a way of asking for help. It means "I want you to come over and help me"

I Point I could use+N …가 있었으면 좋겠다. …이 필요하다

A: **I could use** a little help here. 여기 좀 도와줬으면 해.

B: I'll help you as soon as I finish this.
이거 끝내고 바로 도와줄게.

I could use a hand over here. 누가 좀 도와줬으면 좋겠어.

Looks like you could use an extra hand.
도움이 필요할 것 같아서.

I could use a Coke. 나 콜라 좀 마셔야겠어.

I could use a couple of beers. 나 맥주 좀 마셔야겠어.

013 You're not helping 넌 도움이 안돼

often this is a way to tell someone that they are either doing nothing or else having a negative affect. What the speaker means is "You should be trying to help, but you are not"

I Point I You're not helping me 넌 내게 도움이 되는 게 아니라 반대야

A: That box looks too heavy for you to lift.
네가 들기에 상자가 너무 커 보여.

B: **You're not helping.** Why don't you lift it with me? 넌 도움이 안돼. 나랑 함께 들자.

You're not helping, Terry. It's not your fight.
테리야, 넌 도움이 되지 않아. 그건 네 싸움이 아냐.

I mean, there was at one point you're not helping. 내 말은, 네가 도움이 되지 않는 때가 있었다는거야.

You are perfect exactly the way you are. You're not helping. 넌 전혀 변함이 없네. 넌 도움이 안돼.

You're not helping yourself if you don't talk to me. 네가 말하지 않으면 넌 도움을 받을 수가 없어.

014 I need your help 도움이 필요해

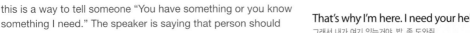

this is a way to tell someone "You have something or you know something I need." The speaker is saying that person should help him

I Point I I need you to do ~ …해줘
Do you need help with that? 그거 도와줄까?

A: **I need your help.** This report is due tomorrow.
네 도움이 필요해. 이 보고서 내일까지 제출해야 돼.

B: Do you want me to write part of it for you?
보고서의 일부분을 나보고 쓰라는거야?

That's why I'm here. I need your help, Bob.
그래서 내가 여기 있는거야. 밥, 좀 도와줘.

I'm sick, and I need your help. 아파서 네 도움이 필요해.

I just need you to go with it, okay?
그냥 잠자코 보고만 있어줘, 알았지?

Folks, I need you to step back, please.
여러분, 제발이지 뒤로 물러서세요.

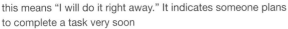

015 Consider it done 기꺼이 그러지, 걱정마, 해놓을게

this means "I will do it right away." It indicates someone plans to complete a task very soon

A: I'd like you to make copies of these files.
이 파일들 복사해.

B: **Consider it done.** I'll bring them to your office this afternoon. 그렇게 할게요. 오후에 사무실에 갖다 놓을게요.

Consider it done. So where you going?
그렇게 할게. 그럼 넌 어디로 가는거야?

Whatever you need, consider it done.
네가 뭘 필요로 하든지 해놓을게.

If you want the files sent to you, consider it done. 네게 파일들을 보내기를 원하면 그렇게 할게.

016 We gotta get help 도움을 받아야 해

often this is said when people really need help. It is a way to say "We can't do this and we need someone to help us"

| Point | Get help! 도움을 청해!

A: We don't have enough employees working here.
여기 일하는 사람이 너무 부족해.

B: I know it. **We have got to get help.**
알아. 도움을 받아야 해.

I need to get help. 도움을 받아야 해.

Run, go get help! 뛰어. 가서 도움을 청해!

John, go down to the beach and get help!
존, 해변으로 가서 도움을 청해!

Get help before you do something else you regret. 네가 후회할 다른 짓을 하기 전에 도움을 받아.

017 What can I do for you? 내가 어떻게 해줄까?, 뭘 도와드릴까요?

this is a way of saying "Can I help you?" People say this when they want to help others

| Point | What else can I do for you? 내가 더 도와줄 일 없어?
So what can I do to help? 그래 뭘 도와줄까?
What can I do? 어쩌겠어?

A: **What can I do for you?** 뭘 도와드릴까요?

B: I would like to open a bank account here.
은행계좌를 만들고 싶어서요.

A: Uhm. Louis? Do you have a minute? B: What can I do for you, Jack?
A: 루이스, 시간있어? B: 뭘 해줄까, 잭?

A: Hello, John. I'm sorry to drop by on you, unannounced. Do you have a moment? B: Sure. So, what can I do for you?
A: 존, 안녕. 갑자기 들이닥쳐 미안. 시간있니? B: 그럼, 뭘 도와줄까?

018 Is there anything I can do for you? 뭐 도와줄 일 없어?

this is very similar to the previous phrase. It is asking if the speaker can do something helpful

| Point | Is there anything I can do to help? 뭐 도와줄 일 없어?
Is there anything I can do to~? 내가 …하는데 도움될 일 없어?

A: I think my brother is getting sick. 형이 아픈 것 같아.

B: That's too bad. **Is there anything I can do to help?** 안됐네. 뭐 도와줄 일 없어?

Is there anything I can do? I am on the board of this hospital. 뭐 도와줄 일 있어? 난 이 병원 이사회 소속이야.

Is there anything I can do for you? Anything at all? 뭐 도와줄 일 있어? 뭐든지?

Is there anything I can do to cheer you up?
널 기운나게 하는데 내가 도움될 일 없어?

019 Let me help you with that 도와줄게

the speaker is offering assistance. He is saying "I'll do some work for you"

| Point | help sb with sth …에게 …의 일을 도와주다
Can I help you with something? 내가 뭐 도와줄까요?

A: Gosh, this suitcase is really heavy.
어휴, 이 가방 정말 무겁네.

B: **Let me help you with** that bag. 가방드는 거 도와줄게.

Excuse me. Can I help you with something?
실례지만 뭐 좀 도와드릴까요?

You want me to help you with that?
그거 내가 도와줄까요?

Sorry, I can't help you with that. 도와주지 못해서 미안.

Your suitcase looks heavy. Let me help you with that. 네 가방이 무거워 보이는데 내가 드는 거 도와줄게.

020 If there's anything you need, don't hesitate to ask 필요한 거 있으면 바로 말해

this is a way of saying "I'll help you if you need it." The speaker wants someone to know he is happy to help if that person has trouble

| Point | If you need anything, just ask 뭐든 필요하면 말만 해

A: Thank you for your help with my wedding.
내 결혼식 도와줘서 고마워.

B: **If there's anything you need, don't hesitate to ask.** 필요한 거 있으면 바로 말해.

미드표현

You let me know if there's anything you need.
필요한 거 있으면 알려줘.

Will you call me if you need anything? My cell will be on. 필요한 거 있으면 전화할래? 핸드폰 켜놓을게.

Call me if you need anything. 필요한 거 있으면 전화해.

021 If you need me, you know where I am

도움이 필요하면 바로 불러

this is used to tell someone that the speaker will help if he is asked to. It is another way of saying "Just call me if you need help, and I'll come"

| Point | You know where to find me 연락처 알고 있지, 나 어디있는지 알지

A: I could use your help when I move.
이사할 때 네 도움이 있으면 좋겠어.

B: **If you need me, you know where I am.**
필요하면 바로 불러.

미드표현

If you need me, you know where to find me.
도움이 필요하면 바로 불러.

Just call me if you need me. 필요하면 전화해.

If you need a little extra, you know where to find it. 더 필요하면 어디있는지 알지.

If you need me, I'll be in my bedroom.
내 도움이 필요하면 나 침실에 있을게.

022 Just say the word! 말만해!

this is a means of expressing "I will help if you ask." We can understand that the speaker is willing to do something to help at any time

A: You can count on my help. **Just say the word.**
내 도움에 의지하라고. 말만해.

B: Thanks Matt. I'll be giving you a call to help out in the future. 고마워 맷. 앞으로 전화해서 도와달라고 할게.

미드표현

Please, just say the word and you'll make me the happiest guy on earth.
빨리 말해, 그럼 난 세계에서 가장 행복한 남자가 될거야.

If you'd like me to deal with him, just say the word. 내가 걔를 손봐주기를 원하면 말만해.

023 She's very supportive 걘 도움이 많이 되고 있어, 걘 무척 협조적이야

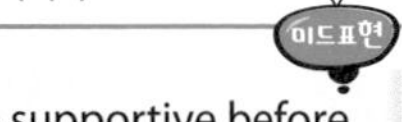

this means the woman is kind and helps others in a big way. It is similar to saying "She treats us very well"

| Point | Be supportive! 좀 도움이 돼라!

A: Why do you like your girlfriend so much?
왜 네 여친을 좋아해?

B: **She's very supportive.** She helps me a lot.
무척 도움을 많이 줘. 날 많이 도와줘.

I'm sorry we weren't more supportive before.
전에 별로 도움이 못돼서 미안해.

He's been incredibly supportive of me.
걘 정말 나에게 큰 도움이 되어왔어.

It's wonderful that your mother is so supportive. 네 엄마가 많이 도와주셔서 정말 잘됐어.

I'm trying to be supportive about this.
난 이 문제에 대해 협조하려고 하고 있어.

024 I'd be happy to help you 기꺼이 도와줄게

this is like saying "Could I help with that?" The person is saying he is ready to help now.

I Point I I'd be happy to~ 기꺼이 …할게

A: I am not sure what gift I should buy for my daughter. 딸에게 무슨 선물을 사줘야 할 지 모르겠어.

B: **I'd be happy to** help you choose one. 기꺼이 고르는 거 도와줄게.

I'd be happy to show you around town.
기꺼이 시내 구경시켜줄게.

I'd be happy to do it. 기꺼이 할게.

I'd be happy to baby-sit for you. 기꺼이 애 봐줄게.

025 I'd do anything for you 널 위해서라면 뭐든 할게

미드표현

this is a way to express "I will do whatever you ask." The speaker is indicating that he really wants to please the person he's talking to

A: Would you mind helping me carry my books? 내 책 나르는 것 좀 도와줄래?

B: Of course. **I'd do anything for you.** 물론. 뭐든지 해줄게.

I would do anything for her. She has already done so much for me.
걔를 위해서라면 뭐든지 할거야. 이미 많은 걸 받았거든.

One of them killed Tammy. You know, they'll do anything for money.
걔네들 중 하나가 태미를 죽였어. 돈을 위해서라면 뭐든지 하잖아.

When I said I'd do anything for the money, obviously I didn't mean it.
돈을 위해서라면 뭐든지 하겠다고 한 말은 정말이지 진심이 아니었어.

026 I'm begging you 부탁이야

미드표현

often this is said when a person has an emergency and needs help very much. It indicates that the speaker could also say "Please help me. I will do anything for help"

I Point I I'm begging you to~ 제발 …좀 해

A: Let me pass your class. **I'm begging you.** 선생님 수업 이수하도록 해주세요. 제발 부탁이에요.

B: Well, I guess I could give you a C as a final grade. 저기, 최종 점수로 C를 줄 수 있을 것 같네.

Look, I'm begging you, don't do it.
이봐, 제발, 그러지마.

I'm begging you, never do that to anyone!
제발, 절대 누구한테도 그러지마!

Oh please eat. Eat. I'm begging you to eat!
좀 먹어, 먹어. 제발 좀 먹으라고!

027 You were a great help 정말 많은 도움이 됐어

미드표현

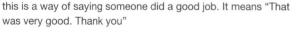

this is a way of saying someone did a good job. It means "That was very good. Thank you"

I Point I You've been a big help 큰 도움이 되었어
It was a great help 큰 도움이 됐어
That's a big help 크게 도움이 돼
This is very helpful 정말 도움돼

A: Thank you. **You were a great help.** 고마워. 정말 큰 도움이 됐어.

B: I was glad to be here for you. 널 위해 여기 있어서 기뻤어.

Actually you were a big help tonight.
사실 오늘 밤 큰 도움이 되었어.

He was a big help to us. 걔가 우릴 많이 도와줬어.

With your experience and connections, you would be a great help.
경력과 인맥으로 넌 크게 도움이 될거야.

Thank you for coming by. You were a great help. 들러줘서 고마워. 정말 많은 도움이 되었어.

028 That will do you good 그게 도움이 될거야, 굉장히 좋을거야

미드표현

this means "You'll feel better after you do it." The speaker thinks something will benefit the person he's talking to

I Point I do sb good 도움이 되다

A: I decided to go to Hawaii with my husband.
남편과 하와이에 가기로 했어.

B: **That will do you good.** The weather is great there. 그게 도움이 될거야. 거기 날씨 정말 좋아.

Fresh air will do you good. 신선한 공기가 도움이 될거야.

A little fruit might do you good, too.
과일을 조금 먹어도 도움이 될거야.

It isn't going to do you any good.
그건 네게 전혀 도움이 되지 않을거야.

029 I don't suppose you know her phone number, do you? 재 전화번호를 좀 알려줄래요?

미드표현

this is a very polite way of getting someone's phone number so that the speaker can call the person later. We can express almost the same thing by asking "What is her number?" or saying "I'd like you to give me her number"

I Point I I don't suppose you~ …을 해줄래요, …은 아니죠?

A: That blonde really liked you.
저 금발여자가 너를 정말 좋아했는데.

B: **I don't suppose** you know her phone number, do you? 재 전화번호를 좀 알려줄래요?

I don't suppose there's any place you can rent cars anywhere around here?
이 근처에 차를 렌트할 수 있는 곳이 있지 않죠?

I don't suppose you have any experience with teenagers? 십대를 가르쳐보거나 길러 본 적이 좀 있나요?

In fact, I don't suppose I could borrow your gun? 사실은 당신 총을 빌려줄래요?

030 Don't be so hard on me 내게 너무 심하게 하지마

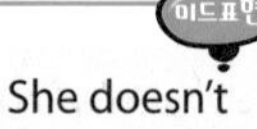

미드표현

this is a way to say "Stop being so unkind to me." The speaker thinks someone is treating him unfairly or badly

I Point I be hard on sb …을 힘들게 하다

A: **Don't be so hard on me.** 내게 너무 심하게 하지마.

B: I have to. You're really lazy. 해야 돼. 넌 정말 게을러.

You shouldn't be so hard on her. She doesn't mean to be hurtful.
넌 걔한테 넘 심하게 하면 안돼. 걘 아프게 하려고 했던 게 아냐.

Right, and maybe he won't be so hard on us.
맞아, 아마 걔가 우리에게 그렇게 심하게 대하지 않을지도 몰라.

031 Cut me some slack 좀 봐줘, 너무 몰아세우지마

미드표현

this indicates the speaker wants to be treated fairly. It is like saying "Stop making my life so difficult"

I Point I cut sb some slack …을 좀 봐주다

A: I don't like the way you've been acting.
너 행동하는 게 마음에 안들어.

B: **Cut me some slack.** I am having a hard time.
좀 봐줘. 난 어려움을 겪고 있단 말야.

Cut me some slack. I was on call last night. I didn't get much sleep.
좀 봐줘. 어젯밤 비상대기였어. 잠을 많이 못 잤다구.

I guess I can cut him some slack.
걔 좀 봐줄 수 있을 것 같아.

Your son's teacher said she cut him some slack. 네 아들 선생님이 걔를 좀 봐주고 있다고 말했어.

I had a hard day. Cut me some slack.
오늘 하루 힘들었어. 좀 봐줘.

032 Give me a break 1. 좀 봐줘 2. 그만 좀 해, 작작 좀 해

this means "That's crazy" or "That doesn't make any sense." It is said to indicate that a person is not doing things in a good or fair way. And this can also be a way to ask for another chance. The speaker is saying "Please let me try again"

A: We need you to stay here for a few days.
며칠간 여기에 머물러줘.

B: **Give me a break.** I'm not going to stay here.
그만 좀 해. 난 여기 머물지 않을거야.

미드표현

Give me a break. I haven't done this before.
좀 봐주라. 나 이런 적 없었잖아.

Give me a break. Did she look like a friend of mine? 그만 좀 해라. 걔가 내 친구처럼 보였다고?

Oh, give me a break. This has nothing to do with saving a life.
그만 좀 해. 이건 목숨을 살리는 일과는 전혀 상관없는 일이야.

033 Cut me a break 나 좀 봐줘

often this is a way to ask someone to give the speaker one more chance to do something correctly. We can understand that the speaker has done something wrong and might be punished for it. It is like saying "Let me do it again and I won't make the same mistake"

| Point | cut sb a break 사정을 봐주다, 기회를 주다

A: I have to give you a ticket for driving fast.
과속으로 딱지를 끊어야겠어요.

B: Come on officer, can't you **cut me a break?**
경관님, 이러지 마요, 좀 봐주시면 안돼요?

미드표현

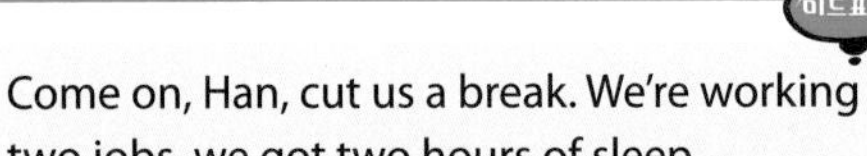

Come on, Han, cut us a break. We're working two jobs, we got two hours of sleep.
그러지마, 한, 우리 좀 봐줘. 투잡을 하고 있고 잠도 두 시간밖에 못자.

So if you could, Susan, cut her a break.
그럼 수잔, 네가 할 수 있으면 걔 좀 봐줘.

They're gonna cut me a break if I turn him in when he contacts me.
걔가 연락해올 때 밀고하면 우리를 봐줄거야.

Why don't you cut me a break, huh?
나 좀 봐주라, 응?

034 Go easy on me 좀 봐줘, 살살 해줘

this means "Be more kind." It is said when someone wants another person to act in a gentle way

| Point | go easy on sb 잘 대해주다, 봐주다
go easy on sth 적당히 하다, 많이 하지 않다

A: Are you ready for the oral test? 구두시험 준비됐니?

B: I guess so. **Go easy on me.** 예, 잘 좀 봐줘요.

미드표현

Tell him to go easy on Jessy, it's her first time.
걔보고 제시한테 살살 하라고 해, 처음이야.

She's never been in any real trouble before. They'll go easy on her.
걔는 진짜 어려움이란 걸 모르고 살았어. 걔들이 잘 대해줄거야.

She's explained that your family has gone through enough, and asked me to go easy on the boy.
걔는 네 가족이 충분히 겪을 걸 겪었으니까 나보고 그 소년을 잘 대해주라고 부탁했어.

035 Have a heart 한번만 봐줘

this is a way to say "Act in a nice way." Like the previous phrase, it is asking for someone to be kind

| Point | have a heart 인정이 있다

A: There will be no vacation this year. 금년에 휴가없어.

B: **Have a heart.** I really need a vacation.
좀 봐줘요. 정말 휴가 가야 돼요.

미드표현

That was a little girl! Don't you have a heart?
조그만 소녀라구? 넌 인정머리도 없냐?

Please, please have a heart! 제발, 제발 인정을 베풀어요!

Can't you give me some money? Have a heart. 나한테 돈 좀 줄 수 없어? 인정을 좀 베풀라고.

036 That's so sweet 고맙기도 해라, 정말 고마워, 너무 친절해

this means "It was a very kind thing to do." Sometimes this is like thanking someone

| Point | It's so sweet of sb (to~) (…하다니) 정말 고마워
You are so sweet 정말 고마워

A: These flowers are for our anniversary.
우리 기념일을 위한 꽃이야.

B: **That's so sweet.** Thank you. 고맙기도 해라. 고마워.

미드표현

So sweet. You are the best. 고맙기도 해라. 네가 최고야.

That's so sweet, but I'm in love with another man. 정말 고마운데 딴 남자를 사랑해.

That was so sweet of you. 정말 고마워.

That was so sweet of you to wait for me!
날 기다려줘서 정말 고마워!

037 It's[That's] very nice of you 너무 고마워, 정말 친절하군

like the previous phrase, this expresses appreciation. It is similar to saying "Thanks for doing that"

| Point | It's very nice of you (to~) (…해서) 정말 고마워

A: I wanted to stop by and see how you are feeling. 잠깐 들러서 네가 어떤지 보려고.

B: **It's nice of you.** I feel OK today.
정말 고마워. 오늘 기분 좋아.

미드표현

It's very nice of you, but I can't accept that.
정말 고맙지만, 이거 받아들일 수가 없어.

I don't think it's very nice of you to park here. You're blocking the entrance.
여기 주차하는 건 좋지 않은 것 같아. 입구를 막고 있잖아.

That's very nice of you, but I do have a boyfriend. 정말 고맙지만, 난 남친이 있어요.

038 That's big of you 친절하기도 하지, 맘이 넓기도 하지, 정말 자상해

often this is used as a sarcastic phrase, which would mean "I think you didn't do enough." It can also mean "It was a nice thing to do"

| Point | How kind (of you)! 이렇게 친절하다니!
You're such a kind person 정말 친절하네
He's got such a good heart 걘 무척 자상한 애야

A: I gave my date money to take the taxi home.
택시타고 집에 가라고 데이트상대에게 돈을 줬어.

B: **That's big of you.** Why didn't you drive her home? 친절하기도 해라. 왜 집에 데려다주지 않았어?

미드표현

I was really touched by your call. It was so big of you. 전화해줘서 감동했어. 친절하기도 하지.

It was big of you to forgive her.
걜 용서한 건 정말 맘이 넓은거였어.

That's very big of you to admit.
인정한 건 정말 통크게 잘한거야.

039 I can't thank you enough 어떻게 감사해야 할지

this means "I'm very grateful to you." The speaker is thanking someone for his kindness

| Point | I can't thank you enough for ~ing …해줘서 뭐라 감사하다고 해야 할지
I don't know how to thank you 뭐라 감사해야 할지
How can we ever thank you? 어떻게 감사를 해야 할지

A: I fixed the problem with your car, Mrs. Krebble.
크레블 씨 차수리 끝났어요.

B: That is great. **I can't thank you enough.**
아주 좋아요. 정말 고마워요.

미드표현

I cannot thank you enough for getting her interested in math.
걜 수학에 관심갖게 해줘서 뭐라 감사해야 할지.

I can't thank you enough for helping me out here. 이걸 도와줘서 뭐라 감사하다고 해야 할지.

I cannot thank you enough for doing this.
이거 해줘서 뭐라 감사해야 할지

040 I really appreciate this 정말 고마워

like the previous phrase, this is a way of saying "Thank you." The speaker is grateful

| Point | I'd appreciate it if you would~ …해주면 고맙겠어

A: These presents are for your kids this Christmas.
이번 성탄절 애들 선물들이야.

B: **I really appreciate this.** 정말 고마워요.

Well I appreciate this, thank you. 정말 고마워, 고마워.

This is great. I really appreciate this.
정말 좋아. 정말 고마워.

It's a wonderful thing and I really appreciate it. 정말 대단해 그리고 정말 고마워.

Andy, that is so amazing, and I really appreciate it, but I can't take it.
앤디, 정말 멋지고 정말 고맙지만, 난 받을 수가 없어.

041 I owe you one 이 은혜를 어떻게 갚아야 할지, 신세가 많아

this means someone has done a favor for the speaker, and the speaker wants to do a favor for that person. It is like saying "I want to do something nice for you soon"

| Point | owe sb sth = owe sth to sb …에게 …을 신세지다

A: Thanks for helping with my homework. **I owe you one.** 숙제 도와줘서 고마워. 신제졌어.

B: Maybe you can buy me dinner tonight.
오늘 저녁 사지 그래.

Now I only owe you $100. 이제 너한테 100달러 빚진거야.

Thanks. I owe you big-time. 고마워. 큰 신세졌어.

You owe me big time for that.
너 나한테 그걸로 신세 많이 진거야.

You don't owe me anything. 넌 나한테 빚진 게 없어.

042 What would I have done without you?
네가 없었더라면 어쩔 뻔했어?

this means "You were very helpful." The speaker is thanking someone for helping

A: You were so nice. **What would I have done without you?** 정말 친절하네. 네가 없었더라면 어쩔 뻔했어?

B: I just wanted to help you out. 그냥 널 도와주고 싶었을 뿐이야.

What would I have done without you? You've been so helpful.
너 없었더라면 어쩔 뻔했어. 너 정말 도움이 많이 됐어.

It's been a trying time. What would I have done without you? 힘든 시기였어. 너 없었더라면 어쩔 뻔했어.

You organized everything. What would I have done without you?
네가 다 정리를 했네. 너 없었더라면 어쩔 뻔했어.

043 You saved the day for us 덕분에 일이 잘 풀렸어

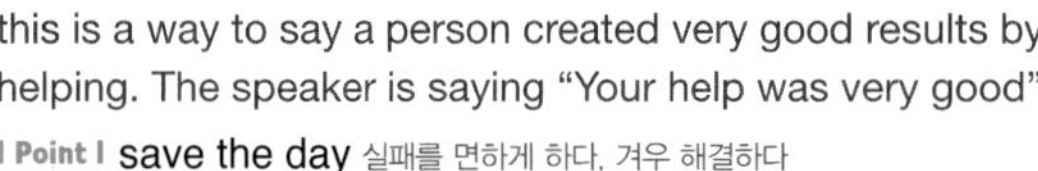

this is a way to say a person created very good results by helping. The speaker is saying "Your help was very good"

| Point | save the day 실패를 면하게 하다, 겨우 해결하다

A: Did you get the money I sent? 내가 보낸 돈 받았어?

B: Yes. **You saved the day for us.** 어. 네 덕에 결과가 좋았어.

I told her that! That was me! I saved the day!
난 걔한테 말했어! 그게 나였다고! 실패를 면하게 해준게!

Hey, looks like we kinda saved the day.
야, 우리가 겨우 문제를 해결한 것처럼 보여.

You made the festival a success. You saved the day for us. 네가 축제를 성공적으로 해냈어. 네 덕에 잘 됐어.

You saved the day for us. What can we do to repay you?
네 덕에 일이 잘 풀렸어. 어떻게 보답하면 되겠어?

044 You shouldn't have 이러지 않아도 되는데, 괜한 수고를 했어

this is often a response when someone is given a present. The real meaning of this phrase is "Thank you very much"

A: Here is a present for your birthday. 여기 네 생일선물.
B: Thank you. You really shouldn't have.
고마워. 정말 이러지 않아도 되는데.

Oh, sweetheart, you shouldn't have! It's so beautiful. 이러지 않아도 되는데, 너무 예뻐.

A: Relax, this didn't cost me a dime.
B: Micheal, you shouldn't have.
A: 걱정마, 돈 하나도 안들었어. B: 마이클, 이러지 않아도 되는데.

You cooked dinner for us? You shouldn't have.
우리를 위해 저녁식사요리를 했다고? 그러지 않아도 되는데.

045 You're (very) welcome 천만에

미드표현

this is a way of saying "I was happy to do something for you. The speaker is responding to someone who thanked him

| Point | You're welcome to~ 편히(마음대로) …해라
Not at all 천만에, 별말씀을, 별것도 아닌데
Don't mention it 천만에요, 그런 말 마세요

A: Thank you for hosting the party. 파티열어줘 고마워.
B: You're very welcome. Come back again.
천만에. 다시 또 와.

I have some work to do, but you're welcome to stay. 할 일이 좀 있지만 편히 있어도 돼.

Now you're welcome to stay as long as you like. 원하는 만큼 편히 머물러.

You're welcome. It's our three-month anniversary. 별것도 아닌데. 우리 3개월 기념일이잖아.

046 (It's) My pleasure 1. 도움이 돼서 기뻐, 별말씀을 2. 반가워

미드표현

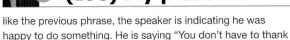

like the previous phrase, the speaker is indicating he was happy to do something. He is saying "You don't have to thank me"

| Point | The pleasure was mine 내가 기쁘지 뭘

A: I appreciate everything you did. 네가 해준 모든 거에 고마워.
B: It's my pleasure. I like to give you a hand.
별 말을. 널 도와주는 게 좋은 걸.

A: Oh, honey, that would be great. Thank you.
B: My pleasure.
A: 자기야, 그러면 정말 좋겠다. 고마워. B: 내가 기쁘지.

A: Thanks for getting this done so quickly.
B: My pleasure.
A: 이거 빨리 끝내줘서 고마워요. B: 별 말씀을요.

A: I want to thank you for taking time to see me. B: My pleasure.
A: 시간내 날 만나줘서 고마워요. B: 도움이 돼서 기뻐요.

047 It's the least I can do 이 정도야 기본이지, 최소한의 내 성의야, 별것도 아닌데

this is used as a response after someone says "Thank you." It is very similar to saying "You're welcome"

A: Thank you for visiting me in the hospital.
병원에 와줘서 고마워.
B: It's the least I can do. 이 정도는 기본이지.

I'm just helping her out. It's the least I can do.
그냥 걜 도와준 거뿐이야. 이 정도야 기본이지.

It's the least I can do to thank you for helping her. 걜 도와줘서 고맙다고 하는데 이 정도는 기본이지.

Let me pay for our drinks. It's the least I can do. 음료수 값은 내가 낼게. 내가 이 정도는 해야지.

Ways of answering a greeting and telling someone goodbye

어떻게 지내냐고 서로 인사를 나눌 때

How're you holding up?

001 How're you holding up? 이제 좀 괜찮아?

this speaker is asking someone how they are doing. It is a question that is asked mostly after a difficult event that may have created problems or sadness within that person's life. We can understand the speaker wants to know "Are you still having serious difficulties?"

| Point | hold up 견디다

A: I heard you've been sick. **How're you holding up?** 아팠다며. 이제는 좀 괜찮아?
B: Well, I spent the whole month in the hospital.
거의 한 달 내내 병원에서 지냈어.

How you holding up? You look good.
이제 좀 괜찮아? 좋아보이는데.

It's good to see you holding up so well.
네가 잘 견디는 걸 보니 좋다.

I'm sorry about your house. How you holding up? 네 집은 정말 안됐어. 어떻게 지내고 있어?

How you holding up since you got fired from temp job? 임시직에서 해고된 후에 어떻게 지내고 있어?

002 How (are) you doing? 안녕?, 잘 지냈어?

미드표현

this is a way to say "Hi." People say this when they greet each other

| Point | How are you? 잘 지내?
How are you doing with[on]~ ? …은 어떻게 돼가?

A: **How are you doing today?** 오늘 어때?
B: I'm fine. How are you? 좋아, 넌 잘 지내?

How are you doing? Are you feeling any better? 잘 지내? 기분 좋아졌어?

Hey, how are you? It's good to see you.
야, 안녕? 반가워.

How are you doing on the prints?
지문은 어떻게 돼가?

How are you doing this? 이거 어떻게 돼가?

003 What's up? 어때?, 무슨 일이야?, 뭐해?

미드표현

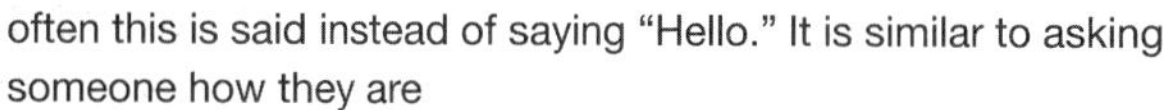

often this is said instead of saying "Hello." It is similar to asking someone how they are

| Point | What's new? 뭐 새로운 일 있어?
What's new with you? (What's new?에 대한 대답) 그러는 넌 별일 있니?

A: Hey there Tom. **What's up?** 야 탐, 뭐해?
B: I'm just going to the store for some beer.
맥주사러 가게 가.

Hey, I know that look. What's up?
야, 왜 그런지 다 알아. 무슨 일이야?

So what's up, you came to see me yesterday.
무슨 일이야, 어제 찾아 왔었다며.

Hey, what's up, dude? You got a problem?
야, 친구야 무슨 일이야? 무슨 문제있어?

So what's up? You've been all weird-acting lately. 그래 무슨 일야? 최근에 너 아주 이상하게 행동하고 있어.

004 How's it going? 잘 지내?, 잘 돼가?, 어떻게 돼가?

미드표현

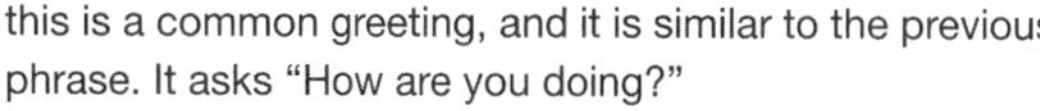

this is a common greeting, and it is similar to the previous phrase. It asks "How are you doing?"

| Point | How's it going with~? …은 잘 돼가?
How's everything going? 다 잘 돼가?
How're things with you? 넌 잘 돼가?
How goes it (with you)? 어떻게 지내?

A: Hello Joan. I haven't seen you in a while.
안녕, 조앤. 한 동안 못봤네.
B: That's right. **How's it going?** 맞아. 넌 잘 지내?

How's it going? You win? 어떻게 돼가? 이겼어?

How's it going with your patient?
네 환자 어떻게 됐어?

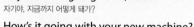

Hey! How's it going so far, babe?
자기야, 지금까지 어떻게 돼가?

How's it going with your new machine?
네 새로운 기계 어때?

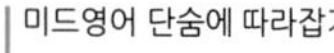

005 How (have) you been? 잘 지냈어?, 잘 있었어?, 어떻게 지냈어?

this is usually said when someone hasn't seen a person for some time. It is a way of asking "How is your life going?"

| Point | So how have you been doing? 어떻게 잘 지냈어?
What have you been doing? 뭐하고 지냈어?

A: Hi Aaron. **How have you been?** 야, 애론. 잘 지냈어?
B: Not so good. I've been sick for a few weeks.
썩 좋지는 않아. 몇 주간 아팠어.

미드표현

I've been great, just great. How have you been? 잘 지냈어. 그냥 잘. 너는 잘 지냈어?

So what have you been doing lately?
그래 최근에 어떻게 지냈어?

How have you been since last we met?
우리가 마지막으로 본 이후에 어떻게 지냈어?

006 What (have) you been up to? 뭐하고 지냈어?, 그간 어떻게 지냈어?

this is usually a way to ask someone "Have you been doing anything interesting lately?" It is often said when a person meets another person after not seeing that person for a while

A: Well Billy, **what have you been up to?**
어 빌리, 그간 어떻게 지냈어?
B: I went on a summer vacation with my parents this year. 금년에 부모님하고 여름휴가 갔었어.

미드표현

A: What have you been up to? B: I've just been sitting here, watching you.
A: 뭐하고 있는거야? B: 여기 앉아서 널 지켜보고 있었어.

So what have you been up to? I haven't seen you since you went off to college.
그간 어떻게 지냈어? 네가 대학에 간 이후로 널 보지 못했어.

I haven't seen you for a while. What have you been up to? 한동안 널 보지 못했네. 그간 어떻게 지냈어?

007 What have you got going on, Bob? 무슨 일이야, 밥?

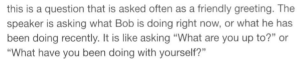

this is a question that is asked often as a friendly greeting. The speaker is asking what Bob is doing right now, or what he has been doing recently. It is like asking "What are you up to?" or "What have you been doing with yourself?"

A: **What have you got going on,** Bob? 밥, 무슨 일이야?
B: I figured that I would do some fishing this afternoon. 오늘 오후에 낚시 좀 할까 생각했었어.

미드표현

Okay, so what do you guys got going on tonight? 그래, 오늘 밤에 무슨 일들이야?

If you can't start respecting what I got going on with Emily, then maybe you shouldn't be here.
나와 에밀리 사이의 일을 존중할 수 없다면 넌 여기 있으면 안되지.

A: What you got going on in there? B: It ain't none of your concern.
A: 거기 너 무슨 일이야? B: 네가 상관할 바가 아냐.

008 How was your day? 오늘 어땠어?

often this is a way to ask a person "What happened during your workday?" It is usually asked at night, when the day has ended

A: You look unhappy Lisa. **How was your day?**
리사, 안 좋아 보여. 오늘 어땠어?
B: We had a lot of problems at my workplace today. 오늘 사무실에서 문제가 많았어.

So, how are you? How was your day?
그래, 오늘 어땠어?

A: Hi, how was your day? B: It was good, but, more importantly, how was yours?
A: : 오늘 어땠어? B: 좋았지만, 너는 어땠는데?

So, how was your day? What did you and your new friend do? 오늘 어땠어? 너와 네 새 친구는 뭐했어?

009 How they hanging? 어떻게 지내?

this is kind of a silly way of asking "How are you doing?" Usually it is only used by people who are teenagers, and it is not common

| Point | How's trick(s)?, What's shaking?, How's it shaking?
모두 6-70년대 표현으로 재미와 우스꽝스러운 표현을 즐겨하는 TV Show 등에서 찾아볼 수 있다.

A: Hi Johnny. **How's it hanging?** 야, 자니. 어떻게 지내?
B: Just fine. Everything is going great.
그냥 좋지. 다 아주 좋아.

미드표현

How they hanging? I haven't seen you in a while. 어떻게 지내? 오랜만이야.

Hey there, Zack. How they hanging?
야, 잭. 어떻게 지내?

How they hanging? Are you getting any action? 어떻게 지내? 데이트는 좀 해?

010 How's life[the world] treating you? 사는 건 어때?, 살만 해?

this asks "How is your life going?" It is a greeting used when seeing a familiar person

| Point | How's A treating you? A가 어때?
How's life~? (어디에서) 사는 게 어때?

A: **How's life treating you?** 살만 해?
B: Things are going well for me at the moment.
현재로선 잘 돼가고 있어.

미드표현

So, Nora, how's married life treating you?
그래, 노라, 결혼생활 어때?

How's the Big Apple treating you? 뉴욕생활이 어때?

How's life on the fifteenth floor? 15층 생활은 어때?

011 How's the[your] family? 가족들 다 잘 지내?

this is a way of asking about the family members that someone lives with. It is like asking "How are they these days?"

| Point | How's the[your] wife? 부인은 잘 지내?
How's your kid? 애들은 잘 지내고?

A: Hello there Elmo. **How's your family doing?**
야, 엘모. 가족들 다 잘 지내고?
B: We had another son since the last time I saw you. 지난 번 본 이후로 아들 하나 더 낳았어.

미드표현

A: How's the family? B: My kid is still out of control. A: 가족들 잘 지내지? B: 애가 아직도 말썽이야.

A : So how's the family? B: Great. Kids are getting so big.
A: 가족들은 잘 지내? B: 아주 좋아. 아이들은 다 컸고.

How's your family in Chicago?
시카고에 있는 네 가족은 다 잘 지내?

012 (Is) Everything okay? 잘 지내지?, 일은 다 잘 되지?

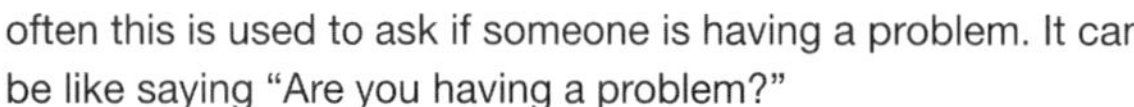

often this is used to ask if someone is having a problem. It can be like saying "Are you having a problem?"

| Point | Is everything okay with sb? …하고는 괜찮아?
Is everything okay in there? 거기는 다 괜찮아?

A: You seem kind of gloomy today. **Is everything okay?** 오늘 좀 우울해보여. 다 잘 되는 거지?
B: I'm having a lot of problems because I don't have enough money. 돈이 부족해 여러 문제가 있어.

미드표현

Everything okay? Need me to call 911?
다 괜찮아? 911 부를까?

Is everything okay? You've been quiet all night. 괜찮아? 밤새 조용하잖아.

Is everything okay with Mom? 엄마하고는 괜찮아?

You look scared. Everything okay?
너 겁이난 것 같아. 무슨 일 있는거야?

013 (You) Doing okay? 잘 지내?, 괜찮아?

like the previous phrase, this is usually asked when someone is worried about another person. It is a way of saying "You look unhappy. Are you alright?"

| Point | (Have) (You) Been okay? 그간 잘 지냈어?

A: What's the matter Ted? **You doing okay?**
테드 무슨 일이야? 괜찮아?

B: I've been fighting a lot with my girlfriend lately.
최근에 여친하고 엄청 싸워.

I know this wasn't easy. You doing okay?
이게 쉽지 않았다는 걸 알고 있어. 너 괜찮아?

Hey, you guys have been in there for a while. You doing okay?
너희들 한동안 여기 있었는데 잘 지내고 있는거야?

I was doing okay till you went off the deep end. 네가 느닷없이 화를 내기까지는 난 잘 지내고 있었어.

014 Look who's here! 아니 이게 누구야!

미드표현

this is an expression of surprise. The speaker is saying "Wow, I'm surprised you're here"

| Point | Fancy meeting you here 이런 데서 만날 줄이야

A: Hey Marge! **Look who's here!** 야 마지! 이게 누구야!

B: Wow, it's Rob! I haven't seen you in a long time.
와, 랍이네! 참 오랜 만이야.

Look who's here. The woman who got Mona fired. 이게 누구야. 모나를 해고한 여자잖아.

Look who's here. Good to see you, welcome back. 이게 누구야. 반가워, 환영해.

Everybody, look who's here! You remember my grandfather!
자 모두들 누가 왔는지 보라고! 내 할아버지 기억하지!

015 What are you doing here? 여긴 어쩐 일이야?, 여기서 뭐 하는거야?

미드표현

often this is a way to ask "Why did you come?" The speaker wants information about why someone came to a place

| Point | What are you doing? 지금 뭐해?

A: **What are you doing here?** 여긴 웬일이야?

B: I come to this bar to have a few drinks sometimes. 가끔 술 좀 마시러 이 바에 와.

What are you doing here? You stay away from us. 여긴 어쩐 일이야? 우리한테 오면 안되잖아.

You have the day off. What are you doing here? 쉬는 날이잖아. 여기서 뭐 하는거야?

What are you doing here? I thought you were both swamped with work.
너 여기서 뭐하는거야? 난 너희 둘 모두 일에 파묻혀 있는 줄 알았는데.

016 I haven't seen you in ages! 오랜 만이야!, 못본지 오래야!

미드표현

the speaker is saying he hasn't met someone for a long time. It is similar to saying "I'm very happy to see you again"

| Point | I haven't seen you in+기간 …동안 못봤다, 오랜 만이다
I haven't seen you in months 오랜 만이야

A: Mr. Johnson! **I haven't seen you in years.**
존슨 선생님! 오랜 만이예요.

B: Yes, not since I was your high school history teacher. 그래, 네 고교 역사 선생님한 이후로 처음이네.

I haven't seen you in a while. Take me to lunch! 한 동안 못 봤었지. 점심 사주라!

What a surprise. We haven't seen you in here in quite some time. 이게 누구야. 꽤 오랜 만이야.

So, how have you been? I feel like I haven't seen you in ages. 어떻게 지냈어? 정말 오랫만에 보는 것 같아.

017 It's been a while 오랜 만이야

usually this is a way to say "I haven't met you for a long time." Many times this is used as a greeting

| Point | It's been a while since~ …한지 오랜 만이다, 오랜 만에 …해봤어
It's been a long time 오랜만이야
Long time no see 오랜만이야

A: Hi Sandy. **It's been a while.** 야 샌디, 오랜 만이야.
B: I'm really surprised to see you right now.
지금 널 보게 되다니 정말 놀라워.

How you doing? It's been a while.
잘 지냈어? 오랜 만이야.

It's been a while since I've driven a sports car.
스포츠 카를 오랫만에 운전해봤어.

It has been a while since I got my prostate checked. 내가 전립선 검사를 한지가 오래 됐어.

018 (I) Never thought I'd see you here 여기서 널 보게 될 줄이야

미드표현

the speaker is indicating he is surprised. He is saying "I am surprised you're here"

| Point | I didn't expect to see you here 여기서 만날 줄은 생각도 못했어

A: **I never thought I'd see you here.**
여기서 널 보게 될 줄이야
B: Oh yes. I come to this restaurant at times.
어 그래, 때때로 이 식당에 와.

Aren't you banned from this place? I never thought I'd see you here.
너 이곳에 오면 안되지 않아? 여기서 널 보게 될 줄이야.

I never thought I'd see you here. What's going on? 여기서 널 보게 될 줄이야. 무슨 일이야?

I never thought I'd see you here. What are you doing in a strip club?
여기서 널 보게 될 줄이야. 스트립 클럽에서 뭐하는거야?

019 I'm doing OK 잘 지내고 있어

미드표현

this often indicates someone feels fine. It is like saying "Everything is good"

| Point | do okay 잘 지내다

A: How have you been doing since you graduated?
졸업한 이후로 어떻게 지냈어?
B: **I'm doing OK.** I got a job working downtown.
잘 지내고 있어. 시내에서 직장도 다니고.

I'm doing okay. Everything seems to be in order here.
나는 잘 지내, 여기는 살기 좋아.

Let her know I'm doing okay.
난 잘 지내고 있다고 걔한테 알려줘.

I was in a car accident, but I'm doing okay.
차사고 났었는데 난 괜찮아.

020 I'm cool 잘 지내, 괜찮아

this is a way for a younger person to say "I'm OK." It is not usually said by adults

| Point | be cool with …가 괜찮다

A: Would you like to have some more soda?
소다 좀 더 마실테야?
B: No, thank you. **I'm cool.** 고맙지만 됐어, 괜찮아.

I'm cool. Casual. 잘 지내, 그냥 그래.

I'm cool. I have a great time.
나는 잘 지내, 멋진 시간을 보내고 있어.

I just want you to know that I'm cool with it.
난 그거 괜찮다는 걸 알려주고 싶어.

I know you're with Chris. And I'm cool with it.
네가 크리스와 함께 있다는 걸 알아. 난 괜찮아.

021 (It) Couldn't be better 최고야, 최고로 좋아

this indicates someone feels very good. It is like saying "It's great."

| Point | (I) Couldn't ask for more 최고야, 더이상 바랄 게 없어

A: How do you like your new car? 새로 산 차 어때?
B: **It couldn't be better.** I love it. 최고야. 정말 좋아.

Your timing couldn't be better.
너 시간 한번 잘 맞춰오네.

A: Is everything okay? B: Couldn't be better.
A: 별 일없어? B: 아주 좋아.

I'm the one who should thank you. You introduced me to all your friends. My business couldn't be better.
내가 너한테 감사해야지. 내게 네 친구들 다 소개시켜줬잖아. 내 사업이 더 없이 잘되고 있어.

022 Never better 최고야, 아주 좋아

like the previous phrase, this is a way to say "Things are very good." People say this to indicate they are doing very well

| Point | A be never been better A가 최고다

A: How are things going at your school?
학교에서 어떻게 지내?
B: **Never better.** My grades have gone up this year.
최고야. 성적이 금년에 올랐어.

I'm fine, never been better. You?
난 괜찮아, 아주 좋아. 넌?

He's perfect, he's never been better.
걘 완벽해, 최고야

A: How you doing? B: Never better.
A: 어때? B: 최고야.

A: How are you this morning? B: Never better.
A: 오늘 아침에 어때? B: 더 없이 좋아.

023 (I) Can't complain 잘 지내, 더 바랄 나위가 없지

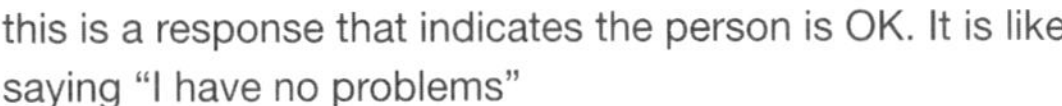

this is a response that indicates the person is OK. It is like saying "I have no problems"

| Point | No complaints 잘 지내
(I have) Nothing to complain about 잘 지내

A: Hey Julie, how are things with you?
야 줄리, 어떻게 지내?
B: **I can't complain.** Everything is okay. 잘 지내. 다 좋아.

Not bad, can't complain. You? 괜찮아. 잘 지내. 넌?

A: Hey, David! How have you been? B: I can't complain.
A: 야 데이빗! 요즘 잘 지내? B: 잘 지내고 있어.

It's only been a week, but I can't complain.
겨우 일주일이 되었지만 더 바랄 나위가 없어.

Can't complain, considering if it weren't for you, I'd be dead--twice.
너 아니었더라면 난 두 번이나 죽었을거라는 걸 고려하면 더없이 잘 지내고 있지.

024 (That's) Not bad 그리 나쁘지 않아, 할만해

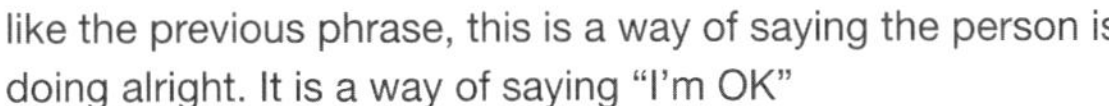

like the previous phrase, this is a way of saying the person is doing alright. It is a way of saying "I'm OK"

| Point | Not bad at all 좋아(=That's good)

A: How are things at your workplace? 사무실에서 어때?
B: **Not bad.** We are always busy with something.
그리 나쁘지 않아. 항상 바빠.

Not bad. I'm impressed. 그리 나쁘지 않아. 감동받았어.

A: How'd it look? B: Not bad. A:어때? B: 나쁘진 않아.

Hey, how about that new cashier at work? Not bad, huh? 새로운 계산대 직원 어때? 괜찮지, 그지?

025 (Just) The usual 늘상 그래, 하던 걸로

this expresses that something is similar and hasn't changed much. It is a way to say "It's the same as it always is." And more commonly this indicates the speaker wants some type of food or drink that he often orders. It is like saying "Please give me what I normally order here"

I Point I Same old same old 늘 그렇지
Same old story[stuff] 항상 똑같은 얘기[것]
Same as always[usual] 맨날 똑같지 뭐
(It's) Business as usual 늘 그렇지 뭐, 언제나처럼 그래

A: What's going on here? 여기 무슨 일이야?
B: You know, **the usual.** Kids yelling at each other over nothing.
알잖아. 늘상 그러는 거. 별 일도 아닌 걸로 서로 소리지르는 애들말야.

미드표현

You know, just writing the column, the usual.
알잖아 나 신문에 칼럼쓰는 거, 늘상 그래.

It's a bunch of the same old, same old errands. The usual. 맨날 하는 같은 심부름들이야, 늘상 그렇듯.

A: So, how's your job? B: Oh, you know. Same old, same old. A: 네 일 어때? B: 알잖아, 맨날 똑같지 뭐.

026 Not (too) much 1. 별일 없어, 그냥 그럭저럭 2. (약한 부정) 별로 (없어)

often this is said after someone asks "What have you been doing?" The speaker wants to say he hasn't done anything special lately

I Point I Nothing much 별로 Nothing special 별일 아냐
Nothing in particular 별일 아냐

A: What's been going on with you? 너 어떻게 지내고 있어?
B: **Not too much.** My life is kind of boring.
그럭저럭. 내 인생이 좀 지루해.

Um. Not much to tell, really. 음, 말할 게 별로 없어, 정말.

A: What's new with you? B: Nothing much. How about you? A: 새로운 일 없니? B: 별일 없어, 넌?

A: What did I miss? B: Not much.
A: 내가 뭘 놓쳤어? B: 별로 없어.

027 Not very well 안 좋아, 별로야

this indicates the person has been having problems. It is like saying "I've had some difficulties"

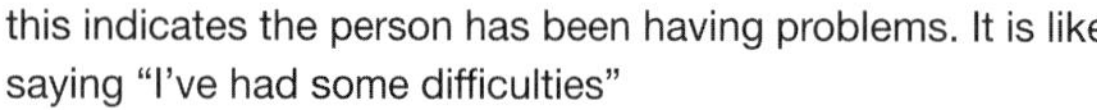

I Point I Not good 별로 안 좋아 Not so great 그렇게 좋진 않아

A: How do you like being married? 결혼하니까 어때?
B: **Not very well.** We argue a lot. 별로야. 많이 싸워.

미드표현

Worst day of my life. Not so great for my wife, either. 내 생애 최악의 하루였어. 아내도 그렇고.

A: How are you? B: Not good. Tammy and I had a huge fight.
A: 잘 지내? B: 안 좋아. 나하고 태미하고 크게 싸웠어.

Not very well personally, but we all respected him very much. 잘은 모르지만 우리는 모두 걔를 무척 존경했어.

028 (Things) Could be better 더 좋았으면 좋겠어, (부정적인 답변) 별로야, 그냥 그래

this is a way of saying "I wish my life would improve." People say this to indicate they have some problems

I Point I What could be better than~? …보다 더 좋은 일이 있을까?

A: How have your investments in the stock market been? 주식에 네가 투자한 거 어때?
B: **Things could be better.** I've lost a lot of money.
별로야. 많이 잃었어.

미드표현

It could be better, but it's gonna be okay, right?
별로야, 하지만 좋아질거야, 알았어?

A: How's it going with you? B: Things could be better. A: 어떻게 지내? B: 그냥 그래.

What could be better than this?
이거보다 더 좋은 일이 있을 수 있을까?

Well, what could be better than drinks with a beautiful woman?
아름다운 여인과 술을 마시는 것보다 더 좋은 일이 있을 수 있을까?

029 (Things) Could be worse (긍정적인 답변) 그럭저럭 잘 지내지, 그나마 다행야

the speaker is saying "My life is alright." He feels that his life has few problems

Point What could be worse than~? …보다 더 나쁜 일이 있을까?

A: I heard you were in the hospital for a while.
한동안 병원에 있었다며.

B: Yeah, but I'm OK now. **Things could be worse.**
어. 하지만 지금은 좋아. 그나마 다행이지.

미드표현

Come on, Jane, things could be worse.
야, 제인, 그나마 다행이지

A: How you doing in there, Mr. O'brien?
B: Could be worse.
A: 오브라이언 씨 어떻게 지내세요? B: 그럭저럭 잘 지내고 있어요.

Our company is losing money, but it could be worse. 우리 회사는 돈을 까먹고 있는데 그나마 다행인 상황이야.

030 I've been better 좀 그래

this is said to indicate the speaker doesn't feel happy. It is a way to express "My situation isn't good"

A: You're looking kind of sad, Ziggy. 지기야 너 좀 슬퍼보여.

B: **I've been better.** The winter weather makes me blue. 좀 그래. 겨울날씨 때문에 우울해.

미드표현

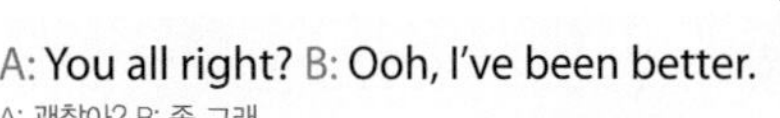

A: You all right? B: Ooh, I've been better.
A: 괜찮아? B: 좀 그래

A: You doing okay? B: I've been better.
A: 잘 지내? B: 좀 그래

A: How you doing? B: I don't know. I guess I've been better. A: 어떻게 지내? B: 몰라. 좀 그래.

A: How you holding up? B: I've been better.
A: 어떻게 지내고 있어? B: 좀 그래.

031 I think I should be going 그만 가봐야겠어

this is a polite way to say "I plan to leave." It is said before a person leaves a place

Point should[had better/must]+be going 가야겠다
I must be going 그만 가봐야 될 것 같아

A: **I should be going now.** 이제 가봐야겠어.

B: Thank you for stopping by our apartment.
우리 집에 들러줘서 고마워.

미드표현

It's time we should be going. 그만 일어나자.

I think I'd better be going. 그만 가봐야 될 것 같아.

I guess I better be going. 가야 될 것 같아.

032 We should get going 자 이제 그만 가봐야 되겠어, 이제 슬슬 가자

this indicates the people think they should leave. It is similar to saying "We'll go soon"

Point should[had better/got to]+get going 그만 일어나야겠다
I should get going 서둘러 가봐야겠어
I've got to get going 가봐야겠어
I better get going 가봐야겠어

A: It's very late. **We should get going.**
늦었네. 그만 가봐야겠어.

B: Please stay for a little while longer. 좀 더 있다 가.

미드표현

Let's get going. 이젠 어서 가자.

I better get going. It was great meeting you.
가야겠어. 만나서 반가웠어.

I've got to get going. Today was great, thanks!
가야겠어. 오늘 정말 좋았어. 고마워!

It's getting late. We should get going.
날이 늦었네. 그만 가봐야겠어.

033 I('ve) Got to get moving 가봐야겠어

often this means the person must go somewhere. It is like saying "I'm going soon"

I Point I should[had better/have to]+get moving 가야겠어
I'd better get moving 난 가봐야겠어요
I'd better get moving 가야겠어
We should get moving 가봐야겠어

A: The party starts soon. **I've got to get moving.**
파티가 곧 시작해. 가봐야겠어.

B: Can I ride with you to the party? 파티하는 곳까지 태워줄래?

미드표현

We should get moving. The next town is a few miles away.
가봐야겠어. 다음 마을은 몇 마일 떨어져있어.

You heard the doctor. Get moving.
의사 말 들었잖아. 얼른 움직여.

Let's get moving, we have to serve dinner in twenty minutes.
어서 가자고, 20분내로 저녁식사를 준비해야 돼.

034 I'm (just) going to take off 그만 일어서야겠어

the speaker is saying "I'm leaving." It indicates he wants to go very soon

I Point I I think I'm gonna take off 일어나야겠어
take off 출발하다, 이륙하다, 옷을 벗다, 쉬다

A: I don't see the hosts. **I'm just going to take off.**
주인들이 안 보이네. 그만 일어서야겠어.

B: I think you should wait and say goodbye to them. 기다렸다가 인사하고 가지.

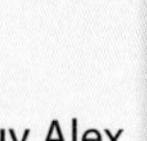

미드표현

Actually, I just think I'm gonna take off.
실은, 난 가야 될 것 같아.

Honey, I'm gonna take off. I'm gonna buy Alex some clothes. 자기야, 나 일어날게. 알렉스 옷 좀 사줄거야.

I need you to stand up and take off your gown. 너 일어나서 네 가운을 벗어봐.

035 I must be off 이제 가봐야겠어

this is a formal way to say that a person will go. It is a way to say "I'll see you later"

I Point I be off 떠나다, 출발하다
(I'd) better be off 나 먼저 갈게
I am off 나 간다

A: **I must be off now.** 이제 가봐야겠어.

B: OK. We'll see you tomorrow. 그래, 내일 보자.

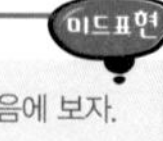

미드표현

I've got to be off, I'll see you. 가야되겠어. 다음에 보자.

I'm off to my audition. How do I look?
오디션보러가. 내 모습 어때?

I'm off to bed. 자러갈거야.

He's off to see his folks. 걔 가족들 만나러 가.

036 (I've) Got to run 서둘러 가봐야겠어, 가야겠어, 빨리 가야 돼

usually this indicates a person has to be somewhere very soon. He is saying "I have to be somewhere else soon"

I Point I (I've) Got to fly 빨리 가야 돼

A: I have a meeting. **I've got to run.**
회의가 있어. 빨리 가야 돼.

B: I'm sorry you must go so soon. 빨리 가야된다니 아쉽네.

미드표현

I've got to run. Tell her I say goodbye.
가야 돼. 걔한테 인사 전해 줘.

Lane, I got to run down to the pharmacy!
레인, 나 약국에 급히 가야 돼!

Look, I got to run out and take care of a few things. 나 빨리 가서 몇가지 일 처리해야 돼.

No, I got to run some errands, I'll meet you there later. 안돼, 심부름 좀 해야 돼. 나중에 거기서 만나.

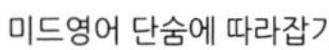

037 I'm outta[out of] here 나 갈게, 난 갈래

the speaker is saying "I'm going right now." Usually this is a way of saying that he is very impatient to go

| Point | I'm getting out of here 여기서 나가야겠어
I'm not here 나 여기 없는거야

A: This sucks. **I'm out of here.** 엿같군. 나 간다.
B: Come on, it isn't so bad. Stick around.
이봐, 그렇게 나쁘지 않아. 좀 있어.

You don't care what I think, so I'm outta here!
내 생각은 신경도 안 쓰잖아. 나 갈게!

I'm getting out of here. Where are my keys?
나 갈게. 열쇠가 어디있지?

If anyone calls, I'm not here. 누가 전화하면, 없다고 해.

038 I'm leaving 나 간다, 이만 가볼게

this is a very simple way to say someone plans to go right now. Another way to say this is "I'll go now"

| Point | I'm gone 나 간다

A: **I am leaving.** I need to get to work. 나 가. 일해야 돼.
B: Don't forget to take your lunch with you.
점심 가지고 가는 거 잊지마.

I'm leaving. Think about what I said.
나 간다. 내가 말한 거 생각해봐.

You don't want me in your life, fine. I'm gone!
네 인생에서 내가 필요없다 이거지, 좋아. 나 간다!

I'm leaving. Thank you for your patience.
나 간다. 참고 기다려줘서 고마워.

I can't do this anymore. I'm leaving.
난 더 이상 이렇게 할 수 없어. 나 간다.

039 If you'll excuse me 양해를 해준다면, 괜찮으면, 실례가 되지 않는다면

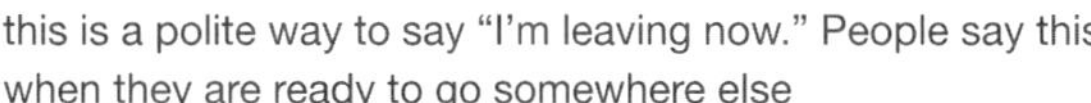

this is a polite way to say "I'm leaving now." People say this when they are ready to go somewhere else

A: **If you'll excuse me,** I must go home.
괜찮으면 나 집에 갈게.
B: Thank you for dropping by. 들러줘서 고마워.

If you'll excuse me now, I have to go to work.
괜찮다면 일하러 갈게.

If you'll excuse me, I have to go. 괜찮으면 갈게.

If you'll excuse me, I have other things to do.
괜찮으면 다른 일이 있어서.

040 Let's hit the road 출발하자고

often this is a way to say "Let's start driving somewhere." Many people say this before they leave on a trip

| Point | hit the road 출발하다, 시작하다

A: It's 6 am. **Let's hit the road.** 6시네. 출발하자고.
B: Did you take our suitcases to the car yet?
짐가방 차에 실었어?

I'd better hit the road. 그만 출발해야겠다.

Let's go. Let's hit the road. 가자. 출발하자고.

Now, let's hit the road and get some cheese steaks! 이제 출발해서 치즈스테이크를 좀 먹자고!

We'd better hit the road so we can get home.
집에 갈 수 있도록 우리 이제 출발하자고.

041 I'm sorry but we were just leaving
미안하지만 나가려는 참이었어

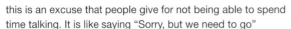

this is an excuse that people give for not being able to spend time talking. It is like saying "Sorry, but we need to go"

A: I have a friend I want to introduce you to.
너에게 소개해주고픈 친구가 있어.

B: **I'm sorry but we were just leaving.**
미안하지만 나가려는 참이야.

미드표현

A: Hey, beautiful. I'm Allan. Can I buy you a drink? B: Um, I'm sorry. We were just leaving.
A: 예쁜 아가씨, 알란인데요. 술한잔 살까요? B: 미안하지만 나가려는 참인데요.

A: What are you doing here? I've been sitting in my apartment all day. I thought you were coming to visit me! B: We were just leaving.
A: 여기서 뭐해? 집에서 하루종일 기다렸는데! 왜 안왔어! B: 막 나가려고 했어.

042 (It was) Nice to see you 만나서 반가워요, 만나서 반가웠어

this indicates the speaker was happy to meet with another person. It is a way to say "I felt happy to talk with you"

| Point | Nice seeing you 만나서 반가웠어
Nice to meet you/ Nice meeting you 만나서 반가워(반가웠어)

A: **It was very nice to see you.** 만나서 반가웠요.
B: Sure. I'll see you again soon. 예. 곧 다시 뵐게요.

미드표현

Nice seeing you again. 다시 봐서 반가워.

Good night, it was very nice to meet you.
잘가. 만나서 정말 반가웠어.

It was really nice meeting you tonight!
오늘 밤 만나서 반가웠어!

043 (It's) Good to see you 만나서 반가워, 만나서 반가웠어

like the previous phrase, this indicates the speaker is happy to see someone. Another way to say this is "I'm happy to spend time with you"

| Point | It's great to see you 만나서 반가워
Good to see again 다시 만나 반가워
It's good to hear your voice 네 목소리 들으니 좋다

A: **It's good to see you** Betty. 베티, 만나서 반가워.
B: Yeah, I was happy to spend time with you.
그래, 함께 시간 보내서 즐거웠어.

Good to see you. How've you been?
만나서 반가워. 어떻게 지냈어?

It's so good to see that he's back.
걔가 돌아와 정말 반가워.

It is so good to see you both. 너희 둘을 만나서 반가웠어.

Hey Donna, alright, good to see you! Got you some pie! 도나야, 만나서 반가워! 파이 좀 줄게!

044 Likewise(, I'm sure) 나도 그래, 나도 마찬가지

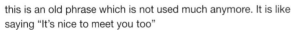

this is an old phrase which is not used much anymore. It is like saying "It's nice to meet you too"

| Point | likewise 똑같이, 마찬가지야

A: I am very charmed to have met you.
널 만나게 돼서 무척 기뻐.

B: Thank you. **Likewise,** I'm sure. 고마워, 정말 나도 그래.

미드표현

A: It will be a pleasure being married to you
B: Uh, likewise.
A: 너와 결혼하면 무척 좋을거야 B: 나도 그래.

A: You must be Annie. Pleasure to meet you
B: Oh, likewise. I hear you're one of the best hairdressers in town.
A: 애니시죠, 만나서 반가워요 B: 저도요, 시내에서 가장 뛰어난 미용사중 한명이시라면서요.

045 Nice talking to you 얘기 즐거웠어

this indicates the speaker is getting ready to leave. He is saying "I enjoyed spending time with you"

| Point | (It was) Nice talking to[with] you 얘기 즐거웠어.

A: Well Jeff, **it's been nice talking to you.**
저기, 제프, 얘기 즐거웠어.

B: Let's do it again sometime. 언제 한번 다시 보자.

All right, nice talking to you Dr. Smith.
알았어요. 얘기 즐거웠어요 스미스 선생님.

A: You're gonna be late for your class. B: Nice talking to you. A: 수업에 늦겠어. B: 얘기 즐거웠어.

Nice talking to you. See you later.
얘기 즐거웠어. 나중에 봐.

046 (I'm) Glad I caught you 때마침 만나게 돼서 반가워

this is a way of saying "Oh, I got here before you left." The speaker is happy he met someone before the person could leave

A: Hey boss, **I'm glad I caught you.**
저기 사장님, 때마침 뵙게 돼 반가워요.

B: Why? Are you having a problem? 왜? 무슨 문제있어?

I'm so glad I caught you, I couldn't find you before. 때마침 봐서 잘 됐네요. 한참을 찾았는데.

I'm glad I caught you before you talked to Tony.. 네가 토니하고 말하기 전에 만나게 돼서 반갑다.

I'm glad I caught you. We need to have a discussion. 때마침 만나게 돼서 반가워. 우리 얘기 좀 해야 돼.

I'm glad I caught you before you left for the day. 네가 퇴근하기 전에 널 만나게 돼서 반가워.

047 Good[Nice] running into you 만나서 반가웠어

usually this is said when a person meets another person by chance. When leaving, he says this, which means "This was a nice surprise"

| Point | run into sb 우연히 만나다
bump into sb 우연히 만나다

A: I've got to go. **Nice running into you.**
가야 돼. 이렇게 만나서 반가웠어.

B: Yeah Joe, it was quite a surprise. 그래 조. 정말 놀랐어.

I just wanted to say it was great running into you today. 오늘 만나서 반가웠다고 말하고 싶을 따름이야.

I should really get home. It was nice running into you. 나 정말 집에 가야 돼. 만나서 반가웠어.

How weird running into you guys here.
여기서 너희들을 만나다니 정말 이상하다.

048 I keep bumping into you 자주 만나네, (우연히) 자주 보네

this means "I keep meeting you by chance." The speaker is surprised to have met someone by chance a few times

| Point | bump into sb = run into sb 우연히 만나다
I ran into her today 오늘 걔하고 우연히 마주쳤어

A: **I keep bumping into you** around here.
이 근처에서 자주 만나네.

B: That's because I work in an office nearby.
주변 사무실에서 일해서 그래.

I know why we keep bumping into each other. This is fate.
우리가 왜 서로 우연히 마주치는지 이유를 알아. 이건 운명야.

We just bumped into each other. I'm doing business in the area.
그냥 우연히 마주친거야. 여기서 사업을 하거든.

This is what I love about this city. You're always bumping into people.
내가 이래서 이 도시가 좋다니까. 항상 사람들과 우연히 만나게 되거든.

049 Have a good time 재미있게 놀아, 즐거운 시간이 되기를 바래

this is a way of telling someone "Enjoy yourself." It is said to someone who is leaving to go to a party or gathering

| Point | Have a good one(day) 좋은 하루 보내

A: I'm going to the party with Megan and Lisa.
메간과 리사와 함께 파티에 가.

B: **Have a good time.** Don't drink too much alcohol. 재미있게 놀아. 술 너무 마시지 말고.

미드표현

Have a good time, and promise to tell me everything. 즐겁게 보내고 이야기 다 해줘야 돼.

You didn't have a good time? 재미있게 못 보냈어?

Did you have a good time with her?
걔하고 재미있었어?

Did you have a good day at school?
학교에서 즐거웠어?

050 Have fun 즐겁게 지내, 재밌는 시간 보내

like the previous phrase, this is telling someone to enjoy what he will do. A similar way to say it is "I hope everything goes well for you"

| Point | have fun with sb[at sth] …와 즐겁게 보내다, …에서 즐겁게 보내다

A: We plan to visit Thailand this winter.
이번 겨울에 태국을 방문할거야.

B: **Have fun.** I hear that the weather there is very nice. 즐겁게 지내. 그곳 날씨가 매우 무척 좋다고 하던데.

미드표현

You guys, have fun! 너희들 재미있게 보내!

You two have fun, and I'll see you at dinner.
둘 재미있게 보내고 저녁먹을 때 보자.

Did you have fun at the bachelor party last night? 지난 밤 총각파티에서 재미좋았어?

051 I'm going to miss you 보고 싶을거야

this is said when people are parting. The speaker means "I wish you wouldn't go away"

| Point | I miss you already 벌써 네가 보고 싶어져
I miss you so much 정말 보고 싶어

A: Goodbye Angie. **I am going to miss you.**
잘 가 앤지. 보고 싶을거야.

B: I think I'll miss you too. 나도 네가 보고 싶을거야.

미드표현

You're moving! We're all going to miss you.
이사간다고! 우리 모두 보고 싶을거야.

I'm going to miss you. I wish you didn't have to go. 보고 싶을거야. 네가 가지 않아도 되면 좋으려만.

I'm going to miss you so much, and I just hope that someday you won't hate me anymore.
네가 정말 보고 싶을거야. 그리고 언젠가는 나를 싫어하지 않기를 바래.

052 (I will) See you around 또 만나, 이따 보자, 다음에 봐, 곧 보자

this is a very casual way to tell someone "I'll meet you again someday soon"

| Point | (I'll) See you soon 조만간 보자
(I'll) Be seeing you! 잘가!, 또 보자!

A: Maybe we can meet up for coffee.
만나서 커피 마시면 어때.

B: Sure we can. **I'll see you around.** 그래 그러자. 이따 보자.

미드표현

Thank you. I'll see you around. 고마워. 다시 보자.

I guess I'll see you around. Next time you're at the inn, find me. 다음에 또 보자. 다음에 여관에 오면 날 찾아.

So how come I never see you around?
어떻게 네가 안보인거야?

Definitely, I'll see you around. 물론이지. 또 보자.

053 (I'll) See you later 나중에 봐

this is the most common way for someone to say "Goodbye"

| Point | (I'll) See you 잘 가
See you later, alligator 안녕, 잘가
See you in the morning 낼 아침에 봐

A: **See you later.** 잘 가.
B: It was good talking to you. 얘기해서 즐거웠어.

I should get back to work. See you. 일해야 돼. 잘 가.

OK sure, go ahead, I'll see you later.
물론 좋아, 그렇게 해. 나중에 봐.

I'm gonna head out now, so I'll see you later.
나 이제 갈게, 나중에 봐.

054 (I'll) Catch you later 나중에 보자

this like slang that tells someone "I'll see you in the future." It is said casually when someone is leaving

| Point | (I'll) Catch up with you later 나중에 봐
I'll try to catch you later 나중에 시간나면 보자구

A: **Catch you later,** Mom. 나중에 봐, 엄마.
B: I'll see you after school. 방과 후에 보자.

I gotta run. Catch you later! 빨리 가야 돼. 나중에 봐.

You go ahead. I'll catch up with you later.
먼저가. 곧 따라 갈게.

Um, okay, I'll catch you later, yeah?
음, 좋아, 나중에 보자고, 알았지?

I got to get ready for a date, so catch you later. 나 데이트 준비해야 되니까 나중에 보자고.

055 Goodbye for now 이만 안녕

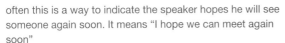

often this is a way to indicate the speaker hopes he will see someone again soon. It means "I hope we can meet again soon"

| Point | Good-bye and good riddance 시원섭섭해

A: **Goodbye for now,** Meredith. 메레디스, 이만 안녕.
B: I hope we meet again soon. 곧 다시 보자.

Goodbye for now. Let's meet up again soon.
이만 안녕. 곧 다시 만나자고.

Goodbye for now. It was nice seeing you.
이만 안녕. 만나서 즐거웠어.

I've got to go home, so goodbye for now.
나 집에 가야 돼, 그러니 이제 안녕.

056 Take care! 몸 조심하고!

this is a common way of saying "Goodbye." People say this to wish each other good luck when they leave each other

| Point | Take care (of yourself) 잘 지내, 몸 건강하게 잘 있어
Be careful 조심해, 잘 지내
take care of sth 처리하다

A: **Take care.** And don't forget to e-mail me.
조심해, 그리고 잊지 말고 내게 이메일보내고.
B: I'll do that when I get home! 집에 가서 보낼게!

Good luck. Take care of yourself.
행운을 빌어. 몸 조심하고.

Be careful. That tea's very hot.
조심해. 그 차는 무척 뜨거워.

Take care of this for me. 내 대신 이것 좀 처리해.

Take care! It was nice seeing you again.
잘가! 다시 보게 돼서 즐거웠어.

057 Don't work too hard 너무 무리하지 말구

often this is a way of saying "Goodbye" to someone and telling them to relax

A: I've got to get going now. **Don't work too hard.**
가야 돼. 너무 무리하지 말고.

B: No, I won't. I'll see you next time you come over.
어, 그럴게. 담에 올 때 보자고.

미드표현

Don't work too hard. I'll see you next week. 너무 무리하지 말고. 담주에 봐.

Thanks for your help, Scott. Don't work too hard. 스캇, 도와줘서 고마워. 너무 무리하지 말고.

I enjoyed our discussion. Don't work too hard. 얘기 즐거웠어. 너무 무리하지 말고.

058 Say hello to your wife 부인한테 안부 전해 줘

this speaker is saying "Tell someone we know that I was thinking of him." It is a way to show respect for someone who they both know

| Point | Say hello[hi] to sb (for me) …에게 안부 전해줘
Give my best to your folks 가족들에게 안부 전해줘
All the best to sb …에게 안부 전해줘
Remember me to sb …에게 안부 전해줘

A: **Say hello to** your dad for me. 네 아빠한테 안부 전해줘.

B: I'll tell him I saw you today. 오늘 널 봤다고 말할게.

미드표현

Let's go say hello to them. 가서 걔들한테 인사하자.

Say hello to your competition. 경쟁자들과 인사해.

There's someone I want you to say hi to. 내가 인사시켜주고 싶은 사람이 있어.

059 Drop me a line 연락해

this is asking someone to get in touch. It is like saying "Contact me"

| Point | I'll drop you a line 편지할게
Drop me a note 편지써라, 연락해
Don't forget to write[e-mail me] 편지(이메일)보내

A: Fred, **drop me a line** when you get the chance.
프레드 기회되면 편지해.

B: I'll call you after work tonight. 오늘 저녁 퇴근 후에 전화할게.

미드표현

A: Drop me a line to let me know how you're doing. B: I will. But I don't have your address.
A: 어떻게 지내는지 궁금하니까 편지나 좀 써. B: 그럴게. 그런데 주소를 모르는데.

Drop me a line when you get to your apartment. 아파트에 도착하게 되면 연락해.

If you have some free time, drop me a line. 시간이 좀 나면 연락해.

Drop me a line. I'd like to stay in contact. 연락해. 서로 연락하고 지내자고.

060 Let's get[keep] in touch! 연락하고 지내자!

this expresses a wish to stay in contact through writing or telephone calls, or something similar. It's like saying "Stay in contact with me"

| Point | get[keep] in touch with …와 연락하다
Keep in touch 연락해
I will be in touch 내가 연락할게
Touch base with her 걔한테 연락해라

A: I liked talking with you. **Let's keep in touch.**
너랑 얘기해서 좋았어. 연락하고 지내자.

B: That's a good idea. Here is my cell phone number. 좋은 생각이야. 이게 내 핸드폰 번호야.

미드표현

You still keep in touch with her? 걔하고 아직 연락해?

We're still trying to get in touch with him. 걔한테 연락을 시도하고 있어.

I can't seem to get in touch with Amy. 에이미한테 연락이 안되는 것 같아.

I just told you to get in touch with your feelings. 내가 너한테 네 감정을 잘 알고 있으라고 말했잖아.

061 Can[Could] you excuse us? 실례 좀 해도 될까요?, 자리 좀 비켜줄래요?

this indicates the speaker wants to talk privately to someone. He is saying "We need privacy to talk about something confidential now"

| Point | Could[May] I be excused? 양해를 구해도 될까요?, 이만 일어나도 될까요?
You're excused 그러세요, 그만 나가 봐
Don't be long = Come back as soon as you can
= Don't take long 오래 걸리지마, 바로 와

A: I must speak with my wife. **Can you excuse us?** 아내하고 얘기 좀 해야겠어. 자리 좀 비켜줄래?
B: Sure. I'll come back in ten minutes. 그래, 10분 후에 올게.

You're excused and you won't have to come to class. 가도 좋아. 수업에 오지 않아도 돼.

Can you excuse us for a moment? I need to speak with her in private.
자리 좀 잠깐 비켜줄래요? 걔하고 사적으로 말할게 있어요.

062 I'll be right with you 잠시만, 곧 돌아올게

this is a way to say "I'll help you soon". It is often said to customers who are waiting for service by a waitress or a clerk who is busy

| Point | I'll be with you in a sec[minute] 잠시만 기다리세요, 곧 도와드리죠
I'll be gone in just a few minutes 잠깐만 갔다 올게
I'll be right back 금방 올게
Be back soon 곧 올게(Back in a sec)

A: I'd like to order some food now. 음식 주문할게요.
B: Of course, sir. **I'll be right with you.**
네, 손님. 바로 오겠습니다.

If you could wait outside I'll be with you soon as we know something.
밖에서 기다리시면 발견 즉시 알려드리죠.

Stay with this nice woman. I'll be back in a minute. 이 멋진 여자와 함께 있어. 곧 돌아올게.

I'll be back in a couple of hours. You're sure you're okay? 두어시간 후에 돌아올게. 괜찮겠지?

Things that are said when they get together and hang out

약속을 정해 만나서 놀거나 초대하거나

Can you make it?

001 Let's make it around six 6시쯤 보기로 하자

this is a way of scheduling an appointment. The speaker is saying "We'll meet at six"

A: When would you like to schedule the meeting?
회의를 몇 시에 하고 싶어?

B: **Let's make it** around four tomorrow afternoon.
내일 오후 4시경에 하자.

미드표현

Yes, I'm free to have dinner. Let's make it around six. 어, 저녁시간 돼. 여섯시 경에 보자.

Let's make it around six. I get off work just before that. 여섯 시경에 보기로 하자. 여섯시 경에 퇴근하거든.

I don't have time now, so let's make the meeting around six.
지금은 시간이 안되니까 여섯시 경에 회의를 하자.

002 Can you make it? 할 수 있겠어?, (제 시간에) 도착할 수 있겠어?

this is a way to ask if a person can come to an event. It is like asking "Will you be there?"

| Point | make it 1. 성공적으로 어떤 일을 해내다 2. …에 시간맞춰 참석하다 (make it to 장소/시간) 3. 생존하다
When can you make it? 몇 시에 도착할 수 있겠니?

A: What time will the movie start? 영화가 언제 시작해?

B: It begins at eight. **Can you make it?**
8시에 시작해. 올 수 있어?

미드표현

I don't think I'm gonna make it to the wedding. 결혼식에 갈 수 없을 것 같아.

Do you think we can make it?
우리가 할 수 있을 것 같아?

You gonna make it? Six miles is pretty far.
제 때 도착할 수 있겠어? 6 마일은 꽤 먼거리인데.

Is the patient gonna make it?
환자가 살아날 수 있을까요?

003 Are you available? 시간 돼?, 지금 바쁘니?

this is asking "Do you have free time?" The speaker wants to know if someone has time to do something

| Point | I'm not available tonight 오늘 밤은 나 안돼
She's not available right now 걔는 지금 시간 안돼
Are you free? 시간 있어? 한가하니?

A: **Are you available** to talk now? 지금 얘기할 시간 있어?

B: Sure. Have a seat in that chair. 물론. 저 의자에 앉아.

Tomorrow, are you free? 내일은 시간 있어?

I need a good chef. You available?
좋은 주방장이 필요한데 네가 해줄 수 있어?

Are you available? I can come by in a few hours. 시간 돼? 내가 몇 시간내로 들를 수 있는데.

004 Let's get together (sometime) (조만간) 한번 보자, 한번 모이자

this is a polite way to say the speaker would like to do something with someone. It means "I want to spend time with you"

| Point | Are you doing anything tonight? 오늘 밤 시간 돼?
(Can we get together tonight?)

A: **Let's get together sometime.** 언제 한번 보자.

B: I'm not sure if I'll be able to. 가능할지 모르겠어.

We should get together sometime.
언제 한번 만나자.

Did you get together with him? 그 사람 만났니?

We must get together and play sometime soon. 우리 언제 한번 만나서 게임 같이 해야지.

005 What do we have going on tonight? 오늘밤 뭐할거야?

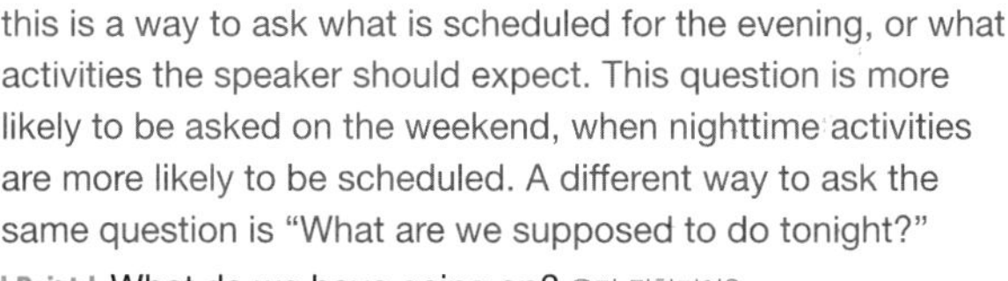

this is a way to ask what is scheduled for the evening, or what activities the speaker should expect. This question is more likely to be asked on the weekend, when nighttime activities are more likely to be scheduled. A different way to ask the same question is "What are we supposed to do tonight?"

I Point I What do we have going on? 우리 뭐할거야?

A: **What do we have going on tonight?**
오늘 밤에 뭐할거야?

B: We are supposed to meet Bill and Heather to see a movie. 빌과 헤더를 만나서 영화보기로 되어 있어.

미드표현

I just got here. What do we have going on tonight? 난 방금 여기 왔어. 오늘 밤 뭐할거야?

What do we have going on tonight? Anything unusual? 오늘 밤 뭐할거야? 뭐 특별한 거 있어?

You better fill me in. What do we have going on tonight? 나한테도 말해줘. 오늘 밤 뭐할건데?

006 I made an appointment with~ …와 약속이 되어 있어

this usually means someone has promised to be somewhere at a certain time. He is saying "I must be ... at ..."

I Point I make an appointment 약속을 정하다

A: **I made an appointment with** the dentist at four o'clock. 4시에 치과 예약되어 있어.

B: Aren't you nervous about having to go there?
거기 가는데 떨리지 않아?

미드표현

I'm calling to make an appointment with Dr. Novak. 노박선생님 예약하려고 전화했는데요.

I'd like to set up an appointment.
약속일정을 정하고 싶어.

I have an appointment. 약속이 있어.

I got an appointment with Brad at lunch time.
브래드와 점심때 약속있어.

007 We('ll) have to do lunch sometime
우리 언제 점심 식사를 같이 하자

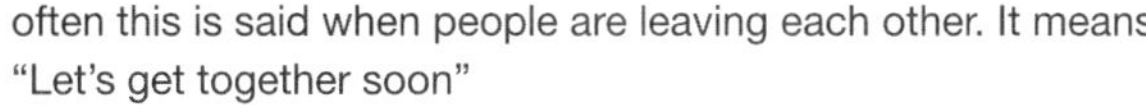

often this is said when people are leaving each other. It means "Let's get together soon"

I Point I do lunch 점심을 하다

A: **We have to do lunch sometime.** 언제 점심 같이 하자.

B: I agree. Call me and we'll schedule it.
좋아. 전화해서 정하자.

미드표현

I liked our conversation. We'll have to do lunch sometime. 얘기 즐거웠어. 언제 점심식사 같이하자.

We'll have to do lunch sometime. Next week maybe? 우리 언제 점심 같이 하자. 다음 주에 할까?

I am busy today, but we'll have to do lunch sometime. 오늘은 바쁘지만 언제 한번 점심 같이 하자.

008 I can make time for you this Friday
이번 주 금요일 시간이 돼

this person is saying "I have free time Friday." He wants someone to know that they can get together that day

I Point I make time for 시간을 내다
I should check my schedule 일정을 확인해봐야 돼

A: When is a good time for you to talk to me?
나랑 얘기하는데 언제 시간이 좋아?

B: **I can make time** for you this Friday. 이번 주 금요일에 시간 낼 수 있어.

Make time. I'll be expecting you.
시간 내. 기다리고 있을게.

I should check my schedule, but I think I can make it. 스케줄을 봐야겠지만 아마 괜찮을거야.

I don't know. I'll have to check my schedule.
잘 모르겠어. 스케줄 좀 확인해봐야 돼.

009 How about Friday? 금요일 어때?

the speaker is suggesting “Friday is a good day to meet.” He is saying this so that someone can choose to say yes or no to meeting on that day

| Point | You want to say 8:00? 8시에 어때?

A: I can’t go there today. **How about Friday?**
오늘 거기 못 가. 금요일은 어때?

B: I won’t be at home on Friday, so it’s impossible.
금요일에는 집에 없어서 안돼.

I'm kind of tied up all day. How about tomorrow?
내가 오늘 하루 온종일 바빠서 꼼짝도 못할 것같아. 내일 어때?

How about tomorrow afternoon around four o'clock? 내일 오후 4시쯤이 어때?

Well, how about if I do it at home?
내가 집에서 그걸 하면 어떨까?

How about you let me take you out to dinner one night? 저녁때 한번 내가 널 데리고 나가 저녁을 사줘도 될까?

010 Hit me up anytime 언제든 연락해

미드표현

this indicates that the speaker is giving someone permission to contact him in the future. It also probably means that the speaker enjoyed communicating with the listener and hopes to do it again. Another way to say this is “Feel free to get in touch with me”

| Point | hit sb up 연락하다, 만나다

A: Is there any chance I could give you a call?
내가 너에게 전화해도 될까?

B: Sure, here’s my number. **Hit me up anytime.**
그럼, 여기 내 전번. 언제든 연락해.

Dude, hit me up anytime. I'm on Facebook.
야, 언제든 연락해. 나 페이스북하니까.

Hit me up if you need some advice about school. 학교에 대해 조언이 필요하면 연락해.

She told me to hit her up when she gets back to the States.
걘 자기가 미국으로 돌아오면 연락하라고 내게 말했어.

011 I’m going 나 갈거야

미드표현

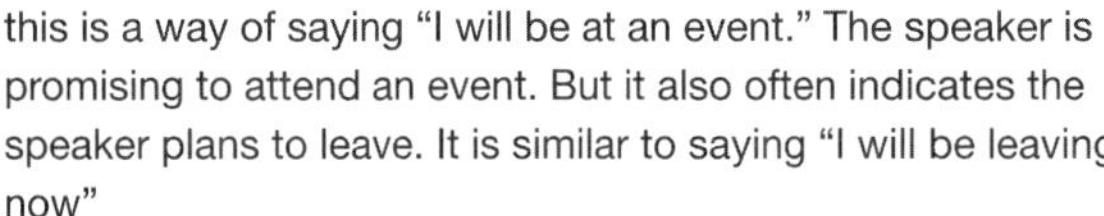
this is a way of saying “I will be at an event.” The speaker is promising to attend an event. But it also often indicates the speaker plans to leave. It is similar to saying “I will be leaving now”

| Point | You’re going? 너 갈거야?

A: Have you heard that Jason is having a Halloween party? 제이슨이 할로윈 파티한다는 거 알아?

B: Yeah, **I’m going.** I’m sure it will be a fun time.
어. 난 갈거야. 재미있을거야.

I'm going. I'll see you tomorrow 갈게. 낼 보자고

I'm not going. I'll finish up all the errands.
난 안가. 잔일들 모두 마칠거야.

Okay. If you're not going, I'm not going.
좋아. 네가 안 간다면, 나도 안가.

The meeting is mandatory, but I'm not going.
회의에 꼭 참석해야 하지만 난 안갈거야.

012 I’ll be there 갈게

this is a way of saying “Yes, that’s a good time for me.” The speaker is agreeing to go somewhere at a certain time

| Point | I’m there 나 갈거야 (I’ll) Be right there 곧 갈게, 지금 가
I’ll be there soon[in a minute] 곧 갈게
I’ll be right down 금방 내려갈게
He has to be there 걘 가야 돼

A: I want you to come to my birthday party.
내 생일파티에 와라.

B: **I’ll be there.** I love going to parties.
갈게. 파티에 가는 거 좋아해.

I say I am there. 나 간다고.

I'll be there. I'll try to be there. 갈게. 가도록 노력할게.

I'll be there as soon as I'm done. 끝나는 대로 갈게.

You bet I'll be there. 꼭 거기에 갈게.

If you send me an invitation, I'll be there.
네가 초대장 보내면 거기에 가도록 할게.

013 They are going to be here 걔네들 이리 올거야

this is a way to say "Those people will come." Usually it is said to confirm people will attend some event

| Point | What time should I be there? 거기에 언제까지 가야 돼?
Where will I find you? 어디 있을 건데?

A: Are Aaron and Emily planning to stop by?
애론과 에밀리가 올까?

B: Yes. **They are going to be here.** 어, 걔네들 이리 올거야.

미드표현

He really wants you to be here. 걘 네가 오길 정말 바래.

She's gonna be here any minute. 걘 곧 올거야.

I told Bob that Jack is going to be here tonight. 밥에게 잭이 오늘밤 올거라고 말했어.

014 I'm on my way 가고 있어, 가는 중이야

this speaker is saying "I'm coming right now." It means he will arrive soon

| Point | I'm on my way to~ …로 가는 중이야
I'm on my way home 집에 가는 중이야
I'm on my way back now 지금 돌아가는 중이야

A: Can you stop at the school and pick up Adam?
학교에 들러서 아담을 데려올 수 있어?

B: Alright. **I'm on my way** right now. 좋아, 지금 가는 중야.

미드표현

Tell them I'm on my way. 내가 가고 있다고 말해.

I'm on my way to the gym, I'll meet you there.
체육관 가는 길이야, 거기서 보자.

No, I'm on my way to the airport right now.
아니, 지금 바로 공항으로 가고 있는 중이야.

I'm on my way to pick him up.
걔를 픽업하러 가는 중이야.

015 I wouldn't miss it (for the world)

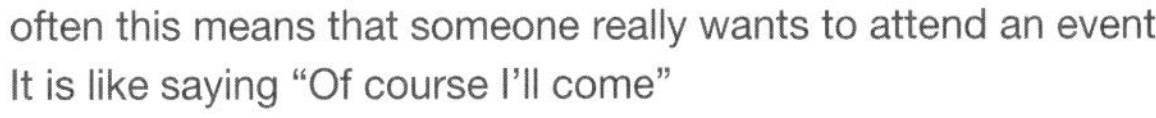

무슨 일이 있어도 꼭 갈게, 꼭 갈게

미드표현

often this means that someone really wants to attend an event. It is like saying "Of course I'll come"

| Point | I'd never miss it 꼭 갈게

A: Would you like to come to the museum with us?
우리랑 박물관에 함께 갈래?

B: Absolutely. **I wouldn't miss it for the world.**
물론, 어떤 일이 있어도 꼭 갈게.

Are we still on for drinks later? I wouldn't miss it. 우리 나중에 같이 술마시는거지? 내가 꼭 갈게.

A: We'll expect you both at the wedding.
B: Wouldn't miss it. A: 너희 둘 다 결혼식에 꼭 와. B: 꼭 갈게.

016 I'm coming with you 너랑 같이 갈게

this means "I'll join you." The speaker plans to travel somewhere with someone

| Point | I'm coming 가고 있어
Who's coming with me? 같이 갈 사람?

A: I must go visit Kathy in the hospital.
캐시 병문안하러 가야 돼.

B: **I'm coming with you.** Let's go now.
나도 너랑 같이 갈게. 자 가자.

미드표현

Jessica, wait, I'm coming with you.
제시카, 잠깐만, 나도 같이 갈게.

I don't think he even knows I'm coming with you today. 오늘 내가 너랑 같이 가는 걸 걔는 모르고 있는 것 같아.

I'm coming with you. Boy, I wish Haley would date some other boys.
너랑 같이 갈게. 어휴, 헤일리가 다른 남자아이들과 데이트하면 좋겠어.

I'm warning you. You run away, I'm coming with you. 내 경고하는데, 너 달아나, 내가 함께 갈게.

017 (You) Wanna come? 올래?, 같이 갈래?

this is very similar to inviting someone. The speaker is saying "Come with me"

A: We're going to the movies. **Want to come?**
우리 영화보러 갈거야. 같이 갈래?

B: I don't know. What movie will you see?
몰라. 무슨 영화 볼건데?

미드표현

Me and the guys are going for a beer. You want to come? 나하고 얘들은 맥주 마시러 갈려고. 같이 갈래?

I was just going to go for a walk. You want to come? 산책하려던 참이었어. 같이 갈래?

We're gonna go to freshman assembly together. Do you wanna come?
우리는 신입생 모임에 함께 갈거야. 너도 같이 갈래?

018 Care to tag along? 따라올테야?

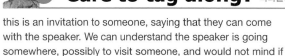

this is an invitation to someone, saying that they can come with the speaker. We can understand the speaker is going somewhere, possibly to visit someone, and would not mind if an extra person comes. It is a way of saying "Would you like to join me when I go?"

| Point | tag along (초대하지 않았는데도) 따라다니다

A: I'm going out to eat. **Care to tag along?**
나 외식할거야. 따라올테야?

B: Sure, I have some time to head to a restaurant.
물론, 식당에 갈 시간이 좀 있어.

미드표현

Want me to tag along? 내가 따라갈까?

Good. Doc, why don't you tag along?
좋아요. 선생님, 따라오세요.

If it's okay with you, I'd like to tag along.
네가 괜찮다면, 따라가고 싶어.

Remember when we were little, and you'd always tag along with me, wherever I went?
우리 어렸을 때 기억나, 내가 어딜 가든 네가 항상 날 따라다녔던 거 말야?

019 (I'll) See you then (약속한 날에 보자며) 그럼 그때 보자

this is a way to confirm that someone will come somewhere. It is like saying "I expect to meet you there"

| Point | (I'll) See you there 거기서 보자

A: I'll be at the park on Thursday. 목요일에 공원에 갈거야.

B: That's great. **I'll see you then.** 좋아. 그럼 거기서 봐.

미드표현

Great, I'll see you then. 좋아. 그때 봐.

All right. See you then, Richard, it was really nice meeting you.
좋아. 그럼 그때 봐, 리차드, 만나서 정말 반가웠어.

I'll see you there tonight around 9:00.
오늘 밤 9시 경에 거기서 봐.

020 You're on time 시간 맞춰왔네, 딱 (시간을) 맞췄네

this speaker is saying that a person isn't late. He wants to say "It's good because you're here when you should be"

| Point | You're just in time 아주 제 시간에 맞췄네

A: Oh my gosh. Am I late for class?
저런. 수업에 제가 늦었나요?

B: No, you aren't. **You're on time.**
아니, 그렇지 않아. 제 시간에 왔어.

미드표현

Just be here and be on time, and get your hair cut. 여기에 제시간에 와서 머리를 깍도록 해.

If they don't make it on time, is there anything you'd like me to tell them?
걔네들이 제 시간에 도착하지 못하면, 내가 걔네들한테 뭐라고 할까?

The broadcast must begin on time. Any problems? 방송은 제 시간에 시작해야 돼. 문제 있는 사람?

021 I can't get ahold of him 연락 정말 안되네

this is a way of saying "There is no way to contact him."This is said when a person can't be communicated with

I Point I get ahold of sth 구하다, 입수하다
get ahold of sb 연락을 취하다

A: Did you tell Paul about the change in the schedule? 폴에게 일정 변경에 대해 말했어?

B: Not yet. **I can't get ahold of him.**
아직 안 했어. 연락이 정말 안돼.

I didn't want to call you, but I can't get hold of the translator.
널 부르고 싶진 않았는데 통역해줄 사람이 없어서.

A: Assuming he fired the gun, how did he get ahold of it? B: Well, maybe Dad give it to him behind Mom's back.
A: 걔가 총을 쐈다고 가정하면 총을 어떻게 구했지? B: 아마 아빠가 엄마몰래 주었겠죠.

022 I('ve) got plans 약속(계획)이 있어

often this is said by someone who won't make an appointment. The person is saying "I have other things to do at that time"

I Point I I('ve) got plans with sb ~와 약속이 있어

A: Are you going to the Halloween party?
할로윈 파티에 갈거야?

B: No. **I've got plans** for that evening.
아니. 그날 저녁에 약속 있어.

I can't do it. I got plans this weekend.
안돼. 이번 주말에 할 일이 있어.

I can't. I've got plans with my parents.
안돼. 부모님과 약속있어.

I'm sorry, I've got plans with my sister.
미안, 누이와 약속이 있어.

A: You got a little time later? B: Not tonight. I got plans. A: 늦게 시간 좀 돼? B: 오늘 밤은 안돼. 계획이 있어.

023 I'll take a rain check 다음으로 미룰게

this is used to say "Let's do it later." This is often said when a person is too busy to do something right away

I Point I rain check 경기가 우천으로 연기시 다음 경기를 볼 수 있도록 해주는 확인표
Can we take a rain check? 미뤄도 돼?
I'll have to beg off 부득이 거절해야겠어

A: Why don't we go golfing today? 오늘 골프치자.

B: I'm busy today, but **I'll take a rain check.**
오늘 바빠, 하지만 다음에 가자.

You mind if I take a rain check? 다음으로 미뤄도 돼?

Could I take a rain check? I am so tired.
미뤄도 돼? 넘 피곤해서.

I'm going to take a rain check on the movie.
영화보는거 미뤄야겠어.

You have to let me take a rain check.
다음으로 미뤄야겠는데요.

024 I don't know what's keeping him
개가 왜 늦어졌는지 모르겠어

the speaker is wondering why someone hasn't arrived. It is a way to say "I'm not sure why he's late"

I Point I What's keeping him? 걔 왜 이렇게 늦지?

A: Why is Sam late for this meeting?
샘이 회의에 왜 늦는거야?

B: I'm not sure. **I don't know what's keeping him.**
글쎄. 왜 늦는지 모르겠어.

The kids left a half hour ago to pick you up. I can't imagine what's keeping them.
애들은 널 픽업하러 반시간 전에 나갔어. 왜 걔네들이 늦어지는지 모르겠네.

Jane should be here by now. I wonder what's keeping her.
제인은 지금쯤이면 도착해야 되는데. 왜 걔가 늦어지는지 모르겠네.

Excuse me, would you mind going in and finding out what's keeping them?
미안하지만 네가 들어가서 뭐 때문에 걔네들이 늦어지는지 알아볼테야?

025 What took you so long? 왜 이렇게 오래 걸렸어?, 왜 이렇게 늦었어?

this is asking "Why were you late?" The speaker wants to know the reason someone didn't come on time

| Point | What took you so long to~? …하는데 왜 이렇게 오래 걸렸어?
What held you up? 왜 늦었어?

A: **What took you so long?** 왜 이리 늦었어?
B: I had to go change my clothes. 옷을 갈아입어야만 했어.

What took you so long to call me?
전화하는데 왜 이렇게 오래 걸렸어?

How come it took you so long to ask me out?
내게 데이트 신청하는데 왜 이렇게 오래 걸렸어?

What's wrong with her? What took you so long? 걔 무슨 문제가 있어? 너 왜 이렇게 오래 걸린거야?

What took you so long? Mr. Kramer, the good news is, your daughter's alive.
왜 이렇게 늦었어요? 크레이머 씨, 좋은 소식은 당신 딸이 살아 있다는 것입니다.

026 Sorry to keep you waiting so long 오래 기다리게 해서 미안해

this is a way to apologize for being late. The person is saying "I feel bad because you had to wait"

| Point | Sorry I kept you waiting so long 오래 기다리게 해서 미안해
Sorry I'm late 늦어서 미안

A: **Sorry to keep you waiting so long.**
오래 기다리게 해서 미안.
B: It's OK. I was just reading a magazine.
괜찮아. 그냥 잡지 읽고 있었어.

I'm sorry I'm late. I got lost. 늦어서 미안해. 길을 잃어서.

I'm sorry to keep you waiting.
오랫동안 기다리게 해서 미안해.

A: Hi, uh, sorry to keep you waiting. B: No problem, I keep myself busy.
A: 오래 기다리게 해서 미안해. B: 괜찮아. 나도 바빴어.

A: Sorry to keep you waiting. B: It's quite all right. A: 오래 기다리게 해서 미안해. B: 정말 괜찮아.

027 I'm running a little late 좀 늦어, 좀 늦을 것 같아

미드표현

this speaker is saying "I'm late for an appointment." He is probably feeling stressed because of this

| Point | You're 30 minutes late 30분 늦었어
I might be about 30 minutes late 30분 정도 늦을거야

A: **I'm running a little late** today. 오늘 좀 늦어.
B: So what time will you be here? 그럼 몇 시에 오는거야?

Take your time. He's just running a little late.
천천히 해. 갠 좀 늦을 것 같아.

I've got to go. I'm running late. 가야 되겠어. 늦었어.

Carol's supposed to be here, but I guess she's running late. 캐롤은 지금쯤 여기 있어야 되는데 늦을건가 보네.

028 Something's come up 일이 좀 생겼어

미드표현

this is used as an excuse not to do something. It is like saying "I have to do something else, so I can't keep our appointment"

| Point | Is there something up? 무슨 일 생겼어?

A: **Something's come up.** I can't come to your office. 일이 좀 생겼어. 네 사무실로 못 가.
B: But you promised you'd meet me here.
하지만 여기서 날 만나기로 약속했잖아.

I'll talk later. Yeah, something's come up.
나중에 얘기할게. 어, 무슨 일이 좀 생겼어.

Listen, something's come up. I think it's a good opportunity. 저기, 일이 좀 생겼어. 좋은 기회인 것 같아.

Um, actually, Claire, something's come up. So... Gotta go. 실은 클레어, 일이 좀 생겼어. 그래서 가야 돼.

029 She's gonna show up 걘 올거야

the speaker is saying a woman will come. He is indicating "I think she will be here"

| Point | show up 모임이나 약속장소에 오다, 나타나다(appear)

A: I don't know if Susan is planning to come.
수잔이 올 건지 모르겠어.

B: **She'll show up.** Believe me. 걘 올거야. 정말야.

She will show up. She always does.
걘 올거야. 항상 그러잖아.

I'm so sorry my daughter didn't show up yet. I'm sure she'll be there any second.
딸이 아직 안와서 미안. 곧 도착할거야.

I'm the first one to show up every morning.
매일 아침 제일 먼저 나오는 사람은 바로 나야.

It makes me angry when you show up late.
네가 늦게 오니까 내가 화가 나네.

030 I'll look you up when I'm in town 시내에 오면 한번 들를게

this person is promising to meet someone the next time he visits an area. It is the same as saying "I'll call you when I come here again"

| Point | look sb up 들르다
Look me up when you're in town 시내에 오면 한번 들러

A: When will you be able to see me again?
다시 언제 날 만나러 올 수 있어?

B: **I'll look you up when I'm in town.** 시내오면 들를게.

Look me up if you're ever on Long Island.
롱 아일랜드에 오게 되면 들러.

I'll look you up next time I'm in New York.
내가 담에 뉴욕가면 들를게.

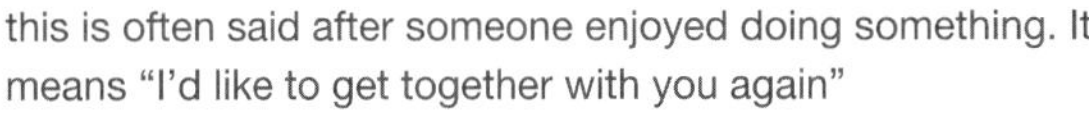

031 Let's do it again 또 만나자, 한번 더 하자

this is often said after someone enjoyed doing something. It means "I'd like to get together with you again"

| Point | Let's do this again sometime 조만간 다시 한 번 보자

A: I had a great time with you. 너랑 정말 즐거웠어.

B: Me too. **Let's do it again soon.**
나도 그래. 곧 다시 한번 만나자.

It's been a lot of fun. Let's do it again.
정말 재미있었어. 우리 또 만나자.

Let's do it again when you have some more time. 네가 시간 좀 날 때 우리 또 만나자.

Let's do it again in the next month.
다음 달에 우리 다시 만나자.

Let's do it again

Blacklist SEASON#1-1

Zamani건을 해결한 Redington이 FBI에 다른 사건을 한 번 더 해보자고 하면서 자신이 갖고 있는 Blacklist에 관해 언급하는 장면.

Reddington: Well, this was fun. Let's do it again. Really, let's do it again. Understand, Zamani was only the first.
Cooper: The first what?
Reddington: Name. On the list.
Cooper: What list?
Reddington: It's called The Blacklist. That sounds exciting. That's why we're all here, of course. My wish list. A list I've been cultivating for over twenty years. Politicians, mobsters, hackers... spies.

레딩턴: 재미있었어요. 우리 다시 한번 합시다. 정말이지, 다시 합시다. 자마니건은 첫 번째에 불과합니다.
쿠퍼: 뭐의 첫 번째요?
레딩턴: 명단. 리스트에 있는 명단요.
쿠퍼: 무슨 리스트요?
레딩턴: 블랙리스트라고 합니다. 흥미롭게 들리네요. 그래서 물론 우리가 여기 다 모인거죠. 내 희망리스트. 내가 20년 넘게 일구어온 리스트 말이죠. 정치가들, 마피아들, 해커들, 그리고 스파이들요.

032 Please keep me company 같이 있어줘, 말[길]동무 해줘

this speaker is asking someone to wait with him. It is like saying "Can you stay with me?"

I Point I We enjoyed your company 같이 있어서 즐거웠어
*It was fun having you가 좀 더 친근한 표현
Would you keep me company? 나하고 이야기하면서 있을래?

A: Please **keep me company** tonight. 오늘밤 말동무 해줘.
B: I can only stay for a few hours. 몇 시간 밖에 못 있어.

I'll come and keep you company.
내가 가서 너와 함께 있어줄게.

Mind if I keep you company for a bit?
잠깐 같이 있어도 돼?

Do you have someone to keep you company tonight? 오늘밤 같이 있을 사람있어?

My parents will keep me company while I'm waiting. 내가 기다리는 동안 부모님이 나와 함께 있을거야.

033 I have company 일행이 있어

often this means someone is busy with friends. It is a way to communicate "I'm busy talking with these people right now"

I Point I have company 손님이 방문해있다

A: Can I come over and see you right now?
네가 지금 너한테 가도 돼?
B: Not yet. **I have company** at the moment.
아직 안돼. 지금 일행이 있어.

We have company right now. Let me call you back later. 지금 누가 와 계셔. 나중에 전화할게.

What, now, do you have company?
뭐라고, 지금 일행이 있다고?

You tell me to put on pants when we have company. 우리가 손님이 있을 때는 바지를 입으라고 했잖아.

034 I'm expecting company 더 올 사람 있어, 누가 오기로 했어

this is a way to say "I think people will come to my house soon." This is used often when a person has invited people to his house

I Point I expect company 손님이 오기로 되어 있다

A: Why is your apartment so clean today?
오늘 네 아파트가 왜 이리 깨끗해?
B: **I'm expecting company** to drop by. 누가 들를거야.

I'm expecting company. Now's not a good time. 누가 오기로 되어있어. 지금은 좀 아닌데.

Oh, Aiden, I would love to, but I'm expecting company. 에이든, 나도 그러고 싶지만 누가 오기로 했어.

Excuse the mess. I didn't expect company today. 지저분해서 미안해. 오늘 누가 올거라 생각하지 않았거든.

035 Do I know you? 저 아세요?, 누구시죠?

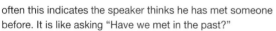

often this indicates the speaker thinks he has met someone before. It is like asking "Have we met in the past?"

I Point I Don't I know you (from somewhere)? 어디서 만난 적이 있지 않나요?
Do you two know each other? 둘 아는 사이야?
How do you know each other? 어떻게 서로 알아?

A: **Do I know you?** You look familiar.
누구시죠? 인상이 낯 익어서요.
B: I think we met each other a few years ago.
몇 년 전에 만난 것 같아요.

I'm sorry. Do I know you? 미안하지만, 누구시죠?

Your voice sounds so familiar. Do I know you?
목소리가 낯익네요. 누구시죠?

Do you two know each other? Well, that saves me an introduction. 둘이 알아? 그럼 소개 안 해도 되겠구만.

036 We are on a first-name basis 우리는 가까운 사이야, 이름부르는 사이야

this is a way of saying "We have a close relationship." It is used to indicate that the two people are friends

| Point | be on a first-name basis 친한 사이야
be on a semi first-name basis 좀 가까운 사이야
be on a last name basis 잘 모르는 사이다

A: Do you know the president well? 사장 잘 알아?
B: Yes I do. **We are on a first name basis.**
어 그래, 친한 사이야.

미드표현

Never a good idea to let people know you're on a first name basis with the bartender.
사람들에게 네가 그 바텐더와 친하다는 걸 말하는 건 좋은 생각같지 않아.

I didn't know you two were on a first name basis. 난 너희들이 가까운 사이인 것을 몰랐어.

Uh, first-name basis? Should I be jealous?
어, 가까운 사이라고? 내가 질투해야 하나?

037 They're really bonding 걔네들 무척 친해, 친해지고 있어

usually this expresses that two people are becoming friends quickly. In other words "They seem to like each other a lot"

| Point | bonding 긴밀한 유대관계, 친한 사이 *male bonding 남자끼리 의기투합

A: Your son and my son are becoming friends.
네 아들과 내 아들이 친구가 됐어.
B: I see that. **They're really bonding together.**
알아. 무척 친해.

미드표현

I'm glad you guys were bonding.
너희들 관계가 좋아서 기뻐.

I'm glad you're bonding with your grandparents. 네가 조부모님들과 좋게 지내서 기뻐.

We were totally bonding as soon as we met each other. 우린 서로 만나자 마자 아주 가까워졌어.

038 We go way back 우리 알고 지낸 지 오래됐어, 우린 오랜 친구야

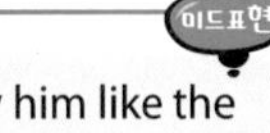

this means two people have known each other for a long time. It's a way to say "He's an old friend of mine"

| Point | go way back 서로 알고 지낸 지 오래되었다
We're not strangers anymore 우리는 이미 아는 사이잖아

A: When did you meet Carl for the first time?
칼을 언제 처음 만났어?
B: A long time ago. **We go way back.**
오래 전에. 알고 지낸 지 오래됐어.

I go way back with Peter. I know him like the back of my hand.
피터와 안 지가 아주 오래됐어. 내 손등만큼 잘 안다고.

Sam, you and I go way back. I know you.
샘, 너와 나는 서로 오랫동안 지내왔어. 난 널 알아.

Come on, tell me. We're not strangers anymore, remember?
이봐, 말해봐. 우린 모르는 사이도 아니잖아. 기억나?

039 How did he fall in with those guys?

걘 어떻게 그 사람들과 친하게 된거야?

this is asking how a person began to be friends with or associate with a certain group of people. It is like asking "When did he start hanging around with those guys?"

| Point | fall in with sb 친해지다, 친구가 되다(be friends with)
fall in with sth 찬성하다(agree)

A: Ed's friends have been getting him into a lot of trouble. 에드는 친구들 때문에 많은 곤경에 빠졌어.
B: That's too bad. **How did he fall in with those guys?** 안됐네. 어쩌다 그런 친구들과 어울리게 된거야?

미드표현

Make sure you fall in with the right crowd.
올바른 사람들과 친구가 되도록 해.

I think I should let her fall in with the bad crowd. 걔가 나쁜 사람들과 친해지도록 해야 될 것 같아.

I was just a kid, 16 or so, and I fell in with the wrong crowd.
난 16세 정도, 어린애였어, 그리고 나쁜 사람들과 어울렸지.

040 What are friends for? 친구 좋다는 게 뭐야?

often this is said as a response to a person saying "Thank you." The speaker is saying "I helped because I'm your friend"

| Point | That's what friends are for 친구 좋다는 게 이런 거지

A: Thank you so much for the wonderful gift.
멋진 선물 줘서 정말 고마워.

B: You are welcome. **What are friends for?**
무슨. 친구 좋다는 게 뭐야?

What're friends for? Don't hesitate to ask me for help, if you're in trouble.
친구 좋다는 게 뭐야? 도울 일 있으면 언제든지 불러.

A: Thanks for helping me carry my stuff. B: Yeah, what are friends for?
A: 내 물건들 들어줘서 고마워. B: 어, 친구 좋다는게 뭐야?

A: I'm so touched you're all willing to do this. B: What are friends for?
A: 너희들이 기꺼이 이 일을 해줘서 감동먹었어. B: 친구 좋다는게 뭐야?

041 Come over to my place [house] 우리 집에 들러, 우리 집에 놀러와

this is an invitation to a person's place. The speaker is saying "Come visit me"

| Point | come over to+장소 …에 들르다, 방문하다, …쪽으로 가다
come over to~ 들러서 …하다

A: **Come over to my place** tomorrow. 낼 우리집에 와.

B: I can't. I have other plans then. 안돼. 낼 다른 계획있어.

I am so glad that you could come over tonight. 오늘 밤에 올 수 있다니 기뻐.

You come over to help Mark move into his new house? 들러서 마크가 이사하는 거 도와주라고?

You should come over to our table.
이쪽 테이블로 와봐.

Come over to my place and have a few drinks.
우리 집으로 와서 술 몇잔 하자.

042 Would you like to come? 같이 갈래?

this is a way to say "Do you want to go with me?" Often it is a way to invite someone to something

| Point | Would you like to come with sb to+장소? …와 함께 …로 갈래?

A: My friends are going scuba diving. **Would you like to come?** 친구들이 스쿠바 다이빙하러 가는데 같이 갈래?

B: That sounds great. I love being in the water.
좋아. 난 물속에 들어가는 걸 좋아해.

John's having a little dinner party tomorrow night. Would you like to come?
오늘밤에 존이 저녁파티하는데 올래?

Would you like to come over for dinner later?
나중에 저녁먹으러 들를래?

What a nice surprise. Would you like to come in? 이게 누구야. 들어와라

043 Drop by for a drink (sometime) (언제) 술 한잔하게 들러

this is a very casual way to say "Come over to my house soon." The speaker wants someone to feel welcome to visit him

| Point | drop by = stop by 예고없이 잠깐 들르다
Drop in sometime 근처에 오면 한 번 들러

A: Can we meet again soon? 조만 간에 다시 볼 수 있어?

B: Sure. **Drop by for a drink sometime.** 그럼. 술 한잔하게 들러.

I told him to drop by for a drink.
걔한테 술 한잔하게 잠깐 들르라고 했어.

You came all the way from Phoenix just to drop by? 걍 들르기 위해 피닉스로부터 그 먼길을 왔다는거야?

Drop by when you're in town, meet your new best friend. 시내에 오면 들러서 네 새로운 베프를 만나라고.

Feel free to drop by any time. 언제든지 편하게 들러.

044 You're gonna come and visit me? 놀러 올 거지?

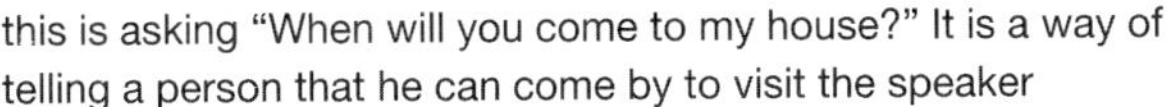

this is asking "When will you come to my house?" It is a way of telling a person that he can come by to visit the speaker

I Point I come and visit = come to visit = come visit
방문하다, 들르다, 놀러가다

A: **You're going to come and visit me?** 놀러 올 거지?
B: Sure. Just tell me when to stop by.
그럼, 언제 와야 되는지 말만 해.

미드표현

You didn't even come and visit me when I was in the hospital.
내가 병원에 있을 때 넌 찾아오지도 않았어.

I should go. May I come and visit you again?
나 가야 돼. 내가 다시 놀러와도 돼?

And call if you're feeling lonely. We will come and visit. 네가 외로우면 전화해. 우리가 놀러갈게.

045 I just had time to pop in 짬내서 잠깐 들렀어

this indicates the speaker is in a hurry. It is like saying "I can stop for a short time but I must go soon"

I Point I pop in 예고없이 잠깐 들르다

A: Hi Randy. I'm surprised to see you here.
야 랜디. 여기서 널 보게 되네.
B: **I just had to pop in** for a visit. 그냥 잠깐 짬내서 들른거야.

미드표현

I'm sorry to just pop in... is it OK if I come in?
갑자기 들러서 미안해. 내가 들어가도 될까?

I just want to pop in and make sure Jessica's okay. 잠깐 들러서 제시카가 괜찮은지 확인하고 싶어.

046 Who is it? 1. (노크, 벨소리에) 누구세요? 2. (전화왔다는 말에) 누군데? 3. 누구야?

this is a way of saying "Tell me who you are." or "Tell me who that person is." It is often said when a person is knocking at the door of a house

I Point I Who's there? 계세요?, 누구 있어요?
Who was it? 누군데?, 누구였어?

A: **Who is it?** 누구세요?
B: It's the mailman. I have a letter for you.
우편배달부입니다. 편지 왔어요.

You like someone. Tell me who it is. Who is it?
너 좋아하는 사람있지. 누군지 말해봐. 누구야?

Just a minute! Who is it? 잠깐만요! 누구세요?

You met someone! Who was it?
누구 만났구나! 누구였어?

047 Buzz him in 들여보내, 문열어 줘

this means "Push the button and let him enter the apartment." People will be allowed in to come and visit

I Point I buzz 인터폰, 초인종 등의 버저를 누르다

A: I think Jimmy is waiting in the lobby. 지미가 복도에서 기다리는 것 같아.
B: **Buzz him in** and have him come upstairs.
문 열어주고 위층으로 올라오게 해.

미드표현

When somebody does not buzz you in, that means go away.
초인종을 눌러도 문을 안 열어주는 건 꺼지란 소리야.

Can you buzz me in, please? Buzz me in! We need to talk.
제발 나 좀 들여보내줘. 날 들여보내줘! 우리 얘기 해.

When Jerry rings the bell, buzz him in.
제리가 벨을 누르면 문열어 줘.

048 Come on in 어서 들어와

this invites someone inside. It is a common way of saying "Welcome"

Point Won't you come in? 들어오지 않을래?
Allow me in 들어가도 되지, 좀 들어갈게

A: Hello Elaine. **Come on in.** 안녕 일레인. 어서 들어와.
B: Thank you. I brought you some wine.
고마워. 와인 좀 가져왔어.

미드표현

Come on in. Turner, you remember Tom?
터너야, 어서 들어와. 너 탐 기억하지?

Honey, it's open. Come on in.
자기야 문 열렸어. 어서 들어와.

Please come on in and make yourself at home. 어서 들어와서 편하게 지내.

049 I like having you here 네가 여기 있어서 좋아

this is a way to say "I enjoy being with you." People say this to someone they like

Point Good to have you here 어서 와, 와줘서 기뻐
Good[nice] to be here 오기를 잘했어, 환영해줘 기뻐

A: It was great of you to invite us.
우릴 초대해줘서 정말 고마웠어.
B: **I like having you here.** 네가 와줘서 좋은 걸.

미드표현

Welcome back. It's very exciting to have you here. 잘 돌아왔어. 네가 와서 얼마나 좋은지 몰라.

Thank you. Good to be here folks.
감사합니다. 여러분과 함께해서 기쁘군요.

I'm so happy to have you here.
네가 여기 와서 난 너무 기뻐.

050 Make yourself at home 편하게 있어, 편히 계세요

this is said to make a person feel comfortable. It means "Relax and enjoy yourself here"

Point make yourself comfortable 편히 하다

A: **Make yourself at home.** My house is like your house. 편하게 해. 네 집처럼 해.
B: Thank you so much. Where can I put my suitcase? 고마워 정말. 이 가방은 어디에 놓을까?

미드표현

Why don't you step into my room and you make yourself at home? 방에 들어와 편하게 있어

Yeah, come in. Make yourself comfortable.
그래, 들어와. 편하게 있어.

051 Where can I freshen up? 화장실이 어디야?

this is a polite way to ask where the toilet is. It is similar to saying "Could you show me the restroom?"

Point Where can I wash up[freshen up]? 화장실[욕실]이 어디야?
Time to make a pit stop (이동중) 화장실 갈 시간

A: **Where can I freshen up?** 화장실이 어디야?
B: The bathroom is down the hall, on the left.
복도 아래 왼쪽에 있어.

미드표현

I think I should use the powder room.
화장실 좀 가야 되겠어.

If you'll excuse me, I have to go to the rest room. 괜찮다면 화장실 좀 가야 되겠어.

I'm thinking that there is no time to make a pit stop. 화장실 들를 시간이 없을 것 같아.

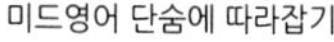

052 I don't want to wear out my welcome

너무 실례되는게 아닌지 몰라

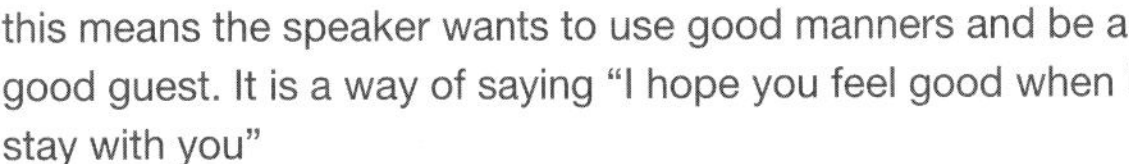

this means the speaker wants to use good manners and be a good guest. It is a way of saying "I hope you feel good when I stay with you"

| Point | wear out one's welcome 너무 오래 머물러 눈총받다
(자신의 환영을 닳아 없어지게 한다는 의미)

A: You can stay as long as you want to.
원하는대로 머물러도 돼.

B: I'll just stay a few days. **I don't want to wear out my welcome.** 며칠 머무를게. 너무 폐 끼치긴 싫거든.

미드표현

I don't want to wear out my welcome. I'll stop by next time I will in town.
너무 폐를 끼치는 것 같아서. 시내에 오면 다음에 또 들를게.

Fine, but I'm kind of worried I might be starting to wear out my welcome a little.
괜찮아. 하지만 내가 너무 폐를 끼치지 않나 좀 걱정돼.

053 (I) Hate to eat and run

(모임에서 빨리 일어나며) 먹자마자 일어나긴 싫지만

this indicates the speaker has to leave after only a short time. He is saying "I'm sorry to leave so soon"

A: **I hate to eat and run,** but I must go.
먹자마자 일어나긴 싫지만 가야 돼.

B: Please come back again soon. 조만간 다시 한번 와.

I hate to eat and run, but I have a prior commitment. 먹자마자 일어나긴 싫지만 선약이 있어서.

I hate to eat and run, so I'll stick around a bit longer. 먹자마자 일어나긴 싫으니 조금만 더 있을게.

Sorry I'm leaving so soon. I really hate to eat and run. 이렇게 일찍 가서 미안해. 정말로 먹자마자 일어나긴 싫은데.

054 Are you leaving so soon [early]?

벌써 가려구?, 왜 이렇게 빨리 가?

미드표현

the speaker is saying "Are you going now?" He is surprised that his guest is leaving so quickly

| Point | Are you leaving? 가는거야?
When are you leaving? 언제 떠나?
Why are you leaving? 왜 떠나?

A: **Are you leaving so soon?** 벌써 가?

B: Yeah, I've got a train to catch. 그래, 기차를 타야 돼.

What are you doing? Are you leaving? Wait.
뭐하는거야? 가는거야? 기다려.

A: Are you leaving so early? B: I've got a plane.
A: 왜 벌써 가? B: 비행기 타야 돼

Wait, wait you guy, what are you doing? W-why are you leaving?
잠깐, 너희들 뭐하는거야? 왜 벌써 가는거야?

055 Are you decent?

들어가도 돼?(들어가도 될 만큼 입을 거 입고 있냐는 말)

this is usually said to ask "Do you have clothes on?" The speaker wants to know if someone is dressed before he enters the room

| Point | decent 품위있는, 옷을 제대로 입고 있는

A: Can I come in? **Are you decent?**
들어가도 돼? 옷 다 입었어?

B: Wait a minute. I'm changing my clothes.
잠깐만. 지금 옷 갈아입는 중이야.

Bob? It's me. Are you decent? 밥? 나야. 들어가도 돼?

Tyler, are you decent? Or more importantly, alone? 타일러, 내가 들어가도 돼? 아님 더 중요한건데 너 혼자 있어?

Are you decent? I need to come into the bathroom. 나 들어가도 돼? 나 화장실에 들어가야 된다고.

056 Just hang out with me 그냥 나랑 놀자

this is asking someone to stay around. It means "Please stay here with me"

| Point | hang out with sb …와 시간을 보내다

A: I'd like you to stay. **Just hang out with me.**
안 갔으면 좋겠어. 나랑 함께 놀자.

B: OK, but I have to go home at nine.
좋아, 하지만 9시에는 집에 가야 돼.

Don't you have any friends to hang out with?
함께 놀 친구가 없는거야?

You need to get out, hang out with your friends more. 나가서 친구들과 더 좀 놀아라.

You don't want to hang out with me anymore? 나랑 더 놀고 싶지 않은거야?

057 We're just hanging around here 그냥 여기서 시간 보내는 중이야

this is expressing "We are relaxing here." The speaker is letting people know he is casually staying somewhere

| Point | hang around 빈둥거리다, 아무 것도 안하고 시간 보내다
hang around with sb …와 함께 놀다, 어울리다

A: What are you guys doing? 너희들 뭐하니?

B: Not much. **We're just hanging around here.**
별로. 그냥 여기서 시간 보내는 중이야.

Maybe I hang around here a little more than I should. 아마 내가 필요 이상으로 여기서 시간을 보내는 것 같아.

He's just really great to hang around with.
걘 정말 같이 지내기 좋은 사람야.

I don't want my daughter hanging around with a guy like that! 내 딸이 저런 자식과 어울리는 게 싫어!

058 We're just goofing around 우린 그냥 빈둥거리고 있어

this indicates the people are doing fun things and not working. It is a way to say "We aren't doing anything serious"

| Point | goof around 할 일없이 빈둥거리다
fool around 빈둥거리다, 바람피다

A: Why are you making so much noise?
왜 그렇게 시끄럽게 굴어?

B: **We're just goofing around.** 그냥 빈둥거리고 있는거야.

That's not funny! Just stop horsing around!
재미없다고! 그만 빈둥거려!

You can't goof around. This is a very serious place of business! 빈둥거리지마. 여기 굉장히 진지한 곳이야!

Come on, I'm just goofing around!
그러지만, 난 그냥 빈둥거리고 있는거야!

059 I had a blast 신나게 놀았어

this is said to express "I had a lot of fun." The speaker wants to tell someone he really liked something

| Point | have a blast = have fun 즐겁고 신나게 보내다

A: Did you like going on your vacation?
너 휴가 간 거 좋았어?

B: Oh sure. **I had a blast** there. 물론. 신나게 놀았어.

It was a blast. 정말 신났었어.

I had such a blast with her the other night.
요전 날 밤 걔하고 흠뻑 즐겼어.

A: Did you two have fun? B: A blast.
A: 너희 둘 재미있었어? B: 신나게 놀았어.

It's going to be a blast. You have to go.
신나게 재미있을거야. 너 꼭 가봐.

060 Go nuts! 실컷 놀아봐!

this is a way to say "Have as much fun as you can." Usually it means someone is telling others to relax and enjoy themselves

| Point | go nuts 미치다, 열중하다, 열광하다

A: Can I use your hot tub tonight? 오늘밤 네 욕조 써도 돼?
B: **Go nuts.** It's really nice to sit in the warm water.
실컷 즐겨. 따뜻한 물에 앉아 있는 건 정말 좋아.

미드표현

If you don't have hobbies you go nuts.
취미가 없으면 돌아버릴걸.

A: Why don't you come downstairs with me? There's some really nice girls down there.
B: I'm fine. Go nuts.
A: 내려가자. 아래층에 예쁜 여자가 있어. B: 아냐, 실컷 놀아.

061 This party rocks! 이 파티 끝내준다!

this expresses that a party is great. The speaker is saying "This is a great time for me"

| Point | That place rocks! 거기 물 좋다!

A: I'm having a great time. **This party rocks!**
정말 재미있어. 이 파티 끝내줘!
B: Yeah, everyone seems to be enjoying themselves. 그래, 다들 즐거하는 것 같아.

미드표현

This menu rocks! 이 메뉴 끝내준다!

Paintball rocks! I had the best day of my life.
페인트볼로 하는 서바이벌 게임 죽여준다! 생애 최고의 날이었어.

This party rocks! Look at all the girls!
이 파티 끝내준다! 저 여자애들 좀 봐!

062 I'm having a good time 재미있어, 재미있게 보내고 있어

this is a way to say "I'm enjoying this." The speaker wants people to know something is fun

| Point | have a good time 즐거운 시간을 보내다
have a wonderful time 정말 즐거운 시간을 보내다

A: How are you doing Linda? 린다 어때?
B: **I'm having a good time.** Thanks for inviting me. 재미있게 보내고 있어. 초대해줘서 고마워.

미드표현

So you're having a good time? 그래 너 재미있어?

Wow! You guys seem to be having a good time. 와! 니네들 재미있게 지내는 것 같아.

I had a good time. Really. Thank you.
재미있었어. 정말이야. 고마워.

063 We're having fun 우린 즐겁게 지내고 있어

this means the people like something. It is like saying "This is terrific"

| Point | have fun (with sb) (…와 함께) 즐거운 시간을 보내다
Go have fun 가서 재미있게 보내
It was really fun 정말 재미있었어

A: Is everything OK at your new house? 새 집 다 괜찮아?
B: Yeah, it's great there. **We're having fun.**
어, 아주 좋아. 즐겁게 지내고 있어.

미드표현

I hope you have fun tonight. 오늘 밤 재미있게 보내.

Do what you like. You go have fun with the guys. 맘대로 해. 가서 애들하고 재미있게 보내.

You didn't have fun today. 너 오늘 재미없었구나.

We're having fun. Let's stay a while longer.
재미좋다. 좀 더 남아 놀자.

064 You're the life of the party 넌 파티에서 분위기 메이커야

this is said to someone that has a fun personality. It is expressing "You help make this party more interesting"

I Point I party pooper 파티의 흥을 깨는 사람

A: I don't know if I can come to the celebration.
축하연에 갈 수 있을 지 모르겠어.

B: You have to come. **You're the life of the party.**
꼭 와야 돼. 넌 분위기 메이커잖아.

It doesn't exactly make you the life of the party. 그렇다고 해서 네가 파티의 분위기 메이커가 되는 건 아냐.

Look at them, though. They're the life of the party. 그래도 걔네들 좀 봐봐. 걔네들 분위기 메이커야.

You have to attend our wedding. You're the life of the party.
넌 우리 결혼식에 꼭 와야 돼. 분위기 메이커잖아.

065 I'm throwing a party 파티를 열거야

this means "I will invite friends to celebrate something." The speaker wants others to know he will host a celebration

I Point I throw a party 파티를 열다
baby shower 출산앞둔 예비모에게 가족, 친구가 모여 선물을 주는 파티

A: **I'm throwing a party** this weekend.
이번 주말에 파티 열거야.

B: Let me know what time I should come over.
몇 시까지 가야 되는지 알려줘.

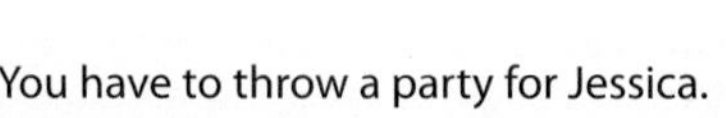

You have to throw a party for Jessica.
제시카에게 파티를 열어줘야지.

I'm gonna be okay, you don't have to throw a party for me. 난 괜찮아, 나 때문에 파티 열 필요없어.

She threw Jim a going-away party.
걘 짐에게 송별회를 열어줬어.

066 Let's get this party started 파티를 시작하자고

usually this is a way to say "Let's start to have fun now." A speaker might say this to indicate that he wants people to do things that make them have more fun

I Point I get ~ started …을 시작하다

A: **Let's get this party started** right now.
이제 파티를 시작하자고.

B: Good idea. I'll put on some dance music.
좋은 생각야. 댄스음악을 틀을게.

Let's get this party started, shall we?
파티를 시작하자고, 그럴까?

Why don't you go inside and get the party started? 들어가서 파티를 시작하자.

Have fun and get this vacation started.
즐겁게 지내, 그리고 이 휴가를 시작하자고.

Okay, grab a seat and let's get the meeting started. 좋아, 자리잡고, 회의를 시작하자고.

067 It's already in full swing! 지금 절정을 이루고 있어!

this expresses that something has already begun. It is similar to saying "It started already"

I Point I be in full swing (특히 파티 등이) 한창이다, 순조롭게 진행 중이다

A: Have you started your birthday celebration?
생일파티를 시작했어?

B: Yeah, I'm having a party. **It's already in full swing.** 어, 파티중이야. 한창하고 있는 중이야.

The party is in full swing, with lots of kids around. 파티가 한창이야 애들도 많고.

Looks like things are in full swing. Everybody showed up this year. 순조로운 것 같아. 금년에는 다들 모였어.

The party was in full swing, and everyone was waiting to surprise the guest of honor. 파티가 절정였고 다들 주빈을 깜짝 놀라게 해주기를 기다리고 있었어.

068 I'll be around 근처에 있을거야, 난 여기 남아 있을게

this often means the speaker will be easy to contact. It is like saying "I'll be close by"

A: Will I be able to meet you again? 다시 만날 수 있을까요?
B: Of course. **I'll be around.** 물론요. 멀리 가지 않을게요.

Just give me the key. I'll be around all day.
열쇠만 줘. 종일 여기 있을게.

If you need me, I'll be around.
내가 필요하면 여기 남아 있을게.

Well, if you'd said yes, maybe they'd still be around. 네가 승낙을 하면 걔네들 아마 남아있을거야.

069 I'm just going to hang back 난 좀 남아 있을거야

this is a way to say that the speaker is not going to rush to go first, but rather he plans to go slower, or possibly stay a little bit longer. Often people hang back so that they can have time to observe what is going on. Another way to say this is "I'll stay back here for a while to see what happens"

| Point | hang back 다른 사람들 가고 나서 남다

A: Would you like to go to a nightclub with us?
우리와 함께 나이트클럽에 갈래?
B: No, **I'm just going to hang back** for a while.
아니, 난 좀 잠시 남아서 기다릴거야.

I'll hang back, too. Where you going?
나도 남을게. 넌 어디 가는데?

You might want to tell them to hang back.
넌 걔네들에게 남아있으라고 하는게 좋을거야.

We're just gonna hang back, search this area another hour. 우리는 남아서 한 시간 정도 이 지역을 뒤져볼게.

Hang back until we breach the door. And give the All-Clear, you copy?
우리가 문을 부수고 들어가서 모두 이상없다고 할 때까지 기다려, 알았지?

070 I'm sticking with you 난 너랑 함께 있겠어

often this is a way of saying "I'll support you or I'll stay with you." The speaker is telling another person that he will try to be helpful

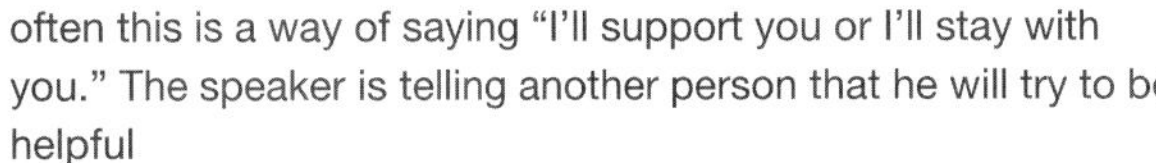

| Point | stick with sb …와 함께 있다, 지원하다
Stick with me 나와 함께 해줘

A: I'm sorry that I caused so much trouble.
문제를 많이 일으켜서 미안해.
B: Never mind that. **I'm sticking with you.**
걱정하지마. 난 네 편이야.

Do you want to stick with that teacher?
그 선생님하고 잘 지내니?

You and I are finished. From now on, I'm sticking with Jack.
너하고 난 끝장났어. 지금부터는 잭하고 함께 다닐거야.

She's not a great secretary, but she did stick with me for five years. I'm gonna call her and hire her again.
걘 뛰어난 비서는 아니지만 나와 5년을 함께 했어. 전화해서 다시 채용하겠어.

071 I'll get out of your hair 널 방해하지 않고 그만 갈게

this speaker is saying that he is going to leave so that the other person can relax or resume whatever they were doing before he arrived. We can understand the speaker interrupted something when he arrived. It's like saying "I'm going to leave so I don't take any more of your time"

| Point | get[be, keep] out of sb's hair 폐끼치지 않고 그만 가다, 괴롭히지 않다
get[keep] ~ out of one's hair …가 괴롭히지 못하게 하다
get in(to) a sb's hair 괴롭히다

A: I'm sorry I don't have time to talk. There's a lot of work to do. 미안하지만 얘기할 시간이 없어. 할 일이 너무 많아서.
B: Okay, I understand. **I'll get out of your hair.**
알았어, 이해해. 그만 방해하고 가볼게.

I will be out of your hair first thing tomorrow.
내일 아침 일찍 사라져줄게.

Now just give us a DNA sample. We'll clear it all up. We'll get out of your hair.
DNA 샘플을 주면 모든 걸 명백히 하고 당신을 괴롭히지 않을게요.

I can't get this out of my hair. 이걸 떨쳐버릴 수가 없어.

My father is hopefully getting the Ryan out of your hair.
아버지는 희망을 갖고 라이언이 너를 괴롭히지 못하도록 하고 계셔.

Ways of asking if there is a problem
상대방에게 무슨 일인지 궁금해서

What's the deal?

001 What's this all about? 도대체 무슨 일이야?

this is usually said when a person wants information. It is like saying "What is going on here?"

I Point I What's that[it] about? = What's it all about?
무엇에 관한 거니?, 왜 그랬니?, 무슨 일이야?
This is what it's all about 이게 다 그거에 관한거야, 그 내용은 이런 것이야

A: **What's this all about?** 도대체 무슨 일이야?
B: The police need to ask you some questions.
경찰이 네게 몇 가지 물어볼 게 있대.

미드표현

What's happening? What's this all about?
무슨 일이야? 도대체 무슨 일이야?

I heard Bill got angry yesterday. What's that about? 빌이 어제 화났다는데 무슨 이유로 그런거야?

So what's this all about? What are you doing?
이게 다 무슨 일이야? 뭐하는 짓이야?

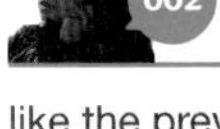

002 What's the deal? 도대체 어떻게 된거야?, 문제가 뭐야?

like the previous phrase, this is asking for information on a situation. The speaker is saying "Explain this to me"

I Point I What's the deal with~? …는 어떻게 된거야?
What is sb's deal? …의 문제가 뭐야?

A: I thought we were leaving. **What's the deal?**
우리가 출발하는 줄 알았는데, 도대체 어떻게 된거야?
B: I decided to stay a while longer. 좀 더 머무르기로 했어.

미드표현

What's the deal with this girl? 이 소녀가 어떻게 된거야?

That is sloppy, reckless work. What, what's the deal? 엉성하고 무모한 일이야, 도대체 어떻게 된거야?

So what's the deal? Are you coming over tonight? 도대체 어떻게 된거야? 오늘밤에 너 오는거야?

What's the deal? I mean you were supposed to be here an hour ago.
어떻게 된거야? 너 한 시간 전에 여기 오기로 되어 있었잖아.

003 What's the matter with you? 1. 무슨 일이야? 2. 도대체 왜 그래?

often this is said when someone is acting strangely. It is a way of saying "What is your problem?"

I Point I What's the matter? 왜 그래?

A: **What's the matter with you?** 무슨 일이야?
B: I think that food made me sick. 음식땜에 아픈 것 같아.

미드표현

What's the matter with you? What is your problem? 무슨 일이야? 무슨 문제야?

Do something! What's the matter with you?
뭔가 좀 해! 도대체 왜 그래?

What's the matter? Are you scared? 왜 그래? 겁나?

004 What's wrong (with you)? 무슨 일이야?, 뭐가 문제야?, 뭐 잘못됐어?

this is very similar to the previous phrase and it is asking about what is troubling someone

I Point I What's wrong? 왜 그래?
What's wrong with sth[sb]? …가 뭐 잘못됐어?
What's wrong with that? 그게 뭐가 문제야?

A: You look terrible. **What's wrong?**
너 무척 안 좋아 보여, 무슨 일이야?
B: I haven't been able to sleep well. 수면장애가 있어.

What's wrong with you? Are you sick?
너 왜 그래? 아파?

I don't know what's wrong with her.
걔한테 무슨 문제가 있는지 모르겠어.

I'm having a lot of sex. What's wrong with that? 난 섹스 많이 해, 그래서 뭐가 문제야?

What's wrong with Tom's heart?
탐의 심장에 무슨 문제가 있는거야?

005 What happened? 무슨 일이야?, 어떻게 된거야?

this is a way to ask "What caused this?" The speaker wants to know why something occurred

| Point | What happened today? 오늘 무슨 일 있었어?
What happened to[with] sb? …에게 무슨 일이야?
What's happening? 무슨 일이야? (가끔) 잘 지내?

A: Your car is really damaged. **What happened?**
네 차 정말 망가졌네. 어떻게 된거야?

B: I had an accident on the way here.
여기 오는 길에 사고가 났어.

미드표현

What happened to Mike's hair? Is he having a nervous breakdown?
마이크 머리는 왜 저래? 신경쇠약증이라도 걸린거야?

What happened with you and Peter?
피터랑 무슨 일 있었어?

Now can you tell me exactly what happened to your husband? 남편한테 무슨 일이 일어난 건지 말해줄래?

What's happening? Are you okay?
무슨 일이야? 괜찮아?

006 What's with you? 뭐 땜에 그래?, 무슨 일이야?

this is indicating that someone isn't acting normally. It is similar to saying "Why are you acting strangely?"

| Point | What is with sth? …가 왜 그래?
What is it with you? 당신 도대체 뭐야?
What is it now? (짜증) 또 무슨 일이야?

A: You are acting strangely. **What's with you?**
너 행동이 이상해. 무슨 일이야?

B: I feel kind of nervous tonight. 오늘 밤 좀 긴장이 돼서.

미드표현

What's with you? You're acting like a kid.
왜 그래? 애처럼 굴고 말아.

What's with your hair? 머리가 왜 그래?

What's with the face? 얼굴이 왜 그래?

What's with you? Are you pissed off?
무슨 일이야? 열받았어?

007 How did this happen? 이게 어떻게 된거야?

here the speaker wants someone to explain an event. He is asking "What was the cause of this thing?"

A: I heard that Willis died last week.
윌리스가 지난 주에 죽었다며.

B: That's terrible. **How did it happen?**
끔찍하네. 어떻게 그런거야?

미드표현

I'm a little confused... How did that happen?
좀 혼란스럽네… 이게 어떻게 된거야?

Yesterday your patient's tumor was 5.8 centimeters. Today it's 4.6. How did that happen?
어제 네 환자의 종양은 5.8센티였어. 오늘은 4.6센티이고. 어떻게 된거야?

She's never done anything like that before. How did it happen?
걘 절대 그런 짓을 한 적이 없어. 어떻게 된거야?

008 What's going on? 무슨 일이야?

this is usually said when someone is confused. It is like saying "Tell me what is happening here"

| Point | What's going on in there? 거기 무슨 일 있어?
What's going on here? 무슨 일이야?
What is going on with you? 어떻게 된 거예요?

A: **What's going on?** I see a lot of police.
무슨 일이야? 경찰이 많이 보이네.

B: I think someone robbed the bank. 누가 은행을 털었나 봐.

미드표현

A: What's going on? B: Peter and I broke up.
A: 무슨 일이야? B: 나 피터하고 깨졌어.

Sam, you're scaring me. What's going on?
샘, 무섭게 왜그래? 무슨 일 있어?

Okay. What's going on? Is this about last night? 좋아. 무슨 일이야? 어젯밤에 관한거야?

What's going on? I heard a loud noise.
무슨 일 있이야? 큰 소리가 들리던데.

009 Where does it come from? 1. 무슨 이유 때문에 그러는거야? 2. 어디서 난거야?

this is a way to ask why a person spoke or acted in a certain way. It is similar to asking "What caused it?" But more commonly, this indicates the speaker wants to know the origin of something. It is very similar to asking "How did it get here?

| Point | Where are you coming from? 너 어떻게 된거야?, 어디 출신이야?

A: You are always angry. **Where does it come from?** 넌 항상 화를 내. 왜 그러는거야?

B: I feel very frustrated about my life.
내 인생에 너무 좌절하고 있어.

미드표현

Look at these books. Where did they come from? 이 책들 좀 봐봐. 이거 어디서 난거야?

You seem angry all the time. Where does it come from?
넌 항상 화가 난 사람같아. 무슨 이유 때문에 그러는거야?

Chris has tons of money. Where does it come from? 크리스는 돈이 엄청 많아. 어디서 난걸까?

010 What's eating you? 뭐가 문제야?, 무슨 걱정거리라도 있어?

this is a very common way to ask "What's bothering you?" It means the speaker wants to know what someone's problem is

| Point | What's bugging you? = What's bothering you?
= What's troubling you? 뭐가 문제야?

A: **What's eating you?** 뭐가 문제야?

B: I don't want to talk about it right now.
지금 말하고 싶지 않아.

미드표현

What's eating you? You've been crabby all day. 뭐가 문제야? 너 종일 괴팍하게 굴어.

Is everything okay? What's eating you?
별일 없어? 무슨 걱정거리라도 있어?

What's eating you? You can always talk to me about problems.
뭐가 문제야? 언제든지 문제거리 얘기하라고.

011 What's gotten into you? 뭐 때문에 이러는거야?

this is usually asked when a person is acting in an odd way. It is asking "Why are you being odd?"

| Point | get into sb[sth] …을 이상한 행동을 하게 하다
What's gotten into your head? 머리가 어떻게 된 거 아냐?, 무슨 생각으로 그래?
What has gotten into you? 대체 왜 그러는거야?

A: You were fighting. **What's gotten into you?**
너 싸웠지. 뭐 때문에 이러는거야?

B: That guy was making me really angry.
저 자식이 정말 날 짜증나게 했어.

미드표현

What a surprise! You excited about shopping. What's gotten into you?
왠일이야! 네가 쇼핑때문에 좋아하고. 뭐 때문에 이러는거야?

What has gotten into you? Skipping school, showing no respect for your father!
뭐 때문에 이러는거야? 학교 빼먹고, 아버지한테 무례하게 행동을 하고!

What has gotten into you? You were being so pleasant. 뭐 때문에 이러는거야? 너 정말 즐거워했는데.

012 What gives? 무슨 일 있어?

this is a way to ask a person what is happening, or what the situation is. It is a way of saying "Explain what is happening"

| Point | Say, what gives? 왜 그러지? , 왠 일이야?

A: **What gives?** Are you planning to move? 무슨 일 있어? 이사할거야?

B: Yeah, I think I'll rent an apartment elsewhere.
어, 다른 곳에 아파트 세를 얻을까 해.

미드표현

She's been waiting for you in the room for 20 minutes. What gives?
걔는 널 방에서 20분이나 기다렸어. 무슨 일이니?

A: What gives? B: I don't know what they're talking about.
A: 무슨 일 있어? B: 걔네들이 무슨 말하는지 모르겠어.

So, what gives? I thought you were the pro at picking up girls.
그래 무슨 일이야? 난 네가 여자 꼬시는데 일가견이 있는 줄 알았는데.

013 What's the problem? 무슨 일인데?

the speaker wants to know "What is causing trouble?" Often this is asked when the speaker is not sure if he is causing the trouble

| Point | What's the problem with~? …가 무슨 문제야?
What's your problem? 무슨 일인데?, 도대체 뭐가 문제지?
You got a problem? 무슨 문제가 있어?

A: **What's the problem,** officer? 경관님, 무슨 일이죠?
B: You were driving much too fast. 속도위반입니다.

Talk to me, what's the problem?
나한테 말해봐, 뭐가 문제야?

What's the problem with it? All the kids are wearing it. 그게 뭐 어때서? 애들 다 입는데.

What about you? What's your problem?
너 왜 그래? 무슨 문제야?

014 What's cooking? 무슨 일이야?

this is old slang that asks "What is going on?" People used this as a greeting at one time

| Point | Let's see what's cooking 어떻게 돼가나 보자

A: Hey Mindy. **What's cooking?** 야 민디, 무슨 일이야.
B: I just thought I'd stop by and say hello. 잠깐 들러서 인사나 하려고.

Hey Alice. What's cooking? 안녕, 앨리스, 무슨 일이야?

What's cooking? How Is your family doing?
무슨 일이야? 네 가족 어떻게 지내?

What's cooking? Anything new going on?
무슨 일이야? 무슨 일 있어?

015 (Is) Something wrong? 뭐 잘못된거야?

this is a simple way to ask "Are you upset?" The speaker would like to know if someone feels unhappy

| Point | (There's) Something wrong with sb[sth] …에 뭔가 문제가 있어
Is there something wrong? 뭐 잘못된 게 있어?
You did something wrong? 너 뭐 잘못한거야?

A: Why do you look unhappy? **Something wrong?**
왜 그리 안 좋아 보여. 뭐 잘못된거야?
B: I don't like the way you've been treating me.
네가 날 대하는 태도가 맘에 안 들어.

Is something wrong? You've been so quiet all evening. 뭐 잘못됐어? 저녁내내 조용하네.

There's something wrong with my husband.
남편한테 문제가 있는 것 같아.

I think there's something wrong with your car.
네 차에 뭔가 문제가 있는 것 같아.

016 That's weird 거 이상하네

this expresses that something unusual happened. It is very similar to saying "I don't understand that"

| Point | This feels (very) weird 이상한 거 같아
That's funny 거참 이상하네

A: Jason just quit school and left the country.
제이슨이 학교를 그만두고 다른 나라로 갔어.
B: **That's weird.** Do you know why he did that?
거 이상하네. 왜 그랬는지 알아?

That's weird. What is that? 거 이상하네. 저게 뭐야?

It feels weird for me. 나한테는 이상한 것 같아.

I don't know, I just had a weird feeling.
모르겠어 기분이 이상했어.

017 You've been acting strange all day 너 오늘 하루종일 이상해

미드표현

this is a way to tell someone "Your actions have been unusual." The speaker may want to know if a problem has caused someone to behave oddly

| Point | It's strange 이봐, 이상하다
It was so strange 정말 이상해

A: **You've been acting strange all day.**
너 하루 종일 이상해.

B: I'm really worried about some things.
정말 어떤 일로 걱정이 많아서.

You've been acting strange all day. Are you having problems with your parents?
너 하루종일 이상해. 부모님과 뭐 문제있어?

I am very worried about you because you've been acting strange all day.
네가 종일 이상해서 무척 걱정돼.

Has your son said anything to you, been acting strange lately?
최근에 당신 아들이 네게 뭔가 얘기를 하거나 좀 이상하게 행동한 적 있어요?

018 What's the story? 어떻게 된거야?

미드표현

this is a way to say "Tell me what is going on." It is asking for information on the situation

| Point | What's your story? 왜 그렇게 행동한거야?, 왜 그런거야?
What's her story? 쟤 왜 저래?

A: You look exhausted. **What's the story?**
너 무척 지쳐 보여. 어떻게 된거야?

B: My boss is making me work a lot of overtime.
사장이 야근을 엄청시켜.

I want to talk about it now. You don't have any money, so what's the story?
지금 얘기하자. 돈이 한 푼도 없다고, 어떻게 된거야?

A: What's your story, bastard? B: Ask me nicely and maybe I'll tell you, dwarf.
A: 어떻게 된거야, 이 자식아? B: 친절하게 물어보면 내가 말해줄지 모르지, 꼬맹아.

019 Why the long face? 왜 시무룩해 보여?, 왜 그렇게 우울한 표정이야?

미드표현

we usually say this when a person looks sad. It is a way of asking "Why do you seem so gloomy?"

| Point | Why is your face so long? 왜 그렇게 우울한 얼굴을 하고 있어?
Don't make a face 이상한 표정 짓지마
(Are) Things getting you down? 골치 아픈 문제라도 있어? 고민 있어?

A: **Why the long face today?** 오늘 왜 시무룩해 보여?

B: I won't have any time to meet my friends this weekend. 이번 주말에 친구들 만날 시간이 조금도 없을거야.

A: Why the long face? B: Someone stole my cellular phone.
A: 왜 그렇게 우울한 표정을 하고 있어? B: 누가 내 핸드폰을 훔쳐갔어.

Hey, why the long face? Are you still sad Dad wouldn't let you go to the bachelor party?
왜 시무룩해? 아빠가 총각 파티에 못가게 해서 아직도 꿀꿀한거야?

Ways of telling people to trust you

서로 믿고 신뢰하고

A deal's a deal

001 [It's a, That's a] Deal 그렇게 하자, 좋아, (합의하에) 그래

this means "I agree to your offer." Often the speaker is saying that he and another person have agreed on the cost of something that is being bought and sold

I Point I [It's a, That's a] Deal? 그럴래?, 좋아?

A: If you pay me $7000, I'll sell you the car.
7천 달러를 주면 너한테 자동차를 팔게.

B: **It's a deal.** I need to go to the bank first.
좋아, 그렇게 하자. 먼저 은행 좀 가야 돼.

We have made the changes you asked for and it's a done deal.
네가 요청한 변화는 다했어, 그러기로 한 거잖아.

Deal. Do you wanna say hello to Mom before you go? 그렇게 하자. 가기 전에 엄마한테 인사할래?

Deal. So, am I seeing you after school?
좋아. 그럼 학교 파한 후에 보는거다.

002 A deal's a deal 약속한거야

this means that a person can't change an agreement that was made. It is a way to say "You have to honor the agreement you made with me"

I Point I (It's a) Done deal 그러기로 한거야

A: I don't want to buy the car now. 지금 차를 사고 싶지 않아.

B: You must. **A deal's a deal.** 사야 돼. 약속은 약속이잖아.

You have to follow through. A deal's a deal.
너 끝까지 따라와야 돼. 약속한거야.

A deal's a deal. I'll give you the money.
약속한거니까 너한테 돈을 줄게.

The contract was signed. A deal's a deal.
계약서에 사인을 했어. 약속한거야.

003 We have a deal? 약속한 거지?, 동의하니?, 그럴래?

this is a way to make certain an agreement was made. It is like saying "Do you agree to this?"

A: **We have a deal?** 그럴래?

B: Sure, I'll agree to that. 물론, 거기에 동의할게.

All right, we have a deal? 좋아, 그렇게 하는거지?

Do we have a deal or not? 그럴래 말래?

A: So, do we have a deal? B: No, I never take first offer. This is what I want.
A: 그럼 우리 약속한거지? B: 아니, 난 절대 첫 번째 제의는 받지 않아. 이게 바로 내가 원하는거야.

004 I thought we had a deal 얘기가 다 됐다고 생각했는데

usually this is said when one person breaks an agreement. The other person may become angry, and this is a way of expressing "I thought I could trust you to honor the agreement"

I Point I We had a deal 그러기로 했잖아, 얘기 다 된 거잖아
That was not the deal 그건 얘기가 다르잖아

A: **I thought we had a deal.** 얘기가 다 된 걸로 생각했는데.

B: Well, I changed my mind about it.
어, 내가 그거에 대해 생각을 바꿨어.

How could you betray me like this? We had a deal, and you stabbed me in the back.
네가 어떻게 이렇게 날 배반할 수 있어? 얘기 다 된 거잖아, 그런데 날 배반했어.

You have to help me out here. I thought we had a deal. 날 도와줘야 돼. 그러기로 얘기 다 된 거잖아.

005 I give you my word 내 약속할게

this is a way of saying "I promise you." The speaker is telling a person to trust him

| Point | I give you my word S+V …을 약속할게
You have my word 내 약속하지
Do I have your word (on~)? (…을) 약속하는 거지?

A: Can I trust you to do this? 네가 이걸 할거라고 믿어도 돼?
B: Yes you can. **You have my word.** 그럼, 내 약속할게.

I give you my word. You will not get a demotion. 내가 약속할게. 넌 강등되지 않을거야.

I give you my word I'll do what I can. 최선을 다한다고 내 약속하지.

Do I have your word on that? 그거 약속하는 거지?

I'll give you a job. I give my word. 네가 일자리 잡아줄게. 내 약속할게.

006 I swear 맹세해, 약속해, 걱정하지마

미드표현

often this means "I promise you this is true." It is said so others will believe the person is being honest

| Point | I swear to God 맹세코
I swear (to God) S+V (맹세코) …을 약속해
I swear on sb (S+V) …걸고 (…을) 맹세해

A: Are you sure you have no money? 정말 너 돈 없어?
B: **I swear.** I forgot to bring my wallet with me. 맹세해. 지갑을 깜박 잊고 안 갖고 왔어.

I swear, it's the truth. 맹세코 그건 사실이야.

I swear I don't know what happened. 어떻게 된 건지 정말 몰라.

I swear on my kids I've never seen that man before in my life. 내 애들을 걸고 맹세하는데 평생 저 남자를 본 적이 없어.

I never kissed your girlfriend. I swear! 난 네 여친에게 절대로 키스하지 않았어. 맹세해!

007 So help me 맹세컨대

미드표현

this is very similar to the previous phrase. The speaker wants to tell someone he is being honest and what he says is true

| Point | So help me God의 줄인 표현

A: **So help me,** I will win this race. 맹세컨대, 경주에서 이길거야.
B: I think you'll need to run faster. 더 빨리 뛰어야 될 걸.

So help me, if you don't back me up on this, I will lose it. 맹세컨대, 네가 이 건을 도와주지 않으면 난 그걸 잃게 돼.

If you ruin this, so help me, I will hurt you! 네가 이걸 망치면, 맹세컨대, 널 해칠거야!

Mom, so help me God, I will not get into this with you. 엄마, 맹세컨대, 엄마와 이 얘기는 하지 않을거야.

008 I'm gonna hold you to that 그 약속 꼭 지켜야 돼

미드표현

the speaker is saying that he expects someone to keep his promise. He is indicating "You must do what you said you would do"

| Point | hold sb to sth …가 …의 약속을 지키게 하다

A: I promise I'll give you the money tomorrow. 내일 너에게 돈을 꼭 줄게.
B: **I am going to hold you to that.** 그 약속 꼭 지켜야 돼.

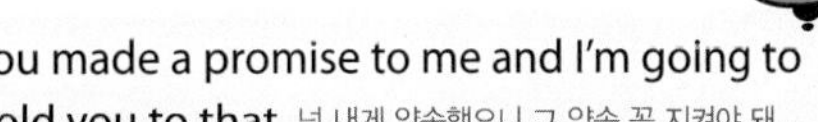

You made a promise to me and I'm going to hold you to that. 넌 내게 약속했으니 그 약속 꼭 지켜야 돼.

Sheila said she'd help me study and I'm going to hold her to that. 쉴라는 내가 공부하는 걸 도와준다고 했고 난 걔의 그 약속을 믿고 있어.

You promised to marry me. I'm going to hold you to that. 나하고 결혼한다고 약속했어. 그 약속 꼭 지켜야 돼.

009 Don't you dare bail on me 약속깨지마

this is often an angry way to say "Don't break your promise." Someone promised to do something with the speaker and the speaker wants the person to keep the promise

| Point | bail on (약속) 어기다, 바람맞히다, 수업(직장) 빼먹다

A: I'm not sure if I can make it to your party.
네 파티에 갈 수 있을런지 모르겠어.

B: **Don't you dare bail on me!** 약속깨지마!

I think we should bail on Friday night dinner.
금요일 저녁 식사 약속은 못지킬 것 같아.

Bad news. I'm afraid I have to bail on you and dad for dinner tonight.
안좋은 소식야. 너와 아빠와 오늘 저녁 먹기로 한 약속 못지킬 것 같아.

I was just thinking I might have to bail on yoga. I have the worst headache all of a sudden.
난 요가수업에 못갈거라고 생각하고 있었어. 갑자기 두통이 아주 심하게 왔거든.

010 I promise you! 정말이야!, 약속해!

미드표현

this indicates the speaker wants another person to trust him. He is telling that person "Believe what I have said"

| Point | I promise S+V …을 약속할게
I promise you that 네게 그거 약속할게
(You) Promise? 약속하는 거지?

A: Are you sure Billy will be here? 빌리가 여기 오는 게 확실해?

B: **I promise you!** He said he was coming.
정말이야! 온다고 했어.

I'll take care of it, I promise. 내가 처리할게, 약속해.

I promise you, I have never done any type of drug. 정말야, 어떤 종류의 약도 한 적이 없어.

I promise I will call you every day.
정말이지 매일 전화할게.

011 You can trust me 날 믿어봐, 난 믿어도 돼

this is a way to say "I am honest." The speaker wants someone to believe he is a good man

| Point | Trust me 내 말을 믿어

A: I am not sure if I want to buy this.
내가 이걸 사야 할지 모르겠어요.

B: **You can trust me.** I won't cheat you.
절 믿어보세요. 손님한테 사기 안쳐요.

I'm your friend, so you can trust me.
난 네 친구야. 날 믿어봐.

Don't worry, all right? You can trust me.
걱정마. 알았어? 날 믿으라고.

You can trust me, Ellen. I'm not going to hurt you. 날 믿어. 엘렌. 널 해치지 않아.

012 Rest assured 안심해도 돼, 걱정하지 말아

미드표현

this usually means "Believe me." It is a way to tell someone that something can be trusted

| Point | rest assured of[that]~ …을 안심해도 된다

A: How can I trust that you will repair my car correctly? 내 차를 제대로 수리한다고 당신을 어떻게 믿죠?

B: **Rest assured** that I will fix it so it works well.
잘 작동하도록 고쳐놓을 테니 안심해도 됩니다.

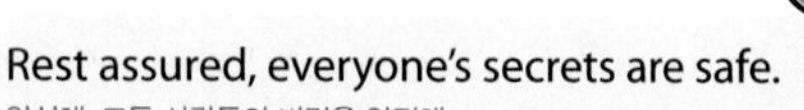

Rest assured, everyone's secrets are safe.
안심해, 모든 사람들의 비밀은 안전해.

Rest assured, we have not forgotten.
안심해, 우린 잊지 않고 있어.

Rest assured, we're gonna take care of it.
걱정마, 우리가 그거 처리할게.

013 I have faith in you 난 널 믿어

usually this is a way to say "I think you will do what you say." The speaker is indicating he trusts someone

Point have[get] faith in sb …을 신뢰하다, 믿다
lose faith in sb …을 신뢰하지 않다
put faith in~ …을 믿다, 신뢰하다

A: You know I'm not a rich man. 내가 부자가 아니라는 걸 알잖아.
B: **I have faith in you.** You'll make me happy.
난 널 믿어. 넌 날 행복하게 해줄거야.

미드표현

She said that even though you don't have faith in yourself, that she has faith in you.
걘 네가 너 스스로를 못 믿는다해도 널 믿는다고 했어.

We got faith in you, buddy. 우린 널 믿어, 친구야.

When you put your faith in people, they reward you. 사람들을 믿게 되면 그 사람들이 네게 보상하게 돼.

014 You can count on me 나한테 맡겨, 날 믿어도 좋아

usually this is expressing that the speaker will do his best. He wants someone to know "I can be trusted"

Point You can count on it 기대해도 좋아
I'm depending on you 너를 믿고 있어
You can lean on me 날 믿어

A: Will you work hard on this project?
이 프로젝트 열심히 할거야?
B: Yes. **You can count on me.** 예, 믿으셔도 됩니다.

In a crisis, you can always count on me.
힘들 땐 항상 날 의지해.

I'm here for you. You can always count on me.
내가 옆에 있잖아. 항상 날 믿어도 돼.

I'm ready for this. You can count on me now.
난 이거 할 준비가 됐어. 이제 날 믿어도 돼.

015 I'll give you the benefit of the doubt
좋은 쪽으로 생각해볼게, 속는 셈치고 믿어볼게

this means "I'll trust what you say." The speaker doesn't know if someone is being honest, but he has decided to trust him anyway

Point give sb the benefit of the doubt 속는 셈치고 믿어보다

A: I promise that I'll pay the money I owe you tomorrow. 내가 빌린 돈 내일 꼭 갚을게.
B: **I'll give you the benefit of the doubt.** But you better bring it tomorrow.
속는 셈치고 믿어보지. 하지만 내일 갚는 게 좋을거야.

I'm willing to give you the benefit of the doubt and say thank you.
좋은 쪽으로 생각할 테니 고맙다고 해.

Why can't you give me the benefit of the doubt that maybe sometimes I'm on your side? 왜 간혹 내가 네 편일 수도 있다고 속는 셈치고 믿지 못하는거야?

I am your husband, and you didn't give me the benefit of the doubt.
난 네 남편인데 넌 날 좋은 쪽으로 생각해보지 않네.

016 I'll be there for you 내가 있잖아, 내가 힘이 되어줄게

this is a way to say "I'll always help you." It indicates the speaker feels a strong responsibility for someone

Point Just be there for her 걔 옆에 있어줘

A: **I'll be there for you** when you have hard times.
네가 어려울 때 내가 힘이 되어줄게.
B: That's good. I need a friend like you.
좋아. 너 같은 친구가 필요해.

미드표현

I'll always be there for you, as a friend and as your brother. 항상 네 곁에 있어줄게, 친구로서 형으로서.

I need to know you'll be there for me.
네가 항상 내 옆에 있어줄지 알아야겠어.

You know, ever since your mother died I promised myself I'd be there for you.
알잖아, 네 엄마가 돌아가신 후로 내가 널 위해 힘이 되어줄거라 다짐했어.

017 I'll make it worth your while

네가 노력한 보람이 헛되지 않게 할게, 보답할게

미드표현

this is a way to say "I'll pay you a lot for the time you work." It is like promising someone a good salary

| Point | make it worth sb's while …의 노고에 답하다, 보답하다

A: I don't know if I can work for you.
너하고 일할 수 있을지 모르겠어.

B: **I'll make it worth your while.**
네 노력을 헛되이 하지 않게 할게.

I'm starting to think that this is about money. So what is it that'll make it worth your while?
이게 돈과 관련돼 있는 것 같다는 생각이 들어. 네 노력을 어떤 식으로 보답하면 될까?

You don't know that. Just wait till everybody's asleep. Seriously. I'll make it worth your while.
너는 모르잖아. 모두가 잘 때까지만 기다려. 정말이지. 내가 너의 노고에 보답할게.

018 I kept up my end of the bargain 난 약속을 지켰어

미드표현

the speaker is saying "I did what I promised to do." He feels he has acted in a fair way

| Point | keep[hold] up one's end of the bargain 약속을 지키다
fulfill one's end of the bargain 약속을 지키다

A: Did you clean the living room like you promised? 네가 약속한 것처럼 응접실을 청소했어?

B: Yes. **I held up my end of the bargain.**
네. 약속을 지켰어요.

I held up my end of the bargain. I was a good friend. 난 내 약속을 지켰어. 난 좋은 친구야.

You better keep up your end of the bargain.
넌 약속을 지키는게 좋을거야.

We have a deal. My domain is the kitchen and the bedroom, his is the office. I held up my end of the bargain.
우리는 거래를 했어. 내 영역은 부엌과 침실이고 걔의 영역은 사무실이야. 난 약속을 지켰어.

019 Sean had a pact with his best friends

션은 친한 친구들과 약속을 했어

미드표현

this means that a man named Sean had come to an agreement with his friends. A pact is a deal where multiple people make a binding promise that they will all do something. We can understand this to mean "Sean and his friends had an agreement to do this"

| Point | make[have] a pack with 의견일치를 보다, 서로 짜다
break one's pack 약속을 깨다

A: Why did Sean donate money to the charity?
션은 왜 자선단체에 돈을 기부했어?

B: Sean **had a pact with** his friends to donate some money every year.
션은 매년 돈을 기부하기로 친구들과 약속을 했거든.

The couple made a pact to stay together.
그 커플은 함께 지내기로 동의했어.

You'll be punished if you break our pact.
네가 합의를 깨면 벌받을거야.

Your nation must take pacts very seriously.
너의 나라는 협약을 지키려고 노력해야 돼.

Two strangers meet on a train, make a pact to get rid of each other's problems.
열차에서 낯선 사람들이 만나서 서로의 문제거리를 제거하기로 서로 짰어.

미드에선 이렇게 쓰인다!

We had a pact

Friends
SEASON#8-9

Rachel이 학창시절 괴롭혔던 Will(브래드 피트)이 추수감사절 식사에 초대받아서 오는데… Ross와 Will은 함께 "I Hate Rachel Club"란 동호회를 공동으로 세웠다는게 밝혀진다.

Rachel: So Ross, we went out for two years and you never told me you were in an "I Hate Rachel Club"?
Will: You went out with her? We had a pact!
Ross: That was in high school. It's not like it was binding forever.
Will: Then why'd it have the word "eternity" in it?

레이첼: 2년간 나랑 사귀면서 네가 "I Hate Rachel Club" 회원이었다는 것을 말하지 않았단 말야?
윌: 너 재랑 데이트를 했다고? 우리 약속 맺었잖아!
로스: 그건 고등학교 때 일이지. 평생 강제성이 있는 것은 아니잖아.
윌: 그럼 "영원"이란 말이 왜 들어있던거야?

020 I'll keep that in mind 명심할게

this speaker is saying "I'll remember that idea." It means that he thinks the idea or knowledge is useful

| Point | keep sth in mind 가슴에 새겨두다, 명심하다

A: You should always do your best in life to succeed. 성공하기 위해서 인생에서 항상 최선을 다 해야 돼.

B: That's good advice. **I'll keep that in mind.** 좋은 조언이야. 명심할게.

Thanks for the advice. I'll keep that in mind. 조언 고마워. 명심할게.

I'll keep that in mind if I ever have problems. 내가 무슨 문제라도 있으면 그걸 명심할게.

You are probably right. I'll keep that in mind. 네가 맞을 지 몰라. 그점 명심할게.

021 I would never do anything to hurt you
결코 너를 다치게 할 어떤 일도 하지 않을거야

this is a literal way of speaking. The speaker wants to say that he would not take any action that would be harmful to the listener. Many times this is said as an expression of affection or love for someone else. It is similar to saying "I will protect you because I won't ever do anything bad to you"

| Point | I'd never do anything to~ 결코 …할 어떤 일도 하지 않을거야

A: It's so hard to trust anyone in a relationship. 관계를 맺을 때 어느 누구도 믿기가 어려워.

B: **I would never do anything to hurt you.** 난 널 다치게 할 어떤 일도 하지 않을거야.

I would never do anything to hurt my research. 난 내 연구를 망칠 어떤 일도 하지 않을거야.

I would never do anything to upset you or to hurt you. 너를 화나게 하거나 다치게 할 어떤 일도 하지 않을거야.

I would never do anything to jeopardize my friendship with Chris. 난 크리스와의 우정을 위험하게 할 어떤 일도 하지 않을거야.

If you were getting married I would never do anything to upset you. 네가 결혼을 한다면 너를 화나게 할 어떤 일도 하지 않을게.

022 You got to give him that 걔 그건 인정해줘야 돼

this is sometimes used as a type of slang, and it means that a person has done or said something that should be recognized as being good or helpful, or possibly even truthful. In other words, "You need to give him credit for something that he said or did that was a positive or true thing"

| Point | I'll give you that 그 점은 인정해. 네 말이 맞아

A: My brother-in-law works 80 hours a week. 처남은 주 80시간 일을 해.

B: He is very ambitious. **You've got to give him that.** 매우 야심만만하구만. 걔 그건 인정해줘야 돼.

Well, he's a sneaky S.O.B. I'll give him that. 갠 엉큼한 개자식이야. 걔 정말 그래.

She's sexy. I'll give you that. And nasty too, I'll bet. 걘 정말 섹시해. 그 점은 인정해. 못된 것도 확실하고.

Rick's gotten us a lot farther than I ever thought he would, I'll give him that. 릭이 내가 예상했던 것보다 훨씬 우리를 앞섰어. 그 점은 인정해.

You got balls. I'll give you that. 넌 배짱이 있어. 그 점은 인정해.

023 We gave Chris a wide berth 우리는 크리스를 멀리했어

this is a way to say that the speaker wanted to avoid Chris and tried to stay away from him whenever it was possible. We can understand maybe he doesn't like Chris, or maybe he is upset or afraid of him. In other words, "We stayed far away from Chris"

| Point | give[keep]~a wide berth 충분한 거리를 두다, 가까이 하지 않다, 피하다
wide berth 충분한 거리

A: Chris was acting drunk and angry at the party. 크리스가 파티에서 술취해 화를 냈어.

B: Yeah, **we gave him a wide berth** so there wouldn't be trouble. 그래, 우린 말썽이 생기지 않도록 걔를 멀리했어.

After the fight, we gave Roberto a wide berth. 싸움 후에 우리는 로베르토를 멀리했어.

Give her a wide berth when she's in the office. 걔가 사무실에 있을 때는 가까이 하지마.

Ways to talk about difficulty

어렵고 힘들고 그래서 엉망이 되어 실패하기도

It's my ass on the line

001 That's where it gets a little tricky 그 부분이 좀 문제야

this is a way to warn others that things are going to change, and they will get more difficult or confusing. The speaker wants to prepare others for problems that may soon occur. It is like saying "We will probably have some difficulty with this"

| Point | that's where it gets a little tricky 그 부분이 좀 까다롭다, 힘들다
tricky 힘든, 곤란한, 교묘한

A: This apartment sucks. Can we buy a new house? 이 아파트는 너무 후져. 새로운 집을 살테야?

B: **That's where it gets a little tricky.** I don't have enough money. 그 부분이 문제야. 돈이 충분하지 않거든.

Well, that's where it gets a little tricky.
그게 좀 까다로운 부분야.

This is going to be a very tricky procedure.
이건 아주 힘든 절차가 될거야.

It's a tricky calculation. 그건 어려운 계산야.

Does this arrangement get a little tricky at times?
이런 방식은 때때로 좀 어려운가?

002 The hard part is still to come 아직 힘든 상황은 오지 않았어

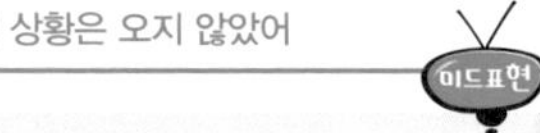

this means "It will get more difficult in the future." The speaker is telling someone to expect things to get harder

| Point | the hard part 쉬운 부분 the fun part 재미있는 부분

A: I think that was very simple. 그건 매우 쉬웠던 것 같아.

B: Yes it was. **The hard part is still to come.**
어 맞아. 아직 힘든 상황이 남아 있어.

You've already done the hard part.
이미 어려운 부분은 마쳤어.

The hard part is truly over. 힘든 상황은 끝났어.

We're through the hard part. 힘든 상황은 끝났어.

003 Don't make this hard for me 이걸 더 힘들게 만들지 말아줘

this means that the speaker is doing something that is difficult, and he is asking the listener not to do anything that would make the task even more difficult. A similar way to say this is "Don't make it tougher than it has to be"

| Point | make it hard to~ …하는 것을 어렵게[힘들게] 하다

A: Please don't take me away to prison.
제발 절 감옥에 넣지 말아줘요.

B: I have to arrest you. **Don't make this hard for me.** 널 체포해야 돼. 더 힘들게 하지마.

They make it hard on purpose.
걔네들은 일부러 그걸 어렵게 만들고 있어.

Don't make it hard on your boyfriend. Let him go. If he loves you, he'll come back.
남친을 너무 힘들게 하지마. 보내줘. 널 사랑한다면 돌아올거야.

They try to make it hard for you.
걔네들은 네가 그것을 힘들어 하게 하려고 해.

That's gonna make it hard to put together a team. 그 때문에 팀을 구성하는게 어려워질거야.

004 He's going through a hard time 걘 힘든 시기를 겪고 있어

this indicates someone has a difficult situation. Another way to say this is "His life is not easy right now"

| Point | go through a hard time 힘든 시기를 보내다
have a hard time ~ing …하느라 힘들다

A: I haven't seen Bill around lately. 최근에 빌을 못 봤어.

B: **He's going through a hard time** and feels sad these days. 걘 어려운 시기를 겪고 있어 요즘 슬픔에 잠겨 있어.

I'm having a hard time keeping it safe.
그거 비밀로 하는게 힘들어.

She got fired. She's going through a hard time.
걘 잘려서 힘든 시기를 보내고 있어.

Jack went through a hard time when he got divorced. 잭은 이혼했을 때 힘든 시기를 보냈어.

005 Please don't give me a hard time 날 힘들게 하지마

미드표현

this is a way to ask someone "Please be nice." The speaker hopes someone won't make his life difficult

Point give sb a hard time …을 힘들게 하다

A: I don't like the way you did your homework.
난 네 숙제하는 방식이 마음에 안 들어.

B: **Please don't give me a hard time.**
제발 날 힘들게 하지마.

I was just giving you a hard time. You've had a tough week. 그냥 너 좀 힘들게 했었어. 힘들게 한 주를 보냈지.

I'm having a hard time figuring it out.
난 그것을 알아내는데 힘든 시간을 보내고 있어.

Most patients have a hard time coping with new surroundings.
대부분 환자들은 새로운 환경에 대처하는데 힘겨워 해.

006 It just kept getting worse and worse
점점 더 나빠지고 있어

미드표현

this is used to say "Everything is bad and it continues to be bad." The speaker is very unhappy because he thinks his life is terrible

Point be getting worse and worse 점점 더 악화되고 있다

A: How is business going at your restaurant?
식당하는 거 어때?

B: **It just keeps getting worse and worse.**
점점 더 나빠지고 있어.

It just keeps getting worse and worse! You know? 점점 더 나빠지고 있어! 알아?

Things got worse and worse.
상황이 점점 더 나빠지고 있어.

His pain's gonna get worse and worse until he dies. 걔의 고통은 죽을 때까지 점점 더 심해질거야.

007 I can't deal with this right now 지금 당장은 나도 어쩔 수가 없어

미드표현

this is a way of saying "I have a difficult time with..." The speaker thinks it is hard to work with something or do something

Point I can't deal with~ …을 할 수가 없어

A: Have you ever eaten sushi? 스시 먹어봤어?

B: Never. **I can't deal with** the raw stuff.
아니. 날 음식은 못 먹어.

I can't deal with being single all over again.
다시 또 독신으로 살 수는 없어.

Let's go. I can't deal with her when she's like this.
가자고. 쟤가 저러면 난 감당이 안돼.

I can't deal with the raw stuff. 날 음식은 못 먹어.

008 It's harder than I thought 생각보다 더 어려워

미드표현

this indicates the speaker thought something would be easy, but it wasn't. It is like saying "It was difficult for me"

Point ~than I thought 내 생각보다 더 …

A: How is your job as a salesman? 영업하는 일이 어때?

B: **It's harder than I thought.** 생각보다 더 어려워.

This is going to be harder than I thought.
생각보다 더 어려워질거야.

This is harder than I thought it would be.
내가 그러리라 생각했던 것보다 더 어려워.

It's been harder than I thought to keep up with schoolwork. 학업을 쫓아가는게 생각보다 더 어려워.

009 It's no picnic 그건 쉬운 일이 아냐

this is a very simple way to indicate that something was not easy to do. Often it is said when something was more difficult than expected. Another way to say this is "We didn't think it would be as hard as it was"

| Point | be no picnic 쉬운 일이 아니다

A: Tell me about your experience in the military.
너 군대 때 얘기해봐.

B: **It's no picnic.** Every soldier I know misses being home. 장난아냐. 병사들 모두 집에 있는 걸 그리워하지.

You know, the flights were no picnic either.
저기, 비행도 역시 쉬운 일은 아니었어.

You wanna be an actor huh? I gotta tell ya, it's no picnic. 배우가 되고 싶다고? 내 말하지만, 그건 쉬운 일이 아냐.

Well, homicide's no picnic, either, right?
그래, 강력반도 쉬운 일이 아냐, 맞지?

I grew up on that side of the world, and it's no picnic. 난 그쪽 세계에서 컸는데 장난 아니야.

010 I'm in big trouble 큰일 났어, 큰 문제가 생겼어

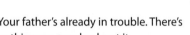

the speaker is expressing that he is worried about something. It is as if he is saying "This is causing me a big problem"

| Point | be[get] in trouble 문제가 있다 get sb in trouble 곤란하게 하다
~will be in trouble if~ 만일 …하면 …가 곤란해질거야

A: I can't find my keys. **I'm in trouble.**
열쇠를 못 찾겠어. 큰일 났어.

B: Yeah, how will you get into your apartment tonight? 어, 오늘 밤에 어떻게 집에 들어갈거야?

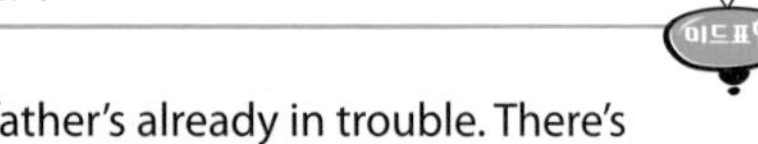

Your father's already in trouble. There's nothing we can do about it.
네 아버지는 이미 문제가 있는 상태야. 우리도 어쩔 수가 없어.

I got in trouble for that before.
전에 그 문제로 곤란한 적 있었어.

I'm not here to get you in trouble.
널 곤란하게 하려고 여기 온 게 아냐.

You're in big trouble. 너 정말 큰일 났다.

011 My life is falling apart 내 인생이 엉망야, 내 인생이 무너지고 있어

미드표현

the speaker is saying he has too many problems in his life. He wants to express "All of my problems are giving me too much stress." Also, when we say 'falling apart,' it can include many major problems, including physical, mental, emotional, financial, social, job-related, and so on.

| Point | fall apart 망치다, 망가지다, (감정)무너지다, (인생) 엉망이 되다
I'm falling apart 너무 힘들어

A: **My life is falling apart.** I have so many problems. 내 인생이 엉망야. 문제가 너무 많아.

B: Calm down. You need time to fix things.
진정해. 시간을 갖고 풀어나가.

My entire body is falling apart. 몸 전체가 엉망이야.

My marriage is falling apart. 결혼이 망가지고 있어.

What's happening to us? We're falling apart.
우리에게 무슨 일이 일어나고 있는거야? 우리 삶이 힘들어지고 있어.

I'm falling apart. My life is too stressful.
나 힘들어. 사는데 스트레스가 너무 많아.

012 I lost my shirt 알거지가 됐어

this is a way of saying that someone lost a lot of his own money on something. Often it refers to an investment that went bad and was a failure, but it can also refer to money losses due to things like gambling. Another way of saying this is "That cost me a lot of money"

| Point | lose one's shirt (투자나 도박 등으로) 무일푼이 되다, 알거지가 되다, 쪽박차다

A: How did you do with your overseas investments? 해외투자건들 어떻게 됐어?

B: They were terrible. **I lost my shirt** on all of them. 끔찍했어. 모두 다 날렸어.

Did you lose your shirt in Vegas?
베거스에서 쪽박찼어?

Many people lost their shirt on Wall Street.
많은 사람들이 월 가에서 알거지가 됐어.

His client's gonna lose his shirt, and Truman's gonna lose his job.
트루먼의 고객은 무일푼이 될거고 본인은 직장을 잃게 될거야.

013 I took the hit for the mistake you made
네가 한 실수로 손해를 봤어

미드표현

this is expressing that the speaker was punished or had some sort of penalty for a problem that someone else created. We can understand that he is probably angry. It is like saying "I had to suffer for what you did"

| Point | take the[a] hit 손해보다, 다치다, 타격을 받다

A: I heard you got fired after I wrecked your car.
내가 네 차를 망가트린 후에 너 해고됐다며.

B: That's right. **I took the hit for the mistake you made.** 맞아. 네가 한 실수로 내가 손해봤어.

The question is do we take the hit?
문제는 우리가 손해를 봤냐는거야?

The company took the hit for the loss of profit.
그 회사는 수익손실로 타격을 받았어

I'm not going to take the hit for the mistake you made. 네가 저지른 실수로 내가 손해를 보지는 않을거야.

Did she take a hit for getting drunk?
걔 술취해서 다쳤어?

014 I'm over the hill 난 한물갔어

미드표현

this is a way for a person to indicate that he is old, and he may not be capable of doing things that a younger person can do. We may also understand that someone who is over the hill is no longer useful. In other words, this person is saying "I'm too old and no longer youthful"

| Point | be over the hill 언덕의 정점을 넘어갔다는 말로 전성기가 지났다, 한물갔다

A: Why aren't you going to run in the marathon?
왜 마라톤을 뛰지 않을거야?

B: **I'm over the hill.** I don't have the energy to run in a race anymore. 나 한물갔어. 더 이상 뛸 수 있는 힘이 없어.

It'd better to be over the hill than buried under it. 완전히 매장되는 것보다는 한물가는게 낫지.

I can't hike with you. I'm over the hill.
난 너랑 등산을 못해. 난 한물갔어.

I'm over the hill. I don't even have sex anymore. 난 한물갔어. 이제 더 이상 섹스조차도 못해.

015 It's gonna put your life on the line 네 생명이 위태롭게 될거야

미드표현

this is a way of saying "You may get killed." When a person puts his life on the line, he does something risky and might get killed

| Point | put sth on the line …을 위태롭게 하다
put oneself[one's neck] on the line (for sb)
(…를 위해) 위험을 감수하다
be on the line[at stake] …가 위태롭게 되다

A: Don't go to Afghanistan. **It's going to put your life on the line.** 아프가니스탄에 가지마. 생명이 위태로와.

B: I don't think it is as dangerous as it seems on the news. 뉴스에 나오는 것처럼 그렇게 위험하지 않은 것 같아.

You put your career on the line.
넌 직장경력을 위태롭게 했어

We put our necks on the line to try to find you. 우린 널 찾기 위해 위험을 감수했어

My reputation is at stake[on the line].
내 명성이 위기에 처해있어

016 It's my ass on the line 내가 큰일나, 잘못되면 내가 다쳐

미드표현

this is a way to say "I'll have trouble if anything goes wrong." The speaker feels that he will be responsible for any problems

| Point | be one's ass on the line …가 위태로와지다
put one's ass on the line …을 위태롭게 하다

A: Why won't you let me into the movie for free?
왜 영화를 공짜로 못 보여주는거야?

B: **It's my ass on the line** if my boss finds out I did that. 사장이 그걸 알아차리면 내가 큰 일나.

That's easy for you to say. It isn't your ass on the line. 너야 말하기 쉽지. 네가 위태로운 건 아니잖아.

You can joke all you want. It's your ass on the line. 맘대로 비웃어. 위태로운 건 너잖아.

Your ass is on the line here, Jane.
네 상황이 어렵게 됐어, 제인.

017 He's gonna ride my ass for the rest of my life

걘 평생 날 힘들게 할거야

this expresses that someone has been bothering the speaker, possibly a policeman who thinks he has committed a crime. The speaker believes the person will continue to bother him throughout his life. It is like saying "He is going to try to cause trouble for me forever"

| Point | ride sb's ass …을 힘들게 하다, 계속 비난을 하다

A: That cop is sure you committed the murder.
저 경찰은 네가 살인을 저질렀다고 확신하고 있어.

B: **He's going to ride my ass for the rest of my life.** 평생 날 힘들게 하겠네.

미드표현

She quit because her boss always rode her ass. 걔는 사장이 늘상 괴롭혀서 그만뒀어.

If you try to ride my ass, I'll hit you.
나를 힘들게 하려고 하면 널 때릴거야.

I think if I were your boss and had to ride your ass every day, you would come home seething with resentment.
만약 내가 네 사장이고 너를 매일 괴롭힌다면 넌 분해서 속이 끓어오른채로 집에 오게 될거라고 생각해.

018 I'm under a lot of pressure

스트레스를 많이 받고 있어, 부담을 많이 느껴

this expresses that "I'm feeling very stressed." Usually people have this afeeling when they have a lot of extra work to do.

| Point | put (a lot of) pressure on~ …에 (많은) 압력을 가하다, 부담을 주다
I'm under the gun 스트레스[압력]에 시달리고 있어

A: **I'm under a lot of pressure** at work.
스트레스를 많이 받고 있어.

B: Oh? Do you have to work on an important project? 그래? 중요한 일을 해야 되는거야?

미드표현

We're under a lot of pressure.
우리는 많은 스트레스를 받고 있어.

I told you, I was under a lot of pressure.
내가 말했잖아, 난 많은 스트레스를 받고 있었어.

I realize you've been under a lot of pressure these past few hours.
지난 몇시간동안 네가 극심한 스트레스를 받고 있었다는 것을 알게 되었어.

019 (It) Couldn't have been easy

(네게) 쉽지 않았을거야

this expresses that "It must've been hard for you." The speaker thinks a person had a hard time with something

| Point | It hasn't been easy 쉽지 않았어
Things haven't been easy 성공했지만 쉽지 않았어

A: How did John become so rich? 어떻게 존이 부자가 됐어?

B: I don't know. **It couldn't have been easy** though. 몰라. 그래도 쉽지는 않았을거야.

미드표현

It must've been hard, trying to keep the family together. Couldn't have been easy.
가족생계를 유지하는데 어려웠을거야. 쉽지 않았을거야.

That certainly could not have been easy for her. 걔한테 분명 쉽지 않았을거야.

020 That's tricky

보기보다 어려워, 까다로와

often this is a way of saying something is difficult, or it's not as easy as it appears to be. It is a way of warning someone that they should be prepared for something that takes effort. A similar way to say this would be "This will be more complicated than you expect"

| Point | That's tricky 어렵네, 까다로와
It's a little tricky 그건 좀 어렵네

A: I need to change my cell phone number.
내 핸드폰 번호를 바꿔야겠어.

B: **That's tricky.** You need to call the cell phone company. 까다로울걸. 통신회사에 전화해야 돼.

미드표현

Diagnosing rape in older females is tricky.
나이든 여자의 강간여부를 진단하는 것은 까다로와.

That's our hope, but the brain's tricky. You never know.
그게 우리의 희망이지만 뇌는 까다로와서 어떻게 될지 모르는거야.

I know it's tricky to keep this a secret.
이걸 비밀로 하는 것은 좀 힘들다는 것을 알아.

Victoria warned me you were a little tricky.
빅토리아가 경고했는데 네가 좀 사기꾼 같대.

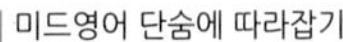

021 He's off the hook 걘 무사히 넘어갔어, 걘 무사해, (상황을) 무사히 넘겼어

this is a way to say "He won't be responsible for that." Often this is used when someone is not punished for something bad that was done

| Point | be off the hook 곤란한 상황을 벗어나다, 무사히 넘기다
get[take] sb off the hook …을 어려운 상황에서 구해주다

A: Did you hear that OJ was arrested again?
OJ 심슨이 다시 체포된 것 들었어?

B: Yeah, I heard. But **he's off the hook** now.
어, 들었어. 하지만 지금은 무사해.

미드표현

You're off the hook. Just as long as nobody finds out about this. 넌 무사해. 아무도 이것을 모르는 한.

Let him off the hook. Show a little kindness.
걜 좀 봐줘. 친절을 좀 베풀라고.

I'm dealing with a lot of things today. My phone has been ringing off the hook.
오늘 많은 일을 하고 있어. 전화가 끊임없이 왔어.

022 She is out of the woods 이제 어려운 고비는 넘겼어

this means "It is not dangerous for her anymore." This is said most often when someone has been very sick, and then that person starts to get well

| Point | be out of the woods 위기를 넘기다, 위험을 벗어나다

A: Tracey was really sick last week.
트레이시는 지난 주에 정말 아팠어.

B: I think **she is out of the woods** now.
지금은 힘든 상황은 넘긴 것 같아.

미드표현

She's not out of the woods yet.
걔는 아직 어려운 고비를 넘기지 못했어.

You survived the surgery, but you're not nearly out of the woods.
수술은 성공적으로 끝났지만 넌 아직 고비를 넘긴 것은 아냐.

It looks like he's out of the woods.
걔가 어려운 고비를 넘긴 것 같아.

023 I don't want to leave you high and dry

네가 힘든데 모른 척하기 싫어

the speaker is indicating he doesn't want to leave his friend when his friend has troubles. It is like saying "I don't want to abandon you"

| Point | leave sb high and dry …을 어려운 처지에 남겨놓다
hold the bag 책임을 혼자 뒤집어쓰다
leave sb holding the bag …에게 책임을 다 지우다, 죄를 뒤집어 씌우다

A: You don't have to help me with this work.
네가 이 일을 도와주지 않아도 돼.

B: **I don't want to leave you high and dry.**
네가 힘든데 모른 척하기 싫어.

미드표현

I feel like I'm leaving you high and dry.
너 힘든데 남겨놓는 것 같아.

You're the one who left me high and dry.
힘든 나를 버려둔 사람은 바로 너야.

Some people might say you're leaving her high and dry.
일부 사람들은 네가 그녀를 어려운 처지에 남겨두었다고 말할 지도 몰라.

024 If worse[worst] comes to worst

최악의 경우라 해도, 아무리 어려워도

this is usually said when someone is thinking of a situation that is very bad. It is like saying "If things become really terrible..."

A: What will you do if a hurricane comes?
허리케인이 오면 넌 어떻게 할거야?

B: **If worst comes to worst,** I'll go stay at my parents' house. 최악의 경우라도 부모님집에서 머물거야.

If worst comes to worst, I'll be your boyfriend.
최악의 경우라 해도 난 네 애인일거야.

If worse comes to worst, you can always hide under the bed. 최악의 경우라 해도 넌 항상 침대 밑에 숨으면 돼.

025 That was a close call 하마터면 큰일날 뻔했네, 위험천만이었어, 굉장히 위험했어

this is used to say "Something bad almost happened." The speaker is happy because he avoided the bad thing

| Point | That was close 아슬아슬했어
Saved by the bell 가까스로 위기를 면했어

A: I thought that policeman was going to give you a ticket. 경찰이 교통위반 딱지를 끊을 거라 생각했어.

B: Me too. **That was a close call.**
나도 그랬는데. 하마터면 큰일날 뻔했네.

It was a close call, but I managed to cover.
위험천만이었지만 내가 겨우 막았어.

Oh, my God, that was close. 맙소사, 아슬아슬했어.

After a close call, she came to her senses and told the man it was over.
큰일날 뻔 했지만 걔는 정신을 차리고 그 남자에게 이젠 끝이라고 말했어.

026 I can ride it out (어려움을) 이겨낼 수 있어

usually this means the speaker will survive some difficult situation. Another way to say it is "It is difficult for me, but I will be OK"

| Point | ride sth out 힘든 상황 등을 견디다, 이겨내다
ride the storm out (곤경) 용감히 맞서다

A: You have been having money problems, right?
너 돈 문제 겪고 있지, 맞지?

B: Yes I have. But I can **ride it out.** 그렇지만 이겨낼 수 있어.

It will be difficult, but I can ride it out.
그게 어렵겠지만 난 이겨 낼 수 있어.

Our business has been doing poorly, but I can ride it out. 우리 사업이 요즘 힘들지만 난 이겨낼 수 있어.

I can ride it out. Don't worry about me.
난 이겨낼 수 있어. 내 걱정마.

027 I can rise to the occasion 난 힘든 상황을 견뎌낼 수 있어

here the speaker is indicating "I can be tough if there is a tough situation." It is a way to say he is strong when it is needed

| Point | rise to the occasion [challenge]
어려움에 직면해 더 열심히 해 잘 이겨내다
You can pull through this 넌 잘 견뎌낼거야, 이겨낼거야

A: Will you be able to work overtime when we have a big job? 아주 중요한 일을 하게 되면 야근할 수 있어?

B: Of course I will. **I can rise to the occasion.**
물론 할 수 있죠. 힘들어도 견뎌낼 수 있어요.

He didn't rise to the occasion.
걘 힘든 상황을 이겨내지 못했어.

I can't seem to rise to the occasion.
이 어려운 상황을 못 벗어날 것 같아.

Neil! Now you're gonna rise to the occasion, son. 닐! 아들아, 이제 넌 어려운 상황을 견뎌낼거야.

028 Something's been nagging me 뭔가 날 성가시게 해

this is usually said when someone has been thinking about something a lot. It is like saying "I've really been bothered by this"

| Point | nag sb 괴롭히다, 성가시게 하다

A: **Something's been nagging me** lately.
최근에 뭔가가 날 힘들게 해.

B: Do you want to talk it over together?
함께 그 얘기 나누어 볼래?

Something's been nagging me. I wanted to talk to you about it.
날 성가시게 하는 게 뭐 있는데 너하고 그 얘기를 해보고 싶었어.

She nagged you? 걔가 널 귀찮게 해?

The question nagged me for days.
그 문제 때문에 며칠간 힘들었어.

029 Why (do you) put me through this?

왜 이렇게 힘들게 하는거야?

미드표현

the speaker is asking why someone is making his life hard. He is saying "You are making my life much more difficult"

| Point | put sb through 어려움을 겪게 하다
put sb through (a school) …의 학비를 대다

A: **Why do you put me through this?**
왜 날 이렇게 힘들게 하는거야?

B: I'm not trying to make things difficult.
힘들게 하려는 게 아니야.

You put me through a lot, too, James, but I forgave you. 제임스, 넌 날 참 많이 힘들게 했지만 널 용서했었어.

I didn't mean to put you through this. I didn't mean to hurt you.
이런 어려움을 겪게 하려는 게 아니었어. 너에게 상처 줄 의도가 아니었어.

My sister will put me through medical school.
내 누이가 내 의과대학 비용을 댈거야.

030 It's such a (real) hassle

성가신 일이야, 힘든 일이야

미드표현

this is commonly used to say "It's difficult to do." Often this refers to a task that people don't like to do

| Point | real hassle 정말 성가신 일

A: Is it easy to get your driver's license?
운전면허를 따는게 쉬워?

B: No, it's not. **It's such a hassle.**
아니, 그렇지 않아. 아주 성가신 일이야.

I thought it would be cool, but it's a bit of a hassle. 난 그게 괜찮다고 생각했지만 좀 성가시네.

If the divorce wasn't a hassle, would you still have gotten back together with her?
이혼이 힘든 일이 아니었다면, 네가 그녀와 다시 합쳤을까?

031 My boss is breathing down my neck

상사가 날 너무 철저히 감시해

미드표현

usually this means a worker is complaining that his boss is watching him too closely. It is similar to saying "He's always checking to see if I've made mistakes"

| Point | breathe down one's neck 바짝 뒤따르다, 철저히 감시하다, 못살게 굴다

A: Tom, you look really unhappy these days.
탐, 너 요즘 정말 우울해 보여.

B: **My boss is breathing down my neck at work.**
사장이 사무실에서 깐깐하게 굴어.

We can't meet up. My boss is breathing down my neck. 우리는 만날 수 없어. 상사가 너무 깐깐하게 굴어.

I'm stressed because my boss is breathing down my neck. 상사가 너무 깐깐해서 스트레스를 받아.

My boss is breathing down my neck. He wants to fire me.
상사가 너무 깐깐하게 굴어. 날 해고하고 싶어해.

032 If anything happens

무슨 일이 생기면, 만일의 사태가 생기면

미드표현

this is often said when someone is worried that an unexpected event will occur. It is a way to say "If something unusual or bad occurs..."

| Point | if anything happens to~ …에게 무슨 일이 생기면

A: I heard you're taking a long airplane flight tomorrow. 내일 장거리 비행 한다며.

B: Right. **If anything happens,** please take care of my kids. 맞아. 무슨 일이 생기면 내 애들 좀 보살펴줘.

If anything happens to him, I swear to God you are never gonna see me again.
걔한테 무슨 일이 생기면 맹세코 넌 날 다시 못 볼 줄 알아.

Now I've warned you. If anything happens to her, you're dead. 충고하는데, 걔한테 무슨 일이 생기면 넌 죽어.

033 I got nothing to show for it 뭐 보여줄 게 없어, 아무런 성과가 없어

when this is said, it means the speaker worked or put effort into doing something, but received no payment or reward for that work. It expresses disappointment, because everyone wants to be paid for working. In other words, "I did the work but got nothing in return"

I Point I have nothing to show for~ 보여줄 성과가 없다
There's nothing to show for ~ 보여줄 게 없다

A: So you retired after working for forty years?
그래 40년간 일한 후에 퇴직하는거야?

B: Yeah, it was a long time but **I've got nothing to show for it.** 어, 긴 세월인데 아무런 성과가 없네.

미드표현

There's nothing to show for all of your effort.
네가 기울인 노력의 결과를 보여줄게 없어.

Nothing! I've got nothing to show for all of this. 아무 것도 없어! 이 모든 것에 대해 보여줄 성과가 하나도 없어.

I've been out here for, like, ten years. I've nothing to show for it.
난 저기 10년간 여기에 있었지만 아무런 성과를 보여주지 못했어.

034 There's always a catch 뭔가 항상 있단말야

when this is said, we can understand the speaker means there is always a hidden cost to everything, and it will be more difficult to do something than expected. A catch refers to the extra cost or difficulty in doing something. It is like saying "There will be more work involved than you think"

I Point I There's always a catch 항상 단점이 있기 마련이야, 항상 뭔가 있기 마련이야

A: Do you think we'll be able to go and collect the money you're owed?
네가 빌려준 돈 우리가 가서 받아올 수 있을 것 같아?

B: Maybe, but **there's always a catch** when dealing with money.
그럴 수도 있지만 돈 문제는 항상 뭔가 문제가 있단 말야.

미드표현

Damn, there's always a catch.
젠장, 항상 뭔가 문제가 있단 말야.

I assume there was a catch? 뭔가 어려운 점이 있겠지?

He's a fantastic boyfriend, really, quite a catch.
걔는 끝내주는 남친이야, 정말 놓쳐서는 안되는 사람이야.

035 I wanna get it out of the way 난 그 문제를 해결하고 싶어

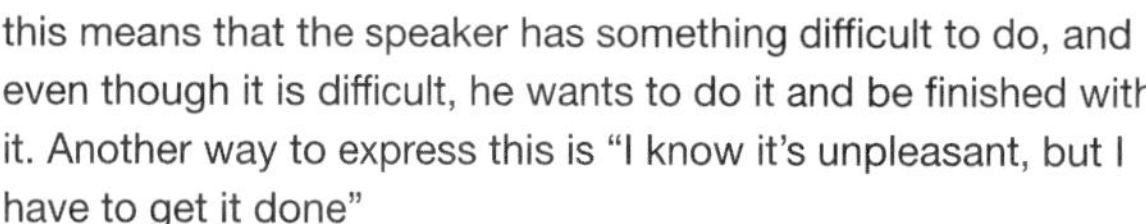

this means that the speaker has something difficult to do, and even though it is difficult, he wants to do it and be finished with it. Another way to express this is "I know it's unpleasant, but I have to get it done"

I Point I get it out of the way (어려운 문제를) 해결하다, 해치우다
get sb out of the way (방해가 되니) 없애다, 빼다

A: I hear that your divorce is happening soon.
너 곧 이혼할거라며.

B: **I want to get it out of the way.** 난 빨리 해치우고 싶어.

미드표현

I'm not gonna be able to relax until I get this out of the way.
내가 이 문제를 해결하기 전에는 쉴 수가 없을거야.

I'm a lawyer, let's just get that out of the way.
난 변호사야, 자 저 문제를 해치우자.

Get him out of the way so I can get her.
걔를 좀 없애봐, 내가 그녀를 갖게.

Or was it your plan all along just to get me out of the way? 그게 나를 제외하기 위한 계획이었던거야?

036 It's a snap 그거 쉬워

this is said when the speaker wants to tell someone that something is very easy to do. Usually it means that it takes very little skill and can be done quickly. In other words, the speaker is saying "Almost anyone will be successful if they try to do this"

I Point I be a snap 매우 쉽다

A: Was it difficult to apply for a visa? 비자 신청하는게 어려웠어?

B: **It's a snap.** Just go to the embassy. 쉬워, 대사관에 가기만 하면 돼.

미드표현

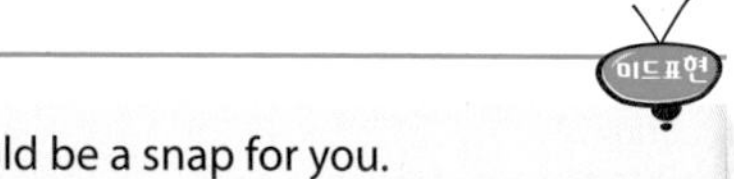

This should be a snap for you.
이거 너한테는 아주 쉬울거야.

Some will be a snap, but there are a few tricky ones. 일부는 아주 쉽겠지만 몇몇은 까다로울거야.

You already know the house. Decorating, planning - it's gonna be a snap for you.
넌 이미 집에 대해서 알고 있어, 집을 장식하고 계획하는 것은 네게 쉬운 일일거야.

MEMO

Ways to talk about something that is possible, or things (un) lucky

운이 들어오고 기회가 찾아오고

I will take my chances

001 That's (just) the way it is 원래 다 그런거야, 다 그런 거지 뭐

this expresses that a situation can't be changed. It is like saying "You can't do anything to change it"

| Point | That's life 그런 게 인생이지
Such is life! 인생이란 그런 것이야!
That's just the facts of life 그게 현실[인생]이야

A: Why is our salary so low here?
왜 여기 급여가 이렇게 적은거야?

B: **That's the way it is.** Some other companies pay more. 다 그런 거지 뭐. 다른 일부 회사들은 더 줘.

I don't know, but it's just the way it is.
잘 모르겠지만 다 그런거지 뭐.

But whether you asked for it or not, that's the way it is.
하지만 네가 그걸 자초했는지 여부를 떠나 원래 다 그런거야.

Why can't you just be satisfied with the way it is? 너 왜 현실을 있는 그대로 만족할 수 없는거야?

002 That's the way the cookie crumbles 사는 게 다 그런 거지

미드표현

this is said to indicate "Sometimes bad things happen like that." Often it is said to indicate that everyone has bad luck at times in life

| Point | That's the way the ball bounces 인생이란 그런거야
That's the way the mop flops 다 그런 거지

A: My girlfriend broke up with me this weekend.
여친하고 이번 주말에 헤어졌어.

B: Sorry to hear that. **That's the way the cookie crumbles.** 안됐구만. 사는 게 다 그렇지 뭐.

You screw up our lives and the best you can do is, that's the way the cookie crumbles?
우리 인생을 망치고 고작하는 말이 인생이 그런거지 라고?

003 When did this fall into your lap? 그게 언제 너한테 굴러 들어온거야?

미드표현

this is a fairly simple way to ask the listener about something that he unexpectedly received. When something falls into someone's lap, it is like getting something good for free, so it is a positive experience. It is somewhat similar to asking "When were you given that?"

| Point | sth fall into sb's lap …가 …에 굴러들어오다

A: The boss said that he is sending me to Hawaii for two weeks. 사장이 2주간 하와이로 날 파견한다고 그랬어.

B: You are so lucky. **When did this fall into your lap?** 너 운도 좋다. 언제 그걸 알게 된거야?

These opportunities fell into Anna's lap.
이 기회들이 애나에게 굴러 들어왔어.

A perfect guy is going to fall into your lap.
한 완벽한 사람이 네게 굴러 들어올거야.

It's everyone's fantasy -- winning the lottery -- untold millions falling into your lap overnight.
모든 이의 환상이지. 로또에 당첨되는거, 하룻밤 사이에 엄청난 양의 돈이 굴러 들어오는거.

004 Shit happens (살다보면) 재수없는 일도 생기는 법이야, 똥 밟을 때도 있는 거지

this is kind of a rude phrase. It is expressing that "Sometimes things happen in life that we can't control"

A: This morning my car broke down on the way to work. 오늘 아침에 출근 길에 차가 고장났어.

B: **Shit happens.** You need to get it fixed soon.
그런 일도 있는 거지 뭐. 빨리 수리해.

My car is damaged, but shit happens.
차가 박살났지만 어쩌겠어.

Shit happens. Let me be here for you.
재수없는 일도 있는 거지. 내가 옆에 있어 줄게.

A: Shit happens, huh? B: I mean, I'm sorry, but I had to do it.
A: 재수없는 일도 있는거라고, 어? B: 내 말은, 미안하지만 나 그래야만 했다고.

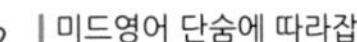

005 Easier said than done 말이야 쉽지

this is usually said when someone suggests something. It is a way to say "It is simple to say that, but much harder to really do it"

| Point | (That's) Easier said than done (그야) 말은 쉽지

A: I want to become rich by the time I'm 40.
마흔 살 때까지는 부자가 되고 싶어.

B: That is **easier said than done.** 말이야 쉽지.

A: You do what's best for you. B: Easier said than done. A: 너에게 좋은 것만 해. B: 말이야 쉽지.

Getting rich is easier said than done.
부자가 된다는 건 말이야 쉽지.

You want a girlfriend? Easier said than done.
여친을 원한다고? 말이야 쉽지.

That will be tricky. It's easier said than done.
그건 어려울거야. 말이야 쉽지.

006 Good things come in small packages
행운은 작은 일에서 시작돼

the speaker wants to say that although something seems small, it may be very important. It expresses that "Sometimes small things are very important"

| Point | Good things come to him[those] who waits
기다리는 사람에겐 복이 내린다

A: These chocolate drops were delicious.
이 초콜릿들은 정말 맛있었어.

B: **Good things come in small packages.**
행운은 원래 작은 일에서 시작되지.

You know what they say. Good things come in small packages.
사람들이 뭐라는지 알지. 좋은 일은 작은 일에서 시작되는거야.

I guess good things don't always come in small packages.
좋은 일이 꼭 작은 일에서부터 시작되는 것 같지는 않아.

Wow, my mama always told me big things come in small packages.
와, 우리 엄마는 항상 큰 일은 작은 일에서부터 시작된다고 하셨어.

007 Rules are rules 규칙은 규칙이니까요

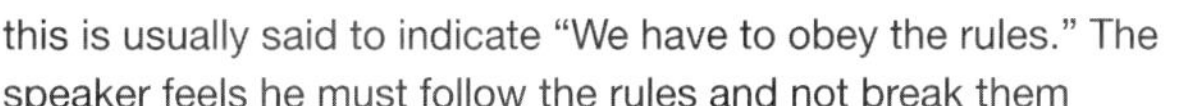

this is usually said to indicate "We have to obey the rules." The speaker feels he must follow the rules and not break them

A: Can I skip the final exam? 기말고사를 안 봐도 돼요?

B: No, you must take it. **Rules are rules.**
안돼. 꼭 봐야 돼. 규칙은 규칙이다.

I'm sorry, I can't help you. See? Rules are rules.
미안, 도와줄 수가 없어. 규칙은 규칙이니까.

Mr. Gill, rules are rules. When you're late, you forfeit the right to take the test.
길씨, 규칙은 규칙입니다. 지각하면, 시험 칠 기회를 잃는거죠.

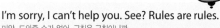

008 You get what you pay for 땀을 흘린 만큼 얻는거야, 지불한 만큼 받아

this is usually said to mean "If you buy something cheaply, it will break easily." In other words, if you want good quality, you need to spend money

| Point | pay for 지불하다

A: The umbrella I bought on the subway broke.
지하철에서 산 우산이 망가졌어.

B: It figures. **You get what you pay for.**
그럴 줄 알았어. 지불한 만큼 받는다니까.

We need to pay more for higher quality because you get what you pay for.
주는 만큼 얻는 것이기 때문에 좋은 품질에는 더 많은 돈을 지불해야 돼.

My old car breaks all the time. I guess you get what you pay for.
내 중고차가 늘상 고장 나. 싼게 비지떡인 것 같아.

009 Live and let live 자신이 알아서 살겠지, 걔네들도 살아야지, 그렇게 살게 냅둬

often this is a way to say "People are free to live their own way, and I am free to live the way I choose." The speaker means he doesn't bother anyone and he doesn't want anyone to bother him

| Point | live and let die 살 때 행복하게 살고 죽을 때 죽자

A: I hate looking at snakes. 뱀을 쳐다보는 게 싫어.

B: **Live and let live.** Don't bother them.
그렇게 살게 놔둬. 방해하지 마.

I don't agree with gay marriage, but I live and let live. 동성결혼에 동의하지 않지만 걔네들도 살아야지 뭐.

You should live and let live when dealing with other cultures.
다른 문화를 상대할 때는 그들만의 것을 인정해야 돼.

010 Look on the bright side 긍정적으로 생각해

this is a very optimistic way to talk. It means "Think about the good things, not the bad things"

A: I can't seem to save any money these days.
요즘 돈을 거의 저축 못하는 것 같아.

B: **Look on the bright side.** At least you're healthy. 긍정적으로 생각해. 적어도 건강하잖아.

Look on the bright side, Peter's having the time of his life.
긍정적으로 생각해야지. 피터는 인생의 황금기를 보내고 있어.

Look on the bright side. At least we're still rich. 긍정적으로 생각해. 적어도 우리는 부자잖아.

Look on the bright side: You're still alive.
긍정적으로 생각하자고. 넌 아직 살아있잖아.

011 What's done is done 이미 끝난 일이야, 이미 엎질러진 물인데

this indicates "It's finished and you can't change it" It is said when something can't be changed at all

| Point | When it's through it's through 끝난 건 끝난거야

A: I really miss being with my ex-wife.
예전 아내와 함께 있는 게 정말 그리워.

B: You're divorced now. **What's done is done.**
이젠 이혼했잖아. 이미 끝난 일이야.

I know I shouldn't have hit him, but what's done is done.
걔를 치지 않았어야 된다는 것을 알지만 이미 엎질러진 물인데.

I'm sorry, but what's done is done.
미안하지만 이미 끝난 일이야.

012 Actions speak louder than words
말보다 행동이 중요해, 백 번 말하는 것보다 한번 행동하는 게 나아

the speaker is saying "Don't just talk, do something." This expresses that it is very important to do more than just talking about something

A: I really love and respect my parents.
난 정말이지 부모님을 사랑하고 존경해.

B: Buy them a gift. **Actions speak louder than words.** 선물을 사드려. 말보다 행동이 중요하지.

If you make a promise, actions speak louder than words. 네가 약속을 하게 되면 말보다는 행동이 중요해.

Actions speak louder than words. You know that. 말보다는 행동이 중요해. 너 알고 있잖아.

In all relationships, actions speak louder than words. 모든 관계에서, 말보다는 행동이 중요해.

013 I'll take my chances 위험부담을 감수하겠어, 모험을 해보겠어

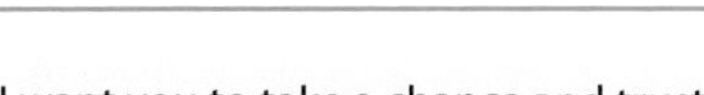

this means "There is a risk but I'll take it." A person says this when he accepts the fact there will be some danger

| Point | take a chance (to~) (…하는) 위험 부담을 감수하다
We'll catch a break 우리에게도 기회가 오겠지

A: I don't think traveling to Africa is a good idea.
아프리카 여행가는 게 좋은 생각 같지 않아.

B: I still want to go. **I'll take my chances.**
그래도 가고 싶어. 모험을 감수할거야.

미드표현

I want you to take a chance and trust me.
운명에 맡기고 날 믿었으면 해.

He will take any chances. 그 녀석 별 짓을 다 할거다.

I'll take my chances with Jimmy.
지미를 만날 기회를 잡을게.

014 I'll give you another chance 한 번 더 기회를 주지

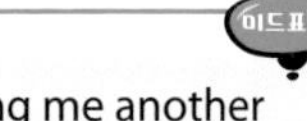

this means someone can try to do something again after failing the first time. It is like saying "You can try again"

| Point | give sb another chance …에게 기회를 한번 더 주다

A: Please don't fire me from this job.
제발 저를 내쫓지 말아주세요.

B: **I'll give you another chance.** But only one time. 한 번 더 기회를 주지. 하지만 딱 한번 만이야.

미드표현

I thank you so much for giving me another chance. 한번 더 기회를 줘서 고마워.

You got to give me another chance.
한 번만 기회를 더 줘.

I've got to give my marriage another chance.
결혼생활 다시 한번 해봐야겠어.

015 Any chance you know where he is? 걔가 어디 있는지 알아?

this is asking "Do you know his location?" The speaker wants to find someone

| Point | Any chance S+V? 혹시 …해?
There is a good chance that S+V …할 가능성은 충분해

A: Bob arrived about an hour ago. 밥이 한시간 전에 왔어.

B: **Any chance you know where he is?**
걔가 어디 있는지 알아?

미드표현

Any chance we can get that little lady to be quiet? 저 아가씨 좀 조용히 시킬 수 있을까?

Any chance you guys found the murder weapon? 너희들 혹 범행도구 발견했어?

There is a good chance you will fail.
실패할 가능성도 있는거야.

016 Chances are he's gonna do this 걔가 아마 그렇게 할거야

this indicates the speaker thinks someone will take some action. He is saying "I think he'll do it"

| Point | Chances are S+V 아마 …일거야
Chances are slim 가능성이 희박하지

A: What will Ray do during the school break?
레이가 학교 쉬는 날에 뭘 할까?

B: **Chances are** he's going to do the report for history class. 역사수업 레포트를 작성할 것 같아.

미드표현

So my chances are the same.
그럼 내 승산도 마찬가지구만.

Chances are my boss will be here without his wife. 사장은 부인없이 혼자 올거야.

Chances are that's our killer.
저 놈이 아마 우리가 찾는 범인일거야.

017 Just try me 나한테 한번 (얘기) 해봐, 기회를 한번 줘봐

this is often said to mean "Believe me." The speaker is telling people he is being sincere

A: Are you sure you really love me? 정말 날 사랑해?

B: **Just try me.** I'd do anything for you.
기회를 한번 줘. 널 위해 뭐든지 할게.

A: You wouldn't believe me. B: Try me.
A: 날 믿지 않을거야. B: 어서 말해봐.

She's not here. Try her at Smith, 456-1258. Don't forget the 212.
부재중이니 456-1258로 스미스에게 전화해서 걜 찾아. 212누르는 거 잊지 말고.

A: You have no idea how bad it is! B: Yeah? Try me. A: 그게 얼마나 으악인지 넌 몰라! B: 그래? 얘기해봐.

A: You're gonna be disappointed. B: Try me.
A: 넌 실망하게 될거야. B: 한번 얘기해봐.

018 It was a long shot 승산이 희박했어, 가능성이 없었어

미드표현

this expresses that someone made a guess, and the guess probably wasn't going to be correct. It is a way to say "I didn't think it was right"

Point It's a bit of a long shot 좀 가능성이 적어

A: Did you win any money from the lottery?
로또에서 돈 좀 땄어?

B: No, I didn't. **It was a long shot anyhow.**
아니, 못 땄어. 어쨌든 승산이 희박했어.

I know it's a long shot, but he might ask me out. 희박하지만 걔가 데이트 신청할지도 몰라.

Getting organs from a body is a long shot.
시신으로부터 장기를 얻는 건 가능성이 희박해.

It's probably be a long shot, but you never know! 가능성이 없을지도 모르겠지만, 누가 알겠어!

019 Eric doesn't have a prayer of passing the math exam today 에릭은 오늘 수학시험을 통과할 가능성이 없어

미드표현

this means "Eric will fail the exam." When someone doesn't have a prayer, they are going to fail

Point don't have a prayer of~ …할 가능성이 없다

A: I heard Eric chose not to study at all last night.
에릭이 지난 밤 내내 공부하지 않았다며.

B: Eric **doesn't have a prayer of** passing the math exam today. 에릭이 오늘 수학시험에 통과할 가능성이 없어.

You do not have a prayer of making the basketball team. 넌 농구팀을 만들 가능성이 전혀 없어.

Karen does not have a prayer of getting that job. 카렌은 그 일자리를 잡을 가능성이 전혀 없어.

I don't have a prayer of getting out of jail.
난 감옥에서 나올 가능성이 전혀 없어.

020 Don't pass up your chance 기회를 놓치지 마라

미드표현

this is usually said to someone who has an opportunity. It means "Try to do it because you may succeed"

Point pass up one's chance …의 기회를 놓치다
screw up one's chance …의 기회를 망치다

A: Do you think I should go to study in France?
내가 공부하러 프랑스에 가야 한다고 생각해?

B: Sure I do. **Don't pass up your chance** to see the world. 물론 그렇지. 견문을 넓힐 수 있는 기회를 놓치지마.

No one wants to pass up a chance for good luck. 아무도 좋은 기회를 놓치고 싶어하지 않아.

It sounds too good to pass up.
기회를 놓치기엔 너무 좋은데.

I screwed up your chance to see your father.
네 아버지를 만날 기회를 내가 망쳤어.

021 It's now or never 기회는 두 번 다시 오지 않을거야, 지금 아니면 안돼

this is indicating someone should take a chance right now. It is like saying "Do this or you may never be able to do it again"

A: I'd like to ask Sue to marry me. 수에게 청혼하고 싶어.

B: **It's now or never.** Go for it.
지금 아니면 기회가 없어. 어서 해봐.

We both knew it was now or never.
우리 모두 지금 아니면 안 된다는 걸 알고 있었어.

If it's now or never, we got to go.
지금 아니면 안 된다면, 가야지.

It's now or never if we want him to live.
걔가 살기를 바란다면 지금 아니면 안돼.

Make up your mind. It's now or never.
결심을 해. 지금 아니면 안돼.

022 This is a huge opportunity 엄청 좋은 기회야

the speaker here is saying "You may be very successful if you try this." Often this is used to say someone has a chance to be promoted or make much more money

| Point | give sb an opportunity to~ …에게 …할 기회를 주다
When opportunity knocks 기회가 왔을 때
Opportunity never knocks twice 기회는 두 번 찾아오지 않는다

A: My dad said I could have a job at his company.
아빠가 그러는데 내가 이 회사에 취직할 수 있을거래.

B: **This is a huge opportunity** for you to become successful. 네가 성공할 수 있는 엄청 좋은 기회야.

I just wanna thank you for this great opportunity. 이런 멋진 기회를 주셔서 고마워요.

Now I have the perfect opportunity to seduce him! 이제 걜 꼬실 완벽한 기회를 가졌어!

I'll give each of you an opportunity to argue your side. 너희 각각에서 자신의 입장을 말할 기회를 주겠어.

023 The coast is clear (두리번거리면서) 이제 안전해, 지금이 기회야

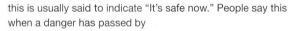

this is usually said to indicate "It's safe now." People say this when a danger has passed by

A: Are there any teachers in the hall? 복도에 선생님 계셔?

B: **The coast is clear.** You can sneak out of school now. 안전해. 이제 학교에서 빠져나와도 돼.

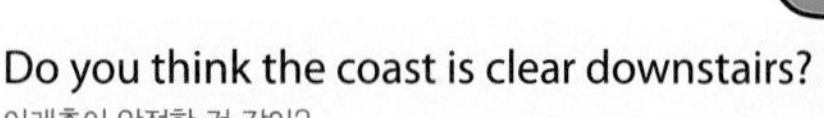

Do you think the coast is clear downstairs?
아래층이 안전한 것 같아?

The coast is clear. Let's get out of here.
지금이 기회야. 여기서 나가자고.

Let me know when the coast is clear.
안전해질 때 내게 알려줘.

The coast is clear for us to sneak away.
우리가 빠져 나가기엔 지금이 기회야.

024 You're missing out on~ …좋은 기회를 놓치고 있는거야

this is a way to tell someone "You need to do this." The idea is that if someone doesn't do something, he will feel unhappy in the future because he didn't

| Point | You really missed out! 넌 정말 좋은 기회를 놓친거야!

A: I don't like hearing classical music.
클래식 음악 듣는 걸 싫어해.

B: **You're missing out on** something beautiful.
넌 아름다운 걸 놓치는거야.

I won't be missing out on anything.
어떤 것도 놓치지 않을거야.

That is so sad. You're missing out on so much.
참 안됐어. 많은 것을 놓쳤어.

I'm missing out on a pretty sweet deal, here.
난 아주 좋은 거래를 할 기회를 놓쳤어.

025 She let it slip through her fingers 걘 기회를 놓쳤어

this expresses that someone had something of value and allowed it to be lost or go away. Usually we think of this happening because the person acted in a careless way. A different way to say this would be "She wasted that opportunity"

| Point | slip through one's fingers 놓치다, 빠져나가다, 기회를 놓치다
let~slip through one's fingers …을 놓치다

A: Jan wasted all of the money she got from her family. 잰은 집에서 물려받은 돈을 다 탕진했어.

B: I know. **She let it slip through her fingers.** 그러게나 말야. 걘 기회를 놓쳐버렸어.

I thought I had a promotion, but it slipped through my fingers.
난 승진되는 줄 알았는데 기회가 날라갔어.

Don't let this opportunity slip through your fingers. 이 기회를 놓치지 않도록 해.

The chance to earn a fortune may slip through his fingers.
많은 돈을 벌 수 있는 기회가 걔한테서 빠져나갈 지도 몰라.

The trip to Paris slipped through my fingers because I had no passport.
여권이 없어서 파리여행갈 기회가 날라가 버렸어.

026 Man, I can't catch a break 어휴, 기회를 잡을 수가 없네

this expresses that the speaker thinks he has been having a lot of bad luck in his life, and nothing good has happened to him. It is a very pessimistic sentiment. In other words, "I haven't had any good luck lately"

| Point | catch a break 기회를 잡다

A: We're going to have to let you go.
우린 너를 내보내야만 될거야.

B: You're firing me? Man, **I can't catch a break.**
나를 해고 한다고? 어휴, 난 운이 지지리도 없네.

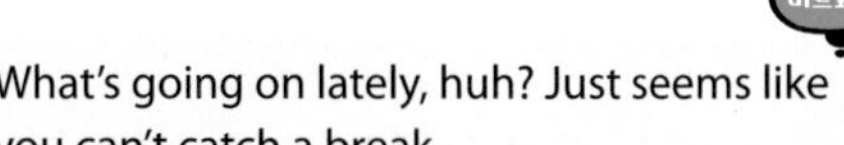

What's going on lately, huh? Just seems like you can't catch a break.
최근에 무슨 일이야? 넌 기회를 잡지 못하는 것 같아 보여.

Is this family ever gonna catch a break?
이 가족은 기회를 잡을 수나 있을까?

You'd think eventually I'd catch a break.
결국에는 내가 기회를 잡을거라 생각하고 싶겠지.

Boy, you cannot catch a break, can you?
어휴, 넌 기회를 잡지 못해, 그지?

027 Fat chance 가망이 별로 없어

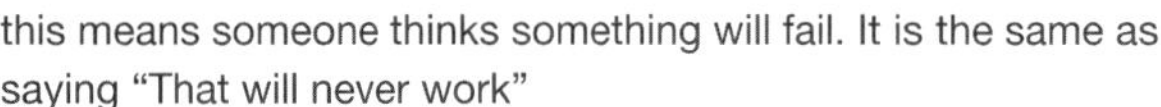

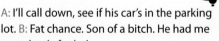

this means someone thinks something will fail. It is the same as saying "That will never work"

A: Andy says he is going to become a policeman.
앤디말로는 경찰관이 될 거래.

B: **Fat chance.** They won't let him join the police force. 가망이 별로 없어. 경찰이 뽑지 않을거야.

A: I'll call down, see if his car's in the parking lot. B: Fat chance. Son of a bitch. He had me completely fooled.
A: 걔차가 주차장에 있는지 확인해볼게. B: 가망이 없군. 개자식, 날 완전히 속였어.

You think you can leave early? Fat chance.
일찍 갈 수 있을 것 같아? 그럴 가망이 없어.

028 That's the one thing~ 그게 …하는거야

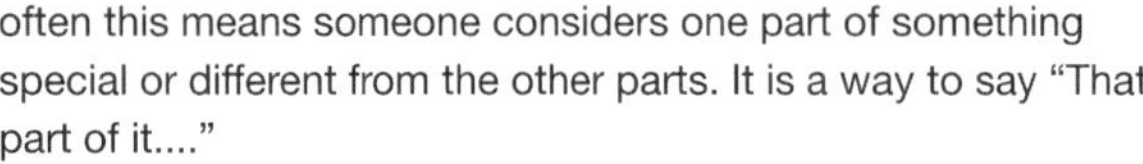

often this means someone considers one part of something special or different from the other parts. It is a way to say "That part of it...."

| Point | That's the one thing (that) S+V 그게 …하는거야
That's the one thing 그럴 수도 있다(It could happen)

A: I heard you owe a lot of money to the government. 정부에 낼 돈이 아주 많다며.

B: **That's the one thing** in my life I am worried about. 그게 내 인생에서 내가 걱정하는거야

That's the one thing that bothered me.
그게 날 괴롭혔던거야.

That's the one thing I can't do.
그게 내가 할 수 없는거야.

That's the one thing about Susan that you must never forget. She is a liar.
그게 네가 절대 수잔에 대해 잊어서는 안 되는거야. 걘 거짓말쟁이야.

029 It's a toss-up 가능성이 반반이야, 예측불허야

this means two things are almost equal. It indicates "They are both very similar"

| Point | toss-up은 앞면(heads)과 뒷면(tails)이 나올 확률이 반반인 동전던지기를 뜻함.
Chances are even = It's fifty-fifty = It's a flip of the coin = It's still up in the air

A: Would you like a sandwich or cereal?
샌드위치 먹을래 아니면 시리얼 먹을래?

B: **It's a toss up.** I'm not sure which I want to eat now. 반반야. 지금 뭘 먹고 싶은지 모르겠어.

It's a toss up whether to go to Tokyo or Seoul.
도쿄로 가느냐 서울로 가느냐는 예측불허야.

It's a toss up who is the better marathon runner. 둘 중 누가 더 훌륭한 마라토너인지 막상막하야.

It's a toss up between the top two contestants. 상위 두 명 경쟁자 사이의 가능성은 반반이야.

030 What are the odds? 가능성은 어때?, 확률이 얼마야?

this speaker is indicating that he is either trying to understand if something will happen, or that he is surprised something happened. It is like saying "I wonder if that will happen or "it's unusual that happened"

| Point | What are the odds S+V[of sth]? …의 가능성은 어때?
What are the odds of sb ~ing? …가 …할 가능성은 어때?

A: Did you hear that Rob won the marathon?
랍이 마라톤에서 우승했다는 거 들었어?

B: But he is so slow. **What are the odds of** him winning? 하지만 걔 무척 느린데. 걔가 우승할 확률이 어떤데?

Oh, man. What're the odds of that happening? 오, 맙소사. 일이 이렇게 겹칠 수가 있어?

What were the odds that you were actually a doctor? 네가 의사였을 가능성은 어땠어?

What are the odds of getting out of this?
이거에서 벗어날 수 있는 기회는 어때?

Give me a percentage. What are the odds of this thing working?
퍼센트로 말해봐. 이 일이 돌아갈 가능성은 어떻게 돼?

031 Lucky for you 다행이야, 잘됐네

미드표현

this is saying that a person had something nice happen. It is similar to saying "It was great that happened"

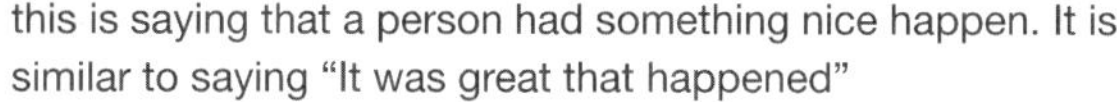

A: This exercise helped me lose weight.
이 운동을 하니까 살이 빠졌어.

B: **Lucky for you.** You look very healthy.
다행이야. 매우 건강해보여.

Then lucky for you, I'm a neurologist.
그럼 너한테 잘 됐네. 난 신경과 전문의야.

Lucky for you I'm in a good mood.
너한테 다행이다, 내가 기분이 좋은 상태거든.

Lucky for you, I know where you can find a little extra.
잘됐다. 난 네가 추가적인 것을 좀 더 어디서 찾아야 하는지 알고 있어.

A: My baby is sick. B: Well, lucky for her, her father's a doctor.
A: 내 아이가 아파. B: 다행이네, 걔 아버지가 의사야.

032 Good luck to you 행운을 빌어, 다 잘 될거야

미드표현

this expresses the hope that things will be good for someone. It's a way to say "I hope your future is good"

| Point | I wish you good luck 행운을 빌어
Good luck with that 행운이 있기를
Good luck, you'll need it 행운을 빌어, 행운이 필요할거야
Break a leg! 행운을 빌어!

A: I'm leaving on a long trip tomorrow. 내일 장거리 여행 가.

B: Really? **Good luck to you.** 정말? 행운을 빌어.

Good luck with everything. 만사 행운 가득하기를.

Best of luck with the wedding. 결혼식 잘 되기를 바래.

But good luck arguing that in court.
법정다툼에서 잘 되기를 빌어.

033 Don't push your luck! 너무 행운을 믿지마!, 너무 설치지마!

this means "If you continue, things may become bad for you." It indicates that a person is doing something risky

| Point | push[press] one's luck 운을 과신하다, 너무 설쳐대다
I don't mean to press my luck, but~
내가 계속 운이 좋을 거라고 생각하는 건 아니지만

A: Maybe I should try to win more money at this casino. 아마 이 카지노에서 돈을 더 많이 따봐야겠어.

B: **Don't push your luck.** Let's go home now.
너무 설치지말고 집에 가자.

미드표현

Don't push your luck. People are getting angry. 너무 설쳐대지마. 사람들이 화를 내잖아.

Walk away while you are winning. Don't push your luck. 네가 이기고 있을 때 그만두라고. 너무 행운을 믿지마.

Everything is going well. Don't push your luck. 모든 일이 다 잘 될거야. 너무 설쳐대지마.

034 I'm out of luck 난 운이 없어

this is a way to say "I don't have a chance to do something." The person feels sad because he was unable to do something he wanted to

| Point | You're out of luck 넌 운이 다 됐어
My luck ran out 운이 다했어
You're SOL(shit out of luck) 넌 운이 없구나

A: Were you able to get a ticket for the concert?
콘서트 표 구할 수 있었어?

B: **I'm out of luck.** The tickets were sold out.
운이 없어. 표가 다 매진되었대.

미드표현

A: I only got 10 dollars left. B: I guess you're out of luck today.
A: 겨우 10달러 남았어. B: 네가 오늘 운이 다했나보군.

Not really good for a match. I think we're out of luck. 경기를 하기에 너무 좋지 않아. 우리가 운이 다한 것 같아.

You're out of luck. Mike's gone.
넌 운이 없네. 마이크는 가버렸는데.

035 I really lucked out 운 끝내주게 좋네

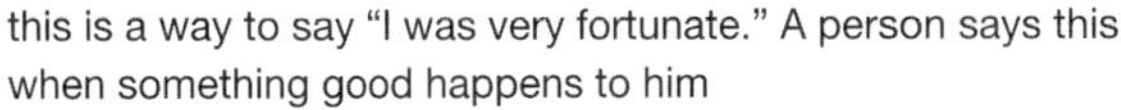

this is a way to say "I was very fortunate." A person says this when something good happens to him

| Point | luck out 운이 좋다

A: How did you buy a jacket so cheaply?
어떻게 자켓을 그렇게 싸게 샀어?

B: **I really lucked out.** The store had a sale.
운이 정말 좋았어. 가게가 세일하더라고.

미드표현

You lucked out with her. 너 걔하고의 운이 끝내주게 좋네.

Wow. You really lucked out. You have a beautiful wife and a gorgeous house.
와, 너 운이 정말 좋다. 아름다운 집과 멋진 집이 있네.

A: Patrol unit spotted it on a routine traffic stop. B: Yeah, we lucked out.
A: 경찰차가 신호등에 섰을 때 그걸 발견했어 B: 그래, 운이 좋았지

036 Tough luck 운이 없네

this expresses the feeling "That's too bad." The speaker is saying he's sorry something bad happened

| Point | Tough break! 재수 옴 붙었군!

A: I wasn't able to win the art contest.
미술 경시대회에서 우승을 못했어.

B: **Tough luck.** You should try again next year.
운이 없구만. 내년에 다시 해봐.

Tough luck. You just missed out on a good thing. 운 정말 없네. 너 좋은 기회 방금 놓쳤어.

Tough break drawing Judge Smith. Who'd ever imagine that?
스미스 판사에게 걸리다니 정말 운이 없네. 누가 상상이나 했겠어?

037 (That's) Just my luck 내가 하는 일이 뭐 그렇지, 내가 무슨 운이 있겠어

this is often said when a person has had something bad happen. It is similar to saying "I always have bad luck"

A: Jamie says he doesn't want to date you.
제이미는 너랑 데이트 원치 않는다고 해.

B: **That's just my luck.** No boys want to date me.
내가 하는 일이 그렇지. 아무도 나하고 데이트 안 하려고 해.

A: Your lower right leg bones are shattered. We need to get you into surgery. B: Oh great just my luck.
A: 오른쪽 아래 다리뼈가 부숴졌어. 곧 수술을 하죠. B: 어, 내 운이 그렇지.

I lost again. That's just my luck.
내가 또 졌어. 내가 하는 일이 그렇지 뭐.

That's just my luck. My car got towed by the cops. 내가 무슨 운이 있겠어. 경찰이 내 차를 또 견인해갔어.

She left me for another guy. That's just my luck. 걔는 날 버리고 딴 놈한테 갔어. 내 운이 그렇지 뭐.

038 Wish me luck! 행운을 빌어줘!

this speaker is asking others to "Hope I succeed." He wants them to send good wishes

| Point | The baby needs shoes 행운을 빌어줘

A: I'm going to try to get an A. **Wish me luck.**
A를 받도록 노력할거야. 행운을 빌어줘.

B: I hope you do really well on the exam.
시험 정말 잘 보기를 바래.

I'm outta here. Wish me luck. 나 갈게. 행운을 빌어줘.

A: Oh, look, wish me luck! B: What for?
A: 오, 행운을 빌어줘! B: 뭘 위해서?

A: Okay, gotta go! Wish me luck! B: Luck!
A: 그래, 가야 돼! 행운을 빌어줘 B: 잘해!

039 My fingers are crossed 행운을 빌어

a person will say this when he is wishing something will happen. He feels that "I really want this to happen"

| Point | My fingers are crossed 잘 되어야 할 텐데
keep one's fingers crossed 행운을 빌어주다

A: I hope my baseball team wins. **My fingers are crossed.** 내가 응원하는 팀이 우승하기를 바래. 행운을 빌거야.

B: They should be able to beat the other team.
상대팀을 이길거야.

Let's keep our fingers crossed and hope that it is sunny. 우리 내일 날씨가 맑도록 행운을 빌어보자.

Let's keep our fingers crossed that the right candidate wins. 올바른 당선자가 나오기를 빌자.

Well, we're gonna keep our fingers crossed for you. 우리는 네가 잘 되라고 행운을 빌어줄거야.

040 Lucky bastard! 그 놈의 자식 운도 좋네

this is often said to express envy when something good occurs to another person. The speaker means "I am jealous of what happened to him"

| Point | Lucky+sb! …가 운 좋네!
Lucky me! 나한테 다행이구만!, 나한테 잘됐네!

A: Several girls want to date Dave.
여러 명의 여자들이 데이브하고 데이트하길 바래.

B: **Lucky bastard!** I wish they wanted to date me.
자식 운도 좋구만! 걔네들이 나랑 데이트하길 바라면 좋을텐데.

Congratulations, you lucky bastard.
축하해, 이 운 좋은 놈아.

A: Hmm? Oh, I'm sorry. I was somewhere else.
B: Lucky bastard.
A: 어? 미안해, 딴생각했었어. B: 자식 운도 좋네.

Lucky bastard! I'm sorry, just tell me what happened. 자식 운도 좋네! 미안, 무슨 일인지 말해봐.

041 Better luck next time 다음엔 더 나아질거야

this is a way to say "Try again in the future." People say this to comfort someone who has failed

A: I was too tired to finish the marathon.
마라톤을 완주하기엔 너무 힘들었어.

B: That's too bad. **Better luck next time.**
정말 안됐어. 다음엔 나아질거야.

Sorry, you didn't win the lottery. Better luck next time. 안됐지만 로또에서 떨어졌어. 다음에 나아지겠지.

Better luck next time. Try studying a little harder. 다음에 더 나아지겠지. 좀 더 열심히 공부하도록 해.

We have no room available. Better luck next time. 빈방이 없어. 다음엔 더 나아지겠지.

042 Break a leg! 행운을 빌어!

미드표현

this is an old expression that actors used to say "Good luck." They said the opposite of what they wished because they were superstitious

| Point | Break a leg! = Good luck 너만 상관없다면

A: I will be acting in the school play.
학교 연극에서 역할을 맡았어.

B: That's terrific. **Break a leg!** 멋져라. 행운을 빌어!

It's your first night on stage. Break a leg!
네 첫 공연이지. 행운을 빌어!

I hope you'll do well. Break a leg! 네가 잘할거라 바래. 행운을 빌어!

Break a leg! Everyone wants you to succeed.
행운을 빌어! 다들 네가 성공하기를 바래.

043 (The) Same to you 너도

미드표현

this speaker wants to say "I hope it happens to you too." He is probably repeating the good wishes someone gave to him

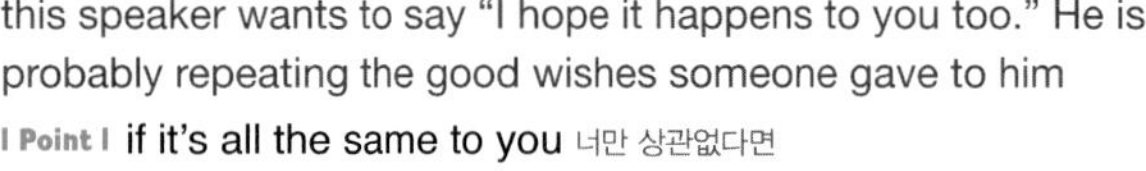

| Point | if it's all the same to you 너만 상관없다면

A: I hope you find a great job. 네가 좋은 직장을 찾길 바래.

B: **Same to you.** It won't be easy for us.
너도. 쉽지는 않을거야.

A: Hey. Good luck. B: Same to you.
A: 행운을 빌어. B: 너도.

A: Fine. Good to see you again. B: Same to you. A: 괜찮아. 널 다시 만나 기뻐. B: 너도.

Well, if it's all the same to you, I'd prefer not to. 저기, 너만 상관없다면, 난 가지 않을래.

044 Knock on wood (행운이) 계속 되길 빌어, (불행이) 그만 되길 빌어

this is said to mean "I'll knock on wood so my good luck continues." It is a very old superstition

| Point | knock on wood 지나친 행.불행의 이야기를 들었을 때 악마가 훼방을 놓지 못하도록 나무를 세 번 두드리는 것을 말함.

A: I heard you've been making a lot of money.
돈을 많이 벌었다고 들었어.

B: Yeah, business has been great, **knock on wood.** 그래, 사업이 잘 되었어. 계속 잘 되길 빌어.

I keep getting richer, knock on wood. 나 돈이 계속 쌓이네, 계속 되길 빌어.

We were lucky at the casino, knock on wood.
우리는 카지노에서 운이 좋았어, 행운이 계속되길 빌어.

I hope to get a job overseas, knock on wood.
난 해외에서 일자리를 얻기를 바래, 그렇게 되기를 빌어.

045 It was[has been] a long day 힘든 하루였어

this means "Today was more difficult than usual." It is a way of telling others the speaker feels tired

| Point | be a long day 힘든 하루다
have a long[rough] day 힘든 하루를 보내다
Rough day for you? 힘든 하루였어?

A: **It has been a long day.** I'm tired. 힘든 하루였어. 피곤해.
B: Sit down and I'll get some dinner for you.
자리에 앉아. 저녁 좀 차려줄게.

You look like you've had a long day.
오늘 하루 힘들었나 보네.

You have a long day ahead of you.
오늘 하루 힘들거야.

I'm sorry honey, I'm just having a rough day.
미안해 자기야, 힘든 하루였어.

046 I had a bad day 진짜 재수없는 날이야, 정말 운없는 하루였어

미드표현

this indicates the speaker had some problems during the day. He is saying "This day was difficult for me"

| Point | have a bad day 재수없는 날을 보내다
Bad hair day 꼬인다 꼬여, 일진이 안 좋아

A: Wow, you look kind of upset. 와, 너 좀 힘들어 보여.
B: I am. **I had a bad day.** 그래. 오늘 재수없는 날이야.

She seems to be having a bad day.
걘 안 좋은 것 같아.

Bad day at work? 직장에서 안 좋았어?

Jack's had a bad day. What happened?
잭의 일진이 안 좋았던 것 같은데. 무슨 일이야?

047 I had a big day 내겐 오늘 중요한 일이 있었어

미드표현

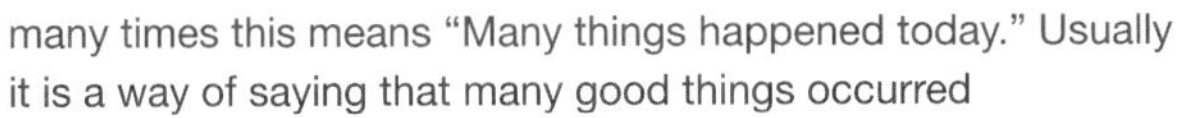

many times this means "Many things happened today." Usually it is a way of saying that many good things occurred

| Point | have a big day 중요한 날이다
Today's a big day for you 오늘은 네게 아주 중요한 날이야
It's a big day for me 내게는 아주 중요한 날이야

A: **It's a big day** for me. I'm going to ask my girlfriend to marry me.
오늘 내게 아주 중요한 날이야. 여친에게 청혼할거야.
B: I hope that she says yes when you propose.
걔가 네 청혼을 받아들이길 바랄게.

We have a big day ahead of us. What do you think? 오늘 우리는 중요한 날을 맞이해. 어때?

I have to go to work. It's a big day, actually.
출근해야 돼. 실은 오늘 중요한 날이거든.

Well, I have a big day ahead of me.
저기, 난 아주 중요한 날이 다가오고 있어.

048 This is not my day 정말 일진 안 좋네

미드표현

a speaker says this after several bad things happen to him in a short time. It is like saying "I think I'm going to have problems today"

| Point | This is not your day 오늘은 네가 되는 게 없는 날이네
My day sucked 하루종일 최악이였어
Today is my day 오늘은 나의 날이다

A: I think someone stole your car, Peter.
피터야, 누가 네 차를 훔쳐간 것 같아.
B: Oh no! **This is not my day!** 어, 안돼! 정말 일진 안 좋네!

I'm gonna be in surgery. Today's my day.
난 오늘 드디어 수술에 들어갈거야.

I didn't want to say anything because it's your day. 오늘은 너의 날이기 때문에 아무 말도 하지 않을래.

Hey lady, your day's over! It's my turn!
이봐 아가씨, 아가씨는 이제 끝났어. 이젠 내 차례야!

049 I had a pretty hectic day 정신없이 바빴어

미드표현

the speaker is expressing "I was very busy." We can understand that he was busier than normal

| Point | hectic 정신없이 바쁜

A: You didn't answer your cell phone when I called.
내가 전화했는데 핸드폰 안 받던데.

B: **I had a pretty hectic day.** There wasn't time to talk on the phone. 정신없이 바빴어. 전화로 얘기할 시간이 없었어.

My life's a little too hectic to be mad about losing a game or two.
내 인생은 너무 바빠 한두 게임 졌다고 화낼 시간이 없어.

This has been one hectic day for me.
오늘은 무척 바쁜 날이었어.

It was a hectic morning. 무척 바쁜 아침이었어.

050 I'm so out of it today! 난 오늘 도통 정신이 없어!

미드표현

often this means someone can't think very clearly on that day. It is a way to say "My mind is working slowly"

| Point | be out of it 정신없다, 집중이 안되다, 소외당하다

A: **I'm so out of it today.** 난 오늘 집중이 안돼.

B: Why? Did you drink a lot last night?
왜? 간밤에 술 많이 마셨어?

She told me someone was after her, that she was being attacked, and as I see it, she just seemed so out of it.
걔는 계속 누군가가 자신을 쫓아와 공격했다고 했는데, 내가 보기에 정신이 없었던 것 같아.

I was really out of it. I'm so tired all the time. It's weird. 난 정신이 없었어. 항상 피곤해. 이상하다고.

051 This is your lucky day 너 오늘 운수 대통이구나

미드표현

this means "Good things have happened to me." The speaker is feeling good because of the things that happened

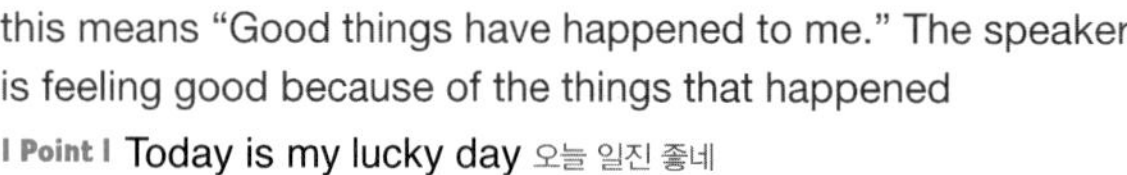

| Point | Today is my lucky day 오늘 일진 좋네

A: This is a prize for being the top student.
최고 학생에게 주는 상이야.

B: Wow! **Today is my lucky day.** 와! 오늘 일진 좋네요.

This is your lucky day. I found someone I think you should go out with.
오늘 운수 좋네. 네가 사귀기 좋은 사람은 찾았어.

Wow, you won 50,000 dollars! This is your lucky day! 5만불이나 따다니! 운수대통이구나!

MEMO

Ways of talking about working hard and saying someone is brave

용기와 배짱으로 최선을 다하니 지치기도

I'll do whatever it takes

001 I'll do whatever it takes 어떻게 해서라도 할게

often this is a way to say "I'll do anything to succeed." The speaker says this to tell others he plans to work as hard as he can

I Point I do whatever it takes to~ 어떻게 해서라도 …을 하다

A: Why do you think you'll get into Yale University?
왜 네가 예일대에 들어갈 거라고 생각하는거야?

B: **I'll do whatever it takes** to become a student there. 어떻게 해서라도 거기에 들어갈거야.

Just do whatever it takes to find that bullet.
어떻게 해서라도 탄환을 찾아.

They're gonna do whatever it takes to get off the Island. 걔네들은 어떻게 해서라도 섬에서 벗어 날려고 할거야.

You gotta do whatever it takes to protect your family. 넌 어떻게 해서라도 가족을 지켜야 돼.

002 I worked my ass off 뼈빠지게 일했어, 죽도록 열심히 일했어

this means "I did things that were very difficult." Usually this expresses that the speaker worked much harder during a period than most other people

I Point I one's ass off 몹시
V+one's ass off (~ing) (…하느라) 죽도록 …하다

A: What was it like being in the military?
군대에 복무한다는 게 어떤 것 같아?

B: It was hard. **I worked my ass off.**
힘들었어. 죽도록 빵빵이 쳤어.

I studied my ass off in law school.
법과대학에서 죽도록 공부했어.

I worked my ass off doing CPR.
심폐소생술하느라 죽도록 힘썼어.

Go home. Take a day off. You've been working your ass off. 집에 가. 하루 쉬어. 죽도록 일했잖아.

003 I busted my ass to get here 여기까지 오려고 안간힘을 썼어

this is a crude way to say "I worked hard." The speaker thinks he has made a strong effort to do something

I Point I bust one's ass 1. 안간힘을 쓰다(주어=one) 2. 혼내다(주어=one 불일치)

A: **I really busted my ass to** buy this house.
난 이 집을 사려고 정말 안간힘을 썼어.

B: Yeah, I know you had to work hard to get the money. 그래, 돈을 벌기 위해 열심히 일해야만 했던 거 알아.

You got nothing to feel guilty about. You bust your ass here every day to get it done.
죄의식 느낄 거 없어. 그걸 끝내려고 여기서 매일 안간힘을 다하고 있잖아.

I still have the right to bust your ass if I see you slipping.
네가 실수를 한다면 혼내줄 권리가 아직 내게 있어.

004 We're working around the clock
우린 최선을 다하고 있어, 쉴틈없이 일하고 있어

this means that the work schedule is 24 hours a day. It is like saying "We never stop working"

I Point I work around the clock 온종일 일하다

A: Have you finished the project you started?
시작한 프로젝트 끝냈어?

B: No, but **we're working around the clock** to get it done. 아니, 하지만 끝내기 위해 최선을 다하고 있어.

Construction crews are working around the clock. 건설인부들이 쉴틈없이 일하고 있어.

He's been working around the clock. He hasn't changed his clothes in three days.
걘 쉴틈없이 일하고 있어. 3일 동안 옷을 갈아 입지도 않았어.

We are working around the clock to find your father. 우리는 네 아버지를 찾기 위해 최선을 다하고 있어.

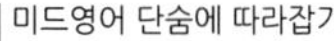

005 I'm doing my best 최선을 다하고 있어

미드표현

this is a way to say "I'm trying very hard." The speaker wants people to know he is doing everything he can do

I Point I do one's best (to~) (…하는데) 최선을 다하다
I'll do my best 최선을 다할게

A: Linda, you are going too slowly. 린다, 너 너무 늦어.
B: **I'm doing my best** to walk as fast as the others. 다른 사람처럼 빨리 걸으려고 최선을 다하고 있어.

I'm doing my best! She's doing her best! And I need you to do your best!
난 최선을 다하고 있어! 걔도 최선을 다하고 있고! 난 네가 최선을 다하길 바래!

I'm going to really do my best to make her happy. 최선을 다해서 걜 행복하게 해줄거야.

I will do my best to remember your birthday next year. 내년엔 네 생일 꼭 기억할게.

006 He goes out of his way to help me 걘 날 돕기 위해 애를 많이 썼어

미드표현

this means someone is very helpful, even if it is hard to be helpful. Usually it is a way to say "He has been very kind to me"

I Point I go out of one's way to~ …하기 위해 애를 많이 쓰다

A: Is Francis being nice to you? 프랜시스가 네게 잘해주던?
B: Yes. **He goes out of his way to help me.**
어. 날 도와주기 위해 애를 많이 썼어.

I went out of my way to give a patient exactly what he wanted.
환자가 원하는 것을 바로 주는데 애를 많이 썼어.

She went out of her way to be cruel to me.
걔는 갖은 애를 써가며 내게 잔인하게 굴었어.

He goes out of his way to make me feel like an idiot. 걘 갖은 애를 써가며 날 바보처럼 느끼게 해.

007 She was firing on all cylinders 걔는 최선을 다했어

미드표현

this means that something was going well. Originally this expression referred to an engine. An engine that is firing on all cylinders is running very well. Similarly, if a person is said to be firing on all cylinders, it means they are doing things in a way that is impressing everyone else. In other words, "She was doing great"

I Point I be firing on all cylinders 전력을 다하다, 효과적으로 일처리하다

A: Laura did a great job when she gave the speech. 로라는 연설을 했을 때 아주 잘했어.
B: I know. **She was firing on all cylinders.**
알아. 걘 최선을 다했어.

Your team is intact and firing on all cylinders.
너희 팀은 변함없이 다 함께 모여서 아주 전력을 다하고 있어.

Our company seems to be firing on all cylinders. 우리 회사는 전력투구를 하고 있는 것 같아.

008 I'm really gonna go all out for this 난 이 일에 최선을 다할거야

미드표현

this speaker is saying he is going to do everything that is possible to succeed at something. We can understand that he will try very hard and not be lazy. When someone goes all out, he puts all of his energy into it. It is like saying "I'll do everything that I can do"

I Point I go all out for~ 전력투구를 다하다

A: You've been training for weeks to run this marathon. 넌 이 마라톤을 뛰기 위해 수주간 연습을 했어.
B: **I'm really gonna go all out** to come in first place. 난 정말 일등하기 위해 전력투구를 할거야.

He is one of my closest casual acquaintances. So I'm gonna go all out for him. 걔는 내가 가장 가깝게 알고 지내는 사람 중 한 명이어서 난 걜 위해 최선을 다할거야.

You really go all out for this holiday, don't you? 넌 정말 이번 휴일에 맘껏 놀거지, 그지 않아?

Linda told me she's going all out for her wedding. 린다는 결혼식을 위해 최선을 다할거라고 내게 말했어.

009 He shot his wad 걘 모든 힘을 쏟아 부었어

this means that the person used all of his energy trying to do something and now he is very tired and has no energy left to do anything more. It does not indicate success or failure. At times, it can also mean that a man has climaxed sexually. Someone who has shot his wad no longer has the ability to be helpful. It is a way to say "He used every means he had to succeed"

Point shoot one's wad 돈, 힘 에너지를 다쓰다, 사정하다(blow one's wad)

A: Why isn't Roger joining us for breakfast?
로저는 왜 함께 아침먹으러 오지 않는거야.

B: He **shot his wad** by staying up all night playing League of Legends. 리그오브레전드를 밤새하느라고 진이 다 빠졌어.

미드표현

If the DA wants to shoot his wad too early, we can't stop him.
검사가 지나치게 빨리 힘을 쏟고 싶다면 말릴 수가 없지.

I already shot my wad earlier in the day.
난 그날 일찍 사정을 이미 했어.

Don't shoot your wad before we finish up.
일 끝내기 전에 먼저 진빼지마.

Bill has no money. He shot his wad on bad investments. 빌은 돈이 없어. 안좋은 투자처에 돈을 쏟아부었어.

010 You're so hell bent on winning the contest

넌 대회에서 우승하기 위해 필사적이야

this expresses that the speaker thinks the listener really wants to win a contest. To be hell bent on something means the person will not stop until he achieves his goal. Another way to express this is "You'll do anything to win that contest"

Point be hell bent on sth[~ing] …하는데 필사적이다, …하려고 작정하다

A: I'll stay up all night to be in first place.
일등이 되기 위해 난 밤을 샐거야.

B: **You're so hell bent on** winning the contest.
넌 대회에서 우승하기 위해 필사적이야.

미드표현

Upon recovery, Chris was bent on revenge.
회복되자마자, 크리스는 복수를 하려고 작정했어.

Nazir is not your average Islamist terrorist bent on bringing down Western civilization.
나지르는 서구문명을 파괴하는데 필사적인 평균적인 이슬람 테러리스트가 아냐.

011 Have you been gunning for a promotion?

승진을 노려왔어?

this means "To work toward getting something." The speaker is talking about working to get a better job

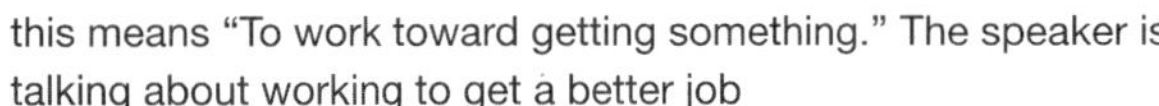

Point be gunning for sth …의 기회를 잡기 위해 필사적이다
be gunning for sb …을 비난할 기회를 노리다

A: **Have you been gunning for** a transfer?
전근을 노리고 있어?

B: Yeah, I've been hoping I can work overseas.
어, 해외근무 할 수 있기를 바라고 있어.

미드표현

Why are you gunning for me? 왜 나를 노리는거야?

There is a mad man gunning for you because of me. 나 때문에 너를 노리는 미친놈이 하나 있어.

They're gunning for any Chicago politician they can find.
걔네들은 시카고 정치가라면 찾을 수 있는 누구든 노리고 있어.

You've been gunning for me the moment you got here!
넌 여기 오자마자 날 비난할 기회를 잡기 위해 필사적이었어!

012 We're pulling out all the stops

최선을 다하고 있어, 모든 수를 다쓰고 있어

this means "We will do everything we can." It indicates that they will make a big effort to do something

Point pull out all the stops 목적을 달성하기 위해 가능한 한 최선을 다하다

A: Our party will be great. **We're pulling out all the stops.** 우리 파티는 멋있을거야. 최선을 다하고 있어.

B: I'll bet you're spending a lot of money on it.
너 정말 거기에 돈을 너무 낭비해.

미드표현

We're pulling out all the stops for the party.
우리는 파티 준비에 최선을 다하고 있어.

Everyone will be impressed. We're pulling out all the stops. 다들 감동을 받을거야. 우리는 최선을 다하고 있어.

For our wedding we're pulling out all the stops. 결혼식을 위해 우리는 최선을 다하고 있어.

013 She's bringing out the big guns 걘 비장의 카드를 꺼냈어

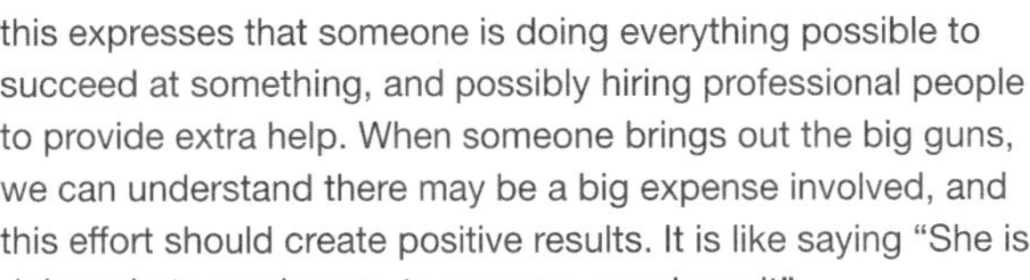

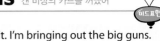

this expresses that someone is doing everything possible to succeed at something, and possibly hiring professional people to provide extra help. When someone brings out the big guns, we can understand there may be a big expense involved, and this effort should create positive results. It is like saying "She is doing whatever she can to ensure a good result"

| Point | bring out the big guns 비장의 카드를 꺼내다
roll out the big guns 비장의 카드를 쓰다
save the big guns 비장의 카드를 아껴두다

A: Fern hired some expensive lawyers for her lawsuit. 펀은 소송에 돈이 많이 드는 변호사를 고용했어.

B: It's getting serious. **She's bringing out the big guns.** 점점 심각해지는구나. 걔가 비장의 카드를 꺼냈네.

미드표현

Okay, that's it. I'm bringing out the big guns.
좋아, 바로 그거야. 내가 비장의 카드를 꺼내야지.

Wouldn't it be better to save Steve for trial? Roll out the big gun later?
재판에서 스티브를 빼는게 낫지 않을까? 비장의 카드는 나중에 써야지?

014 You bend over backwards 넌 최선을 다해, 안간힘을 다 쓰고 있어

this means "You try very hard." Usually people say this when they admire the effort of another person

| Point | bend over backwards 최선을 다해 …하려고 하다, 안간힘을 다 쓰다

A: You're so nice. **You bend over backwards** for everyone. 넌 정말 착해. 모두들 위해 최선을 다하고 있어.

B: Well, I'd like everyone to be happy.
어, 모두들 행복하기를 바래.

미드표현

Why did you bend over backwards defending this woman? 왜 이 여자를 변호하는데 안간힘을 다 쓴거야?

I guess I feel like sometimes we bend over backwards for Dixon, but we don't do the same for Chris.
우리가 때때로 딕슨을 위해서는 최선을 다하는 것 같지만 크리스에게는 그렇게 못하고 있는 것 같아.

I'm not gonna bend over backwards just to please that jerk. 그 멍충이를 만족시키기 위해 최선을 다하지는 않을거야.

015 You work rain or shine 넌 어떤 일이 있어도 일해

this is a way to say that someone is very diligent, and that they are a reliable worker no matter what happens. It is a compliment and has a positive meaning. It is a way to express "You are not lazy and can be depended on to always do your work"

| Point | rain or shine (뭔가 열심히 할 때) 비가오나 눈이오나, 어떤 일이 있어도

A: Frank, you are always here. **You work rain or shine.** 프랭크, 넌 항상 여기 있네. 무슨 일이 있어도 열심히 일하네.

B: Well, I enjoy doing my job and the salary is good too. 어 난 내 일하는게 즐겁고 급여도 좋아.

미드표현

My husband's only hobby is driving around the state looking for bargains, rain or shine.
내 남편의 유일한 취미는 주를 돌아다니면서 비가오나 눈이오나 싼물건 찾아다니는거야.

You work rain or shine. You don't ask for a raise or time off.
무조건 일해. 임금인상이나 휴식은 요구하지도마.

016 I've done everything you asked me to do

네가 시키는 건 다했어

this is a way to say "I completed all of the work." The speaker wants to let someone know that all of the tasks are finished

| Point | I did all I knew 난 최선을 다했어

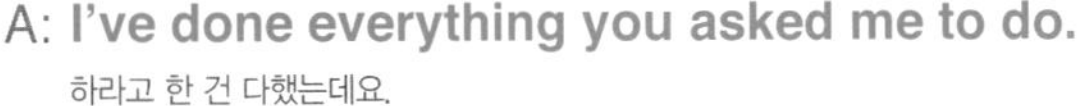

A: **I've done everything you asked me to do.**
하라고 한 건 다했는데요.

B: Alright. You can go leave work and go home now. 좋아. 퇴근하고 집에 가도 좋아.

미드표현

I've done everything you asked me to do. I'm going home now. 네가 시키는 건 다했어. 이제 집에 간다.

Don't criticize me. I've done everything you asked me to do. 나한테 뭐라 하지마. 난 네가 시키는 건 다 했어.

I've done everything you asked me to do. You should be satisfied. 네가 시키는 건 다했어. 만족 좀 해라.

017 I'm tied up all day 하루 온종일 꼼짝달싹 못하고 있어

미드표현

this means "I'm busy during that day." The speaker wants to tell someone that he has no free time on that day

| Point | be tied up 바빠서 꼼짝달싹 못하다

A: Can you attend the meeting tomorrow?
내일 회의에 참석할거야?

B: No. **I'm tied up all day.** 아니. 온종일 꼼짝달싹 못해.

A: Are you going to have any time for lunch this afternoon? B: I don't think so, because I'm all tied up in meetings.
A: 오늘 오후에 점심 시간을 낼 수 있으세요? B: 없을 거예요. 회의 때문에 꼼짝도 못해요.

I'm sorry, but he's tied up all morning on Tuesday. What is the nature of your visit?
죄송하지만 그는 화요일 오전 내내 바빠요. 왜 그러시는데요?

018 I'm up to my ears in work 일 때문에 꼼짝달싹 못해

미드표현

this indicates that the speaker is stressed because he has too much work. He is saying "I have a lot of work waiting to be done"

| Point | be up to one's ears[neck] in work 할 일이 무척 많다

A: **I'm up to my neck in work** these days.
요즘 일이 너무 많아.

B: Do you want someone to help you out?
누가 도와주길 바래?

I have no free time. I'm up to my neck in work.
시간이 안나. 일 때문에 꼼짝달싹못해.

The office is a mess. I'm up to my neck in work. 사무실이 엉망이야. 일 때문에 꼼짝달싹못해.

I'm up to my neck in work. Don't bother me for a while. 일 때문에 꼼짝못하고 있어. 한동안 나 방해하지마.

019 I got held up at work 직장에서 일에 잡혀있었어

미드표현

this is a way to say "I was delayed at my job." We can understand that the speaker had to work for a longer time than he expected to

| Point | I got held up at the office 사무실에 잡혀 있었어
I got held up in traffic 교통이 막혀서 꼼짝 못했어

A: Why are you getting home so late? 왜 이리 늦었어?

B: **I got held up at** my job. I had to stay until everything was finished.
일이 너무 많아서. 다 끝날 때까지 남아있어야 했어.

I got held up behind a traffic accident.
사고때문에 잡혀있었어.

I got held up at Dr. Bergman's office. There was some guy who freaked everybody out. 버그만 박사의 사무실에 잡혀있었어. 어떤 이상한 사람이 있었거든.

A: Sorry, I got held up. B: No, you're just in time. A: 미안, 잡혀있었어. B: 아냐 시간 맞춰왔어.

020 I kept myself busy 그 동안 바빴어, 할 일이 많았어

미드표현

this indicates the speaker was working hard. He is expressing "I did a lot of work"

| Point | keep oneself busy 바쁘게 지내다
I've been keeping myself busy 바빴어

A: How did the conference go last week?
지난 주 회의 어땠어?

B: **I kept myself busy.** It was very useful.
바빴어. 매우 유익했고.

Where have you been keeping yourself?
도대체 어디 있었길래 코빼기도 안보였니?

I kept myself busy when I was staying at her house.걔 집에 있을 때 할 일이 많았어.

I kept myself busy during the cold winter months. 추운 겨울동안 많이 바빴어.

When I was feeling sad, I kept myself busy.
내가 슬플 때는 바쁘게 이것저것을 해.

021 I am swamped 나 엄청 바빠, 눈코 뜰 새없이 바빠

미드표현

this is a way to say "There is a lot of work I must do." Often this means the person is stressed because so much work is waiting to be done

| Point | be swamped with~ …으로 엄청 바쁘다

A: Tom, you seem unhappy these days.
탐, 요즘 울적해 보여.

B: **I am swamped.** I never have time to relax.
엄청 바빠. 쉴 시간도 없어.

I'm so swamped today. My house is a mess and I've got millions of errands to run.
오늘 엄청 바빠. 집이 엉망인데다 볼 일이 너무 많아.

I've been so swamped. I must have forgotten to pay the electric bill.
내가 너무 바빠서 전기세 내는걸 잊었던 것 같아.

If you're swamped, I can cancel my vacation plans. 네가 바쁘면 휴가계획을 취소할게.

022 I'm exhausted 지쳤어

미드표현

this means "I feel very tired." It is usually said after someone has worked for a long time

| Point | I'm extremely exhausted 정말 지쳤어
I'm dead to the world 돌아가시기 일보 직전야

A: How was your trip to the US? 미국 여행이 어땠어?

B: **I'm exhausted.** The flight lasted for 14 hours.
지쳤어. 14시간 동안 비행기를 탔어.

I was injured and I was exhausted.
부상을 당했고 지쳤어.

We are overworked and exhausted.
과다한 업무로 지쳤어.

We're exhausted, and we're not going anywhere. 피곤해, 아무데도 안 갈거야.

023 I'm kind of tuckered out 좀 많이 지쳤어

미드표현

this means the speaker is tired from an activity, and he probably does not want to do anything that will make him more tired. Basically, the speaker is saying "I don't have any more energy and right now I want to rest"

| Point | be tuckered out 지칠대로 지치다, 뻗다
tucker oneself out 많이 지치다

A: Did you enjoy your trip to Paris? 파리여행 즐겁게 했어?

B: It was great, but **I'm kind of tuckered out.**
멋졌지만 좀 힘들어 뻗었어.

I'm kind of tuckered out. 나 완전히 지쳤어.

She'll be tuckered out hiding in a bush somewhere. 걔는 수풀 어딘가에 숨어있으면서 지칠대로 지칠거야.

She really tuckered herself out at the park, huh? 걔는 공원에서 정말 많이 지쳤어 그지?

I'm kind of tuckered out. How are you feeling?
나 좀 많이 지쳤어. 너는 어때?

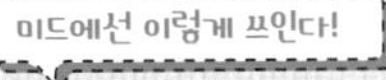

I'm kind of tuckered out

The Big Bang Theory
SEASON#3-21

Sheldon을 방문한 저명한 과학자이자 색녀(?)인 Elizabeth Plimpton 박사는 이미 Leonard와 하룻밤을 보낸다. 그리고 다시 식당에서 만나자 Leonard는 피곤하다며 은근히 어젯밤 일을 자랑하는데 색녀인 Elizabeth는 브라운 색인 인도출신의 Raj를 타겟으로 하고 있다.

Leonard: Boy, I'm kind of tuckered out. How are you feeling, Elizabeth?
Elizabeth: You know what? I am a little tired. Would you be a dear and get me a cup of coffee?
Leonard: Sure. Black, right?
Elizabeth: Actually, now I think I want it hot, brown and sweet.
Leonard: Coming right up.

레너드: 어휴 난 좀 지치네, 엘리자베스, 당신은 어때요?
엘리자베스: 저 말이지, 나도 좀 피곤해요. 커피 한잔 갖다 줄래요?
레너드: 물론요, 블랙이죠?
엘리자베스: 실은 지금은 뜨겁고 달콤한 브라운 커피로 해줘요.
레너드: 바로 가져 올게요.

024 I am totally burned out 완전히 뻗었어

this is said when someone has worked for a long time and now they can't think clearly about it anymore. It is like saying "I'm really tired and I need a rest from this"

| Point | I'm stressed out (at work) (회사에서) 스트레스 엄청 받았어
We were all knocked out 우리 모두 다 지쳤어
I'm all washed out 난 완전히 지쳐버렸어
I'm wiped out 난 완전 녹초야

A: **I am totally burned out** from doing this job.
이 일하느라 완전히 뻗었어.

B: Maybe you need to try a different type of work.
다른 종류의 일을 한번 시도해보는 게 어때.

미드표현

I didn't eat lunch. I can't eat when I'm stressed out. 점심을 안 먹었어. 스트레스 받을 땐 난 못 먹어.

I'm going to have to cancel. I'm totally wiped out. 취소해야 돼. 완전히 녹초가 됐어.

025 I think I pushed myself too hard 내가 너무 무리했나봐

this would likely be said when a person has worked very hard and become very tired, and possibly sick. Many times when we hear this, it means too much hard work and stress have caused mental and physical problems. Essentially, the speaker is saying "I'm exhausted from working so much"

| Point | push oneself too hard 너무 무리하다

A: I have to tell you, you look like shit.
내 말해두는데. 너 정말 똥씹은 표정이야.

B: **I think I pushed myself too hard.**
내가 너무 무리를 한 것 같아.

미드표현

I just hope she doesn't push herself too hard.
난 단지 걔가 너무 무리하지 않기를 바래.

I've been so tired lately. I was pushing myself too hard. 최근에 나 너무 피곤했어. 내가 너무 무리를 했나봐.

I'm ready for bed. I think I pushed myself too hard. 잘 준비됐어. 내가 너무 무리했나봐.

Gina is having a hard time. She's pushing herself too hard.
지나는 힘든 시간을 보내고 있어. 너무 무리했나봐.

026 You put up a good fight 졌지만 잘 싸웠어

this expresses that the speaker thinks someone may have failed, but he tried very hard to have a favorable outcome. In other words, "Your effort was very good, even though it was not successful"

| Point | put up a good fight (목표달성을 못했지만) 잘 싸우다
start[pick] a fight 싸움을 걸다 have a fight with~ …와 싸우다
get into a fight with~ …와 싸우다

A: I wasn't able to win the court case.
법정소송에서 이길 수가 없었어.

B: That's too bad, but **you put up a good fight.**
안됐어. 하지만 잘 싸웠어.

미드표현

Well, you put up a good fight for a freshman.
음. 신입생치고는 잘 싸웠어.

You put up a good fight, Carl. 그래도 선전했어. 칼.

You had a fight with your mother?
너 네 엄마하고 싸웠다고?

Do not pick a fight with me, Dad.
아빠, 내게 싸움걸지마요.

027 Go get some rest 가서 좀 쉬어

usually this is said to someone who has worked for a long time. It means "Go sleep because you are very tired"

| Point | Get some rest 좀 쉬어 You need to get some rest 좀 쉬라고

A: **Go get some rest now.** You look tired.
가서 좀 쉬어. 피곤해 보여.

B: I was up all night working. 밤새 일했다니까.

미드표현

You should go home and get some rest, eat something. 집에 가서 좀 쉬면서 뭐 좀 먹어.

You need to get some rest now. You need to spend some time with friends or family.
좀 쉬라고. 친구나 가족과 좀 시간을 보내.

I'll check back with you later. Try to get some rest. 나중에 확인해볼테니, 가서 좀 쉬어.

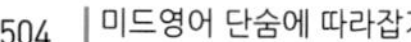

028 I need to take a day off 하루 좀 쉬어야겠어

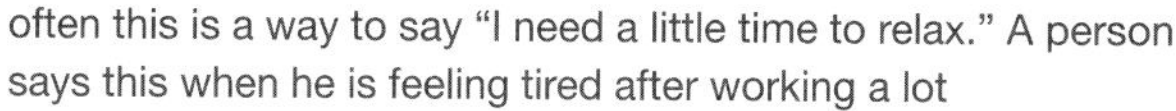

often this is a way to say "I need a little time to relax." A person says this when he is feeling tired after working a lot

I Point I take[get]a day off (of work) 하루 쉬다
give sb a day off 하루 쉬게 하다
I need a day off 하루 쉬고 싶어

A: **I need to take a day off.** 하루 좀 쉬어야겠어.
B: You'll have to wait until next week to do that.
그럴려면 다음 주까지 기다려.

미드표현

Told you he wouldn't take a day off. You owe me $50. 걘 하루 휴가를 쓰지 않을거라고 했잖아. 너 50달러 빚졌어.

I backed you up when you wanted to take a year off school.
네가 학교를 일년 휴학하고 싶다고 했을 때 난 너를 도왔어.

I think I should take a week off work, and we should go on vacation.
내가 일주일 휴가를 내서 우리 휴가를 가자.

029 Let's take a break 잠깐 쉬자

this means "Let's stop for a short time." People say this before they stop for some coffee or a snack. After a while, they start working again

I Point I take five 잠깐 쉬다 Take five 잠깐 쉬어

A: We're worked for hours. **Let's take a break.**
오랫동안 일했으니 잠깐 쉬자.
B: OK. I'm going to make coffee for everyone.
좋아. 내가 다 커피 타 올게.

미드표현

It's time to take a break. 쉴 시간이야.

I can't take a break right now. 지금 당장은 못쉬어.

Okay. Class, take five. 좋아. 얘들아. 5분간 쉬어.

It wasn't until noon that she finally took a break. 걔는 정오가 되어서야 마침내 쉴 수 있었어.

030 I have my hands full! 너무 바빠서 다른 일을 할 겨를이 없어요!

this means "I'm really busy." The speaker wants to tell others he has no free time because of the thing that is making him busy

I Point I have one's hands full 너무 바빠서 다른 일을 못하다
have one's hands full with[~ing] 일이 많아 꼼짝달싹 못하다

A: I can't help you. **I have my hands full.**
못 도와줘. 내가 너무 바빠서.
B: Is there someone else who might give us a little help? 좀 우릴 도와줄 다른 사람 있어?

미드표현

I had my hands full. I don't take my eyes off him ever. 너무 바빴지만 걔에게서 눈을 떼지는 않았어.

Jessica's got her hands full caring her five kids. 제시카는 애를 5명이나 키우기 때문에 바빠.

We've certainly got our hands full. 우리 넘 바빠.

031 You don't have the guts 배짱도 없으면서, 용기도 없으면서

this expresses "You aren't brave enough." The speaker thinks someone doesn't have enough courage to do something

I Point I have the guts to[for+N] …할 배짱이 있다
You've got guts 너 용기있다
You got the guts? 너 그럴 배짱 있어?
You're gutless 배짱도 없어

A: I told my boss he better give me a raise or I'd quit. 사장에게 급여를 올려주지 않으면 그만두겠다고 했어.
B: **You've got guts.** I'd never do that.
용기있네. 난 절대 그렇게 못해.

미드표현

You don't even have the guts to make the decision. 넌 결정할 배짱도 없잖아.

You didn't have the guts for murder.
넌 살인할 배짱도 없었잖아.

You did not have the guts to tell me you were dating her. 넌 걔하고 데이트한다고 말할 용기도 없었잖아.

032 It takes balls to~ …하려면 배짱이 있어야 돼

this is very similar to the previous phrase. It indicates "You must be very brave to do that"

I Point I have[take] the balls 용기 · 배짱이 있다[필요하다]

He takes the bull by the horn 걘 용감하게 나선다

A: I heard that Bobby got into an argument with Jack. 바비가 잭과 논쟁을 했다고 들었어.

B: Really? **It takes balls to** fight with Jack.
정말? 잭과 싸울려면 배짱이 있어야 되는데.

It takes balls to argue with the boss.
사장과 다투려면 배짱이 필요해.

It takes balls to stand up for what you believe in. 네가 믿는 바를 지지하려면 배짱이 필요해.

033 You worked up the nerve to report him

넌 용기를 내서 걔를 신고했어

미드표현

this indicates that something bad happened, and it took time for the listener to become brave enough to disclose the guilty person to authorities. The listener was probably scared that the guilty person would harm him as a form of revenge. We can also say "You got up the courage to turn him in"

I Point I work[get] up the nerve (to~) (…할) 용기를 내다

A: Do you know how they caught Kerry stealing?
케리가 절도하는 걸 어떻게 잡았는지 알아?

B: It's because **you worked up the nerve to** report him. 네가 용기를 내서 신고했기 때문이지.

The night before, as I worked up the nerve to tell Sam, I thought of your mother.
그 전날 밤에, 내가 샘에게 말할 용기를 낼 때 네 엄마 생각을 했어.

I'm trying to get up the nerve to tell her how I feel. 내 기분이 어떤지 용기를 내 걔한테 말하려고 해.

It took me 11 years to get up the nerve to ask out Chris.
크리스에게 데이트 신청을 하는 용기를 내는데 11년이 걸렸어.

034 He took one for the team! 걘 팀을 위해 총대를 맸어!

미드표현

this indicates that a person did something difficult or went through a hardship so that other people could have an advantage. Generally, a person who takes one for the team is considered generous and unselfish. In other words, "He did something hard that allowed us to benefit"

I Point I take one for the team 팀(전체)을 위해 나서다, 희생하다

A: It was nice of Neil to stay in the office so we could have a day off.
우리가 하루 쉴 수 있도록 닐이 사무실에 남아서 너무 고마웠어.

B: I agree. Neil is great. **He took one for the team.** 맞아. 닐은 대단해. 팀을 위해 희생을 했어.

Ah, there he is! The man of the hour! He took one for the team!
아 저기 온다! 우리 주인공! 걘 팀을 위해 희생을 했어!

Sometimes you've got to take one for the team.
때로는 팀을 위해 희생을 해야 돼.

Well, it's always me, take one for the team.
저기, 팀을 위해 희생하는 건 항상 나네.

You could do it without offending her. Come on, Tammy. Take one for the team.
넌 걔를 화나게 하지 않고서도 그걸 할 수 있을거야. 어서, 태미야. 팀을 위해 총대를 매라고.

미드에선 이렇게 쓰인다!

The Big Bang Theory
SEASON#4-15

He took one for the team!

노부인 기부자와 잠자리를 해서 기부를 받은 Leonerd가 식당에 들어서자 총장은 Leonerd가 전체를 위해 몸을 바쳤다면서 박수를 쳐준다.

Seibert: Ah, there he is! The man of the hour! He took one for the team!
Leonard: I didn't do it for the money!
Seibert: Keep telling yourself that, it makes it easier. Trust me, I know.

사이버트: 저기 오네! 화제의 인물! 팀을 위해 희생을 했어!
레너드: 돈 때문에 한게 아녜요!
사이버트: 계속 그렇게 생각해, 그러면 좀 더 쉬워져. 정말야, 내가 알아.

035 I throw caution to the wind 난 대담하게 행동을 해, 모험을 해

this is a way to say "I don't think, I just do it." The speaker wants to say that action is more important than thinking about something

I Point I throw caution to the wind 모험하다

A: Why do you travel all over the world?
왜 전세계를 여행하는거야?

B: **I throw caution to the wind** when I go on vacation. 휴가 갈 때는 모험을 즐겨.

미드표현

I throw caution to the wind when I'm dating.
난 데이트를 할 때 대담하게 행동을 해.

When it comes to risks, I throw caution to the wind. 모험에 관한거라면, 난 대담하게 행동을 해.

I throw caution to the wind when I race cars.
난 자동차 경주를 할 때는 모험을 해.

036 I got cold feet 나 자신없어, 용기를 잃었어

this is indicating "I got scared and I didn't do it." A speaker says this after he changes his mind and doesn't do something

I Point I get cold feet 자신감을 잃다, 겁먹다
*cold feet 두려움에 떨며 두 다리를 움직이지 못하는 상태

A: Angela, why did you decide not to get married?
앤젤라, 왜 결혼하지 않기로 결정했어?

B: **I got cold feet** and couldn't go to the church.
자신이 없어 교회에 갈 수가 없었어.

미드표현

The wedding is about to start when she gets cold feet. 결혼식이 막 시작하려고 하자 걔는 겁이 났어.

Don't get cold feet now, please. All right?
이제 겁먹지마, 제발. 알았어?

What's the matter? Are we getting cold feet?
왜 그래? 우리 겁먹은거야?

037 Don't chicken out 꽁무니 빼지마, 겁먹지마

the speaker is saying "Don't get scared and run away." People say this when they want another person to be brave

I Point I You're a chicken 넌 겁쟁이야
Don't back out on me now! 이제 와서 뒤로 물러서지마!
Don't be such a wimp! 나약하게 굴지마!

A: You have to fight Jeff. **Don't chicken out.**
제프와 붙어. 꽁무니 빼지마.

B: But I'm afraid he will hurt me. 하지만 다칠까봐 걱정돼.

미드표현

A: Well, we will. I'll come back. Okay? B: Okay. Don't chicken out.
A: 저기, 그렇게 할게. 난 돌아올게. 알았지? B: 좋아. 겁먹지는 말고.

I didn't chicken out, man. I just didn't want to drop the news in front of all those people.
난 꽁무니를 뺀게 아냐. 난 단지 그 사람들 앞에 그 소식을 던져주고 싶지 않았어.

038 You just turned tail and ran! 넌 꽁무니를 빼고 달아났어!

this often means that someone acted in a cowardly and shameful way. It is the opposite of being brave and fearless. The speaker is being critical, and he is saying "You should have been bold but you behaved like a coward"

I Point I turn tail 무서워 돌아서 꽁무니를 빼다

A: I thought you were going to help me. **You just turned tail and ran!**
네가 나를 도와줄거라 생각했는데 넌 꽁무니를 빼고 달아났어!

B: I was afraid that those guys were going to beat us up. 저 친구들이 우리를 팰까봐 두려웠어.

He'll turn tail if you hit him.
네가 걜 치면 돌아서 꽁무니를 뺄거야.

We turned tail when we saw the police.
우린 경찰을 보고 꽁무니를 뺐어.

Cowards! You just turned tail and ran!
겁쟁이들! 넌 돌아서 줄행랑을 쳤었지!

039 Don't hold your breath 기대하지마, 기다리지마

미드표현

this means "I don't think it will happen soon." In other words, a person shouldn't hold his breath waiting for something to happen, because it may take a very long time

| Point | hold one's breath 숨을 멈추다, (두려움, 기대 속에) 숨을 죽이다

A: I heard a subway line will be built in this neighborhood. 이 주변에 지하철역이 들어온다며.

B: **Don't hold your breath.** That won't happen for a long time. 기대하지마. 한참 걸릴거야.

I want you to close your eyes and hold your breath. 눈을 감고 숨을 멈춰봐.

So how long can you really hold your breath for? 정말 얼마동안 숨을 멈출 수 있는거야?

This is gonna be tough. Hold your breath. 이건 힘들거야. 긴장하라고.

MEMO

Ways to talk about starting to work or finishing work

내가 능력이 있으니 맡아서 끝낼 수 있다고

I got this

001 I got this covered 내가 알아서 할게

this is a way for the speaker to say he is going to take care of some problem or do work that needs to be done. It is very similar to saying, "Don't worry about it, I can take care of it"

| Point | get sth covered 알아서 처리하다

A: I need to have my medicine by six o'clock.
6시까지는 내 약을 먹어야 돼.

B: I got this covered. I'll pick it up at the pharmacy. 내가 알아서 할게. 약국에서 내가 가져올게.

미드표현

Looks like you got it covered. 네가 알아서 한 것 같구나.

Trust me, we got everything covered.
나를 믿어. 우리가 모두 다 알아서 했어.

She's got it covered? How?
걔가 알아서 처리했다고? 어떻게?

Don't worry. I got it covered. 걱정마. 내가 알아서 할게.

002 I'm on it 내가 할게, 내가 처리 중이야

this is a way to say "I'll try to do it." We can understand that the speaker will try his best to do something

A: I need you to clean these windows.
이 창문들 깨끗이 해놔.

B: I'm on it. They'll be clean by this afternoon.
내가 할게. 오후까지 깨끗이 할게.

미드표현

I will find out if the victim or suspect owned a dog. I'm on it.
피해자나 용의자가 개를 소유했는지 알아볼게. 내가 할게.

A: Find out everything we can on this neighbor. B: I'm on it.
A: 이 이웃에게서 찾을 수 있는 건 다 알아내. B: 네 알겠습니다.

A: Get an ambulance! Right now! Move! B: I'm on it. A: 앰블런스를 불러! 지금 당장! 움직여! B: 알겠습니다.

003 I got this 내가 맡을게

this speaker is saying that he has everything under control and doesn't need any help in fixing a problem or keeping a situation good. It is a simple way of saying "Everything is just fine, and I will take care of it, so don't worry"

| Point | I got this 이해했어, (벨,전화소리) 내가 받을게, (돈을) 내가 낼게, 내가 알아서 (처리)할게

A: We need to rent a new apartment in the next few weeks. 다음 몇 주 안에 새 아파트를 임대해야 돼.

B: I got this. Leave it to me and I'll find a better place to live. 내가 알아서 할게. 내게 맡기면 내가 살기 좋은 집을 찾을게.

미드표현

Just let me see if I got this.
내가 이걸 이해했는지 어디 보자.

I got this. I'll go in and turn on some music.
내가 할게. 내가 들어가서 음악을 좀 틀을게.

I got this, mom. I got this. Just don't answer the door, OK? 엄마, 내가 열게, 문열어주지마, 알았어?

Don't worry, Max, I got this.
맥스야 걱정마, 내가 알아서 할게.

미드에선 이렇게 쓰인다!

I got this

Modern Family SEASON#3-8

둘째 딸 Alex가 Luke와 Manny가 갖고 있던 헬리콥터를 동네 형들에게 뺏기는 장면에서 Alex가 문제를 해결하겠다고 하면서 하는 말.

Cameron: Is there an issue here?
Alex: Uncle Cam, I got this.
Bully: Oh, my God, it's Aex Dunphy. So awesome.
Alex: Problem here, boys?
Luke: These geeks won't give us back our helicopter.

카메론: 무슨 문제 있어?
알렉스: 카메론 삼촌, 내가 알아서 할게요.
불리: 맙소사, 알렉스 던피야, 끝내준다.
알렉스: 얘들아, 뭐 문제있니?
루크: 이 괴짜들이 우리 헬리곱터를 돌려주지 않으려고 해요.

004 I'm working on it 지금 하고 있어

this indicates someone is trying to finish something. It is another way to say "I'm trying to complete it"

| Point | work on ~ …일을 하다, 담당하다, 맡다

A: Have you finished the report yet? 이 보고서 끝냈어?
B: No, but **I'm working on it.** 아뇨, 지금 하고 있어요.

I'm working on your case with Brian.
브라이언과 함께 네 사건을 하고 있어.

She continues working on the photograph.
걔는 계속해서 사진 작업을 하고 있어.

Jack is working on a patient. 잭은 환자를 돌보고 있어.

You wanna work on your interview skills?
인터뷰 기술을 배우고 싶어?

005 We're going in 우리가 맡을게

often this is a way to say "We'll start now." The speaker wants to express he's beginning something

A: Please open the files on the computer.
컴퓨터 파일을 열어봐.
B: Alright. **We're going in** right now. 알았어. 지금 그럴게.

This job has to get started, so we're going in.
이 일이 시작되어야 하니 우리가 시작한다.

We're going in so that everything can be set up. 다 준비되도록 우리가 시작하자.

Can you give us a hand with the equipment? We're going in. 이 장비 좀 도와줄테야. 우리가 시작할테니.

006 I'll go 내가 할게

this is a way to volunteer for something. It means "I will do that"

| Point | I'll go = I'll do that

A: Can someone buy some snacks at the store?
누가 가게에 가서 과자 좀 사올래?
B: **I'll go.** What do you want me to buy there?
내가 갈게. 거기 가서 뭐 사올까?

Do you need someone to run errands? I'll go.
심부름 갈 사람이 필요해? 내가 갈게.

I'll go if you need some extra people to come along. 함께 할 추가인원이 필요하면 내가 갈게.

If you need a volunteer to help out, I'll go.
도움을 줄 자원봉사자가 필요하다면 내가 할게.

007 Let me take care of it 나한테 맡겨

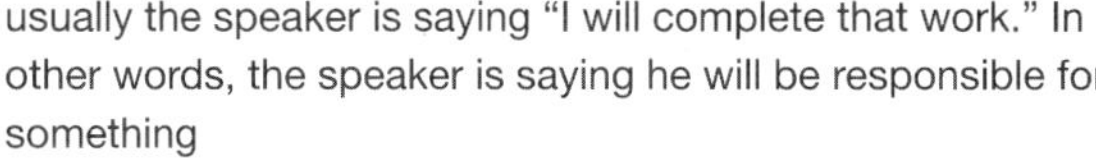

usually the speaker is saying "I will complete that work." In other words, the speaker is saying he will be responsible for something

| Point | I'll take over now 이제 내가 책임지고 할게요

A: This computer needs to be fixed. 이 컴퓨터는 수리해야 돼.
B: **Let me take care of it.** 내가 처리할게.

Let me take care of this. I'm good with kids.
나한테 맡겨. 난 애들을 잘 다뤄.

You gotta take care of yourselves!
너네 몸은 너네가 챙겨!

She's gonna help us take care of the baby!
걔가 아기 돌보는 걸 도와준대!

Let me take care of it. I know how to fix it.
내가 알아서 처리할게. 그거 어떻게 수리하는지 내가 알아.

008 How would I go about doing that?

내가 그걸 어떻게 처리해야 할까?

미드표현

this is a way of asking the method of doing something. A person who asks this wants more information. It is like saying "I'd like to know how to do that so I can try it myself"

| Point | go about+N[~ing] (문제, 상황, 일) 다루기 시작하다

A: I think you should join a club at your school.
너 학교 동아리에 가입해봐라.

B: Good idea. **How would I go about doing that?**
좋은 생각인데. 그거 어떻게 가입하는거야?

And just how are you gonna go about doing that? 그리고 넌 그걸 어떻게 처리할거야?

How do I go about doing that in, like, a non-offensive way?
내가 그걸 불쾌하지 않은 방법으로 어떻게 처리해야 될까?

That doesn't change how we go about finding her killer.
그렇다고 해서 그녀의 살인범을 찾는 방법이 바뀌지 않아.

009 We have an emergency on our hands 지금 우리는 비상시야

미드표현

this indicates something important is happening right now and it must be carefully dealt with or else it could create bigger problems. It can be similar to saying "We have something important that we need to work on immediately"

| Point | have sth[sb] on one's hands 다루어야 될 …가 있다

A: Why are the doctors running toward the hall?
왜 의사들이 복도를 향해서 뛰어들 가는거야?

B: There was an accident. **We have an emergency on our hands.**
사고가 있었대. 지금 우리는 비상사태야.

We could've had a lot more sick people on our hands. 우리는 치료해야 될 더 많은 환자들이 있었을 수도 있어.

We got a real problem on our hands, don't we? 우리는 심각한 문제에 부딪혔어, 안그래?

Maybe the note just means we have a copycat on our hands.
그 노트는 우리가 모방범죄자를 상대해야 한다는 것을 의미할 수도 있어.

010 Leave it to me 내게 맡겨

the speaker is saying he will do something. It is like saying "Trust me, I'll do it"

| Point | leave sth to sb …을 …에게 맡기다

A: Are you sure you can find Darlene?
정말 달린을 찾을 수 있어?

B: **Leave it to me.** She's somewhere in this building. 내게 맡겨. 이 건물 어딘 가에 있을거야.

Let's just leave it to Peter. 피터한테 맡기자.

I'm willing to leave that to fate.
난 기꺼이 운명에 맡길거야.

Good, I'll leave that to you. 좋아, 너한테 맡길게.

011 Let me handle it[this] 내가 알아서 처리할게

미드표현

this is said to mean "I'll do this." It is very similar to the previous phrase. The speaker is taking responsibility to complete something

| Point | handle 다루다, 처리하다

A: The customer is angry because his product didn't arrive. 고객은 제품이 도착하지 않았다고 화를 냈어.

B: **Let me handle this.** I can help him out.
내가 알아서 처리할게. 내가 도와드릴게.

Why don't you let me handle this? 내가 알아서 할게.

I want you to let me handle it. This is for you.
내가 이거 처리하게 해줘. 널 위한거야.

Let me handle this before you screw it up.
네가 망치기 전에 내가 알아서 할게.

It's a problem, but let me handle it.
그게 문제이긴 하지만 내가 알아서 처리할게.

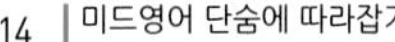

012 Let me do it 내가 할게

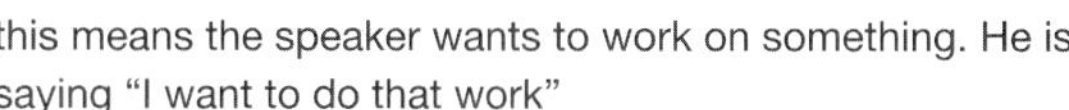

this means the speaker wants to work on something. He is saying "I want to do that work"

I Point I Let me do this[that] 내가 할게
Allow me 나한테 맡겨, 제가 할게요

A: We need someone to make some copies.
누가 좀 복사 좀 해줘.

B: **Let me do it.** I've got some free time.
내가 할게. 시간이 좀 있어.

미드표현

So why don't you just leave me alone and let me do it. 그러니 나 좀 내버려 두고 일 좀 하게 해 줘.

Listen, let me do this alright? I really wanna help you guys out.
자, 이거 내가 할게 어? 정말이지 너네들 도와주고 싶어.

You brought me here to help you. Let me do it. 널 도우라고 이곳에 날 데리고 왔어. 내가 할게.

013 I'm all over it 내가 할게요

this is a way of expressing that the speaker is going to pay attention to something, or labor to do something. It is another way to say "I'm going to do it"

A: Can you move these boxes outside?
이 박스들 좀 밖으로 내다줄래?

B: Of course. **I'm all over it.** 물론. 할게요.

미드표현

Don't worry about the report. I'm all over it.
보고서를 걱정하지마. 내가 잘 파악하고 있어.

I'm all over it. I'll get it done by tomorrow.
잘 알고 있어. 내일까지 그걸 마칠게.

I heard you need software installed. I'm all over it. 소프트웨어를 설치해야 한다며. 내가 잘 알고 있어.

014 Let me try 내가 한번 해볼게

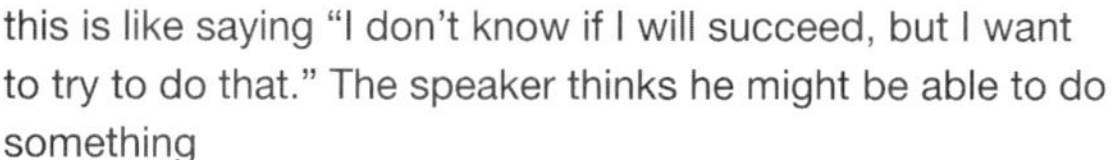

this is like saying "I don't know if I will succeed, but I want to try to do that." The speaker thinks he might be able to do something

I Point I Let me try sth …을 해볼게 *Let me try it on은 한번 입어볼게
Let me try to explain~ …을 설명해보록 할게

A: I can't fix this coffee maker. 이 커피 메이커를 못 고치겠어.

B: **Let me try.** Sometimes I can fix things pretty well. 내가 해볼게. 가끔 물건 수리를 꽤 잘하거든.

미드표현

I believe I can do it. Let me try.
내가 할 수 있을거야. 내가 해볼게.

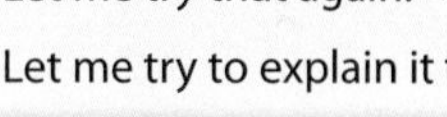

Let me try that again. 다시 한번 해볼게.

Let me try to explain it to you. 내가 너한테 설명해볼게.

015 I'd be the first to go 정말 가고 싶어

this means the speaker is eager to do something. He is indicating "I really want to go"

I Point I be the first to~ 가장 먼저 …하다
Let me be the first to tell you that~ 제일 먼저 내가 …을 얘기할게

A: Would you be willing to take a job overseas?
기꺼이 해외에서 직장을 얻을거야?

B: Sure I would. **I'd be the first to go.**
물론. 몹시 그러고 싶어.

미드표현

I didn't think she'd be the first to go.
걔가 제일 먼저 가리라고는 생각 못했어.

You'll be the first to know. 네게 제일 먼저 알려줄게.

I'm going to resign. I wanted you to be the first to know. 그만 둘거야. 네게 처음 얘기하는거야.

I'd be the first to go if she asked me.
걔가 부탁했다면 내가 가장 먼저 갔을텐데.

016 I'm the one who~ 내가 …했어

this speaker is saying "I'm responsible for that." He wants people to know that he made something happen

| Point | be the one who~ …한 사람은 바로 …야

A: I like the way this room is decorated.
이 방 장식된 거 좋다.

B: Thanks. **I'm the one who** bought the decorations. 고마워. 내가 장식품을 샀어.

I'm the one who said her death was an accident. 걔의 죽음이 사고였다고 말한 사람은 나야.

I'm her boss. I'm the one who hired her.
난 걔 사장야. 내가 바로 걜 채용했어.

I'm the one who operated on him, remember?
내가 그 수술을 했잖아, 기억나?

I'm the one who found it.
내가 바로 그걸 발견한 사람입니다.

017 Could you handle it? 처리할 수 있어?, 감당할 수 있어?, 괜찮겠어?

this means "Will you be able to do it?" The speaker wants to know if a person can do something difficult

| Point | I can handle that 난 그 정도는 할 수 있어

A: Being a doctor is hard. **Could you handle it?**
의사가 되는 건 어려워. 할 수 있겠어.

B: I think I am strong enough to do that job.
그 일을 할 수 있을 정도로 난 강해.

Think you can handle that? 괜찮을 것 같아?

I guess I can handle that. 내가 감당할 수 있을 것 같아.

Now, how do you handle a situation like that?
저런 상황을 어떻게 네가 감당할거야?

018 I can do that 할 수 있어

the speaker is saying he is able to do something. He means "Yes, I'm able to"

| Point | I can do it better 더 잘 할 수 있어

A: Every student has to study very hard here.
여기 학생들은 모두 공부를 열심히 해야 해.

B: **I can do that.** I have done well in school.
난 할 수 있어. 학교에서 공부 잘 했거든.

I don't think I can do that. 나 그거 못할 것 같아.

I can do better than that. 난 그거보다 잘 할 수 있어.

I can do it! I'd like to do it myself.
할 수 있어! 나 혼자 하고 싶어.

019 I can't do this 나 이건 못해

this is a way to say "I'm not able." This indicates the speaker will give up trying to do something

| Point | I can't do that 그럴 수 없어, 그렇게 못해

A: You have looked very stressed lately.
너 최근에 무척 지쳐 보여.

B: **I can't do this.** It is just too difficult.
나 이거 못 하겠어. 정말 너무 어려워.

Sorry, I can't do this right now. I'm driving.
미안, 지금 당장은 못해. 운전 중야.

I can't do this without my husband. I can't do this alone. 남편 없이 못해. 혼자서 못해.

Show you my tits? I can't do that. I barely know you. 가슴을 보여달라고? 그렇게 못해. 잘 알지도 못하는데.

I hate this work. I really can't do this.
이 일을 정말 싫어해. 정말이지 난 이건 못하겠어.

020 I can deal with it 감당할 수 있어, 처리할 수 있어, 그래 가능해

this is said to indicate "I will work on that." Usually it means the speaker feels he can work out some kind of problem

I Point I deal with 처리하다, 감당하다

A: This computer has been broken for a week.
이 컴퓨터는 일주일간 고장나 있었어.

B: **I can deal with it.** It's not hard to fix the problem. 내가 처리할 수 있어. 수리하는 게 어렵지 않아.

Whatever he says, I can deal with it.
걔가 뭐라고 하든 감당할 수 있어.

But we can deal with that. I'll talk to him - or you talk to him.
그건 처리할 수 있어. 우리 둘중 하나가 걔랑 얘기하면 돼.

I'm sure she's fine. If anybody can deal with this, it's Jane. 걔는 괜찮을거야. 제인은 이런걸 잘 감당하거든.

021 I don't feel up to it 나 그거 못할 것 같아

this is expressing that the speaker doesn't think he can do something at a certain time. It is like saying "I probably can't do it right now"

I Point I feel[be] up to+N/~ing …을 해낼 수 있다
I'm not up to it 아직 그 정도는 아냐
Are you up to this? 자신 있어?

A: Why haven't you cleaned the apartment?
아파트를 왜 청소하지 않았어?

B: I'm really tired and **I don't feel up to it.**
정말 피곤해서 못할 것 같아.

Is it okay if the police ask you a few questions? Only if you feel up to it.
경찰이 질문 몇가지 해도 되겠어? 네가 할 수 있을 경우에 한해서 말야.

I'm booked to do a children's party tomorrow, and I don't feel up to it.
내일 아이들 파티를 하기로 되어 있는데 못할 것 같아.

You feel up to talking? 얘기나눌 수 있겠어?

022 It's out of your league 그건 네 능력 밖이야

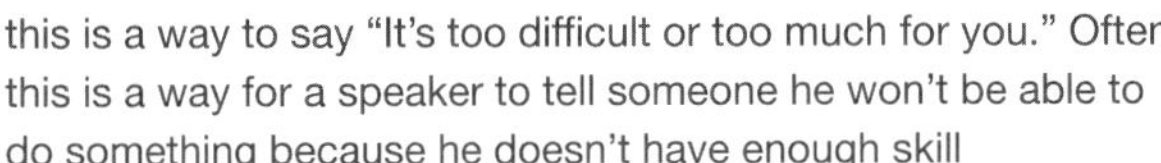

this is a way to say "It's too difficult or too much for you." Often this is a way for a speaker to tell someone he won't be able to do something because he doesn't have enough skill

I Point I be (way) out of one's league …에 비해 수준이 넘 높아, 과분하다

A: Do you think I can get into Harvard University?
내가 하바드에 갈 수 있을 것 같아?

B: No way. **It's out of your league.** 말도 안돼. 네 능력 밖이야.

I think she's a little out of your league.
걘 너한테 좀 과분한 거 같아.

You're way out of my league. Everybody in here knows it.
넌 내게 너무 과분해. 여기 있는 모든 사람이 알고 있어.

I can't do that. He's out of my league.
그렇게는 못해. 걘 내 능력 밖이야.

023 (I'm) Not much of~ …하는 편은 아니야

this means "I don't have a good ability at..." We can understand that the speaker doesn't have a talent for something

A: Cheryl is **not much of** a driver. She's had several accidents.
세릴은 운전을 잘하는 편이 아냐. 사고를 여러 번 냈어.

B: Yeah, I know. I hope that she doesn't get hurt.
어, 나도 알아. 걔가 다치지 않기를 바래.

I'm not much of a dancer. 난 춤을 잘 추는 편이 아냐.

It's not much of a secret. 별로 비밀 같지도 않아.

Not much of a mystery. 별 미스터리도 아니네.

My mom's not much of a cook. 엄마는 요리 잘 못해.

024 I'll never get through this 난 결코 이 일을 해낼 수 없을거야

this means "I can't finish this." The speaker thinks he can't do something until it's complete

| Point | get through …을 이겨내다, 극복하다
How did you get through it? 넌 어떻게 해낸거야?

A: How are you doing on the report you're writing?
네가 쓰고 있는 보고서 어떻게 하고 있어?

B: **I'll never get through this.** There isn't enough information. 절대 이걸 해내지 못할 것 같아. 정보가 충분하지 않아.

미드표현

She'll get through this. She'll find a way to survive. 걘 극복할거야. 생존방법을 찾을거야

It's not your fault. We'll get through this.
네 잘못이 아냐. 우리 함께 이겨낼거야

It's hard, but I'll get through it. 어렵지만, 이겨내야지.

025 I'm good at this 난 이거 잘해

this expresses that the speaker has talent. It is a way to say "I can do this well"

| Point | be good at+N/~ing …에 능숙하다, 잘하다
be not good at = be poor at = be terrible at
…에 서투르다, 잘 못하다

A: Why did you choose to become an airline stewardess? 왜 항공승무원이 되기로 선택했어?

B: **I'm good at this.** People like the service I give them. 내가 잘해서. 사람들이 내가 하는 서비스를 좋아해.

미드표현

She is so good at throwing drinks in people's faces. 걘 사람들 얼굴에 술을 끼얹는 걸 잘해.

This is the part I'm actually good at.
이게 사실 내가 잘하는 부분이야.

I'm not great with figures. 난 숫자에 약해.

I am getting good at that. 난 그것을 점점 잘하고 있어.

026 You suck at this! 너 되게 못하네!

this means "You have no talent for this." It's used when a person tries to do something but fails to do it well

| Point | suck at sth[~ing] …에 서투르다, 젬병이다

A: I hit the golf ball off the course again.
또 골프공을 코스 밖으로 쳐냈어.

B: **You suck at this.** Why not try another sport?
정말 소질이 없네. 다른 운동하지 그래?

미드표현

I really suck at putting my emotions into words. 내 감정을 말로 나타내는데 정말 어눌해

You suck at this game 이런, 완전 망했네.

You suck at being a dad, and you're taking it out on me. 네가 아빠노릇에 서투르다고 내게 화풀이하지마.

027 He's all thumbs 걘 손재주가 너무 없어

this is a way to indicate "He makes many mistakes." We can understand this person has a poor ability to do something

| Point | I'm all thumbs = I'm clumsy 난 서툴러

A: Why was John fired from his job?
존이 왜 직장에서 잘렸어?

B: **He's all thumbs** and his boss got angry at him.
걘 너무 서툴러 사장이 걔한테 화났어.

미드표현

My dad can't repair anything. He's all thumbs.
아빠는 어떤 것도 수리를 못해. 손재주가 없어.

Better let me help him. He's all thumbs.
내가 걸 도와주게 하는게 나아. 걘 손재주가 없어.

I'm all thumbs when it comes to computers.
난 컴퓨터에 관한거라면 젬병이야.

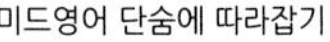

028 He has what it takes 그 사람은 소질이 있어

this is saying someone has ability, and often it also means the person needs to be trained. It is like saying "He has a lot of natural talent"

| Point | have[got] what it takes (to~) (…할) 자격이 있다
I've got what it takes 이길 자격이 있어

A: Will my son be able to become a professor?
내 아들이 교수가 될 수 있을까?

B: **He has what it takes,** but he will need to study a lot. 소질은 있지만 많이 공부해야 돼.

I'll fail. I don't have what it takes.
난 실패할거야. 소질이 없어.

I don't have what it takes to be a surgeon.
외과의사가 되기 위한 소질이 없어.

I don't know what it takes to make a good relationship. 좋은 관계를 만드는 소질이 없나 봐.

029 I know a thing or two about it 그거에 대해 잘 알고 있어

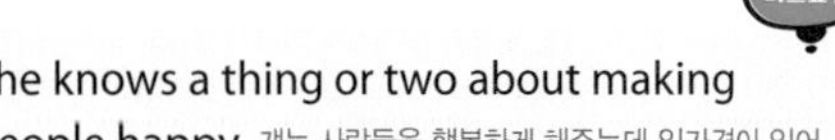

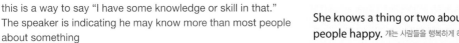

this is a way to say "I have some knowledge or skill in that." The speaker is indicating he may know more than most people about something

| Point | I know something about~ …에 대해 뭐 좀 알아

A: Have you ever been camping in the woods?
숲속에서 캠핑해봤어?

B: **I know a thing or two about** it. I go camping every year. 숲속캠핑은 내가 잘 알아. 매년 캠핑가거든.

She knows a thing or two about making people happy. 걔는 사람들을 행복하게 해주는데 일가견이 있어.

You don't leave another girl's panties in your pocket unless you want your wife to find them. I know a thing or two about affairs.
아내한테 들키지 않으려면 다른 여자의 팬티를 주머니에 넣고 다니면 안돼. 난 바람피는 거에 대해 잘 알고 있거든.

030 Do your stuff! 네 솜씨를 보여줘!, 네가 잘하는거 해봐!

this is a way to say "Start now." The speaker wants someone to begin

| Point | He knows his stuff 그 사람은 능수능란하다

A: I know you play the piano well. **Do your stuff!**
너 피아노 잘 치잖아. 솜씨를 보여줘!

B: Alright. Are there any songs you want me to play for you? 좋아. 내가 연주하길 바라는 노래 뭐 있어?

It's all ready for you. Do your stuff.
너를 위해 모든게 준비됐어. 자 시작해봐.

Do your stuff. I want to see what you're capable of. 시작해봐. 네 솜씨를 보고 싶어.

You think you can do better? Do your stuff.
네가 더 잘 할 수 있을 것 같아? 어서 솜씨를 보여줘봐.

031 Show me what you got 네 실력을 보여줘

the speaker is telling someone "I want to see what your talent is." In other words, he wants to look at the person's ability

| Point | Let me see what you got 네 실력이 어떤지 좀 보자

A: I am the best baseball player on this team.
난 이 팀에서 가장 뛰어난 야구 선수야.

B: Really? **Show me what you've got.**
정말? 네 실력을 보여줘.

Why don't you show me what you got.
네 실력을 보여줘 봐.

Use your something special, kid. Show me what you got. 얘야, 특별한 것을 써봐. 네가 가진 실력을 보여줘.

Hotch, let's check the garage, then show me what you got. 하치, 창고를 확인한 다음 실력을 좀 보여줘요.

032 Look who's got game 너 정말 잘하네

this is said when someone is admiring another person's ability to do something. Originally it was used in the game of basketball, when players with a lot of talent were told they had game. We could say this in a similar way by saying "Wow, you are really good at that"

| Point | got game …을 잘하다, 능숙하다

A: You did very well. **Look who's got game!**
정말 잘했어. 너 정말 잘하는데!

B: Yeah, I've been practicing a lot so I could get better. 그래, 더 잘하도록 연습을 많이 했어.

I'm a lucky man. Guy's got game.
난 운좋은 사람이야. 그 친구가 일을 잘해.

Dave has game and can get any girl here.
데이브는 능숙해서 여기 여자 누구든 취할 수 있어.

Are you telling me you've got game?
네가 능력이 있다고 말하는거야?

Oh yeah, we'll find out if he has got game.
오 그래, 우리는 걔가 능력이 있는지 알아낼거야.

033 Mindy has a way with folks 민디는 사람들을 잘 다루어

this indicates that Mindy has a nice personality, and she is able to make people feel comfortable when she is with them. It is a complimentary thing to say. Another way to say the same thing is "Mindy is very charming when she is with people"

| Point | have[get] a way with sb[sth] …을 잘 다루다

A: Your clerk is very good with customers.
점원이 고객들에게 아주 잘하네요.

B: **Mindy has a way with folks.** 민디는 사람들을 잘 대해요.

She is a good surgeon and she has a way with patients. 걔는 훌륭한 외과의사고 환자들을 잘 다루어.

You've got such a way with words.
너 정말 말솜씨가 엄청 뛰어나.

Kalinda has a way with Cary.
칼린다는 케리를 다룰 수 있는 요령을 알고 있어.

I thought you had a way with women.
난 네가 여자들을 잘 다룬다고 생각했는데.

034 I do this all the time 난 늘상 이래, 늘상 하는 일이야

this expresses that the speaker has a lot of experience. It is similar to saying "This is easy for me to do"

| Point | I do that all day long 난 온종일 그래

A: Wow, you fixed the problem fast. 와, 문제를 빨리 해결했네.

B: **I do this all the time.** It's easy for me.
늘상 이래. 나한테 쉬운 일이야.

Men do this all the time. 남자들은 맨날 그렇다니까.

Don't get me wrong. I do this all the time.
오해하지마. 난 늘상 이래.

You said that you do this all the time.
넌 늘상 그런다고 말했잖아.

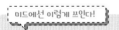

I do it all the time

Modern Family SEASON#1-2

유부남과 자는 등 행실이 좋지 않은 그러나 섹시한 Desiree가 Phil이 자건거를 타고 가는데 인사하며 집 문이 잠겼다고 도와달라고 한다.

Desiree: Hi, uh, this is really embarrassing, but I locked myself out of my house.
Phil: Oh, I do it all the time. Don't be embarrassed.
Desiree: I was.... I was hoping you could help me. There's a window open, but I can't reach it. Would you mind?
Phil: Yeah, sure. Of course.
Desiree: Great.
Phil: You know what they say. Every time God closes a door, he opens a window. Or I guess in this case, every time he locks you out... Okay what do we got here?

데지레: 안녕하세요, 정말 창피하지만, 집안에 열쇠를 두고 문을 잠궈 버렸어요.
필: 어, 난 맨날 그래요. 창피해하지 마세요.
데지레: 좀 도와주셨으면 하는데요, 창문 하나가 열려있지만 제가 닿지가 않아요. 도와줄래요?
필: 그래요, 물론이죠.
데지레: 정말 잘됐네요.
필: 사람들이 그렇게들 말하죠. 신이 문을 잠글 때마다 창문을 열어놓으신다구요. 아니면 이 경우에는 문이 잠겨 못들어갈 때마다… 그래요 어떻게 된거죠?

035 Let's get started 자 시작하자

미드표현

this means "Let's begin." Someone wants to begin working

| Point | get started (…을) 시작하다

A: There is a lot of work to do here. 여기 할 일이 너무 많아.

B: I know. **Let's get started** on it. 알아. 시작하자고.

I'm ready. Let's get started. 난 준비됐어. 시작하자고.

If everybody's ready, we should get started.
다들 준비되면 시작하자고.

I should really get started on this shopping list. 난 정말이지 이 쇼핑 목록을 작성해야 돼.

Let's get started. Our time is limited. 자 시작하자고. 우리 시간은 제한되어 있어.

036 Let's get down to business 자 일을 시작하자

미드표현

this often means that the speaker thinks it is time to do real work. It is a way to say "Let's get serious about this"

| Point | get down to business (진지하게) 일에 착수하다
get down to+a place …로 가다

A: **Let's get down to business.** 자 시작하지

B: What would you like to talk about first?
먼저 뭘 얘기하고 싶어?

Let's get down to business! She needs some makeup! 자 본격적으로 해보자! 쟤 화장 좀 해야 돼!

What're you doing here? Get down to the OR right now. 여기서 뭐해? 빨리 수술실로 가.

The meeting is starting. Let's get down to business. 회의가 시작한다. 이제 진지하게 시작하자고.

037 Let's get cracking 1. 일을 시작하자 2. 빨리 가자

미드표현

this is said to tell people "It's time to work hard." The speaker wants them to know they shouldn't be relaxing

| Point | get cracking 일을 시작하거나 어디로 빨리 가다

A: The coffee break is over. **Let's get cracking.**
커피타임은 끝났어. 일을 시작하자.

B: It's so difficult to start working after a break.
쉬다가 일하는 건 너무 힘들어.

We've got no more than an hour. Let's get cracking. 한 시간도 안 남았어. 어서 서둘러 가자.

We need to get cracking here. 우리는 일을 서둘러야 돼.

Congratulations if you got what you wanted, and if you didn't, I could care less. Get cracking.
네가 원하는 걸 얻었다면 축하해, 그리고 얻지 못했다고 해도 상관없어. 일을 시작하라고.

038 Let's roll 자 시작하자

미드표현

this is a way to say "Let's get started." It tells people that things are beginning

| Point | Let's roll= Let's get started 시작하다, 착수하다

A: Are you ready to leave on our trip?
우리 여행 떠날 준비 됐어?

B: I sure am. I have my suitcases here. **Let's roll.**
물론. 여기 내 짐가방야. 자 가자고.

Everything has been organized. Let's roll.
모든 게 다 준비됐어. 자 시작하자.

I'm anxious to get started. Let's roll.
난 정말이지 시작하고 싶어. 자 시작하자.

Is everyone ready now? Let's roll.
이제 다들 준비됐어? 자 시작하자.

Is everyone here? Good, let's roll.
모두들 모였어요? 좋아요. 이제 시작합시다.

039 I'm going to see it through 난 시작한 일을 끝까지 마무리할거야

this is a way that the speaker is going to make sure something is completed. We might also understand that he is making a vow not to quit doing something. It is like saying "I'm going to keep doing this until it's finished"

| Point | see it through 끝까지 실행하다

A: You know, it will be very difficult to get through medical school. 저 말야, 의대를 마치는게 매우 어려울거야.

B: I know it's tough, but **I'm going to see it through.** 어려운 것은 알지만 난 끝까지 해낼거야.

I finally committed to doing something charitable and I'm going to see it through.
마침내 난 자선관련일에 전념했는데 끝까지 마무리할거야.

He's got five more games in the season. He made a commitment. He's gonna see it through.
이번 시즌에 다섯 게임이 남았는데 헌신적으로 했으니 마무리도 잘 할거야.

When you start something, young man, you see it through. 젊은이, 뭔가 시작했으면 끝내야 돼.

040 I'm gonna get the ball rolling 난 본격적으로 시작할거야

this expresses that the speaker is going to get a process started. We can understand that this is the first step in beginning something. It is very similar to saying "I'm going to start the process so that things can begin"

| Point | get[start] the ball rolling 시작하다, 시작해서 계속하다

A: When are you going to begin the report?
보고서는 언제 쓰기 시작할거야?

B: **I'll get the ball rolling** on Monday morning.
월요일 아침에 본격적으로 시작할거야.

Well, let's just say, I got the ball rolling.
어, 내가 시작했다고 하자고.

You're the one that got this whole ball rolling again. 이 모든 일을 다시 시작한 사람은 바로 너야.

No, it's my fault. I got the ball rolling. I messed with the trial.
아냐, 그건 내 잘못이야. 내가 일을 벌렸어. 내가 재판에 얽혀들었다고.

041 Let's get this show on the road 자 이제 시작하자

this is a fairly common expression, and it simply means that the speaker wants to begin or get things underway. It is a way to signal to everyone that they need to start working now, and is very much like saying "Let's get started"

| Point | get this show on the road 시작하다, 해치우다, 출발하자

A: **Let's get this show on the road.** 자 이제 시작하자.

B: Tell us what to do and we'll do it.
뭘 해야할지 말해주면 우리가 할게.

I'm gonna wash up, and then we'll get this show on the road. 내가 씻고 나서 우리 출발하자고.

A: Let's get this show on the road, all right? B: No, we must wait until your father gets here.
A: 자 이제 출발하자고, 알았어? B: 아니, 우리는 네 아버지가 여기 올 때까지 기다려야 돼.

All right, then. Let's get this show on the road.
좋아 그럼. 우리 시작하자고.

042 Will they be up and running? 걔네들 잘 되고 있어?

this is asking if something will be working at a certain time. It is like asking "Will they be ready to work?"

| Point | be up and running 잘 돌아가다, 잘 작동되다
be up and about[around]
다 나아서 정상적으로 활동하다, 회복해서 건강하게 활동하다
Up and at them! 일어나요!, 적극적으로 해봐!

A: The new computers arrived on Tuesday.
새로운 컴퓨터가 화요일날 도착했어.

B: **Will they be up and running** by next week?
다음 주까지는 제대로 작동될까?

How pretty you look today! It's wonderful that you're up and about!
오늘 너 참 예쁘다! 네가 다시 회복돼서 정말 좋아!

Good to see you up and around.
네 건강한 모습을 봐서 좋아.

043 I'll get right on it 당장 그렇게 할게, 바로 시작할게, 그럴게

this is a way to tell someone "I'll do it now." The speaker wants someone to know that he is going to start work on something

| Point | get right on~ 바로 시작하다, 착수하다

A: Steve, this paperwork has to be finished today.
스티브, 이 서류작업이 오늘 끝나야 돼.

B: I understand. **I'll get right on it.** 알았어요. 바로 시작할게요.

미드표현

A: Doc, I want you to process the body ASAP. B: Yeah, I'll get right on it.
A: 의사선생님, 최대한 이 시신을 빨리 처리해주세요. B: 바로 할게.

A: You should go out, try to find yourself a nice woman. B: Yeah, I'll get right on that.
A: 가서 괜찮은 여자를 만나봐. B: 그럴게.

044 We got off on the wrong foot 시작이 좋지 못했던 것 같아

this indicates someone made a bad impression. It is like saying "We didn't impress each other"

| Point | get off on the wrong foot 시작이 잘못되다, 시작이 순조롭지 않다, 시작부터 어그러지다

A: Why are you and Sally so unkind to each other?
왜 너와 샐리는 서로 안좋아?

B: **We got off on the wrong foot.** She doesn't like me. 시작부터 어그러졌어. 걘 날 안 좋아해.

미드표현

I think we got off on the wrong foot.
우린 시작이 잘못 된 것 같아.

You're starting this case off on the wrong foot. 이 사건을 잘못 시작했어.

But I feel like we got off on the wrong foot this morning. 하지만 오늘 아침 시작이 좋지 못했던 것 같아.

045 It was just like riding a bike 술술 잘 나가더라

this expresses "Once you learn it, you never forget how to do it." People believe that once you learn how to ride a bike, you always remember how to do it

A: Do you remember how to give a presentation?
프리젠테이션 어떻게 하는지 기억해?

B: Sure. **It's just like riding a bike.**
물론. 한번 배우면 잊지 않고 잘할 수 있어.

미드표현

A: How is your relationship with your new boss? B: Once I broke the ice with him, it was just like riding a bike.
A: 새로운 사장과의 관계는 어때? B: 한번 어색한 순간이 깨지니까 술술 잘 돼가.

046 (Are) You done? 다했니?

this is a way of asking "Have you finished?" The speaker wants to know if someone completed something

| Point | It's all done 다 됐어
It's gone 다 끝났어
Are you through? 다했어?

A: I've been waiting to go out with you. **You done?**
너랑 나갈려고 기다리고 있어. 다했니?

B: No, I still have some homework that needs to be finished. 아니. 아직 끝내야 하는 숙제가 좀 있어.

You done? I said, are you done!
다했어? 다했냐고 말했어!

I don't want you to see it until it's all done.
다 끝날 때까진 보지마.

Are you through? I want to add a few comments. 다했어? 몇 가지 말을 더하고 싶은데.

I'm almost through with the docs.
서류 정리 거의 다 끝나가.

047 I'm done with this 이거 다 끝냈어, 그만하겠어, 이제 안해

미드표현

often this means that someone has decided to stop working on something. It either means "I'm finished" or "I don't want to work on this anymore"

I Point I be done (with sth) (…을) 끝내다
be done with sb …와 관계가 끝장나다
be done with+음식 …을 다 먹어치우다

A: I can't understand these directions. **I'm done with this!** 이 지시사항을 이해 못하겠어. 그만할테야!

B: You can't just give up. Try a little harder.
그냥 포기하면 안돼. 좀 더 열심히 해봐.

Bring that back when you're done with it, OK?
그거 끝내면 가져와, 알았지?

We're almost done with this whole thing.
이 모든 일을 거의 끝냈어.

You've crossed the line here, Will. I'm done with you. You hear me? Done!
네가 선을 넘었어, 윌, 너하고 끝이야. 알았어? 끝이라고!

048 Wrap it up 결론을 내자, 이만 끝내자

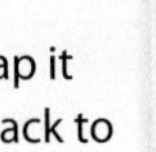

미드표현

this is a way to say "Finish it." The speaker is telling people to complete what they are doing

I Point I wrap sth up …을 끝내다, 마무리하다

A: The store is closing. **Wrap it up.**
가게 문닫습니다. 이만 끝내시죠.

B: But I haven't finished shopping yet.
하지만 아직 쇼핑을 다하지 못했는데요.

Time to wrap it up. 마칠 시간이야.

You got something to say, Scofield? Wrap it up. And all four of you, get your asses back to the block.
할 말이 있어, 스코필드? 끝내자고. 너희 네명은 빨리 돌아가.

049 Game's over 다 끝났어

미드표현

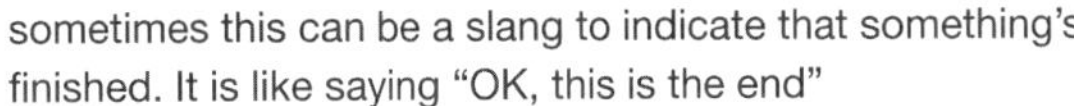

sometimes this can be a slang to indicate that something's finished. It is like saying "OK, this is the end"

A: So I heard your wife found you had a girlfriend.
그래 네 아내가 너 여친이 있는 걸 알아냈다며.

B: Yeah, she knows. **Game's over** for me.
그래, 알게 됐어. 난 다 끝났어.

The game's over just because you're afraid of stupid Mr. White?
네가 멍청한 화이트 씨를 두려워하기 때문에 게임이 끝났다고?

Game's over. It's time to go home.
게임 끝났어. 집에 갈 시간이야.

We lost our chance to win. Game's over.
우리는 승리할 기회를 놓쳤어. 게임 끝났어.

050 We're almost there 거의 다 됐어, 거의 끝났어

미드표현

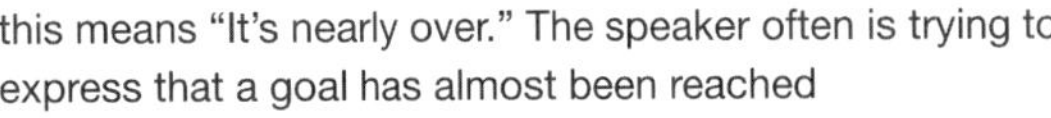

this means "It's nearly over." The speaker often is trying to express that a goal has almost been reached

I Point I be almost there 목표지점에 거의 다다르다, 일을 거의 다 끝마치다

A: How much longer do we have to drive?
얼마나 더 운전을 해야 돼?

B: **We're almost there.** Be patient now.
거의 다 왔어. 조금만 참아.

Hang on a little longer. We're almost there.
조금만 더 기다려봐. 거의 다 됐어.

We're almost there. We'll be finished very soon. 거의 다 됐어. 곧 끝날거야.

Everyone keep working. We're almost there.
다들 계속 일해. 거의 다 됐어.

We're almost there. Nice and easy.
거의 다 왔으니까 천천히 가.

Okay, we're almost there. Here. Put this blindfold on. 좋아, 거의 다 왔어. 여기, 안대를 해.

051 I'm not finished with you 얘기 다 안 끝났어, 아직 할 얘기가 남았어

often this is a way to say "I want to talk more to you about something." Usually the speaker is expressing some anger to the person he is speaking to

I Point I be finished with …을 마치다, …하고 볼 일이 끝나다

A: Can I go back to my office now?
이제 제 사무실로 돌아가도 되나요?

B: No you can't. **I'm not finished with you yet.**
아니 안돼. 아직 할 얘기가 남았어.

We're not finished with the lesson yet.
아직 수업을 끝내지 못했어.

I'm not finished with the report.
보고서 작성 아직 못 끝냈어.

I'm finished with New York. 뉴욕구경 다했어.

052 I just want to get it over with 그냥 빨리 끝냈으면 해

this indicates someone wants to finish something. It is like saying "I want it to end"

I Point I Let's get it over with 빨리 해치워 버리자구

A: Most of us don't want to join the army.
우리들 대부분은 군대에 가기 싫어해.

B: I know. **I just want to get it over with.**
알아. 그냥 빨리 끝냈으면 해.

Just tell her and get it over with.
그냥 걔한테 얘기하고 끝내버려.

If you want me dead, why don't you just shoot me and get it over with?
내가 죽길바라면 그냥 쏘고 끝내버려.

You may as well get it over with as fast as you can, like ripping off a band-aid.
넌 마치 반창고를 떼어내듯 가능한 빨리 그걸 해치우는게 좋을거야.

053 We've been over this 그건 이미 끝난 일이야, 이미 얘기한 일이잖아

this is a way to say "We did or talked about it before." The speaker feels something doesn't need to be done again

I Point I be over 끝나다

A: I need you to give me more money every month. 매달 돈을 좀 더 줘.

B: **We've been over this.** I don't have any extra money to give. 그건 이미 끝난 일이야. 줄 여분의 돈이 없어.

We have been over this before.
그건 다 끝난 이야기잖아.

It's over. You can all go home. 끝났어. 모두 집에 가도 돼.

Wake me up when it's over. 끝나면 깨워.

054 Please get it done by tomorrow 내일까지 마무리해

this is asking someone to complete something by the next day. He is saying "Finish it by the next day"

I Point I get sth done …을 끝내다

A: When is this report going to be due?
이 보고서 언제까지 해야 돼?

B: Please **get it done by** tomorrow. 내일까지 끝내.

If I don't get it done, I'll be fired.
이걸 못 끝내면 난 잘릴거야.

Nobody is leaving until we get this done!
우리가 이걸 끝낼 때까지는 아무도 못 가!

You got to trust me. We're gonna get this done. 날 믿어야 돼. 이걸 끝내야 돼.

055 It works! 제대로 되네!, 효과가 있네!

this is indicating that something is functioning. It means "This is doing what it should"

| Point | It won't work 효과가 없을거야

A: Look at this new remote control I invented.
내가 고안한 새로운 리모트 컨트롤을 봐.

B: **It works!** You must be a genius.
제대로 되네! 넌 정말 천재가봐.

미드표현

I don't care if it works. Why is it so important to you?
그게 제대로 되는 말든 상관없어. 그게 너한테 왜 그렇게 중요한거야?

I don't like the economic plan. It won't work.
경제 계획이 맘에 안들어. 효과가 없을거야.

My key won't work. 내 열쇠가 말을 안 들어.

056 It doesn't work 제대로 안돼, 그렇겐 안돼

this means that something has failed. It is a way to say "Something went wrong"

| Point | It doesn't work that way 그렇게는 안 통해

A: How is the computer you bought? 네가 산 컴퓨터 어때?

B: **It doesn't work.** I think it has a virus.
제대로 안돌아가. 바이러스에 걸렸나봐.

미드표현

You can't just kiss me and think you're gonna make it all go away, okay? It doesn't work that way. 키스만 하면 다 끝난 줄 알아? 절대 아니야.

Please don't push these buttons on the machine because it doesn't work that way.
기계의 이 단추들 누르지마, 그렇게 작동하는게 아니니까.

Don't wear shoes inside of a house. It doesn't work that way. 집안에서 신발을 신지마. 그렇게 하면 안돼.

057 We'll hammer out the details 세부사항에 대한 문제를 해결해야 돼

usually this is said after there has been an agreement to do something together, especially between two businesses or companies. We can understand that they plan to write down the details in a contract that they both agree to. It is like saying "We'll figure out our plan and then write it down in a contract"

| Point | hammer out 오랜 논쟁 끝에 결론에 도달해 문제를 해결하다

A: I'm glad we will be able to merge our businesses. 우리 사업체를 합병할 수 있어 기뻐요.

B: Come to my office Monday and **we'll hammer out the details.** 월요일에 내 사무실로 와서 세부사항을 정리하죠.

미드표현

I have absolutely no idea. Let's go hammer out the details. 난 정말 모르겠어. 세부사항을 결정하자고.

So we have 48 hours to hammer this out.
그럼 우리는 이 문제를 48시간 내로 해결해야 되네.

She's not the one that dragged me to court to hammer out some custody agreement.
걘 양육권 협의를 해결하기 위해 나를 법정으로 끌어들일 사람은 아냐.

058 Problem solved 문제는 해결됐어

very simply, this means that everything is okay and there is no need to worry about the problem anymore. We can understand that the speaker has probably solved whatever bad thing was happing. It is like saying "I took care of everything, so don't worry"

| Point | Problem solved 문제는 해결됐어
End of discussion 토론 끝, 더이상 왈가왈부하지마
End of story 이야기 끝, 더 이상 할 말없음.
Period 이상 끝 Patience 인내하라고, 참아봐

A: There is nowhere that our group can meet tomorrow. 내일 우리 팀이 만날 장소가 없어.

B: Everyone can come over to my apartment. **Problem solved.** 다들 내 아파트로 와. 문제해결.

미드표현

That's it! That's the way to do it! Problem solved. 바로 그거야! 바로 그렇게 하는거야! 문제해결.

I'm your girlfriend, and you should have taken my side. That's it. End of story. Good night.
난 네 여친이니까 넌 내편을 들어줬어야 했어. 그게 다야. 이야기 끝. 잘자.

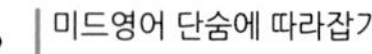

059 I'm working out the kinks 문제점들을 해결하고 있어

미드표현

this means that someone is trying to fix the problems that occur when starting something new. We can understand that the speaker wants to make things better than they are. In other words, "I'm solving the problems so it can be improved"

I Point I work out the kinks (어려운 일의) 문제점을 해결하다, 결함을 해결하다

A: Have you finished the computer program yet?
컴퓨터 프로그램 다 짰어?

B: It's almost done. **I'm working out the kinks.**
거의 다 됐어. 문제점들을 고치고 있어.

Yeah, it's, it's, uh, it's sort of a new tradition. I'm working out the kinks.
어, 이건 새로운 전통이라고 할 수도 있지. 내가 문제점들을 해결하고 있어.

They worked the kinks out of this electrical system years ago.
걔네들은 수년전에 이 전기시스템의 문제점들을 해결했어.

This is a test run. We need to work out all the kinks this weekend so they don't happen again.
이건 시운전이야. 다시는 이런 일이 발생하지 않도록 이번 주말에 모든 문제점들을 해결해야 돼.

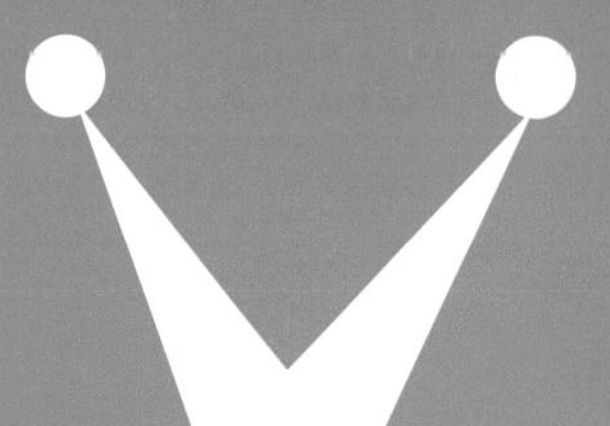

Ways to say you can do something well so things are going well

잘 나가다보니 성공하기도

You nailed it

001 She is on a roll 걔 한창 잘 나가고 있어, 걔 요새 상승세야

this means "She's having good luck." It indicates that many good things have happened to a person over a period of time

| Point | be on a roll 매사가 잘 풀려가고 있다 ↔ be on the skids(죽 쑤고 있다)
You're on the fast track 넌 출세가도를 달리고 있어
He got a hole in one 걔는 단번에 성공을 거두었다

A: Cindy won a lot of money at the casino.
신디는 카지노에서 돈을 많이 땄어.

B: **She is on a roll** tonight. 걔 오늘 밤 잘 나가네.

Don't stop me, I'm on a roll.
나 막지마, 지금 잘 나가고 있다고.

I'm on a roll this week and everything seems to be going my way.
이번주에 나 잘 나가고 있어 만사가 다 내 뜻대로 되고 있어.

I think I'm on a roll because so many good things have happened to me.
많은 좋은 일들이 내게 일어나 내가 아주 잘 풀리는 것 같아.

002 I'm on fire 잘 풀리고 있어

this means "Things are going great for me." The speaker feels he has been having good luck

| Point | be on fire 잘 풀리다

A: How come you've been so lucky?
어떻게 넌 그렇게 운이 좋아?

B: I'm not sure, but **I'm on fire** these days.
나도 몰라 하지만 요즘 일이 잘 풀리고 있어.

It's like they're on fire! 걔네들 잘 풀리는 것 같아!

All of the guys want to date me now. I'm on fire! 다들 나하고 데이트하려고 해. 나 아주 잘 나가고 있어!

Look at my exam score. I'm on fire!
내 시험점수 봐. 나 잘했지!

003 You'll make it happen 너 성공할거야

this expresses that a person will do well because he tries hard. It is similar to saying "You'll be successful"

| Point | make it happen 그 일이 일어나게 하다, 해내다

A: Do you think I can become a pilot?
내가 조종사가 될 수 있을 것 같아?

B: Sure. **You'll make it happen.** 물론, 넌 해낼거야.

I am going to make it happen. 내가 어떻게든 해볼게.

Don't just want it. Make it happen.
원하기만 하지 말고 이루어지게 해봐.

I think I found a way to make this happen.
그걸 해내는 방법을 찾아낸 것 같아.

I'm tired of trying to make things happen!
일이 성공하도록 하는데 지쳤어!

004 I'm going to make something of myself 난 성공할거야

this expresses the feeling that the speaker will work hard and become very successful in the future. It is a type of personal vow to do well. It is very similar to saying "I am sure that I am going to succeed later in life"

| Point | make something of oneself 스스로 노력하여 성공하다

A: **I'm going to make something of myself.**
난 앞으로 성공할거야.

B: Really? Tell me about your long-term goals.
장말? 네 장기적인 목표에 대해서 말해봐.

It's time to make something of myself. 스스로 노력하여 성공해야 할 때야.

This is the year I'm finally going to make something of myself. 올해는 내가 마침내 성공할 해야.

What's so wrong with seeing the potential in somebody and giving them a chance to make something of themselves?
누군가에게서 잠재력을 보고 그들에게 스스로 성공할 수 있는 기회를 주는 게 뭐가 잘못된거야?

005 They made a killing 걔네들 횡재했어, 땡 잡았어

this indicates the people made a lot of money. It is a way of saying "They have a lot more money because of that"

| Point | I made a killing 떼돈 벌었어
make money hand over fist 돈을 왕창 벌다
We hit the jackpot 땡 잡았구나

A: I wish I had invested in Microsoft.
마이크로소프트사에 투자할 걸.

B: Me too. **They made a killing.**
나도 그래. 걔네들 돈 엄청 벌었어.

We are gonna make a killing tonight.
오늘 밤 떼돈 벌겠어.

I'm making money hand over fist.
난 돈을 긁어모으고 있어.

People go to casinos for the same reason they go on blind dates, hoping to hit the jackpot.
사람들은 소개팅에 가는 심정으로 카지노에 가지, 땡잡을 희망을 갖고서.

006 You've got it made 성공했구나, 잘 나가는구나

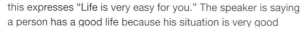

this expresses "Life is very easy for you." The speaker is saying a person has a good life because his situation is very good

A: Your wife is so beautiful. **You've got it made.**
네 아내 정말 예뻐. 잘 나가는구나.

B: Well, each person has different problems.
음, 사람마다 다 다른 문제들이 있지.

You've got it made. This place is so nice.
너 성공했구나. 이 집 정말 좋다.

If you have millions of dollars, you've got it made. 네가 많은 돈을 갖고 있다면 너 성공한거지.

You've got it made. You have a great life.
너 잘나가는구나. 멋지게 사는구나.

007 I did it! 해냈어!

this is often a very happy expression. The speaker is saying "I was successful"

| Point | You did it! 해냈구나!

A: How did your driving test go? 운전면허시험 어떻게 됐어?

B: **I did it!** I passed the test and got my license!
해냈어! 시험에 붙어서 면허증을 땄어!

You did it! You got in. 네가 해냈구나! 합격했어.

Now that wasn't easy, but you did it!
쉽지 않았지만, 넌 해냈어!

I did it! Oh, my God. I won! Who's the best? I'm the best!
내가 해냈어! 맙소사. 내가 이겼어! 누가 최고야? 내가 최고야!

No one believed I'd succeed, but I did it.
아무도 내가 성공할거라 생각한 사람은 없었지만 난 해냈어.

008 I made it! (쉽지 않은 일을) 해냈어!

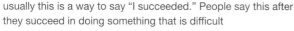

usually this is a way to say "I succeeded." People say this after they succeed in doing something that is difficult

| Point | I'm trying to make it big 크게 성공해볼거야
You made it 너 해냈구나, 왔구나
He made it big 그 사람은 (사업에) 성공했어

A: **I made it!** I got to the top of the mountain.
해냈어! 산 정상에 올랐어.

B: Remember, it's still a long walk down again.
기억해, 다시 내려갈 길이 아직 멀었어.

He made it big in venture capital.
벤처 캐피탈을 해서 크게 성공했어.

I made it! This is better than sex.
내가 해냈어! 이건 섹스보다 더 나아.

009 You nailed it 네가 해냈어, 아주 잘했어

this is a way to express that someone was successful because they did something perfectly. We can understand that this is a way of complimenting someone. It is very much like saying "You did an excellent job"

| Point | nail it 합격하다, 성공하다, 해내다

A: How did I do during the job interview?
취업면접 때 내가 어떻게 했대?

B: **You nailed it.** They want you to work for them.
아주 잘했어. 네가 일하기를 바란대.

I think you nailed it. 난 네가 해낸 것 같아.

She attended Hudson University, two years, and then in 2010 she took the police exam, nailed it.
걘 2년간 허드슨 대학에 다니다 2010년에 경찰시험을 보고 합격했어.

I know, it was amazing! I mean, we totally nailed it, it was beautiful.
알아, 대단했어! 내 말은 우리가 완전히 해냈다고, 정말 아름다웠어.

010 You've come a long way 장족의 발전을 했군

this is usually said when a person has personally developed a lot in life. It means "Your life has changed a lot in a very good way"

| Point | come a long way 장족의 발전을 하다

A: My family was really poor when I was young.
우리 가족은 어렸을 때 정말 가난했어.

B: I know. **You've come a long way.**
알아. 장족의 발전을 한 거지.

You've come a long way since we met 3 months ago.
우리가 3개월 전 만난 이후로 넌 많은 발전을 했어.

It took a long time, and it was painful, and it sucked, but we've come a long way.
시간이 오래 걸렸고 고통스러웠고 또한 엿같았지만 우리는 많은 발전을 했어.

011 He's gonna pull it off 걘 잘 해낼거야

this is a way of saying "He will complete something that people thought was impossible." This is said when the speaker is surprised and happy that a person succeeded at doing something

| Point | pull it off 해내다

A: Do you think Mike can make it work?
마이크가 일을 해낼 것 같아?

B: I do. **He's going to pull it off.** 어. 걘 잘 해낼거야.

I hope you pull it off. 네가 잘 해내길 바래.

I told you, he's going to pull it off.
내가 말했잖아. 걘 잘 해낼거야.

When I pull it off you're going to make me a partner. 내가 잘 해내면 날 파트너로 해줘야 돼.

012 More power to you 더욱 성공하기를

usually this is a way of saying "Good luck, but I think you might fail." People often say this when a person is trying to do something that they wouldn't try to do

A: I don't want to go to Alaska. If you do, **more power to you.** 알래스카에 가고 싶지 않아. 가고 싶으면 성공하길 바래.

B: Why don't you want to go? Are you afraid of the cold weather? 왜 가기 싫어해? 날씨가 추워서?

If you like the culture here, more power to you. 이곳 문화를 좋아한다면 더욱 성공하기를 바래.

More power to you. I'm glad things are going well. 더욱 잘되기를. 일들이 잘 풀려서 기뻐..

If this is the way you can succeed, more power to you.
이게 네가 성공하는 방법이라면 더욱 잘 되기를 바래.

013 I just wanna make things work again

난 일이 다시 제대로 돌아가길 바래

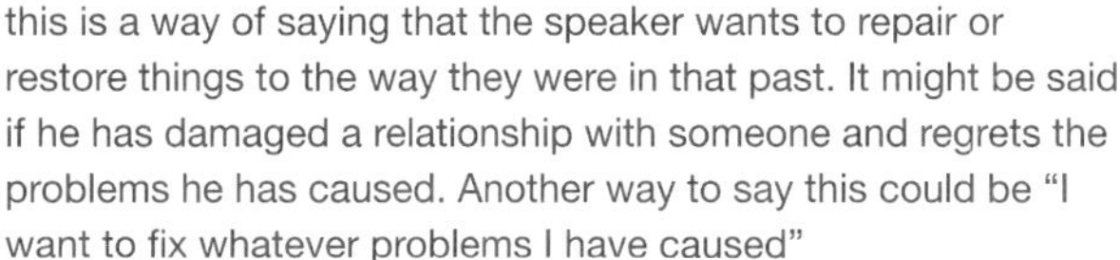

this is a way of saying that the speaker wants to repair or restore things to the way they were in that past. It might be said if he has damaged a relationship with someone and regrets the problems he has caused. Another way to say this could be "I want to fix whatever problems I have caused"

I Point I make things work 일이 돌아가게 하다
make it work 그게 작동하도록 하다

A: People say you've been trying to get together with your ex-wife. 사람들이 그러는데 너 전처와 다시 합치려고 한다며.

B: Yeah, **I just wanna make things work again.**
어, 모든 상황이 다시 제대로 돌아가기를 바래.

미드표현

That's how you make things work, right?
넌 그런 식으로 일이 제대로 돌아가도록 하는구나, 그지?

I am trying to make it work, I swear. I do everything he asks of me.
정말이지 난 그게 잘 돌아가도록 노력하고 있어. 걔가 내게 요구하는 것을 다 하고 있어.

Once I gave Jack up, I wanted to make it work with you.
일단 잭을 포기하고 나서, 난 너와 일을 제대로 하기를 원했어.

014 She has her eyes on the prize 갠 성공하려고 작정했어

this often means that a person is very focused on being successful at something. It indicates that the person is going to try very hard to meet a goal. In other words "She is very determined to succeed, and she won't quit"

I Point I have[get] one's eyes on sb 탐내다, 눈독들이다, 눈여겨보다
have[get] one's eyes on sth 원하다, 갖고 싶어하다

A: My sister is saving all of the money she earns.
내 누이는 버는 돈을 다 저축해.

B: **She has her eyes on the prize** and wants to get rich. 갠 성공해서 부자가 되려고 작정을 했구나.

미드표현

You got eyes on her? What do you see? Walter, talk to me.
너 걔 눈독들이지? 뭐가 좋은데? 월터, 말해봐.

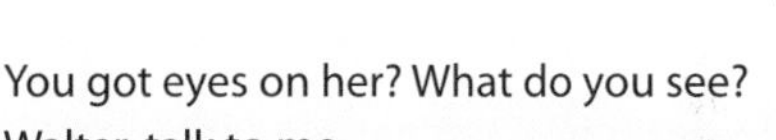

You are the only agency asset to have had eyes on Nazir in seven years.
넌 7년간 나지르를 눈여겨 본 우리 기관의 유일한 자산이야.

015 We might hit[strike] pay dirt 의외로 건수를 올릴 수도 있어

the speaker wants to say "There is a chance this will be very successful." It is a hopeful way to think of something

I Point I hit pay dirt 노다지를 캐다

A: Why are you going to Las Vegas?
라스베거스는 왜 가는거야?

B: **We might strike pay dirt.** You never know.
의외로 건수 올릴 수도 있잖아. 누가 알아.

미드표현

We might strike pay dirt if we keep working at it. 우리가 부단히 노력하면 의외로 건수를 올릴 수도 있을거야.

We might strike pay dirt investing in Internet stocks. 인터넷 주식에 투자를 해서 의외의 건수를 올릴 수도 있어.

We might strike pay dirt if we try harder.
우리가 더 열심히 하면 의외의 건수를 올릴 수도 있어.

016 We're getting somewhere 성과를 거두고 있어, 점점 나아지고 있어

this indicates things are going well. It is like saying "We're making progress"

I Point I get somewhere 성과를 좀 거두다
I'm making progress 발전하고 있어

A: Did you repair the car yet? 벌써 차 수리 했어?

B: **We're getting somewhere.** It should be fixed soon. 잘 되고 있어. 곧 수리가 끝날거야.

미드표현

Now we're getting somewhere. This is good.
이제 성과를 거두고 있어. 좋은 일이야.

I'm sure he's making progress.
갠 나아지고 있을게 확실해.

The show became a large draw.
그 쇼에 관람객이 엄청나게 몰렸어.

017 My life is full of ups and downs 인생이 파란만장했어

this is a way to say "Sometimes my life is happy and sometimes it is sad." It indicates the speaker's life is not always the same

I Point I ups and downs 기복, 부침

A: How have things been since you graduated from university? 대학 졸업 후 어땠어?

B: **My life is full of ups and downs.** It's kind of strange. 파란만장했어. 좀 이상해.

Every relationship has its ups and downs.
모든 관계에는 좋을 때도 있고 나쁠 때도 있는거야.

I'd say we've had our ups and downs.
우리도 인생이 파란만장했다고 할 수 있지.

Luke and I have had our ups and downs over the years. 루크와 나는 오랫동안 부침이 있었어.

018 He wiped the floor with her 걘 그녀를 찍소리 못하게 만들었어

This indicates that someone was able to defeat his opponent without difficulty. When one person wipes the floor with another person, we can understand that it was not a difficult competition. It is like saying "He beat her easily."

I Point I wipe the floor with sb (경기, 논쟁) 패배시키다, 완전히 압도하다

A: Did Lora win the race she ran against Bob?
밥에 맞서서 달렸던 경주에서 로라가 이겼어?

B: No, **Bob wiped the floor with her.** 아니, 밥이 완승했어.

You and me on the same team, we'd wipe the floor with the others.
너와 나는 같은 팀이니, 우리는 다른 팀들을 깔아뭉갤거야.

So, great job. We pretty much wiped the floor with them. 그래, 대단했어. 우리는 걔네들을 완전히 참패시켰어.

The other team? I think you're going to wipe the floor with them.
다른 팀? 난 네가 걔네들을 완패시킬거라 생각해.

019 I know what I'm doing 나도 아니까 걱정하지마, 내가 다 알아서 할게

this means "I can do this well." The speaker is telling someone he doesn't need to be helped

I Point I I know what I'm saying 나도 알고 하는 말이야, 내가 알아서 얘기한다구

A: Would you like me to help you? 내가 도와주길 바래?

B: No, thank you. **I know what I'm doing.**
고맙지만 됐어. 내가 알아서 할게.

Trust me. I know what I'm doing.
날 믿어. 내가 알아서 할게.

You guys, relax, I know what I'm doing.
얘들아, 긴장마, 내가 아니까 걱정마.

Don't worry, mom. I know what I'm doing.
걱정마요, 엄마. 내가 다 알아서 할게.

020 Don't I know it 그런 것쯤은 말 안 해도 나도 알아, 맞아

this is a way to express that the speaker agrees with something. It is similar to saying "That's right"

A: The weather has been very strange this year.
금년에 날씨가 정말 이상해.

B: **Don't I know it.** It's probably due to global warming. 그래, 지구온난화 때문인 것 같아.

Don't I know it. So what's the plan?
맞아. 그래 계획은 뭔데?

A: Shouldn't have to tell them at all. B: Don't I know it. A: 걔네들한테 얘기를 말았어야 하는데 B: 나도 알아

A: Well, we all make mistakes in our youth.
B: Don't I know it.
A: 우린 모두 젊은 시절 실수를 하지. B: 나도 알아.

021 I've paid my dues 내 할 몫(책임)은 다했어, 값을 치뤘어

this indicates the speaker worked a long time to become good at something. It is a way to say "I worked many years to learn this"

I Point I pay one's dues 빚을 갚다, 값을 치루다

A: How did you become such a good jazz musician? 어떻게 그렇게 훌륭한 재즈 음악가가 됐어?

B: I practiced all the time when I was young. **I've paid my dues.** 어렸을 때 항상 연습했지. 값을 치룬거지.

I've paid my dues, and I'm ready to make money. 내가 할 몫을 다 했어. 난 돈을 벌 준비가 됐어.

I don't have to do this anymore. I've paid my dues. 난 더 이상 이렇게 할 필요가 없어. 난 값을 치뤘어.

I'm a senior detective because I've paid my dues. 난 내가 할 건 다했기 때문에 고참형사가 됐어.

022 You'll see 곧 알게 될거야, 두고 보면 알아

미드표현

this indicates the speaker is sure something will happen. He wants to say "You will know I'm right in the future"

I Point I You'll see S+V …을 알게 될거야
(You) Just watch 넌 보고만 있어

A: I don't think you can become a professional baseball player. 네가 프로 야구선수가 될 수 없을 것 같아.

B: I'll be on the Yankees team in a few years. **You'll see.** 몇 년 후에 양키스 선수가 되어 있을거야. 두고 보면 알아.

They're going to find us. We'll get rescued. You'll see. 우리들을 곧 발견할거야. 구조될거야. 두고 봐.

You'll apologize, all will be forgotten. You'll see. 사과하면 다 잊혀질거야. 두고 보면 알아.

You'll see you're the only person I want to be with. 넌 내가 같이 있고 싶어하는 유일한 사람이라는 걸 알게 될거야.

023 You (just) wait and see 두고 봐, 기다려 봐

미드표현

this is very similar to the previous phrase. It means the speaker is certain something will happen in the future

I Point I wait and see 지켜보다

A: This apartment looks very old.
이 아파트는 아주 오래 된 것 같아.

B: I'll make it nice. **Just wait and see.**
정돈 좀 할게. 기다려 봐.

You wait and see. This is gonna fix everything.
두고 봐. 이게 모든 걸 다 고쳐줄거야.

Why don't we just wait and see what she has to say? 걔가 무슨 말을 할지 지켜보자.

We are going to just continue to wait and see what happens. 계속 무슨 일이 일어나는지 지켜볼거야.

024 See, I told you 거봐, 내가 뭐랬어, 내 말이 맞지

미드표현

this is said after something happens like the speaker said it would. It is a way to say "I said that would happen, and I was right"

I Point I See, I told you S+V 거봐, 내가 …라고 했잖아

A: It's snowing outside today. 오늘 밖에 눈이 와.

B: **See? I told you it would.** 거봐? 내가 그럴 거라고 했잖아.

See, I told you. I told you she would do this.
거봐, 내 말이 맞지. 걔가 그럴 거라고 했잖아.

See, I told you they don't swim.
거봐, 걔네들 수영 못한다고 했잖아.

See, I told you he wasn't home. His car's not even here. 거봐, 걔 집에 없다고 했잖아. 여기 걔 차도 없는데.

025 That figures 그럴 줄 알았어, 그럼 그렇지

미드표현

this is an indication that something has happened normally, as the speaker expected it to happen

| Point | That doesn't figure 앞뒤가 안 맞아
So I figured it out 그래서 (연유를) 알게 되었지. 이제 알았어

A: My cousin decided to attend medical school.
사촌이 의대에 가기로 했어.

B: **That figures.** She always was very smart.
그럴 줄 알았어. 걘 항상 무척 똑똑했어.

I think he knows about us. I think he's figured it out. 우리 사이를 걔가 아는 거 같아. 알아낸 거 같아.

A: You just don't like sports. B: That's not true. I've been a baseball fan my whole life. A: Baseball. Well, that figures.
A: 스포츠를 안 좋아하는 구나. B: 아냐, 난 야구를 오랫동안 좋아했어. A: 야구라. 그럼 그렇지.

026 Typical 그럼 그렇지, 뻔할 뻔자야

미드표현

this is said when someone is cynical and not surprised about something bad that happened. It is a way to say "Yeah, I expected that to happen"

A: I think the manager is stealing money from the office. 부장이 사무실에서 돈을 훔치는 것 같아.

B: **Typical.** There is nothing you can do about it.
그럼 그렇지. 네가 어떻게 할 수가 없어.

Sandy came here and insulted everyone. Typical. 샌디가 이리와서 사람들을 모욕했어. 늘 하는 행동이지.

Typical. We can't even get tickets for the concert. 그럼 그렇지. 우리는 콘서트 표를 구할 수도 없어.

It's 6pm and there is a huge traffic jam. Typical. 오후 여섯 시이고 차가 엄청 막혀. 뻔할 뻔자야.

027 (Did) You see that? 봤지?, 내 말이 맞지?

미드표현

often this is a way to say "Look, I knew that would happen." It is very similar to the previous phrase. Sometimes it can also imply "Look at what just happened"

| Point | Can't you see that? 모르겠어?

A: Pam said that she doesn't like me.
팸이 나를 싫어한다고 말했어.

B: **You see that?** I told you not to ask her out.
내 말 맞지? 걔한테 데이트 신청하지 말라고 했잖아.

Did you see that? She was flirting with us.
봤지? 걔가 우리한테 작업걸었어.

Ted, did you see that? This lady just assaulted me. 테드, 봤어? 이 여자가 날 공격했어.

Can't you see that? I'm just trying to make it right. 모르겠어? 나는 단지 그걸 바로 잡으려고 하고 있어.

028 What'd I tell you? 그러게 내가 뭐랬어?

미드표현

this is said to indicate the speaker predicted something would happen. It means "I told you it would happen"

| Point | What did I tell you about~ ? …에 대해 내가 뭐라고 했지?

A: We didn't have enough money to buy a ticket.
표를 구할 돈이 충분하지 않았어.

B: **What'd I tell you?** The tickets are too expensive. 그러게 내가 뭐랬어? 표가 너무 비싸다니까.

What did I tell you? It's perfect! 내가 뭐랬어? 완벽해!

It's working! What did I tell you? 야 된다! 내가 뭐랬어?

What did I tell you about talking to your friends while you're working?
근무 중에 친구와 얘기하는 거에 대해 내가 뭐라고 했지?

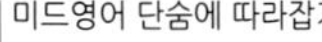

029 You ain't seen nothing yet 지금까지는[이정도는] 아무것도 아니었다구

this is grammatically incorrect, but it is a commonly used phrase which expresses the feeling that the speaker will continue to do difficult or surprising things. It is like saying "I'll do other amazing things in the future"

Point You haven't seen anything yet 이 정도는 약과야

A: I was surprised when you got Sue to agree to date you. 수가 너와 데이트를 하게 만들다니 놀라웠어.

B: **You ain't seen nothing yet.** I'm going to make her my girlfriend. 뭘 이 정도로. 내 여친으로 만들어버릴거야.

미드표현

This is just the beginning. You ain't seen nothing yet. 이건 시작에 불과해. 지금까지 아무것도 아니었어.

You ain't seen nothing yet. I have a lot more ideas. 지금까지는 아무것도 아니었어. 난 더 많은 아이디어가 있어.

The committee is implementing many new rules. You ain't seen nothing yet.
위원회는 많은 새로운 규칙을 시행하려고 해. 지금까지는 아무것도 아녔어.

030 I knew it 내 그럴 줄 알았어, 생각했던 바야

this usually means the speaker thought something was true and was right. It is like saying "I was sure that was true"

Point I knew (that) S+V …일 줄 알고 있었어

A: Andy and Sara are planning to get married.
앤디와 새러가 결혼하기로 했어.

B: **I knew it.** They'll make a great husband and wife. 그럴 줄 알았어. 좋은 남편과 아내가 될거야.

미드표현

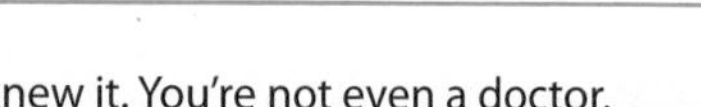

I knew it. You're not even a doctor.
생각했던 대로야. 넌 의사도 아니잖아.

I knew it didn't matter.
그게 문제가 되지 않는다는 걸 알고 있었어.

I knew it was terrible. 끔찍하다는 걸 알고 있었어.

031 I've still got it 나 아직 여전해

this means someone is still able to do something special. It is like saying "I can still do it after many years"

Point We('ve) still got it 우린 아직 여전해

A: Why do all of the girls like you?
왜 모든 여자들이 널 좋아하는거야?

B: It's my charm. **I've still got it.**
내 매력이지. 나 아직 여전하다고.

미드표현

I still got it. Nice and sexy.
나 아직 안 죽었어. 멋지고 섹시하지

I haven't lost the game yet. I've still got it.
나 아직 안졌어. 아직 살아있다고

We're rich and famous. We still got it.
우린 부자고 유명해. 여전하다고

032 You know what got me through it?
내가 그걸 어떻게 이겨냈는지 알아?

we hear this question when a person has gone through a difficult period and wants to explain what kept him strong or what helped him to survive. It is like saying "This is what allowed me to get through that tough time"

Point get sb through~ 어려운 시기를 이겨내거나 어렵게 학교를 마치게 해주다

A: It must have been difficult going through a divorce. 이혼을 겪는 것은 정말 힘든 일임에 틀림없어.

B: **You know what got me through it?** My friends kept cheering me up.
내가 어떻게 이겨냈는지 알아? 친구들이 계속 나를 응원해줬어.

미드표현

That book got me through some tough times.
내가 어려울 때 큰 힘이 되어준 책이지.

It's what got me through university.
그 생각으로 내가 대학교를 견디고 마쳤지.

These are the millions of laughs that got us through all those tough times.
이것들은 내가 그 어려운 시기들을 이겨내도록 해준 많은 재미있는 일들이야.

I've been dragging my ass all day, and you know what got me through it?
온종일 꿀꿀했는데 뭘로 이겨냈는지 알아?

033 Read it and weep 어때 내가 이겼지, 내 말이 맞지

this is often used when a speaker says he is correct. It means "This will show you I'm right"

A: I don't believe Susan gave you a birthday card.
수잔이 네게 생일카드를 줬다는게 안 믿어져.

B: Here it is. **Read it and weep.** 여기 이거 봐. 내 말이 맞지.

This is the contract. Read it and weep.
이게 계약서야. 잘 읽어봐.

Read it and weep. And there's nothing you can do about it.
내 말이 맞지. 네가 그것에 대해 할 수 있는 일이라곤 하나도 없어.

The guilty verdict just came in. Read it and weep. 유죄판결이 내려졌어. 내 말이 맞지.

034 Is he still dating up a storm? 걔 아직 여러 여자와 데이트하고 다녀?

미드표현

this is asking if someone has continued to date many women. It's older slang, but still used. It indicates that the person has been out on a lot of dates, but has not had a serious girlfriend. This can be similar to asking "Is he still going out with various women?"

| Point | up a storm 멋지게, 대단하게

A: Lon has been single for a year now.
론은 일년간 독신으로 지냈어.

B: **Is he still dating up a storm?**
걔 아직도 여러 여자와 데이트하고 다녀?

Did you see us? We've been dancing up a storm. 우리 봤어? 우리 신나게 춤을 추고 있었어.

We hear she was partying up a storm.
걔는 아주 신나게 파티를 했다고 들었는데.

I'm cleaning up a storm before company gets here. 일행들이 여기 오기 전까지 내가 열정적으로 청소를 할게.

MEMO

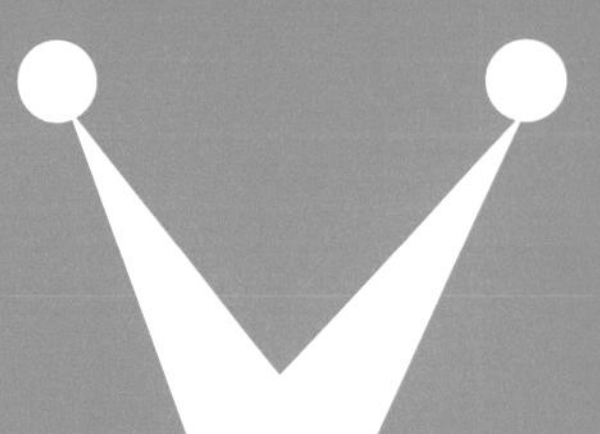

Ways of telling someone to try something

한번해봐 안되면 처음부터 다시 시작해야지

Knock yourself out

001 Go for it 한번 시도해봐

this means "Try it and you may succeed." Often it is said to a person who is not sure whether to try something

| Point | Let's go for it 한번 시도해보자
You'd better go for it 한번 시도해봐

A: Should I travel to Paris during my vacation?
휴가 동안에 파리를 방문해야 할까?
B: **Go for it.** You'll have a great time.
한번 해봐. 멋진 시간 보낼거야.

Go for it. You're the one he wants.
한번 해봐. 넌 걔가 원하는 사람이니.

We just decided to go for it. 한번 시도해보기로 했어.

A: My God, he's really cute. B: Go for it.
A: 와 정말 귀엽다. B: 한번 대시해봐.

I guess we better just go for it. 한번 시도해봐야겠는 걸.

002 Give it a shot 한번 해봐

미드표현

this is a way to say "Do your best." The speaker wants someone to try hard

| Point | Let's give it a shot 한번 해보자

A: I don't think I can get my driver's license.
운전 면허증을 못 딸 것 같아.
B: **Give it a shot.** It's useful to be able to drive.
한번 해봐. 운전할 수 있으면 편리해.

A: Trust me, by the end of the day he'll not only have forgiven me, he'll be thanking me.
B: All right, let's give it a shot.
A: 날 믿어, 나중에는 날 용서하고 고맙다고 할거야. B: 그래 한번 해보자.

I thought I'd give it a shot. 한번 해볼까 생각중이야.

003 Give it a try! 한번 해봐!

미드표현

this is similar to the previous 2 phrases. It is away of telling someone "Do your best"

| Point | Why don't you try it? 한번 해봐
Let's give it a try 해보자구
Give it a whirl! 시험 삼아 한 번 해 봐
Take it for a spin 한번 해봐

A: Do you think IBM will hire me? IBM이 날 뽑을까?
B: You should seek an interview. **Give it a try.**
인터뷰를 해봐. 한번 해보라고.

You want to give it a try? 한번 해보고 싶어?

The girls do it. I thought we'd give it a try.
여자애들이 하니까 우리도 한번 해보려고.

I guess we could give it a try. 한번 해보자.

004 What're you waiting for? 뭘 꾸물대는거야?, 뭘 기다리는거야?

this is a way to say "Go ahead." The speaker wants someone to do something now

| Point | So, why wait? 뭘 기다려?

A: Someday I'm going to meet the girl of my dreams. 언젠가 내 이상형의 여자를 만날거야.
B: **What are you waiting for?** You need to go on some dates. 뭘 기다리는거야? 넌 데이트 좀 해야 돼.

What are you waiting for? Let's go.
뭘 꾸물대? 가자고.

What are you waiting for? She's alone. Go get her. 뭘 꾸물대? 갠 혼자야. 가서 잡아.

I love you and I think I know how you feel about me. So why wait?
널 사랑해 그리고 나에 대한 네 감정도 알아. 그런데 뭘 기다리는거야?

005 It doesn't hurt to ask 물어본다고 나쁠 건 없지, 그냥 한번 물어본거야

usually this means "Ask, and if they say no, it's OK." The speaker is saying it is easy to ask for something, even if the person doesn't say yes

| Point | It can't[won't] hurt to try 한번 해본다고 해서 나쁠 건 없지
It wouldn't hurt (to~) (…을 해도) 밑질 건 없어

A: I might ask Bob out on a date with me.
밥에게 나랑 데이트하자고 해볼까 봐.

B: **It doesn't hurt to ask.** He may really like that.
물어본다고 나쁠 건 없지. 걔가 정말 좋아할 수도 있어.

See if he'll give you a lower price. It doesn't hurt to ask. 깎아줄 수 있는지 알아봐. 손해볼 건 없잖아.

It doesn't hurt to ask. Tell Tim you want a raise. 물어본다고 나쁠 건 없지. 팀에게 임금인상을 원한다고 해.

Did they give you tickets for the show? It doesn't hurt to ask.
걔네들이 너한테 그 쇼티켓을 줬어? 물어본다고 손해볼 건 없잖아.

006 You've got nothing to lose 밑져야 본전인데 뭐

this is a way to say "You risk nothing." The speaker is telling someone to try something because there is no risk

| Point | have (got) nothing to lose 잃을 게 없다, 손해 볼 게 없다

A: Is it a good idea to apply to many colleges?
많은 대학에 지원하는 게 좋은 생각이야?

B: **You've got nothing to lose.** At least one will admit you. 밑져야 본전이지. 적어도 한 대학은 널 받아줄거야.

Come on, do it. You got nothing to lose.
이봐, 해봐. 밑져야 본전이잖아

We have absolutely nothing to lose. Trust me.
우린 손해볼 게 하나도 없어. 날 믿어.

And when you got nothing, you got nothing to lose. 네가 가진게 하나도 없으면 잃을 것도 없는거야.

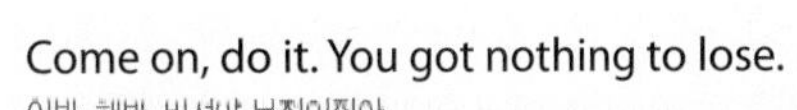

007 What've you got to lose? 손해볼 거 없잖아?

this question is actually more like a statement. It is a way of saying to someone that they should go ahead and try something because they may get benefits if they are successful doing it, but nothing bad will happen if they fail. It is like saying, "Come on try it. You have nothing to worry about if you fail"

| Point | What've you got to lose? 손해볼게 뭐 있어?, 손해볼 것 없잖아

A: Do you really think I should go out on a date with Brad? 내가 브래드하고 데이트를 해야 된다고 생각해?

B: He's a nice guy. **What've you got to lose?**
걔는 착한 사람야. 손해볼 거 없잖아.

Why not at least listen to what the man has to say? What have you got to lose?
적어도 그 남자가 하는 말은 들어보자고. 손해볼 것 없잖아.

Tell him you made the wrong choice, and he's the one you wanna be with. What have you got to lose?
그에게 네가 잘못 선택했다고, 네가 함께 하고픈 사람은 바로 그라고 말해. 손해볼 것 없잖아.

Just ask her on a date. What have you got to lose? 걔한테 데이트 신청해봐. 손해볼 것 없잖아.

008 Have at it 이제 먹어도 돼, 얼른 해, 해봐

this is telling someone to try something. It is like saying "Go ahead"

| Point | have (a go) at~ …을 시작하다, …을 먹다

A: May I try to fix this machine? 이 기계 고쳐도 될까요?

B: **Have at it.** I couldn't fix it. 한번 해봐요. 난 못 고치겠던데.

The files are all here. Have at it.
파일들 모두 여기 있어. 시작해봐.

Have at it. Take all the time you need.
시작해봐. 필요한 만큼 시간을 갖고 해봐.

I told you that you could give it a try. Have at it. 네가 해봐도 된다고 말했잖아. 얼른 해봐.

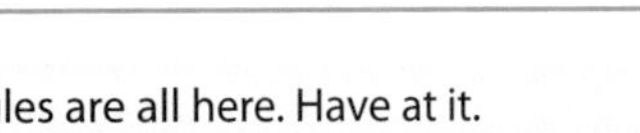

009 Try your luck 한번 해봐

this is similar to the previous phrase. It means "Go ahead with something and see what happens"

| Point | try one's luck 성공여부를 모르지만 성공을 희망하며 한번 해보다
I will try my luck (되든 안되든) 한번 해봐야겠어

A: I want to go to Vegas and gamble.
라스베거스에 가서 도박하고 싶어.

B: **Try your luck.** I think most people lose money there. 한번 해봐. 그 곳에서는 대부분의 사람들이 돈을 잃는 것 같던데.

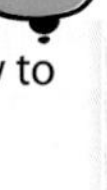

I'm headed back into the casino right now to try my luck again.
지금 바로 카지노에 가서 다시 한번 해봐야겠어.

You can try your luck with the appeals court, counsel. 변호사양반, 항소심을 한번 해보게나.

I'm just gonna be another rich, bored thrill seeker looking to try my luck down there.
난 그곳에서 운에 맡기기를 바라는 또 다른 부유하고 따분한 스릴을 찾는 사람이 될거야.

010 Who's gonna take the first shot? 누가 제일 먼저 해볼거야?

this means "Who will start?" The speaker wants to know which person will begin something

A: This computer game looks too difficult for us.
이 컴퓨터 게임은 내게 너무 어려운 것 같아.

B: It's not difficult. **Who's going to take the first shot** at it? 어렵지 않아. 누가 제일 먼저 해볼거야?

Ready to begin? Who's going to take the first shot? 시작할 준비됐어? 누가 먼저 할거야?

Who's going to take the first shot? Is anyone brave enough? 누가 먼저 해볼거야? 누구 용감한 사람있어?

The fighters are all set. Who's going to take the first shot? 싸울 사람들은 다 준비됐어. 누가 먼저 해볼테야?

011 Why do you get first crack at her?
왜 네가 걔한테 처음으로 시도하는데?

this is asking why another person will have the first option to deal with a woman. Although it can sometimes have different meanings, usually we can understand this to mean that the person wants to have the first opportunity to ask a woman out on a date, before anyone else does. Another way to ask this is "Why do you get to ask her out first?"

| Point | take[have] crack at sth (성공할지는 모르겠지만) …을 시도하다
have[get] first crack at sth[~ing] …을 처음으로 시도하다
*crack 은 명사로 시도란 뜻

A: I get to be the first to ask the new girl out.
새로운 여자애한테 내가 제일 먼저 데이트를 신청해야 돼.

B: **Why do you get first crack at her?**
왜 네가 처음으로 시도하는데?

John, you want to take a crack at that?
존, 너 저거 한번 해볼래?

Look, take a crack at this, for your son.
이봐, 네 아들을 위해서 이거 한번 해봐.

Hang on a sec. Why do you get first crack at her? 잠깐. 왜 네가 걔한테 처음으로 시도하려고 해?

The most critical patients should be getting first crack at these organs.
가장 위급한 환자들의 경우 이 장기들을 먼저 시도해봐야 돼.

012 Just suck it up 좀 참고 해라

this tells someone that he must do something that is hard, even if he doesn't want to. It is like saying "You have to do it"

| Point | suck it up 본격적으로 나서다, 분발하다

A: Being a new employee is very hard.
신입사원이 되는 건 무척 힘들어.

B: **Just suck it up.** You'll have a chance for promotion soon. 참고 해야지. 곧 승진기회가 올거야.

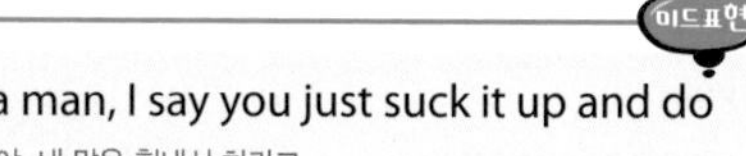

You're a man, I say you just suck it up and do it. 넌 남자야, 내 말은 힘내서 하라고.

You did the crime, why should I have to pay the price? Just suck it up, be a man, and do the time.
네가 범죄를 저질렀는데 내가 왜 그 대가를 치뤄야 돼? 그냥 나서서 남자답게 감옥에 가라고.

So suck it up man. It's a job, it's money.
참고 하라고. 일이잖아, 돈이라고.

013 Pull yourself together 기운 내, 똑바로 잘해, 정신차려

this is a way to say "Be strong and act normally." Usually it's said to someone who is having a difficult time

| Point | pull oneself together 기운차리다, 정신차리다
get one's act together 정신차리다, 마음을 가다듬다
Get your act together 기운차려

A: I've been so gloomy since I broke up with my boyfriend. 내 남친과 헤어진 이후에 너무 우울해.

B: **Pull yourself together.** There are other men to date. 기운차려. 다른 남자들하고 데이트하면 되잖아.

미드표현

I am begging you, pull yourself together, okay? 내 부탁하는데, 정신 차려, 응?

You've got to pull yourself together! She can't see you like this! 정신차려야지! 걘 이런 거 눈뜨고 못봐!

If you don't get your act together and start treating your wife with some respect, I'll take care of you myself.
정신 안 차리고 네 아내를 제대로 대접 안 하면 내가 직접 널 처리하겠어.

014 Cheer up! 기운 내!, 힘내!

this is said to someone who looks sad. It means "Try to be happy"

| Point | (Keep your) Chin up 고개 들어, 낙담하지마

A: Why do you look so unhappy? **Cheer up.**
왜 그리 안 좋아 보여? 힘내라고.

B: I'm really worried because my dad is in the hospital. 아버지가 병원에 계셔서 정말 걱정돼.

미드표현

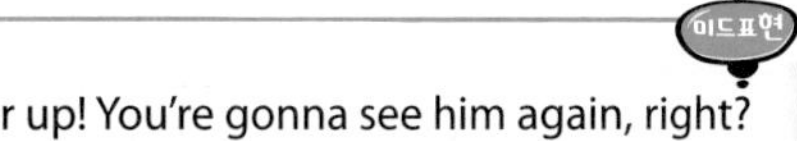

Cheer up! You're gonna see him again, right?
기운내! 다시 걜 만날 거잖아, 맞지?

Deep breath. Chin up. 호흡 크게 들이마시고, 기운 내라고.

Keep your chin up. Tomorrow we'll talk travel.
기운 내. 내일 우린 여행얘기할 거잖아.

015 Stick with it 포기하지마, 계속해

this is a way of saying "Don't give up." The speaker wants someone to continue something

| Point | Stick it out 끝까지 견뎌, 참고 견뎌

A: I don't like my job as a dentist. 치과의사인게 싫어.

B: **Stick with it.** You'll make a lot of money.
포기하지마. 돈을 많이 벌거야.

미드표현

So you think I should stick with it?
그래 네 생각은 내가 포기하면 안 된다는거야?

I wanna quit, but then I think I should stick it out. 그만두고 싶지만 계속 참고 견뎌야 될듯해.

It's difficult at first, but stick with it.
처음에는 어렵지만 포기하지말고 계속해.

016 Go on 1. 어서 말해 2. (동의, 허가) 그래, 어서 계속해 3. (격려) 자 어서 4. 말도 안돼

this is like a command. It means "Continue and don't quit"

| Point | go on+with sth[~ing] 계속해서 …하다
go on+N[to]~ (다음으로) 나아가다, …시작하다
Go ahead 계속해, 그럼, 그렇게 해
Carry on 계속해

A: This hike is too difficult for me to continue.
이 하이킹을 계속 하기에 너무 힘들어.

B: **Go on.** We're almost at the end of it.
계속해. 거의 끝까지 왔는데.

미드표현

Go wash your hands. Go on. 가서 손 씻어. 어서.

Go on, you can do it! 자 어서(힘내), 넌 할 수 있어!

Go ahead, I'm still listening. 계속해, 듣고 있어.

It's alright, you carry on. Carry on.
괜찮아, 계속하라고, 계속해.

017 Get on with it 계속해봐

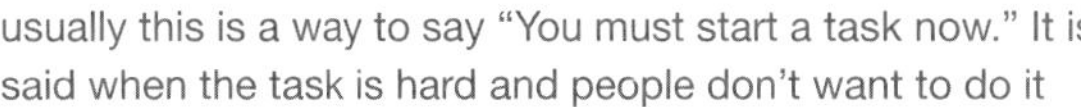

usually this is a way to say "You must start a task now." It is said when the task is hard and people don't want to do it

Point get on with 사이가 좋다, (일) 진척되다, (하던 일) 계속하다
get on with one's life (불행딛고) 다시 일어서다, 다시 정상으로 살아가다
Let's get on with it 계속하자
Get on with it! 서둘러!

A: Why aren't you working? **Get on with it!**
왜 일을 안 해? 계속해!

B: I'm sorry. I was just taking a short break.
죄송해요. 잠깐 쉬는 중이었어요.

미드표현

Let's get on with this. I got an insane amount of work to do today.
이 일 계속하자고. 오늘 할 일이 엄청나게 많아.

You and I need to get on with our special friendship. 너와 난 특별한 우정을 쌓아가야 돼.

I guess I'm just impatient to get on with my life. 어서 빨리 다시 일어서고 싶어.

018 Knock yourself out! 열심히 해!, 지칠 때까지 해봐!

often this means "Try it if you want to." The speaker is telling someone to try something, but he might think it is difficult to do

Point knock out 기절시키다, (경기) 때려눕히다, 깜작 놀라게 하다
knock yourself out (힘들겠지만) 열심히 최선을 다하다, (헤어지면서) 좋은 시간 보내

A: Could I try to ride that horse? 저 말을 타봐도 될까?

B: **Knock yourself out.** I don't think you can get on her. 해볼테면 해봐. 타지 못할 걸.

미드표현

A: Do you mind if I take pictures? B: Knock yourself out. A: 내가 사진을 찍어도 돼? B: 해봐.

A: Mind if we take a look? B:Knock yourself out. A: 한번 봐도 돼? B: 그렇게 해봐.

A: I can have him killed. B: Knock yourself out.
A: 걔를 청부살해할 수 있어. B: 해볼테면 해봐.

019 Keep it up 계속해, 계속 열심히 해

this is a way of telling a person he is doing a good job. It is like saying "You should continue doing it that way"

Point Keep in there! 그 상태로 계속 열심히 해!

A: Do you like the way the food was cooked?
음식 요리한 게 마음에 들어?

B: It was delicious. **Keep it up.** 맛있어. 계속 그렇게 해.

미드표현

Well, keep it up. You might get lucky.
어, 계속 열심히 해. 운이 따를 수도 있으니 말야.

Yeah, keep it up, Jay. There's already one dead person in this room.
그래, 계속해봐, 제이. 이미 이 방에는 한 명 죽은 사람이 있어.

Keep it up, Max, and one day I will show you my penis.
계속해봐, 맥스, 언젠가 내가 너에게 내 거시기를 보여줄게.

020 Keep up the good work (예전처럼) 계속 열심히 해, 계속 수고해

this is almost the same as the previous phrase. It means "Great, continue doing that"

A: You did a wonderful job. **Keep up the good work.** 너 참 일 잘했어. 계속 수고해.

B: I'm really happy to hear you say that.
그렇게 말씀해 주셔서 정말 고마워요.

미드표현

A: I'm having an affair with Danny. B: Well, good for you, honey! He's a good catch, keep up the good work.
A: 나 대니와 바람피고 있어. B: 잘했어, 자기야! 좋은 놈이니 계속 잘해보라고.

A: Keep up the good work. B: I will.
A: 계속 수고하세요. B: 네.

You did great. Keep up the good work.
아주 잘했어. 계속 수고하라고.

021 (You) Hang in there 끝까지 버텨

often this means "Be strong and don't give up." The speaker wants someone to be tough during a difficult time

A: My teachers have given me low grades.
선생님들이 내게 점수를 형편없게 줬어.

B: **Hang in there.** They'll improve if you study a bit. 끝까지 참고 버텨. 네가 공부 좀 하면 점수가 나아질거야.

Hang in there, it's gonna happen.
참고 견뎌. 그렇게 될거야.

Well, hang in there as long as you can, because I still need you.
가능한 한 참고 있어. 네가 필요하니까.

Hang in there. We're gonna get you to the hospital. 잘 견뎌. 병원으로 데려갈게.

022 I'm really rooting for you 정말 널 응원할게

미드표현

this indicates the speaker wants something to succeed. It is like saying "I hope that will go well"

I Point I root for sb (to~) (…가 …하기를) 지지하다, 바래다 (운동경기) 응원하다

A: I heard you were a fan of this year's soccer team. 네가 올해의 축구팀의 팬이라고 들었어.

B: Yeah, **I'm really rooting for this one.**
맞아, 정말 이 팀을 응원해.

Good luck. I'm rooting for you.
행운을 빌어. 널 응원할게.

We're rooting for you. Have a good date.
우린 널 응원할게. 데이트 잘해.

I was always rooting for you two to get together. 난 항상 너희 둘이 함께 하길 바래왔어.

023 Don't give up too easily 너무 쉽게 포기하지마

미드표현

this is a way of telling someone "Be strong." The speaker doesn't want someone to quit

I Point I Don't give up! 포기하지마!
Give it up 당장 때려 치워
Don't give an inch! 한치도 양보하지마!

A: I think this project is going to be a failure.
이 프로젝트가 실패할 것 같아.

B: **Don't give up too easily.** It might be successful. 너무 쉽게 포기하지마. 성공할 수도 있어.

I'm not gonna let you give up.
네가 포기하도록 놔두지 않을거야.

Why give up now? 왜 지금 포기하자는거야?

Don't give up. I mean, if you really like her.
네가 걜 정말 좋아한다면 포기하지마.

I'm just not sure that I'm ready to give up on that yet. 그걸 포기하고 싶은지 아직 모르겠어.

024 You never know 그야 모르잖아, 그야 알 수 없지, 누가 알아

미드표현

usually this is a way to say "It's possible." The speaker is telling someone that something could happen.This can also mean that something is uncertain

I Point I You never know S+V …인지 누가 알아

A: They tell me Paul may become president.
폴이 사장이 될 수도 있다고들 해.

B: **You never know.** He is very popular.
그야 알 수 없지. 걘 인기가 좋으니.

You never know what you need until you find it. 원하는 걸 발견할 때까지는 뭘 원하는지 모르잖아.

You never know when your life's going to change. 언제 너의 인생이 바뀔지는 알 수 없는거야.

I'm just saying you never know what could happen. 무슨 일이 일어날지 몰라서 하는 말이야.

025 We're back to where we started 우린 다시 원점으로 돌아왔어

미드표현

this means that the speaker thinks they have been wasting time doing something wrong, and now they are going to have to start all over again. Often this expresses an unhappy feeling because no progress was made. In other words, "We'll need to start from the beginning"

| Point | be back to where we started 일이 실패해 다시 원점으로 오다

A: It turns out that our suspect is innocent.
우리 용의자가 무죄라고 판명났어.

B: **We're back to where we started.** 우리 그럼 다시 원점이네.

We're not getting anywhere. We've circled right back to where we started.
우리는 아무 성과가 없어. 우리는 맴돌다 다시 원점으로 왔어.

We can't do the surgery. We're back to where we started. 우리는 수술을 할 수 없어. 우린 다시 원점이야.

026 You were like your old self there 넌 예전의 너로 돌아온 것 같았어

미드표현

the meaning of this is that someone may have had a problem that changed their behavior or way of acting, but for a short time, they acted as if they had never had that problem. It is a way of saying "You acted just like you use to in the past"

| Point | be[feel, look] one's old self 예전 모습이다, 상태가 좋다, 회복되다
be back to one's old self (달갑지 않게) 또 저짓이군
usual[normal] self 평상시의 모습　former self 예전의 모습

A: It was nice to be in the gym exercising again.
다시 체육관에서 운동을 하니 좋았어.

B: It's healthy too. **You were like your old self there.** 건강에도 좋고, 넌 예전의 너로 돌아온 것 같았어.

When he came back, he'd be his old self again. 걔가 돌아오면 다시 완전히 회복되어 있을거야.

He seems more like his old self.
상태가 많이 좋아진 것 같아.

He's back to his old self. 걔 또 저 짓야.

I'm back to my I-can-buy-anything-I-want former self.
내가 원하는 건 뭐든지 다 살 수 있다라는 예전의 내모습으로 돌아왔어.

027 You go back out there 다시 뛰어야지

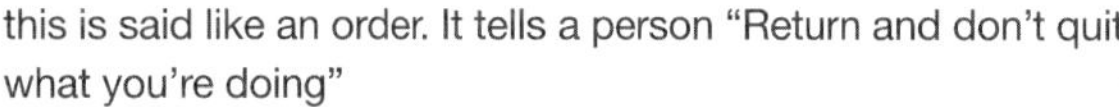

미드표현

this is said like an order. It tells a person "Return and don't quit what you're doing"

| Point | go back out there 그 곳에 다시 가다, 다시 뛰다

A: I don't want to play baseball anymore.
난 더 이상 야구를 하고 싶지 않아.

B: **You go back out there** and try harder.
다시 더 열심히 뛰어야지.

Are you gonna go back out there or what?
다시 뛸거야, 그렇지 않아?

I'm gonna go back out there, see if she knows anything about it.
거기 다시 가서 걔가 뭐 좀 알고 있는 게 있는지 알아볼게.

028 I gotta go back to the drawing board
난 처음부터 다시 시작해야겠어

미드표현

this indicates that a plan to do something has failed, and the speaker has to start figuring out a new way to try to accomplish the same thing. A different way to say this would be "I'm going to have to develop a different strategy."

| Point | go back to the drawing board 처음부터 다시 시작하다

A: So your plan to invent a new machine failed?
새로운 기계를 발명하겠다는 네 계획은 실패했지?

B: Yeah, I guess **I have to go back to the drawing board.** 어, 처음부터 새롭게 다시 시작해야 될 것 같아.

This isn't working so I've got to go back to the drawing board.
이건 작동이 안되니까 처음부터 다시 해야겠어.

I've got to go back to the drawing board and find a better way.
처음부터 다시 시작해서 더 나은 방법을 찾아야겠어.

To figure out a plan, I've got to go back to the drawing board.
좋은 계획을 생각해내기 위해서 처음부터 다시 시작해야 돼.

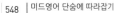

029 You gotta get back in the game 다시 뛰어야지

미드표현

this means that the speaker thinks the listener needs to rejoin something after being away from it for a while. Many times this is used when a person resigns from a job because of stress, and it urges the person to come back to the job. It is like saying "You should try it again."

| Point | get[be, want] back in the game 난관을 극복하고 다시 삶에 뛰어들다

A: I've been so bored since I stopped being a cop.
경찰일을 그만 둔 뒤로 사는게 지겨워졌어.

B: I think **you've got to get back in the game.**
다시 일을 시작해야 될 것 같아.

You've got to get back in the game before you forget how to do it.
어떻게 하는지 방법을 잊기 전에 넌 다시 시작해야 돼.

But at a certain point, you need to get back in the game. 하지만 일정 시점에서 넌 다시 시작해야 돼.

030 I'm back in the saddle 난 다시 시작했어

미드표현

this is a way to say that the speaker has returned to doing something that he had stopped doing in the past. We can understand that the speaker may be happy because he is able to do that thing well or with skill. Another way of saying this would be "I've begun doing it again."

| Point | get[be] back in the saddle 다시복귀[활동]하다(get back on the horse)

A: I thought you retired a few years ago.
너 몇년 전에 퇴직한 걸로 알고 있었는데.

B: I did, but now **I'm back in the saddle again.**
그랬지만 이제 다시 시작했어.

I recovered from my injury and I'm back in the saddle. 난 부상에서 회복되어 다시 시작했어.

Didn't take him long to get back in the saddle. 오래지 않아 걔는 다시 일을 시작했어.

They want you back in the saddle. You ready?
걔네들은 네가 복직하기를 원해. 준비됐어?

031 You should be out and about 다시 활동을 시작해야지

미드표현

this expresses that the speaker thinks someone should be out of the house, and outside doing normal things. Often we can understand the person may have been sick in bed and is now well. It would be similar to say "You should be out doing social things now."

| Point | be out and about (아픈 후에) 다시 활동을 시작하다

A: I need to stay at home for another week.
난 일주일 더 집에 머물러야 돼.

B: No way. **You should be out and about.**
말도 안돼. 다시 활동을 시작해야지.

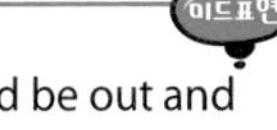

It's beautiful outside. You should be out and about. 밖이 정말 아름다워. 다시 활동을 시작해야지.

You should be out and about so you can get healthy again. 다시 활동을 시작해야지 그래야 다시 건강해지지.

The doctor says I should be out and about as much as possible.
의사는 가능한 많이 활동을 다시 시작하라고 해.

032 He's picking up the pieces 걘 재기 중이야

this is a way to indicate that someone had a bad experience and is recovering now. It is like saying "He is trying to repair the damage in his life"

| Point | pick up the pieces 재기하다, (몸, 마음) 추스리다

A: I heard that Bill and his wife divorced. 빌이 이혼했다며.

B: It's so sad. **He's picking up the pieces now.**
안됐어. 걘 이제 다시 추스리고 있어.

You'll try your best to pick up the pieces.
넌 재기하도록 최선을 다해야 할거야.

His life has been shattered once again. But as always, Jill has come to help pick up the pieces.
걔의 인생이 다시 한번 산산조각났지만 언제나처럼 질이 와서 추스리는 걸 도와줬어.

033 I'm getting back on my feet 난 다시 일어나고 있어, 재기하고 있어

this means "It's getting better after difficult times." We can understand that things are improving for a person or a business. And also this can mean "I'm healing." A person usually says this after being sick or injured

| Point | get[be] back on one's feet 다시 일어서다, 재기하다
stand on my own two feet now 자립하다

A: How has your restaurant been after the fire?
화재 후에 레스토랑이 어땠어?

B: We fixed everything and now **we're getting back on our feet.** 다 고쳤고 이젠 다시 좋아지고 있어.

I want you to hurry up and get back on your feet. 난 네가 빨리 재기하길 바래.

You need to get back on your feet financially.
넌 금전적으로 재기해야 돼.

I'm trying my hardest to stand on my own two feet. 자립하기 위해서 최선을 다하는 중이야.

034 Let's start fresh 새로 다시 시작하자

미드표현

this speaker is telling someone that they need to start all over again. We can infer that there may have been a major problem in the past, and now they need to forget about that problem and start with a new mindset. We can express this as "Let's forget the past and start with a healthy frame of mind"

| Point | start fresh 새롭게 다시 시작하다

A: Can we ever repair the damage to our relationship? 우리 우정이 금간 걸 바로 잡을 수 있을까?

B: It's possible. **Let's start fresh.** 가능하지. 새로 다시 시작하자.

And tomorrow we'll start fresh.
그리고 내일 우리는 다시 새롭게 시작할거야.

We'll start fresh in the morning.
우리는 아침에 다시 새로 시작할거야.

Let's just get some sleep and start fresh tomorrow, huh? 잠 좀 자고 내일 새롭게 출발하자, 응?

035 We just need to get back on the horse
우리는 다시 시작해야 돼

미드표현

most commonly, this is used to say that in spite of a failure, these people need to keep trying until they succeed. This is almost always said when there is a problem and people are pessimistic. The speaker is telling them, "Come on, we have to try again"

| Point | get back on the horse (실패 후) 다시 도전하다, 다시 시작하다

A: It looks like our plan failed completely.
우리 계획이 완전히 실패한 것 같아.

B: We just need to **get back on the horse.**
우리는 다시 시작해야 돼.

You gonna get back on the horse, then?
그럼 넌 다시 시작할거지?

Get back on the horse, Chris. 크리스, 다시 도전하라고.

So why don't you get back on the horse and do what you do best?
그럼 다시 시작해서 네가 가장 잘 하는 걸 하지 그래?

You have to pick yourself up, dust yourself off, and get right back on the horse.
넌 몸을 일으키고, 과거는 잊어버리고 다시 도전을 해야 돼.

미드에선 이렇게 쓰인다!

Get back on the horse

The Big Bang Theory
SEASON#3-23

Penny와 헤어진 Leonerd, Penny는 애인과 함께 있고 낙담한 Leonerd를 위로한다고 Raj가 말을 하기 시작한다.

Raj: I'm telling you, dude, the only way to feel better about Penny going out with other guys is for you to get back on the whores.
Howard: Horse.
Raj: What?
Howard: The phrase is get back on the horse, not whores.
Raj: That's disgusting, dude.

라지: 정말이야, 친구야. 다른 남자와 사귀는 페니에 대해 기분이 나아지게 하는 유일한 방법은 다시 창녀들을 올라타는거야?
하워드: 말.
라지: 뭐라고?
하워드: 그 표현은 창녀가 아니라 말을 다시 타는거야.
라지: 야, 정말 역겹네.

036 We'll pick up where we left off? 중단한 곳에서부터 다시 시작할까요?

미드표현

this is asking if they will be able to continue from the point where things were unexpectedly stopped. Often this is said when a discussion or meeting has to be interrupted. It is like saying "Can we start this again in the same place next time?"

| Point | pick up where we left off yesterday 어제 그만둔데서부터 시작하다

A: Our second meeting is scheduled for next week.
2번째 회의는 다음 주에 열릴거야.

B: Sounds good. **We'll pick up where we left off?**
좋아. 중단된 곳부터 다시 시작할거지?

I'm just afraid I'll pick up where I left off.
아까 멈췄던 부분부터 다시 이어서 해야 될 것 같으네요.

So, we're going to pick up right where we left off huh, Ellie? 그럼 멈췄던 곳에서부터 다시 시작할거지. 엘리?

We need to pick up where Harper left off.
우리는 하퍼가 그만둔데서부터 이어서 해야 돼.

037 Now take it from the top 이제 처음부터 다시 해보자

미드표현

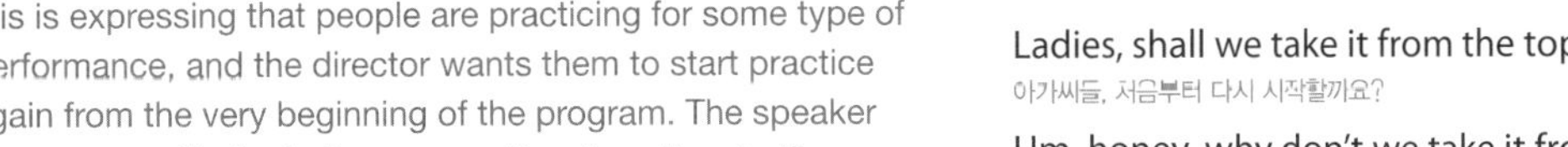

this is expressing that people are practicing for some type of performance, and the director wants them to start practice again from the very beginning of the program. The speaker wants to say "Let's do it one more time from the start"

| Point | take it from the top (공연) 처음부터 다시 하다

A: Do you want us to sing the chorus all over again? 우리가 처음부터 다시 코러스를 부를까요?

B: Yes I do. **Now take it from the top.**
그래요. 자 이제 처음부터 다시 해보죠.

Ladies, shall we take it from the top?
아가씨들, 처음부터 다시 시작할까요?

Um, honey, why don't we take it from the top? 자기야, 처음부터 다시 시작하자.

Break's over, everyone! Let's take it from the top. 자 다들 그만 쉬고 처음부터 다시 해봅시다.

Let's take it from the top of the second act.
2막부터 다시 시작해보자.

038 Keep (on) trying 계속 정진해, 멈추지 말고 계속 노력해

미드표현

this is a way to say "Don't give up." The speaker wants someone to do his best

| Point | keep trying to~ …하려고 계속 노력하다
Keep talking 계속 말해봐
Keep going! 계속 해!(You shouldn't give up)

A: Can you give me advice about how to get rich?
어떻게 부자가 되는지 조언해줄래?

B: **Keep on trying.** You should never give up.
계속 정진해. 절대 포기하면 안돼.

Why do you keep trying to do that?
왜 계속 그렇게 얘기하는거야?

Did I hurt you, or should I keep trying?
내가 아프게 한거야 아님 계속 해야 할까?

Come on, keep going. You can't quit!
이봐, 계속하라고. 그만두면 안돼!

You're doing great. Keep going.
아주 잘하고 있어. 계속 해.

039 Put your hands together 큰 박수를 쳐줘

미드표현

often this is a way to tell people to clap for someone. It is like saying "Please clap to welcome this person"

| Point | put your hands together for …에게 큰 박수를 보내다
Let's give a big hand (for ~) (…에게) 박수를 보냅시다

A: **Put your hands together** for our next singer.
우리 다음 가수에게 큰 박수를 쳐주십시오.

B: I really love this guy's songs. 이 가수의 노래 정말 좋아.

Ladies and gentlemen, please put your hands together for Dr. Laura!
신사숙녀 여러분, 로라 박사께 큰 박수를 부탁드립니다!

All right, ladies and gentlemen, put your hands together for our next lovely young lady.
자, 신사숙녀여러분, 다음 순서인 아리따운 젊은 아가씨에게 큰 박수를 보내주세요.

040 Put yourself out there 당당하고 자신있게 나서봐

usually this means "Go out and try." The speaker wants someone to try to do something

| Point | put oneself out there 자신있게 나서다

A: I haven't been on a date in seven months.
수개 월 동안 데이트를 못해봤어.

B: **Put yourself out there.** You'll meet a nice girl.
자신있게 나서봐. 멋진 여자를 만나게 될거야.

The best chance you have right now is to just completely put yourself out there.
너의 최선의 선택은 모든 걸 백일하에 드러내놓는거야.

I'll put myself out there and act on my instincts. 모든 걸 드러내놓고 본능에 따라 행동할거야.

It took a lot of courage for me to put myself out there like that.
내가 저렇게 나 자신을 드러내놓는 데는 많은 용기가 필요했어.

MEMO

Ways to say that something(someone) is great and congratulate someone

상대방에게 잘했어, 멋지다라고 칭찬하기

Can't top that, Chris

001 Can't top that, Chris 크리스, 난 최고야

this is often a way for a speaker to say that the person he is speaking to can't surpass what another person has done. It is like saying "He was able to do a better job than you will be able to do"

| Point | Can't top that[this] 최고야, 굉장하다, 엄청나다

A: I won the race. **Can't top that,** Chris.
내가 이겼어. 크리스, 난 최고야.

B: I know. You beat me easily. 알아, 날 쉽게 이겼지.

This is solid gold. Can't top that. 이거 순금이야. 최고야.

I'm the winner of the marathon. Can't top that. 나 마라톤 우승했어. 최고야.

She's the most beautiful girl. Can't top that.
걔는 가장 아름다운 여자야. 굉장해.

We are vacationing on the beach. Can't top that. 우리는 해변가에서 휴가보내고 있어. 아주 최고야.

002 (I) Can't beat that 그 보다 더 훌륭할 수는 없어, 완벽해, 끝내준다

this means "I can't do it better." The speaker is saying someone did something very well

| Point | Can you beat that? 어때 보고[듣고] 놀랐지?

A: I won $1500 playing the lottery. 로또해서 1500불을 땄어.

B: **I can't beat that.** I only won $25.
끝내주네. 난 고작 25불 땄는데.

That's a lot of money. I can't beat that.
정말 많은 돈이네. 끝내준다.

I can't beat that. Not even in a million years.
그것보다 더 훌륭할 수는 없어. 절대로.

You should accept their offer. I can't beat that.
걔네들 제의를 받아들여. 완벽하니까.

003 You're amazing 너 정말 놀라워, 대단해, 정말 멋져

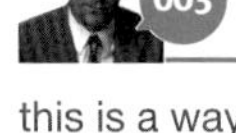

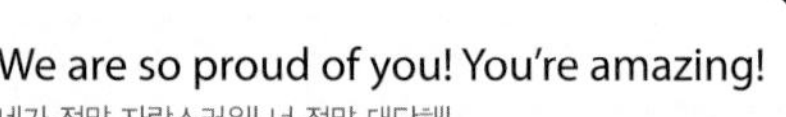

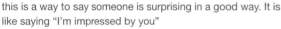

this is a way to say someone is surprising in a good way. It is like saying "I'm impressed by you"

| Point | You were amazing 너 정말 놀라웠어, 대단했어
You look amazing 정말 멋지게 보여
That's[It's] amazing 대단해

A: I was in Africa for several years doing research.
조사하느라 여러 해 동안 아프리카에 있었어.

B: **You're amazing.** Most people just stay in their hometowns.
정말 대단해. 대부분의 사람들은 자기네 고향에 그냥 머무르잖아.

We are so proud of you! You're amazing!
네가 정말 자랑스러워! 너 정말 대단해!

Darling, you are amazing, you know that?
자기야, 자기 정말 대단해, 그거 알아?

Being a model must be so amazing. Why did you stop? 모델이 된다는 건 정말 멋진 일인데, 왜 그만뒀어?

004 That's cool 멋있다, 괜찮은데

this means "I'm impressed." A person says this to indicate he likes something

| Point | That's groovy! 멋지다!
(That's) Far out! 정말 멋지다!
That's nifty! 멋져!

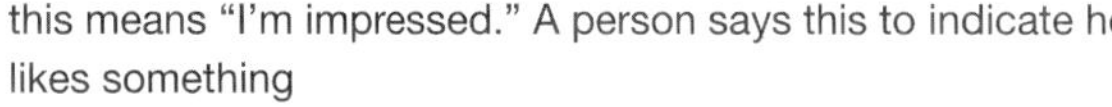

A: I went to see a new action movie this weekend.
이번 주말에 새로 나온 액션영화 보러 갔어.

B: **That's cool.** I like watching action movies.
멋져라. 난 액션영화 보는 것 좋아해.

You're a writer? That's cool. What do you write? 작가라고? 멋지다. 뭘 쓰는데?

I like your watch, man, that's cool.
야 네 시계 좋다, 멋진데.

I didn't know about that, but that's cool.
몰랐는데, 정말 멋지네.

005 Media's gonna go crazy 언론이 열광할거야

this is a way to indicate that the people who report the news are going to be very excited and focused on an interesting story. Here, when it says they will go crazy, it means they will do a lot of reporting on it. A similar way to express this would be "This story is going to be in newspapers and on TV news shows on a lot"

Point go crazy 미치다(go mad), 열중하다, 화내다

A: Apparently the couple was killed while having sex. 명백히 그 커플은 섹스를 하다가 살해당한거야.

B: **The media's gonna go crazy** when they find out. 언론이 알게 되면 난리치겠구만.

You know what? I might just go crazy tonight. 저 말이야, 나 오늘 광란의 밤을 보낼지 몰라.

Sarah will go crazy if she knows that you're down here. 네가 여기 있는거 알면 새라가 화낼거야.

I went crazy when I learned the truth about Danny. 난 대니에 관한 진실을 알았을 때 엄청 화냈어.

He obviously went crazy. He obviously lost his mind. 걘 누가 봐도 미쳤어, 실성했다니까.

006 That's terrific! 끝내주네!

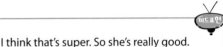

this is a way to say something is really good. It is very similar to saying "Great!"

Point That's super! 정말 잘됐어!, 최고야!, 좋아!
(That's) Awesome! 멋지다!, 죽여주네!

A: I just bought a house to live in. 살 집을 샀어.

B: **That's terrific.** Is it here in Seoul? 잘 됐네, 서울에다 산거야?

I think that's super. So she's really good. 정말 멋지네. 그래, 걘 정말 잘해.

Betty, you're gonna be an awesome Mom. You're caring. You're thoughtful. You're generous. 베티, 넌 정말 멋진 엄마가 될거야. 다정하고 사려깊고 그리고 관대하잖아.

007 Wild! 근사한데!

미드표현

this is like saying "Wow!" The speaker is very impressed about something he heard

Point Classic! 훌륭해 It's neat 훌륭해, 근사해

A: These chocolates were given to me by my boyfriend. 내 남친이 이 초콜릿을 줬어.

B: **Wild.** He must like you a lot. 멋져, 널 무척 좋아하나봐.

Wild, I like it. 근사하다, 맘에 들어.

It's neat to learn about submarines. 잠수함에 대해 배우는 것 멋져.

Are you getting engaged? Wild! 너 약혼해? 야 멋지다!

008 You kick ass! 멋지다!

미드표현

this might be said by teenagers, but usually not adults. Something that kicks ass is supposed to be "Great"

Point kick ass[butt] 강렬한 인상을 주다, 히트치다 *kick(-)ass 인상적인, 강렬한

A: Did you have a good time at the concert? 콘서트가서 재미있었어?

B: Oh yeah! The bands really **kicked ass!** 어, 그럼! 그 그룹 정말 멋지더라!

You are magnificent. How do you know that? You kick ass! 너 대단하다, 그걸 어떻게 알았어? 정말 멋지다!

This is the most fabulous thing I've ever done. I kick ass! This is fantastic! 내가 한 것 중에 가장 멋진 것 같아. 나 되게 멋지다! 굉장해!

What the hell is wrong with that? I kick ass. I'm an excellent resident. 도대체 뭐가 잘못 된거야? 난 멋지고 뛰어난 거주자인데.

009 It's a kick in the pants! 멋지네!

미드표현

this is a way to say "It was enjoyable." In other words, the speaker is expressing that something was interesting or fun

| Point | a kick in the pants 멋진 거, 고무적인 거, 마음에 드는 거
give sb a kick in the pants 꾸짖다, 혼내다

A: How did you like the new amusement park?
새로운 놀이공원 어땠어?

B: **It's a kick in the pants.** I had a lot of fun.
멋져. 재밌었어.

I gave him a kick in the pants. I haven't seen him all morning. 걔한테 모질게 했더니 아침내내 보이질 않아.

Try the new amusement park. It's a kick in the pants. 새로 생긴 놀이공원에 가봐. 정말 멋져.

I like having an energy drink. It's a kick in the pants. 난 에너지 음료마시는 걸 좋아해. 정말 멋져.

It's a kick in the pants. The best thing I ever did. 정말 멋지네. 내가 했던 일 중에서 가장 잘한 일이야.

010 Look at you! (감탄) 얘 좀 봐라!, (비난) 얘 좀 봐!

미드표현

this is usually a way to say "You seem special or impressive." The speaker wants someone to know that something about them seems very good

| Point | look at = take a look at …을 쳐다보다
Look at this! 이것 좀 봐!
Look at that! 저것 좀 봐!

A: **Look at you!** That dress makes you look so pretty. 얘 좀 봐! 이 옷 입으니 너 정말 예뻐 보여.

B: I bought it to wear to the dance tonight.
오늘 밤 댄스할 때 입으려고 샀어..

Look at you all dressed up. Applying for a job here? 멋지게 차려입은 것 좀 봐라. 여기 지원하려고?

Look at you! You turned into such a beautiful woman! 얘 좀 봐라! 너 아주 멋진 여자로 변했구만!

Oh, look at you. More beautiful than ever.
너 좀 봐라. 그 어느 때보다 아름다워.

011 You look great! 좋아 보여!, 멋져 보여!

미드표현

this means the speaker thinks someone has a good style of clothing or haircut. It is similar to saying "I like your appearance"

| Point | How do I look? 내 모습이 어때?

A: **You look great.** Have you been exercising?
너 멋져 보여. 운동했어?

B: Yeah, I lost a lot of weight because I go to a gym to work out. 체육관에서 운동해서 살이 많이 빠졌어.

Look at you. You look great. 얘 좀 봐. 너 멋져 보여.

You know, you look great tonight.
저기 말야, 오늘 밤 너 멋져 보여.

I really appreciate you taking the time to see me. You look great, by the way.
나보러 와줘서 고마워. 너도 좋아보여.

012 You could never disappoint me 넌 참 대단해

미드표현

this means the speaker is saying "I love you so much that I'll always be proud of you." It is typically said to children

A: I'm very sorry I didn't pass the test.
시험에 통과하지 못해서 죄송해요.

B: **You could never disappoint me.** I'm sure you'll pass the next one. 넌 대단한 애야. 다음 시험엔 꼭 합격할거야.

You could never disappoint me. I just want you to be happy. 넌 참 대단해. 네가 행복하기를 바래.

You could never disappoint me. You know what? I'm gonna make your room super pretty. 넌 참 대단해. 그거 알아? 네 방을 멋지게 꾸며줄게.

You made a mistake, but you could never disappoint me. 넌 실수를 했지만 넌 대단한 사람이야.

013 You have good taste 넌 안목이 뛰어나

this is a compliment and it means that a person has a good sense of style or fashion. Usually we think of this as a part of a person's character. Someone with good taste will automatically know what is stylish or good fashion. We can understand the speaker wants to say "You like things that are classy"

| Point | have (got) good taste 뭔가 볼 줄 아는 안목과 감각이 있다
have bad taste 안목이 없다

A: These chairs were imported from Italy. Aren't they nice? 이 의자들은 이태리에서 수입한거였어. 정말 멋지지 않아?

B: They sure are. **You have good taste** in furniture. 정말 그래. 너 가구를 볼 줄 좀 아네.

Well, that's a great movie. You're got good taste. 멋진 영화야. 영화볼 줄 아네.

You want me to be honest? Okay, I kind of think that you have bad taste.
솔직히 말하라고? 좋아. 난 네가 안목이 좀 없는 것 같아.

She has good taste. But how well do you actually know her?
걘 취향이 고급이지만 실제 넌 걔를 얼마나 잘 알고 있어?

014 You're catching on 빨리 이해하는구나

this is said when a speaker wants to tell someone that he is doing a good job learning the correct way to do things. Often it is heard when people are talking to someone who is new and doesn't have a lot of experience. It is very much like saying "You've learned a lot since you began"

| Point | You're catching on 빨리 이해하는구나
I'm not catching on 이해가 잘 안돼
That's catching on 그게 유행이야

A: I organized these files based on when they were submitted. 제출된 순서에 따라 이 파일들을 정리했어요.

B: Very good job. **You're catching on.**
아주 잘했어. 빨리 따라오는구만.

Excellent idea, Sara. You're catching on.
새라, 아주 좋은 생각이야. 아주 빨리 이해하는구나.

I'm catching on to you. 네 말을 빨리 이해하고 있어.

I was wrong, it is catching on.
내가 틀렸어. 그게 유행이야.

Oh good, I'm glad that's catching on.
잘됐어. 그게 유행이어서 기뻐.

015 That has a nice ring to it 말이 그럴 듯해, 그말 참 그럴 듯하다

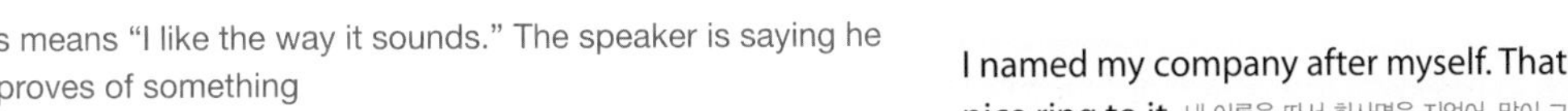

this means "I like the way it sounds." The speaker is saying he approves of something

| Point | have (got) a nice ring to it 멋지다, 어울리다

A: Someday you will be the manager of this office.
언젠가 이 사무실의 매니저가 될거야.

B: I'll be a manager? **That has a nice ring to it.**
내가 매니저가 된다고? 그럴 듯하네.

I named my company after myself. That has a nice ring to it. 내 이름을 따서 회사명을 지었어. 말이 그럴 듯 해.

I'm getting a big raise? That has a nice ring to it. 내 급여가 많이 인상된다고? 말이 그럴 듯하네.

That has a nice ring to it. It will be a hit with everyone. 멋진 이름이네. 다들 좋아하게 될거야.

016 You're the best! 네가 최고야!

often this indicates the speaker really likes someone. It is like saying "I think you're great"

| Point | You're the best (+ N) ~ …에서 네가 최고(의 …) 이다
You're the best(+N) S+have ever had …한 사람 중에 최고(의 …)이다
You're the man! 너무 멋지다!, 근사하다!, 넌 최고야!

A: Here is your birthday gift, Susan. 수잔, 여기 생일선물.

B: **You are the best.** I love you so much!
네가 최고야. 널 정말 사랑해!

Don't worry about it. Everyone knows you're the best. 걱정마. 다들 네가 최고인 걸 알고 있어.

I gotta tell you. You're the best in the business. 정말 말하지만, 넌 이 업계에서 최고야.

You are the best man I have ever known.
내가 겪어본 사람 중에서 넌 최고야.

017 She's a big shot 걘 거물이야

this means the woman has a good job, and is probably powerful. It is similar to saying "She's very important"

| Point | You're a hotshot 넌 대단해

A: What does your sister do at that company?
네 누이는 저 회사에서 하는 일이 뭐야?

B: **She's a big shot.** She advises the president.
걘 거물이야. 사장에게 조언해주고 있어.

She thinks she's a big shot.
자기가 대단하다고 생각하나 봐.

All right, hotshot! Show me what you got!
좋아, 거물! 네 실력을 보여줘!

Well I'm a hotshot doctor. I don't have any problems. 음, 전 잘난 의사라서 문제가 없어요.

018 That's really something 정말 대단해, 거 굉장하네

미드표현

usually this expresses "That is different or special." The speaker wants to indicate that something is interesting because it isn't common

| Point | That's quite[really] something 그거 굉장한데
That was really something 정말 대단했어
You really are something 너 정말 대단해

A: This is a statue I bought in Laos.
이 조각상은 내가 라오스에서 사온거야.

B: **That's really something.** I've never seen anything like it. 정말 굉장하네. 저런 건 처음 봐.

That's something. That's really something.
그거 대단하네. 정말 대단해.

He was really something. You should have seen him. 걔 대단했어. 너도 봤어야 했는데.

Working out on the North Sea for months, that's really something.
북극해에서 몇 달간 일하는거, 그거 정말 대단한거야.

019 You are something else! 정말 대단해!, 잘났어 정말!

this is a way to say someone is unusual. Sometimes it has a positive meaning and sometimes it has a negative meaning. It is like saying "I don't know anyone like you"

| Point | You're something special 넌 특별한 존재야
He's somebody here 걘 이곳 명사야(He's powerful or important)

A: I had dates with four different women this week.
이번 주에 네 명의 다른 여자랑 데이트했어.

B: **You are something else.** I wish I could do that.
너 정말 대단하다. 나도 그랬으면 좋을텐데.

I've studied your theory in recent years. You're something else!
너의 이론을 몇 년동안 봤어. 정말 대단해!

I think you are something else entirely.
난 네가 정말 대단하다고 생각해.

You're something else, you know that?
너 정말 대단해, 그거 알아?

020 I've got to hand it to you! 너 정말 대단하구나!, 나 너한테 두 손 들었어!

미드표현

usually this means "You did a good job." This is often said when someone is surprised that something was successful

| Point | (have) got to hand it to~ …에게 손들다

A: Each of my businesses makes a profit.
내 사업체가 각각 수익을 내고 있어.

B: **I've got to hand it to you.** You are a good businessman. 너 정말 대단해. 넌 훌륭한 사업가야.

I got to hand it to you. How could you know that? 너한테 손 들었다. 어떻게 그걸 알았어?

I got to hand it to these casinos. They got it all figured out. 이 카지노들 대단해. 다 알고 있어.

021 I take credit for it 그건 내가 한거야, 내 능력으로 된거야

this means "I created it." The person is saying he is responsible for something good

| Point | take credit for …의 공을 인정하다, 칭찬하다, …을 자신의 공으로 삼다
give sb credit for …을 …의 공으로 인정하다
get credit for …로 인정받다, 명성을 얻다

A: Which person developed the new schedule?
누가 이 새로운 일정을 만든거야?

B: **I take credit for it.** It took me a long time to plan it out. 내가 한거야. 그거 짜는데 시간 많이 걸렸어.

미드표현

I'm sorry I took credit for your work. I apologized. 네가 한 일을 내 걸로 가로채서 미안해.

I give them credit for searching for a solution.
해결책을 찾은 건 걔네들의 공이야.

She'll be fine. She is a lot smarter than we give her credit for.
걔는 괜찮아질거야. 걘 우리가 생각하는 것보다 더 영리해.

He knows a lot more than you give him credit for. 네가 생각하는 것보다 걘 더 많이 알고 있어.

022 There is nothing like that! 저 만한 게 없지!

this is a way to say something is unique or rare. It means "That thing is very special"

| Point | (It's) Nothing like that 그런 게 아니야

A: Last night I had a great meal of steak and beer.
지난 밤에 고기와 맥주를 많이 먹었어.

B: **There is nothing like that.** I love eating those foods. 그 만한 게 없지. 그 음식들 먹는 걸 좋아해.

미드표현

A cold beer on a hot day. There is nothing like that! 더운 날에 찬 맥주. 그만한 게 없지!

Try this Vietnamese restaurant. There is nothing like that!
여기 베트남 식당을 이용해봐. 저만한 게 없어!

There is nothing like that! You won't be disappointed. 그만한 게 없어! 넌 실망하지 않을거야.

023 Thumbs up! 좋아!

often this means someone likes something. It is very similar to saying "It's good"

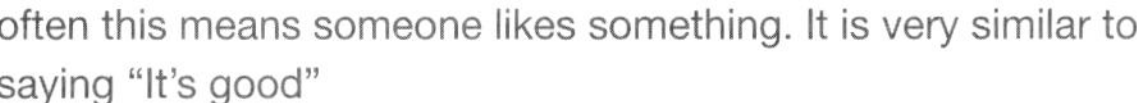

| Point | give (sb) the[a, two] thumbs up 찬성하다, 승낙하다
It gets two thumbs up 대단히 훌륭해

A: What did your boss think about your report?
네 보고서를 사장이 어떻게 생각해?

B: **He said thumbs up.** He thought it had good information in it. 아주 만족해. 좋은 정보가 들어있다고 생각해.

미드표현

I gave her a thumbs up. She smiled.
난 걔한테 찬성의 표시를 하자 걔가 미소지었어.

Tammy gives him the thumbs up while still standing behind the door.
태미는 아직 문 뒤에 서서 엄지손가락을 치켜 들었어.

024 I'm impressed 인상적인데, 놀라운 걸

this is said to indicate the speaker was surprised at how good something was. It is like saying "That is great"

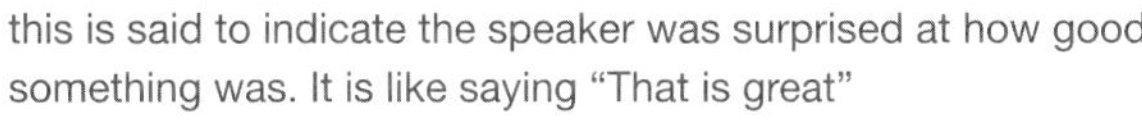

| Point | I'm touched by your effort 너의 노력에 감동받았어

A: I just ran in my first marathon. 처음으로 마라톤을 뛰었어.

B: **I'm impressed.** How long did it take you to finish it? 놀라운 걸. 완주하는데 시간이 얼마나 걸렸어?

미드표현

Not bad. I'm impressed. 괜찮은데, 인상적이야.

I've got to say, I'm impressed. 정말이지, 놀라워.

Well, as your girlfriend, I'm impressed. As your boss, you're a jackass. Don't do it again.
여친으로 감동먹었지만 사장의 입장에서 넌 멍충이야. 다시는 그러지마.

I'm impressed with all the work you did.
네가 한 모든 일에 정말 감동받았어.

025 You did a good[nice] job! 아주 잘했어!

this means "Your work was good." The speaker is saying he liked something that was done

| Point | Good[Nice] job! 잘했어!. 좋았어!

A: Did you like the artwork I made? 내가 만든 공예품 좋았어?
B: **You did a nice job.** It was beautiful.
아주 잘 만들었어. 아름다웠어.

You did such a good job today. 넌 오늘 아주 잘했어.

Good job. Will you be my assistant?
잘했어. 내 비서가 될래?

Good job, you were great! 잘했어!. 넌 대단했어!

026 Good work! 잘했어!, 수고했어!

this is like saying "You did well." This is a way to tell someone that he did something nicely

| Point | Good deal 잘했어. 그렇게 하자. 좋아

A: These are the articles you asked me for.
네가 요청한 물품들이야.
B: **Good work.** They are going to be very useful to me. 수고했어. 내게 매우 유용할거야.

Good work, you guys. Very good.
너희들, 잘했어. 아주 좋아.

That is genius. Good work, Peter. You're a real pro. 천재적이야. 잘했어, 피터. 넌 정말 프로야.

Well, you deserved it. You did good work.
넌 그럴 자격이 충분했어. 일 잘했어.

027 Good for you 잘됐네, 잘했어

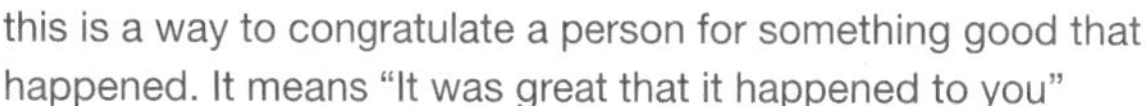

this is a way to congratulate a person for something good that happened. It means "It was great that it happened to you"

| Point | be good for sb …에게 잘된 일이다, …에게 좋다, 어울리다
Good for me 내게 잘된 일이네

A: You know, I've almost finished law school.
저 말야, 난 법대를 거의 끝마쳤어.
B: **Good for you.** I hope you become a successful lawyer. 잘됐네. 네가 훌륭한 변호사가 되기를 바래.

That's great. Good for you. 아주 좋아. 잘됐어.

I think it would be good for me.
그렇게 되면 나한테 좋을 것 같아.

She was not good for me. So I dumped her.
걘 나와 어울리지 않아서 내가 차버렸어.

028 That's great 아주 좋아, 잘됐다, 바로 그거야

this means "Congratulations, good job." It is a way to say that someone did something good

| Point | Very good 아주 좋았어, 잘 알겠습니다
That's good 좋아

A: I fixed the leak in your sink. 싱크대에 물새는 거 고쳤어.
B: **That's great.** Now I can wash dishes.
아주 좋아. 이제 설거지를 할 수 있겠네.

Very good. Good. You made it your own.
아주 좋아. 좋아. 너 스스로 해냈어.

That's great! That's exactly what I'm looking for. 아주 좋아! 내가 찾던게 바로 그거야.

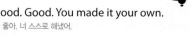

That's great. I'm very happy for you.
아주 좋아. 네가 잘돼서 너무 기뻐.

She invited you to the dance? That's great!
걔가 널 댄스파티에 초대했다고? 잘됐네!

029 Way to go! 잘한다 잘해!, 잘했어!

this is said to tell someone he did well. Like the previous 2 phrases, it means "Congratulations"

A: I got a prize for selling the most products.
내가 판매왕으로 상을 받았어.

B: **Way to go!** You're our best salesman.
잘했다! 넌 우리회사 최고의 영업맨이야.

Way to go! Good job, everybody.
잘했어! 모두들 잘했어.

Way to go son! I knew you'd find it!
잘했어, 아들아! 난 네가 그걸 찾아낼 줄 알았어!

030 Well done 잘했어

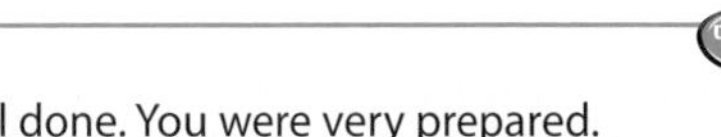

this means "Congratulations, good job." It is very similar to the previous 3 phrases

| Point | Very well done 아주 잘했어
Top notch! 훌륭해!

A: I made this cake just for you. 널 위해 이 케익을 만들었어.
B: **Well done.** It tasted great. 잘했어. 아주 맛이 좋았어.

Well done. You were very prepared.
잘했어. 넌 준비된 사람이었어.

This is great. It's top notch. 아주 좋아. 훌륭해.

Well done. Your patient called his lawyer, threatened to sue us.
잘했다. 네 환자는 변호사에게 전화하고 우리를 고소하겠다고 협박했어.

Well done. You deserve a reward.
잘했어. 넌 보상을 받을 자격이 있어.

031 Nice going! 참 잘했어!, 잘 한다!(비아냥)

this means "Good job." It is another way to say congratulations to someone

A: I was hired at the new GM factory.
새 지엠 공장에 취직했어.

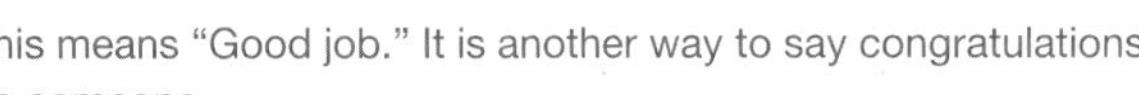

B: **Nice going.** A lot of people want to work there.
잘했어. 많은 사람이 거기서 일하길 원해.

Nice going! You more than deserve it. You've been doing a good job for all the years you were working.
잘했어! 넌 자격이 남아 돌아. 지금까지 열심히 일했잖아.

Nice going, Red. The whole church hates us now. 레드 참 잘도 했다. 이제 교회전체가 우리를 싫어해.

You aced the exam. Nice going!
너 시험을 잘 봤다고. 잘했어!

032 Attaboy! 야, 잘했다!, 잘했어!

this tells someone that he did well. It also is a way to say "Congratulations"

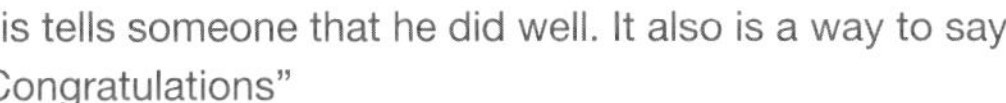

| Point | That's my[a, the] boy! 야 잘했다!, 좋았어!
That a girl! 참 잘했어!

A: Dad, the teacher told me I was her best student.
아빠, 선생님이 선생님이 가르치는 학생 중 제가 최고라고 했어요.

B: **Attaboy!** You're going to do well in school.
야, 잘했어! 넌 학교에서 잘할거야.

Attaboy! We knew you could do it!
잘했어! 우리는 네가 할 수 있을거라는 걸 알고 있었어!

Attaboy! Way to hit a home run! 잘했어! 홈런 잘 쳤어!

Attaboy! You're doing just fine. 잘했어! 넌 잘하고 있어.

Attaboy! We always knew you'd be successful.
잘했어! 우린 네가 성공할거라는 걸 항상 알고 있었어.

033 Nice try (비록 실패했지만) 잘했어, 잘 한거야

this is said when someone has failed to do something. It means "I know you did your best, even if you don't like the result"

A: I just wasn't strong enough to lift that weight.
저 무게를 들어올릴 만큼 강하지 않아.

B: **Nice try.** Maybe you can make yourself stronger. 그래도 잘했어. 더 강해질 수도 있어.

미드표현

Nice try, but you don't get that position anymore! All right? That is my position now!
잘했지만, 더 이상 그 자리는 네꺼가 아니라 내꺼라고!

A: It means I forgive you, please come. B: Nice try. But I'm not going.
A: 널 용서해줄게, 이리와. B: 시도는 좋았지만 난 안 갈거야.

Nice try. You're grounded for two weeks.
시도는 좋았어. 2주간 외출금지야.

034 We can work it out 해결할 방법은 있어, 같이 해결하자

this is a way to say "We can solve the problems." The speaker believes that the problems are not serious

| Point | Let's work it out 제대로 해보자

A: I can't accept this new contract.
이 새로운 계약을 받아들일 수가 없어.

B: **We can work it out.** What do you want to change? 함께 해결하자고. 뭘 바꾸고 싶은데?

미드표현

There's always a solution, we can work it out.
항상 해결책은 있게 마련야. 우린 해결할 수 있어.

Whatever the problem is, you can work it out!
문제가 뭐든지 간에 넌 해결해낼 수 있어!

We're more than friends, Carl. And we've fought before. We always work it out.
칼, 우리는 친구 이상야. 전에도 싸웠지만 우린 항상 해결하잖아.

035 That settles it, then 그럼 해결된거야

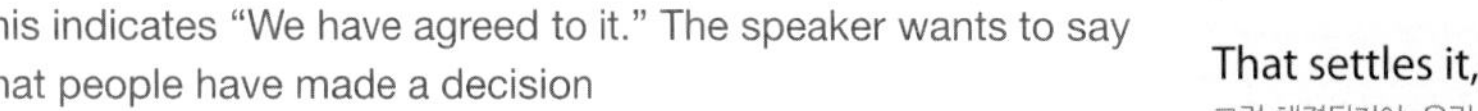

this indicates "We have agreed to it." The speaker wants to say that people have made a decision

A: I'll cook dinner on Monday, Wednesday and Friday, and you cook the other nights.
내가 월,수,금에 저녁할 테니 넌 다른 날 해.

B: **That settles it then.** We'll share the responsibility of cooking.
그럼 그렇게 정하자. 요리하는 걸 반반 나눠서 하자.

미드표현

That settles it, then. We're going home.
그럼 해결된거야. 우린 집에 간다.

Are you quitting the firm? That settles it, then.
회사 그만두는거야? 그럼 해결된거야.

That settles it, then. We all think she's guilty.
그럼 해결된거야. 우리 모두 걔가 유죄라 생각해.

036 Welcome aboard 탑승을 환영합니다, 함께 일하게 된 걸 환영해

this is sometimes used as a greeting when people get on a ship. More commonly, it is said by a boss when a new person is employed. It means "Welcome into our company"

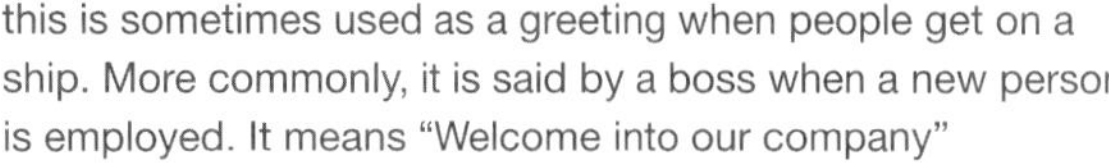

| Point | Welcome home 어서 와
Welcome back 돌아온 걸 환영해
Welcome to the club 클럽에 온 걸 환영해

A: Hi, I'm Bob. I was hired as a new computer technician. 안녕하세요, 밥입니다. 신입 컴퓨터 기사입니다.

B: **Welcome aboard,** Bob. I'm the office manager.
환영해요, 밥. 난 실장예요.

미드표현

This is my new yacht. Welcome aboard!
내 새 요트야. 승선을 축하해!

Welcome to the neighborhood.
이웃이 된 걸 환영해요.

Your boss seems unkind, just like mine. Welcome to my world.
네 사장도 우리 사장처럼 퉁명스럽게 보여. 나와 같은 처지가 됐구만.

Ways to talk about 'time'

시간표현 그리고 서두르거나 천천히 하거나

The clock is ticking

001 I don't have time for this 이럴 시간 없어

미드표현

this is saying "I am too busy to do this now." The speaker wants someone to know he can't do something at that time

| Point | I don't have time for~ …할 시간 없어, …는 집어쳐
I don't have time to (catch my) breath 숨돌릴 시간도 없어

A: I am selling a product that you should buy.
꼭 필요하신 상품을 팔고 있습니다.

B: **I don't have time for this.** I have to focus on my work. 이럴 시간이 없어요. 일에 집중해야 돼요.

I don't have time for this. I'm getting married now. 이럴 시간 없어. 난 이제 결혼한다고.

I don't have time for this crap. I have a party to plan. 이런 말도 안 되는 이야기는 집어쳐. 파티 계획해야 한다고.

I really don't have time for this nonsense.
정말이지 이런 말도 안되는 얘기는 집어쳐.

002 There comes a point when you wanna do bad things 나쁜 짓을 하고 싶을 때도 있는거야

미드표현

this implies that the speaker is saying he has become bored or frustrated and his reaction was to do things that could be harmful or damaging. Another way to say this would be "Sometimes when you are upset, you want to do something hurtful"

| Point | There comes a time[point] when[where]~ …한 때도 있다

A: What happens when you spend years in prison?
감방생활을 하다니 어떻게 된거야?

B: **There comes a point when** you wanna do bad things. 나쁜 짓을 하고 싶을 때도 있는거야.

There comes a time when we must expose our weaknesses. 약점을 노출시켜야 될 때가 있어.

There comes a moment in each of our lives when the control that keeps us sane slips through our fingers.
우리들 모두의 삶에서는 우리가 멀쩡하도록 지켜주는 통제력이 사라지는 때가 있어.

There comes a point where you have to suck it up and stop whining and start living.
싫어도 받아들이고 불평을 그만하고 삶을 시작해야 되는 때가 있어.

003 It'll give us time to figure it out 그렇게 되면 우리가 그걸 해결할 시간을 갖게 될거야

미드표현

this is similar to saying that there is now some extra time to figure out the best solution to a problem. People say this if they have a serious issue that they are not sure how to resolve. Often it is a personal problem. It is like saying "This allows us more time to work on a solution"

| Point | This[It] will give sb time to~ 그렇게 되면 …가 …할 시간을 갖게 될 것이다

A: We have a month before we need to submit our report. 우리가 보고서를 제출해야 될 때까지 한 달 남았어.

B: Good. It has some problems, and **it'll give us time to figure them out.** 좋아. 문제가 좀 있지만 그렇게 되면 우리가 그 문제 해결책을 찾아낼 시간을 갖게 될거야.

That will give us time to locate the missing witness.
그렇게 되면 우리가 실종된 증인의 위치를 찾아낼 시간을 갖게 될거야.

That'll give her time to hook up with some other guy.
그렇게 되면 걔가 어떤 다른 남자와 엮일 시간을 갖게 될거야.

004 You're pushing 50 넌 나이가 50이 다 되어가

this indicates that a person is getting close to fifty years old. Although many people are still quite active at the age of fifty, it also signifies that the person is not so young and some of his physical abilities may not be as good. A way to say the same thing is "You are almost fifty years old"

| Point | be pushing+ age 나이가 …가 다 되어가다 turn+age (in) …에 몇살이 되다

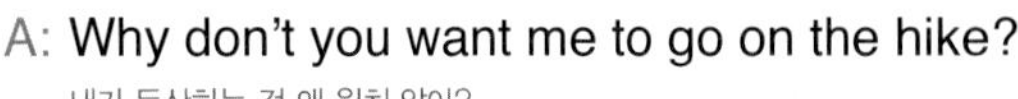

A: Why don't you want me to go on the hike?
내가 등산하는 걸 왜 원치 않아?

B: It's a very difficult hike, and **you're pushing 50.**
등산이라는게 어렵잖아 그리고 넌 50이 다 되어가고.

I mean, you're pushing 70.
내 말은 넌 나이가 70이 다 되어간다는거야.

Well, she's pushing 30. It's time to grow up.
저기, 걔는 30이 다 되어가는데 철들어야지.

I turn 18 in a few weeks. 몇주후면 18세가 돼.

005 You have a lot of time on your hands

너 시간이 남아도는구나

this is a way to say "You have much free time." Sometimes people say this when they envy someone who doesn't have a lot of work to do

| Point | have a lot of time on one's hands …에게 시간이 남아 돌다

A: Every night I play computer games for hours.
매일 밤 몇 시간씩 컴퓨터 게임을 해.

B: **You have a lot of free time on your hands.**
너 시간이 남아도는구나.

미드표현

You must have a lot of time on your hands.
너 시간이 남아도는구나.

Honey, you're going to have a lot of free time on your hands now. Find a hobby.
얘야, 이제 시간이 많이 남아돌거야. 취미생활을 하나 찾으렴.

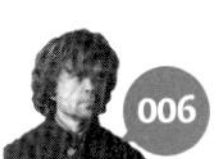

006 I'm running out of time 시간이 얼마 안 남았어, 시간이 다 되어가

often this is a way to say someone has a deadline that is coming soon. It is similar to saying "I have to finish because the deadline is near"

| Point | run out of time = run short of time = be (all) out of time
시간이 모자라다

A: **I'm running out of time.** I need to finish this.
시간이 다 돼가. 이걸 끝마쳐야 돼.

B: I'll make some coffee so you can stay awake. 잠 오지 않게 커피 좀 타줄게.

Come on! Hurry! We're running out of time! 자 어서! 서둘러! 시간이 없다고!

I'm all out of time. 시간이 너무 없어.

The patient was running out of time.
그 환자에게는 시간이 얼마 안 남았어.

Well, let's just hope we haven't run out of time to use it.
시간이 부족해 그걸 사용하지 못하게 되지 않도록 바라자고.

007 I know, the clock is ticking 나도 알아, 시간이 없어

this means "I have a small amount of time to finish." The speaker is saying he knows he has to meet a deadline soon

A: We don't have much time to finish this.
이거 끝마치는데 시간이 얼마 안 남았어.

B: I know. **The clock is ticking.** 알아. 시간이 없어.

미드표현

We've got to get it. The clock is ticking.
그걸 확보해야 돼. 시간이 없어

The clock is ticking. We have no time. 시간이 없어. 시간이 없다고.

The clock is ticking, and we gotta bring him back alive. 시간이 없어, 우리는 걜 산채로 데려와야 돼.

008 I haven't got all day 빨리 좀 해줘, 내가 시간이 없어, 여기서 이럴 시간 없어

this expresses that the speaker doesn't have much time. It is a way of saying "Hurry up!"

| Point | I don't have all day 마냥 이러고 있을 순 없어

A: **I haven't got all day.** Hurry! 이럴 시간이 없어. 서둘러!

B: It takes time to find the files you want.
네가 원하는 파일을 찾는데 시간이 걸려.

미드표현

We haven't got all day to get this done. Keep it moving. 빨리 좀 이거 끝내자고. 어서 서둘러.

Come on, I ain't got all day! Let's go!
자 어서, 이럴 시간이 없어! 어서 가자고!

Carrie? Are you ready? Come on, we don't have all day. 캐리? 준비됐어? 어서, 마냥 이러고 있을 수 없어.

009 Don't drag this out 질질 끌지마

this is meant to tell someone not to make something longer than it needs to be. When someone drags something out, it takes up a lot of extra time. Another way of saying this would be "Don't take up extra time to do it"

| Point | drag sth out …을 질질 끌다
drag sb out 끌어내다

A: I'm going to present the facts of the case to you.
네게 이 사건의 진상을 보여줄게.

B: I don't have much time. **Don't drag this out.**
시간이 별로 없어. 질질 끌지말라고.

미드표현

They're going to drag this out in appeals, so I thought it was going against us.
걔네들은 항소로 이걸 질질 끌려고 할건데, 우리한테는 불리할거라 생각했어.

You drag me out to a park at 3 in the morning to ask me if I wanna stand still with you.
넌 새벽 3시에 나를 공원으로 끌어내 내가 아직도 너와 함께 있고 싶어 하는지를 물어보는거잖아.

010 Time will tell 시간이 지나면 밝혀질거야

the speaker is saying that he will know something in the future. It indicates that "We must wait to find out the answer"

| Point | Time flies 시간이 정말 빨리 간다, 세월이 유수구만
How time flies 시간이 벌써 이렇게 되었네, 시간 정말 잘간다
Times are changing 세월은 변하거든

A: Do you think he will succeed? 걔가 성공할까?

B: I'm not sure. **Time will tell.** 몰라. 시간이 지나면 알겠지.

미드표현

She's youthful and vibrant, thank God, but time flies. 걘 젊고 활기찼지만, 아아, 세월은 유수같지.

I don't think they'll stay married. Time will tell.
걔네들 이혼할 것 같아. 시간이 지나면 알게 될거야.

Time will tell. It may be a good idea.
시간이 지나면 알게 될거야. 그게 좋은 생각일 수도 있어.

Donna may be promoted soon. Time will tell.
도나는 곧 승진될 지도 몰라. 시간이 지나면 밝혀질거야.

011 He wants to take it slow 걔는 천천히 하기를 바래

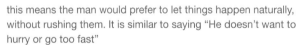

this means the man would prefer to let things happen naturally, without rushing them. It is similar to saying "He doesn't want to hurry or go too fast"

| Point | take it slow 서두르지 않다

A: Has your boyfriend talked to you about marriage? 네 남친이 결혼 이야기 했었어?

B: Not yet. **He wants to take it slow** in this relationship. 아직. 나랑 사귀는데 서두르고 싶지 않은 가봐.

미드표현

I'm gonna take it real slow. 난 천천히 할거야.

I mean we can take it slow.
내 말은 우리가 천천히 해도 된다고.

I think it's good to take it slow.
천천히 하는게 좋다고 생각해.

012 Take your time 천천히 해, 서두르지 마

this means "relax and don't be stressed about a deadline." The speaker is expressing that he is patient about waiting for the person

| Point | take one's time 천천히 하다, 서두르지 않다

A: Should I hurry so we can get to the airport?
공항가는데 서둘러야 돼?

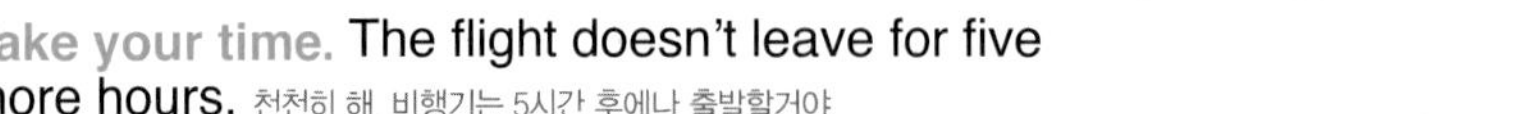

B: **Take your time.** The flight doesn't leave for five more hours. 천천히 해. 비행기는 5시간 후에나 출발할거야.

미드표현

Take your time. It's no big deal. 서두르지마, 별일 아냐.

Take your time. Think about it. 서두르지 말고 생각해봐.

Take your time with that. 그거 서두르지마.

Take your time doing this. 이거 천천히 해.

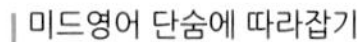

013 What's the[your] rush? 왜 이리 급해

this is asking someone "Why are you hurrying?" The speaker wants a person to explain why he is doing things more quickly

| Point | What's the hurry? 왜 그렇게 서둘러?

A: Oh my God, I need to get to the supermarket right now. 맙소사, 수퍼에 지금 바로 가야 돼

B: **What's your rush?** The supermarket is going to stay open late tonight.
왜 이리 서둘러? 수퍼는 밤 늦게까지 여는데.

What's the rush? The crime scene's not going anywhere. 왜 이리 서두르는거야? 범죄현장은 어디 안 가잖아

You need the report done today? What's the rush? 오늘 보고서를 끝내야 된다고? 왜 그렇게 서둘러?

Hey, slow down a little. What's the rush?
야, 천천히 해. 왜 그렇게 서둘러?

014 There's no rush 바쁠 것 없어, 급할 거 없어, 서두를 필요없어

미드표현

this is used to calm people down. It lets them know "You don't have to be stressed over time limits"

| Point | be in no hurry[rush] …하는 데 서두르지 않다

A: Oh my God! I'll never be able to clean the apartment before the party.
맙소사! 파티시작 전에 아파트 청소를 절대 못할거야.

B: **There's no rush.** You have 5 hours to clean before the party starts.
급할 거 없어. 파티시작하려면 아직 5시간 남았잖아.

Could you please hurry? I'm in a bit of a rush.
빨리 좀 해 주세요, 제가 좀 바쁘거든요.

Take your time. I'm in no rush.
천천히 해. 난 급할 거 없으니까.

Hi, Joe! Where are you going in such a rush?
안녕, 조! 어딜 그렇게 급하게 가는거야?

015 Don't hurry 서두르지마

미드표현

this is used to caution someone, possibly about a problem caused by hurrying. It is like saying "Slow down"

A: **Don't hurry.** You may fall down and hurt yourself. 서두르지 마. 넘어져 다칠 수도 있어.

B: I can't help it. I always walk fast when I feel excited about something.
나도 어쩔 수가 없어. 뭔가 들뜨면 항상 빨리 걸어.

We don't need you right away. Don't hurry.
우린 당장 네가 필요하지 않아. 서두르지마.

Don't hurry. Everything is under control.
서두르지마. 모든 게 다 잘 관리되고 있다고.

Don't hurry. I've already ordered our food.
서두르지마. 내가 이미 음식 주문했어.

016 Not so fast 너무 서두르지마

미드표현

this is similar to the previous phrase. It means "Don't go so quickly"

A: Did you understand the math problem I explained to you? 내가 설명한 수학문제 이해했어?

B: **Not so fast.** You went over it too quickly.
너무 서두르지 마세요. 너무 빨리 지나가셨어요.

Wait, wait. Not so fast. 잠깐, 잠깐, 천천히 하자고.

Not so fast. Isn't there something else that you need to say?
너무 서두르지마. 또 할 말 있다고 하지 않았어?

Not so fast. Where were you gonna change your clothes?
너무 서두르지마. 넌 어디서 옷을 갈아입으려고 했어?

017 Where's the fire? 뭐가 그리 급해?, 왜 그렇게 서두르냐?

this is asking someone "Why're you hurrying?" It doesn't mean there's a fire, but it's asking why someone is acting in an excited way, as if there were a fire

A: Hey Susan, **where's the fire?** You seem to be in a big hurry today.
야 수잔, 어디 불이라도 났어? 오늘 무척 서두르는 것 같아.

B: Yeah, my boss just called and he needs these files right away. 사장이 전화로 이 서류들 당장 가져오래.

Why is everyone running? Where's the fire?
왜 다들 뛰는거야? 왜 그렇게 서두르는거야?

Where's the fire? Just take it easy for a few minutes. 뭐가 그리 급해? 잠깐이라도 천천히 하자고.

Can you slow down? Where's the fire?
천천히 좀 해. 뭐가 그리 급해?

018 This can wait 그건 나중에 해도 돼, 뒤로 미루어도 돼

this means that something is not so important. It is similar to saying "It can be done later"

| Point | That can't wait 이건 급해
Can't that wait? 뒤로 미룰 수 없어?

A: Are these the dishes that you wanted me to clean for the party? 이 접시들이 파티하려고 나보고 닦으라는 것들야?

B: Yeah, but **this can wait.** Right now I need you to help John cook some food.
맞아 하지만 좀 미루어도 돼. 지금은 존이 요리하는 것 좀 도와줘.

It's not that important. This can wait.
그건 그렇게 중요하지 않아. 뒤로 미루어도 돼.

This can wait. We have other things to do.
나중에 해도 돼. 다른 할 일이 있어.

Let's move on from this topic. This can wait.
이 주제부터 건너 뛰자고. 이건 나중에 해도 돼.

019 Pace yourself 서두르지마

this means "Go at a speed that is gentle." The speaker wants to make sure going fast won't make a person overly tired

| Point | pace oneself 서두르지 않다, 페이스를 조절하다

A: I really get tired when I exercise on the machines at the gym. 체육관에서 운동기구로 운동할 때 정말 피곤해.

B: You need to **pace yourself.** It isn't good if you get too exhausted when you exercise.
페이스를 조절해야지. 운동할 때 너무 무리하면 좋지 않아.

Ok, pace yourself everybody. We have a long way to go. 좋아 다들 페이스 조절해. 갈 길이 아직 멀어.

Sweetie, we just got here 5 minutes ago. Pace yourself. 자기야, 여기 온지 이제 5분 됐어. 서두르지마.

020 Don't push (me)! 몰아 붙이지마!, 독촉하지마!

this person is telling another person "Don't try to make me do something." He wants to say that he doesn't want to be pressured

| Point | Don't rush me! 재촉하지마!, 몰아부치지마!(빨리 재촉하는 상대방에게)
Stop pushing! 강요하지마!, 억지로 밀어부치지마!

A: Have you called the company for an interview yet? They aren't going to wait forever.
회사에 면접건으로 전화했어? 마냥 기다려주지 않을 텐데.

B: **Don't push me.** I haven't even decided if I will apply for a job there. 재촉마. 지원여부도 결정못했어.

Don't push your sister! 네 누이를 몰아 붙이지마!

Don't push so hard! 너무 세게 몰아 붙이지마!

You're going to push me on this?
이거 서두르라고 재촉할거야?

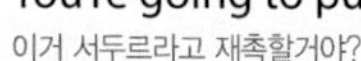

021 Move your ass! 서둘러!, 빨리와!

this is considered very rude. It is telling someone "Go faster" in a very unkind way

| Point | Move it 어서 | Let's move it 가자
Let's move out 떠납시다 | Haul ass! 서둘러!

A: You better **move your ass** or we'll be late for school. 서두르지 않으면 우리 학교에 늦겠다

B: Don't be so unkind to me. I'm hurrying as quickly as I can. 넘 뭐라 하지마. 가능한 한 서두르고 있어.

It's going to be a long ride to Arizona. Move your ass. 애리조나까지 가려면 오래걸릴거야. 서둘러.

A: What? We're never gonna make it! B: Not with that attitude! Now, haul ass!
A: 뭐라고? 우린 절대 시간 맞춰서 도착 못할거야! B: 그런 태도로는 절대 안돼! 빨리 움직여!

022 Make it snappy! 서둘러!, 빠릿빠릿하게 움직여!

미드표현

this is similar to "Move your ass", but it is a little less rude. It is a way to say "Hurry with that"

| Point | Snap out of it 기운내, 정신 차려, 빨리 해

A: Give me a hamburger, french fries and some milk. And **make it snappy!**
햄버거, 프렌치프라이즈와 우유 좀 줘요. 빨리 좀 줘요!

B: You'll have to wait a while. The restaurant is very busy. 좀 기다리셔야 돼요. 식당이 바빠서요.

A: I really think you should hear it. B: Fine. Make it snappy. A: 네가 정말 들어줬으면 해. B: 알았어, 빨리해.

Get me three coffees and make it snappy.
커피 세 잔 빨리 갖다 줘.

Make it snappy. I'm getting impatient.
서둘러. 나 짜증난다고.

023 Snap to it! 빨리해!

미드표현

this is a way of telling someone that they need to complete some task quickly. We can understand that the speaker is probably in a hurry. It is similar to saying "Hurry up and do it"

| Point | snap to it 바로 하다, 서두르다
snap it up (거래) 바로 채가다, 사가다

A: This place needs to be cleaned. **Snap to it!**
이 곳 청소 좀 해야겠다. 어서 서둘러!

B: Relax, we have plenty of time to do it.
진정해, 청소할 시간이 아직 많으니까.

I want you to get to the office fast. Snap to it.
사무실로 빨리 오도록 해. 서둘러.

Get me a fresh cup of coffee. Snap to it.
신선한 커피 좀 가져와. 어서.

These items are on sale. The shoppers will snap them up.
이 상품들은 세일 중이야. 쇼핑하는 사람들이 바로 사갈거야.

If they offer me food, I will snap it up.
걔네들이 음식을 내게 권하면 바로 채갈거야.

024 Hop to it! 가자!, 서둘러!

미드표현

this is a way to say "Get started now." It is not commonly used, but we still hear it said occasionally

| Point | hop to it 서두르다

A: Why haven't you finished your homework for tonight? Come on, **hop to it!**
오늘 밤에 왜 아직 숙제를 못 끝냈냐? 자 서둘러!

B: But Dad, my teacher gave us extra homework so it is taking more time to complete.
하지만 아빠, 선생님이 숙제를 더 내주셔서 끝내려면 시간이 더 필요해요.

I want you to get it done now. Hop to it!
그거 당장 끝내도록 해. 어서 서둘러!

Hop to it! Or would you prefer to get a job elsewhere? 서둘러! 다른 직장 다니고 싶어?

Hop to it! No one told you to sit down.
어서 서둘러! 아무도 네게 앉으라고 한 사람 없어.

025 Hurry up! 서둘러!, 빨리하라구!, 서둘러!

this is a common way of telling people "You need to go faster." The speaker wants them to increase their rate of doing something

| Point | hurry up and+V 서둘러 …하다
Hurry on! 좀 더 속도를 내라고!

A: I still have to clean the kitchen and the bedroom. 아직 부엌하고 침실을 청소해야 돼.

B: **Hurry up.** You are taking way too much time to complete your chores. 서둘러. 넌 잔일하는데 시간 너무 걸리더라.

미드표현

Will you hurry up? Seriously, would you just hurry the hell up! 서둘러줄래? 정말야, 제발 좀 서둘러줄테야!

You better hurry up and find that girl.
넌 어서 서둘러 그 여자 아이를 찾으라고.

Well, hurry up and I'll drive you to school.
서둘러 내가 학교까지 차로 데려다줄게.

026 I'd better get a move on it 빨리 서둘러야겠어

this means "I think I should start now." In some cases, it also means "I should leave now"

| Point | get a move on 서두르다, 가다
We should get a move on 서둘러야겠어
Make a move! 빨리 움직여!, 시작해!

A: It takes 90 minutes for me to get home. **I'd better get a move on it.** 집에 오는데 90분 걸려. 서둘러야 돼.

B: Can't you stay just a little longer? I really enjoy your company. 조금만 더 있지 않을래? 네가 있어서 좋은데.

미드표현

We should get a move on if we wanna make those dinner reservations.
저녁식사 예약을 하려면 서둘러야 돼.

If you guys are finished with the report, we should get a move on.
니네들 레포트 쓰는 거 끝났으면 빨리 움직이자.

If you don't get a move on, we're not gonna make it to the wedding.
우리 서두르지 않으면 결혼식에 못가.

027 There's no time to lose 이러고 있을 때가 아니다

this means "Something should be done right away." The speaker thinks it should be done without any delay or waiting

A: Are you sure we need to leave for the theater right now? 지금 바로 극장으로 출발해야 하는 게 맞아?

B: Absolutely, **there's no time to lose.** If we don't leave now, the tickets will be sold out.
물론이고 말고, 이럴 시간이 없어. 지금 출발 안 하면 표가 없을거야.

미드표현

There's no time to lose. We have to get to the hospital. 이러고 있을 때가 아냐. 우리는 병원에 가야 돼.

Give me your phone! There's no time to lose.
네 핸드폰 이리 줘봐! 이러고 있을 때가 아냐.

There's no time to lose. I have to leave.
이러고 있을 때가 아냐. 나 가야 돼.

028 Look alive! 잠 깨!, 빨리빨리!, 정신차려!

this is a way of telling someone "Be alert and aware of what is going on around you." It is often said in a workplace when a boss comes in

A: Hey Jim, I saw your boss walk into the building a few minutes ago. **Look alive!**
야, 짐, 사장이 건물로 5분 전에 들어갔어. 조심해

B: That's a good idea. I want to be sure he thinks I am working hard.
좋은 생각이야. 사장이 내가 열심히 일한다고 생각하게 해야지.

미드표현

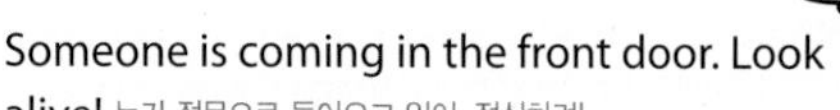

Someone is coming in the front door. Look alive! 누가 정문으로 들어오고 있어. 정신차려!

Is our boss here? Look alive!
사장이 여기 있어? 어서 정신차려!

Look alive! We need to get this work done.
어서 정신차려! 우리 이 일을 마쳐야 돼.

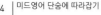

029 This will take a second 잠시만 기다려, 잠시면 돼

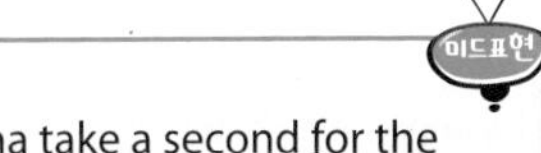

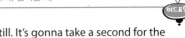

this means something can be completed quickly. It is a way to say "It will be fast"

| Point | This[It] will just take a sec[moment] 금방이면 돼

A: Can you change the dead battery in my watch?
내 시계의 다 된 밧데리 교체 해줄 수 있어?

B: Of course I can. **This will take a second to do.**
물론 할 수 있어. 금방이면 돼.

미드표현

Hold still. It's gonna take a second for the tube to fill. 가만 있어. 관이 차려면 시간이 좀 걸릴거야.

A: This will only take a second. B: Shouldn't somebody help her?
A: 잠시만 기다려. B: 누가 안도와줘도 돼?

A: Uh, Tracy, we're gonna be late. B: Oh. It'll just take a second. I need a recipe.
A: 트레이시, 우리 조금 늦을 것 같아. B: 잠시면 돼. 요리법만 가져오면 돼.

030 Don't waste your time 시간낭비하지마, 시간낭비야

this means "It is worthless." The speaker is saying there is no value in doing something

| Point | Don't waste my time 남의 귀한 시간 축내지마, 그래봐야 소용없어
Don't waste your breath 소용없으니까 그만 둬
You're (just) wasting my time (상대방 말에 무관심) 시간낭비마

A: Did you think the amusement park was fun?
놀이 공원이 재미있었던 것 같아?

B: No. **Don't waste your time** going there.
아니. 거기 가는 시간 낭비하지마.

미드표현

I'm not gonna waste your time, and I'm not gonna waste mine. 너 시간낭비 안 시킬게, 나도 그럴 거고.

Don't waste your time trying to get in my head. There's nothing there.
내 머리 속에 들어 올려고 시간 낭비마. 아무 것도 없으니.

031 How long will it take to fix it? 이거 고치는데 얼마나 걸릴까?

this is asking "How much time to repair this?" It indicates the person wants something to be fixed fast

| Point | How long will[does] it take to~? …하는데 얼마나 걸릴까?
It takes (sb)+시간+to~ (…가) …하는 데 …가 걸린다

A: The engine in your car needs to be repaired.
차의 엔진을 수리해야 돼요.

B: **How long will it take to** fix it? 수리하는데 얼마나 걸려요?

미드표현

How long will it take to find her?
걜 찾는데 얼마나 걸릴까?

How long does it take to get undressed?
옷을 벗는데 얼마나 걸리니?

My husband has a heart attack, and how long does it take them to find me?
내 남편이 심장마비예요, 날 찾는데 얼마나 걸릴까요?

032 How long before you have to leave? 얼마나 있다가 가야 돼?

this is asking how much time remains before the listener must go somewhere else. We can assume the listener has a schedule and must leave at a specific time. A similar way to express this would be "When do you need to go?"

| Point | How long before S+V? 얼마나 있어야 …해?

A: **How long before you have to leave?**
얼마나 있다가 가야 돼?

B: The taxi is going to pick me up in an hour.
택시가 한 시간 후에 날 태우러 올거야.

미드표현

How long before he wakes up?
걔가 일어나려면 얼마나 있어야 돼?

How long before we're able to do that?
우리가 그것을 할 수 있으려면 얼마나 걸릴까?

If I was able to find you, how long before the bad guys find you?
내가 널 찾을 수 있다면 나쁜 놈들은 널 찾는데 얼마나 걸릴까?

How long before he figures it out?
얼마나 있어야 걔가 그걸 알아차릴까?

033 It won't take long 오래 안 걸려

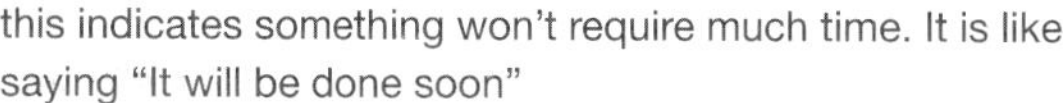

this indicates something won't require much time. It is like saying "It will be done soon"

| Point | It won't take long for sb to~ …가 …하는데 시간이 얼마 걸리지 않다

A: Will you be ready to go soon? 곧 갈 준비 돼?

B: Yeah, **it won't take long** for me to dress.

어, 옷 입는데 오래 안 걸려.

미드표현

Do you have a second? It won't take long.
잠깐 시간 돼? 금방이면 돼.

All right. I'll be back in a few moments with your drink, and the meal won't take long.
좋아요. 음료수는 바로 갖다드리고 식사도 곧 준비하겠습니다.

Just stand over here. This won't take long.
이쪽으로 와서 옆에 서있어. 이거 오래 안 걸려.

034 It's about time 진작에 그랬어야지

this expresses impatience. Often it indicates "It should have been finished sooner"

| Point | It's about[high] time S+V 진작에 …했어야지, 이제서야 …하는구만

A: I think we have finished installing the computer program. 컴퓨터 프로그램 설치를 다한 것 같아.

B: **It's about time.** That took four hours!

진작에 그랬어야지. 네 시간이나 걸리다니!

미드표현

It's about time you learned how to use the Internet. 인터넷를 어떻게 이용해야 되는지를 진작에 배웠어야지.

It's about time Matt paid us a visit.
맷이 우리를 방문해야 될 때인데.

It's about time that you got a haircut.
너 머리를 좀 깍아야 되겠다.

035 I'm working 24-7 온종일 일만해

this is a way to say "I'm doing as much as I can." The speaker wants to express that he is working very hard

| Point | work 24-7 밤낮가리지 않고 일하다

A: Why haven't you completed the writing assignment? 왜 작문 숙제를 다 못한거야?

B: It's very difficult. **I'm working 24-7** to get it all done. 너무 어려워요. 그거 마치는데 온 종일하고 있어요.

미드표현

I have no free time. I'm working 24-7.
난 시간이 없어. 온종일 일만 한다고.

I'm working 24-7. That's why I'm so tired.
난 온종일 일만해. 그래서 나 아주 피곤해.

Sorry, I can't date you. I'm working 24-7.
미안 너와 데이트할 수가 없어. 종일 일하거든.

036 It's a one day job, max 최대 하루치 일이야

this is a way to say that the most time that will be required is one day. It is like saying "I will be finished with this in a day or less

| Point | tops 최대한

I will give you 1 hour tops 최대한 한 시간 주마

A: How long does it take to replace a house's heater? 집의 히터를 교체하는데 얼마나 걸려요?

B: Not so long. **It's a one day job, max.**

그렇게 오래 걸리지 않아요. 최대 하루 걸려요.

The hearing lasts a half hour max.
청문회는 최대 30분 동안 열려.

I was out of my car two, three minutes tops.
2분, 최대한 3분 차를 비웠어.

I've got a surgery, but it shouldn't be more than four hours, five tops.
수술이 있는데 4시간 최대한 5시간을 넘지는 않을거야.

037 Let's just take it one day at a time 그때그때 해결하자고

미드표현

this is a way to say that someone should not get too stressed about the future. In other words, "We need to just think about what happens in each day and not get stressed about what may happen beyond that."

| Point | take it one day at a time 그때그때 해결하다, 천천히 하나씩 해결하다

A: How will I ever recover from going bankrupt?
내가 파산 후에 어떻게 회복할 수 있을까?

B: **Let's just take it one day at a time.**
그때그때 해결하자고.

All I can do is take it one day at a time.
내가 할 수 있는거라고는 그때그때 해결하는거야.

But taking it one day at a time still makes the most sense to me.
하지만 그때그때 해결하는 것이 내게는 이치에 맞아.

Don't get so worked up, Karen. Just take it one day at a time.
카렌, 너무 열받지 말아. 그냥 천천히 하나씩 해결해.

038 When the time is right 때가 되면

미드표현

often this means "I'm waiting for a good opportunity." The speaker wants to wait until he feels it is the moment to do something

| Point | when the time is ripe 적당한 때에, 적합한 시간이 오면

A: When do you plan to buy an apartment?
언제 아파트를 살거야?

B: **When the time is right.** Prices are too high right now. 때가 되면. 가격이 지금은 너무 높아.

When the time is right, maybe I'll finish it.
때가 되면 끝마치겠지.

I'll find a wife when the time is right.
때가 되면 아내를 찾겠지.

I will bring you back when the time is right.
때가 되면 널 다시 데려갈거야.

When the time is right, we'll tell him, and he'll understand. 때가 되면, 우리는 걔한테 말할거고 걔는 이해할거야.

039 You can spend more quality time with your real friends 진정한 친구와 시간을 알차게 보내

미드표현

this is a complex way to say "You can relax with people you like." It means a person will have time to enjoy himself with friends

| Point | spend quality time (with~) (…와 함께) 알찬(값진) 시간을 보내다

A: I don't know what I will do after I retire.
퇴직 후에 뭘 할지 모르겠어.

B: **You can spend more quality time with** your friends. 진정한 친구와 시간을 알차게 보내도록 해.

How about you and me are spending some quality time together?
너와 내가 알찬 시간을 보내는 게 어때?

You need to spend some quality time thinking about the goals in your life.
네 인생목표를 생각하면서 시간을 알차게 보낼 필요가 있어.

040 (You're) All set? 준비 다 됐어?

this is asking "Are you ready?" The speaker wants to know if a person is ready to begin something

| Point | all set to[for+N] …할 준비가 다 되다
I'm all set 준비 다됐어

A: I'm ready to go to the airport. **You're all set?**
공항갈 준비 됐어. 너도 준비됐니?

B: Yes, my suitcases are already packed.
어, 짐가방 다 챙겼어.

All set. Jill's doing the closing. You're ready?
준비됐어. 질은 마무리하고 있는데 넌 준비됐니?

You all set to go? 다들 갈 준비됐어?

You guys ready for the movies? 영화 볼 준비됐어?

It's time to go. Are you all set?
이제 가야 될 시간이야. 준비됐어.

041 She's being prepped for surgery 걔는 수술 준비를 하고 있어

this expresses that a woman is a patient, and she is being prepared to undergo an operation at a hospital. This means her body is likely being cleaned and sterilized. We can also say the same thing as "They are getting her ready for the operation"

| Point | be prepped for …할 준비가 되다

A: Where are the nurses taking my wife?
간호사들이 내 아내를 어디로 데려가는거예요?

B: **She's being prepped for surgery.**
수술할 준비를 하고 있어요.

Let's get you prepped for surgery.
수술 준비를 시켜드릴게요.

You need to stay out here while your husband's prepped for surgery.
남편이 수술준비를 하는 동안 여기에 있으시면 안됩니다.

No way he's prepped for this.
걔가 이것을 준비했을 리가 없어.

042 She's got her bases covered 걘 만반의 준비를 다했어

this is a way to say that a woman has made plans so that she can deal with every possibility. We can understand that she is well prepared for the future. In other words, "She anticipated and planned for problems that could happen"

| Point | cover (all) the bases 모든 준비를 하다, 모든 사태에 대비하다
have all the bases covered 준비를 철저히 하다

A: Do you think Jane will be successful?
제인이 성공할거라 생각해?

B: Sure. **She's got her bases covered.**
물론, 걘 만반의 준비를 다해놓고 있어.

Ron wants to make sure she's got her bases covered. 론은 걔가 만반의 준비를 확실히 하기를 바래.

The way you survive a road trip with my mother is to make sure you have all your bases covered, leave nothing to chance.
내 엄마와의 장거리 여행에서 살아남는 방법은 하나의 빈틈도 없이 모든 사태에 대해 만반의 준비를 확실히 해두는거야.

A: You're treating him for both diseases? B: We're covering all the bases.
A: 두 가지 병으로 그 사람을 치료하고 있는거야? B: 모든 사태에 다 대비하고 있어.

043 Do your homework 사전준비를 해라

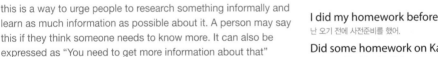

this is a way to urge people to research something informally and learn as much information as possible about it. A person may say this if they think someone needs to know more. It can also be expressed as "You need to get more information about that"

| Point | do one's homework on ~ …에 대한 사전준비를 하다

A: I need to know more information about those suspects. 저 용의자들에 대한 정보를 더 알아야겠어.

B: **Do your homework.** They have been arrested several times. 사전준비를 하라고, 걔네들은 여러번 체포된 적이 있다고.

I did my homework before I showed up.
난 오기 전에 사전준비를 했어.

Did some homework on Kate.
케이트에 대한 사전준비를 했어.

So, those guys did their homework. They picked the perfect time to hit.
그럼, 그놈들은 사전준비를 했어. 걔네들은 치기에 정확한 시간을 골랐어.

044 Let's get set up 어서 준비하자

this is a way to tell people that it is time to organize or put together something. We commonly hear this when people are staging an event like a festival, and they want to get it ready for people to attend. When we hear this, we know the speaker is saying "Let's get everything ready so that we can start"

| Point | get set up 준비하다

A: Everyone has arrived to help with the banquet.
모든 사람들이 연회를 준비하러 왔어.

B: That's good to hear. **Let's get set up.**
반가운 소리네. 자 어서 준비하자.

It's the attorney! Get set up, guys.
변호사다! 자 다들 준비해.

I'll help the blood bank staff get set up.
혈액은행 직원들이 준비하도록 도와줄게.

Morgan, Prentiss, and I will go get set up at the field office with Agent Beeks.
모건, 프렌티스와 나는 가서 빅스 요원과 함께 현장사무실에서 준비를 할게.

045 I'm ready to[for~] …할 준비가 되어있어

this speaker is saying he is prepared for something. It is another way to say "I'm prepared to do..."

| Point | until you're good and ready …할 때가 될 때까지, 완전히 준비될 때까지
We're getting warmed (up) 준비 다 됐어

A: Have you finished watching TV? TV 다 봤어?
B: Yes I have. **I'm ready to** do my homework now.
네 다 봤어요. 이제 숙제할게요.

I'm ready to get drunk and see some strippers. 술마시고 스트립퍼들 볼 준비가 되어 있어.

I'm right here and we're good to go.
여기 있어요. 준비됐습니다.

I'm getting warmed up to play basketball.
농구하려고 준비하고 있어.

046 I was nowhere near ready to be a mother

난 엄마가 되려는 생각이 전혀 없었어

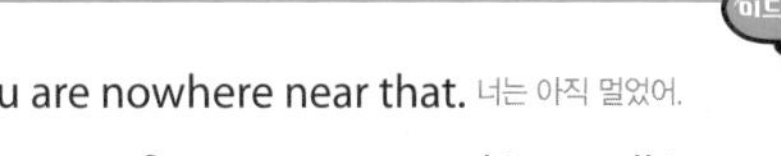

this is a way of saying that the speaker was not mature enough or not interested in getting pregnant and having a child. People say this when they don't want to become parents. It is very similar to saying "I really didn't want to become a mother"

| Point | be nowhere near sth~ …와는 거리가 멀다, 결코 …가 아니다
be nowhere near ready~ …할 준비가 전혀 되어있지 않다

A: Why didn't you marry Andy and have some kids? 왜 앤디와 결혼해서 아이를 낳지 않았어?
B: **I was nowhere near ready to** be a mother.
난 엄마가 되려는 생각이 전혀 없었어.

You are nowhere near that. 너는 아직 멀었어.

There are fine surgeons working well into their 70s, and I am nowhere near 70.
70대에서 일을 잘하는 훌륭한 외과의들이 있는데 난 70이 되려면 아직 멀었어.

I'm the youngest, and my sister's like nowhere near ready for marriage.
내가 막내인데, 누나는 결혼 생각도 없어.

We are nowhere near close to getting engaged, trust me.
우린 약혼 근처에도 가보지 못했어, 정말야.

047 We're good to go 준비 다 됐어

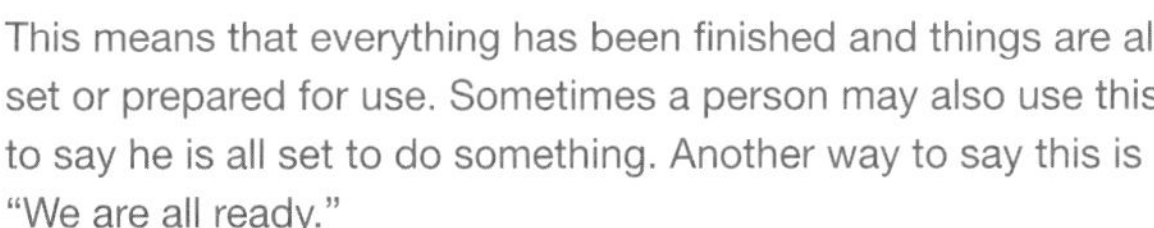

This means that everything has been finished and things are all set or prepared for use. Sometimes a person may also use this to say he is all set to do something. Another way to say this is "We are all ready."

| Point | be good to go 준비가 다 되다

A: Are you finished packing our car? 차에 짐 다 실었어?
B: It's ready for the trip. **We're good to go.**
여행할 준비됐어. 준비 끝.

I'm good to go, man. You know what I'm gonna do? 난 준비가 다 됐어. 내가 뭘 할지 알아?

Then we're good to go. Actually, this is gonna work out well. 그럼 우린 준비가 다 됐어. 실은 이건 잘 될거야.

Oh, let me grab my earrings, and we're good to go. 어, 귀걸이 좀 하면 우린 준비 다 돼.

048 No strings attached 아무런 조건없이

this indicates that there is no hidden cost to an offer or it is without any extra conditions. It is like saying "It has no extra cost"

A: Did your dad give you that car?
아빠가 너에게 저 차를 주신거야?
B: Yes he did. **No strings attached.**
어 그랬어. 아무런 조건도 없이.

I gave you twenty dollars. No strings attached. 네게 20달러를 아무 조건없이 줬어.

One night, just sex. No strings attached?
하룻밤, 그냥 섹스야. 아무 조건 없이?

I want to spend some time with you. No strings attached.
난 너랑 시간을 함께 보내고 싶어. 아무런 조건없이.

049 What's the occasion? 무슨 날이야?

this is asking "What is special?" It is usually said to ask why people are wearing nice clothes

| Point | occasion 특별한 날, 행사

A: That's a nice suit. **What's the occasion?**
옷 멋지다. 무슨 날이야?

B: My best friend is getting married today.
내 친한 친구가 오늘 결혼해.

Ooh, look at you! What's the occasion?
와, 얘 좀 봐! 무슨 날이야?

Wow! You look nice. What's the occasion?
야! 너 멋지다. 무슨 날이야?

A: Things are great. You want some wine? We're celebrating. B: What's the occasion?
A: 일들이 잘 되고 있어. 와인 좀 먹을테야? 축하하자고. B: 무슨 날인데?

050 if that's the case 만약 그렇다면

this is a way to say "If it's true." We can understand that the speaker will act in a certain way if a situation is true

A: I think I'll have free time tonight.
오늘 밤에 시간이 날 것 같아.

B: **If that's the case,** we should go out together.
만약 그렇다면 함께 나가자.

If that's the case, then who's this?
만약 그렇다면 그럼 이 사람은 누구야?

If that's the case there's nothing I can do about it. 만약 그렇다면 내가 어찌할 도리가 없어.

If that's the case, he was shot by somebody 10 to 15 feet tall.
만약 그렇다면 그 남잔 10~15피트 키의 사람에게 총을 맞은거야.

051 (It's) No wonder 어쩐지, 당연하지

this is a way of saying "I'm not surprised S+V." The speaker thinks he understands the reason for something

| Point | (It's) No wonder S+V …하는 게 당연하지, …하는 게 알만해
What do you expect? 당연하지, 뭘 기대한거야?

A: Lisa and Mike argued all of the time.
리사와 마이크가 늘상 다투었어.

B: **No wonder** he left her. 마이크가 걜 떠나는 것도 당연하네.

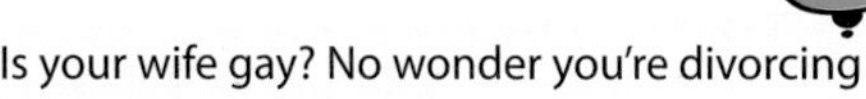

Is your wife gay? No wonder you're divorcing her. 네 마누라가 게이야? 네가 이혼하는 게 당연하지.

No wonder you failed the exam.
네가 왜 시험에 떨어졌는지 알만하네.

No wonder Cindy's never invited you to her birthday party.
신디가 널 생일 파티에 절대 초대하지 않는 것도 알만해.

052 What would you have done (if~) 너라면 어떻게 했겠어?

this is asking "What reaction would you have if...?" The speaker wants to know what someone would do in a specific situation

| Point | What would you have done if S+V …하다면 넌 어떻게 했겠어?

A: I heard you got really angry yesterday.
너 어제 정말 화났다며?

B: **What would you have done if** your friend stole your money? 네 친구가 네 돈을 훔쳤다면 넌 어떻게 했겠어?

What would you have done if you were him?
당신이 저 사람이었다면 어떻게 했겠어?

What would you have done if your dad cheated your mom?
만약 네 아빠가 바람핀다면 어떻게 하겠어?

What would you have done if you would have caught up with him?
네가 걔를 따라 잡았다면 넌 어떻게 하겠어?

053 So, what's your plan B? 그 다음 계획은 뭐야?, 차선책은 뭐야?

this is asking "What will you do if your first plan fails?" The speaker wants to know what might happen if there are problems with an original plan

| Point | Plan B! 작전 2호 개시!

A: I think that I won't get into Yale University.
예일 대학에 못 들어갈 것 같아.

B: **So what's your plan B** for attending a university? 그럼 대학에 들어가는 차선책은 뭐야?

When I got his call, I went to plan B.
걔 전화를 받고 난 차선책을 택했어.

I have no plan B. 예비 계획 따윈 없어.

Time for a plan B. 예비 계획을 발동해야겠네요.

054 The group and Chris mapped out their plan

크리스와 사람들이 계획은 세웠어.

this is expressing that these people are developing a plan to do something. We can understand that they are probably discussing the best way to have a successful plan. A different way to say the same thing is "Chris and the group are organizing their strategy"

| Point | map sth out 준비하다, 세심히 계획하다

A: **The group and Chris are mapping out their plan.** 크리스와 사람들이 계획을 잘 짰어.

B: Well, I hope they are able to finish it soon.
걔네들이 빨리 마무리할 수 있기를 바래.

I know you've got all your moves mapped out. 넌 모든 행동에 계획을 세워놨다는 걸 알고 있어.

It's not exactly what I had mapped out.
그건 내가 계획했던게 전혀 아냐.

She brought the proper identification, she mapped out the correct route, and she brought plenty of cash for emergencies.
걔는 적합한 증명서를 가져왔고, 올바른 길을 잡아놨고 그리고 비상시를 대비해 많은 현금을 가져왔어.

Ways to talk about being happy or excited
기분이 좋거나 안좋거나 감정을 표현할 때

Don't make me feel bad

001 I'm happy for you 네가 잘돼서 나도 기뻐

this is a way to say "Congratulations." The speaker is saying he feels happy that something good happened to someone

A: My boss just recommended me for a promotion.
상사가 날 승진 추천했어.

B: That is great. **I'm so happy for you.**
잘 됐네. 잘 돼서 나도 기뻐.

You look so good! We're so happy for you.
너 정말 좋아 보여! 네가 잘돼서 기뻐.

I'm so glad I could help. Happy for you.
내가 도움이 되어서 정말 기뻐. 네가 잘돼 기뻐.

A: I am getting married. B: I'm happy for you. I am, really. A: 나 결혼해. B: 네가 잘돼서 기뻐. 정말이야.

002 I'm so psyched 정말 신나

this expresses that someone is very interested in something. It is like saying "I feel really excited"

| Point | I'm so excited (about/ (that)S+V) (…가) 정말 신나
I'm thrilled 가슴이 설레

A: How do you feel about the trip to New York?
뉴욕 여행 가는 거 어때?

B: **I'm so psyched.** I love having the chance to visit New York. 너무 신나. 뉴욕을 방문하게 되는 게 너무 좋아.

I was so psyched to hear you're back with my sister! 네가 내 누이와 함께 온다니 너무 신났어!

How psyched are you? 얼마나 신나?

I'm so excited about this wedding.
이 결혼식 생각에 너무 흥분돼.

003 (I'm) Glad to hear it 그것 참 잘됐다, 좋은 소식이라 기뻐

this means "I was happy when someone told me." Often it expresses that something was good news

| Point | (I'm) Glad to[that S+V] …해서 기뻐
(I'm) Glad to hear (that) S+V …하다니 기뻐

A: The newspaper says the highway is being repaired. 신문에 의하면 고속도로가 보수 중이래.

B: **I'm glad to hear it.** It was in bad condition.
그것 참 잘 됐다. 컨디션이 안 좋았거든.

I'm glad to hear you say that, because I'm having a wonderful time.
그거 참 잘됐어. 내가 굉장한 시간을 보내고 있으니 말야.

Glad to hear it. I need someone to accompany me to the wedding.
잘됐네. 결혼식에 같이 갈 사람이 필요하거든.

Oh, I'm so glad to hear you say so.
네가 그렇게 말해주니 참 잘됐어.

004 (That's) Good to know 알게 돼서 기뻐

this is a way to say "I'm happy to get that information" Often people say this when they hear good news

| Point | (That's) Good to hear 듣게 돼서 기뻐

A: I think everyone was impressed by your presentation. 다들 네 프리젠테이션에 감동받았어.

B: **That's good to know.** I worked very hard on it.
기쁘네요. 아주 열심히 준비했거든요.

A: And just so you know, if I was a lesbian, I'd totally do you. B: That's good to know.
A: 그래 저말이야 내가 만약 레즈비언이라면 너랑 사귈거야. B: 기쁘군.

A: Look, I just want to move this place fast. I'll do whatever we have to do. B: Well, that's good to know.
A: 그냥 빨리 이사가고 싶어. 무슨 짓이든 하겠어. B: 그래, 알게 돼서 기뻐.

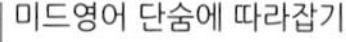

005 I'm walking on air 날아 갈듯이 기뻐, 정말 기뻐

this means the speaker is very happy. It is like saying "I feel great right now"

| Point | I'm on cloud nine 구름 위를 걷는 기분이야

A: I heard that Brad asked you out on a date.
브래드가 너에게 데이트 신청했다며.

B: Yes he did. **I'm walking on air** right now.
어 그랬어. 지금 날 듯이 기뻐.

미드표현

I'm just walking on air at just the thought of suing you.
날 듯이 기뻐. 널 고소한다는 생각에 말야.

Oh, Tina loves me, Kate. I am walking on air.
케이트, 티나가 날 사랑한대. 정말 기뻐.

006 This music really sends me to the moon
이 음악을 듣고 있으면 정말 황홀해져

this is an older saying that means a person really enjoyed some type of music. We can understand the speaker felt very happy when listening to the music, and would like to hear it again. A similar way to say this would be "This music makes me feel so cheerful"

| Point | send sb to the moon …을 황홀하게 해주다, 기분좋게 해주다
send sb to hell 지옥으로 보내다, 골탕먹이다, 힘들게 하다

A: **This music really sends me to the moon.**
이 음악을 들으면 정말이지 황홀해져.

B: I know. Isn't it beautiful? 알아. 정말 아름답지 않아?

미드표현

I could say that your love sends me to the moon. 네 사랑은 날 황홀하게 해주는 것 같아.

The touch of her boyfriend sends her to the moon. 남친의 손길에 걔는 뿅갔어.

I told him that it was Peter who was sending him to hell. 난 걔한테 걔를 골탕먹인 건 바로 피터라고 말했어.

007 It would make me happy 그럼 내가 좋을거야

this is a way to tell someone "That is what I'd like." Sometimes this is said when a speaker expresses something he wishes would happen

| Point | make sb happy …을 기쁘게 해주다
You made me happy 너 때문에 행복했어
Did that make you happy? 그래서 행복했어?

A: How would you feel if I cooked dinner tonight?
오늘 저녁 내가 저녁 해주면 어떻겠어?

B: **It would make me happy.** I like it when you help out. 그러면 내가 좋지. 네가 도와주면 좋더라.

미드표현

I know it would make me happy.
그렇게 하면 내가 행복할거라는 걸 알고 있어.

Living with you would make me happy.
너랑 살면 행복해질거야.

I'll do a lot of things to make you happy.
널 행복하게 해주기 위해 많은 걸 할게.

008 It'll make you feel better 기분이 좀 좋아질거야

this often means "Doing that will make you happier." This might be said to someone who is sad or tired

| Point | make sb feel better …의 기분을 더 좋게 만들어주다
That feels nice (천, 접촉) 기분이 좋은데
I feel great[good] 기분 좋아
That makes me feel better 기분이 더 좋아졌어

A: I heard that tax rates are going down.
세금이 낮아질 거래.

B: **That makes me feel better.** I pay a lot of taxes.
그럼 좋지. 세금 많이 내는데.

미드표현

Would it make you feel better if I did all that?
내가 그걸 다하면 기분이 좋아지겠어?

Dance with us. It'll make you feel better.
우리랑 춤추면 기분 좋아질거야.

I've got something to make you feel better.
네 기분 좋아지게 할 거 갖고 있어.

Go get some sleep. It'll make you feel better.
가서 좀 자. 기분이 더 좋아질거야.

009 Don't make me feel bad 나 기분 나쁘게 하지마

this expresses that the speaker doesn't awant someone to say unkind things. It is another way to say "Be nice to me"

| Point | make sb feel bad …을 언짢게 하다
It makes me feel sad 기분이 나빠지네

A: Your new haircut looks a little strange.
너 새로 이발한 거 이상해.

B: **Don't make me feel bad.** I don't like it either.
기분 나쁘게 하지마. 나도 마음에 안 들어.

You're trying to make me feel bad.
날 기분 나쁘게 하려는구만.

Don't make me feel bad about this.
이걸로 날 기분 나쁘게 하지마.

I'm sorry. I did not mean to make you feel bad. 미안. 널 기분 나쁘게 하려는 건 아니었어.

010 I've never seen him this happy
걔가 이렇게 행복해 하는 것을 본 적이 없어

this indicates "He's very happy these days." The speaker is telling others that someone is in a very good mood

| Point | I've never been this happy 이렇게 행복한 적 없었어
I've never seen you this happy 네가 이렇게 행복해하는 것을 못봤어

A: Henry seems very excited about getting an A in class. 헨리는 반에서 A를 받고 무척 기뻐하는 것 같아.

B: I know. **I've never seen him this happy** before.
알아. 걔가 이렇게 기뻐하는 것을 본 적이 없어.

I've never seen him this mad.
걔가 이렇게 화를 내는 걸 본 적이 없어.

I tell you, I've never seen him this happy.
정말이야. 걔가 이렇게 행복해하는거 처음 봐.

I didn't expect him to be this happy so soon.
이렇게 빨리 걔가 행복해지리라고는 생각도 못했어.

011 I'm (so) flattered 과찬의 말씀을, 그렇게 말해주면 고맙지

this is a way to say that something nice has been done or said about the speaker. It's similar to saying "I'm happy you did that for me." or "I'm happy you said that about me"

| Point | I'm flattered (that) S+V …해서 기분이 좋아
This is very flattering 그런 말을 들으니 기분이 좋네
Don't flatter yourself 잘난 척 좀 그만해, 우쭐대지마

A: Gosh Julie, you look beautiful tonight.
저런 줄리, 오늘 너 정말 예뻐.

B: **I'm flattered.** I just bought this dress you know.
과찬의 말씀을. 그냥 이 옷을 샀을 뿐인데.

I'm flattered, but I'm seeing somebody.
그렇게 말해줘서 고마운데, 나 지금 만나는 사람있어.

Maybe you should be flattered.
아마 어깨가 으쓱했겠구만.

I'm flattered you thought of me.
날 생각하고 있다니 기분이 좋네.

012 That's music to my ears 듣던 중 정말 반가운 말이네

this means "It's really good news." The speaker is happy that he heard something

A: School has been canceled because of the storm. 폭풍 때문에 수업이 취소됐어.

B: Great. **That's music to my ears.**
좋아. 듣던 중 반가운 말이네.

You're going to marry her? That's music to my ears. 너 걔랑 결혼한다고? 듣던 중 반가운 소리네.

That's music to my ears. It's the best thing I ever heard.
듣던 중 반가운 소리네. 이렇게 좋은 얘기를 듣는 건 처음이야.

I heard you are coming home and that's music to my ears.
네가 집에 온다고 들었어. 정말 듣던 중 반가운 말이야.

013 I'm not in the mood 그럴 기분이 아냐

this is expressing "I don't want to do it now." The speaker wants to wait until later to do something

| Point | be in the mood to~[for+N] …할 기분이 든다
I'm in bad mood 기분이 안 좋아
She's moody (감정기복이 심한) 걘 기분파야

A: Would you like to go and see a movie with us?
우리랑 함께 가서 영화볼래?

B: No thank you. **I'm not in the mood.**
고맙지만 됐어. 그럴 기분이 아냐.

I'm really not in the mood to see a movie anymore. 더 이상 영화를 볼 기분이 아냐.

I'm not really in the mood to talk about my mom. 엄마얘기를 할 기분이 아냐.

I don't know why, but I'm in the mood for roast turkey. 이유를 모르겠지만 칠면조구이가 땡기지 않아.

014 You look terrible 안 좋아 보여

this is a way to show worry about someone. It expresses the question "Is there something wrong with you?"

| Point | You don't look (so) good[fine 좋아 보이지 않아
You look down[gloomy] 우울해 보여

A: Did something happen? **You look terrible.**
무슨 일 있어? 안 좋아 보여.

B: I've been very stressed about money problems recently. 최근 돈 문제로 스트레스를 무척 받았어.

Are you sure you're okay? You don't look so good. 정말 너 괜찮은거야? 그렇게 좋아 보이지는 않은데.

A: You don't look good. B: I need to get some air. A: 너 안 좋아 보여. B: 바람 좀 쐬고 와야겠어.

You don't look surprised to see us.
넌 우리를 보고 놀라지 않네.

015 You don't look like it's okay 괜찮아 보이지 않아

this is a complex phrase, which means "You said yes, but I think you mean no." The speaker thinks someone agreed to something, but that person is unhappy about it

| Point | You look like you've had a long day 힘든 하루 보낸 것 같아
You look like shit 너 많이 상했구나. 안 좋아 보여

A: It's okay with me if you go camping with your friends. 네 친구들과 함께 캠핑을 간다면 난 괜찮아.

B: Are you sure? **You don't look like it's okay.**
정말야? 괜찮아 보이지 않는데.

You don't look like it's okay. I think we should say no. 너 괜찮아 보이지 않아. 우리가 거절해야 될 것 같아.

You look unhappy, and you don't look like it's okay. 너 슬퍼 보여 그리고 괜찮아 보이지도 않고.

016 She's really depressed 재는 정말 지쳤어, 의기소침해 있어, 낙담해 있어

often this means someone is very sad. It is like saying "She's very unhappy right now"

| Point | be depressed 울적하다, 우울하다

A: Why hasn't Lisa come to any parties lately?
리사는 왜 최근에 어느 파티에도 오지 않는거야?

B: **She's really depressed** and wants to stay at home. 낙담해 있어 집에 있기를 원해.

He got fat, he's depressed. 갠 살이 쪄서, 낙담해있어.

She's really depressed, so we have to make a quick stop at her place.
걘 정말 지쳐있어서 걔네 집에 잠깐 들려야 해.

I was almost too depressed to come today.
난 오늘 너무 울적해서 거의 올 수가 없었어.

I know how depressed you've been since Jackson was dead. 잭슨이 죽은 후에 네가 얼마나 우울해했는지 알고 있어.

017 I'm not feeling well 기분이 별로 안 좋아, 속이 안 좋아

this expresses that the speaker has a mild sickness. It is a way to say "I feel ill"

| Point | I'm not feeling very good 기분이 그리 좋지 않아
I don't feel right, either 나도 맘이 편하지는 않아

A: Why do you want to go home early?
왜 일찍 집에 가려는거야?

B: **I'm not feeling well** and I need to rest.
몸이 별로 좋지 않아서 쉬어야 되겠어.

I'm not feeling well. I'm going home.
몸이 별로야. 집에 갈래.

A: Vicky! I thought you'd be at work. B: I'm not feeling well. I got a sunburn the other day washing my car.
A: 비키! 너 지금 일하는 줄 알았는데. B: 별로 안좋아. 요전날 세차하다가 살이 탔거든.

018 It's in bad taste 그건 아주 불쾌했어

this indicates that something seems to be insulting or offensive to some people. A thing that is in bad taste is often considered rude or impolite. Another way to say this would be "It will upset some people"

| Point | sth be in bad[poor] taste 상스럽다, 볼가치가 없다, 멋이 없다

A: Rita should not have worn a red dress to the funeral. 리타는 장례식에 빨간색 옷을 입지 말았어야 했는데.

B: I know. I think **it's in bad taste.** 그러게 말이야. 볼썽 사나워.

Honey, that would be in bad taste.
자기야, 그건 흉할거야.

They thought it was in poor taste.
걔네들은 그게 천박하다고 생각했어.

Flo's short skirt was in bad taste in the church.
플로의 짧은 치마는 교회에서 아주 상스러웠어.

I think her behavior was in bad taste.
난 걔의 행동이 천박했다고 생각해.

MEMO

Ways to talk about a special situation

특별한 상황을 말할 때

Let's see what we got here

001 Let's see what we got here 어떤 상황인지 보자

often this is said when a person wants to determine what a situation is like. He is probably wondering what is happening because he has just arrived and doesn't have any information yet. It is a way to say "I want to know what has been going on"

Point what we got here 현재 상황, 현재 갖고 있는 정보나 물건

A: Look, **here's what we got here.** This guy is being charged with murder.
이봐, 우리 상황이 이래. 이 친구는 살인죄로 기소될거야.

B: So you think he's the guy that killed the old lady? 그럼 그가 노부인을 살해한 사람이라고 생각하는거예요?

Let's see what we got here for ya.
네게 어떤 상황인지 한번 보자.

I'll pick you out an outfit. Let's see what we got here. 옷 한벌 골라줄게. 뭐가 있나 보자.

Look, here's what we got here. Cowboy Dan is dead. 저기, 우리가 알고 있는 상황은 카우보이 댄이 죽었다는거야.

002 We're done here 우린 얘기 끝났어

미드표현

this is usually said to indicate things are finished, and whatever was happening is over now. It is also a signal to others that they are allowed to leave. We might understand this to mean "Everything is done, so we can go"

Point We're done here 볼일 다 보다, 더 이상 할 얘기없다
You're done here 넌 끝이야

A: The crew wants to know if they should stay.
그 팀은 계속 남아있어야 하는지 알고 싶어해.

B: No, **we're done here.** Everybody go home.
아니, 다 끝났어. 다들 가도 돼.

It's all circumstantial. We're done here.
그건 모두 다 정황뿐이야. 더 이상 할 얘기 없어.

Just give us their names and we're done here.
걔네들 이름을 대기만해 그럼 여기서 끝낼테니.

I think we are done here. You can go.
볼 일 다본 것 같은데 그만 가도 돼.

I'll be down there when we're done here.
여기 일 끝나면 내가 그리로 갈게.

003 Let's hope it doesn't come to that 그렇게 되지 않기를 바라자

this is said after someone has talked about a very negative possible outcome. It means that the speaker is hoping that the result will be a lot more positive. It is very much like saying "I hope that things in the future will be a lot better than what you described"

Point (sth) come to that (나쁜 상태로) 그렇게 되다

A: We may have to arrest Herman and put him in jail. 우리는 허먼을 체포해서 감방에 넣어야 될지도 몰라.

B: **Let's hope it doesn't come to that.**
그렇게 되지 않기를 바라자고.

I'm glad it didn't come to that.
그게 그렇게 되지 않아서 기뻐.

Do you know it may have come to that?
그게 그렇게 될 수도 있었다는 걸 알고 있어?

As your friend, let's hope it doesn't come to that. 친구로서, 그렇기 되지 않기를 바라자.

004 That's not good 좋지 않은데

미드표현

this is a simple way to express worry or disappointment over something that has happened. For example, a speaker may say this after receiving bad news. It is another way to say "That is something that I am unhappy about"

Point That's[This is] not good 상당이 안좋은
That's not good enough 그걸로 충분하지 않아

A: The teacher said I wasn't doing well in his class.
선생님은 내가 반에서 잘하지 못하고 있다고 말씀하셨어.

B: **That's not good.** You'd better try harder.
그거 안좋은데. 너 더 열심히 하도록 해.

Ron is starting to get attached to Jenna and that's not good.
론은 제나에게 정신적으로 종속되기 시작하는데 그거 좋지 않아.

That's not good enough. We need tangible evidence. 그걸로는 충분하지 않아. 우리는 구체적인 증거가 필요해.

You failed your polygraph? That's not good.
거짓말탐지기를 통과하지 못했다고? 그거 좋지 않은데.

005 I can ill afford a speeding ticket 속도위반벌금을 낼 처지가 아냐

this expresses that the speaker may not have much money, and does not want the police to stop him for driving too fast because he may not be able to pay the fine. It is like saying "Speeding tickets are too expensive and I can't afford to pay for one"

| Point | can ill afford~ …할 입장이 아니다, …할 처지가 아니다

A: Why are you driving so slowly on the highway?
넌 고속도로에서 왜 그렇게 느리게 달리는거야?

B: **I can ill afford** a speeding ticket right now.
속도위반벌금을 낼 형편이 못돼서.

A: My client can ill afford. B: Shut up, Counselor.
A: 제 의뢰인은 그럴 입장이 아닙니다. B: 그만해요, 변호사.

She can ill afford to fail chemistry class.
걘 화학과목을 낙제할 처지가 아냐.

They can ill afford the price of a new computer. 걔네들은 새로운 컴퓨터 가격을 부담할 처지가 아냐.

006 I think things are picking up (사정 · 상황이) 나아질거야

this speaker is saying "Things are getting better." He feels that there is improvement

| Point | pick up 사정이 좋아지다

A: How has business been in your restaurant?
식당사업 어때?

B: It was slow, but **I think things are picking up.**
더디지만 나아질 거라고 생각해.

I think things are picking up at our new restaurant. 우리 식당 사정이 좋아질거야.

Business was slow for a while, but I think things are picking up.
경제가 좀 둔화되었지만 사정이 좋아질거야.

I think things are picking up. It's getting better. 상황이 좋아지는 것 같아. 점점 나아질거야.

I think things are picking up. We're making money. 상황이 나아질 것 같아. 우린 돈을 벌고 있어.

007 That (all) depends 상황에 따라 달라, 경우에 따라 달라

this is usually said when someone thinks something could change. It is like saying "This may change sometime"

| Point | That[It] depends on~ …에 따라 다르다
I guess that[it] depends on~ …따라 다른 것 같아

A: You told me you would move near the ocean someday. 네가 언젠가 바다근처로 이사갈 거라고 말했지.

B: **That all depends.** I might not have enough money to do it. 상황에 따라 달라. 돈이 부족할 수도 있어.

That depends, how much did you hear?
경우에 따라 다르지, 얼마로 들었는데?

That depends on what we buy.
우리가 무엇을 사느냐에 달렸지.

I guess it depends on what you learn.
네가 무엇을 배우냐에 달린 것 같아.

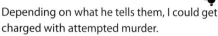

008 Depending on~ …에 따라서

this means "Something may change due to something else." The speaker wants to say that a thing isn't certain

| Point | Depending on the situation 상황에 따라서

A: We may cancel the picnic, **depending on** the weather. 날씨에 따라 피크닉을 취소할 지도 몰라.

B: I hope that it's not going to rain today.
오늘 비가 내리지 않기를 바래.

Depending on what he tells them, I could get charged with attempted murder.
걔가 말하는 거에 따라 난 살인미수죄로 기소될 수도 있어.

Depending on time, I was either gonna meet her back at home or at the church.
시간에 따라, 집에서 혹은 교회에서 걔를 다시 만나거나 할거였어.

009 That's another[a different] story
그건 또 다른 얘기야, 사정이 다른 얘기야

often this is said to indicate that one thing isn't similar to another thing. It is a way to say "It's not the same"

| Point | This is a totally different situation 전혀 다른 상황야

A: Why did you buy a new TV? You already have a TV. 왜 TV를 새로 샀어? TV 있잖아.

B: **That's another story.** I wanted to have a digital TV. 사정이 달라. 디지털 TV를 갖고 싶었거든 .

This is a totally different situation. I'm going to be with this guy forever.
이번은 전혀 달라. 이 남친과 헤어지지 않을거야.

We fought all the time, but that's a different story. 우리는 늘상 싸웠지만 그건 다른 얘기야.

Don't tell the cops about that. That's a different story. 경찰에게 그 얘기를 하지마. 그건 또 다른 얘기야.

010 This is totally getting out of hand
일이 너무 커져 버렸어, 아주 엉망이야

this is a way to say "We can't control this." It indicates that things are becoming crazy or unpredictable

| Point | Things get out of hand 일이 걷잡을 수 없이 되다
This got out of hand 일이 너무 커졌다

A: People keep coming to our house to sell us things. 사람들이 물건들을 팔려고 계속 우리 집에 와.

B: We have to stop that. **This is getting totally out of hand.** 그만 하게 해야 돼. 아주 엉망이야.

Things got out of hand? He changed his mind? 걷잡을 수 없는 상태야? 걘 맘을 바꿨어?

If things get out of hand, 상황이 걷잡을 수가 없게 되면,

I can see how these things can get out of hand. 이 일들이 어떻게 걷잡을 수 없게 될 수 있는지 알겠어.

I guess you could say things got out of hand.
넌 일이 걷잡을 수 없게 되었다고 말할 수 있겠지.

011 It doesn't look good 바람직하진 않아, (사태, 상황) 좋아 보이지 않아

usually this means "I think it will fail." The speaker doubts something will happen

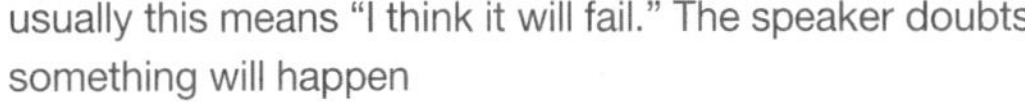

A: How are things at your new business?
너 새로 시작한 사업 어때?

B: **It doesn't look good.** We don't have many customers. 좋아 보이지 않아. 손님이 별로 없어.

You realize that doesn't look good?
그게 바람직하지 않다는 걸 알았어?

I'm not gonna lie to you, it doesn't look good.
거짓말은 못 하겠다. 그래서는 안될 것 같아.

He speaks honestly on the phone to his spouse, and it doesn't look good.
갠 전화로 부인에게 솔직히 말하고 있는데 상황은 좋아 보이지 않아.

012 Now the shoe's on the other foot 이제는 입장이 바뀌었군

this is said to indicate "Things have changed a lot." It is a way to say the situation is reversed from what it was in the past

| Point | Put yourself in my shoes 나랑 입장을 바꿔놓고 생각해 봐
I wouldn't be in your shoes 네 처지는 되고 싶지 않아

A: I used to be a worker. **Now the shoe's on the other foot.** 전에는 근로자였는데 지금은 입장이 바뀌었어.

B: I guess that you like being the company manager. 회사 부장이 된 걸 좋아하는구만.

It seems the shoe is on the other foot now, doesn't it? 이제 입장이 바뀐 것 같구만. 그렇지 않아?

If he were in my shoes he would run.
걔가 내 입장이라면 달아났을거야.

When you're in my shoes, you'll do the same thing. 네가 내 입장이라면 너도 똑같이 그럴거야.

013 That's it 1. 그게 다야 2. 그만 됐어, 이제 못참겠어

often this is a way to say something has finished. It is very similar to saying "It's over." And this also means "I'm upset and I want you to stop something". The speaker is expressing anger over something that is happening

| Point | That's it? 이걸로 끝이야?, 그게 전부야?

A: **That's it.** I've finished working for the day.
그만 됐어. 오늘 일은 끝냈어.

B: But don't you want to finish the work on your desk? 하지만 책상 위에 있는 거 끝내고 싶지 않아?

That's it. That's perfect! 잘했어, 완벽해!

That's it! Get out here, both of you!
그만 됐어! 꺼져 둘 다!

That's it? That's all you're having?
그게 다야? 있는 게 그게 전부야?

014 That was that 일이 그렇게 된거야(that's the story)

this is almost exactly the same as the previous phrase. It means "It is over now"

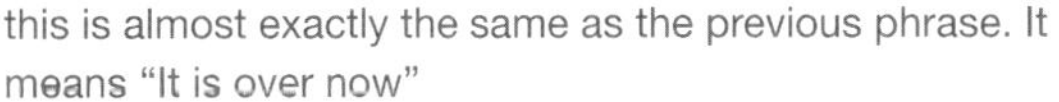

| Point | Here's what's what 사실은 이런거야
That's that 그게 전부야, 그걸로 끝이야

A: I heard you broke up with your girlfriend last night. 지난 밤에 여친과 헤어졌다며.

B: Yeah, it's very sad for me. I guess **that's that.**
그래, 너무 슬퍼. 그게 끝인 것 같아.

You asked me to tell you about Europe. Well, here's what's what.
유럽에 대해 말해달라고 했지. 음, 사실은 이래.

This encyclopedia is great. Here's what's what about almost everything.
백과사전은 엄청나. 거의 모든 거에 대한 정보가 들어있어.

I couldn't make the monthly payments to the bank and that was that.
은행에 할부금을 못 내서 일이 그렇게 된거야.

015 That's all[what] she wrote 더 이상은 없다, 더 이상 할 일이 없다

the speaker is saying everything is over. It is like saying "That is finished"

A: I heard you gave up writing a novel.
소설 쓰는 걸 그만 뒀다며.

B: I ran out of ideas. **That was all she wrote.**
아이디어가 고갈됐어. 다 끝났어.

The campaign is over. That's all she wrote.
선거운동이 끝났어. 더 이상은 할 일이 없어.

That's all she wrote. Let's go home now.
더 이상 할 일이 없어. 이제 집에 가자고.

The computer just stopped working, and that's all she wrote.
컴퓨터가 방금 고장났고 더 이상은 할 일이 없어.

016 That's the whole story 자초지종이 그렇게 된거야

this is a way to say "I told you everything." The speaker is saying he has given all of the details

| Point | the whole story 자초지종
I know the whole story 자초지종을 알아

A: So you became rich because you worked hard seven days a week? 그래 주 7일 열심히 일해 부자 되었다고?

B: **That's the whole story.** It was all hard work.
그렇게 된거야. 정말 열심히 일했었지.

He still doesn't know the whole story, does he? 갠 아직도 사건의 전말을 알지 못하지, 맞지?

I don't have time to tell you the whole story.
자초지종을 다 말할 시간이 없어.

Will you stop? You don't know the whole story.
그만 좀 해라. 자초지종도 모르면서.

017 That's all there is to it 그 뿐이야, 그게 다야

the speaker wants to say that he has told everything. He is indicating "I gave you all of the information"

A: You make cooking look very easy.
넌 요리를 무척 쉬워 보이게 해.

B: Just take your time. **That's all there is to it.**
그냥 시간을 갖고 천천히 해. 그 뿐이야.

I've decided that I need you in my life, and that's all there is to it.
내 인생에 네가 필요하다고 결정했어. 그뿐이야.

You are having dinner with Bob, and that is all there is to it! 넌 밥하고 저녁을 먹는거고 그저 그 뿐이야!

It was a mistake. I'm sure that's all there is to it. 그거 실수였어. 다만 그 뿐이야.

018 I get to the point where~ …하는 정도(지경)까지 이르렀어

usually this means that the speaker does or feels something unusual during a certain time. It is similar to saying "That always makes me S+V

| Point | ~to the point where S+V …할 정도까지
be in a situation where S+V …하는 상황에 놓이다

A: I feel so angry. **I get to the point where everything upsets me.** 화나. 모든 게 다 화나는 지경야.

B: Wow, it sounds like you are having a lot of stress. 와, 스트레스가 엄청난 것 같아.

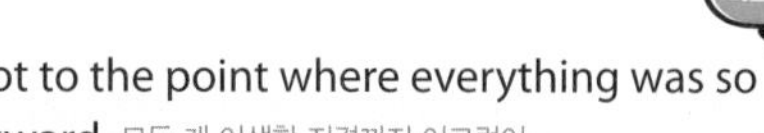

It got to the point where everything was so awkward. 모든 게 어색한 지경까지 이르렀어.

What if it just gets worse, to the point where we can't even look at each other?
만약 상황이 악화되서 서로 바라다 볼 수 없을 정도까지 가면 어떻게 해?

Were you ever in a situation where you could see a thing coming and you didn't do anything?
어떤 일이 벌어질지 뻔히 보면서도 아무런 조치를 취하지 않았던 적이 있어?

MEMO

Ways of talking about jobs and work

직장에서 일을 시작하다

I have a lot on my plate

001 Please cover for me 내 대신 좀 해줘, (경찰) 옹호해줘

often this is way to say "Help me out during the time I'm gone." The speaker wants someone to help while he is away

I Point I cover for sb 다른 사람의 일을 처리해주다

A: I'm leaving early. **Please cover for me.**
나 일찍가니까 내 대신 좀 해줘.

B: I'll tell the teacher you're in the toilet.
선생님한테 너 화장실 갔다고 할게.

미드표현

Can you cover for me? I just got an audition.
내 일 좀 봐줄래? 오디션이 있어서.

I've got to go pick up Linda. Could you cover for me? 린다 데리러 가야 돼. 내 일 좀 봐줄래?

Don't worry. I'll cover for you. 걱정마. 내가 봐줄게.

Is there someone who can fill in for me?
누구 내 일 좀 봐줄 사람있어?

002 Could you fill in for me? 내 대신 일 좀 봐줄래?

this speaker is saying that he is going to work in the place of someone else. We can understand that the missing worker may be sick, injured or on vacation. It is like saying "I am going to do the work he was supposed to do."

I Point I fill in for sb (부재중) …대신 일을 봐주다

A: Where is Richard today? Isn't he working?
오늘 리차드 보이지 않네? 걔 출근안했어?

B: He's sick. **I'm going to fill in for him.**
몸이 아프대. 내가 대신 일을 봐줄거야.

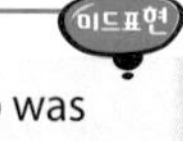

I asked him to fill in for someone who was sick. 난 걔한테 아픈 사람을 대신해서 일을 하라고 했어.

I fill in for him when he isn't available.
난 걔가 일을 할 수 없을 때 대신 일을 봐줬어.

And I'm gonna fill in for him tomorrow night.
그리고 난 내일 저녁 걔를 대신해서 일을 봐줄거야.

I was wondering if you could possibly fill in for me. I would be so grateful.
너, 내 대신 일을 봐줄 수 있을까. 그러면 정말 고맙겠는데.

003 I work for Mr. Truman 트루먼 씨 회사에서 일해

this means "My employer is Mr. Truman." The speaker is talking about who his boss is

I Point I work for …위해서[밑에서] 일하다, …에서 일하다
Who do you work for? 어디서 일해?

A: Who is the head of your department?
네 부서장이 누구셔?

B: **I work for Mr. Truman.** 트루먼 씨 밑에서 일해.

미드표현

I work for the government. 난 공무원이야.

I work for Linda Hamilton and in many ways she's an excellent boss.
난 린다 해밀튼 씨 밑에서 일해. 정말 여러 면에서 뛰어난 상사야.

Does she work for you? 걔가 너 밑에서 일해?

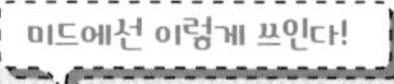

He's working for Abu Nazir

Homeland
SEASON#1-1

미 해병 Brody는 10년 만에 중동에서 구출되지만, 테러에 강박적으로 집착하는 Carrie는 전향한 미군포로가 있다는 첩보를 입수하고 Saul과 얘기를 나눈다.

Saul:	What were his exact words, please?	사울: 정확히 무슨 말이었지?
Carrie:	An American prisoner of war has been turned.	캐리: 한 미군 포로가 전향했대요.
Saul:	He said this in English?	사울: 이걸 영어로 말을 했나?
Carrie:	Yes. He whispered it into my ear right before the guards pulled me away.	캐리: 예. 경비대가 날 끌어내기 직전 내 귀에다 대고 속삭였어요.
Saul:	And when he used the expression "turned..."	사울: 그 사람이 '전향'이라고 말을 했을 때는…
Carrie:	He meant turned..., working for Abu Nazir.	캐리: 전향을 해서 Abu Nazir 밑에서 일한다는 뜻이에요.

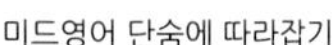

004 I have to call in sick 오늘 결근한다고 전화해야겠어

this is used to say the person didn't work because he was sick. He is saying "I called my boss to say I would stay home"

| Point | call in sick 아파서 출근 못한다고 전화하다, 전화해서 병가내다

A: I feel terrible. **I have to call in sick.**
몸이 정말 안 좋아. 아파서 결근한다고 해야 되겠어.

B: Maybe you should go and see a doctor.
병원가서 진찰 받아 봐.

미드표현

I can't call in sick after eight weeks of sick leave. 8주간의 병가 후에 다시 아파서 출근 못한다고 할 수 없어.

I thought you called in sick to avoid me.
날 피하기 위해 병가 낸 걸로 생각했었어.

What are you doing here? You called in sick this morning. 너 여기 웬일이야? 오늘 아침에 병가 냈잖아.

005 What do you do (for a living)? 직업이 뭐예요?, 하는 일이 뭐예요?

this is a way of asking "What's your job?" The speaker wants to know what kind of work someone does

| Point | What do you do on the side? 뭘 부업으로 해?

A: **What do you do for a living?** 직업이 뭐예요?

B: I work as a lawyer for an insurance company.
보험회사 변호사입니다.

미드표현

Just one more question. What do you do for a living? 질문 하나 더요. 하시는 일이 뭐예요?

A: So, what do you do for a living? B: Right now I'm between jobs.
A: 그럼, 직업이 뭐야? B: 지금은 백수야.

006 I'm my own boss 자영업해, 사업해

this indicates the speaker owns his own business. It is a way to say "I work for myself

| Point | I'm my own boss = I'm self employed
= I run my own business = I work for myself
= I own my own company 사업하다

A: Do you work downtown? 시내에서 일해?

B: No, **I am my own boss.** 아니, 자영업해.

미드표현

I work for myself as a freelance writer.
프리랜서 작가로 혼자 일해.

You work for yourself. You're your own boss.
넌 네 일을 하잖아. 네가 사장이지.

Well, not everyone is cut out to be their own boss. 모든 사람이 다 사장이 되기에 적합한 것은 아냐.

007 Let's call it a day 퇴근하자

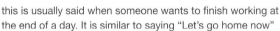

this is usually said when someone wants to finish working at the end of a day. It is similar to saying "Let's go home now"

| Point | call it a day[night] 하던 일 멈추다, 퇴근하다
We've done for the day 그만 하자, 그만 가자
He's gone for the day 걔 퇴근했어
Off we go 그만하고 가자(하자)

A: I think everyone is feeling very tired.
다들 무척 피곤한 것 같아.

B: **Let's call it a day.** We'll start again tomorrow morning. 그만 퇴근하자. 내일 아침 다시 시작하자.

미드표현

Before I simply give up and call it a day, I'd like to ask you one question.
포기하고 그만두기 전에 한가지 물어볼 게 있어.

What do you say we call it a night and get some sleep? 이제 그만 끝내고 잠을 좀 자는 게 어때?

I'm exhausted. You mind if we just call it a night? 지쳤어. 그만 해도 돼?

008 Are you all caught up? 밀린 일은 다 했어?

미드표현

the speaker is asking if someone has done all of the work. A similar question would be "Did you do everything that you needed to do?"

I Point I get[be] caught up …을 따라잡다, …을 마무리하다
I'm behind in my work 일이 밀렸어
I'm way behind 엄청 뒤쳐져서 지금 바빠

A: **Are you all caught up?** 밀린 일은 다 했어?
B: No, I still have some things to do. 아니, 아직 할 일이 있어.

I was just behind. I never caught up with the reading. That's why I got a C.
난 뒤쳐졌어. 독해자료를 다 못해서 C를 받았어.

I'm behind in my work and I have to get it done. 일이 밀려서 끝마쳐야 돼.

009 That should do it 그 정도면 됐어

미드표현

this is a way to say "It's finished." This is said when a job has been completed

A: Have you finished painting the living room?
거실 칠하는 거 끝냈어요?
B: Yes I have. **That should do it.** 네, 끝냈어요. 그 정도면 됐죠.

I was thinking jewelry... so fifty bucks should do it. 귀금속을 생각하고 있었는데… 그럼 50달러면 되겠어.

I think this should do it. 이 정도면 됐어.

Well, that should do it. Thanks for your time.
저기 그 정도면 됐어. 시간 내줘서 고마워.

I printed the report, so that should do it.
난 보고서를 프린터했고 그렇게 일을 끝냈어.

010 That will do (it) 그 정도면 돼, 그만하면 됐어

미드표현

this means something was finished successfully. It is like saying "OK, that worked, now we can leave"

I Point I Will that do (it)? 그거면 충분하지?

A: Is this how you wanted the room organized?
이렇게 방 정리를 하면 되겠어?
B: **That will do.** You guys can go home now.
그만하면 됐어. 이제 집에 가봐.

That will do it. We are all ready now.
그 정도면 됐어. 우리 이제 다 준비됐어.

Is everything in place? That will do it.
다 제대로 됐어? 그만하면 됐어.

That will do it. It's time to wrap things up.
그만하면 됐어. 그만 마무리할 때야.

011 Pack it up 그만두다

미드표현

this indicates that things are finished and everyone can go. It is another way to say "We've all done today"

I Point I pack it up 끝내다, 그만두다
pack it in 일을 그만두다

A: What should I do with this report?
이 보고서 어떻게 해야 돼?
B: **Pack it up** and we'll send it to our boss.
그만해 사장님께 보낼거야.

He decided to pack it in. 걔는 그만 두기로 했어.

Let's just pack it up. The bullet couldn't have gone this far.
그만 두자고. 탄알이 여기까지 날아 왔을리가 없어.

We're going home. Time to pack it up.
우리 집에 간다. 그만 끝낼 시간이야.

It's late and we are ready to pack it in.
늦었어. 우리는 그만 둘 준비가 됐어.

012 I got fired 잘렸어, 해고 당했어

this is a way to say "They told me to stop working there." It's done when a person is not doing a good job

Point I got[was] kicked out 나 잘렸어, 쫓겨났어
You're fired 넌 해고야

A: Why aren't you at your office? 왜 출근 안 한거야?
B: **I got fired.** Now I am looking for a new place to work. 잘렸어. 새로이 일자리를 찾고 있어.

You got fired four times and you still think you are so wonderful.
4번이나 잘렸는데 아직도 네가 대단하다고 생각하는거야.

I don't think that's why you got fired.
네가 잘린 이유는 그게 아닌 것 같은데.

Speaking of which, I heard you got fired a few weeks ago. 말이 나왔으니 말인데, 몇 주전에 잘렸다며.

013 I'm out of a job now 난 지금 백수야

this often indicates a person has been fired or quit. It is a way to say "I don't have work to pay me a salary"

Point be out of a job[work] 실직상태이다(be between jobs)
get the sack[boot, ax] 잘리다
get a pink slip 해고당하다
let sb go 가게 하다, 자르다(fire)

A: The company is cutting employees. 감원 중이래.
B: **I'm out of a job** now because of that.
그 때문에 난 실직했어.

Oh my God, are you out of a job again?
맙소사, 너 또 백수야?

I hate putting people out of work.
사람들을 자르는 게 정말 싫어.

I got fired today for being drunk on the job.
근무 중에 술 먹었다고 오늘 잘렸어.

014 Shape up or ship out 제대로 하지 않으려면 나가라

this is an older phrase which is telling someone that he needs to do a better job on the work he is assigned, or else be prepared to go work somewhere else. It implies that the speaker is the boss, and he has been unhappy with the listener's work in the past. In other words, "Do a better job or get out of here"

A: This is your third mistake. **You better shape up or ship out.** 이게 너 세번째 실수야. 제대로 하지 않으려면 나가라고.
B: Look, I'm sorry. I promise I'll do better in the future. 저기 죄송해요. 앞으로는 더 잘할게요.

This place is a mess. Shape up or ship out.
여기 아주 엉망이구만. 제대로 하지 않으려면 나가.

We're very disappointed in you. You need to shape up or ship out.
우린 네게 엄청 실망했어. 제대로 하지 않으려면 나가라고.

The captain told everyone to shape up or ship out.
대장은 모든 사람에게 제대로 하지 않으려면 나가라고 말했어.

015 He's on leave right now 걔 지금 휴가 중이야

this indicates someone isn't working, possibly because he is sick or on a vacation. It is similar to saying "He'll be away from work for a while"

Point be on leave 휴가 중이다

A: Can I talk to Al Weinstein? 알 와인스타인과 바꿔주세요.
B: I'm sorry, **he's on leave** right now.
죄송하지만 지금 휴가중이세요.

What's gonna happen to us when he goes on leave? 걔가 휴가 가면 우린 어떻게 되는 거지?

A: Does Bill still work in this department?
B: He does, but he's on leave right now.
A: 빌이 이 부서에서 아직 일을 하나요? B: 네, 하지만 지금은 휴가중이에요

As far as I'm concerned, you're still on leave.
내 생각으로는 너 아직 휴가중인데.

016 I've got work to do 할 일이 있어

this indicates "I'm very busy." A person usually is stating he wants to work and doesn't want people to bother him

| Point | have a lot of work to~ 할 일이 많다

A: Do you want to go to lunch together? 같이 점심 먹을래?

B: Not today. **I've got work to do.** 오늘은 안돼. 할 일이 있어.

If you'll excuse me, I have work to do.
괜찮다면, 내가 좀 할 일이 있어서.

Can I go? I've got a lot of work to do.
가도 돼? 할 일이 많아서.

Now that you and Jill are engaged you'll have a lot of work to do.
이제 너하고 질이 결혼하니 할 일이 많을게야.

017 I have a lot on my plate 신경쓸 게 많아, 할 일이 많아

미드표현

this is a way to say that there are many things the speaker has to do. It usually means "My life is more busy than usual"

| Point | have a lot on one's plate 해야 할 일이 많다
have a lot of work left 할 일이 많이 남아있다

A: I see you started another project.
또 다른 프로젝트를 시작했구나.

B: **I have a lot on my plate** these days.
요즘 할 일이 너무 많아.

I think you should go. I got a lot on my plate right now. 너 그만 가라. 지금 할 일이 너무 많아.

I've got a lot on my plate right now that I need to focus on. 지금 신경쓸 게 넘 많아 집중해야 돼.

Well, the FBI Crime Lab does have a lot on its plate. FBI 범죄실험실은 할 일이 많아.

018 I can't do this pro bono work anymore
이런 자원봉사일은 더는 못하겠어

미드표현

this is a way to say "I won't work for free anymore." The speaker is saying he needs to be paid

| Point | pro bono 무료로 행해지는

A: I need money. **I can't do pro bono work anymore.** 돈이 필요해. 자원봉사일은 더 이상 못해.

B: The charity organizations will be unhappy to hear that. 자선단체가 그 얘길 들으면 안좋아하겠네.

He does a lot of pro bono work, huh?
자원봉사일 많이 하나 봐?

I took this case pro bono. 무료로 이 사건을 맡았어.

Well actually, at the moment Alicia is working on a pro bono. 실은, 지금 알리샤는 무료변론사건을 맡고 있어.

019 When is this[it] due? 이게 언제 마감이야?

미드표현

this is a way of asking when the deadline is. The speaker wants to know "When do I need to finish it?"

| Point | be due 마감이다

A: **When is this project due?** 이 프로젝트 마감이 언제야?

B: The professor wants it by Wednesday.
교수님이 수요일까지 끝내래.

Is that your electric bill? When is it due?
전기세 청구서야? 언제까지인데?

Your homework looks very hard. When is it due? 네 숙제가 힘들어보이네. 언제까지야?

When is it due? Will you be able to complete it? 언제까지야? 끝낼 수 있겠어?

When is it due? Is it already late?
언제까지야? 이미 늦은거야?

020 I'm off duty 비번이야

this indicates "I'm done working for today." Often it is a way to say that the speaker won't work anymore at his job during that day

| Point | be off duty 비번이다
go off duty 일을 끝내다(finish work)
be on duty 근무 중이다
go on duty 일을 시작하다(start working)

A: Could you check something on the computer?
컴퓨터에 뭐 좀 확인할 수 있어?

B: Sorry, no. **I'm off duty** now. 미안, 안돼. 나 지금 비번이야.

I seem to be a little bit drunk. I was off duty.
좀 취해 보이지. 근무가 끝나서 그랬어.

A: Come on, man. We're off duty. B: You're off when I say you're off.
A: 이봐, 우리 비번이잖아. B: 내가 비번이라고 하면 그때부터 비번이야.

021 I got called in 호출 받고왔어

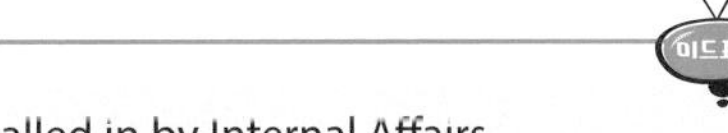

this often means "They called me to work." We can understand the person was asked to work unexpectedly

| Point | be[get] called in 호출 받고 출근하다

A: Hey Sara. I thought today was your day off.
어 새라, 오늘 너 쉬는 날이었잖아.

B: It was. **I got called in** to work. 맞아. 호출 받고 왔어.

I got called in by Internal Affairs.
내사과의 호출을 받고 왔어.

She's upset that she got called in on her day off.
걘 쉬는 날 호출 받아 화가 났어.

I just got called in to Human Resources.
난 방금 인사과로 호출받았어.

022 Put me to work 내게도 일을 줘

this is a way of indicating someone would like to start something. It is like saying "I'm ready right now"

| Point | put sb to work …에게 일을 주다, …에게 일을 시키다

A: I'm ready to go. **Put me to work.**
준비가 됐어. 내게도 일을 줘.

B: I want you to copy these documents. 이 서류들 복사해.

It's time to put you to work. 네게 일을 줄 때가 되었어.

We feed the hungry, we put people to work, and all we ask for in exchange is total devotion.
우리는 배고픈 자에게 밥을 먹이고 사람들에게 일을 주지, 그리고 그 대가로 바라는 건 오직 완전한 충성이야.

Put me to work wherever you need help.
내 도움이 필요하게 되면 내게 일을 줘.

023 What's the hold up? 왜 지체해?, 왜 이리 늦는거야?

this is a way of asking "Why is it taking so long?" The speaker is unhappy because something is taking a lot of time

| Point | hold up 1. 지연, 정체 2. 노상강도

A: **What's the hold up** in here? 여기 왜 이렇게 늦는거야?

B: There is some problem with the fax machine.
팩스기에 좀 문제가 있어.

What's the hold up? You've been in the bathroom for an hour.
왜 이리 늦어? 화장실에 한 시간 있네.

I ordered my lunch but it never came. What's the hold up? 음식주문을 했는데 오질 않네. 왜 이리 늦는거야?

What's the hold up with your homework? It's late! 숙제 왜 이리 늦는거야? 늦었어!

024 You are not cut out to be a physician

자넨 의사로서 적합하지 않아

this is a way to tell someone that he should not do that job. It is like saying "I don't think you should be a physician"

I Point I be cut out for[to be]+N …가 되기에 적합하다
have one's work cut out for~ 힘든 일을 맡다

A: Do you think I should attend medical school?
내가 의과대학에 가야 된다고 생각해?

B: No way. **You are not cut out to be a** physician.
전혀. 넌 의사되기엔 어울리지 않아.

미드표현

I'm not cut out for music. 난 음악하고 거리가 멀지.

Apparently I'm not cut out for that kind of work. 분명히 난 그런 종류의 일에는 어울리지 않아.

I've got my work cut out for me then, don't I? 내가 끝마치기 힘든 일을 맡았어, 그렇지 않아?

025 I'm just doing my job

할 일을 한 것 뿐인데, 내 일을 한 건데

this is usually a way to explain that something was done because it was part of the work. It means "I'm sorry, but I have to do this because it is part of my work." But this also can mean "It's okay, it was my duty." This is usually said as a response after a person that has been helped thanks the person that helped him, and that person is a policeman or fireman

I Point I It's my job 내 일인 걸, 내가 해야 되는 일이야
It's my job to do~ …하는 게 내 일이야
It's your job 그건 네 일이야

A: Why do you have to charge so much money?
왜 그렇게 많은 돈을 청구하는 겁니까?

B: Sorry sir. **I'm just doing my job.**
죄송합니다, 손님. 제 일을 하는 것 뿐인데요.

미드표현

It's my job to teach you. 널 가르치는 게 내 일이야.

It's my job to figure out what happened to your mother.
네 어머니에게 무슨 일이 일어났는지 알아보는 게 내 일이야.

I was just doing my job. I was glad to help out. 제 일을 한 것 뿐인데요. 도와주게 되어 기뻤어요.

026 Let's get to work

일 시작하자

this is telling people "Let's start." The speaker wants to begin doing something

I Point I get to work (on~) (…에 관한) 일을 하다

A: **Let's get to work.** This is important.
자 일 시작하자. 이거 중요한 일이야.

B: Where do you think we should start?
어디부터 시작해야 돼?

미드표현

I gotta get to work. So call me later?
일해야 돼. 나중에 전화할래?

I get to work 60 hours a week for the same salary. 같은 월급받고 주 60시간을 일해야 돼.

Get your ass out of bed and get to work!
침대에서 일어나 일하러 가!

You shouldn't be talking. Get to work!
말하면 안되지. 일해!

027 Work your way up here!

여기까지 열심히 일해서 올라와!

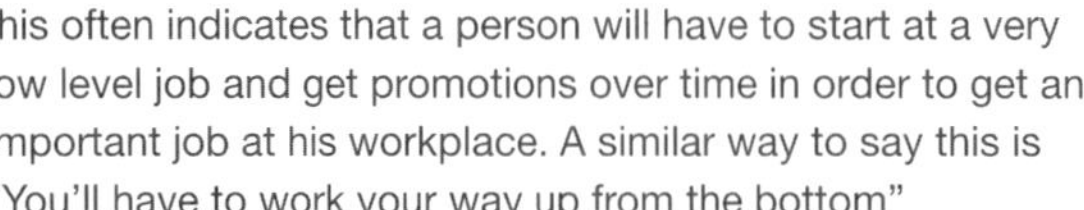

this often indicates that a person will have to start at a very low level job and get promotions over time in order to get an important job at his workplace. A similar way to say this is "You'll have to work your way up from the bottom"

I Point I work one's way up 열심히 일해서 승진하다, 올라가다

A: How can I become president of a company?
내가 어떻게 한 회사의 사장이 될 수 있겠어?

B: You'll need to **work your way up here.**
넌 노력해서 승진해 여기까지 올라와야 돼.

미드표현

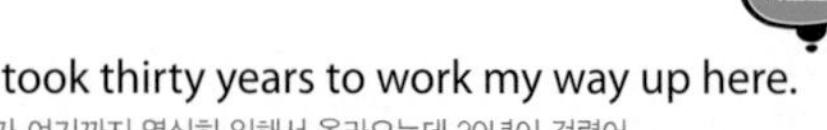

It took thirty years to work my way up here.
내가 여기까지 열심히 일해서 올라오는데 30년이 걸렸어.

You may never be able to work your way up here. 넌 노력해서 이 자리까지 절대 올라올 수 없을 수도 있어.

The mountain climbers are working their way up here. 등산객들이 열심히 노력해서 여기까지 올라오고 있어.

You see how the tumor has worked its way up the spine? 종양이 어떻게 척추까지 전이되었는지 알아?

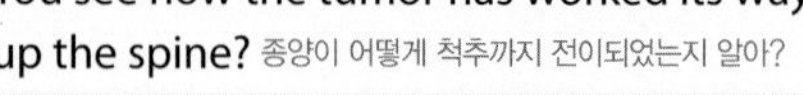

MEMO

Ways of talking about romance and dating

연애하고 사랑하고 그리고 결혼하고 이혼하기

I've got a crush on you

001 She asked me out 걔가 데이트 신청했어

this is a way to say "She invited me on a date." We can understand a woman asked the speaker to go on a date with her

| Point | ask sb out (on a date) 데이트 신청하다
go (out) on a date 데이트하러 가다
be (out) on a date 데이트하다

A: Are you going to the dance with Jill?
질하고 댄스파티에 갈거야?

B: Yes I am. **She asked me out.** 갈거야. 내게 데이트신청했어.

미드표현

Are you asking me out on a date?
지금 데이트 하자는거야?

He finally asked you out? 결국 걔가 데이트 신청했어?

Do you think it would be okay if I asked you out? 너한테 데이트 신청하면 받아 줄래?

I actually came here to ask you out.
실은 데이트 신청하러 왔어.

002 Are you seeing someone? 누구 사귀는 사람 있어?, 만나는 사람있어?

this is a way of asking if someone has a girlfriend or boyfriend. Another way to ask it is "Are you in a relationship with someone?"

| Point | I'm seeing him 걔랑 사귀어
You seeing anyone? 누구 만나?
I'm not seeing anyone 나 지금 사귀는 사람없어

A: **Are you seeing someone** nowadays?
요즘 사귀는 사람 있어?

B: No, I haven't had a boyfriend in a while.
아니, 한 동안 남친 없이 지내고 있어.

미드표현

When you and I broke up I started seeing someone. 우리 헤어지고 난 다른 사람 만나기 시작했어.

I always knew he was seeing someone. I just didn't know who.
걔가 누굴 만난다는 걸 알고 있었는데 누군지는 몰랐어.

When we started dating, I was already kind of seeing someone.
우리가 데이트 시작했을 때, 다른 사람을 만나고 있었어.

003 He's going out with Jane 그 사람은 제인하고 사귀는 중야

this indicates "Jane is his girlfriend." It is a way to say that they are a couple

| Point | go out with sb …와 사귀다
We started going out 우린 교제를 시작했어
We're going steady 우리 교제중이야
He's my steady 쟤가 내가 사귀는 남자야

A: Perry sure looks happy these days.
페리는 정말 요즘 행복해 보여.

B: **He's going out with Jane.** They are a good match. 제인하고 사귀는 중야. 걔네들 잘 어울려.

미드표현

I don't think you should go out with him.
너 걔랑 사귀지 않는 게 좋겠어.

She's been going out with Chris for a few months now. 걔는 크리스랑 몇 달째 사귀고 있어.

He's the hottest guy I've ever gone out with.
내가 데이트 한 사람 중에 최고로 섹시해.

004 This is not some rebound thing 허전한 마음 때문에 만나는 건 아니야

often this is a way to say someone has finished an old relationship and is ready to begin a new relationship. It is similar to saying "I want to date you seriously"

| Point | rebound 헤어진 아픔을 달래려고 혹은 복수심으로 다른 사람을 사귀는 거. 그렇게 사귀게 된 사람은 rebound guy라 한다.

A: I don't know if you are serious about dating me.
네가 나랑 데이트를 진지하게 하는지 모르겠어.

B: I'm serious. **This is not some rebound thing.**
난 진지해. 허전한 마음에 대신 널 사귀는 건 아냐.

미드표현

No don't worry, this is not some rebound thing. I am totally over Anita.
아냐 걱정마, 허전한 맘에 만나는 거 아냐. 애니타는 정말 다 잊었어.

I'm still on the rebound. 아직 실연을 극복하지 못했어.

You don't love him! He's just a rebound guy.
넌 걜 사랑하지 않아. 걘 임시방편으로 만나는 애야.

005 Didn't seem really wild about you

널 그렇게 좋아하는 것 같지 않았어

this is a polite way to indicate that one person did not like another person. This might said when people meet for the first time and learn about each other's personalities. Another way to say this is "He seemed to dislike you"

| Point | be wild about~ …에 대해 무척 들뜨다, 막 흥분되다, 좋아하다
be not wild about~ …을 좋아하지 않다, …을 원치않다

A: Olivia only said a few words to me yesterday.
올리비아는 어제 내게 겨우 몇마디만 했어.

B: I'm afraid **she didn't seem really wild about you.** 걘 널 그렇게 좋아하는 것 같지 않았어.

My girlfriend is wild about chocolate.
내 여친은 초콜릿을 무척 좋아해.

The old man is wild about meeting pretty women. 노친네가 예쁜 여자들을 엄청 좋아해.

I know that you have never been wild about the fact that Teddy married me.
테디가 나하고 결혼했다는 사실에 탐탁치 않게 여겼다는 걸 알아.

006 We are still an item

우린 아직도 사귀어

this is a way to say "We are continuing to date." The speaker wants people to know he still has a relationship with a person

| Point | (복수주어)+be an item 연인사이다

A: Have you broken up with Matt? 맷하고 헤어졌어?

B: No way! **We are still an item.** 무슨! 아직도 사귀고 있어.

We are still an item. Everyone knows that.
우린 아직도 사귀어. 다들 알고 있어.

No, we haven't split up. We are still an item.
응, 우리 헤어지지 않았어. 우린 아직 사귀어.

We've been together for years. We are still an item. 우리는 오랫동안 함께 했어. 아직도 사귀는 사이야.

007 I have feelings for her

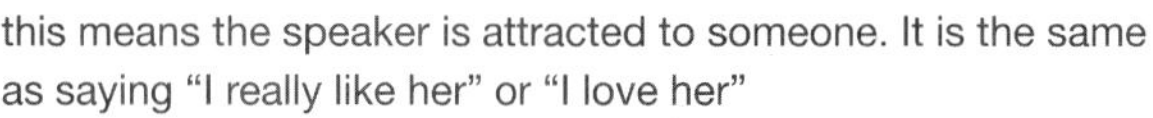

난 걔한테 감정이 있어

this means the speaker is attracted to someone. It is the same as saying "I really like her" or "I love her"

| Point | have a feeling (that) S+V …인 것 같아

A: You seem to like being with Bonita.
너 보니타하고 같이 있는 거 좋아하는 것 같더라.

B: You are right. **I have feelings for** her.
맞아. 걔한테 감정이 있어.

You have strong feelings for Julie, don't you?
너 줄리한테 맘이 많지, 안그래?

I've sort of had feelings for you.
너한테 조금이지만 감정이 생겼어.

To be honest, I still have feelings for you.
솔직히 말해서 난 아직 널 좋아해.

008 He has a thing for her

걘 그 여자를 맘에 두고 있어

this means that a man is very attracted to a woman. It means "He likes her a lot"

| Point | have[get] a thing for[about] …을 무척 좋아하다, …에게 맘이 끌리다
You have a thing for ~ …에게 관심있구나

A: Ted comes to see Mary every day.
테드는 매일 메리를 보기 위해 와.

B: I think **he has got a thing for** her.
걔를 맘에 두고 있는 것 같아.

Do you have a thing for little women?
조그만 여자들을 좋아해?

Did she have a thing for you? You kissed her, right? 걔가 너한테 맘두고 있대? 걔한테 키스했잖아, 맞지?

He used to have a thing for spiked heels.
걘 스파이크 힐을 좋아하곤 했어.

They all had a thing for Tim. 걔들 모두 팀을 좋아했어.

009 I've got a crush on you 난 너한테 반했어

the speaker is saying "I am attracted to you." Often this indicates the speaker wants to date the person he has a crush on

| Point | have[get] a crush on sb …에게 푹 빠지다

A: Why do you look so embarrassed?
왜 그렇게 어쩔 줄 몰라해?

B: **I've got a crush on you.** It makes me shy.
너한테 반했어. 그래서 수줍어.

I had a crush on you when I first met you!
내가 널 첨 봤을 때 너한테 반했어!

I have a crush on you. I am attracted to you.
너한테 푹 빠졌어. 너한테 맘을 빼앗겼어.

Did you hear that? Jerry had a crush on me!!
너 그거 들었어? 제리가 나한테 반했대!!

010 I'm drawn to her 걔한테 끌렸어

this is very similar to the previous phrase. It is a formal way to say "She attracts me"

| Point | be drawn to~ …에 끌리다
Are you drawn to her? 걔한테 끌려?
You're drawn to her! 너 걔한테 끌리는구나!

A: A lot of people seem to like Jennifer.
많은 사람들이 제니퍼를 좋아하는 것 같아.

B: Yeah, **I'm drawn to her** too. 그래, 나도 걔한테 끌렸어.

I was drawn to your honesty. 난 너의 정직함에 끌렸어.

I don't know what it is. I'm strangely drawn to him. 뭔지 모르겠지만, 이상하게 걔한테 끌렸어.

I know why you hired her. Was it because you're drawn to her?
네가 왜 걜 고용했는지 몰라. 걔한테 끌려서 그랬어?

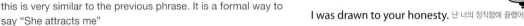

011 I'm crazy for[about] you 난 너한테 빠져있어

often this means "I really like to be around you." The speaker is saying he enjoys the time he spends with someone

| Point | be crazy for[about] = be nuts about = be mad about
= be stuck on …을 무척 좋아하다, 푹 빠지다
He's really stuck on me 걘 정말 나한테 빠졌어

A: Can you tell me how you feel? 네 감정을 말해줄테야?

B: **I'm crazy about you.** I want to spend more time together. 네게 빠졌어. 많은 시간을 같이 보내고 싶어.

I'm crazy about you. Don't you know that?
난 너한테 빠져 있어. 몰랐단 말야?

Look into my eyes. I'm crazy about you.
내 눈을 들여다 봐봐. 난 너한테 빠져 있어.

I'm crazy about you. That's why I got you this ring. 난 너한테 빠져 있어. 그래서 내가 이 반지를 네게 준거야.

012 She can't take her eyes off of Chris 걘 크리스에게 뽕갔어

this is saying that a woman is very interested in Chris. Many times, we can understand it to mean that the woman is romantically attracted, but sometimes it may mean that she is jealous, or that someone looks strange and is drawing her attention. Another way to say this would be "She keeps staring at Chris"

| Point | can't take one's eyes off (of)~ …에 뽕가다, …에게서 눈을 떼지 못하다

A: **She can't take her eyes off of** Chris.
걘 크리스에게 뽕갔어.

B: People say she's in love with him.
걔가 크리스를 사랑한다고들 그래.

They're never going to take their eyes off of me. 걔네들은 절대로 내게서 눈을 떼지 않을거야.

I can't take my eyes off it. You shouldn't, either. 난 그거에서 눈을 뗄 수가 없어. 너도 그럴거야.

He couldn't take his eyes off my boobs that he can never have, now that he's getting married.
걘 이제 결혼하였기 때문에 절대 가져볼 수 없는 내 가슴에서 눈을 떼지를 못했어.

013 I'm so into you 나, 너한테 푹 빠져 있어

usually this means "I like you very much and think about you a lot." It is indicating the speaker has strong feelings for someone

| Point | be into …에 빠지다, 심취하다

A: **I'm so into you** that I can't concentrate on other things. 너한테 너무 빠져서 아무 것도 집중이 안돼.

B: I really like you a lot too. 나도 역시 네가 정말 많이 좋아.

I'm so into you. I can't think of anyone else.
난 너한테 푹 빠져 있어. 다른 사람은 생각할 수 없어.

These days I feel like I'm so into you.
요즘 나 너한테 푹 빠져 있는 것 같아.

Don't you understand that Luke is so into you? 루크가 너한테 푹 빠져 있는걸 몰랐단 말야?

014 She got her hooks in me 난 그녀에게 확 꽂혔어

this is a way of expressing that someone was able to control or influence another person, often when doing things that are bad. It is a way to say "She was able to influence the way I behaved"

| Point | get[have] one's hooks in(to) sb
…을 사로잡다, 컨트롤하다, …에 확 꽂히다

A: Why did you agree to marry Tina? You guys are always arguing. 왜 티나와 결혼하기로 한거야? 너희들 늘상 다투잖아.

B: I know I shouldn't have, but **she got her hooks in me.** 안했어야 하는데 내가 그만 걔한테 확 꽂혔어.

You didn't want her getting her hooks into half your company.
넌 걔가 네 회사의 반을 통제하는 것을 원치 않았어.

We've got our hooks into her. 우리는 걔를 사로잡았어.

You know, she has wanted to get her hooks into Mike for years.
저기, 걘 오랫동안 마이크를 사로잡으려고 했어.

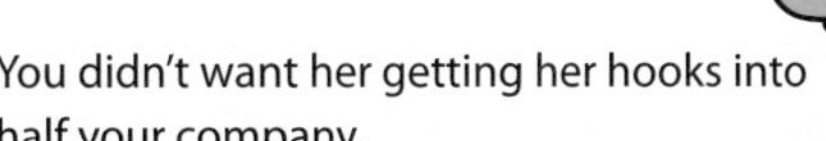

015 He was head over heels about her 걘 그녀에게 푹 빠져있었어

this is often said when a person is in love with another person. It is similar to saying "He is crazy about her" or "He really loves her"

| Point | be[fall] head over heels about sb …에게 홀딱 반하다
be[fall] head over heels in love with sb …에게 푹 빠지다
head over heels 거꾸로

A: Your friend was really in love with his girlfriend.
네 친구는 여친을 정말 사랑했어.

B: I know. **He was head over heels about her.**
알아. 걘 여친에게 완전히 빠져 있었어.

She seems to be head over heels about Chris.
그녀는 크리스에게 홀딱 반한 것 같아.

We're not head over heels in love. We like each other, right?
우리는 사랑에 빠진게 아니라 서로 좋아하는거지, 맞지?

He was head over heels in love with her.
걔는 그녀에게 홀딱 반했어.

How would you feel if your husband fell head over heels in love with a Russian whore?
남편이 러시아 창녀와 사랑에 푹 빠졌다면 네 기분이 어떻겠어?

016 They really hit it off 정말 잘 통하더라고, 걔네들은 바로 좋아하더라고

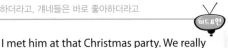

this is a way of saying "They liked each other after they were introduced." We can understand that both people might want to be friends or date

| Point | hit it off 만나자마자 죽이 잘 맞다, 통하다
I really hit it off 만나자마자 좋아해 친구가 됐어
We hit it off 우린 서로 잘 맞았어
It was love at first sight 첫눈에 반했어

A: Jan and Pam have been talking all night.
잰과 팸은 밤새 이야기했어.

B: It looks like **they really hit it off.**
정말 서로 죽이 잘 맞는 것 같아.

I met him at that Christmas party. We really hit it off. 난 걜 그 크리스마스 파티에서 만났고 우린 정말 잘 통했어.

Dick and I really hit it off, and we started making out, and then my boss walked in.
딕과 난 정말 바로 죽이 잘 맞아서 애무하기 시작했는데 사장님이 들어오시더라고.

Is it still possible to believe in love at first sight? 아직 첫눈에 반했다는 걸 믿을 수 있어?

017 You're that serious about this guy?

이 사람을 그렇게 진지하게 사귀는거야?

this is asking if a person has a serious romantic relationship with a man. In other words, we can understand that the couple may be getting ready to get married or move in together. A similar question to ask would be "Are you committing yourself to only be with this guy?"

| Point | get[be] serious about N[~ing] 진지한 감정이다, 진지하게 사귀다

A: John and I are talking about marriage.
존과 난 결혼에 대해 얘기하고 있어.

B: **You're that serious about this guy?**
존과 그렇게 진지하게 사귀는거야?

미드표현

Come on, you can't be serious about this.
그러지마, 너 이건 진심아니지.

There's no way Sam's ever gonna get serious about a woman like that, right?
샘이 여자에 대해 저렇게 진지할 리가 없어, 맞지?

Someday there'll be time to get serious about someone. 언젠가 누군가를 진지하게 사랑하는 때가 있을거야.

So you don't really think he's serious about leaving her?
그럼 넌 걔가 그녀와 헤어지는걸 진지하게 생각하지 않는다는거야?

018 He is Mr. Right 걘 내 이상형이야

this means "He's the man I want to marry." The speaker is saying she thinks a man is perfect for her

| Point | I'm looking for Mr. Right 이상형을 찾고 있어

A: Are you sure you want to marry Richard?
정말 리차드하고 결혼하고 싶어?

B: **He is Mr. Right.** I really love him.
걘 이상형이야. 정말 사랑해.

미드표현

If the guy was Mr. Right she would have told her folks. 걔가 이상형이었다면 자기 가족한테 말했을 텐데.

The next guy you see could turn out to be Mr. Right. 네가 보는 옆 사람이 너의 이상형이 될 수도 있어.

019 You're the one 난 너 뿐이야

this is usually a way for someone to indicate that his partner is the person he wants to be with. In other words, that is the person that he wants to marry and spend his life with. It's like saying "You are a very special person"

| Point | You're the one 난 너 뿐이야

A: Do you really want to marry me?
너 정말 나하고 결혼하고 싶어?

B: Oh yes, I'm sure **you're the one.** 그럼, 난 너 뿐인걸.

미드표현

You're the one. I've waited forever to find you.
넌 내 짝이야. 난 오랫동안 기다리며 너를 찾았어.

All my instincts tell me you're the one.
모든 내 본능이 네가 내게 맞는 짝이라고 말하고 있어.

You're the one. I'm sure of it. 넌 너 뿐이야. 난 확신해.

미드에선 이렇게 쓰인다!

You're the one

Sex and the City
SEASON#6-20

만났다 헤어졌다를 반복하던 Carrie와 Big이 드디어 결합하는 장면.

Carrie: How did you even get here?
Big: It took me a really long time to get here. But I'm here. Carrie you're the one.
Carrie: Kiss me you big crybaby. I miss New York. Take me home.

캐리: 여기는 어떻게 온게 된거야?
빅: 여기까지 오는데 정말 시간이 오래 걸렸지. 하지만 난 여기 있어. 캐리, 너밖에 없어.
캐리: 다 큰 울보쟁이야 키스해줘. 뉴욕이 그리워. 집에 데려다 줘.

020 Anne's a catch 앤은 꼭 붙잡고 싶은 여자야

to call someone a catch means that the person has many good qualities. It is similar to saying "She is a person I really want to date"

| Point | a (good) catch 매력적이거나 돈이 많아 데이트 및 결혼상대로 좋은 상대

A: **Anne's a catch.** She seems popular.
앤은 정말 꼭 잡고 싶은 여자야. 인기가 많아.

B: I know. All of the guys want her as a girlfriend.
알아. 많은 남자 애들이 걔하고 사귀고 싶어해.

I'm hot. I'm a catch. 난 섹시해. 난 완벽해.

Peter is a catch. And he's crazy about you. What is your problem?
피터는 완벽한 상대야. 그리고 걘 너한테 빠졌는데 뭐가 문제야?

021 He's really my type 그 사람 내 타입이네

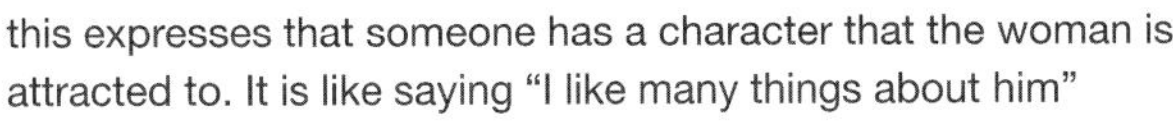

this expresses that someone has a character that the woman is attracted to. It is like saying "I like many things about him"

| Point | What type of woman do you like? 어떤 여자를 좋아해?
She's not my type 걘 내 취향이 아냐

A: How did you like going out with my brother?
내 형하고 데이트 어땠어?

B: **He's really my type.** I think we'll go out again.
정말 내 타입야. 다시 데이트할거야.

Donna and I dated once or twice. She wasn't my type. 도나하고 데이트 한 두번 해봤는데 내 타입이 아녔어.

Good-looking, just not my type.
잘 생겼지만 그냥 내 타입은 아냐.

Maybe not my type, but you're not terrible.
넌 내 타입은 아니지만 으악은 아냐.

I'm not sure she's my type. 걔가 내 타입인지 잘 모르겠어.

022 It was meant to be 운명이었어, 하늘이 정해준거야

this often suggests that something was destiny. It is expressing "This was destined to happen"

| Point | be meant to~ …는 피할 수 없는 운명이다, 운명적으로 …하다
(They're) Meant[Made] for each other 천생연분야(Mate for life)
They are meant to be together 천생연분이야
It's a match made in heaven 천생연분이야

A: Why have you decided to get married?
왜 결혼하기로 결정한거야?

B: I think **it was meant to be** for us. 천생연분인 것 같아서.

Honey we are so meant to be together.
자기야, 우리는 정말 천생연분야.

You two are so meant to be together, everybody thinks so.
너희 둘은 정말 천생연분야, 다들 그렇게 생각해.

He's probably out with Tom. Those two are meant for each other.
걘 아마 탐하고 데이트하나 봐. 걔네들 천생연분야.

023 He took my breath away 걔 때문에 숨 넘어가는 줄 알았어

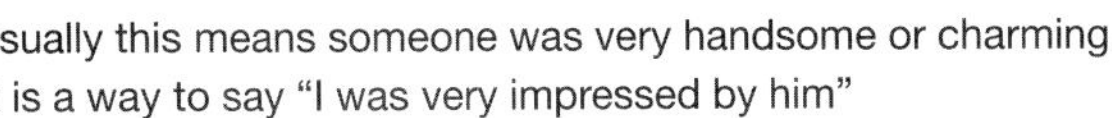

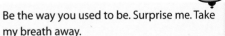

usually this means someone was very handsome or charming. It is a way to say "I was very impressed by him"

| Point | take sb's breath away …을 놀라게 하다, 넋을 빼앗다

A: I heard you met up with Brad Pitt.
브래드 피트를 만났다고 들었어?

B: Yeah, **he took my breath away.** 숨넘어가는 줄 알았어.

Be the way you used to be. Surprise me. Take my breath away.
예전에 그랬던 것처럼 해. 날 놀라게 해봐, 날 깜짝 놀라게 해보라고.

I was sitting across the room, and I saw you, and you took my breath away.
방 건너편에 앉아 있었고 널 봤지. 그리고 놀라서 숨이 막혔지.

When I first saw him, he took my breath away.
걔를 처음 봤을 때 숨넘어가는 줄 알았어.

024 There is a lot of chemistry between you and me 너하고 난 아주 잘 통해.

this means "We have a strong attraction to each other." The speaker is saying the two people like being together

| Point | have good chemistry 잘 통하다, 찰떡 궁합이다

A: Why do we make such a good pair?
우린 왜 이렇게 멋진 커플일까?

B: **There is a lot of chemistry between you and me.** 너하고 내가 아주 잘 통해서 그래.

미드표현

Do you feel there is a lot of chemistry between you and me? 너하고 나 아주 잘 통하는 것 같아?

There is a lot of chemistry between you and me, and that's why we like each other.
우린 서로 잘 통해, 그래서 우리는 서로 좋아하는거야.

Stay here a while. There is a lot of chemistry between you and me.
잠시 기다려봐. 우리 아주 서로 잘 통해.

025 What do you see in her? 그 여자 뭐가 좋아?, 어디가 좋은거야?

this is asking "Why are you attracted to her?" This phrase is usually used when the speaker doesn't like someone and doesn't understand the reason a person is dating her

| Point | What do you see in this guy? 이 사람 어디가 좋은거야?

A: My girlfriend is always yelling at me.
내 여친은 맨날 내게 소리쳐.

B: **What do you see in her?** I don't understand it.
걔 뭐가 좋은거야? 난 이해가 안돼.

미드표현

I don't get it. What do you see in this guy?
모르겠네. 저 자식 어디가 좋은거야?

That guy's like a stupid. What do you see in him anyway? 걔 정말 멍청하잖아. 어디가 좋은거야?

026 I need to hook up with a woman 여자가 있어야겠어

this is used to say "I need to date a woman" or "I need sex with a woman." The speaker would like to find a woman who wants to be with him

| Point | hook up with sb 만나서 친해지다, …와 (성적) 관계하다
hook[set, fix] sb up with~ …을 …에게 소개시켜주다

A: **I need to hook up with a woman.** 여자가 있어야겠어.

B: Be patient and find a girl who is nice.
진정하고 좋은 여자를 찾아봐.

미드표현

Who did you originally want to hook up with?
원래는 누구랑 할려고 했어?

I think I need to hook up with a woman right now. 여자하고 바로 좀 해야 할 것 같아.

I'm not asking you to set me up.
만남을 주선해달라는 얘기가 아니야.

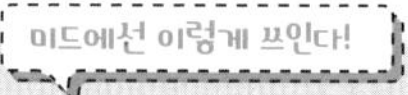

Who did you originally want to hook up with?

Friends
SEASON#7-16

런던에서의 하룻밤으로 서로 연인이 되었지만 실상 런던에서 Monica가 원래 hook up하려고 했던 사람은 Chandler가 아니라 Joey라고 실언하는 Phoebe.

Phoebe: Tell him who you originally wanted to hook up with that night.
Monica: What?!
Chandler: What?
Phoebe: (To Joey) What?!
Chandler: Who did you originally want to hook up with?
Monica: Okay, fine but please don't be upset! Okay? I was really depressed okay? And really drunk! I just wanted something stupid and meaningless. I just wanted just sex. So, when I went to your room that night, I was actually looking for Joey.

피비: 원래 그날 밤에 누구랑 섹스하려고 했는지 챈들러에게 말해.
모니카: 뭐라고?!
챈들러: 뭐라고?
피비: (조이를 보면서) 뭐라고?!
챈들러: 원래 누구와 섹스하려고 했던거야?
모니카: 좋아, 좋아 하지만 제발 화내지마! 알았어? 난 정말 우울했었어. 그리고 정말 취했구! 난 단지 의미없는 바보같은 일을 원했어. 난 단지 섹스를 원했어. 그래서, 내가 그날 저녁 네 방에 갔을 때, 난 실은 조이를 찾고 있었던거야.

027 Are you coming on to me? 지금 날 유혹하는거야?

the speaker is asking if a person is trying to start a relationship with him. It is like asking "Are you trying to become my girlfriend?"

| Point | come on to sb …에게 (성적으로) 끌리다, 유혹하다
come-on 유혹
Are you hitting on me? 지금 날 꼬시는 거냐?
pick-up line 보통 남자가 여자에게 작업 들어갈 때 하는 구절

A: Can I buy you a drink, lady? 술한잔 사드릴까요, 부인?
B: **Are you coming on to me?** 날 유혹하는 거예요?

미드표현

I started to get the feeling that your sister was coming on to me.
네 동생이 날 유혹한다는 생각이 들기 시작했어.

You've got a lot of nerve, coming on to me while my husband is next room.
남편이 옆방에 있는데 날 유혹하다니 너 참 뻔뻔하구나.

Can you stop hitting on me? I'm sitting with my boyfriend. 그만 좀 꼬셔라. 남친하고 앉아있잖아.

028 She made a play for Tom 걘 탐을 유혹하려고 했어

I believe this is a way of saying that a woman attempted to attract a man named Tom, so that he would enter into a romantic relationship with her. The woman is acting in a clever, slightly sneaky way. Another way to say this would be "She tried to interest Tom in romance"

| Point | make a play for sb 상대방과 데이트나 관계를 맺으려 하다
make a play for sth 직장이나 직위 등 중요한 것을 얻으려고 노력하다

A: Why was Angie getting so upset with her sister?
왜 앤지는 자기 언니한테 화나 있었던거야?
B: **Her sister made a play for** Angie's boyfriend.
언니가 앤지의 남친을 유혹하려고 했어.

미드표현

I can't believe she made a play for Jackson.
걔가 잭슨과 관계를 맺으려고 했다는게 놀라워.

What are we talking about? You want to make a play for Chris?
무슨 말 하는거야? 크리스와 맺어지기를 원한다고?

029 He made a move on me 걔 나한테 작업들어오던데, 그 사람 내게 추근대던데

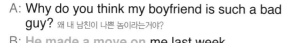

this indicates someone was trying to start a personal relationship. It is a way to say "He seemed to want to begin a relationship"

| Point | make a move on sb = make a pass at sb 추근대다, 찝적대다

A: Why do you think my boyfriend is such a bad guy? 왜 내 남친이 나쁜 놈이라는거야?
B: **He made a move on** me last week.
지난 주에 내게 추근댔어.

미드표현

Eric, he's not gonna make a move on you if he knows you're straight.
에릭, 네가 이성애자인걸 걔가 알면 너한테 찝적대지 않을거야.

Did you think I was making a move on you?
내가 너한테 추근대는 것 같았어?

Hope my new boyfriend doesn't try to make a pass at me. 내 새로운 남친이 내게 추근대지 않기를 바래.

Finn didn't make a pass at me.
핀은 내게 추근대지 않았어.

030 I'm just flirting 좀 추근거린 것 뿐이야, 작업 좀 들어간 것 뿐인데

often this means "I'm just talking with this person for fun." It indicates the speaker isn't trying to start a relationship with someone

| Point | flirt with sb …한테 작업들어가다, 농짓거리하다, 시시덕거리다

A: Do you really want to date Dan?
정말 너 댄과 데이트하고 싶어?
B: No, **I'm just flirting with** him. 아니, 그냥 시시덕거려보는거야.

미드표현

She's flirting with your boyfriend.
걔가 네 남친에게 작업걸고 있어.

James had been flirting with me all night.
제임스는 밤새 나한테 시시덕거렸어.

He probably thought I was flirting with him.
걘 아마도 내가 자기한테 추근거리는 줄 아나봐.

031 We're in a rut 우린 사는게 너무 지루해

this is a way of expressing that people, often a couple, have been doing the same things for a long time and it is getting boring for them. It expresses some frustration and the need for a change. It is similar to saying "We keep doing the same things and I'm getting tired of it"

| Point | be in a rut 틀에 박히다, 지루하다
be stuck in a rut 틀에 박혀있다

A: Are you and your wife having marriage troubles? 너희 부부 결혼상에 뭐 문제있어?

B: **We're in a rut,** and we always argue about the same stuff. 권태기야, 우린 늘상 같은 일로 다퉈.

Is Claire right? Are we in a rut?
클레어 말이 맞는거야? 우리가 권태기에 빠진거야?

I'm trying! We are in a rut!
노력하고 있다고! 우리는 무기력하게 살아가고 있어!

Oh, mama, you're in a rut. We need to spice up your wardrobe.
엄마, 무기력하게 사네. 엄마 옷에 좀 분위기를 띄워야겠어.

She has this idea that we're stuck in a rut.
걔는 우리 삶이 틀에 박혀있다는 생각을 하고 있어.

032 I'll just break it off with her 걔랑 헤어질거야

this indicates the speaker doesn't want to be with a woman. It is another way to say "I'm going to stop my relationship with her"

| Point | break it off 헤어지다, 관계를 끝내다

A: How are you going to stop your relationship with Terri? 테리와의 관계를 어떻게 끝낼거야?

B: **I'll just break it off with her** this week.
이번 주에 그냥 헤어질거야.

I gotta break it off with Sam. 샘과 관계를 끝내야겠어.

I went there to break it off. And then we started fighting. 걔랑 헤어지러 갔다가 싸우기 시작했어.

Well, if you want, I'll just break it off with her.
네가 원한다면 헤어질게.

033 I'm gonna break up with you 우리 그만 만나자, 너랑 헤어질래

this is saying "I'll stop dating you." The speaker wants to stop the relationship with the person he is talking to

| Point | break up with sb …와 헤어지다
We broke up 우리 헤어졌어
We're on a break 잠시 떨어져 있는거야

A: **I'm going to break up with you.** 너랑 헤어질거야.

B: Why? I thought things were good between us.
왜? 우리 사이 좋았던 것 같았는데.

We had a big fight, I had to break up with him. 우린 크게 싸웠고 난 걔와 헤어져야만 했어.

Why did you break up with me?
왜 나하고 헤어진거야?

You're breaking up with me. In my own bedroom. 나랑 헤어지자는 거구만, 내 침실에서말야.

We're on a break. I don't know if we'll get back together. 잠시 냉각중인데 다시 사귈지 모르겠어.

034 I'm trying to play hard to get 튕기고 있는 중야, 일부러 빼고 있어

this is usually done by a woman who wants to date a man, but pretends she isn't interested. It is like saying "I acted like I didn't want to go out with him"

| Point | play hard to get 빼다, 튕기다, 싫은 척하다

A: Has Scott asked you to have dinner with him?
스캇이 너랑 식사하자고 그랬어?

B: Yes, but **I'm still playing hard to get.**
어, 하지만 아직 튕기고 있는 중야.

Don't play hard to get with him. 걔한테 빼지 마.

This playing hard to get thing is not working.
이렇게 튕기는 게 잘 먹히지 않아.

I'm trying a new strategy. I'm playing hard to get. 새 전략을 쓸거야. 싫은 척 튕길거야.

035 You don't want to get involved with me
넌 나와 엮이지 않는게 좋아

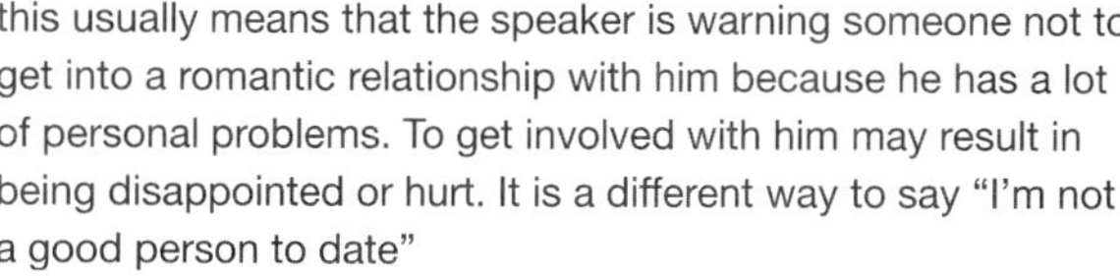

this usually means that the speaker is warning someone not to get into a romantic relationship with him because he has a lot of personal problems. To get involved with him may result in being disappointed or hurt. It is a different way to say "I'm not a good person to date"

| Point | get involved with 끼어들다, 엮이다, 사귀다(with sb)

A: Honestly, I feel very attracted to you.
솔직히 말해서, 나 너한테 무척 끌려.

B: **You don't want to get involved with me.** I'm unreliable. 나와 사귀지 않는게 좋아. 믿을 수 없는 놈이야.

I told you not to get involved with drugs!
내가 마약을 하지 말라고 했잖아!

I think I may be about to get involved with a married man. 유부남과 엮이게 될 지도 모를 것 같아.

It is my job to make sure that you girls don't get involved with a predator.
너희들이 강간범들과 사귀지 않도록 하는게 내 일이야.

036 He's having a lover's spat with Julie
걘 줄리랑 사랑싸움을 하고 있어

this is a relatively simple way of saying that a man and his girlfriend have had an argument and are still angry with one another. Often we can assume the couple will soon make up and be happy together again. A different way to say this would be "He's been fighting with Julie, his girlfriend"

| Point | have a lover's spat with sb …와 사랑싸움하다 *spat 옥신각신, 입씨름

A: Brad looked depressed when I saw him.
내가 브래드를 봤을 때 우울한 모습이었어.

B: **He's having a lover's spat with Julie.**
걔 지금 줄리랑 다투었어.

I think our lover's spat will start a little early this month. 우리의 사랑싸움은 이번달 초에 좀 일찍 시작될거야.

I was just putting out the trash and heard you two having a little spat.
난 쓰레기를 버리다 너희 둘이 입씨름하는 걸 들었어.

Ken, I just had a spat with Penny, and I'm not in the mood. 켄, 나 페니와 방금 싸웠어. 기분이 그래.

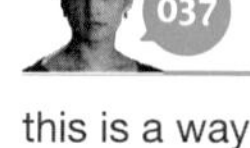

037 We went our separate ways 우리는 갈라섰어

this is a way to say two people had a relationship, but they ended the relationship and no longer are close to one another. Often this expression is used when a boyfriend and girlfriend or husband and wife break up. It is very similar to saying "We are no longer together"

| Point | go one's separate ways 갈라서다, 헤어지다

A: Are you and Tony still seeing each other?
너 토니와 아직도 만나니?

B: No, we fought and then **went our separate ways.** 아니, 싸운 다음에 서로 갈라섰어.

You're just gonna let fate decide whether we go our separate ways?
넌 우리가 갈라설지 여부를 운명에 맡겨둘거야?

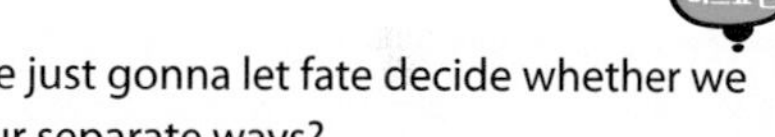

I think the time has come for us to go our separate ways. 우리가 서로 갈라설 때가 왔다고 생각해.

We shared a uterus for nine months, but since then we've pretty much gone our own separate ways.
우리는 9개월간 자궁을 공유했지만 그 이후로는 서로 사뭇 다른 각자의 길을 갔어.

038 We're taking some time apart 우리는 당분간 떨어져 지내고 있어

this expresses that a couple has decided to separate from each other. They may decide not to get back together, or they may decide that they want to be a couple again in the future, but it is uncertain at the moment. It is like saying "We decided that we should break up for a while"

| Point | take[spend] some time apart 당분간 떨어져 지내다

A: Why did you break up with your boyfriend?
너 왜 남친과 헤어진거야?

B: **We're taking some time apart.** 당분간 떨어져 지내고 있어.

We've talked about taking some time apart.
당분간 떨어져 지내는 것에 관해 얘기를 했어.

He's not here. We're taking some time apart. We're separated, not legally.
그는 여기 없어요. 우린 당분간 떨어져 지내요. 별거했는데 법적으로는 아니구요.

039 I dumped him 내가 갤 찼어

the speaker is saying "I ended my relationship with him." She means that she decided to stop it

I Point I dump sb …을 버리다, 차다(ditch)
I'm through with you 너랑은 끝났어
We are history 우린 끝났어, 헤어졌어
He stood me up last night 요전날 걔가 날 바람맞혔어

A: Tom has been looking really sad. 탐은 정말 안돼 보여.
B: That's because **I dumped him** last week.
지난 주에 내가 걜 차서 그래.

She dumped me. 그 여자가 날 찼어.

I got dumped during sex. 섹스 도중에 차였어.

Did you dump a guy because of a bad kiss?
키스 못한다고 찼어?

Forget it. I'm through with you now.
신경쓰지마. 이제 너랑 끝났으니.

040 I split up with my girlfriend 나 여자친구랑 헤어졌어

this is usually said when two people end a relationship. It expresses "We aren't dating anymore"

I Point I split up with sb (…와 관계, 결혼 등을) 끝내다, 갈라서다

A: **I split up with** my girlfriend this year.
금년에 여친하고 헤어졌어.
B: So you mean now you're not seeing anyone?
그럼 지금 사귀는 사람이 없다는 말야?

Did you know that she had recently split up with her husband?
걔가 남편이랑 최근에 헤어진 것 알고 있었어?

I haven't had sex since I split up with my wife.
난 아내와 헤어진 후에 섹스를 못해봤어.

After she split up with her husband, Sam moved to New York.
샘은 남편과 헤어진 후 뉴욕으로 이사왔어.

041 I'm over you (감정적으로) 널 완전히 정리했어, 널 다 잊었어, 너랑 끝이야

this is a way of saying "I don't have romantic feelings for you now." The speaker is expressing he loved someone before but he doesn't love the person now

I Point I It's over between us 우린 끝났어
You're over me? 나하고 끝내자고?

A: **I am over you.** I don't want to see you again.
너랑 끝이야. 다신 널 보고 싶지 않아.
B: Please meet with me one last time.
제발 마지막으로 한번만 만나줘.

I'm over you. Move on with your life.
너랑 끝이야. 이제 네 인생 살아가.

I don't want to see you again. I'm over you.
다시는 널 보고 싶지 않아. 널 다 잊었어.

I'm over you. I have a new boyfriend now.
널 다 잊었어. 지금은 새로운 남친이 있어.

042 He is not boyfriend material 그 사람은 애인감이 아냐

usually this is expressing "He wouldn't be a good boyfriend." This means the man has some problem and would not be nice to date

I Point I be not marriage material 결혼상대는 아니다

A: What do you think about Jack? 잭을 어떻게 생각해?
B: **He is not boyfriend material.** 걘 애인감이 아냐.

You still don't think I'm girlfriend material?
넌 아직도 내가 애인감이 아니라고 생각해?

Tell her she's not marriage material.
걘 결혼상대가 아니라고 걔한테 말해줘.

It's possible that I'm not boyfriend material.
내가 남친감이 아닐 수도 있어.

I don't think Chris is boyfriend material.
내 생각에 크리스는 애인감은 아닌 것 같아.

043 Will you marry me? 나랑 결혼할래?

this is asking if a person will become the speaker's husband or wife. It is a way to say "Please spend your life with me"

| Point | pop the question 청혼하다

A: Will you marry me? 나랑 결혼해줄래?
B: I can't answer that question right now.
지금 당장은 대답못해.

Michael, will you marry me? 마이클, 나랑 결혼할래?

I love you. Will you marry me? 사랑해. 나랑 결혼할래?

Bill is about to pop the question to his girlfriend. 빌이 여친에게 청혼할거야.

Actually, I'm gonna pop the question to her tomorrow night. 실은 내일밤 걔한테 청혼할거야.

044 You and Mike are getting hitched? 너하고 마이크가 결혼해?

미드표현

to get hitched means "get married" We can understand that anyone who gets hitched will be a husband and wife

| Point | get hitched = get married 결혼하다

A: You and Mike are getting hitched?
너하고 마이크가 결혼하는거야?
B: That's right. We've planned our wedding for December. 맞아. 12월에 결혼할 계획이야.

People come to Vegas to get rich or to get hitched. 사람들은 돈을 벌거나 결혼하려고 베거스에 오죠.

Tomorrow, we'll go down to city hall and get hitched. 내일 우리는 시청에 가서 결혼할거야.

Tons of guys get chicks knocked up and don't get hitched.
많은 남자들이 여자들을 임신시켜놓고 결혼을 하지 않아.

You and Mike are getting hitched? Why didn't you tell me? 너와 마이크 결혼해? 왜 말하지 않았어?

045 She's having a baby 걘 임신 중이야

미드표현

often this is a way to say someone is pregnant. It is like saying "She'll give birth soon"

| Point | have a baby 임신 중이다
She had a baby 걔가 애를 낳았어
I'm in labor 진통이 있어

A: Why did Margo go to the hospital?
마고가 왜 병원에 간거야?
B: She's having a baby in about 5 months.
임신 5개월 정도 됐어.

Having a baby is the hardest job in the whole world. 애 낳는 게 이 세상 통틀어 젤 어려운 일이야.

We're having a baby in November.
애기가 11월에 태어나.

Mona is in labor, and she is breathing heavily.
모나는 진통 중이고 숨을 크게 몰아쉬고 있어.

046 I heard Mary is expecting 메리가 임신했대

미드표현

this speaker is indicating that he thinks "Mary is pregnant." He feels she will be a mother soon

| Point | Are you expecting (a child)? 임신했어?
When is the baby due? 예정일이 언제야?
Do you know what it is yet? 아들야 딸야?
It's a baby boy 아들 낳았어

A: I heard Susie is expecting. 수지가 임신했대.
B: Yeah, she and her husband are really happy.
어, 걔네 부부는 정말 행복해.

I heard Mary is expecting. Is that true?
메리가 임신했다며. 정말이야?

I heard Mary is expecting. She's not even married. 메리가 임신했다며. 결혼도 안했는데.

Rumors are going around. I heard Mary is expecting. 소문이 돌고 있어. 메리가 임신했대.

047 You got her pregnant 너 걜 임신시켰어

the speaker wants to say "You had sex and now she will have a baby." Usually this is said in a negative way, when a man and woman aren't married

| Point | get sb pregnant = knock sb up 임신시키다

A: My girlfriend is going to have a baby.
내 여친이 출산할거야.

B: Really? **You got her pregnant?** 정말? 걜 임신시켰어?

I got her pregnant. I admit it. 걜 임신시켰어. 인정할게.

You knocked her up, but you're not going to marry her. 걜 임신시켜놓고 결혼은 안 할거라고.

One of the victims took her own life when she realized the rapist got her pregnant.
피해자 중 한 명은 강간범의 자식을 임신했다는 걸 안 순간 자살했어.

048 You can't move in with me 나랑 같이 못살아

this is a way to tell someone that the speaker doesn't want to live with him. It is very similar to saying "You can't come to my house to live with me"

| Point | move in (with) (…와) 동거하다

A: I would like us to live together. 우리 동거했으면 해.

B: **You can't move in yet with me.** Don't push me on that. 아직 동거 못해. 몰아붙이지 마.

He suggested Julie move in with me.
걘 줄리가 나랑 함께 사는 게 어떠냐고 했어.

We're really going to move in together!
우린 정말 함께 동거할거야!

If I lose my job, I have to move in with my parents! 직장을 잃으면 부모님과 살아야 한다구!

049 I got to have you 너랑 해야겠어

this is not a commonly used phrase. The speaker is telling someone that he wants to have sex with her very much. This is almost always considered rude, although it might be okay if both people are strongly attracted to each other. Another way of expressing the same thing is "I need you to make love with you"

| Point | have sb 함께 하다, (성적으로) 갖다, 취하다

A: **I've got to have you** baby. 자기야 나 너랑 해야겠어.

B: Hold on, this is only our first date.
잠깐, 이제 겨우 우리 첫 데이트인데.

That's all right, baby. I got to have you.
괜찮아, 자기야. 지금 정말 하고 싶어.

What a pleasure it is to have you.
네가 와서 얼마나 기쁜지 몰라.

And those kids are lucky to have you.
저 아이들은 네가 있어 운이 좋아.

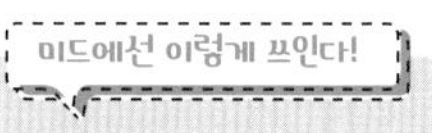

I got to have you

Desperate Housewives
SEASON#1-1

출장을 갔다 와 오래간만에 아내 Lynette를 본 씨내리 Tom이 서둘러 아이들을 밖으로 보내고 아내와 콘돔없이 회포를 풀려다 주먹으로 빰을 얻어맞는 장면.

Lynette:	Oh, you got to be kidding. I'm exhausted. It looks terrible. I'm covered in peaches.	르넷: 오, 진심이야, 난 지쳤다고, 꼴도 말이 아니고 복숭아로 범벅이 되어 있는데.
Tom:	That's all right, baby. I got to have you.	탐: 괜찮아, 자기야, 너랑 해야겠어.
Lynette:	Well, is it okay if I just lie here?	르넷: 그럼 나 여기 그냥 누워있어도 돼?
Tom:	Absolutely.	탐: 물론이고 말고.
Lynette:	I love you.	르넷: 사랑해.
Tom:	And I love you more.	탐: 난 더 사랑해.
Lynette:	Oh, wait, I got to tell you, I was having trouble with swelling, so the doctor took me off the pill, so you're just going to have to put on a condom.	르넷: 잠깐, 말해두는데, 몸이 붓는 증상이 있어서 의사가 피임약을 먹지 말래니까 네가 콘돔을 껴야 될거야.
Tom:	Condom? What's the big deal? Let's risk it.	탐: 콘돔이라고? 뭐 대수라고? 강 하자.
Lynette:	Let's risk it?	르넷: 강 하자고?

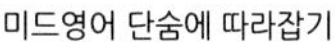

050 He got lucky with Julie 걔, 줄리랑 잤대

usually this indicates "He and Julie had sex for the first time." Most times this is said to indicate the two people don't have a serious relationship

| Point | get lucky with sb …와 섹스하다(= get laid)

A: Joe looks really happy. He has been smiling and chuckling all day. 조는 정말 행복해보여. 종일 싱글벙글야.

B: **He got lucky with Julie** last night. 어제 밤에 줄리랑 했대.

Did you get lucky with your date last night?
지난 밤 데이트한 여자와 성공했어?

You could go get lucky with a hot girl if you want. 원한다면 가서 섹시한 여자와 하라고.

051 He made love to me 그 사람과 난 사랑을 나눴어

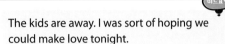

this is usually said to mean the man and woman had a very good sexual encounter. Often it also means the two people are in love and have a good relationship

| Point | make love (to) (…와) 섹스하다, 사랑을 나누다

A: What did you do when you went home with Mark? 마크와 집에 가서 뭐했어?

B: It was romantic. **He made love to me** there.
낭만적이었어. 거기서 사랑을 나눴어.

The kids are away. I was sort of hoping we could make love tonight.
애들도 없으니 우리가 오늘밤 사랑을 나눌 수 있을까 좀 바랬지

You still want to make love to her?
넌 아직도 개랑 하고 싶어?

I just want you to kiss me and make love to me right here, right now.
난 네가 지금 여기서 바로 내게 키스해주고 사랑해주길 바래.

052 I wanna make out with my girlfriend
애인하고 애무하고 싶어

this is a way to indicate the speaker wants to start a physical relationship with his girlfriend. It means "I want to spend time kissing and touching my girlfriend"

| Point | make out (with) (…와) 키스 등 애무하다
fondle 애무하다

A: **I want to make out with my girlfriend.**
여친과 애무하고 싶어.

B: You should just try to be nice to her instead.
대신 걔한테 착하게 대하도록 해.

When he made out with my sister I was so angry at him. 걔가 내 누이랑 애무했을 때 난 엄청 열받았어.

I once made out with a stranger in an elevator. 한번은 엘리베이터에서 모르는 사람과 애무한 적 있어.

053 We're way past second base 우리 진한 애무단계는 훨씬 지났어

this is a way to say that some sexual activity occurred between a man and woman. It is not clear if it means the man felt the woman's breasts or if it was more serious and they had sexual intercourse, but we can understand that it was more than just kissing. In other words, "We did some sexual things together"

| Point | second base 진한 애무 단계
go to second base with sb …와 진한 애무를 하다

A: I heard you and Mindy were kissing last night.
너 민디하고 어젯밤에 키스했다며.

B: It was more than that. **We're way beyond second base.** 그 이상이었어. 우리는 진한 애무단계를 훨씬 넘었어.

He's been stuck on second base forever.
걔는 애무단계에서 벗어나지 못하고 있어.

To be honest, I was hoping at least second base. 솔직히 말해서 진한 애무까지는 희망했었어.

Jill won't let me get past second base, and I really want to explore further.
질은 진한 애무는 못하게 해, 난 정말 더 진도나가고 싶은데.

We got to third base once and that was an accident! 우리는 한번 거의 잘뻔했는데 그건 사고였어!

054 You have no chance of scoring with her

걔랑 섹스할 가능성은 전혀 없어

the speaker is saying "She'll never have sex with you." He means the woman is not attracted to some man

| Point | score 득점하다, 획득하다, 섹스하다

A: I think I'm in love with Angela. 안젤라를 사랑하는 것 같아.

B: Forget it. **You have no chance of scoring with her.** 잊어버려. 걔랑 섹스할 가능성은 전혀 없어.

Let me tell you about this chick I scored with last night! 지난밤에 한 건 올린 여자애 얘기해줄게!

I'm gonna let you even the score, Bob. Go have an affair. 원상태로 돌려놓도록 할게. 밥, 가서 바람펴.

When a stud scores, he announces his victory by putting his spoils on his neighbor's doorknob.
남자가 여자를 취하게 되면 전리품을 이웃집 손잡이에 걸어놓고서 승리를 알리지.

055 You turn me on

넌 내 맘에 쏙 들어, 넌 날 흥분시켜

often this is said when a person wants to tell another person "I'm very attracted to you." It can be considered rude if the other person doesn't like the speaker

| Point | turn sb on ...을 흥분시키다, ...의 몸을 달아오르게 하다 (↔ turn sb off)
You're getting me hard 꼴리게 하네

A: **You really turn me on.** 널 보면 흥분이 돼.

B: Get away from me. I don't like you.
꺼져. 난 널 좋아하지 않아.

Those pictures turn you on? 그런 사진들 보면 꼴려?

Little girls turn you on, big man?
다 큰 양반아, 어린 여자아이들에 흥분돼?

Are you trying to hurt me or turn me on?
날 아프게 하려는거야 흥분시키려는거야?

Your knowledge of these superhero movies is kind of turning me on right now.
이런 수퍼히어로 영화에 대한 너의 지식이 지금 날 좀 꼴리게 해.

056 I wanna get laid

섹스하고파

this is a rude way to say the speaker would like to have sex. It is like saying "I want sex very soon"

| Point | get laid 섹스하다
lay 성적인 대상

A: **I want to get laid** tonight. 오늘 밤 섹스하고 싶어.

B: I don't think that will be possible. 가능할 것 같지 않은데.

You called me to ask me how to get laid?
어떻게 섹스하는 건지 물어보려고 나한테 전화한 거니?

I was trying to get laid. 섹스할려고 그랬어.

Who cares? I wanna get laid.
무슨 상관이야? 그냥 섹스하고파.

057 We ended up cuddling

포옹까지는 했어, 부둥켜 안게 되었어

this means the couple didn't have sex. It is a way to say "We held each other for a long time"

| Point | cuddle 껴안다

A: How was your date with Harriet?
해리엣과의 데이트는 어땠어?

B: **We ended up cuddling** on her sofa.
소파에서 포옹하게 되었어.

She climbed into the bed next to him. They cuddled. 걘 침대로 올라가 그 옆에 눕고 부둥켜안았다.

You are kind, sweet, and want to cuddle a lot.
넌 참 친절하고 자상해. 안는 것을 좋아해.

You wanna get in bed and cuddle for a little while? 침대에 들어가서 잠깐 부둥켜 안을테야?

058 She's really good in bed 걘 정말 밤일 잘해

this is indicating "She is talented at sex." It is unusual to say this, and kind of rude to the woman.

| Point | be good in bed 침대에서 잘하다, 섹스를 잘하다
be good in the sack 섹스를 잘하다

A: How is your sex life with your wife?
아내와 성생활은 어때?

B: **She's really good in bed.** 밤일 정말 잘해.

미드표현

To be completely honest, he's not that good in bed. 정말 정직하게 말해서, 걘 밤일 그렇게 잘 못해.

Men who are too good-looking are never good in bed. 잘 생긴 남자들은 절대로 밤일을 잘 못해.

Let's talk about Charles. Is he good in bed?
찰스에 대해 얘기해 보자고, 걔 밤일 잘해?

059 It was just a one night thing 하룻밤 잔 것뿐이야

this expresses that the speaker had sex once but doesn't plan to start a relationship. It means "We only had sex one time"

| Point | one night thing[stand] = one night together = one night
(사랑없이 그냥) 하룻밤 불장난, 또는 그 상대
quickie 가볍게 빨리 해치우는 섹스

A: Are you going to date Olivia now?
이제 올리비아하고 데이트 할거야?

B: No way. **It was just a one night thing.**
아니. 그냥 하룻밤 잔 것뿐이야.

미드표현

I got her pregnant. But it was just a one night thing, it meant nothing.
걜 임신시켰지만 하룻밤 그 이상의 의민없어.

Mike wasn't a one night stand. I was in love with him. 마이크는 하룻밤 자는 상대가 아니었어. 난 걜 사랑했어.

How about a quickie before I go to work?
출근하기 전에 한번 어때?

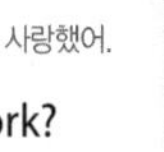

060 They're doing it 쟤네들 그거 해

this is indicating a couple has a sexual relationship. It expresses "They are having sex together"

| Point | do it = have sex

A: Where are Amy and Sid? 에이미하고 시드는 어디있어?

B: **They're doing it** in the other room.
다른 방에서 그거 하고 있어.

미드표현

They're doing it. They are obviously having sex. 쟤네들 그거 한다. 분명히 섹스를 하는데.

They're doing it. Kris isn't a virgin anymore.
쟤네들 그거 해. 크리스는 이제 처녀가 아니네.

You think they are innocent? No, they're doing it. 쟤네들이 순진하다고? 아냐, 쟤네들 섹스하잖아.

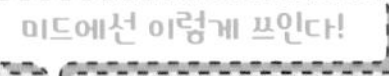

We saw them doing it up against the window

Friends SEASON#5-14

Phoebe와 Rachel이 Joey에게 Chandler와 Monica가 섹스하는 것을 창가를 통해 봤다고 할 때의 장면.

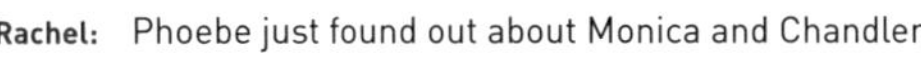

Rachel: Phoebe just found out about Monica and Chandler.
Joey: You mean how they're friends and nothing more?
Rachel: No. Joey, she knows! We were at Ugly Naked Guy's apartment and we saw them doing it through the window. Actually, we saw them doing it up against the window.
Phoebe: You know, we saw them fornicating. Okay, so now they know that you know and they don't know that Rachel knows?
Joey: Yes, but y'know what? It doesn't matter who knows what.

레이첼: 피비가 모니카와 챈들러에 관해서 알아챘어.
조이: 걔네들이 친구 이상은 아니라는 걸 말이지?
레이첼: 아니, 조이, 피비도 안다고! 벌거숭이 집에 있었는데 창문을 통해서 걔네들이 하는 것을 봤어. 실은 걔네들이 창가에 밀어붙이면서 하고 있는 걸 봤어.
피비: 저기, 우린 걔네들이 내통하는 것을 봤어. 좋아, 그럼 이제 걔네들이 네가 알고 있는 것을 알고 있지만 레이첼이 알고 있는 것을 모르고 있지?
조이: 어, 하지만 저 말이야, 누가 무엇을 아는게 무슨 상관이겠어.

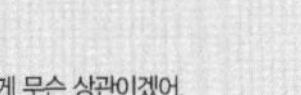

061 Get a room 방 잡아라

this is said when 2 people are acting in a sexual way in public. People think this is bad, and they would use this phrase meaning "Go to a hotel room if you want to do that"

Point go all the way (남녀가) 갈 데까지 가다
How far did you go? 너희들 진도가 어디까지 나갔어?

A: You two should **get a room.** 너희 둘 방 잡아야겠다.
B: I can kiss my girlfriend here if I want to.
내가 원하면 여기서 여친에게 키스할 수 있는거지.

Stop making out here. Get a room.
여기서 깔짝대지 말고 방잡아.

You two look horny. Get a room.
너희 둘 하고 싶어하는 것 같은데 방잡아라.

Get a room. Don't do that in public.
방잡아. 사람보는데서 그러지 말고.

062 Let's get it on 우리 하자

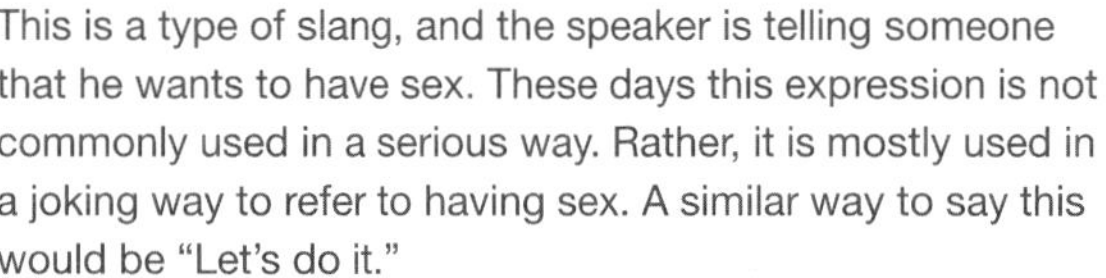

This is a type of slang, and the speaker is telling someone that he wants to have sex. These days this expression is not commonly used in a serious way. Rather, it is mostly used in a joking way to refer to having sex. A similar way to say this would be "Let's do it."

Point get it on 섹스하다(have sex)

A: I've got the condoms. **Let's get it on!**
난 콘돔이 있어. 우리 하자!
B: Slow down. Don't you know anything about romance? 서두르지마. 로맨스의 '로'자도 모르는거야?

Are you ready? Let's get it on!! 준비됐어? 자 하자!!

She just wanted to get it on in front of a fireplace. 걘 단지 난로 앞에서 하길 원했어.

When you spent the night, did we get it on?
네가 밤을 지샜을 때 우리 섹스했어?

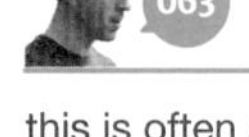

063 Did things get physical? 섹스하는 상황이 된거야?

this is often a subtle way to ask if someone got involved with another person sexually. It can also be a way of asking if a person started to act in a violent way. Similarly, we could ask "Was there sexual contact?"or "Was there any violence?"

Point get physical 물리적 힘을 쓰다, 육체적 관계를 맺다(have sexual relations)

A: I had a terrible date with Brandon.
브랜드과의 데이트는 끔찍했어.
B: He's a loser. Did things **get physical?**
걘 머저리야. 육체적인 관계도 한거야?

So what happened, Jerry? Andy catch you stealing? Things get physical?
그래 무슨 일이야, 제리? 앤디가 네가 절도하는 걸 잡았다고? 쌈질한거야?

It's the second date, you think she'll be expecting things to get physical?
두번째 데이트인데, 걔가 섹스하는 상황을 기대할거라 생각해?

064 I don't make it with guys at concerts
난 콘서트장에서 섹스하지 않아

this is a slangy way to say that the speaker doesn't get sexually involved with men that she meets at concerts. It is not a commonly used phrase. We can express something similar by saying "I don't have sex with people at concerts"

Point make it with sb …와 섹스하다 get off with 섹스하다
be[get] in bed with 잠자리를 같이하다
spend the night with~ …와 함께 밤을 보내다

A: **I don't make it with guys** at concerts.
난 콘서트장에서 섹스하지 않아.
B: Good. So you didn't have sex last night?
좋아. 그럼 너 어젯밤에 섹스하지 않은거지?

I'm your husband. You should make it with me. 네가 네 남편인데 나하고 섹스를 해야지.

Waking up in a stranger's bed every morning, cruising the park at night looking for somebody to get off with, compulsive masturbation every chance you get!
매일 아침 낯선 사람의 침대에서 일어나기, 섹스할 대상을 찾아 밤에 공원을 돌아다니고, 그리고 기회가 있을 때마다 상습적으로 자위를 하고!

065 We're friends with benefits 우리 가끔 섹스하는 친구사이야

this indicates that the speaker has a relationship with someone that is a friendship, but also at times can include sexual contact. The sexual contact is jokingly referred to as a benefit. In other words "We are friends, and sometimes we also sleep together"

Point friends with benefits 섹스도 하는 친구[상대], 섹스친구

A: How would you describe your relationship with Ryan? 라이언과의 관계를 뭐라고 표현할 수 있겠어?

B: It's complex. **We're friends with benefits.**
복잡해. 우린 가끔 섹스도 하는 친구사이야.

미드표현

We've kissed a couple times. It's like friends with benefits without the benefits.
우린 두어차례 키스를 했어. 섹스를 하지 않는 섹스친구같아.

You do it with no strings attached. Friends with benefits. 아무런 조건 없이 해야지. 섹스친구잖아.

We have sex. But I just wanted to do something to say we're more than friends with benefits.
우린 섹스를 해. 하지만 난 우리가 섹스친구 이상이라는 것을 말하기 위해 뭔가 하고 싶었어.

066 This is not a booty call 섹스하자고 전화한거 아냐

this speaker is saying that he has not made contact with someone in order to initiate sex. A booty call is a call or visit specifically to try to find a sex partner right away. This is like saying "I didn't call you because I wanted sex"

Point a booty call 그냥 섹스하자는 전화

A: Are you calling me up for sex? 섹스하자고 전화한거야?

B: No, **this is not a booty call.** 아니, 섹스하자고 전화한게 아냐.

미드표현

You've reached friends with benefits. For a booty call, press one now.
섹스친구입니다. 섹스하자고 하려면 넘버 1을 누르세요.

She's totally running to a booty call with your brother. 걘 네 오빠와의 섹스하자는 전화에 후다닥 달려갔어.

Is this a relationship? A one-night stand? The beginning of a series of late-night booty calls? I think I have the right to know.
우리 사귀는거야? 아님 하룻밤 사랑? 늦은 밤 섹스하자는 전화의 시작야? 난 알아야 될 권리가 있다고 생각해.

067 He had his way with me 걔는 나와 성관계를 맺었어

this is a formal way to say that a man had sex with the person who is speaking. Sometimes it indicates that it was consensual, and sometimes it indicates that a rape occurred. This phrasing is not commonly used because it is so formal. It would be more common to say "He had sex with me"

Point have one's way with sb 작업걸다, (싫어하는 상대와) 성적관계를 맺다

A: So you had sex with your boss? 그럼 너 사장하고 섹스했어?

B: I admit it. **He had his way with me.**
그래. 사장은 나와 성관계를 맺었어.

미드표현

I thought you just wanted me drunk so you could have your way with me.
난 네가 내가 취하길 바란다고 생각했어. 그래야 넌 나와 성적인 관계를 맺을 수 있으니까 말야.

Not wanting to go to prison where bigger men will have their way with me.
덩치가 더 큰 남자들이 나를 성적으로 범할 감옥에는 가고 싶지 않아.

I swear to God, if your sister ever comes to town, I shall have my way with her.
정말이지, 네 누이가 시내에 오기만 하면 난 걔와 성적인 관계를 맺을거야.

068 I don't throw myself at her 난 걔한테 들이대지 않았어

this speaker is saying that he does not make a strong effort to get romantically involved with a woman. We can understand that he may only be a little interested in entering a relationship with her. In other words, "I don't try very hard to become her boyfriend"

Point throw[fling] oneself at sb
찝적대다, 육탄공세를 펼치다, 추파를 던지다, 들이대다

A: How could you sleep with my sister?
너 어떻게 내 누이와 잠을 잘 수 있는거야?

B: It's not my fault. **I didn't throw myself at her.**
내 잘못아냐. 내가 들이댄게 아냐.

미드표현

I'm sorry to throw myself at you like this.
이렇게 추파를 던져서 미안해.

I just wanted to thank you for encouraging me to throw myself at Chris.
나보고 크리스에게 육탄공세를 펼쳐보라고 북돋아줘서 고맙다고 하고 싶었어.

I throw myself at you and you say no, how gay are you?
내가 추파를 던지는데 넌 거절하네, 도대체 넌 얼마나 게이인거야?

069 I want to have a fling 번개 좀 해야겠어

the speaker is saying he wants to have a short romantic relationship. It means "I want to have a relationship that is not serious"

I Point I have a fling 사랑없이 몇번 만나 섹스하다

A: Why are you going alone to Hawaii?
하와이에는 왜 혼자 가?

B: I want to have a fling with a romantic man.
로맨틱한 남자와 즐기고 싶어서.

It isn't dating. It's sex. It's a fling.
그건 데이트가 아냐. 그냥 섹스야 번개 같은거야.

You're just having a fling with a student.
학생하고 불장난 하고 있다는거야.

I wasn't sure if it was just a fling for him.
걔한테는 이게 단지 불장난이었는지 확실히 몰랐었어.

070 I'm hot for you, Chris! 크리스, 난 너와 섹스하고 싶어!

this is not so commonly used, but when we hear it we can understand that the speaker is saying he is very drawn to Chris, and in a sexual way. Another way to say this would be "I'm really attracted to you, and I'm open to starting a relationship"

I Point I be hot for 끌려서 섹스하고 싶어하다
have the hots for sb 설레다, 흥분하다, 하고 싶어 안날나다(오래된 표현)

A: Why do you always follow me around?
왜 항상 날 쫓아다니는거야?

B: I'm hot for you, Chris. I want to be your girlfriend. 크리스, 난 너와 사귀고 싶어. 네 여친이 되고 싶어.

I am so hot for you right now.
나 지금 당장 너랑 하고 싶어.

She's like really sexy....almost dirty hot. And she's hot for you.
걘 정말 더러울 정도로 섹시해. 그리고 너와 하고 싶어 안달이야.

We are not going anywhere until you confess you have the hots for our nanny.
네가 유모와 하고 싶어한다는 고백을 하기 전까지는 우린 아무데도 안갈거야.

Half the patients that come through here have the hots for Chris.
여기오는 절반의 환자들은 크리스 선생님에 안달났는데요.

071 I'm not gonna sneak around with you

난 너랑 바람피우지 않을거야

this often is a way of saying that the speaker is not going to secretly have a romantic relationship with someone who is already married. It may also be a way to say that the listener needs to get a divorce in order to continue the relationship. A similar way to say this is "I'm not going to have a secret affair with you"

I Point I sneak around 몰래 만나다, 바람피우다, 몰래 움직이다

A: I'm not gonna sneak around with you.
난 너랑 바람피우지 않을거야.

B: Do you mean you're ending our affair?
우리의 만남을 끝낸다는 말야?

He's gone. We don't have to sneak around anymore. We can have a real relationship.
걔는 떠났어. 더 이상 몰래 만날 필요가 없어. 떳떳하게 관계를 맺을 수 있어.

Their parents said they couldn't go out, so they had to sneak around.
걔네 부모들이 못만나게 해서 걔네들은 몰래 만나야 했어.

What you're doing is sneaking around behind my back.
네가 지금 하고 있는 것은 나몰래 피하고 다니는거야.

072 Is this how you get your rocks off?

넌 이런 식으로 기쁨을 느끼는거야?

this question is a way to ask someone about doing something he really enjoys. Sometimes we can assume it is asking about something sexual or something else unusual that gives pleasure. It is like asking "Is this how you get enjoyment?"

I Point I get one's rocks off (~ing) 사정하다(ejaculate), 성교하다, 즐기다

A: I invited all of these teenage girls to a party at my house. 난 집에서 하는 파티에 이 모든 십대 소녀들을 초대했어.

B: That seems like a bad idea. Is this how you get your rocks off? 좋은 생각같지 않은데. 이런 식으로 해서 기쁨을 느껴?

He gets his rocks off killing the moms, but the babies he protects.
그는 엄마들을 살해하면서 희열을 느끼지만 아기들은 보호를 해.

He gets his rocks off watching them suffer.
그는 그들이 고통을 당하는 걸 보고 희열을 느껴!

073 I shot my load while I was asleep 나 몽정했어

this is a type of slang, and it has a sexual meaning. The speaker is saying that he ejaculated while he was sleeping, probably because he was having a dream about sex. A similar way to express this would be "I had a wet dream"

| Point | shoot one's load 사정하다(ejaculate)

A: Are you telling me you dream about sex?
섹스에 관한 꿈을 꾼다는 말야?

B: You bet. I **shot my load** while I was asleep.
정말야. 몽정을 했어.

I'm embarrassed to admit that I shot my load while I was asleep. 인정하기 창피하지만 몽정을 했어.

Mike cries after he ejaculates. 마이크는 사정 후에 울어.

If the rapist ejaculated, he was smart enough to use a condom.
강간범이 사정을 했다면 콘돔을 썼을 정도로 영리했을거야.

He ejaculated on her stomach, then made her take a shower.
갠 그녀의 배위에 사정을 한 다음 그녀가 샤워하도록 했어.

074 He forced himself on her 갠 그녀를 성폭행했어

this is a way to say that a man forced a woman to have sex with him, even though she didn't want to do that. We can understand that this was a crime, and is possibly being investigated by the police. In other words, "He raped her"

| Point | force oneself on sb 강제로 성관계를 맺다, 강간하다

A: Why is the woman complaining to the cops?
저 여자는 경찰에 뭘 고소하는거야?

B: See that man? **He forced himself on her.**
저 남자 보이지? 저 사람이 자기를 강간했대.

I didn't force myself on Celine.
난 셀린을 강간하지 않았어.

He broke into their apartments while they slept and he forced himself on them.
갠 걔네들이 자는 사이에 아파트에 침입해서 걔네들을 성폭행했어.

I begged him not to, but he forced himself on me. 난 그사람에게 제발 하지 말아달라고 빌었지만 갠 날 성폭행했어.

075 He cheated on his wife 갠 아내 몰래 바람을 폈어

this is said when a man has sex with a woman who isn't his wife. It is a way to say "He had a girlfriend outside of his marriage"

| Point | cheat on A (with B) A몰래 (B와) 바람피우다, (테스트) 부정행위를 하다
Did you cheat on her? 너 걔몰래 바람피웠어?

A: Why don't you like Gale? 왜 게일을 싫어해?

B: **He cheated on his wife.** 바람폈잖아.

My husband didn't cheat on me, I cheated on him. 남편이 바람을 피운 게 아니라, 내가 바람을 피웠어.

I'm sorry I cheated on you with her.
너 몰래 걔랑 바람나서 미안해.

I never cheated on a test. 시험에서 부정행위 해본 적 없어.

076 He likes to play the field 걔는 여러 여자를 두루 만나는 걸 좋아해

this is a way of saying "He likes to date a lot of girls." We can understand the person doesn't want a wife or a serious girlfriend

| Point | play the field 상대를 바꿔가며 여러 사람과 사귀다, 섹스하다

A: Bob will never get married. **He likes to play the field.** 밥은 절대 결혼 안 할걸. 여러 여자를 만나는 걸 좋아해.

B: Most girls think he is a sleazy guy.
많은 여자들이 밥을 너저분하다고 생각해.

You could play the field for a while, but what you're eventually gonna find out is that I'm the right guy.
잠시 다른 사람들 사귀어봐도 되지만 종국에는 내가 이상형이라는 걸 알게 될거야.

I plan to play the field before getting married.
결혼하기 전에 난 이여자 저여자 두루 만날 생각이야.

077 You were actually fooling around with her
넌 걔하고 재미보고 있었잖아

the speaker is expressing that someone was kissing, touching and maybe having sex with a woman. It is another way to say "You made out with her"

| Point | fool around (with sb) (…와) 재미보다, 바람피다

A: I made out with Michelle the other night.
요전 날 밤 미쉘하고 재미봤어.

B: **You were actually fooling around with her?**
정말 걔하고 재미봤단말야?

미드표현

Jack got fired for fooling around with the manager's wife. 잭은 부장님 부인과 바람피다 잘렸어.

There are certain rules. You don't fool around with your friend's ex-girlfriends or possible girlfriends or girls they're related to.
몇가지 철칙이 있어. 친구들의 옛 여친이나 여친이 될 가능성이 있는 여자 혹은 그들과 연관된 사람들은 안 건드리는게 좋아.

078 Her boyfriend was two-timing her
걔의 남자 친구가 양다리를 걸치고 있어

this means "Her boyfriend also had another girlfriend." This is often said to mean the boyfriend acted badly

| Point | two-time 양다리 걸치다

A: Josie broke up with the guy she was dating.
조시는 데이트하던 남자와 헤어졌어.

B: **Her boyfriend was two-timing her.**
걔 남친이 양다리 걸쳤거든.

미드표현

I was not dumped. It turns out he was two-timing me. 난 차인 게 아니고 걔가 양다리 걸치고 있었던거야.

He's also a bit of a two-timer.
걔 또한 양다리 걸치는 편이야.

079 We'll do a paternity test 우리는 친자확인 검사를 할거야

this simply means that they are going to test a man's DNA to see if he is the father of a child. A paternity test is done when a baby is born and it is uncertain who the father is. This is like saying "We'll check his DNA to see if he got the woman pregnant"

| Point | take[do] a paternity test 친자확인 검사를 하다
foster home 위탁가정

A: The mother isn't sure which man is the father.
엄마는 누가 아버지인지 확실히 몰라.

B: **We'll do a paternity test** to find out.
우리가 친자확인검사를 해서 알아낼거야.

I told him I'd get a paternity test.
난 친자확인검사를 할거라고 걔한테 말했어.

We took the paternity test, and it's official.
우리는 친자확인검사를 했는데 공식적인거야.

There's my son, until we get the results of the paternity test back.
친자확인검사결과를 받아볼 때까지 내 아들이야.

There are 6 kids living in that foster house.
저 위탁가정집에는 6명의 아이가 살고 있어.

080 She's suing me for sole custody
갠 단독양육권을 얻기 위해 나한테 소송을 걸거야

this expresses that someone is going through a divorce, and his wife wants to keep the children for herself. She is asking the divorce court to allow her to be the only parent who has and takes care of the children. In other words, "She wants the court to let her be the only one to raise the children"

| Point | have custody of~ 양육권을 갖다
have[get] sole custody of~ 단독으로 양육권을 갖다

A: Sorry your divorce is going so badly.
네 이혼이 안좋게 돼서 안됐어.

B: I hate my ex. **She's suing me for sole custody.**
전처를 증오해. 갠 단독양육권을 얻기 위해 소송을 하고 있어.

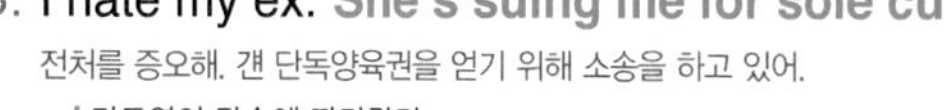

미드표현

We're granting you temporary custody of Wilma. 우리는 당신에게 윌마의 양육권을 임시적으로 부여합니다.

Venessa's filing for custody of Jason.
바네사는 제이슨의 양육권 소송을 제기할거야.

She's blackmailing me to get custody of my son! 걔는 내 아들의 양육권을 갖겠다고 날 협박했어!

MEMO

Things that may be said when a crime happens

범죄를 저질렀으면 재판받고 감방에 가야지

Where was he last seen?

001 I am so busted 딱 걸렸네, 나 큰일났네

this is a way to say "I was caught doing something bad." The speaker knows he may have trouble in the future

I Point I bust 깨부수다, 체포하다, (경찰이) 쳐들어오다, 들키다

A: The teacher knows you skipped class.
선생님이 네가 수업 빠진 거 아셔.

B: She does? **I am so busted.** 그래? 딱 걸렸네.

미드표현

I thought you got busted for armed robbery.
무장강도 건으로 넌 체포된 줄 알았어.

Got busted a few years ago for making fake IDs. 신분증 위조로 수년전에 체포되었어.

Damn it! Busted again. 빌어먹을! 딱 잡혔네.

002 You caught me 들켰네

this is very similar to the previous phrase. It means "You found I did a bad thing"

A: Are you cheating on our test? 시험에 부정행위하는거야?

B: Yeah, **you caught me.** 어, 딱 걸렸네.

미드표현

Oh, you caught me. I am so busted.
아, 들켰네. 딱 걸렸어.

He got caught red-handed.
그 사람은 현장에서 딱 걸렸어.

You caught me sleeping with your wife.
난 네 아내랑 자다가 딱 걸렸어.

I took the money. You caught me.
내가 돈을 가져갔는데 너한테 딱 걸렸네.

003 The murderer was nailed this morning
살인자가 오늘 아침 잡혔어

this is a way to express that a person has been arrested for a criminal offense. It is like saying "He was taken to jail for that crime"

I Point I nail sb = arrest 체포하다
You're under arrest 당신을 체포합니다

A: The man who robbed the bank **was nailed** today. 은행털이범이 오늘 잡혔어.

B: That's great. I don't want dangerous people in this town. 잘됐네. 우리 사는 곳에 위험한 사람이 없으면 해.

미드표현

You're just determined to nail him, aren't you?
너 걔를 체포하기로 결심했구나, 그렇지 않아?

You're under arrest for accessory to murder.
넌 살인방조혐의로 체포한다.

You are under arrest for the rape and murder of Jenifer Lewis.
제니퍼 루이스를 강간하고 살인한 죄로 체포한다.

004 I'm undercover on a drug bust 마약사건으로 위장수사 중이야

this expresses that the speaker is secretly a policeman who is trying to get evidence to arrest criminals for selling illegal drugs. Undercover work is considered dangerous for policemen. Another way to express this would be "I'm working covertly to arrest people who have illegal drugs"

I Point I gun bust 총기사건 drug bust 마약사건

A: Tell me why you are carrying these pills.
너 왜 이 약들을 지니고 있는지 말해봐.

B: **I'm an undercover on a drug bust.**
난 마약사건으로 위장수사 중이야.

미드표현

I'll just tell him I'm undercover on a drug bust.
걔에게 마약사건으로 내가 위장수사 중이라고 말할거야.

She cross-examined me on a drug bust where a cop got killed.
그녀가 경찰이 사망한 마약사건으로 나를 반대심문했어.

It was an isolated incident months ago. And between drug busts and assorted felonies, the gang's been pretty much decimated.
몇 달전에는 서로 관련이 없는 사건였지. 마약사건과 갱의 다수가 사망한 여러가지 중죄들 사이에는.

005 You will get to the perp 넌 범인을 잡게 될거야

this speaker is saying that the police will catch a perpetrator, the criminal who committed a crime. This would be very specific to a conversation between policemen, because normal people don't need to catch a perpetrator. A way to say the same thing would be "You'll find the lawbreaker"

| Point | perp 범인　　unsub[unknown subject] 미확인 용의자

A: We haven't found who the murderer is yet.
아직 범인이 누구인지 알아내지 못했어.

B: Don't worry, **you'll get your perp.**
걱정마. 넌 범인을 잡게 될거야.

미드표현

But you thought he was another perp trying to shoot you.
하지만 넌 걔가 네게 총을 쏘려고 했던 또다른 범인이라고 생각하는거지.

I'd like to hear from the perp how he felt about his mother.
난 범인이 자기 어머니에 대해 어떻게 생각하는지 직접 듣고 싶어.

Only problem is, your Jane Doe was already dead when the perp shot her.
한가지 문제는 미확인시신은 범인이 쏘기 전에 이미 죽어있었다는거야.

006 Where was he last seen? 걔를 마지막으로 본게 어디야?

this literally is asking where a specific person was last seen by people. In many cases we can understand that the person is missing, and people, possibly the police, are looking for clues so they can find where he is. It is similar to asking "What place was that person in before he disappeared?"

| Point | be last seen 마지막으로 목격되다
be last seen ~ing 마지막으로 …하는 것이 목격되다

A: Tommy disappeared three days ago.
타미는 삼일 전에 사라졌어.

B: That is not good. **Where was he last seen?**
좋지 않은데. 걔를 마지막 본게 어디야?

Chris was last seen at choir practice.
크리스는 합창 연습에 마지막으로 목격됐어.

Victim was last seen Friday night.
피해자는 금요일 저녁에 마지막으로 목격됐어.

Last seen wearing a Superman costume.
수퍼맨 복장을 입고 있는 모습이 마지막으로 목격됐어.

007 Let's just hit the street 탐문수사를 하자고

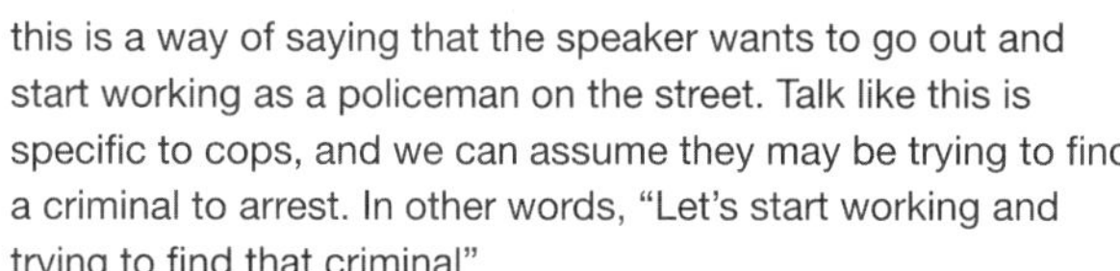
this is a way of saying that the speaker wants to go out and start working as a policeman on the street. Talk like this is specific to cops, and we can assume they may be trying to find a criminal to arrest. In other words, "Let's start working and trying to find that criminal"

| Point | hit the street 탐문수사하다　　finish the sweep 수색을 끝내다

A: Do you want to check the suspect's Facebook page? 용의자의 페이스북을 확인하고 싶어?

B: Not right now. **Let's just hit the street.**
지금은 아냐. 탐문수사를 하자고.

미드표현

Let's just hit the streets, find some girls, question them about Paul.
탐문수사를 해서 여자들을 찾아내고 그들에게 폴에 대해서 물어보자.

I'm gonna need you guys to hit the street and see if you can scare up any of Finch's associates.
너 탐문수사해서 핀치의 동료들 중 누구라도 활용할 수 있는지 알아보도록 해.

We just finished the sweep of Bobby's car.
방금 바비의 자동차 수색을 끝냈어.

008 Sounds like a motive to me 살해동기처럼 들리는데

this is something that could be said by a policeman when he is trying to find out why a crime was committed. If it sounds like the reason given for the crime makes sense, then he has found the motive. In other words, "I think we have found the reason this crime occurred"

| Point | motive (살해) 동기　　ulterior motive 숨은 동기, 저의

A: If the husband dies, she will inherit a fortune.
남편이 죽으면 아내가 많은 재산을 유산으로 받는대.

B: Interesting. **Sounds like a motive to me.**
흥미롭구만. 나한테는 범행동기로 들리는데.

미드표현

Sounds like a motive for murder to me.
살해동기처럼 들리는데.

Why do you have to believe I have an ulterior motive? 왜 내게 숨은 동기가 있다고 믿는거야?

009 I got a tail 미행이 붙었어

미드표현

this expresses that the speaker is walking or driving somewhere, and he has realized that someone is following him and trying to spy on him. He probably wants to get away, because the person following him may try to hurt him.

| Point | have a tail 미행이 붙다　put a tail on 미행을 붙이다
be on tail on 미행중이다　tail sb 미행하다

A: Why are you acting so nervous today?
너 오늘 왜 그렇게 불안하게 행동하는거야?

B: **I've got a tail.** Someone is following me.
미행이 붙었어. 누가 날 미행하고 있어.

Put a tail on him so he can't hurt anyone else.
걔가 아무도 해치지 못하도록 미행을 붙여.

I can't believe Daniel had a tail on me and I didn't know it. 대니얼이 내게 미행을 붙이다니 놀라워. 난 몰랐어.

How did you know I had lunch with Peter, Dad? You have a private investigator tailing me?
내가 피터랑 점심한 걸 어떻게 알아, 아빠? 사설탐정에게 날 미행시킨거야?

010 We found your whole stash 네가 숨겨둔 거 전부를 찾았어

미드표현

this implies that the speaker found the secret hiding place where the listener keeps valuable goods. A stash is often cash or drugs, or something that can be sold for money. The speaker is saying "We found the valuable things that you tried to hide"

| Point | stash 비상금, 숨겨둔 것, 은닉물, 숨겨두다

A: How did you get the gold coins I hid?
내가 숨겨놓은 금화를 어떻게 찾았어?

B: **We found your whole stash.** It's all here.
우린 네가 숨겨둔 거 전부를 찾았어. 여기 다 있어.

I have some thoughts about finding this secret stash. 이 숨겨둔 은밀한 것을 찾는데 내 생각이 좀 있어.

I phoned you to tell you about the stash, didn't I? 내가 전화해서 네게 은닉물에 대해 말했잖아, 그렇지 않아?

I got a little money stashed away for a rainy day. 앞으로 안좋은 날을 대비해 돈을 조금 숨겨놨어.

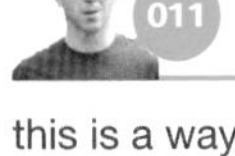

011 He is still unaccounted for 걔는 아직도 행방불명이야

미드표현

this is a way to say that someone is missing, and has not been found. Most often this is used when there has been a big accident, and authorities are checking on injured and dead people. The people who they can't find are unaccounted for. Another way to say this is "He's still missing"

| Point | unaccounted for 행방불명의 *undocumented 밀입국한

A: Did they find Mr. Davis after the train crash?
열차충돌사건 후에 데이비스 씨를 봤어요?

B: I'm sorry, but **he's still unaccounted for.**
미안하지만 아직 실종 중이세요.

She's the only one who's unaccounted for. 실종된 사람은 그녀가 유일해.

Officials have confirmed 246 passenger fatalities in the bombing of the jumbo jet, but the final death toll will likely surge to include many unaccounted-for persons on the ground.
관리들은 점보기의 폭발로 246명의 승객이 사망했음을 확인하였으나 최종 사망자수는 지상에서 실종된 많은 사람들을 포함하면 급증할 것으로 보인다.

012 She was busted for prostitution 걔는 매춘혐의로 체포됐어

미드표현

this indicates that a woman was arrested for taking money and allowing men to have sex with her. Usually when this happens, the woman sells sex as a job, and she may have been arrested several times. We can say the same thing like this "She was arrested for solicitation"

| Point | get busted for 체포되다　bust sb 체포하다
take sb in 체포하다(arrest)　pick sb up 체포하다, 연행하다

A: I think Serena has been arrested before.
세레나가 전에 체포된 적이 있는 것 같아.

B: Yeah, **she was busted for prostitution.** 그래, 매춘혐의로 체포됐었어.

I thought you got busted for armed robbery.
난 네가 무장강도죄로 체포된 줄 알았어.

Three weeks ago, I was busted for pot, okay?
3주전에 난 대마초로 체포됐어, 알았어?

She was busted for prostitution two years ago. 걔는 2년전에 매춘하다 체포됐어.

013 He knows we can't nail him 걘 우리가 자기를 체포할 수 없다는 것을 알아

this is a way to say that a criminal knows police suspect him of committing a crime, but they can't arrest him because they don't have enough evidence. We can assume the criminal feels smug and the police feel frustrated. This can be like saying "They can't arrest him yet because they don't have proof of his guilt"

| Point | nail sb for~ …로 …을 체포하다
nail one's ass to the wall 엄하게 처벌하다, 강력히 벌하다

A: Why is that guy so arrogant? 저 사람 왜 저렇게 거만한거야?
B: **He knows we can't nail him** for the crime.
우리가 그 범죄로 자길 체포할 수 없다는 걸 알아.

Got him now. I would have nailed him fifteen years ago, though.
이제 걜 잡았어. 그래도 15년 전에 체포했었어야 했는데.

DNA can nail you if you don't use a condom.
콘돔을 쓰지 않으면 DNA로 체포될 수 있어.

The cops plan to nail his ass to the wall.
경찰은 그를 강력히 처벌할 계획이야.

014 Book her on blackmail 걜 협박죄로 체포해

this means that the police have arrested a woman who wanted money in exchange for not revealing a damaging secret about someone. People who blackmail have confidential information that can cause problems if it is told to others. A different way to say this is "Arrest her for trying to illegally extort money"

| Point | book 체포하다, 체포해서 피의사실을 기록하다

A: Let us know what Ms. Rosen was arrested for.
로젠 씨가 무슨 일로 체포되었는지 알려주세요.
B: She was extorting money. **Book her on blackmail.** 돈을 갈취했어요. 협박죄로 체포해

Book him on the blackmail till we see what the search turns up.
일단 협박죄로 체포해 그리고 수색결과가 어떤지 보자고.

I don't care if it's a psychic vision, it's enough to book him.
그게 비과학적인 상상이라도 상관없어, 그건 걔를 체포하기에 충분해.

You can't book him here anyhow, detective. Computers are down.
어쨌건 여기서는 걔 체포기록을 할 수가 없어요. 형사님 컴퓨터가 다운됐어요.

015 You have the right to remain silent
묵비권을 행사할 권리가 있다

this is said by police officers. It is like saying to a person who is arrested "You don't have to talk to us"

A: **You have the right to remain silent.**
묵비권을 행사할 권리가 있어.
B: Am I being arrested right now? 지금 체포되는 건가요?

You have the right to remain silent. If you give up that right, anything you say can and will be used against you in a court of law.
당신은 묵비권을 행사할 권리가 있고 법정에서 유리한 진술을 할 권리가 있습니다.

I have a warrant for your arrest. You have the right to remain silent.
체포영장을 가져왔습니다. 묵비권을 행사할 권리가 있습니다.

016 I plead the Fifth 묵비권을 행사할게요

this means that someone refused to talk at a trial because it could have made him seem guilty. The Fifth Amendment is part of the US Constitution, and by law it allows people who are on trial to not speak about things that would make them appear guilty or lead to punishment. Another way to say this is "I refuse to speak about that"

| Point | plead[take] the Fifth (법정에서) 묵비권을 행사하다, 진술을 거부하다

A: Tell us if you robbed the convenience store.
그 편의점을 털었는지 우리에게 말해봐.
B: Can't tell you. **I plead the Fifth.** 말 못해요. 묵비권 행사할게요.

If you bring me into that court, I will plead the Fifth. 날 법정으로 끌고 간다면 묵비권을 행사할거요.

But she'll plead the Fifth.
하지만 걔는 묵비권을 행사할거야.

And you still want to plead the Fifth?
그리고 넌 아직도 묵비권을 행사하고 싶은거야?

That's a battle I am prepared to win. No matter what, you plead the Fifth.
이건 내가 이길 준비를 해놓은 전투야. 어찌됐건, 넌 묵비권을 행사해.

017 We had to post bail 우리는 보석금을 내야했어

this expresses that the speaker gave money to get someone out of jail. The bail money is required to ensure that the person in jail comes to their future court trial. We can also say "The release came after we paid the bail"

| Point | post[put up] bail 보석금을 내다 be (out) on bail 보석으로 풀려나다
release sb on bail 보석으로 풀어주다 bail sb out 보석금을 내고 …을 빼내다

A: How did you get Allen out of jail?
어떻게 앨런을 감옥에서 빼낸거야?

B: **We had to post bail** for him. 걔 보석금을 내야했어.

My lawyers can post bail. 내 변호사가 보석금을 낼 수 있어.

He'll be out on bail by tomorrow afternoon.
걔는 내일 오후에 보석으로 풀려날거야.

They won't release him on bail until they get the passport. 여권을 확보한 후에 걔를 보석으로 풀어줄거야.

She's bailed him out of jail twice in the past 4 years. 그녀는 걔를 지난 4년간 2번이나 보석금을 내고 빼냈어.

018 Turn yourself in to the police 경찰에 자수해

미드표현

this means that the speaker wants someone to go to the police station and allow himself to be arrested for a crime he might have done. Many times, but not always, we can presume the person is guilty. It is like saying "Go to the police and tell them what you did"

| Point | turn sb in (to the police) …을 밀고[신고]하다
turn oneself in 자수하다

A: I should have never stolen the credit cards.
신용카드를 훔치지 말았어야 했는데.

B: Now you have to **turn yourself in** to the police.
이제 넌 경찰에 가서 자수하라고.

Why didn't you turn him in? 왜 걔를 신고하지 않은거야?

I should turn myself in to the police, for God's sake. 맙소사, 내가 경찰에 자수해야겠어.

If I find her I'm gonna try and convince her to turn herself in. 내가 걔를 찾으면 자수하라고 설득해볼거야.

019 I'm gonna lock you up! 널 잡아넣을거야!

미드표현

this would probably only be said by a police officer. It means that the policeman thinks someone is guilty of a crime and plans to arrest him and put him in jail. Another way to say this is "I will arrest you and you'll be locked up in the jail"

| Point | lock sb up 감옥[정신병원]에 가두다
lockup 감옥, 유치장, 구치소 lockdown 구류조치

A: **I'm going to lock you up!** 난 널 잡아넣을거야!

B: You'll never be able to put me in jail.
넌 절대로 날 감옥에 넣지 못할거야.

If you got accused of a crime, they might lock you up for good.
네가 범죄로 기소되면 널 영원히 가둘지도 몰라.

They didn't find me guilty in court because they didn't want to lock me up.
걔네들은 날 가두기를 원치 않기에 내게 무죄판결을 내린거야.

You're going to be spending the next 10 years in lockdown. 넌 앞으로 10년간 교도소에서 시간을 보내게 될거야.

020 We have a suspect in custody 우리는 한 용의자를 구금하고 있어

미드표현

this is said by the police when they have arrested someone that they think has done something that was seriously illegal. In many ways, it is like saying "We have arrested the person that we think is guilty of the crime"

| Point | take sb in custody 수감하다, 구속하다
have[get] sb in custody …을 구류하다, 구금하고 있다
be in custody 구금 중이다

A: What are you doing to solve the murder?
살인사건을 해결하기 위해 어떻게 하고 있어?

B: **We have a suspect in custody.**
우리는 한 용의자를 구금하고 있어.

Do you have David Clark in custody?
데이빗 클락을 구금중에 있습니까?

We're keeping him in custody, for now.
우선은 우리는 그를 구금하고 있어.

We got two suspects in custody and neither of their prints are on the duct tape.
2명의 용의자를 구금하고 있는데 강력접착테입에는 어느 누구의 지문도 없어.

The police had Danny Bolen in custody.
경찰은 대니 볼렌을 구금하고 있어.

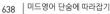

021 We're back to square one 우리 다시 원점이네

this indicates that the speaker thinks they have been wasting time on something, and now they are going to have to start all over again. It can be expressing frustration, since no progress has been made. In other words, "We'll have to begin all over again"

Point be back to square one 원점으로 되돌아가다, 다시 원점이다

A: It looks like all of this effort has been wasted.
이 모든 노력이 수포로 돌아간 것 같아.

B: You're right. **We're back to square one.**
맞아. 우리 다시 원점이야.

But without the confession we're back to square one. 하지만 자백없이는 우린 다시 원점이야.

He's playing us. So we're back to square one?
걘 우릴 갖고 놀고 있어. 그럼 우리는 다시 원점이야?

So we're back to square one? Okay, here's the deal. 그럼 우린 다시 원점이라고? 좋아, 좋은 생각이 있어.

022 Do you swear to tell the truth? 진실만을 말할 것을 맹세합니까?

this is a way of saying "Will you be honest?" It asks if the person will give true answers

Point You may take the stand 증언대에 서 주세요

A: **Do you swear to tell the truth** in court?
법정에서 진실을 말할 것을 맹세합니까?

B: Yes, I promise not to lie. 네, 거짓말하지 않겠습니다.

In the case now pending before this court, do you swear to tell the truth, the whole truth and nothing but the truth?
이 법원안에서 오직 진실만을 말할 것을 맹세합니까?

Do you swear to tell the truth and nothing but the truth so help you God?
하나님 앞에 진실만을 얘기할 것을 맹세합니까?

Raise your right hand. Do you swear to tell the truth, the whole truth, so help you God?
선서를 하십시오. 하나님 앞에서 맹세하고 진실만을 얘기할 것입니까?

023 It was an inside job 내부자소행입니다

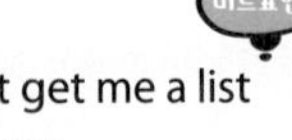

usually this means a crime was done by a person who worked in the place. We can understand it means "The criminal is an employee here"

A: Someone stole millions of dollars from the bank.
누가 은행에서 수백만 달러를 훔쳤어.

B: I'm sure **it was an inside job.** 내부자 소행일거야.

It's probably an inside job. Just get me a list of current and former employees.
아마도 내부자 소행인 것 같아요. 전 현직 직원명단을 주세요.

Maybe it was an inside job. Maybe somebody bought off one of your guys.
아마 내부자 소행인 듯합니다. 아마도 누군가가 당신 직원 중 한 명을 매수했을 겁니다.

024 He is doing time for murder 살인죄로 복역 중이야

the speaker is expressing "That person is in jail for murder." Someone must spend years in jail for killing another person

Point do time (for~) = serve time (for~) (…로) 감방살다
behind bars 투옥되어
put sb in jail 투옥하다

A: What happened to the guy who was arrested?
체포된 사람은 어떻게 됐어?

B: **He's doing time for murder** now. 살인죄로 복역중야.

You're willing to do time for that?
그거 때문에 감방 살고 싶어?

My wife served time for narcotics possession.
내 아내는 마약소지로 감방 살았어.

Jimmy served time for selling drugs and manslaughter. 지미는 마약판매 및 살인으로 감방 살았어.

025 You'll be charged with murder 살인죄로 기소될거야

the speaker is expressing that the police think someone killed another person. He is saying "The police will come and get you because of that"

| Point | charge A with B A를 B로 기소하다 What charge? 무슨 죄목으로?
A be charged with B A는 B로 기소되다

A: **You'll be charged with murder** if you kill someone. 살인하면 살인죄로 기소될거야.

B: I'm not going to kill anyone. 아무도 안 죽일거야.

미드표현

I'm charged with engaging in sexual conduct for a fee. 난 성매매 혐의로 기소되었어.

Sam is charged with attempted murder. 샘은 살인미수로 기소되었어.

The defendant is charged with second-degree murder. 피고는 2급 살인죄로 기소되었습니다.

026 This is a high profile case 이건 주목 받는 사건이야

'high profile' is used to show something is important and many people are watching to see what will happen. A thing that is high profile is "of interest to many people"

| Point | high profile (대중이나 언론으로부터) 많은 관심과 주목을 받는, 주목 받는

A: Can you remember any **high profile court cases?** 주목받았던 법정사건 기억나는거 있어?

B: I think a lot of people thought the OJ Simpson trial was high profile. OJ 심슨재판이 많은 주목을 받았다고 많이들 생각할거야.

미드표현

Is it a high profile case? 주목받는 사건이야?

Victims aren't equal. High profile cases get priority. 희생자는 평등하지 않아. 주목 받는 사건들이 우선권을 갖게 되지.

Nothing I like more than a high profile case. 주목 받는 사건보다 좋은 건 없지.

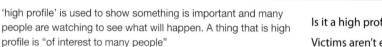

027 I'll have my day in court 법정에서 시시비비를 가릴 날이 올거야

this is a way to say "I'll try to get a fair judgment." It indicates that the speaker will explain his problem and a court will decide whether he is right or not

| Point | have one's day in court 자기 주장이나 소신을 공개적으로 밝히다

A: Have you settled the problem with your neighbor? 이웃주민과 문제 해결했어?

B: Not yet, but **I'll have my day in court** soon. 아직, 하지만 법정에서 곧 밝힐 날이 올거야.

Your honor. I am anxious for my day in court. 재판장님, 저도 하루빨리 재판을 받고 싶습니다.

A: I wanna have my day in court. B: At the risk of having your day in prison? A: 법정에서 시시비비를 가리고 싶어. B: 감방갈 수도 있는데?

028 I'm gonna make a case for temporary insanity 난 일시 정신장애라는 주장을 펼거야

this is something only a lawyer would say. The speaker is saying that he is going to tell the judge that his client was insane at the time of the crime, in the hope that the client will get a lesser punishment. Another way to say this is "We plan to tell the court this man was crazy when he committed the crime"

| Point | make a (strong) case for …을 (강력히) 주장하다

A: How will you save your client from execution? 의뢰인의 사형집행을 어떻게 막을거야?

B: **I'm going to make a case for** temporary insanity. 일시적인 정신장애라는 주장을 펼거야.

미드표현

The lawyer made a case for letting the suspect go. 변호사는 용의자를 풀어주자고 강력히 주장했어.

He made a case for extending the agreement. 걔는 협의안을 연장하자고 주장했어.

I can make a case for a murder charge. 난 살인혐의라는 주장을 할 수 있어.

Our attorney made a case for a monetary settlement. 우리 변호사는 금전적 보상을 주장했어.

029 She's not competent to stand trial 걔는 소송무능력자야

미드표현

this expresses that a woman is crazy or has mental problems, and so she can't be tried in front of a judge in a courtroom. Usually people have to be considered sane when they are arrested for a crime in order to be taken to court. Otherwise, they may be sent to a mental hospital. In other words, "She's too crazy to be tried in court"

I Point I stand trial 재판을 받다　　be on trial 재판중이다
put sb on trial 재판에 회부하다

A: They said the killer will never leave a mental hospital. 살인범은 절대로 정신병원에서 나갈 수가 없을거래.

B: She's completely nuts. **She's not competent to stand trial.** 걘 완전 미친사람이야. 소송무능력자야.

Kate's about to stand trial for murder.
케이트는 살인죄로 재판을 받을거야.

Psych evaluation to see if I'm competent to stand trial. 내가 재판받을 능력이 되는지를 확인하는 심리평가.

James Heller, you have been brought before this court of law to stand trial as a war criminal.
제임스 헬러, 당신은 전범으로 재판을 받기 위해 본 법정에 서게 되었습니다.

030 Has the jury reached a verdict? 배심원 평결이 나왔습니까?

미드표현

this is asking "Did the jury decide if this person is guilty or innocent?" A jury is a group of people at a trial that decides if a person is a criminal

I Point I reach a verdict 평결에 다다르다, 평결이 나오다
The jury is still out (on that) 배심원 평결은 아직 미정이다
foreman [foreperson] 배심원장

A: **Has the jury reached a verdict?**
배심원 평결이 나왔습니까?

B: No, they haven't decided yet. 아뇨, 아직 결정못했어요.

Ladies and gentlemen of the jury, have you reached a verdict? 배심원 여러분, 평결이 나왔습니까?

Has the jury reached a verdict?
배심원은 평결이 나왔습니까?

A: Have you reached a verdict? B: No, Your Honor. We're deadlocked.
A: 평결이 나왔습니까? B: 아닙니다 판사님, 교착상태입니다.

031 Objection! 이의 있습니다!

미드표현

the speaker is probably a lawyer and is saying "I think that is wrong." This is a common way to stop what another lawyer is saying

I Point I All rise 일동기립　　Your Honor! 재판장님!
Sustained 이의 제기를 인정합니다
Overruled [Denied] 이의 기각합니다

A: **Objection,** Your Honor! Leading the witness.
이의 있습니다. 재판장님! 증인을 유도하고 있습니다

B: **Sustained.** The witness will not answer.
인정합니다. 증인은 답변하지 않아도 됩니다.

The objection's overruled. Are you alright, Mr. Caine? 이의 기각합니다. 케인 씨 받아들이겠습니까?

Objection! Detective Munch is not a psychiatrist. 이의있습니다! 먼치 형사는 정신과의사가 아닙니다.

Overruled. The witness may answer the question. 기각합니다. 증인은 질문에 답하십시오.

Sustained. Jury will disregard.
인정합니다. 배심원은 무시하십시오.

032 Still undefeated. Never lost. Never will
난 불패야. 과거에도 안졌고 앞으로도 안질거야

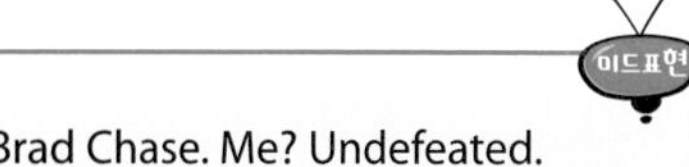

미드표현

this is a rather arrogant thing to say. The speaker is saying that he is very talented, and he has never lost when competing against someone else, and he believes he will always win in the future too. In other words "I am great and I will never be defeated"

I Point I still[stay] undefeated (변호사) 패할 줄 모르는

A: What was the result of your trial? 재판결과가 어땠어?

B: I won the case. **Still undefeated. Never lost. Never will.** 내가 이겼어. 난 불패야. 과거에도 안졌고 앞으로도 안질거야.

You beat Brad Chase. Me? Undefeated.
브래드 체이스를 이겼어. 나? 패한 적이 없어.

Alan, I need to stay undefeated.
알랜, 난 계속 승소를 해야 돼.

Still undefeated. I think my closing made all the difference. 아직 불패야. 내 최후변론이 차이를 가져오는 것 같아.

033 What (do) you got? 뭐야?, 뭐 나온 거 있어?, 무슨 일이야?

this is asking what the result of something is. It is a way to ask "What was the result?" or "What happened?"

| Point | What (do) you got? = What did you get?
= What do we have here? 무슨 일인가?

A: **What did you get** when you went to court?
법원에서 어떻게 됐어?

B: I had to go to jail for a month. 한 달간 감옥가야 됐어.

What do you got there? Is that a pie?
거기 뭐 있어? 파이야?

What do you got? Let's hear it. 뭐야? 들어보자고.

A: Neighbors hear anything? B: We are still canvassing. What do you got?
A: 이웃주민들은 들은게 없대? B: 아직 탐문 조사하고 있어. 뭐 나온 거 있어?

034 What does that prove? 그래서?, 그래서 그게 어쨌다는거야?

usually this is a way to say "It doesn't mean anything." The speaker wants to tell someone that nothing has been proved by some evidence

A: We saw him near the scene of the crime.
우린 그 남자를 범죄현장 부근에서 봤어.

B: **What does that prove?** I think he's innocent.
그래서 어쨌다는거야? 난 그 남자는 무죄인 것 같아.

So you found a knife. What does that prove?
그럼 네가 칼을 찾았다고, 그래서 그게 어쨌다는거야?

What does that prove? I'm still not guilty.
그래서 그게 어쨌다는거야? 난 아직 무죄야.

You say there was lipstick on his shirt. What does that prove?
걔 셔츠에 립스틱이 묻어있었다고, 그래서 그게 어쨌다는건데?

035 That doesn't prove anything 그건 아무런 증거가 되지 않아

this is a way to say that something is not useful evidence because it can't show if a contention is true or false. In other words, it has no value in court, so we can say "That is not useful in showing whether or not someone is lying or being honest"

| Point | That doesn't prove~ 그건 …한 증거가 되지 않아
You can't prove that~ 넌 …을 증명할 수 없어
You can't prove any of this 너 이 어떤 것도 증명할 수 없을거야

A: Ed was seen sneaking away from the apartment. 에드가 아파트에서 몰래 빠져나가는게 목격되었어.

B: **That doesn't prove anything**. He may not be guilty. 그건 아무런 증거가 되지 않아. 걘 무죄일 수도 있어.

I borrowed Kelly's keys. That doesn't prove anything.
난 켈리의 열쇠를 빌렸는데 그건 아무런 증거가 되지 않아.

That doesn't prove he was in the house.
그건 걔가 집에 있었다는 증거가 되지 않아.

You can't prove it was him on that videotape.
넌 비디오에 나오는 사람이 걔라는 걸 증명할 수 없어.

036 The evidence says you did 증거에 의하면 네가 그랬어

this is a way to say that someone seems guilty of something. It is like saying "This indicates you are guilty"

A: I never broke the law. 난 절대 죄를 짓지 않았어요.

B: **The evidence says you did.** 증거가 의하면 네가 그랬어.

I don't care what the evidence says, I didn't kill that man.
증거가 뭐라하든 상관없어, 난 그 남자를 죽이지 않았어.

That's not what the evidence says.
증거에 의하면 그렇지 않아.

You have to listen to the evidence.
증거에 귀를 기울여야 돼.

The evidence was cooked. 증거가 조작되었어.

037 Your fingerprints were all over the gun
네 지문이 총 전체에 묻어있었어

the speaker wants to say "The marks of your fingers are on the gun." It means that the person had the gun in his hands

| Point | fingerprints 지문

A: They can't prove I shot him. 내가 걜 쏜 걸 증명못해.

B: Yes they can. **Your fingerprints were all over the gun.** 아니 할 수 있어. 네 지문이 총 전체에 묻어있었어.

We found your fingerprints on the toilet seat in his bathroom. 그 남자의 욕실 변기에서 네 지문을 발견했어.

We're going to need your fingerprints and a DNA sample. 지문과 DNA 샘플이 필요할거야.

Why are your fingerprints on the necklace? 왜 네 지문이 목걸이에 있는거야?

038 The DNA doesn't match
DNA가 일치하지 않아

this is expressing that a person's body is not the same as the criminal's body. It is like saying "The body type is different so this person is innocent"

| Point | A doesn't match (with) B A가 B와 일치하지 않는다
It's a perfect match 정확히 일치해
Positive for semen 정액에 양성반응이 나왔어

A: How do you know the prisoner is innocent? 그 죄수가 무죄라는 걸 어떻게 알아?

B: **The DNA we found doesn't match his.** 발견한 DNA가 그 사람거하고 일치하지 않아.

The blood doesn't match our victim. 혈액은 피해자의 것과 일치하지 않아.

They're a perfect match. The DNA identical. 정확히 일치해. DNA가 동일해.

He processed the sexual assault kit. Positive for semen. 걔가 성폭행장비를 돌려봤는데 정액이 양성반응 나왔어.

The rapist's semen came back positive for cocaine. 강간범의 정액에서 코가인 양성반응이 나왔어.

039 On what grounds?
무슨 증거로?, 무슨 근거로?

this means "What's the reason for this?" A lawyer says this when he wants to know why something is happening

| Point | On what grounds+의문문? 무슨 근거로 …한거야?

A: We are going to take him to prison. 그 사람을 감옥에 넣을거야.

B: **On what grounds?** You can't do that. 무슨 근거로? 그럴 수는 없지.

On what grounds were you arrested, Mr. Miller? 밀러 씨는 무슨 일로 체포되었습니까?

A: We should get a warrant. B: On what grounds? A: On the grounds that this is a murder investigation.
A: 수색영장을 받아야겠어. B: 무슨 증거로? A: 살인사건 조사라는 근거로.

040 You're off the case
이 환자에서 손떼!, 이 사건에서 손떼

often this is a way of saying "You did a bad job and we don't want you to work on this." The person will be sent to work on something else

| Point | be off the case 이 사건(환자)에서 손떼다

A: I made a mistake during the trial. 재판 중 실수했어.

B: **You're off the case** because of that. 그 때문에 사건에서 손떼.

I'd prefer it if he were taken off the case. 걔가 이번 사건에서 제외되길 바랬어.

I know I'm off the case. 내가 손떼야하는 걸 알고 있어.

You're still in love with him? So, you have to hand off the case. 아직 걜 사랑해? 그럼 이 사건에서 손떼.

You're off the case because you broke the rules. 넌 규칙을 어겼기 때문에 이번 사건에서 손떼.

041 Let me work the case with you 너와 함께 사건을 해결하자

this is likely something that is only said between police and detectives. The speaker is telling someone that he wants to participate with him in order to investigate a crime. It is similar to saying "Let's be partners so we can catch the criminal who did this"

| Point | work the case 사건을 해결하다

A: **Let me work this case with you.**
너와 함께 사건을 해결하자.

B: No, I don't want to have a partner.
됐어, 난 파트너가 필요없어.

Tell Jack I need him working the case.
사건을 해결하는데 잭이 필요하다고 걔한테 얘기해줘.

That was a rough one. Did you work the case?
저건 정말 힘든거였어. 너 그 사건 해결했어?

I need you to work the case with me.
너 나와 함께 사건을 해결하자.

Let me work the case with you until we find a link between our victims.
피해자들간의 연관점을 찾을 때까지 너와 함께 사건을 해결하자.

042 That's what gets him off 그게 그 놈을 흥분시킨거지

미드표현

usually this a way of talking about something unusual that a person enjoys. It means "He really likes doing that"

| Point | What gets me~ 나를 혼란스럽게[화나게] 하는 것은

A: He likes to keep pictures of women without clothes. 걘 발가벗은 여자의 사진을 지니는 것을 좋아해.

B: **It's because that's what gets him off.**
그게 걜 흥분시키니까.

Our rapist is a foot fetishist. That's what gets him off. 이 강간범은 발 성도착증자야. 그게 그 놈을 흥분시키는거야.

I'm sure that's what gets him off, watching them burn.
그게 그 놈을 흥분시킨게 확실해, 그것들이 타는 걸 보는거 말야.

043 The only witness to this alleged murder is you 이 살인혐의의 유일한 증인은 당신이야

미드표현

this is indicating that the person is the only one to see someone killed. The speaker is saying "We need you to talk about the crime you saw"

| Point | eyewitness 목격자

A: **The only witness to** this alleged murder is you.
이 살인혐의의 유일한 증인은 당신이예요.

B: I guess I'll have to testify about it in court.
법정에서 증언해야 될 것 같네요.

These security cameras are the only witnesses we've got.
우리가 갖고 있는 유일한 증인은 이 보안카메라들이야.

You're interrogating our witness without me?
나 없이 우리 증인을 심문한다고?

There is an eyewitness to that murder.
저 살인사건에는 목격자가 있어.

044 Do you have a search warrant? 수색영장 있어요?

this is said by someone whose house is going to be looked at by the police. He wants to know "Do you have legal permission to look in my house?"

| Point | search warrant 수색영장

A: We need to check out your house. 당신 집을 수색해야겠어요.

B: **Do you have a search warrant?** 수색영장있어요?

I got a new warrant that covers his apartment.
그 사람의 아파트를 포함하는 새로운 영장이 있어.

Here's a warrant to search your premises.
당신 집을 수색할 영장이 여기 있습니다.

This is a warrant for all the computers in your possession. 당신 소유의 모든 컴퓨터를 조사할 수색영장입니다.

045 He pleads not guilty 그 사람은 죄를 인정하지 않아

미드표현

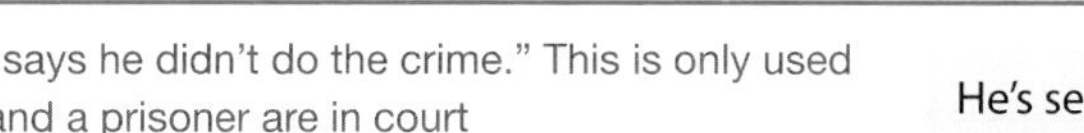

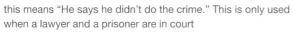

this means "He says he didn't do the crime." This is only used when a lawyer and a prisoner are in court

I Point I plead not guilty 죄를 인정하지 않다

A: How does the prisoner plead? 저 죄수의 주장은 뭡니까?

B: **He pleads not guilty,** Your Honor.
무죄를 주장합니다, 재판장님.

He's setting her up to plead not guilty by reason of mental disease or defect.
걔는 그녀를 꾀여서 정신병 혹은 정신결함으로 무죄를 주장하게끔 했어.

She pleads not guilty, Your Honor.
걔는 무죄를 주장합니다, 재판장님.

Russell Hunter for the defense. My client pleads not guilty.
피고측 변호인 러셀 헌터입니다. 제 고객은 무죄를 주장합니다.

He pleads guilty to the rape and assault three.
그는 세 번의 강간과 폭행죄를 인정합니다.

046 Stay with me 가지마, 침착해, (죽어가는 사람) 정신차려

미드표현

This has 3 meanings. First, this is a way to say "Don't go." The speaker wants someone to stay and not to leave. Second, this means "Don't die." The speaker wants someone to wait because he is badly injured and will die. It is like saying "stay because I don't want to die alone." Third, this means "Calm down and don't be too emotional." The speaker wants someone to act in a professional way in a stressful situation

I Point I You can't die on me(=Don't die on me) 죽지마

A: **Stay with me.** I want to tell you some things.
내 말 계속 들어. 뭔가 얘기해줄게.

B: I'm with you. What do you want to say?
듣고 있어. 무슨 말 하려고?

Don't go please! Just stay with me, please!
가지마 제발! 나하고 함께 있자, 제발!

Mike, this is a crime scene. Stay with me here, okay? Don't lose it.
마이크, 여긴 범죄현장이야. 침착해, 알았지? 망치지 말고.

Mr. Garris, can you see me? Can you hear me? Stay with me!
개리스 씨, 내가 보여요? 내 말 들려요? 정신차려요!

047 They offered a plea bargain 걔네들이 플리바게닝을 제안했어

미드표현

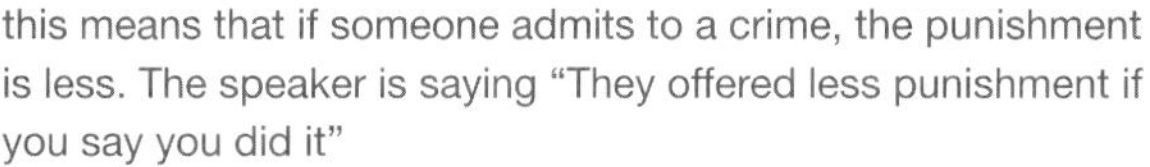

this means that if someone admits to a crime, the punishment is less. The speaker is saying "They offered less punishment if you say you did it"

I Point I plea bargain(ing) 유죄협상제, 유죄답변거래, 자백감형제.
피고가 죄를 시인하는 대가로 형량을 줄여주는 제도

A: I heard that the man will be in jail for two years.
저 사람은 2년간 징역산다며.

B: Yeah, **they offered him a plea bargain.**
어, 죄를 시인하는 대가로 감형받았어.

No! A plea bargain's out of the question. It's not guilty or nothing.
안돼! 유죄협상은 말도 안돼. 무죄가 아니면 아무 것도 안돼.

A plea bargain is our best chance to keep you out of jail. 유죄협상만이 감방에서 나오는 최선의 기회야.

She asked for a meeting to discuss a plea bargain. 그 여자는 유죄협상을 논의할 회의를 하자고 요구했어.

048 We found this on our John Doe 신원미상 시체에서 이걸 찾았어

미드표현

this indicates that something was with a dead person, and the police don't know who the dead person is. It is like saying "Maybe this item will help us find the dead person's name"

I Point I John Doe 남자 신원미상인 Jane Doe 여자 신원미상인

A: **We found this on our John Doe.**
신원미상 시체에서 이걸 찾았어.

B: It looks like an address book. 주소록 같은데.

Look at the bruise marks on John Doe here.
신원미상시체의 멍든 자국을 봐봐.

They're identified your John Doe, his wife is on the way.
신원미상 환자의 신원을 확인했고, 그 부인이 오는 중이야.

I recovered DNA from your Jane Doe skeleton.
신원미상 여자시신의 해골에서 DNA를 복구해냈어.

049 The coroner is beginning an autopsy
검시관이 검시를 시작했어

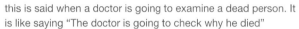

this is said when a doctor is going to examine a dead person. It is like saying "The doctor is going to check why he died"

| Point | coroner 검시관
autopsy 검시
lividity 시반
COD(cause of death) 사망원인
post(ante, peri) mortem 사망후(전, 당시)

A: How did that woman die? 여자의 사인이 뭐예요?
B: **The coroner is beginning an autopsy** to find out. 검시관이 검시를 시작했어요.

미드표현

The coroner is beginning an autopsy of the body of a woman.
검시관이 한 여인의 시신를 부검하기 시작했어.

According to forensic autopsy, she never gave birth.
법의학적 검시에 의하면 그 여자는 아기를 낳아본 적이 없어.

Cause of death was strangulation, but there's no fingerprint bruising.
사인은 교살이지만 지문이 묻은 멍은 없어.

050 He has not committed a crime 걘 죄를 짓지 않았어

this is saying "He is innocent." The speaker believes that someone didn't do something bad

| Point | commit a crime 죄를 짓다

A: Did Jerry do something that was illegal?
제리가 뭐 불법적인 것을 했나요?
B: No. **He has not committed a crime.**
아뇨. 걘 죄를 짓지 않았어요.

You commit a crime, you pay the price.
죄를 지었으니 대가를 치러야지.

He was in prison for one year for the crime he didn't commit. 걘 자기가 저지르지 않은 죄로 1년간 복역했었어.

You did the crime. 넌 죄를 지었어.

051 I'm clean 난 깨끗해(그 일과 상관없어, 무일푼이야), 난 결백해

this is a type of slang. It means "I didn't do anything wrong"

| Point | be clean 결백하다, 약물복용을 하지 않다

A: Have you been using illegal drugs?
불법 약물을 복용했어요?
B: No I haven't. **I'm clean.** 아뇨, 그런 적 없어요. 난 깨끗해요.

I was a drug addict. I'm clean now.
난 마약 중독자였지만 지금은 깨끗해.

I swear I'm clean. 맹세컨대 난 결백해.

I told her I'm clean now and getting my life together.
난 걔한테 난 지금 깨끗하고 다시 기운내서 살고 있다고 말했어.

052 That's our crime scene 여기는 우리가 담당하는 범죄현장이야

this phrase would be used by police officers, and it means "We are checking this area carefully because there was a big crime here"

A: Police officers were sent to 231 Maple Street.
경찰관들이 231 메이플 가로 출동했어.
B: **That's our crime scene.** Someone was murdered. 우리 범죄현장야. 누가 살해됐어.

We're not detectives. We're crime scene analysts. 우린 경찰이 아닙니다. 범죄현장분석가입니다.

I guess it's a good thing I sealed off that crime scene. 범죄현장을 봉쇄한 게 잘한 일 같아.

Your prints were found at a crime scene.
네 지문이 범죄현장에서 발견됐어.

053 I don't get high 난 약 안해

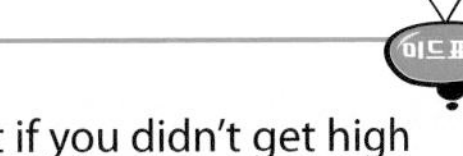

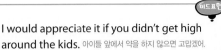

this means that the speaker does not use drugs like marijuana. When people experience the effects of smoking marijuana, we say they are getting high. This speaker is telling us "I don't smoke pot"

Point get high 술, 마약에 취하다 drug high 마약에 흥분한 상태

A: You want to go outside and smoke some dope?
밖에 나가서 약 좀 할테야?

B: No thanks. **I don't get high.** 아니 됐어. 난 약하지 않아.

I would appreciate it if you didn't get high around the kids. 아이들 앞에서 약을 하지 않으면 고맙겠어.

He sniffs chemicals to get high.
걔는 약에 취하기 위해 화약약품의 냄새를 맡아.

That's the same excuse people use to get high. 그건 사람들이 약을 하기 위해 하는 똑같은 변명이야.

They have to get high to have sex.
걔네들은 섹스를 하려면 약을 해야 돼.

054 Am I a suspect? 제가 용의자인가요?

this person is asking if the police think he committed a crime. It is the same as saying "Do you think I did it?"

Point primary suspect 주요용의자

A: We need to ask you some questions about the crime. 범죄에 대해 몇 가지 물어봐야 됩니다.

B: **Am I a suspect?** I swear I didn't do it.
제가 용의자인가요? 정말 난 그러지 않았어요.

I have only one suspect. 용의자가 딱 한 명이야.

Do you consider me a suspect?
나를 용의자로 생각하는 겁니까?

We got a suspect. But it's not who you think.
용의자가 있는데 네가 생각하는 사람이 아냐.

055 You're not gonna buy your way out of this one 넌 이번에는 그냥 넘어가지 못할거야

this speaker is telling someone that he is in trouble, and he will not be able to escape the trouble by using money. Perhaps the money would be used as a bribe, or to hire a powerful lawyer. It is similar to saying "All of your money can't help you now"

Point buy one's way out of sth (자신의 잘못을 뇌물이나 영향력을 발휘해) 곤경에 빠지지 않다, 그냥 넘어가다

A: I'll have my lawyers get me out of jail.
변호사들 시켜서 날 감방에서 빼내게 할거야.

B: **You're not going to buy your way out of this one.** 이번에는 그렇게 넘어가지 못할거야.

He tried to buy his way out of the criminal charges. 갠 범죄혐의에서 그냥 벗어나려고 했어.

Rich people can always buy their way out of trouble. 돈있는 사람들은 언제나 어려움에서 그냥 벗어나.

056 You're not gonna talk your way out of this one 넌 이 일에서 자유롭지 못할거야

this is said in order to tell someone that there will be a punishment for something bad that was done. We can understand that in the past the listener also did something bad, but was able to say things that allowed him to escape punishment. Now, the speaker is saying "This time there will be a penalty for your bad behavior"

Point talk one's way out of~ 어려운 상황을 설득해서 빠져나오다, 피하다

A: I didn't steal the jewelry. I swear it's true.
난 보석을 훔치지 않았어요. 정말이라니까요.

B: **You're not going to talk your way out of this one.** 이번에는 빠져나가지 못할거야.

I'm not talking my way out of this one.
난 변명을 대며 이 일을 피하지 않을거야.

If the other guys hadn't run, I could've talked my way out of it.
다른 사람들이 도망치지 못했다면, 난 말로 설득해서 빠져나올 수 있었을거야.

Depends on who you sold it to. You're not gonna talk your way out of this one.
그걸 누구에게 팔았냐에 따라 다르지. 넌 이 일을 회피하지 못할거야.

057 Give them what's coming to them 받아야 될 당연한 벌을 줘

this is a way to tell someone that he should give people what they are owed. This can mean that a debt is owed, or it can mean that a punishment is owed. We can guess that the people probably did something good to deserve a reward or payment, or something bad to deserve punishment. We can express this similarly by saying "Give them what they are due"

| Point | get[take] what's coming to sb 당연한 벌을 받다

A: The students will be spanked for cheating.
학생들은 부정행위로 체벌받을거야.

B: Okay, **give them what's coming to them.**
그래, 당연한 벌을 내리라고.

미드표현

And as far as the Graysons go, they'll get what's coming to them.
그레이슨 집안에 관한 한, 걔네들은 당연히 벌을 받을거야.

I want you to get exactly what's coming to you. 난 네가 당연한 벌을 받기를 원해.

058 You got him to take the rap for it 넌 걔가 죄를 뒤집어쓰게 했어

this is a way to say that one person committed a crime, but that another person is getting punished for the crime. For example, if a man is arrested for his friend's crime, he is taking the rap for his friend. We can also say "He is getting punished for the bad things someone else did"

| Point | take the rap for~ …대신에 죄를 뒤집어쓰다, 누명을 쓰다

A: I don't think our suspect committed the murder.
우리 용의자가 살인을 저지른 것 같지가 않아.

B: But **you got him to take the rap for it.**
하지만 넌 걔가 죄를 뒤집어 쓰게 했잖아.

미드표현

Why did you take the rap for Zack?
왜 네가 잭의 죄를 뒤집어쓴거야?

I'm gonna have to take the rap for it.
내가 죄를 뒤집어써야 되겠어.

You can't just let her take the rap for you.
걔가 네 대신 죄를 뒤집어쓰게 하면 안돼.

I'm saying that right now Patrick doesn't know that Jill took the rap for him.
패트릭은 질이 자기 대신 누명을 쓴 것을 지금 당장은 모르고 있다는거야.

059 The injuries are not consistent with an accident
상처는 사고와 일치하지 않아

this is used to say someone was hurt in an accident, not in a crime. The speaker means "This probably wasn't a crime"

| Point | be consistent with …와 일치하다
check the stomach contents 위 내용물을 확인하다
bruise 타박상을 입히다, 멍들게 하다 be beaten to death 맞아 죽다

A: Was this person killed by someone?
이 사람은 누군가에 의해 살해된 건가?

B: No, **his injuries are not consistent with an accident.** 아뇨, 부상이 사고와 일치하지 않아요.

미드표현

No other apparent injuries.
다른 눈에 보이는 상처는 없어.

There are bruise on her face and chest.
얼굴과 가슴에 타박상을 입었어.

She was beaten multiple times. 수없이 얻어맞았어.

The victim had been severely beaten.
피해자는 심각하게 얻어맞았어.

060 Let's make a run for it 도망가자, 빨리 피하자

this is a way to say "Let's run away from the police." The speaker hopes they won't be caught and won't have to go to jail

| Point | make a run for it = run for it = run for your life 도망치다
get away from it 도망치다 run off to 도망치다

A: I think we can get away before the cops come.
경찰이 오기 전에 도망갈 수 있을 것 같아.

B: Good. **Let's make a run for it.** 좋아, 빨리 피하자.

미드표현

Run for your life! Get out of the building!
도망쳐! 빌딩에서 나가!

Now, where did he run off to?
그래서 다음에는 그 친구가 어디로 도망쳤는데?

Should you lose your license, we could run off to New York together and become bartenders.
네가 면허를 잃게 되면 뉴욕으로 함께 도망가서 바텐더가 되자고.

061 I'm making a break for it 난 도망갈거야

미드표현

this expresses that the speaker is going to try to escape from some place without being caught. Most commonly we would hear this in reference to a prisoner who wants to escape from jail. A different way to say the same thing would be "I'll try to sneak away without anyone seeing me"

| Point | make a break for it 도망치다, 탈주하다

A: **I'm making a break for it** tonight. 나 오늘밤에 탈주할거야.

B: You'll be punished severely if you get caught. 너 잡히면 가중처벌 될거야.

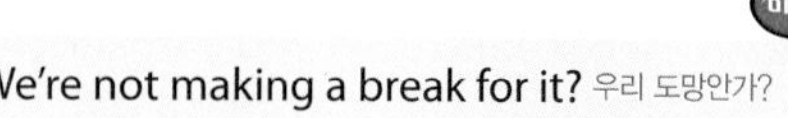

We're not making a break for it? 우리 도망안가?

Ok, I'm makin' a break for it, I'm goin' out the window. 좋아, 난 여길 빠져나가겠어, 창문으로 나갈꺼야.

What do we do? Hide in the back alley till the coast is clear, and when the door opens, make a break for it? 어떻게 하지? 붙잡힐 위험이 없을 때까지 뒷골목에서 숨어있다가 문이 열리면 도망칠까?

062 The killer is on the loose 살인범이 도주 중이야

미드표현

this is something that would be said after a murder has occurred. We can understand that the police have not found or arrested the killer yet, so it may be dangerous to be outside. It is a way to say "Be careful because the killer hasn't been caught by the police"

| Point | be on the loose 도망 중이다, 탈주 중이다

A: Have the cops caught the guy who murdered his wife? 경찰이 부인 살해범을 잡았어?

B: Not yet. **The killer is still on the loose.** 아직, 살인범이 도주중이야.

Well, we know there's a killer on the loose. 그래, 우리는 살인범이 탈주 중이라는 걸 알고 있어.

There is a serial killer on the loose. 한 연쇄살인범이 도주 중이야.

Half the government is going to be in one spot and we've got a terrorist on the loose. 정부인사의 반이 한 장소에 모이는데 테러범이 자유롭게 돌아다니고 있어.

063 Are you packing? 총을 소지하고 있어?

미드표현

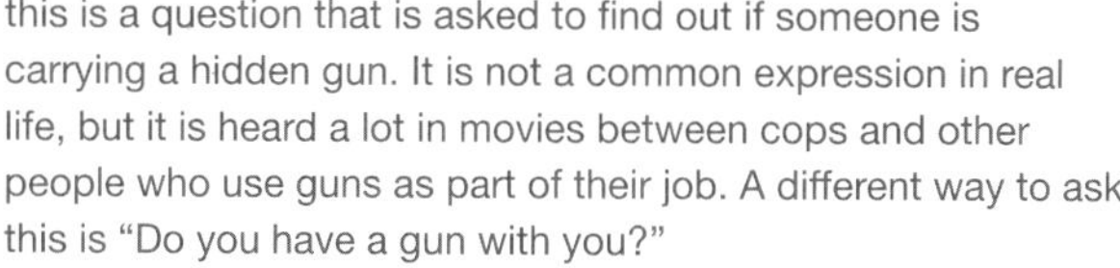

this is a question that is asked to find out if someone is carrying a hidden gun. It is not a common expression in real life, but it is heard a lot in movies between cops and other people who use guns as part of their job. A different way to ask this is "Do you have a gun with you?"

| Point | pack[carry] a gun 총을 지니다 have a gun 총을 가지고 있다
pull (out) a gun 총을 꺼내다
hold[put] a gun to sb's head 머리에 총을 겨누다

A: Those guys look like they want to rob the bank. 저 사람들은 은행을 털고 싶어하는 것 같아.

B: I see them. **Are you packing?** 그들이 보이는데 너 총갖고 있어?

So, why are you packing? 그럼, 왜 총을 갖고 다니는거야?

Do you have a permit for a gun, sir? 선생님, 총기 허가증을 갖고 계십니까?

I didn't know he carried a gun. 난 걔가 총을 지니고 다니는지 몰랐어.

He put a gun to my head and came very close to pulling the trigger. 걘 총을 내 머리에 겨누고 방아쇠를 당기기 바로 직전이었어.

064 Drop your weapon! 총 버려!, 무기 버려!

미드표현

this is telling a person "Let go of your knife or gun!" This is said when a policeman sees a criminal with something dangerous

| Point | Don't move! 꼼짝마!, 움직이지마! Get down! 몸을 낮춰!, 꿇어!

A: **Drop your weapon!** 총 버려!

B: I will put it down right now. 바로 내려놓을게요.

Freeze! Stop right there! Or I'll shoot! 꼼짝마! 움직이지마! 아니면 쏜다!

Stay right where you are! Don't move! 꼼짝마! 움직이지마!

Hands on your head. Down on your knees! 머리에 손 올려. 무릎 꿇어!

065 Stop right there! 꼼짝마!

very simply, this means "Don't move." It is often said by a policeman to a person who is running away

| Point | Stay[Remain] where you are! 꼼짝마!
Hold still! 꼼짝마!
(Get) (Down) On your knees! 무릎꿇어!

A: **Stop right there!** I want to talk to you.
꼼짝마! 얘기 좀 하자.

B: Why? I haven't done anything wrong.
왜? 난 아무 나쁜 짓도 안했어.

Federal agents. Everyone stay where you are.
연방요원이다. 다들 꼼짝마.

Don't even think about it. Don't move!
꿈도 꾸지마. 꼼짝마!

Don't move! Get down on your knees.
움직이지마! 무릎꿇어.

066 (Put your) Hands on your head! 손들어!, 손 머리위로!

this is said by a policeman. He is telling a criminal "I want to see that your hands have nothing bad in them"

| Point | (Put your) Hands on the back of your head! 손 머리뒤로!
Get your hands up! 손들어!
Get out of the truck! 차에서 나와!
Spread your legs! 다리 벌려!

A: Do you need to arrest me? 날 체포해야 돼요?

B: Yes. **Put your hands on your head.** 어. 손 머리 위로.

Police! Get your hands up! 경찰이다! 손들어!

Step away from the truck, put your hands on the back of your head! 트럭에서 떨어지고 손 머리 뒤로해!

Let's see your hands! Get your hands up!
손을 보여봐! 손들어!

Police! Step out of the vehicle with your hands up! 경찰이다! 두손들고 차 밖으로 나와!

067 We're clear in here 여기 안전해, 무사해

It means "We checked and everything is OK." The speaker is saying that he thinks things are safe

| Point | We're (all) clear 안전해, 무사해
clear the house 집을 안전하게 비우다

A: Clear the house. There may be a bomb here.
집을 안전하게 조사해. 폭탄이 있을 지 몰라.

B: **It's clear.** There were no bombs inside.
안전합니다. 안에 폭탄이 없습니다.

Clear. We need medical here. 안전해. 의료진이 필요해.

Clear over here. 이곳은 안전해.

Bathroom's clear. 침실은 안전해.

NYPD! Clear the hall! 뉴욕경찰이다! 복도 다 비켜!

068 This court is adjourned 재판을 휴정합니다

this is a way to say "Court is finished today." We can understand that everyone will leave the courtroom now

| Point | adjourn the court 재판을 휴정하다
We'll take a 10 minute recess 10분간 휴회합니다

A: **This court is adjourned** for today.
오늘 재판을 그만 휴정합니다.

B: Well, I guess we can all go home now.
어, 이제 집에 갈 수 있겠군.

Ladies and gentlemen of the jury, thank you for your service. We're adjourned!
배심원 여러분 감사드립니다. 휴정하겠습니다!

The defendant is free to go. We're adjourned.
피고는 가도 좋습니다. 휴정합니다.

The defendant stays in custody. We are adjourned. 피고를 수감하고 휴정합니다.

Courts recessed until one thirty.
1시 30분까지 휴회합니다.

069 We're a long way from a conviction

유죄판결을 받으려면 아직 멀었어

미드표현

this would be said by a lawyer. It is like saying "It will be hard to show he is guilty"

| Point | conviction 유죄의 판결, 신념 prior conviction 전과
ex-con 전과자 rap sheet 전과기록
larceny 절도죄 felony 중죄
perjury 위증죄

A: I think he's guilty and should go to jail.
난 걔가 유죄이고 감방에 가야 한다고 생각해.

B: **We're a long way from a conviction.**
유죄판결을 받으려면 아직 멀었어.

For a conviction, we're going to need a DNA sample. 유죄판결을 받으려면 DNA샘플이 필요할거야.

He's got six prior convictions for larceny and burglary. 걘 절도죄, 주거침입죄로 6번 전과가 있어.

I'm not that kind of man. I'm an ethical man. A man of conviction.
난 그런 사람이 아냐. 도덕적인 사람이야. 신념있는 사람말야.

070 You are free to go 무죄석방입니다, 가도 됩니다

미드표현

this is something the police say. It means "You can leave now"

A: Do I have to stay here any longer?
더 여기에 있어야 합니까?

B: No. **You are free to go** now. 아뇨. 이제 가도 됩니다.

The jury is dismissed with our thanks. The defendant is free to go.
배심원 여러분 수고에 감사드립니다. 피고는 자유입니다.

I'm dismissing the charges against her. The defendant is free to go.
그 여자에 대한 기소를 취하합니다. 피고는 자유입니다.

071 The court will hold you in contempt

당신을 법정 모독죄로 구속하겠습니다

미드표현

this is a way to say "You may be punished because you didn't cooperate." Sometimes this is said when a witness doesn't want to speak about something

| Point | contempt of court 법정모독
hold sb in contempt 법정모독으로 체포하다

A: I am not going to testify. 증언하지 않을 겁니다.

B: **The court will hold you in contempt** if you don't. 그러면 법정 모독죄로 구속하겠습니다.

If you don't put that phone down, I'm going to hold you in contempt.
그 전화를 내려놓지 않으면 법정모독으로 당신을 체포할 겁니다.

The judge is going to find her in contempt.
판사는 그녀에게 법정모욕죄를 내릴거야.

If I don't give her your name, I will be found in contempt.
내가 걔한테 네 이름을 말하지 않으면 난 법정모독죄를 받을거야.

Before I find you in contempt

The Big Bang Theory
SEASON#3-16

과속으로 걸린 Sheldon은 어쩔 수 없는 상황이었다며 법정에 나와 스스로를 변호하다 특유의 깐죽거림으로 판사의 심기를 불편하게 하는데…

Sheldon: I object. You're completely ignoring the law.
Judge: No, I'm following the law. I'm ignoring you.
Sheldon: Really? I would point out that I am at the top of my profession, while you preside over the kiddy table of yours.
Judge: Dr. Cooper, before I find you in contempt and throw you in jail, I'm going to give you a chance to apologize for that last remark.
Sheldon: I am a scientist. I never apologize for the truth.

쉘든: 이의 있습니다. 판사님은 전적으로 법을 무시하고 계십니다.
판사: 아뇨, 난 법을 따르고 있습니다. 당신을 무시할 뿐입니다.
쉘든: 정말요? 저는 제 직업 최고의 자리에 위치해 있고 판사님은 유치한 테이블에 앉아 있네요.
판사: 쿠퍼 박사, 법정모독죄로 감방에 처넣기 전에 마지막 발언에 사과할 기회를 주겠어요.
쉘든: 전 과학자입니다. 사실에 대해서 사과하지 않습니다.

072 She's on parole 걔는 가석방됐어

this means a woman has been released from prison on the condition that she periodically reports to an officer to make sure she is behaving properly. To be on parole is very similar to being on probation. It is like saying "She was released from jail and was put on parole"

| Point | on parole 가석방되어 parole board 가석방 위원회
parole hearing 가석방 청문회

A: Can Pam travel overseas? 팸은 해외여행을 할 수 있어?
B: She's not allowed. **She's on parole.**
걔는 안돼. 가석방 중이야.

미드표현

He's serving a life sentence without the possibility of parole. 걔는 가석방없는 종신형을 살고 있어.

The judge sentenced me to life with no chance of parole. 판사는 내게 가석방없는 종신형을 선고했어.

Why do I have to do it? I'm on parole, Caroline. 내가 왜 그래야 하는데? 캐롤린, 난 가석방 중이야.

073 He did a year on probation 걘 보호관찰 1년을 살았어

this speaker is saying that a man had gotten in legal trouble, and possibly was in jail, and after being released he had to report to an probation officer at least once a month for a year to make certain he was behaving properly. In other words, "He was on parole for a year"

| Point | be on probation 보호관찰 중이다 probation officer 보호관찰관(PO)
put[place] sb on probation 보호관찰처분을 내리다

A: I think our suspect has been in trouble with the law. 우리 용의자가 법적으로 문제가 있었을거라 생각해.
B: **He did a year on probation.** 그는 보호관찰 1년을 살았어.

미드표현

I heard she freaked out and killed a guy and had to go on probation.
걔가 기겁을 해서 한 남자를 살해해 보호관찰 중이래.

I recently discovered that he is on probation for assault.
걔가 폭행죄로 보호관찰 중이라는 걸 최근에 알게 되었어.

I got a record, and I was on probation.
난 전과가 있었고 보호관찰 중이었어.

074 He paid his debt to society 걔는 죄값을 치렀어

this is something that is said when referring to criminals who have been in jail. To serve time as a punishment in jail is said to be paying a debt to society for doing illegal things. So we can understand that this means "He finished the jail sentence for his crime"

| Point | pay one's debt to society 불법을 저지른 사람이 죄값을 치루다, 복역하다

A: Carlos is getting out of prison after eleven years. 카를로스는 11년만에 출소해.
B: He'll be free. **He paid his debt to society.**
걘 자유의 몸이야. 죄값을 치렀어.

미드표현

My client paid his debt to society.
내 의뢰인은 죄값을 치렀어.

Mr. Danes paid his debt to society. And he pays his rent on time.
데인즈 씨는 죄값을 치렀고 또한 임대료도 제 때에 내고 있어.

He's paid his debt to society, but we know that there's a greater debt.
걔는 죄값을 치렀지만 더 큰 빚이 있다는 것을 우리는 알고 있어.

075 She took her own life 걘 자살했어

this is a way to say that a woman intentionally killed herself. Many times when this happens, it is because the person has been depressed or had mental problems, although sometimes older people do it because they have serious health issues. Another way that we can say this is "She committed suicide"

| Point | take one's own life 자살하다 hang oneself 자살하다

A: Tell me how the old woman died.
그 노부인이 어떻게 죽었는지 말해봐.
B: She had cancer, and **she took her own life.**
암이었는데 자살하셨어.

미드표현

Do you have any idea why your husband wanted to take his own life?
남편이 왜 자살을 원했는지 혹 아십니까?

The last time I spoke to Orson, he intimated that he would take his own life.
내가 지난번에 올슨을 만났을 때 걘 자살을 하겠다고 협박을 했어.

I feel better knowing that he didn't take his own life. 걔가 자살을 하지 않았다는 것을 아니 맘이 편해지네.

076 We came by to pay our respects 조의를 표하기 위해 왔어

미드표현

this is something people say to the family of a dead person when they attend a funeral. It means they have come to honor the memory of that person. Basically, what they are saying is "We want to show how much we respected this person"

| Point | pay one's respects 조의를 표하다(at the wake or funeral)
go to the funeral 장례식에 가다
rest in peace 편히 잠들다

A: **We came by to pay our respects** to your dad.
우리는 네 아버지께 조의를 표하러 왔어.

B: We appreciate you attending his funeral.
아버지 장례식에 와주셔서 감사드려요.

I came to pay my respects to Mrs. Dunford.
던포드 부인께 조의를 표하기 위해 왔어요.

I barely even knew her, but I feel like I had to pay my respects.
그녀를 거의 알지 못하지만 조의를 표해야 될 것 같았어.

I have to go pay my respects. We don't have time for this. 난 가서 조의를 표해야 돼. 이럴 시간이 없어.

I said I'd go to the funeral. I didn't say when.
내가 장례식에 갈거라고 말했지 언제 간다고는 말하지 않았어.

Ways of talking about being sick or injured

아프면 병원에 가서 치료를 받아야

I just had a physical

001 I just had a physical 건강검진을 받았어

this means that someone went to a doctor in order to get his body checked to see if he had any health problems. Many people get a physical once a year. We often see this expressed as "I just had a checkup by my doctor"

I Point I get[do, have] a physical 건강검진받다

A: Have you been to a doctor recently?
너 최근에 병원에 간 적 있어?

B: **I just had a physical.** Everything is fine.
건강검진을 받았는데 다 괜찮대.

미드표현

The admitting intern shipped her off to Psych. Barely did a physical.
입원담당 인턴이 걔를 정신과로 보냈어. 건강상태를 검사하지도 않고 말야.

A: You're dying of kidney failure. B: That's impossible, I just had a physical.
A: 당신은 신부전으로 죽어가고 있어요. B: 말도 안돼요. 얼마전 건강검진을 했는데요.

You need to fill out a detailed medical history. Then we'll schedule you for a physical.
병력을 자세히 적으세요. 그럼 건강검진을 위해 일정을 잡을게요.

002 Does it still hurt? 아직도 아파?

this person is asking "Do you feel pain now?" Often this would be asked about an injury from the past

I Point I 신체+hurts …가 아프다
hurt+신체 …가 아프다, 상처입다
It hurts like hell 너무 아파
Now this may hurt 내가 하는 말이 상처를 줄 수도 있을거야

A: This summer I injured my leg. 이번 여름에 다리 다쳤어.

B: **Does it still hurt** right now? 지금도 여전히 아파?

미드표현

I'm sick. My ankle still hurts. 아파. 발목이 여전히 아파.

It's my foot. It hurts like crazy. I'm gonna need a pain killer. 다리야. 정말 미치게 아파. 진통제가 필요할거야.

My foot is still hurting. Do you have any aspirin? 내 발이 아직도 아파. 아스피린 가진거 있어?

003 I'm under the weather 몸이 별로 안 좋아, 몸이 찌뿌둥해

usually this is a way to say "I'm sick." The speaker wants others to know he isn't feeling well

I Point I be under the weather 몸의 상태가 안 좋다, 아프다
I'm crabby 짜증나다, 심통이 나다
I'm grouchy 난 짜증이 나
He's taken ill 병에 걸렸어

A: Why don't you want to go to the party?
왜 파티에 안 가려고 해?

B: **I'm under the weather** and don't feel good.
몸이 찌뿌둥하고 상태가 안 좋아.

미드표현

She could not be here tonight because she's a little under the weather.
걘 몸이 좀 안 좋아서 오늘밤 여기 올 수 없었어.

I'm not crabby. I'm devastated.
난 짜증이 나는 게 아니라 완전히 망가졌어.

Why are you so crabby? Bad day at the office?
왜 그렇게 짜증부려? 사무실에서 안 좋았어?

004 What're the symptoms? 증상이 어때요?

this is asking "What problems are you having?" The person wants to know what kind of sickness it is

I Point I What seems to be the problem? 어디가 아프십니까?
How (are) you feeling? 몸은 좀 어때요?

A: I feel really sick today. 오늘 정말 몸이 안 좋아.

B: **What are the symptoms** of your sickness?
증상이 어때?

미드표현

A: What seems to be the problem? B: I think I'm about to have a nervous breakdown.
A: 어디가 안 좋아? B: 신경쇠약에 걸릴 것 같아.

It's a symptom of borderline personality disorder. 그건 경계선 인격장애증상이야.

He didn't have any symptoms when she took him to the park.
걔가 그를 공원에 데려갔을 때는 아무런 증상이 없었어.

005 She popped a few vicodin 걘 바이코딘 몇 알을 먹었어

this is a way to say that a woman took several pills that are used as painkillers. Vicodin is a strong drug, and while it's used to stop pain, some people become addicted to it and take it illegally, which can lead to a person being arrested. It is similar to saying "She swallowed several painkillers"

| Point | be popping pills 약을 많이 복용하다
pop a+약물 …약을 먹다

A: Was Jenny in pain after she hurt her leg?
제니는 다리를 다친 후에 아파했어?

B: She was, but then **she popped a few Vicodin.**
그랬는데 바이코딘 몇 알을 먹었어.

Is Sheila popping pills again?
쉴라가 다시 약을 복용하고 있어?

I have no idea what they are but just popping a few can't hurt.
그 약들이 뭔지 모르지만 몇 알 먹는다고 어떻게 되지는 않을거야.

You worried I'm going to be popping more pills? 내가 약을 더 많이 먹을까봐 걱정했구나?

006 She passed out behind the wheel 운전하다 정신을 잃었어

this means a woman was in the driver's seat of a car and then lost control of her body. It might be due to sickness or due to alcohol or drugs. It is saying "She lost consciousness while driving"

| Point | pass[black] out 졸도하다, 기절하다

A: Mary was really drunk at the party last night.
메리는 어제 밤 파티에서 정말 취했어.

B: **She passed out behind the wheel** and crashed her car. 운전하다 정신을 잃고 차를 부셔뜨렸어.

Everything's gonna be fine, Bob. You passed out in my car.
밥, 다 괜찮아요. 내 차에서 네가 의식을 잃었어.

I found her passed out on her front lawn, drunk as a skunk.
걔가 자기 앞마당에 만취해서 쓰러져있는 걸 발견했어.

I don't remember much after that. I blacked out. 그 이후론 기억이 안나. 정신을 잃었거든.

007 I think I'm about to have a nervous breakdown
신경쇠약에 걸릴 것 같아

this is a way to say "Stress is making me crazy." A person who has a nervous breakdown has psychological problems and acts strangely

| Point | nervous breakdown 신경쇠약

A: I think I'm about to **have a nervous breakdown.** 신경 쇠약에 걸릴 것 같아.

B: What is making you so stressed out?
뭐 때문에 그렇게 스트레스를 받는거야?

You're not gonna have a nervous breakdown and kill yourself, are you?
신경쇠약증에 걸려서 자살하지는 않겠지, 그지?

Leave me alone. I'm a woman on the verge of a nervous breakdown.
나 좀 가만히 둬. 나 신경쇠약 직전인 여자야.

008 Do you suffer from insomnia? 불면증에 시달려?

this is asking if a person can't sleep. It is like saying "Can you sleep when you go to bed?"

| Point | suffer from …을 겪다

A: I couldn't get to sleep at all last night.
간밤에 전혀 잠을 잘 수가 없었어.

B: **Do you suffer from insomnia?** 불면증에 시달리는거야?

Do you suffer from headaches, allergies, or diabetes? 두통, 앨러지, 당뇨병을 앓고 있나요?

More than 1.5 million Americans suffer from Alzheimer's Disease.
백 오십만 이상의 미국인이 알츠하이머 병을 앓고 있어.

009 Your blood pressure is stable now 이제 혈압이 안정되었어

this indicates the person's heart is working normally. It is a way to say "Everything seems OK with your heart now"

| Point | blood pressure 혈압
high blood pressure 고혈압

A: How is my overall health, doctor?
전반적인 건강상태가 어떤가요, 선생님?

B: Good. **Your blood pressure is stable now.**
좋습니다. 혈압이 이제 정상입니다.

미드표현

Your blood pressure's higher than it should be. 혈압이 정상보다 높아요.

I had high blood pressure, high cholesterol, and diabetes. 고혈압에 콜레스테롤이 높고 당뇨가 있어.

Well, your blood pressure looks fine. You're free to go. 어, 혈압이 정상으로 보이네요. 가셔도 됩니다.

010 I think you've got a concussion 너 뇌진탕인 것 같아

the speaker thinks someone hit his head hard and it may have damaged something. It's very similar to saying "I think you hurt yourself when you hit your head"

| Point | concussion 뇌진탕

A: Ow! I just hit my head and it hurts!
어! 내가 머리를 부딪혀서 아파!

B: **I think you've got a concussion.** 뇌진탕인 것 같아.

미드표현

The cable guy fell. He hit his head on the tub. He may have a concussion.
케이블설치기사가 떨어졌어. 통에 머리를 부딪혔는데 아마 뇌진탕일지도 몰라.

Mr. Young was very lucky. He only suffered a slight concussion.
영 씨는 아주 운이 좋았어. 약한 뇌진탕이 왔을 뿐이었어.

011 It's just a headache 그냥 머리가 좀 아파

this speaker is expressing "I'm OK, even though my head hurts." He doesn't want people to worry about him

| Point | My head feels heavy 머리가 무거워
My head hurts 머리가 아파
My head is killing me 머리 아파 죽겠어
migraine 편두통

A: You should rest for a while. 너 잠시 쉬어야겠어.

B: I'm OK. **It's just a headache.**
난 괜찮아. 그냥 머리가 좀 아픈거야.

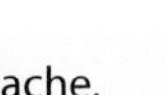

미드표현

She was complaining of a headache.
걔는 머리가 아프다고 호소하고 있었어.

He has no headaches, no neck pain, his CT is clean. 걘 두통도 없고 목통증도 없고 CT도 깨끗해.

By the way, my leg is killing me.
그런데, 내 다리가 아파 죽겠어.

012 I'm gonna get fat again 다시 살찌겠어

we can understand this person was fat in the past, but is thin now. He is saying "I'm doing something that will make me gain weight again"

| Point | I'm getting fat 살이 찌고 있어
I've put on[gained] weight 살이 쪘어

A: Here, have another piece of cake. 케익 한조각 더 먹어.

B: But **I'm going to get fat again** if I eat too much.
하지만 내가 더 먹으면 살이 다시 찔거야.

미드표현

Are you gonna break up with me if I get fat again? 내가 다시 살이 찐다면 나랑 헤어질거야?

Everyone gains weight in college, Mom. It's stressful. 엄마, 대학에서는 다 살쪄요. 스트레스를 많이 받아서.

Some students get fat while at university.
일부 학생들은 대학교 다닐 때 살이 쪄.

013 She's still running a fever 걔 아직 열이나

this indicates "Her body is still too hot." It usually means a sickness is causing the body to heat up

| Point | have[run] a fever = have a high temperature 열이 나다
I think I have a fever 열이 있는 것 같아
I'm running a fever 열이 나요

A: Is Patti feeling better today? 오늘 패티 상태가 좋아?
B: **She's still running a fever.** 여전히 열이 나.

I'm really fine. I just have a fever.
정말 괜찮아. 열이 좀 있을 뿐이야.

The liver temp is 98 degrees which is odd unless she's running a fever.
간 온도가 화씨 98도인데 열이 나지 않았다면 이상한 경우지.

If you have an infection, you'd have a fever.
네가 감염되었으면 열이 났을거야.

014 My foot is cramping 다리에 쥐가 나

the speaker is expressing that his foot hurts from using it too much. It is a way to say "My foot has become painful"

| Point | cramp (손발) 경련(이 나다), 복통(이 나다)
leg cramp 다리에 난 쥐
sprain 삐다, 삠, 접질림
She sprained her knee 무릎에 골절이 생겼어

A: Why are you stopping during the race?
경주 중에 왜 멈추는거야?
B: **My foot is cramping** and I can't run anymore.
다리가 쥐가 나서 더 이상 달릴 수가 없어.

Have you had any cramping, any contractions, anything at all?
경련이라든가, 수축이라든가 뭐 다른 거 걸린 적 있어?

My cramp's still there. I'm gonna take my sock off. 아직 경련이 나. 양말을 벗을게.

I sprained my finger playing tennis.
테니스하다가 손가락을 삐었어.

He said it was just a sprain, and that was it.
그냥 삔 거래. 그게 다고.

015 You fractured a rib 갈비뼈가 부러졌어

this is telling someone "You hurt your chest." The person did something that damaged a bone in his chest

A: Why does my chest hurt so much?
왜 이리 가슴이 아픈거야?
B: **You fractured a rib** during your accident.
사고 중에 갈비뼈가 부러졌어.

You fractured a rib, and you might have a concussion. 갈비뼈가 부러졌어 뇌진탕이 올지 몰라.

The impact of the bullet on your chest fractured a rib. 가슴에 박힌 총알의 충격이 갈비뼈를 부러뜨렸어.

65-year-old man came into the ER with a hip fracture. 65세의 노인이 둔부골절로 응급실에 들어왔어요.

016 He had the runs 걔 설사했어

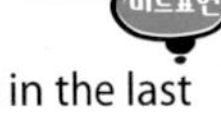

this is a way to say "He had diarrhea." This man had to use the toilet a lot because his stomach was sick

| Point | He has diarrhea = He has the runs = He has the trots
걔 설사야

A: George seemed to have gotten food poisoning.
조지는 식중독에 걸렸던 것 같았어.
B: Yeah, **he had the runs** for a while.
그래, 한동안 설사했었다.

Have you had any bloody diarrhea in the last two weeks? 지난 2주간 피가 섞인 설사를 한 적이 있나요?

I've had no diarrhea, no sweating, no vomiting. 설사도 안하고, 식은 땀도 안나고 구토도 안했어요.

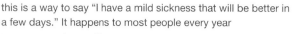

017 I'm coming down with a cold 감기 기운이 있어

this is a way to say "I have a mild sickness that will be better in a few days." It happens to most people every year

| Point | come down with (병)…에 걸리다

A: Why are you staying at home? 왜 집에 있는거야?

B: **I'm coming down with a cold.** 감기 기운이 있어서.

미드표현

I hope he's not coming down with a cold.
걔가 감기에 걸리지 않길 바래.

I think I'm just coming down with a migraine.
편두통이 오는 것 같아.

I'm kinda tired and my wrist hurts and I think I'm coming down with the flu.
좀 피곤하고 팔목이 아파요. 독감에 걸린 것 같아요.

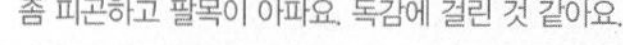

018 My ears are ringing 귀가 멍멍해

often this is said when someone has heard a very loud noise. It indicates "There is a strange sound in my ears"

| Point | My ears are burning (누가 내 얘길 하는지) 귀가 간지럽다
My nose is stuffed up 코가 막혔어
I have a frog in my throat 나 목이 쉬었어

A: **My ears are ringing** right now. 지금 귀가 멍멍해.

B: Mine too. I think the concert was too loud.
나도 그래. 콘서트 소리가 너무 큰 것 같아.

미드표현

I can't hear a word you're saying, my ears are ringing so bad. 네 말 하나도 안 들려. 귀가 너무 멍멍해.

He picked up the telephone, answering it with a frog in his throat.
걘 전화기를 들고서 쉰 목소리로 대답했어.

019 You have bad breath 네 입 냄새 심해

this is said when a person has a bad smell when he breathes. It can mean "You should brush your teeth"

| Point | body odor[BO] 체취, 암내

A: I think **you have bad breath.** 너 입냄새가 심한 것 같아.

B: Should I start using mouthwash?
구강청결제를 쓰기 시작해야 할까?

미드표현

This must be what bad breath tastes like.
이건 입냄새와 같은 걸거야.

Does your girlfriend have B.O.? 네 여친 암내나?

I can't date you because you've got bad breath. 네 입냄새가 너무 심해서 데이트 못하겠다.

020 You need stitches 꿰매야 돼

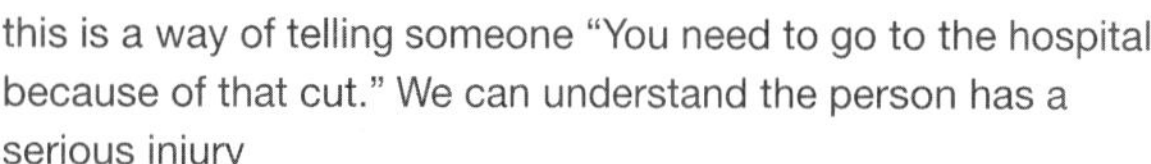

this is a way of telling someone "You need to go to the hospital because of that cut." We can understand the person has a serious injury

| Point | stitch (의학) 상처를 꿰매는 한 바늘
stitch up 꿰매다

A: Do you think this wound on my arm is serious?
내 팔에 난 상처가 심한 것 같아요?

B: Oh yeah. **You need stitches** to close it.
어 그래요. 봉합하기 위해 꿰매야 돼요.

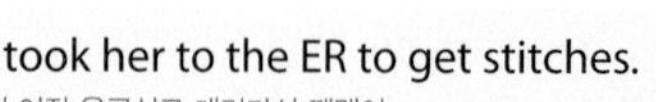

미드표현

I took her to the ER to get stitches.
저 여잘 응급실로 데려가서 꿰맸어.

She needs stitches. Stop the bleeding and stitch her up. 저 여자는 꿰매야 돼. 지혈하고 꿰매도록 해.

You're going to need about six stitches.
6바늘 정도 꿰매야 될 것 같아요.

This is a bad cut. You need stitches.
심하게 베었네. 꿰매야 되겠어.

021 I'm going to be under the knife 수술을 받을거야

미드표현

this person is saying "I will have a serious operation." It is usually said before someone goes to the hospital to be operated on

I Point I go[be] under the knife 수술을 받다, 수술을 받고 있다

A: How serious is the operation you will have?
수술이 얼마나 심각한거야?

B: **I'm going to be under the knife** for several hours. 여러 시간 수술을 받을거야.

Carrie is going under the knife because of the cancer she has. 캐리는 암때문에 수술 받을거야.

A lot of celebrities go under the knife to improve their appearance.
많은 유명인들이 외모를 예쁘게 하기 위해 수술을 받아.

My mom has a great fear of going under the knife. 엄마는 수술받는 걸 무척 무서워하셔.

022 I'm not gonna scrub in for surgery

난 수술에 들어가지 않을거야

미드표현

this is specific to an operating room in a hospital, and the speaker is saying that he is not going to wash his hands for an operation. Because of this, we can presume that he is not going to participate in the operation. A different way to say this is "I'm won't wash up to prepare for the operation"

I Point I scrub in 수술전 손세척하다, 수술에 참여하다
scrub room 수술실

A: Why are you waiting outside the operating room? 너 왜 수술실 밖에서 기다리는거야?

B: **I'm not going to scrub in for surgery.**
난 수술에 들어가지 않을거야.

I'll come out and check on you before I scrub in. 내가 수술들어가기 전에 나와서 널 살펴봐줄게.

You'll scrub in for an adipectomy this afternoon. Congratulations.
오늘 오후에 있는 맹장수술에 들어가게 될거야. 축하해.

He has scrubbed in and is washing his hands in the prep room.
걔는 수술 준비실에서 손을 문질러 깨끗이 닦았어.

023 I have to go make the rounds 회진 돌아야 돼

미드표현

this is used to say that a doctor or nurse must go through the hospital rooms to check on the health of the patients in them. Medical people have to do rounds within a certain time span throughout their work shift. The speaker is saying "I have to go look over my patients now"

I Point I do (one's) rounds 회진하다
make the(one's) rounds 회진하다, 둘러보다, 돌다
go on rounds 회진을 돌다
have rounds 회진이 있다
be on rounds 회진중이다

A: Can you stay and talk with me for a while?
잠시동안 남아서 나랑 얘기 좀 할래?

B: Sorry, **I have to go make the rounds.**
미안, 나 회진 돌아야 돼.

I'll see you on rounds. 회진 때 보자고.

We really should get some sleep before rounds. 회진 전에 정말 잠 좀 자야 돼.

I gotta go. I'm late for rounds. 가야 돼. 회진에 늦었어.

I'm not a patient anymore, so I don't have to be at rounds. 난 이제 환자가 아니니 회진 때 있을 필요가 없어.

Ways of talking about food and drink

먹고 마시고

Want some more?

001 Let's grab a bite 좀 먹자, 뭐 좀 먹으러 가자

this speaker wants to eat a quick meal. He is saying "Let's go to a restaurant and eat something fast"

| Point | grab[take] a bite (to eat) 간단히 먹다, 간단히 요기하다

A: **Let's grab a bite** to eat after the meeting.
회의 후에 간단히 요기하자.

B: Can we get some Chinese food? 중국식으로 먹을까?

Would you like to grab a bite later?
나중에 간단히 좀 먹을래?

Give me a bite! I'm starving. 한 입만! 배고파 죽겠단말야.

We were just going to go grab a bite to eat.
우리 나가서 간단히 요기하려던 참이었어.

002 Let's eat something! 뭘 좀 먹자!

this is a way to express "I'm hungry." The speaker wants to eat some food

A: **Let's eat something** soon. 빨리 뭐 좀 먹자.

B: I didn't realize you were so hungry. 네가 배고픈지 몰랐네.

Let's eat something because I'm getting really hungry. 정말 배고프니 뭐 좀 먹자.

Have you had lunch yet? Let's eat something.
아직 점심 안 먹었어? 뭐 좀 먹자.

Let's eat something at one of these seafood restaurants. 이 씨푸드식당에서 뭐 좀 먹자.

003 Let's dig into this turkey 칠면조 먹자

this speaker is saying "I want to start eating the turkey." We can understand there is turkey being served and the speaker is hungry

| Point | dig in(to) 먹다, (땅을) 파다, 밀어넣다
Dig in 자, 먹자, 들어
Trick or treat! 사탕줄래 골탕먹을래!

A: Happy Thanksgiving everyone. **Let's dig into this turkey.** 다들 추수감사절 축하해. 칠면조 먹자.

B: Everything looks so delicious on the table.
식탁 위에 있는 것들이 다 정말 맛있게 보여.

Well, dig in. I am way too tired to eat.
자 먹어. 난 너무 피곤해서 못 먹겠어.

Trick or treat! I'd like some candy.
사탕줄래 골탕먹을래! 사탕 좀 주세요.

I say screw etiquette. Let's dig in.
예의는 집어치우고. 어서 먹자고.

004 Come and get it 자 와서 먹자, 자 밥먹게 와라

this is a way of telling people "The food is ready." This is said so people come to the table to eat

| Point | Soup's on! 식사준비 다 되었어!
Dinner is served 식사가 준비되었어

A: **Come and get it!** 자 와서 밥먹어!

B: I guess the food is all prepared. 음식이 다 준비된 것 같아.

Come and get it. I have fruit and hard boiled eggs. 와서 밥 먹어라. 과일하고 삶은 달걀야.

Would you please take your seats? Dinner is served. 다들 자리에 좀 앉을래? 식사 준비되었어.

Hey! Hey! You want some?! Come and get it!
야! 더 먹고 싶어?! 어서 와서 먹어!

005 (Do you) Want some more? 더 들래?, 더 먹을래?

usually this is asking if a person wants more food. It is like asking "Are you still hungry?"

| Point | Do you want some more (~)? (…을) 더 들래?
Have some more (sth) (…을) 좀 더 들어
Do you want a bite of this? 이거 들어볼래?, 좀 먹어볼래?

A: This blueberry pie was very good.
이 블루베리 파이는 정말 맛있었어.

B: **Do you want some more?** 더 들래?

You want some more coffee? 커피 좀 더 마실테야?

Want some more wine? 와인 좀 더 마실테야?

A: Do you want some? B: I'll pass.
A: 더 들래? B: 난 됐어.

Do you want some? I got a whole bagful.
더 들래? 한 봉투 가득 들었는데.

006 Take me to lunch 점심 사줘

It is like saying "Let's go eat at a restaurant," and the speaker may expect the person he is talking to pay for the meal

| Point | take sb (out) to lunch 점심을 사주다
go to lunch 점심먹으러 가다
come out to lunch 점심먹으러 나가다

A: How can I thank you for your help?
도와준 거 어떻게 감사해야 할까?

B: **Take me to lunch** someday soon. 조만간에 점심 사.

He took me to lunch at the Greek restaurant.
걔가 그리스 식당에서 점심을 사줬어.

Mona's gone. She went to lunch with her husband. 모나는 갔어. 남편하고 점심먹으러 나갔어.

You take her to lunch and have her get dessert. 걜 데리고 가서 점심하고 디저트도 사줘.

007 Can I get you something? 뭐 좀 사다 줄까?, 뭐 좀 갖다 줄까?

this is usually said by a waitress. She is asking "What do you want to eat?"

| Point | Can I get you a[another] drink? 한 잔 (더) 줄까?
Can I get you anything? 뭐라도 좀 갖다 줄까?
Can I get you a refill? 다시 채워줄까?
What can I get you? 뭘 드릴까요?

A: **Can I get you something** to eat? 먹을 거 좀 갖다 줄까요?

B: I'll have a ham sandwich and some milk.
햄샌드위치하고 우유 먹을래요.

Are you alright? Can I get you anything?
괜찮아? 뭐라도 좀 갖다 줄까?

Can I get you something to drink? Some coffee or something?
뭐 좀 마실 것 갖다 줄까? 커피라든가 뭐 어떤 거?

Before we get started, can I get you anything?
우리가 시작하기 전에 뭐라도 좀 갖다 줄까?

008 That'll really work up your appetite for lunch 그럼 점심 생각이 날거야

this speaker is saying "That activity will make you hungry." We can understand that maybe someone is doing something physical, which makes people hungry

| Point | work up an appetite (운동을 통해) 식욕을 돋구다, 갈증나게 하다
lose one's appetite 식욕을 잃다 spoil one's appetite 식욕을 망치다

A: I plan to run for five miles this morning.
오늘 아침에 5마일을 뛸거야.

B: **That'll really work up your appetite for lunch.**
그러면 점심 먹을 생각이 날거야.

I've lost my appetite. 식욕을 잃었어.

I spoil your appetite. 네 식욕을 망쳤어.

I have a good appetite. 입맛이 돌아, 식욕이 왕성해.

009 Help yourself 1.(음식) 마음껏 들어, 어서 갖다 들어 2. 마음대로 써

this is a polite term. It is said by a host and it means "Take as much food as you want"

| Point | Help yourself to ~ …을 맘껏 들어

A: May I start eating breakfast? 아침 시작해도 돼요?

B: **Help yourself.** I have many kinds of food for you. 어서 들어. 많은 종류의 음식을 준비했어.

Help yourself to whatever's in the fridge.
냉장고에 들어있는 거 다 마음대로 먹어.

There are leftovers in the refrigerator. Help yourself. 냉장고에 음식 남은 거 있으니 갖다 먹어.

A: Do you mind if I use your phone? B: Help yourself. A: 전화기 좀 써도 돼? B: 맘대로.

010 I've got a hankering for Chinese food tonight

오늘밤에는 중국 음식이 당기네

this is simply a way for the speaker to say that he has a very strong desire to eat Chinese food. If a person has a hankering for Chinese food, it is the same as saying "I really am craving Chinese food tonight"

| Point | have a hankering for+N[to~] …하고 싶다, …가 당기다

A: Anything you want to eat for dinner?
저녁으로 뭐 먹고 싶은거 있어?

B: **I've got a hankering for** Chinese food tonight.
오늘밤에는 중국 음식이 당기네.

I have a hankering for Swedish meatballs.
스웨덴식 밋볼이 당기네.

I've got a hankering for Japanese food tonight. 오늘밤에는 일본식이 당겨.

I get a hankering to go out to buy colorful plastic plates. 나가서 다양한 색의 플라스틱 접시를 사고 싶어.

I know I should, but I don't have a hankering for it. 내가 그래야 된다는 것을 알지만 난 그게 별로 당기지 않아.

011 I got a craving that I can't put off

도저히 참을 수 없이 먹고 싶은게 있었어

this is a way for the speaker to say he really wants something and he doesn't want to wait for it. Many times this refers to wanting a specific type of food, but it can also refer to other things, like a craving for cigarettes. Another way to say this is "I really have to have something right now"

| Point | have[get] a craving for[that~]
(주로 먹는 것을) 열망[갈망]하다, 먹고 싶어 죽겠다

A: Why did you go out at midnight to buy ice cream? 넌 왜 자정에 아이스크림을 사러 나간거야?

B: **I got a craving** that I couldn't put off to eat chocolate ice cream. 초콜릿 아이스크림이 먹고 싶어 죽겠는거 있지.

He's getting the attention he's been craving.
걔는 자기가 갈망하던 관심을 얻고 있어.

Yeah, tacos! Ever since you told me that story I've had such a craving for them.
그래, 타코! 네가 그 얘기를 해 준 이후로 타코를 몹시 먹고 싶었어.

Oh man you know what I'm craving right now? Pizza bagels.
내가 지금 뭘 먹고 싶은지 알아? 피자베이글야.

You know what? I am having a serious craving for herbal tea. 저 말이야, 난 지금 허브차 꼭 마시고 싶어.

012 I'm stuffed 배가 불러

this indicates the speaker has a full stomach. It is like saying "I'm so full that I can't eat more food"

| Point | I'm full 배불러

A: How would you like some ice cream?
아이스크림 좀 먹을테야?

B: No, thank you. **I am stuffed** from the dinner.
고맙지만 됐어. 저녁먹어서 배불러.

I'm stuffed. I couldn't eat any more food.
나 배불러. 음식을 더는 못먹겠어.

I'm stuffed. Let's just have some coffee.
나 배불러. 커피 좀 마시자.

Are you really hungry? I'm stuffed.
너 정말 배고파? 난 배부른데.

013 (Would you) Care for some coffee? 커피 들래요?

often this is said when asking people what they want to drink. It means "Do you want to drink a cup of coffee?"

| Point | Would you care for~ ? …을 들래요?, …을 원해요?
How about a cup of coffee? 커피 한잔 할래?

A: I guess we're finished with the meal.
식사를 다 마친 것 같아.

B: **Would you care for some coffee** now?
이제 커피 좀 들래?

Would either of you care for a cup coffee?
너희들 중 누구 커피 마실래?

Would you care for some breakfast? An Omelet? 아침 좀 먹을래? 오믈렛?

Would you care for some water? 물 좀 먹을테야?

014 Let me buy you a drink 술 한잔 살게

미드표현

many times this is a way of being friendly. It is like saying "Let's drink and talk together"

| Point | (Could I) Buy you a drink? 술 한잔 할래?

A: You look tired. **Let me buy you a drink.**
피곤해보여. 술 한잔 살게.

B: Thanks. I'll have a bottle of beer, please.
고마워. 맥주 한잔 할게.

Why don't I buy you a drink instead? First round's on me. 대신 내가 술 사줄까? 일차는 내가 쏠게.

I'll buy you a drink and explain. Meet me in my office at 7:00.
한잔사면서 설명해줄게. 7시에 사무실에서 만나자고.

I'll buy you a drink for second place. What are you having? It's on me.
2차는 내가 쏠게. 뭐 먹을래? 내가 낼게

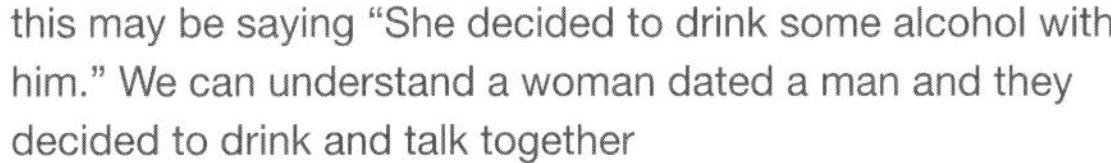

015 She's having drinks with her date

걘 애인과 술을 마시고 있어

미드표현

this may be saying "She decided to drink some alcohol with him." We can understand a woman dated a man and they decided to drink and talk together

| Point | What kind of drinks you got? 무슨 술이 있습니까?
May I freshen your drink? 잔을 다시 채워줄까요?

A: Where is Cheryl at right now? 셰릴이 지금 어디 있어?

B: **She's having drinks with** her date.
애인과 술마시고 있어.

We'll have drinks and bitch about LA.
술마시면서 LA에 대해 욕이나 하자.

I had drinks with opposing counsel last night.
지난밤 상대방 변호사와 술을 마셨어.

I just had a few drinks with my girlfriends.
어제 여자친구들과 간단히 몇 잔했어.

016 Have one for the road 마지막으로 딱 한 잔만 더 하자

미드표현

this is an old phrase that means "Drink one more before you go." Often it is showing friendship

| Point | One for the road? 한 잔 더 할래?

A: I really have to go home now. 이젠 정말 집에 가야 돼.

B: **Have one for the road** before you go.
가기 전에 술 한 잔 더 하자.

Have one for the road. It's on me.
마지막으로 한 잔만 더하자. 내가 낼게.

Here you go Mike. Have one for the road.
자 여기 마지막 잔이야. 마이크. 마지막으로 한 잔 더 하자고.

The bar is closing. Have one for the road.
술집이 문을 닫네. 마지막으로 한 잔 더 하자고.

017 Bottoms up! 위하여!

미드표현

this is used when people are finishing the drinks in their glasses. It means "Drink what remains"

| Point | Cheers! 건배!
Down the hatch! 건배!

A: This is a toast for good luck. **Bottoms up!**
행운을 빌며 건배하자. 위하여!

B: Yeah, good luck everyone! 그래, 다들 행운이 있기를!

You can't drink? Try it. It's very good for you. Bottoms up! 술을 못마신다고? 마셔봐, 굉장히 좋아. 위하여!

I propose a toast to our host. Bottoms up!
호스트를 위해서 건배합시다. 위하여!

Bottoms up! Everyone get a refill now.
위하여! 이제 다들 술잔을 채워요.

Bottoms up! Let's drink to the new staff members. 위하여! 새로운 스태프를 위하여 마십시다.

018 I'd like to propose a toast to~ (…을 위하여) 축배를 할게

미드표현

this speaker wants to express good wishes to someone. He is saying "I want to say something nice about..."

| Point | propose[make] a toast to sb …에게 축배를 들다

A: **I'd like to propose a toast to** the newly married couple. 신혼부부에게 축배를 합시다.

B: Good luck with your marriage. You'll need it!
결혼생활에 행운이 있기를!

I'd like to propose a little toast to the hostess.
안주인에게 축배를 할게.

It's so great seeing you guys again. I'd like to make a toast. 다시 만나 반가워들. 축배를 할게.

I'd like to make a toast to my good friend Michael. 내 좋은 친구 마이클에게 축배를 할게.

019 Hit me (술) 나도 줘

usually when this is used in a bar when drinking alcohol, and it is signaling for the bartender to pour another drink for the speaker. It is not so commonly used these days, although some people still say it. In other words, the speaker is telling the man at the bar "Pour me another of the same drink I just had"

| Point | Hit me (술 더 마시겠냐고 제의를 받을 때) 나도 줘.
(카드) 블랙잭에서 딜러에게 카드 한 장 더 달라고 할 때

A: You want another shot of whiskey?
위스키 한 잔 더 할테야?

B: I sure do. **Hit me.** 물론이지. 따라줘.

Hit me. I'm in the mood to get drunk.
한 잔 따라줘. 취하고 싶네.

I need some whiskey. Hit me.
위스키 좀 먹어야겠어. 따라줘.

Hey bartender, my glass is empty. Hit me.
바텐더, 내 잔이 비었네. 따라줘.

A: More wine? B: Hit me. A: 와인 더 마실래? B: 어 따라줘.

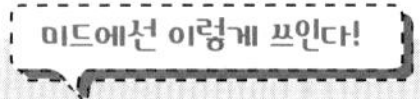

Hit us again

The Big Bang Theory
SEASON#3-11

Leonard의 엄마인 Beverley와 Penny가 바에서 술 마시는 장면으로 술에 취한 Beverley의 모습을 볼 수 있다.

Beverley: Oh, that is fascinating. I'm noticing an immediate lowering of my inhibitions. For example, I'm seriously considering asking that busboy to ravish me in the alleyway, while I eat cheesecake. What do you think?

Penny: Well, we are known for our cheesecake. Hit us again.

Beverley: Yes. If a little is good, more must be better.

베버리: 어, 끝내주네. 나의 억압들이 바로 풀리고 있는 걸 느끼겠어. 예를 들어, 저 웨이터에게 내가 치즈케익을 먹는 동안 뒷골목에서 날 범하라고 하고 싶어져, 어떻게 생각해?

페니: 우리가 치즈케익으로 유명은 하죠. 다시 좀 따라줘요.

베버리: 그래, 조금도 좋지만 많으면 많을수록 좋아

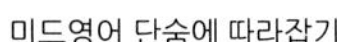

020 Here's to you 1. 당신을 위해 건배! 2. 너한테 주는 선물이야

this is a way to say "I respect you" or "I like you." It is usually a toast made with alcohol

Point Here's to ~! …을 위해 건배!

A: **Here's to you.** You've been very good to me.
당신을 위해 건배. 내게 정말 잘해주었어.

B: Thank you for saying such kind things.
그렇게 좋게 말해줘서 고마워.

Here's to the winners! 승자에게 건배!

Here's to your health! 너의 건강을 위하여!

Here's to your marriage -- our heartfelt congratulations. We also got you a little gift.
네 결혼을 위하여… 우리의 진심어린 축하야. 또 조그마한 선물도 준비했어.

021 While under the influence 술에 취해서

this the speaker is saying something happened after a person drank too much alcohol. It is very similar to saying "When he had been drinking a lot"

Point Under the influence (of alcohol) 술에 취해서
DUI 음주운전(Driving Under the Influence)
He's drunk as a skunk 고주망태로 취해있어

A: Frank did some crazy things **while under the influence.** 프랭크는 술에 취해서 어처구니 없는 짓을 좀 했어.

B: Is that why the police put him in jail?
그 때문에 경찰이 걔를 감옥에 넣은거야?

I wasn't drinking or... under the influence.
난 술을 마시고 있지 않았어. 다시 말해 술에 취하지 않았다고.

We believe you were sexually assaulted while under the influence of a drug.
약에 취한 상태에서 성폭행당하신 것 같습니다.

And Bart was killed in a DUI last year.
바트는 작년에 음주운전 교통사고로 죽었어.

022 I'm off the booze 나 술 끊었어

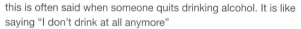

this is often said when someone quits drinking alcohol. It is like saying "I don't drink at all anymore"

Point booze 술 liquor 독주
on the booze 술 많이 먹는 off the booze 술 끊은
How hammered are you? 얼마나 취했어?
Was he hammered? 그 사람 취했었니?

A: You aren't drinking any beer? 맥주 전혀 안 해?

B: **I'm off the booze** for a while. 한 동안 술 끊었어.

Sex is as much an addiction for me as booze.
섹스는 내겐 술만큼 중독성이 강해.

She thinks that her husband's back on the booze. 걘 자기 남편이 다시 술을 많이 먹기 시작했다고 생각해.

Where does she keep the booze?
걘 술을 어디에 두니?

You're crazy! How hammered are you?
미쳤구만! 얼마나 취한거야?

023 Can I bum a smoke? 담배 한 대 얻을 수 있을까?

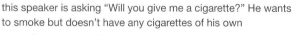

this speaker is asking "Will you give me a cigarette?" He wants to smoke but doesn't have any cigarettes of his own

Point bum n. 떠돌이 v. 갚을 생각없이 빌리다

A: **Can I bum a smoke?** 담배 한 대 얻을 수 있어?

B: No, I don't have any cigarettes. 아니, 담배가 없는데.

I'm out of cigarettes. Can I bum a smoke?
담배가 가 떨어졌네. 한 대 얻을 수 있을까?

Can I bum a smoke? I'll pay you back later.
담배 한 대 줄래? 나중에 갚을게.

Can I bum a smoke? I'm dying for some nicotine. 담대 한 대 줄테야? 니코틴 좀 빨아야겠어.

024 She went cold turkey 걘 담배를 끊었어

this means "She quit suddenly." It is usually used when someone stops drinking alcohol or stops smoking cigarettes

| Point | go cold turkey (술, 담배 등을) 갑자기 끊다
quit cold turkey 갑자기 그만두다

A: How did Liz give up smoking? 리즈가 어떻게 담배를 끊었어?

B: **She went cold turkey.** She just totally stopped one day. 갑자기 끊었어. 어느 날 갑자기 끊었어.

I didn't want to hurt her. I just quit it cold turkey. 걔한테 상처를 주기 싫어 그냥 단칼에 끝냈어.

Just like that? Three packs a day, cold turkey? 그냥 그렇게? 하루에 세 갑씩 피우다가 단번에 끊었다고?

025 Say when 됐으면 말해, 됐으면 그만이라고 말해

미드표현

usually this means "Tell me when to stop pouring your drink." The speaker wants to know how much alcohol he should give someone else

A: Can you pour me some wine? 와인 좀 따라줘.

B: Sure I can. **Say when.** 물론. 됐으면 얘기해.

My wife says "Say when," whenever she pours anything for me.
무언가를 내게 따라줄 때마다 내 아내는 "됐으면 그만"이라는 말을 하라고 해.

I'll pour your wine. Say when.
와인을 따라줄테니 됐으면 말해.

You want some whiskey in your glass? Say when. 네 잔에 위스키 좀 따라줄까? 됐으면 말해.

Say when. I can stop any time.
됐으면 말해. 언제든지 멈출테니.

026 Might I have a sip of water? 물 한 모금만 줄래요?

미드표현

this is a very polite way to ask for water. It is usually said when someone is very thirsty

| Point | take a sip 홀짝홀짝 마시다

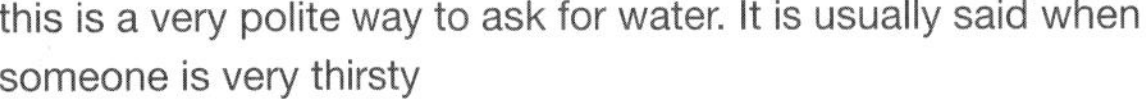

A: **Might I have a sip of water?** 물 한 모금만 줄래요?

B: I'll go get you a glass of it. 물 한 잔 갖다 줄게요.

Can I have a sip of your coffee and a bite of your muffin? 커피 한 모금과 머핀 한 조각 먹어도 돼?

Have a sip of water. 물 좀 마셔.

He takes a sip of coffee from the cup he's holding. 걘 잡고 있는 컵의 커피를 홀짝 마시고 있어.

027 We're not ready to order yet 조금 있다가 주문할게요

미드표현

we can understand the people are reading a menu and didn't decide what to eat yet. It is a way to say "We need more time to decide what to eat"

| Point | Could I take your order (now)? 주문하시겠습니까?
Could you hurry with our orders? 음식 아직 멀었어요?
We'll bring your order right up 주문하신 것 바로 가져다 드릴게요

A: Have you decided what you want to eat?
뭘 드실지 결정하셨나요?

B: **We're not ready to order yet.** 아직 결정 못 했어요.

We're ready to order over here. What's good?
여기 주문할려고요. 뭐가 좋나요?

Good evening. You folks are ready to order?
안녕하세요. 여러분 주문하시겠습니까?

Are we ready to order, or do you need a little more time? 주문하셨나요 아니면 시간이 더 필요하신가요?

028 What'll it be? 뭘로 할래?, 뭘 드시겠습니까?

usually this is asking "What do you want to order to eat or drink?" It is something that is said by a waiter or waitress

Point What are you having? 넌 뭐 먹을래?
What will you have? 뭐 먹을래?
What would you like? 뭘 들래?
What are you going to have? 뭘 들래?
What's yours? 네 거는 뭔대?, 즐겨 마시는 게 뭔대?

A: Hi guys. **What'll it be?** 안녕하세요, 여러분. 뭘 드시겠습니까?
B: We'll have two beers and a shot of whiskey.
맥주 두 잔과 위스키 한 잔 주세요.

You look thirsty. What'll it be?
목마른 것 같네. 뭘로 할래?

What'll it be? We have some good specials today. 뭘로 하시겠습니까? 오늘 좋은 스페셜이 있습니다.

What'll it be? Can I get you a drink?
뭘 드시겠습니까? 마실 것 드릴까요?

029 What are you drinking? 뭘 마실래?, 뭐 마시고 있어?

미드표현

the speaker is asking someone what type of alcohol he wants. It is like saying "Tell me what you'd like to drink"

Point What's your pleasure? 뭘 드시겠습니까?

A: I'll get you a drink. **What are you drinking?**
술 한 잔 갖다 줄게. 뭘 마실래?
B: I'd like to have a dark beer. 흑맥주 먹을래.

Next one is on me. What are you drinking?
다음 건 내가 낼게. 뭐 마실래?

What are you drinking? That looks good.
뭐 마시고 있어? 좋아 보인다.

God, that smells awful. What are you drinking?
와, 냄새 끔찍하다. 뭐 마시고 있어?

030 I'll have the same 같은 걸로 주세요

미드표현

this indicates someone ordered something, and the speaker is saying "I want to order that too"

Point The same for me 같은 걸로 줘요

A: Tonight I'll get the lobster and steak dish.
오늘 밤은 랍스타와 고기요리를 먹을래.
B: That sounds delicious. **I'll have the same.**
맛있겠다. 나도 같은 걸로 할게.

Whatever you're having, I'll have the same.
네가 뭘 먹든 같은 걸로 주세요.

I'll have the same. That meal looks delicious.
같은 걸로 주세요. 저 음식 맛있어 보이네요.

Let's keep this simple. I'll have the same.
간단히 하자고. 같은 걸로 주세요.

That sounds great. Same for me.
그거 괜찮겠네. 나도 같은 걸로 줘요.

031 Make it[that] two 같은 걸로 2개 줘요

미드표현

this is very similar to the previous phrase. It is usually said to mean "I'll get the same thing"

Point Make mine the same 같은 걸로 줘요
Make mine~ …으로 해줘요

A: I'd like to have a salad with my meal.
식사에 샐러드를 같이 주세요.
B: **Make it two.** It's very healthy to eat salads.
같은 걸로 2개 줘요. 샐러드를 먹는게 건강에 아주 좋아요.

Make that two, and a couple of hard-boiled eggs. 같은 걸로 2개 주시고 그리고 삶은 달걀 두어개 줘요.

Make mine well done. 내껀 잘 익혀줘요.

A: Fine, I'll have the Barbecue Burger. B: Make it two. A: 좋아, 난 바비큐 버거를 먹을게. B: 두 개 주세요.

032 (Is that) For here or to go? 여기서 드실 겁니까, 가지고 가실 겁니까?

this is asked by a waiter or waitress. It is a way of asking a customer "Will you eat the food here or do you want it put in a bag so you can take it home to eat?"

I Point I Can I get it to go? 싸가지고 갈 수 있나요?

A: We want three hamburgers, fries, and two sodas. 햄버거 3개, 프라이즈 그리고 음료수 2개 주세요.

B: Alright. **Is that for here or to go?**
네. 여기서 드실 건가요 아니면 포장인가요?

I got your order. For here or to go?
주문 받았는데요, 여기서 드실건가요, 가져가실건가요?

For here or to go? Are you picking it up?
여기서 드실건가요, 가져가실건가요? 픽업하실건가요?

Everything is ready. For here or to go?
다 준비됐습니다. 여기서 드실건가요, 가져가실건가요?

033 I'll pick up the tab 내가 낼게

this is usually said when someone will pay for everything. It means "I'll pay the bill"

I Point I Who's going to pick it up? 술값은 누가 내지?
foot the bill 부담하다, 돈을 내다
Let's split (the bill) 나누어 내자
(Go) Fifty-fifty 반 나누어 내자

A: Don't worry. **I'll pick up the tab.** 걱정마. 내가 낼게.

B: Thank you for taking me out tonight.
오늘 저녁 데리고 나와줘서 고마워.

A: I forgot to bring my wallet. B: I'll foot the bill this time around.
A: 지갑을 놓고 왔어. B: 이번 건 내가 부담할게.

You want to go Dutch, Dick? 각자 내자고, 딕?

034 It's on me 내가 낼게, 내가 쏠게

this speaker is saying "I'll pay for this." He is being polite and buying the meal for everyone

I Point I This one's on me 이번엔 내가 낼게, 이번엔 내가 계산할게
It's on the house (가게) 이건 서비스입니다
This is my round 이번에는 내가 쏠게
I'm buying 내가 쏠게

A: Order what you want. **It's on me.**
원하는 걸 주문해. 내가 낼게.

B: That's very nice. I guess I'll get the steak.
아이 좋아라. 고기 먹을까 봐.

Let's get some breakfast. It's on me!
아침 좀 먹자. 내가 낼게!

If you guys want to get some coffee, it's on the house. 커피 먹으려면 그건 서비스야.

Why don't we go get a couple of beers, chill out a bit? It's on me.
가서 맥주 몇잔하고 긴장을 좀 풀자고. 내가 낼게.

035 How much do I owe you? (식당, 가게 등) 내가 얼마를 내면 되지?, 얼마죠?

this is a way of asking "What is the amount of money I should pay you?" We can understand that someone has paid for something or lent the speaker money in the past

I Point I What do I owe you? 얼마죠? Check, please 계산서 주세요
Could you come down a little? 좀 깎아줄래요?

A: You never paid me the money I lent you.
내가 빌려준 돈 전혀 안 갚네.

B: I'm sorry. **How much do I owe you?** 미안. 얼마였지?

How much do I owe you for the muffin and the latte? 머핀하고 라테 가격이 얼마죠?

Thanks for the faucet. That leak is driving me crazy. What do I owe you?
수도꼭지 갈아줘 고마워요. 물새는 거에 아주 미친다구요. 얼마 드리면 돼죠?

Thanks for buying coffee. How much do I owe you? 커피 사줘서 고마워. 얼마였어?

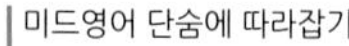

036 (This is) My treat 내가 살게

this means "I will pay the whole bill." The speaker wants to be kind to everyone

Point I'll treat you 내가 한턱 쏠게
This will be my treat 내가 계산할게

A: How much is the restaurant bill? 음식값 얼마 나왔어?
B: Don't worry about it. **This is my treat.**
걱정마. 내가 낼게.

Don't worry about it. This is my treat.
걱정마. 내가 살게.

This is my treat. I hope you like it.
내가 살게. 네가 좋아하길 바래.

This is my treat. Put your wallet away.
내가 살게. 네 지갑은 치워.

037 I gotta take a leak 오줌 좀 싸야겠어

미드표현

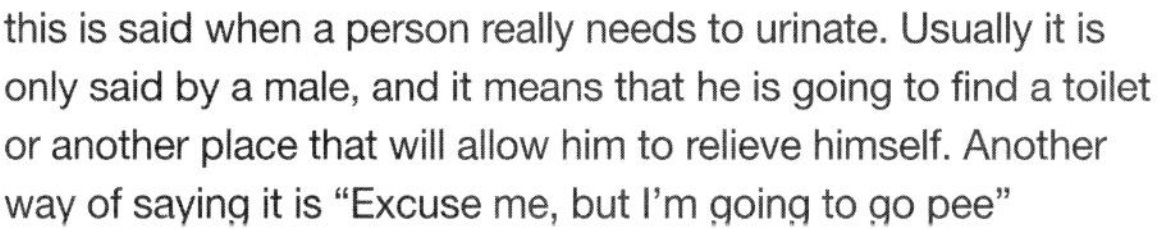

this is said when a person really needs to urinate. Usually it is only said by a male, and it means that he is going to find a toilet or another place that will allow him to relieve himself. Another way of saying it is "Excuse me, but I'm going to go pee"

Point take a leak[piss] (남자) 소변누다, 오줌싸다
relieve oneself 소변누다

A: Pull the car over. **I gotta take a leak.**
차 좀 세워. 오줌 좀 싸야겠어.
B: Wait a minute and I'll stop at the next gas station. 기다려, 다음 주유소에서 설게.

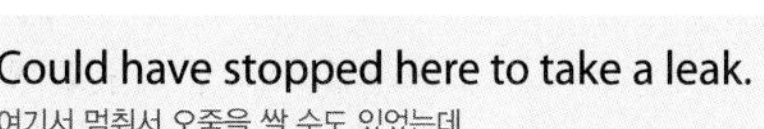

Could have stopped here to take a leak.
여기서 멈춰서 오줌을 쌀 수도 있었는데.

Excuse me, I just got to go take a leak.
미안하지만, 나, 가서 오줌싸야 돼.

I'm going to take a piss. 난 오줌을 쌀거야.

Excuse me, I'm going to relieve myself.
미안하지만 나 소변을 봐야 돼.

Things that are said during telephone calls

전화를 걸거나 받을 때

I'll make some calls

001 I'll make some calls 몇군데 전화 좀 해볼게

this is a way for someone to say that he will call some people in order to ask them for information about something. We can understand that there may be some confusion over an issue, and the speaker wants to confirm or verify or find something. It is very similar to saying "I'll call some people to check on this"

| Point | make some calls 몇 군데 전화를 해보다, 전화 몇 통 해보다

A: My apartment had a fire, and I have to move.
내 아파트에 불이 나서 이사가야 돼.

B: **I'll make some calls.** Maybe I can find you a place to live. 전화 몇군데 좀 해보고, 네게 살 집을 찾아줄 수 있을지 몰라.

미드표현

Actually, I have to make some calls.
실은 나 몇 군데 전화 좀 해봐야 돼.

I'll make some calls, see if I can pull some federal strings. 연방차원의 빽을 쓸 수 있는지 전화 좀 넣어볼게.

I could make some calls if you're looking for work. 네가 일자리를 구한다면 내가 전화 좀 돌려볼 수 있어.

I'm gonna make some calls. I'm gonna get someone there to help you, OK?
내 전화 좀 해볼게. 거기 사람보고 너 도와주도록 할게, 알았어?

002 I just got off with my laywer 방금 내 변호사와 통화했어

this means that the speaker just been speaking with someone on the phone. We can understand that the conversation has finished and he has hung up the phone. In other words "I just got done talking with my lawyer"

| Point | (just) get off with sb (방금) …와 통화를 했어

A: Adam, you look really pissed off.
아담, 너 정말 짜증난 것처럼 보여.

B: **I just got off with** my lawyer. I'm being sued.
방금 변호사와 통화했는데 내가 소송을 당했어.

Jack, I just got off with CTU.
잭, 난 방금전에 CTU와 통화를 했어.

Just got off with Edan. Looks like Dean's on the move. 방금 에단과 통화를 했는데 딘이 움직이는 것 같아.

I just got off with Iowa highway patrol.
방금 아이오와 고속도로 순찰대와 통화를 했어.

003 I hope you don't mind me calling you
내가 전화한거 괜찮겠지

this is a polite way of speaking to someone when you call them unexpectedly. The speaker wants to make sure he isn't being rude by calling when he does. Essentially, he is saying "I hope you don't think it was impolite for me to give you a call"

| Point | I hope you don't mind 괜찮겠지, 그대로 되지
I hope you don't mind, but~ 괜찮길 바래, 하지만…
I hope you don't mind sb ~ing …가 …하는데 괜찮기를 바래

A: Jack, it's after eleven o'clock at night.
잭, 밤 11시가 넘었어.

B: **I hope you don't mind me calling you** so late.
내가 밤늦게 전화해도 괜찮겠지.

I hope you don't mind me crashing.
내가 하룻밤 자도 괜찮겠지.

I hope you don't mind me stopping by.
내가 잠깐 들려도 괜찮겠지.

Hey, Karen. I hope you don't mind, I let myself in. 야, 카렌, 괜찮기를 바래, 나 들어간다.

I hope you don't mind, but I took the liberty of lowering all the shelves in your medicine closet.
괜찮기를 바라지만 내가 멋대로 네 약품선반의 높이를 낮췄어.

004 Are you (still) there? 듣고 있는 거니?, 여보세요?

this is a way for the speaker to ask "Have you hung up?" He wants to know if the other person is listening to him on the phone

| Point | I'm still here 아직 듣고[보고] 있어

A: Howard? **Are you still there?** 하워드? 아직 듣고 있는거야?

B: Yeah, I'm still on the line. 어, 아직 듣고 있어.

Are you still there? Hello? Hello?
듣고 있어? 여보세요? 여보세요?

Margaret, are you still on the line? Are you still there? 마가렛, 아직 통화중이야? 듣고 있어?

Are you still there? Did you hang up?
듣고 있어? 전화끊은거야?

005 Could I leave a message? 메모 좀 전해줄래요?

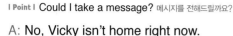

this indicates the speaker can't talk to a person and wants to say something that others will tell that person. It is similar to saying "Please tell him..."

| Point | Could I take a message? 메시지를 전해드릴까요?

A: No, Vicky isn't home right now.
아니, 비키는 지금 집에 없어요.

B: **Could I leave a message** for her?
걔한테 메모 좀 전해줄래요?

미드표현

He's on the line right now. May I take a message? And your phone number?
지금 통화중인데 메모 남기실래요? 전화번호도요?

It's Mike. I'm not here. Leave a message.
마이크입니다. 지금 부재중이니 메시지를 남겨주세요.

Leave a message, and I'll return your call. Thanks. Have a great day.
메시지를 남겨주세요. 바로 연락드리겠습니다. 감사합니다. 즐건 하루 되세요.

006 Hang on a minute 잠깐만, 끊지 말고 기다려

this is saying "Wait." The speaker needs to do something and wants the other person to stay on the telephone line

| Point | Hang on (a minute/ moment/ second)
(전화 및 일반상황에서) 잠시만 기다려
One moment, please 잠시만 기다려 주세요

A: I want to speak to Ron Harris. 론 해리스 있어요?

B: **Hang on a minute.** I'll get him. 잠깐만요. 바꿔줄게요.

미드표현

That's my call waiting. Can you hang on?
전화가 들어 오는데 기다릴래?

Tell her to hang on a minute, will you?
걔보고 잠깐 기다리라고 해, 알았지?

Hang on, hang on. Almost done.
잠깐만 기다려봐. 거의 다 끝났어.

Hang on, what's he doing? 잠깐, 걔 뭐하고 있어?

007 Hold on a second 잠깐만

this is the same as the previous phrase. It means "Wait, I have to do something"

| Point | Hold on (a second/ moment/ minute) (전화 및 일반상황에서) 잠깐만
Hold the wire[line] = Please hold = Hold, please
(끊지 말고) 잠시만 기다려 주세요
Could you hold? 잠시 기다릴래요?

A: Can you find that information for me?
그 정보 좀 찾아줄래?

B: **Hold on a second.** I need to turn on my computer. 잠깐. 컴퓨터 좀 켜고.

미드표현

Can you hold on a moment? I have another call. 잠깐 기다려 줄래? 다른 전화가 왔어.

Hold on a second! I don't work for you!
잠깐만! 난 네 밑에서 일 안해!

Hey! Hold on a minute, hold on a second. Do you think these food are nice?
야, 잠깐만, 잠시만. 이 음식들이 좋다구?

Could you hold for a moment? I'm on a conference call. 잠깐 기다려줄래? 난 전화회의 중이거든.

008 Don't hang up 전화 끊지마

this is telling someone "Stay on the phone line." It is asking that they don't end the phone call

| Point | Don't hang up on me (like that) 전화 끊지마

A: I don't ever want to talk to you again.
다시는 너와 얘기하지 않을거야.

B: **Don't hang up.** Tell me why you're so angry.
전화 끊지마. 왜 그리 화가 났는지 말해 봐.

Why'd you hang up on me? 너 왜 전화를 끊었어?

Samantha, listen to me, don't hang up.
사만다, 내말 들어봐, 전화끊지 말고.

House, don't hang up. We need your help.
하우스, 전화끊지 마요. 선생님 도움이 필요해요.

Mom, it's an important phone call, please hang up. I'll call you back.
엄마, 이건 중요한 전화라고. 전화끊어요. 내가 다시 할게요.

009 I have got another call 다른 전화가 와서

this is a way to say "My phone is telling me someone else is calling." We can understand this is being said to someone the speaker is talking to on the phone now

| Point | I'm getting another call 다른 전화가 오는데
That's my call waiting 다른 전화가 오고 있어
He's on another line 갠 통화 중이야

A: What is that beeping noise? 저 삐삐 소리는 뭐야?
B: **I have got another call** coming in.
다른 전화가 걸려오고 있다는거야.

Can you hang on? I got another call. Hello? 기다릴래? 다른 전화가 와서. 여보세요?

I gotta go, I have another call.
그만 끊어야겠어. 전화가 와서.

Will you hold on a second? I have another call. 잠깐 기다릴래. 다른 전화가 와서.

She gets a call waiting beep on her phone.
갠 통화 중에 전화가 왔다는 신호를 들었다.

010 Give me Rick, please! (전화에서) 릭 부탁합니다

this speaker is asking to talk to Rick. It is a way to say "I want to speak to Rick"

| Point | Could I speak to sb? …좀 바꿔주실래요?, …와 얘기해도 될까?
Is sb there? …씨 계세요?
put sb on the phone …에게 전화를 돌려주다, 연결시키다

A: Hi, this is Sam. Can I help you?
안녕하세요, 샘인데요, 뭘 도와드릴까요?
B: **Give me Rick, please.** I need to talk with him.
릭 부탁해요. 걔하고 얘기해야 돼요.

Can I speak to someone in charge please?
책임자이신분 좀 바꿔주세요?

Could I speak to you for a moment? 잠시 나랑 이야기 좀 할까?

Okay, put her on the phone. Let me talk to her. 좋아, 걔 전화 연결시켜줘. 내가 걔한테 얘기할게.

Well, put her on the phone. I'll tell her I don't wanna sleep with you.
걔 전화연결시켜줘. 내가 걔한테 너하고 자고 싶어하지 않는다고 말할게.

011 I've been meaning to call you 그렇지 않아도 전화하려고 했는데

this is expressing "I didn't call you but I wanted to." It is often said when someone calls another person

A: Hi Bob, it's Mike calling. 안녕. 밥. 나 마이크야.
B: Hi Mike. **I've been meaning to call you.**
안녕 마이크. 안 그래도 전화하려고 했어.

I can't believe it's been so long. I've been meaning to call you.
정말 오래간만이네. 그렇지 않아도 전화하려고 했었는데.

I've been meaning to call you. It's been a while since we talked.
그렇지 않아도 전화하려고 했었어. 우리 이야기 나눈 지 꽤 됐지.

012 Just have him call me 그냥 전화 좀 해달라고 해줘

this expresses that someone is not there and the speaker is asking for a return telephone call. It is like saying "I want a call back from him"

| Point | have A call B A에게 B에게 전화하라고 하다

A: Mr. Gotti isn't here right now. 고티 씨가 지금 안 계세요.
B: OK, **just have him call me** later.
알았어요. 그냥 전화 좀 해달라고 해줘요.

Never mind, just have him call me.
신경 쓰지마. 그냥 걔보고 전화하라고 해.

If he finds it, have him call me immediately.
걔가 그걸 찾으면 내게 바로 전화하라고 해.

When your daddy gets home, have him call me. 아빠가 집에 오시면 바로 내게 전화해달라고 말씀 드려.

013 I dialed your number by mistake 잘못 전화했어요

this is a way to say "I'm sorry, I called accidentally." We can understand that the speaker used the wrong telephone number

| Point | What number are you calling? 몇 번으로 거셨는데요?

A: I'm sorry. **I dialed your number by mistake.**
미안. 다이얼을 잘못 돌렸어.

B: That's OK. Have a nice day. 괜찮아. 잘 지내.

I dialed your number by mistake. Sorry about that. 잘못 전화했네요. 죄송해요.

Is that you Jane? Oops, I dialed your number by mistake. 제인 너야? 아이고, 전화 잘못했네요.

I dialed your number by mistake. My bad.
전화 잘못했네요. 제 잘못예요.

014 Sorry, wrong number 죄송하지만 전화 잘못 거셨네요

this speaker is telling someone "You made a mistake calling here." The caller wanted to talk to another person or call another house

| Point | It's a wrong number 전화 잘못 거셨어요
You have the wrong number 전화 잘못 거셨어요
There's no one here by that name
그런 이름을 가진 사람은 이곳에는 없어요

A: Could you put Rachel on the phone please?
레이첼 좀 바꿔주시겠어요?

B: **Sorry, wrong number.** There is no Rachel living here. 미안해요. 잘못 거셨네요. 레이첼이란 사람 여기 안 살아요.

I'm sorry. Wrong number. 미안하지만 전화잘못하셨는데요.

Hello? Who are you looking for? Did you dial the wrong number?
여보세요? 누구 찾으세요? 전화번호 잘못 돌리셨나요?

I'm sorry, you must have the wrong number.
죄송합니다. 전화를 잘못 거셨네요.

015 (There's a) Phone call for you 너한테 전화왔어

this is telling someone that a person on the phone wants to talk to him. It is like saying "The caller wants to talk to you"

| Point | You have a phone call 전화왔어
Some guy just called for you 방금 어떤 사람한테서 전화왔었어
There's someone on the other line 다른 전화가 와 있어
You're wanted on the telephone 너한테 전화왔어

A: Hey Peter! **Phone call for you!** 야 피터야! 전화왔어!

B: Tell them that I'm coming to the phone.
전화받으러 간다고 말해.

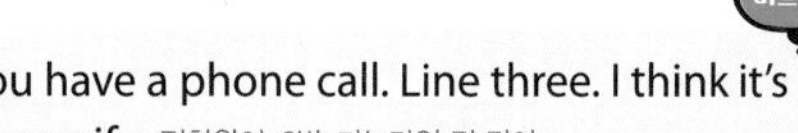

You have a phone call. Line three. I think it's your wife. 전화왔어. 3번. 마누라인 것 같아.

You have a phone call at the front desk.
프론트 데스크에 전화와 있어요.

A: Some guy just called for you. B : Who was it? A: 누가 전화했었어. B: 누구였는데?

016 I'll call back later 내가 나중에 다시 전화할게

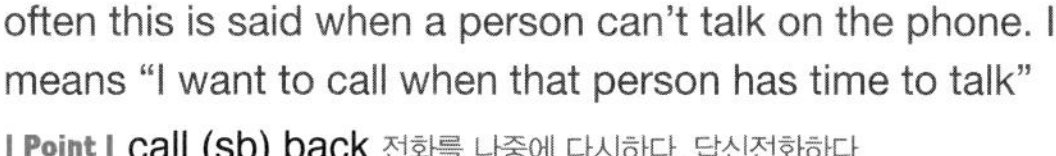

often this is said when a person can't talk on the phone. It means "I want to call when that person has time to talk"

| Point | call (sb) back 전화를 나중에 다시하다, 답신전화하다
call back 답신전화

A: You can't speak to Arnold right now.
아놀드와 지금 통화할 수 없는데요.

B: No problem. **I'll call back later.**
괜찮아요. 나중에 다시 전화하죠.

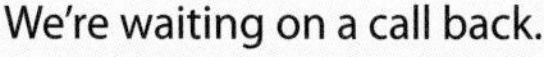

We're waiting on a call back.
우리는 답신전화를 기다리고 있어.

He said he'd call back in an hour, once the family's safe. 걔는 가족이 일단 안전해지면 전화를 다시 하겠다고 했어.

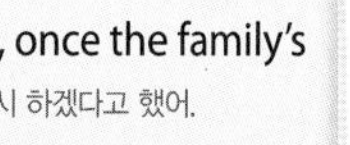

Okay, never mind. I'll call back. Bye.
좋아, 신경쓰지마. 내가 전화다시할게. 안녕.

I'm sorry it took so long to call you back, I just got your message. 전화를 늦게 해서 미안해, 네 메시지를 방금 봤어.

017 It's me 나야

this is like saying "You know who I am." The caller expects someone will know him by the sound of his voice

| Point | Speaking (전화를 받고) 난데요
This is A A인데요
You got Michael 마이클인데요

A: Hi, this is Bruce speaking. Can I help you?
안녕하세요. 브루스입니다. 무엇을 도와드릴까요?

B: **It's me,** Jeff. I have some stuff to deliver to you.
나야, 제프. 네게 보낼 물건이 있어서.

미드표현

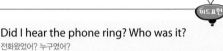

Hello? It's me. Wait, don't hang up, please. I just need to see you, please?
여보세요? 나야. 기다려, 끊지마. 제발. 너 좀 봐야 돼, 응?

It's me. Do you have some time to talk?
나야. 잠깐 얘기할 시간 있어?

It's me. I have something important to tell you.
나야. 너한테 할 중요한 얘기가 있어.

It's me. I missed you and had to call.
나야. 네가 보고 싶어서 전화해야 했어.

018 Who was it? 누군데? 누구였어?

this speaker is asking "What person called?" He wants information about who the caller was

| Point | Who is it? 누구세요?
Who's calling(, please)? 누구세요?
Can I ask who's calling? 누구시죠?
Who's on the phone? 누구 전화야?, 누구예요?

A: I heard the phone ring. **Who was it?**
전화소리 들었는데. 누구였어?

B: It was a salesman for an insurance company.
보험회사 세일즈맨이었어.

미드표현

Did I hear the phone ring? Who was it?
전화왔었어? 누구였어?

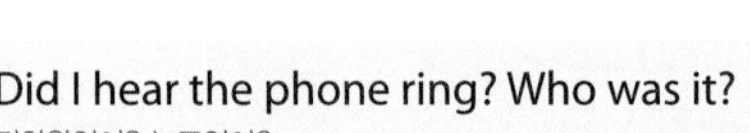

A: Who's on the phone, Jill? B: It's just a boy from my school.
A: 질, 누구 전화야? B: 그냥 같은 학교 남학생이야.

A: May I ask who's calling? B: The woman he happens to be living with. Is he there?
A: 누구시죠? B: 걔하고 우연히 함께 사는 여자요. 걔 있어요?

019 Who is this? 누구세요?, (면전에서) 이사람 누구야?

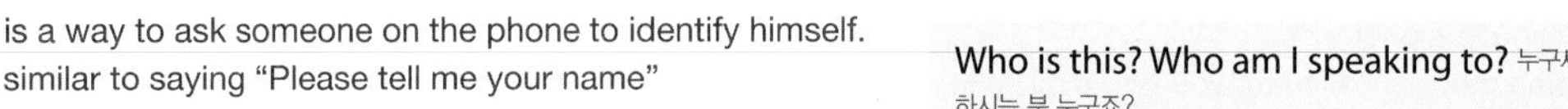

this is a way to ask someone on the phone to identify himself. It is similar to saying "Please tell me your name"

| Point | Who is this? 통화 중에 "지금 전화하는 사람은 누구세요?" 혹은 대면한 상태에서 "이 사람 누구야?"라고 묻는 말.

A: Hi, it's Tracey. **Who is this?** 안녕, 트레이시인데, 누구세요?

B: It's Steve. Don't you recognize my voice?
스티브야. 내 목소리 모르겠어?

미드표현

Who is this? Who am I speaking to? 누구세요? 통화하시는 분 누구죠?

Who is this guy? Why is he writing down everything I say?
이 사람 누구야? 왜 내가 하는 말을 다 받아 적는거야?

This is Michael. Who is this? 마이클인데 누구시죠?

020 Would you get that? 문 좀 열어줄래?, 전화 좀 받아줄래?

this indicates the speaker wants someone to answer the phone or to answer the door. He is asking "Can you pick up the phone?" or "Can you open the door?"

| Point | answer the phone 전화를 받다
I'll get it 내가 전화 받을게, 내가 문 열어줄게

A: I'm in the shower. **Would you get that?**
나 샤워 중인데 전화 좀 받아줄래?

B: Sure. Are you expecting someone to call?
그래. 누구 전화 올 사람 있어?

미드표현

Would you get that please? People have been calling to congratulate me all day.
전화 좀 받아줄래? 종일 사람들이 전화해서 날 축하해주고 있어.

I'll get it. I'm sure it's Julie. 내가 문 열어줄게. 줄리일거야.

021 Give me a call 전화해, 나중에 연락해

미드표현

this is a way of saying "Call me." The speaker wants to talk to someone in the future

| Point | give me a call[ring] 전화하다

A: Would you like to go out with me? 나하고 데이트할래?

B: Sure. **Give me a call** later on tonight.
물론, 오늘 밤 늦게 전화해.

My number is on this business card. Give me a call. 내 전번은 이 명함에 있으니 전화 줘.

Give me a call if you want. 하고 싶을 때 전화해.

You've got my number, give me a call.
내 전번 아니까 전화해.

Why did you give me a ring? 왜 내게 전화한거야?

022 I have (got) to go 이제 가봐야겠어, 이제 끊어야겠어

미드표현

the speaker is expressing he can't talk anymore. It is similar to saying "I can't talk to you now"

| Point | (I) Gotta go (전화) 끊어야겠다

A: I have many things to do. **I have to go.**
할 일이 많아. 이제 끊어야겠어.

B: Alright. I'll give you a call tomorrow night.
좋아. 내일 저녁에 전화할게.

I haven't got any time. I have to go.
나 시간이 없어. 그만 끊어야 돼.

I have to go. My mom just got home.
그만 끊어야 돼. 엄마가 방금 오셨어.

I have to go. I'll talk to you later.
이제 끊어야겠어. 나중에 통화하자고.

You are a jerk. I have to go. 넌 머저리야. 나 끊는다.

023 (I'll) Talk to you soon 또 걸게, 다음에 이야기하자

미드표현

usually this is a way to end a phone conversation. It is like saying "Goodbye, I'll call you again"

| Point | Talk to you tomorrow 낼 얘기하자
Talk to you later 나중에 얘기하자

A: It was very nice hearing from you.
네 얘기 들어서 아주 좋았어.

B: Thank you. **Talk to you soon.** 고마워. 다음에 이야기하자.

Goodbye for now. Talk to you soon.
이제 안녕. 나중에 전화할게.

Talk to you soon. I can call again tomorrow.
또 걸게. 내일 다시 전화할게.

Talk to you soon. I have to hang up.
또 걸게. 끊어야 돼.

I got to get back inside and shower. So I'll talk to you later. 이제 들어가서 샤워해야겠어. 나중에 하기로 하자고.

I gotta go. So, I'll talk to you later.
이런, 이제 가야겠어. 나중에 얘기해.

024 He won't take my calls 내 전화를 안 받으려고 해

미드표현

this means "That person won't answer the phone if I call." It indicates that person may be upset with the speaker

| Point | take one's call …의 전화를 받다

A: Why don't you just apologize to Ted?
테드에게 그냥 잘못했다고 하지.

B: I tried. **He won't take my calls** anymore.
그랬는데. 더 이상 내 전화를 안 받으려고 해.

He won't take my calls. He'll only talk to you.
걘 내 전화를 안 받아. 너하고만 얘기하려고 해.

You refused to take my calls and told security at your firm not to let me in!
넌 내 전화를 안 받고 회사경비보고 날 못 들어오게 막으라고 했다고!

I'll be right back, I just gotta take this call.
곧 돌아올게, 나 이 전화 받아야 돼.

She's not gonna take my calls.
걔는 내 전화를 받지 않을거야.

025 She's been on the horn with all of her friends

종일 전화통을 붙잡고 친구들과 통화하고 있어

usually this is saying the woman has called many friends. Another way to say it is "She made many calls to talk to friends"

| Point | be on the horn with~ …와 통화중이다

A: Why is your phone line always busy?
왜 네 전화는 항상 통화 중이야?

B: It's my daughter. **She's been on the horn with** all of her friends.
딸 때문에. 종일 전화통을 붙잡고 친구들과 수다떨고 있어.

미드표현

She's been on the horn with every member of the school board all day long.
걘 오늘 온종일 전화통을 붙잡고 학교 이사진들 모두와 통화했다구.

She's been on the horn with all of her friends. Can you believe it?
종일 전화통을 붙잡고 친구들과 통화하고 있어. 그게 말이나 돼?

I didn't talk to her. She's been on the horn with all of her friends.
난 걔랑 얘기 못했어. 종일 전화통을 붙잡고 친구들과 통화하고 있던데.

026 My phone's been ringing off the hook with job offers

일자리를 주겠다는 전화가 줄창 오고 있어

the speaker wants to say "Many people called to try to hire me." It indicates he will take a job soon

| Point | ring off the hook 전화기가 떨어질 정도로 전화가 불티나게 오다

A: Have you had success sending out your resume? 네 이력서 다 잘 발송했어?

B: Oh yes. **My phone's been ringing off the hook with** job offers. 그럼. 일자리 준다는 전화가 불티나게 와.

미드표현

Jim's phone's been ringing off the hook with sympathy calls. 짐에게 위로전화가 줄창 오고 있어.

My phone's been ringing off the hook with telemarketers. 텔레마케터들이 내게 줄창 전화를 하고 있어.

Our phone's been ringing off the hook with relatives calling. 우리 전화로 친척들 전화가 줄창 들어오고 있어.

027 The first name on my speed dial is you

스피드 단축번호의 첫 이름은 너야

this indicates the speaker's mother is important to him. He is saying "My mom's number is the first one on my telephone"

| Point | have sb on speed dial …을 스피드 단축번호로 해놓다

A: My family is very important. **The first name on my speed dial** is Mom.
내 가족은 무척 소중해. 단축키의 1번은 엄마야.

B: Wow. You must like to talk with her a lot.
와, 엄마하고 얘기하는 걸 무척 좋아하나 보다.

미드표현

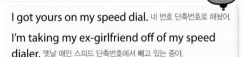

I got yours on my speed dial. 네 번호 단축번호로 해놨어.

I'm taking my ex-girlfriend off of my speed dialer. 옛날 애인 스피드 단축번호에서 빼고 있는 중야.

028 Call me on your cell phone 핸드폰으로 전화해

this speaker wants someone to call him with a mobile phone. Often this means the caller should be free to call anytime

| Point | be on a cell phone 핸드폰으로 통화중이다

A: How can I reach you this afternoon?
오늘 오후에 어떻게 너한테 연락해?

B: **Call me on your cell phone** when you are free.
시간 날 때 핸드폰으로 전화해.

미드표현

She is on a cell phone, talking to Dad.
걘 핸드폰으로 아빠에게 전화 중이야.

He's at my parents. His cell phone's probably out of range.
걘 우리 부모님 댁에 있어. 핸드폰이 안 되는 지역일거야.

Have him call you back on your cell phone.
걔보고 네 핸드폰으로 전화하도록 해.

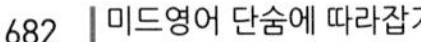

029 I always have my phone on vibrate
난 항상 핸드폰을 진동으로 해놔

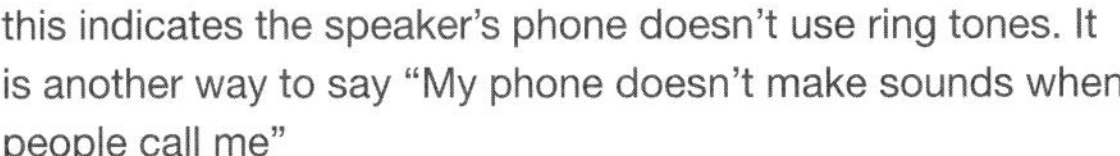

this indicates the speaker's phone doesn't use ring tones. It is another way to say "My phone doesn't make sounds when people call me"

| Point | Mine is on silent mode 내 휴대폰은 진동으로 돼 있어

A: **I always have my phone on vibrate.** It's more polite. 난 항상 핸드폰을 진동으로 해놔. 이게 더 예절을 지키는 거지.

B: I know. I hate the sounds of phones ringing.
알아. 전화벨소리 정말 싫어.

I had my phone on vibrate, I was a little busy.
전화를 진동으로 해놔서, 좀 바빴거든.

I always have my phone on vibrate so I don't get disturbed.
난 항상 전화기를 진동으로 해놔, 방해받지 않도록 말야.

That's not my phone ringing. I always have my phone on vibrate.
저건 내 전화소리가 아냐. 난 항상 진동으로 해놔.

I always have my phone on vibrate, so I can take it to class.
난 전화기를 항상 진동으로 해놔. 수업시간에 가져갈 수 있도록 말야.

030 Why didn't you answer your cell phone?
왜 핸드폰 안 받았어?

this person is saying "I called but you never answered." He wants to know why the other person didn't answer

| Point | answer one's cell phone …의 핸드폰을 받다

A: **Why didn't you answer your cell phone?**
왜 네 핸드폰 안 받았어?

B: I forgot it in my office today. 오늘 사무실에 두고 왔어.

He's not answering his cell phone.
걘 핸드폰을 받지 않아.

I turned my cell phone off. 핸드폰을 꺼놨어.

A: Why didn't you answer your cell phone?
B: It was in my car.
A: 왜 네 핸드폰받지 않은거야? B: 차에 뒀거든.

031 She said her cell phone isn't getting good reception
걘 자기 전화수신상태가 안 좋대

this is usually said when a person has problems getting calls. It is like saying "The signal to her call phone is weak"

| Point | You're breaking up! 소리가 끊겨서 들려!
We have a bad connection 전화상태가 안 좋아 잘 안 들려

A: I'm getting into an elevator right now.
지금 엘리베이터 안으로 들어가고 있어.

B: Call when you get out of it. **You're breaking up.**
나오면 전화해. 소리가 끊기네.

A: I've been calling your cell. B: Well, we get bad reception at CIA.
A: 핸드폰으로 계속 전화했었는데. B: 저기, CIA에서는 수신상태가 안 좋아.

A: You're breaking up and I can't hear you.
B: The reception is really lousy in this area.
A: 소리가 끊겨서 잘 안들려. B: 이 지역 수신상태가 정말 안좋아.

032 My battery went dead
배터리가 닳았어

this is a way to say "There was no more power." It is said when a cell phone has no more electrical charge

| Point | The phone [battery] is dead 배터리가 다 됐어, 전화기가 먹통이야
My battery's dying 배터리가 닳아서 전화가 끊어지려고 해
It eats up the batteries 배터리가 빨리 닳아
Keep your cell phone charged 핸드폰 충전시키고 다녀

A: Did you break your cell phone? 핸드폰 망가졌어?

B: No. **My battery went dead** and it stopped working. 아니, 배터리가 다 돼서 작동이 안돼.

The boss has been looking for you. Is your cell not working? 사장이 계속 찾았어. 핸드폰 안돼?

My battery went dead after I lost my charger.
내가 충전기를 잃어버린 후에 내 배터리가 죽었어.

My battery went dead in the middle of the conversation. 통화 중에 내 배터리가 죽었어.

Can I borrow your phone? My battery went dead. 네 전화기 좀 빌려줄테야? 내 전화가 죽었어.

033 Your cell phone's ringing 네 핸드폰 전화울려, 너 핸드폰 온다

this speaker is saying "Someone is calling you." He wants the phone's owner to know a call is coming in

| Point | I like your ring tone 너 핸드폰 벨소리 좋더라

A: **Your cell phone's ringing.** 네 핸드폰 전화온다.
B: Do you mind if I answer this call? 이 전화 받아도 돼지?

It's ringing, but she's not picking up.
전화기가 울리는데 걔는 전화를 받지 않고 있어.

Curtis' phone is ringing and he's not answering it?
커티스의 핸드폰이 울리는데 받지를 않는다고?

Why do you think the phone keeps ringing?
왜 전화기가 계속 울린다고 생각해?

We got home just before 10:00, uh, and the phone was ringing.
우리는 10시 바로 전쯤 집에 도착했는데 전화기가 울리고 있었어.

034 I'll send it to you in a text message
그 내용을 문자 메시지로 보내줄게

미드표현

this indicates the person will write something and send it on a cell phone. It is another way to say "I'll send the message with my cell phone"

| Point | text 문자를 보내다

A: What is the name of that book's author?
그 책의 저자 이름이 뭐야?
B: I can't remember, but **I'll send it to you in a text message** later. 기억 안 나지만 나중에 문자로 알려줄게.

Most exchanges take place by email, text message, or IM.
모든 거래는 이메일, 문자, 혹은 인터넷 메신저로 이뤄지고 있어.

I kept emailing her. I kept texting her.
난 계속 걔한테 이메일과 문자를 보내고 있었어.

Are you okay? I've been texting you all day.
너 괜찮아? 난 종일 너에게 문자를 보냈는데.

035 I'll friend you on Facebook 페이스북에 친추할게

미드표현

this literally means that the speaker is going to go on the Internet and become a friend on the listener's Facebook page, where they will be able to keep in touch. It is like saying "I'm going to join the list of people you are in contact with on Facebook"

| Point | friend (인터넷) …와 친구하다

A: Will we be able to stay in contact?
우리 연락하고 지낼 수 있을까?
B: **I'll friend you on Facebook.** 페이스북에 친추할게.

Oh, you're on facebook? You should friend me. 어, 너 페이스북하니? 그럼 나 친추해줘.

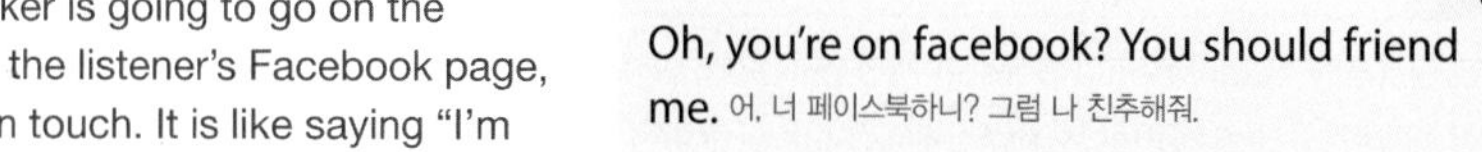

Why won't you friend me on Facebook?
페이스북에서 날 친추하지 않을거야?

If you friend me online, we can keep in touch.
네가 인터넷에서 나를 친구로 해놓으면 서로 연락할 수 있어.

The teachers decided to friend each other on Facebook. 선생님들은 페이스북에서 서로 친추하기로 했어.

MEMO

Things that are said when going somewhere

차를 타거나 차에서 내리거나

I'm stuck in traffic

001 Where am I? (장소) 여기가 어디죠?, (관계 등) 우리 무슨 관계야?

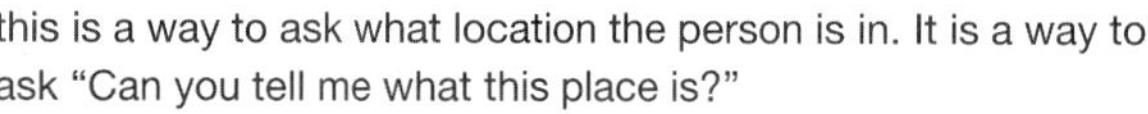

this is a way to ask what location the person is in. It is a way to ask "Can you tell me what this place is?"

Point Where are we? 여기가 어디지?
Where are we on[with]~? …은 어떻게 됐어?

A: Can you help me? **Where am I?**
도와줄래요? 여기가 어디죠?

B: You are at the corner of Main Street and Pearl Avenue. 여기는 메인 가와 펄 거리가 만나는 코너예요.

미드표현

Where are we? Who the hell are you?
여기가 어디야? 넌 도대체 누구고?

Where are we? Where is this relationship going?
우리 무슨 관계야? 너와 나의 관계가 어디로 가고 있는거야?

Where are we on unsolved rapes?
미해결된 강간사건들 어떻게 됐어?

Where are we with missing persons?
실종된 사람들 어떻게 됐어?

002 I think I'm lost 길을 잃은 것 같아

this speaker is saying "I don't know where I am." He probably wants someone to help him find the right way

Point I got lost 길을 잃었어
Are you lost? 길을 잃었어?
*I'm lost는 어떻게 해야 할 지 모르겠다라는 의미로도 쓰임

A: Where are you driving to now?
지금 어디로 차를 몰고 가는거야?

B: I'm not sure. **I think I'm lost.** 잘 몰라. 길을 잃은 것 같아.

미드표현

Hey, I'm lost. You from around here?
저기요, 길을 잃었는데, 이 근처에 살아요?

We got lost. We took the wrong bridge.
길을 잃었어. 다른 다리로 들어섰어.

We only went 1/4 of a mile, and we almost got lost. 우린 단지 4분의 1마일을 갔는데 거의 길을 잃을뻔 했어.

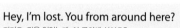

003 Which way is the Stock Exchange? 증권거래소가 어느 쪽예요?

this speaker is asking for directions. He wants to know how to get to the stock exchange

Point Which way is it? 그건 어느 쪽에 있어?
Which way is west? 어느 쪽이 서쪽야?
I'll show you the way 길 안내해드릴게요
This way 이쪽이예요
Please come this way 이쪽으로 따라 오세요

A: **Which way is the stock exchange?**
증권거래소가 어느 쪽예요?

B: It's a mile ahead, on your left hand side.
1마일 전방, 왼편에 있어요.

미드표현

Can you tell me which way Broadway is?
브로드웨이가 어느 쪽에 있는지 말해줄래요?

Which way is the bathroom? 화장실이 어느 쪽예요?

Which way is out? 어느 쪽이 출구인가요?

004 Coming through 좀 지나갈게요, 실례합니다

often this is used to say "I need to pass by you." A person might say this when moving out of a crowded place

Point Let me through 지나가게 길 좀 비켜주세요
Make way 길 좀 내주세요
Clear the way! 길 좀 비켜주세요!

A: Excuse me. **Coming through.** 실례해요. 좀 지나갈게요.

B: Hey, you shouldn't push me. 이봐요, 밀치면 안돼죠.

미드표현

Excuse me! Look out! Coming through!
실례해요! 조심해요! 지나갈게요!

Excuse me! Coming through behind you!
실례해요! 뒤에 좀 지나갈게요!

Clear the way! Coming through.
길 좀 비켜주세요. 지나갑니다.

005 Outta[out of] the way 길 좀 비켜

this is a rude way to tell someone "Move." The speaker wants someone to move so he can pass

I Point I Keep out of my way 비키세요 Step aside 비켜주세요
Out, please (엘리베이터) 저 내려요. 저 좀 내릴게요

A: I'm leaving this place. **Out of the way.**
여기를 나갈거야. 길 좀 비켜.

B: You need to try to be more polite. 좀 더 예의바르게 해야지.

미드표현

Coming through. Out of my way! Handicapped.
지나갈게요. 비켜주세요! 장애인예요.

Okay! Everybody out, please! 좋아! 모두 나가주세요!

Step aside, ladies! 아가씨들, 옆으로 비켜주세요!

006 I got held up behind a traffic accident

교통사고로 꼼짝달싹 못했어

this speaker wants to say "I was late because an accident made people drive slow." Usually it is a way to explain why a person was late

I Point I got held up~ …에 잡혀있다, 붂여있다
got held up at work 일에 묶여있다
got held up in traffic 차가 막혀 꼼짝달싹 못하다

A: Why were you so late getting to work?
왜 이렇게 출근이 늦은거야?

B: **I got held up behind** a traffic accident on the highway. 고속도로에서 사고가 나 꼼짝달싹 못했어.

미드표현

Uh, sorry I was late. I got held up at the office.
미안, 늦었네. 사무실에 잡혀 있었어.

Sorry I took so long. Got held up in the bathroom by the two girls.
시간이 오래 걸려 미안해. 욕실에서 2명의 여자에게 꼼짝 못하게 잡혀 있었어.

I got held up, and there was traffic and anyway, sorry. 길이 막혀 꼼짝 못하고 있었어, 어쨌든 미안해.

007 I'm stuck in traffic 차가 막혀, 길이 막혀서 꼼짝도 못했어, 정체야

usually this means that the cars on a street are moving very slowly. The speaker might be indicating "I will be late because I can't drive quickly"

I Point I I'm in traffic 차가 막혀
The traffic was terrible 끔찍하게 막혔어
Traffic on the strip 시내가 막혀 *strip은 간판이 즐비한 거리
It's usually jammed 거긴 늘상 꽉 막혀

A: Where are you calling from? 어디서 전화하는거야?

B: I'm downtown and **I'm stuck in traffic.**
시내에 있는데 교통 때문에 꼼짝 못하고 있어.

미드표현

Friday night. Traffic on the strip.
금요일 저녁. 시내가 막혀.

I'm in traffic. They're paving Fifth Avenue!
차가 막혀. 5번가를 포장하고 있어!

It took a long time. The traffic was terrible.
시간이 오래 걸렸어. 길이 정말 막혔어.

How was the traffic coming over here?
여기 오는데 교통 어때?

008 Going down? 내려 가세요?

this is used mainly on elevators. It is a way of asking "Are you traveling to lower floors?"

This is my floor (엘리베이터) 저 내려요. 내려야하니까 좀 비켜주세요
Going up? 올라 가세요?
Going up or down? (엘리베이터) 올라갑니까 내려갑니까?
Up or down? 올라가요? 아니면 내려가요?

A: Hello Mr. Tyler. **Going down?**
안녕하세요 타일러 씨. 내려가세요?

B: Why yes, I am going down. 물론, 내려갑니다.

미드표현

Which floor are you going to? Going down?
몇층 가세요? 내려가세요?

Going down? This elevator is descending.
내려가세요? 이거 내려가는데요.

Which button can I press? Going down?
몇층 눌러드릴까요? 내려가세요?

Glad you got on the elevator with me. Going down? 같이 엘리베이터를 타서 기뻐. 내려가?

009 You can't miss it 꼭 찾으실 거예요, 뻔히 보이니까 찾을 수 있어요

미드표현

often this indicates "It is easy to see." People say this when they give directions to some place

A: The supermarket is very big. **You can't miss it.**
슈퍼마켓이 아주 커. 바로 찾을거야.

B: Well, I think I'll go there to buy some groceries.
어, 식료품 좀 사려고 거기 갈 생각야.

You can't miss it. It's right off the main road.
쉽게 찾을 거예요. 큰길지나면 바로 있어요.

You can't miss it. It's right off the main road.
큰 도로를 지나면 바로 보여.

Just go downtown and it's right across from City Hall. You can't miss it.
조금 더 시내로 들어오면 시청 바로 맞은 편이야. 바로 보여.

010 I'll give you a ride 태워다 줄게

미드표현

this speaker is offering to drive a person somewhere. It means "We can go in my car"

| Point | Can I give you a ride[lift]? 태워다 줄까?
Can I have a ride[lift]? 태워줄래?
You wanna go for a ride? 드라이브시켜줄까?

A: It is a long subway ride to my house.
집에까지 지하철로 오래 걸려.

B: Don't worry. **I'll give you a ride.** 걱정마. 내가 태워다 줄게.

You know what? Let me give you a ride home.
저기 말야? 내가 집까지 태워다 줄게.

Hey, hang around for about a minute or two, okay? I'll give you a ride home.
야, 1, 2분 여기서 기다려봐, 응? 집까지 태워줄게.

How about I give you a ride home?
집에 데려다 줄까?

Wanna go for a ride in my Porsche?
내 포르쉐타고 드라이브하고 싶어?

011 I'll pick you up at seven 7시에 데리러 갈게

미드표현

the speaker wants to say "I will drive to your house by seven." We can understand the two people are going to travel together after they leave the house

| Point | pick sb up …을 차로 데리러 가다

A: When will you be arriving? 언제 도착할거야?

B: **I'll pick you up at** eight tomorrow night.
내일 저녁 8시에 데리러 갈게.

I'll pick you up at about seven. We have reservations at Michelle's.
한 7시경에 데리러 갈게. 미셸식당에 예약해두었어.

Why don't you call Mona to see if she can pick you up tomorrow morning?
모나한테 내일 아침 데리러 올 수 있는지 전화해보지, 그래?

012 (Are you) Going my way? 혹시 같은 방향으로 가니?, 같은 방향이면 태워줄래?

미드표현

this is a way of asking if the person wants to go to the same location. It is like asking "Do you want to go to the same place as me?"

A: I need a ride home. **Are you going my way?**
집에 차로 가야 하는데 혹시 나랑 같은 방향이니?

B: No, my house is in the other direction.
아니, 내 집은 다른 방향이야.

I'm headed downtown. Are you going my way? 난 시내가는데 같은 방향이야?

Are you going my way? I need a ride home.
같은 방향이야? 집에 차로 가야하는데.

Are you going my way? Can you give me a lift? 나랑 같은 방향이야? 나 좀 태워줄래?

013 Hop in 어서 타

often this is a way to say "Get into my car and I'll drive you somewhere." The speaker is offering to give someone a ride

| Point | Get in 차에 타
Step out of the vehicle = Get out of the car 차에서 어서 내려

A: Are you going downtown right now? 지금 시내에 가?
B: Yes I am. Hop in and I'll give you a ride.
어 그래. 어서 타. 데려다 줄게.

미드표현

I'll take you to school. Hop in.
학교 데려다줄테니 어서 타.

Hop in. I'm going to the same place.
어서 타. 나도 같은 곳에 가.

You want to get something to eat? Hop in.
먹을 거 좀 사고 싶어. 어서 타.

014 Please fill it[her] up (기름) 가득 채워주세요

the speaker wants to have his car filled with gas. He is at a gas station and is saying "Put as much gas in as possible"

| Point | Don't fill up the tank 가득 채우지 마세요
I ran out of gas 기름이 모자라

A: How much gas would you like? 기름 얼마나 넣어드릴까요?
B: It's nearly empty. **Please fill her up.**
거의 바닥이니 가득 채워주세요.

미드표현

This is the end of the road, and you're out of gas. 막다른 길이고 기름도 모자라.

We ran out of gas, and we don't know where we are, so we can't get a tow truck.
기름이 떨어졌어, 여기가 어딘지도 몰라서 견인차도 부를 수가 없어.

You sure you're not out of gas?
기름 안모자르는거 확실해?

015 Step on it! 빨리 해, (엑셀) 더 밟아

this is usually said when a person wants the driver to go fast. It is the same as saying "Drive quickly"

| Point | Ease it up 천천히 가요, 속도를 낮춰요
Why don't you slow down a bit? 좀 천천히 가자, 천천히 하자
Punch it! 더 밟아!

A: We're very late now. **Step on it.** 우리 아주 늦었어. 더 밟아.
B: I can't go much faster than this. 이것보다 더 빨리는 못가.

미드표현

I think maybe we should slow down a little.
조금 속도를 줄이는 게 좋을 것 같아.

Step on it! I'm really late! 더 밟아! 나 정말 늦었다고!

We've got to get out of here. Step on it!
우리 여기서 빨리 빠져나가야 돼. 어서 밟아!

Step on it! We're about to get robbed!
어서 밟아! 강도당하겠어!

016 It's about ten minutes' ride 차로 약 10분 거리예요

this indicates a location takes 10 minutes to drive to. It is a way to say "It will be 10 minutes to get there if we drive a car"

| Point | How far is it from here? 여기서 얼마나 걸려요?
Is it within walking distance? 걸어서 가도 되는 거리인가요?
It's not far from here 여기서 그리 멀지 않아요

A: Where is the historical museum?
역사 박물관이 어디에 있어요?
B: **It's about ten minutes' ride** from here.
여기서 차로 한 10분이면 갈 수 있어요.

미드표현

A: I heard that this city has a good art museum. B: That's right. It's not far from here.
A: 이 도시에 멋진 미술관이 있다면서. B: 맞아. 여기서 멀지 않아.

We can go to John's house. It's not far from here. 존의 집에 가자. 여기서 안 멀어.

My apartment is nearby. It's about 10 minutes' ride on the subway.
내 아파트가 이 근처야. 전철로 약 10분 가면 돼.

How far is it from here? Would taking a taxi be very expensive? 얼마나 멀어? 택시타면 많이 나올까?

017 I'll get off 내릴게요

often this is said when a person leaves a bus, train, plane or boat. It expresses "I'm leaving this vehicle"

I Point I get off 버스나 기차에서 내리다
get on 버스나 기차를 타다

A: Are you riding this bus for a long distance?
버스로 장거리 가나요?

B: No. **I'll get off** at the next stop.
아뇨. 다음 정거장에서 내립니다.

Will you tell me when[where] to get off?
언제[어디서] 내려야 하는지 알려줄래요?

I'll drop you. (가다) 내려드리죠.

When the time came to get on the bus, I couldn't do it. 버스를 탈 때가 되었을 때 난 그렇게 할 수 없었어.

018 Pull over right here 바로 여기에 차를 세워요

the speaker wants to say "Stop the car here." He is telling the driver where to stop

I Point I pull over 길가에 차를 세우다, 차를 옆으로 대다
pull up (신호등 등에) 차를 세우다

A: OK Joe, **you can pull over right here.**
좋아, 조, 여기에 차를 세워.

B: Is this the house you just bought?
네가 이번에 산 집이 이거야?

This is it, pull over right here.
여기예요, 여기에 차 세워요.

Why did you pull over to the side of the road?
왜 길 한쪽에 차를 세웠어?

Just pull over and let me out of the car!
차를 세우고 날 내려줘!

019 Get a speeding ticket? 속도위반 딱지 끊겼어?

this person is asking "Did the police stop you for driving too fast?" A speeding ticket makes people pay money because they drove fast and a policeman caught them

I Point I She got pulled over for speeding 속도위반으로 단속에 걸리다
I got caught for speeding 속도위반으로 걸렸어
Did you get a ticket? 딱지 끊겼어?

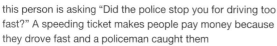

A: The police stopped me when I was on the highway. 고속도로를 달리는데 경찰이 날 세웠어.

B: Oh really? Did you **get a speeding ticket** from them? 어 정말? 속도위반 딱지 끊겼어?

Worst thing I've done is get a speeding ticket.
내가 한 가장 나쁜 짓은 교통위반야.

I got pulled over for a speeding ticket.
속도위반으로 잡혀 차를 길가에 댔어.

No rap sheet, not even a speeding ticket.
아무런 전과기록도 없어요, 속도위반 딱지조차도 없어요.

MEMO

Phrases that are used a lot in American dramas

기타 미드에 자주 나오는 표현들

I wouldn't put it past her

001 I wouldn't put it past her 걔는 능히 그러고도 남을 사람이야

this is a way to indicate that the speaker thinks someone is capable of doing something that is bad. When we hear this said, we know that the speaker is talking about something that he disapproves of. It is like saying "I wouldn't be surprised if he did that bad thing"

| Point | I wouldn't put it past sb (to+V~) …는 …을 하고도 남을 사람이야

A: The rumor is Ted stole the money.
테드가 돈을 훔쳤다는 소문이 있어.

B: **I wouldn't put it past him.** He's very greedy.
걔는 그러고도 남아. 욕심이 너무 많거든.

I wouldn't put it past her to hurt her own family. 걔는 자기 가족을 해치고도 남을 사람이야.

A: So what are you saying, that the twins murdered Martin? B: Well, I wouldn't put it past them.
A: 그럼 쌍둥이가 마틴을 살해한 거에 대해 네 생각은 어때? B: 개네들 그러고도 남지.

002 You're not that way 넌 그런 사람 아니잖아

this is often said when a speaker wants to express surprise about the way that someone has behaved. The speaker thinks that person's actions are unusual or out of the ordinary. In other words, the speaker is saying "That is not the way that you normally behave"

| Point | not that way 그런 식이 아닌

A: I got into a huge fight at a restaurant last night.
지난밤에 한 식당에서 큰 싸움을 벌였어.

B: But **you're not that way.** You hate conflict.
하지만 너 원래 그렇지 않잖아. 너 싸우는거 싫어하잖아.

We're not that way, I'm afraid. We need each other. 안됐지만 우리는 그런 사람들 아냐. 우리는 서로를 필요로 해.

You are not that way. So I suggest you think long. 넌 그런 사람이 아냐. 아주 진지하게 고민해봐.

I learned that I'll never win, not that way.
난 그런 식으로는 절대 이길 수 없다는 것을 배웠어.

003 You're still on that? 아직도 그 얘기야?

this is indicating that the speaker thinks someone has brought up the same subject over and over again, and it is not interesting or useful to do so. In other words, the speaker wants to know "Why do you always want to talk about that? No one else cares about it"

| Point | You still on that? 너 계속 그럴꺼야?, 아직도 그 얘기야?, 아직도 그 상태야?

A: My songs aren't good enough for your restaurant? 내 노래가 네 식당수준에 못미친다는 얘기지?

B: OK, **we're still on that.** 좋아, 계속 얘기하자는거지.

You're still on that? Why haven't you advanced? 아직도 그 상태야? 왜 나아가지 못한거야?

Most of the students are on level 3. You're still on that? 대다수 학생들은 레벨 3인데 넌 아직도 거기야?

You're still on that? Come on, hurry it up a little. 너 아직도 그 상태야? 어서, 좀 서둘러.

004 Who was on the receiving end of it?
그걸 당하는 쪽은 누구였어?

this is often asked to find out who suffered the unpleasant effects of something, often caused by another person. It is usually not good to be on the receiving end of something, because it is something negative. This can be like saying "Who had to deal with the problems that occurred?"

| Point | be on[at] the receiving end (of~)
(선물, 비난 등을) …받는 입장[쪽]이 되다, 당하는 쪽이 되다

A: Mr. White said some workers are going to be cut. 화이트 씨는 일부 직원들이 감원될거라고 했어.

B: **Who is going to be on the receiving end of the cuts?** 감원을 당하는 사람들이 누구일까?

미드표현

So who was on the receiving end of the 100 grand? 그럼 누가 10만 달러를 받는 쪽이 누구였어?

You guys have no idea what it's like to be on the receiving end. 당하는 입장이 어떤 건지 너희들은 몰라.

I just never thought you'd be on the receiving end of it. 난 네가 그것을 당하는 쪽일거라 전혀 생각해본 적이 없어.

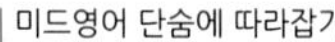

005 You really are a piece of work 너 참 괴짜다

this means that someone is very unique, but often it has a negative meaning and is not a compliment. Sometimes it is even an insult that indicates a person is bad. A person who says this often means "You do some very strange things that I don't understand"

| Point | a piece of work 독특한 사람, 특이한 사람, 괴짜

A: I tricked some kids into giving me this money.
몇몇 아이들 속여서 이 돈을 받아냈어.

B: That's terrible. **You really are a piece of work.**
심하구만. 넌 정말 괴짜야.

You're really a piece of work. 넌 정말 문제있는 사람이야.

She is a piece of work, and I don't know what to do. 걘 괴짜고 난 어떻게 해야 할지 모르겠어.

Your new mother-in-law's a piece of work.
네 새 장모는 괴짜야.

006 How is this gonna work out? 이 결과가 어떻게 될까?

미드표현

this is said when someone is unsure what the end result of something will be. It means the person wants another person to predict what may happen. It is very similar to asking "What do you think is going to happen next?"

| Point | how ~ work out 결과가 …하게 되다

A: The stock market fell by ten percent today.
오늘 주식이 10% 하락했어.

B: I don't like it. **How is this going to work out?**
맘에 안드네. 결과가 어떻게 될까?

You've committed to raising a baby with her. How is this gonna work out?
넌 헌신적으로 걔와 아이를 키워왔어. 그 결과가 어떻게 될 것 같아?

I was a little worried about how this was gonna work out, but you came through.
이게 어떻게 될지 좀 걱정을 했는데 넌 잘 헤쳐나왔어.

We hate each other. How is this going to work out? 우린 서로 싫어하는데 이 결과가 어떻게 되겠어?

007 X marks the spot! 바로 그 자리[지점]이야!

미드표현

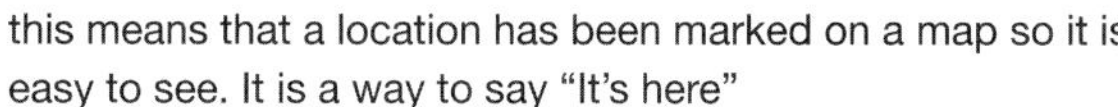

this means that a location has been marked on a map so it is easy to see. It is a way to say "It's here"

| Point | That hits the spot 바로 그거야

A: **X marks the spot.** Can you see where it is?
바로 여기야. 그게 어디 있는지 보여?

B: Oh yes. It is on the right side of this map.
어 그래. 이 지도의 오른편에 있어.

Really. it's very creative. Sort of like X marks the spot. 정말이야. 굉장히 창의적이야. 바로 그거야.

No, I'm not confused. X marks the spot.
아니 이해됐어. 바로 그 자리야.

008 It never happened 그런 일 없어, 이런 적 한번도 없었어

the speaker is saying "That didn't occur." He is expressing a blunt denial of some event

| Point | That (has) never happened (to me) (before)
이런 경험 처음이야, 난생 첨 겪는 일이야

A: Were you around when our teacher came to class drunk? 선생님이 술취해 수업에 왔을 때 있었니?

B: No way. That's a lie. **It never happened.**
아녜요. 거짓예요. 그런 적 없어요.

I never did anything like that before.
난 이런 거 해본 적이 없어요.

He said it never happened before.
걔는 이런 적 한번도 없었다고 했어.

I know it's never happened before.
이런 적 한번도 없었다는거 알아.

This has never happened to me before.
이런 경험 처음이야.

009 What is it gonna take to make you happy?

어떻게 해야 널 행복하게 해줄 수 있을까?

미드표현

this is said when a person wants to know what must be done in order to satisfy another person. It can be used in a romantic relationship where one person is unhappy. It can also be used in a business negotiation, when one person wants to know what he will need to do to reach an agreement. In other words, "How can I meet your needs?"

| Point | What is it going to take to~? 어떻게 해야 …하겠어?

A: **What is it gonna take to** make you happy?
어떻게 해야 만족하겠어요?

B: I want a much higher price for the property I'm selling. 내가 매도하는 부동산가격을 높게 쳐줘요.

What's it gonna take to get you to relax?
어떻게 해야 널 편하게 해줄 수 있을까?

What is it gonna take to get you dressed and through that door?
어떻게 해야 네가 옷을 입고 문밖으로 나가겠니?

I am tired of you judging me. What is it gonna take to get rid of you?
네가 날 비난하는데 지쳤어. 어떻게 해야 널 없앨 수 있을까?

010 It is written all over your face 네 얼굴에 다 써있어

미드표현

this means "I can see the answer by looking at your face. When a person's face shows his emotion strongly, this phrase is used

A: How did you know that I was feeling nervous?
내가 긴장하고 있는 줄 어떻게 알았어?

B: **It's written all over your face.** You seem uptight. 네 얼굴에 다 써있어. 초조해 보여.

Don't give me that look, because it's written all over your faces.
그런 표정짓지마, 네 얼굴에 다 적혀있으니까.

It's written all over your face. Today was a good day. 네 얼굴에 다 써 있어. 오늘은 좋았구나.

The jury found Gary guilty. It's written all over your face. 배심원은 게리에게 유죄판결을 내렸어. 네 얼굴에 다 써있어.

011 How'd you get your hands on this drug?

어떻게 이 약물을 손에 넣었어?

this is a way of asking how a person obtained something. In many cases, we can understand that the item was rare or illegal, and so it was not easy to acquire. In other words, "How were you able to get this unusual thing?"

| Point | get[lay] one's hands on sth …을 얻다, 구하다, 손에 넣다

A: **How'd you get your hands on this drug?**
어떻게 이 약물을 손에 넣었어?

B: A guy on the street sold it to me for fifty dollars.
거리에서 한 남자가 50달러에 그걸 내게 팔았어.

I'm trying to get my hands on an invoice, but it's gonna take some time.
송장을 손에 넣으려고 하는데, 시간이 좀 걸릴거야.

He managed to get his hands on his father's gun. 걔는 아버지의 총을 손아귀에 어찌어찌해서 넣었어.

How did a terror cell get its hands on anthrax without a single lab reporting a security breach? 테러범들이 탄저균을 손아귀에 넣었는데 어떻게 단 한군데 연구소에서도 보안침입에 대한 보고서가 없는거지?

012 That's (very) me 그게 나야, 나 원래 그런놈야

this is way for the speaker to express that something is an aspect of his character. He is telling people that this is how he normally behaves or acts, even if they disapprove of him. In other words "This is how I am"

| Point | That's (very) me 그게 나야, 나 원래 그런놈야, (호명에) 접니다

A: People don't think you should work in a bar.
넌 바에서 일하면 안된다고들 해.

B: **But that's me.** I like working there.
하지만 그게 나인걸. 난 거기서 일하는 걸 좋아해.

Actually, that's me. That's what I want.
실은 나 그런 사람야. 그게 내가 원하는거야.

He said he wished I wasn't gay, Grace. That's me. I'm gay.
그레이스, 걔는 내가 게이가 아니길 바랬었다고 해. 그게 나인걸. 난 게이야.

That's me. That's why I'm here now.
그게 나야. 그래서 내가 지금 여기에 있는거야.

I know it's pretty selfish, but that's me.
정말 이기적이라는 걸 알지만, 나 원래 그런 놈야.

013 I got[have] something for you 네게 줄게 있어

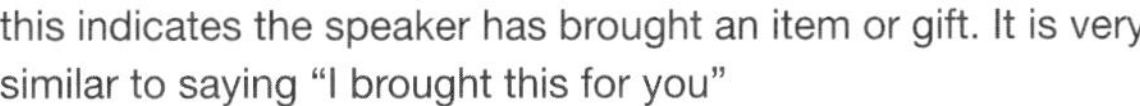

this indicates the speaker has brought an item or gift. It is very similar to saying "I brought this for you"

| Point | This is for you 널 위해 준비했어, 이건 네거야
Here's something for you 이거 너 줄려고
Here's to you 여기 너 줄려고

A: **I have something for you.** 네게 줄게 있어.
B: Oh really? Did you bring me a present?
어 정말? 내게 선물 가져 왔어?

미드표현

First, I have a little something for you.
첫째, 네게 뭐 좀 줄게 있어.

Come up to my apartment because I have something for you. 내 아파트로 와, 네게 줄게 있어.

So here's to you, Wilma. Happy birthday.
윌마야 이거 너 줄려고, 생일 축하해.

014 You're gonna have to suck up to him 걔한테 아부떨어야 돼

This means a person should be very nice to a boss or superior so that the person will gain some advantage

| Point | suck up to sb 잘 보이다, 아첨하다

A: Darlene always **sucks up to the boss.**
달린은 늘상 사장한테 아첨해.
B: Yeah, I think she wants him to promote her.
그래, 사장이 자길 승진시켜주길 바라나봐.

미드표현

Yeah, which surgeon are we going to have to suck up to today? 오늘은 어떤 외과의한테 비위를 맞춰야 할까?

That's right. You're gonna have to suck up to Edie Britt. 맞아. 넌 에디 브리트에게 잘 보여야 돼.

015 You're a great-looking guy and all 게다가 넌 아주 멋지게 생겼어

this is a somewhat complex phrase and is not easy to explain in a simple way. It means that the speaker acknowledges everything that is associated with the subject, but that the subject itself is in some way not impressive to the speaker. In other words, the speaker wants to say "I understand that, but I'm not impressed"

| Point | ~ and all 게다가, …까지 one and all 모두(everyone)

A: I find that some women are attracted to me.
나한테 끌리는 여자들이 좀 있는 것 같아.
B: Well, **you're a good looking guy and all.**
그리고 게다가 넌 아주 멋지게 생겼잖아.

미드표현

You should've turned your cell phone off completely with GPS and all.
넌 핸드폰을 완전히 껐어야 했어, GPS까지 말야.

Sure, I get that. I mean, he's your first boyfriend and all.
그래, 알겠어. 내 말은 게다가 걔가 네 첫번째 남친이라는거야.

016 I'm gonna miss you, you little cunt
네가 보고 싶어 질거야, 이 더러운 년아

this is a very impolite and sarcastic way of speaking. We can understand that the speaker is really not going to miss the person because he is using a very strong insult by calling her a cunt. It would be like saying "You are a bitch and I hope I never see you again"

| Point | you (little) cunt 이 더러운 년아
you prick 이 더러운 놈아 you bastard 이 나쁜 새끼야

A: I wish I had fired you before I resigned.
내가 그만 두기 전에 널 해고했어야 했는데.
B: Oh, I'm gonna miss you, **you little cunt.**
이 더러운 년아, 보고 싶을거야.

미드표현

You're spoiling everything! I'll gut you, you little cunt! 넌 모든 걸 망치고 있어! 널 작살낼거야, 이 더러운 년아!

All right? We're done! I did it for you, you prick. 알았어? 우리 끝이라고! 난 널 위해서 그랬어, 이 더러운 놈아.

You'd better run, you bastard!
도망가는게 좋아, 이 나쁜 새끼야!

017 It looks as if~ 마치 …인 것처럼 보여

this is like saying "It seems like S+V." The speaker is saying he thinks something is true

Point It looks as if she doesn't know that S+V
걔는 …을 몰랐던 것처럼 보여
It looks as if S+V 마치 …인 것처럼 보여

A: **It looks as if** Sara didn't know that the party was tonight. 새라는 파티가 오늘밤이었다는 걸 몰랐던 것 같아.
B: You're right. I don't think she came.
맞아. 걔가 안온 것 같아.

It looks as if you're expecting someone for dinner. 네가 저녁식사 같이 할 사람을 기다리는 것처럼 보여.

He does look as if he has something else on his mind. 걘 뭔가 다른 생각을 품고 있는 것처럼 보여.

018 Not that~, but~ …은 아니지만 그래도…

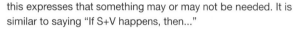

this expresses that something may or may not be needed. It is similar to saying "If S+V happens, then..."

A: **Not that** you need help, **but** we could study together. 네가 도움이 필요하지는 않겠지만 그래도 함께 공부할 수도 있어.
B: Yeah, it would be great if you and I could study.
그래, 너와 내가 함께 공부할 수 있다면 많은 도움이 될거야.

Not that I will come to the party, but if I do I'll come late. 파티에 가는 건 아니지만 가더라도 늦을거야.

Not that you need it, but here is some extra money. 네가 필요하지는 않겠지만 이거 여분의 돈이야.

Not that I ever saw it, but I heard it was a great movie. 본 적은 없지만 아주 좋은 영화라 들었어.

019 You've got me beat 나보다 낫네, 금시초문인 걸, 몰랐어

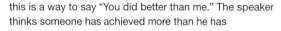

this is a way to say "You did better than me." The speaker thinks someone has achieved more than he has

A: I only sold three computers from our store.
가게에서 겨우 컴퓨터 3대를 팔았어.
B: **You've got me beat.** I didn't sell any today.
나보다 낫네. 난 오늘 한 대도 못 팔았어.

I just can't top that. You've got me beat. 완전 짱이다. 나보다 낫네.

You've got me beat. I won't even try to compete. 나보다 낫네. 경쟁할 시도도 못하겠네.

Your work is amazing. You've got me beat.
너 정말 일 잘하네. 나보다 나아.

020 We have something in common 우린 공통점이 있어

this means "We are similar in some way." Speakers say this when they think they would enjoy talking to someone who has similar interests

Point have something in common 뭔가 공통점이 있다

A: **We have got something in common.** We are both from California. 우린 공통점이 있어. 둘 다 캘리포니아 출신이야.
B: Oh yeah? I didn't know you came from there.
어 그래? 네가 거기 출신인지 몰랐어.

It looks like we've got something in common after all. 결국 우린 닮은 데가 있는 것 같아.

I don't really have anything in common with Karen. 난 카렌과 공통점이 정말이지 하나도 없어.

So that's one more thing we have in common.
그럼 우린 공통점이 하나 더 있는거네.

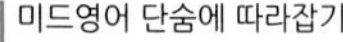

021 I'm way ahead of you 이미 다 알고 있어, 이미 하고 있어, 이미 앞서가고 있어

the speaker is indicating he has already thought of something. It is like saying "I considered that already"

| Point | be ahead of me[us] 내(우리) 앞에 …가 있다
Get ahead of~ …을 앞서가다

A: We need snacks for the party. 파티에 쓸 스낵이 필요해.
B: **I'm way ahead of you.** I bought chips and soda last night. 알고 있어. 지난 밤에 칩하고 음료수 사놨어.

Let's not get ahead of ourselves.
너무 앞서서 생각하지 말자.

Well, let's not get ahead of the evidence.
증거보다 앞서 생각하지 말자고.

You are always one step ahead of me. I hate that about you! 넌 늘 나보다 한발 앞서가. 그런 네가 싫어!

022 Not a big leap to lying 거짓말과 같은 셈이야

this is a way to indicate that someone is behaving in a bad way, and although he may not be lying, it would be easy for him to begin lying. We can understand the speaker has a low opinion of the person he's talking about. In other words, "I'm sure he could also be a liar"

| Point | not a big leap to~ …와 거의 마찬가지인 셈이다

A: She has tried to avoid answering our questions.
걔는 우리의 질문에 답을 하지 않으려고 했어.
B: I know, and **it's not a big leap to lying.**
알아, 거짓말하는 것과 마찬가지인 셈이야.

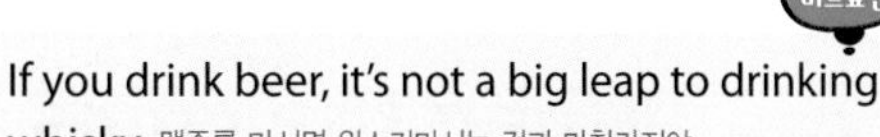

If you drink beer, it's not a big leap to drinking whisky. 맥주를 마시면 위스키마시는 것과 마찬가지야.

It's not a big leap to leave your job and start another. 직장을 그만두고 새롭게 시작하는 것과 마찬가지인 셈이야.

It won't be a big leap to move from your hometown to the city.
네 고향에서 도시로 이사하는 것과 같은 셈일거야.

023 The same goes for you 너도 마찬가지야

this usually means that the same rules will apply to one person in the same way they apply to other people. The speaker wants to say that the treatment of the person he is talking to is equal to the others. We can express something similar as "That means for you it's identical"

| Point | The same goes for~ …도 마찬가지야

A: Kevin is not allowed in. **The same goes for you.** 케빈은 출입금지야. 너도 마찬가지이고.
B: You mean I have to stand outside?
그럼 밖에서 기다려야 된다는 말야?

And the same goes for you if you stick with him. 걔랑 계속 같이 한다면 너도 마찬가지야.

No one is allowed to leave. The same goes for you. 아무도 나가지 못해. 이건 너도 마찬가지야.

Ron is prohibited from the club, and the same goes for you. 론은 클럽출입이 금지되었는데 너도 마찬가지야.

024 He's not gonna to pull the plug on his wife
걘 아내의 생명유지장치를 떼지 않을거야

this tells us that a man has a wife who is in the hospital, and she is being kept alive by medical machines. The man doesn't want to turn off or pull the plug on the machines, because then his wife would die. This can also be expressed as "He's not going to stop life support for his wife"

| Point | pull the plug (on sth[sb])
(자금부족으로) 그만두다, 손떼다, 중단시키다, 생명유지장치를 떼다

A: Ted's wife has been kept alive in the hospital for years. 테드의 부인은 오랫동안 병원에서 생명을 연명해왔어.
B: He's not going to **pull the plug on** his wife.
걔가 아내의 생명유지장치를 떼지는 않을거야.

They were getting ready to pull the plug.
걔네들은 손뗄 준비가 되어 있었어.

We decided it would be best to pull the plug, though, and let her rest in peace.
그렇다 해도 생명유지장치를 떼고 걔가 편안히 잠들게 하는게 최선일거라 결정했어.

I'll pull the plug on the settlement agreement, divorce you. 난 합의서를 그만두고 너와 이혼할거야.

025 You're stuck with me 넌 싫어도 나와 함께 있어야 돼

this is expressing that the speaker is going to stay with someone, and that person has no choice in the matter. In other words, the listener must tolerate the speaker even if he doesn't like him. It is like saying "I'm staying with you, no matter what"

| Point | be[get] stuck with sb[sth]
억지로 사귀거나, 싫은 일을 하다, 원치 않지만 함께 붙어 있다

A: Can't I choose to work with another partner?
내가 파트너를 바꿔서 일할 선택권이 없나?

B: No way. **You're stuck with me.**
전혀 없어. 너 나랑 함께 해야 돼.

Why do we always get stuck with looking for the needle in the haystack?
왜 우리는 항상 건초더미 속에서 바늘을 계속 찾아야 하는걸까?

You're stuck with me till the end of the week.
주말이 시작되기 전까지 싫어도 넌 나와 함께 있어야 돼.

You gonna be stuck with this people for the next five hours!
넌 앞으로 5시간 동안 이 사람들과 함께 있어야 될거야!

026 When the chips are down, you come through
위기가 닥치면 네가 해내잖아

this is a way to say that the person is dependable, even when things are tough to deal with. The speaker is also saying that he trusts this person. It is very much like saying "I can count on you when things become difficult"

| Point | when the chips are down 막상 일이 닥치면, 위기가 오면

A: Why did you choose to work with me?
넌 왜 나하고 일하겠다고 한거야?

B: **When the chips are down,** you come through.
위기가 닥치면 네가 해내잖아.

Can I trust you when the chips are down?
막상 일이 닥치면 내가 널 믿을 수 있을까?

I plan to get out of here when the chips are down. 위기가 오면 난 여기를 벗어날 계획이야.

He does his best work when the chips are down. 막상 일이 닥치면 걔는 자기 일에 최선을 다해.

027 I'm wired into the DA's office 난 검사실에 연줄이 있어

this is an unusual phrase and it means that the speaker has a relationship with the district attorney's office, which is in charge of prosecuting criminals when they have been arrested. We might presume the speaker has some influence in criminal cases. It is like saying "I have leverage with the district attorney"

| Point | be wired into~ (고위직과) …에 연줄이 있다,
…에 열중하다[빠져있다](be devoted to), 송금되다

A: How were you able to influence the prosecution? 너 어떻게 검찰에 힘을 쓸 수 있었던거야?

B: **I'm wired into** the DA's office. 난 검사실에 연줄이 있거든.

I know a lot of cops and detectives, and inspectors. And of course I am wired into the D.A.'s office.
난 경찰과 형사들 그리고 조사관들을 알고 있어. 물론 난 검사실에도 연줄이 있어.

I trust the rest of my money will be wired into my account shortly?
내 나머지 돈은 바로 내 계좌로 송금되는거죠?

That $10,000 was wired into Amir's account.
저 만 달러는 아미르의 계좌로 송금됐어.

028 (I'm) All better 좋아졌어

this indicates someone is healed or not sick anymore. It is the same as saying "I feel good now"

| Point | make it all better 좋게 하다

A: How do you feel after having the flu?
독감 걸린 후에 몸 상태가 어때?

B: **I'm all better.** I am as healthy as I've ever been.
좋아졌어. 그 어느 때보다 건강해.

You got that, Mom? Dad made it all better.
알았어요, 엄마? 아빠가 그걸 더 좋게 했어요.

You had an accident, remember? But the doctors made you all better.
너 사고를 당했어, 기억나? 하지만 의사들이 널 나아지게 했어.

I'm all better now that I'm with you.
너와 함께 있으니 좋아졌어.

029 We're in the middle of nowhere 우린 아주 외진 곳에 있어

미드표현

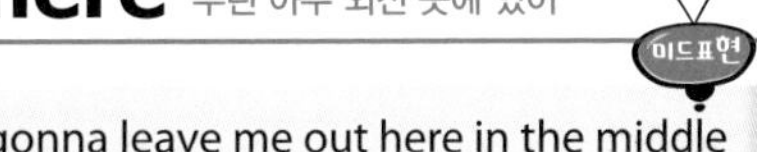

this usually means the people are in the country, away from buildings and people. It is often said when people get lost while driving

| Point | be in the middle of nowhere 외딴 곳에 있다, 아주 멀리 있다

A: **We're in the middle of nowhere.**
우린 아주 외진 곳에 있어.

B: I know. I think we need to look at a map.
알아. 지도를 봐야 될 것 같아.

You're gonna leave me out here in the middle of nowhere? 이런 외진 곳에 날 버려둘거야?

I dropped him off in the middle of nowhere.
난 걜 외딴 곳에 내려주었어.

You won't get cell coverage. We're in the middle of nowhere.
핸드폰이 안 될거야. 우린 아주 외진 곳에 있는거야.

030 There you have it 네 말이 옳아, 그렇게 된거야, 자 볼까, 자 됐어

미드표현

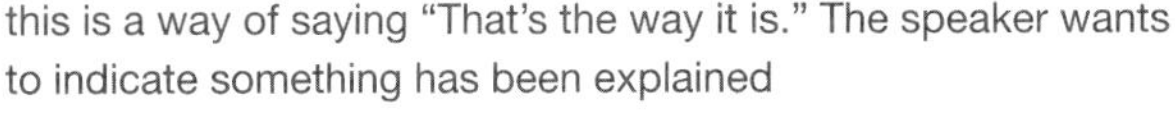

this is a way of saying "That's the way it is." The speaker wants to indicate something has been explained

A: So you spent several years in Australia?
호주에서 몇 년 있었다며?

B: **There you have it.** I owned an import business there. 맞아. 거기서 수입업을 했었어.

There you have it. Now we know the truth.
네 말이 옳아. 이제 우리는 진실을 알아.

I'm telling you everything I know. There you have it. 내가 아는 걸 다 말하는거야. 그렇게 된거야.

There you have it. We're all done now.
그렇게 된거야. 우린 이제 다 끝났어.

031 It's like you're hiding something 뭔가 숨기는 것 같아

미드표현

this indicates the speaker thinks someone isn't being honest about something. It is similar to saying "I think you're not being truthful"

| Point | It's like+N[~ing, S+V] …하는 것과 다름없어

A: You never let me see your e-mail. **It's like you're hiding something.**
이메일을 내겐 전혀 안 보여주네. 뭔가 숨기는 것 같아.

B: My e-mail messages are my own private business. 내 이메일 메시지는 내 사생활이라고.

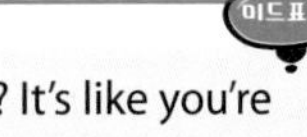

Why are you acting so weird? It's like you're hiding something.
왜 그렇게 이상하게 행동해? 뭔가 숨기는 것 같아.

It's like saying, "Hi, I just killed my wife."
마치 "안녕, 방금 마누라 죽였어"라고 말하는 것 같아.

032 She's gonna mooch off us 걔는 우리에게 빌붙어살거야

미드표현

this indicates that the speaker thinks a woman will use their things without sharing the cost of buying them. We can understand that the woman is probably a visitor, and the speaker thinks she is selfish. We can say something similar like this "She'll use our stuff, but she won't help pay for it"

| Point | mooch off 돈도 안주고 빌붙어살다(sponge off 빌붙어지내다), 빈대붙다

A: Why don't you want her to stay with us?
걔가 우리와 함께 남는 걸 원치 않아?

B: **She's going to mooch off us.** 걔는 우리에게 빌붙어 살거야.

I've already mooched dinner off you guys.
난 이미 너희들로부터 저녁빈대붙었잖아.

We're supposed to just get him a ticket?! That guy is always mooching off of us!
걔한테 표를 줘야 된다고?! 저 자식 늘상 우리한테 빈대붙잖아.

You know what her plan is, she's gonna stay here and mooch off us.
걔 계획인 뭔지 알아, 걘 여기 남아서 우리한테 빌붙어살거래.

She's gonna stay here and mooch off us forever? 걘 영원히 여기 남아 우리한테 빌붙어산다는거야?

033 She treats you like shit 걘 널 개떡같이 여겨

this indicates that the speaker thinks a woman treats the listener very poorly. Often it is a way to say that the speaker thinks the listener needs to end the relationship with the woman. In other words, "She acts very unkind toward you"

| Point | treat sb like shit …을 개떡같이 여기다, 못되게 대하다
look like shit 꼴이 말이 아니다, 똥씹은 표정이다

A: Why don't you like my new girlfriend?
왜 내 새여친을 좋아하지 않는거야?

B: Ralph, **she treats you like shit.**
랄프, 걘 너를 개떡같이 대한다고.

What happened to you? You look like shit.
너 무슨 일이야? 똥씹은 표정인데.

I can't believe you let him treat you like shit.
걔가 너를 개떡같이 대하도록 놔두다니 믿기지 않네.

I looked like shit after drinking all night.
밤새 술을 마셔대니 꼴이 말이 아냐.

If you treat people like shit, they will hate you.
사람들을 그렇게 못되게 대하면 사람들이 널 싫어하게 될거야.

034 Just like that 그냥 그렇게

this means "It happened quickly." The speaker is saying something was fast

A: Did you have a long interview? 인터뷰가 길었어?

B: No, it was over **just like that.** 아니, 그냥 그렇게 끝났어.

I'm supposed to forgive you, just like that?
내가 널 용서하기로 되어 있는거야, 그냥 그렇게?

So that's it? It's over? Just like that?
그래서 그게 다야? 정말 끝이란 말야? 그냥 이렇게?

I cannot believe you broke up with her just like that. 네가 걔하고 그냥 그렇게 끝낸 게 믿을 수가 없어.

035 Let's just call it even 비긴 셈치자

this is a way to say "We don't owe each other anything." It implies that the people don't have a debt to each other

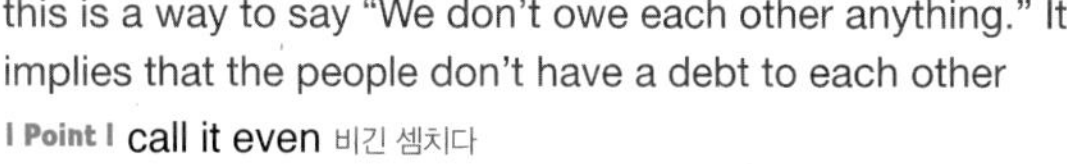

| Point | call it even 비긴 셈치다

A: Do I owe you some money for the movie tickets? 영화표 값 내가 줘야지?

B: No, you bought dinner. **Let's just call it even.**
아니, 네가 저녁 샀잖아. 비긴 셈치자.

Forget about what you owe me. Let's just call it even. 내게 빚진 건 잊어. 비긴 셈 치자.

Let's just call it even. I don't want anything else. 비긴 셈 치자. 다른 거 원하는 거 없어.

Everything is cool now. Let's just call it even.
모든 게 다 잘됐네. 비긴 셈 치자.

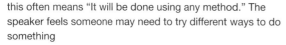

036 One way or another 어떻게든, 어떻게 해서든, 무슨 짓을 해서라도

this often means "It will be done using any method." The speaker feels someone may need to try different ways to do something

A: It is taking forever to build this new subway.
이 새로운 지하철을 만드는데 시간이 엄청 걸릴거야.

B: They will complete it, **one way or another.**
어떻게 해서든 완공될거야.

One way or another, you got to pay what you owe. 어떻게 해서든 빚진 건 갚아.

She's the only family I have, and one way or another, I will make it better.
걔는 내 유일한 가족이야. 어떻게든 더 좋아지게 할거야.

No, I'm going to do this one way or another.
아니, 난 어떻게든 이걸 할거야.

One way or another, you will get that girl pregnant. 어떻게든, 넌 저 여자애를 임신시킬거야.

037 It's a guy thing 남자들 이야기야

this speaker is saying something is understood more by men. It indicates "It's something that men think more about than women do"

| Point | We're doing guy stuff 남자들 하는 일하고 있어

A: I don't know why you like watching sports so much. 왜 네가 그렇게 많이 스포츠경기 보는 걸 좋아하는지 모르겠어.

B: **It's a guy thing.** Women don't understand it. 남자들이 좋아하는거야. 여자들은 이해 못해.

미드표현

I don't know. Maybe it's a guy thing. 잘 모르지만 아마 남자들 얘길거야.

Betty kept a secret. It's because it's a guy thing. 베티가 비밀로 하는데 남자 문제니까 그러는거야.

It's a guy thing, you couldn't possibly understand. 그건 남자들 얘기야. 넌 거의 이해할 수가 없을거야.

038 Fork over some cash 현금 좀 내

this is a very simple way to tell a person that he has to pay for something, or that he must pay what he owes. It is a demand, and does not give the person the option of refusing to pay. It is very similar to saying "Okay, it's time for you to pay the money you owe"

| Point | fork (it) over 돈을 주다[내다]

A: You need to **fork over some cash** for the tickets. 티켓을 사려면 현금을 좀 내야 돼.

B: Okay, I'll stop at the bank and pick up some money. 알았어. 은행에 들러서 돈 좀 찾을게.

미드표현

Come on everybody, fork over your cash. 자 여러분, 현금을 내세요.

Well, it's gonna hurt a lot more if you don't sign it. Fork it over. 그럼 서명을 하지 않으면 더 많이 아플거야. 돈을 내라고.

Come on, we always share. Fork it over. 그러지마. 우린 항상 공유하잖아. 돈을 줘봐.

Now just shut up and fork over some cash. 자 그만 입다물고 현금이나 내라고.

039 We even raised a toast to good old Mike

우린 그리운 옛 마이클을 위해 건배하기도 했어

this is a way of saying that someone or something has been around for a long time and that it is liked by many people. Generally we can understand it is a show respect for the reliability and trustworthiness of the person or thing. It is similar to saying "It has been around a long time and we are very fond of it[him]"

| Point | good old 그리운, 지나간, 예전의, (반어적) 그 잘난

A: I heard everyone had a good time down at the pub. 술집에서 다들 즐거웠다며.

B: Yes, we even raised a toast to **good old** Mike. 어, 그리운 마이크를 위해 건배하기도 했어.

미드표현

I'm sure good old Mike was ready and able twenty-four seven. 난 그리운 마이크가 언제든지 준비가 되어있었을거라 확신해.

When good old Chris came home with some whore's baby, did you pretend to love it? 그 잘난 크리스가 어떤 매춘부 아이와 함께 집에 왔을 때 아이를 좋아하는 척 했어?

040 He died in a state of grace 갠 은총을 받고 죽었어

this is a religious reference that means the person died with God's love and favor surrounding him. To religious people, this is considered the best way to die, because whatever sins they have will be forgiven. It would be similar to saying "He died knowing that he was going to heaven"

| Point | be in a state of+명사 …한 상태이다

A: Was it sad when your grandfather died? 네 할아버지가 돌아가셨을 때 슬펐어?

B: Yes, but we believe that he **died in a state of grace.** 어, 하지만 할아버지는 은총을 받고 돌아가셨다고 믿고 있어.

미드표현

Well, he was in a state of severe agitation. 음, 갠 심각하게 동요했어.

Steven came to me three years ago in a state of confusion. 스티븐은 혼란에 빠진 상태로 3년전에 날 찾아왔어.

After receiving a report about the Gallagher home, I found the children under Francis Gallagher's care in a state of neglect. 갤러거홈에 관한 보고서를 본 후에 난 프랜시스 갤러거의 보호하에 있는 아이들이 방임상태에 있다는 것을 알게 됐어.

041 Would you scoot a little? 조금만 옆으로 가줄래?

this is a very informal way to ask another person to move over. Often this is said when people are sitting in a small area and someone arrives and needs extra room to be able to sit down too. It is like saying "Shove over so I can sit next to you"

| Point | scoot over 옆으로 자리를 살짝 비켜주다
scoot sth over 옆으로 좀 이동시키다

A: **Would you scoot a little?** I need to sit down.
옆으로 좀 가줄테야. 나 좀 앉게.

B: Sure. Does this give you enough room?
그래. 이제 공간 충분해?

미드표현

Excuse me. Can I just scoot in front of you?
미안하지만 네 앞으로 가도 될까?

Scoot over a little bit, you're blocking the clock. 옆으로 조금만 비켜봐, 네가 시계를 가리고 있어.

You mind if I take a look? Scoot over a little so Sam can see. 내가 봐도 될까? 샘이 볼 수 있도록 좀 옆으로 가봐.

Dad, here. Sit here. Jennifer, scoot over, please. 아빠, 여기요. 여기 앉아요. 제니퍼 옆으로 좀 가봐.

042 You better believe she's tired 정말로 걔는 지쳤어

this expresses that someone is very tired, and that feeling tiredness is genuine. People often say you'd better believe it when they want to emphasize that something is true or real. Another way to say this is "She is really tired now"

| Point | You'd better believe that~ 정말이지 …해, 틀림없이 …해

A: How is Angie after she worked all night?
앤지가 밤새 일한 후에 어때?

B: **You better believe she's tired.** 정말로 걘 지쳤어.

미드표현

You better believe it. 틀림없어, 정말이야.

If I see you coming in, I'll kill her! You better believe that! 네가 들어오면 걜 죽여버릴거야! 정말이야!

You better believe he's tired, after the day we had! 우리가 보낸 하루를 생각해보면 걘 정말 지쳤어.

043 I've come this close to winning 난 거의 승리 할 뻔했어

this means the speaker has almost won something, but not quite. Perhaps he is speaking of running in a race or being in a contest and finishing in second or third place. Another way to express the same thing is "I nearly was a winner"

| Point | be[come] this close to~ 거의 …할 뻔하다, …할 지경이다

A: Have you ever hit a casino jackpot?
카지노에서 대박 터트린 적 있어?

B: No, but **I've come close to winning.**
아니, 하지만 거의 딸뻔 한 적이 있어.

I am this close to robbing you guys.
너희들을 거의 털 뻔 했어.

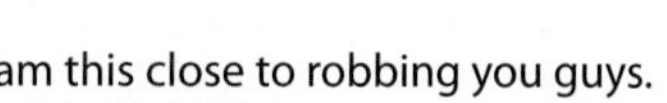

I've never been this close to suicide.
난 이처럼 거의 자살할 뻔한 적이 없어

I was this close to dying for two weeks.
지난 2주 동안 난 거의 죽을 뻔 했어.

Emily was this close to getting her life back.
에밀리는 거의 자기 삶을 다시 되찾을 뻔했어.

044 I can hold my head high 난 떳떳할 수 있어

this implies that the speaker has nothing to be ashamed of and can be proud of whatever happened. Sometimes when a scandal occurs, people's reputations are hurt. If a person still has a good reputation, he can still hold his head high. Another way to say this is "I am not ashamed"

| Point | hold one's head high 떳떳하다, 자랑스럽게 여기다, 거만[도도]하게 굴다

A: You were acquitted of all charges.
너는 모든 혐의를 벗었어.

B: **I can hold my head high** now. 난 이제 떳떳할 수 있겠구만.

I can walk down the street and hold my head high! 난 거리를 자랑스럽게 활보할 수 있어!

Well as long as I give it my best shot, I can hold my head high.
내가 최선을 다하는 한 난 떳떳할 수 있어.

I held my head high after being found innocent. 난 무죄로 판명난 뒤에 떳떳했어.

045 It's a fine line 거의 차이 없어, 매한가지야

this is a way of saying "This thing can be very similar to that thing." Often it is a way of warning someone not to get the two things confused

| Point | It's a fine line between A and B A와 B사이의 차이가 거의 없다

A: Sometimes my boyfriend makes me hate him.
때때로 남친이 내가 자기를 미워하게 만들어.

B: **It's a fine line** between love and hate when you are passionate. 열정적일 때는 사랑과 증오는 거의 같은 거지.

It's a fine line between a cop and a criminal.
경찰과 범죄자는 거의 차이가 없어.

Don't be rude. It's a fine line to cross over.
무례하게 행동하지마. 받아들일 수 없는 그런 행동을 하는 것과 매한가지야.

It's a fine line between love and hatred.
사랑과 증오사이의 차이는 거의 없어.

046 That's all I need 내가 필요한 건 그게 다야

미드표현

the speaker is saying that things are complete. It means "It's everything I have to have"

| Point | That's all I need to do~ 내가 필요한 건 …하는 것 뿐이야
All I need is ~ 내가 필요한 건 …야

A: I heard you don't have much money these days.
너 요즘에 돈이 많지 않다며.

B: But I have enough food. **That's all I need.**
하지만 식량은 충분해. 난 그거면 돼.

Thank you so much. That's all I needed to hear. 고마워. 내가 듣고 싶었던 건 그게 다야

All I need is the opportunity for you to hear me out. All right?
내가 바라는 건 네가 내 얘길 끝까지 다 들어주는 기회를 달라는거야, 알겠어?

All I need is five minutes. 내가 필요로 하는 건 5분이야.

047 (It) Doesn't fit 아귀가 들어맞지 않아, 앞뒤가 맞지 않아

미드표현

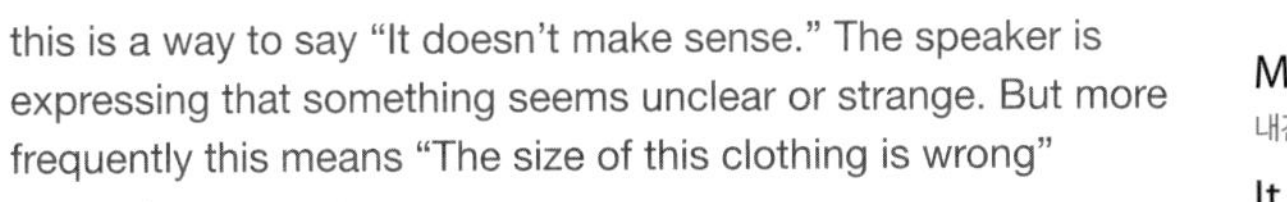

this is a way to say "It doesn't make sense." The speaker is expressing that something seems unclear or strange. But more frequently this means "The size of this clothing is wrong"

| Point | fit 적합하다, 어울리다

A: Your wife said she went to visit her sister.
네 아내가 그러던데 동생 만나러 갔었대.

B: **It doesn't fit.** My wife and her sister don't like each other. 말도 안돼. 내 처와 처제는 사이가 안좋아.

Mine doesn't fit. The pants are a little tight.
내건 안 맞아. 바지가 너무 꽉 끼어.

It doesn't fit into my life. 내 인생에 안 맞아.

You were right, it doesn't fit the symptoms.
네 말이 맞았어, 그건 증상과 맞지가 않아.

Admirable work, but I'm afraid it doesn't fit with my agenda.
훌륭하게 일을 했는데 내 일정과 맞지가 않는 것 같아.

048 What is this fuss about? 왜들 이 난리야?

미드표현

this is a way to ask why something is causing a problem or disturbance. It is like asking "Why is this happening?"

| Point | fuss 야단법석, 호들갑
make a fuss about~ …에 불필요한 소란을 떨다

A: **What is this fuss about?** 왜들 이 난리야?

B: I think that two schoolboys started fighting.
남학생 두 명이 싸우기 시작한 것 같아.

I just feel kind of silly that I made such a big fuss about my ring.
귀걸이 갖고 야단법석을 떨다니 내가 좀 어리석었어.

He's going to be up all night and fussy all day.
걘 오늘 밤새며 소란스러울거야.

049 Take it up with your boss 사장하고 이야기해봐

미드표현

the speaker is saying "This is the responsibility of your boss." In other words, he thinks the person should talk to his boss about the matter

| Point | take it up with sb (문제, 제안)…와 상의하다, 이야기하다

A: We are always being asked to work late.
늘상 우리에게 야근을 시켜.

B: I know. **Take it up with your boss.**
알아. 사장하고 이야기해봐.

If she gets mad, have her take it up with me.
걔가 화를 내면 나하고 이야기하게 끔 해.

Take it up with the D.A. 검사님하고 말씀해보시지요.

Why didn't you just take it up with me?
왜 나한테 직접 털어놓지 않았어?

050 It's for a good cause 좋은 일로 그러는거야

미드표현

this is a way to say "There is a good reason for doing this." The speaker feels that it is important to do something

A: Are you saying you want me to donate money?
내가 돈을 기부하라는 말이야?

B: **It's for a good cause.** It will help poor children.
좋은 일로 그러자는거야. 가난한 아이들을 도와줄거야.

I will donate an $5 million check that I was saving for a good cause.
좋은 일에 쓰려고 모아둔 5백만불을 기부할게요.

A: I really appreciate you donating this stuff. B: Anything for a good cause.
A: 이것들을 기부해줘서 정말 고마워. B: 좋은 일에 쓰이는 거라면야.

051 Stay put 그대로 있어

미드표현

this indicates the speaker wants someone to remain in a place. It is like saying "Don't move"

| Point | Stay like this 계속 이렇게 해
Stick around 가만히 있어(Stay here)

A: **Stick around** and we'll have some fun together.
가만히 있어, 함께 재미있게 놀자.

B: Oh really? What do you want us to do?
정말? 우리가 어떻게 하면 되는데?

You two stay put right there. We'll meet you there. 너희 둘 거기 그대로 있어. 우리가 가서 만날 테니.

Stay put till I need you.
내가 널 필요로 할 때까지 그대로 있어.

Try again. Things can't stay like this.
다시 해 봐. 이렇게 지낼 순 없잖아.

Come on, honey, stick around. It's fun here.
자, 자기야, 가만히 있어. 여기 재미있다고.

052 This one's for you 이건 너를 위한거야

미드표현

this is said to dedicate something to someone. It indicates "I'm doing it to honor you"

A: I dedicate this soccer match to my dad. **This one's for you.**
이 축구게임을 아버지께 바칠게요. 이건 아버지를 위한 게임예요.

B: That is a very nice thing to do, son.
그렇게 해줘서 참 고맙구나, 아들아.

I dedicate this to my sweetheart. This one's for you. 난 이걸 내 사랑하는 이에게 바쳐. 이건 너를 위한거야.

This one's for you. I'll always remember our time together.
이건 너를 위한거야. 우리 함께 한 시간을 항상 기억할거야.

I'll play you a song. This one's for you.
네게 노래를 연주할게. 이건 너를 위한거야.

053 I'm going to take the high road 내 소신대로 행동할거야

this speaker is expressing that he is going to do things in a respectful way. It is very similar to saying "I'll act with dignity"

| Point | take the high road 소신에 맞는 길을 택하다, 소신에 따라 행동하다

A: I heard your ex-girlfriend has been saying you are bad. 헤어진 여친이 네가 나쁜 놈이라고 하고 다닌다며.

B: **I'm going to take the high road** and say nothing about her.
난 소신대로 행동하면서 걔에 대해 아무 말도 하지 않을거야.

미드표현

I'm gonna take the high road and I'm gonna ignore your nastiness.
난 내 신념대로 행동할거고 너의 비열함을 무시하겠어.

I won't argue. I'm going to take the high road.
난 다투지 않을거야. 난 내 소신대로 행동할거야.

I'm going to take the high road. No more profanity. 난 옳은 길을 갈거야. 불경한 말은 쓰지 않을거야.

I won't stoop. I'm going to take the high road.
난 비뚤어지지 않고 바른 길로 갈거야.

054 I'm trying to keep it that way 그렇게 하려고 해

this is usually said when someone doesn't want things to change. It is a way to say "I want it to continue to be the same"

| Point | keep it that way 계속 그렇게 지내다[하다]

A: The garden that you planted looks very beautiful. 네가 가꾼 정원이 정말 아름다워 보여.

B: **I'm trying to keep it that way,** though it's hard work. 힘든 일이지만, 계속 그렇게 유지하려고 해.

미드표현

Louis and I are happy. Can we just keep it that way for a while?
루이스와 난 행복해. 잠시 동안 그냥 그렇게 지낼 수 있을까?

We're gonna do our best to keep it that way, okay? 우리는 그렇게 하려고 최선을 다할거야, 알았어?

And I need to keep it that way.
그리고 난 계속 그렇게 하는게 필요해.

055 That fits the bill 그게 요구를 충족시켜줘

this means "It's just fine." It indicates that something is good and works well

| Point | fit the bill 필요한 것을 가져다주다, 요구를 충족시켜주다

A: This new copier will help you work faster.
새로운 복사기로 일을 더 빨리 할 수 있을거야.

B: **That fits the bill.** It will be great to be able to use it. 그렇게 돼. 이걸 사용하게 돼서 정말 좋아.

미드표현

Thanks for the advice. That fits the bill.
조언 고마워. 그게 딱 맞았어.

That fits the bill. It's exactly what I need.
그게 딱 맞았어. 내가 필요한게 바로 그거야.

That fits the bill. How much do I owe you?
그게 딱 맞았어. 내가 얼마 줘야 돼?

056 I'll go along for the ride 같이 갈게

this is usually said when someone wants to get in a car. It means "I'll travel in your car with you." But to "be along for the ride" can also mean that someone is present but not active or participating. It is like saying someone is "going somewhere to watch what will happen"

| Point | go along for the ride 부담없이 함께하다
be along for the ride 소극적으로 가담하다

A: Do you want to go shopping with me? 나랑 쇼핑갈래?

B: Sure. **I'll go along for the ride.** 물론, 네 차로 갈게.

미드표현

Do not expect him to just go along for the ride. 걔가 그냥 따라올거라 기대하지마.

He's calling the shots and Tina's just along for the ride. 걔가 결정하면 티나는 그냥 따라가.

057 I got back in one piece 무사히 돌아왔어

usually this is expressing "I wasn't harmed." The speaker had a dangerous experience but wasn't injured

| Point | in one piece 무사히, 온전히

A: I heard you went to Iraq. Was it dangerous?
이라크에 갔다며. 위험했어?

B: Yes, but **I got back in one piece.**
어, 하지만 무사히 돌아왔어.

Just promise me you'll bring her back in one piece. 무사히 걜 다시 데려온다고 약속해줘.

I'm going to help her get through Princeton in one piece. 걔가 무사히 프린스턴을 졸업할 수 있도록 도울게.

Glad to see you in one piece. 네가 무사히 돌아와 기뻐.

058 It's just a phase 그냥 한때 저러는거야

미드표현

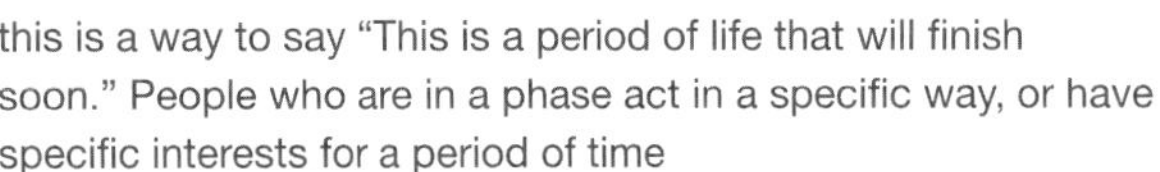

this is a way to say "This is a period of life that will finish soon." People who are in a phase act in a specific way, or have specific interests for a period of time

| Point | This is probably just a phase 일시적인 현상일거야
That does not sound like a phase to me
일시적으로 저러는 게 아닌 것 같아

A: I'm worried that my son plays too many computer games. 아들이 컴퓨터 게임을 너무 많이 해서 걱정야.

B: **It's just a phase.** He'll get interested in other things soon. 한때 그러는 거지. 곧 다른 거에 관심을 가질거야.

Scott hates talking with girls. I'm sure it's just a phase.
스캇이 여자애들하고 말하는 걸 싫어하는데 한때 저러는 걸거야.

You're overreacting. Tina's just going through a phase. That's what girls her age do.
네가 과민반응하는거야. 티나는 일시적인 현상을 겪는거야. 걔 또래의 여자애들이 그러는 거잖아.

You hope that Sam being gay is just a phase.
넌 샘의 게이다움이 일시적일거라고 바라고 있어.

059 I'm just thinking out loud 혼자 해본 소리야, 그냥 혼잣말이야

미드표현

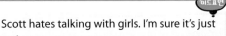

this is a way to say "Don't listen to me, I'm talking to myself." This is said when a person is talking, but only talking to help him think better

| Point | think out loud 생각을 입밖으로 내서 말하다, 혼잣말을 하다

A: Were you talking to me about something?
나한테 뭐라고 했어?

B: No, I'm sorry. **I was just thinking out loud.**
아니, 미안. 혼잣말이었어.

Don't worry, I'm just thinking out loud.
걱정마, 그냥 혼잣말해본거야.

I'm just thinking out loud. I'll find a solution soon. 혼자 해본 소리야. 난 곧 해결책을 찾을거야.

You don't have to answer me. I'm just thinking out loud. 나한테 답할 필요없어. 혼자 해본 소리야.

060 There's more to it than that 다른 뭔가가 있어, 그것보다는 더 깊은 뜻이 있어

미드표현

this indicates that there is more information than most people know. It is very similar to saying "You don't know everything yet"

| Point | I think there's more to it than that 뭔가 그보다는 다른 뜻이 있는 것 같아

A: I heard you quit your job because you were unhappy. 불행해서 직장을 그만뒀다며.

B: **There's more to it than that.** I'll tell you about it later. 다른 뭔가가 있지. 나중에 얘기해줄게.

Don't believe what she said. There's more to it than that. 걔가 하는 말 믿지마. 다른 뭔가가 더 있어.

There's more to it than that. Trust me, I know.
다른 뭔가가 더 있어. 날 믿어. 내가 안다고.

I'll explain everything. There's more to it than that. 내가 모든 걸 설명할게. 그것보다는 더 깊은 뜻이 있어.

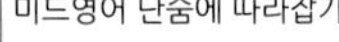

061 Just put me out of my misery

날 비참하게 내버려두지마, (듣고 싶은 말을 해줘서) 편하게 해줘

미드표현

this indicates the speaker is very stressed. It is a way to say "I hate feeling so bad"

Point put sb out of sb's misery …을 편하게 해주다

A: Jason, you look terrible today. 제이슨, 너 오늘 끔찍해보인다.

B: I feel terrible. **Just put me out of my misery.** 으악야. 날 좀 편하게 해줘.

Put me out of my misery. This stress is too much to deal with. 나 좀 편하게 해줘. 스트레스가 너무 많아.

I wish you've put me out of my misery. I feel terrible. 나 좀 편하게 해줬으면 해. 기분 으악야.

I feel so sick today. Please put me out of my misery. 오늘 좀 아파. 나 좀 편하게 해줘.

062 I can't afford it

그럴 형편이 안돼, 그럴 여유가 없어

미드표현

usually this means "It's too much money". Sometimes this can also mean "It will create too many problems for you"

Point I can't afford to~ …할 형편이 안돼
I'm dead[flat] broke 거덜났어, 빈털터리야
Is the money good? 돈벌이는 괜찮아?, 돈 많이 줘?
chip in 돈을 각출하다
cost a fortune[an arm and a leg] 돈이 상당히 들다

A: You really want to buy that gold necklace, right? 정말 저 금목걸이 사고 싶지, 맞아?

B: Yeah, but **I can't afford it.** 어, 하지만 그럴 형편이 안돼.

You're gonna be making money hand over fist! 너 벼락부자 되겠다!

Maybe we could all chip in and buy him some perfume. 우리 돈을 조금씩 모아서 걔한테 향수를 사주자.

It will cost a fortune to get that dental work done. 치과치료받으려면 거덜나겠다.

I heard you work at the hotel. Is the money good? 호텔에서 일한다며? 돈은 많이 받아?

063 Rise and shine!

(잠자리에서) 일어나

미드표현

this means "Wake up." It is a simple way to tell someone to get out of bed in the morning

Point I didn't sleep a wink 한숨도 못 잤어
Let's hit the hay[sack] 자러 가자
sleep in 늦잠자다(wake up late) crash in (다른 사람 집에서) 밤을 지새다

A: **Rise and shine!** It's time to get up and go to school. 일어나! 일어나 학교 갈 시간야.

B: Mom, can I sleep for ten more minutes? 엄마, 10분만 더 자게 해줘요.

Well you get a good night's sleep. I'll come back in the morning. 잘 잘자. 낼 아침에 올게.

You barely slept last night. Come on. Take a nap. 어제 한 숨도 못잤잖아. 자, 낮잠 좀 자라고.

You gotta stay here tonight. Look, you can crash in my bedroom. 오늘밤 여기 머물러도 돼. 내 침실에서 자도 돼.

064 It's your turn

네 차례야

미드표현

this expresses that someone should try to do something now. It's similar to saying "This is your chance"

Point It's your turn to~ 이제 네가 …해야 할 차례야
Wait your turn 차례를 기다려 Your turn now 네 차례야
Get in line 줄서요 You're up 네 차례야(Your turn is next)

A: We all have the chance to hit some golf balls. **It's your turn.** 모두 골프공을 칠 기회가 있어. 네 차례야.

B: I'm nervous. I've never played golf before. 떨려. 골프 처음 치는 거거든.

Now it's your turn to make an effort to make Kate happy. 이제 네가 노력해서 케이트를 기쁘게 해줄 차례야.

Whose turn is it? I can't remember who began first. 누구 차례지? 누가 먼저 시작했는지 기억이 안나.

Yeah, well, get in line behind all the other ladies! 저기, 다른 여자들 뒤에 줄서요!

065 I make jokes when I'm nervous 난 긴장하면 농담을 해

this is a way of saying "I try to be humorous when I feel uncomfortable." We can understand that when the speaker is stressed, he tries to make others laugh

| Point | make a joke[make jokes] 농담하다
make a joke of[about]~ …을 우습게 만들다
Can't you take a joke? 농담도 못하냐?

A: **I make jokes when I'm nervous.** 난 긴장하면 농담을 해.
B: Really? When I'm nervous, I become very quiet.
정말? 난 긴장하면 조용해지는데.

Don't make jokes now. 농담하지마.

Okay, fine! Make jokes, I don't care!
좋아! 맘껏 비웃어. 난 상관없어!

Don't make a joke of your life. 인생을 낭비하지 마세요.

This is no joking[laughing] matter! 농담할 일이 아냐!

066 We used to skip school together 우린 학교를 빼먹곤 했어

this indicates the speaker used to not attend school classes when he was supposed to. It is something that teachers consider bad behavior

| Point | skip school = play hooky = be truant 학교를 땡땡이 치다
He went to Yale 걘 예일대 나왔어
We don't have class today 오늘 수업없어

A: Why did you and Susan get punished?
왜 너하고 수잔이 혼났어?
B: **We used to skip school together** and we got caught. 같이 학교 땡땡이치다 잡혔어.

Sometimes she would just play hooky and spend the day with me.
때론 수업을 빼먹고 나와 시간을 보내곤 했어.

Mary must be smart. She went to Yale.
메리는 무지 똑똑한가봐. 예일대에 갔잖아.

067 For Pete's sake! 제발!, 지독하네!, 너무하는구만!

this is a polite way to express surprise or mild anger. It is like saying "Wow!" or "Come on!"

| Point | For Pete's[God's, Heaven's, Christ's] sake
제발, 지독하네, 너무하는구만!

A: I just need a few more minutes to get ready.
준비하는데 몇 분 더 걸려.
B: **For Pete's sake!** We're already late right now!
제발! 벌써 우린 늦었다구!

For God's sake. Why would I care if you end up with a man I despise?
너무하는구만. 내가 경멸하는 인간과 네가 결국 맺어지는데 왜 내가 신경써야해?

For God's sake, he just woke up from a coma.
와, 걔가 방금 혼수상태에서 깨어났어.

Eric, for God's sakes, that's no language for a woman to hear!
에릭, 그러지 말라고, 그건 여자가 들어야 할 말이 아냐.

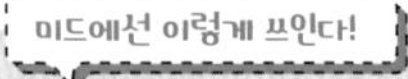

For God's sake, have mercy

Gotham SEASON#1-1

Fish의 버림을 받은 Oswald의 뒤처리를 맡은 Harvey 형사는 파트너인 James Gordon형사에게 Oswald를 죽이라고 한다. For God's sake는 죽음을 앞에 둔 Oswald가 James에게 생명을 구걸하는 장면에서 나오는 말.

Oswald: Please, Mr. Gordon, just let me live. I'll do whatever you say. I-I'll be your slave for life. Listen to me, there is a war coming. A-a terrible war. Falcone is losing his grip, and his rivals are hungry. There-there will be chaos. Rivers of blood in the streets. I know it! I-I can see it coming. See, I'm clever that way. And I can help you. I-I can be a spy.
James: Shut up! Turn around.
Oswald: For God's sake, have mercy.
James: Don't ever come back to Gotham.

오스왈드: 고든 형사님, 제발요, 살려주세요. 시키는 건 뭐든지 할게요. 평생 노예가 될게요. 제 말 좀 들어봐요. 전쟁이 다가오고 있어요. 아주 끔찍한 전쟁요. 팔콘의 장악력은 떨어져가고 라이벌들은 굶주려해요. 대혼란이 있을거예요. 거리에는 핏물이 강물처럼 흐를거에여. 난 알고 있어요. 난 그렇게 될게 보여요. 난 그쪽으로 잘 알잖아요. 난 형사님을 도울 수 있어요. 당신의 스파이가 될 수 있어요.
제임스: 입닥쳐! 돌아서.
오스왈드: 제발, 자비를 베풀어주세요.
제임스: 고담으로는 다시 돌아올 생각하지마.

068 God forbid! 그럴 리가!, 어림도 없는 소리!, 그런 일이 없기를!

this means "I really hope that doesn't happen." The speaker is talking about something that he is afraid might occur

| Point | God[Heaven] forbid (that) S+V …라니 당치않아, …라니 그럴리가

A: Wear your coat today. **God forbid** you might get sick. 오늘 코트 입어. 아프게 될지 모르니까.

B: But Mom, it isn't very cold outside.
하지만, 엄마, 밖이 그다지 춥지 않아요.

You want to quit school? God forbid!
학교를 그만두겠다고? 어림도 없는 소리!

I hope you never have health problems. God forbid! 네가 건강에 전혀 이상이 없기를 바래. 그런 일이 없기를!

Don't ever insult your father. God forbid!
네 아버지를 모욕하지마라. 그런 일이 없기를!

069 For crying out loud! (화나거나 조급할 때) 이거 참!, 제발 좀!

usually this expresses anger or frustration about something. It is similar to saying "I can't believe this!"

A: I don't know which food I want to eat.
어느 음식을 먹어야 할지 모르겠어.

B: **For crying out loud!** Just pick one of them!
이거 참! 아무 거나 골라 먹어!

She was all over me! She kissed me for crying out loud! 걔가 나한테 들이댔다고! 키스도 했다고 이거 참!

Oh, for crying out loud! I'm surprised you even passed your intern exam.
이거 참! 네가 인턴 시험을 통과하다니 놀랍다.

For crying out loud, I was at my girlfriend's place. 이거 참, 난 여친집에 있었어요.

070 There you are 1. (물건 주며) 여기 있어 2. 그것봐, 내가 뭐랬어 3. 그렇게 된 거였어

this usually is said either when someone is giving something to another person, or when people are arriving somewhere

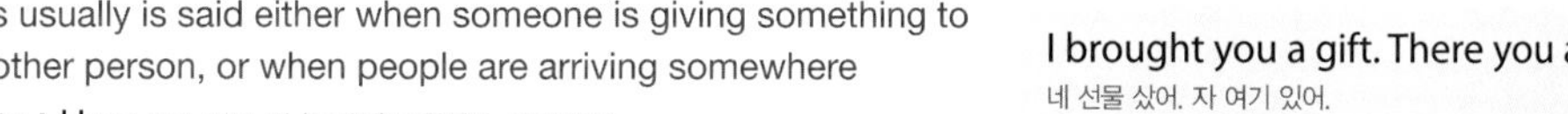

| Point | Here we are 자 (드디어) 도착했다, 여기 있다

A: The meal is ready. **There you are.**
음식이 준비됐어. 자 여기 있어.

B: Wow! All of the food looks delicious.
와! 음식이 다 맛나게 보여.

I brought you a gift. There you are.
네 선물 샀어. 자 여기 있어.

Well, here we are. Let me unload your luggage for you. 자, 다 왔습니다. 짐을 내려 드리죠.

Here we are. Her house is the yellow one in front of us. 다 왔어. 정면에 있는 노란 집이야.

071 There it is 자 여기 있어

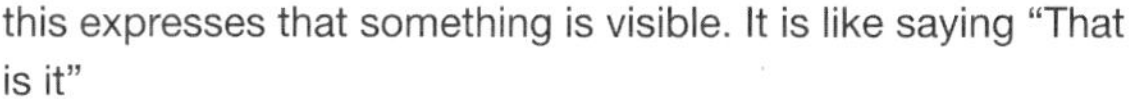

this expresses that something is visible. It is like saying "That is it"

| Point | Here it is 저것봐라, 저기있네, 바로 그거야

A: I'm here to pick up my prescription. It's Michelle Stewart. 처방전 받으러 왔어요. 미셸 스튜어트예요.

B: **Here it is.** 여기 있습니다.

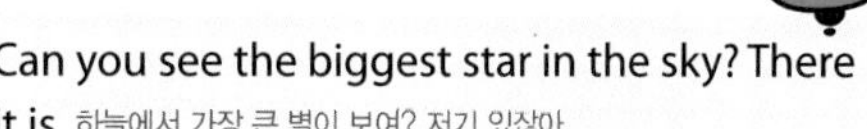

Can you see the biggest star in the sky? There it is. 하늘에서 가장 큰 별이 보여? 저기 있잖아.

I like you, too. But we don't have sex. Okay? There it is. I'd like to be having sex with the woman I cook for.
나도 네가 좋지만 우리는 섹스를 하지 않아. 맞지? 바로 그거야. 난 내가 요리를 해주는 여자와 섹스를 하고 싶다고.

072 Here he comes 저기 오는구만

this is a way of saying that a person is either arriving or leaving. It is saying either "He's coming" or "He's leaving"

| Point | There he goes 걔 저기 온다

A: Jack is supposed to be here soon. **Here he comes.** 잭이 곧 여기 올거야. 저기 오네.

B: Yeah, I can see him walking down the sidewalk. 그래, 보도를 걸어오는게 보이네.

Here he comes. What the hell is he doing?! 저기 오는 구만. 걔가 도대체 뭘하고 있는거야?!

Just wait for it. Okay, here he comes. 좀 기다리자고. 그래, 저기 오네.

Oh! Here he comes, okay, please do something. 걔가 저기 오네. 어떻게 좀 해봐.

073 Here it comes 1. 자 여기 있어 2. 또 시작이군, 올 것이 오는 구만

usually this means something is approaching from the distance. It can also be someone who is bringing something like food to another room and announcing that the food is being brought.

A: Why is our food taking so long? 우리 음식이 왜 그리 오래 걸려?

B: **Here it comes.** I think the waitress is bringing it over. 자 여기 오네. 여종업원이 가지고 오고 있어.

I see the bus has almost arrived. Here it comes. 버스가 거의 도착했을거야. 여기 오네.

Here it comes. I'm bringing your dinner in to you. 자 여기 있어. 너 먹을 점심 가져왔어.

The bus is arriving. Here it comes. 버스가 온다. 여기 오네.

074 There you go 여기 있어, 잘했어

these phrases is said when giving someone something. It is like saying "This is for you"

| Point | Here you go (물건 등을 건네며) 여기 있습니다

A: Can I borrow five dollars from you? 5달러 빌려줄래?

B: Sure you can. **There you go.** 물론이지. 자 여기 있어.

There you go! Last to know again! 그럼 그렇지! 또 내가 제일 늦게 아는구나!

Well, there you go. He was doing the same thing. 잘했어. 걔는 똑같이 하고 있었어.

There you go. Go on upstairs. Put on a dress -- a black dress. 여기 있어. 이층으로 가서 검은 드레스를 입어.

075 There you go again 또 시작이군

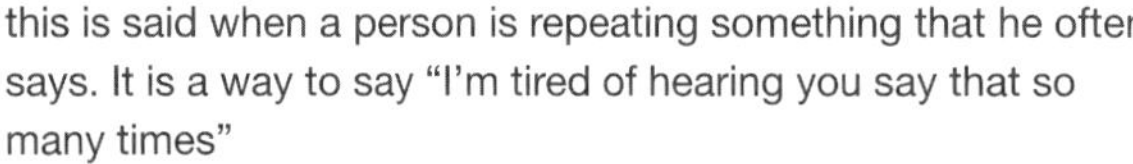

this is said when a person is repeating something that he often says. It is a way to say "I'm tired of hearing you say that so many times"

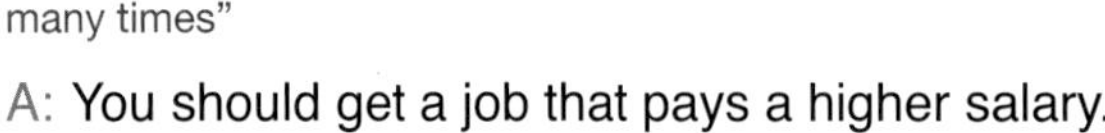

A: You should get a job that pays a higher salary. 급여가 더 많은 직장을 찾아봐.

B: **There you go again.** You always complain about money. 또 시작이군. 넌 늘상 돈타령야.

There you go again. I'm getting sick of your nonsense. 또 시작이군. 난 네 헛소리에 지쳤어.

There you go again. Always gossiping about your co-workers. 또 시작이군. 항상 동료들 뒷담화를 하는구만.

There you go again, eating. You should stick to your diet. 또 시작이군, 먹는거. 다이어트 좀 지켜라.

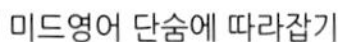

076 Here we go 자 간다, 여기 있다

this often indicates that some common behavior or pattern is starting again. It is similar to saying "It is about to start." It can also mean "we're going to start now" and additionally, it can be a way to say "I found it"

I Point I Here we go again 또 시작이군

A: We're all ready to start the trip. 여행출발할 준비됐어.

B: That's great. **Here we go.** 잘됐다. 자 이제 가자.

Here we go. We're on our way to Chicago.
자 간다. 우린 시카고로 가고 있어.

Everything is ready. Here we go.
다 준비됐어. 자 출발하자.

Here we go again. You are always complaining. 또 그러네. 늘상 불평야.

077 Here goes (어렵고 힘든 일을) 한번 해봐야지, 자 간다

미드표현

this means "I'm going to try to do it." The speaker is indicating he will attempt to do something, but he is not sure if he will succeed or fail. And "there goes that" means that something has failed or isn't possible to do. The speaker is admitting "It can't be done"

I Point I There goes that 어쩔 수 없네

A: It is too rainy to have a picnic today.
오늘 비가 너무 많이 와서 피크닉 못가겠어.

B: **There goes that.** Maybe we can go to the movies instead. 어쩔 수 없네. 대신 영화보러갈까.

I'm not sure if this will work. Here goes.
이게 될지 모르겠어. 한번 해봐야지.

I guess the company decided not to hire me. There goes that.
회사가 날 고용하지 않기로 했나봐. 어쩔 수 없지.

I'm going to try to draw a picture. Here goes.
그림을 그려볼려고. 한번 해봐야지.

078 Jane felt really bad about the whole bachelor party thing 제인은 이 총각파티로 기분 엿짢았어

미드표현

this is a way to express "event" or "occasion." The speaker is trying to say something in a short and simple way, without using a lot of words to describe something

I Point I ~ thing 이미 상대방이 알고 있거나 혹은 바로 앞에서 언급한 내용을 다시 반복하지 않기 위해서 간단히 '대표단어+thing'을 쓴다. 여기서 bachelor party thing이라고 말할 때는 whore와 함께 광란하는 파티의 모습까지 말하지 않으면서 말하는 방법이다.

A: **How was your blind date thing?** 소개팅 어땠어?

B: The girl was cute but she was really unfriendly.
여자애가 이뻤지만 정말 무뚝뚝했어.

My firm is having its annual dinner thing.
회사가 연례 만찬하는거 하고 있어.

I have a meeting thing with my department.
부서회의 하는게 있어.

I probably should've checked earlier, but I'm new to this whole dinner party thing.
내가 더 일찍 확인을 했어야 했는지 몰라. 하지만 난 이 저녁파티일이 처음이어서.

079 I gave up, like, everything. And for what?
음, 다 포기했어, 뭘 위해?

미드표현

The best way to describe 'like,' it is as a pause in conversation, while someone thinks of what to say. It is similar to the function of "um" or "uh", which also have no meaning

I Point I like는 별 의미없는 말하는 습관의 하나로 우리 말로 치면 음…, 어… 이런 정도의 의미이다. 원래는 it's like인데 빨리 발음하다보면 like가 들리게 된다.

A: Your boyfriend is, **like,** the hottest guy in our school. 네 남친은 어, 학교에서 가장 섹시해.

B: I know it. He's so handsome. 알아. 너무 잘 생겼지.

Ross, is he gonna live with you, like, in your apartment? 로스, 같이 살꺼야, 아파트에서?

I've been waiting for like, forever to go out with Lorraine.
내가 로레인하고 데이트하려고, 얼마나 기다려왔는데.

080 Don't blow it out of proportion

지나치게 부풀리지마, 너무 과장하지마

This means that someone is making a small issue into a very big issue. We can understand the person is upset, and is exaggerating how bad or important something is. It is like saying "You are making this seem more serious than it really is."

| Point | blow sth out of proportion 과장하다

A: I'll never forget how you insulted me.
네가 어떻게 날 그렇게 모욕할 수 있는거야?

B: That was a joke. **Don't blow it out of proportion.** 농담인데. 너무 부풀리지마.

And you're the one who blew it out of proportion. 그리고 그걸 지나치게 부풀린 건 바로 너야.

Sheldon, you do this all the time. You fixate on some crazy idea and then blow it way out of proportion.
쉘든, 넌 항상 이러잖아. 말도 안되는 생각에 사로잡혀서 지나치게 부풀리는거 말야.

I'm probably just blowing this out of proportion. 아마 내가 너무 지나치게 부풀리는 걸 수도 있어.

081 They gang up on me

걔네들이 날 괴롭혀

This indicates that the larger kids are working together to intimidate or control the kids who are not as strong. They are showing their power over others as they work as a group. Another way to say this is "The big kids joined up to intimidate the small kids."

| Point | gang up on sb 집단으로 공격하다, 무리지어 괴롭히다

A: Why did you let the punks steal your money?
너 왜 불량배들한테 돈을 뺏긴거야?

B: **They ganged up on me.** There was nothing I could do. 집단으로 협박했어. 나도 어쩔 수가 없었어.

Don't let those bastards gang up on you.
저 나쁜 놈들이 널 괴롭히지 못하게 해.

They really ganged up on her at the meeting.
걔네들은 회의에서 집단으로 걔를 괴롭혔어.

The criminals ganged up on Steve outside the subway station.
범죄자들이 지하철 역 밖에서 스티브를 집단으로 공격했어.

MEMO

FBI

MORE EXPRESSIONS

01 General

- ☐ **Sort of** 어느 정도는, 다소(kind of)
- ☐ **Just for fun** 재미로(for kicks)
- ☐ **For the hell of it** 그냥 아무 의미없이
- ☐ **It's the real thing** 진짜야, 진심야
- ☐ **What's the use?** 무슨 소용이야?
- ☐ **What was all that banging?** 대체 무슨 소리야?
- ☐ **What is it you need?** 원하는게 뭔데?
- ☐ **He has a one-track mind** 걘 한가지 밖에 몰라
- ☐ **I wear the pants in my house** 이 집의 주인은 나야
- ☐ **We need to straighten it out** 바로 잡아야 해
- ☐ **It's an open and shut case** 불을 보듯 뻔하다
- ☐ **It was next to nothing** 거의 제로야
- ☐ **So far, so good** 지금까지는 괜찮아
- ☐ **So it seems** 그런 것 같아
- ☐ **Some night, huh?** 대단한 밤야, 안 그래?
- ☐ **Get your ass in here!** 이쪽으로 와!
- ☐ **I'm doing my hair** 머리 손질 중이야
- ☐ **Let me live vicariously** 간접경험좀 하자
- ☐ **Thanks for the history lesson** 뒷북치지마
- ☐ **He's still going strong** 아직도 건재해
- ☐ **I try to treat you with respect** 난 널 존중하려고 해
- ☐ **I'm being helped now** 다른 사람이 봐주고 있어요
- ☐ **I'm just looking[browsing]** 그냥 구경하고 있는 거예요
- ☐ **I always get my money's worth** 난 항상 본전은 찾아
- ☐ **They are all the rage these days** 요새 그게 대유행이야
- ☐ **To each his own!** 사람마다 취향은 서로 달라!
- ☐ **(There's) Nothing to it** 식은 죽 먹기야, 해보면 아무 것도 아니야
- ☐ **It's a piece of cake = It's a cinch = It's a breeze = It's a snap** 쉬운 일이야
- ☐ **You haven't changed a bit** 너 정말 하나도 안 변했구나
- ☐ **(It's) Time for a change** 바꿀 때도 됐잖아
- ☐ **James lived up to his promise** 제임스는 약속에 따라 행동했어 ▶ live up to …에 부응하다
- ☐ **That is a photo op(opportunity)** 사진이라도 찍어둬야할 거리인 걸
- ☐ **This problem runs in the family** 이 문제는 우리 집안 내력이야
- ☐ **Everything but the kitchen sink** 없는 것 빼놓고는 전부다
- ☐ **That's a sight for sore eyes** 피곤한 눈에 정말 보기 좋은 광경인데
- ☐ **That's giving me goosebumps** 그러니 소름이 끼치는군
- ☐ **We've grown apart** 지내다 보니 멀어졌어, 성장하면서 멀어졌어
- ☐ **What an imagination you have!** 상상력도 풍부하군!
- ☐ **What are you all dressed up for?** 웬일로 그렇게 쫙 빼입은 거야?
- ☐ **Completely identical. You can't tell them apart** 완벽하게 똑같아. 구분 못할 거야
- ☐ **Have a seat** 앉아 ▶ Please be seated 착석하세요 ▶ (Is) This (seat) taken? 자리 있어요?
- ☐ **You've always been on the go** 너 항상 바쁘게 지내왔잖아
- ☐ **She always butters him up** 그 여자는 항상 그 남자에게 입에 발린 소리만 한다
- ☐ **I'm laying low** 조용히 지내고 있어(I'm staying away from most people)
- ☐ **Will that be all?** 달리 더 필요한 것은 없으십니까? ▶ Is that everything? (Is there) Anything else? (상점에서) 더 필요한건 없어요?
- ☐ **Can you break a hundred?** 100불짜리 잔돈 좀 바꿔줄 수 있어? ▶ I can't break that (택시기사가) 거슬러드릴 잔돈이 없는데요. Do you have anything smaller? 잔돈 없으세요?, Keep the change 거스름돈은 가져요
- ☐ **What's the damage[price]?** 얼마예요?
- ☐ **Do you carry Colombian coffee?** 콜럼비아산 커피 팔아요? ▶ Do you carry something …를 파나요?, …있어요?
- ☐ **It's a bargain (price)** 싸다, 싸잖아 ▶ You can't beat that 정말 잘 샀다, That's a steal 거저나 마찬가지예요, 정말 싸구나!
- ☐ **That's a rip-off** 바가지야 바가지 ▶ That's too steep! 너무 비싼데요!
- ☐ **It's all sold out** 매진예요 ▶ It sells like hot cakes! 날개돋힌 듯 팔려요!
- ☐ **Don't I get a discount?** 할인은 안되나요? ▶ Can you give me a discount?, Can you come down a little? 좀더 깎아주세요
- ☐ **Charge it please** 신용카드로 낼게요 ▶ Cash or charge? 현금으로요 아니면 신용카드로요, Cash, please = I'll charge it, please 현금으로요, I'll pay by check = I'm gonna pay for this with check 수표로 낼게요, I'd like to buy it on credit 신용카드로 낼게요
- ☐ **Put it on my tab** 외상으로 달아놔 ▶ Be sure to pay up front 반드시 선불하도록 하세요
- ☐ **I'd like to get a refund, please** 환불해주세요

- ☐ **They're having a going-out-of-business sale** 점포 정리 세일을 한대
- ☐ **I'm in the red** 난 적자야(↔ in the black)
- ☐ **Need I say more?** 더 말해야 하나?, 더 말하지 않아도 알겠지?
- ☐ **Am I getting through on this?** 이 문제에 관해서는 내 말을 잘 알겠지?, 내 말 이해되니?
- ☐ **Are you catching my drift?** 내 말 이해했어?
- ☐ **(Do you) get my drift?** 무슨 말인지 알겠어?, 이해돼?
- ☐ **Fancy that!** 정말!(Wow!) 설마!
- ☐ **Imagine that!** 놀라워라!
- ☐ **My eye[foot]!** 맙소사!, 말도 안돼!(I don't believe it)
- ☐ **She almost had a fit** 까무라칠 뻔했다
- ☐ **Isn't that something?** 별 일이 다 있네
- ☐ **I almost jumped out of my skin** 거의 까무라치는 줄 알았어
- ☐ **If I say no, that means no** 난 한번 안한다고 하면 안해
- ☐ **I have got to put my foot down** 난 결사 반대야
- ☐ **I'm not going to lift a finger** 손 하나 까딱 안 할거야(I won't give any assistance)
- ☐ **The answer is no** 대답은 아냐 야.
- ☐ **That's not true (is it?)** 그렇지 않아
- ☐ **You couldn't (do that)!** 절대 못할걸!, 그렇게 못할거면서!
- ☐ **When hell freezes over** 절대로 아니야(Absolutely never), 그런 일은 죽었다 깨어나도 안 일어나
- ☐ **Please don't shut me out** 날 거절하지마
- ☐ **That will be the day** 그런 일은 절대로 없을 거야(I think that something will never happen)
- ☐ **You don't have a leg to stand on** 넌 그런 주장을 할 수 있는 근거가 없어 (Your idea or argument is completely wrong)
- ☐ **Better to be safe than sorry** 유비무환, 후회하느니 신중하는 게 낫다
- ☐ **Never let your emotions get the best of you** 감정적으로 말하지마
- ☐ **Your reputation is getting trashed** 네 명예가 산산조각 나게 생겼단 말야.
- ☐ **It shouldn't be this way** 이래선 안되는데
- ☐ **That doesn't make the grade** 그렇게 해서는 안돼(make the grade 필요한 기준에 다다르다, 성공하다)
- ☐ **You're not getting any younger** 그런다고 해서 조금도 더 젊어지지는 않아
- ☐ **You shouldn't just lie down and take it** 당하고만 있으면 안돼
- ☐ **Don't rock the boat** 공연히 평지풍파 일으키지 마
- ☐ **Don't make waves** 풍파 일으키지 마
- ☐ **Don't put all your eggs in one basket** 한가지 일에 목숨 걸지 마
- ☐ **Wake up and smell the coffee** 정신차려(You need to be aware of something that is happening)
- ☐ **Things change, roll with the punches** 변화에 순응해 (You should expect surprises in life)
- ☐ **That's a mean thing to say!** 그건 야비해!
- ☐ **I'm not a kid anymore** 난 더 이상 어린애가 아니라구
- ☐ **I wasn't born yesterday!** 난 어리숙하지 않아!
- ☐ **Do you think I was born yesterday?** 내가 그렇게 어리숙해보이냐?, 누굴 바보로 아나?
- ☐ **You read my mind** 내 마음을 읽었구만(you suggested something that I really want to do)
- ☐ **I'm on to you** 네 속셈을 알고 있어(I know what you're after)
- ☐ **Can we not talk about that?** 그 얘기 안하면 안될까?
- ☐ **Catch me later[some other time]** 나중에 다시 얘기할래?
- ☐ **Go ahead, make my day!** 그래 어서 덤벼봐, 내 기꺼이 상대해 주지
- ☐ **You really made my day** 너 때문에 오늘 아주 기분이 좋아졌어
- ☐ **Don't speak ill of him** 그 사람 욕하지 마
- ☐ **I won't give up without a fight** 순순히 물러나진 않을 거야
- ☐ **Let's bury the hatchet** 오랜 불화를 끝내자, 싸움을 그만두자
- ☐ **We made up** 우린 화해했어
- ☐ **flunk something** …을 실패하다
- ☐ **It's a wild goose chase** 헛수고야
- ☐ **You can't pull the wool over my eyes** 날 속일 수는 없어
- ☐ **I'm drawing a (complete) blank** 난 완전히 무시당하고 있어
- ☐ **I got a raw deal** 불공평한 처우를 받았어 ▶ raw deal 부당한 처사
- ☐ **I got ripped off** 이용당했어

- ☐ **flunk something** …을 실패하다
- ☐ **It's a wild goose chase** 헛수고야
- ☐ **You can't pull the wool over my eyes** 날 속일 수는 없어
- ☐ **I'm drawing a (complete) blank** 난 완전히 무시당하고 있어
- ☐ **I got a raw deal** 불공평한 처우를 받았어 ▶ raw deal 부당한 처사
- ☐ **I got ripped off** 이용당했어

- ☐ **Where do we go from here?** 여기서 어디로 가야되는 거지?

- ☐ **I did not know where to turn** 뭘 어떻게 해야할지 모르겠어
- ☐ **What's the answer?** 어쩌지?, 어떻게 하지?
- ☐ **I hope I haven't disturbed you** 방해가 안되었길 바래
- ☐ **Sorry's not enough** 죄송하다는 말만으로는 해결되지 않아
- ☐ **Pardon my language** 거친 표현 미안해
- ☐ **If you'll pardon the expression** 이런 표현을 써도 될지 모르겠습니다만,
- ☐ **Pardon[Excuse] my French** 상스러운 말을 해서 죄송합니다, 욕해서 미안해
- ☐ **Please don't be sorry** 미안해 할 필요 없어
- ☐ **I'm not that kind** 난 그런 사람 아니예요
- ☐ **I'll turn the other cheek** 다른쪽 뺨도 돌려댈거야, 용서할 거야
- ☐ **I'll let you off this time** 이번엔 용서해줄게
- ☐ **I want to set the record straight** 오해를 바로 잡고 싶어
- ☐ **There's got to be some misunderstanding** 뭔가 오해가 있는 게 분명해
- ☐ **You're twisted my words** 넌 내 말을 곡해했어
- ☐ **You know** 말야, 알지
- ☐ **I'm here to tell you that~** 내 생각은 ….이래
- ☐ **So to speak** 말하자면
- ☐ **In other words** 달리 말하자면
- ☐ **Needless to say** 말할 필요도 없지만
- ☐ **To tell the truth** 사실을 말하자면
- ☐ **To begin with** 우선 말씀 드리자면
- ☐ **I mean to say** 더 정확하게 말하면
- ☐ **shoot the breeze** 가볍게 대화하다
- ☐ **Do you have (some) time?** 시간 있어요?
- ☐ **Let's just talk turkey** 본론으로 들어가죠
- ☐ **I'll come to the point** 단도직입적으로 말할게
- ☐ **I'll come to that** 나중에 얘기할게
- ☐ **That[which] brings me to the (main) point** 본론으로 들어가면
- ☐ **Regardless to say** 말할 필요도 없이
- ☐ **She clammed up** 그 여자는 입을 꾹 다물고 있었다
- ☐ **Think before you speak[act]** 말하기 전에 생각해 보고 말해
- ☐ **What's your opinion?** 네 의견은 뭐야?
- ☐ **I need your opinion** 네 의견이 필요해
- ☐ **I would like your opinion** 네 의견을 듣고 싶어
- ☐ **I'd like to think it over** 잘 검토해볼게
- ☐ **What are your thoughts here?** 이걸 어떻게 생각해?
- ☐ **I'm trying to keep an open mind** 편견을 갖지 않으려 해
- ☐ **I was somewhere else** 잠시 딴 생각했어(I wasn't paying attention)
- ☐ **I was lost in thought** 생각에 빠져 있었어
- ☐ **You're just the way I pictured you** 생각했던 대로군
- ☐ **Nine times out of ten** 십중팔구
- ☐ **It's in the cards** 예상했던 거야, 있을 수 있는 일이야
- ☐ **I took a shot in the dark** 막연하게 추측한 거야
- ☐ **Why didn't it work?** 왜 들통났어?
- ☐ **What's so crazy about that?** 그럼 안되나?, 게 난리야?
- ☐ **(There's) no reason (to)** 그럴 이유가 없어
- ☐ **I think there must be a reason** 뭔가 이유가 있겠지
- ☐ **That's the name of the game** 그건 매우 중요한 일이야 (That is the main idea of this)
- ☐ **First things first** 중요한 것부터 먼저 하자(Let's do what is important first)
- ☐ **Spare me the details** (쓸데없는 소리 말고) 요점이나 말해
- ☐ **It carries no weight** 그건 전혀 중요하지 않아
- ☐ **Nothing matters anymore** 더 이상 중요한 것은 없어
- ☐ **That doesn't tell me much** 그건 별 의미가 없는데
- ☐ **You're all missing my point** 그 얘기가 아냐.
- ☐ **First thing we have to do is do~** 우리가 우선적으로 해야 할 일은 …이야
- ☐ **Don't place[put] such a premium on that** 그렇게 그걸 중요시하지 마라
- ☐ **Everything's up in the air** 아직 모든 것이 미정이야(Anything could happen)
- ☐ **I('ll) pass** 난 됐어, 난 안 먹을[할]래
- ☐ **Heads or tails!** (동전을 던지면서) 앞면일까 뒷면일까!
- ☐ **Let's flip a coin for it** 동전던지기하자
- ☐ **Let's bring this matter to a close** 이 문제에 대해 결정을 내리자
- ☐ **You are free to choose for yourself** 네 것은 네가 마음대로 결정해
- ☐ **I'll be the judge of that** 내가 판단할 일이야
- ☐ **I'm done with my choices** 선택을 했어
- ☐ **What are my choices?** 뭐가 있나요?
- ☐ **I wanted to thank you for everything** 여러모로 고마워
- ☐ **Thank you for your trouble** 수고해줘서 고마워

- ☐ **Thank you for the tip** 귀띔해줘서 고마워
- ☐ **Thank you for telling me the truth** 사실을 말해줘서 고마워
- ☐ **Thank you in advance** 미리 감사해
- ☐ **Thanks anyway** 하여간 고마워
- ☐ **Thanks for reminding me about it** 생각나게 해줘서 고마워
- ☐ **Thanks for the reminder** 생각나게 해줘서 고마워
- ☐ **Thanks for your support** 도와줘서 고마워
- ☐ **Thanks for walking me home** 집까지 같이 걸어와줘서 고마워
- ☐ **Thanks for coming. I love you** 와줘서 고마워. 사랑해
- ☐ **Thanks for the lift[ride]** 태워다 줘서 고마워요
- ☐ **Thanks for catching[pointing out] my mistake** 내 실수를 지적해줘서 고마워
- ☐ **I'll stand by you** 네게 힘이 되어줄게. 네 옆에 있어줄게(I'll help you if you need it)
- ☐ **That should help** 도움이 될거야
- ☐ **It won't help anything** 별로 도움이 되지 않을거야
- ☐ **Would you please?** 그래 줄래요?
- ☐ **What's the good word?** 잘 지내지?
- ☐ **(Have you) been keeping out of trouble?** 별일 없지?
- ☐ **Nice weather, huh?** 날씨 좋지, 그지?
- ☐ **Where are you headed?** 어디 가?(Where're you going?, Where're you off to?)
- ☐ **How's business?** 잘 지내?, 하는 일은 어때?
- ☐ **I must say good bye[night] now** 이제 가봐야겠어
- ☐ **It's time to wrap up, folks** 마칠 시간입니다, 여러분
- ☐ **Time to pack** (여행) 떠날 시간이야
- ☐ **Time is up** (시험시간 등 제한된 시간의 상황에서)시간 다 됐다
- ☐ **(It's) Time to move[split]** 이제 그만 가봐야겠어(= I've got to go)
- ☐ **I really have to be somewhere but it was nice meeting you** 어디 좀 가봐야 돼서. 정말 반가웠어
- ☐ **When's convenient[good] for you?** 언제가 편해?
- ☐ **What time is[would be] good for you?** 몇 시가 좋겠어?
- ☐ **What time is okay for you?** 몇 시가 괜찮아?
- ☐ **I'd like to meet him** 걜 만나고 싶어
- ☐ **Does this afternoon work for you?** 오후 괜찮아?
- ☐ **I'm afraid I have another appointment** 미안하지만 다른 약속이 있어서
- ☐ **I have no time available** 시간이 안돼
- ☐ **I have no time to see you** 널 만날 시간이 없어
- ☐ **I hope to see you again (sometime)** 조만간에 다시 한번 보자, 나중에 얼굴 한번 봐
- ☐ **Everyone's waiting for us** 다들 우릴 기다리고 있어
- ☐ **I've been out of touch** 사람들과 접촉을 못했지
- ☐ **You look kind of familiar** 어디서 많이 뵌 분 같은데
- ☐ **What was the name again?** 이름이 뭔지 한번 더 말씀해 주세요
- ☐ **Can I have your name?** 이름이 뭐예요?
- ☐ **Let's just be friends** 그냥 친구하자
- ☐ **I'm glad we got to know each other** 친하게 지냈으면 좋겠어
- ☐ **I had a nice[lovely] time** 즐거웠어, 좋았어(I enjoyed it)
- ☐ **Is someone there?** 거기 누구 있어?
- ☐ **Please answer the door** 누가 왔나 나가 봐라
- ☐ **Can I come see you?** 찾아가도 돼?
- ☐ **I'm glad you could drop by** 들러줘서 기뻐
- ☐ **Nice place you have here** 좋은 곳이네요, 정말 좋군요
- ☐ **Come back and see me sometime** 또 놀러 와
- ☐ **I hope I'm not intruding on you** 방해가 되지 않기를 바래.
- ☐ **My[Our] house is your house** 내 집이라 생각하고 편히 계세요
- ☐ **Don't stay away so long** 자주 좀 와(Let's meet again very soon)
- ☐ **Scratch my back and I'll scratch yours** 오는 정이 있으면 가는 정도 있지
- ☐ **It's like chewing somebody else's gum** 꼭 남의 껌을 씹는 기분이야
- ☐ **Speak of the devil!** 호랑이도 제 말 하면 온다더니!
- ☐ **The sooner the better** 빠르면 빠를 수록 좋아
- ☐ **What goes around comes around** 인생은 돌고 돌아
- ☐ **There are no free lunches** 세상엔 공짜가 없는 법
- ☐ **Stop trying to keep up with the Joneses** 뱁새가 황새 따라가려다 가랑이 찢어져
- ☐ **You win some and you lose some** 딸 때도 있고 잃을 때도 있는 거지 뭐
- ☐ **Win a few, lose a few** 얻는게 있으면 잃는 것도 있는 법이지
- ☐ **(You) can't win them all** 질 수도 있는거야, 늘 잘될 수는 없지

- ☐ **You can't judge a book by its cover** 겉만 보고 판단하면 안돼
- ☐ **People aren't always what they appear to be, kid. Remember it** 사람들이 모두 겉모습처럼 선량한 건 아니란다, 얘야. 내 말 명심해.
- ☐ **It ain't over till it's over** 완전히 끝날 때까진 아직 끝이 아니야
- ☐ **Where there's smoke there's fire** 아니 땐 굴뚝에 연기날까
- ☐ **You can't take it with you** 무덤속까지 가지고 갈 수도 없잖아, 죽으면 돈도 다 소용없다구
- ☐ **It's like having the fox guard the henhouse** 고양이한테 생선가게를 맡긴 격이야
- ☐ **Old enough to know better** 나잇살이나 먹었으니 알 건 알아야지
- ☐ **It cuts both ways** 좋은 면도 있고 나쁜 면도 있어
- ☐ **When it rains, it pours** 왔다 하면 장대비야
- ☐ **My days are numbered** 좋은 시절 다 갔어(Something bad will happen to me soon)
- ☐ **It's not a good sign** 좋은 징조가 아니야
- ☐ **He's in a mess** 그 사람, 쩔쩔매고 있어
- ☐ **I'm really in a fix** 제가 아주 곤란한 상황에 처했어요
- ☐ **I'm between a rock and a hard place** 첩첩산중이야
- ☐ **Save it for a rainy day** 어려울 때를 대비해 저축해둬
- ☐ **He is going to be in hot water** 그 사람 어려워질 거야
- ☐ **It's hard to keep up** 따라 잡기 어려워, 힘들어
- ☐ **I'm in a bind** 난처한 상황에 처해 있어(This is causing a problem for me)
- ☐ **They're in harm's way** 위험한 상황에 놓여있어(They're in a dangerous situation)
- ☐ **There wasn't time** 시간이 없었어
- ☐ **I have no time to call my own** 정신없이 바빠
- ☐ **My ass is dragging** 완전히 지쳤어, (힘들어서) 꼼짝도 못하겠어
- ☐ **I was dead to the world** 난 완전히 녹초가 됐어
- ☐ **Just kicking it** 그냥 쉬고 있어(I'm just relaxing)
- ☐ **I need to kick back and relax** 쉬어야겠어(I want some free time)
- ☐ **I can't compete with that** 도저히 못 당하겠군
- ☐ **He kicks my butt in math** 걔가 수학은 나보다 잘해 ▶ kick my butt 나보다 잘하다
- ☐ **She has an eye for it** 걔도 안목이 있어
- ☐ **I have good taste** 나도 안목이 있어
- ☐ **I know all the tricks of the trade** 필요한 지식과 기술을 갖췄어
- ☐ **He's really stuck up!** 쟤 정말 건방져!
- ☐ **What makes you so special?** 넌 뭐가 그리 특별해?
- ☐ **Don't be arrogant** 잘난 척 하지마
- ☐ **I know right from wrong** 옳고 그른 것은 가릴 줄 알아
- ☐ **I know it all from A to Z** 처음부터 끝까지 다 알아
- ☐ **I know it backwards and forwards** 낱낱이 알아
- ☐ **You are always putting on airs** 넌 항상 뻐기냐, 넌 항상 으시대(You are too proud around others)
- ☐ **He's always blowing his own horn** 걘 항상 자화자찬이야(He is always talking about how great he is)
- ☐ **Rock on!** 멋지군!, 좋아!
- ☐ **Fucking A** 대단하군, 굉장하군, 물론이지
- ☐ **They are the cream of the crop** 그 사람들이 최고야
- ☐ **Tanya has an ass that won't quit** 타냐는 정말 엉덩이가 멋져("~that won't quit" is often considered a rude way to say something, and shouldn't be used. It means something is very nice)
- ☐ **This is second to none** 비교할 수 없을 정도로 좋아(It's the best)
- ☐ **How about that!** 거 근사한데!, 그거 좋은데!, 놀라운데!(Wow, that is very interesting)
- ☐ **It doesn't get any better than this** 이보다 나은 건 없어
- ☐ **take a turn for the worse[better]** 악화되다(좋아지다)
- ☐ **You did it very well** 아주 잘 했어.
- ☐ **Go get them** 이겨라, 힘내라
- ☐ **Go to it!** 힘내!, 해보는 거야!
- ☐ **That'll be good** 잘 될 거야
- ☐ **You're headed in the right direction** 제대로 가고 있어
- ☐ **Bon voyage!** 즐거운 여행해!(Have a nice trip!)
- ☐ **You know, strickly BYOB(Bring Your Own Beer)** 각자 술은 알아서 가져와
- ☐ **I'm (really) enjoying myself.** 정말 신나게 놀고 있어
- ☐ **I had a ball** 즐거웠어
- ☐ **He doesn't have a care in the world** 걘 천하태평이야
- ☐ **I wanna rock and roll all night!** 밤새 신나게 놀고 싶어!(this is not used in conversation. It is a line from a song. It indicates someone wants to go to parties and drink a lot of alcohol and have fun)
- ☐ **Hold your horses** 서두르지마, 닥달하지마, 재촉하지마
- ☐ **Haste makes waste** 서두르다가 일을 그르치기 마련이야
- ☐ **Get the lead out** 일에 착수해

- ☐ **Shake a leg!** 서둘러!
- ☐ **Sooner than you think** 생각보다 빨리 그렇게 될 거야, 이러고 있을 여유가 없어
- ☐ **in a split second** 눈 깜짝할 사이에
- ☐ **sooner or later** 조만간
- ☐ **Just in the nick of time** 아슬아슬하게 때를 맞추어
- ☐ **now and then** 어쩌다
- ☐ **Every minute[moment] counts** 시간이 매우 중요해
- ☐ **I'm just killing time** 그냥 시간이나 죽이고 있는 거예요
- ☐ **You got the time?** 몇시에요?(What time is it?)
- ☐ **Since when?** 언제부터?
- ☐ **I couldn't be happier** 정말이지 아주 행복해
- ☐ **I feel like a fish out of water** 어쩔 줄을 모르겠어, 불편해
- ☐ **I feel like shit** 기분 엉망이니까 건드리지마.
- ☐ **I feel like a million dollars[bucks]** 난 아주 건강해
- ☐ **I feel like throwing up** 토할 것 같아
- ☐ **I feel a bit lost suddenly** 갑자기 좀 멍한 느낌이야, 어떻게 해야 할지 모르겠어
- ☐ **I have no feeling (one way or the other) about that** 난 아무 감정 없어
- ☐ **I'm [feeling] on top of the world!** 기분이 무척 좋아!(Everything seems great)
- ☐ **I'm out of sorts** 기운이 없어, 기분이 안 좋아(I don't feel normal)
- ☐ **The situation went from bad to worse** 설상가상이야 (We kept having more and more problems)
- ☐ **All hell broke loose** 모든 게 엉망진창이야
- ☐ **So it goes** 자, 일이 이렇게 되었다
- ☐ **It was touch and go there for a while** 한동안은 심각한 상황이었어
- ☐ **Touch and go** 위급한 상황
- ☐ **They're walking a fine line here** 걔네들은 지금 아슬아슬한 줄타기를 하고 있어
- ☐ **That's not the end of the story** 얘기가 끝난 게 아냐
- ☐ **That's a far cry from~** …와 전혀 별개의 것이야
- ☐ **He is out on business** 외근 중이야(He had to travel to a place to do work)
- ☐ **I've got some business** 돈벌이 하고 있어(I'm doing something for money)
- ☐ **Business is business** 일은 일이고, 계산은 계산이야
- ☐ **That business is really cut-throat** 그 쪽 일은 정말 치열해
- ☐ **I have to run an errand** 심부름해야 돼, 볼 일이 있어
- ☐ **He stepped out of the office** 방금 사무실에서 나가셨어요
- ☐ **He's out in the field** 걔는 현장에 나가 있어
- ☐ **I'm home** 나 왔어
- ☐ **He's always on the go** 그는 늘 바삐 돌아다녀
- ☐ **The gun is loaded** 총은 장전되어 있어
- ☐ **Police have no leads** 경찰에선 단서를 찾지 못했대
- ☐ **I won't have him subjected to scrutiny and ridicule** 그가 뒷조사나 조롱받는 것을 원치않아.
- ☐ **He's asking a leading question** 그는 유도 심문을 하고 있습니다
- ☐ **I smell a rat** 뭔가 냄새가 나, 수상해
- ☐ **Get him out of my sight** 데려가
- ☐ **He could have been coerced, maybe brain washed** 강압수사를 받았거나 세뇌를 받았을 지도 몰라
- ☐ **The good news is he confessed, though he now wants to recant** 비록 지금 부인하고 있지만 좋은 소식은 그가 자백을 했다는 거야. ▶ recant (자기 주장, 자백 등을) 부인하다
- ☐ **CPR : cardiopulmonary resuscitation** (심폐 기능 소생) I performed CPR, and he didn't respond 심폐소생술을 했지만 그 남자는 아무 반응이 없었어
- ☐ **ICU : Intensive care unit** 중환자실 ▶ That guy's in the ICU with respiratory paralysis 그 남자는 호흡마비로 중환자실에 있어 She just came up from the ICU. She's in room 208 걘 중환자실에서 방금 나왔어. 208호실에 있어 The ICU's on the fourth floor. People die all the time. She's in the ICU. There's nothing I can do 중환자실은 4층야. 항상 사람들이 죽어나가지. 걔가 중환자실에 있는데 내가 할 수 있는 게 아무 것도 없어
- ☐ **OR : Operating Room** 수술실 ▶ We'll get you to the OR as soon as possible 가능한 한 빨리 수술실로 옮길게요 We need to get her into the OR immediately 저 여자를 즉시 수술실로 옮겨야 돼
- ☐ **DOA : Dead On Arrival** 도착시 이미 사망 ▶ He's DOA 병원에 도착했을 때 이미 사망했었어
- ☐ **OD : overdose** 약물을 과다복용하다(과거형은 OD'd) ▶ There's plenty of drugs around here. You think he OD'd? 여기 많은 약물이 있는데, 약물과다복용한 것 같아?
- ☐ **Enjoy your meal!** 맛있게 들어!
- ☐ **I could eat a horse** (너무 배가 고파서) 뭐든지 먹겠다
- ☐ **You eat like a bird!** 넌 정말 적게 먹는구나!
- ☐ **It tastes good** 참 맛있다
- ☐ **Drink up** 쭉 들이켜
- ☐ **The usual, please** 항상 하는 걸로요
- ☐ **He eat us out of house and home** 걘 우리집 음식을 완전히 거덜냈어

- [ ] **My mouth is watering already** 벌써부터 군침이 도네
- [ ] **It's a fancy restaurant** 여긴 고급 음식점이야
- [ ] **There are around the clock restaurants over there** 저쪽에 24시간 여는 음식점들이 있다
- [ ] **I had one too many** 난 취했어
- [ ] **Where can I reach him?** 걔에게 어디로 연락해야 돼?
- [ ] **I can't make outgoing calls** 전화가 거는 건 안 돼
- [ ] **Is he around?** 걔 있어?
- [ ] **I was expecting your call** 전화 기다리고 있었어
- [ ] **Hi, you've reached Bill Sanford** (전화에서) 여보세요, 빌 샌포트네 집입니다
- [ ] **Could I call you?** 나중에 전화해도 될까?
- [ ] **I won't keep you any longer** (전화통화에서) 네 시간 그만 뺏어야겠어
- [ ] **You called?** 전화했었니?
- [ ] **The line's busy** 통화중입니다
- [ ] **How can I direct your call?** 어디로 바꿔 드릴까요?
- [ ] **It's just a stone's throw from here** 엎어지면 코 닿을 거리야
- [ ] **I have a flat tire** 타이어가 펑크났어
- [ ] **I had a little fender-bender** 작은 접촉 사고가 있었어
- [ ] **Drive safely** 운전 조심해
- [ ] **Where to?** 어디로 가십니까?, 어디로 가?
- [ ] **Where do you want to go?** 어디를 가려는데?
- [ ] **I am a stranger here myself** 여기가 초행길이라서요, 여기는 처음 와봐서요

02 감탄사

- [ ] **Come on!** 1. 어서 2. 그러지마, 제발 3. 자 덤벼
- [ ] **My goodness!** 이런 세상에! ▶ (Sweet) Mother of God! 저런!, 맙소사!
- [ ] **(Oh, my) Gosh** 세상에나!, 맙소사! ▶ (Oh, my) God 세상에! Oh, lord 맙소사
- [ ] **Oh, dear! / Dear me!** 저런, 이를 어째 ▶ Oh, shit 아니, 이런 Oh, shoot! 오, 맙소사!
- [ ] **Oh, boy[man]** 우와, 이런, 맙소사 ▶ Oh man 이런, Oops! 아이쿠!
- [ ] **Holy crap! / Holy cow! / Holy shit!** 맙소사!, 제기랄
- [ ] **Good God** 어머나, 맙소사 ▶ Good grief! 아이고, 이를 어쩌나, 야단났네 Good heavens! 이거 큰일이군
- [ ] **(God) Damn it** 제기랄!, 빌어먹을 ▶ You poor thing 이런 가엾게도
- [ ] **God bless you!** 1. 고마워라 2. 상대방이 재채기했을 때 해주는 말
- [ ] **Blah blah blah** 어쩌구 저쩌구

03 사람표현

- [ ] **You freak!** 미친 놈 같으니!
- [ ] **You're a (such) a loser** 한심한 놈 같으니, 넌 골통야
- [ ] **He's a has-been** 걘 한물갔어 ▶ You're history 넌 끝장났어
- [ ] **He's a movie buff** 그 사람은 영화광이야 ▶ buff (영화나 뮤지컬 등) 팬, 광
- [ ] **What a geek!** 이런 얼간이 같은놈! ▶ geek 괴짜, 얼간이 geeky 이상한, 괴짜의
- [ ] **She was a nerd when she was at school** 걘 학교다닐 때 괴물였어 ▶ nerd 1. 컴퓨터나 과학에 심취한 괴짜 2. 멍청이, 촌스런 놈
- [ ] **My teacher is a kook** 우리 선생님은 기인야 ▶ kook 괴짜, 미치광이
- [ ] **You're a moron** ▶ moron 멍청이, 얼간이
- [ ] **Maybe you think I'm a weirdo** 날 이상한 놈이라 생각하겠죠 ▶ weirdo 이상하게 행동하는 사람
- [ ] **I'm not a jerk** 난 멍청하지 않아 ▶ jerk 바보, 멍청이
- [ ] **You're a dork** 넌 바보야 ▶ dork 싫은 녀석, 바보 dorky 어리석은, 바보 같은
- [ ] **You little creep!** 이 재수없는 자식아! ▶ creep 재수없는 자식, 밥맛없는 놈 creepy 재수없는, 비굴한

- ☐ **My wife thinks I'm a wimp!** 마누라는 내가 겁쟁이라 생각하고 있어 ▶ wimp 소심쟁이, 겁쟁이
- ☐ **He's s schmuck** 아무 것도 모르는 놈이지 ▶ schmuck 얼간이, 바보 같은 녀석
- ☐ **He's kind of an asshole** 걘 좀 머저리야
- ☐ **You're a sick bastard, you know that?** 넌 재수없는 개자식야, 그거 알아? ▶ bastard 개자식, 후레자식
- ☐ **She's a knockout** 그 여자는 대단한 미인이다
- ☐ **He's dating a chick** ▶ chick 보통 남자들끼리 대화할때 여자를 가리키는 말
- ☐ **You look like a bimbo** ▶ bimbo 멍청하고 성적으로 쉬운 여자
- ☐ **What's going on, babe?** ▶ babe 여자를 친근하게 부르는 말이거나 섹시한 여자를 가리키는 말
- ☐ **Nobody wants to marry a whore!** 아무도 매춘부랑은 결혼하려 하지 않아! ▶ whore 매춘부
- ☐ **You fucking bitch!** 이 죽일년! ▶ son of bitch 개자식
- ☐ **Shut up, you slut!** 아가리 닥쳐, 이 걸레야! ▶ slut 매춘부, 암캐 slutty 추잡한, 걸레 같은
- ☐ **He got caught with a hooker** 걘 매춘부랑 있다 걸렸어 ▶ hooker 매춘부
- ☐ **She's dressed to kill** 죽이게 입었군
- ☐ **She's hip** 저 여자 멋지다
- ☐ **She's a real looker[What a looker]** 그 여자는 진짜 몸매가 끝내 줘
- ☐ **He's a pretty tough cookie** 그 사람 아주 만만치 않은 사람이야 ▶ You're sharp 예리하군 You're quick 눈치 하난 빠르단 말이야
- ☐ **You're the picture of health** 넌 건강의 화신이야 ▶ He has a strong constitution 걘 체력이 강해
- ☐ **He's an easy-going person** 성격이 좋은 사람야, 걘 성격이 무던해
- ☐ **She's a smooth talker** 쟤는 정말 말 잘해(남을 설득 잘하는 사람)
- ☐ **He's a back-seat driver** 걘 오지랖이 넓어
- ☐ **He's a good mixer** 걘 친구들을 잘 사귀어 ▶ mixer 사교적인 사람, 잘 어울리는 사람

SUPPLEMENT

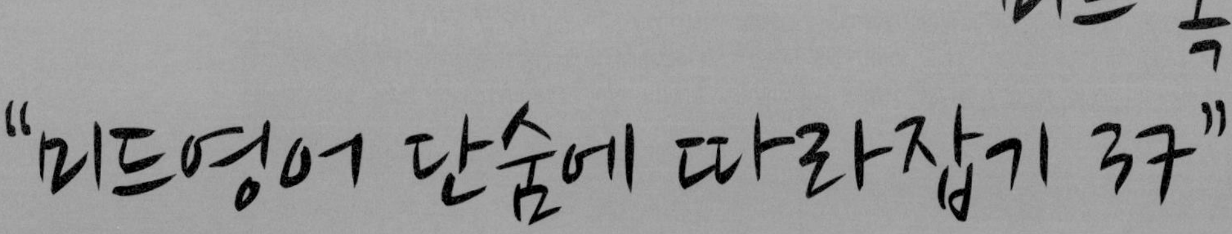
미드 속
"미드영어 단숨에 따라잡기 37"

01 What can I say?

뭐랄까?, 할 말이 없어, 낸들 어쩌겠어?

<Friends 2-18>

모니카는 아버지 친구인 리차드와 사귀는 중에 서로 몇명의 이성과 사귀었는지 얘기를 나누고 있다.

Monica: Alright, before I tell you, uh, why don't you tell me how many women you've been with.

Richard: Two.

Monica: Two? TWO? **How is that possible?** I mean, have you seen you?

Richard: Well, I mean **what can I say?** I, I was married to Barbara for 30 years. She was my high school sweetheart, now you, that's two.

Monica: Two it is. Okay, time for bed, I'm gonna go brush my teeth.

Richard: Woah, woah, no **wait a minute** now. **C'mon it's your turn.** Oh c'mon. Ya know, I don't need the actual number, just a ballpark.

Monica: Okay, it is definitely less than a ballpark.

모니카: 좋아요. 내가 말하기 전에, 몇명의 여자와 사귀었는지 말해봐요.
리차드: 두명
모니카: 두명, 두명요? 어떻게요? 내 말은 당신같은 멋진 사람이?
리차드: 내 말은 낸들 어쩌겠어? 난 고등학교 때 바바라와 만나서 30년간 바바라와 결혼했고, 이제는 너, 그래서 둘이야.
모니카: 두명이네요. 그래요. 잘 시간이네요. 가서 양치질 할게요.
리차드: 어어, 안돼, 잠깐만. 이제 네 차례야, 어서, 정확한 숫자보다 대강만 말해봐.
모니카: 그래요, 분명히 말하지만 대강의 수(야구장에 모인 대략의 관중수)보다는 적어요.

02 What do you want from me?

내가 뭘 더 어떻게 해야 되는데?, 더 뭘 원하는데?, 나더러 어쩌라는거야?

<Sex and the City 1-7>

캐리는 빅의 자유분망한 연애생활을 보면서 파티에서 빅에게 짜증을 부린다.

Carrie: How many women are you dating?

BIG: In the tri-state area?

Carrie: Well, let's see, there's me, um, Julia, and let's not forget international Melissa.

BIG: **I'm not doing this here.**

Carrie: Fine.

BIG: Can't we just enjoy the party?

Carrie: I don't know.

BIG: Come on, **I mean, what do you want from me?**

캐리: 몇명의 여자와 데이트를 하는거야?
빅: 인근 3개주에서?
캐리: 어디보자, 내가 있고, 줄리아, 그리고 국제적인 멜리사를 빼놓으면 안되지.
빅: 여기서 이러지 말자.
캐리: 좋아.
빅: 그냥 파티를 즐기면 안될까?
캐리: 모르겠어.
빅: 그러지말고, 내 말은 나더러 어쩌라고?

Says who?

누가 그래?, 그걸 말이라고 해!

<Sex and the City 1-11>

캐리는 빅과 한 침대에 있을 때 방귀를 뀌게 되고 그 이후로 3번의 데이트에서 섹스를 못했다고 자책한다.

Carrie: I farted. I farted in front of my boyfriend. And we're no longer having sex. And he thinks of me as one of the boys. And I'm gonna have to move to another city where the shame of this won't follow me.

Miranda: You farted. You're human.

Carrie: I don't want him to know that. **I mean** he's this perfect guy. **You know**, he walks around in his perfect apartment with his perfect suit. And he's just perfect, perfect, perfect, and I'm the girl who farts. **No wonder** we're not having sex.

Miranda: **You're insane!** It's been 3 times. It's perfectly normal.

Carrie: **Says who?** I mean, say it's not the... then what else is going on? I mean, is it normal to be in the same bed and not do it?

캐리: 방귀를 뀌었어. 남친 앞에서 방귀를 뀌었어. 그리고 우리는 더 이상 섹스를 하지 않아. 빅은 나를 남자취급하는 것 같아. 너무 창피해서 다른 도시로 이사가야 할까 봐.

미란다: 넌 방귀를 뀐거야. 넌 인간이야.

캐리: 빅이 모르기를 원해. 내 말은 그는 그 정도로 완벽한 남자야. 완벽한 아파트에서 완벽한 복장을 한 채로 걸어다니는데 난 방귀를 뀌는 여자야. 섹스를 하지 않는 것도 당연하지.

미란다: 미쳤구만! 겨우 3번 걸러놓고. 그건 극히 정상이야.

캐리: 누가 그래? 내 말은 그게 아니라면 그럼 무슨 일인거야? 내 말은 같은 침대에 있으면서도 섹스를 하지 않는게 정상이라는거야?

I'll make it work

그게 돌아가게 할게, 난 해낼 수 있어

<Walking Dead 2-6>

릭은 아내는 임신을 하게 되고 유산하려다 릭이 알아차린다.

Laurie: **You want me to** bring a baby into this? To live a short, cruel life?

Rick: **How can you think like that?**

Laurie: We can't even protect the son we already have.

Rick: So this is the solution?

Laurie: Rick, I threw them up. **I screwed up**. I don't know how we do this.

Rick: **We can make it work.**

Laurie: How? Tell me how.

Rick: **We'll figure it out.**

로리: 이런 상황에서 아기를 낳으라고? 잔인하게 짧게 살다 가라고?

릭: 어떻게 그렇게 생각해?

로리: 우린 이미 있는 아이조차도 보호하지 못하잖아.

릭: 그래서 이게 해결책이야?

로리: 릭, 토해버렸어. 내가 망쳐버렸어. 어떻게 해야 할지 모르겠어?

릭: 우리는 해낼 수 있어.

로리: 어떻게? 어떻게 할 수 있는지 말해줘.

릭: 우리가 알아낼거야.

05

I'm all yours

뭐든지 말해, 편하게 말해

<Sex and the City 1-1>

캐리는 옛 애인 커트를 상대로 남자처럼 섹스하기 도전에 성공했는데 다시 바에서 만나게 된다.

Curt: **Lucky me,** twice in one week.

Carrie: You may not be getting that lucky.

Curt: I **was pissed off** the way you left.

Carrie: You were?

Curt: Yeah. Then I thought how great! You finally understand that we can have sex without commitment.

Carrie: Yeah, right. **Sure, I guess.** So whenever **I feel like it**, I'll **give you a call**.

Curt: Yeah, whenever you feel like it. **I mean**, if I'm alone, **I'm all yours**.

Carrie: **Alright.**

Curt: I like this new you. - Call me.

Carrie: Yup.

커트: 내가 운이 좋네, 일주일에 두번이나 보고 말야.
캐리: 그렇게 운이 좋지 않을지도 몰라.
커트: 네가 휙 가버려서 화가 났었어.
캐리: 그랬어?
커트: 어. 그리고 나서 아주 좋았다고 생각했어. 네가 드디어, 서로 얽매임없이 섹스를 할 수 있다는 것을 이해했잖아.
캐리: 어, 맞아. 그럼. 그럼 내가 내키면 전화줄게.
커트: 아, 내키면 언제든지. 내 말은 내가 혼자 있을 때는 난 당신꺼야.
캐리: 좋아.
커트: 이런 새로운 네가 좋아. 전화해.
캐리: 그래.

06

I screwed up

내가 일을 망쳤어

<Breaking Bad 5-10>

월터는 스카일러에게 자신이 마약제조를 해서 번 돈을 받고 자식에게 물려주기를 바란다.

Walter: Skyler, I'll make this easy. **I'll give myself up.** If you promise me one thing. You keep the money. Never speak of it. **Never give it up.** You pass it on to our children. Give them everything. Will you do that? Please? Please don't let me have done all this **for nothing**.

Skyler: How did Hank find out? Did-- did somebody talk?

Walter: No, no one talked. It was me. **I screwed up.**

월터: 스카일러, 내가 일을 쉽게 해줄게. 내가 자수할게. 내게 한가지 약속해주면. 돈을 가져. 절대 알려서도 안되고 절대 포기해서도 안돼. 우리 아이에게 넘겨줘. 다 넘겨줘. 그래줄래? 제발? 지금까지 한 일을 의미없게 만들지 말아줘.
스카일러: 행크는 어떻게 알아낸거야? 누가 얘기한거야?
월터: 아니, 아무도 말하지 않았어. 그건 나였어. 내가 다 망쳤어.

07

Is that what I think it is?

이게 내가 생각하는게 맞아?

<Modern Family 2-14>

발렌타인 데이를 맞아 필과 클레어는 호텔에서 롤플레이를 해보기로 한다. 필은 클라이브로, 클레어는 줄리아나라는 가명으로 처음 만나서

Claire: **Why do I get the feeling** you're not really a salesman?

Phil: Ohh... Pretty and smart. Or should I say "pretty smart"? I might do some high-risk work for Uncle Sam that takes me clear around the country.

Claire: Mm, so you could say you're a... national man of mystery.

Phil: Never did catch what you do.

Claire: Didn't you?

Phil: Surprising, I know. **I'm usually pretty good at** catching things from women in bars.

Claire: Well... Clive, I am just a bored housewife with a dark side and an hour to kill.

Phil: **Is that what I think it is?**

Claire: It's not a gift card. Or maybe it is. I'll be upstairs, Clive. **Don't take too long.**

Phil: I never do.

클레어: 왜 당신이 진짜 세일즈맨이 아니라는 생각이 들죠?
필: 어.. 예쁜데 똑똑하기까지 하고. 아니면 꽤 똑똑하다고 해야 되나요? 국가를 위해서 아주 위험한 일을 할지도 모르죠. 그 때문에 전국을 쭉 돌아다니죠.
클레어: 그럼 당신은 미스테리한 국가적인 인물이라는 말이군요.
필: 당신의 직업은 캐치 못했어요.
클레어: 그랬어요?
필: 놀랍게도, 난 알아요. 보통 바에서 만난 여자들의 속셈을 캐치하는데 능하거든요.
클레어: 클라이브, 난 단지 지루한 전업주부예요. 어두운 이면이 있고 한시간 재미볼 시간이 있어요.
필: 그게 내가 생각하는 그건가요?
클레어: 기프트 카드가 아녜요. 혹은 그거일 수도 있죠. 올라가 있을게요, 클라이브. 바로 올라와요.

08

Put yourself out there

당당하게 나서봐, 자신있게 시도해봐

<Friends 8-17>

챈들러와 모니카는 레이첼을 좋아하게 된 조이에게 한번 시도는 해보라고 하는데...

Monica: Honey, you gotta talk to her.

Joey: I can't! **Y'know? You guys don't know what it's like to put yourself out there** like that and just get shot down.

Chandler: I don't know what that's like?! Up until I was 25 I thought the only response to, "I love you," was, **"Oh crap!"**

모니카: 자기야, 레이첼에게 얘기해봐.
조이: 난 못해! 저 말이야? 너희들은 그렇게 자신있게 나섰다가 거절당하는게 어떤건지 몰라서 그래.
챈들러: 내가 그게 어떤 건지 모른다고? 25살까지 "널 사랑해"에 대한 답은 "오, 젠장!"이라는 것 뿐였어.

09

I'm good to go

만반의 준비가 다 되었어

<The Big Bang Theory 2-18>

레슬리는 레너드의 집에서 4중주 연습을 끝내고 레너드를 유혹하는 장면이다.

Lesley: **Just so we're clear,** you understand that me hanging back to practice with you is a pretext for letting you know that I'm sexually available.

Leonard: Really?

Lesley: Yeah, **I'm good to go.**

Leonard: I thought **you weren't interested in me**.

Lesley: That was before I saw you handling that beautiful piece of wood between your legs.

Leonard: You mean my cello?

Lesley: No, **I mean** the obvious crude double entendre. I'm seducing you.

Leonard: **No kidding?**

Lesley: **What can I say**, I'm a passionate and impulsive woman. **So how about it?**

레슬리: 확실히 하고자 하는데 내가 남아서 연습을 하고자 한 것은 네가 나와 섹스를 할 수 있다는 것을 알려주기 위한 구실인 거 알고 있지.
레너드: 정말?
레슬리: 그럼, 난 준비됐어.
레너드: 넌 나한테 관심없는 줄 알았는데.
레슬리: 너의 두 다리사이에 아름다운 목재품을 다르는 것을 보기 전이었지.
레너드: 내 첼로를 말하는거야?
레슬리: 아니, 내 말은 누가봐도 뻔한 중의법을 쓴 것이야. 지금 널 유혹하는 중이야.
레너드: 정말?
레슬리: 어쩌겠어. 난 열정적이고 충동적인 여자인걸. 그럼 하는게 어때?

10

You lost me

이해 못했어, 다시 분명히 말해줘

<Friends 5-18>

조이는 오디션에 떨어지는데...

Ross: Yeah **y'know what?** Maybe-maybe you didn't **mess up** your audition because **you suck**, maybe you messed up because you care more about uh, your godson.

Joey: **What you do mean?**

Ross: I think, sub-consciously…

Joey: Wait-whoa-whoa, **you lost me.**

로스: 저기 말야. 아마도 네가 실력이 없어서 오디션에 떨어진게 아니라 벤의 대부로서 벤을 더 사랑한다는 뜻일 수도 있겠어.
조이: 그게 무슨 말이야?
로스: 내 생각에 무의식적으로...
조이: 잠깐, 난 이해 못했어.

11

We're done here

우리 얘기 그만해

<Breaking Bad 4-6>

월터의 목숨이 위험에 처해 있다는 것을 알고 스카일러는 경찰에 가서 자주하자고 한다.

Skyler: A schoolteacher, cancer, desperate for money?

Walter: Okay, **we're done here.**

Skyler: Roped into working for-- Unable to even quit? You told me that yourself, Walt. Jesus, **what was I thinking?** Walt, please. Let's both of us stop trying to justify this whole thing and admit you're in danger.

Walter: **Who are you talking to right now?** Who is it you think you see? Do you know how much I make a year? **I mean**, even if I told you, **you wouldn't believe it.** Do you know what would happen if I suddenly decided to stop going in to work? A business big enough that it could be listed on the NASDAQ **goes belly-up**, disappears. It ceases to exist without me. No. You clearly don't know who you're talking to, so let me clue you in. I am not in danger, Skyler. I am the danger.

스카일러: 학교 교사가 암에 걸려서 돈이 절박해져서 그런거라고?

월터: 좋아, 얘기 그만하자고.

스카일러: 꾀임에 속아 일을 시작했는데 그만 둘 수 없었다? 그렇게 내게 말했잖아, 월트. 맙소사, 내가 무슨 생각이었지? 월트, 제발. 우리 둘 다 이 모든 일을 합리화하지 말고 네가 위험에 처해있다는 것을 인정하자.

월터: 지금 누구랑 얘기하는 줄이나 알아? 네가 보는 사람이 누구라고 생각해? 내가 일년에 얼마를 버는 줄 알아? 말해도 믿지 못할거야. 내가 일을 관두면 어떤 일이 생길 줄 알아? 나스닥에 상장될 정도의 큰 기업체가 망해서 없어질거야. 나 없이는 존재하지도 않아. 안되지. 당신이 지금 누구하고 얘기하는 줄 모르니 힌트를 줄게. 난 위험에 빠진 게 아냐. 내 자신이 바로 위험이라고.

12

I will take you down

널 혼내줄거야

<Desperate Housewives 2-9>

카톨릭 단체의 도움으로 석방된 카를로스는 성당에 몸과 마음이 기울고 이를 제지하기 위해서 수녀에게 도움을 처하지만 단칼에 거절당하자...

Gabrielle: **What the hell kind of** nun are you? Look, if you try to come between me and my husband, **I will take you down.**

Sister Mary: I grew up on the south side of Chicago. If you wanna threaten me, **you're gonna have to do a lot better than that.**

Gabrielle: **You listen to me**, you little bitch. **You do not want to** start a war with me.

Sister Mary: Well, I have God on my side. Bring it on.

가브리엘: 무슨 수녀가 이래요? 이봐요. 나와 내 남편 사이에 끼려고 하면 가만두지 않을거예요.

메리수녀: 난 시카고 남부에서 자랐어요. 날 협박하려면 그거 갖고는 부족하죠.

가브리엘: 내 말들어. 이 못된 년아. 나와 싸움을 시작하지 않는게 좋을거야.

메리수녀: 하나님이 내 편인 걸요. 어디 한번 해봐요.

13

Just go with it

그냥 참고 지내

<Friends 4-20>

로스가 에밀리와 한달 후에 결혼식을 올린다고 하자 레이첼은 네번 밖에 만나지 않은 조슈아에게 정서불안인 상태에서 결혼하자고 하는데...

Rachel: 'Cause **I am really happy about** us. I think we are, I think we are so on the right track! **Y'know?** I mean, I think we are working, **I think we are clicking.** Y'know?

Joshua: Yeah, sure-sure, yeah, we're-we're-we're-we're-we're clicking.

Rachel: Yeah-yeah, y'know if-if there was just like one little area where I think we would need to **work on**; I-I would think it was we're just not crazy enough!

Joshua: **I gotta say,** I'm not too sure I agree with that.

Rachel: Well, yeah, right, **y'know what?** Yeah, **you're right**, I mean, **we have our fun**. Yeah! But if I mean, I mean like crazy! Y'know? **Okay, all right.** This is gonna, this is gonna sound y'know, a little hasty, but uh, **just go with it**. What if we got married?

레이첼: 난 정말 우리 만남에 기쁘기 때문이야. 난 우리가 제대로 가고 있다고 생각해! 내 말은 우리가 잘 돌아가고 마음이 서로 통한다고 생각해.

조슈아: 어, 물론, 그래. 우리는 서로 마음이 통하지.

레이첼: 근데 우리 사이에 아쉬운 부분이 있다면 우리가 그렇게 열정적이지는 않다는거야.

조슈아: 근데 말야, 난 동의하기가 그렇게 쉽지 않은데.

레이첼: 저기, 그래 저말야? 네 말이 맞아. 우리 나름대로 재미있게 지내고 있어. 하지만 내 말은, 내 말은 좀 열정적으로란 말야! 좋아. 이건 좀 성급하게 들릴지 모르겠지만 그냥 참고 있으라고. 우리 결혼하면 어때?

14

There goes my weekend!

내 주말이 날라갔네

<CSI: Las Vegas 2-5>

사인을 찾기 위해 시신 앞에 로빈슨 박사와 닉, 캐서린이 대화를 나누고 있다.

Nick: Oh, he was dumped, all right ... out of a chopper. Right, doctor?

Robbins: Victim's injuries **are not inconsistent with** a fall of that magnitude. No fracture of the pelvis no compression of the lumbar vertebrae no shortening of the body.

Catherine: **There goes your theory,** Nick. **Good try, though.** So what was the cause of death?

닉: 그가 버려진 것은 맞죠, 헬리콥터에서요. 맞죠, 박사님?

로빈슨: 피살자의 상처는 그 정도의 높이에서 떨어질 때의 상처와 일치하지 않아. 골반의 골절도 없고, 요추에 압박도 없고, 몸이 줄어들지도 않았어.

캐서린: 닉, 네 생각이 틀렸네. 그래도 시도는 좋았어. 그럼 사인은 뭐예요?

Deal with it!

정신차려!, 받아들여!

<Desperate Housewives 3-7>

식료품점에서의 인질극 장면. 노라가 죽자 르넷을 분노해서 캐롤린을 쳐다본다.

Carolyn: Oh, **don't look at me that way**. You know you wanted her dead.

Lynette: **How can you say that?**

Carolyn: Well, you told me about her and your husband after I made it pretty clear **where I stand on** whores.

Lynette: I did not want this. **Don't you dare say** that I wanted this.

Carolyn: Shut up!

Lynette: No, I will not shut up! What's the matter with you?!

Carolyn: Have you not been paying attention? My husband **cheated on** me!

Lynette: **Who cares?!** Who cares? We all have pain! Everyone in here has pain, but **we deal with it**! We swallow it and **get going with our lives**! What we don't do is go around shooting strangers!

캐롤린: 그런 식으로 날 쳐다보지마. 쟤가 죽기를 바란걸 알아.
르넷: 어떻게 그렇게 말할 수 있어?
캐롤린: 내가 창녀들을 어떻게 생각하는지 분명히 말한 후에 넌 쟤와 남편에 대해서 말했어.
르넷: 난 이걸 원하지 않았어. 어떻게 감히 내가 이걸 원했다고 말하는거야?
캐롤린: 닥쳐!
르넷: 아니, 난 입다물지 않을거야. 넌 도대체 뭐가 문제야?
캐롤린: 지금까지 내 말 못들었어? 내 남편이 바람을 폈다고!
르넷: 누가 신경이나 쓴대? 우리 모두 아픔을 갖고 있어. 여기 있는 모든 사람은 아픔이 있지만 헤쳐나가고 있다고. 우리는 맘속으로 삼키고 삶을 살아가고 있다고. 우리가 하지 않는 일은 돌아다니면서 총을 쏘는 일이라고!

16

What does that tell us?

이게 무슨 말이겠어?

<CSI: Las Vegas 1-18>

그리썸과 닉이 얘기를 나누고 있는데 브래스 경감이 들어온다.

Grissom: I think Shepherd planned the murder of his wife.

Nick: **I'm with you.** Why'd he **end up dead**?

Brass: Bad karma. Jessica and this Shepherd guy had been phoning each other day and night for the past two years. **What does that tell you?**

그리썸: 쉐퍼드가 자기 아내의 살인을 계획한 것 같아.
닉: 저도 그런데요 왜 그도 죽었죠?
브래스: 악연이네. 제시카와 이 쉐퍼드란 작자는 지난 2년간 밤낮으로 서로 통화를 하고 있었네. 이게 어떻게 생각해?

17

What have you done?

도대체 무슨 짓을 한거야?

<The Big Bang Theory 3-23>

쉘든이 소개팅으로 하게 해서 에이미라는 괴짜를 만나는데... 두 괴짜가 서로 잘 어울리자 하워드가 탄식하듯 내뱉는 말이...

Amy: If that was slang, **I'm unfamiliar with it.** If it was literal, I share your aversion to soiled hosiery. In any case, I'm here because my mother and I have agreed that I will date at least once a year.

Sheldon: Interesting. My mother and I have the same agreement about church.

Amy: I don't object to the concept of a deity, but I'm baffled by the notion of one that takes attendance.

Sheldon: Well, then **you might want to** avoid East Texas.

Amy: **Noted.** Now, before this goes any further, you should know that all forms of physical contact up to and including coitus **are off the table.**

Sheldon: May I buy you a beverage?

Amy: Tepid water, please.

Howard: Good God, **what have we done?**

에이미: 그게 슬랭이라면 난 처음 들어봐요. 그리고 그게 말그대로라면 더러운 양말은 나도 질색이예요. 어쨌건 내가 여기에 나온 이유는 엄마와 일년에 한번씩 데이트하기로 약속해서예요.

쉘든: 흥미롭군요. 저희 엄마와 저도 교회에 대해서 같은 약속을 했는데요.

에이미: 신이라는 개념에 반대하지는 않지만, 교회에 출석을 해야 된다는 생각에는 당황스럽네요.

쉘든: 그럼 동부 텍사스는 피하는게 좋겠어요.

에이미: 알았어요. 이제 우리가 더 진전되기 전에 성교를 포함한 모든 신체적 접촉은 없는거예요.

쉘든: 음료수 내가 사도 될까요?

에이미: 미지근한 물로 부탁해요.

하워드: 맙소사, 우리가 무슨 짓을 한거야?

18

That rings a bell

그러니까 기억이 나네

<Desperate Housewives 3-21>

교통사고로 기억상실증에 걸린 마이크가 병원에 와서 자신의 물건들을 챙

Meter Man: **You know,** I could give you another ticket for littering.

Gabrielle: You could try, but **you might not want to.** See, **I'm engaged to** Victor Lang. **Ring a bell?** The mayor? Your new boss?

Meter Man: I don't follow politics.

주차요원: 쓰레기 무단투기로 딱지 한장 더 끊을 수도 있어요.

가브리엘: 그럴 수는 있겠지만, 안그러는게 좋을거요. 봐요, 난 빅터 랭과 약혼했어. 기억나는 것 없어요? 시장? 당신의 새로운 보스?

주차요원: 정치에 관심없어요.

19 This is where I draw the line

여기까지가 내 한계야

<Desperate Housewives 3-18>

톰이 허리를 다치자 맥컬스키 부인에게 다섯 아이와 톰을 맡기고 피자가게를 혼자 운영하는데...

Mrs. McCluskey: Well, **here's a surprise for you**... I quit.
Lynette: What? What? Why? Why? **What happened?**
Mrs. McCluskey: Five kids are tough enough, but your husband makes six. **And that's where I draw the line.**
Lynette: Okay, **I know that,** uh, Tom has been a little cranky lately.
Mrs. McCluskey: "No, I'm cranky. He's insufferable. **I hate to admit this,** Lynette, but every time that man screams out in pain, I do a little jig inside.
Lynette: Look, I'll talk to Tom--
Mrs. McCluskey: No, my mind's made up.
Lynette: Wait, wait, wait! **Please don't do this.** Please. I am at the end of my rope.

맥클러스키 부인: 저기, 깜짝 선물이야... 나 그만뒀어.
르넷: 뭐라구요? 왜요? 무슨 일인데요?
맥클러스키 부인: 아이 다섯도 아주 힘든 일인데, 자네 남편까지 합하면 여섯이야. 그리고 여기까지가 내 한계야.
르넷: 그래요, 알고 있어요. 톰이 최근에 좀 괴팍하게 굴죠.
맥클러스키 부인: 아니, 내가 괴팍한거고 톰은 참을 수 없을 정도야. 이걸 인정하기 싫지만, 르넷, 그 인간이 아프다고 소리지를 때다마 난 속이 부글부글 끓어.
르넷: 톰에게 얘기를 할게요.
맥클러스키 부인: 아냐, 내 맘은 결정됐어.
르넷: 잠깐만요! 제발 이러지 마세요. 제발요. 저도 죽을 지경예요.

20 We'll see how it goes

어떻게 돌아가는지 지켜보자

<The Big Bang Theory 2-10>

스테파니와 동거중인 레너드는 페니에게 동거를 취소할 수 있는 방법을 물어본다.

Leonard: Okay, **here's the thing,** I'm afraid that if I ask her to move out, she'll just **dump me.**
Penny: Well, **it's a chance you have to take. I mean,** look, **if it's meant to be,** it'll be.
Leonard: Very comforting. Okay, so what do I say to her?
Penny: I don't know. **I mean,** what have women said to you when they wanted to slow a relationship down?
Leonard: really like you, but I want to see how things go with Mark?
Penny: Yeah, that'll slow it down.

레너드: 그래, 문제는 이거야. 집에서 나가라고 한다면 걔가 날 차버릴 것 같아.
페니: 그 정도 위험은 감수해야지. 어차피 그렇게 될거라면 언제가는 그렇게 될 일이야.
레너드: 참 위로가 된다. 그래, 그럼 내가 그녀에게 뭐라고 해야 돼?
페니: 몰라. 내 말은 여자들이 너와 관계를 천천히 하자고 할 때 뭐라고 네게 말했어?
레너드: 정말 네가 좋지만, 마크와도 잘 맞을지 알고 싶어?
페니: 그러면 되겠네.

21

Don't fall for it

속지마라

<Friends 8-9>

조이가 임신한 레이첼을 골려 먹고 있는 장면.

Joey: Hey, Rach, **did you know that** during pregnancy, your hands can swell up to twice their size and never go back?

Rachel: **Oh my God**, lemme see that!!

Joey: **You fall for it** every time!

조이: 레이첼, 임신하게 되면 손이 두배로 부어올라 예전으로 다시 안돌아간다는거 알고 있어?
레이첼: 맙소사, 어디 보자!!
조이: 넌 매번 넘어가더라!

22

I could do with a cold beer

시원한 맥주 마시고 싶어

<Modern Family 2-18>

제이는 게이인 아들 친구들과 술을 먹다 술김에 한 친구인 페퍼와 쇼핑을 하기로 한다. 담날 아침 이를 안 제이는 글로리아에게 응급상황이 발생한 것처럼 해달라고 부탁하는데...

Gloria: Ay, Jay! I... I think you'll have to take me now to the hospital. My head is in pain. **Do you mean like that?**

Jay: Yes, thank you. Okay, it's showtime. And with this guy, I mean that literally.

Pepper: I'm here! **Oh, my God. What I could do with this house.** Hello, Jay. Mwah. Mwah. Chop, chop... it's a two-hour drive, not counting our stop at the outlet mall.

Jay: Oh, okay. Um, Gloria, **we're leaving!**

Gloria: Hello. You must be Pepper. Ay, ay, ay. My head.

Jay: **What's the matter**, Gloria?

Gloria: Oh, nothing. I just had a little ice cream. He hasn't stopped talking about you all day long.

글로리아: 아, 제이! 나 병원에 데려가야 될 것 같아. 머리가 아파요. 이렇게 말야?
제이: 어, 고마워. 자 이제 쇼우타임이야. 그리고 이 친구와는 말그대로 의미하는거야.
페퍼: 저 왔어요! 맙소사. 이런 집이 있었으면 좋겠다. 안녕하세요, 제이. 차로 2시간예요, 우리가 아울렛 매장에 들르는 걸 뺀 시간예요.
제이: 좋아, 글로리아, 우리 간다!
글로리아: 안녕하세요. 페퍼 씨군요. 아, 머리가.
제이: 글로리아, 무슨 문제야?
글로리아: 아무 것도 아냐. 아이스크림을 좀 먹었어. 하루종일 당신 얘기를 끊이지 않고 했어요.

I'll get out of your hair

널 방해하지 않고 그만 갈게

<Desperate Housewives 3-15>

회상장면으로 배관공 마이크가 올슨의 집에 와서 싱크대를 수리하려고 한다.

Orson: I'm Monique's boyfriend. She's upstairs lying down. She **wasn't feeling well.**

Mike: Well, I'll just **finish up with** the sink and **get out of your hair.**

Orson: Look, **why don't you** let me **take care of** that? **I mean,** I'm pretty handy, and it's getting late.

올슨: 난 모니크의 남친예요. 그녀는 위층에서 쉬고 있어요. 몸이 좀 안좋아서요.
마이크: 그럼 싱크대 빨리 고치고 가겠습니다.
올슨: 저기, 내가 하는게 어떨까요? 내 말은 내가 손재수가 있고 또 너무 늦어져서요.

We've got bigger fish to fry

더 중요한 문제가 있어

<Breaking Bad 5-1>

마약제조 영상이 경찰의 증거물 보관소에 있다는 사실을 알게 된 그들은 Gustavo의 수하인 Mike를 찾아가 이 영상을 제거할 계획을 세우는데…

Mike: **I am done** listening to this asshole talk. Now **get out of my way.**

Jesse: He's got something you need to hear, **all right?**

Mike: What did you do, Jesse? Do you even know? Do you even know what you've done?

White: **He saves your own life.**

Mike: One more word--

Jesse: Mike. Mike. If you kill him, you're going to have to kill me. **Come on.**

Mike: Oh, Jesse. Jesus. **What is it with** you guys?

White: **Honest to God.** May I? Look. Whatever differences you and I have, **they'll keep.** Right now **we've got bigger fish to fry.**

Mike: Bigger fish.

Jesse: The video cameras.

White: Gus kept cameras on us at the lab, at the laundry, **God only knows** where else. And, of course, when I say "us," including you.

마이크: 이 자식의 말도 안되는 얘기는 다 들었어. 그러니 그만 꺼져.
제시: 월트는 당신이 들어야하는 것을 갖고 있어요. 알겠어요?
마이크: 무슨 짓을 한거야, 제시? 알기나 해? 무슨 짓을 했는지 알기나 해?
월터: 그가 너를 구해줬지.
마이크: 한마디만 더 하면…
제시: 마이크, 마이크, 당신을 월트를 죽인다면 나도 죽여야 할거예요. 그러지 마요.
마이크: 오, 제시, 맙소사, 도대체 너희 둘은 왜 그러는거야?
월터: 내가 말해도 될까? 자, 우리 서로 다른 점은 무엇이든 접어두고 현재는 더 큰 문제가 있어.
마이크: 더 큰 문제라.
제시: 비디오 카메라.
월터: 거스는 실험실, 세탁소 그리고 어딘지 모를 곳에서 우리들을 카메라에 담았고, 물론 내가 '우리'라고 할 때는 당신도 포함해.

Can't argue with that

물론이지, 당연하지, 두말하면 잔소리지

<The Big Bang Theory 5-9>

레너드와 페니가 영화관에서 표를 사고 있다.

Penny: Oh, hey, if we hurry, we can make the new Jennifer Aniston movie.

Leonard: **Oh, yeah, sure.** There's also an amazing documentary about building a dam on river in South America.

Penny: Okay, but the Jennifer Aniston movie has Jennifer Aniston, and she's not building a dam.

Leonard: **Can't argue with that.** I'll get the tickets.

Penny: Okay.

Leonard: Actually, **you know what? I think it's about time** I pick a movie we see.

Penny: You pick plenty of movies.

페니: 서두르면 제니퍼 애니스톤의 신작 영화를 볼 수 있어.
레너드: 그래 물로. 남아메리카 강에 댐 건설에 관한 멋진 도큐멘타리도 있는데.
페니: 그래, 하지만 제니퍼 애니스톤의 영화에는 제니퍼 애니스톤이 있어. 그리고 그녀는 댐을 건설하지는 않아.
레너드: 두말하면 잔소리지. 내가 표를 사올게.
페니: 좋아.
레너드: 실은, 저기 말야? 내가 볼 영화를 고를 차례인 것 같은데.
페니: 네가 지금까지 많은 영화 골랐잖아.

26

I got to put my foot down

난 반대야, 절대 안돼

<Friends 7-2>

모니카는 성대한 결혼식을 원해서 챈들러가 모은 돈을 다 쓰자고 하는데...

Chandler: I realize that honey, but I'm not gonna spend all of the money on one party.

Monica: Honey, I love you, but if you call our wedding a party one more time, you may not **get invited**. Okay? Listen, we could always earn more money, okay? But uh, we're only gonna get married once.

Chandler: Look, I understand, but **I have to put my foot down**. Okay? The answer is no.

Monica: You-you're gonna have to put your foot down?

챈들러: 그건 나도 알아 하지만 한 파티에 돈을 다 쓰지는 않을거야.
모니카: 자기야, 널 사랑하지만, 우리의 결혼식을 파티라고 한번 더 부르면 넌 초대받지 못할 수도 있어. 알았어? 이봐, 우리는 앞으로 계속 더 많은 돈을 모을 수 있지만, 결혼은 오직 한번 뿐이야.
챈들러: 저기, 이해해 하지만 난 반대야. 알겠어? 대답은 노야.
모니카: 네가 반대할거라고?

Don't bring me into this

나까지 끌고 들어가지마

<Sex and the City 3-5>

사만의 흑인 애인이 Chivon의 누나가 둘의 만남을 용인하지 않는다.

Charlotte: Maybe you should **stop seeing him**, Samantha. Race is a very big issue.

Samantha: No. **There is no reason to bring race into this.** Chivon is a sweet man. We have great sex, and he happens to have the biggest...

Charlotte: Black cock! We know he has a big black cock!

Samantha: **I was about to** say biggest heart. But **now that** you're so interested, yes. He does have a big black cock.

Miranda: It's big African-American cock. Right, Charlotte?

Charlotte: Don't make fun of me. My chin hurts.

샬롯: 사만다, 그를 그만 만나는게 어때. 인종은 큰 문제잖아.
사만다: 아니. 우리 사귀는데 인종문제를 끌어드릴 이유는 없어. 쉬본은 달콤한 남자야. 우리는 아주 멋진 섹스를 했고 공교롭게도 아주 큰...
샬롯: 흑인의 고추! 우리는 그가 커다란 흑인고추를 갖고 있는 것을 알아!
사만다: 난 아주 맘이 넓다고 말하려고 했는데. 하지만 관심이 그렇게 있다면야, 그는 커다란 흑인 고추를 갖고 있어.
미란다: 커다란 아프리카 미국인 고추라고 해야지. 맞지, 샬롯?
샬롯: 나 놀리지마. 턱이 아프네.

You dig?

알겠어?

<Modern Family 3-5>

헤일리가 돈을 빌려준 피터를 찾아가 돈을 받아내려는 제이와 필.

Jay: You Peter?

Peter: **What do you want?**

Jay: You know Haley Dunphy? You owe her $900. We're here to collect.

Phil: **You dig?**

Peter: I tried to call that girl, **like**, ten times, but her voice mail was always... full.

Phil: **That does sound like** Haley.

제이: 네가 피터냐?
피터: 뭘 원하시죠?
제이: 너 헤일리 던피라고 알지. 걔한테 900달러 빚졌다며. 우리 수금하러 왔다.
필: 알겠어?
피터: 전화하려고 했는데, 열번이나, 근데 음성사서함은 항상 꽉차있더라구요.
필: 헤일리답네.

What have you got going on?

무슨 일이야?

<Desperate Housewives 2-12>

음주운전으로 유치장에 있는 브리에게 옆에 있던 창녀가 오해하고 언제부터 일을 시작했냐는 묻는다.

Prostitute: **I bet** the guys **go crazy with** your whole classy, repressed thing you **got going on**, huh? **I mean,** your skin has, like, no pores.

Bree: **I am not sure, but** I think there was a compliment in there somewhere, so thank you. But I am not an escort.

매춘부: 당신한테서 풍기는 고상하고 억제된거에 남성네들이 미칠거예요? 당신 피부에는 저기, 모공도 없잖아요.
브리: 잘모르겠지만, 그래도 칭찬하는 것 같으니 고마워요. 하지만 난 고급접대부가 아녜요.

I wouldn't say that

그렇지는 않을 걸

<Sex and the City 6-19>

캐리는 파리로 떠났고 뒤늦게 자신의 실수를 깨달은 빅이 남은 친구들을 찾아와 조언을 구한다.

Big: Well, I know I haven't been your favorite over the few years.

Charlotte: **I wouldn't say that.**

Samantha: I would.

Big: Well, **god knows I've made a lot of mistakes with** Carrie. **I fucked it up.** Many times. **I know that.** Look, I need your advice.

빅: 지난 몇 년간 날 좋게 보지 않은 걸 알고 있어요.
샬롯: 그렇지 않은 걸요.
사만다: 난 그렇게 생각해요.
빅: 정말이지 캐리에게 많은 실수를 했어요. 내가 망쳐버렸죠. 여러번요. 알고 있어요. 저기, 여러분의 조언이 필요해요.

Don't get hung up on it

너무 신경쓰지마

<Desperate Housewives 1-9>

정원사 존의 집 앞에서 존이 친구와 자신의 연애사에 대해 얘기하고 있다.

Friend: **I still don't get** while you're not with Danielle anymore. She looked so slutty at Ray's party.

John: **She's not my type, I guess.**

Friend: What? Oh, **you still hung up on** your mysterious married lady?

친구: 네가 더 이상 다니엘과 사귀지 않는 걸 이해못하겠어. 레이의 파티에서는 헤프게 보이던데.
존: 내 타입이 아닌가봐.
친구: 뭐라고? 네 숨겨둔 유부녀를 잊지 못하고 있는거야?

32 Who put you up to it?

누가 부추긴거야?

<The Big Bang Theory 5-2 >

쉘든은 페니의 지저분한 의자를 버리게 하려고 에이미를 이용하는데...

Amy: I just have one question about the chair.
Penny: And what's that?
Amy: Aren't you worried about it being unhygienic?
Penny: No, it's completely fine. Hmm. I get it. Sheldon sent you. He put you up to this.

에이미: 의자에 대해 물어볼게 하나 있어.
페니: 그게 뭔데?
에이미: 의자가 비위생적이라고 생각하지 않아?
페니: 응. 전혀 괜찮어. 음. 알겠어. 쉘든이 널 보냈구나. 쉘든이 너보고 이렇게 하라고 시켰어.

33 He's picking up the pieces

걘 재기하고 있어

<Game of Thrones 1-4>

세르세이가 네드 스타크를 찾아온다.

Stark: The King **called on me** to serve him and the realm, and **that's what I'll do until** he tells me otherwise.
Cersei: You can't change him. You can't help him. He'll do what he wants, which is all he's ever done. **You'll try your best to pick up the pieces.**
Stark: If that's my job, then **so be it**.

스타크: 왕이 제가 왕과 왕국을 위해 일하라고 하셨습니다. 다른 말씀이 있기 전까지는 그 일을 할 겁니다.
세르세이: 왕을 변화시킬 수는 없어요. 왕을 도울 수도 없어요. 왕은 지금까지 그래왔던 것처럼 자기 맘대로 할거예요. 당신은 최선의 노력을 다해서 사태를 수습하는게 다일거예요.
스타크: 그게 저의 일이라면 그렇게 하지요.

34 It's not all it's cracked up to be

그게 항상 좋은 것만은 아냐

<Modern Family 1-16>

미첼과 카메론은 릴리에게 엄마가 없는거에 고민하다 소아과 의사인 미우라 박사와 대화를 나눈다.

Dr. Miura: Guys, listen. I had a very complicated relationship with my mother. She was born in Japan crazy-traditional. **She didn't want me to** become a doctor. She wanted me to **get married** and have kids. But my father... we would talk, and he would **actually listen to what I wanted**. **Anyway, what I'm trying to say is**, having a mother **isn't always what it's cracked up to be**.

미우라 박사: 들어봐요. 난 엄마와 매우 복잡한 관계였어요. 엄마는 일본태생으로 아주 전통적이셨어요. 엄마는 제가 의사가 되는 걸 원치 않았죠. 결혼해서 아이들 낳는 것을 바랬어요. 하지만 아버지는, 우린 대화를 하게 되었고 아버지는 마침내 내가 원하는 것에 귀를 기울이셨죠. 어쨌든, 내가 말하려고 하는 것은 엄마가 있다는게 항상 좋은 것만은 아니에요.

35 Duly noted

잘 알아 들었어

<The Big Bang Theory 4-12>

쉘든은 어플을 개발하자고 하고 친구들에게 일을 분담하는데...

Raj: Hey, why **am I in charge of** phone support? **Seems** a bit racist.

Sheldon: A customer service representative with an Indian accent will create the impression we're a vast enterprise that uses overseas call centers.

Raj: Oh. Very clever. But still racist.

Sheldon: **Duly noted.**

라지: 왜 내가 전화지원 담당이야? 인종차별같은데.
쉘든: 인도 억양의 고객지원 담당자가 있으면 해외 콜센터를 이용하는 커다란 기업이라는 인상을 줄 수 있을거야.
라지: 아. 알겠어. 그래도 인종차별적이야.
쉘든: 잘 알아들었어.

36 I wouldn't be caught dead at that show

난 절대로 그 쇼에 가지 않을거야

<Desperate Housewives 1-9>

개비는 자선행사로 집에서 패션쇼를 연다.

Bree: So, why isn't Mrs. Huber here?

Edie: **Last I heard**, she went to visit her sister. **I just can't believe** that Martha would **agree to** wear this. She always said **she'd never be caught dead in** black.

브리: 왜 후버 부인은 왜 안오는거야?
이디: 최근에 듣기론 언니 만나러 갔어. 후버부인이 이걸 입겠다고 했다니 놀랍네. 항상 검은 색 옷은 절대 안입을거라고 했는데.

37 Don't go overboard with it

오버하지마

<Friends 6-10>

송년파티에서 조이는 라이벌 남자를 내쫓기 위해 화장실에서 그 남자 중요부위에 물을 뿌리는데...

Joey: Uh, **take a look at** the guy's pants! I mean, I know you told us to show excitement, but don't you think he **went a little overboard**?

Director: **What's the matter with you? Get out of here!**

Joey: Yeah, **take a hike**, wet pants!

조이: 저 친구의 바지를 봐요! 내 말은 열띤 분위기를 만들라고 했지만 저 친구는 너무 지나쳤다고 생각하지 않아요?
감독: 당신 왜그래? 나가요!
조이: 그래, 가버려, 오줌싸개야!

MEMO

MEMO